Arguing About Law

Arguing About Law introduces philosophy of law in an accessible and engaging way. It includes articles ranging over a wide array of topics, and covers the key questions in general jurisprudence, topics in normative legal theory, as well as the theoretical foundations of public law and private law. In addition to including many classics, such as selections by Joseph Raz, Ronald Dworkin and John Gardner, *Arguing About Law* also includes non-traditional selections, such as Martin Luther King Jr.'s "Letter from a Birmingham Jail", and discussion of contemporary issues, including terrorism and torture, and the law and sexual morality.

The volume is divided into eleven sections, helping the student get to grips with both the classic and core arguments and emerging debates in:

- the nature of law
- legality and morality
- the rule of law
- the duty to obey the law
- the legal enforcement of sexual morality
- the nature of rights
- rights, terrorism and torture
- criminal law theory
- constitutional theory
- tort theory
- critical approaches to law

Each selected article is clear, interesting and free from unnecessary jargon. The editors provide lucid introductions to each section in which they give an overview of the debate and outline the arguments of the papers. *Arguing About Law* is an inventive and stimulating reader for students new to philosophy of law, legal theory and jurisprudence.

Aileen Kavanagh is Reader in Law at the University of Leicester, UK.

John Oberdiek is Associate Professor of Law at the Rutgers University School of Law-Camden, USA and Co-Director of the Rutgers Institute for Law and Philosophy.

This exciting and lively series introduces key subjects in philosophy with the help of a vibrant set of readings. In contrast to many standard anthologies which often reprint the same technical and remote extracts, each volume in the *Arguing About Philosophy* series is built around essential but fresher philosophical readings, designed to attract the curiosity of students coming to the subject for the first time. A key feature of the series is the inclusion of well-known yet often neglected readings from related fields, such as popular science, film and fiction. Each volume is edited by leading figures in their chosen field and each section carefully introduced and set in context, making the series an exciting starting point for those looking to get to grips with philosophy.

Arguing About Knowledge
Edited by Duncan Pritchard and Ram Neta

Arguing About Law
Edited by Aileen Kavanagh and John Oberdiek

Arguing About Metaethics
Edited by Andrew Fisher and Simon Kirchin

Arguing About the Mind
Edited by Brie Gertler and Lawrence Shapiro

Arguing About Art 3rd Edition
Edited by Alex Neill and Aaron Ridley

Forthcoming titles:

Arguing About Language
Edited by Darragh Byrne and Max Kolbel

Arguing About Metaphysics
Edited by Michael Rea

Arguing About Political Philosophy
Edited by Matt Zwolinski

Arguing About Religion
Edited by Kevin Timpe

Arguing About Law

Edited by

Aileen Kavanagh and John Oberdiek

Routledge
Taylor & Francis Group

LONDON AND NEW YORK

First published 2009
by Routledge
2 Park Square, Milton Park, Abingdon, Oxon OX14 4RN

Simultaneously published in the USA and Canada
by Routledge
711 Third Avenue, New York, NY 10017

Routledge is an imprint of the Taylor & Francis Group, an informa business

Typeset in Joanna and Bell Gothic by
RefineCatch Limited, Bungay, Suffolk

British Library Cataloguing in Publication Data
A catalogue record for this book is available from the British Library

Library of Congress Cataloging-in-Publication Data
A catalog record has been requested for this book

ISBN 10: 0–415–46241–X (hbk)
ISBN 10: 0–415–46242–8 (pbk)
ISBN 13: 978–0–415–46241–9 (hbk)
ISBN 13: 978–0–415–46242–6 (pbk)

Dedication

For Our Parents

Contents

GENERAL INTRODUCTION

LAW FIGURES PROMINENTLY in our lives, for law is nearly everywhere, everywhere it addresses the widest range of human affairs, and everywhere it claims authority. Consider each of these facts in turn. Law's reach is nearly inescapable, in that we all live under legal regimes and cannot easily travel to places that lack them. There may be some lawless parts of the world, like lands riven by civil war, but otherwise the entire globe is governed by some legal system or other. Legal systems just are ubiquitous, and law, as a result, just is a fact of life. Law is thus *pervasive* and this jurisdictional fact partly explains the prominence of law in our lives. But it does not fully explain it. Also important to that explanation is the fact that the vast majority of modern legal systems recognize laws that bear on almost every aspect of life. Although a legal regime recognizing only the rudiments of, say, contract law is possible, the legal regimes under which we all in fact live recognize a far richer panoply of laws. There is little in our lives that law does not regulate in some way. It is true that law has a long arm, but a less often noticed yet no less important fact is that its fingerprints are also all over everything. In this respect, law is *comprehensive*. That law is both pervasive and comprehensive in these ways helps to explain why law figures prominently in our lives. Even in combination, however, these two key determinants of law's prominence are not enough. Necessary to the explanation of that prominence is the further fact that law claims *authority*. Indeed, it is this fact that underwrites the explanatory relevance of law's pervasiveness and comprehensiveness to begin with – absent claimed authority, after all, it would not matter that law is pervasive and comprehensive. We all know, though, that law is hard to ignore: we typically conform our conduct to the law's requirements and prohibitions and we frequently do as the law says precisely because the law says so. Law purports to be authoritative and we often treat it as such. It is no wonder, then, that law figures so prominently in our lives – it aspires to so much – and the fact that it does gives us good reason to explore and understand it. This is legal philosophy's aim.

This thumbnail explanation of law's centrality to our lives, moreover, stimulates most of the questions addressed in this anthology, which taken together constitute the fundamental questions of legal philosophy. Like any branch of philosophy, legal philosophy (or philosophy of law as it is also known) involves exacting inquiry into fundamental but deceptively simple questions. Legal philosophy in particular, unsurprisingly, focuses on those basic questions about law and legal systems that may seem to yield easy answers but, upon careful reflection, do not. It is probably not an exaggeration to say that everything one might think about law is contested in legal philosophy. (Even the question of how to situate legal philosophy within the broader discipline of philosophy is contested, though it is safe to say that legal philosophy most commonly draws on or overlaps with political philosophy, moral philosophy, philosophy of social science, and philosophy of language.) The controversies that occupy legal philosophy are on full display in this anthology, and it is one of this volume's distinguishing features that its constitutive sections are organized to highlight those controversies. Contemporary legal philosophy is dynamic and rigorous, and it is the aim of the readings herein to introduce the major debates that have been joined, canvass the major positions that have been staked out within those debates, and convey a sense of the philosophical depth as well as the practical importance and even urgency of the questions that legal philosophy asks.

This anthology is divided into five parts comprising eleven separate sections, with each section revolving around at least one key debate within philosophy of law. Each section, in turn, has a substantive introduction to the debate that it addresses. No detailed discussion of those specific debates is therefore warranted in advance. An overview of the volume as a whole, however, is in order, and in providing one we also seek to provide a synoptic view of legal philosophy as a whole.

It is common to distinguish between two broad kinds of inquiry within legal philosophy – general jurisprudence and normative legal theory – and Part 1 encompasses two sections that focuses on the first of these. General jurisprudence, as its name suggests, takes up the most general questions about law, namely, those concerning the very nature of law. This is a highly abstract and difficult topic. And while understanding the nature of law is worthwhile in its own right, it also has practical importance. This practical importance is underscored by the fact that inquiry into the nature of law tends to concentrate on the relationship that law bears to morality. The first section, "The Nature of Law: Framing the Debate," introduces the historical antecedents to the contemporary debate over the relationship between legality and morality. The only fully historical set of readings in the anthology, this section's selections all are classics: Oliver Wendell Holmes's 1897 "The Path of the Law", the paired *Harvard Law Review* articles from 1958 by H. L. A. Hart and Lon Fuller that spawned the so-called Hart/Fuller Debate, and then Ronald Dworkin's earliest criticism of Hart, which initiated the Hart/Dworkin Debate that still shapes the field of general jurisprudence. Several influential movements in philosophy of law are represented here, and legal positivism in particular, which sharply distinguishes between law's existence and its moral merit, is highlighted for critical examination.

The second section, "Legality and Morality," follows closely on the heels of the first and features a series of articles that provide an accurate picture of the going positions in the current debate over law and morality's relationship. As the readings make clear, and as the introduction to the section elaborates, general jurisprudence as it now stands is dominated by four positions, each of which countenances a different relationship between legality and morality: inclusive legal positivism, articulated by Jules Coleman; exclusive legal positivism, by Joseph Raz; interpretivism, by Dworkin; and natural law theory, by Robert George. John Gardner's recent "Legal Positivism: 5½ Myths" is a fitting denouement to Part 1, cleaning up discussion of legal positivism and distinguishing its true commitments from its imagined ones.

Part 2, "Law, the State, and the Individual," ventures into normative legal theory and comprises three sections that bear on the state's role in alternately protecting and constraining individual liberty through law. This Part begins, in Section 3, with a set of readings on the rule of law, which constitutes perhaps the most basic protection that a legal system can provide to the individuals who live under its dominion. While the rule of law is universally valorized and often held to be a pre-condition of the realization of most of what is valuable in organized society, the articles in this section make clear that the content of the rule of law remains a matter of deep disagreement. Raz, true to his legal positivism, offers a spare account of the rule of law in his well-known essay "The Rule of Law and its Virtue." Dworkin, true to his jurisprudential views, offers a morally richer competing conception in "Political Judges and the Rule of Law." Finally, Jeremy Waldron takes aim at Dworkin's conception of the rule of law and foreshadows his own influential work on constitutional judicial review in "The Rule of Law as a Theater of Debate." As even this much makes clear, although the debates around which this anthology is organized are discrete and largely self-contained, they nevertheless bear on one another in various ways, and in the introductions to each section we point out those links.

Where Section III's touchstone is the protection of individual liberty through law, it is the constraints that law seeks to impose on liberty that animates Section IV, "The Duty to Obey the Law." Here Raz articulates his novel and influential account of authority and its upshot that there is no general obligation to obey the law, John Rawls appeals to his celebrated social contract theory of justice to delineate the conditions of civil disobedience, and slain American civil rights leader Martin Luther King, Jr. offers a poignant defense of disobedience from behind the walls of a Birmingham, Alabama jail. The limits of law's authority to constrain liberty are also the focus of the charged and long-standing debate in Section V over the legal enforcement of sexual morality. The two articles reprinted here provide a concise and dispassionate introduction to this often personal matter of dispute. John Finnis, the leading living exponent of natural law theory, offers a spirited defense of the state's right to discriminate against gay men and women on the basis of the judgment that homosexuality is base. Stephen Macedo responds forcefully (and with a touch of humor) that Finnis's arguments fail and, further, that they are inconsistent with the broader commitments of natural law theory.

In the background of these various debates, and indeed sometimes in the fore-ground, are claims and assumptions about rights, and in the two sections comprising Part 3, rights take center stage. Section VI deals with the fundamental question of the nature of rights, and the four readings therein are coupled to represent opposing positions on two distinct and more specific debates about the nature of rights. The first pairing illustrates what is known as the will or choice theory of rights, defended by Hart, on the one hand, and the so-called interest or benefit theory of rights, defended by Neil MacCormick, on the other. At issue in this more specific debate between Hart and MacCormick is what it is that a right protects – a choice by the right holder or a right holder's interest? A different debate over the nature of rights is at issue in the second pairing of articles, by Dworkin and Raz, and it revolves around the individualism of rights. Famously invoking the metaphor of a trump card, Dworkin maintains that rights are at bottom individualistic and thus exist to prevent considerations of social expediency from running roughshod over the claims of individuals. Raz, in contrast, argues that rights are justified in part by their protection of the common good and so are not so thoroughly pitted against the interests of the community as, for example, Dworkin contends. Together, the two sub-debates that are introduced in this section provide the foundations necessary to understand fully what rights are and so what their implications are to political life. And there is perhaps no more timely and pressing debate at the political ground level than the one that is at the core of section seven, "Rights, Terrorism, and Torture". Waldron opens the section by addressing the general question of how to weigh the values of security and liberty – a question that has attracted concentrated and sustained attention since the terrorist attacks of September 11th, 2001. This more general discussion is followed by Henry Shue's and Jeff McMahan's compressed but trenchant arguments that torture ought never to be legal, whatever its moral status.

Part 4 shifts focus away from law as such, as well as from particular debates in normative legal theory, detailing instead the philosophical foundations of three substantive bodies of law: constitutional law, criminal law, and tort law. An increasingly common mode of analysis in legal philosophy, examining the philosophical content of doctrinal areas of law involves both conceptual and normative spadework, and each of the substantive areas of law that are explored here has been the subject of extensive conceptual and normative theorizing in recent years. Constitutional law has probably garnered the most philosophical attention over the longest span and it is examined in Section VIII by fixing on two related problems in constitutional theory: first, the interpretation of constitutions; and second, the legitimacy of constitutions themselves and of the institutions that implement them. The debate surrounding the authority of constitutions is represented in the selections by Waldron and Cécile Fabre, while the debate surrounding how best to read constitutions is captured in the readings by Andrei Marmor and United States Supreme Court Justice Antonin Scalia. Section 9 turns from constitutional to criminal law, and examines the perennial controversy over the justification of punishment. This debate was irrevocably altered by Hart's entry into it, as the introduction to the section explains, and each of the three articles reprinted in the section, by Daniel Farrell, John Gardner, and R. A. Duff, owe much to Hart for the broad orientation towards the problem of punishment that they share. The last area of law examined, in Section X, is tort law. The least mature subject of philosophical scrutiny of the three areas discussed here, tort theory has seen an explosion of activity in the last two decades. A. M. Honoré offers a wide-ranging primer of many of the philosophical issues surrounding tort law, including its basis in corrective justice. Where Honoré sees overtones also of distributive justice in tort law's foundations, however, Stephen Perry argues for a corrective justice account of tort law shorn of considerations of distributive justice, and along the way illustrates what is distinctive about tort law.

Finally, in Part 5, three strands of "critical" accounts of law are introduced. Beginning with Roberto Unger's manifesto for Critical Legal Studies (CLS), a self-consciously politicized research program that began in the United States in the 1970s emphasizing both the indeterminacy of law and the way in which conservative political ideology deviously fills in the law's gaps, the section tracks the trajectory and permutations that this and similar lines of inquiry into law have taken. Perhaps the most significant off-shoot of CLS has been Critical Race Theory, and in the article reprinted here, Richard Delgado articulates what a race-conscious understanding of the law involves and how it differs from the CLS movement, notably in its position on the importance of legal rights. Similarly, Anne Phillips is concerned to expose inequalities in the law, but her essay focuses on the legal and political oppression of women, not racial minorities. Even as these three critical movements dissent from mainstream treatments of law, it is worth noting that they are hardly total outsider theories. For, as discussed in the introduction to this last section, their respective platforms sometimes share various planks with those of more established (and even establishment) movements, notably legal realism and legal positivism.

As this survey makes plain, this anthology covers a vast amount of terrain, a fact that reflects just how wide-ranging legal philosophy is. But of course it could have covered more ground, or indeed covered the same ground differently. In choosing this volume's contents, we have been guided by a number of factors, but two stand out. First, we have chosen topics in virtue of their centrality to the field, and pieces by virtue of their intrinsic excellence and their relationship to the other pieces chosen – our aim has been to offer the reader a window into the field's important and sophisticated debates. Second, we have sought to include pieces that could be reprinted in their entirety without editing or excerpting. We set this as a goal for a few reasons. Philosophical arguments do not lend themselves to cutting-and-pasting, as each step in an argument builds upon the previous one, with few sentences or even words to spare. It was important to us not to alter, where possible, the character of the selections we included here. Beyond that, we also sought to expose students to as unfiltered a picture of legal philosophy as possible, allowing them to appreciate first-hand how vibrant and deep the subject is. A final advantage that we identified to including as many fully-reprinted articles as possible was the anthology's viability as a citable scholarly resource. Collecting so many first-rate works of legal philosophy, it is our hope that this anthology streamlines the research of active scholars in philosophy of law. Thus, aside from two book excerpts, only three of the thirty-six pieces are at all edited – in the case of Holmes's essay, to isolate the philosophically important material, and in the cases of Fuller's and Unger's classic articles, to rein in their standard American law review lengths. Meeting this desideratum unfortunately necessitated passing over many excellent articles that were simply too long to be fully reprinted.

There is no question that there are many interesting topics and many outstanding works in legal philosophy that this anthology does not include. Most of our choices regarding both topic and essay, all of which we made together, were exceedingly difficulty to make. We do not have sections devoted to the recent methodology debate in general jurisprudence, for example, to the growing and increasingly important literature on the philosophical foundations of international law, or to basic questions about legal reasoning and interpretation, among others. And this is to say nothing of the first-class legal philosophers whose work is not at all represented here. The chief reasons for these omissions were our goal of including as many fully reprinted pieces as possible and the constraints of overall length that we were working under – if Routledge had thrown caution to the wind and permitted it, this volume could easily have topped 1000 pages. Still, we are delighted with what we have. For we are confident that, despite its omissions, every topic and selection that made the cut deserves its place.

We chose all of the topics and selections together, but we divided the task of writing the various introductions between us. Aileen Kavanagh wrote the introductions to sections seven, eight, and eleven, while John Oberdiek wrote this main introduction as well as the introductions to Sections I through VI and IX and X. We could not have done any of these things without each other's help, nor could we have done them or many other publication-related tasks without the invaluable advice and assistance of a host of people: Grant Berger, Jules Coleman, Sylvie Delacroix, Antony Duff, Cécile Fabre, Kim Ferzan, Samuel Freeman, John Gardner, Doug Husak, George Letsas, Paul Litton, Stephen Macedo, Panu Minkkinen, Hans Oberdiek, Dennis Patterson, Stephen Perry, Tommie Shelby, Wil Waluchow, and the proposal's anonymous reviewers. Thank you all. There are also three people from Routledge, past and present, to whom we are indebted: Pri Pathak, who first initiated the project and was a pleasure to work with through the reviewing stages; Tony Bruce, who shepherded it after Pri moved on and who oversaw the entire process; and, finally and especially, Gemma Dunn, whose blend of competence and concern was both professionally and personally indispensable in getting this anthology published. Thank you. Finally, and most importantly, we would like to thank our respective spouses, Matthew Robinson and Patty Oberdiek, for being so supportive throughout the long process of putting this anthology together.

PART 1

General Jurisprudence

I. THE NATURE OF LAW: FRAMING THE DEBATE

Introduction

GENERAL JURISPRUDENCE is that branch of legal philosophy that considers the most abstract questions about law, and its central focus is the nature of law. Asking "What is law?," general jurisprudence seeks an answer that is true not merely of one or another set of laws, but of all law as law. In this respect, *the* law of any particular jurisdiction, being local and contingent, is inapposite, for querying the nature of law aims to reveal those features that all law possesses but that only law possesses. This terrain is fraught – even characterizing the methodology of the inquiry is contested[1] – but it is also of fundamental importance. Law is a complex and inescapable social phenomenon purporting to guide and indeed direct the conduct of those over whom it claims authority, and understanding any matter relating to law presupposes understanding what law itself is.

Law is a normative phenomenon in that it (at least) purports to provide binding reasons for action to its subjects, and explaining the normative purport of law, and specifically law's relationship to the *bona fide* normative order of morality, has long nourished general jurisprudence. The selections in this section and the next are largely occupied with analyzing this relationship. The present section introduces the historical precursors to the contemporary debate about the nature of law, and specifically the debate about the relation between legality and morality, while the next section provides a map of the positions currently staked out in that debate.

A basic, if crude, dividing line between competing theories of the nature of law concerns whether legality depends to some degree upon morality. There are multiple camps on both sides of this divide, but, historically speaking, the two most prominent are *natural law theory* and *legal positivism*, with the former affirming and the latter denying the dependence at issue. Contrast the unofficial slogan of traditional natural law theory, associated most closely with the medieval theologian and philosopher St. Thomas Aquinas, that "lex iniusta non est lex" – unjust law is not law – with the unofficial slogan of legal positivism, articulated in the 19th century by legal philosopher John Austin, that "[t]he existence of law is one thing; its merit or demerit is another."[2] These are of course only slogans, which are open to (mis)interpretation, but they nevertheless do reflect significantly different accounts of the nature of law. And their most fundamental cleavage is over the relation of legality to morality.

This dividing line is, again, a crude one. But it can be sharpened by focusing on the way that Austin framed his slogan on behalf of legal positivism, namely, in terms of the *existence* of law. The question then becomes, "What must obtain for law to exist?" Austin's own prominent answer was that law was whatever the sovereign commanded: law was essentially coercive and existed wherever there was, and in virtue of there being, an order by a sovereign backed by a threat of sanction. In light of this, it is not hard to see why Austin did not believe law's existence was necessarily something to be celebrated. On his view, law was merely a matter of unadorned social fact, not of morality.

A central tenet of legal positivism even today, the thesis that the existence of law is a matter of social fact alone – the so-called *social thesis* – has found advocates beyond legal positivism's traditional boundaries. The American legal realists of the early 20th Century, for example, regarded law as a matter of pure social fact shorn of moral trimmings.[3] This much is clear in future US Supreme Court Justice Oliver Wendell Holmes, Jr.'s 1897 *Harvard Law Review* article, "The Path of the Law", where he established himself as legal realism's most influential forebear by contending that "[t]he prophecies of what the courts will do in fact, and nothing more pretentious, are what I mean by the law."[4] Much as Austin distinguished legality from morality and identified law with a sovereign's orders backed by threats, Holmes argued that "[o]ne of the many evil effects of the confusion between legal and moral ideas . . . is that theory is apt to get the cart before the horse, and to consider the right or the duty as something existing apart from and independent of the consequences of its breach, to which certain sanction are added afterward."[5] Far from recognizing any moral conditions for legality, Holmes argued that a clear-eyed understanding of law was to be gained by taking up the perspective of a "bad man", for "a bad man has as much reason as a good one for wishing to avoid an encounter with the public force, and therefore you can see the practical importance of the distinction between morality and law."[6] Understanding law and law alone, then, involved understanding not morality, but what triggers legal sanction by the courts.

Although contemporary legal positivists share Austin's belief that the existence of law is a matter of social fact alone, they have not endorsed the particulars of Austin's position. H. L. A. Hart, the dominant figure in 20th Century legal philosophy and a legal positivist himself, famously disparaged Austin's account of law for its likeness to an account of a gunman's hold-up. Hart argued in his 1961 masterpiece *The Concept of Law*[7] that Austin's command theory (as well as Holmes's nascent realism) failed to take account of the perspective of those who *accepted* the law that purported to bind them. From this so-called "internal point of view", persons obey the law not out of mere habit, nor for fear of sanction; rather, they consider themselves to be obligated – not merely obliged, as by a gunman – to obey the law, and thus to be following a rule which they can rely on in justification of their obedience and in criticism of those who disobey. Accounting for this internal point of view in a theory of the nature of law has been considered essential ever since Hart, but doing so requires acknowledging a complex relationship between law and morality: Hart's account recognized that people take themselves to be morally obligated to obey the law, yet sharply distinguished between law and morality.

This latter commitment was the focal point of the famous debate between Hart and Lon Fuller – the Hart/Fuller Debate – that began in the pages of the *Harvard Law Review* in 1958. In "Positivism and the Separation of Law and Morals," Hart defended legal positivism's so-called separation thesis, which is a corollary of its social thesis, explaining the sense in which law and morality were conceptually distinct. In "Positivism and Fidelity to Law: A Reply to Professor Hart", Fuller defended a conception of natural law theory, arguing that law necessarily possessed an "internal morality" (see the Introduction to Section III) that undermined the separation thesis. Adding heat to the debate, as well as illustrating the real-world implications of the philosophical dispute, was the fact that both Hart and Fuller cited the Nazi regime's legal system (or lack thereof) and the fallout from its destruction in support of their respective positions.

If the Hart/Fuller Debate refocused general jurisprudence's attention on the relation of law and morality, the Hart/Dworkin Debate about that relation set an agenda that continues to occupy the field. Ronald Dworkin, a student of Fuller's at Harvard and of Hart's at Oxford, first attacked Hart's separation thesis in 1967's "The Model of Rules", where he argued that the law was constituted not merely of rules, as legal positivism supposedly held, but of legal principles as well. Whereas rules either did or did not *determine* the outcome to a case and existed in virtue of their social *pedigree*, principles, where they applied, merely *guided* judges in deciding cases and depended in part for their validity on their *content* – specifically and crucially, legal principles had moral content. Thus, unless a judge was faced with an easy case where a rule simply determined the outcome, judges had to appeal to extra-institutional and morally laden principles to resolve legal controversies. As such, Dworkin argued, legality depended in part upon morality.

Now, the accuracy of Dworkin's characterization of legal positivism has been subject to widespread doubt, as has the role that he believes adjudication plays in the explication of the nature of law,[8] but his early criticisms of legal positivism nevertheless spawned a great deal of innovation – even fissure – within that camp, as positivists attempted either to absorb or to deflect Dworkin's various charges (see Section II). Beyond his role as foil, however, Dworkin is due much credit for pointing the way towards a comprehensive account of law's nature that competes with legal positivism, which remains today in some form or another, despite Fuller's and Dworkin's efforts, the dominant position in general jurisprudence.

Notes

1 For synopses of the so-called methodology debate in general jurisprudence, see Julie Dickson, "Methodology in Jurisprudence: A Critical Survey," *Legal Theory* 10, 2004, 117–156, and John Oberdiek and Dennis Patterson, "Moral Evaluation and Conceptual Analysis in Jurisprudential Methodology," in Michael Freeman and Ross Harrison (eds.) *Current Legal Issues: Law and Philosophy*, Oxford: Oxford University Press, 2007, pp. 60–75.

2 John Austin, *The Province of Jurisprudence Determined* (1832), W. E. Rumble (ed.), Cambridge: Cambridge University Press, 1995, p. 157.

3   Brian Leiter has argued powerfully that American legal realism, far from representing a position on the nature of law in competition with legal positivism, in fact presupposes legal positivism. See Brian Leiter, "Legal Realism and Legal Positivism Reconsidered", *Ethics* 111, 2001, 278–301. Nothing here contradicts that interpretation of legal realism.

4   Oliver Wendell Holmes, Jr., "The Path of the Law", p. 17.

5   Ibid., p. 15.

6   Ibid., p. 16.

7   H. L. A. Hart, *The Concept of Law*, Oxford: Oxford University Press, 1961.

8   According to Dworkin, "no firm line divides jurisprudence from adjudication or any other aspect of legal practice." Ronald Dworkin, "Legal Theory and the Problem of Sense", in Ruth Gavison (ed.), *Issues in Contemporary Legal Philosophy*, Oxford: Oxford University Press, 1987, pp. 9–20, p. 14.

Further reading

John Austin, *The Province of Jurisprudence Determined* (1832), W. E. Rumble (ed.), Cambridge: Cambridge University Press, 1995.

Stephen Burton (ed.), *The Path of the Law and its Influence: The Legacy of Oliver Wendell Holmes, Jr.*, New York: Cambridge University Press, 2000.

Julie Dickson, "Methodology in Jurisprudence: A Critical Survey", *Legal Theory* 10, 2004, 117–156.

Ronald Dworkin, *Taking Rights Seriously*, Cambridge, MA: Harvard University Press, 1977.

Ronald Dworkin, "Legal Theory and the Problem of Sense", in Ruth Gavison (ed.), *Issues in Contemporary Legal Philosophy*, Oxford: Oxford University Press, 1987, pp. 9–20.

Lon Fuller, *The Morality of Law*, revised edition, New Haven, CT: Yale University Press, 1964.

P. M. S. Hacker and Joseph Raz (eds) *Law, Morality, and Society: Essays in Honour of H. L. A. Hart*, Oxford: Oxford University Press, 1977.

Hans Kelsen, *The Pure Theory of Law*, Max Knight (trans.), Berkeley, CA: University of California Press, 1967.

Brian Leiter, "Legal Realism and Legal Positivism Reconsidered", *Ethics* 111, 2001, 278–301.

John Oberdiek and Dennis Patterson, "Moral Evaluation and Conceptual Analysis in Jurisprudential Methodology", in Michael Freeman and Ross Harrison (eds), *Current Legal Issues: Law and Philosophy*, Oxford: Oxford University Press, 2007, pp. 60–75.

Scott Shapiro, "The Hart-Dworkin Debate: A Short Guide for the Perplexed", in Arthur Ripstein (ed.), *Ronald Dworkin*, New York: Cambridge University Press, 2007, pp. 22–55.

Questions

1. How is Holmes's view similar to Hart's, and how is it different?
2. In what ways do Hart and Fuller actually disagree about the nature of law, and in what ways do they simply fail to engage with each other's position?
3. Is Hart committed to denying that there are conceptual links between legality and morality?

4. Did the Nazis have law?
5. How might a legal positivist respond to Dworkin's criticisms?
6. Is it fruitful or misguided to approach the question of the nature of law through adjudication, as Dworkin does?

Chapter 1

Oliver Wendell Holmes

THE PATH OF THE LAW[1]

WHEN WE STUDY law we are not studying a mystery but a well known profession. We are studying what we shall want in order to appear before judges, or to advise people in such a way as to keep them out of court. The reason why it is a profession, why people will pay lawyers to argue for them or to advise them, is that in societies like ours the command of the public force is intrusted to the judges in certain cases, and the whole power of the state will be put forth, if necessary, to carry out their judgments and decrees. People want to know under what circumstances and how far they will run the risk of coming against what is so much stronger than themselves, and hence it becomes a business to find out when this danger is to be feared. The object of our study, then, is prediction, the prediction of the incidence of the public force through the instrumentality of the courts.

The means of the study are a body of reports, of treatises, and of statutes, in this country and in England, extending back for six hundred years, and now increasing annually by hundreds. In these sibylline leaves are gathered the scattered prophecies of the past upon the cases in which the axe will fall. These are what properly have been called the oracles of the law. Far the most important and pretty nearly the whole meaning of every new effort of legal thought is to make these prophecies more precise, and to generalize them into a thoroughly connected system. The process is one, from a lawyer's statement of a case, eliminating as it does all the dramatic elements with which his client's story has clothed it, and retaining only the facts of legal import, up to the final analyses and abstract universals of theoretic jurisprudence. The reason why a lawyer does not mention that his client wore a white hat when he made a contract, while Mrs. Quickly would be sure to dwell upon it along with the parcel gilt goblet and the sea-coal fire, is that he foresees that the public force will act in the same way whatever his client had upon his head. It is to make the prophecies easier to be remembered and to be understood that the teachings of the decisions of the past are put into general propositions and gathered into text-books, or that statutes are passed in a general form. The primary rights and duties with which jurisprudence busies itself again are nothing but prophecies. One of the many evil effects of the confusion between legal and moral ideas, about which I shall have something to say in a moment, is that theory is apt to get the cart before the horse, and to consider the right or the duty as something existing apart from and independent of the consequences of its breach, to which certain sanctions are added afterward. But, as I shall try to show, a legal duty so called is nothing but a prediction that if a man does or omits certain things he will be made to suffer in this or that way by judgment of the court;—and so of a legal right.

The number of our predictions when generalized and reduced to a system is not unmanageably large. They present themselves as a finite body of dogma which may be mastered within a reasonable time. It is a great mistake to be frightened by the ever increasing number of reports. The reports of a given jurisdiction in the course of a generation take up pretty much the whole body of the law, and restate it from the present point of view. We could reconstruct the corpus from them if all that went before were burned. The use of the earlier reports is mainly historical, a use about which I shall have something to say before I have finished.

I wish, if I can, to lay down some first principles for the study of this body of dogma or systematized prediction which we call the law, for men who want to use it as the instrument of their business to enable them to prophesy in their turn, and, as bearing upon the study, I wish to point out an ideal which as yet our law has not attained.

The first thing for a business-like understanding of the matter is to understand its limits, and therefore I think it desirable at once to point out and dispel a confusion between morality and law, which sometimes rises to the height of conscious theory, and more often and indeed constantly is making trouble in detail without reaching the point of consciousness. You can see very plainly that a bad man has as much reason as a good one for wishing to avoid an encounter with the public force, and therefore you can see the practical importance of the distinction between morality and law. A man who cares nothing for an ethical rule which is believed and practiced by his neighbors is likely nevertheless to care a good deal to avoid being made to pay money, and will want to keep out of jail if he can.

I take it for granted that no hearer of mine will misinterpret what I have to say as the language of cynicism. The law is the witness and external deposit of our moral life. Its history is the history of the moral development of the race. The practice of it, in spite of popular jests, tends to make good citizens and good men. When I emphasize the difference between law and morals I do so with reference to a single end, that of learning and understanding the law. For that purpose you must definitely master its specific marks, and it is for that that I ask you for the moment to imagine yourselves indifferent to other and greater things.

I do not say that there is not a wider point of view from which the distinction between law and morals becomes of secondary or no importance, as all mathematical distinctions vanish in presence of the infinite. But I do say that that distinction is of the first importance for the object which we are here to consider,—a right study and mastery of the law as a business with well understood limits, a body of dogma enclosed within definite lines. I have just shown the practical reason for saying so. If you want to know the law and nothing else, you must look at it as a bad man, who cares only for the material consequences which such knowledge enables him to predict, not as a good one, who finds his reasons for conduct, whether inside the law or outside of it, in the vaguer sanctions of conscience. The theoretical importance of the distinction is no less, if you would reason on your subject aright. The law is full of phraseology drawn from morals, and by the mere force of language continually invites us to pass from one domain to the other without perceiving it, as we are sure to do unless we have the boundary constantly before our minds. The law talks about rights, and duties, and malice, and intent, and negligence, and so forth, and nothing is easier, or, I may say, more common in legal reasoning, than to take these words in their moral sense, at some stage of the argument, and so to drop into fallacy. For instance, when we speak of the rights of man in a moral sense, we mean to mark the limits of interference with individual freedom which we think are prescribed by conscience, or by our ideal, however reached. Yet it is certain that many laws have been enforced in the past, and it is likely that some are enforced now, which are condemned by the most enlightened opinion of the time, or which at all events pass the limit of interference as many consciences would draw it. Manifestly, therefore, nothing but confusion of thought can result from assuming that the rights of man in a moral sense are equally rights in the sense of the Constitution and the law. No doubt simple and extreme cases can be put of imaginable laws which the statute-making power would not dare to enact, even in the absence of written constitutional prohibitions, because the community would rise in rebellion and fight; and this gives some plausibility to the proposition that the law, if not a part of morality, is limited by it. But this limit of power is not coextensive with any system of morals. For the most part it falls far within the lines of any such system, and in some cases may extend beyond them, for reasons drawn from the habits of a particular people at a particular time. I once heard the late Professor Agassiz say that a German population would rise if you added two cents to the price of a glass of beer. A statute in such a case would be empty words, not because it was wrong, but because it could not be enforced. No one will deny that wrong statutes can be and are enforced, and we should not all agree as to which were the wrong ones.

The confusion with which I am dealing besets confessedly legal conceptions. Take the fundamental question, What constitutes the law? You will find some text writers telling you that it is something different from what is decided by the courts of Massachusetts or England, that it is a system of reason, that it is a deduction from principles of ethics or admitted axioms or what not, which may or may not coincide with the decisions. But if we take the view of our friend the bad man we shall find that he does not care two straws for the axioms or deductions, but that he does want to know what the Massachusetts or English courts are likely to do in fact. I am much of his mind. The prophecies of what the courts will do in fact, and nothing more pretentious, are what I mean by the law.

Take again a notion which as popularly understood is the widest conception which the law contains;—the notion of legal duty, to which already I have referred. We fill the word with all the content which we draw from morals. But what does it mean to a bad man? Mainly, and in the first place, a prophecy that if he does certain things he will be subjected to disagreeable consequences by way of imprisonment or compulsory payment of money. But from his point of view, what is the difference between being fined and being taxed a certain sum for doing a certain thing? That his point of view is the test of legal principles is shown by the many discussions which have arisen in the courts on the very question whether a given statutory liability is a penalty or a tax. On the answer to this question depends the decision whether conduct is legally wrong or right, and also whether a man is under compulsion or free. Leaving the criminal law on one side, what is the difference between the liability under the mill acts or statutes authorizing a taking by eminent domain and the liability for what we call a wrongful conversion of property where restoration is out of the question? In both cases the party taking another man's property has to pay its fair value as assessed by a jury, and no more. What significance is there in calling one taking right and another wrong from the point of view of the law? It does not matter, so far as the given consequence, the compulsory payment, is concerned, whether the act to which it is attached is described in terms of praise or in terms of blame, or whether the law purports to prohibit it or to allow it. If it matters at all, still speaking from the bad man's point of view, it must be because in one case and not in the other some further disadvantages, or at least some further consequences, are attached to the act by the law. The only other disadvantages thus attached to it which I ever have been able to think of are to be found in two somewhat insignificant legal doctrines, both of which might be abolished without much disturbance. One is, that a contract to do a prohibited act is unlawful, and the other, that, if one of two or more joint wrongdoers has to pay all the damages, he cannot recover contribution from his fellows. And that I believe is all. You see how the vague circumference of the notion of duty shrinks and at the same time grows more precise when we wash it with cynical acid and expel everything except the object of our study, the operations of the law.

Nowhere is the confusion between legal and moral ideas more manifest than in the law of contract. Among other things, here again the so called primary rights and duties are invested with a mystic significance beyond what can be assigned and explained. The duty to keep a contract at common law means a prediction that you must pay damages if you do not keep it,—and nothing else. If you commit a tort, you are liable to pay a compensatory sum. If you commit a contract, you are liable to pay a compensatory sum unless the promised event comes to pass, and that is all the difference. But such a mode of looking at the matter stinks in the nostrils of those who think it advantageous to get as much ethics into the law as they can. It was good enough for Lord Coke, however, and here, as in many other cases, I am content to abide with him. In Bromage v. Genning,[2] a prohibition was sought in the King's Bench against a suit in the marches of Wales for the specific performance of a covenant to grant a lease, and Coke said that it would subvert the intention of the covenantor, since he intends it to be at his election either to lose the damages or to make the lease. Sergeant Harris for the plaintiff confessed that he moved the matter against his conscience, and a prohibition was granted. This goes further than we should go now, but it shows what I venture to say has been the common law point of view from the beginning, although Mr. Harriman, in his very able little book upon Contracts has been misled, as I humbly think, to a different conclusion.

I have spoken only of the common law, because there are some cases in which a logical justification can be found for speaking of civil liabilities as imposing duties in an intelligible sense. These are the relatively few in which equity will grant an injunction, and will enforce it by putting the defendant in prison or otherwise punishing him unless he complies with the order of the court. But I hardly think it advisable to shape general theory from the exception, and I think it would be better to cease troubling ourselves about primary rights and sanctions altogether, than to describe our prophecies concerning the liabilities commonly imposed by the law in those inappropriate terms.

I mentioned, as other examples of the use by the law of words drawn from morals, malice, intent, and negligence. It is enough to take malice as it is used in the law of civil liability for wrongs,—what we lawyers call the law of torts,—to show you that it means something different in law from what it means in morals, and also to show how the difference has been obscured by giving to principles which have little or nothing to do with each other the same name. Three hundred years ago a parson preached a sermon and told a story out of Fox's Book of Martyrs of a man who had assisted at the torture of one of the saints, and afterward died, suffering compensatory inward torment. It happened that Fox was wrong. The man was alive and chanced to hear the sermon, and thereupon he sued the parson. Chief Justice Wray instructed the jury that the defendant was not liable, because the story was told innocently, without malice. He took malice in the moral sense, as importing a malevolent motive. But nowadays no one doubts that a man may be liable, without any malevolent motive at all, for false statements manifestly calculated to inflict temporal damage. In stating the case in pleading, we still should call the defendant's conduct malicious; but, in my opinion at least, the word means nothing about motives, or even about the defendant's attitude toward the future, but only signifies that the tendency of his conduct under the known circumstances was very plainly to cause the plaintiff temporal harm.[3]

In the law of contract the use of moral phraseology has led to equal confusion, as I have shown in part already, but only in part. Morals deal with the actual internal state of the individual's mind, what he actually intends. From the time of the Romans down to now, this mode of dealing has affected the language of the law as to contract, and the language used has reacted upon the thought. We talk about a contract as a meeting of the minds of the parties, and thence it is inferred in various cases that there is no contract because their minds have not met; that is, because they have intended different things or because one party has not known of the assent of the other. Yet nothing is more certain than that parties may be bound by a contract to things which neither of them intended, and when one does not know of the other's assent. Suppose a contract is executed in due form and in writing to deliver a lecture, mentioning no time. One of the parties thinks that the promise will be construed to mean at once, within a week. The other thinks that it means when he is ready. The court says that it means within a reasonable time. The parties are bound by the contract as it is interpreted by the court, yet neither of them meant what the court declares that they have said. In my opinion no one will understand the true theory of contract or be able even to discuss some fundamental questions intelligently until he has understood that all contracts are formal, that the making of a contract depends not on the agreement of two minds in one intention, but on the agreement of two sets of external signs,—not on the parties' having *meant* the same thing but on their having *said* the same thing. Furthermore, as the signs may be addressed to one sense or another,—to sight or to hearing,—on the nature of the sign will depend the moment when the contract is made. If the sign is tangible, for instance, a letter, the contract is made when the letter of acceptance is delivered. If it is necessary

that the minds of the parties meet, there will be no contract until the acceptance can be read,—none, for example, if the acceptance be snatched from the hand of the offerer by a third person.

This is not the time to work out a theory in detail, or to answer many obvious doubts and questions which are suggested by these general views. I know of none which are not easy to answer, but what I am trying to do now is only by a series of hints to throw some light on the narrow path of legal doctrine, and upon two pitfalls which, as it seems to me, lie perilously near to it. Of the first of these I have said enough. I hope that my illustrations have shown the danger, both to speculation and to practice, of confounding morality with law, and the trap which legal language lays for us on that side of our way. For my own part, I often doubt whether it would not be a gain if every word of moral significance could be banished from the law altogether, and other words adopted which should convey legal ideas uncolored by anything outside the law. We should lose the fossil records of a good deal of history and the majesty got from ethical associations, but by ridding ourselves of an unnecessary confusion we should gain very much in the clearness of our thought.

So much for the limits of the law. The next thing which I wish to consider is what are the forces which determine its content and its growth. You may assume, with Hobbes and Bentham and Austin, that all law emanates from the sovereign, even when the first human beings to enunciate it are the judges, or you may think that law is the voice of the Zeitgeist, or what you like. It is all one to my present purpose. Even if every decision required the sanction of an emperor with despotic power and a whimsical turn of mind, we should be interested none the less, still with a view to prediction, in discovering some order, some rational explanation, and some principle of growth for the rules which he laid down. In every system there are such explanations and principles to be found. It is with regard to them that a second fallacy comes in, which I think it important to expose.

The fallacy to which I refer is the notion that the only force at work in the development of the law is logic. In the broadest sense, indeed, that notion would be true. The postulate on which we think about the universe is that there is a fixed quantitative relation between every phenomenon and its antecedents and consequents. If there is such a thing as a phenomenon without these fixed quantitative relations, it is a miracle. It is outside the law of cause and effect, and as such transcends our power of thought, or at least is something to or from which we cannot reason. The condition of our thinking about the universe is that it is capable of being thought about rationally, or, in other words, that every part of it is effect and cause in the same sense in which those parts are with which we are most familiar. So in the broadest sense it is true that the law is a logical development, like everything else. The danger of which I speak is not the admission that the principles governing other phenomena also govern the law, but the notion that a given system, ours, for instance, can be worked out like mathematics from some general axioms of conduct. This is the natural error of the schools, but it is not confined to them. I once heard a very eminent judge say that he never let a decision go until he was absolutely sure that it was right. So judicial dissent often is blamed, as if it meant simply that one side or the other were not doing their sums right, and, if they would take more trouble, agreement inevitably would come.

This mode of thinking is entirely natural. The training of lawyers is a training in logic. The processes of analogy, discrimination, and deduction are those in which they are most at home. The language of judicial decision is mainly the language of logic. And the logical method and form flatter that longing for certainty and for repose which is in every human mind. But certainty generally is illusion, and repose is not the destiny of man. Behind the logical form lies a judgment as to the relative worth and importance of competing legislative grounds, often an inarticulate and unconscious judgment, it is true, and yet the very root and nerve of the whole proceeding. You can give any conclusion a logical form. You always can imply a condition in a contract. But why do you imply it? It is because of some belief as to the practice of the community or of a class, or because of some opinion as to policy, or, in short, because of some attitude of yours upon a matter not capable of exact quantitative measurement, and therefore not capable of founding exact logical conclusions. Such matters really are battle grounds where the means do not exist for determinations that shall be good for all time, and where the decision can do no more than embody the preference of a given body in a given time and place. We do not realize how large a part of our law is open to reconsideration upon a slight change in the habit of the public mind. No concrete proposition is self-evident, no matter how ready we may be to accept it, not even Mr. Herbert Spencer's. Every man has a right to do what he wills, provided he interferes not with a like right on the part of his neighbors.

Why is a false and injurious statement privileged, if it is made honestly in giving information about a servant? It is because it has been thought more important that information should be given freely, than that a man should be protected from what under other circumstances would be an actionable wrong. Why is a man at liberty to set up a business which he knows will ruin his neighbor? It is because the public good is supposed to be best subserved by free competition. Obviously such judgments of relative importance may vary in different times and places. Why does a judge instruct a jury that an employer is not liable to an employee for an injury received in the course of his employment unless he is negligent, and why do the jury generally find for the plaintiff if the case is allowed to go to them? It is because the traditional policy of our law is to confine liability to cases where a prudent man might have foreseen the injury, or at least the danger, while the inclination of a very large part of the community is to make certain classes of persons insure the safety of those with whom they deal. Since the last words were written, I have seen the requirement of such insurance put forth as part of the program of one of the best known labor organizations. There is a concealed, half conscious battle on the question of legislative policy, and if any one thinks that it can be settled deductively, or once for all, I only can say that I think he is theoretically wrong, and that I am certain that his conclusion will not be accepted in practice *semper ubique et ab omnibus*.

Indeed, I think that even now our theory upon this matter is open to reconsideration, although I am not prepared to say how I should decide if a reconsideration were proposed. Our law of torts comes from the old days of isolated, ungeneralized wrongs, assaults, slanders, and the like, where the damages might be taken to lie where they fell by legal judgment. But the torts with which our courts are kept busy to-day are mainly the incidents of certain well known businesses. They are injuries to person or property by railroads, factories, and the like. The liability for them is estimated, and sooner or later goes into the price paid by the public. The public really pays the damages, and the question of liability, if pressed far enough, is really the question how far it is desirable that the public should insure the safety of those whose work it uses. It might be said that in such cases the chance of a jury finding for the defendant is merely a chance, once in a while rather arbitrarily interrupting the regular course of recovery, most likely in the case of an unusually conscientious plaintiff, and therefore better done away with. On the other hand, the economic value even of a life to the community can be estimated, and no recovery, it may be said, ought to go beyond that amount. It is conceivable that some day in certain cases we may find ourselves imitating, on a higher plane, the tariff for life and limb which we see in the Leges Barbarorum.

I think that the judges themselves have failed adequately to recognize their duty of weighing considerations of social advantage. The duty is inevitable, and the result of the often proclaimed judicial aversion to deal with such considerations is simply to leave the very ground and foundation of judgments inarticulate, and often unconscious, as I have said. When socialism first began to be talked about, the comfortable classes of the community were a good deal frightened. I suspect that this fear has influenced judicial action both here and in England, yet it is certain that it is not a conscious factor in the decisions to which I refer. I think that something similar has led people who no longer hope to control the legislatures to look to the courts as expounders of the Constitutions, and that in some courts new principles have been discovered outside the bodies of those instruments, which may be generalized into acceptance of the economic doctrines which prevailed about fifty years ago, and a wholesale prohibition of what a tribunal of lawyers does not think about right. I cannot but believe that if the training of lawyers led them habitually to consider more definitely and explicitly the social advantage on which the rule they lay down must be justified, they sometimes would hesitate where now they are confident, and see that really they were taking sides upon debatable and often burning questions.

So much for the fallacy of logical form. Now let us consider the present condition of the law as a subject for study, and the ideal toward which it tends. We still are far from the point of view which I desire to see reached. No one has reached it or can reach it as yet. We are only at the beginning of a philosophical reaction, and of a reconsideration of the worth of doctrines which for the most part still are taken for granted without any deliberate, conscious, and systematic questioning of their grounds. The development of our law has gone on for nearly a thousand years, like the development of a plant, each generation taking the inevitable next step, mind, like matter, simply obeying a law of spontaneous growth. It is perfectly natural and right that it should have been so. Imitation is a necessity of human nature, as has been illustrated by a remarkable French writer, M. Tarde, in an admirable book, "Les Lois de l'Imitation." Most of the things we do, we do for no better reason than that our fathers have done them or that our neighbors do them, and the same is true of a larger part than we suspect of what we think. The reason is a good one, because our short life gives us no time for a better, but it is not the best. It does not follow, because we all are compelled to take on faith at second hand most of the rules on which we base our action and our thought, that each of us may not try to set some corner of his world in the order of reason, or that all of us collectively should not aspire to carry reason as far as it will go throughout the whole domain. In regard to the law, it is true, no doubt, that an evolutionist will hesitate to affirm universal validity for his social ideals, or for the principles which he thinks should be embodied in legislation. He is content if he can prove them best for here and now. He may be ready to admit that he knows nothing about an absolute best in the cosmos, and even that he knows next to nothing about a permanent best for men. Still it is true that a body of law is more rational and more civilized when every rule it contains is referred articulately and definitely to an end which it subserves, and when the grounds for desiring that end are stated or are ready to be stated in words.

At present, in very many cases, if we want to know why a rule of law has taken its particular shape, and more or less if we want to know why it exists at all, we go to tradition. We follow it into the Year Books, and perhaps beyond them to the customs of the Salian Franks, and somewhere in the past, in the German forests, in the needs of Norman kings, in the assumptions of a dominant class, in the absence of generalized ideas, we find out the practical motive for what now best is justified by the mere fact of its acceptance and that men are accustomed to it. The rational study of law is still to a large extent the study of history. History must be a part of the study, because without it we cannot know the precise scope of rules which it is our business to know. It is a part of the rational study, because it is the first step toward an enlightened scepticism, that is, toward a deliberate reconsideration of the worth of those rules. When you get the dragon out of his cave on to the plain and in the daylight, you can count his teeth and claws, and see just what is his strength. But to get him out is only the first step. The next is either to kill him, or to tame him and make him a useful animal. For the rational study of the law the black-letter man may be the man of the present, but the man of the future is the man of statistics and the master of economics. It is revolting to have no better reason for a rule of law than that so it was laid down in the time of Henry IV. It is still more revolting if the grounds upon which it was laid down have vanished long since, and the rule simply persists from blind imitation of the past. I am thinking of the technical rule as to trespass *ab initio*, as it is called, which I attempted to explain in a recent Massachusetts case.[4] . . .

I look forward to a time when the part played by history in the explanation of dogma shall be very small, and instead of ingenious research we shall spend our energy on a study of the ends sought to be attained and the reasons for desiring them. As a step toward that ideal it seems to me that every lawyer ought to seek an understanding of economics. The present divorce between the schools of political economy and law seems to me an evidence of how much progress in philosophical study still remains to be made. In the present state of political economy, indeed, we come again upon history on a larger scale, but there we are called on to consider and weigh the ends of legislation, the means of attaining them, and the cost. We learn that for everything we have to give up something else, and we are taught to set the advantage we gain against the other advantage we lose, and to know what we are doing when we elect.

There is another study which sometimes is undervalued by the practical minded, for which I wish to say a good word, although I think a good deal of pretty poor stuff goes under that name. I mean the study of what is called jurisprudence. Jurisprudence, as I look at it, is simply law in its most generalized part. Every effort to reduce a case to a rule is an effort of jurisprudence, although the name as used in English is confined to the broadest rules and most fundamental conceptions. One mark of a great lawyer is that he sees the application of the broadest rules. There is a story of a Vermont justice of the peace before whom a suit was brought by one farmer against another for breaking a churn. The justice took time to consider, and then said that he had looked through the statutes and could find nothing about churns, and gave judgment for the defendant. The same state of mind is shown in all our common digests and text-books. Applications of rudimentary rules of contract or tort are tucked away under the head of Railroads or Telegraphs or go to swell treatises on historical subdivisions, such as Shipping or Equity, or are gathered under an arbitrary title which is thought likely to appeal to the practical mind, such as Mercantile Law. If a man goes into law it pays to be a master of it, and to be a master of it means to look straight through all the dramatic incidents and to discern the true basis for prophecy. Therefore, it is well to have an accurate notion of what you mean by law, by a right, by a duty, by malice, intent, and negligence, by ownership, by possession, and so forth. . . .

We cannot all be Descartes or Kant, but we all want happiness. And happiness, I am sure from having known many successful men, cannot be won simply by being counsel for great corporations and having an income of fifty thousand dollars. An intellect great enough to win the prize needs other food beside success. The remoter and more general aspects of the law are those which give it universal interest. It is through them that you not only become a great master in your calling, but connect your subject with the universe and catch an echo of the infinite, a glimpse of its unfathomable process, a hint of the universal law.

Notes

1   Excerpted from 10 *Harvard Law Review* 457 (1897).
2   1 Roll. Rep. 368.
3   See Hanson v. Globe Newspaper Co., 159 Mass. 293, 302.
4   Commonwealth v. Rubin, 165 Mass. 453.

Chapter 2

H. L. A. Hart

POSITIVISM AND THE SEPARATION OF LAW AND MORALS

IN THIS ARTICLE I shall discuss and attempt to defend a view which Mr. Justice Holmes, among others, held and for which he and they have been much criticized. But I wish first to say why I think that Holmes, whatever the vicissitudes of his American reputation may be, will always remain for Englishmen a heroic figure in jurisprudence. This will be so because he magically combined two qualities: one of them is imaginative power, which English legal thinking has often lacked; the other is clarity, which English legal thinking usually possesses. The English lawyer who turns to read Holmes is made to see that what he had taken to be settled and stable is really always on the move. To make this discovery with Holmes is to be with a guide whose words may leave you unconvinced, sometimes even repelled, but never mystified. Like our own Austin, with whom Holmes shared many ideals and thoughts, Holmes was sometimes clearly wrong; but again like Austin, when this was so he was always wrong clearly. This surely is a sovereign virtue in jurisprudence. Clarity I know is said not to be enough; this may be true, but there are still questions in jurisprudence where the issues are confused because they are discussed in a style which Holmes would have spurned for its obscurity. Perhaps this is inevitable: jurisprudence trembles so uncertainly on the margin of many subjects that there will always be need for someone, in Bentham's phrase, "to pluck the mask of Mystery" from its face.[1] This is true, to a preeminent degree, of the subject of this article. Contemporary voices tell us we must recognize something obscured by the legal "positivists" whose day is now over: that there is a "point of intersection between law and morals,"[2] or that what *is* and what *ought* to be are somehow indissolubly fused or inseparable,[3] though the positivists denied it. What do these phrases mean? Or rather which of the many things that they *could* mean, *do* they mean? Which of them do "positivists" deny and why is it wrong to do so?

I.

I shall present the subject as part of the history of an idea. At the close of the eighteenth century and the beginning of the nineteenth the most earnest thinkers in England about legal and social problems and the architects of great reforms were the great Utilitarians. Two of them, Bentham and Austin, constantly insisted on the need to distinguish, firmly and with the maximum of clarity, law as it is from law as it ought to be. This theme haunts their work, and they condemned the natural-law thinkers precisely because they had blurred this apparently simple but vital distinction. By contrast, at the present time in this country and to a lesser extent in England, this separation between law and morals is held to be superficial and wrong. Some critics have thought that it blinds men to the true nature of law and its roots in social life.[4] Others have thought it not only intellectually misleading but corrupting in practice, at its worst apt to weaken resistance to state tyranny or absolutism,[5] and at its best apt to bring law into disrespect. The nonpejorative name "Legal Positivism," like most terms which are used as missiles in intellectual battles, has come to stand for a baffling multitude of different sins. One of them is the sin, real or alleged, of insisting, as Austin and Bentham did, on the separation of law as it is and law as it ought to be.

How then has this reversal of the wheel come about? What are the theoretical errors in this distinction? Have the practical consequences of stressing the distinction as Bentham and Austin did been bad? Should we now reject it or keep it? In considering these questions we should recall the social philosophy which went along with the Utilitarians' insistence on this distinction. They stood firmly but on their own utilitarian ground for all the principles of liberalism in law and government. No one has ever combined, with such even-minded sanity as the Utilitarians, the passion for reform with respect for law together with a due recognition of the need to control the abuse of power even when power is in the hands of reformers. One by one in Bentham's works you can identify the elements of the *Rechtstaat* and all the principles for the defense of which the terminology of natural law has in our day been revived. Here are liberty of speech, and of press, the right of association,[6] the need that laws should be published and made widely known before they are enforced,[7] the need to control administrative agencies,[8] the insistence that there should be no criminal liability without fault,[9] and the importance of the principle of legality, *nulla poena sine lege*.[10] Some, I know, find the political and moral insight of the Utilitarians a very simple one, but we should not mistake this simplicity for superficiality nor forget how favorably their simplicities compare with the profundities of other thinkers. Take only one example: Bentham on slavery. He says the

question at issue is not whether those who are held as slaves can reason, but simply whether they suffer.[11] Does this not compare well with the discussion of the question in terms of whether or not there are some men whom Nature has fitted only to be the living instruments of others? We owe it to Bentham more than anyone else that we have stopped discussing this and similar questions of social policy in that form.

So Bentham and Austin were not dry analysts fiddling with verbal distinctions while cities burned, but were the vanguard of a movement which laboured with passionate intensity and much success to bring about a better society and better laws. Why then did they insist on the separation of law as it is and law as it ought to be? What did they mean? Let us first see what they said. Austin formulated the doctrine:

The existence of law is one thing; its merit or demerit is another. Whether it be or be not is one enquiry; whether it be or be not conformable to an assumed standard, is a different enquiry. A law, which actually exists, is a law, though we happen to dislike it, or though it vary from the text, by which we regulate our approbation and disapprobation. This truth, when formally announced as an abstract proposition, is so simple and glaring that it seems idle to insist upon it. But simple and glaring as it is, when enunciated in abstract expressions the enumeration of the instances in which it has been forgotten would fill a volume.

Sir William Blackstone, for example, says in his "Commentaries," that the laws of God are superior in obligation to all other laws; that no human laws should be suffered to contradict them; that human laws are of no validity if contrary to them; and that all valid laws derive their force from that Divine original.

Now, he *may* mean that all human laws ought to conform to the Divine laws. If this be his meaning, I assent to it without hesitation. . . . Perhaps, again, he means that human lawgivers are themselves obliged by the Divine laws to fashion the laws which they impose by that ultimate standard, because if they do not, God will punish them. To this also I entirely assent. . . .

But the meaning of this passage of Blackstone, if it has a meaning, seems rather to be this: that no human law which conflicts with the Divine law is obligatory or binding; in other words, that no human law which conflicts with the Divine law *is a law.* . . .[12]

Austin's protest against blurring the distinction between what law is and what it ought to be is quite general: it is a mistake, whatever our standard of what ought to be, whatever "the text by which we regulate our approbation or disapprobation." His examples, however, are always a confusion between law as it is and law as morality would require it to be. For him, it must be remembered, the fundamental principles of morality were God's commands, to which utility was an "index": besides this there was the actual accepted morality of a social group or "positive" morality.

Bentham insisted on this distinction without characterizing morality by reference to God but only, of course, by reference to the principles of utility. Both thinkers' prime reason for this insistence was to enable men to see steadily the precise issues posed by the existence of morally bad laws, and to understand the specific character of the authority of a legal order. Bentham's general recipe for life under the government of laws was simple: it was "*to obey punctually; to censure freely.*"[13] But Bentham was especially aware, as an anxious spectator of the French revolution, that this was not enough: the time might come in any society when the law's commands were so evil that the question of resistance had to be faced, and it was then essential that the issues at stake at this point should neither be oversimplified nor obscured.[14] Yet, this was precisely what the

confusion between law and morals had done and Bentham found that the confusion had spread symmetrically in two different directions. On the one hand Bentham had in mind the anarchist who argues thus: "This ought not to be the law, therefore it is not and I am free not merely to censure but to disregard it." On the other hand he thought of the reactionary who argues: "This is the law, therefore it is what it ought to be," and thus stifles criticism at its birth. Both errors, Bentham thought, were to be found in Blackstone: there was his incautious statement that human laws were invalid if contrary to the law of God,[15] and "that spirit of obsequious *quietism* that seems constitutional in our Author" which "will scarce ever let him recognise a difference" between what is and what ought to be.[16] This indeed was for Bentham the occupational disease of lawyers: "[I]n the eyes of lawyers—not to speak of their dupes—that is to say, as yet, the generality of non-lawyers— the *is* and *ought to be* . . . were one and indivisible."[17] There are therefore two dangers between which insistence on this distinction will help us to steer: the danger that law and its authority may be dissolved in man's conceptions of what law ought to be and the danger that the existing law may supplant morality as a final test of conduct and so escape criticism.

In view of later criticisms it is also important to distinguish several things that the Utilitarians did not mean by insisting on their separation of law and morals. They certainly accepted many of the things that might be called "the intersection of law and morals." First, they never denied that, as a matter of historical fact, the development of legal systems had been powerfully influenced by moral opinion, and, conversely, that moral standards had been profoundly influenced by law, so that the content of many legal rules mirrored moral rules or principles. It is not in fact always easy to trace this historical causal connection, but Bentham was certainly ready to admit its existence; so too Austin spoke of the "frequent coincidence"[18] of positive law and morality and attributed the confusion of what law is with what law ought to be to this very fact.

Secondly, neither Bentham nor his followers denied that by explicit legal provisions moral principles might at different points be brought into a legal system and form part of its rules, or that courts might be legally bound to decide in accordance with what they thought just or best. Bentham indeed recognized, as Austin did not, that even the supreme legislative power might be subjected to legal restraints by a constitution[19] and would not have denied that moral principles, like those of the fifth amendment, might form the content of such legal constitutional restraints. Austin differed in thinking that restraints on the supreme legislative power could not have the force of law, but would remain merely political or moral checks;[20] but of course he would have recognized that a statute, for example, might confer a delegated legislative power and restrict the area of its exercise by reference to moral principles.

What both Bentham and Austin were anxious to assert were the following two simple things: first, in the absence of an expressed constitutional or legal provision, it could not follow from the mere fact that a rule violated standards of morality that it was not a rule of law; and, conversely, it could not follow from the mere fact that a rule was morally desirable that it was a rule of law.

The history of this simple doctrine in the nineteenth century is too long and too intricate to trace here. Let me summarize it by saying that after it was propounded to the world by Austin it dominated English jurisprudence and constitutes part of the framework of most of those curiously English and perhaps unsatisfactory productions—the omnibus surveys of the whole field of jurisprudence. A succession of these were published after a full text of Austin's lectures finally appeared in 1863. In each of them the utilitarian separation of law and morals is treated as something that enables lawyers to attain a new clarity. Austin was said by one of his

English successors, Amos, "to have delivered the law from the dead body of morality that still clung to it";[21] and even Maine, who was critical of Austin at many points, did not question this part of his doctrine. In the United States men like N. St. John Green,[22] Gray, and Holmes considered that insistence on this distinction had enabled the understanding of law as a means of social control to get off to a fruitful new start; they welcomed it both as self-evident and as illuminating—as a revealing tautology. This distinction is, of course, one of the main themes of Holmes' most famous essay "The Path of the Law,"[23] but the place it had in the estimation of these American writers is best seen in what Gray wrote at the turn of the century in *The Nature and Sources of the Law*. He said:

> The great gain in its fundamental conceptions which Jurisprudence made during the last century was the recognition of the truth that the Law of a State . . . is not an ideal, but something which actually exists. . . . [I]t is not that which ought to be, but that which is. To fix this definitely in the Jurisprudence of the Common Law, is the feat that Austin accomplished.[24]

II.

So much for the doctrine in the heyday of its success. Let us turn now to some of the criticisms. Undoubtedly, when Bentham and Austin insisted on the distinction between law as it is and as it ought to be, they had in mind *particular* laws the meanings of which were clear and so not in dispute, and they were concerned to argue that such laws, even if morally outrageous, were still laws. It is, however, necessary, in considering the criticisms which later developed, to consider more than those criticisms which were directed to this particular point if we are to get at the root of the dissatisfaction felt; we must also take account of the objection that, even if what the Utilitarians said on this particular point were true, their insistence on it, in a terminology suggesting a general cleavage between what is and ought to be law, obscured the fact that at other points there is an essential point of contact between the two. So in what follows I shall consider not only criticisms of the particular point which the Utilitarians had in mind, but also the claim that an essential connection between law and morals emerges if we examine how laws, the meanings of which are in dispute, are interpreted and applied in concrete cases; and that this connection emerges again if we widen our point of view and ask, not whether every particular rule of law must satisfy a moral minimum in order to be a law, but whether a system of rules which altogether failed to do this could be a legal system.

There is, however, one major initial complexity by which criticism has been much confused. We must remember that the Utilitarians combined with their insistence on the separation of law and morals two other equally famous but distinct doctrines. One was the important truth that a purely analytical study of legal concepts, a study of the meaning of the distinctive vocabulary of the law, was as vital to our understanding of the nature of law as historical or sociological studies, though of course it could not supplant them. The other doctrine was the famous imperative theory of law—that law is essentially a command.

These three doctrines constitute the utilitarian tradition in jurisprudence; yet they are distinct doctrines. It is possible to endorse the separation between law and morals and to value analytical inquiries into the meaning of legal concepts and yet think it wrong to conceive of law as essentially a command. One source of great confusion in the criticism of the separation of law and morals was the belief that the falsity of any one of these three doctrines in the utilitarian tradition showed the other two to be false; what was worse was the failure to see that there were three quite separate doctrines in this tradition. The indiscriminate use of the label "positivism"

to designate ambiguously each one of these three separate doctrines (together with some others which the Utilitarians never professed) has perhaps confused the issue more than any other single factor.[25] Some of the early American critics of the Austinian doctrine were, however, admirably clear on just this matter. Gray, for example, added at the end of the tribute to Austin, which I have already quoted, the words, "He may have been wrong in treating the Law of the State as being the command of the sovereign"[26] and he touched shrewdly on many points where the command theory is defective. But other critics have been less clearheaded and have thought that the inadequacies of the command theory which gradually came to light were sufficient to demonstrate the falsity of the separation of law and morals.

This was a mistake, but a natural one. To see how natural it was we must look a little more closely at the command idea. The famous theory that law is a command was a part of a wider and more ambitious claim. Austin said that the notion of a command was "the *key* to the sciences of jurisprudence and morals,"[27] and contemporary attempts to elucidate moral judgments in terms of "imperative" or "prescriptive" utterances echo this ambitious claim. But the command theory, viewed as an effort to identify even the quintessence of law, let alone the quintessence of morals, seems breathtaking in its simplicity and quite inadequate. There is much, even in the simplest legal system, that is distorted if presented as a command. Yet the Utilitarians thought that the essence of a legal system could be conveyed if the notion of a command were supplemented by that of a habit of obedience. The simple scheme was this: What is a command? It is simply an expression by one person of the desire that another person should do or abstain from some action, accompanied by a threat of punishment which is likely to follow disobedience. Commands are laws if two conditions are satisfied: first, they must be general; second, they must be commanded by what (as both Bentham and Austin claimed) exists in every political society whatever its constitutional form, namely, a person or a group of persons who are in receipt of habitual obedience from most of the society but pay no such obedience to others. These persons are its sovereign. Thus law is the command of the uncommanded commanders of society—the creation of the legally untrammelled will of the sovereign who is by definition outside the law.

It is easy to see that this account of a legal system is threadbare. One can also see why it might seem that its inadequacy is due to the omission of some essential connection with morality. The situation which the simple trilogy of command, sanction, and sovereign avails to describe, if you take these notions at all precisely, is like that of a gunman saying to his victim, "Give me your money or your life." The only difference is that in the case of a legal system the gunman says it to a large number of people who are accustomed to the racket and habitually surrender to it. Law surely is not the gunman situation writ large, and legal order is surely not to be thus simply identified with compulsion.

This scheme, despite the points of obvious analogy between a statute and a command, omits some of the most characteristic elements of law. Let me cite a few. It is wrong to think of a legislature (and a fortiori an electorate) with a changing membership, as a group of persons habitually obeyed: this simple idea is suited only to a monarch sufficiently long-lived for a "habit" to grow up. Even if we waive this point, nothing which legislators do makes law unless they comply with fundamental accepted rules specifying the essential lawmaking procedures. This is true even in a system having a simple unitary constitution like the British. These fundamental accepted rules specifying what the legislature must do to legislate are not commands habitually obeyed, nor can they be expressed as habits of obedience to persons. They lie at the root of a legal system, and what is most missing in the utilitarian scheme is an analysis of what it is for a

social group and its officials to accept such rules. This notion, not that of a command as Austin claimed, is the "key to the science of jurisprudence," or at least one of the keys.

Again, Austin, in the case of a democracy, looked past the legislators to the electorate as "the sovereign" (or in England as part of it). He thought that in the United States the mass of the electors to the state and federal legislatures were the sovereign whose commands, given by their "agents" in the legislatures, were law. But on this footing the whole notion of the sovereign outside the law being "habitually obeyed" by the "bulk" of the population must go: for in this case the "bulk" obeys the bulk, that is, it obeys itself. Plainly the general acceptance of the authority of a lawmaking procedure, irrespective of the changing individuals who operate it from time to time, can be only distorted by an analysis in terms of mass habitual obedience to certain persons who are by definition outside the law, just as the cognate but much simpler phenomenon of the general social acceptance of a rule, say of taking off the hat when entering a church, would be distorted if represented as habitual obedience by the mass to specific persons.

Other critics dimly sensed a further and more important defect in the command theory, yet blurred the edge of an important criticism by assuming that the defect was due to the failure to insist upon some important connection between law and morals. This more radical defect is as follows. The picture that the command theory draws of life under law is essentially a simple relationship of the commander to the commanded, of superior to inferior, of top to bottom; the relationship is vertical between the commanders or authors of the law conceived of as essentially outside the law and those who are commanded and subject to the law. In this picture no place, or only an accidental or subordinate place, is afforded for a distinction between types of legal rules which are in fact radically different. Some laws require men to act in certain ways or to abstain from acting whether they wish to or not. The criminal law consists largely of rules of this sort: like commands they are simply "obeyed" or "disobeyed." But other legal rules are presented to society in quite different ways and have quite different functions. They provide facilities more or less elaborate for individuals to create structures of rights and duties for the conduct of life within the coercive framework of the law. Such are the rules enabling individuals to make contracts, wills, and trusts, and generally to mould their legal relations with others. Such rules, unlike the criminal law, are not factors designed to obstruct wishes and choices of an antisocial sort. On the contrary, these rules provide facilities for the realization of wishes and choices. They do not say (like commands) "do this whether you wish it or not," but rather "if you wish to do this, here is the way to do it." Under these rules we exercise powers, make claims, and assert rights. These phrases mark off characteristic features of laws that confer rights and powers; they are laws which are, so to speak, put at the disposition of individuals in a way in which the criminal law is not. Much ingenuity has gone into the task of "reducing" laws of this second sort to some complex variant of laws of the first sort. The effort to show that laws conferring rights are "really" only conditional stipulations of sanctions to be exacted from the person ultimately under a legal duty characterizes much of Kelsen's work.[28] Yet to urge this is really just to exhibit dogmatic determination to suppress one aspect of the legal system in order to maintain the theory that the stipulation of a sanction, like Austin's command, represents the quintessence of law. One might as well urge that the rules of baseball were "really" only complex conditional directions to the scorer and that this showed their real or "essential" nature.

One of the first jurists in England to break with the Austinian tradition, Salmond, complained that the analysis in terms of commands left the notion of a right unprovided with a place.[29] But he confused the point. He argued

first, and correctly, that if laws are merely commands it is inexplicable that we should have come to speak of legal rights and powers as conferred or arising under them, but then wrongly concluded that the rules of a legal system must necessarily be connected with moral rules or principles of justice and that only on this footing could the phenomenon of legal rights be explained. Otherwise, Salmond thought, we would have to say that a mere "verbal coincidence" connects the concepts of legal and moral right. Similarly, continental critics of the Utilitarians, always alive to the complexity of the notion of a subjective right, insisted that the command theory gave it no place. Hägerström insisted that if laws were merely commands the notion of an individual's right was really inexplicable, for commands are, as he said, something which we either obey or we do not obey; they do not confer rights.[30] But he, too, concluded that moral, or, as he put it, commonsense, notions of justice must therefore be necessarily involved in the analysis of any legal structure elaborate enough to confer rights.[31]

Yet, surely these arguments are confused. Rules that confer rights, thought distinct from commands, need not be moral rules or coincide with them. Rights, after all, exist under the rules of ceremonies, games, and in many other spheres regulated by rules which are irrelevant to the question of justice or what the law ought to be. Nor need rules which confer rights be just or morally good rules. The rights of a master over his slaves show us that. "Their merit or demerit," as Austin termed it, depends on how rights are distributed in society and over whom or what they are exercised. These critics indeed revealed the inadequacy of the simple notions of command and habit for the analysis of law; at many points it is apparent that the social acceptance of a rule or standard of authority (even if it is motivated only by fear or superstition or rests on inertia) must be brought into the analysis and cannot itself be reduced to the two simple terms. Yet nothing in this showed the utilitarian insistence on the distinction between the existence of law and its "merits" to be wrong.

III.

I now turn to a distinctively American criticism of the separation of the law that is from the law that ought to be. It emerged from the critical study of the judicial process with which American jurisprudence has been on the whole so beneficially occupied. The most skeptical of these critics—the loosely named "Realists" of the 1930's—perhaps too naïvely accepted the conceptual framework of the natural sciences as adequate for the characterization of law and for the analysis of rule-guided action of which a living system of law at least partly consists. But they opened men's eyes to what actually goes on when courts decide cases, and the contrast they drew between the actual facts of judicial decision and the traditional terminology for describing it as if it were a wholly logical operation was usually illuminating; for in spite of some exaggeration the "Realists" made us acutely conscious of one cardinal feature of human language and human thought, emphasis on which is vital not only for the understanding of law but in areas of philosophy far beyond the confines of jurisprudence. The insight of this school may be presented in the following example. A legal rule forbids you to take a vehicle into the public park. Plainly this forbids an automobile, but what about bicycles, roller skates, toy automobiles? What about airplanes? Are these, as we say, to be called "vehicles" for the purpose of the rule or not? If we are to communicate with each other at all, and if, as in the most elementary form of law, we are to express our intentions that a certain type of behavior be regulated by rules, then the general words we use—like "vehicle" in the case I consider—must have some standard instance in which no doubts are felt about its application. There must be a core of settled meaning, but there will be, as well, a penumbra of debatable

cases in which words are neither obviously applicable nor obviously ruled out. These cases will each have some features in common with the standard case; they will lack others or be accompanied by features not present in the standard case. Human invention and natural processes continually throw up such variants on the familiar, and if we are to say that these ranges of facts do or do not fall under existing rules, then the classifier must make a decision which is not dictated to him, for the facts and phenomena to which we fit our words and apply our rules are as it were *dumb*. The toy automobile cannot speak up and say, "I am a vehicle for the purpose of this legal rule," nor can the roller skates chorus, "We are not a vehicle." Fact situations do not await us neatly labeled, creased, and folded, nor is their legal classification written on them to be simply read off by the judge. Instead, in applying legal rules, someone must take the responsibility of deciding that words do or do not cover some case in hand with all the practical consequences involved in this decision.

We may call the problems which arise outside the hard core of standard instances or settled meaning "problems of the penumbra"; they are always with us whether in relation to such trivial things as the regulation of the use of the public park or in relation to the multidimensional generalities of a constitution. If a penumbra of uncertainty must surround all legal rules, then their application to specific cases in the penumbral area cannot be a matter of logical deduction, and so deductive reasoning, which for generations has been cherished as the very perfection of human reasoning, cannot serve as a model for what judges, or indeed anyone, should do in bringing particular cases under general rules. In this area men cannot live by deduction alone. And it follows that if legal arguments and legal decisions of penumbral questions are to be rational, their rationality must lie in something other than a logical relation to premises. So if it is rational or "sound" to argue and to decide that for the purposes of this rule an airplane is not a vehicle, this argument must be sound or rational without being logically conclusive. What is it then that makes such decisions correct or at least better than alternative decisions? Again, it seems true to say that the criterion which makes a decision sound in such cases is some concept of what the law ought to be; it is easy to slide from that into saying that it must be a moral judgment about what law ought to be. So here we touch upon a point of necessary "intersection between law and morals" which demonstrates the falsity or, at any rate, the misleading character of the Utilitarians' emphatic insistence on the separation of law as it is and ought to be. Surely, Bentham and Austin could only have written as they did because they misunderstood or neglected this aspect of the judicial process, because they ignored the problems of the penumbra.

The misconception of the judicial process which ignores the problems of the penumbra and which views the process as consisting pre-eminently in deductive reasoning is often stigmatized as the error of "formalism" or "literalism." My question now is, how and to what extent does the demonstration of this error show the utilitarian distinction to be wrong or misleading? Here there are many issues which have been confused, but I can only disentangle some. The charge of formalism has been leveled both at the "positivist" legal theorist and at the courts, but of course it must be a very different charge in each case. Leveled at the legal theorist, the charge means that he has made a theoretical mistake about the character of legal decision; he has thought of the reasoning involved as consisting in deduction from premises in which the judges' practical choices or decisions play no part. It would be easy to show that Austin was guiltless of this error; only an entire misconception of what analytical jurisprudence is and why he thought it important has led to the view that he, or any other analyst, believed that the law was a closed logical system in which judges deduced their decisions from premises.[32] On the contrary,

he was very much alive to the character of language, to its vagueness or open character;[33] he thought that in the penumbral situation judges must necessarily legislate,[34] and, in accents that sometimes recall those of the late Judge Jerome Frank, he berated the common-law judges for legislating feebly and timidly and for blindly relying on real or fancied analogies with past cases instead of adapting their decisions to the growing needs of society as revealed by the moral standard of utility.[35] The villains of this piece, responsible for the conception of the judge as an automaton, are not the Utilitarian thinkers. The responsibility, if it is to be laid at the door of any theorist, is with thinkers like Blackstone and, at an earlier stage, Montesquieu. The root of this evil is preoccupation with the separation of powers and Blackstone's "childish fiction" (as Austin termed it) that judges only "find," never "make," law.

But we are concerned with "formalism" as a vice not of jurists but of judges. What precisely is it for a judge to commit this error, to be a "formalist," "automatic," a "slot machine"? Curiously enough the literature which is full of the denunciation of these vices never makes this clear in concrete terms; instead we have only descriptions which cannot mean what they appear to say: it is said that in the formalist error courts make an excessive use of logic, take a thing to "a dryly logical extreme,"[36] or make an excessive use of analytical methods. But just how in being a formalist does a judge make an excessive use of logic? It is clear that the essence of his error is to give some general term an interpretation which is blind to social values and consequences (or which is in some other way stupid or perhaps merely disliked by critics). But logic does not prescribe interpretation of terms; it dictates neither the stupid nor intelligent interpretation of any expression. Logic only tells you hypothetically that if you give a certain term a certain interpretation then a certain conclusion follows. Logic is silent on how to classify particulars—and this is the heart of a judicial decision.

So this reference to logic and to logical extremes is a misnomer for something else, which must be this. A judge has to apply a rule to a concrete case—perhaps the rule that one may not take a stolen "vehicle" across state lines, and in this case an airplane has been taken.[37] He either does not see or pretends not to see that the general terms of this rule are susceptible of different interpretations and that he has a choice left open uncontrolled by linguistic conventions. He ignores, or is blind to, the fact that he is in the area of the penumbra and is not dealing with a standard case. Instead of choosing in the light of social aims, the judge fixes the meaning in a different way. He either takes the meaning that the word most obviously suggests in its ordinary nonlegal context to ordinary men, or one which the word has been given in some other legal context, or, still worse, he thinks of a standard case and then arbitrarily identifies certain features in it—for example, in the case of a vehicle, (1) normally used on land, (2) capable of carrying a human person, (3) capable of being self-propelled—and treats these three as always necessary and always sufficient conditions for the use in all contexts of the word "vehicle," irrespective of the social consequences of giving it this interpretation. This choice, not "logic," would force the judge to include a toy motor car (if electrically propelled) and to exclude bicycles and the airplane. In all this there is possibly great stupidity but no more "logic," and no less, than in cases in which the interpretation given to a general term and the consequent application of some general rule to a particular case is consciously controlled by some identified social aim.

Decisions made in a fashion as blind as this would scarcely deserve the name of decisions; we might as well toss a penny in applying a rule of law. But it is at least doubtful whether any judicial decisions (even in England) have been quite as automatic as this. Rather, either the interpretations stigmatized as automatic have resulted from the conviction that it is fairer in a criminal statute to take a meaning which would jump to the mind of the ordinary man at the cost even of defeating other values, and this itself is a social policy (though possibly a bad one); or much more frequently, what is stigmatized as "mechanical" and "automatic" is a determined choice made indeed in the light of a social aim but of a conservative social aim. Certainly many of the Supreme Court decisions at the turn of the century which have been so stigmatized[38] represent clear choices in the penumbral area to give effect to a policy of a conservative type. This is peculiarly true of Mr. Justice Peckham's opinions defining the spheres of police power and due process.[39]

But how does the wrongness of deciding cases in an automatic and mechanical way and the rightness of deciding cases by reference to social purposes show that the utilitarian insistence on the distinction between what the law is and what it ought to be is wrong? I take it that no one who wished to use these vices of formalism as proof that the distinction between what is and what ought to be is mistaken would deny that the decisions stigmatized as automatic are law; nor would he deny that the system in which such automatic decisions are made is a legal system. Surely he would say that they are law, but they are bad law, they ought not to be law. But this would be to use the distinction, not to refute it; and of course both Bentham and Austin used it to attack judges for failing to decide penumbral cases in accordance with the growing needs of society.

Clearly, if the demonstration of the errors of formalism is to show the utilitarian distinction to be wrong, the point must be drastically restated. The point must be not merely that a judicial decision to be rational must be made in the light of some conception of what ought to be, but that the aims, the social policies and purposes to which judges should appeal if their decisions are to be rational, are themselves to be considered as part of the law in some suitably wide sense of "law" which is held to be more illuminating than that used by the Utilitarians. This restatement of the point would have the following consequence: instead of saying that the recurrence of penumbral questions shows us that legal rules are essentially incomplete, and that, when they fail to determine decisions, judges must legislate and so exercise a creative choice between alternatives, we shall say that the social policies which guide the judges' choice are in a sense there for them to discover; the judges are only "drawing out" of the rule what, if it is properly understood, is "latent" within it. To call this judicial legislation is to obscure some essential continuity between the clear cases of the rule's application and the penumbral decisions. I shall question later whether this way of talking is salutary, but I wish at this time to point out something obvious, but likely, if not stated, to tangle the issues. It does not follow that, because the opposite of a decision reached blindly in the formalist or literalist manner is a decision intelligently reached by reference to some conception of what ought to be, we have a junction of law and morals. We must, I think, beware of thinking in a too simple-minded fashion about the word "ought." This is not because there is no distinction to be made between law as it is and ought to be. Far from it. It is because the distinction should be between what is and what from many different points of view ought to be. The word "ought" merely reflects the presence of some standard of criticism; one of these standards is a moral standard but not all standards are moral. We say to our neighbour, "You ought not to lie," and that may certainly be a moral judgment, but we should remember that the baffled poisoner may say, "I ought to have given her a second dose." The point here is that intelligent decisions which we oppose to mechanical or formal decisions are not necessarily identical with decisions defensible on moral grounds. We may say of many a decision: "Yes, that is right; that is as it ought to be," and we may mean only that some accepted purpose or policy has been thereby advanced; we may not mean to endorse the moral propriety of the policy or the decision. So the contrast between the mechanical decision and the intelligent one can be reproduced inside a system dedicated to the pursuit of the most evil aims. It does not exist as a contrast to be found only in legal systems which, like our own, widely recognize principles of justice and moral claims of individuals.

An example may make this point plainer. With us the task of sentencing in criminal cases is the one that seems most obviously to demand from the judge the exercise of moral judgment. Here the factors to be weighed seem clearly to be moral factors: society must not be exposed to wanton attack; too much misery must not be inflicted on either the victim or his dependents; efforts must be made to enable him to lead a better life and regain a position in the society whose laws he has violated. To a judge striking the balance among these claims, with all the discretion and perplexities involved, his task seems as plain an example of the exercise of moral judgment as could be; and it seems to be the polar opposite of some mechanical application of a tariff of penalties fixing a sentence careless of the moral claims which in our system have to be weighed. So here intelligent and rational decision is guided however uncertainly by moral aims. But we have only to vary the example to see that this need not necessarily be so and surely, if it need not necessarily be so, the Utilitarian point remains unshaken. Under the Nazi regime men were sentenced by courts for criticism of the regime. Here the choice of sentence might be guided exclusively by consideration of what was needed to maintain the state's tyranny effectively. What sentence would both terrorize the public at large and keep the friends and family of the prisoner in suspense so that both hope and fear would cooperate as factors making for subservience? The prisoner of such a system would be regarded simply as an object to be used in pursuit of these aims. Yet, in contrast with a mechanical decision, decision on these grounds would be intelligent and purposive, and from one point of view the decision would be as it ought to be. Of course, I am not unaware that a whole philosophical tradition has sought to demonstrate the fact that we cannot correctly call decisions or behavior truly rational unless they are in conformity with moral aims and principles. But the example I have used seems to me to serve at least as a warning that we cannot use the errors of formalism as something which per se demonstrates the falsity of the utilitarian insistence on the distinction between law as it is and law as *morally* it ought to be.

We can now return to the main point. If it is true that the intelligent decision of penumbral questions is one made not mechanically but in the light of aims, purposes, and policies, though not necessarily in the light of anything we would call moral principles, is it wise to express this important fact by saying that the firm utilitarian distinction between what the law is and what it ought to be should be dropped? Perhaps the claim that it is wise cannot be theoretically refuted for it is, in effect, an *invitation* to revise our conception of what a legal rule is. We are invited to include in the "rule" the various aims and policies in the light of which its penumbral cases are decided on the ground that these aims have, because of their importance, as much right to be called law as the core of legal rules whose meaning is settled. But though an invitation cannot be refuted, it may be refused and I would proffer two reasons for refusing this invitation. First, everything we have learned about the judicial process can be expressed in other less mysterious ways. We can say laws are incurably incomplete and we must decide the penumbral cases rationally by reference to social aims. I think Holmes, who had such a vivid appreciation of the fact that "general propositions do not decide concrete cases," would have put it that way. Second, to insist on the utilitarian distinction is to emphasize that the hard core of settled meaning is law in some centrally important sense and that even if there are borderlines, there

must first be lines. If this were not so the notion of rules controlling courts' decisions would be senseless as some of the "Realists"—in their most extreme moods, and, I think, on bad grounds—claimed.[40]

By contrast, to soften the distinction, to assert mysteriously that there is some fused identity between law as it is and as it ought to be, is to suggest that all legal questions are fundamentally like those of the penumbra. It is to assert that there is no central element of actual law to be seen in the core of central meaning which rules have, that there is nothing in the nature of a legal rule inconsistent with *all* questions being open to reconsideration in the light of social policy. Of course, it is good to be occupied with the penumbra. Its problems are rightly the daily diet of the law schools. But to be occupied with the penumbra is one thing, to be preoccupied with it another. And preoccupation with the penumbra is, if I may say so, as rich a source of confusion in the American legal tradition as formalism in the English. Of course we might abandon the notion that rules have authority; we might cease to attach force or even meaning to an argument that a case falls clearly within a rule and the scope of a precedent. We might call all such reasoning "automatic" or "mechanical," which is already the routine invective of the courts. But until we decide that this is what we want, we should not encourage it by obliterating the Utilitarian distinction.

IV.

The third criticism of the separation of law and morals is of a very different character; it certainly is less an intellectual argument against the Utilitarian distinction than a passionate appeal supported not by detailed reasoning but by reminders of a terrible experience. For it consists of the testimony of those who have descended into Hell, and, like Ulysses or Dante, brought back a message for human beings. Only in this case the Hell was not beneath or beyond earth, but on it; it was a Hell created on earth by men for other men.

This appeal comes from those German thinkers who lived through the Nazi regime and reflected upon its evil manifestations in the legal system. One of these thinkers, Gustav Radbruch, had himself shared the "positivist" doctrine until the Nazi tyranny, but he was converted by this experience and so his appeal to other men to discard the doctrine of the separation of law and morals has the special poignancy of a recantation. What is important about this criticism is that it really does confront the particular point which Bentham and Austin had in mind in urging the separation of law as it is and as it ought to be. These German thinkers put their insistence on the need to join together what the Utilitarians separated just where this separation was of most importance in the eyes of the Utilitarians; for they were concerned with the problem posed by the existence of morally evil laws.

Before his conversion Radbruch held that resistance to law was a matter for the personal conscience, to be thought out by the individual as a moral problem, and the validity of a law could not be disproved by showing that its requirements were morally evil or even by showing that the effect of compliance with the law would be more evil than the effect of disobedience. Austin, it may be recalled, was emphatic in condemning those who said that if human laws conflicted with the fundamental principles of morality then they cease to be laws, as talking "stark nonsense."

> The most pernicious laws, and therefore those which are most opposed to the will of God, have been and are continually enforced as laws by judicial tribunals. Suppose an act innocuous, or positively beneficial, be prohibited by the sovereign under the penalty of death; if I commit this act, I shall be tried and condemned, and if I object to the sentence, that it is contrary to the law of God . . . the

court of justice will demonstrate the inconclusiveness of my reasoning by hanging me up, in pursuance of the law of which I have impugned the validity. An exception, demurrer, or plea, founded on the law of God was never heard in a Court of Justice, from the creation of the world down to the present moment.[41]

These are strong, indeed brutal words, but we must remember that they went along—in the case of Austin and, of course, Bentham—with the conviction that if laws reached a certain degree of iniquity then there would be a plain moral obligation to resist them and to withhold obedience. We shall see, when we consider the alternatives, that this simple presentation of the human dilemma which may arise has much to be said for it.

Radbruch, however, had concluded from the ease with which the Nazi regime had exploited subservience to mere law—or expressed, as he thought, in the "positivist" slogan "law as law" (*Gesetz als Gesetz*)—and from the failure of the German legal profession to protest against the enormities which they were required to perpetrate in the name of law, that "positivism" (meaning here the insistence on the separation of law as it is from law as it ought to be) had powerfully contributed to the horrors. His considered reflections led him to the doctrine that the fundamental principles of humanitarian morality were part of the very concept of *Recht* or Legality and that no positive enactment or statute, however clearly it was expressed and however clearly it conformed with the formal criteria of validity of a given legal system, could be valid if it contravened basic principles of morality. This doctrine can be appreciated fully only if the nuances imported by the German word *Recht* are grasped. But it is clear that the doctrine meant that every lawyer and judge should denounce statutes that transgressed the fundamental principles not as merely immoral or wrong but as having no legal character, and enactments which on this ground lack the quality of law should not be taken into account in working out the legal position of any given individual in particular circumstances. The striking recantation of his previous doctrine is unfortunately omitted from the translation of his works, but it should be read by all who wish to think afresh on the question of the interconnection of law and morals.[42]

It is impossible to read without sympathy Radbruch's passionate demand that the German legal conscience should be open to the demands of morality and his complaint that this has been too little the case in the German tradition. On the other hand there is an extraordinary naïveté in the view that insensitiveness to the demands of morality and subservience to state power in a people like the Germans should have arisen from the belief that law might be law though it failed to conform with the minimum requirements of morality. Rather this terrible history prompts inquiry into why emphasis on the slogan "law is law," and the distinction between law and morals, acquired a sinister character in Germany, but elsewhere, as with the Utilitarians themselves, went along with the most enlightened liberal attitudes. But something more disturbing than naïveté is latent in Radbruch's whole presentation of the issues to which the existence of morally iniquitous laws give rise. It is not, I think, uncharitable to say that we can see in his argument that he has only half digested the spiritual message of liberalism which he is seeking to convey to the legal profession. For everything that he says is really dependent upon an enormous overvaluation of the importance of the bare fact that a rule may be said to be a valid rule of law, as if this, once declared, was conclusive of the final moral question: "Ought this rule of law to be obeyed?" Surely the truly liberal answer to any sinister use of the slogan "law is law" or of the distinction between law and morals is, "Very well, but that does not conclude the question. Law is not morality; do not let it supplant morality."

However, we are not left to a mere academic discussion in order to evaluate the plea which Radbruch made for the revision of the distinction between law and morals. After the war Radbruch's conception of law as containing in itself the essential moral principle of humanitarianism was applied in practice by German courts in certain cases in which local war criminals, spies, and informers under the Nazi regime were punished. The special importance of these cases is that the persons accused of these crimes claimed that what they had done was not illegal under the laws of the regime in force at the time these actions were performed. This plea was met with the reply that the laws upon which they relied were invalid as contravening the fundamental principles of morality. Let me cite briefly one of these cases.[43]

In 1944 a woman, wishing to be rid of her husband, denounced him to the authorities for insulting remarks he had made about Hitler while home on leave from the German army. The wife was under no legal duty to report his acts, though what he had said was apparently in violation of statutes making it illegal to make statements detrimental to the government of the Third Reich or to impair by any means the military defense of the German people. The husband was arrested and sentenced to death, apparently pursuant to these statutes, though he was not executed but was sent to the front. In 1949 the wife was prosecuted in a West German court for an offense which we would describe as illegally depriving a person of his freedom (*rechtswidrige Freiheitsberaubung*). This was punishable as a crime under the German Criminal Code of 1871 which had remained in force continuously since its enactment. The wife pleaded that her husband's imprisonment was pursuant to the Nazi statutes and hence that she had committed no crime. The court of appeal to which the case ultimately came held that the wife was guilty of procuring the deprivation of her husband's liberty by denouncing him to the German courts, even though he had been sentenced by a court for having violated a statute, since, to quote the words of the court, the statute "was contrary to the sound conscience and sense of justice of all decent human beings." This reasoning was followed in many cases which have been hailed as a triumph of the doctrines of natural law and as signaling the overthrow of positivism. The unqualified satisfaction with this result seems to me to be hysteria. Many of us might applaud the objective—that of punishing a woman for an outrageously immoral act—but this was secured only by declaring a statute established since 1934 not to have the force of law, and at least the wisdom of this course must be doubted. There were, of course, two other choices. One was to let the woman go unpunished; one can sympathize with and endorse the view that this might have been a bad thing to do. The other was to face the fact that if the woman were to be punished it must be pursuant to the introduction of a frankly retrospective law and with a full consciousness of what was sacrificed in securing her punishment in this way. Odious as retrospective criminal legislation and punishment may be, to have pursued it openly in this case would at least have had the merits of candour. It would have made plain that in punishing the woman a choice had to be made between two evils, that of leaving her unpunished and that of sacrificing a very precious principle of morality endorsed by most legal systems. Surely if we have learned anything from the history of morals it is that the thing to do with a moral quandary is not to hide it. Like nettles, the occasions when life forces us to choose between the lesser of two evils must be grasped with the consciousness that they are what they are. The vice of this use of the principle that, at certain limiting points, what is utterly immoral cannot be law or lawful is that it will serve to cloak the true nature of the problems with which we are faced and will encourage the romantic optimism that all the values we cherish ultimately will fit into a single system, that no one of them has to be sacrificed or compromised to accommodate another.

"All Discord Harmony not understood
All Partial Evil Universal Good"

This is surely untrue and there is an insincerity in any formulation of our problem which allows us to describe the treatment of the dilemma as if it were the disposition of the ordinary case.

It may seem perhaps to make too much of forms, even perhaps of words, to emphasize one way of disposing of this difficult case as compared with another which might have led, so far as the woman was concerned, to exactly the same result. Why should we dramatize the difference between them? We might punish the woman under a new retrospective law and declare overtly that we were doing something inconsistent with our principles as the lesser of two evils; or we might allow the case to pass as one in which we do not point out precisely where we sacrifice such a principle. But candour is not just one among many minor virtues of the administration of law, just as it is not merely a minor virtue of morality. For if we adopt Radbruch's view, and with him and the German courts make our protest against evil law in the form of an assertion that certain rules cannot be law because of their moral iniquity, we confuse one of the most powerful, because it is the simplest, forms of moral criticism. If with the Utilitarians we speak plainly, we say that laws may be law but too evil to be obeyed. This is a moral condemnation which everyone can understand and it makes an immediate and obvious claim to moral attention. If, on the other hand, we formulate our objection as an assertion that these evil things are not law, here is an assertion which many people do not believe, and if they are disposed to consider it at all, it would seem to raise a whole host of philosophical issues before it can be accepted. So perhaps the most important single lesson to be learned from this form of the denial of the Utilitarian distinction is the one that the Utilitarians were most concerned to teach: when we have the ample resources of plain speech we must not present the moral criticism of institutions as propositions of a disputable philosophy.

V.

I have endeavored to show that, in spite of all that has been learned and experienced since the Utilitarians wrote, and in spite of the defects of other parts of their doctrine, their protest against the confusion of what is and what ought to be law has a moral as well as an intellectual value. Yet it may well be said that, though this distinction is valid and important if applied to any particular law of a system, it is at least misleading if we attempt to apply it to "law," that is, to the notion of a legal system, and that if we insist, as I have, on the narrower truth (or truism), we obscure a wider (or deeper) truth. After all, it may be urged, we have learned that there are many things which are untrue of laws taken separately, but which are true and important in a legal system considered as a whole. For example, the connection between law and sanctions and between the existence of law and its "efficacy" must be understood in this more general way. It is surely not arguable (without some desperate extension of the word "sanction" or artificial narrowing of the word "law") that every law in a municipal legal system must have a sanction, yet it is at least plausible to argue that a legal system must, to be a legal system, provide sanctions for certain of its rules. So too, a rule of law may be said to exist though enforced or obeyed in only a minority of cases, but this could not be said of a legal system as a whole. Perhaps the differences with respect of laws taken separately and a legal system as a whole are also true of the connection between moral (or some other) conceptions of what law ought to be and law in this wider sense.

This line of argument, found (at least in embryo form) in Austin, where he draws attention to the fact that every developed legal system contains certain fundamental notions which are "necessary" and "bottomed in the common nature of man,"[44] is worth pursuing—

up to a point—and I shall say briefly why and how far this is so.

We must avoid, if we can, the arid wastes of inappropriate definition, for, in relation to a concept as many-sided and vague as that of a legal system, disputes about the "essential" character, or necessity to the whole, of any single element soon begin to look like disputes about whether chess could be "chess" if played without pawns. There is a wish, which may be understandable, to cut straight through the question whether a legal system, to be a legal system, must measure up to some moral or other standard with simple statements of fact: for example, that no system which utterly failed in this respect has ever existed or could endure; that the normally fulfilled assumption that a legal system aims at some form of justice colours the whole way in which we interpret specific rules in particular cases, and if this normally fulfilled assumption were not fulfilled no one would have any reason to obey except fear (and probably not that) and still less, of course, any moral obligation to obey. The connection between law and moral standards and principles of justice is therefore as little arbitrary and as "necessary" as the connection between law and sanctions, and the pursuit of the question whether this necessity is logical (part of the "meaning" of law) or merely factual or causal can safely be left as an innocent pastime for philosophers.

Yet in two respects I should wish to go further (even though this involves the use of a philosophical fantasy) and show what could intelligibly be meant by the claim that certain provisions in a legal system are "necessary." The world in which we live, and we who live in it, may one day change in many different ways; and if this change were radical enough not only would certain statements of fact now true be false and vice versa, but whole ways of thinking and talking which constitute our present conceptual apparatus, through which we see the world and each other, would lapse. We have only to consider how the whole of our social, moral, and legal life, as we understand it now, depends on the contingent fact that though our bodies do change in shape, size, and other physical properties they do not do this so drastically nor with such quicksilver rapidity and irregularity that we cannot identify each other as the same persistent individual over considerable spans of time. Though this is but a contingent fact which may one day be different, on it at present rest huge structures of our thought and principles of action and social life. Similarly, consider the following possibility (not because it is more than a possibility but because it reveals why we think certain things necessary in a legal system and what we mean by this): suppose that men were to become invulnerable to attack by each other, were clad perhaps like giant land crabs with an impenetrable carapace, and could extract the food they needed from the air by some internal chemical process. In such circumstances (the details of which can be left to science fiction) rules forbidding the free use of violence and rules constituting the minimum form of property—with its rights and duties sufficient to enable food to grow and be retained until eaten —would not have the necessary nonarbitrary status which they have for us, constituted as we are in a world like ours. At present, and until such radical changes supervene, such rules are so fundamental that if a legal system did not have them there would be no point in having any other rules at all. Such rules overlap with basic moral principles vetoing murder, violence, and theft; and so we can add to the factual statement that all legal systems in fact coincide with morality at such vital points, the statement that this is, in this sense, necessarily so. And why not call it a "natural" necessity?

Of course even this much depends on the fact that in asking what content a legal system must have we take this question to be worth asking only if we who consider it cherish the humble aim of survival in close proximity to our fellows. Natural-law theory, however, in all its protean guises, attempts to push the argument much further and to assert that human beings are equally devoted to and united in their conception of aims (the pursuit of knowledge, justice to their fellow men) other than that of survival, and these dictate a further necessary content to a legal system (over and above my humble minimum) without which it would be pointless. Of course we must be careful not to exaggerate the differences among human beings, but it seems to me that above this minimum the purposes men have for living in society are too conflicting and varying to make possible much extension of the argument that some fuller overlap of legal rules and moral standards is "necessary" in this sense.

Another aspect of the matter deserves attention. If we attach to a legal system the minimum meaning that it must consist of general rules— general both in the sense that they refer to courses of action, not single actions, and to multiplicities of men, not single individuals— this meaning connotes the principle of treating like cases alike, though the criteria of when cases are alike will be, so far, only the general elements specified in the rules. It is, however, true that *one* essential element of the concept of justice is the principle of treating like cases alike. This is justice in the administration of the law, not justice of the law. So there is, in the very notion of law consisting of general rules, something which prevents us from treating it as if morally it is utterly neutral, without any necessary contact with moral principles. Natural procedural justice consists therefore of those principles of objectivity and impartiality in the administration of the law which implement just this aspect of law and which are designed to ensure that rules are applied only to what are genuinely cases of the rule or at least to minimize the risks of inequalities in this sense.

These two reasons (or excuses) for talking of a certain overlap between legal and moral standards as necessary and natural, of course, should not satisfy anyone who is really disturbed by the Utilitarian or "positivist" insistence that law and morality are distinct. This is so because a legal system that satisfied these minimum requirements might apply, with the most pedantic impartiality as between the persons affected, laws which were hideously oppressive, and might deny to a vast rightless slave population the minimum benefits of protection from violence and theft. The stink of such societies is, after all, still in our nostrils and to argue that they have (or had) no legal system would only involve the repetition of the argument. Only if the rules failed to provide these essential benefits and protection for anyone—even for a slave-owning group—would the minimum be unsatisfied and the system sink to the status of a set of meaningless taboos. Of course no one denied those benefits would have any reason to obey except fear and would have every moral reason to revolt.

VI.

I should be less than candid if I did not, in conclusion, consider something which, I suspect, most troubles those who react strongly against "legal positivism." Emphasis on the distinction between law as it is and law as it ought to be may be taken to depend upon and to entail what are called "subjectivist" and "relativist" or "non-cognitive" theories concerning the very nature of moral judgments, moral distinctions, or "values." Of course the Utilitarians themselves (as distinct from later positivists like Kelsen) did not countenance any such theories, however unsatisfactory their moral philosophy may appear to us now. Austin thought ultimate moral principles were the commands of God, known to us by revelation or through the "index" of utility, and Bentham thought they were verifiable propositions about utility. Nonetheless I think (though I cannot prove) that insistence upon the distinction between law as it is and ought to be has been, under the general head of "positivism," confused with a moral theory according to which statements of what is the case ("statements of fact") belong to a category or type radically different from statements of what ought to be ("value statements"). It may therefore be well to dispel this source of confusion.

There are many contemporary variants of this type of moral theory: according to some, judgments of what ought to be, or ought to be done, either are or include as essential elements expressions of "feeling," "emotion," or "attitudes" or "subjective preferences"; in others such judgments both express feelings or emotions or attitudes and enjoin others to share them. In other variants such judgments indicate that a particular case falls under a general principle or policy of action which the speaker has "chosen" or to which he is "committed" and which is itself not a recognition of what is the case but analogous to a general "imperative" or command addressed to all including the speaker himself. Common to all these variants is the insistence that judgments of what ought to be done, because they contain such "non-cognitive" elements, cannot be argued for or established by rational methods as statements of fact can be, and cannot be shown to follow from any statement of fact but only from other judgments of what ought to be done in conjunction with some statement of fact. We cannot, on such a theory, demonstrate, e.g., that an action was wrong, ought not to have been done, merely by showing that it consisted of the deliberate infliction of pain solely for the gratification of the agent. We only show it to be wrong if we add to those verifiable "cognitive" statements of fact a general principle not itself verifiable or "cognitive" that the infliction of pain in such circumstances is wrong, ought not to be done. Together with this general distinction between statements of what is and what ought to be go sharp parallel distinctions between statements about means and statements of moral ends. We can rationally discover and debate what are appropriate means to given ends, but ends are not rationally discoverable or debatable; they are "fiats of the will," expressions of "emotions," "preferences," or "attitudes."

Against all such views (which are of course far subtler than this crude survey can convey) others urge that all these sharp distinctions between is and ought, fact and value, means and ends, cognitive and noncognitive, are wrong. In acknowledging ultimate ends or moral values we are recognizing something as much imposed upon us by the character of the world in which we live, as little a matter of choice, attitude, feeling, emotion as the truth of factual judgments about what is the case. The characteristic moral argument is not one in which the parties are reduced to expressing or kindling feelings or emotions or issuing exhortations or commands to each other but one by which parties come to acknowledge after closer examination and reflection that an initially disputed case falls within the ambit of a vaguely apprehended principle (itself no more "subjective," no more a "fiat of our will" than any other principle of classification) and this has as much title to be called "cognitive" or "rational" as any other initially disputed classification of particulars.

Let us now suppose that we accept this rejection of "noncognitive" theories of morality and this denial of the drastic distinction in type between statements of what is and what ought to be, and that moral judgments are as rationally defensible as any other kind of judgments. What would follow from this as to the nature of the connection between law as it is and law as it ought to be? Surely, from this alone, nothing. Laws, however morally iniquitous, would still (so far as this point is concerned) be laws. The only difference which the acceptance of this view of the nature of moral judgments would make would be that the moral iniquity of such laws would be something that could be demonstrated; it would surely follow merely from a statement of what the rule required to be done that the rule was morally wrong and so ought not to be law or conversely that it was morally desirable and ought to be law. But the demonstra-

tion of this would not show the rule not to be (or to be) law. Proof that the principles by which we evaluate or condemn laws are rationally discoverable, and not mere "fiats of the will," leaves untouched the fact that there are laws which may have any degree of iniquity or stupidity and still be laws. And conversely there are rules that have every moral qualification to be laws and yet are not laws.

Surely something further or more specific must be said if disproof of "noncognitivism" or kindred theories in ethics is to be relevant to the distinction between law as it is and law as it ought to be, and to lead to the abandonment at some point or some softening of this distinction. No one has done more than Professor Lon Fuller of the Harvard Law School in his various writings to make clear such a line of argument and I will end by criticizing what I take to be its central point. It is a point which again emerges when we consider not those legal rules or parts of legal rules the meanings of which are clear and excite no debate but the interpretation of rules in concrete cases where doubts are initially felt and argument develops about their meaning. In no legal system is the scope of legal rules restricted to the range of concrete instances which were present or are believed to have been present in the minds of legislators; this indeed is one of the important differences between a legal rule and a command. Yet, when rules are recognized as applying to instances beyond any that legislators did or could have considered, their extension to such new cases often presents itself not as a deliberate choice or fiat on the part of those who so interpret the rule. It appears neither as a decision to give the rule a new or extended meaning nor as a guess as to what legislators, dead perhaps in the eighteenth century, would have said had they been alive in the twentieth century. Rather, the inclusion of the new case under the rule takes its place as a natural elaboration of the rule, as something implementing a "purpose" which it seems natural to attribute (in some sense) to the rule itself rather than to any particular person dead or alive. The Utilitarian description of such interpretative extension of old rules to new cases as judicial legislation fails to do justice to this phenomenon; it gives no hint of the differences between a deliberate fiat or decision to treat the new case in the same way as past cases and a recognition (in which there is little that is deliberate or even voluntary) that inclusion of the new case under the rule will implement or articulate a continuing and identical purpose, hitherto less specifically apprehended.

Perhaps many lawyers and judges will see in this language something that precisely fits their experience; others may think it a romantic gloss on facts better stated in the Utilitarian language of judicial "legislation" or in the modern American terminology of "creative choice."

To make the point clear Professor Fuller uses a nonlegal example from the philosopher Wittgenstein which is, I think, illuminating.

> Someone says to me: "Show the children a game." I teach them gaming with dice and the other says "I did not mean that sort of game." Must the exclusion of the game with dice have come before his mind when he gave me the order?[45]

Something important does seem to me to be touched on in this example. Perhaps there are the following (distinguishable) points. First, we normally do interpret not only what people are trying to do but what they say in the light of assumed common human objectives so that unless the contrary were expressly indicated we would not interpret an instruction to show a young child a game as a mandate to introduce him to gambling even though in other contexts the word "game" would be naturally so interpreted. Second, very often, the speaker whose words are thus interpreted might say: "Yes, that's what I mean [or "that's what I meant all along"] though I never thought of it until you put this particular case to me." Third, when we thus

recognize, perhaps after argument or consultation with others, a particular case not specifically envisaged beforehand as falling within the ambit of some vaguely expressed instruction, we may find this experience falsified by description of it as a mere decision on our part so to treat the particular case, and that we can only describe this faithfully as coming to realize and to articulate what we "really" want or our "true purpose"— phrases which Professor Fuller uses later in the same article.[46]

I am sure that many philosophical discussions of the character of moral argument would benefit from attention to cases of the sort instanced by Professor Fuller. Such attention would help to provide a corrective to the view that there is a sharp separation between "ends" and "means" and that in debating "ends" we can only work on each other nonrationally, and that rational argument is reserved for discussion of "means." But I think the relevance of his point to the issue whether it is correct or wise to insist on the distinction between law as it is and law as it ought to be is very small indeed. Its net effect is that in interpreting legal rules there are some cases which we find after reflection to be so natural an elaboration or articulation of the rule that to think of and refer to this as "legislation," "making law," or a "fiat" on our part would be misleading. So, the argument must be, it would be misleading to distinguish in such cases between what the rule is and what it ought to be —at least in some sense of ought. We think it ought to include the new case and come to see after reflection that it really does. But even if this way of presenting a recognizable experience as an example of a fusion between is and ought to be is admitted, two caveats must be borne in mind. The first is that "ought" in this case need have nothing to do with morals for the reasons explained already in section III: there may be just the same sense that a new case will implement and articulate the purpose of a rule in interpreting the rules of a game or some hideously immoral code of oppression whose immorality is appreciated by those called in to interpret it. They too can see what the "spirit" of the game they are playing requires in previously unenvisaged cases. More important is this: after all is said and done we must remember how rare in the law is the phenomenon held to justify this way of talking, how exceptional is this feeling that one way of deciding a case is imposed upon us as the only natural or rational elaboration of some rule. Surely it cannot be doubted that, for most cases of interpretation, the language of choice between alternatives, "judicial legisla-tion" or even "fiat" (though not arbitrary fiat), better conveys the realities of the situation.

Within the framework of relatively well-settled law there jostle too many alternatives too nearly equal in attraction between which judge and lawyer must uncertainly pick their way to make appropriate here language which may well describe those experiences which we have in interpreting our own or others' principles of conduct, intention, or wishes, when we are not conscious of exercising a deliberate choice, but rather of recognizing something awaiting recognition. To use in the description of the interpretation of laws the suggested terminology of a fusion or inability to separate what is law and ought to be will serve (like earlier stories that judges only find, never make, law) only to conceal the facts, that here if anywhere we live among uncertainties between which we have to choose, and that the existing law imposes only limits on our choice and not the choice itself.

Notes

71 *Harvard Law Review* 593 (1958).
1 Bentham, *A Fragment on Government*, in 1 Works 221, 235 (Bowring ed. 1859) (preface, 41st para.).
2 D'Entrèves, *Natural Law* 116 (2nd ed. 1952).
3 Fuller, *The Law in Quest of Itself* 12 (1940); Brecht, *The Myth of Is and Ought*, 54 Harv. L. Rev. 811 (1941); Fuller, *Human Purpose and Natural Law*, 53 J. Philos. 697 (1953).

4 See Friedmann, *Legal Theory* 154, 294–95 (3rd ed. 1953). Friedmann also says of Austin that "by his sharp distinction between the science of legislation and the science of law," he "inaugurated an era of legal positivism and self-sufficiency which enabled the rising national State to assert its authority undisturbed by juristic doubts." Id. at 416. Yet, "the existence of a highly organised State which claimed sovereignty and unconditional obedience of the citizen" is said to be "the political condition which makes analytical positivism possible." Id. at 163. There is therefore some difficulty in determin-ing which, in this account, is to be hen and which egg (analytical positivism or political condition). Apart from this, there seems to be little evidence that any national State rising in or after 1832 (when the *Province of Jurisprudence Determined* was first published) was enabled to assert its authority by Austin's work or "the era of legal positivism" which he "inaugurated."
5 See Radbruch, *Die Erneuerung des Rechts*, 2 Die Wand-lung 8 (Germany 1947); Radbruch, *Gesetzliches Unrecht und Übergesetzliches Recht*, 1 Süddeutsche Juristen-Zeitung 105 (Germany 1946) (reprinted in Radbruch, *Rechtsphilosophie* 347 (4th ed. 1950)). Radbruch's views are discussed at pp. 617–21 infra.
6 Bentham, *A Fragment on Government*, in 1 Works 221, 230 (Bowring ed. 1859) (preface, 16th para.); Bentham, *Principles of Penal Law*, in 1 Works 365, 574–75, 576–78 (Bowring ed. 1859) (pt. III, c. XXI, 8th para., 12th para.).
7 Bentham, *Of Promulgation of the Laws*, in I Works 155 (Bowring ed. 1859); Bentham, *Principles of the Civil Code*, in 1 Works 297, 323 (Bowring ed. 1859) (pt. I, c. XVII, 2nd para.); Bentham, *A Fragment on Government*, in 1 Works 221, 233 n.[m] (Bowring ed. 1859) (preface, 35th para.).
8 Bentham, *Principles of Penal Law*, in 1 Works 365, 576 (Bowring ed. 1859) (pt. III, c. XXI, 10th para., 11th para.).
9 Bentham, *Principles of Morals and Legislation*, in 1 Works 1, 84 (Bowring ed. 1859) (c. XIII).
10 Bentham, *Anarchical Fallacies*, in 2 Works 489, 511–12 (Bowring ed. 1859) (art. VIII); Bentham, *Principles of Morals and Legislation*, in 1 Works 1, 144 (Bowring ed. 1859) (c. XIX, 11th para.).
11 Id. at 142 n.§ (c. XIX, 4th para. n.§).
12 Austin, *The Province of Jurisprudence Determined* 184–85 (Library of Ideas ed. 1954).

13 Bentham, *A Fragment on Government*, in 1 Works 221, 230 (Bowring ed. 1859) (preface, 16th para.).

14 See Bentham, *Principles of Legislation*, in The Theory of Legislation 1, 65 n.* (Ogden ed. 1931) (c. XII, 2nd para. n.*).

  Here we touch upon the most difficult of questions. If the law is not what it ought to be; if it openly combats the principle of utility; ought we to obey it? Ought we to violate it? Ought we to remain neutral between the law which commands an evil, and morality which forbids it?

  See also Bentham, *A Fragment on Government*, in 1 Works 221, 287–88 (Bowring ed. 1859) (c. IV, 20th–25th paras).

15 1 Blackstone, *Commentaries* *41. Bentham criticized "this dangerous maxim," saying "the natural tendency of such a doctrine is to impel a man, by the force of conscience, to rise up in arms against any law whatever that he happens not to like." Bentham, *A Fragment on Government*, in 1 Works 221, 287 (Bowring ed. 1859) (c. IV, 19th para.). See also Bentham, *A Comment on the Commentaries* 49 (1928) (c. III). For an expression of a fear lest anarchy result from such a doctrine, combined with a recognition that resistance may be justified on grounds of utility, see Austin, op. cit. supra note 12, at 186.

16 Bentham, *A Fragment on Government*, in 1 Works 221, 294 (Bowring ed. 1859) (c. V, 10th para.).

17 Bentham, *A Commentary on Humphreys' Real Property Code*, in 5 Works 389 (Bowring ed. 1843).

18 Austin, op. cit. supra note 12, at 162.

19 Bentham, *A Fragment on Government*, in 1 Works 221, 289–90 (Bowring ed. 1859) (c. IV, 33rd–34th paras.).

20 See Austin, op. cit. supra note 12, at 231.

21 Amos, *The Science of Law* 4 (5th ed. 1881). See also Markby, *Elements of Law* 4–5 (5th ed. 1896):

  Austin, by establishing the distinction between positive law and morals, not only laid the foundation for a science of law, but cleared the conception of law . . . of a number of pernicious consequences to which . . . it had been supposed to lead. Positive laws, as Austin has shown, must be legally binding, and yet a law may be unjust. . . . He has admitted that law itself may be immoral, in which case it may be our moral duty to disobey it. . . . Cf. Holland, Jurisprudence 1–20 (1880).

22 See Green, Book Review, 6 *Am. L. Rev.* 57, 61 (1871) (reprinted in Green, *Essays and Notes on the Law of Tort and Crime* 31, 35 (1933)).

23 10 *Harv. L. Rev.* 457 (1897).

24 Gray, *The Nature and Sources of the Law* 94 (1st ed. 1909) (§ 213).

25 It may help to identify five (there may be more) meanings of "positivism" bandied about in contemporary jurisprudence:

  (1) the contention that laws are commands of human beings, see pp. 602–06 infra,

  (2) the contention that there is no necessary connection between law and morals or law as it is and ought to be, see pp. 594–600 supra,

  (3) the contention that the analysis (or study of the meaning) of legal concepts is (a) worth pursuing and (b) to be distinguished from historical inquiries into the causes or origins of laws, from sociological inquiries into the relation of law and other social phenomena, and from the criticism or appraisal of law whether in terms of morals, social aims, "functions," or otherwise, see pp. 608–10 infra,

  (4) the contention that a legal system is a "closed logical system" in which correct legal decisions can be deduced by logical means from predetermined legal rules without reference to social aims, policies, moral standards, see pp. 608–10 infra, and

  (5) the contention that moral judgments cannot be established or defended, as statements of facts can, by rational argument, evidence, or proof ("noncognitivism" in ethics), see pp. 624–26 infra.

  Bentham and Austin held the views described in (1), (2), and (3) but not those in (4) and (5). Opinion (4) is often ascribed to analytical jurists, see pages pp. 608–10 infra, but I know of no "analyst" who held this view.

26 Gray, *The Nature and Sources of the Law* 94–95 (2nd ed. 1921).

27 Austin, op. cit. supra note 12, at 13.

28 See, e.g., Kelsen, *General Theory of Law and State* 58–61, 143–44 (1945). According to Kelsen, all laws, not only those conferring rights and powers, are reducible to such "primary norms" conditionally stipulating sanctions.

29 Salmond, *The First Principles of Jurisprudence* 97–98 (1893). He protested against "the creed of what is termed the English school of jurisprudence," because it "attempted to deprive the idea of law of that ethical significance which is one of its most essential elements." Id. at 9, 10.

30 Hägerström, *Inquiries Into the Nature of Law and Morals* 217 (Olivecrona ed. 1953): "[T]he whole theory of the subjective rights of private individuals . . . is incompatible with the imperative theory." See also id. at 221:

> The description of them [claims to legal protection] as rights is wholly derived from the idea that the law which is concerned with them is a true expression of rights and duties in the sense in which the popular notion of justice understands these terms.

31 Id. at 218.

32 This misunderstanding of analytical jurisprudence is to be found in, among others, Stone, *The Province and Function of Law* 141 (1950):

> In short, rejecting the implied assumption that all propositions of all parts of the law must be logically consistent with each other and proceed on a single set of definitions . . . he [Cardozo, J.] denied that the law is actually what the analytical jurist, *for his limited purposes*, assumes it to be.

See also id. at 49, 52, 138, 140; Friedmann, *Legal Theory* 209 (3rd ed. 1953). This misunderstanding seems to depend on the unexamined and false belief that analytical studies of the meaning of legal terms would be impossible or absurd if, to reach sound decisions in particular cases, more than a capacity for formal logical reasoning from unambiguous and clear predetermined premises is required.

33 See the discussion of vagueness and uncertainty in law, in Austin, op. cit. supra note 12, at 202–05, 207, in which Austin recognized that, in consequence of this vagueness, often only "fallible tests" can be provided for determining whether particular cases fall under general expressions.

34 See Austin, op. cit. supra note 12, at 191: "I cannot understand how any person who has considered the subject can suppose that society could possibly have gone on if judges had not legislated. . . ." As a corrective to the belief that the analytical jurist must take a "slot machine" or "mechanical" view of the judicial process it is worth noting the following observations made by Austin:

(1) Whenever law has to be applied, the " 'competition of opposite analogies' " may arise, for the case "may resemble in some of its points" cases to which the rule has been applied in the past and in other points "cases from which the application of the law has been withheld." 2 Austin, *Lectures on Jurisprudence* 633 (5th ed. 1885).

(2) Judges have commonly decided cases and so derived new rules by "building" on a variety of grounds including sometimes (in Austin's opinion too rarely) their views of what law ought to be. Most commonly they have derived law from pre-existing law by "consequence founded on analogy," i.e., they have made a new rule "in *consequence* of the existence of a similar rule applying to subjects which are *analogous*. . . ." 2 id. at 638–39.

(3) "[I]f every rule in a system of law were perfectly definite or precise," these difficulties incident to the application of law would not arise. "But the ideal completeness and correctness I now have imagined is not attainable in fact. . . . though the system had been built and ordered with matchless solicitude and skill." 2 id. at 997–98. Of course he thought that much could and should be done by codification to eliminate uncertainty. See 2 id. at 662–81.

35 2 id. at 641:

> Nothing, indeed, can be more natural, than that legislators, direct or judicial (especially if they be narrow-minded, timid and unskillful), should lean as much as they can on the examples set by their predecessors.

See also 2 id. at 647:

But it is much to be regretted that Judges of capacity, experience and weight, have not seized every opportunity of introducing a new rule (a rule beneficial for the future). . . . This is the reproach I should be inclined to make against Lord Eldon. . . . [T]he Judges of the Common Law Courts would not do what they ought to have done, namely to model their rules of law and of procedure to the growing exigencies of society, instead of stupidly and sulkily adhering to the old and barbarous usages.

36 Hynes v. New York Cent. R.R., 231 N.Y. 229, 235, 131 N.E. 898, 900 (1921); see Pound, *Interpretations of Legal History* 123 (2nd ed. 1930); Stone, op. cit. supra note 32, at 140–41.

37 See McBoyle v. United States, 283 U.S. 25 (1931).

38 See, *e.g.*, Pound, *Mechanical Jurisprudence*, 8 Colum. L. Rev. 605, 615–16 (1908).

39 See, *e.g.*, Lochner v. New York, 198 U.S. 45 (1905). Justice Peckham's opinion that there were no reasonable grounds for interfering with the right of free contract by determining the hours of labor in the occupation of a baker may indeed be a wrongheaded piece of conservatism but there is nothing automatic or mechanical about it.

40 One recantation of this extreme position is worth mention in the present context. In the first edition of *The Bramble Bush*, Professor Llewellyn committed himself wholeheartedly to the view that "what these officials do about disputes is, to my mind, the law itself" and that "*rules* . . . are important so far as they help you . . . predict what judges will do. . . . That is all their importance, except as pretty playthings." Llewellyn, *The Bramble Bush* 3, 5 (1st ed. 1930). In the second edition he said that these were "unhappy words when not more fully developed, and they are plainly at best a very partial statement of the whole truth. . . . [O]ne office of law is to control officials in some part, and to guide them even . . . where no thoroughgoing control is possible, or is desired. . . . [T]he words fail to take proper account . . . of the office of the institution of law as an instrument of conscious shaping. . . ." Llewellyn, *The Bramble Bush* 9 (2nd ed. 1951).

41 Austin, *The Province of Jurisprudence Determined* 185 (Library of Ideas ed. 1954).

42 See Radbruch, *Gesetzliches Unrecht und Übergesetzliches Recht*, 1 *Süddeutsche Juristen-Zeitung* 105 (Germany 1946) (reprinted in Radbruch, *Rechtsphilosophie* 347 (4th ed. 1950)). I have used the translation of part of this essay and of Radbruch, *Die Erneuerung des Rechts*, 2 *Die Wandlung* 8 (Germany 1947), prepared by Professor Lon Fuller of the Harvard Law School as a mimeographed supplement to the readings in jurisprudence used in his course at Harvard.

43 Judgment of July 27, 1949, Oberlandesgericht, Bamberg, 5 *Süddeutsche Juristen-Zeitung* 207 (Germany 1950), 64 *Harv. L. Rev.* 1005 (1951); see Friedmann, *Legal Theory* 457 (3rd ed. 1953).

44 Austin, *Uses of the Study of Jurisprudence*, in *The Province of Jurisprudence Determined* 365, 373, 367–69 (Library of Ideas ed. 1954).

45 Fuller, *Human Purpose and Natural Law*, 53 J. Philos. 697, 700 (1956).

46 Id. at 701, 702.

Chapter 3

Lon L. Fuller

POSITIVISM AND FIDELITY TO LAW

A reply to Professor Hart

PROFESSOR HART has made an enduring contribution to the literature of legal philosophy. I doubt if the issues he discusses will ever again assume quite the form they had before being touched by his analytical powers. His argument is no mere restatement of Bentham, Austin, Gray, and Holmes. Their views receive in his exposition a new clarity and a new depth that are uniquely his own.

I must confess that when I first encountered the thoughts of Professor Hart's essay, his argument seemed to me to suffer from a deep inner contradiction. On the one hand, he rejects emphatically any confusion of "what is" with "what ought to be." He will tolerate no "merger" of law and conceptions of what law ought to be, but at the most an antiseptic "intersection." Intelligible communication on any subject, he seems to imply, becomes impossible if we leave it uncertain whether we are talking about "what is" or "what ought to be." Yet it was precisely this uncertainty about Professor Hart's own argument which made it difficult for me at first to follow the thread of his thought. At times he seemed to be saying that the distinction between law and morality is something that exists, and will continue to exist, however we may talk about it. It expresses a reality which, whether we like it or not, we must accept if we are to avoid talking nonsense. At other times, he seemed to be warning us that the reality of the distinction is itself in danger and that if we do not mend our ways of thinking and talking we may lose a "precious moral ideal," that of fidelity to law. It is not clear, in other words, whether in Professor Hart's own thinking the distinction between law and morality simply "is," or is something that "ought to be" and that we should join with him in helping to create and maintain.

These were the perplexities I had about Professor Hart's argument when I first encountered it. But on reflection I am sure any criticism of his essay as being self-contradictory would be both unfair and unprofitable. There is no reason why the argument for a strict separation of law and morality cannot be rested on the double ground that this separation serves both intellectual clarity and moral integrity. If there are certain difficulties in bringing these two lines of reasoning into proper relation to one another, these difficulties affect also the position of those who reject the views of Austin, Gray, and Holmes. For those of us who find the "positivist" position unacceptable do ourselves rest our argument on the double ground that its intellectual clarity is specious and that its effects are, or may be, harmful. On the one hand, we assert that Austin's definition of law, for example, violates the reality it purports to describe. Being false in fact, it cannot serve effectively what Kelsen calls "an interest of cognition." On the other hand, we assert that under some conditions the same conception of law may become dangerous, since in human affairs what men mistakenly accept as real tends, by the very act of their acceptance, to become real.

It is a cardinal virtue of Professor Hart's argument that for the first time it opens the way for a truly profitable exchange of views between those whose differences center on the distinction between law and morality. Hitherto there has been no real joinder of issue between the opposing camps. On the one side, we encounter a series of definitional fiats. A rule of law is—that is to say, it really and simply and always is—the command of a sovereign, a rule laid down by a judge, a prediction of the future incidence of state force, a pattern of official behavior, etc. When we ask what purpose these definitions serve, we receive the answer, "Why, no purpose, except to describe accurately the social reality that corresponds to the word 'law.' " When we reply, "But it doesn't look like that to me," the answer comes back, "Well, it does to me." There the matter has to rest.

This state of affairs has been most unsatisfactory for those of us who are convinced that "positivistic" theories have had a distorting effect on the aims of legal philosophy. Our dissatisfaction arose not merely from the impasse we confronted, but because this impasse seemed to us so unnecessary. All that was needed to surmount it was an acknowledgment on the other side that its definitions of "what law really is" are not mere images of some datum of experience, but direction posts for the application of human energies. Since this acknowledgment was not forthcoming, the impasse and its frustrations continued. There is indeed no frustration greater than to be confronted by a theory which purports merely to describe, when it not only plainly prescribes, but owes its special prescriptive powers precisely to the fact that it disclaims prescriptive intentions. Into this murky debate, some shafts of light did occasionally break through, as in Kelsen's casual admission, apparently never repeated, that his whole system might well rest

on an emotional preference for the ideal of order over that of justice.[1] But I have to confess that in general the dispute that has been conducted during the last twenty years has not been very profitable.

Now, with Professor Hart's paper, the discussion takes a new and promising turn. It is now explicitly acknowledged on both sides that one of the chief issues is how we can best define and serve the ideal of fidelity to law. Law, as something deserving loyalty, must represent a human achievement; it cannot be a simple fiat of power or a repetitive pattern discernible in the behavior of state officials. The respect we owe to human laws must surely be something different from the respect we accord to the law of gravitation. If laws, even bad laws, have a claim to our respect, then law must represent some general direction of human effort that we can understand and describe, and that we can approve in principle even at the moment when it seems to us to miss its mark.

If, as I believe, it is a cardinal virtue of Professor Hart's argument that it brings into the dispute the issue of fidelity to law, its chief defect, if I may say so, lies in a failure to perceive and accept the implications that this enlargement of the frame of argument necessarily entails. This defect seems to me more or less to permeate the whole essay, but it comes most prominently to the fore in his discussion of Gustav Radbruch and the Nazi regime.[2] Without any inquiry into the actual workings of whatever remained of a legal system under the Nazis, Professor Hart assumes that something must have persisted that still deserved the name of law in a sense that would make meaningful the ideal of fidelity to law. Not that Professor Hart believes the Nazis' laws should have been obeyed. Rather he considers that a decision to disobey them presented not a mere question of prudence or courage, but a genuine moral dilemma in which the ideal of fidelity to law had to be sacrificed in favor of more fundamental goals. I should have thought it unwise to pass such a judgment without first inquiring with more particularity what "law" itself meant under the Nazi regime.

I shall present later my reasons for thinking that Professor Hart is profoundly mistaken in his estimate of the Nazi situation and that he gravely misinterprets the thought of Professor Radbruch. But first I shall turn to some preliminary definitional problems in which what I regard as the central defect in Professor Hart's thesis seems immediately apparent.

I. The definition of law

Throughout his essay Professor Hart aligns himself with a general position which he associates with the names of Bentham, Austin, Gray, and Holmes. He recognizes, of course, that the conceptions of these men as to "what law is" vary considerably, but this diversity he apparently considers irrelevant in his defense of their general school of thought.

If the only issue were that of stipulating a meaning for the word "law" that would be conducive to intellectual clarity, there might be much justification for treating all of these men as working in the same direction. Austin, for example, defines law as the command of the highest legislative power, called the sovereign. For Gray, on the other hand, law consists in the rules laid down by judges. A statute is, for Gray, not a law, but only a source of law, which becomes law only after it has been interpreted and applied by a court. Now if our only object were to obtain that clarity which comes from making our definitions explicit and then adhering strictly to those definitions, one could argue plausibly that either conception of the meaning of "law" will do. Both conceptions appear to avoid a confusion of morals and law, and both writers let the reader know what meaning they propose to attribute to the word "law."

The matter assumes a very different aspect, however, if our interest lies in the ideal of fidelity to law, for then it may become a matter of capital importance what position is assigned to the judiciary in the general frame of government. Confirmation for this observation may be found in the slight rumbling of constitutional crisis to be heard in this country today. During the past year readers of newspapers have been writing to their editors urging solemnly, and even apparently with sincerity, that we should abolish the Supreme Court as a first step toward a restoration of the rule of law. It is unlikely that this remedy for our governmental ills derives from any deep study of Austin or Gray, but surely those who propose it could hardly be expected to view with indifference the divergent definitions of law offered by those two jurists. If it be said that it is a perversion of Gray's meaning to extract from his writings any moral for present controversies about the role of the Supreme Court, then it seems to me there is equal reason for treating what he wrote as irrelevant to the issue of fidelity to law generally.

Another difference of opinion among the writers defended by Professor Hart concerns Bentham and Austin and their views on constitutional limitations on the power of the sovereign. Bentham considered that a constitution might preclude the highest legislative power from issuing certain kinds of laws. For Austin, on the other hand, any legal limit on the highest lawmaking power was an absurdity and an impossibility. What guide to conscience would be offered by these two writers in a crisis that might some day arise out of the provision of our constitution to the effect that the amending power can never be used to deprive any state without its consent of its equal representation in the Senate?[3] Surely it is not only in the affairs of everyday life that we need clarity about the obligation of fidelity to law, but most particularly and urgently in times of trouble. If all the positivist school has to offer in such times is the observation that, however you may choose to define law, it is always something different from morals, its teachings are not of much use to us.

I suggest, then, that Professor Hart's thesis as it now stands is essentially incomplete and that before he can attain the goals he seeks he will have to concern himself more closely with a definition of law that will make meaningful the obligation of fidelity to law.

II. The definition of morality

It is characteristic of those sharing the point of view of Professor Hart that their primary concern is to preserve the integrity of the concept of law. Accordingly, they have generally sought a precise definition of law, but have not been at pains to state just what it is they mean to exclude by their definitions. They are like men building a wall for the defense of a village, who must know what it is they wish to protect, but who need not, and indeed cannot, know what invading forces those walls may have to turn back.

When Austin and Gray distinguish law from morality, the word "morality" stands indiscriminately for almost every conceivable standard by which human conduct may be judged that is not itself law. The inner voice of conscience, notions of right and wrong based on religious belief, common conceptions of decency and fair play, culturally conditioned prejudices—all of these are grouped together under the heading of "morality" and are excluded from the domain of law. For the most part Professor Hart follows in the tradition of his predecessors. When he speaks of morality he seems generally to have in mind all sorts of extralegal notions about "what ought to be," regardless of their sources, pretensions, or intrinsic worth. This is particularly apparent in his treatment of the problem of interpretation, where uncodified notions of what ought to be are viewed as affecting only the penumbra of law, leaving its hard core untouched.

Toward the end of the essay, however, Professor Hart's argument takes a turn that seems to depart from the prevailing tenor of his thought. This consists in reminding us that there is such a thing as an immoral morality and that there are many standards of "what ought to be" that can hardly be called moral.[4] Let us grant, he says, that the judge may properly and inevitably legislate in the penumbra of a legal enactment, and that this legislation (in default of any other standard) must be guided by the judge's notions of what ought to be. Still, this would be true even in a society devoted to the most evil ends, where the judge would supply the insufficiencies of the statute with the iniquity that seemed to him most apt for the occasion. Let us also grant, says Professor Hart toward the end of his essay, that there is at times even something that looks like discovery in the judicial process, when a judge by restating a principle seems to bring more clearly to light what was really sought from the beginning. Again, he reminds us, this could happen in a society devoted to the highest refinements of sin, where the implicit demands of an evil rule might be a matter for discovery when the rule was applied to a situation not consciously considered when it was formulated.

I take it that this is to be a warning addressed to those who wish "to infuse more morality into the law." Professor Hart is reminding them that if their program is adopted the morality that actually gets infused may not be to their liking. If this is his point it is certainly a valid one, though one wishes it had been made more explicitly, for it raises much the most fundamental issue of his whole argument. Since the point is made obliquely, and I may have misinterpreted it, in commenting I shall have to content myself with a few summary observations and questions.

First, Professor Hart seems to assume that evil aims may have as much coherence and inner logic as good ones. I, for one, refuse to accept that assumption. I realize that I am here raising, or perhaps dodging, questions that lead into the most difficult problems of the epistemology of ethics. Even if I were competent to undertake an excursus in that direction, this is not the place for it. I shall have to rest on the assertion of a belief that may seem naïve, namely, that coherence and goodness have more affinity than coherence and evil. Accepting this belief, I also believe that when men are compelled to explain and justify their decisions, the effect will generally be to pull those decisions toward goodness, by whatever standards of ultimate goodness there are. Accepting these beliefs, I find a considerable incongruity in any conception that envisages a possible future in which the common law would "work itself pure from case to case" toward a more perfect realization of iniquity.

Second, if there is a serious danger in our society that a weakening of the partition between law and morality would permit an infusion of "immoral morality," the question remains, what is the most effective protection against this danger? I cannot myself believe it is to be found in the positivist position espoused by Austin, Gray, Holmes, and Hart. For those writers seem to me to falsify the problem into a specious simplicity which leaves untouched the difficult issues where real dangers lie.

Third, let us suppose a judge bent on realizing through his decisions an objective that most ordinary citizens would regard as mistaken or evil. Would such a judge be likely to suspend the letter of the statute by openly invoking a "higher law"? Or would he be more likely to take refuge behind the maxim that "law is law" and explain his decision in such a way that it would appear to be demanded by the law itself?

Fourth, neither Professor Hart nor I belong to anything that could be said in a significant sense to be a "minority group" in our respective countries. This has its advantages and disadvantages to one aspiring to a philosophic view of law and government. But suppose we were both transported to a country where our beliefs were anathemas, and where we, in turn, regarded the prevailing morality as thoroughly evil. No doubt in this situation we would have reason to fear that the law might be covertly manipulated to our disadvantage; I doubt if either of us would be apprehensive that its injunctions would be set aside by an appeal to a

morality higher than law. If we felt that the law itself was our safest refuge, would it not be because even in the most perverted regimes there is a certain hesitancy about writing cruelties, intolerances, and inhumanities into law? And is it not clear that this hesitancy itself derives, not from a separation of law and morals, but precisely from an identification of law with those demands of morality that are the most urgent and the most obviously justifiable, which no man need be ashamed to profess?

Fifth, over great areas where the judicial process functions, the danger of an infusion of immoral, or at least unwelcome, morality does not, I suggest, present a real issue. Here the danger is precisely the opposite. For example, in the field of commercial law the British courts in recent years have, if I may say so, fallen into a "law-is-law" formalism that constitutes a kind of belated counterrevolution against all that was accomplished by Mansfield.[5] The matter has reached a stage approaching crisis as commercial cases are increasingly being taken to arbitration. The chief reason for this development is that arbitrators are willing to take into account the needs of commerce and ordinary standards of commercial fairness. I realize that Professor Hart repudiates "formalism," but I shall try to show later why I think his theory necessarily leads in that direction.[6]

Sixth, in the thinking of many there is one question that predominates in any discussion of the relation of law and morals, to the point of coloring everything that is said or heard on the subject. I refer to the kind of question raised by the Pope's pronouncement concerning the duty of Catholic judges in divorce actions.[7] This pronouncement does indeed raise grave issues. But it does not present a problem of the relation between law, on the one hand, and, on the other, generally shared views of right conduct that have grown spontaneously through experience and discussion. The issue is rather that of a conflict between two pronouncements, both of which claim to be authoritative; if you will, it is one kind of law against another. When this kind of issue is taken as the key to the whole problem of law and morality, the discussion is so denatured and distorted that profitable exchange becomes impossible. In mentioning this last aspect of the dispute about "positivism," I do not mean to intimate that Professor Hart's own discussion is dominated by any *arrière-pensée*; I know it is not. At the same time I am quite sure that I have indicated accurately the issue that will be uppermost in the minds of many as they read his essay.

In resting content with these scant remarks, I do not want to seem to simplify the problem in a direction opposite to that taken by Professor Hart. The questions raised by "immoral morality" deserve a more careful exploration than either Professor Hart or I have offered in these pages.

III. The moral foundations of a legal order

Professor Hart emphatically rejects "the command theory of law," according to which law is simply a command backed by a force sufficient to make it effective. He observes that such a command can be given by a man with a loaded gun, and "law surely is not the gunman situation writ large."[8] There is no need to dwell here on the inadequacies of the command theory, since Professor Hart has already revealed its defects more clearly and succinctly than I could. His conclusion is that the foundation of a legal system is not coercive power, but certain "fundamental accepted rules specifying the essential lawmaking procedures."[9]

When I reached this point in his essay, I felt certain that Professor Hart was about to acknowledge an important qualification on his thesis. I confidently expected that he would go on to say something like this: I have insisted throughout on the importance of keeping sharp the distinction between law and morality. The question may now be raised, therefore, as to the nature of these fundamental rules that furnish the frame-

work within which the making of law takes place. On the one hand, they seem to be rules, not of law, but of morality. They derive their efficacy from a general acceptance, which in turn rests ultimately on a perception that they are right and necessary. They can hardly be said to be law in the sense of an authoritative pronouncement, since their function is to state when a pronouncement is authoritative. On the other hand, in the daily functioning of the legal system they are often treated and applied much as ordinary rules of law are. Here, then, we must confess there is something that can be called a "merger" of law and morality, and to which the term "intersection" is scarcely appropriate.

Instead of pursuing some such course of thought, to my surprise I found Professor Hart leaving completely untouched the nature of the fundamental rules that make law itself possible, and turning his attention instead to what he considers a confusion of thought on the part of the critics of positivism. Leaving out of account his discussion of analytical jurisprudence, his argument runs something as follows: Two views are associated with the names of Bentham and Austin. One is the command theory of law, the other is an insistence on the separation of law and morality. Critics of these writers came in time to perceive—"dimly" Professor Hart says—that the command theory is untenable. By a loose association of ideas they wrongly supposed that in advancing reasons for rejecting the command theory they had also refuted the view that law and morality must be sharply separated. This was a "natural mistake," but plainly a mistake just the same.

I do not think any mistake is committed in believing that Bentham and Austin's error in formulating improperly and too simply the problem of the relation of law and morals was part of a larger error that led to the command theory of law. I think the connection between these two errors can be made clear if we ask ourselves what would have happened to Austin's system of thought if he had abandoned the command theory.

One who reads Austin's Lectures V and VI[10] cannot help being impressed by the way he hangs doggedly to the command theory, in spite of the fact that every pull of his own keen mind was toward abandoning it. In the case of a sovereign monarch, law is what the monarch commands. But what shall we say of the "laws" of succession which tell who the "lawful" monarch is? It is of the essence of a command that it be addressed by a superior to an inferior, yet in the case of a "sovereign many," say, a parliament, the sovereign seems to command itself since a member of parliament may be convicted under a law he himself drafted and voted for. The sovereign must be unlimited in legal power, for who could adjudicate the legal bounds of a supreme lawmaking power? Yet a "sovereign many" must accept the limitation of rules before it can make law at all. Such a body can gain the power to issue commands only by acting in a "corporate capacity"; this it can do only by proceeding "agreeably to the modes and forms" established and accepted for the making of law. Judges exercise a power delegated to them by the supreme lawmaking power, and are commissioned to carry out its "direct or circuitous commands." Yet in a federal system it is the courts which must resolve conflicts of competence between the federation and its components.

All of these problems Austin sees with varying degrees of explicitness, and he struggles mightily with them. Over and over again he teeters on the edge of an abandonment of the command theory in favor of what Professor Hart has described as a view that discerns the foundations of a legal order in "certain fundamental accepted rules specifying the essential lawmaking procedures." Yet he never takes the plunge. He does not take it because he had a sure insight that it would forfeit the black-and-white distinction between law and morality that was the whole object of his Lectures—indeed, one

may say, the enduring object of a dedicated life. For if law is made possible by "fundamental accepted rules"—which for Austin must be rules, not of law, but of positive morality—what are we to say of the rules that the lawmaking power enacts to regulate its own lawmaking? We have election laws, laws allocating legislative representation to specific geographic areas, rules of parliamentary procedure, rules for the qualification of voters, and many other laws and rules of similar nature. These do not remain fixed, and all of them shape in varying degrees the lawmaking process. Yet how are we to distinguish between those basic rules that owe their validity to acceptance, and those which are properly rules of law, valid even when men generally consider them to be evil or ill-advised? In other words, how are we to define the words "fundamental" and "essential" in Professor Hart's own formulation: "certain fundamental accepted rules specifying the essential lawmaking procedure"?

The solution for this problem in Kelsen's theory is instructive. Kelsen does in fact take the plunge over which Austin hesitated too long. Kelsen realizes that before we can distinguish between what is law and what is not, there must be an acceptance of some basic procedure by which law is made. In any legal system there must be some fundamental rule that points unambiguously to the source from which laws must come in order to be laws. This rule Kelsen called "the basic norm." In his own words,

> The basic norm is not valid because it has been created in a certain way, but its validity is assumed by virtue of its content. It is valid, then, like a norm of natural law. . . . The idea of a pure positive law, like that of natural law, has its limitations.[11]

It will be noted that Kelsen speaks, not as Professor Hart does, of "fundamental rules" that regulate the making of law, but of a single rule or norm. Of course, there is no such single rule in any modern society. The notion of the basic norm is admittedly a symbol, not a fact. It is a symbol that embodies the positivist quest for some clear and unambiguous test of law, for some clean, sharp line that will divide the rules which owe their validity to their source and those which owe their validity to acceptance and intrinsic appeal. The difficulties Austin avoided by sticking with the command theory, Kelsen avoids by a fiction which simplifies reality into a form that can be absorbed by positivism.

A full exploration of all the problems that result when we recognize that law becomes possible only by virtue of rules that are not law, would require drawing into consideration the effect of the presence or absence of a written constitution. Such a constitution in some ways simplifies the problems I have been discussing, and in some ways complicates them. In so far as a written constitution defines basic lawmaking procedure, it may remove the perplexities that arise when a parliament in effect defines itself. At the same time, a legislature operating under a written constitution may enact statutes that profoundly affect the lawmaking procedure and its predictable outcome. If these statutes are drafted with sufficient cunning, they may remain within the frame of the constitution and yet undermine the institutions it was intended to establish. If the "court-packing" proposal of the 'thirties does not illustrate this danger unequivocally, it at least suggests that the fear of it is not fanciful. No written constitution can be self-executing. To be effective it requires not merely the respectful deference we show for ordinary legal enactments, but that willing convergence of effort we give to moral principles in which we have an active belief. One may properly work to amend a constitution, but so long as it remains unamended one must work with it, not against it or around it. All this amounts to saying that to be effective a written constitution must be accepted, at least provisionally, not just as law, but as good law.

What have these considerations to do with the ideal of fidelity to law? I think they have a great deal to do with it, and that they reveal the essential incapacity of the positivistic view to serve that ideal effectively. For I believe that a realization of this ideal is something for which we must plan, and that is precisely what positivism refuses to do.

Let me illustrate what I mean by planning for a realization of the ideal of fidelity to law. Suppose we are drafting a written constitution for a country just emerging from a period of violence and disorder in which any thread of legal continuity with previous governments has been broken. Obviously such a constitution cannot lift itself unaided into legality; it cannot be law simply because it says it is. We should keep in mind that the efficacy of our work will depend upon general acceptance and that to make this acceptance secure there must be a general belief that the constitution itself is necessary, right, and good. The provisions of the constitution should, therefore, be kept simple and understandable, not only in language, but also in purpose. Preambles and other explanations of what is being sought, which would be objectionable in an ordinary statute, may find an appropriate place in our constitution. We should think of our constitution as establishing a basic procedural framework for future governmental action in the enactment and administration of laws. Substantive limitations on the power of government should be kept to a minimum and should generally be confined to those for which a need can be generally appreciated. In so far as possible, substantive aims should be achieved procedurally, on the principle that if men are compelled to act in the right way, they will generally do the right things.

These considerations seem to have been widely ignored in the constitutions that have come into existence since World War II. Not uncommonly these constitutions incorporate a host of economic and political measures of the type one would ordinarily associate with statutory law. It is hardly likely that these measures have been written into the constitution because they represent aims that are generally shared. One suspects that the reason for their inclusion is precisely the opposite, namely, a fear that they would not be able to survive the vicissitudes of an ordinary exercise of parliamentary power. Thus, the divisions of opinion that are a normal accompaniment of lawmaking are written into the document that makes law itself possible. This is obviously a procedure that contains serious dangers for a future realization of the ideal of fidelity to law.

I have ventured these remarks on the making of constitutions not because I think they can claim any special profundity, but because I wished to illustrate what I mean by planning the conditions that will make it possible to realize the ideal of fidelity to law. Even within the limits of my modest purpose, what I have said may be clearly wrong. If so, it would not be for me to say whether I am also wrong clearly. I will, however, venture to assert that if I am wrong, I am wrong significantly. What disturbs me about the school of legal positivism is that it not only refuses to deal with problems of the sort I have just discussed, but bans them on principle from the province of legal philosophy. In its concern to assign the right labels to the things men do, this school seems to lose all interest in asking whether men are doing the right things.

IV. The morality of law itself

Most of the issues raised by Professor Hart's essay can be restated in terms of the distinction between order and good order. Law may be said to represent order *simpliciter*. Good order is law that corresponds to the demands of justice, or morality, or men's notions of what ought to be. This rephrasing of the issue is useful in bringing to light the ambitious nature of Professor Hart's undertaking, for surely we would all agree that it is no easy thing to distinguish order from good order. When it is said, for example, that law simply represents that public order which obtains under all governments—democratic,

Fascist, or Communist[12]—the order intended is certainly not that of a morgue or cemetery. We must mean a functioning order, and such an order has to be at least good enough to be considered as functioning by some standard or other. A reminder that workable order usually requires some play in the joints, and therefore cannot be too orderly, is enough to suggest some of the complexities that would be involved in any attempt to draw a sharp distinction between order and good order.

For the time being, however, let us suppose we can in fact clearly separate the concept of order from that of good order. Even in this unreal and abstract form the notion of order itself contains what may be called a moral element. Let me illustrate this "morality of order" in its crudest and most elementary form. Let us suppose an absolute monarch, whose word is the only law known to his subjects. We may further suppose him to be utterly selfish and to seek in his relations with his subjects solely his own advantage. This monarch from time to time issues commands, promising rewards for compliance and threatening punishment for disobedience. He is, however, a dissolute and forgetful fellow, who never makes the slightest attempt to ascertain who have in fact followed his directions and who have not. As a result he habitually punishes loyalty and rewards disobedience. It is apparent that this monarch will never achieve even his own selfish aims until he is ready to accept that minimum self-restraint that will create a meaningful connection between his words and his actions.

Let us now suppose that our monarch undergoes a change of heart and begins to pay some attention to what he said yesterday when, today, he has occasion to distribute bounty or to order the chopping off of heads. Under the strain of this new responsibility, however, our monarch relaxes his attention in other directions and becomes hopelessly slothful in the phrasing of his commands. His orders become so ambiguous and are uttered in so inaudible a tone that his subjects never have any clear idea what he wants them to do. Here, again, it is apparent that if our monarch for his own selfish advantage wants to create in his realm anything like a system of law he will have to pull himself together and assume still another responsibility.

Law, considered merely as order, contains, then, its own implicit morality. This morality of order must be respected if we are to create anything that can be called law, even bad law. Law by itself is powerless to bring this morality into existence. Until our monarch is really ready to face the responsibilities of his position, it will do no good for him to issue still another futile command, this time self-addressed and threatening himself with punishment if he does not mend his ways.

There is a twofold sense in which it is true that law cannot be built on law. First of all, the authority to make law must be supported by moral attitudes that accord to it the competency it claims. Here we are dealing with a morality external to law, which makes law possible. But this alone is not enough. We may stipulate that in our monarchy the accepted "basic norm" designates the monarch himself as the only possible source of law. We still cannot have law until our monarch is ready to accept the internal morality of law itself.

In the life of a nation these external and internal moralities of law reciprocally influence one another; a deterioration of the one will almost inevitably produce a deterioration in the other. So closely related are they that when the anthropologist Lowie speaks of "the generally accepted ethical postulates underlying our . . . legal institutions as their ultimate sanction and guaranteeing their smooth functioning,"[13] he may be presumed to have both of them in mind.

What I have called "the internal morality of law" seems to be almost completely neglected by Professor Hart. He does make brief mention of "justice in the administration of the law," which consists in the like treatment of like cases, by whatever elevated or perverted standards the

word "like" may be defined.[14] But he quickly dismisses this aspect of law as having no special relevance to his main enterprise.

In this I believe he is profoundly mistaken. It is his neglect to analyze the demands of a morality of order that leads him throughout his essay to treat law as a datum projecting itself into human experience and not as an object of human striving. When we realize that order itself is something that must be worked for, it becomes apparent that the existence of a legal system, even a bad or evil legal system, is always a matter of degree. When we recognize this simple fact of everyday legal experience, it becomes impossible to dismiss the problems presented by the Nazi regime with a simple assertion: "Under the Nazis there was law, even if it was bad law." We have instead to inquire how much of a legal system survived the general debasement and perversion of all forms of social order that occurred under the Nazi rule, and what moral implications this mutilated system had for the conscientious citizen forced to live under it.

It is not necessary, however, to dwell on such moral upheavals as the Nazi regime to see how completely incapable the positivistic philosophy is of serving the one high moral ideal it professes, that of fidelity to law. Its default in serving this ideal actually becomes most apparent, I believe, in the everyday problems that confront those who are earnestly desirous of meeting the moral demands of a legal order, but who have responsible functions to discharge in the very order toward which loyalty is due.

Let us suppose the case of a trial judge who has had an extensive experience in commercial matters and before whom a great many commercial disputes are tried. As a subordinate in a judicial hierarchy, our judge has of course the duty to follow the law laid down by his supreme court. Our imaginary Scrutton has the misfortune, however, to live under a supreme court which he considers woefully ignorant of the ways and needs of commerce. To his mind, many of this court's decisions in the field of commercial law simply do not make sense. If a conscientious judge caught in this dilemma were to turn to the positivistic philosophy what succor could he expect? It will certainly do no good to remind him that he has an obligation of fidelity to law. He is aware of this already and painfully so, since it is the source of his predicament. Nor will it help to say that if he legislates, it must be "interstitially," or that his contributions must be "confined from molar to molecular motions."[15] This mode of statement may be congenial to those who like to think of law, not as a purposive thing, but as an expression of the dimensions and directions of state power. But I cannot believe that the essentially trite idea behind this advice can be lifted by literary eloquence to the point where it will offer any real help to our judge; for one thing, it may be impossible for him to know whether his supreme court would regard any particular contribution of his as being wide or narrow.

Nor is it likely that a distinction between core and penumbra would be helpful. The predicament of our judge may well derive, not from particular precedents, but from a mistaken conception of the nature of commerce which extends over many decisions and penetrates them in varying degrees. So far as his problem arises from the use of particular words, he may well find that the supreme court often uses the ordinary terms of commerce in senses foreign to actual business dealings. If he interprets those words as a business executive or accountant would, he may well reduce the precedents he is bound to apply to a logical shambles. On the other hand, he may find great difficulty in discerning the exact sense in which the supreme court used those words, since in his mind that sense is itself the product of a confusion.

Is it not clear that it is precisely positivism's insistence on a rigid separation of law as it is from law as it ought to be that renders the positivistic philosophy incapable of aiding our judge? Is it not also clear that our judge can never achieve a satisfactory resolution of his dilemma unless he views his duty of fidelity to law in a context which also embraces his responsibility for making law what it ought to be?

The case I have supposed may seem extreme, but the problem it suggests pervades our whole legal system. If the divergence of views between our judge and his supreme court were less drastic, it would be more difficult to present his predicament graphically, but the perplexity of his position might actually increase. Perplexities of this sort are a normal accompaniment of the discharge of any adjudicative function; they perhaps reach their most poignant intensity in the field of administrative law.

One can imagine a case—surely not likely in Professor Hart's country or mine—where a judge might hold profound moral convictions that were exactly the opposite of those held, with equal attachment, by his supreme court. He might also be convinced that the precedents he was bound to apply were the direct product of a morality he considered abhorrent. If such a judge did not find the solution for his dilemma in surrendering his office, he might well be driven to a wooden and literal application of precedents which he could not otherwise apply because he was incapable of understanding the philosophy that animated them. But I doubt that a judge in this situation would need the help of legal positivism to find these melancholy escapes from his predicament. Nor do I think that such a predicament is likely to arise within a nation where both law and good law are regarded as collaborative human achievements in need of constant renewal, and where lawyers are still at least as interested in asking "What is good law?" as they are in asking "What is law?"

V. The problem of restoring respect for law and justice after the collapse of a regime that respected neither

After the collapse of the Nazi regime the German courts were faced with a truly frightful predicament. It was impossible for them to declare the whole dictatorship illegal or to treat as void every decision and legal enactment that had emanated from Hitler's government. Intolerable dislocations would have resulted from any such wholesale outlawing of all that occurred over a span of twelve years. On the other hand, it was equally impossible to carry forward into the new government the effects of every Nazi perversity that had been committed in the name of law; any such course would have tainted an indefinite future with the poisons of Nazism.

This predicament—which was, indeed, a pervasive one, affecting all branches of law— came to a dramatic head in a series of cases involving informers who had taken advantage of the Nazi terror to get rid of personal enemies or unwanted spouses. If all Nazi statutes and judicial decisions were indiscriminately "law," then these despicable creatures were guiltless, since they had turned their victims over to processes which the Nazis themselves knew by the name of law. Yet it was intolerable, especially for the surviving relatives and friends of the victims, that these people should go about unpunished, while the objects of their spite were dead, or were just being released after years of imprisonment, or, more painful still, simply remained unaccounted for.

The urgency of this situation does not by any means escape Professor Hart. Indeed, he is moved to recommend an expedient that is surely not lacking itself in a certain air of desperation. He suggests that a retroactive criminal statute would have been the least objectionable solution to the problem. This statute would have punished the informer, and branded him as a criminal, for an act which Professor Hart regards as having been perfectly legal when he committed it.[16]

On the other hand, Professor Hart condemns without qualification those judicial decisions in which the courts themselves undertook to declare void certain of the Nazi statutes under which the informer's victims had been con-

victed. One cannot help raising at this point the question whether the issue as presented by Professor Hart himself is truly that of fidelity to law. Surely it would be a necessary implication of a retroactive criminal statute against informers that, for purposes of that statute at least, the Nazi laws as applied to the informers or their victims were to be regarded as void. With this turn the question seems no longer to be whether what was once law can now be declared not to have been law, but rather who should do the dirty work, the courts or the legislature.

But, as Professor Hart himself suggests, the issues at stake are much too serious to risk losing them in a semantic tangle. Even if the whole question were one of words, we should remind ourselves that we are in an area where words have a powerful effect on human attitudes. I should like, therefore, to undertake a defense of the German courts, and to advance reasons why, in my opinion, their decisions do not represent the abandonment of legal principle that Professor Hart sees in them. In order to understand the background of those decisions we shall have to move a little closer within smelling distance of the witches' caldron than we have been brought so far by Professor Hart. We shall have also to consider an aspect of the problem ignored in his essay, namely, the degree to which the Nazis observed what I have called the inner morality of law itself.

Throughout his discussion Professor Hart seems to assume that the only difference between Nazi law and, say, English law is that the Nazis used their laws to achieve ends that are odious to an Englishman. This assumption is, I think, seriously mistaken, and Professor Hart's acceptance of it seems to me to render his discussion unresponsive to the problem it purports to address.

Throughout their period of control the Nazis took generous advantage of a device not wholly unknown to American legislatures, the retroactive statute curing past legal irregularities. The most dramatic use of the curative powers of such a statute occurred on July 3, 1934, after the "Roehm purge." When this intraparty shooting affair was over and more than seventy Nazis had been—one can hardly avoid saying—"rubbed out," Hitler returned to Berlin and procured from his cabinet a law ratifying and confirming the measures taken between June 30, and July 1, 1934, without mentioning the names of those who were now considered to have been lawfully executed.[17] Some time later Hitler declared that during the Roehm purge "the supreme court of the German people . . . consisted of myself,"[18] surely not an overstatement of the capacity in which he acted if one takes seriously the enactment conferring retroactive legality on "the measures taken."

Now in England and America it would never occur to anyone to say that "it is in the nature of law that it cannot be retroactive," although, of course, constitutional inhibitions may prohibit certain kinds of retroactivity. We would say it is normal for a law to operate prospectively, and that it may be arguable that it ought never operate otherwise, but there would be a certain occult unpersuasiveness in any assertion that retroactivity violates the very nature of law itself. Yet we have only to imagine a country in which *all* laws are retroactive in order to see that retroactivity presents a real problem for the internal morality of law. If we suppose an absolute monarch who allows his realm to exist in a constant state of anarchy, we would hardly say that he could create a regime of law simply by enacting a curative statute conferring legality on everything that had happened up to its date and by announcing an intention to enact similar statutes every six months in the future.

A general increase in the resort to statutes curative of past legal irregularities represents a deterioration in that form of legal morality without which law itself cannot exist. The threat of such statutes hangs over the whole legal system, and robs every law on the books of some of its significance. And surely a general threat of this sort is implied when a government is willing

to use such a statute to transform into lawful execution what was simple murder when it happened.

During the Nazi regime there were repeated rumors of "secret laws." In the article criticized by Professor Hart, Radbruch mentions a report that the wholesale killings in concentration camps were made "lawful" by a secret enactment.[19] Now surely there can be no greater legal monstrosity than a secret statute. Would anyone seriously recommend that following the war the German courts should have searched for unpublished laws among the files left by Hitler's government so that citizens' rights could be determined by a reference to these laws?

The extent of the legislator's obligation to make his laws known to his subjects is, of course, a problem of legal morality that has been under active discussion at least since the Secession of the Plebs. There is probably no modern state that has not been plagued by this problem in one form or another. It is most likely to arise in modern societies with respect to unpublished administrative directions. Often these are regarded in quite good faith by those who issue them as affecting only matters of internal organization. But since the procedures followed by an administrative agency, even in its "internal" actions, may seriously affect the rights and interests of the citizen, these unpublished, or "secret," regulations are often a subject for complaint.

But as with retroactivity, what in most societies is kept under control by the tacit restraints of legal decency broke out in monstrous form under Hitler. Indeed, so loose was the whole Nazi morality of law that it is not easy to know just what should be regarded as an unpublished or secret law. Since unpublished instructions to those administering the law could destroy the letter of any published law by imposing on it an outrageous interpretation, there was a sense in which the meaning of every law was "secret." Even a verbal order from Hitler that a thousand prisoners in concentration camps be put to death was at once an administrative direction and a validation of everything done under it as being "lawful."

But the most important affronts to the morality of law by Hitler's government took no such subtle forms as those exemplified in the bizarre outcroppings I have just discussed. In the first place, when legal forms became inconvenient, it was always possible for the Nazis to bypass them entirely and "to act through the party in the streets." There was no one who dared bring them to account for whatever outrages might thus be committed. In the second place, the Nazi-dominated courts were always ready to disregard any statute, even those enacted by the Nazis themselves, if this suited their convenience or if they feared that a lawyer-like interpretation might incur displeasure "above."

This complete willingness of the Nazis to disregard even their own enactments was an important factor leading Radbruch to take the position he did in the articles so severely criticized by Professor Hart. I do not believe that any fair appraisal of the action of the postwar German courts is possible unless we take this factor into account, as Professor Hart fails completely to do.

These remarks may seem inconclusive in their generality and to rest more on assertion than evidentiary fact. Let us turn at once, then, to the actual case discussed by Professor Hart.[20]

In 1944 a German soldier paid a short visit to his wife while under travel orders on a reassignment. During the single day he was home, he conveyed privately to his wife something of his opinion of the Hitler government. He expressed disapproval of (*sich abfällig geäussert über*) Hitler and other leading personalities of the Nazi party. He also said it was too bad Hitler had not met his end in the assassination attempt that had occurred on July 20th of that year. Shortly after his departure, his wife, who during his long absence on military duty "had turned to other men" and who wished to get rid of him, reported his remarks to the local leader of the

Nazi party, observing that "a man who would say a thing like that does not deserve to live." The result was a trial of the husband by a military tribunal and a sentence of death. After a short period of imprisonment, instead of being executed, he was sent to the front again. After the collapse of the Nazi regime, the wife was brought to trial for having procured the imprisonment of her husband. Her defense rested on the ground that her husband's statements to her about Hitler and the Nazis constituted a crime under the laws then in force. Accordingly, when she informed on her husband she was simply bringing a criminal to justice.

This defense rested on two statutes, one passed in 1934, the other in 1938. Let us first consider the second of these enactments, which was part of a more comprehensive legislation creating a whole series of special wartime criminal offenses. I reproduce below a translation of the only pertinent section:

> The following persons are guilty of destroying the national power of resistance and shall be punished by death: Whoever publicly solicits or incites a refusal to fulfill the obligations of service in the armed forces of Germany, or in armed forces allied with Germany, or who otherwise publicly seeks to injure or destroy the will of the German people or an allied people to assert themselves stalwartly against their enemies.[21]

It is almost inconceivable that a court of present-day Germany would hold the husband's remarks to his wife, who was barred from military duty by her sex, to be a violation of the final catch-all provision of this statute, particularly when it is recalled that the text reproduced above was part of a more comprehensive enactment dealing with such things as harboring deserters, escaping military duty by self-inflicted injuries, and the like. The question arises, then, as to the extent to which the interpretive principles applied by the courts of Hitler's government should be accepted in determining whether the husband's remarks were indeed unlawful.

This question becomes acute when we note that the act applies only to *public* acts or utterances, whereas the husband's remarks were in the privacy of his own home. Now it appears that the Nazi courts (and it should be noted we are dealing with a special military court) quite generally disregarded this limitation and extended the act to all utterances, private or public.[22] Is Professor Hart prepared to say that the legal meaning of this statute is to be determined in the light of this apparently uniform principle of judicial interpretation?

Let us turn now to the other statute upon which Professor Hart relies in assuming that the husband's utterance was unlawful. This is the act of 1934, the relevant portions of which are translated below:

(1)   Whoever publicly makes spiteful or provocative statements directed against, or statements which disclose a base disposition toward, the leading personalities of the nation or of the National Socialist German Workers' Party, or toward measures taken or institutions established by them, and of such a nature as to undermine the people's confidence in their political leadership, shall be punished by imprisonment.

(2)   Malicious utterances not made in public shall be treated in the same manner as public utterances when the person making them realized or should have realized they would reach the public.

(3)   Prosecution for such utterances shall be only on the order of the National Minister of Justice; in case the utterance was directed against a leading personality of the National Socialist German Workers' Party, the Minister of Justice shall order

prosecution only with the advice and consent of the Representative of the Leader.

(4)   The National Minister of Justice shall, with the advice and consent of the Representative of the Leader, determine who shall belong to the class of leading personalities for purposes of Section 1 above.[23]

Extended comment on this legislative monstrosity is scarcely called for, overlarded and undermined as it is by uncontrolled administrative discretion. We may note only: first, that it offers no justification whatever for the death penalty actually imposed on the husband, though never carried out; second, that if the wife's act in informing on her husband made his remarks "public," there is no such thing as a private utterance under this statute. I should like to ask the reader whether he can actually share Professor Hart's indignation that, in the perplexities of the postwar reconstruction, the German courts saw fit to declare this thing not a law. Can it be argued seriously that it would have been more beseeming to the judicial process if the postwar courts had undertaken a study of "the interpretative principles" in force during Hitler's rule and had then solemnly applied those "principles" to ascertain the meaning of this statute? On the other hand, would the courts really have been showing respect for Nazi law if they had construed the Nazi statutes by their own, quite different, standards of interpretation?

Professor Hart castigates the German courts and Radbruch, not so much for what they believed had to be done, but because they failed to see that they were confronted by a moral dilemma of a sort that would have been immediately apparent to Bentham and Austin. By the simple dodge of saying, "When a statute is sufficiently evil it ceases to be law," they ran away from the problem they should have faced.

This criticism is, I believe, without justification. So far as the courts are concerned, matters certainly would not have been helped if, instead of saying, "This is not law," they had said, "This is law but it is so evil we will refuse to apply it." Surely moral confusion reaches its height when a court refuses to apply something it admits to be law, and Professor Hart does not recommend any such "facing of the true issue" by the courts themselves. He would have preferred a retroactive statute. Curiously, this was also the preference of Radbruch.[24] But unlike Professor Hart, the German courts and Gustav Radbruch were living participants in a situation of drastic emergency. The informer problem was a pressing one, and if legal institutions were to be rehabilitated in Germany it would not do to allow the people to begin taking the law into their own hands, as might have occurred while the courts were waiting for a statute. . . .

VI. The moral implications of legal positivism

We now reach the question whether there is any ground for Gustav Radbruch's belief that a general acceptance of the positivistic philosophy in pre-Nazi Germany made smoother the route to dictatorship. Understandably, Professor Hart regards this as the most outrageous of all charges against positivism.

Here indeed we enter upon a hazardous area of controversy, where ugly words and ugly charges have become commonplace. During the last half century in this country no issue of legal philosophy has caused more spilling of ink and adrenalin than the assertion that there are "totalitarian" implications in the views of Oliver Wendell Holmes, Jr.

German legal positivism not only banned from legal science any consideration of the moral ends of law, but it was also indifferent to what I have called the inner morality of law itself. The German lawyer was therefore peculiarly prepared to accept as "law" anything that called itself by that name, was printed at government expense, and seemed to come "*von oben herab.*"

In the light of these considerations I cannot

see either absurdity or perversity in the suggestion that the attitudes prevailing in the German legal profession were helpful to the Nazis. Hitler did not come to power by a violent revolution. He was Chancellor before he became the Leader. The exploitation of legal forms started cautiously and became bolder as power was consolidated. The first attacks on the established order were on ramparts which, if they were manned by anyone, were manned by lawyers and judges. These ramparts fell almost without a struggle.

Professor Hart and others have been understandably distressed by references to a "higher law" in some of the decisions concerning informers and in Radbruch's postwar writings. I suggest that if German jurisprudence had concerned itself more with the inner morality of law, it would not have been necessary to invoke any notion of this sort in declaring void the more outrageous Nazi statutes.

To me there is nothing shocking in saying that a dictatorship which clothes itself with a tinsel of legal form can so far depart from the morality of order, from the inner morality of law itself, that it ceases to be a legal system. When a system calling itself law is predicated upon a general disregard by judges of the terms of the laws they purport to enforce, when this system habitually cures its legal irregularities, even the grossest, by retroactive statutes, when it has only to resort to forays of terror in the streets, which no one dares challenge, in order to escape even those scant restraints imposed by the pretence of legality— when all these things have become true of a dictatorship, it is not hard for me, at least, to deny to it the name of law.

I believe that the invalidity of the statutes involved in the informer cases could have been grounded on considerations such as I have just outlined. But if you were raised with a generation that said "law is law" and meant it, you may feel the only way you can escape one law is to set another off against it, and this perforce must be a "higher law." Hence these notions of "higher law," which are a justifiable cause for alarm, may themselves be a belated fruit of German legal positivism. . . .

But as an actual solution for the informer cases, I, like Professors Hart and Radbruch, would have preferred a retroactive statute. My reason for this preference is not that this is the most nearly lawful way of making unlawful what was once law. Rather I would see such a statute as a way of symbolizing a sharp break with the past, as a means of isolating a kind of cleanup operation from the normal functioning of the judicial process. By this isolation it would become possible for the judiciary to return more rapidly to a condition in which the demands of legal morality could be given proper respect. In other words, it would make it possible to plan more effectively to regain for the ideal of fidelity to law its normal meaning.

VII. The problem of interpretation: the core and the penumbra

It is essential that we be just as clear as we can be about the meaning of Professor Hart's doctrine of "the core and the penumbra,"[25] because I believe the casual reader is likely to misinterpret what he has to say. Such a reader is apt to suppose that Professor Hart is merely describing something that is a matter of everyday experience for the lawyer, namely, that in the interpretation of legal rules it is typically the case (though not universally so) that there are some situations which will seem to fall rather clearly within the rule, while others will be more doubtful. Professor Hart's thesis takes no such jejune form. His extended discussion of the core and the penumbra is not just a complicated way of recognizing that some cases are hard, while others are easy. Instead, on the basis of a theory about language meaning generally, he is proposing a theory of judicial interpretation which is, I believe, wholly novel. Certainly it has never been put forward in so uncompromising a form before.

As I understand Professor Hart's thesis (if we add some tacit assumptions implied by it, as well as some qualifications he would no doubt wish his readers to supply) a full statement would run something as follows: The task of interpretation is commonly that of determining the meaning of the individual words of a legal rule, like "vehicle" in a rule excluding vehicles from a park. More particularly, the task of interpretation is to determine the range of reference of such a word, or the aggregate of things to which it points. Communication is possible only because words have a "standard instance," or a "core of meaning" that remains relatively constant, whatever the context in which the word may appear. Except in unusual circumstances, it will always be proper to regard a word like "vehicle" as embracing its "standard instance," that is, that aggregate of things it would include in all ordinary contexts, within or without the law. This meaning the word will have in any legal rule, whatever its purpose. In applying the word to its "standard instance," no creative role is assumed by the judge. He is simply applying the law "as it is."

In addition to a constant core, however, words also have a penumbra of meaning which, unlike the core, will vary from context to context. When the object in question (say, a tricycle) falls within this penumbral area, the judge is forced to assume a more creative role. He must now undertake, for the first time, an interpretation of the rule in the light of its purpose or aim. Having in mind what was sought by the regulation concerning parks, ought it to be considered as barring tricycles? When questions of this sort are decided there is at least an "intersection" of "is" and "ought," since the judge, in deciding what the rule "is," does so in the light of his notions of what "it ought to be" in order to carry out its purpose.

If I have properly interpreted Professor Hart's theory as it affects the "hard core," then I think it is quite untenable. The most obvious defect of his theory lies in its assumption that problems of interpretation typically turn on the meaning of individual words. Surely no judge applying a rule of the common law ever followed any such procedure as that described (and, I take it, prescribed) by Professor Hart; indeed, we do not normally even think of his problem as being one of "interpretation." Even in the case of statutes, we commonly have to assign meaning, not to a single word, but to a sentence, a paragraph, or a whole page or more of text. Surely a paragraph does not have a "standard instance" that remains constant whatever the context in which it appears. If a statute seems to have a kind of "core meaning" that we can apply without a too precise inquiry into its exact purpose, this is because we can see that, however one might formulate the precise objective of the statute, this case would still come within it.

Even in situations where our interpretive difficulties seem to head up in a single word, Professor Hart's analysis seems to me to give no real account of what does or should happen. In his illustration of the "vehicle," although he tells us this word has a core of meaning that in all contexts defines unequivocally a range of objects embraced by it, he never tells us what these objects might be. If the rule excluding vehicles from parks seems easy to apply in some cases, I submit this is because we can see clearly enough what the rule "is aiming at in general" so that we know there is no need to worry about the difference between Fords and Cadillacs. If in some cases we seem to be able to apply the rule without asking what its purpose is, this is not because we can treat a directive arrangement as if it had no purpose. It is rather because, for example, whether the rule be intended to preserve quiet in the park, or to save carefree strollers from injury, we know, "without thinking," that a noisy automobile must be excluded.

What would Professor Hart say if some local patriots wanted to mount on a pedestal in the park a truck used in World War II, while other citizens, regarding the proposed memorial as an eyesore, support their stand by the "no vehicle"

rule? Does this truck, in perfect working order, fall within the core or the penumbra?

Professor Hart seems to assert that unless words have "standard instances" that remain constant regardless of context, effective communication would break down and it would become impossible to construct a system of "rules which have authority."[26] If in every context words took on a unique meaning, peculiar to that context, the whole process of interpretation would become so uncertain and subjective that the ideal of a rule of law would lose its meaning. In other words, Professor Hart seems to be saying that unless we are prepared to accept his analysis of interpretation, we must surrender all hope of giving an effective meaning to the ideal of fidelity to law. This presents a very dark prospect indeed, if one believes, as I do, that we cannot accept his theory of interpretation. I do not take so gloomy a view of the future of the ideal of fidelity to law.

An illustration will help to test, not only Professor Hart's theory of the core and the penumbra, but its relevance to the ideal of fidelity to law as well. Let us suppose that in leafing through the statutes, we come upon the following enactment: "It shall be a misdemeanor, punishable by a fine of five dollars, to sleep in any railway station." We have no trouble in perceiving the general nature of the target toward which this statute is aimed. Indeed, we are likely at once to call to mind the picture of a disheveled tramp, spread out in an ungainly fashion on one of the benches of the station, keeping weary passengers on their feet and filling their ears with raucous and alcoholic snores. This vision may fairly be said to represent the "obvious instance" contemplated by the statute, though certainly it is far from being the "standard instance" of the physiological state called "sleep."

Now let us see how this example bears on the ideal of fidelity to law. Suppose I am a judge, and that two men are brought before me for violating this statute. The first is a passenger who was waiting at 3 A.M. for a delayed train. When he was arrested he was sitting upright in an orderly fashion, but was heard by the arresting officer to be gently snoring. The second is a man who had brought a blanket and pillow to the station and had obviously settled himself down for the night. He was arrested, however, before he had a chance to go to sleep. Which of these cases presents the "standard instance" of the word "sleep"? If I disregard that question, and decide to fine the second man and set free the first, have I violated a duty of fidelity to law? Have I violated that duty if I interpret the word "sleep" as used in this statute to mean something like "to spread oneself out on a bench or floor to spend the night, or as if to spend the night"?

Testing another aspect of Professor Hart's theory, is it really ever possible to interpret a word in a statute without knowing the aim of the statute? Suppose we encounter the following incomplete sentence: "All improvements must be promptly reported to . . ." Professor Hart's theory seems to assert that even if we have only this fragment before us we can safely construe the word "improvement" to apply to its "standard instance," though we would have to know the rest of the sentence before we could deal intelligently with "problems of the penumbra." Yet surely in the truncated sentence I have quoted, the word "improvement" is almost as devoid of meaning as the symbol "X."

The word "improvement" will immediately take on meaning if we fill out the sentence with the words, "the head nurse," or, "the Town Planning Authority," though the two meanings that come to mind are radically dissimilar. It can hardly be said that these two meanings represent some kind of penumbral accretion to the word's "standard instance." And one wonders, parenthetically, how helpful the theory of the core and the penumbra would be in deciding whether, when the report is to be made to the planning authorities, the word "improvement" includes an unmortgageable monstrosity of a house that lowers the market value of the land on which it is built.

It will be instructive, I think, to consider the effect of other ways of filling out the sentence. Suppose we add to, "All improvements must be promptly reported to . . ." the words, "the Dean of the Graduate Division." Here we no longer seem, as we once did, to be groping in the dark; rather, we seem now to be reaching into an empty box. We achieve a little better orientation if the final clause reads, "to the Principal of the School," and we feel completely at ease if it becomes, "to the Chairman of the Committee on Relations with the Parents of Children in the Primary Division."

It should be noted that in deciding what the word "improvement" means in all these cases, we do not proceed simply by placing the word in some general context, such as hospital practice, town planning, or education. If this were so, the "improvement" in the last instance might just as well be that of the teacher as that of the pupil. Rather, we ask ourselves, What can this rule be for? What evil does it seek to avert? What good is it intended to promote? When it is "the head nurse" who receives the report, we are apt to find ourselves asking, "Is there, perhaps, a shortage of hospital space, so that patients who improve sufficiently are sent home or are assigned to a ward where they will receive less attention?" If "Principal" offers more orientation than "Dean of the Graduate Division," this must be because we know something about the differences between primary education and education on the postgraduate university level. We must have some minimum acquaintance with the ways in which these two educational enterprises are conducted, and with the problems encountered in both of them, before any distinction between "Principal" and "Dean of the Graduate Division" would affect our interpretation of "improvement." We must, in other words, be sufficiently capable of putting ourselves in the position of those who drafted the rule to know what they thought "ought to be." It is in the light of this "ought" that we must decide what the rule "is.". . .

VIII. The moral and emotional foundations of positivism

If we ignore the specific theories of law associated with the positivistic philosophy, I believe we can say that the dominant tone of positivism is set by a fear of a purposive interpretation of law and legal institutions, or at least by a fear that such an interpretation may be pushed too far. I think one can find confirmatory traces of this fear in all of those classified as "positivists" by Professor Hart, with the outstanding exception of Bentham, who is in all things a case apart and who was worlds removed from anything that could be called *ethical* positivism.

Now the belief that many of us hold, that this fear of purpose takes a morbid turn in positivism, should not mislead us into thinking that the fear is wholly without justification, or that it reflects no significant problem in the organization of society.

Fidelity to law *can* become impossible if we do not accept the broader responsibilities (themselves purposive, as all responsibilities are and must be) that go with a purposive interpretation of law. One can imagine a course of reasoning that might run as follows: This statute says absinthe shall not be sold. What is its purpose? To promote health. Now, as everyone knows, absinthe is a sound, wholesome, and beneficial beverage. Therefore, interpreting the statute in the light of its purpose, I construe it to direct a general sale and consumption of that most healthful of beverages, absinthe.

If the risk of this sort of thing is implicit in a purposive interpretation, what measures can we take to eliminate it, or to reduce it to bearable proportions? One is tempted to say, "Why, just use ordinary common sense." But this would be an evasion, and would amount to saying that although we know the answer, we cannot say what it is. To give a better answer, I fear I shall have to depart from those high standards of clarity Professor Hart so rightly prizes and so generally exemplifies. I shall have to say that the answer lies in the concept of *structure*. A statute or a rule of common law has, either explicitly, or by virtue of its relation with other rules, something that may be called a structural integrity. This is what we have in mind when we speak of "the intent of the statute," though we know it is men who have intentions and not words on paper. Within the limits of that structure, fidelity to law not only permits but demands a creative role from the judge, but beyond that structure it does not permit him to go. Of course, the structure of which I speak presents its own "problems of the penumbra." But the penumbra in this case surrounds something real, something that has a meaning and integrity of its own. It is not a purposeless collocation of words that gets its meaning on loan from lay usage.

It is one of the great virtues of Professor Hart's essay that it makes explicit positivism's concern for the ideal of fidelity to law. Yet I believe, though I cannot prove, that the basic reason why positivism fears a purposive interpretation is not that it may lead to anarchy, but that it may push us too far in the opposite direction. It sees in a purposive interpretation, carried too far, a threat to human freedom and human dignity.

Let me illustrate what I mean by supposing that I am a man without religious beliefs living in a community of ardent Protestant Christian faith. A statute in this community makes it unlawful for me to play golf on Sunday. I find this statute an annoyance and accept its restraints reluctantly. But the annoyance I feel is not greatly different from that I might experience if, though it were lawful to play on Sunday, a power failure prevented me from taking the streetcar I would normally use in reaching the course. In the vernacular, "it is just one of those things."

What a different complexion the whole matter assumes if a statute compels me to attend church, or, worse still, to kneel and recite prayers! Here I may feel a direct affront to my integrity as a human being. Yet the purpose of both statutes may well be to increase church attendance. The difference may even seem to be that the first statute seeks its end slyly and by indirection, the second, honestly and openly. Yet surely this is a case in which indirection has its virtues and honesty its heavy price in human dignity.

Now I believe that positivism fears that a too explicit and uninhibited interpretation in terms of purpose may well push the first kind of statute in the direction of the second. If this is a basic concern underlying the positivistic philosophy, that philosophy is dealing with a real problem, however inept its response to the problem may seem to be. For this problem of the impressed purpose is a crucial one in our society. One thinks of the obligation to bargain "in good faith" imposed by the National Labor Relations Act.[27] One recalls the remark that to punish a criminal is less of an affront to his dignity than to reform and improve him. The statutory preamble comes to mind: the increasing use made of it, its legislative wisdom, the significance that should be accorded to it in judicial interpretation. The flag salute cases[28] will, of course, occur to everyone. I myself recall the splendid analysis by Professor von Hippel of the things that were fundamentally wrong about Nazism, and his conclusion that the grossest of all Nazi perversities was that of coercing acts, like the putting out of flags and saying, "Heil Hitler!" that have meaning only when done voluntarily, or, more accurately, have a meaning when coerced that is wholly parasitic on an association of them with past voluntary expressions.[29]

Questions of this sort are undoubtedly becoming more acute as the state assumes a more active role with respect to economic activity. No significant economic activity can be organized exclusively by "don'ts." By its nature economic production requires a co-operative effort. In the economic field there is special reason, therefore, to fear that "This you may not do" will be transformed into "This you must

do—but willingly." As we all know, the most tempting opportunity for effecting this transformation is presented by what is called in administrative practice "the prehearing conference," in which the negative threat of a statute's sanctions may be used by its administrators to induce what they regard, in all good conscience, as "the proper attitude."

I look forward to the day when legal philosophy can address itself earnestly to issues of this sort, and not simply exploit them to score points in favor of a position already taken. Professor Hart's essay seems to me to open the way for such a discussion, for it eliminates from the positivistic philosophy a pretense that has hitherto obscured every issue touched by it. I mean, of course, the pretense of the ethical neutrality of positivism. That is why I can say in all sincerity that, despite my almost paragraph-by-paragraph disagreement with the views expressed in his essay, I believe Professor Hart has made an enduring contribution to legal philosophy.

Notes

Lon L. Fuller, excerpts from "Positivism and Fidelity to Law: A Reply to Professor Hart", 71 *Harvard Law Review* 630 (1958) 630–649. Reprinted by kind permission of the Estate of Lon L. Fuller.

1 Kelsen, *Die Idee des Naturrechtes*, 7 Zeitschrift für Öffentliches Recht 221, 248 (Austria 1927).

2 Hart, *Positivism and the Separation of Law and Morals*, 71 *Harv. L. Rev.* 593, 615–21 (1958).

3 U.S. Const. art. V.

4 Hart, supra note 2, at 624.

5 For an outstanding example, see G. Scammell and Nephew, Ltd. v. Ouston, [1941] A.C. 251 (1940). I personally would be inclined to put under the same head Victoria Laundry, Ltd. v. Newman Industries, Ltd., [1949] 2 K.B. 528 (C.A.).

6 See Hart, supra note 2, at 608–12.

7 See N.Y. Times, Nov. 8, 1949, p. 1, col. 4 (late city ed.) (report of a speech made on November 7, 1949 to the Central Committee of the Union of Catholic Italian Lawyers).

8 Hart, supra note 2, at 603.

9 Ibid.

10 1 Austin, *Lectures on Jurisprudence* 167–341 (5th ed. 1885).

11 Kelsen, *General Theory of Law and State* 401 (3rd ed. 1949).

12 *E.g.*, Friedmann, *The Planned State and the Rule of Law*, 22 *Austr. L.J.* 162, 207 (1948).

13 Lowie, *The Origin of the State* 113 (1927).

14 Hart, supra note 2, at 623–24.

15 Southern Pac. Co. v. Jensen, 244 U.S. 205, 221 (1917) (Holmes, J., dissenting), paraphrasing Storti v. Commonwealth, 178 Mass. 549, 554, 60 N.E. 210, 211 (1901) (Holmes, C.J.), in which it was held that a statute providing for electrocution as a means of inflicting the punishment of death was not cruel or unusual punishment within the Massachusetts Declaration of Rights, Mass. Const. pt. First, art. XXVI, simply because it accomplished its object by molecular, rather than molar, motions.

16 See Hart, supra note 2, at 619–20.

17 N.Y. Times, July 4, 1934, p. 3, col. 3 (late city ed.).

18 See N.Y. Times, July 14, 1934, p. 5, col. 2 (late city ed.).

19 Radbruch, *Die Erneuerung des Rechts*, 2 Die Wandlung 8, 9 (Germany 1947). A useful discussion of the Nazi practice with reference to the publicity given laws will be found in Giese, *Verkündung und Gesetzeskraft*, 76 Archiv des öffentlichen Rechts 464, 471–72 (Germany 1951). I rely on this article for the remarks that follow in the text.

20 Judgment of July 27, 1949, Oberlandesgericht, Bamberg, 5 *Süddeutsche Juristen-Zeitung* 207 (Germany 1950), 64 *Harv. L. Rev.* 1005 (1951).

21 The passage translated is § 5 of a statute creating a Kriegssonderstrafrecht. Law of Aug. 17, 1938, [1939] 2 *Reichsgesetzblatt* pt. 1, at 1456. The translation is mine.

22 See 5 *Süddeutsche Juristen-Zeitung* 207, 210 (Germany 1950).

23 The translated passage is article II of A Law Against Malicious Attacks on the State and the Party and for the Protection of the Party Uniform, Law of Dec. 20, 1934, [1934] 1 *Reichsgesetzblatt* 1269. The translation is mine.

24 See Radbruch, *Die Erneuerung des Rechts*, 2 Die Wandlung 8, 10 (Germany 1947).

25 Hart, supra note 2, at 606–08.

26 See id. at 607.

27 § 8(d), added by 61 Stat. 142 (1947), 29 U.S.C. § 158(d) (1952); see NLRA §§ 8(a)(5), (b)(3), as amended, 61 Stat. 141 (1947), 29 U.S.C. §§ 158(a)(5), (b)(3) (1952).

28 Minersville School Dist. v. Gobitis, 310 U.S. 586 (1940), overruled, West Virginia State Bd. of Educ. v. Barnette, 319 U.S. 624 (1943).

29 Von Hippel, *Die Nationalsozialistische Herrschaftsordnung als Warnung und Lehre* 6–7 (1946).

Chapter 4

Ronald Dworkin

THE MODEL OF RULES

I. Embarrassing questions

LAWYERS LEAN HEAVILY on the connected concepts of legal right and legal obligation. We say that someone has a legal right or duty, and we take that statement as a sound basis for making claims and demands, and for criticizing the acts of public officials. But our understanding of these concepts is remarkably fragile, and we fall into trouble when we try to say what legal rights and obligations are. We say glibly that whether someone has a legal obligation is determined by applying "the law" to the particular facts of his case, but this is not a helpful answer, because we have the same difficulties with the concept of law.

We are used to summing up our troubles in the classic questions of jurisprudence: What is "the law"? When two sides disagree, as often happens, about a proposition "of law," what are they disagreeing about, and how shall we decide which side is right? Why do we call what "the law" says a matter of legal "obligation"? Is "obligation" here just a term of art, meaning only "what the law says"? Or does legal obligation have something to do with moral obligation? Can we say that we have, in principle at least, the same reasons for meeting our legal obligations that we have for meeting our moral obligations?

These are not puzzles for the cupboard, to be taken down on rainy days for fun. They are sources of continuing embarrassment, and they nag at our attention. They embarrass us in dealing with particular problems that we must solve, one way or another. Suppose a novel right-of-privacy case comes to court, and there is no statute or precedent either granting or denying the particular right of anonymity claimed by the plaintiff. What role in the court's decision should be played by the fact that most people in the community think that private individuals are "morally" entitled to that particular privacy? Suppose the Supreme Court orders some prisoner freed because the police used procedures that the Court now says are constitutionally forbidden, although the Court's earlier decisions upheld these procedures. Must the Court, to be consistent, free all other prisoners previously convicted through these same procedures?[1] Conceptual puzzles about "the law" and "legal obligation" become acute when a court is confronted with a problem like this.

These eruptions signal a chronic disease. Day in and day out we send people to jail, or take money away from them, or make them do things they do not want to do, under coercion of force, and we justify all of this by speaking of such persons as having broken the law or having failed to meet their legal obligations, or having interfered with other people's legal rights. Even in clear cases (a bank robber or a willful breach of contract), when we are confident that someone had a legal obligation and broke it, we are not able to give a satisfactory account of what that means, or why that entitles the state to punish or coerce him. We may feel confident that what we are doing is proper, but until we can identify the principles we are following we cannot be sure that they are sufficient, or whether we are applying them consistently. In less clear cases, when the issue of whether an obligation has been broken is for some reason controversial, the pitch of these nagging questions rises, and our responsibility to find answers deepens.

Certain lawyers (we may call them "nominalists") urge that we solve these problems by ignoring them. In their view the concepts of "legal obligation" and "the law" are myths, invented and sustained by lawyers for a dismal mix of conscious and subconscious motives. The puzzles we find in these concepts are merely symptoms that they are myths. They are unsolvable because unreal, and our concern with them is just one feature of our enslavement. We would do better to flush away the puzzles and the concepts altogether, and pursue our important social objectives without this excess baggage.

This is a tempting suggestion, but it has fatal drawbacks. Before we can decide that our concepts of law and of legal obligation are myths, we must decide what they are. We must be able to state, at least roughly, what it is we all believe that is wrong. But the nerve of our problem is that we have great difficulty in doing just that. Indeed, when we ask what law is and what legal obligations are, we are asking for a theory of how we use those concepts and of the conceptual commitments our use entails. We cannot conclude, before we have such a general theory, that our practices are stupid or superstitious.

Of course, the nominalists think they know how the rest of us use these concepts. They think that when we speak of "the law," we mean a set of timeless rules stocked in some conceptual warehouse awaiting discovery by judges, and that when we speak of legal obligation we mean the invisible chains these mysterious rules

somehow drape around us. The theory that there are such rules and chains they call "mechanical jurisprudence," and they are right in ridiculing its practitioners. Their difficulty, however, lies in finding practitioners to ridicule. So far they have had little luck in caging and exhibiting mechanical jurisprudents (all specimens captured—even Blackstone and Joseph Beale—have had to be released after careful reading of their texts).

In any event, it is clear that most lawyers have nothing like this in mind when they speak of the law and of legal obligation. A superficial examination of our practices is enough to show this, for we speak of laws changing and evolving, and of legal obligation sometimes being problematical. In these and other ways we show that we are not addicted to mechanical jurisprudence.

Nevertheless, we do use the concepts of law and legal obligation, and we do suppose that society's warrant to punish and coerce is written in that currency. It may be that when the details of this practice are laid bare, the concepts we do use will be shown to be as silly and as thick with illusion as those the nominalists invented. If so, then we shall have to find other ways to describe what we do, and either provide other justifications or change our practices. But until we have discovered this and made these adjustments, we cannot accept the nominalists' premature invitation to turn our backs on the problems our present concepts provide.

Of course the suggestion that we stop talking about "the law" and "legal obligation" is mostly bluff. These concepts are too deeply cemented into the structure of our political practices—they cannot be given up like cigarettes or hats. Some of the nominalists have half-admitted this and said that the myths they condemn should be thought of as Platonic myths and retained to seduce the masses into order. This is perhaps not so cynical a suggestion as it seems; perhaps it is a covert hedging of a dubious bet.

If we boil away the bluff, the nominalist attack reduces to an attack on mechanical jurisprudence. Through the lines of the attack, and in spite of the heroic calls for the death of law, the nominalists themselves have offered an analysis of how the terms "law" and "legal obligation" should be used which is not very different from that of more classical philosophers. Nominalists present their analysis as a model of how legal institutions (particularly courts) "really operate." But their model differs mainly in emphasis from the theory first made popular by the nineteenth century philosopher John Austin, and now accepted in one form or another by most working and academic lawyers who hold views on jurisprudence. I shall call this theory, with some historical looseness, "positivism." I want to examine the soundness of positivism, particularly in the powerful form that Professor H. L. A. Hart of Oxford has given to it. I choose to focus on his position, not only because of its clarity and elegance, but because here, as almost everywhere else in legal philosophy, constructive thought must start with a consideration of his views.

II. Positivism

Positivism has a few central and organizing propositions as its skeleton, and though not every philosopher who is called a positivist would subscribe to these in the way I present them, they do define the general position I want to examine. These key tenets may be stated as follows:

(a) The law of a community is a set of special rules used by the community directly or indirectly for the purpose of determining which behavior will be punished or coerced by the public power. These special rules can be identified and distinguished by specific criteria, by tests having to do not with their content but with their *pedigree* or the manner in which they were adopted or developed. These tests of pedigree can be used to distinguish valid legal rules from spurious legal rules (rules which lawyers and litigants wrongly argue are rules of law) and also

from other sorts of social rules (generally lumped together as "moral rules") that the community follows but does not enforce through public power.

(b) The set of these valid legal rules is exhaustive of "the law," so that if someone's case is not clearly covered by such a rule (because there is none that seems appropriate, or those that seem appropriate are vague, or for some other reason) then that case cannot be decided by "applying the law." It must be decided by some official, like a judge, "exercising his discretion," which means reaching beyond the law for some other sort of standard to guide him in manufacturing a fresh legal rule or supplementing an old one.

(c) To say that someone has a "legal obligation" is to say that his case falls under a valid legal rule that requires him to do or to forbear from doing something. (To say he has a legal right, or has a legal power of some sort, or a legal privilege or immunity, is to assert, in a shorthand way, that others have actual or hypothetical legal obligations to act or not to act in certain ways touching him.) In the absence of such a valid legal rule there is no legal obligation; it follows that when the judge decides an issue by exercising his discretion, he is not enforcing a legal obligation as to that issue.

This is only the skeleton of positivism. The flesh is arranged differently by different positivists, and some even tinker with the bones. Different versions differ chiefly in their description of the fundamental test of pedigree a rule must meet to count as a rule of law.

Austin, for example, framed his version of the fundamental test as a series of interlocking definitions and distinctions.[2] He defined having an obligation as lying under a rule, a rule as a general command, and a command as an expression of desire that others behave in a particular way, backed by the power and will to enforce that expression in the event of disobedience. He distinguished classes of rules (legal, moral or religious) according to which person or group is the author of the general command the rule represents. In each political community, he thought, one will find a sovereign—a person or a determinate group whom the rest obey habitually, but who is not in the habit of obeying anyone else. The legal rules of a community are the general commands its sovereign has deployed. Austin's definition of legal obligation followed from this definition of law. One has a legal obligation, he thought, if one is among the addressees of some general order of the sovereign, and is in danger of suffering a sanction unless he obeys that order.

Of course, the sovereign cannot provide for all contingencies through any scheme of orders, and some of his orders will inevitably be vague or have furry edges. Therefore (according to Austin) the sovereign grants those who enforce the law (judges) discretion to make fresh orders when novel or troublesome cases are presented. The judges then make new rules or adapt old rules, and the sovereign either overturns their creations, or tacitly confirms them by failing to do so.

Austin's model is quite beautiful in its simplicity. It asserts the first tenet of positivism, that the law is a set of rules specially selected to govern public order, and offers a simple factual test—what has the sovereign commanded?—as the sole criterion for identifying those special rules. In time, however, those who studied and tried to apply Austin's model found it too simple. Many objections were raised, among which were two that seemed fundamental. First, Austin's key assumption that in each community a determinate group or institution can be found, which is in ultimate control of all other groups, seemed not to hold in a complex society. Political control in a modern nation is pluralistic and shifting, a matter of more or less, of compromise and cooperation and alliance, so that it is often impossible to say that any person or group has that dramatic control necessary to qualify as an Austinian sovereign. One wants to say, in the United States for example, that the "people" are sovereign. But this means almost nothing, and in itself provides no test for determining what the "people" have commanded, or distinguishing their legal from their social or moral commands.

Second, critics began to realize that Austin's analysis fails entirely to account for, even to recognize, certain striking facts about the attitudes we take toward "the law." We make an important distinction between law and even the general orders of a gangster. We feel that the law's strictures—and its sanctions—are different in that they are obligatory in a way that the outlaw's commands are not. Austin's analysis has no place for any such distinction, because it defines an obligation as subjection to the threat of force, and so founds the authority of law entirely on the sovereign's ability and will to harm those who disobey. Perhaps the distinction we make is illusory—perhaps our feelings of some special authority attaching to the law is based on religious hangover or another sort of mass self-deception. But Austin does not demonstrate this, and we are entitled to insist that an analysis of our concept of law either acknowledge and explain our attitudes, or show why they are mistaken.

H. L. A. Hart's version of positivism is more complex than Austin's, in two ways. First, he recognizes, as Austin did not, that rules are of different logical kinds (Hart distinguishes two kinds, which he calls "primary" and "secondary" rules). Second, he rejects Austin's theory that a rule is a kind of command, and substitutes a more elaborate general analysis of what rules are. We must pause over each of these points, and then note how they merge in Hart's concept of law.

Hart's distinction between primary and secondary rules is of great importance.[3] Primary rules are those that grant rights or impose obligations upon members of the community. The rules of the criminal law that forbid us to rob, murder or drive too fast are good examples of primary rules. Secondary rules are those that stipulate how, and by whom, such primary rules may be formed, recognized, modified or extinguished. The rules that stipulate how Congress is composed, and how it enacts legislation, are examples of secondary rules. Rules about forming contracts and executing wills are also secondary rules because they stipulate how very particular rules governing particular legal obligations (i.e., the terms of a contract or the provisions of a will) come into existence and are changed.

His general analysis of rules is also of great importance.[4] Austin had said that every rule is a general command, and that a person is obligated under a rule if he is liable to be hurt should he disobey it. Hart points out that this obliterates the distinction between being *obliged* to do something and being *obligated* to do it. If one is bound by a rule he is obligated, not merely obliged, to do what it provides, and therefore being bound by a rule must be different from being subject to an injury if one disobeys an order. A rule differs from an order, among other ways, by being *normative*, by setting a standard of behavior that has a call on its subject beyond the threat that may enforce it. A rule can never be binding just because some person with physical power wants it to be so. He must have *authority* to issue the rule or it is no rule, and such authority can only come from another rule which is already binding on those to whom he speaks. That is the difference between a valid law and the orders of a gunman.

So Hart offers a general theory of rules that does not make their authority depend upon the physical power of their authors. If we examine the way different rules come into being, he tells us, and attend to the distinction between primary and secondary rules, we see that there are two possible sources of a rule's authority.[5]

(a) A rule may become binding upon a group of people because that group through its practices *accepts* the rule as a standard for its conduct. It is not enough that the group simply conforms to a pattern of behavior: even though most Englishmen may go to the movies on Saturday evening, they have not accepted a rule requiring that they do so. A practice constitutes the acceptance of a rule only when those who follow the practice regard the rule as binding, and recognize the rule as a reason or justification for their own behavior and as a reason for criticizing the behavior of others who do not obey it.

(b) A rule may also become binding in quite a different way, namely by being enacted in conformity with some *secondary* rule that stipulates that rules so enacted shall be binding. If the constitution of a club stipulates, for example, that by-laws may be adopted by a majority of the members, then particular by-laws so voted are binding upon all the members, not because of any practice of acceptance of these particular by-laws, but because the constitution says so. We use the concept of *validity* in this connection: rules binding because they have been created in a manner stipulated by some secondary rule are called "valid" rules. Thus we can record Hart's fundamental distinction this way: a rule may be binding (a) because it is accepted or (b) because it is valid.

Hart's concept of law is a construction of these various distinctions.[6] Primitive communities have only primary rules, and these are binding entirely because of practices of acceptance. Such communities cannot be said to have "law," because there is no way to distinguish a set of legal rules from amongst other social rules, as the first tenet of positivism requires. But when a particular community has developed a fundamental secondary rule that stipulates how legal rules are to be identified, the idea of a distinct set of legal rules, and thus of law, is born.

Hart calls such a fundamental secondary rule a "rule of recognition." The rule of recognition of a given community may be relatively simple ("What the king enacts is law") or it may be very complex (the United States Constitution, with all its difficulties of interpretation, may be considered a single rule of recognition). The demonstration that a particular rule is valid may therefore require tracing a complicated chain of validity back from that particular rule ultimately to the fundamental rule. Thus a parking ordinance of the city of New Haven is valid because it is adopted by a city council, pursuant to the procedures and within the competence specified by the municipal law adopted by the state of Connecticut, in conformity with the procedures and within the competence specified by the constitution of the state of Connecticut, which was in turn adopted consistently with the requirements of the United States Constitution.

Of course, a rule of recognition cannot itself be valid, because by hypothesis it is ultimate, and so cannot meet tests stipulated by a more fundamental rule. The rule of recognition is the sole rule in a legal system whose binding force depends upon its acceptance. If we wish to know what rule of recognition a particular community has adopted or follows, we must observe how its citizens, and particularly its officials, behave. We must observe what ultimate arguments they accept as showing the validity of a particular rule, and what ultimate arguments they use to criticize other officials or institutions. We can apply no mechanical test, but there is no danger of our confusing the rule of recognition of a community with its rules of morality. The rule of recognition is identified by the fact that its province is the operation of the governmental apparatus of legislatures, courts, agencies, policemen, and the rest.

In this way Hart rescues the fundamentals of positivism from Austin's mistakes. Hart agrees with Austin that valid rules of law may be created through the acts of officials and public institutions. But Austin thought that the authority of these institutions lay only in their monopoly of power. Hart finds their authority in the background of constitutional standards against which they act, constitutional standards that have been accepted, in the form of a fundamental rule of recognition, by the community

which they govern. This background legitimates the decisions of government and gives them the cast and call of obligation that the naked commands of Austin's sovereign lacked. Hart's theory differs from Austin's also, in recognizing that different communities use different ultimate tests of law, and that some allow other means of creating law than the deliberate act of a legislative institution. Hart mentions "long customary practice" and "the relation [of a rule] to judicial decisions" as other criteria that are often used, though generally along with and subordinate to the test of legislation.

So Hart's version of positivism is more complex than Austin's, and his test for valid rules of law is more sophisticated. In one respect, however, the two models are very similar. Hart, like Austin, recognizes that legal rules have furry edges (he speaks of them as having "open texture") and, again like Austin, he accounts for troublesome cases by saying that judges have and exercise discretion to decide these cases by fresh legislation.[7] (I shall later try to show why one who thinks of law as a special set of rules is almost inevitably drawn to account for difficult cases in terms of someone's exercise of discretion.)

III. Rules, principles, and policies

I want to make a general attack on positivism, and I shall use H. L. A. Hart's version as a target, when a particular target is needed. My strategy will be organized around the fact that when lawyers reason or dispute about legal rights and obligations, particularly in those hard cases when our problems with these concepts seem most acute, they make use of standards that do not function as rules, but operate differently as principles, policies, and other sorts of standards. Positivism, I shall argue, is a model of and for a system of rules, and its central notion of a single fundamental test for law forces us to miss the important roles of these standards that are not rules.

I just spoke of "principles, policies, and other sorts of standards." Most often I shall use the term "principle" generically, to refer to the whole set of these standards other than rules; occasionally, however, I shall be more precise, and distinguish between principles and policies. Although nothing in the present argument will turn on the distinction, I should state how I draw it. I call a "policy" that kind of standard that sets out a goal to be reached, generally an improvement in some economic, political, or social feature of the community (though some goals are negative, in that they stipulate that some present feature is to be protected from adverse change). I call a "principle" a standard that is to be observed, not because it will advance or secure an economic, political, or social situation deemed desirable, but because it is a requirement of justice or fairness or some other dimension of morality. Thus the standard that automobile accidents are to be decreased is a policy, and the standard that no man may profit by his own wrong a principle. The distinction can be collapsed by construing a principle as stating a social goal (i.e., the goal of a society in which no man profits by his own wrong), or by construing a policy as stating a principle (i.e., the principle that the goal the policy embraces is a worthy one) or by adopting the utilitarian thesis that principles of justice are disguised statements of goals (securing the greatest happiness of the greatest number). In some contexts the distinction has uses which are lost if it is thus collapsed.[8]

My immediate purpose, however, is to distinguish principles in the generic sense from rules, and I shall start by collecting some examples of the former. The examples I offer are chosen haphazardly; almost any case in a law school casebook would provide examples that would serve as well. In 1889 a New York court, in the famous case of *Riggs v. Palmer*,[9] had to decide whether an heir named in the will of his grandfather could inherit under that will, even though he had murdered his grandfather to do so. The

court began its reasoning with this admission: "It is quite true that statutes regulating the making, proof and effect of wills, and the devolution of property, if literally construed, and if their force and effect can in no way and under no circumstances be controlled or modified, give this property to the murderer."[10] But the court continued to note that "all laws as well as all contracts may be controlled in their operation and effect by general, fundamental maxims of the common law. No one shall be permitted to profit by his own fraud, or to take advantage of his own wrong, or to found any claim upon his own iniquity, or to acquire property by his own crime."[11] The murderer did not receive his inheritance.

In 1960, a New Jersey court was faced, in *Henningsen v. Bloomfield Motors, Inc.*,[12] with the important question of whether (or how much) an automobile manufacturer may limit his liability in case the automobile is defective. Henningsen had bought a car, and signed a contract which said that the manufacturer's liability for defects was limited to "making good" defective parts—"this warranty being expressly in lieu of all other warranties, obligations or liabilities." Henningsen argued that, at least in the circumstances of his case, the manufacturer ought not to be protected by this limitation, and ought to be liable for the medical and other expenses of persons injured in a crash. He was not able to point to any statute, or to any established rule of law, that prevented the manufacturer from standing on the contract. The court nevertheless agreed with Henningsen. At various points in the court's argument the following appeals to standards are made: (a) "[W]e must keep in mind the general principle that, in the absence of fraud, one who does not choose to read a contract before signing it cannot later relieve himself of its burdens."[13] (b) "In applying that principle, the basic tenet of freedom of competent parties to contract is a factor of importance."[14] (c) "Freedom of contract is not such an immutable doctrine as to admit of no qualification in the area in which we are concerned."[15] (d) "In a society such as ours, where the automobile is a common and necessary adjunct of daily life, and where its use is so fraught with danger to the driver, passengers and the public, the manufacturer is under a special obligation in connection with the construction, promotion and sale of his cars. Consequently, the courts must examine purchase agreements closely to see if consumer and public interests are treated fairly."[16] (e) " '[I]s there any principle which is more familiar or more firmly embedded in the history of Anglo-American law than the basic doctrine that the courts will not permit themselves to be used as instruments of inequity and injustice?' "[17] (f) " 'More specifically, the courts generally refuse to lend themselves to the enforcement of a "bargain" in which one party has unjustly taken advantage of the economic necessities of other. . . .' "[18]

The standards set out in these quotations are not the sort we think of as legal rules. They seem very different from propositions like "The maximum legal speed on the turnpike is sixty miles an hour" or "A will is invalid unless signed by three witnesses." They are different because they are legal principles rather than legal rules.

The difference between legal principles and legal rules is a logical distinction. Both sets of standards point to particular decisions about legal obligation in particular circumstances, but they differ in the character of the direction they give. Rules are applicable in an all-or-nothing fashion. If the facts a rule stipulates are given, then either the rule is valid, in which case the answer it supplies must be accepted, or it is not, in which case it contributes nothing to the decision.

This all-or-nothing is seen most plainly if we look at the way rules operate, not in law, but in some enterprise they dominate—a game, for example. In baseball a rule provides that if the batter has had three strikes, he is out. An official cannot consistently acknowledge that this is an accurate statement of a baseball rule, and decide that a batter who has had three strikes is not out. Of course, a rule may have exceptions (the batter who has taken three strikes is not out if the catcher drops the third strike). However, an accurate statement of the rule would take this exception into account, and any that did not would be incomplete. If the list of exceptions is very large, it would be too clumsy to repeat them each time the rule is cited; there is, however, no reason in theory why they could not all be added on, and the more that are, the more accurate is the statement of the rule.

If we take baseball rules as a model, we find that rules of law, like the rule that a will is invalid unless signed by three witnesses, fit the model well. If the requirement of three witnesses is a valid legal rule, then it cannot be that a will has been signed by only two witnesses and is valid. The rule might have exceptions, but if it does then it is inaccurate and incomplete to state the rule so simply, without enumerating the exceptions. In theory, at least, the exceptions could all be listed, and the more of them that are, the more complete is the statement of the rule.

But this is not the way the sample principles in the quotations operate. Even those which look most like rules do not set out legal consequences that follow automatically when the conditions provided are met. We say that our law respects the principle that no man may profit from his own wrong, but we do not mean that the law never permits a man to profit from wrongs he commits. In fact, people often profit, perfectly legally, from their legal wrongs. The most notorious case is adverse possession—if I trespass on your land long enough, some day I will gain a right to cross your land whenever I please. There are many less dramatic examples. If a man leaves one job, breaking a contract, to take a much higher paying job, he may have to pay damages to his first employer, but he is usually entitled to keep his new salary. If a man jumps bail and crosses state lines to make a brilliant investment in another state, he may be sent back to jail, but he will keep his profits.

We do not treat these—and countless other counter-instances that can easily be imagined—as showing that the principle about profiting from one's wrongs is not a principle of our legal system, or that it is incomplete and needs qualifying exceptions. We do not treat counter-instances as exceptions (at least not exceptions in the way in which a catcher's dropping the third strike is an exception) because we could not hope to capture these counter-instances simply by a more extended statement of the principle. They are not, even in theory, subject to enumeration, because we would have to include not only those cases (like adverse possession) in which some institution has already provided that profit can be gained through a wrong, but also those numberless imaginary cases in which we know in advance that the principle would not hold. Listing some of these might sharpen our sense of the principle's weight (I shall mention that dimension in a moment), but it would not make for a more accurate or complete statement of the principle.

A principle like "No man may profit from his own wrong" does not even purport to set out conditions that make its application necessary. Rather, it states a reason that argues in one direction, but does not necessitate a particular decision. If a man has or is about to receive something, as a direct result of something illegal he did to get it, then that is a reason which the law will take into account in deciding whether he should keep it. There may be other principles or policies arguing in the other direction—a policy of securing title, for example, or a principle limiting punishment to what the legislature has stipulated. If so, our principle may not prevail, but that does not mean that it is not a principle of our legal system, because in the next case, when these contravening considerations are absent or less weighty, the principle may be decisive. All that is meant, when we say that a particular principle is a principle of our law, is

that the principle is one which officials must take into account, if it is relevant, as a consideration inclining in one direction or another.

The logical distinction between rules and principles appears more clearly when we consider principles that do not even look like rules. Consider the proposition, set out under "(d)" in the excerpts from the *Henningsen* opinion, that "the manufacturer is under a special obligation in connection with the construction, promotion and sale of his cars." This does not even purport to define the specific duties such a special obligation entails, or to tell us what rights automobile consumers acquire as a result. It merely states—and this is an essential link in the *Henningsen* argument—that automobile manufacturers must be held to higher standards than other manufacturers, and are less entitled to rely on the competing principle of freedom of contract. It does not mean that they may never rely on that principle, or that courts may rewrite automobile purchase contracts at will; it means only that if a particular clause seems unfair or burdensome, courts have less reason to enforce the clause than if it were for the purchase of neckties. The "special obligation" counts in favor, but does not in itself necessitate, a decision refusing to enforce the terms of an automobile purchase contract.

This first difference between rules and principles entails another. Principles have a dimension that rules do not—the dimension of weight or importance. When principles intersect (the policy of protecting automobile consumers intersecting with principles of freedom of contract, for example), one who must resolve the conflict has to take into account the relative weight of each. This cannot be, of course, an exact measurement, and the judgment that a particular principle or policy is more important than another will often be a controversial one. Nevertheless, it is an integral part of the concept of a principle that it has this dimension, that it makes sense to ask how important or how weighty it is.

Rules do not have this dimension. We can speak of rules as being *functionally* important or unimportant (the baseball rule that three strikes are out is more important than the rule that runners may advance on a balk, because the game would be much more changed with the first rule altered than the second). In this sense, one legal rule may be more important than another because it has a greater or more important role in regulating behavior. But we cannot say that one rule is more important than another within the system of rules, so that when two rules conflict one supercedes the other by virtue of its greater weight. If two rules conflict, one of them cannot be a valid rule. The decision as to which is valid, and which must be abandoned or recast, must be made by appealing to considerations beyond the rules themselves. A legal system might regulate such conflicts by other rules, which prefer the rule enacted by the higher authority, or the rule enacted later, or the more specific rule, or something of that sort. A legal system may also prefer the rule supported by the more important principles. (Our own legal system uses both of these techniques.)

It is not always clear from the form of a standard whether it is a rule or a principle. "A will is invalid unless signed by three witnesses" is not very different in form from "A man may not profit from his own wrong," but one who knows something of American law knows that he must take the first as stating a rule and the second as stating a principle. In many cases the distinction is difficult to make—it may not have been settled how the standard should operate, and this issue may itself be a focus of controversy. The first amendment to the United States Constitution contains the provision that Congress shall not abridge freedom of speech. Is this a rule, so that if a particular law does abridge freedom of speech, it follows that it is unconstitutional? Those who claim that the first amendment is "an absolute" say that it must be taken in this way, that is, as a rule. Or does it merely state a principle, so that when an abridgement of

speech is discovered, it is unconstitutional unless the context presents some other policy or principle which in the circumstances is weighty enough to permit the abridgement? That is the position of those who argue for what is called the "clear and present danger" test or some other form of "balancing."

Sometimes a rule and a principle can play much the same role, and the difference between them is almost a matter of form alone. The first section of the Sherman Act states that every contract in restraint of trade shall be void. The Supreme Court had to make the decision whether this provision should be treated as a rule in its own terms (striking down every contract "which restrains trade," which almost any contract does) or as a principle, providing a reason for striking down a contract in the absence of effective contrary policies. The Court construed the provision as a rule, but treated that rule as containing the word "unreasonable," and as prohibiting only "unreasonable" restraints of trade.[19] This allowed the provision to function logically as a rule (whenever a court finds that the restraint is "unreasonable" it is bound to hold the contract invalid) and substantially as a principle (a court must take into account a variety of other principles and policies in determining whether a particular restraint in particular economic circumstances is "unreasonable").

Words like "reasonable," "negligent," "unjust," and "significant" often perform just this function. Each of these terms makes the application of the rule which contains it depend to some extent upon principles or policies lying beyond the rule, and in this way makes that rule itself more like a principle. But they do not quite turn the rule into a principle, because even the least confining of these terms restricts the *kind* of other principles and policies on which the rule depends. If we are bound by a rule that says that "unreasonable" contracts are void, or that grossly "unfair" contracts will not be enforced, much more judgment is required than if the quoted terms were omitted. But suppose a case in which some consideration of policy or principle suggests that a contract should be enforced even though its restraint is not reasonable, or even though it is grossly unfair. Enforcing these contracts would be forbidden by our rules, and thus permitted only if these rules were abandoned or modified. If we were dealing, however, not with a rule but with a policy against enforcing unreasonable contracts, or a principle that unfair contracts ought not to be enforced, the contracts could be enforced without alteration of the law.

IV. Principles and the concept of law

Once we identify legal principles as separate sorts of standards, different from legal rules, we are suddenly aware of them all around us. Law teachers teach them, lawbooks cite them, legal historians celebrate them. But they seem most energetically at work, carrying most weight, in difficult lawsuits like *Riggs* and *Henningsen*. In cases like these, principles play an essential part in arguments supporting judgments about particular legal rights and obligations. After the case is decided, we may say that the case stands for a particular rule (*e.g.*, the rule that one who murders is not eligible to take under the will of his victim). But the rule does not exist before the case is decided; the court cites principles as its justification for adopting and applying a new rule. In *Riggs*, the court cited the principle that no man may profit from his own wrong as a background standard against which to read the statute of wills and in this way justified a new interpretation of that statute. In *Henningsen*, the court cited a variety of intersecting principles and policies as authority for a new rule respecting manufacturer's liability for automobile defects.

An analysis of the concept of legal obligation must therefore account for the important role of principles in reaching particular decisions of law. There are two very different tacks we might take.

(a) We might treat legal principles the way we treat legal rules and say that some principles are binding as law and must be taken into account by judges and lawyers who make decisions of legal obligation. If we took this tack, we should say that in the United States, at least, the "law" includes principles as well as rules.

(b) We might, on the other hand, deny that principles can be binding the way some rules are. We would say, instead, that in cases like *Riggs* or *Henningsen* the judge reaches beyond the rules that he is bound to apply (reaches, that is, beyond the "law") for extra-legal principles he is free to follow if he wishes.

One might think that there is not much difference between these two lines of attack, that it is only a verbal question of how one wants to use the word "law." But that is a mistake, because the choice between these two accounts has the greatest consequences for an analysis of legal obligation. It is a choice between two *concepts* of a legal principle, a choice we can clarify by comparing it to a choice we might make between two concepts of a legal rule. We sometimes say of someone that he "makes it a rule" to do something, when we mean that he has chosen to follow a certain practice. We might say that someone has made it a rule, for example, to run a mile before breakfast because he wants to be healthy and believes in a regimen. We do not mean, when we say this, that he is *bound* by the rule that he must run a mile before breakfast, or even that he regards it as binding upon him. Accepting a rule as binding is something different from making it a rule to do something. If we use Hart's example again, there is a difference between saying that Englishmen make it a rule to see a movie once a week, and saying that the English have a rule that one must see a movie once a week. The second implies that if an Englishman does not follow the rule, he is subject to criticism or censure, but the first does not. The first does not exclude the possibility of a *sort* of criticism—we cay say that one who does not see movies is neglecting his education—but we do not suggest that he is doing something wrong just in not following the rule.[20]

If we think of the judges of a community as a group, we could describe the rules of law they follow in these two different ways. We could say, for instance, that in a certain state the judges make it a rule not to enforce wills unless there are three witnesses. This would not imply that the rare judge who enforces such a rule is doing anything wrong just for that reason. On the other hand we can say that in that state a rule of law requires judges not to enforce such wills; this does imply that a judge who enforces them is doing something wrong. Hart, Austin and other positivists, of course, would insist on this latter account of legal rules; they would not at all be satisfied with the "make it a rule" account. It is not a verbal question of which account is right. It is a question of which describes the social situation more accurately. Other important issues turn on which description we accept. If judges simply "make it a rule" not to enforce certain contracts, for example, then we cannot say, before the decision, that anyone is "entitled" to that result, and that proposition cannot enter into any justification we might offer for the decision.

The two lines of attack on principles parallel these two accounts of rules. The first tack treats principles as binding upon judges, so that they are wrong not to apply the principles when they are pertinent. The second tack treats principles as summaries of what most judges "make it a principle" to do when forced to go beyond the standards that bind them. The choice between these approaches will affect, perhaps even determine, the answer we can give to the question whether the judge in a hard case like *Riggs* or *Henningsen* is attempting to enforce pre-existing legal rights and obligations. If we take the first tack, we are still free to argue that because such judges are applying binding legal standards they are enforcing legal rights and obligations. But if we take the second, we are out of court on that issue, and we must acknowledge that the

murderer's family in *Riggs* and the manufacturer in *Henningsen* were deprived of their property by an act of judicial discretion applied *ex post facto*. This may not shock many readers—the notion of judicial discretion has percolated through the legal community—but it does illustrate one of the most nettlesome of the puzzles that drive philosophers to worry about legal obligation. If taking property away in cases like these cannot be justified by appealing to an established obligation, another justification must be found, and nothing satisfactory has yet been supplied.

In my skeleton diagram of positivism, previously set out, I listed the doctrine of judicial discretion as the second tenet. Positivists hold that when a case is not covered by a clear rule, a judge must exercise his discretion to decide that case by what amounts to a fresh piece of legislation. There may be an important connection between this doctrine and the question of which of the two approaches to legal principles we must take. We shall therefore want to ask whether the doctrine is correct, and whether it implies the second approach, as it seems on its face to do. En route to these issues, however, we shall have to polish our understanding of the concept of discretion. I shall try to show how certain confusions about that concept, and in particular a failure to discriminate different senses in which it is used, account for the popularity of the doctrine of discretion. I shall argue that in the sense in which the doctrine does have a bearing on our treatment of principles, it is entirely unsupported by the arguments the positivists use to defend it.

V. Discretion

The concept of discretion was lifted by the positivists from ordinary language, and to understand it we must put it back *in habitat* for a moment. What does it mean, in ordinary life, to say that someone "has discretion"? The first thing to notice is that the concept is out of place in all but very special contexts. For example, you would not say that I either do or do not have discretion to choose a house for my family. It is not true that I have "no discretion" in making that choice, and yet it would be almost equally misleading to say that I do have discretion. The concept of discretion is at home in only one sort of context: when someone is in general charged with making decisions subject to standards set by a particular authority. It makes sense to speak of the discretion of a sergeant who is subject to orders of superiors, or the discretion of a sports official or contest judge who is governed by a rule book or the terms of the contest. Discretion, like the hole in a doughnut, does not exist except as an area left open by a surrounding belt of restriction. It is therefore a relative concept. It always makes sense to ask, "Discretion under which standards?" or "Discretion as to which authority?" Generally the context will make the answer to this plain, but in some cases the official may have discretion from one standpoint though not from another.

Like almost all terms, the precise meaning of "discretion" is affected by features of the context. The term is always colored by the background of understood information against which it is used. Although the shadings are many, it will be helpful for us to recognize some gross distinctions.

Sometimes we use "discretion" in a weak sense, simply to say that for some reason the standards an official must apply cannot be applied mechanically but demand the use of judgment. We use this weak sense when the context does not already make that clear, when the background our audience assumes does not contain that piece of information. Thus we might say, "The sergeant's orders left him a great deal of discretion," to those who do not know what the sergeant's orders were or who do not know something that made those orders vague or hard to carry out. It would make perfect sense to add, by way of amplification, that the lieutenant had ordered the sergeant to take his five most experienced men on patrol but that it was hard to determine which were the most experienced.

Sometimes we use the term in a different weak sense, to say only that some official has final authority to make a decision and cannot be reviewed and reversed by any other official. We speak this way when the official is part of a hierarchy of officials structured so that some have higher authority but in which the patterns of authority are different for different classes of decision. Thus we might say that in baseball certain decisions, like the decision whether the ball or the runner reached second base first, are left to the discretion of the second base umpire, if we mean that on this issue the head umpire has no power to substitute his own judgment if he disagrees.

I call both of these senses weak to distinguish them from a stronger sense. We use "discretion" sometimes not merely to say that an official must use judgment in applying the standards set him by authority, or that no one will review that exercise of judgment, but to say that on some issue he is simply not bound by standards set by the authority in question. In this sense we say that a sergeant has discretion who has been told to pick any five men for patrol he chooses or that a judge in a dog show has discretion to judge airedales before boxers if the rules do not stipulate an order of events. We use this sense not to comment on the vagueness or difficulty of the standards, or on who has the final word in applying them, but on their range and the decisions they purport to control. If the sergeant is told to take the five most experienced men, he does not have discretion in this strong sense because that order purports to govern his decision. The boxing referee who must decide which fighter has been the more aggressive does not have discretion, in the strong sense, for the same reason.[21]

If anyone said that the sergeant or the referee had discretion in these cases, we should have to understand him, if the context permitted, as using the term in one of the weak senses. Suppose, for example, the lieutenant ordered the sergeant to select the five men he deemed most experienced, and then added that the sergeant had discretion to choose them. Or the rules provided that the referee should award the round to the more aggressive fighter, with discretion in selecting him. We should have to understand these statements in the second weak sense, as speaking to the question of review of the decision. The first weak sense—that the decisions take judgment—would be otiose, and the third, strong sense is excluded by the statements themselves.

We must avoid one tempting confusion. The strong sense of discretion is not tantamount to license, and does not exclude criticism. Almost any situation in which a person acts (including those in which there is no question of decision under special authority, and so no question of discretion) makes relevant certain standards of rationality, fairness, and effectiveness. We criticize each other's acts in terms of these standards, and there is no reason not to do so when the acts are within the center rather than beyond the perimeter of the doughnut of special authority. So we can say that the sergeant who was given discretion (in the strong sense) to pick a patrol did so stupidly or maliciously or carelessly, or that the judge who had discretion in the order of viewing dogs made a mistake because he took boxers first although there were only three airedales and many more boxers. An official's discretion means not that he is free to decide without recourse to standards of sense and fairness, but only that his decision is not controlled by a standard furnished by the particular authority we have in mind when we raise the question of discretion. Of course this latter sort of freedom is important; that is why we have the strong sense of discretion. Someone who has discretion in this third sense can be criticized, but not for being disobedient, as in the case of the soldier. He can be said to have made a mistake, but not to have deprived a participant of

a decision to which he was entitled, as in the case of a sports official or contest judge.

We may now return, with these observations in hand, to the positivists' doctrine of judicial discretion. That doctrine argues that if a case is not controlled by an established rule, the judge must decide it by exercising discretion. We want to examine this doctrine and to test its bearing on our treatment of principles; but first we must ask in which sense of discretion we are to understand it.

Some nominalists argue that judges always have discretion, even when a clear rule is in point, because judges are ultimately the final arbiters of the law. This doctrine of discretion uses the second weak sense of that term, because it makes the point that no higher authority reviews the decisions of the highest court. It therefore has no bearing on the issue of how we account for principles, any more than it bears on how we account for rules.

The positivists do not mean their doctrine this way, because they say that a judge has no discretion when a clear and established rule is available. If we attend to the positivists' arguments for the doctrine we may suspect that they use discretion in the first weak sense to mean only that judges must sometimes exercise judgment in applying legal standards. Their arguments call attention to the fact that some rules of law are vague (Professor Hart, for example, says that all rules of law have "open texture"), and that some cases arise (like *Henningsen*) in which no established rule seems to be suitable. They emphasize that judges must sometimes agonize over points of law, and that two equally trained and intelligent judges will often disagree.

These points are easily made; they are commonplace to anyone who has any familiarity with law. Indeed, that is the difficulty with assuming that positivists mean to use "discretion" in this weak sense. The proposition that when no clear rule is available discretion in the sense of judgment must be used is a tautology.

It has no bearing, moreover, on the problem of how to account for legal principles. It is perfectly consistent to say that the judge in *Riggs*, for example, had to use judgment, and that he was bound to follow the principle that no man may profit from his own wrong. The positivists speak as if their doctrine of judicial discretion is an insight rather than a tautology, and as if it does have a bearing on the treatment of principles. Hart, for example, says that when the judge's discretion is in play, we can no longer speak of his being bound by standards, but must speak rather of what standards he "characteristically uses."[22] Hart thinks that when judges have discretion, the principles they cite must be treated on our second approach, as what courts "make it a principle" to do.

It therefore seems that positivists, at least sometimes, take their doctrine in the third, strong sense of discretion. In that sense it does bear on the treatment of principles; indeed, in that sense it is nothing less than a restatement of our second approach. It is the same thing to say that when a judge runs out of rules he has discretion, in the sense that he is not bound by any standards from the authority of law, as to say that the legal standards judges cite other than rules are not binding on them.

So we must examine the doctrine of judicial discretion in the strong sense. (I shall henceforth use the term "discretion" in that sense.) Do the principles judges cite in cases like *Riggs* or *Henningsen* control their decisions, as the sergeant's orders to take the most experienced men or the referee's duty to choose the more aggressive fighter control the decisions of these officials? What arguments could a positivist supply to show that they do not?

(1) A positivist might argue that principles cannot be binding or obligatory. That would be a mistake. It is always a question, of course, whether any particular principle is *in fact* binding upon some legal official. But there is nothing in the logical character of a principle that renders it incapable of binding him. Suppose that the judge

in *Henningsen* had failed to take any account of the principle that automobile manufacturers have a special obligation to their consumers, or the principle that the courts seek to protect those whose bargaining position is weak, but had simply decided for the defendant by citing the principle of freedom of contract without more. His critics would not have been content to point out that he had not taken account of considerations that other judges have been attending to for some time. Most would have said that it was his duty to take the measure of these principles and that the plaintiff was entitled to have him do so. We mean no more, when we say that a *rule* is binding upon a judge, than that he must follow it if it applies, and that if he does not he will on that account have made a mistake.

It will not do to say that in a case like *Henningsen* the court is only "morally" obligated to take particular principles into account, or that it is "institutionally" obligated, or obligated as a matter of judicial "craft," or something of that sort. The question will still remain why this type of obligation (whatever we call it) is different from the obligation that rules impose upon judges, and why it entitles us to say that principles and policies are not part of the law but are merely extralegal standards "courts characteristically use."

(2) A positivist might argue that even though some principles are binding, in the sense that the judge must take them into account, they cannot determine a particular result. This is a harder argument to assess because it is not clear what it means for a standard to "determine" a result. Perhaps it means that the standard *dictates* the result whenever it applies so that nothing else counts. If so, then it is certainly true that individual principles do not determine results, but that is only another way of saying that principles are not rules. Only rules dictate results, come what may. When a contrary result has been reached, the rule has been abandoned or changed. Principles do not work that way; they incline a decision one way, though not

conclusively, and they survive intact when they do not prevail. This seems no reason for concluding that judges who must reckon with principles have discretion because a set of principles *can* dictate a result. If a judge believes that principles he is bound to recognize point in one direction and that principles pointing in the other direction, if any, are not of equal weight, then he must decide accordingly, just as he must follow what he believes to be a binding rule. He may, of course, be wrong in his assessment of the principles, but he may also be wrong in his judgment that the rule is binding. The sergeant and the referee, we might add, are often in the same boat. No one factor dictates which soldiers are the most experienced or which fighter the more aggressive. These officials must make judgments of the relative weights of these various factors; they do not on that account have discretion.

(3) A positivist might argue that principles cannot count as law because their authority, and even more so their weight, are congenitally *controversial*. It is true that generally we cannot *demonstrate* the authority or weight of a particular principle as we can sometimes demonstrate the validity of a rule by locating it in an act of Congress or in the opinion of an authoritative court. Instead, we make a case for a principle, and for its weight, by appealing to an amalgam of practice and other principles in which the implications of legislative and judicial history figure along with appeals to community practices and understandings. There is no litmus paper for testing the soundness of such a case—it is a matter of judgment, and reasonable men may disagree. But again this does not distinguish the judge from other officials who do not have discretion. The sergeant has no litmus paper for experience, the referee none for aggressiveness. Neither of these has discretion, because he is bound to reach an understanding, controversial or not, of what his orders or the rules require, and to act on that understanding. That is the judge's duty as well.

Of course, if the positivists are right in another of their doctrines—the theory that in each legal system there is an ultimate *test* for binding law like Professor Hart's rule of recognition—it follows that principles are not binding law. But the incompatibility of principles with the positivists' theory can hardly be taken as an argument that principles must be treated any particular way. That begs the question; we are interested in the status of principles because we want to evaluate the positivists' model. The positivist cannot defend his theory of a rule of recognition by fiat; if principles are not amenable to a test he must show some other reason why they cannot count as law. Since principles seem to play a role in arguments about legal obligation (witness, again, *Riggs* and *Henningsen*), a model that provides for that role has some initial advantage over one that excludes it, and the latter cannot properly be inveighed in its own support.

These are the most obvious of the arguments a positivist might use for the doctrine of discretion in the strong sense, and for the second approach to principles. I shall mention one strong counter-argument against that doctrine and in favor of the first approach. Unless at least some principles are acknowledged to be binding upon judges, requiring them as a set to reach particular decisions, then no rules, or very few rules, can be said to be binding upon them either.

In most American jurisdictions, and now in England also, the higher courts not infrequently reject established rules. Common law rules—those developed by earlier court decisions—are sometimes overruled directly, and sometimes radically altered by further development. Statutory rules are subjected to interpretation and reinterpretation, sometimes even when the result is not to carry out what is called the "legislative intent."[23] If courts had discretion to change established rules, then these rules would of course not be binding upon them, and so would not be law on the positivists' model. The positivist must therefore argue that there are standards, themselves binding upon judges, that determine when a judge may overrule or alter an established rule, and when he may not.

When, then, is a judge permitted to change an existing rule of law? Principles figure in the answer in two ways. First, it is necessary, though not sufficient, that the judge find that the change would advance some policy or serve some principle, which policy or principle thus justifies the change. In *Riggs* the change (a new interpretation of the statute of wills) was justified by the principle that no man should profit from his own wrong; in *Henningsen* certain rules about automobile manufacturers' liability were altered on the basis of the principles and policies I quoted from the opinion of the court.

But not any principle will do to justify a change, or no rule would ever be safe. There must be some principles that count and others that do not, and there must be some principles that count for more than others. It could not depend on the judge's own preferences amongst a sea of respectable extra-legal standards, any one in principle eligible, because if that were the case we could not say that any rules were binding. We could always imagine a judge whose preferences amongst extra-legal standards were such as would justify a shift or radical reinterpretation of even the most entrenched rule.

Second, any judge who proposes to change existing doctrine must take account of some important standards that argue against departures from established doctrine, and these standards are also for the most part principles. They include the doctrine of "legislative supremacy," a set of principles and policies that require the courts to pay a qualified deference to the acts of the legislature. They also include the doctrine of precedent, another set of principles and policies reflecting the equities and efficiencies of consistency. The doctrines of legislative supremacy and precedent incline toward the *status quo*, each within its sphere, but they do not command it. Judges are not free, however, to pick and choose amongst the principles and policies that make up these doctrines—if they were, again, no rule could be said to be binding.

Consider, therefore, what someone implies who says that a particular rule is binding. He may imply that the rule is affirmatively supported by principles the court is not free to disregard, and which are collectively more weighty than other principles that argue for a change. If not, he implies that any change would be condemned by a combination of conservative principles of legislative supremacy and precedent that the court is not free to ignore. Very often, he will imply both, for the conservative principles, being principles and not rules, are usually not powerful enough to save a common law rule or an aging statute that is entirely unsupported by substantive principles the court is bound to respect. Either of these implications, of course, treats a body of principles and policies as law in the sense that rules are; it treats them as standards binding upon the officials of a community, controlling their decisions of legal right and obligation.

We are left with this issue. If the positivists' theory of judicial discretion is either trivial because it uses "discretion" in a weak sense, or unsupported because the various arguments we can supply in its defense fall short, why have so many careful and intelligent lawyers embraced it? We can have no confidence in our treatment of that theory unless we can deal with that question. It is not enough to note (although perhaps it contributes to the explanation) that "discretion" has different senses that may be confused. We do not confuse these senses when we are not thinking about law.

Part of the explanation, at least, lies in a lawyer's natural tendency to associate laws and rules, and to think of "the law" as a collection or system of rules. Roscoe Pound, who diagnosed this tendency long ago, thought that English speaking lawyers were tricked into it by the fact that English uses the same word, changing only the article, for "a law" and "the law."[24] (Other languages, on the contrary, use two words: "loi" and "droit," for example, and "Gesetz" and "Recht.") This may have had its effect, with the English speaking positivists, because the expression "a law" certainly does suggest a rule. But the principal reason for associating law with rules runs deeper, and lies, I think, in the fact that legal education has for a long time consisted of teaching and examining those established rules that form the cutting edge of law.

In any event, if a lawyer thinks of law as a system of rules, and yet recognizes, as he must, that judges change old rules and introduce new ones, he will come naturally to the theory of judicial discretion in the strong sense. In those other systems of rules with which he has experience (like games), the rules are the only special authority that governs official decisions, so that if an umpire could change a rule, he would have discretion as to the subject matter of that rule. Any principles umpires might mention when changing the rules would represent only their "characteristic" preferences. Positivists treat law like baseball revised in this way.

There is another, more subtle consequence of this initial assumption that law is a system of rules. When the positivists do attend to principles and policies, they treat them as rules *manqué*. They assume that if they are standards of law they must be rules, and so they read them as standards that are trying to be rules. When a positivist hears someone argue that legal principles are part of the law, he understands this to be an argument for what he calls the "higher law" theory, that these principles are the rules of a law above the law.[25] He refutes this theory by pointing out that these "rules" are sometimes followed and sometimes not, that for every "rule" like "no man shall profit from his own wrong" there is another competing "rule" like "the law favors security of title," and that there is no way to test the validity of "rules" like these. He concludes that these principles and policies are not valid rules of a law above the law, which is true, because they are not rules at all. He also concludes that they are extralegal standards which each judge selects according to his own lights in the exercise of his discretion, which is false. It is as if a zoologist had proved that fish are not mammals, and then concluded that they are really only plants.

VI. The rule of recognition

This discussion was provoked by our two competing accounts of legal principles. We have been exploring the second account, which the positivists seem to adopt through their doctrine of judicial discretion, and we have discovered grave difficulties. It is time to return to the fork in the road. What if we adopt the first approach? What would the consequences of this be for the skeletal structure of positivism? Of course we should have to drop the second tenet, the doctrine of judicial discretion (or, in the alternative, to make plain that the doctrine is to be read merely to say that judges must often exercise judgment). Would we also have to abandon or modify the first tenet, the proposition that law is distinguished by tests of the sort that can be set out in a master rule like Professor Hart's rule of recognition? If principles of the *Riggs* and *Henningsen* sort are to count as law, and we are nevertheless to preserve the notion of a master rule for law, then we must be able to deploy some test that all (and only) the principles that do count as law meet. Let us begin with the test Hart suggests for identifying valid *rules* of law, to see whether these can be made to work for principles as well.

Most rules of law, according to Hart, are valid because some competent institution enacted them. Some were created by a legislature, in the form of statutory enactments. Others were created by judges who formulated them to decide particular cases, and thus established them as precedents for the future. But this test of pedigree will not work for the *Riggs* and *Henningsen* principles. The origin of these as legal principles lies not in a particular decision of some legislature or court, but in a sense of appropriateness developed in the profession and the public over time. Their continued power depends upon this sense of appropriateness being sustained. If it no longer seemed unfair to allow people to profit by their wrongs, or fair to place special burdens upon oligopolies that manufacture potentially dangerous machines, these principles would no longer play much of a role in new cases, even if they had never been overruled or repealed. (Indeed, it hardly makes sense to speak of principles like these as being "overruled" or "repealed." When they decline they are eroded, not torpedoed.)

True, if we were challenged to back up our claim that some principle is a principle of law, we would mention any prior cases in which that principle was cited, or figured in the argument. We would also mention any statute that seemed to exemplify that principle (even better if the principle was cited in the preamble of the statute, or in the committee reports or other legislative documents that accompanied it). Unless we could find some such institutional support, we would probably fail to make out our case, and the more support we found, the more weight we could claim for the principle.

Yet we could not devise any formula for testing how much and what kind of institutional support is necessary to make a principle a legal principle, still less to fix its weight at a particular order of magnitude. We argue for a particular principle by grappling with a whole set of shifting, developing and interacting standards (themselves principles rather than rules) about institutional responsibility, statutory interpretation, the persuasive force of various sorts of precedent, the relation of all these to contemporary moral practices, and hosts of other such standards. We could not bolt all of these together into a single "rule," even a complex one, and if we could the result would bear little relation to Hart's picture of a rule of recognition, which is the picture of a fairly stable master rule specifying "some feature or features possession of which by a suggested rule is taken as a conclusive affirmative indication that it is a rule . . ."[26]

Moreover, the techniques we apply in arguing for another principle do not stand (as Hart's rule of recognition is designed to) on an entirely different level from the principles they support. Hart's sharp distinction between acceptance and validity does not hold. If we are arguing for the principle that a man should not profit from his own wrong, we could cite the acts of courts and legislatures that exemplify it, but this speaks as much to the principle's acceptance as its validity. (It seems odd to speak of a principle as being valid at all, perhaps because validity is an all-or-nothing concept, appropriate for rules, but inconsistent with a principle's dimension of weight.) If we are asked (as we might well be) to defend the particular doctrine of precedent, or the particular technique of statutory interpretation, that we used in this argument, we should certainly cite the practice of others in using that doctrine or technique. But we should also cite other general principles that we believe support that practice, and this introduces a note of validity into the chord of acceptance. We might argue, for example, that the use we make of earlier cases and statutes is supported by a particular analysis of the point of the practice of legislation or the doctrine of precedent, or by the principles of democratic theory, or by a particular position on the proper division of authority between national and local institutions, or something else of that sort. Nor is this path of support a one-way street leading to some ultimate principle resting on acceptance alone. Our principles of legislation, precedent, democracy, or federalism might be challenged too; and if they were we should argue for them, not only in terms of practice, but in terms of each other and in terms of the implications of trends of judicial and legislative decisions, even though this last would involve appealing to those same doctrines of interpretation we justified through the principles we are now trying to support. At this level of abstraction, in other words, principles rather hang together than link together.

So even though principles draw support from the official acts of legal institutions, they do not have a simple or direct enough connection with these acts to frame that connection in terms of criteria specified by some ultimate master rule of recognition. Is there any other route by which principles might be brought under such a rule?

Hart does say that a master rule might designate as law not only rules enacted by particular legal institutions, but rules established by *custom* as well. He has in mind a problem that bothered other positivists, including Austin. Many of our most ancient legal rules were never explicitly created by a legislature or a court. When they made their first appearance in legal opinions and texts, they were treated as already being part of the law because they represented the customary practice of the community, or some specialized part of it, like the business community. (The examples ordinarily given are rules of mercantile practice, like the rules governing what rights arise under a standard form of commercial paper.)[27] Since Austin thought that all law was the command of a determinate sovereign, he held that these customary practices were not law until the courts (as agents of the sovereign) recognized them, and that the courts were indulging in a fiction in pretending otherwise. But that seemed arbitrary. If everyone thought custom might in itself be law, the fact that Austin's theory said otherwise was not persuasive.

Hart reversed Austin on this point. The master rule, he says, might stipulate that some custom counts as law even before the courts recognize it. But he does not face the difficulty this raises for his general theory because he does not attempt to set out the criteria a master rule might use for this purpose. It cannot use, as its only criterion, the provision that the community regard the practice as *morally* binding, for this would not distinguish legal customary rules from moral customary rules, and of course not all of the

community's long-standing customary moral obligations are enforced at law. If, on the other hand, the test is whether the community regards the customary practice as *legally* binding, the whole point of the master rule is undercut, at least for this class of legal rules. The master rule, says Hart, marks the transformation from a primitive society to one with law, because it provides a test for determining social rules of law other than by measuring their acceptance. But if the master rule says merely that whatever other rules the community accepts as legally binding are legally binding, then it provides no such test at all, beyond the test we should use were there no master rule. The master rule becomes (for these cases) a non-rule of recognition; we might as well say that every primitive society has a secondary rule of recognition, namely the rule that whatever is accepted as binding is binding. Hart himself, in discussing international law, ridicules the idea that such a rule could be a rule of recognition, by describing the proposed rule as "an empty repetition of the mere fact that the society concerned . . . observes certain standards of conduct as obligatory rules."[28]

Hart's treatment of custom amounts, indeed, to a confession that there are at least some rules of law that are not binding because they are valid under standards laid down by a master rule but are binding—like the master rule—because they are accepted as binding by the community. This chips at the neat pyramidal architecture we admired in Hart's theory: we can no longer say that only the master rule is binding because of its acceptance, all other rules being valid under its terms.

This is perhaps only a chip, because the customary rules Hart has in mind are no longer a very significant part of the law. But it does suggest that Hart would be reluctant to widen the damage by bringing under the head of "custom" all those crucial principles and policies we have been discussing. If he were to call these part of the law and yet admit that the only test of their force lies in the degree to which they are accepted as law by the community or some part thereof, he would very sharply reduce that area of the law over which his master rule held any dominion. It is not just that all the principles and policies would escape its sway, though that would be bad enough. Once these principles and policies are accepted as law, and thus as standards judges must follow in determining legal obligations, it would follow that *rules* like those announced for the first time in *Riggs* and *Henningsen* owe their force at least in part to the authority of principles and policies, and so not entirely to the master rule of recognition.

So we cannot adapt Hart's version of positivism by modifying his rule of recognition to embrace principles. No tests of pedigree, relating principles to acts of legislation, can be formulated, nor can his concept of customary law, itself an exception to the first tenet of positivism, be made to serve without abandoning that tenet altogether. One more possibility must be considered, however. If no rule of recognition can provide a test for identifying principles, why not say that principles are ultimate, and form the rule of recognition of our law? The answer to the general question "What is valid law in an American jurisdiction?" would then require us to state all the principles (as well as ultimate constitutional rules) in force in that jurisdiction at the time, together with appropriate assignments of weight. A positivist might then regard the complete set of these standards as the rule of recognition of the jurisdiction. This solution has the attraction of paradox, but of course it is an unconditional surrender. If we simply designate our rule of recognition by the phrase "the complete set of principles in force," we achieve only the tautology that law is law. If, instead, we tried actually to list all the principles in force we would fail. They are controversial, their weight is all important, they are numberless, and they shift and change so fast that the start of our list would be obsolete before we reached the middle. Even if we succeeded, we would not have a key for law

because there would be nothing left for our key to unlock.

I conclude that if we treat principles as law we must reject the positivists' first tenet, that the law of a community is distinguished from other social standards by some test in the form of a master rule. We have already decided that we must then abandon the second tenet—the doctrine of judicial discretion—or clarify it into triviality. What of the third tenet, the positivists' theory of legal obligation?

This theory holds that a legal obligation exists when (and only when) an established rule of law imposes such an obligation. It follows from this that in a hard case—when no such established rule can be found—there is no legal obligation until the judge creates a new rule for the future. The judge may apply that new rule to the parties in the case, but this is *ex post facto* legislation, not the enforcement of an existing obligation.

The positivists' doctrine of discretion (in the strong sense) required this view of legal obligation, because if a judge has discretion there can be no legal right or obligation—no entitlement—that he must enforce. Once we abandon that doctrine, however, and treat principles as law, we raise the possibility that a legal obligation might be imposed by a constellation of principles as well as by an established rule. We might want to say that a legal obligation exists whenever the case supporting such an obligation, in terms of binding legal principles of different sorts, is stronger than the case against it.

Of course, many questions would have to be answered before we could accept that view of legal obligation. If there is no rule of recognition, no test for law in that sense, how do we decide which principles are to count, and how much, in making such a case? How do we decide whether one case is better than another? If legal obligation rests on an undemonstrable judgment of that sort, how can it provide a justification for a judicial decision that one party had a legal obligation? Does this view of obligation square with the way lawyers, judges and laymen speak, and is it consistent with our attitudes about moral obligation? Does this analysis help us to deal with the classical jurisprudential puzzles about the nature of law?

These questions must be faced, but even the questions promise more than positivism provides. Positivism, on its own thesis, stops short of just those puzzling, hard cases that send us to look for theories of law. When we reach these cases, the positivist remits us to a doctrine of discretion that leads nowhere and tells nothing. His picture of law as a system of rules has exercised a tenacious hold on our imagination, perhaps through its very simplicity. If we shake ourselves loose from this model of rules, we may be able to build a model truer to the complexity and sophistication of our own practices.

Notes

35 *University of Chicago Law Review* 14 (1967)

1 See Linkletter v. Walker, 381 U.S. 618 (1965).

2 J. Austin, *The Province of Jurisprudence Determined* (1832).

3 See H. L. A. Hart, *The Concept of Law* 89–96 (1961).

4 Id. at 79–88.

5 Id. at 97–107.

6 Id. passim, particularly ch. VI.

7 Id. ch. VII.

8 See Dworkin, *Wasserstrom: The Judicial Decision*, 75 Ethics 47 (1964), reprinted as *Does Law Have a Function?*, 74 Yale L.J. 640 (1965).

9 115 N.Y. 506, 22 N.E. 188 (1889).

10 Id. at 509, 22 N.E. at 189.

11 Id. at 511, 22 N.E. at 190.

12 32 N.J. 358, 161 A.2d 69 (1960).

13 Id. at 386, 161 A.2d at 84.

14 Id.

15 Id. at 388, 161 A.2d at 86.

16 Id. at 387, 161 A.2d at 85.

17 Id. at 389, 161 A.2d at 86 (quoting Frankfurter, J., in United States v. Bethlehem Steel, 315 U.S. 289, 326 (1942)).

18 Id.

19 Standard Oil v. United States, 221 U.S. 1, 60 (1911); United States v. American Tobacco Co., 221 U.S. 106, 180 (1911).

20 The distinction is in substance the same as that made by Rawls, *Two Concepts of Rules*, 64 *Philosophical Rev.* 3 (1955).

21 I have not spoken of that jurisprudential favorite, "limited" discretion, because that concept presents no special difficulties if we remember the relativity of discretion. Suppose the sergeant is told to choose from "amongst" experienced men, or to "take experience into account." We might say either that he has (limited) discretion in picking his patrol, or (full) discretion to either pick amongst experienced men or decide what else to take into account.

22 H. L. A. Hart, *The Concept of Law* 144 (1961).

23 See Wellington & Albert, *Statutory Interpretation and the Political Process: A Comment on Sinclair v. Atkinson*, 72 Yale L.J. 1547 (1963).

24 R. Pound, *An Introduction to the Philosophy of Law* 56 (rev. ed. 1954).

25 See, *e.g.*, Dickinson, *The Law Behind Law* (pts 1 & 2), 29 Colum. L. Rev. 112, 254 (1929).

26 H. L. A. Hart, *The Concept of Law* 92 (1961).

27 See Note, *Custom and Trade Usage: Its Application to Commercial Dealings and the Common Law*, 55 Colum. L. Rev. 1192 (1955), and materials cited therein at 1193 n.1. As that note makes plain, the actual practices of courts in recognizing trade customs follow the pattern of applying a set of general principles and policies rather than a test that could be captured as part of a rule of recognition.

28 H. L. A. Hart, *The Concept of Law* 230 (1961).

II. LEGALITY AND MORALITY

Introduction

AS THE PREVIOUS SECTION makes clear, the relationship between legality and morality is the central focus of debate about the nature of law, which is itself the fundamental question of general jurisprudence. Where the previous section charted important early salvos in that debate, the present section introduces the most prominent "live" positions regarding legality's relationship to morality. There are basically four such positions: inclusive legal positivism, exclusive legal positivism, natural law theory, and interpretivism.

Towards articulating the central tenets of these positions, it is worth glancing back to the Hart/Dworkin Debate (see Section I), as it was Dworkin's early criticism of Hart that prompted the articulation and defense of more refined accounts of legal positivism, which in turn have served as foils in the development of non-positivist alternatives. Dworkin's fundamental early criticism of Hart was that moral principles could be legally binding in virtue of their moral content but that legal positivism could not agree because it held that law consisted only in rules whose validity depended upon their social pedigree and not their content. Legal positivists responded to Dworkin in turn, but, strikingly, they did not do so with one voice. Instead, two quite different legal positivisms emerged.

On the one hand, some have attempted to blunt the force of Dworkin's challenge by accommodating it, defending *inclusive legal positivism* (also known as "soft" positivism). They agree with Dworkin that a norm's legal validity can depend upon its moral content, but they nevertheless remain committed legal positivists because they hold that legality can depend upon moral criteria only if a social or conventional rule underwrites the dependence. The Eighth Amendment to the U.S. Constitution banning "cruel and unusual punishment," for example, refers to the moral idea of cruelty in its key phrase. Inclusive legal positivism holds that the moral content therein is among the Eighth Amendment's criteria of legal validity, but it is so only because it is incorporated by the Constitution, which is itself a thoroughly social or conventional source of law. According to inclusive legal positivism, then, legal validity does not *necessarily* depend upon morality, but crucially, legal validity can depend upon morality as a contingent matter in a particular jurisdiction if that jurisdiction's positive law makes it so depend. This is the conception of legal positivism that Jules

Coleman defends in "Negative and Positive Positivism," and it is his view that it "can do justice to Dworkin's insights while rendering his objections harmless."[1] It is also the position, notably, that Hart himself consciously embraced as a response to Dworkin in his posthumously published "Postscript" to the second edition of *The Concept of Law*.[2]

Exclusive legal positivism (also known as "hard" positivism), on the other hand, offers a more radical response to Dworkin's challenge. Far from attempting to accommodate it, exclusive legal positivism faces Dworkin's challenge head-on and attempts to turn it back, holding that legal validity can never depend upon moral criteria, *pace* both Dworkin as well as inclusive legal positivism. As Joseph Raz characterizes exclusive legal positivism's central thesis in "Legal Positivism and the Sources of Law," "the existence and content of every law is fully determined by social sources."[3] Raz's argument for this "sources thesis"[4] revolves, most fundamentally, around law's authoritative guidance function. "Since it is of the very essence of the alleged authority that it issues rulings which are binding regardless of any other justification," Raz contends, "it follows that it must be possible to identify those rulings without engaging in a justificatory argument, i.e. as issuing from certain activities and interpreted in the light of publicly ascertainable standards not involving moral argument."[5] Legal systems can only hope to make good on the authority that they necessarily claim for themselves, according to Raz, if their rulings conclusively resolve the problems that they address. This kind of authority is possible, however, only if a legal system's rulings can be ascertained in light of those rulings alone, without recourse to the underlying (possibly moral) matters that the rulings purport to resolve. Legal validity cannot depend upon moral criteria, in short, without undermining the claim to authority that is a necessary feature of law. Raz's defense of exclusive legal positivism thus hinges on his influential account of authority (see Section IV). Indeed, in an important sense Raz's theory of the relation between legality and morality is just an implication of his more fundamental theory of authority.

For his own part, Dworkin's views about the relation between legality and morality have evolved considerably since he first criticized Hart's legal positivism, and that more developed position has come to be known as *interpretivism*. Dworkin's mature jurisprudential views are systematically presented in his important 1986 book *Law's Empire*,[6] but they are previewed in "Law as Interpretation," published just four years earlier. Dworkin opens "Law as Interpretation" with the claims that "legal practice is an exercise in interpretation" and that "law so conceived is deeply and thoroughly political."[7] The animating idea of his view is that, when they decide hard cases, judges must heed the legal history of the controversies before them, but they must at the same time make the best of that history in the decisions that they render: "A plausible interpretation of legal practice must . . . satisfy a test with two dimensions: it must both fit that practice and show its point or value."[8] No judge adjudicates cases in a vacuum because every judge "has a responsibility to advance the enterprise in hand," and in this way, Dworkin maintains, judges must *interpret* the existing legal enterprise before determining what to decide. In interpreting the law, however, judges are guided not merely by considerations of fit, but by what would make the enterprise of law the best enterprise it can be. Morality – or as Dworkin characterizes it, politics – thus enters the picture because the judicial interpretation of law will be driven at least in part by a conception of what makes law valuable. What the law is thus depends in part upon what the law ought to be.

While legality and morality are closely allied in Dworkin's view, it is probably a mistake to characterize interpretivism as a version of *natural law theory*, for in its modern incarnations – developed most systemically by John Finnis in *Natural Law and Natural Rights*[9] – natural law theory envisages a quite different relationship between legality and morality than does interpretivism. Natural law theory also, of course, conceives of the relationship between legality and morality differently than any stripe of legal positivism. These distinctions, as well as misconceived differences, are clarified in Robert George's "Natural Law and Positive Law".

Just as Raz's exclusive legal positivism is founded upon an account of authority, George argues that communities depend upon an authority to coordinate individual and collective conduct in pursuit of the common good. But where Raz's focus is on claimed authority, George's is on legitimate authority: "morally valid authority", George maintains, "translates natural principles of justice and political morality into rules and principles of positive law."[10] Sometimes this translation is straightforward, as with laws prohibiting murder. Other times, and indeed in the vast majority of cases, however, it requires the significant creative exercise of moral judgment. In either case, though, creating positive law is a mandate of natural law. Thus, while "the body of law created by the legislator is not itself the natural law", it remains the case that "the creation of law (and a system of law) has a moral purpose."[11] Still, in contrast to Dworkin's conception of law, where a judge must invoke moral judgments to decide hard cases in any jurisdiction, George contends that law is almost fully "analyzable in technical terms" and that a judge has no "plenary authority to substitute his own understanding of the requirements of the natural law for the contrary understanding of the legislator or constitution maker in deciding cases at law."[12] To engage in such substitution would violate the rule of law in a legal regime that, as a matter of positive law, withholds law-making power from judges (see Section III). The various allocations of responsibility between judiciary and legislature are defined by positive constitutional law, which is morally valid to the extent that it is founded upon principles of natural law, and thus, according to George's natural law theory, a judge would actually violate the natural law by ignoring positive law's allocative strictures and proceeding to create law through Dworkinian constructive interpretation. The relationship between legality and morality that natural law theory recognizes is complex and varied, bearing some similarities to interpretivism but also to legal positivism, while at once and ultimately remaining distinct from either.

It is a sociological fact about the discipline of general jurisprudence today that legal positivism of some variety or other is the dominant position about the nature of law. But despite its dominance within the circle of general jurisprudence scholars, legal positivism nevertheless remains a view that is much misunderstood and even maligned by many. There is perhaps no clearer statement of what legal positivism does, and equally importantly, does *not* stand for than John Gardner's "Legal Positivism: 5½ Myths". By hiving off claims that legal positivism simply does not entail (or at least does not entail simply) – that there is value in law's positivity; that a formal rule of law is especially important; that judges may only rely on valid legal sources in adjudication; that judges must legislate from the bench; that only textualist or intentionalist legal interpretation is defensible; and that there is no necessary connection between law and morality – Gardner isolates legal positivism's central claim. And it is nothing more than this: "In any legal system, whether a given norm is legally valid, and hence whether it forms part of the law of that system, depends on its sources, not its merits (where its merits, in the relevant sense, include the merits of its sources."[13] This is a sharper if more cumbersome claim than Austin's famous one that "[t]he existence of law is one thing; its merit or demerit is another",[14] but it is also not too distant a descendent. And it clarifies the nature of debate over the nature of law for the next generation of general jurisprudence scholars.

Notes

1 Jules Coleman, "Negative and Positive Positivism", p. 115.
2 H. L. A. Hart, "Postscript" in *The Concept of Law* (P. A. Bulloch and J. Raz, eds, 2nd ed.), New York: Oxford University Press, 1994, p. 250.
3 Joseph Raz, "Legal Positivism and the Sources of Law", p. 122.
4 Ibid., p. 123.
5 Ibid., p. 125.
6 Ronald Dworkin, *Law's Empire*, Cambridge, MA: Harvard University Press and London: Fontana Press, 1986.
7 Ronald Dworkin, "Law as Interpretation", p. 127.
8 Ibid., p. 137.
9 John Finnis, *Natural Law and Natural Rights*, Oxford: Oxford University Press, 1980.
10 Robert P. George, "Natural Law and Positive Law", p. 148.
11 Ibid., p. 149.
12 Ibid., p. 150.
13 John Gardner, "Legal Positivism: 5½ Myths", p. 154.
14 John Austin, *The Province of Jurisprudence Determined* (1832), W. E. Rumble (ed.), Cambridge: Cambridge University Press, 1995, p. 157.

Further reading

John Austin, *The Province of Jurisprudence Determined* (1832), W. E. Rumble (ed.), Cambridge: Cambridge University Press, 1995.
Brian Bix, "On the Dividing Line Between Natural Law Theory and Legal Positivism", *Notre Dame Law Review* 75, 2000, 1613–1624.
Jules Coleman, *The Practice of Principle*, New York: Oxford University Press, 2001.
Jules Coleman (ed.), *Hart's Postscript: Essays on the* Postscript *to* The Concept of Law, New York: Oxford University Press, 2001.
Ronald Dworkin, *Law's Empire*, Cambridge, MA: Harvard University Press; and London: Fontana Press, 1986.
John Finnis, *Natural Law and Natural Rights*, Oxford: Oxford University Press, 1980.

Robert George (ed.), *Natural Law Theory: Contemporary Essays*, New York: Oxford University Press, 1992.

Robert George (ed.), *The Autonomy of Law: Essays on Legal Positivism*, New York: Oxford University Press, 1996.

Leslie Green, "Positivism and Conventionalism", *Canadian Journal of Law and Jurisprudence* 12, 1999, 35–52.

H. L. A. Hart, "Postscript" in *The Concept of Law* (P. A. Bulloch and J. Raz, eds, 2nd ed.), New York: Oxford University Press, 1994.

Matthew Kramer, *In Defense of Legal Positivism: Law Without Trimmings*, Oxford: Oxford University Press, 1999.

Andrei Marmor, *Positive Law and Objective Values*, Oxford: Oxford University Press, 2001.

Andrei Marmor, "Legal Positivism: Still Descriptive and Morally Neutral", *Oxford Journal of Legal Studies*, 26, 2006, 683–704.

Dennis Patterson, *Law and Truth*, Oxford: Oxford University Press, 1996.

Stephen Perry, "The Varieties of Legal Positivism", *Canadian Journal of Law and Jurisprudence* 9, 1996, 361–374.

Gerald Postema, " 'Protestant' Interpretation and Social Practices", *Law and Philosophy* 6, 1987, 283–319

Joseph Raz, *The Authority of Law: Essays on Law and Morality*, Oxford: Oxford University Press, 1979.

Joseph Raz, *The Morality of Freedom*, Oxford: Oxford University Press, 1986.

Joseph Raz, *Ethics in the Public Domain: Essays in the Morality of Law and Politics*, New York: Oxford University Press, 1994.

Roger Shiner, *Norm and Nature: The Movements of Legal Thought*, New York: Oxford University Press, 1992.

Philip Soper, "Legal Theory and the Obligation of a Judge: The Hart/Dworkin Dispute", *Michigan Law Review* 75, 1977, 473–519.

Nicos Stavropoulos, *Objectivity in Law*, New York: Oxford University Press, 1996.

Wil Waluchow, *Inclusive Legal Positivism*, Oxford: Oxford University Press, 1994.

Questions

1. Is Coleman correct that inclusive legal positivism "can do justice to Dworkin's insights while rendering his objections harmless"?
2. Can inclusive legal positivism meet the challenge posed by Raz's exclusive legal positivism?
3. Does Dworkin's interpretivism mark a departure from his earlier views, or is it continuous with them?
4. How, if at all, are inclusive and exclusive legal positivism aligned against interpretivism, and how, if at all, are exclusive legal positivism and interpretivism aligned against inclusive legal positivism?
5. How, if at all, is natural law theory, as George presents it, aligned with legal positivism on the one hand, and interpretivism on the other?
6. How many of the doubts about legal positivism are based on "myths" about the view, and how many are well-founded?

Chapter 5

Jules L. Coleman

NEGATIVE AND POSITIVE POSITIVISM

EVERY THEORY ABOUT the nature or essence of law purports to provide a standard, usually in the form of a statement of necessary and sufficient conditions, for determining which of a community's norms constitute its law. For example, the naive version of legal realism maintains that the law of a community is constituted by the official pronouncements of judges. For the early positivists like Austin, law consists in the commands of a sovereign, properly so-called. For substantive natural law theory, in every conceivable legal system, being a true principle of morality is a necessary condition of legality for at least some norms. Legal positivism of the sort associated with H. L. A. Hart maintains that, in every community where law exists, there exists a standard that determines which of the community's norms are legal ones. Following Hart, this standard is usually referred to as a rule of recognition. If all that positivism meant by a rule of recognition were "the standard in every community by which a community's legal norms were made determinate," every theory of law would be reducible to one or another version of positivism. Which form of positivism each would take would depend on the particular substantive conditions of legality that each theory set out. Legal positivism would be true analytically, since it would be impossible to conceive of a theory of law that did not satisfy the minimal conditions for a rule of recognition. Unfortunately, the sort of truth legal positivism would then reveal would be an uninteresting one.

In order to distinguish a rule of recognition in the positivist sense from other statements of the conditions of legality, and therefore to distinguish positivism from alternative jurisprudential theses, additional constraints must be placed on the rule of recognition. Candidates for these constraints fall into two categories: restrictions on the conditions of legality set out in a rule of recognition; and constraints on the possible sources of authority (or normativity) of the rule of recognition.

An example of the first sort of constraint is expressed by the requirement that in every community the conditions of legality must be ones of pedigree or form, not substance or content. Accordingly, for a rule specifying the conditions of legality in any society to constitute a rule of recognition in the positivist sense, legal normativity under it must be determined, for example, by a norm's being enacted in the requisite fashion by a proper authority.

The claim that the authority of the rule of recognition is a matter of its acceptance by officials, rather than its truth as a normative principle, and the related claim that judicial duty under a rule of recognition is one of conventional practice rather than critical morality, express constraints of the second sort.

Ronald Dworkin expresses this second constraint as the claim that a rule of recognition in the positivist sense must be a social, rather than a normative, rule. A social rule is one whose authority is a matter of convention; the nature and scope of the duty it imposes is specified or constituted by an existing, convergent social practice. In contrast, a normative rule may impose an obligation or confer a right in the absence of the relevant practice or in the face of a contrary one. If a normative rule imposes an obligation, it does so because it is a correct principle of morality, not, *ex hypothesi*, because it corresponds to an accepted practice.

Dworkin, for one, conceives of the rule of recognition as subject to constraints of both sorts. His view is that only pedigree standards of legality can constitute rules of recognition, and that a rule of recognition must be a social rule.[1] Is legal positivism committed to either or both of these constraints on the rule of recognition?

I. Negative positivism

Candidates for constraints on the rule of recognition are motivated by the need to distinguish legal positivism from other jurisprudential theses: in particular, natural law theory. Positivism denies what natural law theory asserts: namely, a necessary connection between law and morality. I refer to the denial of a necessary or constitutive relationship between law and morality as the separability thesis. One way of asking whether positivism is committed to any particular kind of constraint on the rule of recognition is simply to ask whether any constraints on the rule are required by commitment to the separability thesis.

To answer this question we have to make some preliminary remarks concerning how we are to understand both the rule of recognition and the separability thesis. The notion of a rule of recognition is ambiguous; it has both an epistemic and a semantic sense. In one sense, the rule of recognition is a standard which one can use to identify, validate, or discover a community's law. In another sense, the rule of

recognition specifies the conditions a norm must satisfy to constitute part of a community's law. The same rule may or may not be a rule of recognition in both senses, since the rule one employs to determine the law need not be the same rule as the one that makes law determinate. This ambiguity between the epistemic and semantic interpretations of the rule of recognition pervades the literature and is responsible for a good deal of confusion about the essential claims of legal positivism. In my view, legal positivism is committed to the rule of recognition in the semantic sense at least; whether it is committed to the rule of recognition as a standard for identifying law (epistemic sense) is a question to which we shall return later.

In the language that is fashionable in formal semantics, to say that the rule of recognition is a semantic rule is to say that it specifies the truth conditions for singular propositions of law of the form, "it is the law in C that P," where C is a particular community and P a putative statement of law. The question whether the separability thesis imposes substantive constraints on the rule of recognition is just the question whether the separability thesis restricts the conditions of legality for norms or the truth conditions for propositions of law.

The separability thesis is the claim that there exists at least one conceivable rule of recognition (and therefore one possible legal system) that does not specify truth as a moral principle among the truth conditions for any proposition of law.[2] Consequently, a particular rule of recognition may specify truth as a moral principle as a truth condition for some or all propositions of law without violating the separability thesis, since it does not follow from the fact that, in one community in order to be law a norm must be a principle of morality, being a true principle of morality is a necessary condition of legality in all possible legal systems.

It is tempting to confuse the separability thesis with the very different claim that the law of a community is one thing and its morality another. This last claim is seriously ambiguous. In one sense, the claim that the law of a community is one thing and its morality another may amount to the very strong assertion that there exists no convergence between the norms that constitute a community's law and those that constitute its morality. Put this way, the thesis is an empirical one whose inadequacies are demonstrated by the shared legal and moral prohibitions against murder, theft, battery, and the like.

Instead, the claim may be that one can identify or discover a community's law without having recourse to discovering its morality. This is an epistemic claim about how, in a particular community, one might go about learning the law. It may well be that in some communities—even those in which every legal norm is a moral principle as well—one can learn which norms are law without regard to their status as principles of morality. Whether in every community this is the case depends on the available sources of legal knowledge, not on the existence of a conceptual relationship, if any, between law and morality.

A third interpretation of the thesis that a community's law is one thing and its morality another, the one Dworkin is anxious to ascribe to positivism, is that being a moral principle is not a truth condition for any proposition of law (in any community). Put this way the claim would be false, just in case "it is the law in C that P" (for any community, C, and any proposition of law, P) were true only if P stated a (true) principle of morality. Were the separability thesis understood this way, it would require particular substantive constraints on each rule of recognition, that is, no rule of recognition could specify truth as a moral principle among its conditions of legality. Were legal positivism committed to both the rule of recognition and to this interpretation of the claim that the law and morality of a community are distinct, Dworkin's arguments in Model of Rules I (MOR-I) would suffice to put it to rest.

However, were the claim that the law of a community is one thing and its morality another understood, not as the claim that in every community law and morality are distinct, but as the assertion that they are conceptually distinguishable, it would be reducible to the separability thesis, for it would assert no more than the denial of a constitutive relationship between law and morality.

In sum, "the law of a community is one thing and its morality another," makes either a false factual claim, an epistemic claim about the sources of legal knowledge, or else it is reducible to the separability thesis. In no case does it warrant substantive constraints on particular rules of recognition.

Properly understood and adequately distinguished from the claim that the law and morality of a community are distinct, the separability thesis does not warrant substantive constraints on any particular rule of recognition. It does not follow, however, that the separability thesis imposes no constraints at all on any rule of recognition. The separability thesis commits positivism to the proposition that there exists at least one conceivable legal system in which the rule of recognition does not specify being a principle of morality among the truth conditions for any proposition of law. Positivism is true, then, just in case we can imagine a legal system in which being a principle of morality is not a condition of legality for any norm: that is, just as long as the idea of a legal system in which moral truth is not a necessary condition of legal validity is not self-contradictory.

The form of positivism generated by commitment to the rule of recognition as constrained by the separability thesis I call negative positivism to draw attention both to the character and the weakness of the claim it makes.[3] Because negative positivism is essentially a negative thesis, it cannot be undermined by counterexamples, any one of which will show only that, in some community or other, morality is a condition of legality at least for some norms.

II. Positive positivism: law as hard facts

In MOR-I, Dworkin persuasively argues that in some communities moral principles have the force of law, though what makes them law is their truth or their acceptance as appropriate to the resolution of controversial disputes rather than their having been enacted in the appropriate way by the relevant authorities. These arguments would suffice to undermine positivism were it committed to the claim that truth as a moral principle could never constitute a truth condition for a proposition of law under any rule of recognition. The arguments are inadequate to undermine the separability thesis, which makes no claim about the truth conditions of any particular proposition of law in any particular community. The arguments in MOR-I therefore, are inadequate to undermine negative positivism.

However, Dworkin's target in MOR-I is not really negative positivism; it is that version of positivism one would get by conjoining the rule of recognition with the requirement that the truth conditions for any proposition of law could not include reference to the morality of a norm. Moreover, in fairness to Dworkin, one has to evaluate his arguments in a broader context. In MOR-I Dworkin is anxious to demonstrate, not only the inadequacy of the separability thesis, but that of other essential tenets of positivism— or at least what Dworkin takes to be essential features of positivism—as well.

The fact that moral principles have the force of law, because they are appropriate, true, or accepted even though they are not formally enacted, establishes for Dworkin that: (1) the positivist's conception of law as rules must be abandoned; as must (2) the claim that judges exercise discretion—the authority to extend beyond the law to appeal to moral principles—to resolve controversial cases; and (3) the view that the law of every community can be identified by use of a noncontroversial or pedigree test of legality.

The first claim of positivism must be abandoned because principles, as well as rules, constitute legal norms; the second because, while positivists conceive of judges as exercising discretion by appealing to moral principles, Dworkin rightly characterizes them as appealing to moral principles, which, though they are not rules, nevertheless may be binding legal standards. The third tenet of positivism must be abandoned because the rule of recognition in Dworkin's view must be one of pedigree, that is, it cannot make reference to the content or truth of a norm as a condition of its legality; and any legal system that includes moral principles among its legal standards cannot have as its standard of authority a pedigree criterion.[4]

The question, of course, is whether positivism is committed to either judicial discretion, the model of rules, or to a pedigree or uncontroversial standard of legality. We know at least that it is committed to the separability thesis from which only negative positivism appears to follow. Negative positivism is committed to none of these claims. Is there another form of positivism that is so committed?

Much of the debate between the positivists and Dworkin appears rather foolish, unless there is a version of positivism that makes Dworkin's criticisms, if not compelling, at least relevant. That version of positivism, whatever it is, cannot be motivated by the separability thesis alone. The question then is whether anything other than its denial of the central tenet of natural law theory motivates positivism?

One easy, but ultimately unsatisfying, response is to maintain that Dworkin's objections are to Hart's version of positivism. While this is no doubt true, such a remark gives no indication of what it is in Hart's version of positivism that is essential to positivism generally. Dworkin, after all, takes his criticisms of Hart to be criticisms of positivism generally, and the question remains whether positivism is committed to the essentials of Hart's version of it.

A more promising line of argument is the following. No doubt positivism is committed to the separability thesis. Still, one can ask whether commitment to the separability thesis is basic or derivative from some other, perhaps programmatic, commitments of legal positivism. That is, one can look at the separability thesis in isolation or as a component, perhaps even a derivative element, of a network of commitments of legal positivism.[5] We are led to negative positivism when we pursue the former route. Perhaps there is a more interesting form of positivism in the cards if we pursue the latter.

Certainly one reason some positivists have insisted upon the distinction between law and morality is the following: While both law and morality provide standards by which the affairs of people are to be regulated, morality is inherently controversial. People disagree about what morality prescribes, and uncertainty exists concerning the limits of permissible conduct and the nature and scope of one's moral obligations to others. In contrast, for these positivists at least, law is apparently concrete and uncontroversial. Moreover, when a dispute arises over whether or not something is law, there exists a decision procedure that, in the bulk of cases, settles the issue. Law is knowable and ascertainable, so that, while a person may not know the range of his moral obligations, he is aware of (or can find out) what the law expects of him. Commitment to the traditional legal values associated with the rule of law requires that law consist in knowable, largely uncontroversial fact; and it is this feature of law that positivism draws attention to and which underlies it.

One can reach the same characterization of law as consisting in uncontroversial, hard facts by ascribing to legal positivism the epistemological and semantic constraints of logical positivism on legal facts. For the logical positivists, moral judgments were meaningless because they could not be verified by a reliable and essentially uncontroversial test. In order for statements of law to be meaningful, they must be verifiable by such a test (the epistemic conception of the rule of recognition). To be meaningful, therefore, law cannot be essentially controversial.

Once positivism is characterized as the view of law as consisting in hard facts, Dworkin's ascription of certain basic tenets to it is plausible, and his objections to them are compelling. First, law for positivism consists in rules rather than principles, because the legality of a rule depends on its formal characteristics—the manner and form of its enactment—whereas the legality of a moral principle will depend on its content. The legality of rules, therefore, will be essentially uncontroversial; the legal normativity of principles will be essentially controversial. Second, adjudication takes place in both hard and simple cases. Paradigm or simple cases are uncontroversial. The answer to them as a matter of law is clear, and the judge is obligated to provide it. Cases falling within the penumbra of a general rule, however, are uncertain. There is no uncontroversial answer as a matter of law to them, and judges must go beyond the law to exercise their discretion in order to resolve them. Controversy implies the absence of legal duty and, to the extent to which legal rules have controversial instances, positivism is committed to a theory of discretion in the resolution of disputes involving them. Third, positivism must be committed to a rule of recognition in both the epistemic and the semantic senses, for the rule of recognition not only sets out the conditions of legality, it provides the mechanism by which one settles disputes about what, on a particular matter, the law is. The rule of recognition for the positivist is the principle by which particular propositions of law are verified. Relatedly, the conditions of legality set forth in the rule of recognition must be ones of pedigree or form, otherwise the norm will fail to provide a reliable principle for verifying and adjudicating competing claims about the law. Finally, law and morality are distinct (the separability thesis) because law consists in hard facts, while morality does not.

Unfortunately for positivism, if the distinction between law and morality is motivated by commitment to law as uncontroversial, hard facts, it must be abandoned because, as Dworkin rightly argues, law is controversial, and even where it is, law may involve matters of obligation and right rather than discretion.

There is no more plausible way of understanding Dworkin's conception of positivism and of rendering his arguments against it (at least those in MOR-I) persuasive. The result is a form of positive positivism that makes an interesting claim about the essence of law—that by and large law consists in hard, concrete facts—a claim that Dworkin neatly shows is mistaken. The entire line of argument rests, however, on ascribing to legal positivism either a programmatic or metaphysical thesis about law. It is the thesis of law as hard facts—whether motivated by semantic, epistemic, or normative arguments— that explains not only positivism's commitment to the separability thesis, but its adherence to other claims about law, that is, discretion, the model of rules, and the noncontentful standard of legality.

The argument for law as hard facts that relies on the positivist program of knowable, ascertainable law is straightforwardly problematic. Legal positivism makes a conceptual or analytic claim about law, and that claim should not be confused with programmatic or normative interests certain positivists, especially Bentham, might have had. Ironically, to hold otherwise is to build into the conceptual account of law a particular normative theory of law; it is to infuse morality, or the way law ought to be, into the concept of law (or the account of the way law is). In other words, the argument for ascribing certain tenets to positivism in virtue of the positivist's normative ideal of law is to commit the very mistake positivism is so intent on drawing attention to and rectifying.

The argument for law as hard facts that relies, not on the programmatic interests of some positivists, but on the semantics and epistemology of logical positivism is both more plausible and interesting. Hart's characterization of his inquiry as an analysis both of the concept of law and of how one determines if a norm constitutes valid law as if these were one and the same thing suggests a conflation of semantic and epistemic inquiries of the sort one associates with logical positivism. Recall, in this regard, Hart's discussion of the move from the "prelegal" to the "legal." The move from the prelegal to the legal is accomplished by the addition of secondary rules to the set of primary social rules of obligation: in particular, by the addition of a rule of recognition that solves the problem of uncertainty, that is, the epistemic problem of determining which norms are law. Moreover Hart's discussion of judicial discretion—that is, the absence of legal duty—as arising whenever the application of a general term in a rule of law is controversial further suggests the identification, for Hart at least, of law with fact ascertainable by the use of a reliable method of verification. Still, in order to justify the ascription to positivism of the view that law consists in hard facts, we need an argument to the effect that part of what it means to be a legal positivist is to be committed to some form of verificationism.

The problem with any such argument is that the separability thesis can stand on its own as a fundamental tenet of positivism without further motivation. After all, verificationism may be wrong and the separability thesis right; without fear of contradiction one can assert both a (metaphysical) realist position about legal facts and the separability thesis. (As an aside, this fact alone should suffice to warrant caution in ascribing logical positivism to legal positivism on the grounds that they are both forms of positivism; otherwise one might be tempted to ascribe metaphysical or scientific realism to legal realism on similar grounds, which, to say the least, would be preposterous[6]). In short, one alleging to be a positivist can abandon the metaphysics of verificationism, hang on to the separability thesis, and advance the rather plausible position that the motive for the separability thesis—if indeed there is one—is simply that the distinction it insists on between law and morality is a valid one; and, just in case that is not enough, the positivist can point out that there is a school of jurisprudence that denies the existence of the distinction. In effect, the positivist can retreat to negative positivism and justify his doing so by pointing out that the separability thesis needs no further motivation, certainly none that winds up committing the advocate of a sound jurisprudential thesis to a series of dubious metaphysical ones.

While I am sympathetic to this response, it is not going to satisfy Dworkin. There is something unsatisfactory about a theory of law that does not make an affirmative claim about law. Indeed, one might propose as an adequacy condition that any theory of law must have a point about law. Negative positivism fails to satisfy this adequacy condition. Natural law theory satisfies this adequacy condition by asserting that in every conceivable legal system moral truth is a necessary condition of legality—at least for some norms. Since it consists in the denial of this claim, negative positivism makes no assertion about what is true of law in every conceivable legal system. The view Dworkin rightly ascribes to Hart, but wrongly to positivism generally, that the point of positivism is that law consists in hard facts, meets the adequacy condition and makes the kind of claim, mistaken though it may be, that one can sink one's teeth into.

I want to offer an alternative version of positivism, which, like the "law-as-hard-facts" conception, is a form of positive positivism. The form of positive positivism I want to characterize and defend has, as its point, not that law is largely uncontroversial—it need not be—but that law is ultimately conventional: That the authority of law is a matter of its acceptance by officials.

III. Positive positivism: law as social convention

It is well known that one can meet the objections to positivism Dworkin advances in MOR-I by constructing a rule of recognition (in the semantic sense) that permits moral principles as well as rules to be binding legal standards.[7] Briefly the argument is this: Even if some moral principles are legally binding, not every moral principle is a legal one. Therefore, a test must exist for distinguishing moral principles that are legally binding from those that are not. The characteristic of legally binding moral principles that distinguishes them from nonbinding moral principles can be captured in a clause in the relevant rule of recognition. In other words, a rule is a legal rule if it possesses characteristic C; and a moral principle is a legal principle if it possesses characteristic C_1. The rule of recognition then states that a norm is a legal one if and only if it possesses either C or C_1. Once this rule of recognition is formulated, everything Dworkin ascribes to positivism, other than the model of rules, survives. The (semantic) rule of recognition survives, since whether a norm is a legal one does not depend on whether it is a rule or a principle, but on whether it satisfies the conditions of legality set forth in a rule of recognition. The separability thesis survives just so long as not every conceivable legal system has in its rule of recognition a C_1 clause; that is, a clause that sets out conditions of legality for some moral principles, or if it has such a clause, there exists at least one conceivable legal system in which no principle satisfies that clause. Finally, one argument for judicial discretion—the one that relies not on controversy but on the exhaustibility of legal standards—survives. That is, only a determinate number of standards possess either C or C_1, so that a case may arise in which no legal standard under the rule of recognition is suitable or adequate to its resolution. In such cases, judges must appeal to nonlegal standards to resolve disputes.[8]

Given Dworkin's view of positivism as law consisting in hard facts, he might simply object to this line of defense by noting that the "rule of recognition" formed by the conjunction of the conditions of legality for both principles and rules could not be a rule of recognition in the positivist's sense because its reference to morality would make it inherently controversial. Put another way, a controversial rule of recognition could not be a rule of recognition in the epistemic sense; it could not provide a reliable verification principle. For that reason, it could not be a rule of recognition in the positivist sense. Interestingly, that is not quite the argument Dworkin advances. To be sure, he argues that a rule of recognition of this sort could not constitute a rule of recognition in the positivist's sense. Moreover, he argues that such a rule would be inherently controversial. But the argument does not end with the allegation that such a rule would be controversial. The controversial character of the rule is important for Dworkin, not because it is incompatible with law as hard fact or because a controversial rule cannot be a reliable verification principle, but because a controversial rule of recognition cannot be a social rule. A controversial rule of recognition cannot be a conventional one, or one whose authority depends on its acceptance.

At the outset of the essay I distinguished between two kinds of constraints that might be imposed on the rule of recognition: those having to do with substantive conditions of legality and those having to do with the authority of the rule of recognition itself. The difference between Dworkin's arguments against positivism in MOR-I and MOR-II is that, in the former essay, the version of positivism he objects to is constrained in the first way—legality must be determined by a noncontentful (or pedigree) test—whereas the version of positivism he objects to in MOR-II is constrained in the second way—the rule-of-recognition's authority must be a matter of convention.

Against the law-as-convention version of positivism, Dworkin actually advances four related arguments, none of which, I want to argue, is ultimately convincing. These are what I will refer to as: (1) the social rule argument; (2) the pedigree argument; (3) the controversy argument; and (4) the moral argument.[9]

A. The social rule argument

Legal obligations are imposed by valid legal norms. A rule or principle is a valid one provided it satisfies the conditions of legality set forth in the rule of recognition. The question Dworkin raises in MOR-II concerns the nature of duties under rule of recognition itself. Does the rule of recognition impose duties on judges because they accept it or because the rule is defensible within a more comprehensive moral theory of law? For Dworkin this is the question of whether the rule of recognition is a social or a normative rule.

Dworkin's first argument in MOR-II against law-as-convention positivism is that the social rule theory provides an inadequate general theory of duty. The argument is this: According to the social rule theory an individual has an obligation to act in a particular way only if (1) there is a general practice of acting in that way; and (2) the rule that is constructed or built up from the practice is accepted from an internal point of view. To accept a rule from an internal point of view is to use it normatively as providing reasons both for acting in accordance with it and for criticizing departures from it. But, as Dworkin rightly notes, there may be duties even where no social practice exists, or where a contrary practice prevails. This is just another way of saying that not every duty is one of conventional morality.

If the positivist's thesis is that the social rule theory provides an adequate account of the source of all noninstitutional duties or of the meaning of all claims about such duties, it is surely mistaken. Not all duties imposed by rules are imposed by conventional rules. Fortunately, the law-as-convention version of positivism makes no such claim. The question is not whether the social rule theory is adequate to account for duties generally; it is whether the theory accounts for the duty of judges under a rule of recognition. An inadequate general theory of obligation may be an adequate theory of judicial duty. Were one to take the social rule argument seriously, it would amount to the odd claim that the rule of recognition cannot be a social rule and, therefore, that obligations under it could not be ones of conventional morality, simply because not every duty-imposing rule is a social rule.

B. The pedigree argument

The first serious argument Dworkin makes against the social rule theory of judicial obligation relies, in part, on the arguments in MOR-I. In meeting the objection to MOR-I, I constructed a rule of recognition that set out distinct conditions of legality for both rules (C) and moral principles (C_1). Let us abbreviate this rule as "C and C_1." Dworkin's claim is that such a rule cannot be a social rule.

The argument is this: The truth conditions in "$C + C_1$" make reference to moral principles as well as to legal rules. Unlike legal rules, moral principles cannot be identified by their pedigree. Because to determine which of a community's moral principles are legal ones will rely on the content of the principles, it will be a matter of some controversy. But if there is substantial controversy, then there cannot be convergence of behavior sufficient to specify a social rule. The social rule theory requires convergency of behavior, that is, a social practice. A nonpedigree standard implies controversy; controversy implies the absence of a social practice; the absence of the requisite social practice means that the rule cannot be a social rule. A rule of recognition that made reference to morality— the kind of rule of recognition we constructed to overcome Dworkin's objections in MOR-I—

could not be a social rule and, therefore, could not be a rule of recognition in the positivist's sense.

The argument moves too quickly. Not every reference that a rule of recognition might make to morality would be inherently controversial. It does not follow from the fact that $C + C_1$ refers to moral principles that this rule cannot determine legality in virtue of some noncontent characteristic of moral principles. For example, C_1 could be an "entrenchment" requirement of the sort Rolf Sartorius has proposed, so that whether a moral principle is a legal principle will depend on whether it is mentioned in preambles to legislation and in other authoritative documents: The more mentions, the more weight the principle receives.[10] Or C_1 could state that a moral principle is a legal principle only if it is widely shared by members of the community. In short, the legality of a moral principle could be determined by some of its noncontentful characteristics. In such cases, to determine which moral principles are legally binding would be no more troublesome or controversial than to determine which rules are legal ones.

Though not every reference to morality will render a rule of recognition controversial, some ways of identifying which of a community's moral principles are law will. Suppose C_1 makes moral truth a condition of legality, so that a moral principle could not be part of a community's law unless it were true. Whereas its entrenchment is not a controversial characteristic of a moral principle, its truth is. Any rule of recognition that made moral truth a condition of legality would be controversial. A controversial rule of recognition results in divergence of behavior sufficient to undermine its claim to being a social rule. If a rule of recognition is not a social rule, it cannot be a rule of recognition in the positivist's sense.

Not every possible rule of recognition, therefore, would be a social rule. For example, "the law is whatever is morally right" could never be a rule of recognition in the positivist's sense. Because positivism of the sort I want to defend holds that law is everywhere conventional—that (in the language of this discussion) the rule of recognition in every community is a social rule—it must be mistaken.

C. The controversy argument

Dworkin's view is that the rule of recognition in any jurisdiction is either a social rule or a normative rule; it imposes a duty, in other words, either because it is accepted or because it is true. Law-as-convention positivism is the view that, in every community, the rule of recognition is a social rule. At this level, negative positivism is the view that, in at least one conceivable community, the rule of recognition is a social rule. Natural law theory would then be the view that, in every conceivable legal system, the rule of recognition is a normative rule. Dworkin's claim is that the rule of recognition is a normative rule, and therein lies the justification for placing him within the natural law tradition.

The argument in the previous section is compatible with some rules of recognition being normative rules and others being social rules. For example, a rule of recognition that made no reference to morality or, if it did, referred only to noncontentful features of moral principles, might, for all that the previous argument shows, still be a social rule. If it were, Dworkin's arguments, based on the controversial nature of rules of recognition that refer to morality, would be inadequate to establish the normative theory of law.

What Dworkin needs is an argument that no rule of recognition can be a social rule: That regardless of the conditions of legality it sets forth, no rule of recognition can account for certain features of law unless it is a normative rule. Dworkin has such an argument and it appears to be this: Regardless of the specific conditions of legality it sets forth, every rule of recognition will give rise to controversy at some

point. For example, a rule that made no reference to morality could still give rise to controversy concerning either the weight to be given to precedent, or the question of whether—and if so, to what extent—the present legislature could bind a future one. Though the rule itself would not be controversial, particular instances of it would be. Were the rule of recognition a social rule, it could not impose duties on judges in such controversial cases. The existence of judicial duties in controversial cases can only be explained by interpreting the rule of recognition as a normative rule.

This argument relies on the fact that even rules of recognition which are by and large uncontroversial will have controversial applications. In those controversial cases, the social rule interpretation of the rule of recognition could not account for the rule's imposing an obligation on judges. That is because, in the social rule theory, obligations derive from convergent practice; and in both the controversial, as well as the as yet unresolved, cases there exists no convergent practice or opinion from which an obligation might derive.

The rule of recognition is either a social rule or a normative rule. If it imposes obligations in controversial cases, it cannot be a social rule. Therefore, if the rule of recognition imposes a duty upon judges in controversial cases, it must be a normative rule. Because the rule of recognition in every community is a normative rule, the obligations of judges under it are ones of critical rather than conventional morality; and the ultimate authority of law is a matter of morality, not convention.

The argument from controversy presupposes that judges are bound by duty, even in controversial cases, under the rule of recognition. Positivism, it appears, is committed to judicial discretion in such cases and is, therefore, unable to explain either the source or nature of the duty. Because the social rule theory of judicial obligation is unable to explain the fact of judicial obligation in controversial cases, it must be false and, therefore, its alternative, the normative rule theory, true.

One response a positivist might make to Dworkin's argument is to deny that in such cases judges are bound by duty, in which case the failure of the social rule theory to account for judicial duty would not be troublesome. Dworkin quickly dismisses the plausibility of this response with the offhand remark that such a view likens law to a game in which the participants agree in advance that there are no right answers and no duties where sufficient controversy or doubt exists regarding the requirements of a rule. The analogy to a game is supposed to embarrass positivism, but it need not. Anyone even superficially familiar with Hart's work knows that the bulk of examples he draws upon to illustrate his claims about rules, law, and the nature of adjudication are drawn from games like baseball and chess. So the positivist might welcome, rather than eschew, the analogy to games.

Whether it is advanced to support or to criticize positivism, the alleged analogy to games is unsatisfying. The more interesting tack is to suppose along with Dworkin that judges may be obligated by a rule of recognition, even in its controversial applications, and then ask whether, in spite of Dworkin's arguments to the contrary, the social rule theory can explain this feature of law.

D. The moral argument

That Dworkin takes judicial obligations in cases involving controversial applications of the rule of recognition to be ones of critical morality rather than conventional practice is illustrated by the moral argument. Unlike the previous arguments I have outlined, the moral argument is direct and affirmative in the sense that, instead of trying to establish the inadequacies of the social rule theory, its purpose is to provide direct support for the normative interpretation of the rule of recognition. The argument is simply this:

In resolving hard or controversial cases that arise under the rule of recognition, judges do not typically cite the practice or opinions of other judges. Because these cases are controversial, there exists no convergent practice among judges to cite. Instead, in order to resolve these disputes, judges typically appeal to principles of political morality. For example, in determining how much weight to give precedent, judges may apply alternative conceptions of fairness. If, as the social rule theory claims, the source of a judge's duty depends on the rule or principle he cites as its basis, the sources of judicial obligation in these controversial cases are the principles of political morality judges cite as essential to the resolution of the dispute. The duty of judges in controversial cases can only be explained if the rule of recognition is a normative one whose authority depends on its moral merits; whose normativity, in other words, depends on moral argument of precisely the sort judges appear to engage in.

E. Summary

Dworkin has three distinct, powerful arguments against law-as-convention positivism. Each argument has a slightly different character and force. The point of the pedigree argument is that a rule of recognition that makes reference to the content of moral principles as a condition of their legality will spur controversy and, because it will, it cannot be a social rule, or, therefore, a rule of recognition in the positivist's sense. The argument is weak in the sense that, even if sound, it would be inadequate to establish the normative account of the rule of recognition. Only controversial rules of recognition fail to be social rules; for all the argument shows, uncontroversial rules of recognition may be social rules.

The more general argument from controversy appears to fill the gap left by the pedigree argument. Here the argument is not that every rule of recognition will be systematically controversial.

Instead, the argument relies on the plain fact that even basically uncontroversial rules of recognition will have controversial instances. The social rule theory cannot account for judicial obligation in the face of controversy. If the rule of recognition imposes an obligation on judges in controversial cases, as Dworkin presumes it does, the obligation can be accounted for only if the rule is a normative one whose capacity to impose a duty does not depend on widespread convergence of conduct or opinion. The point of the argument can be put in weaker or stronger terms. One can say simply that obligations in controversial cases exist and positivism cannot account for them; or one can put the point in terms of natural law theory as the claim that the duties that exist are ones of critical morality, rather than conventional practice.

The point of the moral argument is that, in resolving hard cases, judges appear to rely on principles of political morality rather than on convergent social practice. Judges apparently believe that they are bound to resolve these controversies and, more important, that their duty to resolve them in one way rather than another depends on the principles of morality to which they appeal.

IV. Convention and controversy

Each of the objections to the social rule theory can be met.[11] Consider the pedigree argument first, that is, the claim that a rule of recognition which refers to morality—which has a C_1 clause satisfied by some norm—will be controversial and, therefore, cannot be a social rule of recognition. Suppose the clause in the rule of recognition states: The law is whatever is morally correct. The controversy among judges does not arise over the content of the rule of recognition itself. It arises over which norms satisfy the standards set forth in it. The divergence in behavior among officials as exemplified in their identifying different standards as legal ones does not establish their failure to accept the same rule

of recognition. On the contrary, judges accept the same truth conditions for propositions of law, that is, that law consists in moral truth. They disagree about which propositions satisfy those conditions. While there may be no agreement whatsoever regarding which standards are legal ones—since there is no agreed upon standard for determining the truth of a moral principle—there is complete agreement among judges concerning the standard of legality. That judges reach different conclusions regarding the law of a community does not mean that they are employing different standards of legality. Since disagreement concerning which principles satisfy the rule of recognition presupposes that judges accept the same rule of recognition, the sort of controversy envisaged by the pedigree argument is compatible with the conventionalist account of the authority of the rule of recognition.

Notice, however, that were we to understand the rule of recognition epistemically, as providing a reliable test for identifying law, rather than as specifying truth conditions for statements of law, the sort of controversy generated by a rule of recognition like the law is whatever is morally right would be problematic, since the proposed rule of recognition would be incapable of providing a reliable test for identifying legal norms. This just draws our attention once again both to the importance of distinguishing between the epistemic and semantic interpretations of the rule of recognition, and to the necessity of insisting upon the semantic interpretation of it.

Even on the semantic interpretation, the phrase "controversy in the rule of recognition" is ambiguous. Controversy may arise, as it does in the previous case, over which norms satisfy the conditions of legality set forth in the rule of recognition; or it can arise over the conditions of legality set out in the rule of recognition. Cases of the first sort are the ones Dworkin envisions arising from a rule of recognition that includes a clause specifying legality conditions for moral principles. These cases are not problematic because controversy presupposes agreement about and acceptance of the rule of recognition. In contrast, the claim that every rule of recognition will be controversial in some of its details is precisely the claim that, in some cases, controversy will arise over the content or proper formulation of the rule of recognition itself. The question that these cases pose is not whether judges agree about which norms satisfy the same rule of recognition; rather, it is whether judges can be said to be applying the same rule. Since the social rule theory requires of the rule of recognition that its formulation be specified by convergence of behavior or belief, the controversy concerning the proper formulation of the rule means that the rule cannot be a social rule and, therefore, not a rule of recognition in the positivist's sense.

One way of interpreting Dworkin's claim is that, wherever controversy exists in the proper formulation of a rule, the rule cannot be a conventional or social rule. This is counterintuitive, since all rules—those of conventional as well as critical morality—are vague at points and, therefore, their application in some contexts will be controversial. If we take Dworkin to be making the argument that the existence of controversy is straightforwardly incompatible with the idea of a social rule, then no rule could ever be a social rule. Certainly, in spite of the controversial nature of all rules governing behavior, we are able to distinguish (at least in broad terms) the conventional rules from those whose authority depends on their truth.

A more sympathetic and plausible reading of Dworkin is that he does not mean to contest the existence of social rules. Instead his claim is that social rules cannot account for duties beyond the range of convergent practice. Social rules cannot explain duties in controversial cases. With respect to the rule of recognition, the social rule theory cannot account for the obligation of judges to give the correct formulation of the rule of recognition in its controversial instances. On

the assumption that judges have such an obligation, the social rule theory fails. Only a normative interpretation of the rule of recognition can explain the duty in cases of divergent opinions or conduct, since the duty, according to the normative theory, does not derive from convergent practice but from sound moral argument.

Schematically, Dworkin's argument is as follows:

1   Every rule of recognition will be controversial with respect to its scope and, therefore, with respect to the nature and scope of the obligations it imposes.

2   Nevertheless, in resolving disputes involving controversial aspects of the rule, judges are under an obligation, as they are in the uncontroversial cases, to give the right answer.

3   The social rule theory which requires convergence of behavior as a condition of an obligation cannot account for the obligation of judges in 2.

4   Therefore, positivism cannot account for judicial obligation in 2.

5   Therefore, only a normative theory of law in which the duty of judges depends on moral argument rather than convergent practice can account for judicial duty in 2.

As I suggested earlier, a positivist might respond by denying the truth of 2, that is, that judges are obligated in controversial cases in which behavior and opinion diverge. Hart, for one, denies 2, and he appears to do so because he accepts 3. That he denies 2 is made evident by his characterizing these kinds of cases as involving "uncertainty in the rule of recognition" in which "all that succeeds is success." If a positivist were to deny 2 to meet Dworkin's objections on the grounds that he (the positivist) accepts 3, it would be fair to accuse him of begging the question. He would be denying the existence of judicial obligation simply because his theory cannot account for it. Moreover, from a strategic point of view, it would be better to leave open the question of whether such duties exist, rather than to preclude the very possibility of their existence as a consequence of the theory; otherwise any argument that made the existence of such duties conceivable would have the effect of completely undermining the theory. Notice, however, that Dworkin is led to an analogous position, since his argument for the normative theory of law (i.e., 5) requires that judges are under obligations in every conceivable controversial case (i.e., 2). The social rule theory logically precludes judicial obligation in such cases; the normative theory requires it. Both theories of law will fail, just in case the existence of judicial duty in controversial cases involving the rule of recognition is a contingent feature of law. In other words, if it turns out that in some legal systems judges have an obligation to provide a particular formulation of the rule of recognition when controversy arises over its proper formulation, whereas in other legal systems no such duty exists and judges are free to exercise discretion—at least until one or another formulation takes hold—both the theory that logically precludes judicial duties in all controversial cases, and that which logically entails such duties, will fail.

Denying the existence of the duties to which Dworkin draws attention is a strategy that will not serve the positivist well. One alternative would be to admit the existence of the duty in some cases, but to give up the social rule theory according to which the nature and scope of a duty are completely specified by convergent practice in favor of some other theory concerning the way in which conventional or social rules give rise to duties. This is a promising line of argument I am not prepared to discuss here. However, it seems to me that the discussion of conventions in David Lewis's brilliant book, *Convention*,[12] might provide the theoretical foundations for an alternative to the standard social rule theory. Briefly, the idea is that the

duties imposed by social rules or conventions are the results of expectations that arise from efforts to coordinate behavior. Vested, warranted expectations may extend beyond the area of convergent practice, in which case the obligations to which a social rule gives rise might cover controversial, as well as uncontroversial, cases.[13]

Another alternative strategy, the one I have been trying to develop, follows the social rule theory in restricting the duty imposed by a conventional rule to the area of convergent practice. In this view, if controversy arises in the rule of recognition itself, it does not follow that the judges are free to exercise discretion in providing a formulation of the rule. What counts is not whether controversy exists, but whether there exists a practice among judges of resolving the controversy in a particular way. And to answer the question of whether such a practice exists, we do not look to the rule of recognition—whose conditions of legality are presumably in dispute—but to the social rule constituted by the behavior of judges in applying the rule of recognition. Whether a duty exists will depend, in part, on whether the judges have developed an accepted social practice of resolving these controversies in a particular way.

Suppose that, in applying the rule of recognition, judges have developed a practice of resolving controversial instances of it. Suppose further that in some jurisdictions, for example, the United States and England, judges, by and large, resolve such disputes, as Dworkin believes they do, by providing arguments of principle; so that in determining, for example, whether and to what extent the Supreme Court can review the constitutionality of federal legislation, judges argue from principles of political morality, for example, the separation of powers and so on. According to Dworkin, we would have a controversy in the rule of recognition itself that judges would be required to resolve in the appropriate way; and the obligation of judges would derive from principles of morality that constitute the best argument. This is the essence of what I referred to as the "moral argument," and it would show that the rule of recognition is a normative, not a social, rule.

For the traditional positivist, we would have a case in which no obligation existed, where all that succeeded was success: A case in which the judges' recourse to the principles of political morality necessarily involved an exercise of discretion.

Both of these positions are mistaken. If, as Dworkin supposes, judges as a general rule look to moral principles in resolving controversial features of the rule of recognition, then there exists a practice among them of resolving controversial aspects of the rule of recognition in that way; that is, as the moral argument suggests judges in the United States and Britain do. If this is, in fact, the practice of judges in constitutional democracies like ours—as it must be if Dworkin's arguments are to be taken seriously—and if the practice is critically accepted by judges, then there is a legal duty even in controversial cases: A duty that does not derive from the principles judges cite (as in Dworkin) but from their acceptance of the practice of resolving these disputes by offering substantive moral arguments. All Dworkin's arguments really show is that judges have adopted critically the practice that the best moral argument wins, which explains both their appeal to substantive moral principles and, contrary to the traditional positivist, their duty to do so.

What, in Dworkin's view, is evidence for the normative theory of the rule of recognition— that is, general and widespread appeal to moral principle to resolve controversies in it—is, in my view, evidence of the existence of a social practice among judges of resolving such disputes in a particular way; a practice that specifies part of the social rule regarding judicial behavior. The appeal to substantive moral argument is, then, perfectly compatible with the conventionalist account of law.

To argue that the appeal to moral argument is compatible with the conventionalist account is not to establish that account, since the appeal to moral argument as a vehicle of dispute resolution is also consistent with the normative theory of law. One could argue that, at most, my argument shows only that Dworkin's arguments, which rely on both the controversial nature of law and the appeal to moral principle to resolve controversy, are inadequate to undermine positivism. We need some further reasons to choose between the normative and conventional theories of law.

Dworkin has taken the "acid test" for positivism to be whether it can account for judicial behavior in jurisdictions, such as the United States and England, in which both prospective litigants and judges believe that disputes which arise because of controversy in the rule of recognition are to be resolved, not by discretion, but by principled argument. His arguments are all to the effect that positivism cannot account for either the expectations of litigants or the behavior of judges, because positivism is committed to discretion whenever controversy arises. If controversy arises in a rule subordinate to the rule of recognition, positivism is committed to discretion in virtue of the theory of language it adopts that makes so much of the difference between "core" and "penumbra" instances of general terms. If controversy arises in the rule of recognition itself, positivism is committed to discretion because the rule of recognition is a social rule specified by the behavior of judges; and a social rule can impose an obligation only to the extent behavior converges, that is, only in the absence of controversy. I have argued that, contrary to Dworkin, positivism can, in fact, account for the obligations of judges in controversial instances of the rule of recognition, since the existence of controversy does not preclude the existence of conformity of practice in resolving it. If I am correct, neither the existence of controversy nor the appeal to moral argument in certain jurisdictions as necessary to its resolution is incompatible with law-as-convention positivism. What then is the acid test?

For the normative theory of law to be correct, judges must be under a legal obligation to resolve controversies arising in every conceivable rule of recognition by reliance on substantive moral argument. That is because Dworkin's version of the normative theory entails the existence of judicial duty in all cases, and because the resolution of the dispute must involve moral argument. After all, if the rule of recognition is, as Dworkin claims, a normative rule, then its authority rests on sound moral argument and the resolution of disputes concerning its scope must call for moral argument. Were judges to rely on anything else, the authority of the rule of recognition will not be a matter of its moral merits; or if they appeal to nothing at all, then in such jurisdictions we would have reason to believe that judges are under no particular obligation to resolve a controversy in the rule of recognition.

The real acid test seems to be not whether positivism of the sort I am developing can account for judicial obligations in the kinds of cases we are discussing, but whether these obligations constitute a necessary feature of law which, in every jurisdiction, is imposed by moral principle. As long as the existence of such duties is a contingent feature of law, as is the duty to resolve disputes by appealing to moral argument, the normative theory of law is a less plausible account than is the conventionalist theory. Indeed, it seems straightforwardly false, since we can imagine immature legal systems (which are legal systems nonetheless) in which no practice for resolving disputes in the rule of recognition has as yet developed—where all that succeeds is success. Or we could imagine the development of considerably less attractive practices for resolving such disputes, for example, the flip of a coin: heads, defendant wins; tails, plaintiff does. In the first sort of legal system, it would seem odd to say judges were legally bound to resolve such disputes (though

they might always be morally bound to do so), since no practice had as yet developed. Eventually, such a practice is likely to develop, and the range of judicial discretion will narrow as the practice becomes widespread and critically accepted. As the second example shows, the practice that finally develops need not conform to judicial practice in the United States and England. Though judicial discretion narrows as the range of judicial obligation expands, it may do so in a way that is considerably less attractive than the moral argument envisions; in a way that is, in fact, less attractive than a system in which all that succeeded was success.

Unlike traditional positivism, which has trouble explaining judicial behavior in mature legal systems, and the normative theory of law, which has difficulty explaining developing and immature legal systems (for the reasons that the first precludes obligations in controversial cases, while the second requires them), law-as-convention positivism understands such duties to be a contingent feature of law that can be explained as arising from the critical acceptance of a practice of dispute resolution, rather than from the principles of morality which judges under one kind of practice might cite.

V. Conclusion

Dworkin makes three correct observations about the controversial nature of some legal standards.

1. A legal system can (and does in the United States and Britain) recognize certain standards as part of the law even though they are "essentially controversial" in the sense that there may be disagreements among judges as to which these are, and there is no decision procedure which, even in principle, can demonstrate what they are, and so settle disagreements.

2. Among such essentially controversial legal standards are moral principles owing their status as law to their being "true" moral principles, though their "truth" cannot be demonstrated by any agreed upon test.

3. The availability of such controversial principles fills the "gaps" left by ordinary sources of law, which may be partially indeterminate, vague, or conflicting. So that, at least with respect to the resolution of disputes involving standards subordinate to the rule of recognition, a judge never has to exercise law-making power or "discretion" to fill the gaps or remove the indeterminacy if such moral principles are a part of the law.

In this essay, I have drawn distinctions among three versions of positivism and have discussed their relationship to Dworkin's claims: (1) "Negative positivism," the view that the legal system need not recognize as law "controversial" moral standards; (2) "positive, hard-facts positivism," the view that controversial standards cannot be regarded as law and, hence, rejects Dworkin's three points; (3) "positive, social rule positivism," which insists only on the conventional status of the rule of recognition but accepts Dworkin's three points.

Since the inclusion of controversial moral principles is not a necessary feature of the concept of law, Dworkin's arguments to the effect that such principles figure in judicial practice in the United States and in Britain, are inadequate to undermine the very weak claim of negative positivism. On the other hand, if Dworkin is right—and I am inclined to think that he is—in thinking that controversial moral principles sometimes figure in legal argument, then any form of positivism that is committed to the essentially noncontroversial nature of law is mistaken. Finally, what I have tried to do is to develop a form of positivism which accepts the controversial nature of some legal reasoning, while denying that this is incompatible with the essential, affirmative claim of the theory that law is everywhere conventional in nature. If I am correct, there is a form of positivism which can do justice to Dworkin's insights while rendering his objections harmless.

Notes

Marshall Cohen (ed.), *Ronald Dworkin and Contemporary Jurisprudence* (Duckworth 1983), pp. 28–48

1 Dworkin's claim that positivism is committed to a pedigree standard of legality is too narrow. What he means to argue, I believe, is that positivism is committed to some form of "noncontentful" criterion of legality, of which a pedigree standard would be one. For ease of exposition, I will use "pedigree test" broadly to mean any sort of noncontentful criterion of legality.

2 The phrase "truth as a moral principle as a condition of legality" does seem a bit awkward. However, any other phrase, such as "morality as a condition of legality" or "moral contents as a condition of legality," would be ambiguous, since it would be unclear whether the separability thesis was a claim about the relationship between law and critical morality or between law and conventional morality. My understanding of the separability thesis is a denial of a constitutive relationship between law and critical morality.

3 This seems to be in the form of positivism David Lyons advances to meet Dworkin's objections to positivism. Cf. David Lyons, "Review: *Principles, Positivism, and Legal Theory*," *Yale Law Journal* 87 (1977): 415.

4 But see Rolf Sartorius, "Social Policy and Judicial Legislation," *American Philosophical Quarterly* 8 (1971): 151; Jules Coleman, "Review, *Taking Rights Seriously*," *California Law Review* 66 (1978): 885.

5 The following characterization of positivism in virtue of motivations for the separability thesis was developed after numerous discussions with Professor Dworkin. I am particularly grateful to him for remarks, but it is likely that I have not put the characterizations as well as he would have.

6 That is because legal realism is skeptical about the existence of legal facts. Legal facts are "created" by official action; they are not "out there" to be discovered by judges. Scientific or metaphysical realism maintains exactly the opposite view of facts.

7 See note 4.

8 Often overlooked is the fact that there are two distinct arguments for discretion: One relies on the controversial nature of penumbra cases involving

general terms; the other relies on the finiteness of legal standards. The first argument is actually rooted in a theory of language; the second, which would survive a rejection of that theory, relies on gaps in the law. See Coleman, "Review, *Taking Rights Seriously*."

9 Dworkin does not explictly distinguish among these various arguments, nor does he label any of them. The labels and distinctions are mine.

10 Sartorius, "Social Policy," p. 151; Dworkin himself discusses, but wrongly rejects this possibility; see "Model of Rules I" in *Taking Rights Seriously* (1977), p. 977. See also C. L. Ten's useful discussion, "The Soundest Theory of Law," *Mind* 88 (1979): 522.

11 There are two ways in which we might understand the notion of a social rule. Under one interpretation, not every rule of recognition would be a social rule; under the other, each would be. As both Hart and Dworkin use the term, a social rule is specified by behavior. It cannot be formulated in the absence of a practice, and the nature of the practice determines the scope of the rule and the extent of the duties it imposes. The rule that men must doff their hats upon entering church is a social rule in this sense. Not every rule of recognition, however, is a social rule in this sense for two reasons. First, at least in some jurisdictions, the content of the rule may be specified prior to the existence of an appropriate practice. For example, the formulation of the Constitution of the United States did not require the existence of the relevant judicial practice; it preceded the practice. No doubt ambiguities and other uncertainties in the rule are resolved through judicial practice; nevertheless, the general form and nature of the rule had been specified without regard to practice. Second, whereas Dworkin's contrast between social rule and normative rule theories of law turns on the manner in which legal rules give rise to duties, the rule of recognition is not itself a duty-imposing rule. We might construct a broader notion of a social rule. In this sense a rule will be a social rule if its existence or authority depends, in part, on the existence of a social practice. Here the requirement is not that the rule's proper formulation be specified by practice. Instead, the claim is that the authority of the rule depends on the existence of a practice. The rule itself may be specifiable, at least in general terms and at some points in time, without regard to the practice. However, in the absence of the practice, the rule is empty in that it is incapable of providing justifications for action. In short, its normativity depends on the practice, though its content need not be specified by it. Every rule of recognition for the positivist is a social rule in this sense.

12 David Lewis, *Convention: A Philosophical Study* (1969).

13 Gerald Postema has been trying to develop an alternative to the social rule theory that relies heavily on Lewis's theory of conventions. See Gerald J. Postema, "Coordination and Convention at the Foundations of Law," *Journal of Legal Studies* 11 (1982): 165.

Chapter 6

Joseph Raz

LEGAL POSITIVISM AND THE SOURCES OF LAW

1. The nature of legal positivism

THE PERENNIAL and inexhaustible nature of the controversy concerning the positivist analysis of the law is due in no small measure to the elusive meaning of 'positivism' in legal philosophy. True, it is well established that legal positivism is essentially independent (even though not historically unrelated) both of the positivism of nineteenth-century philosophy and of the logical positivism of the present century. But the great variation between different positivist theories of law and the large variety of philosophical motivations permeating the work of the non-positivists indicates the difficulty, perhaps the impossibility, of identifying legal positivism at its source—in a fundamental positivist philosophical outlook. The easiest approach to the continuing controversy concerning legal positivism is through the particular theses or groups of theses round which it revolves.

Three areas of dispute have been at the centre of the controversy: the identification of the law, its moral value, and the meaning of its key terms. We could identify these as the social thesis, the moral thesis, and the semantic thesis respectively. It should be understood, however, that in each area positivists (and their opponents) are identified by supporting (or rejecting) one or more of a whole group of related theses rather than any particular thesis.

In the most general terms the positivist social thesis is that what is law and what is not is a matter of social fact (that is, the variety of social theses supported by positivists are various refinements and elaborations of this crude formulation). Their moral thesis is that the moral value of law (both of a particular law and of a whole legal system) or the moral merit it has is a contingent matter dependent on the content of the law and the circumstances of the society to which it applies. The only semantic thesis which can be identified as common to most positivist theories is a negative one, namely, that terms like 'rights' and 'duties' cannot be used in the same meaning in legal and moral contexts. This vague formulation is meant to cover such diverse views as: (1) 'moral rights' and 'moral duties' are meaningless or self-contradictory expressions, or (2) 'rights' and 'duties' have an evaluative and a non-evaluative meaning and they are used in moral contexts in their evaluative meaning whereas in legal contexts they are used in their non-evaluative meaning, or (3) the meaning of 'legal rights and duties' is not a function of the meaning of its component terms—as well as a whole variety of related semantic theses.

Of these the social thesis is the more fundamental. It is also responsible for the name 'positivism' which indicates the view that the law is posited, is made law by the activities of human beings. The moral and semantic theses are often thought to be necessitated by the social thesis. In crude outline the arguments run as follows: Since by the social thesis what is law is a matter of social fact, and the identification of law involves no moral argument, it follows that conformity to moral values or ideals is in no way a condition for anything being a law or legally binding. Hence, the law's conformity to moral values and ideals is not necessary. It is contingent on the particular circumstances of its creation or application. Therefore, as the moral thesis has it, the moral merit of the law depends on contingent factors. There can be no argument that of necessity the law has moral merit. From this and from the fact that terms like 'rights' and 'duties' are used to describe the law—any law regardless of its moral merit—the semantic thesis seems to follow. If such terms are used to claim the existence of legal rights and duties which may and sometimes do contradict moral rights and duties, these terms cannot be used in the same meaning in both contexts.

I have argued elsewhere[1] that both arguments are fallacious and that neither the moral nor the semantic theses follow from the social one. The claim that what is law and what is not is purely a matter of social fact still leaves it an open question whether or not those social facts by which we identify the law or determine its existence do or do not endow it with moral merit. If they do, it has of necessity a moral character. But even if they do not, it is still an open question whether, given human nature and the general conditions of human existence, every legal system which is in fact the effective law of some society does of necessity conform to some moral values and ideals. As for the semantic thesis, all the positivist has reason to maintain is that the use of normative language to describe the law does not always carry the implication that the speaker endorses the law described as morally binding. Put somewhat more precisely this means that normative language when used to state the law does not always carry its full normative force. To this even the non-positivist can agree. This does not justify the view that

terms like rights and duties are used with a different meaning in legal and moral contexts.

It is not the purpose of the present essay to explore these arguments. I mention them only to indicate the extent to which the version of positivism that will be argued for here is a moderate one which need not conflict with the natural lawyer's view concerning the semantic analysis of normative terms and the relation between law and morality. The following are but some examples of views usually associated with natural law theories which are comparable with the version of positivism defended below:

(a) 'A legal duty' means a duty which one has because the law requires the performance of that action.

(b) There is a necessary connection between law and popular morality (i.e. the morality endorsed and practised by the population).

(c) Every legal system's claim to authority is justified.

Whether or not these views are true, they are certainly compatible with the social thesis which is the backbone of the version of positivism I would like to defend. The social thesis is best viewed not as a 'first-order' thesis but as a constraint on what kind of theory of law is an acceptable theory—more specifically it is a thesis about some general properties of any acceptable test for the existence and identity of legal systems.

The (Strong) Social Thesis. A jurisprudential theory is acceptable only if its tests for identifying the content of the law and determining its existence depend exclusively on facts of human behaviour capable of being described in value-neutral terms, and applied without resort to moral argument.

This formulation is less clear than it might be. A more clear and lucid statement requires a fuller theoretical elaboration and is likely, therefore, to be more controversial. The above formulation strives to get at the core motivation and the basic idea underlying the various formulations of the social thesis and accepts the inevitable cost in lack of precision. Some clarification may nevertheless be called for.

First, the thesis assumes that any complete theory of law includes tests for the identification of the content and determination of the existence of the law. This seemed self-evident to many philosophers of law who saw it as one of their main tasks to provide such tests. Other equally influential legal philosophers were never stirred to do so and felt that such tests are no part of legal philosophy or are fruitless or impossible. Lon Fuller is the most eminent of those contemporary philosophers who have taken such a view. The reasons for dissenting from such positions will be indicated briefly in the next section. It is best to regard such theories as incomplete theories of law. For one reason or another most, if not all, theories of law are incomplete in that they do not propose answers to some questions which fall within the province of jurisprudence.

Secondly, the thesis assumes that there is a sufficiently rich vocabulary of value-neutral terms. It does not assume that there is a clear and sharp break between value-laden and value-free terms. Nor is it committed to any side in the naturalist/anti-naturalist dispute. That the test is *capable* of being described in value-neutral terms does not mean that no value or deontic conclusions are entailed by it. To assert that is to take an anti-naturalist position.

Thirdly, the thesis does not require disregarding the intentions, motivations, and moral views of people. Value-neutrality does not commit one to behaviourism.

Finally, it is worth noting that the social thesis can be divided into two: A—A social condition is necessary for identifying the existence and content of the law: A rule is a legal rule only if it meets a social condition. B—A social condition is sufficient for identifying the existence and content of the law: A rule is a legal rule if it meets the social condition.

2. The social thesis

I have claimed that the social thesis has always been at the foundation of positivist thinking about the law and that its semantic and moral consequences have all too often been misunderstood. It is not to my purpose here to expound and defend any particular view about the tests by which the existence and content of law is to be identified.[2] But since acceptance of the social thesis does give shape to theories of law which endorse it, it is important to reflect once again upon the reasons supporting the social thesis. In so doing I will inevitably commit myself to certain more definite views about the social conditions for the existence and identity of legal systems.

A. The most general and non-theoretical justification of the social thesis is that it correctly reflects the meaning of 'law' and cognate terms in ordinary language. This claim can be and has been illustrated often enough. It seems fundamentally sound as an essential part of every defence of the social thesis and yet in itself it is inconclusive. The word 'law' has non-legal uses: laws of nature, moral laws, laws of various institutions, the laws of thought, etc. Several of these have problematical status; moreover there are no clear demarcation lines in linguistic usage between the different kinds of law. Hence the dispute about the character of international law, for example, cannot be determined by appeal to ordinary language.

For similar reasons usage is too amorphous to give adequate support for the social thesis. It certainly suggests that law has a social base, that Nazi Germany had a legal system, etc. But it is not sufficiently determinate to establish beyond dispute that social facts are both sufficient and necessary conditions for the existence and identity of the law.

Finally, we do not want to be slaves of words. Our aim is to understand society and its institutions. We must face the question: is the ordinary sense of 'law' such that it helps identify facts of importance to our understanding of society?

B. The social thesis is often recommended on the ground that it clearly separates the description of the law from its evaluation. This, it is alleged, prevents confusion and serves clarity of thought. This is true, but it presupposes the thesis rather than supports it. If the law is to be identified by social tests then trying to identify it without clearly separating social facts from evaluative considerations is misleading and often downright wrong. But if the identification of the law involves, as many natural lawyers believe it does, evaluative as well as social conditions then to distinguish between the two in identifying the law is misleading and wrong.

C. Adhering to the social thesis eliminates investigator's bias. It requires that the investigator should put aside his evaluative and deontic views and rely exclusively on considerations which can be investigated and described in a value-neutral way. This again, though true, presupposes the social thesis and is one of its results rather than its foundation. For in this respect too it must be admitted that if those natural lawyers who reject the social thesis are right then involving the investigator's sense of values (it will not then be called bias) is the only proper way for identifying the law. This does not mean that on this view the law is what it is because the investigator believes in certain values. It does, however, mean that the proper way for identifying the law is to inquire into the validity and implications of certain values.

D. There are, no doubt, many other reasons and variations on reasons which have been proposed in support of the social thesis and many of them have at least some truth in them. But the main justification of the social thesis lies in the character of law as a social institution. Some social institutions may have to be understood in ways which are incompatible with an analogous

social thesis applied to them. But the law, like several others, is an institution conforming to the social thesis. To see this, it is necessary to specify in a general way the main ingredients of the tests for existence and identity for a legal system and to identify those with which the social thesis is concerned. The tests for identity and existence of a legal system contain three basic elements: efficacy, institutional character, and sources.

Efficacy is the least controversial of these conditions. Oddly enough it is also the least studied and least understood. Perhaps there is not much which legal philosophy can contribute in this respect. Though I believe there are at least some, however elementary, difficulties which need to be explored.[3] Since this essay is not concerned with the precise details of the efficacy condition these difficulties can be overlooked. Suffice it that all agree that a legal system is not the law in force in a certain community unless it is generally adhered to and is accepted or internalized by at least certain sections of the population. This condition is simply designed to assure that the law referred to is the actual law of a given society and not a defunct system or an aspiring one. It is the least important of the conditions. It is not disputed by natural lawyers. And it does not help to characterize the essence of law as a kind of human institution. It distinguishes between effective and non-effective law and not between legal and non-legal systems. Consider, by way of analogy, social morality. The same condition applies. No morality is the social morality of a population unless it is generally conformed to and accepted by that population. Here the condition of efficacy does not illuminate the nature of morality. It merely tells an effective morality from one which is not.

More important and also more controversial is the second component of the tests for existence and identity—the institutionalized character of the law. Again, the many controversies about the precise nature of the institutional aspect of law can be side-stepped here. It is widely agreed (and by many natural lawyers as well) that a system of norms is not a legal system unless it sets up adjudicative institutions charged with regulating disputes arising out of the application of the norms of the system. It is also generally agreed that such a normative system is a legal system only if it claims to be authoritative and to occupy a position of supremacy within society, i.e. it claims the right to legitimize or outlaw all other social institutions.

These institutionalized aspects of law identify its character as a social type, as a kind of social institution. Put in a nutshell, it is a system of guidance and adjudication claiming supreme authority within a certain society and therefore, where efficacious, also enjoying such effective authority. One may think that there is much more that can be said about the sort of social institution that law is. Why be so sparing and abstract in its description? No doubt the features of law mentioned can and should be elaborated in much greater detail. But when articulating a general test for existence and identity for the law one probably should not go beyond this bare characterization. The rest belongs properly to the sociology of law, for it characterizes some specific legal systems or some types of legal systems (modern capitalist, feudal, etc.), and not necessarily all legal systems.[4]

'Law', as was mentioned already, is used in many different contexts and is applied to norms of great variety and diversity. Lawyers quite naturally focus their professional attention on a certain range of uses: those which are tied to institutions of the type described. Many legal philosophers have suggested that the philosophical analysis of law should follow the legal profession and should pin its analysis to this kind of institution. This is quite natural and completely justified. Given even the very sketchy and rudimentary characterization proposed above, it is amply clear that law thus understood is an institution of great importance to all those who live in societies governed by law, which

nowadays means almost everybody. There is more than enough justification to make it a subject of special study (which need not and should not neglect its complex interrelations with other institutions and social forces). There is also sufficient reason to encourage the general public's consciousness of law as a special type of institution.

Many natural law theories are compatible with all that was said above concerning the institutional nature of law. Yet it must be pointed out that such an institutionalized conception of law is incompatible with certain natural law positions; and this for two reasons. In the first place, it is a consequence of the institutionalized character of the law that it has limits. Legal systems contain only those standards which are connected in certain ways with the operation of the relevant adjudicative institutions.[5] This is what its institutionalized character means. Hence the law has limits: it does not contain all the justifiable standards (moral or other) nor does it necessarily comprise all social rules and conventions. It comprises only a subset of these, only those standards having the proper institutional connection.[6] This is incompatible with the view that law does not form a separate system of standards and especially with the claim that there is no difference between law and morality or between it and social morality.

A second and perhaps more radical consequence of the conception of law as an institutional system is that one cannot impose moral qualifications as conditions for a system or a rule counting as legal which are not reflected also in its institutional features. If law is a social institution of a certain type, then all the rules which belong to the social type are legal rules, however morally objectionable they may be. Law may have necessary moral properties, but if so, then only on the ground that all or some of the rules having the required institutional connections necessarily have moral properties. To impose independent moral conditions on the identity of law will inevitably mean either that not all the rules forming a part of the social institution of the relevant type are law or that some rules which are not part of such institutions are law. Either way 'law' will no longer designate a social institution.

3. The sources of law

Most positivists are ambiguous concerning one interesting point. While their general terms suggest an endorsement of the strong social thesis, their actual doctrines rest on efficacy and institutionality as the only conditions concerning the social foundation of the law. Let the combination of these two conditions be called the weak social thesis. It is easy to show that the weak and the strong theses are not equivalent. Suppose that the law requires that unregulated disputes (i.e. those with respect to which the law is unsettled) be determined on the basis of moral considerations[7] (or a certain subclass of them, such as considerations of justice or moral considerations not fundamentally at odds with social morality). Suppose further that it is argued that in virtue of this law moral considerations have become part of the law of the land (and hence the law is never unsettled unless morality is). This contention runs directly counter to the strong thesis. If it is accepted, the determination of what is the law in certain cases turns on moral considerations, since one has to resort to moral arguments to identify the law. To conform to the strong thesis we will have to say that while the rule referring to morality is indeed law (it is determined by its sources) the morality to which it refers is not thereby incorporated into law. The rule is analogous to a 'conflict of law' rule imposing a duty to apply a foreign system which remains independent of and outside the municipal law.

While all this is clear enough, it is equally clear that the contrary view (according to which morality becomes part of the law as a consequence of the referring law) does not offend against the requirement of efficacy. For here too

the bulk of the legal system may be conformed to. Nor is this view inconsistent with the institutional aspect of law: morality becomes law, on this view, by being tied to the relevant institutions. Finally, the allegation that morality can be thus incorporated into law is consistent with the thesis of the limits of law, for it merely asserts that source-based laws may from time to time incorporate parts of morality into law while imposing perhaps various conditions on their applicability. Having said that I should add that the result of admitting the view under consideration is that some non-source-based moral principles are part of almost every legal system, since most legal systems require judges to apply moral considerations on various occasions.

The difference between the weak and the strong social theses is that the strong one insists, whereas the weak one does not, that the existence and content of every law is fully determined by social sources. On the other hand, the weak thesis, but not the strong one, builds into the law the conditions of efficacy and institutionality. The two theses are logically independent. The weak thesis though true is insufficient to characterize legal positivism. It is compatible with—

(a) Sometimes the identification of some laws turns on moral arguments,

but also with—

(b) In all legal systems the identification of some laws turns on moral argument.

The first view is on the borderline of positivism and may or may not be thought consistent with it. But whereas the first view depends on the contingent existence of source-based law making moral considerations into the criteria of validity in certain cases (as in the example above), the second view asserts a conceptual necessity of testing law by moral argument and is clearly on the natural law side of the historical positivist/natural law divide.

I will argue for the truth of the strong social thesis (thus excluding both (a) and (b)).[8] I shall rename the strong social thesis 'the sources thesis'. A 'source' is here used in a somewhat technical sense (which is, however, clearly related to traditional writings on legal sources). A law has a source if its contents and existence can be determined without using moral arguments (but allowing for arguments about people's moral views and intentions, which are necessary for interpretation, for example). The sources of a law are those facts by virtue of which it is valid and which identify its content. This sense of 'source' is wider than that of 'formal sources' which are those establishing the validity of a law (one or more Acts of Parliament together with one or more precedents may be the formal source of one rule of law). 'Source' as used here includes also 'interpretative sources', namely all the relevant interpretative materials. The sources of a law thus understood are never a single act (of legislation, etc.) alone, but a whole range of facts of a variety of kinds.

What are the reasons for accepting the sources thesis? Two arguments combine to support it. The one shows that the thesis reflects and explicates our conception of the law; the second shows that there are sound reasons for adhering to that conception.

When discussing appointments to the Bench, we distinguish different kinds of desirable characteristics judges should possess. We value their knowledge of the law and their skills in interpreting laws and in arguing in ways showing their legal experience and expertise. We also value their wisdom and understanding of human nature, their moral sensibility, their enlightened approach, etc. There are many other characteristics which are valuable in judges. For present purposes these two kinds are the important ones. The point is that while it is generally admitted that both are very important for judges as judges, only the first group of characteristics

mentioned is thought of as establishing the legal skills of the judge. The second group, though relevant to his role as a judge, is thought of as reflecting his moral character, not his legal ability. Similarly, when evaluating judgments as good or bad, lawyers and informed laymen are used to distinguishing between assessing judicial arguments as legally acceptable or unacceptable and assessing them as morally good or bad. Of many legal decisions we hear that they are legally defective, being based on a misinterpretation of a statute or a case, etc. Of others it is said that though legally the decisions are acceptable, they betray gross insensitivity to current social conditions, show how conservative judges are, that they are against trade unions, or that in their zeal to protect individuals they go too far in sacrificing administrative efficiency, etc.

These distinctions presuppose that judges are, at least on occasion, called upon to rely on arguments revealing their moral character rather than their legal ability. (It is unreasonable to suppose that the judge's moral character reveals itself only when he is wrong in law. It affects decisions too often for that to be a reasonable hypothesis.) As indicated above, the use of moral judgment is regarded not as a special case of applying law or legal arguments, but is contrasted with them. This is manifested in the way the two kinds of tests evaluating judges and judgments are related to two further distinctions. The first is that between applying the law and creating, innovating, or developing the law. It is a common view that judges both apply the law and develop it. And though their two functions are extremely hard to disentangle in many cases, yet sometimes, at least, it is clear of a case that it breaks new ground, while of many others it may be equally clear that they merely apply established law. The important point is that it is our normal view that judges use moral arguments (though perhaps not only such arguments) when developing the law and that they use legal skills when applying the law (though not only legal skills are used when they have to decide whether to apply a precedent or distinguish or overrule it. I shall disregard this problem in the sequel and will return to it in Essay 10 [in the original] below).[9]

Finally there is the distinction between settled and unsettled law. All lawyers know that on some questions the law is unsettled. Sometimes they say on such cases that no one knows what the law is—as if there is law on the question which is very difficult to discover. But most of the time they express themselves more accurately, saying that this is an open question, that the law is unsettled, etc. (On the interpretation of these expressions, see Essay 4 [in the original].[10]) It is primarily in deciding cases regarding which the law is unsettled (as well as in distinguishing and reversing settled law) that judges are thought to develop the law using moral, social, and other non-legal arguments. It is when deciding cases where the law is settled that the judges are thought of as using their legal skills in applying the law.

The sources thesis explains and systemizes these distinctions. According to it, the law on a question is settled when legally binding sources provide its solution. In such cases judges are typically said to apply the law, and since it is source-based, its application involves technical, legal skills in reasoning from those sources and does not call for moral acumen. If a legal question is not answered by standards deriving from legal sources then it lacks a legal answer—the law on the question is unsettled. In deciding such cases courts inevitably break new (legal) ground and their decision develops the law (at least in precedent-based legal systems). Naturally, their decisions in such cases rely at least partly on moral and other extra-legal considerations.

One need not assume complete convergence between the distinctions mentioned above and the sources thesis. If, in fact, the sources thesis coincides with the way these distinctions are generally applied, it has explanatory power and is supported to that extent. It can then be regarded as being a systemizing or a tidying-up thesis where it goes beyond the ordinary use of these distinctions. This argument for the sources thesis is not an argument from the ordinary sense of 'law' or any other term. It relies on fundamental features of our understanding of a certain social institution, the primary examples of which are contemporary municipal legal systems but which extend far beyond them. It is not part of the argument that a similar conception of legal systems is to be found in all cultures and in all periods. It is part of our ways of conceiving and understanding the working of social institutions. There is nothing wrong in interpreting the institutions of other societies in terms of our typologies. This is an inevitable part of any intelligent attempt to understand other cultures. It does not imply that in interpreting alien institutions you disregard the intentions, beliefs, or value-schemes of their participants. It only means that at some stage you classify their activities, thus interpreted, in terms of a scheme for analysing social institutions of which the participants themselves may have been ignorant.

Still, it may be reassuring to know that the sources thesis is not merely a reflection of a superficial feature of our culture. I shall argue briefly that the sources thesis captures and highlights a fundamental insight into the function of law. It is a commonplace that social life requires and is facilitated by various patterns of forbearances, co-operation, and co-ordination between members of the society or some of them. The same is true of the pursuits of goals which the society or sections in it may set themselves. Different members and different sections of a society may have different views as to which schemes of co-operation, co-ordination, or forbearance are appropriate. It is an essential part of the function of law in society to mark the point at which a private view of members of the society, or of influential sections or powerful groups in it, ceases to be their private view and becomes (i.e. lays a claim to be) a view binding on all members notwithstanding their disagreement with it. It does so and can only do so by providing publicly ascertainable ways of guiding behaviour and regulating aspects of social life.[11] Law is a public measure by which one can measure one's own as well as other people's behaviour. It helps to secure social co-operation not only through its sanctions providing motivation for conformity but also through designating in an accessible way the patterns of behaviour required for such co-operation. This fact has been emphasized by many a natural lawyer for it forms part of the justification of the need for positive law. Locke is a prominent and well-known example. Hart more than anybody else emphasized the point among legal positivists.

To prevent misunderstanding let me elaborate some of the crucial steps in the argument. Many societies (large or small) have a relatively formal way of distinguishing between expressions of views, demands, etc., and authoritative rulings. Such a distinction is an essential element in our conception of government, be it in a family, in a loosely organized community, or in the state. Not all authoritative rulings are laws, not all systems of such rules are legal systems. But marking a rule as legally binding is marking it as an authoritative ruling. This marking-off of authoritative rulings indicates the existence in that society of an institution or organization claiming authority over members of the society that is holding them bound to conform to certain standards just because they were singled out by that purported authority regardless of whether or not they are justifiable standards on other grounds. Since it is of the very essence of the alleged authority that it issues rulings which are binding regardless of any other justification, it follows that it must be possible to identify those rulings without engaging in a justificatory argument, i.e. as issuing from certain activities and interpreted in the light of publicly ascertainable standards not involving moral argument.

If the first argument for the sources thesis was that it reflects and systemizes several interconnected distinctions embedded in our conception of the law, the second argument probes deeper and shows that the distinctions and the sources thesis which explicates them help to identify a basic underlying function of the law: to provide publicly ascertainable standards by which members of the society are held to be bound so that they cannot excuse non-conformity by challenging the justification of the standard. (Though, of course, in many countries they are free to act to change it.) This is the reason for which we differentiate between the courts' applying the law, i.e. those standards which are publicly ascertainable and binding beyond a moral argument open to the litigants, and the activity of the courts in developing the law relying on moral and other rational considerations. In making this a test for the identification of law, the sources thesis identifies it as an example of a kind of human institution which is of decisive importance to the regulation of social life.

Notes

Joseph Raz, *The Authority of Law* (Oxford 1979), pp. 37–52
My thinking on the problems discussed in this essay was greatly influenced by conversations with R. M. Dworkin and J. M. Finnis, who disagree with many of my conclusions.

1 *Practical Reason and Norms*, pp. 162 ff.
2 See my *Practical Reason and Norms*, Sections 4.3–5.2, where I suggested various modifications and elaborations on Hart's ideas as expounded in *The Concept of Law* (Oxford, 1961).
3 See my *The Concept of a Legal System* (Oxford, 1970), ch. 9, for some of the puzzling aspects of many common views about efficacy.
4 The main possible addition to the facts I mentioned are sanctions, the use of coercion or of force, and the existence of institutions for law-enforcement. See on this H. Oberdiek, 'The Role of Sanctions and Coercion in Understanding Law and Legal Systems', *American Journal of Jurisprudence* (1975), p. 71; Raz, *Practical Reason and Norms*, pp. 154–62.

5 Kelsen thought the relation is simple: Laws are norms addressed to courts (see, for example, *The General Theory of Law and State* (New York, 1945), p. 29. Others suggest more indirect connections. Most notable is Hart's idea that laws are standards courts are bound to apply and use in adjudication: *The Concept of Law*, pp. 89 ff.

6 Cannot a society have judicial institutions instructed to apply all social rules and cannot we envisage such a society lacking a clear differentiation between social morality and ideal or critical morality? Such societies are possible and probably have existed. This, however, merely shows that from their point of view there was no distinction between law and morality (unless they were made conscious of the distinction by observing other communities). We who have the distinction can still apply it to them when judging that, as things stand in their community, law encompasses the whole of their social morality. But things could have been different even for them.

7 Note that the reference is to morality, not to social morality. Social morality is based on sources: the customs, habits, and common views of a community.

8 The weak social thesis provides all the ingredients by which one determines whether a normative system is a legal system and whether it is in force in a certain country. In other words, the weak social thesis provides a complete test of existence of legal systems, a test by which one determines whether there is a legal system in force in a country. It also contributes (that is, the institutional character of law contributes) some of the ingredients which make up the test of identity of a legal system (i.e. the test by which one determines whether two norms belong to the same legal system), but here it is insufficient and has to be supplemented by the strong social thesis, i.e. by the claim that all laws have social sources.

E. P. Soper, 'Legal Theory and the Obligation of the Judge: The Hart/Dworkin Dispute', *Michigan L. Rev.* 75 (1977) p. 511 f., and D. Lyons, 'Principles, Positivism and Legal Theory', *Yale L.J.* 87 (1977) p. 424 f., argue that legal positivism is consistent with (a). Supporters of such a conception of the law have to provide an adequate criterion for separating legal references to morality, which make its application a case of applying pre-existing legal rules from cases of judicial discretion in which the judge, by resorting to moral consideration, is changing the law. I am not aware of any serious attempt to provide such a test.

9 See 'Law and Value in Adjudication', in Raz, *The Authority of Law* (Oxford: Oxford University Press, 1979), ch. 10.

10 See 'Legal Reasons, Sources, and Gaps', in Raz, *The Authority of Law* (Oxford: Oxford University Press, 1979), ch. 4.

11 I do not mean to suggest that all laws are open. Secret laws are possible provided they are not altogether secret. Someone must know their content some of the time. They are publicly ascertainable and they guide the behaviour of the officials to whom they are addressed or who are charged with their enforcement by being so.

Chapter 7

Ronald Dworkin

LAW AS INTERPRETATION

I N THIS ESSAY I shall argue that legal practice is an exercise in interpretation not only when lawyers interpret particular documents or statutes, but generally. Law so conceived is deeply and thoroughly political. Lawyers and judges cannot avoid politics in the broad sense of political theory. But law is not a matter of personal or partisan politics, and a critique of law that does not understand this difference will provide poor understanding and even poorer guidance. I propose that we can improve our understanding of law by comparing legal interpretation with interpretation in other fields of knowledge, particularly literature. I also expect that law, when better understood, will provide a better grasp of what interpretation is in general.

I. Law

The central problem of analytical jurisprudence is this: What sense should be given to propositions of law? By propositions I mean the various statements lawyers make reporting what the law is on some question or other. Propositions of law can be very abstract and general, like the proposition that states of the United States may not discriminate on racial grounds in supplying basic services to citizens, or they can be relatively concrete, like the proposition that someone who accepts a check in the normal course of business without notice of any infirmities in its title is

entitled to collect against the maker, or very concrete, like the proposition that Mrs. X is liable in damages to Mr. Y in the amount of $1150 because he slipped on her icy sidewalk and broke his hip. In each case a puzzle arises. What are propositions of law really about? What in the world could make them true or false?

The puzzle arises because propositions of law seem to be descriptive—they are about how things are in the law, not about how they should be—and yet it has proved extremely difficult to say exactly what it is that they describe. Legal positivists believe that propositions of law are indeed wholly descriptive: they are in fact pieces of history. A proposition of law, in their view, is true if some event of a designated law-making kind has taken place, and otherwise not. This seems to work reasonably well in very simple cases. If the Illinois Legislature enacts the words, "No will shall be valid without three witnesses," then the proposition of law, that an Illinois will needs three witnesses, seems to be true only in virtue of that historical event.

But in more difficult cases the analysis fails. Consider the proposition that a particular affirmative action scheme (not yet tested in the courts) is constitutionally valid. If that is true, it cannot be so just in virtue of the text of the Constitution and the fact of prior court decisions, because reasonable lawyers who know exactly what the Constitution says and what the courts have done may yet disagree whether it is true. (I am doubtful that the positivists' analysis holds even in the simple case of the will; but that is a different matter I shall not argue here.)

What are the other possibilities? One is to suppose that controversial propositions of law, like the affirmative action statement, are not descriptive at all, but are rather expressions of what the speaker wants the law to be. Another is more ambitious: controversial statements are attempts to describe some pure objective or natural law, which exists in virtue of objective moral truth rather than historical decision. Both these projects take some legal statements, at least, to be purely evaluative as distinct from descriptive: they express either what the speaker prefers—his personal politics—or what he believes is objectively required by the principles of an ideal political morality. Neither of these projects is plausible, because someone who says that a particular untested affirmative action plan is constitutional does mean to describe the law as it is rather than as he wants it to be or thinks that, by the best moral theory, it should be. He might, indeed, say that he regrets that the plan is constitutional and thinks that according to the best moral theory, it ought not to be.

There is a better alternative: propositions of law are not simply descriptive of legal history in a straightforward way, nor are they simply evaluative in some way divorced from legal history. They are interpretive of legal history, which combines elements of both description and evaluation but is different from both. This suggestion will be congenial, at least at first blush, to many lawyers and legal philosophers. They are used to saying that law is a matter of interpretation; but only, perhaps, because they understand interpretation in a certain way. When a statute (or the Constitution) is unclear on some point, because some crucial term is vague or because a sentence is ambiguous, lawyers say that the statute must be interpreted, and they apply what they call "techniques of statutory construction." Most of the literature assumes that interpretation of a particular

document is a matter of discovering what its authors (the legislators, or the delegates to the Constitutional Convention) meant to say in using the words they did. But lawyers recognize that on many issues the author had no intention either way and that on others his intention cannot be discovered. Some lawyers take a more skeptical position. They say that whenever judges pretend they are discovering the intention behind some piece of legislation, this is simply a smoke screen behind which the judges impose their own view of what the statute should have been.

Interpretation as a technique of legal analysis is less familiar in the case of the common law, but not unfamiliar. Suppose the Supreme Court of Illinois decided, several years ago, that a negligent driver who ran down a child was liable for the emotional damage suffered by the child's mother, who was standing next to the child on the road. Now an aunt sues another careless driver for emotion when she heard, on the telephone many miles from the accident, that her niece had been hit. Does the aunt have a right to recover for damage? Lawyers often say that this is a matter of interpreting the earlier decision correctly. Does the legal theory on which the earlier judge actually relied, in making his decision about the mother on the road, cover the aunt on the telephone? Once again skeptics point out that it is unlikely that the earlier judge had in mind any theory sufficiently developed so as to decide the aunt's case either way, so that a judge "interpreting" the earlier decision is actually making new law the way he or she thinks best.

The idea of interpretation cannot serve as a general account of the nature or truth of propositions of law, however, unless it is cut loose from these associations with the speaker's meaning or intention. Otherwise it becomes simply one version of the positivists' thesis that propositions of law describe decisions made by people or institutions in the past. If interpretation is to form the basis of a different and more plausible theory about propositions of law, then we must develop a more inclusive account of what interpretation is. But that means that lawyers must not treat legal interpretation as an activity *sui generis*. We must study interpretation as a general activity, as a mode of knowledge, by attending to other contexts of that activity.

Lawyers would do well to study literary and other forms of artistic interpretation. That might seem bad advice (choosing the fire over the frying pan) because critics themselves are thoroughly divided about what literary interpretation is, and the situation is hardly better in the other arts. But that is exactly why lawyers should study these debates. Not all of the battles within literary criticism are edifying or even comprehensible, but many more theories of interpretation have been defended in literature than in law, and these include theories that challenge the flat distinction between description and evaluation that has enfeebled legal theory.

II. Literature

A. *The aesthetic hypothesis*

If lawyers are to benefit from a comparison between legal and literary interpretation, however, they must see the latter in a certain light, and in this section I shall try to say what that is. (I would prefer the following remarks about literature to be uncontroversial among literary scholars, of course, but I am afraid they will not be.) Students of literature do many things under the titles of "interpretation" and "hermeneutics," and most of them are also called "discovering the meaning of a text." I shall not be interested, except incidentally, in one thing these students do, which is trying to discover the sense in which some author used a particular word or phrase. I am interested instead in arguments that offer some sort of interpretation of the meaning of a work as a whole. These sometimes take the form of assertions about

characters: that Hamlet really loved his mother, for example, or that he really hated her, or that there really was no ghost but only Hamlet himself in a schizophrenic manifestation. Or about events in the story behind the story: that Hamlet and Ophelia were lovers before the play begins (or were not). More usually they offer hypotheses directly about the "point" or "theme" or "meaning" or "sense" or "tone" of the play as a whole: that *Hamlet* is a play about death, for example, or about generations, or about politics. These interpretive claims may have a practical point. They may, for example, guide a director staging a new performance of the play. But they may also be of more general importance, helping us to an improved understanding of important parts of our cultural environment. Of course, difficulties about the speaker's meaning of a particular word in the text (a "crux" of interpretation) may bear upon these larger matters. But the latter are about the point or meaning of the work as a whole, rather than the sense of a particular phrase.

Critics much disagree about how to answer such questions. I want, so far as is possible, not to take sides but to try to capture the disagreements in some sufficiently general description of what they are disagreeing about. My apparently banal suggestion (which I shall call the "aesthetic hypothesis") is this: an interpretation of a piece of literature attempts to show which way of reading (or speaking or directing or acting) the text reveals it as the best work of art. Different theories or schools or traditions of interpretation disagree on this hypothesis, because they assume significantly different normative theories about what literature is and what it is for and about what makes one work of literature better than another.

I expect that this suggestion, in spite of its apparent weakness, will be rejected by many scholars as confusing interpretation with criticism or, in any case, as hopelessly relativistic, and therefore as a piece of skepticism that really denies the possibility of interpretation altogether. Indeed the aesthetic hypothesis might seem simply another formulation of a theory now popular, which is that since interpretation creates a work of art, and represents only the fiat of a particular critical community, there are only interpretations and no best interpretation of any particular poem or novel or play. But the aesthetic hypothesis is neither so wild nor so weak nor so inevitably relativistic as might first appear.

Interpretation of a text attempts to show it as the best work of art it can be, and the pronoun insists on the difference between explaining a work of art and changing it into a different one. Perhaps Shakespeare could have written a better play based on the sources he used for *Hamlet* than he did, and in that better play the hero would have been a more forceful man of action. It does not follow that *Hamlet*, the play he wrote, really is like that after all. Of course, a theory of interpretation must contain a subtheory about identity of a work of art in order to be able to tell the difference between interpreting and changing a work. (Any useful theory of identity will be controversial, so this is one obvious way in which disagreements in interpretation will depend upon more general disagreements in aesthetic theory.)

Contemporary theories of interpretation all seem to use, as part of their response to that requirement, the idea of a canonical text (or score, in the case of music, or unique physical object in the case of most art). The text provides one severe constraint in the name of identity: all the words must be taken account of and none may be changed to make "it" a putatively better work of art. (This constraint, however familiar, is not inevitable. A joke, for example, may be the same joke though told in a variety of forms, none of them canonical; an interpretation of a joke will choose a particular way in which to put it, and this may be wholly original, in order to bring out its "real" point or why it is "really" funny.) So any literary critic's style of interpretation will be sensitive to his theoretical beliefs about the nature of and evidence for a canonical text.

An interpretive style will also be sensitive to the interpreter's opinions about coherence or integrity in art. An interpretation cannot make a work of art more distinguished if it makes a large part of the text irrelevant, or much of the incident accidental, or a great part of the trope or style unintegrated and answering only to independent standards of fine writing. So it does not follow, from the aesthetic hypothesis, that because a philosophical novel is aesthetically more valuable than a mystery story, an Agatha Christie novel is really a treatise on the meaning of death. This interpretation fails, not only because an Agatha Christie novel, taken to be a treatise on death, is a poor treatise less valuable than a good mystery, but because the interpretation makes the novel a shambles. All but one or two sentences would be irrelevant to the supposed theme; and the organization, style, and figures would be appropriate not to a philosophical novel but to an entirely different genre. Of course some books originally offered to the public as mysteries or thrillers (and perhaps thought of by their authors that way) have indeed been "reinterpreted" as something more ambitious. The present critical interest in Raymond Chandler is an example. But the fact that this reinterpretation can be successful in the case of Chandler, but not Christie, illustrates the constraint of integrity.

There is nevertheless room for much disagreement among critics about what counts as integration, about which sort of unity is desirable and which irrelevant or undesirable. Is it really an advantage that the tongue of the reader, in reading a poem aloud, must "mime" motions or directions that figure in the tropes or narrative of the poem? Does this improve integrity by adding yet another dimension of coordination? Is it an advantage when conjunctions and line endings are arranged so that the reader "negotiating" a poem develops contradictory assumptions and readings as he goes on, so that his understanding at the end is very different from what it was at discrete points along the way? Does this add another dimension of complexity to unity, or does it rather compromise unity because a work of literature should be capable of having the same meaning or import when read a second time? Schools of interpretation will rise or fall in response to these questions of aesthetic theory, which is what the aesthetic hypothesis suggests.

The major differences among schools of interpretation are less subtle, however, because they touch not their quasi-formal aspects of art but the function or point of art more broadly conceived. Does literature have (primarily or substantially) a cognitive point? Is art better when it is in some way instructive, when we learn something from it about how people are or what the world is like? If so, and if psychoanalysis is true (please forgive that crude way of putting it), then a psychoanalytic interpretation of a piece of literature will show why it is successful art. Is art good insofar as it is successful communication in the ordinary sense? If so, then a good interpretation will focus on what the author intended, because communication is not successful unless it expresses what a speaker wants it to express. Or is art good when expressive in a different sense, insofar as it has the capacity to stimulate or inform the lives of those who experience it? If so, then interpretation will place the reader (or listener or viewer) in the foreground. It will point out the reading of the work that makes it most valuable—best as a work of art—in that way.

Of course theories of art do not exist in isolation from philosophy, psychology, sociology, and cosmology. Someone who accepts a religious point of view will probably have a different theory of art from someone who does not, and recent critical theories have made us see how far interpretive style is sensitive to beliefs about meaning, reference, and other technical issues in the philosophy of language. But the aesthetic hypothesis does not assume that anyone who interprets literature will have a fully developed and self-conscious aesthetic theory. Nor that everyone who interprets must subscribe entirely to one or another of the schools I crudely described. The best critics, I think, deny that there is one unique function or point of literature. A novel or a play may be valuable in any number of ways, some of which we learn by reading or looking or listening, rather than by abstract reflection about what good art must be like or for.

Nevertheless anyone who interprets a work of art relies on beliefs of a theoretical character about identity and other formal properties of art, as well as more explicitly normative beliefs about what is good in art. Both sorts of beliefs figure in the judgment that one way of reading a text makes it a better text than another way. These beliefs may be inarticulate (or "tacit"). They are still genuine beliefs (and not merely "reactions") because their force for any critic or reader can be seen at work not just on one isolated occasion of interpretation, but in any number of other occasions, and because they figure in and are amenable to argument.[1] (These weak claims do not, of course, take sides in the running debate on whether there are any necessary or sufficient "principles of value" in art, or whether a theory of art could ever justify an interpretation in the absence of direct experience of the work being interpreted.[2])

None of this touches the major complaint I anticipated against the aesthetic hypothesis: that it is trivial. Obviously (you might say) different interpretive styles are grounded in different theories of what art is and what it is for and what makes art good art. The point is so banal that it might as well be put the other way around: different theories of art are generated by different theories of interpretation. If someone thinks stylistics are important to interpretation, he will think a work of art better because it integrates pronunciation and trope; if someone is attracted by deconstruction, he will dismiss reference in its familiar sense from any prominent place in an account of language. Nor does my elaboration of the hypothesis in any way help to adjudicate amongst theories of interpretation or to rebut the charge of nihilism or relativism. On the contrary, since people's views about what makes art good art are inherently subjective, the aesthetic hypothesis abandons hope of rescuing objectivity in interpretation except, perhaps, among those who hold very much the same theory of art, which is hardly very helpful.

No doubt the aesthetic hypothesis is in important ways banal—it must be abstract if it is to provide an account of what a wide variety of theories disagree about—but it is perhaps not so weak as all that. The hypothesis has the consequence that academic theories of interpretation are no longer seen as what they often claim to be—analyses of the very idea of interpretation—but rather as candidates for the best answer to the substantive question posed by interpretation. Interpretation becomes a concept of which different theories are competing conceptions. (It follows that there is no radical difference but only a difference in the level of abstraction between offering a theory of interpretation and offering an interpretation of a particular work of art.) The hypothesis denies, moreover, the sharp distinctions some scholars have cultivated. There is no longer a flat distinction between interpretation, conceived as discovering the real meaning of a work of art, and criticism, conceived as evaluating its success or importance. Of course some distinction remains because there is always a difference between saying how good a particular work can be made to be and saying how good that is. But evaluative beliefs about art figure in both these judgments.

Objectivity is another matter. It is an open question, I think, whether the main judgments we make about art can properly be true or false, valid or invalid. This question is part of the more general philosophical issue of objectivity, presently much discussed in both ethics and the philosophy of language, and no one is entitled to a position who studies the case of aesthetic judgment alone. Of course no important aesthetic claim can be "demonstrated" to be true or false; no argument can be produced for any interpretation that we can be sure will commend itself to everyone, or even everyone with experience and training in the appropriate form of art. If this is what it means to say that aesthetic judgments are subjective—that they are not demonstrable—then of course they are subjective. But it does not follow that no normative theory about art is better than any other, nor that one theory cannot be the best that has so far been produced.

The aesthetic hypothesis reverses (I think to its credit) a familiar strategy. E. D. Hirsch, for example, argues that only a theory like his can make interpretation objective and particular interpretations valid.[3] This seems to me a mistake on two connected grounds. Interpretation is an enterprise, a public institution, and it is wrong to assume, a priori, that the propositions central to any public enterprise must be capable of validity. It is also wrong to assume much about what validity in such enterprises must be like—whether validity requires the possibility of demonstrability, for example. It seems better to proceed more empirically here. We should first study a variety of activities in which people assume that they have good reasons for what they say, which they assume hold generally and not just from one or another individual point of view. We can then judge what standards people accept in practice for thinking that they have reasons of that kind.

Nor is the point about reversibility—that a theory of art may depend upon a theory of interpretation as much as vice versa—an argument against the aesthetic hypothesis. I am not defending any particular explanation of how people come to have either theories of interpretation or theories of art, but only a claim about the argumentative connections that hold between these theories however come by. Of course, even at the level of argument, these two kinds of theories are mutually reinforcing. It is plainly a reason for doubting any theory of what an object of art is, for example, that the theory generates an obviously silly theory of interpretation. My point is exactly that the connection is reciprocal, so that anyone called upon to defend a particular approach to interpretation would be forced to rely on more general aspects of a theory of art, whether he realizes it or not. And this may be true even though the opposite is, to some extent, true as well. It would be a mistake, I should add, to count this fact of mutual dependence as offering, in itself, any reason for skepticism or relativism about interpretation. This seems to be the burden of slogans like "interpretation creates the text," but there is no more immediate skeptical idea that what we take to be a work of art must comport with what we take interpreting a work of art to be than in the analogous idea that what we take a physical object to be must sit well with our theories of knowledge; so long as we add, in both cases, that the connection holds the other way around as well.

B. *Author's intention*

The chief test of the aesthetic hypothesis lies, however, not in its resistance to these various charges, but in its explanatory and particularly its critical power. If we accept that theories of interpretation are no independent analyses of what it means to interpret something but are rather based in and dependent upon normative theories of art, then we must accept that they are vulnerable to complaints against the normative theory in which they are based. It does seem to me, for example, that the more doctrinaire author's intention theories are vulnerable in this way. These theories must suppose, on the present hypothesis, that what is valuable in a work of art, what should lead us to value one work of art more than another, is limited to what the author in some narrow and constrained sense intended to put there. This claim presupposes, as I suggested earlier, a more general thesis that art must be understood as a form of

speaker–audience communication; but even that doubtful thesis turns out, on further inspection, not to support it.

Of course the "intentionalists" would object to these remarks. They would insist that their theory of interpretation is not an account of what is valuable in a book or poem or play but only an account of what any particular book or poem or play means and that we must understand what something means before we can decide whether it is valuable and where its value lies. And they would object that they do not say that only intentions of the author "in some narrow and constrained sense" count in fixing the meaning of his work.

In the first of these objections, the author's intention theory presents itself not as the upshot of the aesthetic hypothesis—not as the best theory of interpretation within the design stipulated by that hypothesis—but rather as a rival to it, a better theory about what kind of thing an interpretation is. But it is very difficult to understand the author's intention theory as any sort of rival to the present hypothesis. What question does it propose to answer better? Not, certainly, some question about the ordinary language or even technical meaning of the words "meaning" or "interpretation." An intentionalist cannot suppose that all his critics and those he criticizes mean, when they say "interpretation," the discovery of the author's intention. Nor can he think that his claims accurately describe what every member of the critical fraternity in fact does under the title "interpretation." If that were so, then his strictures and polemics would be unnecessary. But if his theory is not semantic or empirical in these ways, what sort of a theory is it?

Suppose an intentionalist replies:

It points out an important issue about works of literature, namely: What did the author of the work intend it to be? This is plainly an important question, even if its importance is preliminary to other equally or more important questions about significance or value. It is, in fact, what most people for a long time have called "interpretation." But the name does not matter, so long as the activity is recognized as important and so long as it is understood that scholars are in principle capable of supplying objectively correct answers to the question it poses.

This reply comes to this: we can discover what an author intended (or at least come to probabilistic conclusions about this) and it is important to do so for other literary purposes. But why is it important? What other purposes? Any answer will assume that value or significance in art attaches primarily to what the author intended, just because it is what the author intended. Otherwise, why should we evaluate what this style of interpretation declares to be the work of art? But then the claim that interpretation in this style is important depends on a highly controversial, normative theory of art, not a neutral observation preliminary to any coherent evaluation. Of course no plausible theory of interpretation holds that the intention of the author is always irrelevant. Sometimes it is plainly the heart of the matter, as when some issue turns on what Shakespeare meant by "hawk" as distinguished from "handsaw." But it is nevertheless controversial that we must know whether Shakespeare thought Hamlet was mad or sane pretending to be mad in order to decide how good a play he wrote. The intentionalist thinks that we do, and that is exactly why his theory of interpretation is not a rival to the aesthetic hypothesis but rather a suitor for the crown that hypothesis holds out. The second objection to my charge against author's intention theories may prove to be more interesting. Intentionalists make the author's state of mind central to interpretation. But they misunderstand, so far as I can tell, certain complexities in that state of mind; in particular they fail to appreciate how intentions for a work and beliefs about it interact. I have in mind an experience familiar to anyone who creates anything, of suddenly seeing something "in" it that he did not previously know was there. This is sometimes (though I think not very well) expressed in the author's cliché, that his characters seem to have minds of their own. John Fowles provides an example from popular fiction.

When Charles left Sarah on her Cliff edge, I ordered him to walk straight back to Lyme Regis. But he did not; he gratuitously turned and went down to the Dairy.

Oh, but you say, come on—what I really mean is that the idea crossed my mind as I wrote that it might be more clever to have him stop and drink milk . . . and meet Sarah again. That is certainly one explanation of what happened; but I can only report—and I am the most reliable witness—that the idea seemed to me to come clearly from Charles, not myself. It is not only that he has begun to gain an autonomy; I must respect it, and disrespect all my quasi-divine plans for him, if I wish him to be real.[4]

Fowles changed his mind about how the story in *The French Lieutenant's Woman* "really" goes in the midst of writing it, if we are to credit this description. But he might also have changed his mind about some aspect of the novel's "point" years later, as he is rumored to have done after seeing the film made from his book. He might have come to see Sarah's motives very differently after reading Harold Pinter's screenplay or watching Meryl Streep play her; Pinter and Streep were interpreting the novel, and one or both of their interpretations might have led Fowles to change his interpretation once again. Perhaps I am wrong in supposing that this sort of thing happens often. But it happens often enough, and it is important to be clear about what it is that happens.

The intentionalist wants us to choose between two possibilities. Either the author suddenly realizes that he had a "subconscious intention" earlier, which he only now discovers, or he has simply changed his intention later. Neither of those explanations is at all satisfactory. The subconscious is in danger of becoming phlogiston here, unless we suppose some independent evidence, apart from the author's new view of his work, to suggest that he had an earlier subconscious intention. I do not mean that features of a work of art of which an author is unaware must be random accidents. On the contrary, if a novel is both more interesting and more coherent if we assume the characters have motives different from those the novelist thought of when he wrote (or if a poet's tropes and style tend to reinforce his theme in ways he did not appreciate at the time), the cause of this must in some way lie in the artist's talent. Of course there are unsolved mysteries in the psychology of creation, but the supposition of subconscious *intentions*, unsupported by other evidence of the sort a psychoanalyst would insist on, solves no mysteries and provides no explanation. This is not crucial to the point, however, because whether or not Fowles had a subconscious intention to make Charles or Sarah different characters from the "quasi-divine plan" he thought he had, his later decisions and beliefs neither consist in nor are based on any discovery of that earlier intention. They are produced by confronting not his earlier self but the work he has produced.

Nor is any new belief Fowles forms about his characters properly called (as in the intentionalist's second suggestion) a new and discrete intention. It is not an intention about what sort of characters to create because it is a belief about what sort of characters he has created; and it is not an intention about how others should understand the book, though it may or may not include an expectation of that sort. Fowles changed his view in the course of writing his book, but he changed it, as he insists, by confronting the text he had already written, by treating its characters as real in the sense of detachable from his own antecedent designs, in

short by interpreting it, and not by exploring the subconscious depths of some previous plan or finding that he had a new plan. If it is true that he changed his mind again, after seeing the film, then this was, once again, not a retrospective new intention or a rediscovered old one. It was another interpretation.

An author is capable of detaching what he has written from his earlier intentions and beliefs, of treating it as an object in itself. He is capable of reaching fresh conclusions about his work grounded in aesthetic judgments: that his book is both more coherent and an analysis of more important themes read in a somewhat different way from what he thought when he was writing it. This is, I think, a very important fact for a number of reasons; but I want, for my present purpose, only to emphasize one. Any full description of what Fowles "intended" when he set out to write *The French Lieutenant's Woman* must include the intention to produce something capable of being treated that way, by himself and therefore by others, and so must include the intention to create something independent of his intentions. I quote Fowles once again, and again as a witness rather than for his metaphysics: "Only one reason is shared by all of us [novelists]: *we wish to create worlds as real as, but other than, the world that is.* Or was. That is why we cannot plan. . . . We also know that a genuinely created world must be independent of its creator . . ."[5]

I suspect that regarding something one has produced as a novel or poem or painting, rather than a set of propositions or marks, depends on regarding it as something that can be detached and interpreted in the sense I described. In any case, this is characteristically how authors themselves regard what they have done. The intentions of authors are not simply conjunctive, like the intentions of someone who goes to market with a shopping list, but structured, so that the more concrete of these intentions, like intentions about the motives of a particular character in a novel, are contingent on interpretive beliefs whose soundness varies with what is produced and which might be radically altered from time to time.

We can, perhaps, isolate the full set of interpretive beliefs an author has at a particular moment (say at the moment he sends final galleys to the printer) and solemnly declare that these beliefs, in their full concreteness, fix what the novel is or means. (Of course, these beliefs would inevitably be incomplete, but that is another matter.) But even if we (wrongly) call this particular set of beliefs "intentions," we are, in choosing them, ignoring another kind or level of intention, which is the intention to create a work whose nature or meaning is not fixed in this way, because it is a work of art. That is why the author's intention school, as I understand it, makes the value of a work of art turn on a narrow and constrained view of the intentions of the author.

III. Law and literature

A. The chain of law

These sketchy remarks about literary interpretation may have suggested too sharp a split between the role of the artist in creating a work of art and that of the critic in interpreting it later. The artist can create nothing without interpreting as he creates; since he intends to produce art, he must have at least a tacit theory of why what he produces is art and why it is a better work of art through this stroke of the pen or the brush or the chisel rather than that. The critic, for his part, creates as he interprets; for though he is bound by the fact of the work, defined in the more formal and academic parts of his theory of art, his more practical artistic sense is engaged by his responsibility to decide which way of seeing or reading or understanding that work shows it as better art. Nevertheless there is a difference between interpreting while creating and creating while interpreting, and therefore a recognizable difference between the artist and the critic.

I want to use literary interpretation as a model for the central method of legal analysis, and I therefore need to show how even this distinction between artist and critic might be eroded in certain circumstances. Suppose that a group of novelists is engaged for a particular project and that they draw lots to determine the order of play. The lowest number writes the opening chapter of a novel, which he or she then sends to the next number who adds a chapter, with the understanding that he is adding a chapter to that novel rather than beginning a new one, and then sends the two chapters to the next number, and so on. Now every novelist but the first has the dual responsibilities of interpreting and creating, because each must read all that has gone before in order to establish, in the interpretivist sense, what the novel so far created is.[6] He or she must decide what the characters are "really" like; what motives in fact guide them; what the point or theme of the developing novel is; how far some literary device or figure, consciously or unconsciously used, contributes to these, and whether it should be extended or refined or trimmed or dropped in order to send the novel further in one direction rather than another. This must be interpretation in a non-intention-bound style because, at least for all novelists after the second, there is no single author whose intentions any interpreter can, by the rules of the project, regard as decisive.

Some novels have in fact been written in this way (including the soft-core pornographic novel *Naked Came the Stranger*[7]), though for a debunking purpose, and certain parlor games for rainy weekends in English country houses have something of the same structure. But in my imaginary exercise the novelists are expected to take their responsibilities seriously and to recognize the duty to create, so far as they can, a single, unified novel rather than, for example, a series of independent short stories with characters bearing the same names. Perhaps this is an impossible assignment; perhaps the project is doomed to produce not simply a bad novel but no novel at all, because the best theory of art requires a single creator or, if more than one, that each have some control over the whole. (But what about legends and jokes?) I need not push that question further because I am interested only in the fact that the assignment makes sense, that each of the novelists in the chain can have some idea of what he or she is asked to do, whatever misgivings each might have about the value or character of what will then be produced.

Deciding hard cases at law is rather like this strange literary exercise. The similarity is most evident when judges consider and decide "common-law" cases; that is, when no statute figures centrally in the legal issue, and the argument turns on which rules or principles of law "underlie" the related decisions of other judges in the past. Each judge is then like a novelist in the chain. He or she must read through what other judges in the past have written not simply to discover what these judges have said, or their state of mind when they said it, but to reach an opinion about what these judges have collectively *done*, in the way that each of our novelists formed an opinion about the collective novel so far written. Any judge forced to decide a law suit will find, if he looks in the appropriate books, records of many arguably similar cases decided over decades or even centuries past by many other judges of different styles and judicial and political philosophies, in periods of different orthodoxies of procedure and judicial convention. Each judge must regard himself, in deciding the new case before him, as a partner in a complex chain enterprise of which these innumerable decisions, structures, conventions, and practices are the history; it is his job to continue that history into the future through what he does on the day. He must interpret what has gone before because he has a responsibility to advance the enterprise in hand rather than strike out in some new direction of his own. So he must determine, according to his own judgment, what the earlier decisions come to,

what the point or the practice so far, taken as a whole, really is.

The judge in the hypothetical case I mentioned earlier, about an aunt's emotional shock, must decide what the theme is, not only of the particular precedent of the mother in the road, but of accident cases, including that precedent, as a whole. He might be forced to choose, for example, between these two theories about the "meaning" of that chain of decisions. According to the first, negligent drivers are responsible to those whom their behavior is likely to cause physical harm, are responsible to these people for whatever injury—physical or emotional—they in fact cause. If this is the correct principle, then the decisive difference between that case and the aunt's case is just that the aunt was not within the physical risk, and therefore she cannot recover. On the second theory, however, negligent drivers are responsible for any damage they can reasonably be expected to foresee if they think about their behavior in advance. If that is the right principle, then the aunt may yet recover. Everything turns on whether it is sufficiently foreseeable that a child will have relatives, beyond his or her immediate parents, who may suffer emotional shock when they learn of the child's injury. The judge trying the aunt's case must decide which of these two principles represents the better "reading" of the chain of decisions he must continue.

Can we say, in some general way, what those who disagree about the best interpretation of legal precedent are disagreeing about? I said that a literary interpretation aims to show how the work in question can be seen as the most valuable work of art, and so must attend to formal features of identity, coherence, and integrity as well as more substantive considerations of artistic value. A plausible interpretation of legal practice must also, in a parallel way, satisfy a test with two dimensions: it must both fit that practice and show its point or value. But point or value here cannot mean artistic value because law, unlike literature, is not an artistic enterprise.

Law is a political enterprise, whose general point, if it has one, lies in coordinating social and individual effort, or resolving social and individual disputes, or securing justice between citizens and between them and their government, or some combination of these. (This characterization is itself an interpretation, of course, but allowable now because relatively neutral.) So an interpretation of any body or division of law, like the law of accidents, must show the value of that body of law in political terms by demonstrating the best principle or policy it can be taken to serve.

We know from the parallel argument in literature that this general description of interpretation in law is not license for each judge to find in doctrinal history whatever he thinks should have been there. The same distinction holds between interpretation and ideal. A judge's duty is to interpret the legal history he finds, not to invent a better history. The dimension of fit will provide some boundaries. There is, of course, no algorithm for deciding whether a particular interpretation sufficiently fits that history not to be ruled out. When a statute or constitution or other legal document is part of the doctrinal history, the speaker's meaning will play a role. But the choice of which of several crucially different senses of speaker's or legislator's intention is the appropriate one cannot itself be referred to anyone's intention but must be decided, by whoever must make the decision, as a question of political theory.[8] In the common-law cases the question of fit is more complex. Any particular hypothesis about the point of a string of decisions ("These decisions establish the principle that no one can recover for emotional damage who did not lie within the area of physical danger himself.") is likely to encounter, if not flat counter-examples in some earlier case, at least language or argument that seems to suggest the contrary. So any useful conception of interpretation must contain a doctrine of mistake—as must any novelist's theory of interpretation for the chain novel. Sometimes a legal argument will explicitly recognize such mistakes: "Insofar as the cases of A v. B and C v. D may have held to the contrary, they were, we believe, wrongly decided and need not be followed here." Sometimes the doctrine of precedent forbids this crude approach and requires something like: "We held, in E v. F, that such-and-such, but that case raised special issues and must, we think, be confined to its own facts" (which is not quite so disingenuous as it might seem).

This flexibility may seem to erode the difference on which I insist, between interpretation and a fresh, clean-slate decision about what the law ought to be. But there is nevertheless this overriding constraint. Any judge's sense of the point or function of law, on which every aspect of his approach to interpretation will depend, will include or imply some conception of the integrity and coherence of law as an institution and this conception will both tutor and constrain his working theory of fit—that is, his convictions about how much of the prior law an interpretation must fit, and which of it, and how. (The parallel with literary interpretation holds here as well.)

It should be apparent, however, that any particular judge's theory of fit will often fail to produce a unique interpretation. (The distinction between hard and easy cases at law is perhaps just the distinction between cases in which they do and do not.) Just as two readings of a poem may each find sufficient support in the text to show its unity and coherence, so two principles may each find enough support in the various decisions of the past to satisfy any plausible theory of fit. In that case substantive political theory (like substantive consideration of artistic merit) will play a decisive role. Put bluntly, the interpretation of accident law, that a careless driver is liable to those whose damage is both substantial and foreseeable, is probably a better interpretation, if it is, only because it states a sounder principle of justice than any principle that distinguishes between physical and emotional damage or that makes recovery for emotional damage depend on whether the plaintiff was in danger of physical damage. (I should add that this issue as an issue of political morality, is in fact very complex, and many distinguished judges and lawyers have taken each side.)

We might summarize these points this way. Judges develop a particular approach to legal interpretation by forming and refining a political theory sensitive to these issues on which interpretation in particular cases will depend; they call this their legal philosophy. It will include both structural features, elaborating the general requirement that interpretation must fit doctrinal history, and substantive claims about social goals and principles of justice. Any judge's opinion about the best interpretation will therefore be the consequence of beliefs other judges need not share. If a judge believes that the dominant purpose of a legal system, the main goal it ought to serve, is economic, then he will see in past accident decisions some strategy for reducing the economic costs of accidents overall. Other judges, who find any such picture of the law's function distasteful, will discover no such strategy in history but only, perhaps, an attempt to reinforce conventional morality of fault and responsibility. If we insist on a high order of neutrality in our description of legal interpretation, therefore, we cannot make our description of the nature of legal interpretation much more concrete than I have.

B. *Author's intention in law*

I want instead to consider various objections that might be made not to the detail of my argument but to the main thesis, that interpretation in law is essentially political. I shall not spend further time on the general objection already noted: that this view of law makes it irreducibly and irredeemably subjective, just a matter of what particular judges think best or what they had for breakfast. Of course, for some lawyers and legal scholars this is not an objection at all, but only the beginnings of skeptical wisdom about law. But it is the nerve of my argument that the flat distinction between description and evaluation on which this skepticism relies—the distinction between finding the law just "there" in history and making it up wholesale—is misplaced here because interpretation is something different from both.

I shall want, therefore, to repeat the various observations I made about subjectivity and objectivity in literary interpretation. There is no obvious reason in the account I gave of legal interpretation to doubt that one interpretation of law can be better than another and that one can be best of all. Whether this is so depends on general issues of philosophy not peculiar to law any more than to literature; and we would do well, in considering these general issues, not to begin with any fixed ideas about the necessary and sufficient conditions of objectivity (for example, that no theory of law can be sound unless it is demonstrably sound, unless it would wring assent from a stone). In the meantime we can sensibly aim to develop various levels of a conception of law for ourselves, to find the interpretation of a complex and dramatically important practice which seems to us at once the right kind of interpretation for law and right as that kind of interpretation.

I shall consider one further, and rather different, objection in more detail: that my political hypothesis about legal interpretation, like the aesthetic hypothesis about artistic interpretation, fails to give an adequate place to author's intention. It fails to see that interpretation in law is simply a matter of discovering what various actors in the legal process—constitutional delegates, members of Congress and state legislatures, judges, and executive officials—intended. Once again it is important to see what is at stake here. The political hypothesis makes room for the author's intention argument as a conception of interpretation, a conception which claims that the best political theory gives the intentions of legislators and past judges a decisive role in interpretation. Seen this way, the author's intention theory does not challenge the political hypothesis but contests for its authority. If the present objection is really an objection to the argument so far, therefore, its claim must be understood differently, as proposing, for example, that the very "meaning" of interpretation in law requires that only these officials' intentions should count or that at least there is a firm consensus among lawyers to that effect. Both of these claims are as silly as the parallel claims about the idea or the practice of interpretation in art.

Suppose, therefore, that we do take the author's intention theory, more sensibly, as a conception rather than an explication of the concept of legal interpretation. The theory seems on firmest ground, as I suggested earlier, when interpretation is interpretation of a canonical legal text, like a clause of the Constitution, or a section of statute, or a provision of a contract or will. But just as we noticed that a novelist's intention is complex and structured in ways that embarrass any simple author's intention theory in literature, we must now notice that a legislator's intention is complex in similar ways. Suppose a delegate to a constitutional convention votes for a clause guaranteeing equality of treatment without regard to race in matters touching peoples' fundamental interests; but he thinks that education is not a matter of fundamental interest and so does not believe that the clause makes racially segregated schools unconstitutional. We may sensibly distinguish an abstract and a concrete intention here: the delegate intends to prohibit discrimination in whatever in fact is of fundamental interest and also intends not to prohibit segregated schools. These are not isolated, discrete intentions; our descriptions, we might say, describe the same intention in different ways. But it matters very much which description a theory of legislative intention accepts as canonical. If we accept the first description, then a judge who wishes to

follow the delegate's intentions, but who believes that education is a matter of fundamental interest, will hold segregation unconstitutional. If we accept the second, he will not. The choice between the two descriptions cannot be made by any further reflection about what an intention really is. It must be made by deciding that one rather than the other description is more appropriate in virtue of the best theory of representative democracy or on some other openly political ground. (I might add that no compelling argument has yet been produced, so far as I am aware, in favor of deferring to a delegate's more concrete intentions, and that this is of major importance in arguments about whether the "original intention" of the Framers requires, for example, abolishing racial discrimination, or capital punishment.)

When we consider the common-law problems of interpretation, the author's intention theory shows in an even poorer light. The problems are not simply evidentiary. Perhaps we can discover what was "in the mind" of all the judges who decided cases about accidents at one time or another in our legal history. We might also discover (or speculate) about the psychodynamic or economic or social explanations of why each judge thought what he or she did. No doubt the result of all this research (or speculation) would be a mass of psychological data essentially different for each of the past judges included in the study, and order could be brought into the mass, if at all, only through statistical summaries about which proportion of judges in which historical period probably held which opinion and was more or less subject to which influence. But this mass, even tamed by statistical summary, would be of no more help to the judge trying to answer the question of what the prior decisions, taken as a whole, really come to than the parallel information would be to one of our chain novelists trying to decide what novel the novelists earlier in the chain had collectively written. That judgment, in each case, requires a fresh exercise of interpretation which is neither brute historical research nor a clean-slate expression of how things ideally ought to be.

A judge who believed in the importance of discerning an author's intention might try to escape these problems by selecting one particular judge or a small group of judges in the past (say, the judges who decided the most recent case something like his or the case he thinks closest to his) and asking what rule that judge or group intended to lay down for the future. This would treat the particular earlier judges as legislators and so invite all the problems of statutory interpretation including the very serious problem we just noticed. Even so, it would not even escape the special problems of common-law adjudication after all, because the judge who applied this theory of interpretation would have to suppose himself entitled to look only to the intentions of the particular earlier judge or judges he had selected, and he could not suppose this unless he thought that it was the upshot of judicial practice as a whole (and not just the intentions of some *other* selected earlier judge) that this is what judges in his position should do.

IV. Politics in interpretation

If my claims about the role of politics in legal interpretation are sound, then we should expect to find distinctly liberal or radical or conservative opinions not only about what the Constitution and laws of our nation should be but also about what they are. And this is exactly what we do find. Interpretation of the equal protection clause of the Constitution provides especially vivid examples. There can be no useful interpretation of what that clause means independent of some theory about what political equality is and how far equality is required by justice, and the history of the last half-century of constitutional law is largely an exploration of exactly these issues of political morality, Conservative lawyers argued steadily (though not consistently) in favor of an author's intentions style of interpreting this clause, and they accused others, who used a different style with more egalitarian results, of inventing rather than interpreting law. But this was bluster meant to hide the role their own political convictions played in their choice of interpretive style, and the great legal debates over the equal protection clause would have been more illuminating if it had been more widely recognized that reliance on political theory is not a corruption of interpretation but part of what interpretation means.

Should politics play any comparable role in literary and other artistic interpretation? We have become used to the idea of the politics of interpretation. Stanley Fish, particularly, has promoted a theory of interpretation which supposes that contests between rival schools of literary interpretation are more political than argumentative: rival professoriates in search of dominion. And of course it is a truism of the sociology of literature, and not merely of the Marxist contribution to that discipline, that fashion in interpretation is sensitive to and expresses more general political and economic structures. These important claims are external: they touch the causes of the rise of this or that approach to literature and interpretation.

We are now concerned with the internal question, about politics in rather than the politics of interpretation.[9] How far can principles of political morality actually count as arguments for a particular interpretation of a particular work or for a general approach to artistic interpretation? There are many possibilities and many of them are parasitic on claims developed or mentioned in these essays. It was said that our commitment to feminism, or our fidelity to nation, or our dissatisfaction with the rise of the New Right, ought to influence our evaluation and appreciation of literature. Indeed it was the general (though not unanimous) sense of the conference that professional criticism must be faulted for its inattention to such political issues. But if our convictions about these particular political issues count in deciding how good some novel or play or poem is, then they must also count in deciding, among particular interpretations of these works, which is the best interpretation. Or so they must if my argument is sound.

We might also explore a more indirect connection between aesthetic and political theory. Any comprehensive theory of art is likely to have, at its center, some epistemological thesis, some set of views about the relations that hold among experience, self-consciousness, and the perception or formation of values. If it assigns self-discovery any role in art, it will need a theory of personal identity adequate to mark off the boundaries of a person from his or her circumstances, and from other persons, or at least to deny the reality of any such boundaries. It seems likely that any comprehensive theory of social justice will also have roots in convictions about these or very closely related issues. Liberalism, for example, which assigns great importance to autonomy, may depend upon a particular picture of the role that judgments of value play in people's lives; it may depend on the thesis that people's convictions about value are beliefs, open to argument and review, rather than simply the givens of personality, fixed by genetic and social causes. And any political theory that gives an important place to equality also requires assumptions about the boundaries of persons, because it must distinguish between treating people as equals and changing them into different people.

It may be a sensible project, at least, to inquire whether there are not particular philosophical bases shared by particular aesthetic and particular political theories so that we can properly speak of a liberal or Marxist or perfectionist or totalitarian aesthetics, for example, in that sense. Common questions and problems hardly guarantee this, of course. It would be necessary to see, for example, whether liberalism can indeed be traced, as many philosophers have supposed, back into a discrete epistemological base, different from that of other political

theories, and then ask whether that discrete base could be carried forward into aesthetic theory and there yield a distinctive interpretive style. I have no good idea that this project could be successful, and I end simply by acknowledging my sense that politics, art, and law are united, somehow, in philosophy.

Notes

9 Critical Inquiry 179 (1982)

1   See Evans, *Semantic Theory and Tacit Knowledge*, in L. Wittgenstein, *To Follow a Rule* (S. Holtzman & C. Leich, eds) (1981).

2   It may be one of the many important differences between interpretation in art and law, which I do not examine in this essay, that nothing in law corresponds to the direct experience of a work of art, though some lawyers of the romantic tradition do speak of a good judge's "sixth sense," which enables him to grasp which aspects of a chain of legal decisions reveal the "immanent" principle of law even though he cannot fully explain why.

3   E. Hirsch, *Validity in Interpretation* (1967).

4   J. Fowles, *The French Lieutenant's Woman* 96–97 (1969).

5   Id. at 96 (emphasis in original)

6   Even the first novelist has the responsibility of interpreting to the extent that any writer must which includes not only interpreting as he writes but interpreting the genre in which he sets out to write. Will novelists with higher numbers have less creative "freedom" than those with lower? In one sense, no novelist has any freedom at all, because each is constrained to choose that interpretation which (he believes) makes the continuing work of art the best it can be. But we have already seen (and the discussion of law below will elaborate) two different dimensions along which any interpretation can be tested: the "formal" dimension, which asks how far the interpretation fits and integrates the text so far completed, and the "substantive" dimension, which considers the soundness of the view about what makes a novel good on which the interpretation relies. It seems reasonable to suppose that later novelists will normally—but certainly not inevitably—believe that fewer interpretations can survive the first of these tests than would have

survived had they received fewer chapters. Most interpreters would think that a certain interpretation of *A Christmas Carol*—that Scrooge was inherently evil, for example—would pass the test of integrity just after the opening pages, but not towards the end of the novel. Our sense that later novelists are less "free" may reflect just that fact. This does not mean, of course, that there is more likely to be consensus about the correct interpretation later rather than earlier in the chain, or that a later novelist is more likely to find an argument that "proves" his interpretation right beyond rational challenge. Reasonable disagreement is available on the formal as well as the substantive side, and even when most novelists would think only a particular interpretation could fit the novel to a certain point, some novelists of imagination might find some dramatic change in plot that (in his opinion) unexpectedly unifies what had seemed disparate and unnecessary, and redeems what had

seemed wrong or trivial. Once again, we should be careful not to confuse the fact that consensus would rarely be reached, at any point in the process, with the claim that any particular novelist's interpretation must be "merely subjective." No novelist, at any point, will be able simply to read in a mechanical way the correct interpretation off the text he receives but it does not follow from that fact alone that one interpretation is not superior to others overall. In any case, it will nevertheless be true, for all novelists beyond the first, that the assignment to find (what they believe to be) the correct interpretation of the text so far is a different assignment from the assignment to begin a novel of their own. For a fuller discussion, see Dworkin, "*Natural*" *Law Revisited*, 34 A. Fla. L. Rev. 165 (1982).

7 P. Ashe, *Naked Came the Stranger* (1969).

8 See Dworkin, *The Forum of Principle*, 56 N.Y.U. L. Rev. 469 (1981).

9 See *Politics of Interpretation*, 9 *Critical Inquiry* I (1982).

Chapter 8

Robert P. George

NATURAL LAW AND POSITIVE LAW

1. Natural law

A S I UNDERSTAND the natural law,[1] it consists of three sets of principles: first, and most fundamentally, a set of principles directing human choice and action toward intelligible purposes, i.e. basic human goods which, as intrinsic aspects of human well-being and fulfilment, constitute reasons for action whose intelligibility as reasons does not depend on any more fundamental reasons (or on sub-rational motives such as the desire for emotional satisfactions) to which they are mere means; second, a set of 'intermediate' moral principles which specify the most basic principle of morality by directing choice and action toward possibilities that may be chosen consistently with a will toward integral human fulfilment and away from possibilities the choosing of which is inconsistent with such a will;[2] and third, fully specific moral norms which require or forbid (sometimes with, sometimes without exceptions) certain specific possible choices.[3]

2. Basic practical principles

The first, and, as I say, most fundamental, principles of natural law are not, strictly speaking, moral norms. They do not resolve questions of which option(s) may uprightly be chosen in situations of morally significant choice. Indeed, the multiplicity of these most basic practical principles *creates* situations of morally significant choice, and makes it necessary for us to identify norms of morality in order to choose uprightly in such situations.

The most basic practical principles refer to ends or purposes which provide non-instrumental reasons for acting. These principles identify intrinsic human goods (such as knowledge, friendship, and health) as ends to be pursued, promoted, and protected, and their opposites (ignorance, animosity, illness) as evils to be avoided or overcome.

Of course, not all ends to which action may be directed are provided by reasons, much less non-instrumental reasons. All of us sometimes want things we have no reason to want. Such desires, though not rationally grounded, are perfectly capable of motivating us to act. One may, for example, experience thirst and desire a drink of water. It may well be that no intelligible good is to be advanced or protected by one's having a drink. One desires a drink not for the sake of health, or friendship, or any other intelligible good which would provide a *reason* for going to the water fountain. Still, one has a motive, albeit a sub-rational motive, to have a drink. One's acting on this motive is perfectly explicable and may, depending on other factors, be perfectly reasonable.[4]

In addition to the distinction between reasons and (non-rationally grounded) desires (and other sub-rational motives), there is the distinction between instrumental and non-instrumental reasons for action. Instrumental goods provide reasons for acting only in so far as they are means to other ends. Money, for example, is a purely instrumental good. It is of value only in so far as one can buy or do things with it. Intrinsic goods, on the other hand, though they may, to be sure, also have considerable instrumental value, are worthwhile for their own sakes. As ends-in-themselves, intrinsic goods provide reasons for action whose intelligibility as reasons does not depend on more fundamental reasons (or on ends ultimately provided by sub-rational motives) to which they are mere means.

Following Germain Grisez, I (and others) refer to intrinsic goods as 'basic human goods'. We do so to stress the point that such goods are not 'platonic forms' somehow detached from the persons in and by whom they are instantiated. Rather, they are intrinsic aspects of the well-being and fulfilment of flesh and blood human beings in their manifold dimensions (that is to say, as animate beings, as rational beings, and as agents through deliberation and choice). Basic human goods provide reasons for action precisely in so far as they are constitutive aspects of human flourishing.

3. Moral principles

Taken together, the first principles of practical reason that direct action to the basic human goods outline the (vast) range of possible rationally motivated actions, and point to an ideal of 'integral human fulfilment'. This is the ideal of the complete fulfilment of all human persons (and their communities) in all possible respects. The first principle of morality, which is no mere ideal, directs that our choosing be compatible with a will toward integral fulfilment. The specifications of this principle, in, for example, the Golden Rule of fairness or the Pauline Principle that evil may not be done even that good might come of it, take into account

the (necessarily sub-rational) motives people may have for choosing or otherwise willing incompatibility with such a will.

Moral principles—whether the most basic and general principle prior to its specification, or those specifications which are intermediate between the most basic principle and fully specific moral norms, or the fully specific norms themselves—are intelligible as principles of action and relevant to practical thinking only because, at the most basic level of practical reflection, rational human beings are capable of grasping a multiplicity of intelligible ends or purposes that provide reasons for action. Paradigmatically, moral principles govern choice by providing conclusive second-order reasons to choose one rather than another, or some rather than other, possibilities in cases in which one has competing first-order reasons, i.e., where competing possibilities each offer some true human benefit and, thus, hold some genuine rational appeal.[5] Paradigmatically, moral norms exclude the choosing of those possibilities which, though rationally grounded, fall short of all that reason requires.

This conception of the role of moral norms in practical reasoning is captured in the tradition of natural law theorizing by the notion of *recta ratio*—'right reason'. Right reason is reason unfettered by emotional or other impediments to choosing consistently with what reason fully requires. Often enough, a possibility for choice may be rationally grounded (i.e., for a (first-order) *reason* provided by the possibility of realizing or participating in some true human benefit, some basic human good) yet, at the same time, be contrary to *right* reason (i.e., contrary to at least one conclusive (second-order) reason provided by a moral norm which excludes the choosing of that possibility).

Of course, most of our choices are not between right and wrong options, but rather between incompatible right options. Where a choice is between or among morally acceptable possibilities, one has a reason to do X and a reason to do Y, the doing of which is incompatible here and now with doing X, yet no conclusive reason provided by a moral norm to do X or not to do X for the sake of doing Y. In situations of this sort, one is considering possibilities made available by the practical intellect's grasp of the most basic principles of practical reason and precepts of natural law. These pertain to the first set of principles of natural law I identified at the beginning of this chapter. Yet practical reason is unable to identify principles in the second and third sets (i.e., second order principles or norms) to determine one's choice. One's choice, then, though rationally grounded, is in a significant sense rationally underdetermined.[6] Doing X or not doing X in order to do Y are both fully reasonable, are both fully compatible with *recta ratio*.

4. Natural law, practical reason, and morality

As choosing subjects, or 'acting persons', we make the natural law effective by bringing the principles of natural law into our practical deliberation and judgement in situations of morally significant choice. This task is not merely a job for the natural law theorist or for believers in natural law. It is something that every rational agent does to some extent, and every responsible agent does to a large extent.

Even in the most mundane aspects of our lives, in matters of no great moral moment, we regularly and effortlessly identify and act upon the first-order reasons that constitute the most basic principles of natural law. In fact, countless choices in which these principles centrally figure are so commonplace that ordinary people would be shocked to learn that they were acting on principles at all. They would characterize their choices as merely 'doing what comes naturally', or even 'doing what I like'. And, in a sense, they would be absolutely right. They are choosing and acting, with minimal reflection or

deliberation, for the sake of reasons (and, thus, on principles) that are so patently obvious, that are grasped so effortlessly, that fit into the established patterns of their lives so easily, that they require hardly any thought at all.

Beyond this, everyone who deliberates among competing possibilities each or all of which have at least some rational appeal, and who, upon reflection, identifies a principle of rectitude in choosing which will enable him to judge correctly that one of those options is, uniquely, right (and should therefore be chosen) and others are wrong (and therefore, despite their elements of rational appeal, should not be chosen) makes the second and third sets of principles of natural law effective in his own willing and choosing. In cases of this sort, one is acting not only on the *prima principii*, the most basic precepts of natural law that are, as it were, the foundations of any sort of rational action (whether morally upright or defective), but also on the basis of moral norms that distinguish fully reasonable from practically unreasonable, morally upright from immoral, choosing.

Now, here it is worth pausing to avert a misunderstanding. By saying that the choosing subject 'makes the natural law effective' I do not mean to imply that the subject creates the natural law or confers upon it its morally binding nature or its force. No one should infer from my willingness to put the choosing subject in an active role with respect to the natural law ('making it effective') that the natural law, as I understand it, is somehow subjective. On the contrary, the reasons constitutive of each of the three sets of principles of natural law are, in a stringent sense, *objective*. They are grasped (only) by *sound* practical judgment and missed (only) when enquiry and judgment miscarry. They correspond to aspects of the genuine fulfilment of human persons, as such, and to the real (and strictly non-optional) requirements of reasonableness in human willing and choosing (i.e., the norms of morality) that obtain for human beings, as such, and which do not depend upon, or vary with, people's beliefs, wishes, desires, or subjective interests or goals. The principles of natural law possess and retain their normative and prescriptive force independently of anyone's decision to adopt or refuse to adopt them in making the practical choices to which they apply.[7]

That being said, it remains true that we make the natural law effective in our lives precisely by grasping and acting on these principles. In doing so, we exercise the human capacity for free choice. A free choice is a choice between open practical possibilities (to do X or not to do X, perhaps for the sake of doing Y) such that nothing but the choosing itself settles the matter.[8] The existence of basic reasons for action (and, thus, of the primary principles of natural law) are conditions of free choice. If there were no such reasons, then all of our actions would be determined—determined either by external causes or by internal (sub-rational) factors such as feeling, emotion, desire, etc.[9] The denial of free choice, which is central to the various modern reductionisms in philosophy, psychology, and the social sciences, is, then, closely connected to the denial of the possibility of rationally motivated action. To deny free choice and the existence of the basic goods, reasons, and principles that are its conditions, is to suppose that people are nothing more than animals with a well-developed capacity for theoretical and instrumentally practical rationality. If people were nothing more than that, then natural law could never be effective for them and would, indeed, hardly be intelligible conceptually.

Because persons can make free choices, they are self-constituting beings. In freely choosing—that is, in choosing for or against goods that provide non-instrumental reasons—one integrates the goods (or the damaging and consequent privation of the goods, i.e., the evils) one intends into one's will. Thus, one effects a sort of synthesis between oneself as an acting

person and the object of one's choices (i.e., the goods and evils one intends—either as ends-in-themselves or as means to other ends). One's choices perdure in one's character and personality as a choosing subject unless or until, for better or worse, one reverses one's previous choice by choosing incompatibly with it or, at least, resolves to choose differently should one face the same or relevantly similar choices in the future.[10]

Of course, ethical theory is a complicated business in part because different types of willing bear on human goods and evils in interestingly and importantly different ways. Thus it is necessary to distinguish, as the tradition of natural law theorizing does, as distinct modes of voluntariness, 'intending' a good or evil (as an end or as a means to some other end) from 'accepting as a side-effect' a good or evil that one foresees as a consequence of one's action but does not intend. Although one is morally responsible for the bad side-effects one knowingly brings about, one is not responsible for them in the same way one is responsible for what one intends. Often, one will have an obligation in justice or fairness to others (and thus a conclusive moral reason) not to bring about a certain evil that one knows or believes would likely result, albeit as an unintended side-effect, from one's action. Sometimes, though, one will have no obligation to avoid bringing about a certain foreseen bad side-effect of an action one has a reason (perhaps even a conclusive reason) to perform.

5. Natural law, positive law, and the common good

Communities, like individual persons, make choices. Their choices have to do with the ordering of the common lives of members of communities. Sometimes, especially in small communities, many of these choices or decisions are made by consensus, by achieving unanimity about what to do. It is the rare community, however, that can rely exclusively on unanimity. Most communities must rely on authority to co-ordinate the action of individuals and sub-communities within the larger community for the sake of the common good. This is obviously true of political communities. Although there are many different forms of government, all political communities must create and rely upon authority of some sort.[11]

Political authorities serve the common good in large measure by creating, implementing, and enforcing laws. Where the laws are just (and expedient), authorities serve their communities well; where they are unjust (or inexpedient), they serve their communities badly. The moral purpose of a system of laws is to make it possible for individuals and sub-communities to realize for themselves important human goods that would not be realizable (or would not be realizable fully) in the absence of the laws. Hence, according to Aquinas, 'the end of the law is the common good'.[12]

It is tempting to think of authority and law as necessary only because of human selfishness, inconstancy, weakness or intransigence. The truth, however, is that the law would be necessary to co-ordinate the behaviour of members of the community for the sake of the common good even in a society of angels. Of course, in such a society legal sanctions—the threat of punishment for law-breaking—would be unnecessary; but laws themselves would still be needed. Given that no earthly society is a society of angels, legal sanctions are—quite reasonably—universal features of legal systems. They are not, however, essential to the very concept of law.

But, someone might object, certain familiar laws would not be necessary in a society of angels—laws against murder, rape, theft, etc. The actions forbidden by such laws are plainly immoral—contrary to natural law—and would never be performed by perfectly morally upright beings. True. And since the moral point of law is to serve the good of people as they are—with

all their (perhaps I should say our) faults—laws against these evils are necessary and proper. The natural law itself requires that someone (or some group of persons or some institution) exercise authority in political communities and the authority fulfils his (or their or its) moral function by translating certain principles of natural law into positive law and reinforcing and backing up these principles with the threat of punishment for law-breaking. Thus, a morally valid authority, in a sense, derives the positive law from the natural law; or, as I have said, translates natural principles of justice and political morality into rules and principles of positive law.

Aquinas, following up a lead from Aristotle, observed that the positive law is derived from the natural law in two different ways. In the case of certain principles, the legislator translates the natural law into the positive law more or less directly. So, for example, a conscientious legislator will prohibit grave injustices such as murder, rape, and theft by moving by a process akin to deduction[13] from the moral proposition that, say, the killing of innocent persons is intrinsically unjust to the conclusion that the positive law must prohibit (and punish) such killing.

In a great many cases, however, the movement from the natural law to the positive law in the practical thinking of the conscientious legislator cannot be so direct. For example, it is easy to understand the basic principle of natural law that identifies human health as a good and the preservation and protection of human health as important purposes. A modern legislator will therefore easily see, for example, the need for a scheme of co-ordination of traffic that protects the safety of drivers and pedestrians. The common good, which it is his responsibility to foster and serve in this respect, requires it. Ordinarily, however, he cannot identify a uniquely correct scheme of traffic regulation which can be translated from the natural law to the positive law. Unlike the case of murder, the natural law does not determine once and for all the perfect scheme of traffic regulation. A number of different schemes—bearing different and often incommensurable costs and benefits, risks and advantages—are consistent with the natural law. So the legislator must exercise a kind of creativity in choosing a scheme. He must move, not by deduction, but rather by an activity of the practical intellect that Aquinas called *determinatio*.[14]

Unfortunately, no single word in English captures the meaning of *determinatio*. 'Determination' captures some of the flavour of it; but so does 'implementation', 'specification', 'concretization'. The key thing to understand is that in making *determinationes*, the legislator enjoys a kind of creative freedom that may be analogous to that of the architect. An architect must design a building that is sound and sensible for the purposes to which it will be put. He cannot, however, identify an ideal form of a building that is uniquely correct. Ordinarily, at least, a range of possible buildings differing in a variety of respects will satisfy the criteria of soundness and usability. Obviously, a building whose 'doors' are no more than 3' high ordinarily fails to meet an important requirement for a usable building. No principle of architecture, however, sets the proper height of a door as such at 6' 2" as opposed to 6' 8". In designing any particular building, the conscientious architect will strive to make the height of the doors make sense in light of a variety of other factors, some of which are themselves the fruit of something akin to a *determinatio* (e.g. the height of the ceilings); but even here he will typically face a variety of acceptable but incompatible design options.

It is meaningful and correct to say that the legislator (including the judge to the extent that the judge in the jurisdiction in question exercises a measure of law-creating power) makes the natural law effective for his community by deriving the positive law from the natural law. The natural law itself requires that

such a derivation be accomplished and that someone (or a group or institution) be authorized to accomplish it. Because no human individual (or group or institution) is perfect in moral knowledge or virtue, it is inevitable that even conscientious efforts to translate the natural law into positive law, whether directly or by *determinationes*, will sometimes miscarry. None the less, the natural law itself sets this as the task of the legislator and it is only through his efforts that the natural law can become effective for the common good of his community.

Of course, the body of law created by the legislator is not itself the natural law. The natural law is in no sense a human creation. The positive law (of any community), however, *is* a human creation. It is an object—a vast cultural object composed of sometimes very complicated rules and principles, but an object none the less. Metaphysically, the positive law belongs to the order Aristotle identified as the order of 'making' rather than of 'doing'. For perfectly good reasons, it is made to be subject to technical application and to be analyzed by a kind of technical reasoning—hence the existence of law schools that teach students not (or not just) moral philosophy, but the distinctive techniques of legal analysis, e.g., how to identify and understand legal sources, how to work with statutes, precedents, and with the (often necessarily) artificial definitions that characterize any complex system of law.

At the same time, the creation of law (and a system of law) has a moral purpose. It is in the order of 'doing', (the order, not of technique, but rather of free choice, practical reasoning, and morality—the order studied in ethics and political philosophy) that we identify the need to create law for the sake of the common good. The lawmaker creates an object—the law—deliberately and reasonably subject to technical analysis—for a purpose that is moral, and not itself merely technical. To fail to create this object (or to create unjust laws) would be inconsistent with the requirements of the natural law, it would be a failure of legislative duty precisely in the moral order.

6. Natural law, positive law, and the judicial role

The fact that the law is a cultural object that is created for a moral purpose generates a great deal of the confusion one encounters today in debates about the role of moral philosophy in legal reasoning. The vexed question of American constitutional interpretation is the scope and limits of the power of judges to invalidate legislation under certain allegedly vague or abstract constitutional provisions. Some constitutional theorists, such as Professor Ronald Dworkin, who wish to defend an expansive role of the judge, argue that the conscientious judge must bring judgments of moral and political philosophy to bear in deciding hard cases.[15] Others, such as Judge Robert Bork, who fear such a role for the judge, and hold, in any event, that the Constitution of the United States does not give the judge such a role, maintain that moral philosophy has little or no place in judging, at least in the American system.[16]

Some people who are loyal to the tradition of natural law theorizing are tempted to suppose that Professor Dworkin's position, whatever its faults in other respects, is the one more faithful to the tradition. This temptation should, however, be resisted. While the role of the judge as a law-creator reasonably varies from jurisdiction to jurisdiction[17] according to each jurisdiction's own authoritative *determinationes*—that is to say, each jurisdiction's positive law—Judge Bork's idea of a body of law that is properly and fully (or almost fully) analyzable in technical terms is fully compatible with classical understandings of natural law theory.

Natural law theory treats the role of the judge as itself fundamentally a matter for *determinatio*, not for direct translation from the natural law. It does not imagine that the judge enjoys (or should enjoy) as a matter of natural law a plenary

authority to substitute his own understanding of the requirements of the natural law for the contrary understanding of the legislator or constitution maker in deciding cases at law. On the contrary, for the sake of the Rule of Law, understood as ordinarily a necessary (albeit not a sufficient) condition for a just system of government, the judge (like any other actor in the system) is morally required (that is, obligated as a matter of natural law) to respect the limits of his own authority as it has been allocated to him by way of an authoritative *determinatio*. If the law of his system constrains his law-creating power in the way that Judge Bork believes American fundamental law does, then, for the sake of the Rule of Law, he must respect these constraints, even where his own understanding of natural justice deviates from that of the legislators or constitution makers and ratifiers whose laws he must interpret and apply. None of this means that Judge Bork is more nearly correct than Professor Dworkin on the question of what degree of law-creating power *our* law places in the hands of the judge; it merely means that the question whether Dworkin or Bork is more nearly correct is properly conceived as itself a question of positive law—not natural law.

Bork, who is understood by some of his critics as denying the existence of natural law or any type of objective moral order, has recently clarified his position: 'I am far from denying that there is a natural law, but I do deny both that we have given judges the authority to enforce it and that judges have greater access to that law than do the rest of us.'[18]

If Bork's view is sound (and subject, perhaps, to one or two minor qualifications I am prepared to believe that it is sound), that leaves us with the question whether the natural law itself— quite independently of what the Constitution may say—confers upon the judge a sort of plenary power to enforce it. One of my central aims in this essay has been to argue that the correct answer to this question is 'no'. To the extent that judges are not given power under the Constitution to translate principles of natural justice into positive law, that power is not one they enjoy; nor is it one they may justly exercise. For judges to arrogate such power to themselves in defiance of the Constitution is not merely for them to exceed their authority under the positive law; it is to violate the very natural law in whose name they purport to act.

Notes

Robert George (ed.), *The Autonomy of Law* (Oxford 1996), pp. 321–34

1 For a fuller account of the understanding of natural law set forth in this paragraph, see Joseph M. Boyle, Jr., Germain Grisez, and John Finnis, 'Practical Principles, Moral Truth and Ultimate Ends', *American Journal of Jurisprudence* 32 (1987) 99–151. I have defended this understanding against various criticisms in 'Recent Criticism of Natural Law Theory', *University of Chicago Law Review* 55 (1988) 1371–1492; 'Human Flourishing as a Criterion of Morality: A Critique of Perry's Naturalism', *Tulane Law Review* 63 (1989) 1455–1474; 'Does the Incommensurability Thesis Imperil Common Sense Moral Judgments?' *American Journal of Jurisprudence* 37 (1992) 185–195; and 'Natural Law and Human Nature' in Robert P. George (ed.), *Natural Law Theory: Contemporary Essays* (Oxford: Clarendon Press, 1992), 31–41.

2 Examples of moral principles in this category are the 'Golden Rule' of fairness and the 'Pauline Principle' which forbids the doing of evil even as a means of bringing about good consequences.

3 Examples of norms in this category are those forbidding such specific possible choices as wilfully refusing to return borrowed property to its owner upon his request (which is a good example of a moral norm which admits of exceptions) and directly killing an innocent person (which is a good example of an exceptionless moral norm). Note that 'direct' killing refers to the intending of death—one's own or someone else's—as an end in itself (as in killing for revenge) or as a means to another end (as in terror bombing the civilian population of an unjust aggressor nation). It is sometimes, though not always, morally permis-

sible to accept the bringing about of death—one's own or someone else's—as the foreseen and accepted side effect of a choice in which one does not intend death (either as end or means).

4 To act on one's sub-rational motive is not necessarily unreasonable or morally wrong. Moral questions arise only when one has a reason not to do something which one has a non-rationally grounded desire to do. So, to stay with the example, where one is thirsty and has no reason not to slake one's thirst, then there is nothing wrong with having a drink. Visiting the water fountain, in these circumstances, is an innocent pleasure.

5 I defend this conception of the role of moral principles in 'Does the Incommensurability Thesis Imperil Common Sense Moral Judgments?'.

6 See Joseph Raz, *The Morality of Freedom* (Oxford: Clarendon Press, 1986), 388–9.

7 On the objectivity of the principles of natural law, see John Finnis, *Natural Law and Natural Rights* (Oxford: Clarendon Press, 1980), 69–75; and *Fundamentals of Ethics* (Oxford: Oxford University Press, 1983), 56–79.

8 For a thorough explanation and defence of this conception of free choice, see Joseph M. Boyle, Jr., Germain Grisez, and Olaf Tollefsen, *Free Choice: A Self-Referential Argument* (Notre Dame, Indiana: University of Notre Dame Press, 1976).

9 I explain this point at length in 'Free Choice, Practical Reason, and Fitness for the Rule of Law', in *Social Discourse and Moral Judgment*, Daniel N. Robinson (ed.) (New York: Academic Press, 1992).

10 On the lastingness and character-forming consequences of free choices, see J. Finnis, *Fundamentals of Ethics*.

11 See Finnis, *Natural Law and Natural Rights*, 231–59.

12 *Summa theologiae*, I–II, q. 96, a. 1.

13 *Summa theologiae*, I–II, q. 95, a. 2.

14 Ibid. For a sound exposition and valuable development of Aquinas's understanding of *determinatio*, see Finnis, *Natural Law and Natural Rights*, 285–90. Also see Finnis, 'On "The Critical Legal Studies Movement"', *American Journal of Jurisprudence*, 30 (1985), 21–42.

15 For the most fully developed articulation of Dworkin's position, see his *Law's Empire* (Cambridge, Massachusetts: Harvard University Press, 1986).

16 See Robert H. Bork, *The Tempting of America: The Political Seduction of the Law* (New York: The Free Press, 1990), esp. 251–9.

17 I am concerned here with the role and duty of judges in basically just legal systems, i.e., systems which do not deserve to be subverted and which judges and others would do wrong to subvert. Different considerations apply in sorting out the obligations of judges in fundamentally unjust legal systems. I do not take up these considerations in this essay.

18 Bork, *The Tempting of America*, 66.

Chapter 9

John Gardner[1]

LEGAL POSITIVISM

5½ Myths

I. Isolating legal positivism

THE LABEL "LEGAL POSITIVISM" is sometimes attached to a broad intellectual tradition, distinguished by an emphasis on certain aspects of legal thought and experience (namely the empirical aspects). This way of using the label is well-suited to work in the history of ideas, in which the object of the exercise is to trace the ways in which philosophical themes were reprised and reworked as they were handed down from one generation to the next. In such work there is no need to identify any distinctive proposition that was advanced or accepted by all those designated as "legal positivists," for the label attaches by virtue of common themes rather than common theses. But things are different when the label "legal positivism" is used in philosophical argument. In philosophical debate our interest is in the truth of propositions, and we always need to know which proposition we are supposed to be debating. So there is nothing philosophical to say about "legal positivists" as a group unless there is some distinctive proposition or set of propositions that was advanced or assumed by all of them. In philosophical argument, to put it another way, "legal positivists" stand or fall together only if they are united by thesis rather than merely by theme. There is neither guilt by association nor redemption by association in philosophy.

In this paper, I intend to treat one and only one proposition as the distinctive proposition of "legal positivism," and to designate as "legal positivists" all and only those who advance or endorse this proposition. The proposition is:

(LP) In any legal system, whether a given norm is legally valid, and hence whether it forms part of the law of that system, depends on its sources, not its merits.

In philosophical argument it matters not which proposition is given which name; it matters only which is true. On the other hand, I obviously did not choose this proposition (LP) at random to carry the famous "legal positivism" branding. In the first place, I wanted to bring my use of the label into a tolerable extensional alignment with the use of the label familiar from the history of ideas. Those commonly said to constitute the dominant historical figures of the "legal positivist tradition"—Thomas Hobbes, Jeremy Bentham, John Austin, Hans Kelsen, and Herbert Hart—do not converge on many propositions about law. But subject to some differences of interpretation, they do converge unanimously on proposition (LP). Secondly, proposition (LP) is the one that contemporary self-styled "legal positivists"—such as Joseph Raz and Jules Coleman—bill themselves as subscribing to qua legal positivists, and the correct interpretation of which they debate when they debate among themselves *qua* legal positivists. Finally, my use of the label makes literal sense of the label itself. What should a "legal positivist" believe if not that laws are *posited*? And this, roughly, is what (LP) says of laws. It says, to be more exact, that in any legal system, a norm is valid as a norm of that system solely in virtue of the fact that at some relevant time and place some relevant agent or agents announced it, practiced it, invoked it, enforced it, endorsed it, or otherwise engaged with it. It is no objection to its counting as a law that it was an appalling norm that those agents should never have engaged with. Conversely, if it was never engaged with by any relevant agents, then it does not count as a law even though it may be an excellent norm that all the relevant agents should have engaged with unreservedly. As Austin famously (if perhaps too brashly) expressed the point, "the existence of law is one thing; its merit or demerit is another."[2]

We see here how the contrast between "sources" and "merits" in (LP) is meant to be read. "Source" is to be read broadly such that any intelligible argument for the validity of a norm counts as source-based if it is not merits-based. The two categories, in other words, are jointly exhaustive of the possible conditions of validity for any norm. But are they also mutually exclusive? You may say that there is a problem of overlap which prevents us from classifying some arguments for the validity of a norm as either source-based or merits-based, for they mention conditions of both types. On the one hand (i) we have arguments that attempt to validate certain norms by relying on *merit-based tests of their sources*, e.g. by relying on the fact that they were announced or practiced by Rex, together with the fact that Rex is a noble king. On the other hand (ii) we have arguments that attempt to validate certain norms by relying on *source-based tests of their merits*, e.g. by relying on the fact that they are reasonable norms, together with the fact that some other norm (validated only by its source) instructs us to apply all and only reasonable norms.

The legal positivist tradition has been united in regarding arguments of type (i) as invoking merit conditions of a type which cannot possibly be among the conditions of a norm's legal validity. The question of whether Rex is a noble king (or whether the regime in Lilliput is a just one, etc.) obviously bears on the moral significance of his (its) pronouncements and practices, but the answer to such questions cannot, according to legal positivists, affect the legal status of those pronouncements and practices. This is not to deny, of course, that they can make a merely *causal* difference to legal status: maybe the fact that Rex is a noble King explains why his subjects, or his officials, have come to regard his word as law. But it is *his word* that they regard as law. For his word to be regarded as law it must be possible to regard his word as law without reopening the question, when his word is heard, of whether he is a noble king. Thus Rex's nobility, according to legal positivists, cannot make a *constitutive* difference to Rex's ability to affect legal validity. So our approximation (LP) should be reformulated more exactly to read:

(LP*) In any legal system, whether a given norm is legally valid, and hence whether it forms part of the law of that system, depends on its sources, not its merits (where its merits, in the relevant sense, include the merits of its sources).

As far as arguments of type (ii) are concerned, the tradition has been more divided. Those who have come to be known as "soft" or "inclusive" legal positivists allow that in some legal systems norms may be legally valid in virtue of their merits (e.g. their reasonableness), but only if other legally valid norms happen to pick out those merits as relevant to legal validity.[3] Others, known correspondingly as "hard" or "exclusive" legal positivists, deny this. They hold that a law which declares that (say) all and only reasonable laws shall be valid does not legally validate any further norms, in spite of appearances. Rather, it delegates to some official (say, a judge) the task of validating further norms himself or herself by *declaring* them reasonable. On this "hard legal positivist" view, the validity of the further laws in question comes not of their reasonableness (their merit) but rather of the fact that some relevant agent declared them reasonable (their source).[4]

In what follows, I will for the most part bracket the internecine debate between "hard" and "soft" legal positivists and leave (LP*) ambiguous in respect of it. Where necessary, I will default to the "hard" version, since that is the version I support myself. I will leave it to the reader to make the modifications needed to accommodate the soft version, where relevant. These modifications should not alter much what I have to say. That is because the problems I will be surveying—and it will largely be a second-hand survey—are apt to afflict hard and soft legal positivists alike. In general, they are not problems of legal positivism's own making. They are problems of systematic misrepresentation by others. Have the members of any tradition of thought ever had their actual philosophical commitments so comprehensively mauled, twisted, second-guessed, crudely psychoanalyzed, and absurdly reinvented by ill-informed gossip and hearsay, as the legal positivists? Has any other thesis in the history of philosophy been so widely and so contemptuously misstated, misinterpreted, misapplied, and misappropriated as (LP*)? Well, actually, I can think of a few. Something like this is apt to happen whenever a label is used in both philosophy and, relatedly, in the history of ideas. "Natural lawyers" will feel some sympathy, as they often suffer similar indignities. Nevertheless, there are special and interesting lessons to be learnt from the catalog of myths about legal positivism that have gradually built up to give it a whipping-boy status in so much legally-related literature.[5] Some of these lessons, not surprisingly, are lessons about law itself.

II. Why so misunderstood?

But before we come to the myths, let's just stop to ask ourselves what it is about legal positivism that made it so ripe for misrepresentation. I think there are two principal factors.

First: Proposition (LP*), although a proposition about the conditions of validity of certain norms that may be used in practical reasoning, is itself normatively inert. It does not provide any guidance at all on what anyone should do about anything on any occasion. Sometimes, like any proposition, it does of course serve as the minor (or informational) premise in a practical syllogism. If someone happens to acquire a duty to determine what the law of Indiana says on some subject on some occasion, then the truth of (LP*) affects how she should proceed. According to (LP*), she should look for sources of Indiana law, not ask herself what it would be most meritorious for people in Indiana to do. On the other hand, (LP*) is never a major (or operative) premise of any practical syllogism. That means that *by itself* it does not point in favor of or against doing anything at all. I don't just mean that it provides no moral guidance. It provides no legal guidance either. It merely states one feature that all legal guidance necessarily has, viz. that if valid *qua* legal it is valid in virtue of its sources, not its merits.[6] Lawyers and law teachers find this comprehensive normative inertness in (LP*) hard to swallow. They think (rightly) that legal practice is a practical business, and they expect the philosophy of law to be the backroom activity of telling front-line practitioners how to do it well, with their heads held high. When a philosopher of law asserts a proposition that neither endorses nor criticizes what they do, but only identifies some necessary feature of what they do, lawyers and law teachers are often frustrated. They automatically start to search for hidden notes of endorsement or criticism, secret norms that they are being asked to follow. They refuse to believe that there are none.[7] They cannot accept that legal philosophy is not wholly (or even mainly) the backroom activity of identifying what is good or bad about legal practice, and hence of laying on practical proposals for its improvement (or failing that, abandonment). In this fundamentally anti-philosophical climate, a thesis like (LP*), which is inertly informative, is bound to become egregiously distorted.

Second: To make (LP*) a revealing proposition about law one has to believe that there is some *alternative* to validating norms according to their sources. One has to believe that some norms are valid depending on their merits, or else one won't see the contrastive purchase of (LP*). Instead, (LP*) will just strike one as rehearsing a general truth about norms—that all norms are made valid by somebody's engagement with them—and hence as revealing nothing special about law. All the torchbearers for the legal positivist tradition that were mentioned above agreed that, by default, the validity of a norm depends on its merits: the fact that a norm would be a good one to follow is, by default, what makes it valid. All agreed, for instance, that this is true of moral norms.[8] Legal norms, they agreed, are special (although not unique) in defying this default logic of norm-validation. How on earth do they defy it? It is a matter of deep wonderment to many philosophers.[9] Alas, many lawyers and law teachers and students do not share the wonderment. For many in these lines of work think—being especially affected by a feature they see every day and take for granted in legal norms—that whether *any* norm is valid can depend only on its sources. They assume that moral and aesthetic norms are the same: just like legal norms, they can only be validated by the beliefs or endorsements of their users, or by social conventions or practices, etc. When one proposes a moral or aesthetic norm, such people often react in classic positivist fashion by asking "Who says?" or "On whose authority?" (as if the validity of a moral or aesthetic norm would depend on somebody *saying* it or *authorizing* it) rather that by asking what is the merit of the norm. Such general normative

positivists—and they have always dominated the Critical Legal Studies movement and similar pseudo-radical camps—naturally cannot see what (LP*) has to offer in illuminating the distinctive nature of law.[10] So if legal positivism is to illuminate the distinctive nature of law, the thinking goes, (LP*) cannot be all there is to it. There must be more. And there begins the myth-spinning.

III. The myths

A. *The value of positivity*

My title says I will cover 5½ myths about legal positivism, and I will begin with the half-myth. At the inception of the legal positivist tradition—in the work of Hobbes and arguably that of Bentham—we find an (LP*)-inspired optimism about the value of law. Insofar as legal norms are valid on their sources rather than their merits, this fact alone is held to endow legal norms with some redeeming merit even when they are (in every other respect) unmeritorious norms.[11] Their redeeming merit is their special ability to settle matters that cannot be settled one way or the other on their merits. Believers in this claim are sometimes known as "normative legal positivists" but here I will call them "positivity-welcomers."[12] That is because they need not endorse (LP*) and hence need not be legal positivists in the sense I am exploring. As positivity-welcomers they merely endorse

> (PW) To the extent that (LP*) is sound, it identifies something not only true about legal norms, but meritorious about legal norms as well.

Those who are both legal positivists and positivity-welcomers are less frustrating to lawyers and law-school-dwellers than other legal positivists. For such people give (LP*) some immediate and invariant practical significance of a kind that warms our legal hearts. They tell us that the positivity of law is not only something we have to live with, but also something we can be proud of. Thanks to the truth of (LP*) combined with the truth of (PW), they say, it is always in one respect meritorious—and hence *ceteris paribus* justifiable—to advance a legal solution (however otherwise unmeritorious) to a moral or economic problem that would be intractable on its merits alone.

This rather self-congratulatory conclusion has not been common ground among the leading figures of the legal positivist tradition, and in particular the philosophical maturing of the tradition in the twentieth century led to its abandonment by the tradition's most important modern torchbearers, among them Kelsen, Hart, and Raz. Hart is an especially interesting case. Hart agreed with those who say that all laws have a redeeming merit which comes of their very nature as laws. However, he did not trace this redeeming merit of all laws to their positivity. He traced it instead to the fact that, in his view, laws are not merely norms but *rules*, i.e. norms capable of repeated application from case to case. This fact of their normative generality, he thought, means that wherever laws go a kind of justice (and hence a kind of merit) automatically follows, for the correct re-application of any law entails that like cases are treated alike.[13] My own view, contrary to Hart's, is that there is no justice (and more generally no merit) to be found in the mere fact that like cases are treated alike.[14] But be that as it may, Hart's belief that all laws have some redeeming merit has everything to do with the fact that in his view laws are general norms and nothing to do with the fact that in his view they are posited norms. These two qualities are unconnected.[15] Notice that as it stands, (LP*) is not a proposition specifically about *laws*. It is a proposition about what makes norms valid as *legal norms*, and hence as part of the law. It includes within its scope nongeneral legal norms such as the ruling that Tice must pay $50 to Summers in damages. This too is valid as a legal norm on its sources, according to (LP*), even though it is

not a norm capable of repeated application and hence would not be a law, according to Hart—and hence would not share in the value that Hart ascribes to all laws.

Some legal positivists go further, as Raz does, and deny that there is any built-in merit in all laws, let alone in all legal norms.[16] Observers of such debates often ask: If legal positivists disagree among themselves about whether the positivity of legal norms lends them any value, why is it that they all mysteriously agree in making such a *fuss* about the positivity of law? Doesn't it reveal that they all think it *important* that legal norms are posited norms? True enough. Philosophers who defend (LP*), like all other philosophers, are offering an interpretation of their subject matter that plays up the true and important and plays down the true but unimportant.[17] But what is important about legal norms, even what is important for their evaluation, need not be something that lends value or merit to them. Notice that the positivity of law could also be evaluatively important as a ground of *abhorrence* for law, as something that automatically drains merit out of each legal norm rather than adding merit to it. Anarchists, for example, can turn their arguments against submission to authority into arguments against respect for law only by endorsing (LP*) as a stepping stone. Only if legal norms are posited by someone do they count as exercises of authority. Anarchists who do not endorse (LP*) therefore should not have a blanket opposition to respecting legal norms *qua* legal. That anarchists do typically have a blanket opposition to respecting legal norms *qua* legal shows that they are typically legal positivists. Would one suppose that this in turn showed a secret belief, on the part of all such anarchists, that all legal norms, or all laws, have a built-in redeeming merit?

If not, then one should not jump to that conclusion regarding non-anarchistic legal positivists either. It is open to them to hold, for example, that the truth of (LP*) is evaluatively important precisely because (LP*) brings out a single feature of legal norms that leads anarchists to find laws invariably (in one respect) repugnant and some of their opponents to find laws invariably (in one respect) attractive. Nor are these—invariable repugnance and invariable attraction—the only possible evaluative reactions to law's positivity. Perhaps the positivity of law sometimes makes law more repugnant and sometimes makes it more attractive and sometimes makes no difference at all to law's value, depending on what other conditions hold. Only if a law is meritorious in some other ways, say, does its positivity lend it additional merit. I am not advocating this position. I am only saying that the truth of (LP*) must be granted, at least *arguendo*, before the argument over this position can even begin. This shows why philosophers of law might regard the positivity of legal norms as evaluatively important without thereby being predisposed to the (LP*)-inspired but not (LP*)-entailed thesis (PW).

B. The rule of law

Legal positivists are sometimes identified as placing a particular emphasis on the ideal of the rule of law (or *Rechtstaat*) as opposed to other ideals of government. No doubt on some occasions this is just another way of saying that legal positivists are relative enthusiasts for law, in that they see some built-in redeeming merit in legal norms *qua* posited. This is the half-myth that we already considered under heading (A), involving the extra thesis (PW). But on at least some occasions the association of legal positivism with the rule of law is clearly supposed to suggest a different point not implicating (PW). It is supposed to suggest that legal positivists insist on the evaluation of laws according to their form (e.g. their clarity, certainty, prospectivity, generality, and openness) as opposed to their content (e.g. what income tax rate they set, or what limits on freedom of speech they authorize). The label

"rule of law" is used to designate the former clutch of "content-independent" evaluative criteria.[18]

It is hard to disentangle the various confusions that underlie this myth. The simplest and commonest confusion seems to be this one. Thanks to the sloppy multi-purpose way in which the word "formal" is bandied around by lawyers, the distinction just drawn between the form of a law and its content is often conflated with the distinction drawn in (LP*) between source-based criteria of normative validity and merits-based criteria. Thus, those who think that norms are legally valid according to their sources and not their merits are then herded together with those who think that norms are legally valid according to their form rather than their content.[19] This herding-together is muddled. While the former position is the legal positivist one captured in (LP*), the latter is a classic anti-legal-positivist position often associated (fairly or unfairly) with Lon Fuller.[20] To hold a norm legally valid according to its formal merits rather than according to the merits of its content is still to hold it valid according to its merits, and this puts one on a collision course with (LP*).

This point is spelled out by Hart in a passage towards the end of *The Concept of Law*.[21] Alas, Hart later went on to court confusion on the same point by suggesting that legal reasons (including legal norms) are distinctive in being reasons of a content-independent type.[22] Unlike moral and economic norms, their validity cannot be affected by their content. In saying this, Hart cooked up a red herring the scent of which still lingers.[23] The validity of legal norms *can* depend on their content so long as it does not depend on the *merits* of their content. That a certain authority has legal jurisdiction only to change the criminal law means that, by virtue of their content, its measures purporting to create new causes of action in tort do not create valid legal reasons. Conversely, and by the same token, the validity of legal norms cannot depend on their merits even if their merit does not lie in their content but lies rather in their form, e.g. in the extent of their compliance with rule-of-law standards. Hart should have said, to get to the real point, that legal reasons (including legal norms) are reasons of a distinctively merit-independent type. They take their legal validity from their sources, not from their merits, and their merits for these purposes include not only the merits of their content but also the merits of their form (as well as the merits of the person or people who purported to make them or the merits of the system within which they were purportedly made etc.). Thus, as Hart had correctly explained in his earlier engagements with Fuller, a legal norm that is retroactive, radically uncertain, and devoid of all generality, and hence dramatically deficient relative to the ideal of the rule of law, is no less valid *qua* legal, than one that is prospective, admirably certain, and perfectly general.[24]

The conflation of the form–content distinction with the source–merit distinction is compounded, in many discussions of the relationship between legal positivism and the rule of law, by numerous other confusions. In the background of such discussions seems often to lurk the further assumption that the apt ways of evaluating any norm are dictated by the conditions of its validity. Thus, if we suppose that all conditions of legal validity are source-based, we are limited to source-based criticisms of the law; if we endorse "formal" conditions of legal validity, we are limited to "formal" criticisms of the law, and so forth. Why should this be so? It implies that the only criticism one can properly make of a supposed legal norm is that it is legally invalid. But far from being the only proper criticism of a supposed legal norm, *this need not be any criticism at all*. Agreeing that a norm is legally valid is not incompatible with holding that it is entirely worthless and should be universally attacked, shunned, ignored, or derided. There are substantive moral debates to be had—independently of the normative inert (LP*)—about the attitude one should have to

legally valid norms. In these debates that whole gamut of possible attitudes is on the table. Remember the anarchists we encountered above, who went as far as to regard the fact that a norm is posited as actually part of the case for attacking it, shunning it, ignoring it, or deriding it? Even for positivity-welcoming legal positivists, who combine (LP*) and (PW) and conclude that legally valid norms necessarily have some redeeming merit, this is still only a *redeeming* merit. It does not affect the possibility of attacking, shunning, ignoring, or deriding the same legal norm on the ground of its many more striking and important demerits. Those demerits may obviously include the demerits of its content (e.g. what income tax rate it sets or what limits on freedom of speech it authorizes) as well as the demerits of its form (e.g. its unclarity, uncertainty, retroactivity, ungenerality, and obscurity).

And why, to bring out one final confusion under this heading, should these last two dimensions of criticism be regarded as rivals? That one believes that unclarity, uncertainty, retroactivity, ungenerality, obscurity and so forth are demerits of a legal norm does not entail that one denies that there are further demerits in the same norm's content (e.g. that it sets a too-low rate of income tax or a too-high protection for freedom of speech). Nor does it suggest that one regards the former demerits as more important than the latter. One may well think, to be sure, that the former demerits are in a sense *more peculiarly legal* demerits than the others. As a believer in (LP*), one is committed to agreeing with Hart that the law's living up to the rule-of-law values that Fuller called the "inner morality of law" cannot be among the conditions for the legal validity of any norm. But so long as they are not held to be among the conditions for the legal validity of any norm, one is not debarred from agreeing with Fuller that these values constitute law's special inner morality, endowing law with its own distinctive objectives and imperatives.[25] Legal positivism is not a whole theory of law's nature, after all. It is a thesis about legal validity, which is compatible with any number of further theses about law's nature, including the thesis that all valid law is by its nature subject to special moral objectives and imperatives of its own. It is a long way from this thesis, however, to the conclusion that valid law answers *only* to its own special objectives and imperatives, and not to the rest of morality. A more credible assumption is that law's inner morality, if it has one, adds *extra* moral objectives and imperatives for legal norms to live up to, *on top* of the regular moral objectives and imperatives (e.g. avoiding the infliction of pain, not deceiving its addressees) that every practice or activity should live up to as a matter of course. Naturally, this addition of extra moral objectives and imperatives can give rise to extra conflicts. Sometimes laws that have meritorious content can accordingly be made morally questionable by the fact that there is no way to make them sufficiently clear, certain, prospective, general, or open. Thus—true enough—the pursuit of some other sound governmental ideals may sometimes be slowed down by adherence to the ideal of the rule of law.

But this is no reason to imagine that those who subscribe to the ideal of the rule of law have no commitment to any potentially conflicting ideals of government, or that they automatically regard potentially conflicting ideals as subordinate, or that they do not regard the law as answering to any ideals apart from the specialized ideal of the rule of law.[26] In particular, none of the leading figures of the legal positivist tradition subscribed to any views resembling any of these. And even if they had, for the reasons I have given, this could have had no philosophical connection with their being legal positivists.

C. *Positivistic adjudication*

In some quarters legal positivists are thought to be committed to a distinctive view about the proper way of adjudicating cases, according to which judges should not have regard to the merits of cases when deciding them. This conclusion generally comes of combining an endorsement of (LP*) with the widespread assumption that judges are under a professional (i.e. a role-based moral) obligation to decide cases only by applying valid legal norms to them.[27] But the latter assumption is not shared by legal positivists in general and is directly challenged by several of the tradition's leading figures. The simplest way to challenge it is to rely on its systematic and unavoidable collision with another pressing professional obligation of judges, namely their obligation not to refuse to decide any case that is brought before them and that lies within their jurisdiction. If judges are professionally bound to decide cases only by applying valid legal norms to them, the argument goes, then there are necessarily some cases that they should refuse to decide, for there are necessarily some cases not decidable only by applying valid legal norms. This in turn is so precisely because of the positivity of legal norms. There are inherent limitations on the ability of agents to anticipate future cases in which the norms they create may be relied upon, and to shape the norms they create in such a way as to settle across the board which cases they apply to.[28] Insofar as legal norms are the creations of agents—i.e. insofar as they are the posited norms that (LP*) tells us they are—these inherent limitations inevitably give rise to some gaps in the law.

When I speak of "gaps" here, I do not mean that the law is silent regarding some cases. Closure rules (such as "everything not forbidden by law is permitted by law") are perfectly capable of preventing legal silence.[29] Rather, the gaps I have in mind arise (i) in cases in which a given legal norm is neither applicable nor inapplicable, but rather indeterminate in its application, and (ii) in cases in which valid legal norms conflict so that two rivals (e.g. one forbidding a certain action and the other requiring the same action) are both applicable at once and there exists no third legal norm that resolves the conflict. No closure rule, however ingenious, can guarantee to eliminate these latter types of gaps.[30] They are endemic to law, in all legal systems, thanks to the positivity of law. This makes it inevitable that if judges are to decide all cases validly brought before them, they will sometimes have to go beyond the mere application of posited (including legal) norms. And once they have exhausted all the normative resources of posited norms, what else is there for them to rely on but the merits of the case and hence of the various norms that might *now* be posited in order to resolve it?

The picture presented here—which is mainly attributable to the work of Hart and Raz, but also owes something to Kelsen—makes legal positivists the natural enemies of the mytho-logical "legal positivist" view that judges should not have regard to the merits of cases when deciding them. Except by withdrawing from judges the requirement to decide every case validly brought before them, legal positivists cannot but ascribe to judges the role of deter-mining at least some cases at least partly on their merits, and hence cannot but expect of them that they will go beyond the task of merely applying valid law. This brings out the important fact that, in dealing with the full gamut of human decision, source-based and merit-based norms are apt to call upon each other's services at frequent intervals. At least sometimes, relying on source-based norms is warranted because it provides one way of resolving cases that cannot be completely resolved on their merits. On any view, this provides at least part of the justification (such as it is) for having legal systems. It is this fact, you will recall, that positivity-welcomers inflate to yield their conclusion that all laws have some redeeming merit just in virtue of their positivity. What they less often notice, however, is that the reverse point also holds with similar force and on similar grounds. At least some-times relying on some or all of the merits of a case is warranted because it provides a way of resolving cases that cannot be completely

resolved according to the applicable source-based norms. This does not necessarily turn into a constant buck-passing exercise. The source-based norms may obviously narrow the issue such that it can now be resolved on the merits even though, without the intervention of source-based norms, it would not have been resolvable on the merits.

This proposal invites a modification of the myth under consideration. Are legal positivists at the very least committed to the view that judges should, if *possible*, decide cases by applying source-based norms? Should judges resort to deciding on the merits only as a fallback, when legal norms cannot settle the matter? This idea has some moral appeal. But it is still not one that has any natural affinity with legal positivism. As I explained, (LP*) is normatively inert. It only tells us that, insofar as judges should apply legal norms when they decide cases, the norms they should apply are source-based norms. But that leaves completely open the vexed questions of whether and when judges should only apply legal norms. Some legal positivists—one thinks particularly of Bentham—happen to be enthusiasts for limiting the role of judges in developing the law.[31] It would be better, on this Benthamite view, if judges stuck to merely applying the law, so far as possible, and left law-making activities by and large to the legislature. Is (LP*) implicated in this view in any way? No. Bentham's preference for the legislature to make the law and judges to apply it is in fact totally independent of his legal positivism. One could equally be a legal positivist enthusiast for judges to be the main lawmakers. Moreover, endorsing (PW) changes nothing on this front. Unlike (LP*), (PW) is obviously not normatively inert. It does have some implications, even taken on its own, for what some people should sometimes do. But it still does not bring us any closer to the conclusion that legislatures should make the law and judges should so far as possible only apply it. For (PW), like (LP*), is completely indifferent as between legislative and judicial sources.[32] It holds that the positivity of legal norms endows them with some redeeming merit, whatever their demerits. If it is truly the *positivity* of legal norms that supposedly endows them with this redeeming merit (and not some other feature), then the merit in question necessarily remains constant as between enacted and judge-made legal norms. For judge-made legal norms are no less posited than their enacted counterparts. This is acknowledged in the very idea that judge-made law is judge-*made*, i.e. is legally valid because some judge or judges at some relevant time and place announced it, practiced it, invoked it, enforced it, endorsed it, accepted it, or otherwise engaged with it.

D. Judicial legislation

Legal positivism militates against the assumption that judges should only and always apply valid legal norms. This is sometimes held to be a reason to abandon legal positivism. This suggestion lay at the heart of Ronald Dworkin's first critique of Hart's work. Dworkin agreed with Hart that judges cannot but decide some cases at least partly on their merits. However, he refused to concede that this could possibly involve judges in doing anything other than applying valid legal norms. If they did anything other than applying valid legal norms they would be part-time legislators, Dworkin said, and that would lay to waste the important doctrine of the separation of powers between the legislature and the judiciary. It would also condemn the law to violations of the rule-of-law ban on retroactive legislation, for the law made by judges would necessarily be applied by them retroactively to the cases before them. On these twin grounds Dworkin felt impelled to reject (LP*). He famously concluded that the validity of *some* legal norms depends on their merits rather than their sources. It depends, in his view, on their merits as moral justifications for other (source-based) legal norms.[33]

Even if we grant the premises, we may marvel at the conclusion. Why should the fact that the law would inevitably fail to live up to certain ideals if (LP*) were true be a reason to deny (LP*), rather than a reason to admit that law inevitably fails to live up to certain ideals, or perhaps a reason to wonder whether one has exaggerated the ideals themselves?[34] But never mind that familiar challenge to Dworkin's conclusion. Instead, I want to focus on Dworkin's premise according to which (LP*), at least in Hart's hands, turns judges into part-time legislators. Here we see a fresh myth that is sometimes wheeled out, in combination with the myth just considered under heading (C), to effect a kind of pincer movement against legal positivists as a group. Either legal positivists agree that judges should not decide cases on their merits (absurd!), or they become committed to the view that judges are part-time legislators (intolerable!).

The latter myth—Dworkin's myth—has at its source the mistaken assumption that all law-making is necessarily *legislative* law-making. It is fair to point out that Hart accidentally encouraged this mistaken assumption. He said that, in cases in which a case cannot be decided by applying only valid legal norms, the judge has "discretion" to decide the case either way.[35] Technically this is correct. The case is *ex hypothesi* unregulated by law in respect of its result and that makes the result legally discretionary. But talk of "discretion" is also misleading here. It suggests a judge who is entitled, consistently with his or her professional obligations, to give up legal reasoning and instead simply to reason morally or economically or aesthetically, or maybe even not to reason at all any more but simply go with his or her gut instinct, the toss of a coin, etc. But giving up legal reasoning in this way, at least at this early stage in the game, would admittedly be a violation of a judge's professional obligations. For judges admittedly have a professional obligation to reach their decisions by legal reasoning. And even in a case which cannot be decided by applying only existing legal norms it is possible to use legal reasoning to arrive at a new norm that enables (or constitutes) a decision in the case, and this norm is validated as a new legal norm in the process.

Obviously, legal reasoning, in this sense, is not simply reasoning about what legal norms already apply to the case. It is reasoning that has already-valid legal norms among its major or operative premises, but combines them non-redundantly in the same argument with moral or other merit-based premises. To forge a (legally simplified) example: (1) the Civil Rights Act of 1964 gives everyone the legal right not to be discriminated against in respect of employment on the ground of his or her sex (source-based legal norm); (2) denying a woman a job on the ground of her pregnancy is morally on a par with discriminating against her on the ground of her sex, even though there is no exact male comparator to a pregnant woman that would allow the denial to count as sex-discriminatory in the technical sense (merits-based moral claim); thus (3) women have a legal right not to be denied a job on the ground of their pregnancies (new legal norm); now (4) this woman P has been denied a job by D on the ground of her pregnancy (proven fact); thus (5) D owes P a job (a further new legal norm, but a nongeneral one).

This is a classic example of legal reasoning. Naturally, I have sidelined some possible complications. In particular I have ignored conflicting legal norms that may inhibit judicial delivery of new legal norms by this kind of reasoning. If a previous judicial decision establishes norms inconsistent with (3), then the rules of *stare decisis* applicable in the legal system in question may affect what a judge faced with the facts in (4) has the legal power to do. Perhaps she may overrule the earlier decision. Or perhaps she has scope to distinguish the earlier decision, i.e. to rely on and hence validate a norm narrower than (3) which is consistent with the earlier decision, but which still reflects the moral force of (2), and which still yields (5). Or

perhaps not. These questions depend on the local legal norms establishing her powers as a judge. These norms set source-based constraints on the judge's use of merits-based legal reasoning. If the judge violates these constraints, different legal systems cope differently with the violation. Some may have a *per incuriam* doctrine similar to the common law one that eliminates the legal validity of norm (3) but leaves norm (5) legally valid until the case is appealed. Others may have different solutions. The possibilities are endless.

But none of this detracts from the main point. The main point is that the reasoning from (1) to (5) is an example of specifically legal reasoning—reasoning *according to law*—because the existing legal norm in premise (1) plays a non-redundant but also nondecisive role in the argument. Because the existing law is not decisive the judge necessarily ends up announcing, practicing, invoking, enforcing, or otherwise engaging with some new norm or norms (which may of course be modifications of existing legal norms), in this case the norms in (3) and (5). In virtue of (and subject to) the judge's legal powers to decide cases on this subject, these new norms become legally valid in the process, at least for the purposes of the present case. If the judge sits in a sufficiently elevated court, then, depending on the workings of the local *stare decisis* doctrine, the new norms may also become legally valid for the purposes of future cases, subject always to future judicial powers of overruling and distinguishing. But that future validity does not turn these new norms into legislated norms even if they have exactly the same legal effects as legislated norms. In creating new legal norms by legal reasoning, or according to law, the judge plays a different role from that of a legislature. For a legislature is entitled to make new legal norms on entirely nonlegal grounds, i.e. without having any existing legal norms operative in its reasoning. A legislature is entitled to think about a problem purely on its merits. Thus, it can enact laws against pregnancy-related denials of employment without having to rely on the existing norms of the Civil Rights Act (or other specifically legal materials) to do so. But not so a judge. Barring special circumstances, a judge may only create this new legal norm on legal grounds, i.e. by relying on already valid legal norms in creating new ones.

This is not the only difference between legislative and judicial law-making, but for our purposes it is the most important.[36] Dworkin may object that it is a merely verbal quibble. His arguments were directed against judicial law-making, he may say, whether we bless it with the name of "legislation" or not. But that is not true. Dworkin's arguments were based respectively on the moral importance of the separation of powers, and the rule of law's ban on retroactivity. What is really morally important under the heading of the separation of powers is not the separation of law-making powers from law-applying powers, but rather the separation of *legislative* powers of law-making (i.e. powers to make legally unprecedented laws) from judicial powers of law-making (i.e. powers to develop the law gradually using existing legal resources). Similarly, the only morally credible rule-of-law ban on retroactive legislation is just that, namely a ban on retroactive *legislation*, not a ban on the retroactive change of legal norms even when that change is made in accordance with law. In short, the distinction I drew between legislation and judicial law-making, far from being a merely verbal one, is a distinction of great significance in many moral (and some legal) arguments— notably the classic moral arguments based on the separation of powers and the rule of law that Dworkin himself invokes.

It is also entirely consistent with (LP*). According to (LP*), norms are made legally valid by someone's having engaged with them. A judge's engagement with norms by mounting a defense of them partly in terms of other legal norms is one such type of engagement. It differs in deeply important ways from the legislative engagement that consists in the norm's straightforward (legally undefended) pronouncement. So it is a myth that legal positivists must become believers in judicial legislation as soon as they agree that legal norms do not settle every case.

E. Interpretation

It is sometimes hinted by critics, and widely believed by students, that legal positivists must favor particular methods of legal interpretation. They must be supporters of interpretation using only the resources of the legal text itself.[37] Or maybe believers in interpretation according to the original intention of the law-maker.[38] Why these particular methods of interpretation? Because presumably the act of positing that legally validates a norm under (LP*) must also identify the norm that it validates. And it may seem that there are only two aspects of the positing act that are suitable candidates for this identificatory role: the text in which the norm is posited and the intention of the agent who posits it. So presumably legal positivists have to choose between the rock of "textualism" and the hard place of "originalism." Or so the popular mythology goes.

A preliminary but telling objection to confronting legal positivists with this Hobson's choice is that it already assumes that the legally valid norms mentioned in (LP*) must be posited *articulately* (i.e. in words) and *intentionally* (i.e. with a view to positing a norm). But that is by no means the shared assumption of believers in (LP*). The "command" versions of (LP*) espoused by Bentham and Austin admittedly did embrace this assumption. But Hart went to great pains to distance himself from it. He argued (I think successfully) that in all legal systems at least some valid legal norms are posited and hence validated by being practiced or used rather than by being articulated, and that the relevant uses of these norms need not be regarded or intended as norm-positing acts by the relevant users.[39] Yet presumably these norms often need to be interpreted too. When that is so, what would it mean to interpret them "using only the resources of the text itself" or "according to original intention"? Neither proposal makes sense. So presumably there are other proposals for the interpretation of practice-validated norms that *do* make sense. Why not apply these other proposals, whatever they may be, to articulate and intentional acts of law-making, such as legislation, too? Why not, for example, interpret all these acts, in their norm-creating aspect, just as they were interpreted by others at the time when they were performed (which need neither be a textualist nor an originalist interpretation)? That meets the condition that the act of positing that legally validates a norm under (LP*) must also identify the norm that it validates. The norm is identified as the norm that certain others, observing the acts of positing in question, took those acts to be creating.

The reason why this won't do regarding legislation and other acts of intentional law-making, it may be said, is this. To have the power to make law intentionally—as it is sometimes put, to be an *authority*—one must surely have the power intentionally to determine what law one makes, at least up to a point.[40] And that surely requires interpreters to give credence to what one meant (originalism) or, alternatively, to limit attention to the words one chose to convey what one meant (textualism). It will not do to give the power to determine what norm one created entirely to others who observed one's norm-positing act, by making their interpretation authoritative rather than one's own. But *why* will this not do? So long as one can work out more or less how the relevant others will read what one says or does, one can also adapt what one says or does to anticipate their readings. If one can work out that the relevant others are perverse types who will always read "cat" to mean "dog," one can make the dog-regulating laws one means to make by passing a Cat Regulation Act. By this feedback route, one has the power intentionally to determine what law one makes even though

the norm for interpreting that law does not refer to one's intentions (i.e. is not originalist), and gives one's text a quirky meaning (i.e. is not textualist). All of this depends, to be sure, on the assumption that one can work out more or less how the relevant others will read what one said or did. But in a legal system this condition can normally be met by having (source-based) legal rules of interpretation. These rules will be used by interpreters (e.g. by judges) and can therefore be relied upon in advance by legislators and other lawmakers to work out, backwards, how they should speak or behave in order to be held to have made the law that they are trying to make.

So the widely different norms of interpretation adopted and practiced in different legal systems need not differ in the measure of ability they give to lawmakers intentionally to shape the laws that they make. So long as the local norms of interpretation can be grasped by the lawmakers (or by those drafting statutes or judgments on their behalf), the laws can be intentionally shaped by anticipating how they will be interpreted by others and drafting them accordingly. It does not follow, of course, that we should be indifferent as between different possible norms of interpretation—that we should not care, for example, whether traditional British strict construction in reading statutes prevails over the more relaxed American approach. Possibly one of these approaches makes for all-round better judicial decisions than the other, or possibly neither is as good as some third approach, or possibly a mixture of approaches would be best of all, etc. My point is only that *this* desideratum—the achievement of all-round better judicial decision—is the proper basis for selecting (and legally validating) norms of interpretation. In selecting such norms one need not be inhibited by the need to build in a special respect for the law-maker's words or the law-maker's intentions because, thanks to the feedback loop I mentioned, that can largely look after itself whatever norm one adopts or practices.

I say "largely" because of course there is a proviso. Since legislators and other lawmakers are no more clairvoyant than the rest of us, they can only adapt their law-making to norms of interpretation already in use or proposed. So the considerations just mentioned do have a certain conservative leaning. Insofar as law-making agents are to be treated as *authorities* regarding the norms they made, there is a reason to apply to those norms the interpretative norms that were knowably applicable to them *at the time when they were made*.[41] But how significant a constraint is this? One must remember that most legal norms, even when intentionally made, were not made by just one agent in one fell swoop. They were made by a succession of legal engagements. When people ask their lawyer or their law teacher "What does the First Amendment have to say about this problem?" they don't normally mean to restrict attention to the norm created by the original agreement on the text back in 1789. They mean to ask about the *law* of the First Amendment, which includes the original 1789 sources *plus* the often conflicting pronouncements, arguments, and practices of countless judges in First Amendment cases over the intervening centuries. Since a great deal of this intervening law-making was itself intentional, the question is not only one of treating the Congress of 1789 as an authority, but also one of treating the Supreme Court of 1926 as an authority, and indeed as an authority regarding how to treat the Congress of 1789 as an authority, and then of treating the Supreme Court of 1968 as an authority regarding both the Congress of 1789 and the Supreme Court of 1926, and regarding the legally proper way to relate them, and so forth. It follows that the limited conservative implications of the principle of deference to authority are so limited as to be rarely worthy of any real moral anxiety. They point to nothing like "originalism" or "textualism" conceived as interpretative doctrines that would freeze the First Amendment or the Civil Rights Act at the time of enactment, or limit the range of background context that could bear upon its meaning.

In all of this I have been granting another very common assumption that supporters of (LP*) need not, and often do not, share. I have been granting that the interpretation of legal norms belongs exclusively to the law-applying stage of legal reasoning, as opposed to the law-making stage. Recall that we started with the question of how (LP*) would have us *identify* the norms that are validated according to source-based criteria, and we took this to be where the question of interpretation fits in. But that is already a mistake. Interpretative activity straddles the distinction between the identification of existing legal norms and the further use of them to make new legal norms. To the extent that a judge can determine what the First Amendment means by relying exclusively on the relevant source-based norms (i.e. by relying on the text of the First Amendment together with judicial interpretations of it and judicial interpretations of those interpretations and applicable laws of precedent and interpretation), that judge is merely identifying the First Amendment in interpreting it. But to the extent that the judge is left with conflicts among or indeterminacies in the applicable source-based norms—including those of precedent and interpretation—the process of legal interpretation necessarily takes him beyond the law. The assembled ranks of source-based norms took the judge so far, but at a certain point they left the meaning of the First Amendment unclear, to be settled on the merits. At that point, settling the meaning of the First Amendment means *giving* it a meaning. It necessarily goes beyond norm-application to norm-alteration.

Remember our example of legal reasoning about sex discrimination under the Civil Rights Act? There our imaginary judge started with (1) an interpretation of the Act according to which it gives people a legal right not to be discriminated against on grounds of sex in employment. From that starting point, in combination with a moral premise, our imaginary judge ruled (and thereby made it the law) that (3) a woman has a legal right not to be denied a job because she is pregnant. Was this in turn an interpretation of (1)? Maybe. Maybe we forgot to mention that, according to our imaginary judge, (3A) a woman has a legal right *under the Civil Rights Act* not to be denied a job because she is pregnant. That judges talk like this has been understood by Dworkin and many others to suggest that all they are doing is applying the norms in the Civil Rights Act when they arrive at conclusion (3A).[42] But it does not suggest that at all. It suggests that they are *interpreting* the norms in the Civil Rights Act when they arrive at (3A), and that could mean *either* applying them or developing them. Some acts of interpretation are concerned with settling the law in the sense of identifying what it already says, but other acts of interpretation, like that captured in (3A), are concerned with settling the law in the sense of getting it to say something new.[43] According to (LP*), the difference between the two cases is the difference between wholly *source-based* modes of interpretation (looking to existing conventions of interpretation, or to some person's or constituency's actual understanding, etc.) and partly or wholly *merits-based* modes of interpretation (looking to what would make the norm morally defensible, or more fit for its intended purpose, etc.). Predictably—and much to the frustration of lawyers and law teachers all over the world—(LP*) has nothing at all to say on the subject of what the balance ought to be between these two families of interpretative considerations, for, here as elsewhere, (LP*) has nothing to say on the subject of where law-making should end and law-applying should begin. It merely says that whatever law is applied also has to be made, for unless it is made (either beforehand or in the process of application) there is nothing valid to apply. Interpreting it, however, can be making it and/or applying it.[44]

F. The "no necessary connection" thesis

Finally, I come to the jurisprudence student's favorite myth about legal positivism. Apparently legal positivists believe:

> (NNC) there is no necessary connection between law and morality.

This thesis is absurd and no legal philosopher of note has ever endorsed it as it stands.[45] After all, there is a necessary connection between law and morality if law and morality are necessarily *alike* in any way. And of course they are. If nothing else, they are necessarily alike in both necessarily comprising some valid norms. But there are many other necessary connections between law and morality on top of this rather insubstantial one, and legal positivists have often taken great pains to assert them. Hobbes, Bentham, Austin, Kelsen, Hart, Raz, and Coleman all rely on at least some more substantial necessary connections between law and morality in explaining various aspects of the nature of law (although they do not all rely on the same ones).

So how arises the myth that, as the leading legal positivists, they must all deny all such connections? It seems to arise from Hart's early work. In a much-cited footnote, Hart mistook Bentham's and Austin's ringing endorsements of (LP*)—notably Austin's remark that "the existence of law is one thing; its merit or demerit is another"—for endorsements of (NNC). Then by hint and emphasis he seemed to endorse (NNC) himself.[46] But a few pages later he admitted that he did not really endorse it. For even in this early work he advanced the proposal (mentioned under heading (A) above) that every law necessarily exhibits a redeeming moral merit, a dash of justice that comes of the mere fact that a law is a general norm that would have like cases treated alike.[47] For Hart this built-in dash of moral merit in every law clearly forges a necessary connection between law and morality. So his apparent endorsements of (NNC) must be read as bungled preliminary attempts to formulate and defend (LP*), which, like Bentham and Austin, he really did endorse.

How does (NNC) differ from (LP*)? In two respects (LP*) is the broader of the two propositions and in two respects the narrower. Let me begin by explaining how it is narrower. First, (LP*) is narrower than (NNC) in that it is concerned only with the conditions of legal *validity*. Studying the nature of law involves—as my remarks over the last few pages have amply demonstrated—studying much more than the conditions of legal validity. That some people mistake an account of the conditions of legal validity for an account of the whole nature of law (and hence mistake legal positivism's distinctive *thesis about law* for a comprehensive *theory of law*) may come of the fact that one can question the validity of a certain putatively valid law by asking "Is this really a law?" and that question in turn is easily confused with the much more abstract (and pretentious) question "What is law?"[48] But, in fact, once one has tackled the question of whether a certain law is valid there remain many relatively independent questions to address concerning its meaning, its fidelity to law's purposes, its role in sound legal reasoning, its legal effects, and its social functions, to name but a few. To study the nature of law one needs to turn one's mind to the philosophical aspects of these further questions too. To these further questions there is no distinctively "legal positivist" answer, because legal positivism is a thesis only about the conditions of legal validity.

Proposition (LP*) narrows (NNC) further in that it restricts its attention to one specific connection that is sometimes thought to hold between a law's validity and its moral merits, namely a relationship in which the former *depends* upon the latter. This is a one-way relationship. Legal positivists deny that laws are valid because of their moral merits. But they do not deny the converse proposition that laws might be morally meritorious because of their validity. As we saw, some legal positivists—Hobbes, Bentham, and Hart the most prominent among them—have regarded valid laws as necessarily endowed with some moral value just in virtue of being valid laws, never mind how morally odious in other respects. (NNC) rules this view out. On the other hand, (LP*) is compatible with it but does not require it.

At the same time, (LP*) is broader than (NNC) in that it is concerned not only with the connection between a law's validity and its *moral* merits, but with the connection between a law's validity and *any* of its merits. Legal positivists line up equally against views according to which the validity of a law depends upon, for example, its economic or aesthetic merits. Moreover—as we saw under heading (B) above—legal positivists must also reject views according to which the validity of a law depends upon its merits purely as a means, i.e. its fitness for its purpose (be that purpose meritorious or unmeritorious). Thus, as we saw, the thesis that insufficiently clear or insufficiently certain norms lack validity is a classic *anti*-positivist thesis.

Finally, unlike (NNC), (LP*) does not limit its embargo to supposedly *necessary* connections between a law's validity and its merits, i.e. to those that are supposed to exist by law's very nature. At any rate, it does not do so as I have expressed it. But here we have, you will recall, the most important point at which legal positivists differ in their interpretation of (LP*), so I had best say that in this respect (LP*) is only *arguably* broader than (NNC). According to the so-called "soft" legal positivists, there may be laws, the validity of which depends on their merits, but only if the "merits" test in question is set by some other law, the validity of which does *not* depend on its merits. Thus, according to soft legal positivists, there is no law that depends for its validity on its merits just in virtue of the nature of law, i.e. necessarily. However, there can be laws that depend for their validity on their merits in particular legal systems because other laws of those legal systems so dictate, i.e. contingently. Hart endorsed this view. But personally, as I mentioned near the beginning, I side with those "hard" legal positivists who reject it. In my view, no law depends for its validity on its merits *full stop*, whether owing to the very nature of law (necessarily) or merely owing to what other laws say (contingently). To capture the hard as well as the soft legal positivist position—quite apart from its other dimensions of over- and underinclusiveness—(NNC) should not discriminate between necessary and contingent connections.

IV. Legal positivism for natural lawyers

The myths I have been concerned with here are myths often peddled about legal positivism as an intellectual tradition. My first aim has been to counteract the common but philosophically disreputable tendency to find leading writers in that tradition guilty by association. Since they are legal positivists, the thinking goes, they must espouse such-and-such a silly "legal positivist" thesis. But by and large, as we have seen, the leading figures found guilty by this method do not espouse the silly theses with which they are thus associated. What they do espouse in common is thesis (LP*), which is often misrepresented by critics as some quite different and much sillier thesis, or at least held out as having some much sillier theses among its implications. That is why my second aim here, and perhaps the philosophically more important of the two, has been to identify what is and what is not an implication of (LP*). The main tendency we encountered—running through several of our myths—was a tendency to assume that (LP*) must have implications of its own for what at least some people (e.g. judges, governments) should do. In fact, it has no such implications. It tells us how the legal validity of any norm in any legal system falls to be determined—namely, by its sources—but leaves open whether and when and why any of us should ever bother to have or to follow any valid legal norms. To show that

valid legal norms are ever worth having or following, and in what way, always requires a separate argument, regarding which (LP*) is in itself entirely agnostic.

Our friends in the natural law tradition tend to balk at the idea that we can study the validity of legal norms in the agnostic way envisaged by (LP*), i.e. without deciding in advance whether (at least some) valid legal norms are going to be worth having or following. It is not that natural lawyers cannot see the possibility of, or interest in, studying the validity-conditions of certain norms in the practically noncommittal sense of "validity." Sure, the rules of a game can be valid *qua* rules of the game without having any significance for what anyone should do except to the extent that they fancy playing the game. But law is not a game. It purports to bind us morally, i.e. in a way that binds even those of us who do not fancy playing. So why not go straight to the question of whether it succeeds in doing so? Why begin by asking about its legal validity in the thin, practically noncommittal sense found in (LP*), and only then go on to ask whether it is valid law in the thicker sense of being morally binding on at least some people? According to this critique, the problem with legal positivism is not that it has silly answers of the kind peddled in its name by the myth-spinners. The problem, rather, is that it has a distracting and prevaricating *question*, which is the question of what determines legal validity in the thin, practically noncommittal sense of "legal validity."

There are indeed two inflexions of "legally valid," and they correspond to two senses of "legal." In most European languages other than English there are two words for law corresponding conveniently to these two senses of "legal": *lex* and *ius*, *Gesetz* and *Recht*, *loi* and *droit*, and so on. Legal positivists need not deny that there is a moralized notion of law captured in the second term in each of these pairs.[49] They need not deny that in some contexts "legality" accordingly names a moral value, such that in the second moralized sense of "valid law," laws may be more or less valid depending on the extent to which they exhibit legality, and hence depending on their merits. Nor need they deny that one must capture this moral value of legality, whatever it is, in order to tell the whole story of law's nature. As in any other field of human endeavor, understanding the nature of the endeavor in full admittedly means having an ability to tell success in the endeavor from failure. Perhaps law does have a special way of succeeding, as these European languages seem to suggest. Maybe the ideal of the rule of law, for example, does represent a moral ideal distinctively for law, such that one does not fully understand the nature of law until one understands that at least part of its success, if it were ever successful, would lie in conformity to this ideal. Or maybe the relevant ideal of legality is something quite different. But picking out the relevant ideal(s) is irrelevant to the truth or the importance of (LP*). For (LP*) tries to answer a logically prior question. What is this field of human endeavor, to which the natural lawyer's proposed criteria of success and failure apply? What makes something a candidate for being accounted a success or failure in these terms? What is this *lex*, such that it ought to be *ius*? Legal positivism naturally supplies only part of the answer. To be exact, legal positivism explains what it takes for a law to be legally valid in the thin *lex* sense, such that the question arises of whether it is also legally valid in the thicker *ius* sense, i.e. morally binding *qua* law. In doing so legal positivism admittedly does not distinguish law from a game, which is also made up of posited norms. To distinguish law from a game one must add, among other things, that law, unlike a game, purports to bind us morally. That has implications, no doubt, for what counts as successful law, and hence for what one might think of as law's central case.[50] But this does not detract from the truth or the importance of (LP*), which is not a thesis about law's central case but about the validity-conditions for all legal norms, be they central (morally successful) or peripheral (morally failed) examples.

Notes

46 *American Journal of Jurisprudence* 199 (2001)

2 Austin, *The Province of Jurisprudence Determined* (1832; ed. W. E. Rumble, Cambridge: Cambridge University Press, 1995), 157.

3 This possibility was clearly envisaged by Hart in *The Concept of Law* (Oxford: Clarendon Press, 1961), 204, and was relied upon in the postscript to the book's second edition (Oxford: Clarendon Press, 1994) at 250. (Subsequent references are to the first edition unless otherwise specified.) In the meantime "soft" legal positivism had been proposed by Philip Soper in "Legal Theory and the Obligation of a Judge: The Hart/Dworkin Dispute," *Michigan Law Review* 75 (1977) 473; David Lyons, "Principles, Positivism, and Legal Theory," *Yale Law Journal* 87 (1977) 415; and perhaps most influentially by Jules Coleman in "Negative and Positive Positivism," *Journal of Legal Studies* 11 (1982) 139.

4 This was clearly Kelsen's view: see *The General Theory of Law and State* (New York: Russell and Russell, 1961), e.g. at 134–6. The most influential contemporary exponent of the "hard" legal positivist view is Joseph Raz: see his "Authority, Law and Morality," *The Monist* 68 (1985) 295, further defended in Scott Shapiro, "On Hart's Way Out," *Legal Theory* 4 (1998) 469.

5 See Fred Schauer, "Positivism as Pariah" in Robert P. George (ed.), *The Autonomy of Law* (Oxford: Clarendon Press, 1996).

6 Dworkin's talk of "the grounds of law" in *Law's Empire* (Cambridge, Mass.: Harvard University Press, 1986), at 4ff, intentionally elides the distinction I am drawing here. Both the claim that legal norms are valid on their sources and the claim that legislation constitutes a source of valid legal norms are treated by Dworkin as *legal* claims. But only the second is a legal claim. The first is a claim about what *makes* the second a legal claim. To be exact, "legislation is a source of valid legal norms" is a legal claim only if the norm it mentions (viz. the norm of legislation-following) is itself being held out as valid on the strength of its sources rather than its merits (e.g. on the strength of the fact that legislation is identified as a source of law in a constitutional document or judicial practice.)

7   For a particularly clear expression of this refusal, see Gerald J. Postema, "Jurisprudence as Practical Philosophy," *Legal Theory* 4 (1998) 329.

8   Kelsen is an apparent exception. He normally reserved the label "morality" for a specialized order of posited (conventionally- or ecclesiastically-validated) norms rivaling law. Nevertheless, his work always presupposed the possibility of genuine moral norms valid on their merits. I have defended this reading of Kelsen in "Law as a Leap of Faith," in Peter Oliver, Sionaidh Douglas Scott and Victor Tadros (eds.), *Faith in Law* (Oxford: Hart Publishing, 2000).

9   As Hart expressed the wonderment: "How are the creation, imposition, modification and extinction of obligations and other operations on other legal entities such as rights possible? How can such things be done?" See Hart, "Legal and Moral Obligation" in Melden (ed.), *Essays in Moral Philosophy* (Seattle: University of Washington Press, 1958), 82 at 86.

10 When legal positivists are labeled simply as "positivists," or it is otherwise insinuated that they tend to share the broader philosophical positions of e.g. Comte or Ayer—beware! It is usually the pot calling the kettle black. And nowhere more spectacularly than in the work of Stanley Fish: e.g. "Wrong Again," *Texas Law Review* 62 (1983) 299 at 309ff, especially note 31.

11 See e.g. Hobbes, "Questions Concerning Liberty, Necessity, and Chance" in W. Molesworth (ed.), *The English Works of Thomas Hobbes* (London: Bohn, 1839–1845), vol. v, at 194. For thorough documentation of Bentham's complex views on the built-in merit of law, see Gerald Postema, *Bentham and the Common Law Tradition* (Oxford: Clarendon Press, 1986).

12 Prominent examples of positivity-welcomers today: Neil MacCormick, "A Moralistic Case for A-moralistic Law," *Valparaiso Law Review* 20 (1985) 1; Tom Campbell, *The Legal Theory of Ethical Positivism* (Aldershot: Dartmouth, 1996); Jeremy Waldron, "Normative (or Ethical) Positivism" in Jules Coleman (ed.), *Hart's Postscript* (Oxford: Oxford University Press, 2001), 410. I erred on the side of excess in the list of legal positivists I classified as positivity-welcomers in my review of Campbell's book in *King's College Law Journal* 9 (1998) 180.

13 See Hart's 1958 essay "Positivism and the Separation of Law and Morals" in his *Essays in Jurisprudence and Philosophy* (Oxford: Clarendon Press, 1983), 49 at 81; also *The Concept of Law*, supra, note 3, chapter 8.

14 See my lecture "The Virtue of Justice and the Character of Law" in *Current Legal Problems* 53 (2000) 1.

15 Some of Bentham's remarks cited by Postema, note 11, supra, suggest that for him the only built-in merit of laws lies in their *combination* of generality and positivity, which is why I said that he was only *arguably* a supporter of (PW).

16 See Raz's assembled arguments in chapters 12 and 13 of *The Authority of Law* (Oxford: Clarendon Press, 1979). These add up to a rebuttal not only of law's built-in rational appeal but also (by the same token) of its built-in merit.

17 Which shows that it is a mistake to follow Ronald Dworkin in contrasting "interpretive" accounts of law's nature with "descriptive" ones, unless one happens to share Dworkin's idiosyncratic "constructive" view of interpretation. Cf. Dworkin, "Legal Theory and the Problem of Sense" in Ruth Gavison (ed.), *Issues in Contemporary Legal Philosophy* (Oxford: Clarendon Press, 1987), 9 at 13–14.

18 See e.g. Hugh Collins, "Democracy and Adjudication" in Neil MacCormick and Peter Birks (eds), *The Legal Mind* (Oxford: Clarendon Press, 1986), 67 at 68; Kenneth Winston, "Constructing Law's Mandate" in David Dyzenhaus (ed.), *Recrafting the Rule of Law* (Oxford: Hart Publishing, 1999), 290ff.

19 See e.g. Dworkin, *Taking Rights Seriously* (London: Duckworth, 1977), 17: legal positivists' criteria of legal validity have to do "not with [the] content [of norms] but with . . . the manner in which they were adopted or developed."

20 "Positivism and Fidelity to Law: A Reply to Professor Hart," *Harvard Law Review* 71 (1958) 630. I say "fairly or unfairly" because arguably Fuller is not talking about the conditions of legal validity at all, and so is not engaging with (LP*). Arguably he is talking about the conditions under which (admittedly valid) law deserves no respect among legal officials.

21 In *The Concept of Law*, supra, note 3, 202–7.

22 "Commands and Authoritative Legal Reasons" in his *Essays on Bentham* (Oxford: Clarendon Press, 1982), 243 at 254–5.

23 I am not doubting the value of the idea of content-independence in framing or solving other philosophical problems. For example, the notion does help to illuminate (as Hart observes) the difference between norms and other reasons. For more sweeping (although I think unsuccessful) objections to the philosophical value of the idea of content-independence, see P. Markwick, "Law and Content-Independent Reasons," *Oxford Journal of Legal Studies* 20 (2000) 579.

24 But isn't this insistence on the possibility of legal validity without conformity to the rule of law at odds with Hart's view, already mentioned at note 13, supra, that all laws (being not only norms but rules) have a built-in element of generality? No, it isn't. For the absence of this element of generality, as we saw, does not affect the legal validity of any norm, in Hart's view. It only affects whether it is a valid *law* as opposed to a legally valid norm of a nongeneral type (e.g. Tice must pay $50 to Summers). Either way, its legal validity turns on its source not its generality. Apart from which, the minimal generality required to achieve "rulishness" clearly falls well short of the measure of generality expected by any credible version of the rule-of-law ideal. One cannot congratulate oneself on having conformed to the generality clause of the rule of law merely by virtue of the fact that the norm one made was a rule.

25 Hart, *The Concept of Law*, supra, note 3, 202.

26 Friedrich Hayek did much to encourage the view that allegiance to the rule of law requires a suppression of all other ideals for government and law: cf. *The Road to Serfdom* (London: George Routledge, 1944), 54ff. However, Hayek's arguments to this effect were uniformly fallacious.

27 Cf. Dworkin, *Law's Empire*, supra, note 6, 6–8.

28 As explained at length by Hart in *The Concept of Law*, supra, note 3, 121–32.

29 Cf. Kelsen's denial of the possibility of legal gaps in the *sense of silences* in "On the Theory of Interpretation," *Legal Studies* 10 (1990) 127 at 132. As Kelsen rightly observes, deontic logic supplies automatic closure rules for cases in which the law fails to do so. Since these defaults are not valid on their sources but are necessary truths they are not valid as legal norms according to (LP*). This reminds us that the view according to which judges should only apply legal norms is in one

respect absurd. At the very least, they also need to apply the norms of logic, which are valid on their (intellectual) merits.

30 Joseph Raz, *The Authority of Law*, supra, note 16, 70ff.

31 See Postema, supra, note 11, at 197, citing Bentham's manuscript remark that "[no] degree of wisdom . . . can render it expedient for a judge . . . to depart from pre-established rules."

32 This remains true when it is formulated as the thesis that "the law ought to be such that legal decisions can be made without the exercise of moral judgment": Jeremy Waldron, "The Irrelevance of Moral Objectivity" in Robert George (ed.), *Natural Law Theory* (Oxford: Clarendon Press, 1992). Judges can help to make the law like this no less than legislatures.

33 *Taking Rights Seriously*, supra, note 19, chapter 2. I omit the further and independent claim that source-based legal norms are "rules" and merit-based ones are "principles." Hart used the word "rule" in its ordinary sense simply to mean "general norm." Principles are general norms and hence count as rules in Hart's sense. Dworkin, on the other hand, gave "rules" a special technical meaning: they are general norms that cannot be either more or less weighty. His claim that all source-based norms must be rules in this special technical sense is mistaken. Source-based norms are more or less weighty in proportion to the importance of their source: one owed to the Supreme Court has greater weight than one owed to the Court of Appeals, etc.

34 For (LP*)-independent reasons to think that law inevitably fails to live up to the ideal of the rule of law, properly understood, see my "Rationality and the Rule of Law in Offences Against the Person," *Cambridge Law Journal* 53 (1994) 502. For (LP*)-independent reasons to think that some people exaggerate the ideal of the rule of law, and so read conformity as violation, see Timothy Endicott, "The Impossibility of the Rule of Law," *Oxford Journal of Legal Studies* 19 (1999) 1.

35 *The Concept of Law*, supra, note 3, 128.

36 It is explored most fully in Raz, *Ethics in the Public Domain* (Oxford: Clarendon Press, 1994), chapters 11 and 13 (chapters 12 and 14 in the paper edition).

37 See e.g. Fish, "Wrong Again," supra, note 10, 309–10. Cf. Dworkin, *A Matter of Principle* (Cambridge,

Mass.: Harvard University Press, 1986), who kindly observes at 37 that "not even" legal positivists sign up to this "textualist" view—even though they "seem the most likely" to do so!

38 See e.g. Michael Freeman, "Positivism and Statutory Construction: An Essay in the Retrieval of Democracy" in Stephen Guest (ed.), *Positivism Today* (Aldershot: Dartmouth, 1996), 11 at 21.

39 *The Concept of Law*, supra, note 3, e.g. 113, 149–150.

40 Raz, "Intention in Interpretation" in *The Autonomy of Law*, supra, note 5, 249 at 256–60.

41 Ibid, 271.

42 See e.g. Dworkin, *Law's Empire*, supra, note 6, at 6.

43 As Bentham explains robustly in *Of Laws in General*, H. L. A. Hart (ed.) (London: Athlone Press, 1970), 162ff.

44 Some student resistance to this picture seems to come of the following line of thought: (i) one must identify what norm one is interested in before one can ask about its validity according to (LP*), but (ii) one cannot identify what norm one is interested in without first eradicating the indeterminacies and other gaps in its application that (LP*) makes inevitable, and hence without completing its interpretation. But this argument works only if there can be no such thing as an identifiable norm with built-in indeterminacies. If one says, as all legal positivists who have thought about the matter must say, that one is interested in the validity of norms complete with their indeterminacies then one assumes the opposite. There is of course a genuine dispute to be had about just how indeterminate a norm can be before it stops being a norm at all. But clearly it does not stop being a norm merely because there are some actions, the normative status of which it leaves unclear. This is the respect in which it is misleading (although not false) to frame (LP*) as a thesis about the identification of legal norms, rather than their validity.

45 Although it is helpfully billed as "the quintessence of legal positivism" in student textbook Howard Davies and David Holdcroft, *Jurisprudence: Texts and Commentary* (London: Butterworths, 1991), 3.

46 "Positivism and the Separation of Law and Morals," supra, note 13, 57–8.

47 Ibid, 81. See text at note 13, supra.

48 This confusion is another one that is courted in Dworkin's opaque question "what are the grounds of law?": *Law's Empire*, supra, note 6, at 4.

49 Hart explicitly pointed it out in *The Concept of Law*, supra, note 3, at 203–7.

50 The most important study of which—taking (LP*) for granted although remaining studiously unexcited by it—is John Finnis's *Natural Law and Natural Rights* (Oxford: Clarendon Press, 1981).

PART 2

Law, the State, and the Individual

III. THE RULE OF LAW

Introduction

WHILE CITIZENS and political leaders debate the relative importance of values like liberty, equality, and the general welfare, there is a political ideal that commands allegiance across nearly the entire political spectrum and that is widely thought to underlie these other values, and it is the rule of law. The Universal Declaration of Human Rights, adopted by the United Nations in 1948, is emblematic of this common view, holding that "it is essential, if man is not to be compelled to have recourse, as a last resort, to rebellion against tyranny and oppression, that human rights should be protected by the rule of law."[1] The UN's avowed position is that respect for the rule of law is a precondition of respect for human rights, a belief that has for years served as a basis for criticizing anti-democratic and despotic governments and is increasingly invoked today in criticism of, for example, the United States's treatment of terrorism suspects (see Section VII). Even its link to human rights, however, underplays the value that the rule of law is commonly thought to possess, for it is widely believed that establishing it is necessary to realize myriad desirable aspects of a decent society well beyond the protection of basic human rights. So understood, the rule of law is the cornerstone of any reasonably just or good government.

What, then, is the rule of law that it could be considered by so many to be so fundamentally important? Despite its near-universal valorization, what the rule of law consists in is a matter of significant philosophical dispute. In his 1964 book, *The Morality of Law,*[2] Lon Fuller offered eight "principles of legality" that taken together characterize one prominent conception of the rule of law: laws should be (1) general, (2) public, (3) prospective, (4) clear, (5) compatible with one another, (6) possible to obey, (7) stable, and (8) consistently applied. While Fuller famously believed these eight principles to constitute the "internal morality" of law, imbuing law itself with moral value (see Sections I and II above), what is worth noting at present is that the rule of law on this conception is a *formal* ideal—the content of laws is left open. So for example while secure human rights might require the rule of law, on this view, the rule of law does not require secure human rights. Why the formality? As Joseph Raz maintains in "The Rule of Law and its Virtue", "[i]f the rule of law is the rule of the good law then to explain its nature is to propound a complete social philosophy. But if so the term lacks any useful function."³

The formality of the rule of law on this conception likely has much to do with the ideal's appeal across the political spectrum. For in leaving the content of laws open, it is seemingly compatible with and can therefore be put in the service of the widest range of political moralities and legal systems. It is precisely this fact, however, that calls into question the value of the rule of law so conceived. What, after all, is the value in the rule of law in a wicked legal system? As Ronald Dworkin points out, "compliance with the rule book is plainly not sufficient for justice; full compliance will achieve very great injustice if the rules are unjust."⁴ The consistent application of morally bankrupt law, in other words, is morally worse than its inconsistent application. Given the repugnant ends to which his eight principles of legality can seemingly be turned, Fuller's claim that they represent law's inner morality is questionable. What is clear, however, is that if the rule of law is conceived formally, its value cannot reside in the substance of the laws with which it is compatible. Thus Raz holds that "conformity to the rule of law is an *inherent* value of laws, indeed it is their most important inherent value."⁵ What exactly is that inherent value, according to Raz? It is the value, and more specifically the "negative value", of avoiding the evils of arbitrary, lawless rule.⁶

As this suggests, debate about the rule of law implicates the fundamental concerns of general jurisprudence and in particular the relation between legality and morality (see Sections I and II). This is clear in "The Rule of Law and its Virtue", where Raz directly challenges Fuller's claim about the internal morality of law and defends legal positivism, arguing that the value of the rule of law does not itself impart any moral value whatsoever to legal systems. The sense in which debate over the rule of law can be understood as a proxy war between positivists and anti-positivists is further underscored in Dworkin's "Political Judges and the Rule of Law", where he distinguishes between the "rule book" and "rights" conceptions of the rule of law, associating the former primarily with legal positivism while himself adopting the latter.⁷ As noted above, Dworkin believes that the rule of law, on the rule book conception, is an insufficient guarantor of justice, and that fact counts against the adequacy of such a formal conception of the rule of law. The rights conception, by Dworkin's lights, has an advantage in this regard because "[i]t does not distinguish, as the rule-book conception does, between the rule of law and substantive justice; on the contrary it requires, as part of the ideal of law, that the rules in the rule book capture and enforce moral rights."⁸ This, it should be clear, is a *substantive* conception of the rule of law if anything is. Indeed, where Raz warns of turning an account of the rule of law into a complete social philosophy, Dworkin unapologetically embraces that project. Upon reflection, perhaps this difference in approach should not be surprising in light of Raz's and Dworkin's deeply opposed views on the relation between legality and morality.

On Dworkin's view, again, the rule of law has value because it protects the moral rights of those persons over whom it has dominion. The rule of law so conceived is therefore praiseworthy precisely because it is substantively accurate—it gets rights right. In "The Rule of Law as a Theater of Debate", Jeremy Waldron presses Dworkin on just this point, arguing that Dworkin overstates the importance of getting ante-cedently defined rights right. Waldron poses the following question: "If the rule of law is identified—as it is in Dworkin's conception—with law's getting it right so far as moral rights are concerned, does any importance attach to the procedures by which this happens or the means by which we as a society make the attempt to get moral rights right?"[9] This is not an idle question from Waldron. He has powerfully argued against judicial review of legislation adopted by democratic procedures (see Section VIII), and his question for Dworkin is clearly motivated by his own commitment to what we can call a *procedural* conception of the rule of law. Waldron devotes his essay to uncovering the "proceduralist element" in Dworkin's understanding of the rule of law, which he believes is present but obscured by what Waldron calls the "objectivist element" in Dworkin's account, which emphasizes getting the morally best outcomes regardless of how those outcomes are achieved.

The procedural conception of the rule of law that is latent in Waldron's exposition of Dworkin's position is not necessarily at odds with either a formal conception like Raz's or, for that matter, Dworkin's substantive conception. Procedures are after all typically formal in the relevant sense, and they can also play a major role in a robustly substantive political morality.[10] The procedural conception nevertheless sounds dis-tinctive notes—or at any rate notes that do not resonate as much in either of the other accounts—and for that reason it probably warrants separate billing alongside the formal and substantive conceptions. And the very existence of conceptions of the rule of law as diverse as these three proves that while it is a powerful and widely venerated if politically elusive ideal, the rule of law remains at least as philosophically elusive.

Notes

1 *Universal Declaration of Human Rights*, G.A. res. 217A (III), U.N. Doc A/810 (1948).
2 Lon L. Fuller, *The Morality of Law*, New Haven: Yale University Press, 1964.
3 Joseph Raz, "The Rule of Law and its Virtue", p. 181.
4 Ronald Dworkin, "Political Judges and the Rule of Law", p. 195.
5 Raz, "Rule of Law", p. 189 (emphasis added).
6 Ibid., p. 191.
7 Dworkin, "Political Judges", p. 194–195.
8 Ibid., p. 195.
9 Jeremy Waldron, "The Rule of Law as a Theater of Debate", p. 214.
10 This latter point is expressly made by Dworkin in his reply to Waldron: "I take questions of proper legal procedure to be themselves questions of political morality that themselves have right answers. I am, that is, an objectivist about procedures." Ronald Dworkin, "Replies", in Justine Burley (ed.), *Dworkin and His Critics*, Oxford: Blackwell Publishing, 2004, p. 387.

Further reading

David Dyzenhaus (ed.), *Recrafting the Rule of Law: Limits of the Legal Order*, Oxford: Hart Publishing, 1999.

Ronald Dworkin, "Replies", in Justine Burley (ed.), *Dworkin and His Critics*, Oxford: Blackwell Publishing, 2004.

Lon L. Fuller, *The Morality of Law*, New Haven: Yale University Press, 1964.

Allan C. Hutchinson and Patrick J. Monahan (eds), *The Rule of Law: Ideal or Ideology*, Toronto: Carwell Publishers, 1987.

David Lyons, *Ethics and the Rule of Law*, New York: Cambridge University Press, 1984.

Andrei Marmor, "The Rule of Law and its Limits", *Law and Philosophy* 23, 2004, 1–43.

Ian Shapiro, *The Rule of Law*, New York: NYU Press, 1994.

Universal Declaration of Human Rights, G.A. res. 217A (III), U.N. Doc A/810 (1948).

Questions

1. Is the rule of law an independent ideal, or does it instead represent a comprehensive ideal of the good and just society?
2. Can the rule of law be upheld in a wicked legal regime?
3. If the rule of law is an inherent value of any legal system, does it follow that all law is valuable?
4. Dworkin maintains that "compliance with the rule book is plainly not sufficient for justice", but can he hold it to be even necessary?

Chapter 10

Joseph Raz

THE RULE OF LAW AND ITS VIRTUE

F. A. HAYEK HAS PROVIDED one of the clearest and most powerful formulations of the ideal of the rule of law: 'stripped of all technicalities this means that government in all its actions is bound by rules fixed and announced beforehand—rules which make it possible to foresee with fair certainty how the authority will use its coercive powers in given circumstances, and to plan one's individual affairs on the basis of this knowledge'.[1] At the same time the way he draws certain conclusions from this ideal illustrates one of the two main fallacies in the contemporary treatment of the doctrine of the rule of law: the assumption of its overriding importance. My purpose is to analyse the ideal of the rule of law in the spirit of Hayek's quoted statement of it and to show why some of the conclusions which he drew from it cannot be thus supported. But first we must be put on our guard against the other common fallacy concerning the rule of law.

Not uncommonly when a political ideal captures the imagination of large numbers of people its name becomes a slogan used by supporters of ideals which bear little or no relation to the one it originally designated. The fate of 'democracy' not long ago and of 'privacy' today are just two examples of this familiar process. In 1959 the International Congress of Jurists meeting in New Delhi gave official blessing to a similar perversion of the doctrine of the rule of law.

The function of the legislature in a free society under the Rule of Law is to create and maintain the conditions which will uphold the dignity of man as an individual. This dignity requires not only the recognition of his civil and political rights but also the establishment of the social, economic, educational and cultural conditions which are essential to the full development of his personality.[2]

The report goes on to mention or refer to just about every political ideal which has found support in any part of the globe during the post-war years.

If the rule of law is the rule of the good law then to explain its nature is to propound a complete social philosophy. But if so the term lacks any useful function. We have no need to be converted to the rule of law just in order to discover that to believe in it is to believe that good should triumph. The rule of law is a political ideal which a legal system may lack or may possess to a greater or lesser degree. That much is common ground. It is also to be insisted that the rule of law is just one of the virtues which a legal system may possess and by which it is to be judged. It is not to be confused with democracy, justice, equality (before the law or otherwise), human rights of any kind or respect for persons or for the dignity of man. A non-democratic legal system, based on the denial of human rights, on extensive poverty, on racial segregation, sexual inequalities, and religious persecution may, in principle, conform to the requirements of the rule of law better than any of the legal systems of the more enlightened Western democracies. This does not mean that it will be better than those Western democracies. It will be an immeasurably worse legal system, but it will excel in one respect: in its conformity to the rule of law.

Given the promiscuous use made in recent years of the expression 'the rule of law' it is hardly surprising that my claim will alarm many. We have reached the stage in which no purist can claim that truth is on his side and blame the others for distorting the notion of the rule of law. All that I can claim for my account is, first, that it presents a coherent view of one important virtue which legal systems should possess and, secondly, that it is not original, that I am following in the footsteps of Hayek and of many others who understood 'the rule of law' in similar ways.

1. The basic idea

'The rule of law' means literally what it says: the rule of the law. Taken in its broadest sense this means that people should obey the law and be ruled by it.[3] But in political and legal theory it has come to be read in a narrower sense, that the government shall be ruled by the law and subject to it. The ideal of the rule of law in this sense is often expressed by the phrase 'government by law and not by men'. No sooner does one use these formulas than their obscurity becomes evident. Surely government must be both by law and by men. It is said that the rule of law means that all government action must have foundation in law, must be authorized by law. But is not that a tautology? Actions not authorized by law cannot be the actions of the government as a government. They would be without legal effect and often unlawful.

It is true that we can elaborate a political notion of government which is different from the legal one: government as the location of real power in the society. It is in this sense that one can say that Britain is governed by The City or by the trade unions. In this sense of 'government' it is not a tautology to say that government should be based on law. If the trade union ruling a country breaks an industrial relations law in order to impose its will on the Parliament or if the President or the F.B.I. authorize burglaries and conspire to pervert justice they can be said to violate the rule of law. But here 'the rule of law' is used in its original sense of obedience to law. Powerful people and people in government, just like anybody else, should obey the law. This is no doubt correct, and yet does it exhaust the meaning of the rule of law? There is more to the rule of law than the law and order interpretation allows. It means more even than law and order applied to the government. I shall proceed on the assumption that we are concerned with government in the legal sense and with the conception of the rule of law which applies to government and to law and is no mere application of the law and order conception.

The problem is that now we are back with our initial puzzle. If government is, by definition, government authorized by law the rule of law seems to amount to an empty tautology, not a political ideal.

The solution to this riddle is in the difference between the professional and the lay sense of 'law'. For the lawyer anything is the law if it meets the conditions of validity laid down in the system's rules of recognition or in other rules of the system.[4] This includes the constitution, parliamentary legislation, ministerial regulations, policemen's orders, the regulations of limited companies, conditions imposed in trading licences, etc. To the layman the law consists only of a subclass of these. To him the law is essentially a set of open, general, and relatively stable laws. Government by law and not by men is not a tautology if 'law' means general, open, and relatively stable law. In fact, the danger of this interpretation is that the rule of law might set too strict a requirement, one which no legal system can meet and which embodies very little virtue. It is humanly inconceivable that law can consist only of general rules and it is very undesirable that it should. Just as we need government both by laws and by men, so we need both general and particular laws to carry out the jobs for which we need the law.

The doctrine of the rule of law does not deny that every legal system should consist of both general, open, and stable rules (the popular conception of law) and particular laws (legal orders), an essential tool in the hands of the executive and the judiciary alike. As we shall see, what the doctrine requires is the subjection of particular laws to general, open, and stable ones. It is one of the important principles of the doctrine that *the making of particular laws should be guided by open and relatively stable general rules.*

This principle shows how the slogan of the rule of law and not of men can be read as a meaningful political ideal. The principle does not, however, exhaust the meaning of 'the rule of law' and does not by itself illuminate the reasons for its alleged importance. Let us, therefore, return to the literal sense of 'the rule of law'. It has two aspects: (1) that people should be ruled by the law and obey it, and (2) that the law should be such that people will be able to be guided by it. As was noted above, it is with the second aspect that we are concerned: the law must be capable of being obeyed. A person conforms with the law to the extent that he does not break the law. But he obeys the law only if part of his reason for conforming is his knowledge of the law. Therefore, if the law is to be obeyed it *must be capable of guiding the behaviour of its subjects.* It must be such that they can find out what it is and act on it.

This is the basic intuition from which the doctrine of the rule of law derives: the law must be capable of guiding the behaviour of its subjects. It is evident that this conception of the rule of law is a formal one. It says nothing about how the law is to be made: by tyrants, democratic majorities, or any other way. It says nothing

about fundamental rights, about equality, or justice. It may even be thought that this version of the doctrine is formal to the extent that it is almost devoid of content. This is far from the truth. Most of the requirements which were associated with the rule of law before it came to signify all the virtues of the state can be derived from this one basic idea.

2. Some principles

Many of the principles which can be derived from the basic idea of the rule of law depend for their validity or importance on the particular circumstances of different societies. There is little point in trying to enumerate them all, but some of the more important ones might be mentioned:

(1) *All laws should be prospective, open, and clear.* One cannot be guided by a retroactive law. It does not exist at the time of action. Sometimes it is then known for certain that a retroactive law will be enacted. When this happens retroactivity does not conflict with the rule of law (though it may be objected to on other grounds). The law must be open and adequately publicized. If it is to guide people they must be able to find out what it is. For the same reason its meaning must be clear. An ambiguous, vague, obscure, or imprecise law is likely to mislead or confuse at least some of those who desire to be guided by it.

(2) *Laws should be relatively stable.* They should not be changed too often. If they are frequently changed people will find it difficult to find out what the law is at any given moment and will be constantly in fear that the law has been changed since they last learnt what it was. But more important still is the fact that people need to know the law not only for short-term decisions (where to park one's car, how much alcohol is allowed duty free, etc.) but also for long-term planning. Knowledge of at least the general outlines and sometimes even of details of tax law and company law are often important for

business plans which will bear fruit only years later. Stability is essential if people are to be guided by law in their long-term decisions.[5]

Three important points are illustrated by this principle. First, conformity to the rule of law is often a matter of degree, not only when the conformity of the legal system as a whole is at stake, but also with respect to single laws. A law is either retroactive or not, but it can be more or less clear, more or less stable, etc. It should be remembered, however, that by asserting that conformity to the principles is a matter of degree, it is not meant that the degree of conformity can be quantitatively measured by counting the number of infringements, or some such method. Some infringements are worse than others. Some violate the principles in a formal way only, which does not offend against the spirit of the doctrine. Secondly, the principles of the rule of law affect primarily the content and form of the law (it should be prospective, clear, etc.) but not only them. They also affect the manner of government beyond what is or can usefully be prescribed by law. The requirement of stability cannot be usefully subject to complete legal regulation. It is largely a matter for wise governmental policy. Thirdly, though the rule of law concerns primarily private citizens as subject to duties and governmental agencies in the exercise of their powers (on which more below), it is also concerned with the exercise of private powers. Power-conferring rules are designed to guide behaviour and should conform to the doctrine of rule of law if they are to be capable of doing so effectively.

(3) *The making of particular laws (particular legal orders) should be guided by open, stable, clear, and general rules.* It is sometimes assumed that the requirement of generality is of the essence of the rule of law. This notion derives (as noted above) from the literal interpretation of 'the rule of law' when 'law' is read in its lay connotations as being restricted to general, stable, and open law. It is also reinforced by a belief that the rule of law is particularly relevant to the protection of equality and that equality is related to the generality of law. The last belief is, as has often been noted before, mistaken. Racial, religious, and all manner of discrimination are not only compatible but often institutionalized by general rules.

The formal conception of the rule of law which I am defending does not object to particular legal orders as long as they are stable, clear, etc. But of course particular legal orders are mostly used by government agencies to introduce flexibility into the law. A police constable regulating traffic, a licensing authority granting a licence under certain conditions, all these and their like are among the more ephemeral parts of the law. As such they run counter to the basic idea of the rule of law. They make it difficult for people to plan ahead on the basis of their knowledge of the law. This difficulty is overcome to a large extent if particular laws of an ephemeral status are enacted only within a framework set by general laws which are more durable and which impose limits on the unpredictability introduced by the particular orders.

Two kinds of general rules create the framework for the enactment of particular laws: those which confer the necessary powers for making valid orders and those which impose duties instructing the power-holders how to exercise their powers. Both have equal importance in creating a stable framework for the creation of particular legal orders.

Clearly, similar considerations apply to general legal regulations which do not meet the requirement of stability. They too should be circumscribed to conform to a stable framework. Hence the requirement that much of the subordinate administrative law-making should be made to conform to detailed ground rules laid down in framework laws. It is essential, however, not to confuse this argument with democratic arguments for the close supervision of popularly elected bodies over law-making by non-elected ones. These further arguments may be valid but have nothing to do with the rule of law, and though sometimes they reinforce rule of law type arguments, on other occasions they support different and even conflicting conclusions.

(4) *The independence of the judiciary must be guaranteed.* It is of the essence of municipal legal systems that they institute judicial bodies charged, among other things, with the duty of applying the law to cases brought before them and whose judgments and conclusions as to the legal merits of those cases are final. Since just about any matter arising under any law can be subject to a conclusive court judgment, it is obvious that it is futile to guide one's action on the basis of the law if when the matter comes to adjudication the courts will not apply the law and will act for some other reasons. The point can be put even more strongly. Since the court's judgment establishes conclusively what is the law in the case before it, the litigants can be guided by law only if the judges apply the law correctly.[6] Otherwise people will only be able to be guided by their guesses as to what the courts are likely to do—but these guesses will not be based on the law but on other considerations.

The rules concerning the independence of the judiciary—the method of appointing judges, their security of tenure, the way of fixing their salaries, and other conditions of service—are designed to guarantee that they will be free from extraneous pressures and independent of all authority save that of the law. They are, therefore, essential for the preservation of the rule of law.

(5) *The principles of natural justice must be observed.* Open and fair hearing, absence of bias, and the like are obviously essential for the correct application of the law and thus, through the very same considerations mentioned above, to its ability to guide action.

(6) *The courts should have review powers over the implementation of the other principles.* This includes review of both subordinate and parliamentary legislation and of administrative action, but in itself it is a very limited review—merely to ensure conformity to the rule of law.

(7) *The courts should be easily accessible.* Given the central position of the courts in ensuring the rule of law (see principles 4 and 6) it is obvious that their accessibility is of paramount importance. Long delays, excessive costs, etc., may effectively turn the most enlightened law to a dead letter and frustrate one's ability effectively to guide oneself by the law.

(8) *The discretion of the crime-preventing agencies should not be allowed to pervert the law.* Not only the courts but also the actions of the police and the prosecuting authorities can subvert the law. The prosecution should not be allowed, for example, to decide not to prosecute for commission of certain crimes, or for crimes committed by certain classes of offenders. The police should not be allowed to allocate its resources so as to avoid all effort to prevent and detect certain crimes or prosecute certain classes of criminals.

This list is very incomplete. Other principles could be mentioned and those which have been mentioned need further elaboration and further justification (why—as required by the sixth principle—should the courts and not some other body be in charge of reviewing conformity to the rule of law? etc.).[7] My purpose in listing them was merely to illustrate the power and fruitfulness of the formal conception of the rule of law. It should, however, be remembered that in the final analysis the doctrine rests on its basic idea that the law should be capable of providing effective guidance. The principles do not stand on their own. They must be constantly interpreted in the light of the basic idea.

The eight principles listed fall into two groups. Principles 1 to 3 require that the law should conform to standards designed to enable it effectively to guide action. Principles 4 to 8 are designed to ensure that the legal machinery of enforcing the law should not deprive it of its ability to guide through distorted enforcement and that it shall be capable of supervising conformity to the rule of law and provide effective remedies in cases of deviation from it. All the principles directly concern the system and method of government in matters directly relevant to the rule of law. Needless to say, many other aspects in the life of a community may, in more indirect ways, either strengthen or weaken the rule of law. A free press run by people anxious to defend the rule of law is of great assistance in preserving it, just as a gagged press or one run by people wishing to undermine the rule of law is a threat to it. But we need not be concerned here with these more indirect influences.

3. The value of the rule of law

One of the merits of the doctrine of the rule of law I am defending is that there are so many values it does not serve. Conformity to the rule of law is a virtue, but only one of the many virtues a legal system should possess. This makes it all the more important to be clear on the values which the rule of law does serve.

The rule of law is often rightly contrasted with arbitrary power. Arbitrary power is broader than the rule of law. Many forms of arbitrary rule are compatible with the rule of law. A ruler can promote general rules based on whim or self-interest, etc., without offending against the rule of law. But certainly many of the more common manifestations of arbitrary power run foul of the rule of law. A government subjected to the rule of law is prevented from changing the law retroactively or abruptly or secretly whenever this suits its purposes. The one area where the rule of law excludes all forms of arbitrary power is in the law-applying function of the judiciary where the courts are required to be subject only to the law and to conform to fairly strict procedures.[8] No less important is the restraint imposed by the rule of law on the making of particular laws and thus on the powers of the executive. The arbitrary use of power for personal gain, out of vengeance or favouritism, is most commonly manifested in the making of particular legal orders. These

possibilities are drastically restricted by close adherence to the rule of law.

'Arbitrary power' is a difficult notion. We have no cause to analyse it here. It seems, however, that an act which is the exercise of power is arbitrary only if it was done either with indifference as to whether it will serve the purposes which alone can justify use of that power or with belief that it will not serve them. The nature of the purposes alluded to varies with the nature of the power. This condition represents 'arbitrary power' as a subjective concept. It all depends on the state of mind of the men in power. As such the rule of law does not bear directly on the extent of arbitrary power. But around its subjective core the notion of arbitrary power has grown a hard objective edge. Since it is universally believed that it is wrong to use public powers for private ends any such use is in itself an instance of arbitrary use of power. As we have seen the rule of law does help to curb such forms of arbitrary power.

But there are more reasons for valuing the rule of law. We value the ability to choose styles and forms of life, to fix long-term goals and effectively direct one's life towards them. One's ability to do so depends on the existence of stable, secure frameworks for one's life and actions. The law can help to secure such fixed points of reference in two ways: (1) by stabilizing social relationships which but for the law may disintegrate or develop in erratic and unpredictable ways; (2) by a policy of self-restraint designed to make the law itself a stable and safe basis for individual planning. This last aspect is the concern of the rule of law.

This second virtue of the rule of law is often, notably by Hayek, identified as the protection of individual freedom. This is right in the sense of freedom in which it is identified with an effective ability to choose between as many options as possible. Predictability in one's environment does increase one's power of action.[9] If this is freedom well and good. The important thing is to remember that this sense of freedom differs from what is commonly meant by political freedom. Political freedom consists of: (1) the prohibition of certain forms of behaviour which interfere with personal freedom and (2) the limits imposed on the powers of public authorities in order to minimize interference with personal freedom. The criminal offences against the person are an example of the first mode of protecting personal freedom, the disability of the government to restrict freedom of movement—an example of the second. It is in connection with political freedom in this sense that constitutionally guaranteed rights are of great importance. The rule of law may be yet another mode of protecting personal freedom. But it has no bearing on the existence of spheres of activity free from governmental interference and is compatible with gross violations of human rights.

More important than both these considerations is the fact that observance of the rule of law is necessary if the law is to respect human dignity. Respecting human dignity entails treating humans as persons capable of planning and plotting their future. Thus, respecting people's dignity includes respecting their autonomy, their right to control their future. A person's control over his life is never complete. It can be incomplete in any one of several respects. The person may be ignorant of his options, unable to decide what to do, incapable of realizing his choices or frustrated in his attempts to do so, or he may have no choice at all (or at least none which is worth having). All these failures can occur through natural causes or through the limitations of the person's own character and abilities.

Naturally, there are many ways in which one person's action may affect the life of another. Only some such interferences will amount to an offence to the dignity or a violation of the autonomy of the person thus affected. Such offences can be divided into three classes: insults, enslavement, and manipulation. (I am using the last two terms in a somewhat special sense.) An insult offends a person's dignity if it consists of or implies a denial that he is an autonomous person or that he deserves to be treated as one. An action enslaves another if it practically denies him all options through the manipulation of the environment. (Though it may be for a length of time—as in real slavery—I mean to include here also coercing another to act in a certain way on a single occasion.) One manipulates a person by intentionally changing his tastes, his beliefs or his ability to act or decide. Manipulation—in other words—is manipulation of the person, of those factors relevant to his autonomy which are internal to him. Enslavement is the elimination of control by changing factors external to the person.

The law can violate people's dignity in many ways. Observing the rule of law by no means guarantees that such violations do not occur. But it is clear that deliberate disregard for the rule of law violates human dignity. It is the business of law to guide human action by affecting people's options. The law may, for example, institute slavery without violating the rule of law. But deliberate violation of the rule of law violates human dignity. The violation of the rule of law can take two forms. It may lead to uncertainty or it may lead to frustrated and disappointed expectations. It leads to the first when the law does not enable people to foresee future developments or to form definite expectations (as in cases of vagueness and most cases of wide discretion). It leads to frustrated expectations when the appearance of stability and certainty which encourages people to rely and plan on the basis of the existing law is shattered by retroactive law-making or by preventing proper law-enforcement, etc. The evils of uncertainty are in providing opportunities for arbitrary power and restricting people's ability to plan for their future. The evils of frustrated expectations are greater. Quite apart from the concrete harm they cause they also offend dignity in expressing disrespect for people's autonomy. The law in such cases encourages autonomous action only in order to frustrate its purpose. When such frustration is the result of human action or the result of the activities of social institutions then it expresses disrespect. Often it is analogous to entrapment: one is encouraged innocently to rely on the law and then that assurance is withdrawn and one's very reliance is turned into a cause of harm to one. A legal system which does in general observe the rule of law treats people as persons at least in the sense that it attempts to guide their behaviour through affecting the circumstances of their action. It thus presupposes that they are rational autonomous creatures and attempts to affect their actions and habits by affecting their deliberations.

Conformity to the rule of law is a matter of degree. Complete conformity is impossible (some vagueness is inescapable) and maximal possible conformity is on the whole undesirable (some controlled administrative discretion is better than none). It is generally agreed that general conformity to the rule of law is to be highly cherished. But one should not take the value of the rule of law on trust nor assert it blindly. Disentangling the various values served by the rule of law helps to assess intelligently what is at stake in various possible or actual violations. Some cases insult human dignity, give free rein to arbitrary power, frustrate one's expectations, and undermine one's ability to plan. Others involve only some of these evils. The evil of different violations of the rule of law is not always the same despite the fact that the doctrine rests on the solid core of its basic idea.

4. The rule of law and its essence

Lon Fuller[10] has claimed that the principles of the rule of law which he enumerated are essential for the existence of law. This claim if true is crucial to our understanding not only of the rule of law but also of the relation of law and morality. I have been treating the rule of law as an ideal, as a standard to which the law ought to conform but which it can and sometimes does

violate most radically and systematically. Fuller, while allowing that deviations from the ideal of the rule of law can occur, denies that they can be radical or total. A legal system must of necessity conform to the rule of law to a certain degree, he claims. From this claim he concludes that there is an essential link between law and morality. Law is necessarily moral, at least in some respects.

It is, of course, true that most of the principles enumerated in section 2 above cannot be violated altogether by any legal system.[11] Legal systems are based on judicial institutions. There cannot be institutions of any kind unless there are general rules setting them up. A particular norm can authorize adjudication in a particular dispute, but no number of particular norms can set up an institution. Similarly retroactive laws can exist only because there are institutions enforcing them. This entails that there must be prospective laws instructing those institutions to apply the retroactive laws if the retroactive laws are to be valid. In the terminology of H. L. A. Hart's theory one can say that at least some of the rules of recognition and of adjudication of every system must be general and prospective. Naturally they must also be relatively clear if they are to make any sense at all, etc.

Clearly, the extent to which generality, clarity, prospectivity, etc., are essential to the law is minimal and is consistent with gross violations of the rule of law. But are not considerations of the kind mentioned sufficient to establish that there is necessarily at least some moral value in every legal system? I think not. The rule of law is essentially a negative value. The law inevitably creates a great danger of arbitrary power—the rule of law is designed to minimize the danger created by the law itself. Similarly, the law may be unstable, obscure, retrospective, etc., and thus infringe people's freedom and dignity. The rule of law is designed to prevent this danger as well. Thus the rule of law is a negative virtue in two senses: conformity to it does not cause good except through avoiding evil and the evil which is avoided is evil which could only have been caused by the law itself. It is thus somewhat analogous to honesty when this virtue is narrowly interpreted as the avoidance of deceit. (I do not deny that honesty is normally conceived more broadly to incorporate other virtuous acts and inclinations.) The good of honesty does not include the good of communication between people, for honesty is consistent with a refusal to communicate. Its good is exclusively in the avoidance of the harm of deceit—and not deceit by others but by the honest person himself. Therefore, only a person who can deceive can be honest. A person who cannot communicate cannot claim any moral merit for being honest. A person who through ignorance or inability cannot kill another by poison deserves no credit for it. Similarly, that the law cannot sanction arbitrary force or violations of freedom and dignity through total absence of generality, prospectivity, or clarity is no moral credit to the law. It only means that there are some kinds of evil which cannot be brought about by the law. But this is no virtue in the law just as it is no virtue in the law that it cannot rape or murder (all it can do is sanction such actions).

Fuller's attempt to establish a necessary connection between law and morality fails. In so far as conformity to the rule of law is a moral virtue it is an ideal which should but may fail to become a reality. There is another argument, however, which establishes an essential connection between the law and the rule of law, though it does not guarantee any virtue to the law. Conformity to the rule of law is essential for securing whatever purposes the law is designed to achieve. This statement should be qualified. We could divide the purposes a law is intended to serve into two kinds: those which are secured by conformity with the law in itself and those further consequences of conformity with the law or of knowledge of its existence which the law is intended to secure.[12] Thus a law prohibiting racial discrimination in government employment has as its direct purpose the establishment of racial equality in the hiring, promotion, and conditions of service of government employees (since discriminatory action is a breach of law). Its indirect purposes may well be to improve race relations in the country in general, prevent a threat of a strike by some trade unions, or halt the decline in popularity of the government.

Conformity to the rule of law does not always facilitate realization of the indirect purposes of the law, but it is essential to the realization of its direct purposes. These are achieved by conformity with the law which is secured (unless accidentally) by people taking note of the law and guiding themselves accordingly. Therefore, if the direct purposes of the law are not to be frustrated it must be capable of guiding human behaviour, and the more it conforms to the principles of the rule of law the better it can do so.

In section 2 we saw that conformity to the rule of law is one among many moral virtues which the law should possess. The present consideration shows that the rule of law is not merely a moral virtue—it is a necessary condition for the law to be serving directly any good purpose at all. Of course, conformity to the rule of law also enables the law to serve bad purposes. That does not show that it is not a virtue, just as the fact that a sharp knife can be used to harm does not show that being sharp is not a good-making characteristic for knives. At most it shows that from the point of view of the present consideration it is not a moral good. Being sharp is an inherent good-making characteristic of knives. A good knife is, among other things, a sharp knife. Similarly, conformity to the rule of law is an inherent value of laws, indeed it is their most important inherent value. It is of the essence of law to guide behaviour through rules and courts in charge of their application. Therefore, the rule of law is the specific excellence of the law. Since conformity to the rule of law is the virtue of law in itself, law as law regardless of the purposes it serves, it is understandable and right that the rule of law is thought of as among the few virtues of law which are the special responsibility of the courts and the legal profession.

Regarding the rule of law as the inherent or specific virtue of law is a result of an instrumental conception of law. The law is not just a fact of life. It is a form of social organization which should be used properly and for the proper ends. It is a tool in the hands of men differing from many others in being versatile and capable of being used for a large variety of proper purposes. As with some other tools, machines, and instruments a thing is not of the kind unless it has at least some ability to perform its function. A knife is not a knife unless it has some ability to cut. The law to be law must be capable of guiding behaviour, however inefficiently. Like other instruments, the law has a specific virtue which is morally neutral in being neutral as to the end to which the instrument is put. It is the virtue of efficiency; the virtue of the instrument as an instrument. For the law this virtue is the rule of law. Thus the rule of law is an inherent virtue of the law, but not a moral virtue as such.

The special status of the rule of law does not mean that conformity with it is of no moral importance. Quite apart from the fact that conformity to the rule of law is also a moral virtue, it is a moral requirement when necessary to enable the law to perform useful social functions; just as it may be of moral importance to produce a sharp knife when it is required for a moral purpose. In the case of the rule of law this means that it is virtually always of great moral value.

5. Some pitfalls

The undoubted value of conformity to the rule of law should not lead one to exaggerate its importance. We saw how Hayek noted correctly its relevance for the protection of freedom. We also saw that the rule of law itself does not provide sufficient protection of freedom. Consider, however, Hayek's position. He begins with a grand statement which inevitably leads to exaggerated expectations:

> The conception of freedom under the law that is the chief concern of this book rests on the contention that when we obey laws, in the sense of general abstract rules laid down irrespective of their application to us we are not subject to another man's will and are therefore free. It is because the lawgiver does not know the particular cases to which his rules will apply, and it is because the judge who applies them has no choice in drawing the conclusions that follow from the existing body of rules and the particular facts of the case, that it can be said that laws and not men rule. . . . As a true law should not name any particulars, so it should especially not single out any specific persons or group of persons.[13]

Then, aware of the absurdity to which this passage leads, he modifies his line, still trying to present the rule of law as the supreme guarantor of freedom:

> The requirement that the rules of true law be general does not mean that sometimes special rules may not apply to different classes of people if they refer to properties that only some people possess. There may be rules that can apply only to women or to the blind or to persons above a certain age. (In most instances it would not even be necessary to name the class of people to whom the rule applies: only a woman, for example, can be raped or got with child.) Such distinctions will not be arbitrary, will not subject one group to the will of others, if they are equally recognized as justified by those inside and those outside the group. This does not mean that there must be unanimity as to the desirability of the distinction, but merely that individual views will not depend on whether the individual is in the group or not.[14]

But here the rule of law is transformed to encompass a form of government by consent and it is this which is alleged to guarantee freedom. This is the slippery slope leading to the identification of the rule of law with the rule of the good law.

Hayek's main objection is to governmental interference with the economy:

We must now turn to the kinds of governmental measures which the rule of law excludes in principle because they cannot be achieved by merely enforcing general rules but, of necessity, involve arbitrary discrimination between persons. The most important among them are decisions as to who is to be allowed to provide different services or commodities, at what prices or in what quantities—in other words, measures designed to control the access to different trades and occupations, the terms of sale, and the amounts to be produced or sold.

There are several reasons why all direct control of prices by government is irreconcilable with a functioning free system, whether the government actually fixes prices or merely lays down rules by which the permissible prices are to be determined. In the first place, it is impossible to fix prices according to long-term rules which will effectively guide production. Appropriate prices depend on circumstances which are constantly changing and must be continually adjusted to them. On the other hand, prices which are not fixed outright but determined by some rule (such as that they must be in a certain relation to cost) will not be the same for all sellers and, for this reason, will prevent the market from functioning. A still more important consideration is that, with prices different from those that would form on a free market, demand and supply will not be equal, and if the price control is to be effective, some method must be found for deciding who is to be allowed to buy or sell. This would necessarily be dis-

cretionary and must consist of *ad hoc* decisions that discriminate between persons on essentially arbitrary grounds.[15]

Here again it is clear that arguments which at best show that certain policies are wrong for economic reasons are claimed to show that they infringe the rule of law and the making of supposedly misguided but perfectly principled particular orders is condemned as an arbitrary exercise of power.

Since the rule of law is just one of the virtues the law should possess, it is to be expected that it possesses no more than prima facie force. It has always to be balanced against competing claims of other values. Hence Hayek's arguments, to the extent that they show no more than that some other goals inevitably conflict with the rule of law, are not the sort of arguments which could, in principle, show that pursuit of such goals by means of law is inappropriate. Conflict between the rule of law and other values is just what is to be expected. Conformity to the rule of law is a matter of degree, and though, other things being equal, the greater the conformity the better— other things are rarely equal. A lesser degree of conformity is often to be preferred precisely because it helps realization of other goals.

In considering the relation between the rule of law and other values the law should serve, it is of particular importance to remember that the rule of law is essentially a negative value. It is merely designed to minimize the harm to freedom and dignity which the law may cause in its pursuit of its goals however laudable these may be. Finally, regarding the rule of law as the inherent excellence of the law means that it fulfills essentially a subservient role. Conformity to it makes the law a good instrument for achieving certain goals, but conformity to the rule of law is not itself an ultimate goal. This subservient role of the doctrine shows both its power and its limitations. On the one hand, if the pursuit of certain goals is entirely incompatible with the rule of law, then these goals should not be pursued by legal means. But on the other hand one should be wary of disqualifying the legal pursuit of major social goals in the name of the rule of law. After all, the rule of law is meant to enable the law to promote social good, and should not be lightly used to show that it should not do so. Sacrificing too many social goals on the altar of the rule of law may make the law barren and empty.

Notes

Joseph Raz, *The Authority of Law* (Oxford 1979), pp. 210–29

1 *The Road to Serfdom* (London, 1944), p. 54.

2 Clause 1 of the report of Committee I of the International Congress of Jurists at New Delhi, 1959.

3 Cf., on this sense of the phrase, Jennings, *The Law and the Constitution* (London, 1933), pp. 42–5.

4 I am here following Hart, *The Concept of Law* (Oxford, 1961), pp. 97–107.

5 Of course, uncertainty generated by instability of law also affects people's planning and action. If it did not, stability would not have any impact either. The point is that only if the law is stable are people guided by their knowledge of the context of the law.

6 I am not denying that courts also make law. This principle of the rule of law applies to them primarily in their duty to apply the law. As law-makers they are subject to the same principles as all law-makers.

7 Similar lists of principles have been discussed by various authors. English writers have been mesmerized by Dicey's unfortunate doctrine for too long. For a list similar to mine see Lon Fuller's *The Morality of Law*, 2nd ed., ch. 2. His discussion of many of the principles is full of good sense. My main reason for abandoning some of his principles is a difference of views on conflicts between the laws of one system.

8 The rule of law itself does not exclude all the possibilities of arbitrary law-making by the courts.

9 But then welfare law and governmental manipulation of the economy also increase freedom by increasing—if successful—people's welfare. If the rule of law is defended as the bulwark of freedom in this sense, it can hardly be used to oppose in principle governmental management of the economy.

10 In *The Morality of Law*, 2nd ed. (Yale, 1969), Fuller's argument is complex and his claims are numerous and hard to disentangle. Many of his claims are weak and unsupportable. Others are suggestive and useful. It is not my purpose to analyse or evaluate them. For a sympathetic discussion see R. E. Sartorius, *Individual Conduct and Social Norms* (Encino, California, 1975), ch. 9.

11 I am not adopting here Fuller's conception of the law, but rather I am following my own adaptation of Hart's conception. Cf. Hart's *The Concept of Law* and my *Practical Reason and Norms* (1975), pp. 132–54. Therefore, the discussion which follows is not a direct assessment of Fuller's own claims.

12 See further on this distinction Essay 9 [in the original] above.

13 F. A. Hayek, *The Constitution of Liberty* (Chicago, 1960), pp. 153–4.

14 Ibid., p. 154.

15 F. A. Hayek, *The Constitution of Liberty*, pp. 227–8.

Chapter 11

Ronald Dworkin

POLITICAL JUDGES AND THE RULE OF LAW

Two questions and two ideals

THIS ESSAY IS ABOUT two questions, and the connections between them. The first is a practical question about how judges do and should decide hard cases. Do judges in the United States and Great Britain make political decisions? Should their decisions be political? Of course the decisions that judges make must be political in one sense. In many cases a judge's decision will be approved by one political group and disliked by others, because these cases have consequences for political controversies. In the United States, for example, the Supreme Court must decide important constitutional issues that are also political issues, like the issue whether accused criminals have procedural rights that make law enforcement more difficult. In Britain the courts must decide cases that demand an interpretation of labor legislation, like cases about the legality of secondary picketing, when the Trades Union Congress favors one interpretation and the Confederation of British Industries another. I want to ask, however, whether judges should decide cases on political *grounds*, so that the decision is not only the decision that certain political groups would wish, but is taken on the ground that certain principles of political morality are right. A judge who decides on political grounds is not deciding on grounds of party politics. He does not decide in favor of the interpretation sought by the unions because he is

(or was) a member of the Labour party, for example. But the political principles in which he believes, like, for example, the belief that equality is an important political aim, may be more characteristic of some political parties than others.

There is a conventional answer to my question, at least in Britain. Judges should not reach their decisions on political grounds. That is the view of almost all judges and barristers and solicitors and academic lawyers. Some academic lawyers, however, who count themselves critics of British judicial practice, say that British judges actually do make political decisions, in spite of the established view that they should not. J. A. G. Griffiths of the London School of Economics, for example, in a polemical book called *The Politics of the Judiciary*, argued that several recent decisions of the House of Lords were political decisions, even though that court was at pains to make it appear that the decisions were reached on technical legal rather than political grounds.[1] It will be helpful briefly to describe some of these decisions.

In *Charter*[2] and *Dockers*[3] the House of Lords interpreted the Race Relations Act so that political clubs, like the West Ham Conservative Club, were not obliged by the Act not to discriminate against coloured people. In *Tameside* the House overruled a Labour minister's order reversing a local Conservative council's decision not to change its school system to the comprehensive plan favored by the Labour government.[4] In the notorious *Shaw's Case*, the House of Lords sustained the conviction of the publisher of a directory of prostitutes.[5] It held that he was guilty of what it called the common law crime of "conspiracy to corrupt public morals," even though it conceded that no statute declared such a conspiracy to be a crime. In an older case, *Liversidge v. Anderson*, the House upheld the decision of a minister who, in the Second World War, ordered someone detained without trial.[6] Griffiths believes that in each of these cases (and in a great many other cases he discusses) the House acted out of a particular political attitude, which is defensive of established values or social structures and opposed to reform. He does not say that the judges who took these decisions were aware that, contrary to the official view of their function, they were enforcing a political position. But he believes that that was nevertheless what they were doing.

So there are those who think that British judges do make political decisions. But that is not to say that they should. Griffiths thinks it inevitable, as I understand him, that the judiciary will play a political role in a capitalist or semi-capitalist state. But he does not count this as a virtue of capitalism; on the contrary, he treats the political role of judges as deplorable. It may be that some few judges and academics—including perhaps Lord Justice Denning—do think that judges ought to be more political than the conventional view recommends. But that remains very much an eccentric—some would say dangerous—minority view.

Professional opinion about the political role of judges is more divided in the United States. A great party of academic lawyers and law students, and even some of the judges in the prestigious courts, hold that judicial decisions are inescapably and rightly political. They have in mind not only the grand constitutional decisions of the Supreme Court but also the more ordinary civil decisions of state courts developing the common law of contracts and tort and com-mercial law. They think that judges do and should act like legislators, though only within what they call the "interstices" of decisions already made by the legislature. That is not a unanimous view even among sophisticated American lawyers, nor is it a view that the public at large has fully accepted. On the contrary, politicians sometimes campaign for office promising to curb judges who have wrongly seized political power. But a much greater part of the public accepts political jurisprudence now than did, say, twenty-five years ago.

My own view is that the vocabulary of this debate about judicial politics is too crude, and that both the official British view and the "progressive" American view are mistaken. The debate neglects an important distinction between two kinds of political arguments on which judges might rely in reaching their decisions. This is the distinction (which I have tried to explain and defend elsewhere) between arguments of political principle that appeal to the political rights of individual citizens, and arguments of political policy that claim that a particular decision will work to promote some conception of the general welfare or public interest.[7] The correct view, I believe, is that judges do and should rest their judgments on controversial cases on arguments of political principle, but not on arguments of political policy. My view is therefore more restrictive than the progressive American view but less restrictive than the official British one.

The second question I put in this essay is, at least at first sight, less practical. What is the rule of law? Lawyers (and almost everyone else) think that there is a distinct and important political ideal called the rule of law. But they disagree about what that ideal is. There are, in fact, two very different conceptions of the rule of law, each of which has its partisans. The first I shall call the "rule-book" conception. It insists that, so far as is possible, the power of the state should never be exercised against individual citizens except in accordance with rules explicitly set out in a public rule book available to all. The government as well as ordinary citizens must play by these public rules until they are changed, in accordance with further rules about how they are to be changed, which are also set out in the rule book. The rule-book conception is, in one sense, very narrow, because it does not stipulate anything about the content of the rules that may be put in the rule book. It insists only that whatever rules are put in the book must be followed until changed. Those who have this conception of the rule of law do care about the content of the rules in the rule book, but they say that this is a matter of substantive justice, and that substantive justice is an independent ideal, in no sense part of the ideal of the rule of law.

I shall call the second conception of the rule of law the "rights" conception. It is in several ways more ambitious than the rule-book conception. It assumes that citizens have moral rights and duties with respect to one another, and political rights against the state as a whole. It insists that these moral and political rights be recognized in positive law, so that they may be enforced *upon the demand of individual citizens* through courts or other judicial institutions of the familiar type, so far as this is practicable. The rule of law on this conception is the ideal of rule by an accurate public conception of individual rights. It does not distinguish, as the rule-book conception does, between the rule of law and substantive justice; on the contrary it requires, as part of the ideal of law, that the rules in the rule book capture and enforce moral rights.

That is a complex ideal. The rule-book conception of the rule of law has only one dimension along which a political community might fall short. It might use its police power over individual citizens otherwise than as the rule book specifies. But the rights conception has at least three dimensions of failure. A state might fail in the *scope* of the individual rights it purports to enforce. It might decline to enforce rights against itself, for example, though it concedes citizens have such rights. It might fail in the

accuracy of the rights it recognizes: it might provide for rights against the state, but through official mistake fail to recognize important rights. Or it might fail in the *fairness* of its enforcement of rights: it might adopt rules that put the poor or some disfavored race at a disadvantage in securing the rights the state acknowledges they have.

The rights conception is therefore more complex than the rule-book conception. There are other important contrasts between the two conceptions; some of these can be identified by considering the different places they occupy in a general theory of justice. Though the two conceptions compete as ideals of the legal process (because, as we shall see, they recommend different theories of adjudication), they are nevertheless compatible as more general ideals for a just society. Any political community is better, all else equal, if its courts take no action other than is specified in rules published in advance, and also better, all else equal, if its legal institutions enforce whatever rights individual citizens have. Even as general political ideals, however, the two conceptions differ in the following way. Some high degree of compliance with the rule-book conception seems necessary to a just society. Any government that acts contrary to its own rule book very often—at least in matters important to particular citizens—cannot be just, no matter how wise or fair its institutions otherwise are. But compliance with the rule book is plainly not sufficient for justice; full compliance will achieve very great injustice if the rules are unjust. The opposite holds for the rights conception. A society that achieves a high rating on each of the dimensions of the rights conception is almost certainly a just society, even though it may be mismanaged or lack other qualities of a desirable society. But it is widely thought, at least, that the rights conception is not necessary to a just society, because it is not necessary, in order that the rights of citizens be protected, that citizens be able to demand adjudication and enforcement of these rights as individuals. A government of wise and just officers will protect rights (so the argument runs) on its own initiative, without procedure whereby citizens can dispute, as individuals, what these rights are. Indeed, the rights conception of the rule of law, which insists on the importance of that opportunity, is often dismissed as legalistic, as encouraging a mean and selfish concern with individual property and title.

The two conceptions also differ in what might be called their philosophical neutrality. The rights conception seems more vulnerable to philosophical objections. It supposes that citizens have moral rights—that is, rights other than and prior to those given by positive enactment—so that a society can sensibly be criticized on the ground that its enactments do not recognize the rights people have. But many philosophers doubt that people have any rights that are not bestowed on them by enactments or other official decisions; or even that the idea of such rights makes sense. They doubt particularly that it is sensible to say that people have moral rights when (as the rights conception must concede is often the case) it is controversial within the community what moral rights they have. The rights conception must suppose, that is, that a state may fail along the dimension of accuracy even when it is controversial whether it has failed; but that is just what philosophers doubt makes sense. The rights conception therefore seems open to the objection that it presupposes a philosophical point of view that is itself controversial, and which will therefore not be accepted by all members of the community.

The last contrast I shall mention will join the two issues of this essay. For the two conceptions of the rule of law offer very different advice on the question of whether judges should make political decisions in hard cases—that is, cases in which no explicit rule in the rule book firmly decides the case either way. Though the two conceptions, as general political ideals, may both have a place in a full political theory, it makes a great difference which is taken to be the ideal

of law because it is that ideal which governs our attitudes about adjudication. The rule-book conception has both negative and positive advice about hard cases. It argues, positively, that judges should decide hard cases by trying to discover what is "really" in the rule book, in one or another sense of that claim. It argues, negatively, that judges should never decide such cases on the ground of their own political judgment, because a political decision is not a decision about what is, in any sense, in the rule book, but rather a decision about what ought to be there. The rule-book conception supports the conventional British view about political judges.

I must now pause to explain the idea this positive advice uses: the idea that it makes sense to ask, in a hard case, about what is "really" in the rule book. In a modern legal system hard cases typically arise, not because there is nothing in the rule book that bears on the dispute, but because the rules that are in the book speak in an uncertain voice. *Charter*, for example, was a hard case because it was unclear whether the rule Parliament put in the rule book—the rule that organizations that serve "a section of the public" must not discriminate—forbade a political club to deny membership to blacks. It is, in that sense, "unclear" what the rule book really, properly understood, provides. A lawyer who speaks this way treats the rule book as an attempt at communication and supposes that an unclear rule can be better understood by applying techniques that we use to improve our understanding of other sorts of communication.

Different generations of rule-book lawyers—and different lawyers within each generation—advocate different techniques for this purpose. Some prefer semantic questions. They argue in the following way. "The legislature uses words when it enacts a rule, and the meaning of these words fix what rules it has enacted. So any theory about the meaning of the phrase 'a section of the public' is a theory that makes the Race Relations Act more precise. The rule-book conception therefore directs judges to try to form semantic theories. They should ask, for example, what the phrase 'a section of the public' would be taken to mean in a similar context in ordinary discourse. Or what the most natural meaning of some component of the phrase, like the word 'public,' is. Or what similar phrases were taken to mean in other statutes. It is understood that different judges will give different answers to these semantic questions; no one answer will be so plainly right that everyone will agree. Nevertheless each judge will be trying, in good faith, to follow the rule-book ideal of the rule of law, because he will be trying, in good faith, to discover what the words in the rule book really mean."

These semantic questions are very popular in Britain. A different set of questions—group-psychological questions—are now more popular in the United States. Those who favor group-psychological questions rather than semantic questions take decisions rather than words to be the heart of the matter. "Why are the particular rules that a legislature enacts (rather than, for example, the rules that law professors prefer) the rules that form the rule book for law? Because legislators have been given authority by the community as a whole to *decide* what rules shall govern. The words they choose are normally the best evidence of what they have decided, because it is assumed that legislators use words in their standard meanings to report their decisions. But if, for some reason, the words used do not uniquely report a particular decision, then it is necessary to turn to whatever other evidence of what they intended to do we can find. Did the legislators—or some important group of them—suppose that their Race Relations Act would apply to political clubs so as to forbid racial discrimination there? If so, then the Act represents that decision, and it is that decision that is embedded in the rule book properly understood. But if they supposed that the Act would not apply to political clubs, then the rule book, properly understood, contains that decision instead."

Once again there is no assumption here that all reasonable lawyers will agree about what the legislators intended. On the contrary, defenders of the rule-book model know that even skilled lawyers will disagree over inferences of legislative intention drawn from the same evidence. They insist that the question of intention is nevertheless the right question to ask, because each judge who asks it is at least doing his best to follow the rule-book model and therefore (on this conception) to serve the rule of law.

The semantic and psychological questions these different groups propose are historical rather than political. A third (and more sophisticated) set of historical questions has recently gained in popularity. "Suppose a hard case cannot be decided on semantic grounds. Perhaps the phrase 'a section of the public' might just as properly be used to include as to exclude associations like political clubs. Suppose it cannot be decided by asking what the legislators who enacted that statute intended to accomplish. Perhaps very few legislators had even thought of the question whether political clubs should be included. We must then ask a question different from either the semantic or the psychological question, which is this. What would the legislature have decided if, contrary to fact, it *had* decided whether or not political clubs were to be included?" Lawyers who want to answer this counterfactual question might consider, for example, other decisions the same legislators reached in other areas of law. Or they might consider more broadly the pattern of legislation about race relations or freedom of association in recent years. They might use such evidence to argue, for example, that if Parliament had for some reason been forced to debate a clause explicitly extending the acts to political clubs, it would have approved that clause.

It is even more obvious in the case of this counterfactual historical question than in the case of the semantic or psychological question that reasonable lawyers will disagree about the conclusions to be drawn from the same evidence. But once again the rule-book conception deems it better that they try to answer this question, even though they disagree, than that they ask the different and political question, about which they will surely disagree, of what Parliament *should* have done. For the counterfactual question, like the semantic and psychological questions but unlike the political question, is supported by a theory that also supports and explains the rule-book conception itself. We follow the rule book, on this theory, because we assign to a political institution the responsibility and the power to decide how the police power of the state shall be used. If, on some occasion, that institution has in fact not decided that question (because it did not realize that a decision was necessary) but would have decided one way rather than the other if it had, then it is more in keeping with the rationale of the rule book that the power be used that way than the contrary way. If neither of the two decisions that a court might reach is actually recorded in the rule book, it is fairer, on this argument, to take the decision that would have been in the rule book but for a historical accident.

This argument for the counterfactual question concedes that the rule that is to be applied is not in the actual rule book. In this respect the counterfactual question is different from the semantic and psychological questions, each of which can more plausibly be said to reveal what is in the actual rule book "properly understood." But the three sorts of questions have a more fundamental unity. Each aims at developing what might be called a "rectified" rule book in which the collection of sentences is improved so as more faithfully to record the will of the various institutions whose decisions put those sentences into the rule book. The questions are all, in themselves, politically neutral questions, because they seek to bring to the surface a historical fact—the will of responsible lawmakers—rather than to impose a distinct and contemporary political judgment upon that will. It is

perfectly true—and conceded, as I said, by the rule-book model—that any particular judge's answer to these politically neutral questions may well be different from another judge's answer. It is the virtue of the different historical questions, not the certainty or predictability of the answer, that recommends these questions to the rule-book model. That conception of the rule of law opposes political questions, like the question of what the legislators should have done, not because these questions admit of different answers, but because they are simply the wrong questions to ask.

The rights conception, on the other hand, will insist that at least one kind of political question is precisely the question that judges faced with hard cases must ask. For the ultimate question it asks in a hard case is the question of whether the plaintiff has the moral right to receive, in court, what he or she or it demands. The rule book is *relevant* to that ultimate question. In a democracy, people have at least a strong *prima facie* moral right that courts enforce the rights that a representative legislature has enacted. That is why some cases are easy cases on the rights model as well as on the rule-book model. If it is clear what the legislature has granted them, then it is also clear what they have a moral right to receive in court. (That statement must be qualified in a democracy whose constitution limits legislative power. It must also be qualified (though it is a complex question how it must be qualified) in a democracy whose laws are fundamentally unjust.

But though the rights model concedes that the rule book is in this way a source of moral rights in court, it denies that the rule book is the exclusive source of such rights. If, therefore, some case arises as to which the rule book is silent, or if the words in the rule book are subject to competing interpretations, then it is right to ask which of the two possible decisions in the case best fits the background moral rights of the parties. For the ideal of adjudication, under the rights model, is that, so far as is practicable, the moral rights that citizens actually have should be available to them in court. So a decision that takes background rights into account will be superior, from the point of view of that ideal, to a decision that instead speculates on, for example, what the legislation would have done if it had done anything.

It is important to notice, however, that the rule book continues to exert an influence on the question of what rights the parties have, under the rights model, even when background moral rights also exert an influence.[8] A judge who follows the rights conception of the rule of law will try, in a hard case, to frame some principle that strikes him as capturing, at the appropriate level of abstraction, the moral rights of the parties that are pertinent to the issues raised by the case. But he cannot apply such a principle unless it is, as a principle, consistent with the rule book, in the following sense. The principle must not conflict with other principles that must be presupposed in order to justify the rule he is enforcing, or any considerable part of the other rules. Suppose a judge himself approves what might be called a radical Christian principle: that each citizen is morally entitled that those who have more wealth than he does make available to him the surplus. He might wish to apply that principle to hard cases in tort or contract so as to refuse damages against a poor defendant, on the ground that the richer plaintiff's right to damages must be set off against the defendant's right to charity. But he cannot do so, because (for better or for worse) that principle is inconsistent with the vast bulk of the rules in the rule book. No adequate justification of what is in the rule book could be given, that is, without presupposing that the radical Christian principle has been rejected. The rights conception supposes that the rule book represents the community's efforts to capture moral rights and requires that any principle rejected in those efforts has no role in adjudication.

So a judge following the rights conception must not decide a hard case by appealing to any

principle that is in that way incompatible with the rule book of his jurisdiction. But he must still decide many cases on political grounds, because in these cases contrary moral principles directly in point are each compatible with the rule book. Two judges will decide such a hard case differently because they hold different views about the background moral rights of citizens. Suppose a case applying a commercial statute requires a choice between a moral principle enforcing *caveat emptor* and a competing principle stressing the moral rights of contractual partners against each other, as members of a cooperative enterprise. It may well be—at a given stage of development of commercial law—that neither answer is in the sense described plainly incompatible with the British rule book taken as a whole. Each judge deciding that issue of principle decides as he does, not because all alternatives are excluded by what is already in the rule book, but because he believes his principle to be correct, or at least closer to correct than other principles that are also not excluded. So his decision is a political decision in the sense described. It is precisely that sort of political decision that the rule-book conception steadily condemns.

The two topics of this essay are in that way joined. The practical question, which asks whether judges should make political decisions in hard cases, is joined to the theoretical question of which of two conceptions of the rule of law is superior. The connection is threatening to the rights conception, because many people are convinced that it is wrong for judges to make political decisions and they will be anxious to reject any theory about the ideals of law that recommends them. So I shall pursue the two topics, now joined, by asking whether the conviction that judges should stay out of politics is sound.

The argument from democracy

Why is it wrong for judges to make political decisions of the sort I say the rights conception requires them to make? One argument will seem to many of you decisive against judicial political decisions. Political decisions, according to this argument, should be made by officials elected by the community as a whole, who can be replaced from time to time in the same way. That principle applies to all political decisions, including the decision what rights individuals have, and which of these should be enforceable in court. Judges are not elected or reelected, and that is wise because the decisions they make *applying* the rule book as it stands to particular cases are decisions that should be immune from popular control. But it follows that they should not make independent decisions about changing or expanding the rule book, because these decisions should be made in no way *other* than under popular control.

That is the familiar argument from democracy. There is a short answer to that argument, at least in Britain. If Parliament, which is elected by the people, is dissatisfied with a particular political decision made by judges, then Parliament can override that decision by appropriate legislation. Unfortunately that short answer is too short. Legislative time is a scarce resource, to be allocated with some sense of political priorities, and it may well be that a judicial decision would be overruled if Parliament had time to pass every law it would like to pass, but will not be overruled because Parliament does not. In some cases there is a further difficulty in the short answer. When an issue is the subject of great controversy, then Parliament may be disabled from changing a judicial decision, for practical political reasons, because any change would infuriate some powerful section of the community or alienate some parts of a governing coalition. It may be that the issue of whether the Race Relations Act should apply to certain sorts of clubs is an issue like that. Either decision would provoke such effective political opposition that Parliament is effectively saddled with whatever decision the courts reach.

So we cannot be content with the short answer to the argument from democracy. But there are more serious defects in that argument. It assumes, in the first place, that the rule-book solution to hard cases—which urges judges to ask historical questions of the sort I described rather than political questions—does serve democracy in some way that the rights conception does not. It assumes that these historical questions do bring to the surface decisions that an elected legislature has actually made. But if we look more closely at the questions, we shall find that the assumption has no basis.

Suppose a statute can be interpreted in two ways, one of which requires one decision in a hard case and the other of which requires the other. The phrase "a section of the public," for example, may be interpreted so that the statute includes only facilities open to anyone who can afford them, in which case a political club which is not open to members of other parties does not fall within the statute. Or it may be interpreted so as to exclude only intimate or domestic occasions, like private parties, in which case a political club is covered by the statute. The semantic and group-psychological questions assume that Parliament decided to adopt one or the other of these two different statutes; they aim to provide techniques for deciding which of the two decisions it (probably) took.

The semantic questions argue that if the critical words of the statute are words more likely to be used by someone who has taken one of these decisions than someone who has taken the other, then that is evidence, at least, that the legislature has taken that decision. So if the words "the public or a section of the public" are more likely to be used by someone who had decided to exclude political clubs from the Act than by someone who has decided to include them, then Parliament probably took the former decision. But this is fallacious. For, though it is sensible to argue that if the legislature has taken one or other of these decisions, it is more likely to have taken the one more naturally expressed by the words it used, it is not sensible to argue in the other direction, that because it used these words it must have taken one or the other of these decisions. It may have taken neither. Indeed the fact that the words used are compatible with either decision makes it more likely that it has not taken either decision, unless there is some independent evidence that it has.

The group-psychological questions do not supply that independent evidence, except in very rare cases, because the strategy they recommend also presupposes, rather than shows, that the individuals whose intentions are in play had any pertinent intention at all. The rare exceptions are cases in which the legislative history contains some explicit statement that the statute being enacted had one rather than the other consequence, a statement made under circumstances such that those who voted for the statute must have shared that understanding. In most cases the legislative history contains nothing so explicit. The group-psychological questions then fix on peripheral statements made in legislative hearings, or on the floor of the legislature, or on other provisions of the statute in question, or on provisions of statutes in related areas, attempting to show that these statements or provisions are inconsistent with an intention to create a statute under one interpretation of the unclear phrase, though consistent with an intention to create a statute under the other interpretation. That is not an argument in favor of the claim that key legislators intended to adopt that second statute, unless it is assumed that these legislators must have intended to enact one or the other. But they may not have intended to enact either; and the fact that they did not enact their statute in words that clearly put either intention into effect is a very strong argument that they did not.

We must be careful to avoid a trap here. We may be tempted to say, of any particular legislator, that he either intended to enact a particular statute (that is, a particular interpretation of the words that form the bill he votes for) or intended not to enact that statute. If that were so, then

evidence that suggests that he did not intend to enact a statute that would include political clubs would suggest that he did intend to enact a statute that did not include them. But it is not so. A legislator may vote with great enthusiasm for a bill because he knows that it will force hotels and restaurants to cease discrimination without thereby having either the intention that the same prohibition should apply to semipublic institutions like political clubs or the intention that it should not. He may simply have failed to consider the issue of whether it should. Or he may positively have intended that the statute be inconclusive on whether such institutions should be covered, because either decision, if explicit, would anger an important section of the public or otherwise prove impolitic.

In either case, the argument that it would be more consistent for him to have had the intention to exclude political clubs than to include them—more consistent with what he had voted for elsewhere in the present statute or in other statutes, or more consistent with the arguments given in hearings or on the legislative floor—is beside the point. That may be an argument about what he *should* have intended on the question of political clubs. It is no argument that he *did* so intend, because he may have been ignorant of, or had good reason for ignoring, what consistency required.

The counterfactual questions I mentioned are not open to the same objection. They do not assume that particular members of the legislature took a decision or had an intention one way or the other. They concede that no one may even have thought of the relevant issue. They ask what legislators would have decided or intended if, contrary to fact, they had been forced to attend to the issue. They insist that that question admits of an answer in principle, even though in particular cases it might be hard to discover what the answer is, and even though any particular judge's answer will be controversial. The argument that counterfactual historical questions respect democracy is therefore different from the argument that semantic and psychological questions do. It runs as follows. "Suppose we decide that it is likely, on the balance of probabilities, that Parliament would have brought political clubs within the statute if, for some reason, it had been forced to decide whether they were to be within or without. Then it is just an accident that Parliament did not actually decide to include them. It is (we might say) the latent will of Parliament that they be within, and even though a latent will is not an actual will, it is nevertheless closer to the spirit of democracy to enforce the latent will of Parliament than to encourage judges to impose their own will on the issue."

This argument is unsound, for a number of reasons. First, it is at least arguable that in many cases there is no answer, even in principle, to a counterfactual historical question. Philosophers divide on whether it is necessarily true that if Parliament had been forced to vote on the issue of political clubs, it would either have voted to include them or not voted to include them. But let us set that philosophical point aside and assume that, in at least enough cases to support the argument from democracy, counterfactual historical questions have a right answer, even when it is controversial what that right answer is. It is nevertheless true that a great number of different counterfactual questions can be asked about any particular legislative decision, and the answers to these different questions will be different, because how Parliament would have decided if it had been forced to decide will depend on the way in which it was forced to decide.

It may be, for example, that if the Parliamentary draftsman had put a clause including political clubs into the first draft of the bill, that clause would have survived, because no amendment would have been proposed that would have succeeded; but also true that if the draftsman had included a clause excluding political clubs, that clause would have survived, again because no amendment would have been

proposed that would have succeeded. What is the latent Parliamentary will then, assuming that neither clause was in fact put into the bill at any stage? The counterfactual technique cannot work unless it stipulates some canonical form of the counterfactual question. But why should one form of the question—one hypothesis about the conditions in which Parliament might have been forced to decide—be superior to another from the standpoint of the argument from democracy?

There is a further objection. No canonical form of the counterfactual question that makes that question genuinely historical would be acceptable to lawyers and judges in practice. For though counterfactual questions have found their way into legal practice, they are used as political rather than historical questions. The answer they would receive if they were really historical questions would be rejected by lawyers as irrelevant to adjudication. Consider the following (arbitrary) form for the counterfactual question: Suppose that just before the Race Relations Act had its final hearing one member of the Cabinet convinced his colleagues that the Act must take a position, one way or the other, on political clubs, and that in consequence Parliament finally took a position. What position would it have taken? If a historian were asked that question, he would reject any a priori restrictions on the kind of evidence that would be relevant. Suppose he discovered that a Minister of the day had written a letter to his mistress on the subject of political clubs, describing the special vulnerability of one or the other of his colleagues to pressure from such clubs. Suppose he discovered that the party had commissioned a secret political poll on the public's attitudes on this or related issues. He would insist on seeing that letter or the results of that poll, if at all possible, and if he were fortunate enough to see these, he would insist that they were of dramatic relevance to the historical counterfactual question he had been asked. He would be right, if the question were really a historical one, because it is less likely that the Cabinet would have proposed including political clubs if some member were vulnerable or if the public strongly opposed their inclusion.

But a judge asking the question of what Parliament would have done had it attended to the problem of political clubs is distinctly not interested in letters to mistresses or in secret political polls. His argument is, not that Parliament would actually have taken the decision in question if it had taken any decision on the matter, but rather that Parliament would have taken that decision if it were acting consistently with some assumed justification for what it did do. That is a very different matter, and history has little to do with it. The argument I composed in favor of the counterfactual question insisted that, if Parliament would have included political clubs had it been forced to choose, then it is only an accident, from the standpoint of democracy, that political clubs are not explicitly included. But it does not follow, from the different claim that Parliament out of consistency should have included political clubs, that it is only an accident that it did not explicitly include them. Suppose it is true that Parliament should have included them out of consistency, but also true that for political reasons it would in fact have excluded them if it had done anything. Then the supposed theory of democracy, that decisions on political matters should be made by Parliament, hardly argues that political clubs should be included.

It might now be said, however, that a different theory of democracy does make relevant the question of what Parliament, in consistency, should have done. The legislature elected by the people does more (according to this theory) than enact the particular provisions that make up the statute books. It chooses the general policies the state is to pursue and the general principles it is to respect. If, in a hard case, one decision follows more naturally from the principles that the legislature served in enacting a statute, then the judges should take that decision, even though it is true that, as a matter of historical fact, the legislature itself would have taken the other one if it had taken either. The legislature endorses principles by enacting legislation these principles justify. The spirit of democracy is served by respecting these principles. It is not served by speculating whether the legislature itself, on some particular occasion, would have kept the faith.

This argument is meant to defend the counterfactual questions as they are used in practice. It concedes that these questions are evaluative, at least in the sense described, rather than just historical, but argues that questions that are evaluative in that sense do serve democracy. Perhaps a similar argument could be made to justify the group-psychological questions. It might be said that these questions do not really suppose that individual legislators have an intention that the statute be construed one way rather than another. Instead they ask what principles a legislator who voted for the statute would be presumed to have thereby endorsed, so that the decision in a hard case may be governed by those principles. If the group-psychological questions are understood and defended in this way, then they are not after all different from the counterfactual questions. When a judge asks what the legislators must have intended to accomplish, he means to ask what policies or principles most naturally fit the statute they approved. When he asks what they would have done if required to answer the question before him, he means to ask what answer flows from policies or principles that most naturally fit the statute they approved. Neither question is really psychological or historical; they ask the same basic question in either a psychological or a historical disguise.

But if the psychological and counterfactual questions are understood in this way, then it is no longer plausible to suppose that a judge who puts these questions in order to decide a hard case is not making a political decision. For the evaluations these questions, so understood, require are not different in character from the evaluations recommended by the rights conception of the rule of law. If only one set of principles is consistent with a statute, then a judge following the rights conception will be required to apply these principles. If more than one is consistent, the question of which interpretation more "naturally" flows from the statute as a whole requires a choice among ways to characterize the statute that must reflect the judge's own political morality. That is the source of the complaint I mentioned at the outset of this essay, which is that British judges really make political judgments according to their own lights disguised as judgments about legislative intentions or history. This is true; though the suggestion of hypocrisy is, for the most part, unfair. If psychological or counterfactual questions are put as genuine historical questions, then they will supply no useful answers. If they are to be useful, then they must be understood as questions that call for the sort of political judgment that they, in practice, force from the judges who use them. Judges may not acknowledge these judgments, but that is a failure of recognition not a failure of integrity.

Rights and democracy

The argument from democracy, therefore, does not provide an argument in favor of the rulebook conception of adjudication. So far I have not contested the root assumption of that argument, that it is offensive to democracy if matters of political principle are decided by courts rather than elected officials. We must now ask whether that assumption is sound. Do judicial decisions on matters of principle (as distinct from policy) offend any plausible theory of democracy?

The argument that they do supposes that the decision of a legislature elected by the majority of the public is, in the last analysis, the best way of deciding questions about the rights that individual citizens have against each other and against the society as a whole. But this might be

so for two different kinds of reasons, or some combination of the two. Legislation might be a more accurate procedure for deciding what people's rights are than alternative procedures, or it might be a better procedure for reasons other than accuracy. We rely, to some degree, on both sorts of justifications for other institutional theories, like the theory that a jury trial is a good method for testing accusations of crime. We think that trial by jury is a reasonably accurate method, but we also think that it is a good method for reasons that are not reasons of accuracy.

So we must consider the argument for democracy, as a strategy for deciding questions about rights, under two aspects. Are there, first, institutional reasons why a legislative decision about rights is likely to be more accurate than a judicial decision? It is difficult to assess the question of accuracy in the abstract, that is, apart from some particular theory of rights. But I cannot imagine what argument might be thought to show that legislative decisions about rights are inherently more likely to be correct than judicial decisions. Obviously, on any theory of rights, decisions about rights are better if they are based on more rather than less information about a variety of facts. But I know of no reason why a legislator is more likely to have accurate beliefs about the sort of facts that, under any plausible conception of rights, would be relevant to determining what people's rights are. On any plausible theory of rights, moreover, questions of speculative consistency—questions that test a theory of rights by imagining circumstances in which that theory would produce unacceptable results—are likely to be of importance in an argument about particular rights, because no claim of right is sound if it cannot stand the test of hypothetical counter-example. But the technique of examining a claim of right for speculative consistency is a technique far more developed in judges than in legislators or in the bulk of the citizens who elect legislators.

In some cases, moreover, the public that elects

legislators will be in effect a party to the argument whether someone has a right to something, because that public's own interests oppose the concession of a right. That will typically be true when the argument lies in a politically sensitive area, like that of race relations. Politically powerful groups may prefer that political clubs discriminate, and no countervailing force, except the politically impotent minority itself, may very much care. It would be wrong to assume that in such circumstances the legislators will lack the independent judgment to identify the right at stake or the courage to enforce it. But it is nevertheless true that in such cases legislators are subject to pressures that judges are not, and this must count as a reason for supposing that, at least in such cases, judges are more likely to reach sound conclusions about rights. I am now arguing only that legislators are not institutionally better placed to decide questions about rights than judges are. Someone might object that as things are, in Britain for example, judges will do a worse job because they hold worse theories about rights. They are drawn from a particular class, educated in a particular way, and members of a particular profession such that they are very likely not to appreciate the rights of people from very different classes. Nothing I have so far said meets that argument. I shall consider its force later.

Second, are there other reasons of fairness, apart from reasons of accuracy, why legislation should be the exclusive strategy for deciding what right people have? We must consider a familiar argument that appeals to the importance of respect for the law and other aspects of political stability. "Legislatures are unlikely to reach a decision about rights that will offend some powerful section of the community so much that it will shake the political order. If the legislature does make this mistake, the government will fall, and the orderly process of democracy will replace the foolish legislature with another. Courts have no similar built-in defense against very unpopular decisions,

because judges have no direct fear of popular dissatisfaction with their performance. On the contrary, some judges may take pleasure in their freedom to disregard popular views. So if judges reach a political decision that is outrageous, the public will not be able to vindicate itself by replacing them. Instead it will lose a measure of its respect, not only for them, but for the institution and processes of the law itself, and the community will be less cohesive and less stable as a result. Surely that has been the consequence of the ill-judged experiment that brought courts into the political process through the Industrial Relations Act."

This argument urges that judges should not make political judgments, including political judgments about rights, because the effect of their being seen to make such judgments will lessen respect for the law. This particular argument, unlike the others I discuss, does not assume that the "historical" questions a judge might ask in lieu of political questions are nonpolitical. It assumes only that they will be *seen* to be nonpolitical. But that assumption is in fact equally dubious. For in all but a few of the cases in which a judicial decision has been widely and publicly criticized for being political, the judges set out historical rather than political grounds in their opinions. The law was brought into disrespect (whatever that means) by the content of the decision, not the character of the arguments provided. Political stability may argue against legislation that either deliberately or inadvertently leaves politically sensitive issues open for judges to decide. It is not an argument that, if judges are in fact forced to decide such issues, they should decide them on historical rather than political grounds.

Moreover the factual basis of the argument is at best unproved. Groups of citizens who intensely dislike a judicial decision will complain, not only about the decision but also about the nature of the institution that produced it. They may even be moved to disobey the decision, particularly if they have the political power to do so with impunity. But there is so far no evidence that the inclination to disobey will be general rather than local. There were grave predictions, for example, that political hostility to the American war in Vietnam and the disobedience to laws pursuing that war would lead to a general breakdown of law and order. That danger was seen, by different groups, both as an argument against the war and an argument in favor of prosecuting dissidents. But though crime continues to rise in the United States at a depressingly orderly rate, there is no evidence whatsoever that these political events were in any way contributory.

In any case, if the argument is taken to be an argument specifically against frankly political decisions by courts, it fails for a reason I have so far not mentioned. For it assumes that the public discriminates between political decisions taken by legislatures and those taken by courts, and that the public believes that the former are legitimate and the latter are not. But even if this is so now, the public sense of illegitimacy would presumably disappear if it were recognized by lawyers and other officials that such decisions are consistent with democracy and recommended by an attractive conception of the rule of law. So the present argument begs the question whether lawyers and officials should embrace that conclusion. It provides only an argument that any professional endorsement of such decisions should be followed—as inevitably it would be followed—by a change in the public's attitudes toward the law as well.

I recognize that there are many differences between Britain and the United States (I shall mention some of these later) that make any quick comparison between public attitudes in the two countries suspect. But it is worth noticing that a shift in the Supreme Court's attitude toward constitutional interpretation a few decades ago—a shift from reliance on historical arguments toward political arguments—was not followed by any sharp loss in the public's respect for that Court's decisions, as measured by the public's disposition to comply. On the contrary, the Warren Court achieved almost miraculous compliance with extremely unpopular decisions when popular understanding of the Court's role still insisted on historical rather than political interpretation of the Constitution, certainly to a greater degree than it does now. Popular opinion, in this case, has followed the Court.

Political stability, however, is not the main reason—apart from reasons of accuracy—why most people want decisions about rights to be made by legislatures. The reason is one of fairness. Democracy supposes equality of political power, and if genuine political decisions are taken from the legislature and given to courts, then the political power of individual citizens, who elect legislators but not judges, is weakened, which is unfair. Learned Hand gave this reason, in his famous Holmes lectures, for resisting political decisions by the Supreme Court. He said that he would not want to be ruled by "a bevy of Platonic Guardians," even if he knew how to choose them, which he did not.[9]

If all political power were transferred to judges, democracy and equality of political power would be destroyed. But we are now considering only a small and special class of political decisions. It is not easy to see how we are to test whether and how much individual citizens lose, in political power, if courts are assigned some of these decisions. But it seems plausible that—however gains or losses in political power are measured—some citizens gain more than they lose.

It is no doubt true, as a very general description, that in a democracy power is in the hands of the people. But it is all too plain that no democracy provides genuine equality of political power. Many citizens are for one reason or another disenfranchised entirely. The economic power of large business guarantees special political power for its managers. Interest groups, like unions and professional organizations, elect officers who also have special power. Members of entrenched minorities have, as individuals, less power than individual members of other groups that are, as groups, more powerful. These defects in the egalitarian character of democracy are well known and perhaps in part irremedial. We must take them into account in judging how much individual citizens lose in political power whenever an issue about individual rights is taken from the legislature and given to courts. Some lose more than others only because they have more to lose. We must also remember that some individuals gain in political power by that transfer in institutional assignment. For individuals have powers under the rights conception of the rule of law that they do not have under the rule-book conception. They have the power to demand, as individuals, a fresh adjudication of their rights. If their rights are recognized by a court, these rights will be enforced in spite of the fact that no Parliament had the time or the will to enforce them.

It may be a nice question whether any particular individual gains in power more than he loses when courts undertake to decide what political rights he has. Access to courts may be expensive, so that the right of access is in that way more valuable to the rich than the poor. But since, all else equal, the rich have more power over the legislature than the poor, at least in the long run, transferring some decisions from the legislature may for that reason be more valuable to the poor. Members of entrenched minorities have in theory most to gain from the transfer, for the majoritarian bias of the legislature works most harshly against them, and it is their rights that are for that reason most likely to be ignored in that forum. If courts take the protection of individual rights as their special responsibility, then minorities will gain in political power to the extent that access to the courts is in fact available to them, and to the extent to which the courts' decisions about their rights are in fact sound. The gain to minorities, under these conditions, would be greatest under a system of judicial review of legislative decisions, such as

holds in the United States and would hold in Britain under some versions of the proposed constitutional Bill of Rights. But it may nevertheless be substantial, even if the court's power to adjudicate political rights is limited to cases, like *Charter*, in which the legislature has not plainly settled the issue of what rights they shall be deemed to have. I assume, of course, favorable conditions that may not hold. But there is no reason to think, in the abstract, that the transfer of decisions about rights from the legislatures to courts will retard the democratic ideal of equality of political power. It may well advance that ideal.

Conservative judges

My argument thus far has been theoretical and institutional. Some will think it therefore beside the point, because they believe that the main arguments against encouraging judges to take political decisions are practical and personal. "British judges are intensely conservative and protective of established forms of authority. Perhaps that is only an accident of history, or perhaps it is the inevitable consequence of other institutional arrangements and traditions. But it is in any case a fact; and it would be perverse to ignore that fact in considering, for example, whether minorities and the poor would gain if judges were more explicitly political, or whether these judges are likely to do a better or worse job than Parliament in identifying genuine political rights."

I do not dispute that characterization of the present generation of judges in Great Britain. With some distinguished exceptions, it seems to me correct. But it does not follow that judges, however conservative, will reach less attractive decisions under a regime that encourages them to make political decisions about individual rights than a regime that obliges them to make "neutral" decisions by posing the "historical" questions I described. The various decisions cited by Griffiths and others to show the conservative character of British judges were all ostensibly justified on these "historical" grounds. Though critics suppose, for example, that the *Tameside* decision reflects the judge's disapproval of comprehensive education, and *Shaw's Case* shows their conviction that sexual license should be discouraged, each of these decisions reads as if the judges were obliged by neutral considerations of statutory construction and the interpretation of precedent to reach the conclusions they did. It is therefore hard to see how the explicit direction to judges, to make decisions about rights on political grounds, would produce more "conservative" decisions. The point is not that judges deliberately ignore their duty to reach decisions on historical rather than political grounds. It is rather that "historical" decisions must in the nature of the case be political.

If the explicit direction had any effect on the decisions produced by conservative judges, it might well be to make these decisions *less* rather than more conservative. The obligation to show the political character of the decision as a decision about individual rights *rather than the general welfare* must act as a general liberal influence. In Shaw's case, for example, the House held itself obliged, by its view of the precedents, to consider whether the publication of Shaw's *Ladies Directory* tended to corrupt public morals. That is a question, considered in itself, about the character of the general welfare (Viscount Simonds called it the "moral welfare") of society, and conservative judges may naturally be expected to take a conservative view of the public's welfare. Suppose, however, that reigning legal theory required the House to ask itself first whether the precedents unambiguously required them to recognize such a crime, and, if not, whether the theory that such a crime existed was more consistent with Shaw's rights as an individual than the theory that it did not. It would then have been strenuously argued that individuals have a moral right, at least in principle, not to be punished except for committing a crime clearly published in advance, and that in virtue of that right it would be unjust to punish Shaw. I very much doubt that even "conservative" judges would wish to deny the inherent appeal of such a right or that any competent judge would argue that it would be incompatible with British legal and political practice to recognize it. But a judge asked to take the decision on grounds of political principle could not have jailed Shaw unless he rejected the right as a matter of moral principle or argued that British practice denied it.

The *Charter* case, which I have been using as my leading example, was decided in what might be called a conservative way, and that is why it is taken by critics to be a political decision. Certainly the opinions of the Law Lords do not describe their decision as political: these opinions apply semantic questions to the phrase "a section of the public." But it is no doubt a fair comment that less conservative judges might have assigned a more powerful meaning to that phrase, because they would have had a different opinion on the question whether it is in the public interest that semipublic institutions lose a measure of control over the character of their membership. Suppose, however, that their Lordships had put to themselves, instead of the semantic question that invites the influence of the judgment about the general welfare, an explicitly political question about the competing rights of members of minorities not to suffer from discrimination and of club members to choose their own associates on criteria reasonable to them. The Race Relations Act embodies a compromise between those two rights: it holds that the right to be free from discrimination is sufficiently strong so that fully public institutions may not discriminate, but not so strong as to annihilate the competing right to choose associates in fully private settings like domestic entertainment or exclusive clubs. How should the balance be struck in intermediate cases not explicitly settled by the Act, like nonexclusive societies open in general to everyone with a particular political affiliation?

It is not inconceivable that a conservative judge would disagree with the initial judgment of the Act. He might think the Act undervalues freedom of association, or that it is bad policy to legislate morality in race relations (though it is sound to do so in sex). But if he is told he must decide a case like *Charter* on principles of political morality, compatible with the principles of the Act, he would be forced to set aside these convictions, because they are *not* compatible. He cannot hold that there is a morally relevant difference between the degree to which freedom of association is constrained by requiring Claridges not to discriminate and the degree to which that freedom is constrained by similar requirements on the West Ham Conservative Club. Even though he disapproves the way the balance was struck in the Act, he cannot plausibly suppose that a different political principle, striking the balance so as to couple the Conservative Club with private homes, is compatible with that Act. The more frankly political the subject matter of a case—the more that case is like *Charter* rather than the commercial case discussed abstractly earlier—then the more the explicitly political character of the statute or precedent in question will constrain the judge's own political morality in the way just described.

Here again the supposedly neutral semantic questions the House of Lords used permitted a decision that gave more effect to the judge's personal convictions than a frankly political jurisprudence would have allowed. The semantic questions, precisely because they are not political in form, do not discriminate among the kinds of political judgments that will, inevitably, influence the answers judges give them. They attract hidden political judgments that may be inconsistent in principle with the legislation supposedly being enforced. The political questions the rights model recommends, however, require that the political answers they receive be both explicit and principled, so that their appeal and their compatibility with principles more generally endorsed can be tested.

So even those who think that the political principles of the present judges are unsound do not have, in that belief, good reason to oppose the rights model and the style of adjudication it recommends. That model is likely to decrease the number of decisions they deplore. There is, however, a further and perhaps more important reason why we should reject the argument that appeals to the conservative character of the present judges. For the character of judges is a consequence of the theory of adjudication in force; therefore it cannot reasonably be urged as a reason for not changing that theory. If the rights conception of the rule of law were to become more popular in this country than it has been, legal education would almost certainly become broader and more interesting than it is now, and men and women who would never think of a legal career, because they want a career that will make a difference to social justice, will begin to think differently. The profession would change, as it did dramatically in the United States earlier in this century, and the lawyers whom that profession values and sends to the bench would be different. The argument that political jurisprudence would be a misfortune in Britain because judges are too firmly welded to established order begs the question. If law had a different place here, different people would have a place in the law.

Two ideals and two countries

Many people will resist the comparison I have made between Britain and the United States and argue that the role of law is so different in the two countries as to make comparisons unreliable. I agree with the spirit of the objection; but the differences do not touch the present point. I do not argue that it is likely that Britain will move toward a more openly political jurisprudence, but only that its judges and lawyers would be different if it did. I concede that the differences in legal culture reflect more fundamental differences that make the United States more fertile ground for the rights conception. Americans are still fascinated by the idea of individual rights, which is the zodiac sign under which their country was born. Their record in recognizing and protecting these rights has been less than spectacular. But public debate in the United States is dominated, to a degree British commentators find surprising, by discussion of what rights people have.

In Britain political debate centers on the different idea I have several times referred to, though not discussed, which is the nineteenth-century idea of the general welfare or collective good. When political debate talks of fairness, it is generally fairness to classes or groups within the society (like the working class or the poor), which is a matter of the collective welfare of these groups. American debate has insisted that rights belong to individuals rather than groups and has resisted measuring fairness by classes rather than people.

This difference in the vocabulary of political debate reflects and contributes to a difference in the general attitude toward lawyers and judges and their place in government. In the United States lawyers have often been scoundrels, and Americans give them no public honor, as they do give doctors and even some teachers. But America assigns lawyers, as a group, power and influence in a wide variety of matters, notably including government. In Britain lawyers are treated very well. They are dressed up in costumes—though principally middle-aged drag—and when they become judges their dignity is protected by very wide powers of contempt. But they have very little real power.

I have so far said very little directly in support of the rights conception as a political ideal. I have been too occupied with its defense. The positive case for that conception is straightforward. I conceded that a society devoted to that conception of the rule of law may pay a price, certainly in efficiency and possibly in the communitarian spirit that too much concern with law is supposed to cripple. But that society makes an important promise to each individual, and the value of that promise seems to me worth the cost. It encourages each individual to suppose that his relations with other citizens and with his government are matters of justice, and it encourages him and his fellow citizens to discuss as a community what justice requires these relationships to be. It promises a forum in which his claims about what he is entitled to have will be steadily and seriously considered at his demand. It cannot promise him that the decision will suit him, or even that it will be right. But that is not necessary to make the promise and the sense of justice that it creates valuable. I may have made it seem as if democracy and the rule of law were at war. That is not so; on the contrary, both of these important political values are rooted in a more fundamental ideal, that any acceptable government must treat people as equals. The rule of law, in the conception I support, enriches democracy by adding an independent forum of principle, and that is important, not just because justice may be done there, but because the forum confirms that justice is in the end a matter of individual right, and not independently a matter of the public good.[10]

Notes

Originally published in the *Proceedings of the British Academy*, 64 (1978). © 1980 British Academy.

1 J. A. G. Griffiths, *The Politics of the Judiciary* (Manchester University Press, 1977; paperback ed., New York: Fontana Books, 1977).

2 Charter v. Race Relations Board (1973), A.C. 868.

3 Dockers' Labour Club v. Race Relations Board (1975), A.C. 259.

4 Secretary of State for Education and Science v. Tameside Metropolitan Borough Council (1976), 3 W.L.R. 641.

5 Shaw v. D.P.P. (1961), 2 W.L.R. 897.

6 Liversidge v. Anderson (1942), A.C. 206.

7 *Taking Rights Seriously* (Cambridge, Mass.: Harvard

University Press, 1977; London: Duckworth, 1978.

8 I explain why at greater length in ibid., ch. 4.

9 Learned Hand, *The Bill of Rights* (Cambridge, Mass.: Harvard University Press, 1962).

10 Some of the issues discussed in this essay—in particular the group-psychological theory of statutory construction—are developed below in Chapter 16, "How to Read the Civil Rights Act" [Dworkin, *A Matter of Principle* (Cambridge, Mass.: Harvard University Press, 1985)].

Chapter 12

Jeremy Waldron

THE RULE OF LAW AS A THEATER OF DEBATE

THE RULE OF LAW is one of a cluster of ideals that constitute the core of modern political morality: the others include democracy, human rights, and perhaps also the principle of free markets. These ideals are so tightly clustered that there is a tendency to use any one of them as surrogate for all the others: "democracy" becomes code for human rights too, or "the rule of law" becomes code for rights, democracy, and markets.[1] That's a nuisance from an analytical point of view, because it prevents us seeing the distinctive light cast in our political morality by each of the separate stars in this constellation. And it can mislead us about the history and dialectics of these ideals. In some ways, the rule of law is more fundamental than the others. Democracy cannot exist unless procedures of election and accountability are secured by law; markets presuppose the integrity of legal rules defining property and contracts; and as the Universal Declaration of Human Rights states in its preamble, it is widely thought to be "essential, if man is not to be compelled to have recourse, as a last resort, to rebellion against tyranny and oppression, that human rights should be protected by the rule of law."[2] Moreover, the rule of law is arguably the oldest and most enduring theme in Western political thought. From Aristotle to Antonin Scalia, from Sir John Fortescue to John Locke, from Dicey to Dworkin, the rule of law has provided a perennial topic for political and legal writing for more than 2,500 years, as jurists and statesmen explore and elaborate the idea that laws might rule instead of men, and that "King Nomos" might prevail over the power of tyrants, mobs, and absolute monarchs.[3]

The prominence of this theme in our thought is in part a reflection of the fact that we can never quite agree what it amounts to.[4] To some the rule of law refers to the authoritative imposition of order in a society: clear rules are laid down whose likely impact in various situations can be ascertained well in advance, and these rules – which one can find in the texts of statutes and precedents – are enforced rigorously in every situation to which they apply, without fear or favor.[5] To others, the essence of the rule of law is reasoned deliberation, particularly as it is exercised in judicial settings.[6] On this account, the rule of law is the very opposite of the imperious imposition of a posited set of rules. A society is ruled by law in this sense when power is not exercised arbitrarily, but only pursuant to intelligent and open exercises of public reason in institutions and forums set up for that purpose. The function of legal texts is to frame and facilitate those processes, not short-circuit them. Settlement and predictability matter less on this second account than they do on the rule-book conception; that is, it matters less that we know in advance what the final determination of a given issue is going to be, more that we have some assurance about the procedures and activities that will attend that determination. I shall call these two conceptions of the rule of law "the rule-book model" and "the proceduralist model."

There are, of course, other conceptions in the literature as well.[7] Ronald Dworkin introduced what might be regarded as a third conception in his essay "Political Judges and the Rule of Law," when he contrasted what I have already referred to (following his example) as "the rule-book conception" with what he called "the rights conception."

It assumes that citizens have moral rights and duties with respect to one another, and political rights against the state as a whole. It insists that these moral and political rights be recognized in positive law, so that they may be enforced upon the demand of the individual citizens through courts or other judicial institutions of the familiar type, so far as this is practicable. The rule of law on this conception is the ideal of rule by an accurate public conception of individual rights.[8]

Now, if the rights conception referred only to *legal* rights, then there might be a case for regarding it as a subspecies of the rule-book conception. The argument has often been made that individual rights depend on clear rules of positive law, that legal predictability is key to the liberty that rights protect, and that the essence of legal rights is that law keep faith with the expectations that were established when it laid down its rules. After all, how can I be said to have a legal right unless the provision securing that right is clear, settled, and determinate in some public legal text?[9] I say a case *might* be made to that effect. But I doubt that Professor Dworkin would accept it. For him the existence of rights in law is so tightly bound up with moral argument about justice and argument about how we are required as a matter of principle to respond to antecedent legal materials, that any rule-book conception of them would make a mockery of

the moral standing that these rights are supposed to have.

Anyway, the conception of the rule of law defended by Professor Dworkin in "Political Judges and the Rule of Law" is distinguished by its emphasis on *moral* rights, and by the directness of the link that it seeks to establish between that idea and the idea of legality. A society committed to the rights conception of the rule of law makes an important promise to each citizen, according to Dworkin: "It encourages each individual to suppose that his relations with other citizens and with his government are matters of justice."[10]

The rule of law on this conception is the ideal of rule by an accurate public conception of individual rights. It does not distinguish, as the rule-book conception does, between the rule of law and substantive justice; on the contrary it requires, as part of the ideal of law, that the rules in the rule-book capture and enforce moral rights.[11]

The reference to "accuracy" seems particularly important. Moral rights are there – objectively – to be captured and enforced. There is a truth about rights and justice that our public conceptions ought to embody, but that they might or might not embody accurately. No doubt people will disagree about which propositions concerning moral rights are true and which false; consequently, on this conception, they will disagree about whether their society is in fact keeping faith with the rule of law ideal. But Dworkin makes much of the point that objectivity is not incompatible with disagreement:[12] "The rights conception must suppose that a state may fail along the dimension of accuracy even when it is controversial whether it has failed."[13] Anyway, *every* conception of the rule of law is going to require that some controversial judgments be made in the application of the ideal – judgments that may be impossible to prove to the satisfaction of everyone and that may be true or false nonetheless. The only difference in the case of this third conception – which I shall call the objectivist conception of the rule of law[14] – is the link between legality and what purport to be objective judgments about moral rights (as opposed to objective judgments about the enactment of texts or the integrity of procedures).[15]

But here's a question. If the rule of law is identified – as it is in Dworkin's conception – with law's getting it right so far as moral rights are concerned, does any importance attach to the procedures by which this happens or the means by which we as a society make the attempt to get moral rights right? Is it important for the rule of law that we try to establish the truth about rights and justice by *legalistic* means – such as procedures of litigation and deliberation and decision by judges? Does it matter that we use procedures like these – as opposed to, say, divination or appeals to tradition? I am asking in other words: is Dworkin's conception of the rule of law a purely objectivist conception, or are there also important elements in it of what we have called the proceduralist approach?

In "Political Judges and the Rule of Law," Professor Dworkin considers the possibility that "[a] government of wise and just officers will protect rights . . . on its own initiative, without procedure whereby citizens can dispute, as individuals, what these rights are."[16] That might seem to suggest that if he ever had to choose between familiar legal procedures, on the one hand, and, on the other hand, more accurate determinations of rights by entirely nonlegalistic means – for example, Solomonic judgments for particular cases by a philosopher-king – he would choose the latter. It is perhaps not entirely a silly dilemma to pose. There have been those who have urged us to turn away from procedural legalism if we ever want to reach a society ruled by enlightened values.[17] Admittedly, many who take this view also repudiate talk of moral rights as among the values they want us to be accurately ruled by, and some repudiate talk of justice as well. They suggest that law should

respond to other values, like efficiency, compassion, or progress, and it is in the service of these that they propose we should deploy political methods other than legalistic procedures. But it is not hard to imagine that someone might think this about moral rights as well. For all we know, moral rights may be better served by nonlegalistic than by legalistic means; perhaps we should aim at the outcomes rights call for by discretion, command, and administration rather than through the more laborious processes of courts and litigation.[18] Or, if the critics were right that rights and justice were hopeless as moral ideals and should be replaced by other values, then presumably anyone who wholeheartedly accepted the objectivist conception would have to follow them in that.[19]

The general point is this. Some critics say we can reach better outcomes – *whatever* "better" turns out to mean – by using procedures other than those that are stressed in the proceduralist conception of the rule of law.[20] They say that when procedures and morally desirable outcomes diverge, we should follow the outcomes. And maybe they are right. So my question for Professor Dworkin is this: will he follow them in that, if he is ever put to the choice? Or, to focus the matter slightly differently: does he think a commitment to the rule of law permits one to follow outcomes rather than procedures in a dilemma like this? Or putting it yet another way, and mindful of the point we began with, that the rule of law is not supposed to epitomize the sum of all good things: does a commitment to the rule of law represent at least in part a belief that public power should be exercised in a particular way, rather than just *any* way that offers the morally best outcomes?

My hunch is that there is in fact a very substantial proceduralist element in Ronald Dworkin's conception of the rule of law, and that at times it is ascendant over the objectivist element that we have been discussing. That is what I shall argue in the rest of this chapter. Indeed, I shall try to show that, throughout officials refuse to defer to a determination that they judge has not been duly arrived at, either because of some procedural defect or because in their opinion the institution that reached the decision was not competent to do so.) And it is true that in the broader legal process school, the Hart and Sacks principle of settlement was complemented by theories of institutional competence, claiming, for example, that courts are better at settling certain kinds of issues than others.[24] As I read the materials, however, it is important not to conflate institutional settlement and institutional competence.[25] Claims of institutional competence are contributions to disputes about the allocation of institutional authority – disputes that themselves require settlement. Suppose an official believes that a certain type of issue would be better settled by a judicial than by a legislative process. If the constitution in fact entrusts such issues to the legislature, then the principle of institutional settlement requires respect for *that* determination, and it follows from this that the legislature's decision on the matter counts as "duly arrived at," irrespective of anyone's opinion about its merits or about the merits of the prior decision that allocated authority in this way.[26]

As I said, this approach can therefore quickly bridge the apparent gap between rule-book and proceduralist conceptions of legality. After all, the rule-book conception doesn't just privilege any old set of rules. At least in its positivist manifestations, it privileges the rules that have emerged from certain institutional *sources* of law,[27] which means rules that have emerged as a result of the operation of specific institutional procedures – the judgments of *this* set of courts or the deliberations and votes of *this* legislature. So if a proceduralist conception of the rule of law is to avoid degenerating into a rule-book conception, there must be elements in it that in some sense privilege the continuing operation of the procedures over the specification of the rulings that, at particular times, have emerged from their operation. Somehow the dynamics of

the procedure must be kept alive. But that is a tall order because – it may be thought (and this, surely, was what Hart and Sacks meant about institutional settlement) – the point, surely, of setting up and operating procedures is to secure outcomes. We deliberate and vote in the legislature so that bills become law. We litigate in order to settle disputes and allocate liability. These are not processes we initiate for the fun of it. So what would it mean to privilege procedure over outcome? What sense could there be in it? And even if it made sense, how could it be done?

Two (rather abstract) analogies come to mind. The first is from the theory of justice, specifically the historic entitlement theory of Robert Nozick. Nozick is famous for contrasting his historical entitlement conception of justice with what he calls "current time-slice conceptions."[28] A time-slice conception focuses on the profile of individuals' holdings of wealth and resources at a given time (and judges it in terms of equality or the maximization of utility or conformity to some pattern), whereas an historical entitlement conception judges individual holdings on the basis of how they came about. Nozickian historical entitlement is mostly procedural.[29] But it is not just procedural in the sense that the procedures run and then there's an outcome, and the justice of that outcome is simply its having resulted from these procedures. It is procedural also in the sense that the procedures are ongoing, and one does violence to them by concentrating on distribution-at-a-time at all. What is wrong with the current time-slice approach, according to Nozick, is that it treats as static a situation that is inherently dynamic. The distribution of resources through markets and so forth is not like a race where there is an activity followed by a finishing line and a result, and that's that. Each result immediately becomes the basis for further activity. The goods I bought yesterday – the justice of whose being in my possession is defined by procedures of sale and purchase – are goods I may sell tomorrow. And the overall distribution of resources that results from whatever

Professor Dworkin's work, he has really responded to his main adversaries – the defenders of the rule-book conception (whom he regards as mainly legal positivists) – with a version of the proceduralist conception rather than with a version of the objectivist conception. He says that it is the objectivist conception that he is really working with, but I think he works comfortably with it only so long as it keeps company with the proceduralist conception. When they threaten to part – as they did in the dilemma I posited – Dworkin is as likely to go with the conception of the rule of law that stresses commitment to certain procedures as with a conception that is open to any political procedures provided they reach the right result.

Before going on, I would like to warn readers that this chapter is almost entirely expository, which doesn't mean that it gets Dworkin right necessarily, but that its aim is mainly to understand what I think of as a very interesting conception of the rule of law emerging from his work. I think it is mainly a proceduralist conception, and I want to clear away some other stands of Dworkinian jurisprudence – like "the right answer thesis" – that, if interpreted in the wrong way, are in danger of obscuring our view of it. I have no particular objection to the position that I am attributing to Dworkin. In a tangle like this, clarification is task enough.

I

Proceduralist views inevitably face two ways. On the one hand, respecting the integrity of a given set of procedures means trusting them to determine outcomes rather than specifying an outcome in advance and pursuing it by any means necessary. On the other hand, respecting the integrity of a given set of procedures also seems to mean respecting the outcome that they yield, and once it is determined that that is the outcome, it may mean abiding by it in a spirit rather like that of the rule-book conception. From this point of view, the procedures are a way

of defining what gets into the rule-book, and so the distinction between these first two conceptions of the rule of law may not be so clear after all.

We see this in the account of the rule of law that emerges from the classic Legal Process materials of Henry Hart and Albert Sacks.[21] Though many jurists associate this work – naturally enough, in view of its title – with a normative emphasis on procedures,[22] the leading principle of the Hart and Sacks materials is actually a principle of settlement. Hart and Sacks begin by stressing the need for processes of social decision, interpretation, and change, but the terms in which they do so refer insistently to people's need for settled understandings. And they proceed quickly to identify legality, not so much with the processes themselves as with the determinations that might emerge from them:

> Implicit in every such system of procedures is the central idea of law – an idea which can be described as *the principle of institutional settlement*. The principle builds upon the basic and inescapable facts of social living: . . . namely the fact that human societies are made up of human beings striving to satisfy their respective wants under conditions of interdependence, and the fact that this common enterprise inevitably generates questions of common concern which have to be settled, one way or another, if the enterprise is to maintain itself . . . The principle of institutional settlement expresses the judgment that decisions which are the duly arrived at result of duly established procedures of this kind ought to be accepted as binding upon the whole society unless and until they are duly changed.[23]

Admittedly the Hart and Sacks principle can be read in two ways – one emphasizing the sheer fact of settlement, the other emphasizing "duly arrived at." (On the second reading, the rule of law is perhaps not violated when citizens or procedures run tomorrow will in turn be itself just a momentary phase in the continuous operation of the economy. Nozick's procedural principles of historic entitlement are recursive: they operate restlessly and repeatedly upon the outcomes that their operation generates.[30]

I suppose the analogue of this would be a legal system that allowed for repeated and indefinite appeals of a given outcome, or repeated litigation on the same subject. This is something we know legal systems try to avoid – precisely in the interests of what Hart and Sacks would call settlement. They allow for only one or two levels of appeal and they have doctrines like *res judicata*, issue-preclusion, and double jeopardy. Interestingly, though, the Hart and Sacks principle of institutional settlement takes possibility of recursion into account: "[D]ecisions which are the duly arrived at result of duly established procedures . . . ought to be accepted as binding . . . *unless and until they are duly changed.*"[31] Even if a *particular* outcome cannot be litigated and relitigated indefinitely, general issues implicated in that outcome can be revisited. Supreme courts can overturn their own precedents and bills that have failed in one legislative session may be reintroduced in the sessions that follow.

Equally interesting is the way that Ronald Dworkin seizes on this possibility in elaborating his conception of the rule of law. In his early writing on civil disobedience, Dworkin considered the predicament of citizens who believe that the law allows something that most of their fellow citizens and most officials believe it prohibits.[32] One common analysis of this predicament is that these citizens may appeal the decision they disagree with, but that they are bound to accept the authoritative word of the official body empowered to render a final determination – the highest competent court, for example – and that once that court has ruled, respect for the rule of law requires the citizens to simply comply with its ruling. Dworkin rejects this, in part because it ignores aspects of our

legal practice that allow the same issue – if not the same particular case – to be argued and reargued over and over again.

> [A]ny court, including the Supreme Court, may overrule itself. In 1940 the Court decided that a West Virginia law requiring students to salute the Flag was constitutional.[33] In 1943 it reversed itself, and decided that such a statute was unconstitutional after all.[34] . . . We cannot assume, in other words, that the Constitution is always what the Supreme Court says it is. Oliver Wendell Holmes, for example, did not follow such a rule in his famous dissent in the *Gitlow* case.[35] A few years before, in *Abrams*,[36] he had lost his battle to persuade the court that the First Amendment protected an anarchist who had been urging general strikes against the government. A similar issue was presented in *Gitlow* and Holmes once again dissented. "It is true," he said, "that in my opinion this criterion was departed from [in *Abrams*] but the convictions that I expressed in that case are too deep for it to be possible for me as yet to believe that it . . . settled the law." Holmes voted for acquitting Gitlow, on the ground that what Gitlow had done was no crime, even though the Supreme Court had recently held that it was.[37]

There is no departure here from the rule of law, Dworkin implies, even though the position seems unsatisfactory from the point of view of rule-books and settlements.[38]

A second analogy reinforces the point. Think of the procedures of scientific inquiry. A given hypothesis in physics or biology may be supported by the evidence; it may withstand rigorous testing; the results may be replicated in laboratories all over the world; the hypothesis may fit with the surrounding science; it may be fruitful for further discoveries; and so it may take its place in the pantheon of currently accepted scientific laws. But no law is ever so well-established by these procedures that it cannot be revisited, and subjected again to critical tests in the light of new evidence or new structures of inquiry. And this is not just because scientists enjoy running these procedures. It is because they are committed to the idea of objective truth on the matters that any given hypothesis addresses, truth that is supposed to stand independent of any attempt we might make to get at that truth. Thus the ultimate acceptability of a given hypothesis is not just a function of its having survived any finite amount of testing and scientific scrutiny – and, in that sense, of being the outcome of the operation of certain procedures. Its acceptability is supposed to be a matter of objective truth and falsity, which means that there is always something beyond our procedures in the light of which it makes sense – and can sometimes be sensible – to run the procedures yet again, to see whether the hypothesis can be falsified.[39] The idea of objective truth is capable then of reproaching what our procedures have generated. But at the same time, since the procedures are all we have, the idea of objective truth underwrites any attempt to block the repeated running of the procedures in the interest of settlement or "knowing where we stand." Now it is true that the idea of objective truth also provides us with some basis for criticizing and revising the procedures we use, not merely revisiting their outcomes. But that just reinforces the point. Objectivity subverts settlement – whether it is the settlement implicit in a given outcome or the settlement implicit in the view that a given set of procedures are the ones we ought to use to determine outcomes.

Throughout his work, Dworkin has used the idea of objective right answers in just this way, to subvert conceptions of the rule of law oriented towards settlement, predictability, and determinacy.[40] I said at the start of this chapter that he believes – as most of us do – that objectivity is not incompatible with disagreement.[41] And one might go further than this. On some accounts, an assumption of objectivity is *necessary* for disagreement: otherwise what would people

think they were disagreeing about?[42] If moral positions were purely subjective, there might be *opposition* between one person's attitudes and another's, but there would not be anything that one person was affirming and another denying, or anything that one person thought true and the other thought false.[43] Now it is no doubt silly to suppose as a general matter that the only point of talking about objective truth or falsity in a given field is to *facilitate* disagreement in that field – to keep the argument alive, as it were, and stop people disengaging on the grounds of *de gustibus non disputandum*. Those who insist, for example, on the objective truth of the proposition that torture is always wrong do so because they care about *torture*, not because they care to have a jolly good debate on the subject. Still, when one reads what Professor Dworkin writes about objectivity, it is striking how much of what he says is directed at those who would discredit argumentation about the matters that Dworkin thinks are objective, as opposed to those who in his view have got some issue objectively wrong. The skeptics and postmodernists who come under attack in his article "Objectivity and Truth – You'd Better Believe It," for example, are attacked for thinking that philosophical debate on moral and other objective-sounding matters is a waste of time.[44] They are not trying to discredit our convictions – some (like Richard Rorty, for example) say they share them[45] – but rather our methods and practices of defending them. Indeed the gist of Dworkin's case in this article is to treat these as "pointless, unprofitable, wearying interruptions . . ."[46] and to deny to them – as far as possible – the availability of any argument about the objective status of moral truth that could be isolated from first-order moral issues themselves. There may be a debate to be had about whether people have an absolute moral right not to be tortured, but Dworkin suggests there is no separate debate to be had about whether our judging that people have an absolute moral right not to be tortured corresponds to moral reality. There is just first-order moral debate, and the article is as strident against those realists who invite a second-order debate by talking about moral facts and moral reality as it is against those antirealists who would take up the invitation and perhaps seek to discredit our practices of (first-order) argumentation.[47]

Again, the effect of the commitment to objectivity in shaking loose the grip of settlement is evident in Professor Dworkin's early writings on civil disobedience. He acknowledges some sort of need for settlement in the law – "It is of course inevitable that some department of government have the final say on what law will be enforced. When men disagree about moral rights, there will be no way for either side to prove its case and some decision must stand if there is not to be anarchy"[48] – and he recognizes that, whatever their jurisprudence, citizens may have to come to terms with the decisions of powerful institutions as a matter of individual prudence.[49] But still, to the extent that legality depends on moral argument, there is always a basis for refusing to accept any particular determination as final: "A citizen's allegiance is to the law, not to any particular person's view of what the law is." In fact, Dworkin's insistence on the existence of objective right answers to constitutional and legal questions (not just to moral questions) has exactly this effect of undermining settlement. "[N]o judicial decision," he says, "is necessarily the right decision."[50] True, a determination by a court may make a difference to what the law is, as a matter of precedent.[51] But the difference it is supposed to make is itself a matter of moral argument – I shall say more about Dworkin's view of this in section II – and that too is an argument about an objective issue, an argument that any particular fallible human decision maker may get wrong. So citizens who believe a court has made a legal or moral mistake (about this or anything else) are not morally required to accept its determination as conclusive. Particularly where they conceive the matter to be one of moral importance, they must be allowed to persevere with their challenge:

It is one thing to say that an individual must sometimes violate his conscience when he knows that the law commands him to do it. It is quite another to say that he must violate his conscience even when he reasonably believes that the law does not require it, because it would inconvenience his fellow citizens if he took the most direct, and perhaps the only, method of attempting to show that he is right and they are wrong.[52]

Indeed, Dworkin defends the practice of citizens' continuing to defy the courts when they think the courts have made a mistake precisely as a way of galvanizing the procedures that define our legal system:

If our practice were that whenever a law is doubtful . . . one must act as if it were valid, then the chief vehicle we have for challenging the law on moral grounds would be lost. . . . [C]onsider . . . what society gains when people follow their own judgment in cases like this. When the law is uncertain . . . the reason usually is that different legal principles and policies have collided, and it is unclear how best to accommodate these conflicting principles and policies. Our practice, in which different parties are encouraged to pursue their own understanding, provides a means of testing relevant hypotheses. . . . The record a citizen makes in following his own judgment, together with the arguments he makes supporting that judgment when he has the opportunity, are helpful in creating the best judicial decision possible. This remains true even when, at the time the citizen acts, the odds are against his success in court.[53]

One comes away from reading these early articles with the impression that what matters, in Dworkin's view of the rule of law, is that the avenues of argument and challenge remain open. Any principle of settlement is subordinated to the importance of the procedures that allow citizens as much as judges to pursue the possibility that the law is not what it says on the rule-books and that society has not kept faith – as its authoritative determinations claim to have kept faith – with principles of right and justice.

I have said that this emphasis in Professor Dworkin's work is underwritten by his commitment to the principle of objective right answers to moral and legal questions. But in the papers we have been discussing, he is at pains to distance himself from any reification of the objectivity criterion. He rejects as "nonsense" the view that "there is always a 'right answer' to a legal problem to be found ... locked up in some transcendental strongbox."[54] Moreover – and quite strikingly, from our point of view in this chapter – he insists that his own talk of right answers is meant "only to summarize as accurately as I can many of the practices that are part of our legal process."[55]

> Lawyers and judges make statements of legal right and duty, even when they know these are not demonstrable, and support them with arguments even when they know that these arguments will not appeal to everyone. They make these arguments to one another, in the professional journals, in the classrooms, and in the courts.[56]

Skeptics may criticize those practices as fatuous, and as we have seen, Dworkin uses the idea of objective right answers as a vehicle for responding to such skepticism. But the point is not to get any particular legal position accepted as objectively true. The point is to understand the purposes that are served by legal argumentation.

> I understand those purposes to be ... the development and testing of law through experimentation by citizens and through the adversary process. Our legal system pursues these goals by inviting citizens to decide the strengths and weaknesses of legal arguments

for themselves, or through their own counsel, and to act on these judgments, although that permission is qualified by the limited threat that they may suffer if the courts do not agree.[57]

Right answers as such do very little work in this picture; but they frame and underwrite Dworkin's sense of the argumentative practices, procedures, and activities whose ascendancy in a society is, he thinks, definitive of the rule of law.

II

Turning now from Dworkin's discussion of civil disobedience to his main work in legal theory, we find something very similar. The "right answer thesis," when it was introduced into his jurisprudence, was not there to vindicate the claims of any particular legal proposition. It was there, and Professor Dworkin argued for it, in order to counter the suggestion explicit in H. L. A. Hart's legal positivism that in hard cases the sources of law may run out, leaving the decision maker – usually a judge – to come up with a determination on some basis other than legal argument.[58] On Hart's positivist account, there may have to be an end to the process of *legal* argumentation, and if a decision is reached it may have to be reached on some other basis. But the case that Dworkin makes – a case that we will not examine here – is supposed to show that the possibilities for the methods and processes of legal argumentation are much deeper and more extensive than that.[59] This position is expressed using the idea of "the right answer" and associating it with the thesis that even in a hard case one of the parties has a right to win.[60] But since Dworkin denies – here as much as in the writings on civil disobedience – that any alleged right answer is self-certifying as such, what we have is actually an account of how and why we should persist in arguing about the answer to hard cases, underwritten by the notion of an objectively true outcome. We have, in short, a technique for lawyers and judges — a technique that is supposed to be made compelling by Dworkin's account of how his ideal judge proceeds rather than by his account of where his ideal judge ends up.[61]

In interpreting his position this way, I have no particular investment in showing that Professor Dworkin really does or really does not believe in right answers to hard legal questions. As we have seen, he says he doesn't believe in one particular version of the right answer thesis — the transcendental strongbox account.[62] In other places, the thesis that there are right answers seems to be something that he does want to defend. But what he mainly wants to defend it from, I think, are denials that would have the consequence of crippling or blocking the procedures of legal argumentation. So Dworkin's repeated insistence that there can be right answers even though there is protracted disagreement among members of the community as to what these right answers are, is not, as it seems to be, an attempt to protect the right answer thesis from a particularly troubling objection. It is, rather, very close to the heart of the matter: if claims of objectivity and the persistence of argument were not associated in this way, the right answer thesis would not be doing the work that he wants it to do in his jurisprudence.

In *Law's Empire*, the right answer thesis is notable by its absence. I am not saying it is explicitly denied. But the book is mainly given over to an account of how lawyers and judges proceed and what justifies requiring them to proceed in that way. Again, how they proceed, Dworkin says, is by *arguing*, and the book "tries to grasp the argumentative character of our legal practice. . . ."[63]

> Legal practice, unlike many other social phenomena, is *argumentative*. . . . People who have law make and debate claims about what law permits and forbids that would be impossible — because senseless — without law and a good

part of what their law reveals about them cannot be discovered except by noticing how they ground and defend these claims.[64]

Having said that, I should add that Professor Dworkin does not treat legal argumentation simply as an aesthetic. Another way he characterizes legal practice is in terms of its "propositional" character,[65] which reminds us that the argument is *about* something and about something that matters.[66] But there is less emphasis on objectivity in *Law's Empire* than there is in some of Dworkin's other writings. His tactic, in an interesting section on "external skepticism" is to defuse the debate about objectivity, rather than take one side in that debate and defend it.[67] Metaphysical issues, he says, should not be allowed to distract us from the practice of argumentation about law and justice, and it must not be allowed to infect our explication of the issues at stake in such argumentation.

The conception of law defended in *Law's Empire* is a particular account of the connection between the way we justify present exercises of power and the relation between past decisions that have been made in the community. The general idea of the rule of law, Dworkin says, is this: "Law insists that force not be used or withheld, no matter how useful that would be to ends in view, no matter how beneficial or noble those ends, except as licensed or required by individual rights and responsibilities flowing from past political decisions about when collective force is justified."[68] Now, it would not be hard to put a gloss on that which accorded with the rule-book conception — under the rule of law, force may not be used unless licensed in advance by antecedently posited rules (laid down in statutes or precedents, for example) — and that conception would justify the doctrine in terms of the importance of notice and predictability for those upon whom force is likely to be used. But Dworkin's gloss on the idea of law again emphasizes the *argumentative* character of the relation between present force and antecedent decisions. It isn't just a matter of pointing to a justification in the existing materials; it's a matter of arguing from those materials, arguing about their interpretation and arguing about the general principles that they (arguably) presuppose. He notes as a matter of fact that lawyers and judges tend to worry away at statutes and precedents long after they have exhausted any possible significance these could have as bases of predictability: "[O]ur judges actually pay more attention to so-called conventional sources of law like statutes and precedents than conventionalism allows them to do."[69] And he believes that it is the task of jurisprudence to explain this persistence in argumentation.

The explanation he offers – law as integrity – is not something whose details we will examine here. Briefly: it is the idea of a certain sort of community, where people accept that they are bound together by reciprocal obligations that run deep and pervasively through their existing practices of mutual concern and respect. They treat particular obligations that they may have been found to have to one another in particular cases not as limited to those circumstances but "as derivative from and expressing a more general responsibility active throughout [their] association in different ways."[70] To honor this commitment, when any particular issue comes up for present decision, they are bound to delve relentlessly into the established terms of their association to ascertain how the present issue would best be decided in view of the deep commitments they think of themselves as having already taken on. That is what Professor Dworkin means by the rule of law – decision making in the context of that sort of practice. He believes it gives a distinctive flavor to a community's political culture:

Politics has a different character for such a people. It is *a theater of debate* about which principles the community should adopt as a system, which view it should take of justice,

fairness, and due process. . . . Members of a community of principle accept that their political rights and duties are not exhausted by the particular decisions their political institutions have reached, but depend, more generally, on the scheme of principles those decisions presuppose and endorse.[71]

Of course, this "theater of debate" is likely to be characterized by disagreement. People will disagree about what principles our existing decisions presuppose, and they will disagree too about what would be attractive or eligible principles to consider for this role. And Professor Dworkin as always wants to resist any skeptical claim that such disagreement makes the argument futile or inconsequential. Once again, if there is a role for the idea of "right answers" in *Law's Empire*, it is to block this move – that is, as before, to underwrite, with the idea of objectivity, the point of persisting with argument in the absence of consensus. Mostly, though, "law as integrity consists in an approach, in questions rather than answers."[72] Whatever its role in the book, the idea of objective right answers is not supposed to condemn as violations of the rule of law political arguments that in an objective sense *fail to get it right* about the principled relation between present issues and antecedent decisions. Instead it seems as though the demands of integrity are satisfied, on Dworkin's view, in the *attempt* to ascertain and work from deeper principles implicit in existing decisions.

We want our officials to treat us as tied together in an association of principle, and we want this for reasons that do not depend on any identity of conviction among these officials, either about fit or about the more substantive principles an interpretation engages. Our reasons endure when judges disagree, at least in detail, about the best interpretation of the community's political order, because each judge still confirms and reinforces the principled character of our association by *striving* in spite of the disagreement, to reach his own opinion instead of turning to the usually simpler task of fresh legislation.[73]

The expressive value of integrity is confirmed, he says, "when people in good faith *try* to treat one another in a way appropriate to common membership in a community . . . and to see each other as making *this attempt*, even when they disagree about exactly what integrity requires in particular circumstances."[74]

All of this argues, in my view, for a conception of the rule of law that is, in the last analysis, proceduralist rather than objectivist. A society ruled by law, according to Dworkin, is a society committed to a certain method of arguing about the exercise of public power. A society shows its allegiance to the rule of law by dint of its commitment to asking certain questions and approaching them in the right way. And it is distinguished, ultimately, from societies that lack such a commitment not by the substance of what it does – substantively respecting moral rights, for example – but by the procedures that it unflinchingly follows. "Law is not exhausted by any catalogue of rules or principles [or] . . . by any roster of officials . . . Law's empire is defined by attitude, not territory or power or process."[75]

III

My characterization of Dworkin's account of the rule of law as a proceduralist conception may be misunderstood. In modern constitutional theory, terms like "proceduralism" and "legal process" are associated with views that confine constitutional review to procedural or quasi-procedural issues. According to John Hart Ely, for example, judges may review legislation for defects in the procedures involved in its enactment or in order to maintain the integrity of the democratic process; but they should not address issues of substance in exercising what is in fact quite a problematic power, from a democratic point of view.[76] Now Professor Dworkin is a critic of this view: he does not believe that procedural issues can be separated from substantive issues in the way that Ely implies, nor does he accept that there is a serious issue about the democratic status of judicial review that needs to be addressed in this way.[77] On Dworkin's theory, judges have no choice but to follow the instruction of the Constitution and address substantive issues of moral right. And a regime in which they are empowered to do this may well be a better democracy precisely because of their ability to address substantive as well as procedural issues in this way.[78] But none of this detracts from what I have referred to as the proceduralist aspect of Dworkin's own jurisprudence. In constitutional law, Dworkin's position is that important issues of rights must be dealt with through a set of procedures appropriate to their character as issues of principle, and this applies whether the issues themselves are issues about political procedures or not.

Reference to constitutional theory, however, does give us the opportunity to consider more closely the kind of procedures that Professor Dworkin has in mind in his conception of the rule of law. I have used the words "argument" and "argumentation" over and over again to refer to these procedures. But we need to pin things down a little. The complaint is often heard that Dworkin's proceduralism does not necessarily imply any commitment to participatory values. Allan Hutchinson is one of the severest critics on this score: "Despite paying lip-service to 'a theater of debate,' *Law's Empire* is about accepting and assuming political obligations and not about participating in the making of them. . . . In *Law's Empire*, judges have been elevated to the rank of moral prophets and philosopher monarchs. For citizens, politics has become a spectator sport."[79] And Silas Wasserstrom says something similar about Dworkin's legalistic "theater of debate":

Nor am I at all sure what the "theater of debate about which principles the community should adopt as a system" is supposed to be like, but I suspect it would not be very moving or dramatic, even for the community's few moral philosophers who attend or participate. . . . I have no clear idea what the politics of the community of principle would be like, but I suspect its politics would be rather rarified and effete, and would involve very few ordinary citizens as active participants.[80]

I have my own doubts about Dworkin's commitment to democratic politics,[81] but I think this is a little unfair. Several times in *Law's Empire*, Dworkin indicates that it is the responsibility of each citizen, not just each judge, to try to figure out what integrity requires: in a community governed by the rule of law "each citizen has a responsibility to identify, ultimately, [a scheme of principle] for himself, as his community's scheme," and to organize his dealings with other citizens on that basis.[82] Indeed Professor Dworkin appears to think that one of the advantages of an American-style system of judicial review is that it actually improves the quality of debate among members of the public:

> When an issue is seen as constitutional, . . . and as one that will ultimately be resolved by courts applying general constitutional principles, the quality of public argument is often improved, because the argument concentrates from the start on questions of political morality. . . . When a constitutional issue has been decided by the Supreme Court, and is important enough so that it can be expected to be elaborated, expanded, contracted, or even reversed by future decisions, a sustained national debate begins, in newspapers and other media, in law schools and classrooms, in public meetings and around dinner tables. That debate better matches [the] conception of republican government,

in its emphasis on matters of principle, than almost anything the legislative process on its own is likely to produce.[83]

He may or may not be right about this.[84] But so far as the characterization of his conception of the rule of law is concerned, it is evident that Dworkin does not think citizens are required to submit to oligarchic nonparticipatory determinations of what law, rights, and principles add up to. The discussion of civil disobedience that we studied in section II of this chapter makes that quite clear, and it indicates that the proceduralism of Dworkin's may not be regarded as a purely spectator sport.

We have seen that throughout Dworkin's writings, the idea that there are objective right answers to the conundrums that legality poses for us helps invigorate and keep open the legal and political processes that he favors. It is true that this gives a particular objectivist spin to Dworkin's theory of institutional competence, and sometimes he says things like this: "The best institutional structure is the one best calculated to produce the best answers to the essentially moral question of what the democratic conditions actually are, and to secure stable compliance with those conditions."[85] He uses this also as a basis for some skepticism about legislative procedures, which he says may not be "the safest vehicle for protecting the rights of politically unpopular groups."[86] But he is also sometimes willing to say that "[l]egislatures are guardians of principle too,"[87] and that if lawmakers ask themselves the right questions and proceed in the right, responsive to concerns about integrity and principle in their deliberations, then their procedures too are constitutive of the rule of law.[88]

I have mostly shied away from asserting that Dworkin's conception of the rule of law is unequivocally proceduralist. We have seen throughout that there are elements of the objectivist and the rule-book conception, and no doubt other conceptions too. It is a delicate exercise in triangulation, as it were, to see how a given conception responds to the interlocking concerns about settlement, process, and objectivity that are implicated in the rule of law ideal. All of them in various ways pay tribute to the needs and concerns of ordinary people and what they expect from their law.[89] What I have tried to do, however, is to emphasize those parts of Professor Dworkin's conception of legality that find respect for individuals and their rights in the manner in which we proceed in our legal system, not just in the notion of objective principles or in the reality of established settlements. The rule of law prevails in a community, according to Dworkin, when its "collective decisions [are] made by political institutions whose structure, composition, and practices treat all members of the community, as individuals with equal concern and respect."[90] A society committed to the rule of law in this sense may well use courts more than a society without such a commitment. But that is not merely because – and I think not mainly because – courts are more likely to get things right. It is rather that courts are supposed to exhibit in their forms, structures, and procedures a determination to take seriously the issues of right that they are addressing. A society committed to the rule of law

> encourages each individual to suppose that his relations with other citizens and with his government are matters of justice, and it encourages him and his fellow citizens to discuss as a community what justice requires those relations to be. It promises a forum in which his claims about what he is entitled to have will be steadily and seriously considered at his demand.[91]

For these purposes, taking rights seriously is not so much a matter of getting rights right; it is a matter of conveying in the *way* in which we make our decisions that we understand that rights are involved. Personally, I believe that the same argument can be made, on certain

favorable assumptions, for legislatures too: they too have their own way of respecting in their structures and procedures the equality of respect due to the opinions of ordinary men and women.[92] But I shall not try to persuade Professor Dworkin of that now. This chapter, as I said at the beginning, is supposed to be an exposition of his account of the rule of law, and it is intended to bring out proceduralist themes in that account that are in danger of being downplayed in a jurisprudential environment that continues to be obsessed with the right answer thesis.

Notes

Justine Burley (ed.) *Dworkin and His Critics* (Blackwell 2004) pp. 319–36

1 For this observation, see Joseph Raz, "The Rule of Law and its Virtue," in his collection *The Authority of Law: Essays on Law and Morality* (Oxford: Clarendon Press, 1979), p. 210.

2 Universal Declaration of Human Rights (1948), Preamble, para. 3.

3 For these references: see Aristotle, *Politics*, Bk. III, chs. 10–11, 15–16; Antonin Scalia, "The Rule of Law as a Law of Rules," *University of Chicago Law Review*, vol. 56, 1989, p. 1175; Sir John Fortescue, In Praise of the Laws of England (1468) from Fortescue, *On the Laws and Governance of England* (Cambridge, UK: Cambridge University Press, 1997), p. 17; John Locke, *Second Treatise*, ch. 11; A. V. Dicey, *Introduction to the Study of the Law of the Constitution Eighth Edition of 1915* (Indianapolis, IN: Liberty Press, 1982), pp. 110–22; Ronald Dworkin, "Political Judges and the Rule of Law," in *A Matter of Principle* (Cambridge, MA: Harvard University Press, 1985), ch. 1. For "King Nomos," see Donald Kelley, *The Human Measure: Social Thought in the Western Legal Tradition* (Cambridge, MA: Harvard University Press, 1990), p. 283.

4 See the discussion in Jeremy Waldron, "Is the Rule of Law an Essentially Contested Concept (in Florida)?" *Law and Philosophy*, vol. 21, 2002, p. 137, and Richard Fallon, "The Rule of Law as a Concept in Constitutional Discourse," *Columbia Law Review*, vol. 97, 1997, p. 1.

5 See Scalia, "The Rule of Law as a Law of Rules," op. cit., and also F. A. Hayek, *The Constitution of Liberty* (London: Macmillan, 1960), chs. 9–10, for versions of the "rule-book" view.

6 See Fallon, "The Rule of Law as a Concept in Constitutional Discourse," op. cit., pp. 18–21, for a fine account of this proceduralist view.

7 One that is very important, but that I shall not spend much time discussing in this paper, links the rule of law to equality before the law. For example, see Dicey, *Law of the Constitution*, op. cit, p. 114:

    We mean . . . when we speak of the "rule of law" as a characteristic of our country, not only that with us no man is above the law, but (what is a different thing) that here every man, whatever be his rank or condition, is subject to the ordinary law of the realm and amenable to the jurisdiction of the ordinary tribunals.

8 Dworkin, "Political Judges and the Rule of Law," op. cit., pp. 11–12. (This essay was first published as a Maccabaean Lecture in the *Proceedings of the British Academy*, vol. 64, 1978, p. 259.)

9 For a powerful version of this argument, see Jeremy Bentham, *Principles of the Civil Code*, in C. B. Macpherson (ed.), *Property: Mainstream and Critical Positions* (Oxford: Blackwell, 1977), p. 41.

10 Dworkin, "Political Judges and the Rule of Law," op. cit., p. 32.

11 Ibid., p. 12.

12 Compare J. L. Mackie, *Ethics: Inventing Right and Wrong* (Harmondsworth, UK: Penguin, 1977), p. 21 with Michael Moore, "Moral Reality," *Wisconsin Law Review*, 1982, at pp. 1089–90.

13 Dworkin, "Political Judges and the Rule of Law," op. cit., p. 13.

14 Here I differ slightly from Fallon, who calls this sort of conception "a substantive conception" of the rule of law: see Fallon, "The Rule of Law as a Concept in Constitutional Discourse," op. cit., pp. 21–4. That term can be misleading for it is also used to refer to noninstrumental conceptions: see Margaret Jane Radin, "Reconsidering the Rule of Law," *Boston University Law Review*, vol. 69, 1989, pp. 781–819, at pp. 787–8.

15 See Fallon, "The Rule of Law as a Concept in Constitutional Discourse," op. cit., pp. 23–4.

16 Dworkin, "Political Judges and the Rule of Law," op. cit., p. 12.

17 For a long time, this was a theme of Marxist jurisprudence: see, e.g., Evgenii Pashukanis, *Law and Marxism: A General Theory* (London: Ink Links, 1978). See also Mark Tushnet, "An Essay on Rights," *Texas Law Review*, vol. 62, 1984, p. 1363.

18 For the possibility of this disjunction between moral rights and legalistic means, see Jeremy Waldron, "A Right-Based Critique of Constitutional Rights," *Oxford Journal of Legal Studies*, vol. 13, 1993, pp. 18–51, at p. 30; see further Jeremy Waldron, *Law and Disagreement* (Oxford: Clarendon Press, 1999), pp. 217–21.

19 After all, morality is not rights-based just because we think it is. That too is an objective question, and anyone defending what I have called the objectivist conception of the rule of law surely believes that we should be ruled by an accurate conception of moral rights only on condition that the idea of moral rights is a good idea. Otherwise we should seek to capture in our public policy and public decisions whatever other moral ideas are objectively better.

20 See, e.g., Edward L. Rubin, "Law and Legislation in the Administrative State," *Columbia Law Review*, vol. 89, 1989, p. 369.

21 Henry M. Hart and Albert M. Sacks, *The Legal Process: Basic Problems in the Making and Application of Law*, ed. William N. Eskridge and Philip P. Frickey (Westbury, NY: Foundation Press, 1994).

22 See, e.g., Fallon, "The Rule of Law as a Concept in Constitutional Discourse," op. cit., pp. 18–19.

23 Hart and Sacks, *The Legal Process*, op. cit., p. 4.

24 See, e.g., Lon Fuller, "Forms and Limits of Adjudication," *Harvard Law Review*, vol. 92, 1978, p. 353.

25 I discuss this also in Jeremy Waldron, "Authority for Officials," in Lukas Meyer, Stanley Paulson, and Thomas W. Pogge (eds), *Rights, Culture, and the Law — Essays After Joseph Raz* (Oxford: Oxford University Press, 2003), pp. 45–70.

26 Thus Hart and Sacks say, for example, that the principle of institutional settlement "forbids a court to substitute its own ideas for what the legislature has duly enacted" (Hart and Sacks, *The Legal Process*, op. cit., p. 1194). And they say it also commands respect for precedent: "Respect for the principle of institutional settlement demands . . . [that what] a legislature has duly determined ought

not to be set at naught by any other agency or person. What earlier judicial decisions have duly settled ought not to come unsettled" (ibid., p. 147).

27 For the sources thesis, see Raz, *The Authority of Law*, op. cit., pp. 47 ff.

28 Robert Nozick, *Anarchy, State and Utopia* (Oxford: Basil Blackwell, 1974), pp. 153–60.

29 For the distinction between pure-procedural and other approaches to justice, see John Rawls, *A Theory of Justice* (Oxford: Oxford University Press, 1971), pp. 73–7.

30 For this feature of Nozick's theory, see Lawrence Davis, "Comments on Nozick's Entitlement Theory," *Journal of Philosophy*, vol. 73, 1976, pp. 836–44, at pp. 838–9.

31 Hart and Sacks, *The Legal Process*, op, cit., p. 4.

32 Ronald Dworkin, "Civil Disobedience," in *Taking Rights Seriously*, rev. edn (London: Duckworth, 1977), p. 210.

33 [*Minersville School District* v. *Gobitis*, 310 U.S. 586 (1940).]

34 [*West Virginia State Board of Education* v. *Barnette*, 319 U.S. 624 (1943).]

35 [*Gitlow* v. *New York* 268 U.S. 652, 672 (1925).]

36 [*Abrams* v. *United States* 250 U.S. 616, 624 (1919).]

37 Dworkin, "Civil Disobedience," op. cit., pp. 213 and 211; I have reversed the order of these two excerpts, but it does not affect the gist of Professor Dworkin's argument.

38 But compare the statement in Ronald Dworkin, *Freedom's Law: The Moral Reading of the American Constitution* (Cambridge, MA: Harvard University Press, 1996), pp. 124–5, supporting *stare decisis* on the issue of abortion.

39 It will be evident that this paragraph is heavily influenced by a Popperian view of scientific method. See, e.g., Karl Popper, *Conjectures and Refutations: The Growth of Scientific Knowledge* (New York: Basic Books, 1962). But I do not think that any of the issues between Popper and his critics are relevant here, except for those critics who deny the existence of objective truth and perhaps also those inductivists who believe that certain methods are capable of establishing general propositions finally and conclusively. I don't think there are very many people in that latter group; but there are of course thousands in the former category.

40 There is also an element of substantive justice in the

Hart and Sacks conception, as when they say (Hart and Sacks, *The Legal Process*, op. cit., p. 6):

> [T]he principle of institutional settlement operates not merely as a principle of necessity but as a principle of justice. This means attention to the constant improvement of all the procedures which depend upon the principle in the effort to assure that they yield decisions which are not merely preferable to the chaos of no decision but are calculated as well as may be affirmatively to advance the larger purposes of society.

But it does not appear to do the same work as it does in Dworkin's writing.

41 See note 12 above.

42 The classic version of this argument is found in G. E. Moore, "The Nature of Moral Philosophy," in his book *Philosophical Studies* (London: Routledge and Kegan Paul, 1922), pp. 333–4. See also Oliver A. Johnson, "On Moral Disagreements," *Mind*, vol. 68, 1959, p. 482.

43 Arguably, this does not apply to projectivist or quasi-realist positions like that of Simon Blackburn, which – though rejecting objectivity – do not present moral judgments as mere reports of attitudes; see Simon Blackburn, *Essays in Quasi-Realism* (New York: Oxford University Press, 1983).

44 Ronald Dworkin, "Objectivity and Truth – You'd Better Believe It," *Philosophy and Public Affairs*, vol. 25 (1996), p. 87.

45 See, e.g., Richard Rorty, "Human Rights, Rationality and Sentimentality," in S. Shute and S. Hurley (eds), *On Human Rights: The 1993 Oxford Amnesty Lectures* (New York: Basic Books, 1993), pp. 115–16; "Solidarity or Objectivity?" in his collection, *Objectivity, Relativism and Truth: Philosophical Papers Volume I* (Cambridge, UK: Cambridge University Press, 1991), p. 33.

46 Dworkin, "Objectivity and Truth," op. cit., p. 139.

47 Ibid., pp. 104–5.

48 Dworkin, "Taking Rights Seriously," in *Taking Rights Seriously*, op. cit., p. 186.

49 Dworkin, "Civil Disobedience," op. cit., p. 213: "[A] man must consider what the courts will do when he decides whether it would be prudent to follow his own judgment. He may have to face jail, bankruptcy, or opprobrium if he does."

50 Dworkin, "Taking Rights Seriously," op. cit.,

p. 185. The view that what the courts finally determine is law by definition, Dworkin regards as "wrong, and in the end deeply corrupting of the idea and rule of law" – see Ronald Dworkin, "Civil Disobedience and Nuclear Protest" in *A Matter of Principle*, op. cit., pp. 115–16.

51 Dworkin, "Civil Disobedience," in *Taking Rights Seriously*, op. cit., pp. 211 and 214.

52 Ibid., p. 214.

53 Ibid., pp. 212–13. Again, I have altered the order of some of the passages in the excerpt without, I think, altering their sense.

54 Ibid., p. 216.

55 Ibid.

56 Ibid.

57 Ibid., pp. 216–17.

58 H. L. A. Hart, *The Concept of Law*, 2nd edn (Oxford: Clarendon Press, 1994).

59 See especially "The Model of Rules I and 'Hard Cases'," in *Taking Rights Seriously*, op. cit.

60 Ibid., p. 82.

61 For Hercules' "technique" see ibid., pp. 129–30.

62 See text accompanying note 54 above; see also Dworkin, *Taking Rights Seriously*, op. cit., p. 337.

63 Ronald Dworkin, *Law's Empire* (Cambridge, MA: Harvard University Press, 1986), p. 14.

64 Ibid., p. 13.

65 Ibid., p. 14.

66 *Law's Empire* opens with the words "It matters how judges decide cases" (ibid., p. 1).

67 Ibid., pp. 76–86.

68 Ibid., p. 93.

69 Ibid., p. 130.

70 Ibid., p. 200.

71 Ibid., p. 211.

72 Ibid., p. 239. See also ibid., p. 412: "I have not devised an algorithm for the courtroom. No electronic magician could design from my arguments a computer program that would supply a verdict everyone would accept once the facts of the case and the text of all past statutes and judicial decisions were put at the computer's disposal."

73 Ibid., p. 264 (my emphasis).

74 Ibid., p. 190 (my emphasis).

75 Ibid., p. 413.

76 John Hart Ely, *Democracy and Distrust: A Theory of Judicial Review* (Cambridge, MA: Harvard University Press, 1981).

77 Dworkin, "The Forum of Principle," in *A Matter of Principle*, op. cit., pp. 33–71, pp. 57–69.

78 See Dworkin, *Freedom's Law*, op. cit., ch. 1. For a critique of this position, see Jeremy Waldron, "Judicial Review and the Conditions of Democracy," *Journal of Political Philosophy*, vol. 6, 1998, p. 335, and *Law and Disagreement*, op. cit., ch. 13.

79 Allan C. Hutchinson, "Indiana Dworkin and Law's Empire," *Yale Law Journal*, vol. 96, 1987, pp. 637–55, at p. 654. For "theater of debate," see Dworkin, *Law's Empire*, op. cit., p. 211 and the passage cited at text accompanying note 71 above.

80 Silas Wasserstrom, "The Empire's New Clothes," *Georgetown Law Journal*, vol. 75, 1986, pp. 199–314 at p. 265.

81 See Waldron, *Law and Disagreement*, op. cit., ch. 13.

82 Dworkin, *Law's Empire*, op. cit., pp. 190, 213.

83 Dworkin, *Freedom's Law*, op. cit., p. 345.

84 For a critique, see Waldron, *Law and Disagreement*, op. cit., pp. 289–91.

85 Dworkin, *Freedom's Law*, op. cit., p. 34.

86 Ibid.

87 Ibid., p. 31.

88 See Dworkin, *Law's Empire*, op. cit., pp. 167, 176, and 217–19.

89 For an interesting discussion of the values associated with legality, see also Ronald Dworkin, "Hart's Postscript and the Character of Political Philosophy," pp. 24–8, available at http://www.law.nyu.edu/clppt/program2001/readings/readingshart/rdhartcolloquium2.pdf.

90 Dworkin, *Freedom's Law*, op. cit., p. 17.

91 Dworkin, "Political Judges and the Rule of Law," op. cit., p. 32.

92 See Waldron, *Law and Disagreement*, op. cit., chs 3–5 and 10–11. See also Jeremy Waldron, *The Dignity of Legislation* (Cambridge, UK: Cambridge University Press, 1999)

IV. THE DUTY TO OBEY THE LAW

Introduction

SOCRATES WAS TRIED and convicted on a trumped up charge of impiety in 399 BCE and sentenced to death. As recounted in Plato's *Crito*, Socrates knew himself to be innocent of the charge, but he nevertheless considered it his duty to accept the final determination of the law and not to flee Athens. Remaining faithful to the law and indeed to its unjust punishment until the end, Socrates was put to death three days after the events described in the *Crito*. As even this much makes plain, whether and to what extent there is a duty to obey the law has been a matter of philosophical debate from the beginning. It remains, moreover, one of the central topics of legal philosophy today. And this is to say nothing of its political relevance: Mahatma Gandhi, Martin Luther King, Jr., and Nelson Mandela, to take three prominent examples, each made his respective indelible mark on the twentieth century in large part by self-consciously and publicly disobeying the law.

Philosophical debate concerning the existence and contours of the duty to obey the law—also known as the issue of political obligation—has several facets. This is in part because it implicates debate about the nature of law (discussed above in Sections I and II). If one adopts a form of natural law or Dworkinian interpretivism, for example, then the very identification of law will be morally-laden and, as a result, the case for a robust duty to obey the law will be strong. If, however, one adopts some version of legal positivism, which strictly distinguishes between a law's validity and merit, then the case for the duty will be harder to make. Debate about political obligation is, in this way, related to deep questions in general jurisprudence. But the question of political obligation has yet further dimensions, for it is also intertwined with questions about both political authority and civil disobedience. On the one hand, if there is no duty to obey the law, then given the plausible supposition that a state has authority only if its citizens have such a duty, it follows that the state must lack authority over those whom it purports to rule rightfully. On the other hand, even if there is a duty to obey, it is nevertheless implausible to suppose that it is absolute, holding however repugnant the law, and this limitation calls for an account of the conditions under which disobedience is permitted. Examining the duty to obey thus proceeds in tandem with the examinations of authority and civil disobedience. In light of these many interconnections, it is difficult to explore thoroughly the duty to obey the law in total isolation from other topics.

None of this, though, should suggest that the question of political obligation is not a distinctive question. And one way of posing that distinctive question is this: Is there a general moral obligation to obey the law? This question can itself be analyzed by noting, first and most obviously, that it is a *moral* and not a *legal* obligation that is at issue. For of course a citizen of a particular state has a general legal obligation to obey that state's law. What is sought instead is whether that legal obligation is morally binding. Second, it is a *general* moral obligation to obey the law that is at issue. The fact that there may be some marginal cases where some person subject to legal authority has or lacks a moral duty to obey the law is therefore inapposite. Third and finally, it is *obedience* to the law that is at issue. To obey the law is not merely to conform one's behavior to the law, but to conform one's behavior to it (at least in part) because it is the law – one must do what the law says because the law says so. If one were to respond with a comprehensive affirmative answer to the question Is there a general moral obligation to obey the law?, then, one would say that a given state's citizens all are morally required to conform their conduct to the core laws of their state in virtue of its being the law.

As it happens, a significant number of contemporary philosophers of law provide a negative response to the question of political obligation, denying that there is a general moral obligation to obey the law. Most prominent among these philosophical anarchists is Joseph Raz. His rejection of political obligation is a corollary of his influential "service conception" of normative authority, wherein the state does not merely claim to have but actually possesses authority if and only if it provides the service to its citizens of mediating between them and right reason, such that its citizens are more likely to do what they have reason to do if they follow the state's commands than if they act on their own reasoning about what to do. On Raz's view, states do not uniformly provide this service—some people are better than the state is at determining what they have reason to do on various matters—and thus no state has general authority. Consequently, while some people may be obligated to obey the law some of the time, it is never the case that all people always are so obligated. As Raz puts it, "the extent of the obligation to obey varies from person to person. In no case is the moral obligation as extensive as the legal obligation."[1] There are, to be sure, circumstances in which Raz recognizes a duty to obey the law. But, paradoxically, they are not the circumstances where the law is just, for "[T]he more just and valuable the law is . . . the more reason one has *to conform to it*, and the less *to obey it*."[2] No brief introduction can do justice to the sophistication of Raz's argument on this score, but suffice it to say, to the extent that there is any duty to obey the law on Raz's account of political obligation, it is highly circumscribed.

There are, of course, a host of arguments on the other side of this debate. A general moral duty to obey the law has been variously defended on grounds of consent, fairness, the benefits that the state confers on its citizens, a duty of beneficence that citizens owe to each other, or some combination of these or further considerations. But it is important to repeat that no one defends absolute political obligation, the thesis that one must obey the law whatever its content. John Rawls, probably the most influential political philosopher of the twentieth century, nicely sounds several of these ideas in "The Justification of Civil Disobedience":

> Assuming that the constitution is just and that we have accepted and plan to continue to accept its benefits, we then have both an obligation and a natural duty (and in any case the duty) to comply with what the majority enacts even though it may be unjust. In this way we become bound to follow unjust laws, not always, of course, but provided the injustice does not exceed certain limits. . . . [But if] the enactments of the majority exceed certain bounds of injustice, the citizen may consider civil disobedience.[3]

The defense of civil disobedience that Rawls goes on to mount, and which is largely incorporated into his magisterial 1971 treatise *A Theory of Justice*,[4] is explicated against the background of and in fact relies upon his wider social contract theory of justice. In recognizing a role for civil disobedience in even his ideal theory of the just constitutional democracy, Rawls highlights the important fact that states with a just constitution may nevertheless fall short of their ideals in practice — "even under a just constitution unjust laws may be passed and unjust policies enforced."[5] On this picture, civil disobedience is a fundamentally loyal political act. For it represents a final attempt by citizens who are committed to the conception of justice embodied in their constitution to sway the majority to bring the law and its enforcement sufficiently in line with that conception.

It is surely not coincidental that this is an apt description of those acts of civil disobedience that Martin Luther King, Jr. led in the American civil rights movement of the 1950s and 1960s. In King's famous and eloquent words, "I submit that an individual who breaks a law that conscience tells him is unjust, and who willingly accepts the penalty of imprisonment in order to arouse the conscience of the community over its injustice, is in reality expressing the highest respect for law."[6] The justifiability of King's disobedience is of course beyond dispute. What remains a matter of fundamental philosophical dispute, however, is whether King owed the law the respect that he paid it.

Notes

1   Joseph Raz, "The Obligation to Obey: Revision and Tradition", p. 237.
2   Ibid., p. 234.
3   John Rawls, "The Justification of Civil Disobedience", p. 247.
4   John Rawls, *A Theory of Justice*, Cambridge, MA: Harvard University Press, 1971.
5   Rawls, "Justification", p. 247.
6   Martin Luther King, Jr., "Letter from a Birmingham Jail", p. 258.

Further reading

Richard Dagger, "Membership, Fair Play, and Political Obligation", *Political Studies* 48, 2000, 104–17.
William Edmundson, *Three Anarchical Fallacies*, Cambridge: Cambridge University Press, 1998.

William Edmundson (ed.), *The Duty to Obey the Law: Selected Philosophical Readings*, Lanham, MD: Rowman and Littlefield Publishers, 1999.

Margaret Gilbert, *A Theory of Political Obligation*, New York: Cambridge University Press, 1992.

Leslie Green, *The Authority of the State*, Oxford: Oxford University Press, 1988.

George Klosko, *The Principle of Fairness and Political Obligation*, Lanham, MD: Rowman and Littlefield Publishers, 1992.

John Rawls, *A Theory of Justice*, Cambridge, MA: Harvard University Press, 1971.

Joseph Raz, *The Authority of the State: Essays on Law and Morality*, New York: Oxford University Press, 1979.

Joseph Raz, *The Morality of Freedom*, New York: Oxford University Press, 1986.

Joseph Raz, *Ethics in the Public Domain: Essays in the Morality of Law and Politics*, New York: Oxford University Press, 1994.

Joseph Raz (ed.), *Authority*, New York: NYU Press, 1990.

Christopher Heath Wellman and A. John Simmons, *Is There a Duty to Obey the Law?*, New York: Cambridge University Press, 2005.

Robert Paul Wolff, *In Defense of Anarchism*, 3rd edition, Berkeley, CA: University of California Press, 1998.

Questions

1. What is the best argument for there being a general duty to obey the law?
2. What accounts for Raz's paradoxical claim that the duty to obey the law is inversely related to the justice of the laws whose obedience is in question?
3. If there is no general duty to obey the law, as Raz maintains, does it follow that one is morally permitted to break the law?
4. Do you agree with Rawls and King that civil disobedience is an expression of respect for the law?

Chapter 13

Joseph Raz

THE OBLIGATION TO OBEY
Revision and tradition

THE TURBULENT 1960s, years of the civil-rights movement and of the Vietnam War, brought, as a by-product of civil strife and widespread discontent, renewed interest in the question of the duties an individual owes his society. It was soon to give way to a preoccupation with what society owes to its members, that is, to the swelling of interest in theories of justice and individual rights. But before it did so, a good deal of common ground seemed to have been established among many of the political and moral theorists who did and still do attend to the issue. It is summed up by the view that every citizen has a prima-facie moral obligation to obey the law of a reasonably just state. Its core intuition is the belief that denying an obligation to obey its laws is a denial of the justice of the state. This is believed to be so either on instrumentalist grounds or on grounds of fairness. The instrumentalist contends that the state will not be able to function if its citizens are not obligated to obey its laws and respect that obligation for the most part. The fairness argument has it that anyone who denies an obligation to obey in a just state takes unfair advantage of others who submit to such an obligation.

I have joined several theorists who challenge this consensus.[1] There have, of course, always been those who deny the existence of an obligation to obey the law on the ground that no state can be just. Their most powerful philosophical spokesman in recent years has been Robert Paul Wolff.[2] The challenge posed by the arguments referred to is that they claim that even in a just state, if there can be such, there is no general obligation to obey the law. Not even all those who deny the existence of a general obligation to obey the law have realized its full implications. If there is no general obligation to obey, then the law does not have general authority, for to have authority is to have a right to rule those who are subject to it. And a right to rule entails a duty to obey. I shall contend below that in a very real sense this conclusion returns to the main line of thought of the founders of modern political theory. However, it appears to be a novel position and not surprisingly has led to a number of misunderstandings as typified in Dr Finnis's article.[3] This essay aims to help dispel some of the misunderstandings.

I. Government without authority

Let us start by considering the (apparent) paradox of the just government. Most political theorists acknowledge that there is no general obligation to obey the law of an unjust state. But, it is contended, there is an obligation to obey the law of a reasonably just state, and the greater its justice the stricter, or at any rate the clearer, the obligation. But is this so? Isn't the reverse the case? The morality of a government's laws measures, in part, its justice. Its laws are moral only if there is a moral obligation to perform the actions which they impose a legal obligation to perform. That moral obligation cannot be due to the existence of an obligation to obey the law. To establish an obligation to obey the law one has to establish that it is relatively just. It is relatively just only if there is a moral obligation to do that which it imposes legal obligations to do. So the moral obligations on which the claim that the law is just is founded are prior to and independent of the moral obligation to obey the law. The alleged moral obligation to obey arises from these independent obligations to act as the law requires.

Since the obligation to obey the law derives from these other moral obligations, its weight or strictness reflects their weight. The stricter they are the stricter is the obligation to obey. But if so, then the obligation to obey the law is at best redundant. It may make a moral difference if it exists in an unjust state, for there it imposes a moral obligation where none exists. But in a just state, it is at best a mere shadow of other moral duties. It adds nothing to them. Since the obligation to obey exists only in a just state, it is at best redundant.

Consider the question whether there is a legal obligation to obey the law. The obligation exists, but it is hardly ever mentioned, for it is the shadow of all the specific legal obligations. The law requires one to pay tax, refrain from murder, assault, theft, libel, breach of contract, etc. Hence, tautologically, one has a legal obligation to pay tax, refrain from murder, assault, theft, libel, breach of contract, etc. A short, though empty and uninformative, way of describing one's legal duties is to say that one has a legal duty to obey the law. One has a legal duty to obey the law because one has a legal duty to obey this law and that, and so on, until one exhausts their list. It is likewise, the paradox can be interpreted as alleging, with the moral duty to obey the law. It exists only to the extent that there are other, independent moral duties to obey each of the laws of the system. It is merely their shadow.

In fact the paradox is even worse. The obligation to obey the law is no mere shadow. It would be, were it to exist, a moral perversion. Consider legal duties such as the duty not to commit murder and not to rape. Clearly there are moral duties to refrain from murder and from rape. Equally clearly we approve, if we do, of the laws prohibiting such acts, because the acts they forbid are morally forbidden.[4] Moreover, we expect morally conscientious people to comply with these laws because the acts they forbid are immoral. I would feel insulted if it were suggested that I refrain from murder and rape because I recognize a moral obligation to obey the law. We expect people to avoid such actions whether or not they are legally forbidden, and for reasons which have nothing to do with the law. If it turns out that those reasons fail, that it is only respect for the law which restrains them from such acts, then those people lose much of our respect.

But if the obligation to obey the law is not a morally correct reason by which the morally conscientious person should guide his action, at least not in such elementary and fundamental areas of the law as those mentioned, then can there be such an obligation? Can there be a moral obligation to perform an action if to take the existence of the obligation as one's reason for the action it enjoins would be wrong, or ill-fitting?

So much for the apparent paradox of the just law. The more just and valuable the law is, it says, the more reason one has to *conform to* it, and the less *to obey* it. Since it is just, those considerations which establish its justice should be one's reasons for conforming with it, i.e. for acting as it requires. But in acting for these reasons one would not be obeying the law, one would not be conforming because that is what the law requires. Rather, one would be acting on the doctrine of justice to which the law itself conforms.

I called the paradox merely 'apparent' because it is overstated. For reasons we will examine in the next section, sometimes the law makes a moral difference. In particular, sometimes the law is just, although no independent obligation attaches to what it requires. In these cases it is morally obligatory to act as the law requires because it so requires. But even though over-stated, the alleged paradox is instructive. It challenges the existence of a general obligation to obey the law. To succeed, it need only establish that in some fairly central cases there is no such obligation. From this point of view it matters not that some laws are not like the laws against murder and rape. If a legal prohibition of murder neither imposes an independent moral obliga-tion nor makes the duty not to murder stricter or weightier than it was without the law, then the case is made. The prohibitions of murder, rape, enslavement, imprisonment, and similar legal prohibitions are central to the laws of all just legal systems. Their existence cannot be dismissed as marginal or controversial. If these laws do not make a difference to our moral obligations, then there is no *general* obligation to obey the law. There may be a moral obligation to obey some laws, but this was never in contention.

The argument so far depends on two assump-tions, both of which are open to challenge. First, the argument assumes that to refrain from murder or any other moral perversion solely because the law proscribes it is morally distorted and undesirable. It may be objected that while this is not the best motive for refraining from murder it is not the worst either. It is better, for example, than sparing a person's life because he will then suffer a more painful death. Second, it assumes that the reasons for obeying the law, when such can be found, must derive from the reasons for having laws with that particular content. It may be objected that the reasons for obedience normally thought of as constituting the obligation to obey have nothing to do with the desirability of any particular law but with the desirability of the existence of a legal system and a structure of government by law as a whole.

The argument of the following pages will help rebut these objections and will bolster the assumptions, especially the second one.[5] My present purpose is more modest. Even if the alleged paradox fails to disprove the existence of an obligation to obey, it succeeds in making us re-examine some of our assumptions about the functions of law in society. It reveals that much of the good that the law can do does not presuppose any obligation to obey.

Once more, a simplified picture will help bring out the point more clearly. Let us assume that in its sole proper function, the law prohibits murder, neglect of children by their parents, and other similar immoralities. On this assumption it is plausible to claim that the law's direct function is to motivate those who fail to be sufficiently moved by sound moral considerations. The con-scientious, knowledgeable person will do what the law requires of him regardless of whether the law exists or not. The law is not for him. It is for those who deny their moral duties. It forces them to act as they should by threatening sanctions if they fail to do so. By addressing the self-interest of those who fail to be properly moved by moral considerations, the law reassures the morally conscientious. It assures him that he will not be taken advantage of, will not be exploited by the unscrupulous.

This oversimplified picture demonstrates the good a government without authority can do.[6] One can threaten and penalize people without having authority over them. One can also have an organization to issue and carry out threats with-out authority over them either. We can imagine the law-enforcement functions we have in mind being carried out by people who are paid salaries, or given other incentives to enforce and to administer the laws. The personnel in charge of the implementation of the law need not necessarily be subject to the authority or the government or its law; they may be doing a job under a contract. Their actions are morally permissible for reasons independent of the law. Even when they encroach on the personal liberty of the offender, they need not invoke the law in justification. They treat offenders in ways morally appropriate for those who renege on their moral duties.

The picture is oversimplified. But it is so in what it leaves out, not in what it says. Governments fulfil the functions we described, but they do much else besides. Some of their other functions do not presuppose the recognition of authority either. It is an important fact about the modern state that to an ever greater extent it affects our fortunes by means other than exercising, or claiming to exercise, authority over us. In many states the government, or public authorities generally, are the largest employer in the country, control much of the infrastructure through a state monopoly on the provision of mail, telephone, airport and seaport services, and the like. The armed forces are the largest clients for many high-technology industries, and so on. The details vary from state to state, but the overall picture is rather similar.

The effects of this concentration of economic power are evident in the state's growing use of its economic muscle to achieve aims which in previous times would have required legislation or administrative actions. Governments attempt to affect the direction of industrial development, the level of economic activity, the rate of inflation, the level of unemployment, the regional distribution of wealth in the country, and other objectives through their economic power alone. Even non-economic objectives such as racial equality in employment are sometimes pursued by the use of economic power, rather than by the exercise of authority. It is often argued that the awarding of governmental contracts only to equal-opportunity employers is the best way of pursuing such objectives.

Many of these developments are relatively recent, and raise difficult questions about the adequacy of the existing machinery for controlling governmental powers. The machinery evolved primarily as a check on the government's exercise of legislative and administrative power. It is ill-suited today to supervise the economic activities of public authorities. Nevertheless, it is clear that only the degree to which governments affect their populations by non-governmental means is new, for governments have always affected individuals by changing their physical or economic environment by means which do not invoke its authority. Governments have built roads, dug canals, constructed state buildings and monuments, employed people, and the like for as long as political society has existed.

II. On the foundation of political authority

Governments affect us through their intervention in the market by changing the physical environment, and by providing the morally unscrupulous or misguided with self-interested reasons to do that which they ought to do, but which moral reasons fail to make them do. Focusing on these aspects of governmental activity helps dispel the myth that denying the existence of an obligation to obey the law amounts to denying the possibility of a just government. This myth is based on a misperception of the aims and means of governmental action. If in principle governments can discharge all the mentioned functions without authority, then they can do so justly as well as unjustly. From our perspective it does not matter if the same ends can be achieved by other means, ones which do not involve the existence of governments. I am not challenging the justice of alternative modes of social organization, nor comparing their precise merits. I only seek to establish that those who favour the continued exercise of many of the existing functions of governments cannot argue from that to the existence of a general obligation to obey the law. For those functions can be discharged by governments independently of such an obligation.

One objection may be that the argument overlooks that at least government officials must accept governmental authority for government to function as described. If the officials do not obey the law, then the morally unscrupulous, for example, will have no fear that legal sanctions may be applied to them. The contract model answered this objection, because officials would serve the government by consent rather than because they recognize its authority. This may not be a very practical arrangement in some cases. A more important objection may be that, where governments do not exercise any authority, not even over their officials, one may well doubt whether they are governments at all rather than corporations who voluntarily undertake some good social services. Be that as it may, the functions described which are normally carried out by governments can in principle be carried out without authority. Furthermore, let us remind ourselves that the argument does not require that nobody is under the authority of government. It only claims there is no general obligation to obey the law, i.e. that not everyone is under an obligation to obey all the laws, not even in a relatively just society.

My basic position is not that no one has any moral reason ever to take account of the existence of the law. I argue that the extent of the obligation to obey varies from person to person. In no case is the moral obligation as extensive as the legal obligation. Consider three typical situations in which ordinary citizens do find themselves under an obligation to obey.

First, imagine that I use in the course of my employment tools which may create a safety hazard to passers-by. The government has issued safety regulations detailing the equipment which may be used and the safety measures that I must take to make their use safe. The government experts who laid down these safety regulations are experts in their field. Their judgment is much more reliable than mine. I am therefore duty-bound to obey the regulations which they have adopted.

Second, we all have reason to preserve the countryside. In areas visited by many people, this goal would be enhanced if no one had barbecues. In fact everyone had barbecues in those areas. The damage is done, and my refraining from a barbecue will not help. The situation is so bad that my having a barbecue will not make even a small difference. At long last the government steps in and forbids having barbecues except in a few designated locations. Because the regulation might reverse the trend, I have an obligation to obey this law.

Third, I disagree with the government's policy of allowing the construction of nuclear-power plants. I can try to block the roads leading to the construction sites to stop building material and machinery from reaching the workers. Doing so will be against the law. It will also, if successful to any degree, encourage other people to take the law into their own hands when they think they can force the government to change its policies. This will undermine the ability of the government to discharge its functions. Despite this lapse on the government's part, I still regard it as a relatively just and moral government. I have an obligation to obey the law and avoid breaking it in the way described.

In one respect the last case differs from the first two. Though I am obligated to obey the law, the obligation does not show that the law or government had authority over me regarding the issue in question. In the first two cases my obligation to obey results from the law's authority. It knows best, or it can best arrange matters. Hence, I had better accept its instructions and obey. In the last case there are no such assumptions. It is merely that I will undermine the government's ability to do good. That reason can, and often does, apply to people not subject to the authority of the government. A foreign state may restrain its action in order not to undermine the ability of my government to fulfil its useful functions. But a foreign state is not subject to the authority of the government.[7]

More important are the features the three cases have in common. 1. They are typical cases. Much of planning law, laws concerning safety at work, regulations regarding standards of manufactured goods such as cars, pharmaceuticals, and the like, rules concerning the safe maintenance of cars, or concerning standards of safe driving, qualifications required for engaging in certain occupations, and many more, all belong to the first category. Standards for the preservation of the environment, for the protection of scarce resources, for the raising of revenue through taxation to finance public projects, welfare services, or other valuable projects, and many more belong in most cases to the second category. Any act aimed at forcing public authorities to change their policies or actions by unlawful means belongs to the third category. Some laws are more likely to be broken for these reasons than others, but the violation of any law can, on occasion, be used for such a purpose.

2. In all the examples, the law makes a difference to one's moral obligations. The moral obligation is a prima-facie one; it may be overridden by contrary considerations. But for the law, I might well have adopted different safety precautions. I accept the superior reliability of the law on such issues, and defer to its judgment. I would not have had any reason to avoid having barbecues in the beauty spots of the second example, but for the introduction of the law which gives rise to the expectation that the widespread but damaging practice will come to an end, or at least that it will be sufficiently reduced so that my self-restraint will make a difference, however little. Finally, had the blockade of the nuclear-power plant site not been against the law, it would not have been an act tending to undermine the ability of the government to carry out its proper functions. That is why it is proper to talk in all these cases of my obligation to obey some laws.

3. None of the cases separately nor all of them together offer an argument capable of being generalized to point to a general obligation to obey. The contrary is the case. They highlight the degree to which the obligation is limited and varies in accordance with circumstances. The first case depends on the law's

superior knowledge. But if I am the greatest living expert on pharmaceuticals, then the law has no authority over me regarding the safety of pharmaceuticals. Sometimes I have the option of investing time, money, and mental effort in a problem to solve it myself, or to go to a knowledgeable friend and follow his advice. The law, in cases of the first type, is like a knowledgeable friend and the same range of options are available. So that in such matters the range of the law's authority over individuals varies from one person to another.

The second example concerns not the law's superior knowledge but its ability to achieve goals which individuals have reason to pursue, but cannot do so effectively on their own, because their realization requires co-ordinating the actions of large numbers of people. Although central to the normal functioning of the law, such cases cannot be generalized to generate an obligation to obey the law of a relatively just state. First, not all laws purport to fulfil such a function. Laws of the kind involved in the first class of cases, as well as laws like the prohibition of rape and murder, differ from laws which co-ordinate the efforts of large groups. In the former cases, the reasons for acting in accord with the law apply with the same stringency in each case regardless of the degree of general conformity with the law. Every time someone murders or recklessly engages in a risky activity he acts wrongly, harming or risking others. Not so in our second example. Here the existence of reasons for the action, and their weight, depend on general conformity, or the likelihood of it. Some laws are of this character, others are not. The reasons which lead one to acknowledge the law's authority in cases of co-ordination do not apply elsewhere. Second, laws striving to achieve co-ordination address masses of people, and are designed to be enforced and regulated through the activities of judicial and administrative institutions. They are drafted not merely to state most accurately the actions required if co-ordination is to be achieved, but also to be easily comprehended, and to avoid giving rise to administrative corruption, the harassment of individuals, and other undesirable by-products of the operation of the legal machine. A person who understands the situation will often have reason to go beyond the law, and to do more than the law requires in pursuit of the same co-ordinating goal. Alternatively, he may find that on occasion he has no reason to follow certain aspects of the law. They may be the inevitable simplifications the law has to embrace to be reasonably understood and efficiently enforced. There is no reason for an individual not faced with the same considerations to conform to the law on such occasions.

The third type of example is often invoked to supplement the previous two and plug the remaining holes. It is argued that, if the law is reasonably just, cases like those of the first two types exist in large numbers. In other cases one ought to obey the law, for otherwise one would undermine its ability to function effectively. The argument is based on a false premiss. Law breaking is liable to undermine the effectiveness of the government in many cases. In others, violations of law have no such effect. Offences never known to anyone or violating the interests of one private individual only, as with many torts and breaches of contract, generally do not diminish the government's effectiveness. There may be other reasons for conforming with the law in some of these cases, but the threat to the effectiveness of government and the law is not among them.

These three types of argument illustrated by our examples are not the only ones which lead to obligations to obey some laws or others. I have discussed them because, other than consent and voluntary commitments, they most commonly give rise to an obligation to obey. They usefully illustrate the main points which need emphasizing. First, that the extent of the duty to obey the law in a relatively just country varies from person to person and from one range of cases to another. There is probably a common core of

cases regarding which the obligation exists and applies equally to all. Some duties based on the co-ordinative argument (e.g. duty to pay tax) and on the bad-example argument (e.g. avoiding political terrorism) are likely to apply equally to all citizens. Beyond this core, the extent of the obligation to obey will vary greatly. Second, the extent of the obligation depends on factors other than whether the law is just and sensible. It may depend on the expertise of the individual citizen, as in cases of the first kind, or on the circumstances of the occasion for the violation, as often in cases of the third kind.

III. Revisionism is traditionalism

Dr Finnis's article[8] exemplifies some of the confusions which pervade our reflections on the obligation to obey. His central claim is that the law presents itself as a seamless web: its subjects are not allowed to pick and choose.[9] This is certainly the case. But Finnis does not even pause to indicate that he draws from this the conclusion that we are not allowed to pick and choose, let alone present any reason in support of it. For him, if this is how the law presents itself, then this is how we ought to take it. To be sure, if we have an obligation to obey the law, then the conclusion does indeed follow. But one cannot presuppose that we have such an obligation in order to provide the reason ('the law is a seamless web') for claiming that we have an obligation to obey. This would be a most vicious circle indeed. Does he perchance imply that we cannot pick and choose, for if we do the whole system of law and order will be undermined and will eventually collapse? He certainly does not argue to that effect, nor does he consider the case to the contrary which I have presented above and previously.[10] Under these circumstances one hesitates to foist any particular interpretation on Finnis's statement.

Dr Finnis's intriguing article contains similar throwaway points which leave the reader wondering how they are meant to be taken. Does he really believe that 'apart from the law' a person 'could reasonably be relatively indifferent to the concerns and interests of persons whose activities . . . do not affect him or at least do not benefit him'?[11] There are no doubt people who do hold that we have no moral obligations to people who do not benefit us. But such a broad statement has no hope of carrying conviction without any word in its defence. Moreover, most of those people will take the point as militating against there being an obligation to obey the law, at least to the extent that it requires us to benefit strangers. Finnis regards it as a further reason to believe in an obligation to obey.

Finnis tells us that, even if farmers have a duty not to pollute the river, they may misguidedly dispute this, and that therefore the way to get them to do their moral duty is to have a moral obligation to obey the law. They will then refrain from pollution, because the law requires them to do so. But that will be the case only if they will not make a mistake about their obligation to obey the law, and only if the law makers will not make a mistake about the obligation not to pollute the rivers. Even if these conditions are met, they constitute an argument for the existence of an obligation to obey the law only if the law-makers are not likely to make fewer mistakes than the farmers on other issues as well. For the obligation to obey is general, and what is won in the absence of pollution can easily be lost in the maltreatment of old-age pensioners or of the mentally ill.

Those who emphasize the danger of every person deciding for himself whether the case for the law's authority over any range of questions is good or not often overlook this last point. Human judgment errs. It falls prey to temptations and bias distorts it. This fact must affect one's considerations. But which way should it incline one? The only general answer which I find persuasive is that it depends on the circumstances. In some areas and regarding some people, caution requires submission to authority. In others it leads to denial of authority. There are risks, moral and other, in uncritical acceptance of authority. Too often in the past, the fallibility of human judgment has led to submission to authority from a misguided sense of duty where this was a morally reprehensible attitude.

Finnis's elegant discussion of the river-pollution case illustrates one way in which the law can do good, and when it does it should certainly be obeyed.[12] It is a good illustration of an occasion on which the existence of the law makes a difference. While some laws make a difference, I doubt that all do. Some of the examples used above show how greatly many legal rules, all equally central to the law, differ from the river-pollution example. One should not be so captivated by one paradigm that others go unnoticed. Consider the river-pollution case itself. Finnis quite reasonably directs our attention to a time when co-ordination, though desirable, does not obtain and the law steps in to secure it. But travel ten years on. By now (let us simplify), either the scheme introduced by the law has taken root and is the general practice or it has long since been forgotten and is honoured only in the breach. In the second case, my conforming with the law will serve no useful purpose unless it happens to protect me from penalties, or to stop my behaviour being misunderstood by others. There is then no point in obeying the law. There is reason to conform with it if the scheme is in general effective. But, as is evident by comparing this case with the previous one, where the law is the same but the practice of conformity is missing, that reason is not the law but the actual practice.

All the questions I raise can be answered. I have stated my answers in previous publications and supplemented them above. Finnis seems to disagree, but he fails to tell us why. He properly explains why the law is a way of achieving co-ordination,[13] but he never even attempts to show that coordination requires general obedience to law.[14]

I should make clear my agreement with Finnis

in his doubts about the value of social choice and game theory as guides to moral decisions. This is not the occasion to go into such issues. But we should remember that all the arguments concerning an obligation to obey which have been canvassed so far were essentially instrumental arguments. They assumed that we have reason to promote or protect certain states of affairs, and examined whether recognition of an obligation to obey the law, or obedience to law, is a way of doing so. But are there not non-instrumental reasons for obeying the law?

Non-instrumental reasoning is central to a distinguished tradition in political philosophy. Today one of the most common arguments, often repeated in different forms, is based on alleged considerations of fairness. It is unfair, it is claimed, to enjoy benefits derived from the law without contributing one's share to the production of those benefits. As has been pointed out many times before, this argument is of dubious validity when one has no choice but to accept the benefits, or even more generally, when the benefits are given to one who does not request them, and in circumstances which do not imply an understanding concerning the conditions attached to their donation and receipt. Besides, even where it is unfair not to reciprocate for services received, or not to contribute one's share to the production of a good of general public value, it cannot be unfair to perform innocuous acts which neither harm any one nor impede the provision of any public good. Many violations of law are such innocuous acts. Therefore, appeals to fairness can raise no general obligation to obey the law.

The more traditional, non-instrumental justification of the obligation to obey the law relies on contract and consent. Not all consent theorists base either the validity of the consent or the reasons for giving it on non-instrumental reasons. Hobbes wished to derive it all from enlightened self-interest. Locke allowed moral reasons to enter the argument, but they are instrumental reasons. Consent to obey is designed to bring greater conformity with the natural law and greater respect for the natural rights of men than is likely to be achieved in a state of nature. Rousseau was the most important eighteenth-century thinker to highlight the intrinsic value of the social contract as the act which constitutes civil society, as well as the personality of those who belong to it.

Consent to obey the law of a relatively just government indeed establishes an obligation to obey the law.[15] The well-known difficulty with consent as the foundation of political authority is that too few have given their consent. This argument in its customary form can be right and wrong at the same time. Consent or agreement requires a deliberate, performative action, and to be binding it has to be voluntarily undertaken. Many people, however, have never performed anything remotely like such an action. The only time I did was during my national military service, in circumstances where failure to take the oath would have led to being court-martialled. I would not have made the oath but for these circumstances, and I do not think I was ever bound to observe this coerced undertaking.

Nevertheless, this objection is also misguided. There are other ways of incurring voluntary or semi-voluntary obligations. Consider a family or a friendship. There are obligations which friends owe each other, and which are in a sense voluntary obligations, as it is obligatory neither to form friendships nor to continue with them once formed. Yet we do not undertake these obligations by an act of promise or consent. As does friendship, these obligations arise from the developing relations between people. Loyalty is an essential duty arising from any personal relationship. The content of this duty helps us to identify the character of the relationship. If the duty precludes your having sex with another person, then your relations are of one character; and if it precludes publicizing disagreements between you, then you have relations of another kind, and so on. In other words, duties of loyalty are semi-voluntary, because the relationship itself is not obligatory. Moreover, they are non-instrumentally justified because they are part of what makes the relationship into the kind of relationship it is. (I am assuming that having the particular relationship, friendship, is itself of intrinsic value.)

What has this excursion into the normative aspect of personal relations to do with the obligation to obey the law? It demonstrates the possibility of one kind of obligation to obey which arises out of a sense of identifying with or belonging to the community. Such an attitude, if directed to a community which deserves it, is intrinsically valuable. It is not, however, obligatory. One does not have a moral duty to feel a sense of belonging in a community; certainly there is no obligation to feel that one belongs to a country (rather than one's village, or some other community). I talk of a feeling that one belongs, but this feeling is nothing other than a complex attitude comprising emotional, cognitive, and normative elements. Feeling a sense of loyalty and a duty of loyalty constitutes, here too, an element of such an attitude.

The government and the law are official or formal organs of the community. If they represent the community or express its will justly and accurately, then an entirely natural indication of a member's sense of belonging is one's attitude toward the community's organization and laws. I call such an attitude respect for law. It is a belief that one is under an obligation to obey because the law is one's law, and the law of one's country. Obeying it is a way of expressing confidence and trust in its justice. As such, it expresses one's identification with the community. Respect for law does not derive from consent. It grows, as friendships do; it develops, as does one's sense of membership in a community. Nevertheless, respect for law grounds a quasi-voluntary obligation. An obligation to obey the law is in such cases part and parcel of one's attitude toward the community. One feels that one betrays the community if one breaks the law to gain advantage, or out of convenience, or thought-

lessness, and this regardless of whether the violation actually harms anyone, just as one can be disloyal to a friend without harming him or any of his interests, without even offending him.

An obligation to obey which is part of a duty of loyalty to the community is a semi-voluntary obligation, because one has no moral duty to identify with this community. It is founded on non-instrumental considerations, for it constitutes an attitude of belonging which has intrinsic value, if addressed to an appropriate object. Vindicating its existence does not, therefore, establish the existence of a general obligation to obey the law. For good or ill, there are many who do not feel this way about their country, and many more who do not feel like this about its formal legal organization. It is sometimes said that the denial of a general obligation to obey is of recent vintage. It is in many ways the opposite. At the birth of modern political theory in the seventeenth and eighteenth centuries, there was one clear orthodoxy: if there is a general obligation to obey the law, it exists because it was voluntarily undertaken. That is the view defended here. The fathers of modern political theory also believed that such obligations were indeed voluntarily undertaken. If this view is no longer true today, it is because the societies we live in are less homogeneous, more troubled about their own identity and about the role of government and the law in the social fabric. Society has changed, not political theory.

Notes

First published in Notre Dame Journal of Law, Ethics and Public Policy, 1 (1984).
1 See M. B. E. Smith, 'Is There a Prima Facie Obligation to Obey the Law?', Yale Law Journal, 82 (1973); A. Woozley, Law and Obedience (London: Duckworth, 1979); Raz, The Authority of Law; R. Sartorius, 'Political Authority and Political Obligation', Virginia Law Review, 67 (1981).
2 In Defense of Anarchism (New York: Harper and Row, 1970).

3 J. M. Finnis, 'The Authority of Law in the Predicament of Contemporary Social Theory', *Notre Dame Journal of Law, Ethics and Public Policy*, 1 (1984).

4 Here, as elsewhere in this essay, I am assuming that the immorality of an action, even if a necessary condition of the justice of a law prohibiting it, is never a sufficient condition.

5 The first objection is indecisive. The fact that some motives for action according to law are worse than the desire to obey may be nothing more than the ranking of evils. It may show merely that we normally regard intellectual confusion (the belief in an obligation to obey and action for it) as a lesser evil than cruelty, hatred, etc.

6 My analysis here is loose and informal. It runs parallel to the ingenious discussion of the pre-state existence of voluntary protection associations in R. Nozick's *Anarchy, State and Utopia* (New York: Basic Books, 1974). I do not share his picture of the working of the invisible hand, nor his understanding of people's moral rights and duties. But my argument parallels his in the emphasis on the extent to which governments do or can carry out functions which do not presuppose possession of authority.

7 In other words, I agree with R. P. Wolff's contention that sometimes one has reason to obey someone who claims authority for reasons which do not amount to submission to his authority. See *In Defense of Anarchism*, 15–16.

8 'The Authority of Law in the Predicament of Contemporary Social Theory'.

9 Ibid. 120.

10 *The Authority of Law*, ch. 12.

11 *The Authority of Law*.

12 Ibid. 134–7.

13 Ibid. 134–5.

14 Throughout I am using 'co-ordination' in its ordinary signification, rather than in the narrow and artificial sense it has been given in some recent writings in game theory.

15 I discuss the issue at some length in my 'Authority and Consent', *Virginia Law Review*, 67 (1981).

Chapter 14

John Rawls

THE JUSTIFICATION OF CIVIL DISOBEDIENCE

I. Introduction

I SHOULD LIKE to discuss briefly, and in an informal way, the grounds of civil disobedience in a constitutional democracy. Thus, I shall limit my remarks to the conditions under which we may, by civil disobedience, properly oppose legally established democratic authority; I am not concerned with the situation under other kinds of government nor, except incidentally, with other forms of resistance. My thought is that in a reasonably just (though of course not perfectly just) democratic regime, civil disobedience, when it is justified, is normally to be understood as a political action which addresses the sense of justice of the majority in order to urge reconsideration of the measures protested and to warn that in the firm opinion of the dissenters the conditions of social cooperation are not being honored. This characterization of civil disobedience is intended to apply to dissent on fundamental questions of internal policy, a limitation which I shall follow to simplify our question.

II. The social contract doctrine

It is obvious that the justification of civil disobedience depends upon the theory of political obligation in general, and so we may appropriately begin with a few comments on this question. The two chief virtues of social institutions are justice and efficiency, where by the efficiency of institutions I understand their effectiveness for certain social conditions and ends the fulfillment of which is to everyone's advantage. We should comply with and do our part in just and efficient social arrangements for at least two reasons: first of all, we have a natural duty not to oppose the establishment of just and efficient institutions (when they do not yet exist) and to uphold and comply with them (when they do exist); and second, assuming that we have knowingly accepted the benefits of these institutions and plan to continue to do so, and that we have encouraged and expect others to do their part, we also have an obligation to do our share when, as the arrangement requires, it comes our turn. Thus, we often have both a natural duty as well as an obligation to support just and efficient institutions, the obligation arising from our voluntary acts while the duty does not.

Now all this is perhaps obvious enough, but it does not take us very far. Any more particular conclusions depend upon the conception of justice which is the basis of a theory of political obligation. I believe that the appropriate conception, at least for an account of political obligation in a constitutional democracy, is that of the social contract theory from which so much of our political thought derives. If we are careful to interpret it in a suitably general way, I hold that this doctrine provides a satisfactory basis for political theory, indeed even for ethical theory itself, but this is beyond our present concern.[1] The interpretation I suggest is the following: that the principles to which social arrangements must conform, and in particular the principles of justice, are those which free and rational men would agree to in an original position of equal liberty; and similarly, the principles which govern men's relations to institutions and define their natural duties and obligations are the principles to which they would consent when so situated. It should be noted straightaway that in this interpretation of the contract theory the principles of justice are understood as the outcome of a hypothetical agreement. They are principles which would be agreed to if the situation of the original position were to arise. There is no mention of an actual agreement, nor need such an agreement ever be made. Social arrangements are just or unjust according to whether they accord with the principles for assigning and securing fundamental rights and liberties which would be chosen in the original position. This position is, to be sure, the analytic analogue of the traditional notion of the state of nature, but it must not be mistaken for a historical occasion. Rather it is a hypothetical situation which embodies the basic ideas of the contract doctrine; the description of this situation enables us to work out which principles would be adopted. I must now say something about these matters.

The contract doctrine has always supposed that the persons in the original position have equal powers and rights, that is, that they are symmetrically situated with respect to any arrangements for reaching agreement, and that coalitions and the like are excluded. But it is an essential element (which has not been sufficiently observed although it is implicit in Kant's version of the theory) that there are very strong restrictions on what the contracting parties are presumed to know. In particular, I interpret the theory to hold that the parties do not know their position in society, past, present,

or future; nor do they know which institutions exist. Again, they do not know their own place in the distribution of natural talents and abilities, whether they are intelligent or strong, man or woman, and so on. Finally, they do not know their own particular interests and preferences or the system of ends which they wish to advance: they do not know their conception of the good. In all these respects the parties are confronted with a veil of ignorance which prevents any one from being able to take advantage of his good fortune or particular interests or from being disadvantaged by them. What the parties do know (or assume) is that Hume's circumstances of justice obtain: namely, that the bounty of nature is not so generous as to render cooperative schemes superfluous nor so harsh as to make them impossible. Moreover, they assume that the extent of their altruism is limited and that, in general, they do not take an interest in one another's interests. Thus, given the special features of the original position, each man tries to do the best he can for himself by insisting on principles calculated to protect and advance his system of ends whatever it turns out to be.

I believe that as a consequence of the peculiar nature of the original position there would be an agreement on the following two principles for assigning rights and duties and for regulating distributive shares as these are determined by the fundamental institutions of society: first, each person is to have an equal right to the most extensive liberty compatible with a like liberty for all; second, social and economic inequalities (as defined by the institutional structure or fostered by it) are to be arranged so that they are both to everyone's advantage and attached to positions and offices open to all. In view of the content of these two principles and their application to the main institutions of society, and therefore to the social system as a whole, we may regard them as the two principles of justice. Basic social arrangements are just insofar as they conform to these principles, and we can, if we like, discuss questions of justice directly by reference to them. But a deeper understanding of the justification of civil disobedience requires, I think, an account of the derivation of these principles provided by the doctrine of the social contract. Part of our task is to show why this is so.

III. The grounds of compliance with an unjust law

If we assume that in the original position men would agree both to the principle of doing their part when they have accepted and plan to continue to accept the benefits of just institutions (the principle of fairness), and also to the principle of not preventing the establishment of just institutions and of upholding and complying with them when they do exist, then the contract doctrine easily accounts for our having to conform to just institutions. But how does it account for the fact that we are normally required to comply with unjust laws as well? The injustice of a law is not a sufficient ground for not complying with it any more than the legal validity of legislation is always sufficient to require obedience to it. Sometimes one hears these extremes asserted, but I think that we need not take them seriously.

An answer to our question can be given by elaborating the social contract theory in the following way. I interpret it to hold that one is to envisage a series of agreements as follows: first, men are to agree upon the principles of justice in the original position. Then they are to move to a constitutional convention in which they choose a constitution that satisfies the principles of justice already chosen. Finally they assume the role of a legislative body and, guided by the principles of justice, enact laws subject to the constraints and procedures of the just constitution. The decisions reached in any stage are binding in all subsequent stages. Now whereas in the original position the contracting parties have no knowledge of their society or of their own position in it, in both a constitutional

convention and a legislature, they do know certain general facts about their institutions, for example, the statistics regarding employment and output required for fiscal and economic policy. But no one knows particular facts about his own social class or his place in the distribution of natural assets. On each occasion the contracting parties have the knowledge required to make their agreement rational from the appropriate point of view, but not so much as to make them prejudiced. They are unable to tailor principles and legislation to take advantage of their social or natural position; a veil of ignorance prevents their knowing what this position is. With this series of agreements in mind, we can characterize just laws and policies as those which would be enacted were this whole process correctly carried out.

In choosing a constitution the aim is to find among the just constitutions the one which is most likely, given the general facts about the society in question, to lead to just and effective legislation. The principles of justice provide a criterion for the laws desired; the problem is to find a set of political procedures that will give this outcome. I shall assume that, at least under the normal conditions of a modern state, the best constitution is some form of democratic regime affirming equal political liberty and using some sort of majority (or other plurality) rule. Thus it follows that on the contract theory a constitutional democracy of some sort is required by the principles of justice. At the same time it is essential to observe that the constitutional process is always a case of what we may call imperfect procedural justice: that is, there is no feasible political procedure which guarantees that the enacted legislation is just even though we have (let us suppose) a standard for just legislation. In simple cases, such as games of fair division, there are procedures which always lead to the right outcome (assume that equal shares is fair and let the man who cuts the cake take the last piece). These situations are those of perfect procedural justice. In other cases it does not matter what the outcome is as long as the fair procedure is followed: fairness of the process is transferred to the result (fair gambling is an instance of this). These situations are those of pure procedural justice. The constitutional process, like a criminal trial, resembles neither of these; the result matters and we have a standard for it. The difficulty is that we cannot frame a procedure which guarantees that only just and effective legislation is enacted. Thus even under a just constitution unjust laws may be passed and unjust policies enforced. Some form of the majority principle is necessary but the majority may be mistaken, more or less willfully, in what it legislates. In agreeing to a democratic constitution (as an instance of imperfect procedural justice) one accepts at the same time the principle of majority rule. Assuming that the constitution is just and that we have accepted and plan to continue to accept its benefits, we then have both an obligation and a natural duty (and in any case the duty) to comply with what the majority enacts even though it may be unjust. In this way we become bound to follow unjust laws, not always, of course, but provided the injustice does not exceed certain limits. We recognize that we must run the risk of suffering from the defects of one another's sense of justice; this burden we are prepared to carry as long as it is more or less evenly distributed or does not weigh too heavily. Justice binds us to a just constitution and to the unjust laws which may be enacted under it in precisely the same way that it binds us to any other social arrangement. Once we take the sequence of stages into account, there is nothing unusual in our being required to comply with unjust laws.

It should be observed that the majority principle has a secondary place as a rule of procedure which is perhaps the most efficient one under usual circumstances for working a democratic constitution. The basis for it rests essentially upon the principles of justice and therefore we may, when conditions allow, appeal to these principles against unjust legislation. The justice of the constitution does not ensure the justice of laws enacted under it; and while we often have both an obligation and a duty to comply with what the majority legislates (as long as it does not exceed certain limits), there is, of course, no corresponding obligation or duty to regard what the majority enacts as itself just. The right to make law does not guarantee that the decision is rightly made; and while the citizen submits in his conduct to the judgment of democratic authority, he does not submit his judgment to it.[2] And if in his judgment the enactments of the majority exceed certain bounds of injustice, the citizen may consider civil disobedience. For we are not required to accept the majority's acts unconditionally and to acquiesce in the denial of our and others' liberties; rather we submit our conduct to democratic authority to the extent necessary to share the burden of working a constitutional regime, distorted as it must inevitably be by men's lack of wisdom and the defects of their sense of justice.

IV. The place of civil disobedience in a constitutional democracy

We are now in a position to say a few things about civil disobedience. I shall understand it to be a public, nonviolent, and conscientious act contrary to law usually done with the intent to bring about a change in the policies or laws of the government.[3] Civil disobedience is a political act in the sense that it is an act justified by moral principles which define a conception of civil society and the public good. It rests, then, on political conviction as opposed to a search for self or group interest; and in the case of a constitutional democracy, we may assume that this conviction involves the conception of justice (say that expressed by the contract doctrine) which underlies the constitution itself. That is, in a viable democratic regime there is a common conception of justice by reference to which its citizens regulate their political affairs and interpret the constitution. Civil disobedience is a public act which the dissenter believes to be justified by this conception of justice, and for this reason it may be understood as addressing the sense of justice of the majority in order to urge reconsideration of the measures protested and to warn that, in the sincere opinion of the dissenters, the conditions of social cooperation are not being honored. For the principles of justice express precisely such conditions, and their persistent and deliberate violation in regard to basic liberties over any extended period of time cuts the ties of community and invites either submission or forceful resistance. By engaging in civil disobedience a minority leads the majority to consider whether it wants to have its acts taken in this way, or whether, in view of the common sense of justice, it wishes to acknowledge the claims of the minority.

Civil disobedience is also civil in another sense. Not only is it the outcome of a sincere conviction based on principles which regulate civic life, but it is public and nonviolent, that is, it is done in a situation where arrest and punishment are expected and accepted without resistance. In this way it manifests a respect for legal procedures. Civil disobedience expresses disobedience to law within the limits of fidelity to law, and this feature of it helps to establish in the eyes of the majority that it is indeed conscientious and sincere, that it really is meant to address their sense of justice.[4] Being completely open about one's acts and being willing to accept the legal consequences of one's conduct is a bond given to make good one's sincerity, for that one's deeds are conscientious is not easy to demonstrate to another or even before oneself. No doubt it is possible to imagine a legal system in which conscientious belief that the law is unjust is accepted as a defense for noncompliance, and men of great honesty who are confident in one another might make such a system work. But as things are such a scheme would be unstable; we must pay a price

in order to establish that we believe our actions have a moral basis in the convictions of the community.

The nonviolent nature of civil disobedience refers to the fact that it is intended to address the sense of justice of the majority and as such it is a form of speech, an expression of conviction. To engage in violent acts likely to injure and to hurt is incompatible with civil disobedience as a mode of address. Indeed, an interference with the basic rights of others tends to obscure the civilly disobedient quality of one's act. Civil disobedience is nonviolent in the further sense that the legal penalty for one's action is accepted and that resistance is not (at least for the moment) contemplated. Nonviolence in this sense is to be distinguished from nonviolence as a religious or pacifist principle. While those engaging in civil disobedience have often held some such principle, there is no necessary connection between it and civil disobedience. For on the interpretation suggested, civil disobedience in a democratic society is best understood as an appeal to the principles of justice, the fundamental conditions of willing social cooperation among free men, which in the view of the community as a whole are expressed in the constitution and guide its interpretation. Being an appeal to the moral basis of public life, civil disobedience is a political and not primarily a religious act. It addresses itself to the common principles of justice which men can require one another to follow and not to the aspirations of love which they cannot. Moreover, by taking part in civilly disobedient acts one does not foreswear indefinitely the idea of forceful resistance; for if the appeal against injustice is repeatedly denied, then the majority has declared its intention to invite submission or resistance and the latter may conceivably be justified even in a democratic regime. We are not required to acquiesce in the crushing of fundamental liberties by democratic majorities which have shown themselves blind to the principles of justice upon which justification of the constitution depends.

V. The justification of civil disobedience

So far we have said nothing about the justification of civil disobedience, that is, the conditions under which civil disobedience may be engaged in consistent with the principles of justice that support a democratic regime. Our task is to see how the characterization of civil disobedience as addressed to the sense of justice of the majority (or to the citizens as a body) determines when such action is justified.

First of all, we may suppose that the normal political appeals to the majority have already been made in good faith and have been rejected, and that the standard means of redress have been tried. Thus, for example, existing political parties are indifferent to the claims of the minority, and attempts to repeal the laws protested have been met with further repression since legal institutions are in the control of the majority. While civil disobedience should be recognized, I think, as a form of political action within the limits of fidelity to the rule of law, at the same time it is a rather desperate act just within these limits, and therefore it should, in general, be undertaken as a last resort when standard democratic processes have failed. In this sense it is not a normal political action. When it is justified there has been a serious breakdown; not only is there grave injustice in the law but a refusal more or less deliberate to correct it.

Second, since civil disobedience is a political act addressed to the sense of justice of the majority, it should usually be limited to substantial and clear violations of justice and preferably to those which, if rectified, will establish a basis for doing away with remaining injustices. For this reason there is a presumption in favor of restricting civil disobedience to violations of the first principle of justice, the principle of equal liberty, and to barriers which contravene the second principle, the principle of open offices which protects equality of opportunity. It is not, of course, always easy to tell whether these principles are satisfied. But if we think of them as guaranteeing the fundamental equal political and civil liberties (including freedom of conscience and liberty of thought) and equality of opportunity, then it is often relatively clear whether their principles are being honored. After all, the equal liberties are defined by the visible structure of social institutions; they are to be incorporated into the recognized practice, if not the letter, of social arrangements. When minorities are denied the right to vote or to hold certain political offices, when certain religious groups are repressed and others denied equality of opportunity in the economy, this is often obvious and there is no doubt that justice is not being given. However, the first part of the second principle which requires that inequalities be to everyone's advantage is a much more imprecise and controversial matter. Not only is there a problem of assigning it a determinate and precise sense, but even if we do so and agree on what it should be, there is often a wide variety of reasonable opinion as to whether the principle is satisfied. The reason for this is that the principle applies primarily to fundamental economic and social policies. The choice of these depends upon theoretical and speculative beliefs as well as upon a wealth of concrete information, and all of this mixed with judgment and plain hunch, not to mention in actual cases prejudice and self-interest. Thus unless the laws of taxation are clearly designed to attack a basic equal liberty, they should not be protested by civil disobedience; the appeal to justice is not sufficiently clear and its resolution is best left to the political process. But violations of the equal liberties that define the common status of citizenship are another matter. The deliberate denial of these more or less over any extended period of time in the face of normal political protest is, in general, an appropriate object of civil disobedience. We may think of the social system as divided roughly into two parts, one which incorporates the fundamental equal liberties (including equality of opportunity) and another which embodies social and economic policies properly aimed at promoting the advantage of everyone. As a rule civil disobedience is best limited to the former where the appeal to justice is not only more definite and precise, but where, if it is effective, it tends to correct the injustices in the latter.

Third, civil disobedience should be restricted to those cases where the dissenter is willing to affirm that everyone else similarly subjected to the same degree of injustice has the right to protest in a similar way. That is, we must be prepared to authorize others to dissent in similar situations and in the same way, and to accept the consequences of their doing so. Thus, we may hold, for example, that the widespread disposition to disobey civilly clear violations of fundamental liberties more or less deliberate over an extended period of time would raise the degree of justice throughout society and would ensure men's self-esteem as well as their respect for one another. Indeed, I believe this to be true, though certainly it is partly a matter of conjecture. As the contract doctrine emphasizes, since the principles of justice are principles which we would agree to in an original position of equality when we do not know our social position and the like, the refusal to grant justice is either the denial of the other as an equal (as one in regard to whom we are prepared to constrain our actions by principles which we would consent to) or the manifestation of a willingness to take advantage of natural contingencies and social fortune at his expense. In either case, injustice invites submission or resistance; but submission arouses the contempt of the oppressor and confirms him in his intention. If straightaway, after a decent period of time to make reasonable political appeals in the normal way, men were in general to dissent by civil disobedience from infractions of the fundamental equal liberties, these liberties would, I believe, be more rather than less secure. Legitimate civil disobedience properly exercised is a stabilizing device in a constitutional regime, tending to make it more firmly just.

Sometimes, however, there may be a complication in connection with this third condition. It is possible, although perhaps unlikely, that there are so many persons or groups with a sound case for resorting to civil disobedience (as judged by the foregoing criteria) that disorder would follow if they all did so. There might be serious injury to the just constitution. Or again, a group might be so large that some extra precaution is necessary in the extent to which its members organize and engage in civil disobedience. Theoretically the case is one in which a number of persons or groups are equally entitled to and all want to resort to civil disobedience, yet if they all do this, grave consequences for everyone may result. The question, then, is who among them may exercise their right, and it falls under the general problem of fairness. I cannot discuss the complexities of the matter here. Often a lottery or a rationing system can be set up to handle the case; but unfortunately the circumstances of civil disobedience rule out this solution. It suffices to note that a problem of fairness may arise and that those who contemplate civil disobedience should take it into account. They may have to reach an understanding as to who can exercise their right in the immediate situation and to recognize the need for special constraint.

The final condition, of a different nature, is the following. We have been considering when one has a right to engage in civil disobedience, and our conclusion is that one has this right should three conditions hold: when one is subject to injustice more or less deliberate over an extended period of time in the face of normal political protests; where the injustice is a clear violation of the liberties of equal citizenship; and provided that the general disposition to protest similarly in similar cases would have acceptable consequences. These conditions are not, I think, exhaustive, but they seem to cover the more obvious points; yet even when they are satisfied and one has the right to engage in civil disobedience, there is still the different question of whether one should exercise this right, that is, whether by doing so one is likely to further one's ends. Having established one's right to protest, one is then free to consider these tactical questions. We may be acting within our rights but still foolishly if our action only serves to provoke the harsh retaliation of the majority; and it is likely to do so if the majority lacks a sense of justice, or if the action is poorly timed or not well designed to make the appeal to the sense of justice effective. It is easy to think of instances of this sort, and in each case these practical questions have to be faced. From the standpoint of the theory of political obligation we can only say that the exercise of the right should be rational and reasonably designed to advance the protester's aims, and that weighing tactical questions presupposes that one has already established one's right, since tactical advantages in themselves do not support it.

VI. Conclusion: several objections considered

In a reasonably affluent democratic society justice becomes the first virtue of institutions. Social arrangements irrespective of their efficiency must be reformed if they are significantly unjust. No increase in efficiency in the form of greater advantages for many justifies the loss of liberty of a few. That we believe this is shown by the fact that in a democracy the fundamental liberties of citizenship are not understood as the outcome of political bargaining, nor are they subject to the calculus of social interests. Rather these liberties are fixed points which serve to limit political transactions and which determine the scope of calculations of social advantage. It is this fundamental place of the equal liberties which makes their systematic violation over any extended period of time a proper object of civil disobedience. For to deny men these rights is to infringe the conditions of social cooperation among free and rational persons, a fact which is

evident to the citizens of a constitutional regime since it follows from the principles of justice which underlie their institutions. The justification of civil disobedience rests on the priority of justice and the equal liberties which it guarantees.

It is natural to object to this view of civil disobedience that it relies too heavily upon the existence of a sense of justice. Some may hold that the feeling for justice is not a vital political force, and that what moves men are various other interests, the desire for wealth, power, prestige, and so on. Now this is a large question the answer to which is highly conjectural, and each tends to have his own opinion. But there are two remarks which may clarify what I have said: first, I have assumed that there is in a constitutional regime a common sense of justice the principles of which are recognized to support the constitution and to guide its interpretation. In any given situation particular men may be tempted to violate these principles, but the collective force in their behalf is usually effective since they are seen as the necessary terms of cooperation among free men; and presumably the citizens of a democracy (or sufficiently many of them) want to see justice done. Where these assumptions fail, the justifying conditions for civil disobedience (the first three) are not affected, but the rationality of engaging in it certainly is. In this case, unless the costs of repressing civil dissent injures the economic self-interest (or whatever) of the majority, protest may simply make the position of the minority worse. No doubt as a tactical matter civil disobedience is more effective when its appeal coincides with other interests, but a constitutional regime is not viable in the long run without an attachment to the principles of justice of the sort which we have assumed.

Then, further, there may be a misapprehension about the manner in which a sense of justice manifests itself. There is a tendency to think that it is shown by professions of the relevant principles together with actions of an altruistic nature requiring a considerable degree of self-sacrifice. But these conditions are obviously too strong, for the majority's sense of justice may show itself simply in its being unable to undertake the measures required to suppress the minority and to punish as the law requires the various acts of civil disobedience. The sense of justice undermines the will to uphold unjust institutions, and so a majority despite its superior power may give way. It is unprepared to force the minority to be subject to injustice. Thus, although the majority's action is reluctant and grudging, the role of the sense of justice is nevertheless essential, for without it the majority would have been willing to enforce the law and to defend its position. Once we see the sense of justice as working in this negative way to make established injustices indefensible, then it is recognized as a central element of democratic politics.

Finally, it may be objected against this account that it does not settle the question of who is to say when the situation is such as to justify civil disobedience. And because it does not answer this question, it invites anarchy by encouraging every man to decide the matter for himself. Now the reply to this is that each man must indeed settle this question for himself, although he may, of course, decide wrongly. This is true on any theory of political duty and obligation, at least on any theory compatible with the principles of a democratic constitution. The citizen is responsible for what he does. If we usually think that we should comply with the law, this is because our political principles normally lead to this conclusion. There is a presumption in favor of compliance in the absence of good reasons to the contrary. But because each man is responsible and must decide for himself as best he can whether the circumstances justify civil disobedience, it does not follow that he may decide as he pleases. It is not by looking to our personal interests or to political allegiances narrowly construed, that we should make

up our mind. The citizen must decide on the basis of the principles of justice that underlie and guide the interpretation of the constitution and in the light of his sincere conviction as to how these principles should be applied in the circumstances. If he concludes that conditions obtain which justify civil disobedience and conducts himself accordingly, he has acted conscientiously and perhaps mistakenly, but not in any case at his convenience.

In a democratic society each man must act as he thinks the principles of political right require him to. We are to follow our understanding of these principles, and we cannot do otherwise. There can be no morally binding legal interpretation of these principles, not even by a supreme court or legislature. Nor is there any infallible procedure for determining what or who is right. In our system the Supreme Court, Congress, and the President often put forward rival interpretations of the Constitution.[5] Although the Court has the final say in settling any particular case, it is not immune from powerful political influence that may change its reading of the law of the land. The Court presents its point of view by reason and argument; its conception of the Constitution must, if it is to endure, persuade men of its soundness. The final court of appeal is not the Court, or Congress, or the President, but the electorate as a whole. The civilly disobedient appeal in effect to this body. There is no danger of anarchy as long as there is a sufficient working agreement in men's conceptions of political justice and what it requires. That men can achieve such an understanding when the essential political liberties are maintained is the assumption implicit in democratic institutions. There is no way to avoid entirely the risk of divisive strife. But if legitimate civil disobedience seems to threaten civil peace, the responsibility falls not so much on those who protest as upon those whose abuse of authority and power justifies such opposition.

Notes

John Rawls, "The Justification of Civil Disobedience", in *Collected Papers* (Harvard 1999) 176–189. Reprinted by kind permission of the Estate of John Rawls.

1 By the social contract theory I have in mind the doctrine found in Locke, Rousseau, and Kant. I have attempted to give an interpretation of this view in Chapters 3–5 [of the original].

2 On this point see A. E. Murphy's review of Yves Simon's *The Philosophy of Democratic Government* (Chicago: University of Chicago Press, 1951) in the *Philosophical Review*, 61 (April 1952): 198–211.

3 Here I follow H. A. Bedau's definition of civil disobedience. See his "On Civil Disobedience," *Journal of Philosophy*, 58 (October 1961).

4 For a fuller discussion of this point, to which I am indebted, see Charles Fried, "Moral Causation," *Harvard Law Review*, 77 (May 1964): 1258–1270.

5 For a presentation of this view to which I am indebted, see A. M. Bickel, *The Least Dangerous Branch* (Indianapolis: Bobbs-Merrill, 1962), especially chs 5 and 6.

Chapter 15

Martin Luther King, Jr.

LETTER FROM A BIRMINGHAM JAIL

16 April 1963

MY DEAR FELLOW CLERGYMEN:
While confined here in the Birmingham city jail, I came across your recent statement calling my present activities "unwise and untimely." Seldom do I pause to answer criticism of my work and ideas. If I sought to answer all the criticisms that cross my desk, my secretaries would have little time for anything other than such correspondence in the course of the day, and I would have no time for constructive work. But since I feel that you are men of genuine good will and that your criticisms are sincerely set forth, I want to try to answer your statement in what I hope will be patient and reasonable terms.

I think I should indicate why I am here in Birmingham, since you have been influenced by the view which argues against "outsiders coming in." I have the honor of serving as president of the Southern Christian Leadership Conference, an organization operating in every southern state, with headquarters in Atlanta, Georgia. We have some eighty five affiliated organizations across the South, and one of them is the Alabama Christian Movement for Human Rights. Frequently we share staff, educational and financial resources with our affiliates. Several months ago the affiliate here in Birmingham asked us to be on call to engage in a nonviolent direct action program if such were deemed necessary. We readily consented, and when the hour came we lived up to our promise. So I, along with several members of my staff, am here because I was invited here. I am here because I have organizational ties here.

But more basically, I am in Birmingham because injustice is here. Just as the prophets of the eighth century B.C. left their villages and carried their "thus saith the Lord" far beyond the boundaries of their home towns, and just as the Apostle Paul left his village of Tarsus and carried the gospel of Jesus Christ to the far corners of the Greco Roman world, so am I compelled to carry the gospel of freedom beyond my own home town. Like Paul, I must constantly respond to the Macedonian call for aid.

Moreover, I am cognizant of the interrelatedness of all communities and states. I cannot sit idly by in Atlanta and not be concerned about what happens in Birmingham. Injustice anywhere is a threat to justice everywhere. We are caught in an inescapable network of mutuality, tied in a single garment of destiny. Whatever affects one directly, affects all indirectly. Never again can we afford to live with the narrow, provincial "outside agitator" idea. Anyone who lives inside the United States can never be considered an outsider anywhere within its bounds.

You deplore the demonstrations taking place in Birmingham. But your statement, I am sorry to say, fails to express a similar concern for the conditions that brought about the demonstrations. I am sure that none of you would want to rest content with the superficial kind of social analysis that deals merely with effects and does not grapple with underlying causes. It is unfortunate that demonstrations are taking place in Birmingham, but it is even more unfortunate that the city's white power structure left the Negro community with no alternative.

In any nonviolent campaign there are four basic steps: collection of the facts to determine whether injustices exist; negotiation; self purification; and direct action. We have gone through all these steps in Birmingham. There can be no gainsaying the fact that racial injustice engulfs this community. Birmingham is probably the most thoroughly segregated city in the United States. Its ugly record of brutality is widely known. Negroes have experienced grossly unjust treatment in the courts. There have been more unsolved bombings of Negro homes and churches in Birmingham than in any other city in the nation. These are the hard, brutal facts of the case. On the basis of these conditions, Negro leaders sought to negotiate with the city fathers. But the latter consistently refused to engage in good faith negotiation.

Then, last September, came the opportunity to talk with leaders of Birmingham's economic community. In the course of the negotiations, certain promises were made by the merchants— for example, to remove the stores' humiliating racial signs. On the basis of these promises, the Reverend Fred Shuttlesworth and the leaders of the Alabama Christian Movement for Human Rights agreed to a moratorium on all demonstrations. As the weeks and months went by, we realized that we were the victims of a broken promise. A few signs, briefly removed, returned; the others remained. As in so many past experiences, our hopes had been blasted, and the shadow of deep disappointment settled upon us. We had no alternative except to prepare for direct action, whereby we would present our very bodies as a means of laying our case before the conscience of the local and the national community. Mindful of the difficulties involved, we decided to undertake a process of self purification. We began a series of workshops on nonviolence, and we repeatedly asked ourselves: "Are you able to accept blows without retaliating?" "Are you able to endure the ordeal of jail?" We decided to schedule our direct action program for the Easter season, realizing that except for Christmas, this is the main shopping period of the year. Knowing that a strong economic-withdrawal program would be the by product of direct action, we felt that this would be the best time to bring pressure to bear on the merchants for the needed change.

Then it occurred to us that Birmingham's mayoral election was coming up in March, and we speedily decided to postpone action until after election day. When we discovered that the Commissioner of Public Safety, Eugene "Bull" Connor, had piled up enough votes to be in the run off, we decided again to postpone action until the day after the run off so that the demonstrations could not be used to cloud the issues. Like many others, we waited to see Mr. Connor defeated, and to this end we endured postponement after postponement. Having aided in this community need, we felt that our direct action program could be delayed no longer.

You may well ask: "Why direct action? Why sit ins, marches and so forth? Isn't negotiation a better path?" You are quite right in calling for negotiation. Indeed, this is the very purpose of direct action. Nonviolent direct action seeks to create such a crisis and foster such a tension that a community which has constantly refused to negotiate is forced to confront the issue. It seeks so to dramatize the issue that it can no longer be ignored. My citing the creation of tension as part of the work of the nonviolent resister may sound rather shocking. But I must confess that I am not afraid of the word "tension." I have earnestly opposed violent tension, but there is a type of constructive, nonviolent tension which is necessary for growth. Just as Socrates felt that it was necessary to create a tension in the mind so that individuals could rise from the bondage of myths and half truths to the unfettered realm of creative analysis and objective appraisal, so must we see the need for nonviolent gadflies to create the kind of tension in society that will help men rise from the dark depths of prejudice and racism to the majestic heights of understanding and brotherhood. The purpose of our direct action program is to create a situation so crisis packed that it will inevitably open the door to negotiation. I therefore concur with you in your call for negotiation. Too long has our beloved Southland been bogged down in a tragic effort to live in monologue rather than dialogue.

One of the basic points in your statement is that the action that I and my associates have taken in Birmingham is untimely. Some have asked: "Why didn't you give the new city administration time to act?" The only answer that I can give to this query is that the new Birmingham administration must be prodded about as much as the outgoing one, before it will act. We are sadly mistaken if we feel that the election of Albert Boutwell as mayor will bring the millennium to Birmingham. While Mr. Boutwell is a much more gentle person than Mr. Connor, they are both segregationists, dedicated to maintenance of the status quo. I have hope that Mr. Boutwell will be reasonable enough to see the futility of massive resistance to desegregation. But he will not see this without pressure from devotees of civil rights. My friends, I must say to you that we have not made a single gain in civil rights without determined legal and nonviolent pressure. Lamentably, it is an historical fact that privileged groups seldom give up their privileges voluntarily. Individuals may see the moral light and voluntarily give up their unjust posture; but, as Reinhold Niebuhr has reminded us, groups tend to be more immoral than individuals.

We know through painful experience that freedom is never voluntarily given by the oppressor; it must be demanded by the oppressed. Frankly, I have yet to engage in a direct action campaign that was "well timed" in the view of those who have not suffered unduly from the disease of segregation. For years now I have heard the word "Wait!" It rings in the ear of every Negro with piercing familiarity. This "Wait" has almost always meant "Never." We must come to see, with one of our distinguished jurists, that "justice too long delayed is justice denied."

We have waited for more than 340 years for our constitutional and God given rights. The nations of Asia and Africa are moving with jetlike speed toward gaining political independence, but we still creep at horse and buggy pace toward gaining a cup of coffee at a lunch counter. Perhaps it is easy for those who have never felt the stinging darts of segregation to say, "Wait." But when you have seen vicious mobs lynch your mothers and fathers at will and drown your sisters and brothers at whim; when you have seen hate filled policemen curse, kick and even kill your black brothers and sisters; when you see the vast majority of your twenty million Negro brothers smothering in an airtight cage of poverty in the midst of an affluent society; when you suddenly find your tongue twisted and your speech stammering as you seek to explain to your six year old daughter why she can't go to the public amusement park that has just been advertised on television, and see tears welling up in her eyes when she is told that Funtown is closed to colored children, and see ominous clouds of inferiority beginning to form in her little mental sky, and see her beginning to distort her personality by developing an unconscious bitterness toward white people; when you have to concoct an answer for a five year old son who is asking: "Daddy, why do white people treat colored people so mean?"; when you take a cross county drive and find it necessary to sleep night after night in the uncomfortable corners of your automobile because no motel will accept you; when you are humiliated day in and day out by nagging signs reading "white" and "colored"; when your first name becomes "nigger," your middle name becomes "boy" (however old you are) and your last name becomes "John," and your wife and mother are never given the respected title "Mrs."; when you are harried by day and haunted by night by the fact that you are a Negro, living constantly at tiptoe stance, never quite knowing what to expect next, and are plagued with inner fears and outer resentments; when you are forever fighting a degenerating sense of "nobodiness"—then you will understand why we find it difficult to wait. There comes a time when the cup of endurance runs over, and men are no longer willing to be plunged into the abyss of despair. I hope, sirs, you can understand our legitimate and unavoidable impatience. You express a great deal of anxiety over our willingness to break laws. This is certainly a legitimate concern. Since we so diligently urge people to obey the Supreme Court's decision of 1954 outlawing segregation in the public schools, at first glance it may seem rather paradoxical for us consciously to break laws. One may well ask: "How can you advocate breaking some laws and obeying others?" The answer lies in the fact that there are two types of laws: just and unjust. I would be the first to advocate obeying just laws. One has not only a legal but a moral responsibility to obey just laws. Conversely, one has a moral responsibility to disobey unjust laws. I would agree with St. Augustine that "an unjust law is no law at all."

Now, what is the difference between the two? How does one determine whether a law is just or unjust? A just law is a man made code that squares with the moral law or the law of God. An unjust law is a code that is out of harmony with the moral law. To put it in the terms of St. Thomas Aquinas: An unjust law is a human law that is not rooted in eternal law and natural law. Any law that uplifts human personality is just. Any law that degrades human personality is unjust. All segregation statutes are unjust because segregation distorts the soul and damages the personality. It gives the segregator a false sense

of superiority and the segregated a false sense of inferiority. Segregation, to use the terminology of the Jewish philosopher Martin Buber, substitutes an "I it" relationship for an "I thou" relationship and ends up relegating persons to the status of things. Hence segregation is not only politically, economically and sociologically unsound, it is morally wrong and sinful. Paul Tillich has said that sin is separation. Is not segregation an existential expression of man's tragic separation, his awful estrangement, his terrible sinfulness? Thus it is that I can urge men to obey the 1954 decision of the Supreme Court, for it is morally right; and I can urge them to disobey segregation ordinances, for they are morally wrong.

Let us consider a more concrete example of just and unjust laws. An unjust law is a code that a numerical or power majority group compels a minority group to obey but does not make binding on itself. This is difference made legal. By the same token, a just law is a code that a majority compels a minority to follow and that it is willing to follow itself. This is sameness made legal. Let me give another explanation. A law is unjust if it is inflicted on a minority that, as a result of being denied the right to vote, had no part in enacting or devising the law. Who can say that the legislature of Alabama which set up that state's segregation laws was democratically elected? Throughout Alabama all sorts of devious methods are used to prevent Negroes from becoming registered voters, and there are some counties in which, even though Negroes constitute a majority of the population, not a single Negro is registered. Can any law enacted under such circumstances be considered democratically structured?

Sometimes a law is just on its face and unjust in its application. For instance, I have been arrested on a charge of parading without a permit. Now, there is nothing wrong in having an ordinance which requires a permit for a parade. But such an ordinance becomes unjust when it is used to maintain segregation and to deny citizens the First-Amendment privilege of peaceful assembly and protest.

I hope you are able to see the distinction I am trying to point out. In no sense do I advocate evading or defying the law, as would the rabid segregationist. That would lead to anarchy. One who breaks an unjust law must do so openly, lovingly, and with a willingness to accept the penalty. I submit that an individual who breaks a law that conscience tells him is unjust, and who willingly accepts the penalty of imprisonment in order to arouse the conscience of the community over its injustice, is in reality expressing the highest respect for law.

Of course, there is nothing new about this kind of civil disobedience. It was evidenced sublimely in the refusal of Shadrach, Meshach and Abednego to obey the laws of Nebuchadnezzar, on the ground that a higher moral law was at stake. It was practiced superbly by the early Christians, who were willing to face hungry lions and the excruciating pain of chopping blocks rather than submit to certain unjust laws of the Roman Empire. To a degree, academic freedom is a reality today because Socrates practiced civil disobedience. In our own nation, the Boston Tea Party represented a massive act of civil disobedience.

We should never forget that everything Adolf Hitler did in Germany was "legal" and everything the Hungarian freedom fighters did in Hungary was "illegal." It was "illegal" to aid and comfort a Jew in Hitler's Germany. Even so, I am sure that, had I lived in Germany at the time, I would have aided and comforted my Jewish brothers. If today I lived in a Communist country where certain principles dear to the Christian faith are suppressed, I would openly advocate disobeying that country's antireligious laws.

I must make two honest confessions to you, my Christian and Jewish brothers. First, I must confess that over the past few years I have been gravely disappointed with the white moderate. I have almost reached the regrettable conclusion that the Negro's great stumbling block in his stride toward freedom is not the White Citizen's Counciler or the Ku Klux Klanner, but the white moderate, who is more devoted to "order" than to justice; who prefers a negative peace which is the absence of tension to a positive peace which is the presence of justice; who constantly says: "I agree with you in the goal you seek, but I cannot agree with your methods of direct action"; who paternalistically believes he can set the timetable for another man's freedom; who lives by a mythical concept of time and who constantly advises the Negro to wait for a "more convenient season." Shallow understanding from people of good will is more frustrating than absolute misunderstanding from people of ill will. Lukewarm acceptance is much more bewildering than outright rejection.

I had hoped that the white moderate would understand that law and order exist for the purpose of establishing justice and that when they fail in this purpose they become the dangerously structured dams that block the flow of social progress. I had hoped that the white moderate would understand that the present tension in the South is a necessary phase of the transition from an obnoxious negative peace, in which the Negro passively accepted his unjust plight, to a substantive and positive peace, in which all men will respect the dignity and worth of human personality. Actually, we who engage in nonviolent direct action are not the creators of tension. We merely bring to the surface the hidden tension that is already alive. We bring it out in the open, where it can be seen and dealt with. Like a boil that can never be cured so long as it is covered up but must be opened with all its ugliness to the natural medicines of air and light, injustice must be exposed, with all the tension its exposure creates, to the light of human conscience and the air of national opinion before it can be cured.

In your statement you assert that our actions, even though peaceful, must be condemned because they precipitate violence. But is this a logical assertion? Isn't this like condemning a robbed man because his possession of money precipitated the evil act of robbery? Isn't this like condemning Socrates because his unswerving commitment to truth and his philosophical inquiries precipitated the act by the misguided populace in which they made him drink hemlock? Isn't this like condemning Jesus because his unique God consciousness and never ceasing devotion to God's will precipitated the evil act of crucifixion? We must come to see that, as the federal courts have consistently affirmed, it is wrong to urge an individual to cease his efforts to gain his basic constitutional rights because the quest may precipitate violence. Society must protect the robbed and punish the robber. I had also hoped that the white moderate would reject the myth concerning time in relation to the struggle for freedom. I have just received a letter from a white brother in Texas. He writes: "All Christians know that the colored people will receive equal rights eventually, but it is possible that you are in too great a religious hurry. It has taken Christianity almost two thousand years to accomplish what it has. The teachings of Christ take time to come to earth." Such an attitude stems from a tragic misconception of time, from the strangely irrational notion that there is something in the very flow of time that will inevitably cure all ills. Actually, time itself is neutral; it can be used either destructively or constructively. More and more I feel that the people of ill will have used time much more effectively than have the people of good will. We will have to repent in this generation not merely for the hateful words and actions of the bad people but for the appalling silence of the good people. Human progress never rolls in on wheels of inevitability; it comes through the tireless efforts of men willing to be co workers with God, and without this hard work, time itself becomes an ally of the forces of social stagnation. We must use time creatively, in the knowledge that the time is always ripe to do right. Now is the time to make real the promise of democracy and transform our pending national elegy into a creative psalm of brotherhood. Now is the time to lift our national policy from the quicksand of racial injustice to the solid rock of human dignity.

You speak of our activity in Birmingham as extreme. At first I was rather disappointed that fellow clergymen would see my nonviolent efforts as those of an extremist. I began thinking about the fact that I stand in the middle of two opposing forces in the Negro community. One is a force of complacency, made up in part of Negroes who, as a result of long years of oppression, are so drained of self respect and a sense of "somebodiness" that they have adjusted to segregation; and in part of a few middle-class Negroes who, because of a degree of academic and economic security and because in some ways they profit by segregation, have become insensitive to the problems of the masses. The other force is one of bitterness and hatred, and it comes perilously close to advocating violence. It is expressed in the various black nationalist groups that are springing up across the nation, the largest and best known being Elijah Muhammad's Muslim movement. Nourished by the Negro's frustration over the continued existence of racial discrimination, this movement is made up of people who have lost faith in America, who have absolutely repudiated Christianity, and who have concluded that the white man is an incorrigible "devil."

I have tried to stand between these two forces, saying that we need emulate neither the "do nothingism" of the complacent nor the hatred and despair of the black nationalist. For there is the more excellent way of love and nonviolent protest. I am grateful to God that, through the influence of the Negro church, the way of nonviolence became an integral part of our struggle. If this philosophy had not emerged, by now many streets of the South would, I am convinced, be flowing with blood. And I am further convinced that if our white brothers dismiss as "rabble rousers" and "outside agitators" those of us who employ nonviolent direct action, and if they refuse to support our nonviolent efforts, millions of Negroes will, out of frustration and despair, seek solace and security in black nationalist ideologies—a development that would inevitably lead to a frightening racial nightmare.

Oppressed people cannot remain oppressed forever. The yearning for freedom eventually manifests itself, and that is what has happened to the American Negro. Something within has reminded him of his birthright of freedom, and something without has reminded him that it can be gained. Consciously or unconsciously, he has been caught up by the Zeitgeist, and with his black brothers of Africa and his brown and yellow brothers of Asia, South America and the Caribbean, the United States Negro is moving with a sense of great urgency toward the promised land of racial justice. If one recognizes this vital urge that has engulfed the Negro community, one should readily understand why public demonstrations are taking place. The Negro has many pent up resentments and latent frustrations, and he must release them. So let him march; let him make prayer pilgrimages to the city hall; let him go on freedom rides—and try to understand why he must do so. If his repressed emotions are not released in non-violent ways, they will seek expression through violence; this is not a threat but a fact of history. So I have not said to my people: "Get rid of your discontent." Rather, I have tried to say that this normal and healthy discontent can be channeled into the creative outlet of nonviolent direct action. And now this approach is being termed extremist. But though I was initially disappointed at being categorized as an extremist, as I continued to think about the matter I gradually gained a measure of satisfaction from the label. Was not Jesus an extremist for love: "Love your enemies, bless them that curse you, do good to them that hate you, and pray for them which despitefully use you, and persecute you." Was not Amos an extremist for justice: "Let justice roll down like waters and righteousness like an ever flowing stream." Was not Paul an extremist

for the Christian gospel: "I bear in my body the marks of the Lord Jesus." Was not Martin Luther an extremist: "Here I stand; I cannot do otherwise, so help me God." And John Bunyan: "I will stay in jail to the end of my days before I make a butchery of my conscience." And Abraham Lincoln: "This nation cannot survive half slave and half free." And Thomas Jefferson: "We hold these truths to be self evident, that all men are created equal . . ." So the question is not whether we will be extremists, but what kind of extremists we will be. Will we be extremists for hate or for love? Will we be extremists for the preservation of injustice or for the extension of justice? In that dramatic scene on Calvary's hill three men were crucified. We must never forget that all three were crucified for the same crime—the crime of extremism. Two were extremists for immorality, and thus fell below their environment. The other, Jesus Christ, was an extremist for love, truth and goodness, and thereby rose above his environment. Perhaps the South, the nation and the world are in dire need of creative extremists.

I had hoped that the white moderate would see this need. Perhaps I was too optimistic; perhaps I expected too much. I suppose I should have realized that few members of the oppressor race can understand the deep groans and passionate yearnings of the oppressed race, and still fewer have the vision to see that injustice must be rooted out by strong, persistent and determined action. I am thankful, however, that some of our white brothers in the South have grasped the meaning of this social revolution and committed themselves to it. They are still all too few in quantity, but they are big in quality. Some—such as Ralph McGill, Lillian Smith, Harry Golden, James McBride Dabbs, Ann Braden and Sarah Patton Boyle—have written about our struggle in eloquent and prophetic terms. Others have marched with us down nameless streets of the South. They have languished in filthy, roach infested jails, suffering the abuse and brutality of policemen who view them as "dirty nigger-lovers." Unlike so many of their moderate brothers and sisters, they have recognized the urgency of the moment and sensed the need for powerful "action" antidotes to combat the disease of segregation. Let me take note of my other major disappointment. I have been so greatly disappointed with the white church and its leadership. Of course, there are some notable exceptions. I am not unmindful of the fact that each of you has taken some significant stands on this issue. I commend you, Reverend Stallings, for your Christian stand on this past Sunday, in welcoming Negroes to your worship service on a nonsegregated basis. I commend the Catholic leaders of this state for integrating Spring Hill College several years ago.

But despite these notable exceptions, I must honestly reiterate that I have been disappointed with the church. I do not say this as one of those negative critics who can always find something wrong with the church. I say this as a minister of the gospel, who loves the church; who was nurtured in its bosom; who has been sustained by its spiritual blessings and who will remain true to it as long as the cord of life shall lengthen.

When I was suddenly catapulted into the leadership of the bus protest in Montgomery, Alabama, a few years ago, I felt we would be supported by the white church. I felt that the white ministers, priests and rabbis of the South would be among our strongest allies. Instead, some have been outright opponents, refusing to understand the freedom movement and misrepresenting its leaders; all too many others have been more cautious than courageous and have remained silent behind the anesthetizing security of stained glass windows.

In spite of my shattered dreams, I came to Birmingham with the hope that the white religious leadership of this community would see the justice of our cause and, with deep moral concern, would serve as the channel through which our just grievances could reach the power structure. I had hoped that each of you would understand. But again I have been disappointed.

I have heard numerous southern religious leaders admonish their worshipers to comply with a desegregation decision because it is the law, but I have longed to hear white ministers declare: "Follow this decree because integration is morally right and because the Negro is your brother." In the midst of blatant injustices inflicted upon the Negro, I have watched white churchmen stand on the sideline and mouth pious irrelevancies and sanctimonious trivialities. In the midst of a mighty struggle to rid our nation of racial and economic injustice, I have heard many ministers say: "Those are social issues, with which the gospel has no real concern." And I have watched many churches commit themselves to a completely other worldly religion which makes a strange, un-Biblical distinction between body and soul, between the sacred and the secular.

I have traveled the length and breadth of Alabama, Mississippi and all the other southern states. On sweltering summer days and crisp autumn mornings I have looked at the South's beautiful churches with their lofty spires pointing heavenward. I have beheld the impressive outlines of her massive religious education buildings. Over and over I have found myself asking: "What kind of people worship here? Who is their God? Where were their voices when the lips of Governor Barnett dripped with words of interposition and nullification? Where were they when Governor Wallace gave a clarion call for defiance and hatred? Where were their voices of support when bruised and weary Negro men and women decided to rise from the dark dungeons of complacency to the bright hills of creative protest?"

Yes, these questions are still in my mind. In deep disappointment I have wept over the laxity of the church. But be assured that my tears have been tears of love. There can be no deep disappointment where there is not deep love. Yes, I love the church. How could I do otherwise? I am in the rather unique position of being the son, the grandson and the great grandson of preachers. Yes, I see the church as the body of Christ. But, oh! How we have blemished and scarred that body through social neglect and through fear of being nonconformists.

There was a time when the church was very powerful—in the time when the early Christians rejoiced at being deemed worthy to suffer for what they believed. In those days the church was not merely a thermometer that recorded the ideas and principles of popular opinion; it was a thermostat that transformed the mores of society. Whenever the early Christians entered a town, the people in power became disturbed and immediately sought to convict the Christians for being "disturbers of the peace" and "outside agitators." But the Christians pressed on, in the conviction that they were "a colony of heaven," called to obey God rather than man. Small in number, they were big in commitment. They were too God-intoxicated to be "astronomically intimidated." By their effort and example they brought an end to such ancient evils as infanticide and gladiatorial contests. Things are different now. So often the contemporary church is a weak, ineffectual voice with an uncertain sound. So often it is an archdefender of the status quo. Far from being disturbed by the presence of the church, the power structure of the average community is consoled by the church's silent—and often even vocal—sanction of things as they are.

But the judgment of God is upon the church as never before. If today's church does not recapture the sacrificial spirit of the early church, it will lose its authenticity, forfeit the loyalty of millions, and be dismissed as an irrelevant social club with no meaning for the twentieth century. Every day I meet young people whose disappointment with the church has turned into outright disgust.

Perhaps I have once again been too optimistic. Is organized religion too inextricably bound to the status quo to save our nation and the world? Perhaps I must turn my faith to the inner spiritual church, the church within the church, as the true ekklesia and the hope of the world. But again I am thankful to God that some noble souls from the ranks of organized religion have broken loose from the paralyzing chains of conformity and joined us as active partners in the struggle for freedom. They have left their secure congregations and walked the streets of Albany, Georgia, with us. They have gone down the highways of the South on tortuous rides for freedom. Yes, they have gone to jail with us. Some have been dismissed from their churches, have lost the support of their bishops and fellow ministers. But they have acted in the faith that right defeated is stronger than evil triumphant. Their witness has been the spiritual salt that has preserved the true meaning of the gospel in these troubled times. They have carved a tunnel of hope through the dark mountain of disappointment. I hope the church as a whole will meet the challenge of this decisive hour. But even if the church does not come to the aid of justice, I have no despair about the future. I have no fear about the outcome of our struggle in Birmingham, even if our motives are at present misunderstood. We will reach the goal of freedom in Birmingham and all over the nation, because the goal of America is freedom. Abused and scorned though we may be, our destiny is tied up with America's destiny. Before the pilgrims landed at Plymouth, we were here. Before the pen of Jefferson etched the majestic words of the Declaration of Independence across the pages of history, we were here. For more than two centuries our forebears labored in this country without wages; they made cotton king; they built the homes of their masters while suffering gross injustice and shameful humiliation—and yet out of a bottomless vitality they continued to thrive and develop. If the inexpressible cruelties of slavery could not stop us, the opposition we now face will surely fail. We will win our freedom because the sacred heritage of our nation and the eternal will of God are embodied in our echoing demands. Before closing I feel impelled to mention one other point in your statement that has troubled me profoundly. You warmly commended the Birmingham police force for keeping "order" and "preventing violence." I doubt that you would have so warmly commended the police force if you had seen its dogs sinking their teeth into unarmed, nonviolent Negroes. I doubt that you would so quickly commend the policemen if you were to observe their ugly and inhumane treatment of Negroes here in the city jail; if you were to watch them push and curse old Negro women and young Negro girls; if you were to see them slap and kick old Negro men and young boys; if you were to observe them, as they did on two occasions, refuse to give us food because we wanted to sing our grace together. I cannot join you in your praise of the Birmingham police department.

It is true that the police have exercised a degree of discipline in handling the demonstrators. In this sense they have conducted themselves rather "nonviolently" in public. But for what purpose? To preserve the evil system of segregation. Over the past few years I have consistently preached that nonviolence demands that the means we use must be as pure as the ends we seek. I have tried to make clear that it is wrong to use immoral means to attain moral ends. But now I must affirm that it is just as wrong, or perhaps even more so, to use moral means to preserve immoral ends. Perhaps Mr. Connor and his policemen have been rather nonviolent in public, as was Chief Pritchett in Albany, Georgia, but they have used the moral means of nonviolence to maintain the immoral end of racial injustice. As T. S. Eliot has said: "The last temptation is the greatest treason: To do the right deed for the wrong reason."

I wish you had commended the Negro sit inners and demonstrators of Birmingham for their sublime courage, their willingness to suffer and their amazing discipline in the midst of great provocation. One day the South will recognize its real heroes. They will be the James Merediths, with the noble sense of purpose that enables them to face jeering and hostile mobs, and with the agonizing loneliness that characterizes the life of the pioneer. They will be old, oppressed, battered Negro women, symbolized in a seventy two year old woman in Montgomery, Alabama, who rose up with a sense of dignity and with her people decided not to ride segregated buses, and who responded with ungrammatical profundity to one who inquired about her weariness: "My feets is tired, but my soul is at rest." They will be the young high school and college students, the young ministers of the gospel and a host of their elders, courageously and nonviolently sitting in at lunch counters and willingly going to jail for conscience' sake. One day the South will know that when these disinherited children of God sat down at lunch counters, they were in reality standing up for what is best in the American dream and for the most sacred values in our Judaeo Christian heritage, thereby bringing our nation back to those great wells of democracy which were dug deep by the founding fathers in their formulation of the Constitution and the Declaration of Independence.

Never before have I written so long a letter. I'm afraid it is much too long to take your precious time. I can assure you that it would have been much shorter if I had been writing from a comfortable desk, but what else can one do when he is alone in a narrow jail cell, other than write long letters, think long thoughts and pray long prayers?

If I have said anything in this letter that overstates the truth and indicates an unreasonable impatience, I beg you to forgive me. If I have said anything that understates the truth and indicates my having a patience that allows me to settle for anything less than brotherhood, I beg God to forgive me.

I hope this letter finds you strong in the faith. I also hope that circumstances will soon make it possible for me to meet each of you, not as an integrationist or a civil-rights leader but as a fellow clergyman and a Christian brother. Let us all hope that the dark clouds of racial prejudice will soon pass away and the deep fog of misunderstanding will be lifted from our fear drenched communities, and in some not too distant tomorrow the radiant stars of love and brotherhood will shine over our great nation with all their scintillating beauty.

Yours for the cause of Peace and Brotherhood,
Martin Luther King, Jr.

V. THE LEGAL ENFORCEMENT OF SEXUAL MORALITY

Introduction

TOLERANCE AND INDEED ACCEPTANCE of all manner of diversity has perhaps never been more common than it is today, and in such a climate, the idea that the state should regulate the sex lives and lifestyles of gay adults might strike many as unjust and hopelessly retrograde. That idea has, however, not always been harshly judged. In fact, consensual gay sex was actually criminalized in both Britain and the United States up through most of the twentieth century—conviction of "buggery" even carried the death penalty in Britain until 1861, while only in 2003 were the statutes of those U.S. states that still criminalized "sodomy" held to be unconstitutional by the Supreme Court. Criminalization of consensual gay sex between adults is now a thing of the past in Anglo-American law. But the idea that the state may enforce traditional sexual morality remains even today a politically formidable one that continues to influence the content of Anglo-American law, even if not its criminal codes.

The modern jurisprudential debate over the legal enforcement of sexual morality was prompted by the 1957 Wolfenden Report, which was a set of recommendations prepared at the behest of the British Parliament by its Committee on Homosexual Offences and Prostitution. The Report recommended, among other things, that "homosexual behaviour between consenting adults in private should no longer be a criminal offence."[1] Drawing on John Stuart Mill's famous claim in *On Liberty* that "the only purpose for which power can be rightfully exercised over any member of a civilized community, against his will, is to prevent harm to others",[2] the Wolfenden Report based its recommendation to decriminalize homosexual conduct on the general claim that "there must remain a realm of private morality and immorality which is, in brief and crude terms, not the law's business."[3]

The Wolfenden Report was not without its critics. In a much publicized lecture delivered to the British Academy in 1959 called "The Enforcement of Morals",[4] English High Court judge Patrick Devlin attacked the Report's recommendation concerning homosexual conduct. Devlin argued that a society's prevailing norms of sexual morality were partly constitutive of the society itself, and that the enforcement of such norms through the criminal law was thus necessary to preserve the society's very existence (see Section IX). Homosexual behavior, in Devlin's view, threatened this essential social cohesion because it conflicted with prevailing moral norms and could therefore be permissibly criminalized. That the behavior was in some sense private was irrelevant, according to Devlin, as one could not "define inflexibly areas of morality into which the law is in no circumstances to be allowed to enter."[5] The criminalization of homosexual behavior was born of necessity, Devlin believed, and self-preservation outweighed privacy.

Devlin's criticisms of the Wolfenden Report were immediately met with criticisms of their own. None were more famous than H. L. A. Hart's, delivered first in a weekly periodical and then more fully a few years later as a set of lectures at Stanford University, which would became the book *Law, Liberty, and Morality*. Hart maintained that Devlin had failed to substantiate what Hart called the "disintegration thesis", namely, that society would dissolve unless its prevailing sexual moral norms were enforced by the criminal law. Addressing two interpretations of Devlin's thesis in turn, Hart argued first that it was empirically unfounded: "no evidence is produced to show that deviation from accepted sexual morality, even by adults in private, is something which, like treason, threatens the existence of society."[6] If instead the thesis were understood as an *a priori* conceptual claim and not an empirical one, furthermore, it also foundered, for such a claim would rely on the "absurd" proposition that "a society is identical with its morality as that is at any given moment in its history, so that a change in its morality is tantamount to the destruction of a society."[7] In neither case, Hart argued, had Devlin established the truth of the disintegration thesis or the conclusion supposedly following from it that homosexual behavior may be criminalized.

The Hart/Devlin Debate, as it came to be known, concerned not just the legal enforcement of traditional sexual morality, but its legal enforcement through the criminal law. History, at least in Western democracies, has sided with Hart on the permissibility of criminalizing consensual gay sex between adults. But what Hart called "legal moralism" remains very much alive. John Finnis, the leading exponent of natural law jurisprudence (detailed in Robert George's "Natural Law and Positive Law" in Section II), for example, maintains in "Law, Morality, and 'Sexual Orientation' " that while the state may not be authorized to criminalize consensual homosexual conduct, "states do have the authority to discourage . . . homosexual conduct and 'orientation' (i.e. overtly manifested active willingness to engage in homosexual conduct)."[8] Though he disagrees with Devlin about the proper scope of the criminal law, then, Finnis nevertheless recognizes that the criminal law is not the only tool in the state's toolbox and steadfastly maintains that the state may use its other ones to steer people away from homosexuality.

Perhaps the most fundamental way in which Finnis's defense of legal moralism parts from Devlin's consists in its reliance on what Hart called "critical" and not "positive" morality. For Devlin, the morality to be enforced by so-called "morals legislation" was society's prevailing morality—it was society's "positive" morality in virtue of being posited or simply accepted. The key to Finnis's view, in contrast, is "critical" morality, or the true morality that one employs (or takes oneself to be employing) in criticizing prevailing moral norms. Thus, according to Finnis, the state may discourage homosexual conduct because gay sex is *in fact* morally wrong and worthless, whether or not it is taken to be by the majority of society.

Finnis devotes considerable attention in "Law, Morality, and 'Sexual Orientation'" to explaining why he believes that homosexual conduct is base. His argument need not be explicated here, but a broader point about it is worth making: the kind of legal moralism that Finnis advocates is a function of his commitment to natural law jurisprudence. Central to that theory of law are moral and, more broadly, value judgments that are grounded in an account of human nature. In this way, the defensibility of any particular version of natural law theory depends upon the defensibility of the value judgments that figure centrally in it.

Taking these up in "Against the Old Sexual Morality of the New Natural Law", Stephen Macedo contends that Finnis cannot defend his disapproval of at least certain kinds of gay sexual relationships. Confronting Finnis's argument that only sexual relationships that are potentially procreative have value, Macedo maintains that Finnis cannot find the value that he does in a sexual relationship between sterile heterosexuals while rejecting as worthless one between homosexuals—after all, neither are potentially procreative. Consistency aside, Macedo further objects to Finnis's dim view of gay relationships, arguing that it is "simplistic and implausible to portray the essential nature of *every form* of non-procreative sexuality as no better than the *least valuable* form."[9]

Some criticisms of legal moralism reject that position's premises, holding that the state has no authority to legislate based on inevitably controversial value judgments. Part of what makes Macedo's arguments powerful is that he shares with Finnis a crucial premise, accepting in principle the authority of the state to base its laws on such judgments. Macedo does not criticize morals legislation so much as the conservative conception of morality, historically antagonistic to homosexuality, that often is taken for granted by proponents of morals legislation.

What legal rights gay people should have is one of the most contentious issues facing Western democracies today, and in that respect, sexual morality continues to be an object of legal regulation. The consensus that gay sex ought not to be criminalized has not yielded any further consensus—for example, about whether gay people may reveal their sexual orientation at work without being fired, about whether gay people may adopt children, or about whether they may marry. There are of course many factors that shape these more specific debates about the law, but surely one of them is the perceived nature and value of gay relationships. In addition to fruitfully engaging with one another, the sophisticated and dispassionate accounts that Finnis and Macedo each provide of that nature and value (or lack thereof) also join, clarify, and ultimately advance the wider debate about the legal enforcement of sexual morality.

Notes

1 *Report of the Committee on Homosexual Offences and Prostitution* (1957), Cmd. 247, para. 62.

2 John Stuart Mill, *On Liberty* (1859, 4th edition 1869), in Michael L. Morgan (ed.) *Classics of Moral and Political Theory*, Indianapolis: Hackett Publishing Company, 1992, p. 1050.

3 *Report*, para. 61.

4 Patrick Devlin, "The Enforcement of Morals," Maccabaean Lecture in Jurisprudence, *Proceedings of the British Academy* 45, 1959, 129–51; reprinted as "Morals and the Criminal Law" in Patrick Devlin, *The Enforcement of Morals*, Oxford: Oxford University Press, 1965, pp. 1–25.

5 Devlin, *The Enforcement of Morals*, p. 13.

6 H. L. A. Hart, *Law, Liberty, and Morality*, Stanford, CA: Stanford University Press, 1963, p. 50.

7 Ibid., p. 51.

8 John Finnis, "Law, Morality, and 'Sexual Orientation' ", this volume, p. 269.

9 Stephen Macedo, "Against the Old Sexuality of the New Natural Law", p. 294.

Further reading

Patrick Devlin, *The Enforcement of Morals*, Oxford: Oxford University Press, 1965.

Robert George, *Making Men Moral: Civil Liberties and Public Morality*, New York: Oxford University Press, 1993.

Robert George (ed.), *Natural Law, Liberalism, and Morality*, New York: Oxford University Press, 1996.

H. L. A. Hart, *Law, Liberty, and Morality*, Stanford, CA: Stanford University Press, 1963.

John Stuart Mill, *On Liberty* (1859, 4th edition 1869), in Michael L. Morgan (ed.) *Classics of Moral and Political Theory*, Indianapolis: Hackett Publishing Company, 1992, pp. 1044–1115.

Report of the Committee on Homosexual Offences and Prostitution (1957), Cmd. 247, para. 62.

US Cases

Romer v. Evans, 517 U.S. 620 (1996).

Lawrence v. Texas, 539 U.S. 558 (2003).

UK Law

The Equality Act 2006 (2006 c3).

Questions

1. Can a state be justified in discriminating amongst its citizens on the basis of their sexual orientation?

2. Is Finnis's moral distinction between a gay relationship and a heterosexual relationship that has no prospect of being procreative defensible?

3. Do you agree with Macedo that it is "simplistic and implausible to portray the essential nature of *every form* of non-procreative sexuality as no better than the *least valuable* form"?

Chapter 16

John M. Finnis

LAW, MORALITY, AND "SEXUAL ORIENTATION"

I.

DURING THE PAST thirty years there has emerged in Europe a standard form of legal regulation of sexual conduct. This standard form or scheme, which I shall call the "standard modern [European] position," is accepted by the European Court of Human Rights and the European Commission of Human Rights (the two supra-national judicial and quasi-judicial institutions of the European Convention for the Protection of Human Rights and Fundamental Freedoms (1950), to which almost all European states are party, whether or not they are also party to the European [Economic] Community now known as the European Union). The standard modern European position has two limbs. On the one hand, the state is not authorized to, and does not, make it a punishable offence for adult consenting persons to engage, in private, in immoral sexual acts (for example, homosexual acts). On the other hand, states do have the authority to discourage, say, homosexual conduct and "orientation" (i.e. overtly manifested active willingness to engage in homosexual conduct). And typically, though not universally, they do so. That is to say, they maintain various criminal and administrative laws and policies which have as part of their purpose the discouraging of such conduct. Many of these laws, regulations, and policies discriminate (i.e. distinguish) between hetero-

sexual and homosexual conduct adversely to the latter.

In England, for example, well after Parliament's decriminalization of private adult homosexual conduct by the Sexual Offences Act 1967, the highest court (the House of Lords) reaffirmed that a jury may lawfully convict on a charge of conspiring to corrupt public morals by publishing advertisements by private individuals of their availability for (non-commercial) private homosexual acts.[1] The Court of Appeal has constantly reaffirmed, notably in 1977, 1981 and 1990,[2] that public soliciting of adult males by adult males falls within the statutory prohibition of "importun[ing] in a public place for an immoral purpose."[3] Parliament has peacefully accepted both these judicial interpretations of the constitutional, statutory and common law position. It has also voted more than once to maintain the legal position whereby the age of consent for lawful intercourse is 21 for homosexual but 16 for heterosexual intercourse;[4] in February 1994 the House of Commons voted to make the homosexual age of consent 18, which would reduce but retain the differentiation between homosexual and heterosexual conduct.[5] In 1988, Parliament specifically prohibited local governments in England from doing anything to "intentionally promote homosexuality" or "promote the teaching in any maintained school of the acceptability of homosexuality as a pretended family relationship."[6]

The provisions of English law relating to marriage and to adoption similarly manifest a purpose or at least a willingness to discourage homosexual conduct and impede its promotion by any form of invitatory activity other than between consenting adults and in a truly private milieu.

The English position as outlined above is in full conformity with the position upheld by the European human rights institutions. When the European Court of Human Rights in 1981 adopted (and in 1988 reaffirmed) the position which Parliament in England had taken in 1967, it ruled that penal prohibition of private adult homosexual activity is not necessary for the securing of the state's legitimate aim of protecting morals.[7] In doing so, the court expressly left unscathed, and in principle confirmed, the decision of March 13, 1980 of the European Commission of Human Rights (and of the Commission on October 12, 1978 and the Council of Ministers by Resolution DH (79) 5 of June 12, 1979) that states can properly prohibit private consensual homosexual acts involving a male under 21 notwithstanding the Convention right of non-discrimination in the legal protection of rights and notwithstanding that the state law in question made 16 the "age of consent" for heterosexual intercourse (and 18 the age of majority for other purposes).

The Commission has subsequently reaffirmed that decision and has declared unarguable ("inadmissible" for further judicial process) complaints made, under the Convention's anti-discrimination provisions, against the long-standing Swiss law which criminalizes homosexual prostitution (male or female) but not heterosexual prostitution.[8]

II.

The standard modern [European] position is consistent with the view that (apart perhaps from special cases and contexts) it is unjust for A to impose any kind of disadvantage on B simply because A believes (perhaps correctly) that B has sexual inclinations (which he may or may not act on) towards persons of the same sex. (Special cases are more likely to arise, for example, where B's inclination is towards "man-boy love," i.e. pederasty.) The position does not give B the widest conceivable legal protection against such unjust discrimination (just as it generally does not give wide protection against needless acts of adverse private discrimination in housing or employment to people with unpopular or eccentric political views). But the position does not itself encourage, sponsor or impose any such unjust burden. (And it is accompanied by many legal protections for homosexual persons with respect to assaults, threats, unreasonable discrimination by public bodies and officials, etc.)

The concern of the standard modern position itself is not with inclinations but entirely with certain *decisions* to *express* or *manifest* deliberate promotion of, or readiness to engage in, homosexual *activity* or *conduct*, including promotion of forms of life (e.g. purportedly marital cohabitation) which both encourage such activity and present it as a valid or acceptable alternative to the committed heterosexual union which the state recognizes as marriage. Subject only to the written or unwritten constitutional requirement of freedom of discussion of ideas, the state laws and state policies which I have outlined are intended to discourage decisions which are thus deliberately oriented towards homosexual conduct and are manifested in public ways.

The standard modern position differs from the position which it replaced, which made adult consensual sodomy and like acts crimes per se. States which adhere to the standard modern position make it clear by laws and policies such as I have referred to that the state has by no means renounced its legitimate concern with public morality and the education of children and young people towards truly worthwhile and against alluring but bad forms of conduct and life. Nor have such states renounced the judgment that a life involving homosexual conduct is bad even for anyone unfortunate enough to have innate or quasi-innate homosexual inclinations.

The difference between the standard modern position and the position it has replaced can be expressed as follows. The standard modern position considers that the state's proper responsibility for upholding true worth (morality) is a responsibility *subsidiary* (auxiliary) to the *primary* responsibility of parents and non-political voluntary associations. The subsidiary character of government is widely emphasized and increasingly accepted, at least in principle, in contemporary European politics. (It was, for example, a cornerstone of the Treaty of Maastricht of 1992.) This conception of the proper role of government has been taken to exclude the state from assuming a directly parental disciplinary role in relation to consenting *adults*. That role was one which political theory and practice formerly ascribed to the state on the assumption that the role followed by logical necessity from the truth that the state should encourage true worth and discourage immorality. That assumption is now judged to be mistaken (a judgment for which I shall argue in the final part of this lecture).

So the modern theory and practice draws a distinction not drawn in the former legal arrangements—a distinction between (a) supervising the truly private conduct of adults and (b) supervising the *public realm or environment*. The importance of the latter includes the following considerations: (1) this is the environment or public realm in which young people (of whatever sexual inclination) are educated; (2) it is the context in which and by which everyone with responsibility for the well being of young people is helped or hindered in assisting them to avoid bad forms of life; (3) it is the milieu in which and by which all citizens are encouraged and helped, or discouraged and undermined, in their own resistance to being lured by temptation into falling away from their own aspirations

to be people of integrated good character, and to be autonomous, self-controlled persons rather than slaves to impulse and sensual gratification.

While the type (a) supervision of truly private adult consensual conduct is now considered to be outside the state's normally proper role (with exceptions such as sado-masochistic bodily damage, and assistance in suicide), type (b) supervision of the moral-cultural-educational environment is maintained as a very important part of the state's justification for claiming legitimately the loyalty of its decent citizens.

III.

The standard modern position is part of a politico-legal order which systematically outlaws many forms of discrimination. Thus the European Convention on Human Rights (model for several dozen constitutions enacted over the past thirty-five years by the British authorities, for nations gaining independence) provides that the protection of the rights it sets out is to be enjoyed without discrimination on any ground such as "sex, race, colour, language, religion, political or other opinion, national or social origin, association with a national minority, property, birth or other status."

But the standard modern position deliberately rejects proposals to include in such lists the item "sexual orientation." The explanation commonly given (correctly, in my opinion) is this. The phrase "sexual orientation" is radically equivocal. Particularly as used by promoters of "gay rights," the phrase ambiguously assimilates two things which the standard modern position carefully distinguishes: (I) a psychological or psychosomatic disposition inwardly orienting one *towards* homosexual activity; (II) the deliberate decision so to orient one's public *behavior* as to express or *manifest* one's active interest in and endorsement of homosexual *conduct* and/or forms of life which presumptively involve such conduct.

It is also widely observed that laws or proposed laws outlawing "discrimination based on sexual orientation" are always interpreted by "gay rights" movements as going far beyond discrimination based merely on A's belief that B is sexually attracted to persons of the same sex. Instead (it is observed), "gay rights" movements interpret the phrase as extending full legal protection to public activities intended specifically to promote, procure and facilitate homosexual conduct.

It has been noticed in public circles in Europe that such laws have indeed been interpreted by American courts as having just such an implication. An example which has been widely reported is the Georgetown University case,[9] requiring a religiously affiliated educational institution to give equal access to its facilities to organizations "participating in and promoting homosexual lifestyles [which necessarily include homosexual conduct]" in manifest opposition to the moral beliefs and teachings of the religion with which that institution professed an association.

So, while the standard position accepts that acts of type (I) discrimination are unjust, it judges that there are compelling reasons both to deny that such injustice would be appropriately remedied by laws against "discrimination based on sexual orientation," and to hold that such a "remedy" would work significant discrimination and injustice against (and would indeed damage) families, associations and institutions which have organized themselves to live out and transmit ideals of family life that include a high conception of the worth of truly conjugal sexual intercourse.

It is in fact accepted by almost everyone, on both sides of the political debate, that the adoption of a law framed to prohibit "discrimination on grounds of sexual orientation" would require the prompt abandonment of all attempts by the political community to discourage homosexual conduct by means of educational policies, restrictions on prostitution, non-recognition of

homosexual "marriages" and adoptions, and so forth. It is judged (and in my view soundly) that the law itself would perforce have changed from teaching, in many ways, that homosexual conduct is bad to teaching, massively, that it is a type of sexual activity as good as any other (and per se much less involved with onerous responsibilities than is the sexual union of husband and wife or, in perhaps other ways, the life of those who live in unmarried chastity).

IV.

The standard modern position involves a number of explicit or implicit judgments about the proper role of law and the compelling interests of political communities, and about the evil of homosexual conduct. Can these be defended by reflective, critical, publicly intelligible and rational arguments? I believe they can. Since even the advocates of "gay rights" do not seriously assert that the state can never have any compelling interests in public morality or the moral formation of its young people or the moral environment in which parents, other educators, and young people themselves must undertake this formation, I shall in this lecture focus rather on the underlying issue which receives far too little public discussion: What is wrong with homosexual conduct? Is the judgment that it is morally wrong inevitably a manifestation either of mere hostility to a hated minority, or of purely religious, theological, and sectarian belief which can ground no constitutionally valid determination disadvantaging those who do not conform to it?

I have been using and shall continue to use the terms "homosexual activity," "homosexual acts" and "homosexual conduct" synonymously, to refer to bodily acts, on the body of a person of the same sex, which are engaged in with a view to securing orgasmic sexual satisfaction for one or more of the parties.

Let me begin by noticing a too little noticed fact. All three of the greatest Greek philosophers,

Socrates, Plato and Aristotle, regarded homosexual *conduct* as intrinsically shameful, immoral, and indeed depraved or depraving. That is to say, all three rejected the linchpin of modern "gay" ideology and lifestyle.

Socrates is portrayed by Plato (and by Xenophon) as having strong homosexual (as well as heterosexual) inclinations or interest, and as promoting an ideal of homosexual romance between men and youths, but at the same time as utterly rejecting homosexual conduct. This is made clear in Sir Kenneth Dover's book *Greek Homosexuality*;[10] in Dover's summarizing words: "Xenophon's Socrates lacks the sensibility and urbanity of the Platonic Socrates, but there is no doubt that both of them condemn homosexual copulation."[11] It is also made clear by Gregory Vlastos in his last book, precisely on Socrates: In Socratic *eros* involving relationships of affection between men and boys or youths, intimacy is limited to mind- and eye-contact and "terminal gratification" is forbidden[12] (and *a fortiori* in relationships between adult males, since virtually all Athenians regarded sex acts between adult males as intrinsically shameful).[13] Vlastos thus makes it clear that Socrates forbids precisely what I have been calling homosexual conduct.

In the recent Amendment 2 case in Colorado, *Evans v. Romer*,[14] the widely influential classical philosopher Professor Martha Nussbaum gave oral and written evidence on these matters, as expert witness for plaintiffs who seek to overturn a provision of the Colorado Constitution which provides that no official body in Colorado may adopt any law or policy "whereby homosexual, lesbian or bisexual orientation, conduct, practices or relationships shall constitute or otherwise be the basis of . . . a claim to minority status, quota preferences, protected status or claim of discrimination." In her oral testimony (on October 15, 1993), she flatly denied that Dover's book *Greek Homosexuality* came to the conclusion that Socrates condemned homosexual copulation. Dover concluded only, she said, that Socrates condemned the seduction of students. A

few days later, the Princeton legal and political-theoretical scholar Professor Robert George gave evidence to show that Dover's book unequivocally concludes that Socrates, as portrayed by our two sources Plato and Xenophon, condemned homosexual copulation as such, and did not confine the prohibition to any particular relationships. Professor Nussbaum promptly wrote[15] to George asserting that that was false testimony given in reckless disregard of the truth. Demanding peremptorily that George retract before the close of the trial on October 22, 1993, she claimed that Dover himself would personally support her reading of his conclusion about Socrates. In the event, Dover wrote to me on January 23, 1994, and authorizes me to quote him:

> It is certainly my opinion that the Socrates of Plato and Xenophon condemned homosexual copulation as such, and did not confine the prohibition to any particular relationships. I certainly meant to say that on pp. 159f. of my book.[16]

What, then, about Plato? Well, the same Plato who in his *Symposium* wrote a famous celebration of *romantic* and *spiritual* man-boy erotic relationships, made very clear that all forms of sexual *conduct* outside heterosexual marriage are shameful, wrongful and harmful. This is particularly evident from his treatment of the matter in his last work, the *Laws*, but is also sufficiently clear in the *Republic* and the *Phaedrus*, and even in the *Symposium* itself. This is affirmed unequivocally both by Dover and by Vlastos, neither of whom has any favor for these views of Plato. According to Vlastos, for example, Plato:

> saw anal intercourse as 'contrary to nature,' [footnote: Ph[ae]dr[us] 251A1, L[aws] 636–7] a degradation not only of man's humanity, but even of his animality . . .[17]

It is for Plato, Vlastos adds, a type of act far more serious than any mere going "contrary to the rules."[18]

On Plato, Martha Nussbaum's oral evidence took a remarkable course. She claimed that the translation of Laws 636[19] which had been quoted to the court in my affidavit was inaccurate; instead of the phrase "those guilty of such enormities," it should have read, in morally neutral terms, "those who first ventured to do these things." Therefore, none of the translations of or references to Plato in my affidavit could be relied upon, and Plato in fact approved of homosexual conduct. Robert George then gave evidence that all the existing English translations, without exception, translate the relevant Greek phrase with some pejorative term, or use a pejorative term about the same conduct at an equivalent point in the previous sentence; and that in particular the philologist Sir Kenneth Dover translates the relevant Greek word, tolmema, as "crime" (meaning moral crime). So in her affidavit, delivered on the last day of the trial, Professor Nussbaum stated that Liddell & Scott, "the authoritative Greek dictionary relied on by all scholars in this area," translates tolmema with only the favorable or neutral terms "an adventure, enterprise, deed of daring."[20] In fact, however, Liddell & Scott translates it "adventure, enterprise, daring or shameless act."[21] What Nussbaum had done was quote from the 1897 edition of the dictionary, an edition entirely superseded in 1940, doing so without disclosing to the court the date or edition. In short, she put a dictionary before the court precisely as "the authoritative dictionary relied on by all scholars in the area," but the quotation which she said was from that dictionary was in fact from a dictionary which is not authoritative or relied upon by any scholars. And she did so because to have quoted from the real "authoritative dictionary" would have destroyed the fundamental contention of her oral evidence about Plato, while to have allowed the court to know the truth about the long-superseded nineteenth century source of her lexicography would have deprived her testimony of the appearance of authoritative support which it so badly needed

to offset the devastating counter-witness of Dover.

In her oral testimony, she flatly denied that Dover's study of Plato concludes that Plato condemned all homosexual copulation. No, she said, Dover concluded only that Plato condemned sex involving bribery or prostitution. Once again, Dover, having been put on notice of that contention, permits me to quote his letter of January 23, 1994: "Plato condemns all homosexual copulation (pp. 165–8 in my book)."[22]

A key element in Plato's condemnation of homosexual conduct is his repeated judgment, in the Phaedrus and the Laws, that it is para phusin, contrary to nature. On this matter, Professor Nussbaum's testimony was clear:

> the terms tendentiously translated "according to nature" and "unnatural" or "contrary to nature" actually refer (in my own expert opinion and the consensus of recent scholars such as Price, whose study of the passage [in the Laws] has been widely accepted) to "birth" and not "nature" in any normative moral sense.[23]

This claim about a consensus of recent scholars rejecting as tendentious the translation "unnatural" or "contrary to nature," or supporting Nussbaum's outlandish translation of para phusin, was pure fabrication. According to Nussbaum herself, the "modern consensus" on the matter formed itself around Price's "widely accepted" study. Very well. But what Nussbaum says about Price's study of the passage is, shockingly, the exact reverse of the truth. That study unhesitatingly translates para phusin, in Laws 636 and 841, as "unnatural". For example, its translation of 636c is: "homosexual intercourse, between males or females, seems to be an unnatural [para phusin] crime [tolmema] of the first rank."[24]

Let me summarize how Professor Nussbaum treated Price's "widely accepted" study. Price's book translates these uses of para phusin as "unnatural," and yet her statements under oath unambiguously imply that it rejects that translation as tendentious. The conclusions of the book's long appendix on "Plato's Sexual Morality" are squarely based on Price's reasoned judgment that "unnatural" in these passages both conveyed and entailed Plato's essential *moral* judgments on sexual conduct, yet Nussbaum swears that it supports her denial that the term had "any normative moral sense" and her assertion that it signified for Plato no more than inconsistency with a temporary pro-natalist colonial politics. Nussbaum implicitly claims the support of Price's book for her fundamental contention that the sexual morality put to the court by Robert George and by me is purely theological, Catholic and indeed narrowly Thomist in origin, and "simply has no precedent in the ancient Greek secular exemplars of natural law argumentation"[25] including Plato;[26] yet Price's book in fact argues, prominently and very explicitly, that Plato's main positions on the morality of sexual conduct, evidenced by the *Republic* and the *Phaedrus* as well as by the *Laws*, were (rather to Price's regret) substantially the same as the positions maintained in the Catholic tradition's understanding of natural law.[27]

The fabrication of the imaginary "modern consensus" about *para phusin* also required Professor Nussbaum to withhold from the court the fact that the other scholarly authorities most prominently and frequently appealed to in her testimony—Dover, Price, Vlastos, Winkler—all concur in using the terms "unnatural" or "contrary to nature" to translate *para phusin* as predicated of homosexual acts in *Laws*.[28] All treat this translation as entirely uncontroversial. All judge that *para phusin*, as used by Plato in the *Laws*, must be understood as the core of a very firm and unqualified condemnation of homosexual conduct. All explicitly or implicitly reject out of hand Nussbaum's assertion that "the passage" in the *Laws* "says nothing at all about sexual acts among non-married people." Like even Halperin and Winkler (the openly "gay"

scholars also appealed to in Nussbaum's affidavit), Dover, Price, and (as we shall see) Vlastos all judge that to know or tell Plato's views on the morality, the immorality, of all such non-marital conduct as homosexual sex acts, one need go no further than these unmistakably clear passages in the *Laws*, texts with which every other text of Plato can readily be seen to be consistent.[29]

As for Aristotle, Dover's discussion is less satisfactory; it neglects a number of relevant passages. Still, it does not contradict the scholarly consensus that Aristotle rejected homosexual conduct. In fact, such conduct is frequently represented by Aristotle (in some cases directly and in other cases by a lecturer's hint) as intrinsically perverse, shameful and harmful both to the individuals involved and to society itself.[30]

On Aristotle, the manipulations in Nussbaum's affidavit were as thoroughgoing as we should by now expect. She associated Price's book with her affidavit's assertions that Aristotle approved and endorsed homosexual acts. But in reality the Aristotle of Price's book is "rather shocked" even by Plato's *Republic*'s carefully and famously restricted suggestion that "the lover may kiss and touch the beloved, with his consent, *just like a son.*"[31] The final sentences of Price's reflections on Aristotle's view of erotic love conclude that, for Aristotle, such love is properly either marital or pederastic; on the same page Price reminds us that for Aristotle pederasty is not only as transient as boyhood but also "should keep to its higher forms, 'looking rather than loving' as Plato had put it."[32] It is not to include homosexual sex acts. What do we find Nussbaum saying? "I agree with Price's conclusion," she says, proceeding to quote Price's final sentences, but slicing off, without any indication, the first fourteen words so that in place of Price's reference to marriage and "pederasty" (thus understood as *excluding* sex acts) she can substitute her own words "heterosexual and homosexual relations" (understood as *including* sex acts between males *of any age*). A similar falsifying and unsignalled truncation occurs in her affidavit's only quotation from Aristotle himself, and all the other passages of Aristotle that she cites are manifestly abused and misrepresented.

Although the ideology of homosexual love (with its accompanying devaluation of women) continued to have philosophical defenders down to the end of classical Greek civilization, there equally continued to be influential philosophical writers, wholly untouched by Judaeo-Christian tradition, who taught that homosexual conduct is not only intrinsically shameful but also inconsistent with a proper recognition of the equality of women with men in intrinsic worth. (The ancients did not fail to note that Socrates' homo-erotic orientation, for all its admirable chastity— abstention from homosexual conduct—went along with a neglect to treat his wife as an equal.) A good example of such late classical writing is Plutarch's Erotikos,[33] written probably some time in the early second century, but certainly free from Judaeo-Christian influence. Plutarch's vast literary-historical and philosophical corpus of writings is an effort to recapture and recapitulate the highest achievements of classical civilization, and had a very substantial influence on Western thought down to recent times. I shall say more about Plutarch's thought on these matters below.

Another example is the Stoic, Musonius Rufus (who taught at Rome circa 80 A.D. and again was not influenced by Jewish or Christian thought). He rejects all homosexual conduct as shameful. Sexual conduct is decent and acceptable only within marriage. The point of marriage includes not only procreation and the raising of children, but also, integrally and essentially, a complete community of life and mutual care and affection between husband and wife.[34]

At the heart of the Platonic-Aristotelian and later ancient philosophical rejections of all homosexual conduct, and thus of the modern "gay" ideology, are three fundamental theses: (1) The commitment of a man and woman to each other in the sexual union of marriage is intrinsically good and reasonable, and is incompatible with sexual relations outside marriage. (2) Homosexual acts are radically and peculiarly non-marital, and for that reason intrinsically unreasonable and unnatural. (3) Furthermore, according to Plato, if not Aristotle, homosexual acts have a special similarity to solitary masturbation, and both types of radically non-marital act are manifestly unworthy of the human being and immoral.

V.

I want now to offer an interpretation of these three theses which articulates them more clearly than was ever attempted by Plato or, so far as we can tell, by Aristotle. It is, I think, an interpretation faithful to what they do say, but takes up suggestions in Plutarch and in the eighteenth century Enlightenment philosophy of Immanuel Kant (who likewise rejected all homosexual conduct), though even these writers' indications, too, remain relatively terse. My account also articulates thoughts which have historically been implicit in the judgments of many non-philosophical people, and which have been held to justify the laws adopted in many nations and states both before and after the period when Christian beliefs as such were politically and socially dominant. And it is an application of the theory of morality and natural law developed over the past thirty years by Germain Grisez and others. A fuller exposition can be found in the chapter on marriage, sexual acts, and family life, in the new second volume of Grisez's great work on moral theology.[35]

Plato's mature concern, in the *Laws*, for familiarity, affection and love between spouses in a chastely exclusive marriage, Aristotle's representation of marriage as an intrinsically desirable friendship between quasi-equals, and as a state of life even more natural to human beings than political life,[36] and Musonius Rufus's conception of the inseparable double goods of marriage, all find expression in Plutarch's celebration of marriage—as a union not of mere instinct but of reasonable love, and not merely for procreation but for mutual help, goodwill and cooperation for their own sake.[37] Plutarch's severe critiques of homosexual conduct (and of the disparagement of women implicit in homosexual ideology),[38] develop Plato's critique of homosexual and all other extra-marital sexual conduct. Like Musonius Rufus, Plutarch does so by bringing much closer to explicit articulation the following thought. Genital intercourse between spouses enables them to actualize and experience (and in that sense express) their marriage itself, as a single reality with two blessings (children and mutual affection).[39] Non-marital intercourse, especially but not only homosexual, has no such point and therefore is unacceptable.

The core of this argument can be clarified by comparing it with Saint Augustine's treatment of marriage in his *De Bono Coniugali*. The good of marital communion is here an instrumental good, in the service of the procreation and education of children so that the intrinsic, non-instrumental good of friendship will be promoted and realized by the propagation of the human race, and the intrinsic good of inner integration be promoted and realized by the "remedying" of the disordered desires of concupiscence.[40] Now, when considering sterile marriages, Augustine had identified a further good of marriage, the natural *societas* (companionship) of the two sexes.[41] Had he truly integrated this into his synthesis, he would have recognized that in sterile and fertile marriages alike, the communion, companionship, *societas* and *amicitia* of the spouses—their being married—is the very good of marriage, and is an intrinsic, basic human good, not merely instrumental to any other good. And this communion of married life, this integral amalgamation of the lives of the two persons (as Plutarch[42] put it before John Paul II),[43] has as its intrinsic elements, as essential *parts* of one and the same good, the goods and ends to which the theo-logical tradition, following Augustine, for a long time subordinated that communion. It took a long and gradual process of development of doctrine, through the Catechism of the Council of Trent, the teachings of Pius XI and Pius XII, and eventually those of Vatican II—a process brilliantly illuminated by Germain Grisez[44]—to bring the tradition to the position that procreation and children are neither the *end* (whether primary or secondary) to which marriage is instrumental (as Augustine taught), nor instrumental to the good of the spouses (as much secular and "liberal Christian" thought supposes), but rather: Parenthood and children and family are the intrinsic fulfillment of a communion which, because it is not merely instrumental, can exist and fulfill the spouses even if procreation happens to be impossible for them.

Now if, as the recent encyclical on the foundations of morality, *Veritatis Splendor*, teaches, "the communion of persons in marriage" which is violated by every act of adultery is itself a "fundamental human good,"[45] there fall into place not only the elements of the classic philosophical judgments on non-marital sexual conduct but also the similar judgments reached about such conduct by decent people who cannot articulate explanatory premises for those judgments, which they reach rather by an insight into what is and is not *consistent* with realities whose goodness they experience and understand at least sufficiently to will and choose. In particular, there fall into place the elements of an answer to the question: Why cannot non-marital friendship be promoted and expressed by sexual acts? Why is the attempt to express affection by orgasmic non-marital sex the pursuit of an illusion? Why did Plato and Socrates, Xenophon, Aristotle, Musonius Rufus, and Plutarch, right at the heart of their reflections on the homoerotic culture around them, make the very deliberate and careful judgment that homosexual *conduct* (and indeed all extra-marital sexual gratification) is radically incapable of participating in, actualizing, the common good of friendship?

Implicit in the philosophical and common-sense rejection of extra-marital sex is the answer: The union of the reproductive organs of husband and wife really unites them biologically (and their biological reality is part of, not merely an instrument of, their *personal* reality); reproduction is one function and so, in respect of that function, the spouses are indeed one reality, and their sexual union therefore can *actualize* and allow them to *experience* their *real common good*—their *marriage* with the two goods, parenthood and friendship, which (leaving aside the order of grace) are the parts of its wholeness as an intelligible common good even if, independently of what the spouses will, their capacity for biological parenthood will not be fulfilled by that act of genital union. But the common good of friends who are not and cannot be married (for example, man and man, man and boy, woman and woman) has nothing to do with their having children by each other, and their reproductive organs cannot make them a biological (and therefore personal) unit.[46] So their sexual acts together cannot do what they may hope and imagine. Because their activation of one or even each of their reproductive organs cannot be an actualizing and experiencing of the *marital good*—as marital intercourse (intercourse between spouses in a marital way) can, even between spouses who *happen* to be sterile—it can do no more than provide each partner with an individual gratification. For want of a *common good* that could be actualized and experienced *by and in this bodily union*, that conduct involves the partners in treating their bodies as instruments to be used in the service of their consciously experiencing selves; their choice to engage in such conduct thus dis-integrates each of them precisely as acting persons.[47]

Reality is known in judgment, not in emotion, and *in reality*, whatever the generous hopes and dreams and thoughts of *giving* with which some same-sex partners may surround their sexual acts, those acts cannot express or do more than is expressed or done if two strangers engage in such activity to give each other pleasure, or a prostitute pleasures a client to give him pleasure in return for money, or (say) a man masturbates to give himself pleasure and a fantasy of more human relationships after a gruelling day on the assembly line. This is, I believe, the substance of Plato's judgment—at that moment in the *Gorgias* which is also decisive for the moral and political philosophical critique of hedonism[48]—that there is no important distinction in essential moral worthlessness between solitary masturbation, being sodomized as a prostitute, and being sodomized for the pleasure of it. Sexual acts cannot in *reality* be self-giving unless they are acts by which a man and a woman actualize and experience sexually the real giving of themselves to each other—in biological, affective and volitional union in mutual commitment, both open-ended and exclusive—which like Plato and Aristotle and most peoples we call marriage.

In short, sexual acts are not unitive in their significance unless they are marital (actualizing the all-level unity of marriage) and (since the common good of marriage has two aspects) they are not marital unless they have not only the generosity of acts of friendship but also the procreative significance, not necessarily of being intended to generate or capable in the circumstances of generating but at least of being, as human conduct, acts of the reproductive kind—actualizations, so far as the spouses then and there can, of the reproductive function in which they are biologically and thus personally one.

The ancient philosophers do not much discuss the case of sterile marriages, or the fact (well known to them) that for long periods of time (e.g. throughout pregnancy) the sexual acts of a married couple are naturally incapable of resulting in reproduction. They appear to take for granted what the subsequent Christian tradition certainly did, that such sterility does not render the conjugal sexual acts of the spouses non-marital. (Plutarch indicates that intercourse with a sterile spouse is a desirable mark of marital esteem and affection.)[49] For: A husband and wife who unite their reproductive organs in an act of sexual intercourse which, so far as they then can make it, is of a kind suitable for generation, do function as a biological (and thus personal) unit and thus can be actualizing and experiencing the two-in-one-flesh common good and reality of marriage, even when some biological condition happens to prevent that unity resulting in generation of a child. Their conduct thus differs radically from the acts of a husband and wife whose intercourse is masturbatory, for example sodomitic or by fellatio or coitus interruptus.[50] In law such acts do not consummate a marriage, because in reality (whatever the couple's illusions of intimacy and self-giving in such acts) they do not actualize the one-flesh, two-part marital good.

Does this account seek to "make moral judgments based on natural facts"?[51] Yes and no. No, in the sense that it does not seek to infer normative conclusions or theses from non-normative (natural-fact) premises. Nor does it appeal to any norm of the form "Respect natural facts or natural functions." But yes, it does apply the relevant practical reasons (especially that marriage and inner integrity are basic human goods) and moral principles (especially that one may never intend to destroy, damage, impede, or violate any basic human good, or prefer an illusory instantiation of a basic human good to a real instantiation of that or some other human good) to facts about the human personal organism.

VI.

Societies such as classical Athens and contemporary England (and virtually every other) draw a distinction between behavior found merely (perhaps extremely) offensive (such as eating excrement), and behavior to be repudiated as destructive of human character and relationships. Copulation of humans with animals is repudiated because it treats human sexual activity and satisfaction as something appropriately sought in a manner as divorced from the actualizing of an intelligible common good as is the instinctive coupling of beasts—and so treats human bodily life, in one of its most intense activities, as appropriately lived as merely animal. The deliberate genital coupling of persons of the same sex is repudiated for a very similar reason. It is not simply that it is sterile and disposes the participants to an abdication of responsibility for the future of humankind. Nor is it simply that it cannot *really* actualize the mutual devotion which some homosexual persons hope to manifest and experience by it, and that it harms the personalities of its participants by its dis-integrative manipulation of different parts of their one personal reality. It is also that it treats human sexual capacities in a way which is deeply hostile to the self-understanding of those members of the community who are willing to commit themselves to real marriage in the understanding that its sexual joys are not mere instruments or accompaniments to, or mere compensations for, the accomplishment of marriage's responsibilities, but rather enable the spouses to *actualize and experience* their intelligent commitment to share in those responsibilities, in that genuine self-giving.

Now, as I have said before, "homosexual orientation," in one of the two main senses of that highly equivocal term, is precisely the deliberate willingness to promote and engage in homosexual acts—the state of mind, will, and character whose self-interpretation came to be expressed in the deplorable but helpfully revealing name "gay." So this willingness, and the whole "gay" ideology, treats human sexual capacities in a way which is deeply hostile to the self-understanding of those members of the community who are willing to commit themselves to real marriage.

Homosexual orientation in this sense is, in fact, a standing denial of the intrinsic aptness of sexual intercourse to actualize and in that sense give expression to the exclusiveness and open-ended commitment of marriage as something good in itself. All who accept that homosexual acts can be a humanly appropriate use of sexual capacities must, if consistent, regard sexual capacities, organs and acts as instruments for gratifying the individual "selves" who have them. Such an acceptance is commonly (and in my opinion rightly) judged to be an active threat to the stability of existing and future marriages; it makes nonsense, for example, of the view that adultery is per se (and not merely because it may involve deception), and in an important way, inconsistent with conjugal love. A political community which judges that the stability and protective and educative generosity of family life is of fundamental importance to that community's present and future can rightly judge that it has a compelling interest in denying that homosexual conduct—a "gay lifestyle"—is a valid, humanly acceptable choice and form of life, and in doing whatever it *properly* can, as a community with uniquely wide but still subsidiary functions, to discourage such conduct.

VII.

I promised to defend the judgment that the government of political communities is subsidiary, and rationally limited not only by constitutional law and by the moral norms which limit every decent person's deliberation and choice, but also by the inherent limits of its general justifying aim, purpose or rationale. That rationale is, of course, the common good of the political community. And that common good, I shall argue, is not basic, intrinsic or constitutive, but rather is instrumental.

Every community is constituted by the communication and cooperation between its members. To say that a community has a common good is simply to say that communication and cooperation have a point which the members more or less concur in understanding, valuing and pursuing. There are three types of

common good which each provide the constitutive point of a distinctive type of open-ended community and directly instantiate a basic human good: (1) the affectionate mutual help and shared enjoyment of the friendship and *communio* of "real friends"; (2) the sharing of husband and wife in married life, united as complementary, bodily persons whose activities make them apt for parenthood—the *communio* of spouses and, if their marriage is fruitful, their children; (3) the *communio* of religious believers cooperating in the devotion and service called for by what they believe to be the accessible truths about the ultimate source of meaning, value and other realities, and about the ways in which human beings can be in harmony with that ultimate source. Other human communities *either* are dedicated to accomplishing a specific goal or set of goals (like a university or hospital) and so are not in the open-ended service of their members, *or* have a common good which is instrumental rather than basic. One should notice here that association and cooperation, even when oriented towards goals which are both specific and instrumentally rather than basically and intrinsically good (as, e.g., in a business enterprise), have a more than merely instrumental character inasmuch as they instantiate the basic good of friendship in one or other of its central or non-central forms.

The political community—properly understood as one of the forms of collaboration needed for the sake of the basic goods identified in the first principles of natural law—is a community cooperating in the service of a common good which is instrumental, not itself basic. True, it is a good which is "great and god-like"[52] in its ambitious range: "to secure the whole ensemble of material and other conditions, including forms of collaboration, that tend to favor, facilitate, and foster the realization by each individual [in that community] of his or her personal development"[53] (which will in each case include, constitutively, the flourishing of the family, friendship and other communities to which that person belongs). True too, its proper range includes the regulation of friendships, marriage, families, and religious associations, as well as of all the many organizations and associations which are dedicated to specific goals or which, like the state itself, have only an instrumental (e.g. an economic) common good. But such regulation of these associations should never (in the case of the associations with a non-instrumental common good) or only exceptionally (in the case of instrumental associations) be intended to take over the formation, direction or management of these personal initiatives and interpersonal associations. Rather, its purpose must be to carry out the *subsidiary* (i.e. helping, from the Latin *subsidium*, help) function[54] of assisting individuals and groups to coordinate their activities for the objectives and commitments they have chosen, and to do so in ways consistent with the other aspects of the common good of this community, uniquely complex, far-reaching and demanding in its rationale, its requirements of cooperation, and its monopolization of force: the political community.[55]

The fundamentally instrumental character of the political common good is indicated by both parts of the Second Vatican Council's teaching about religious liberty, a teaching considered by the Council to be a matter of natural law (i.e. of "reason itself").[56] The first part of the teaching is that everyone has the right not to be coerced in matters of religious belief and practice. For, to know the truth about the ultimate matters compendiously called by the Council "religious," and to adhere to and put into practice the truth one has come to know, is so significant a good and so basic a responsibility, and the attainment of that "good of the human spirit"[57] is so inherently and non-substitutably a matter of *personal* assent and *conscientious* decision, that if a government intervenes coercively in people's search for true religious beliefs, or in people's expression of the beliefs they suppose true, it will harm those people and violate their dignity even when

its intervention is based on the correct premise that their search has been negligently conducted and/or has led them into false beliefs. Religious acts, according to the Council, "transcend" the sphere which is proper to government; government is to care for the temporal common good, and this includes [the subsidiary function of] acknowledging and fostering the religious life of its citizens; but governments have no responsibility or right to direct religious acts, and "exceed their proper *limits*" if they presume to do so.[58]

The *second* part of the Council's teaching concerns the proper restrictions on religious freedom, namely those restrictions which are

> required for [i] the effective *protection of the rights* of all citizens and of their peaceful coexistence, [ii] a sufficient care for the authentic *public peace* of an ordered common life in true justice, and [iii] a proper upholding of *public morality*. All these factors constitute the fundamental part of the common good, and come under the notion of *ordre public*.[59]

Here, too, the political common good is presented as instrumental, serving the protection of human and legal rights, *public* peace and *public* morality—in other words, the preservation of a social environment conducive to virtue. Government is precisely not presented here as dedicated to the commanding of virtue and the repressing of vice, as such, even though virtue (and vice) are of supreme and constitutive importance for the well-being (or otherwise) of individual persons and the worth (or otherwise) of their associations.

Is the Council's natural law teaching right? Or should we rather adhere to the uncomplicated theory of Aquinas's treatise *On Princely Government*, that government should command whatever leads people towards their ultimate (heavenly) end, forbid whatever deflects them from it, and coercively deter people from evil-doing and induce them to morally decent conduct?[60]

Perhaps the most suasive short statement of that teaching is still Aristotle's famous attack on theories which, like the sophist Lycophron's, treat the state as a mere mutual insurance arrangement?[61] But in two crucial respects, at least, Aristotle (and with him the tradition) has taken things too easily.

First: If the object, point or common good of the political community were indeed a self-sufficient life, and if self-sufficiency (autarcheia) were indeed what Aristotle defines it to be—a life lacking in nothing, of complete fulfillment[62]—then we would have to say that the political community has a point it cannot hope to achieve, a common good utterly beyond its reach. For subsequent philosophical reflection has confirmed what one might suspect from Aristotle's own manifest oscillation between different conceptions of eudaimonia (and thus of autarcheia): Integral human fulfillment is nothing less than the fulfillment of (in principle) all human persons in all communities and cannot be achieved in any community short of the heavenly kingdom, a community envisaged not by unaided reason (natural law theory) but only by virtue of divine revelation and attainable only by a divine gift which transcends the capacities of nature. To be sure, integral human fulfillment can and should be a conception central to a natural law theory of morality and thus of politics, and should be envisaged as a kind of ideal community (to which will answer the reality of the Kingdom which Christian faith's first moral norm directs us to seek).[63] But that ideal community is not, as early natural law theories such as Aristotle's prematurely proposed, the political community.

Second: When Aristotle speaks of "making" people good, he constantly[64] uses the word poiesis which he has so often contrasted with praxis and reserved for techniques ("arts") of manipulating matter.[65] But helping citizens to choose and act in line with integral human fulfillment must involve something which goes beyond any art or technique. For only individual acting persons can by their own choices make themselves good or evil. Not that their life should or can be individualistic; their deliberating and choosing will be shaped, and helped or hindered, by the language of their culture, by their family, their friends, their associates and enemies, the customs of their communities, the laws of their polity, and by the impress of human influences of many kinds from beyond their homeland. Their choices will involve them in relationships just or unjust, generous or illiberal, vengeful or charitable, with other persons in all these communities. And as members of all these communities they have some responsibility to encourage their fellow-members in morally good and discourage them from morally bad conduct.

To be sure, the political community is a cooperation which undertakes the unique tasks of giving coercive protection to all individuals and lawful associations within its domain, and of securing an economic and cultural environment in which all these persons and groups can pursue their own proper good. To be sure, this common good of the political community makes it far more than a mere arrangement for "preventing mutual injury and exchanging goods." But it is one thing to maintain, as reason requires, that the political community's rationale requires that its public managing structure, the state, should deliberately and publicly identify, encourage, facilitate and support the truly worthwhile (including moral virtue), should deliberately and publicly identify, discourage and hinder the harmful and evil, and should, by its criminal prohibitions and sanctions (as well as its other laws and policies), assist people with parental responsibilities to educate children and young people in virtue and to discourage their vices. It is another thing to maintain that that rationale requires or authorizes the state to direct people to virtue and deter them from vice by making even secret and truly consensual adult acts of vice a punishable offence against the state's laws.[66]

So there was a sound and important distinction of principle which the Supreme Court of the United States overlooked in moving from *Griswold v. Connecticut*[67] (private use of contraceptives by *spouses*) to *Eisenstadt v. Baird* (*public distribution of contraceptives to unmarried people*).[68] The truth and relevance of that distinction, and its high importance for the common good, would be overlooked again if laws criminalizing private acts of sodomy between adults were to be struck down by the Court on any ground which would also constitutionally require the law to tolerate the advertising or marketing of homosexual services, the maintenance of places of resort for homosexual activity, or the promotion of homosexualist "lifestyles" via education and public media of communication, or to recognize homosexual "marriages" or permit the adoption of children by homosexually active people, and so forth.

Notes

69 Notre Dame University Law Review 1049 (1994)

1 Knuller (Publishing, Printing and Promotions) Ltd. v. Director of Pub. Prosecutions, [1973] A.C. 435 (1972).

2 Regina v. Goddard, 92 Crim. App. R. 185 (1990); Regina v. Gray 74 Crim. App. R. 324 (1981); Regina v. Ford, 66 Crim. App. R. 46 (1977).

3 Sexual Offences Act 1956, 4 & 5 Eliz. 2, ch. 69, § 32 (Eng.).

4 Id. § 6(1) (heterosexual acts: age of consent 16); Sexual Offences Act, 1967, ch. 60, § 1(1) (Eng.) (homosexual acts: age of consent 21).

5 The bill has yet to be passed by the House of Lords.

6 The statute states:

2A(1) A local authority shall not—

(a)   intentionally promote homosexuality or publish material with the intention of promoting homosexuality;

(b)   promote the teaching in any maintained school of the acceptability of homosexuality as a pretended family relationship.

Local Government Act 1986, ch. 10, § 2A (Eng.), *inserted by* Local Government Act 1988, ch. 9, § 28 (Eng.).

A "maintained school" is any school funded by a local governmental authority and includes most of the schools in England.

7 Dudgeon v. United Kingdom, 45 Eur. Ct. H.R. 21 (ser.A) (1981); Norris v. Ireland, 142 Eur. Ct. H.R. 20 (ser.A) (1988).

8 Application 11680/85, decision of March 10, 1988, unpublished; *see* Mireille Delmas-Marty, *The European Convention for the Protection of Human Rights: International Protection Versus National Restrictions* 253–54 (1992).

9 Gay Rights Coalition of Georgetown Univ. Law Ctr. v. Georgetown Univ., 536 A.2d 1 (D.C. 1987).

10 Kenneth J. Dover, *Greek Homosexuality* 154–59 (1978).

11 Id. at 159.

12 Gregory Vlastos, *Socrates, Ironist and Moral Philosopher* 38–39 (1991).

13 Clifford Hindley & David Cohen, *Debate: Law, Society, and Homosexuality in Classical Athens*, 133 *Past & Present* 167, 179–80, 188 n.14 (1991).

14 No. 92CV7223 (D. Den., filed Nov. 12, 1992).

15 Letter from Martha Nussbaum, Professor of Philosophy and Classics, Brown University (Oct. 20, 1993). The letter was faxed on October 21, 1993.

16 Letter from Kenneth J. Dover (Jan. 23, 1994) (on file with author).

17 Gregory Vlastos, *Platonic Studies* 25 (2d ed. 1981). In the footnote, Vlastos complains that by *para phusin*, "contrary to nature," Plato here and in 836B-C meant something "far stronger" than the phrase "against the rules," which Dover had used in a 1966 article on *eros* and *nomos*. Sometime before the revised edition, Vlastos and Dover corresponded about this complaint, and Vlastos records a letter from Dover:

What [Plato] did believe was that the act was "unnatural", in the sense "against the rules"; it was a morally ignorant exploitation of pleasure beyond what was "granted" (*kata phusin apodedosthai*, [*Laws*] 636C4), the product of an *akrateia*, ([636]C6), which can be aggravated by habituation and bad example. His comparison of homosexuality with incest ([Laws] 837E8–838E1) is particularly revealing.

Id. at 424. And Vlastos immediately remarks that Dover's allusion to Plato's comparison of homosexuality with incest shows that Dover acknowledges the great force with which Plato is condemning what Vlastos called "anal intercourse" and Dover, loosely, "the act" and "homosexuality". Id. at 25, 424.

18 Id. at 25. I want to add, out of respect for Plato, that Anthony Price's valuable book firmly rejects Vlastos' theory that Socrates and Plato, though forbidding homosexual acts, accepted that lovers could nevertheless rightly engage in the sort of petting spoken of in Phaedrus 255e. Anthony W. Price, Love and Friendship in Plato and Aristotle 89–94 (1989).

19 "When male unites with female for procreation the pleasure experienced is held to be natural, but unnatural when male mates with male or female with female, and those first guilty of these enormities were impelled by their weakness for pleasure." Plato, Laws I, 636C, at 41 (R.G. Bury trans., 1926).

20 Affidavit of Martha C. Nussbaum, at 1¶ 10, Evans v. Romer, No. 92CV7223 (D.Den., filed Nov. 12, 1992) (Oct. 21, 1993) (served Oct. 22, 1993).

21 Liddell & Scott, A Greek-English Lexicon 1803 (Sir Henry Stuart Jones & Roderick McKenzie eds, 9th ed. 1940, Supp. 1968) (1992).

22 Dover, supra note 16.

23 Nussbaum, supra note 20, at 1¶ 54. This "consensus of recent scholars such as Price" becomes in the opening sentence of the following paragraph "the modern consensus". An earlier reference makes it clear that the reference to Price's "widely accepted" study of the passage is to his book, Love and Friendship in Plato and Aristotle, supra note 18. The book was reviewed by Professor Nussbaum in the Times Literary Supplement in February, 1990. Throughout her discussion of the Laws in ¶¶ 51–55, Nussbaum refers to "the passage," without ever identifying it or attending to the fact that in my affidavit dated October 8, 1993, I had cited four passages, and had quoted two widely separated passages each of which applies to homosexual acts the phrase on which she is commenting in ¶ 54,

para phusin. The only passage she has explicitly cited to the court is the Laws 636 passage in book I, but some confused remarks in ¶ 52, and the drift of ¶ 54, suggest that she may have had Laws VIII, 841 uppermost in her mind in ¶ 54. It should not be overlooked that the discordance between homosexual acts and phusis is plainly asserted by Plato's mouthpiece also in Laws VIII, 836 & 838.

24 Price, supra note 18, at 230.

25 Nussbaum, supra note 20, at ¶ 14.

26 Id. at ¶ 67.

27 Price, supra note 18, at 229–235 (note the references to Paul VI and John Paul II, at 233, 235).

28 Dover, supra note 10, at 165–68; Vlastos, supra note 17, at 25, 425; John J. Winkler, The Constraints of Desire 18, 21n. (1990).

29 See David M. Halperin, One Hundred Years of Homosexuality 91 (1990); Winkler, supra note 28, at 18, 21.

30 See Aristotle, Nicomachean Ethics VII, 5:1148b29; Aristotle, Politics II, 1:1252a33–39, together with the hints in II, 6:1269b28 and II, 7:1272a25.

31 Price, supra note 18, at 224–25 (citing Plato, Republic 403b4–6 and Aristotle, Politics, 1262a32–7).

32 Id. (quoting Plato, Laws VIII, 837C4–5).

33 Plutarch, Erotikos, Dialogue on Love, 751C–D, 766E–771D.

34 Musonius Rufus, Discourses XII and XIIA, in Cora E. Lutz, Musonius Rufus "the Roman Socrates," X Yale Classical Studies 85–89 (1947).

35 2 Germain Grisez, The Way of the Lord Jesus, Living a Christian Life 555–574, 633–680 (1993).

36 Aristotle, Nicomachean Ethics, VIII,12: 1162a16–30; see also the probably pseudo-Aristotle, Oeconomica I, 3–4: 1343b12–1344a22; III.

37 Plutarch reads this conception back to the dawn of Athenian civilization and, doubtless anachronistically, ascribes it to the great original Athenian law-giver, Solon: Marriage should be "a union of life between man and woman for the delights of love and the getting of children." Plutarch, Life of Solon 20, 4. See also Plutarch, Erotikos 769:

In the case of lawful wives, physical union is the beginning of friendship, a sharing, as it were, in great mysteries. [The] pleasure is short [or unimportant: mikron], but the respect and kindness and mutual affection and loyalty that daily spring from it [conjugal sex] convicts neither the Delphians of raving when they call Aphrodite 'Harmony' nor Homer when he designates such a union 'friendship'. It also proves that Solon was a very experienced legislator of marriage laws. He prescribed that a man should consort with his wife not less than three times a month—not for the pleasure surely, but as cities renew their mutual agreements from time to time, just so he must have wished this to be a renewal of marriage and with such an act of tenderness to wipe out the complaints that accumulate from everyday living.

38 *See* Plutarch, *Erotikos* 768D–770A; IX *Moralia* 427 (Loeb ed., 1961); *see also* the fine translation in D.A. Russell, *Plutarch* 92 (1973).

39 Plutarch speaks of the union of husband and wife as an "integral amalgamation" [*di' holon krasis*]. Plutarch, *Erotikos* 769F; *Coniugalia Praecepta* 142F.

40 St. Augustine, *De Bono Coniugali*, 9.9.

41 Id. at 3.3.

42 Plutarch, *Erotikos* 769f; *Coniugalia Praecepta* 142f.

43 John Paul II, Address to Young Married Couples at Taranto (October 1989), quoted in Grisez, supra note 35, at 571 n.46 ("a great project: fusing your persons to the point of becoming 'one flesh' ").

44 Grisez, supra note 35, at 556–569.

45 John Paul II, *Veritatis Splendor* ¶¶ 13, 48 (1984); *see also* id. at ¶¶ 50, 67, 78, 79.

46 Steven Macedo, *The New Natural Lawyers*, The Harv. Crimson, Oct. 28, 1993, writes:

> In effect, gays can have sex in a way that is open to procreation, and to new life. They can be, and many are, prepared to engage in the kind of loving relations that would result in procreation—were conditions different. Like sterile married couples, many would like nothing better.

Here, fantasy has taken leave of reality. Anal or oral intercourse, whether between spouses or between males, is no more a biological union "open to procreation" than is intercourse with a goat by a shepherd who fantasizes about breeding a faun; each "would" yield the desired mutant "were conditions different". Biological union between humans is the inseminatory union of male genital organ with female genital organ; in most circumstances it does not result in generation, but it is the behavior that unites biologically because it is the behavior which, as behavior, is suitable for generation.

47 For the whole argument, see Grisez, supra note 35, at 634–39, 648–54, 662–4.

48 Plato, *Gorgias* 494–5, especially 494el–5, 495b3.

49 Plutarch, *Life of Solon*, 20,3. The post-Christian moral philosophy of Kant identified the wrongfulness of masturbation and homosexual (and bestial) conduct as consisting in the instrumentalization of one's body, and thus ("since a person is an absolute unity") the "wrong to humanity in our own person." But Kant, though he emphasizes the equality of husband and wife (impossible in concubinage or more casual prostitution), did not integrate this insight with an understanding of marriage as a single two-part good involving, inseparably, friendship as well as procreation. Hence he was puzzled by the question why marital intercourse is right when the woman is pregnant or beyond the menopause. *See* Immanuel Kant, *The Metaphysics of Morals* 277–79, 424–26 (Mary Gregor trans., Cambridge Univ. Press 1991, 96–97, 220–22) (1797). The deep source of his puzzlement is his refusal to allow intelligible goods any structural role in his ethics, a refusal which sets him against a classical moral philosophy such as Aristotle's, and indeed against any adequate theory of natural law, and in turn is connected with his dualistic separation of body from mind and body, a separation which conflicts with his own insight, just quoted, that the person is a real unity.

50 Or deliberately contracepted, which I omit from the list in the text only because it would no doubt not now be accepted by secular civil law as preventing consummation—a failure of understanding. *See* discussion, supra note 46.

51 Macedo, supra note 46, at 2:

> All we can say is that conditions would have to be more radically different in the case of gay and lesbian couples than sterile married couples for new life to result from sex . . . but what is the moral force of that? The new natural law theory does not make moral judgments based on natural facts.

Macedo's phrase "based on" equivocates between the first premises of normative arguments (which must be normative) and the other premise(s) (which can and normally should be factual and, where appropriate, can refer to natural facts such as that the human mouth is not a reproductive organ).

52 Aristotle, *Nicomachean Ethics*, I, 1: 1094b9.

53 John Finnis, *Natural Law and Natural Rights* 147 (1980). As I indicate, this account of the common good of the political community is close to that worked out by French commentators on Aquinas in the early mid-twentieth century. Id. at 160. A similar account was adopted by the Second Vatican Council: "the sum of those conditions of social life which allow social groups and their individual members relatively thorough and ready access to their own fulfillment." *Gaudium et Spes* ¶ 26 (1965); *see also Dignitatis Humanae* ¶ 6 (1965).

54 *See* Finnis, supra note 53, at 146–47, 159.

55 Of course, the common good of the political community has important elements which are scarcely shared with any other community within the polity: for example, the restoration of justice by punishment of those who have offended against just laws; the coercive repelling and restraint of those whose conduct (including negligent omissions) unfairly threatens the interests of others, particularly those interests identified as moral ("human") or legal rights, and corresponding compulsory measures to secure restitution, compensation or reparation for violations of rights; and the specifying and upholding of a system of holding or property rights which respects the various interests, immediate and vested or remote and contingent, which everyone has in each holding. But the fact that these and various other elements of the political common good are peculiar to the political community and the proper responsibility of its leaders, the government, in no way entails that these elements are basic human goods or that the political common good is other than in itself instrumental.

56 *Dignitatis Humanae* ¶ 2. In the succeeding part, the Declaration treats the matter as one of divine revelation. Id. at ¶¶ 9–14.

57 It is one of the *animi humani bona* mentioned in id. ¶ 1.

58 "Potestas igitur civilis, cuius finis proprius est bonum commune temporale curare, religiosam quidem civium vitam agnoscere eique favere debet, sed *limites suos excedere* dicenda est, si actus religiosos dirigere vel impedire praesumat." Id. at ¶ 3.

59 Id. at ¶ 7.

60 *De Regimine Principum* c.14 (... ab iniquitate coerceat et ad opera virtuosa inducat). This thesis is qualified, though not abandoned, in other works of Aquinas. Thus *Summa Theologiae* II–II q.104 a.5c teaches that human government has no authority over people's minds and the interior motions of their wills. Id. I–II q.96 a.2 teaches that governmental pursuit of virtue should be gradual and should not ask too much of the average citizen (who is not virtuous).

61 It states:

> [T]he *polis* was formed not for the sake of life only but rather for the good life ... and ... its purpose is not [merely] military alliance for defence ... and it does not exist [merely] for the sake of trade and business relations ... any *polis* which is truly so called, and is not one merely in name, must have virtue/excellence as an object of its care [*peri aretes epimeles einai*: be solicitous about virtue]. Otherwise a polis sinks into a mere alliance, differing only in space from other forms of alliance where the members live at a distance from each other. Otherwise, too, the law becomes a mere social contract [*syntheke*: covenant]—or (in the phrase of the sophist Lycophron) 'a guarantor of justice as between one man and another'—instead of being, as it should be, such as will make [*poiein*] the citizens good and just. ... The polis is not merely a sharing of a common locality for the purpose of preventing mutual injury and exchanging goods. These are necessary preconditions of the existence of a polis ... but a polis is a *communio* [*koinonia*] of clans [and neighborhoods] in living well, with the object of a full and self-sufficient [*autarkous*] life ... it must therefore be for the sake of truly good (*kalon*) actions, not of merely living together." Aristotle, *Politics*, III.5: 1280a32, a35, 1280b7–13, b30–31, b34, 1281a1–4.

62 Aristotle, *Nicomachean Ethics*, I, 7:1097b8. This, incidentally, differs widely from what Stephen Macedo, *Liberal Virtues* 215–17 (1990), means by "an autarchic person."

63 For nothing less than integral human fulfillment, the fulfillment of all persons in all the basic human goods, answers to reason's full knowledge of, and the will's full interest in, the human good in which one can participate by action. And so the first principle of a sound morality must be: In voluntarily acting for human goods and avoiding what is opposed to them, one ought to choose and will those and only those possibilities 'whose willing is compatible with integral human fulfillment. To say that immorality is constituted by cutting back on, fettering, reason by passions is equivalent' to saying that the sway of feelings over reason constitutes immorality by deflecting one to objectives not in line with integral human fulfillment. This ideal community is thus the good will's most fundamental orientating ideal.

64 Apart from the passage just cited, see Aristotle, *Nicomachean Ethics*, I, 10; 1099b32; II, 1: 110364; X, 9: 1180b24.

65 E.g. Aristotle, *Nicomachean Ethics*, VI, 5: 1140a2; Aristotle, *Politics*, 1, 2: 1254a5.

66 So a third way in which Aristotle takes things too easily is his slide from upholding government's responsibility to assist or substitute for the direct parental discipline of youth, to claiming that this responsibility continues, and in the same direct coercive form, "to cover the whole of a lifetime, since most people obey necessity rather than argument, and punishments rather than the sense of what is truly worthwhile." Aristotle, *Nicomachean Ethics*, X.9:1180a1–3.

67 381 U.S. 479 (1965).

68 405 U.S. 438 (1972). The law struck down in *Griswold* was the law forbidding use of contraceptives even by married persons; Griswold's conviction as an accessory to such use fell with the fall of the substantive law against the principals in such use. Very different, in principle, would have been a law directly forbidding Griswold's activities as a public promoter of contraceptive information and supplies. If American constitutional law fails to recognize such distinctions, it shows, I suggest, its want of sound principle.

Chapter 17

Stephen Macedo

AGAINST THE OLD SEXUAL MORALITY OF THE NEW NATURAL LAW

I. Introduction

I T IS SAID THAT when he was on his death-bed, W. C. Fields was seen by his daughter reading the Bible. Dumbfounded, she asked whether he had experienced a last minute conversion. 'No,' he replied, 'I'm just looking for loopholes.'

I hope that what follows is not the philosophical equivalent of looking for loopholes. I mean to take seriously the possibility that the new natural law's radical critique of contemporary sexual attitudes and conduct might be true. Consider Germain Grisez's challenge to the libertarianism which certainly characterizes an extreme form of liberalism that came to the fore in the 1960s:

> The promoters of sexual liberation thought it would eliminate the pain of sexual frustration and make society as a whole more joyful. What has happened instead shows how wrong they were. The pain of sexual frustration is slight in comparison with the misery of abandoned women and unwanted children, of people lonely for lack of true marital intimacy, of those dying wretchedly from sexually transmitted disease. Moreover, unchastity's destructive effects on so many families impact on the wider society, whose stability depends on families ... Boys and girls coming to maturity

without a solid foundation in a stable family are ill prepared to assume adult social responsibilities.[2]

I do not believe that this is true—I feel sure that it is not the whole truth—but it may well represent an important and neglected part of the truth. Such charges need to be taken seriously, both on their own terms and as part of the broader conservative critique of the cultural changes accelerated by the sexual revolution of the 1960s.

The argument of this chapter is that while we should reject the sexual teachings of the new natural law—ably represented by John Finnis's important contribution to this volume—we also have something to learn from it. The natural lawyers are fundamentally right in their insistence that we must make value judgements in the realm of sexual morality. They are also right, I believe, to insist on the continuing validity of important aspects of traditional morality, especially the value of married life. The new natural law goes badly wrong, however, in its very narrow view of the legitimate forms of sexual expression. In particular, I will argue, the new natural law's own moral stance, properly understood, provides grounds for affirming the good of sexual relationships between committed, loving homosexual partners, and for extending the institution of marriage to homosexuals.

I also mean this chapter to make a larger point about liberalism. Contrary to the suggestions of Michael Sandel and others, liberalism properly understood is not committed to a stance of neutrality on questions of the good life. There is no inconsistency between a robust commitment to liberalism (or perhaps I should say a commitment to a robust liberalism) and support for an institution such as marriage, which certainly expresses a judgement about better and worse lives. While liberal principles support a wide range of individual freedoms, they also allow space for political judgements to be made about better and worse ways of using our freedom. Public policies may encourage the better ways without coercing people or infringing on their basic rights.

The new natural lawyers correctly perceive that liberalism has less to do with neutrality than its critics allege. The natural lawyers are prepared to be judgemental, and liberal public policy can and should incorporate some of their judgements. Unfortunately, as we shall see in Parts III–V below, the natural law strictures about sexual morality are unreasonably narrow and arbitrary.

II. Natural law and limited government

We can begin, however, by conceding that there are many ways in which natural law and limited government are compatible. Finnis points out in his contribution to this volume that natural lawyers have long affirmed the importance of such standard features of legally limited constitutional government as the rule of law and orderly rotation in office. Finnis also mentions the Second Vatican Council's momentous if somewhat belated embrace, in 1965, of a principled case for religious liberty, even for those with false beliefs. The Council allowed that the pursuit of religious truth is so 'inherently and inimitably a matter of *personal* assent and *conscien-*

tious decision,' as Finnis puts it, that government intervention here both harms individuals and violates their dignity.[3] In these ways, and no doubt in many others, natural law theory endorses certain garden variety limits on government power.

There are also resources for limiting government power more specific to the natural law tradition: useful antidotes, for example, to civic republicanism and other doctrines that inflate the importance of political life. Natural lawyers emphasize the principle of subsidiarity, with its insistence that the state's function is instrumental with respect to those associations which directly promote basic human goods, such as the family, friendship, and religious communities. The state regulates and facilitates these associations but should not supplant them.[4] For the new natural lawyers, the goods of politics are instrumental rather than basic.

Finnis also describes the ideal community, 'the good will's most fundamental orienting ideal,' as one that transcends politics: it is 'nothing less than . . . the fulfilment of all persons in all the basic human goods'. The ideal community is not the political community, as Aristotle supposed, but rather the 'heavenly kingdom . . . attainable only by virtue of divine revelation'.[5] This too has the effect of putting politics in its place: as an affair about very important goods (peace, prosperity, freedom, order) but not about the whole good nor directly about the highest goods.

By emphasizing that politics is of essentially instrumental importance, and that the ideal community transcends what can be achieved in politics, natural law provides for a political moderation that may be lacking in theories sometimes more closely associated with liberal democracy. Totalistic democratic theories, such as that of John Dewey for example, posit political ends that embrace man's highest and most complete ideals, and encourage people to transfer all moral and religious aspirations onto the shared political project.[6] Concentrating moral energies in this way seems to me not only politically dangerous but a disservice to the complexity of the moral life. Finnis, in contrast, limits political aspirations, and insists that room be left for extra-political associations in which to pursue important parts of the good life, for Finnis the most important parts.

The new natural law certainly has resources for limiting political power. Indeed, in some respects its limitations are excessively strict. Finnis levels harsh criticisms at Leo Strauss for allowing that governments may sometimes do intrinsically nasty things when the safety of the whole people is at stake.[7] Strauss's sin is to have justified NATO's threat to use nuclear weapons against innocent civilians in order to deter aggression by Stalin's Soviet Union. Finnis argues, to the contrary, that the strategic deterrent (established around the time Strauss was writing *Natural Right and History*) was immoral.

Strauss was hardly eccentric in arguing that the normal rules of good conduct might justifiably be relaxed in extreme circumstances. Locke made similar allowances in his discussion of executive prerogative, and so have many other friends of limited government.[8] That a reasonably just nation like the United States might feel compelled to threaten innocent civilians to ward off an unjust and potentially devastating attack is deeply unfortunate. It is also, it seems to me, clearly justifiable in some circumstances. What is unclear is how to justify the absolute prohibition on threats against the innocent that Finnis espouses.

The new natural law's absolutism depends on the 'incommensurability thesis', which holds that basic goods are plural, and that it is always wrong to choose against basic goods. That values are plural is common ground among many contemporary moral philosophers, including Isaiah Berlin, Thomas Nagel, and Bernard Williams.[9] On this ground, one can agree with the natural lawyers that utilitarians are wrong to posit a simple scale according to which moral trade offs can be made in hard cases. Value pluralism does not, however, yield the new natural law's absolute prohibitions on choosing against basic goods—such as innocent life—no matter what other values hang in the balance. It is a terrible thing to be forced to threaten innocent lives in order to preserve ourselves from unjust aggression, as Strauss conceded. Catastrophic consequences do matter, however, and they can matter enough to justify the sort of threat involved in the nuclear deterrent posed by the United States.[10]

It is hard to see how one vindicates absolute prohibitions against the kinds of threats involved in the strategic deterrent, unless one believes in a providential deity who is prepared to sort out the consequences for us in the end.[11] Absent such a faith, we should ourselves take the responsibility for making hard trade offs, even though we cannot fully specify, aside from particular decisions and circumstances, exactly how we do so, even though we cannot define precisely in advance when it is justifiable to break the normal moral rules and limits. If rule-like procedures were available to us in hard cases the moral world would be simpler than it is. As things stand (and as Strauss suggested, following Aristotle) the ultimate contours of moral rightness 'reside in concrete decisions rather than in general rules'.[12] Neither utilitarian reductionism nor the absolutist strictures of the new natural law are adequate to the complexity of the moral realm.

There are, clearly, a number of reasons to think that contemporary natural law of the Finnis, Grisez, and George variety is not only compatible with but supportive of various limitations on government power. This is no great revelation. The important question is: how well does the new natural law view stack up against its rivals when it comes to justifying and delimiting the proper role of government? Let us turn to the greatest point of contention: the realm of personal privacy and sexual freedom.

III. Sexual morality and the new natural law

Finnis manages to blunt liberal objections to natural law teachings on sexuality by arguing that while 'public morality' is a legitimate political concern, this does not mean that government should promote virtue and punish vice 'as such'. Governments should maintain a 'social environment conducive to virtue,' not coercively deter evil-doing or legally mandate decent conduct.[13] Governments should not, that is, be especially concerned to punish private vices through the criminal law. With respect to homosexuality, for example, the law should not criminally prosecute homosexual acts among consenting adults committed in secret, but it should supervise 'the *public realm or environment*,' within which young and old are morally educated and encouraged toward good or bad lives. It should do this by 'denying that "gay lifestyles" are a valid, humanly acceptable choice and form of life, and in doing whatever it properly can . . . to discourage such conduct.'[14] Finnis suggests that the United States Supreme Court should have overturned the criminal prosecution of private homosexual acts in *Bowers v. Hardwick*, but only while distinguishing such permissibly private conduct from 'the advertising or marketing of homosexual services, the maintenance of places of resort for homosexual activity, or the promotion of homosexualist "lifestyles" '. The law should prohibit the public promotion and facilitation of homosexual activity, along with homosexual marriages and the 'adoption of children by homosexually active people'.[15]

In all this, Finnis advocates for society at large a stance not unlike the 'don't ask, don't tell' policy recently adopted for the military in the United States. The aim is to maintain a public, morally educative environment hospitable to what is deemed good conduct, not to engage in zealous witch-hunts against those who keep their homosexuality private. While it is all to the good that neither Professor Finnis nor the Clinton Administration advocates witch-hunts against homosexuals, we must pause before celebrating the proposed policies.

Finnis argues that natural law, properly understood, shows that homosexual acts are a distraction from the good life properly understood, and so should be discouraged by public policy. Given the tenor of recent discussions of homosexuality in American politics, it is worth noting at the outset that Finnis goes out of his way to distinguish his position from the narrow prejudice and mere 'disgust' which characterize much popular opposition to equal rights for gays and lesbians. Most significantly, neither Finnis nor Grisez suggests that homosexual acts are unique in being distractions from real human goods, or in justly being subject to legal discouragement. Indeed, these new natural lawyers strikingly treated gay and lesbian sexual activity like most forms of heterosexual activity: just like all recreational sex, all sex outside of marriage, all contracepted sex and sex not open to the good of procreation, including all contracepted sex within a stable, permanent marriage.[16]

The new natural law's prohibitions on 'recreational' sexual activity are very broad, and are based on the contention that the only valuable sexual activity is activity that is open to procreation in heterosexual marriage. Openness to new life within stable, permanent marriage is what gives sex value and meaning: it is uniquely capable of making sex more than the mere use of bodies for pleasure.

> The union of the reproductive organs of husband and wife really unites them biologically (and their biological reality is part of, not merely an instrument of, their *personal* reality). Reproduction is one function and so, in respect of that function, the spouses are indeed one reality, and their sexual union therefore can *actualize* and allow them to *experience* their *real common good*—*their marriage* with two goods, parenthood and friendship . . .'[17]

For Finnis, Grisez, and other new natural lawyers, all non-procreative, recreational sex amounts to the mere instrumentalization of bodies for mutual use and pleasure, all are the moral equivalent of mutual masturbation: simultaneous individual gratifications with no shared good in common.[18] This is as true of contracepted sex in marriage as it is of homosexual sodomy: all sex acts not open to procreation in marriage are incapable of participating in or expressing any shared goods such as friendship, and are not only valueless but distractions from real human goods.

Indeed, the case against recreational heterosexual sex may be even stronger than that against gay and lesbian sex. Uncontracepted heterosexual sex risks the great evil of bringing unwanted children into the world. Even when effectively contracepted, it is a choice against the great good of new life. Gay and lesbian sex does not share in either of these evils. Finnis and Grisez allow that people may be homosexual by nature, and so the goods of procreation and child rearing are not open to them.[19] Homosexual conduct is not, then, a choice against the great integrating goods of heterosexual marriage (as are wrongful heterosexual acts) because these goods are not open to gays and lesbians.

The wrongfulness of gay sex is merely its 'self-disintegrity': the purported failure to act in a way that is consistent with a desire for the real goods that homosexual couples may share in common, goods such as friendship and mutual helping. Real goods can be embodied in homosexual as well as heterosexual friendships, but sex only distracts from them. When sex is chosen it is as a source of 'subjective satisfactions' through the use and instrumentalization of each other's bodies.[20]

The foregoing analysis (which we can accept for the moment in order to consider its implications) casts a very interesting light on contemporary popular attitudes toward sexuality. Natural law analysis reveals the gross and unreflective arbitrariness of public policies and proposals that, in the name of family values, fix their scornful attention on gays and lesbians. There is a crisis of the family in America, but what could be easier in the face of rampant heterosexual promiscuity, premarital sex, teenage pregnancy, and sky-rocketing divorce rates than to fasten our attention on a long despised class of people who bear no children?

One might reply that nowhere is promiscuity greater than in the gay male population. This could be true, though I have no empirical evidence to support this assertion and Finnis cites none. Richard Posner (who has studied a wide range of evidence) argues that there may be natural grounds for supposing that homosexual male couples will tend, on average, to have a harder time than heterosexual couples maintaining long-term relationships (though he does not, so far as I can see, compare homosexual and sterile childless heterosexual couples).[21] Lesbian couples, on the other hand, are very stable. Supposing, as is possible, that lesbians have the lowest rates of infidelity, would we then be justified in establishing a three-tiered public moral pecking order with special honours for lesbian couples?

It would be hard to see how the mere fact (if it is one) that gay men have a harder time settling down in stable relationships could furnish a ground for discriminating against them. No doubt, there is promiscuity among gay men: too much, as elsewhere in society. Before we condemn these people we should consider how promiscuous men in general would be were their sexual desires not harnessed and controlled by their wives, children, and family life. If these inducements to stability were not available to heterosexual men—or imposed upon them as the case may be—how promiscuous would they be? So long as we refuse to extend to gay men the inducements to stability and self-control (such as marriage) available to heterosexuals, we should regard promiscuous gay men as victims of fate, circumstance, and public policy (at least in important part) rather than of any special moral depravity.

In any case, civilized societies have abandoned the notion of collective guilt. The fact is that not all homosexuals are promiscuous and not all promiscuous people are homosexual. If promiscuity is a social evil, let society oppose promiscuity wherever it appears. Indeed, if promiscuity is self-destructive and homosexual men are prone to it by nature, homosexuality might be regarded as a disability (albeit a fairly mild one). Rather than singling out people with this disability for special discrimination (something we do not normally regard as decent or proper) would it not be more honourable to try and improve these people's lives as best we can?

The great merit of the new natural law's position is its fair-mindedness and broad sweep. If Finnis, Grisez and others criticize those who would seek to 'normalize' homosexuality and equalize our legal treatment of it (as I would), he poses an even greater challenge to the *conventional wisdom* that would single out homosexuality as peculiarly perverse and 'unnatural'. Finnis shows that on reflection such attitudes embody a double standard of permissiveness toward straights and censoriousness toward gays engaging in acts that are essentially the same. For Finnis, the wrongness of homosexuality is captured by its similarity with much heterosexual activity: all sexual activity which is not between married couples and open to procreation shares with homosexuality the essential characteristics of masturbation, the use of bodies for mere physical pleasure, the disengagement of sexuality from real, shared goods. Contracepted sexual acts between happily married couples are essentially the same as homosexual sodomy.

An important implication of the foregoing account is that governments have just as much reason to act against all premarital and contracepted heterosexual sex as they do against homosexuality. The new natural law speaks in favour only of very broadly based public actions against sexual immorality in general: divorce, contraception, and all sex outside of marriage, along with homosexuality. A government that rejects natural law teachings with respect to illicit heterosexual activity thereby jettisons the only natural law grounds for passing laws that discriminate against homosexual conduct. This is a great—and I would have thought insuperable—obstacle to any state that would rely on natural law as a ground for prohibiting homosexual conduct but not contraception, extra-marital sex, and so on.

Now, a possible rejoinder would be that simply because some justifiable moral strictures (against heterosexuals) have been relaxed, that is no reason to relax them all. But it is a reason when the strictures arbitrarily maintained are directed against a long despised minority. It is a reason when the majority is unwilling to impose on itself contraints that it imposes on a discrete and insular minority like homosexuals. It is a reason when a small minority is selectively saddled with restrictions that should apply with the same force to the majority.

The argument so far has entertained a hypothetical, namely, the plausibility of the new natural law's sexual teaching. Now we must turn to the core issue: are there good reasons to confine valuable sexual activity as narrowly as the natural lawyers would have it?

As we have seen, Finnis and Grisez argue that homosexual sex acts lack the 'unitive' quality of sex open to procreation in marriage. The choice of gays and lesbians 'to activate their reproductive organs' (and the same goes for heterosexuals using contraception or engaging in sodomy or other deliberately non-procreative sex) 'cannot be an actualizing and experiencing of the marital good—as marital intercourse can, even between spouses who happen to be sterile—it can do no more than provide each partner with an individual gratification'.[22] Homosexual sex not only foregoes opportunities to participate in real goods, it positively undermines the goods that homosexual friends may share in their non-sexual relations: goodwill and affection can be expressed far more intelligibly and effectively by acts such as conversation, or mutually beneficial help in work, domestic tasks, etc. Those who openly proclaim their active homosexuality must be seen, Finnis concludes, as 'deeply hostile to the self-understanding of those members of the community who are willing to commit themselves to real marriage'.[23] Society should do what it can to discourage and stigmatize such conduct, short of criminalizing truly private acts.

What are we to make of all this? It seems quite wrong to say that the essential nature of non-procreative sexual acts engaged in by couples in committed relationships—or even by people who have recently fallen in love—is necessarily as private, incommunicable, and subjective, as Finnis and Grisez maintain. The new natural lawyers exaggerate the purely subjective, self-centred character of all non-procreative sexuality. And so, Finnis insists that 'whatever the generous hopes and dreams' of 'some same-sex partners,' their sexual acts

> cannot express or do more than is expressed or done if two strangers engage in such activity to give each other pleasure, or a prostitute gives pleasures to a client in return for money, or (say) a man masturbates to give himself a fantasy of more human relationships after a gruelling day on the assembly line.[24]

Finnis's contention is that homosexual acts at their best (between loving couples in committed relationships) can express and embody nothing more than anonymous bathhouse sex, a quick trip to a prostitute, or masturbation. Is it even remotely plausible that there are no distinctions to be drawn here? And how can Finnis announce such confident and sweeping conclusions without any inquiry into the actual nature of homosexual relationships?

My guess is that most committed loving couples—whether gay or straight—are quite sensitive to the difference between loving sexual acts and mere mutual masturbation, and that they would regard the latter, with Finnis, as a real failure. Finnis is not all wrong: promiscuous, casual sex engaged in with strangers may well have the valueless character he describes.

It is, however, simplistic and implausible to portray the essential nature of *every form* of non-procreative sexuality as no better than the *least valuable* form.

The great virtue of the new natural law's position on sexuality, I said above, is its fair-mindedness and broad sweep. While this is generally true, the position is plagued by a major and unexplained inconsistency. As we have seen, an essential condition of good sex for the new natural lawyers is the biological unity of heterosexual couples whose acts are open to procreation. And yet, Finnis and Grisez argue that sexual union within a *sterile* marriage has intrinsic value: 'marital union itself fulfills the spouses,' as Grisez puts it.[25] But as Andrew Koppelman asks, how can such a position be justified when the bodies of the elderly or sterile can form no 'single reproductive principle', no 'real unity'?[26] Sterile couples can only imitate the procreative act: there is for them no possibility of procreation. And yet, the new natural lawyers regard sex between involuntarily sterile or elderly married couples as not only permissible but good.[27]

What is the point of sex in an infertile marriage? Not procreation: the partners know they are infertile. If they have sex, it is for pleasure and to express their love or friendship or some other shared good. It will be for precisely the same reasons that committed, loving gay couples have sex. Why are these good reasons for sterile or elderly married couples but not for gay and lesbian couples? And if, on the other hand, sex detracts from the real goods shared by homosexual couples, and indeed undermines their friendship, why is that not the case for infertile heterosexual couples as well? Why is not their experience of sexual intimacy as 'private and incommunicable' as that of gays?

How do we make sense of this rather glaring double standard? Perhaps because sterility is a condition beyond the control of couples rather than a choice? Because sterile heterosexual couples can do things that, were it not for conditions beyond their control, would result in procreation? But Grisez and Finnis allow that homosexuality is also an unchosen condition. So if the natural lawyers say that sterile heterosexual couples can have loving sex that is good, why not gays and lesbians in committed relations?

For the natural lawyers, the presence of the appropriate, complementary physical equipment is an essential condition of valuable sexual activity. The problem for homosexuals and those using contraceptives is that 'their reproductive organs cannot make them a biological (and therefore personal) unit,' whereas sterile heterosexuals who 'unite their sexual organs in an act of sexual intercourse which, so far as they can make it, is of a kind suitable for generation, do function as a biological (and thus personal) unit,' and thus actualize and experience real goods in common.[28]

Of course, gays and lesbians do not have the physical equipment such that anyone could have children by doing what they can do in bed. They can, Finnis and Grisez repeatedly tell us, only imitate or fantasize the real procreative acts, and the real goods of marital sex. What the new natural lawyers fail to see is that exactly the same thing is true, albeit less vividly, of sterile married couples: their reproductive organs *do not unite them biologically*, they only appear to do so. Finnis simply denies this: sterile heterosexuals *can* be united biologically, he insists, because their equipment allows them 'to engage in the behaviour which, as behaviour, is suitable for generation'.[29]

Is sterile heterosexual intercourse 'as behaviour' suitable for generation? Pointing a gun at someone and pulling the trigger is behaviour that is suitable for murder. Are such acts still suitable for murder, and do they share murder's moral significance, if the gun is unloaded? If it is a water gun or a gun made of licorice? The National Rifle Association might have said, 'guns don't kill people, bullets kill people.'[30] Likewise, penises and vaginas don't unite biologically, sperm and eggs do (at least in a healthy uterus and under the right conditions). For the new natural lawyers, however, the crucial thing is penises and vaginas—whether they work or not!

Suppose one gay male has a sex-change operation (has his penis removed and a vagina installed). Is he then permitted on natural law grounds to have sex with another man? Or—leave aside the sex change operation—suppose a gay male eschews oral or anal sex in favour of inter-crural sex (inserting the penis between the thighs of the partner) does this resemble sterile heterosexual behaviour closely enough to have 'procreative significance'?[31]

Is not all this a bit silly? Sex between sterile couples can in truth have no more 'procreative significance' than gay or lesbian sex. Sterile heterosexual sex has only the appearance but not the reality of biological unity. Finnis makes everything of the fact that heterosexual intercourse is in general the sort of behaviour appropriate to procreation. But such behaviour is not suitable for procreation in many cases and in some cases (the very old) it may bear less resemblance than gay sex to behaviour 'suitable for generation'.

Many classes of people cannot experience the good of procreation. All of these can only imitate 'procreative' relations as best they can (if imitating procreation is still a moral imperative for them, which is certainly questionable). It seems simply arbitrary to ascribe such overwhelming moral significance to brute facts of biology, especially when those brute facts represent appearances (of biological unity) rather than reality. Is this really the ground upon which to erect so crucial a moral distinction?

All this reveals a strange feature of the new natural law's version of teleological ethics, namely, its overbreadth. The new natural law asserts the universal validity of ends that are in general good for the species, even when those ends make no sense as applied to particular individuals.[32] Consider the analogy between sex and eating. We eat and have sex to sustain and reproduce human life, but also because both activities are also pleasurable in themselves, and especially when shared with others: social dining cements friendships, expresses affection, and so on. But suppose eating and nourishment are severed? Is eating for the sake of mere pleasure unnatural or irrational? Koppelman suggests that chewing sugarless gum is to eating as masturbation is to sex. Is it immoral? Or as Andy Sabl has suggested to me, suppose a person lost his capacity to digest but not the capacity to eat. Nutrition could be delivered intravenously, but would it then be immoral to eat for the sake of pleasure, or perhaps for the sake of pleasure as well as the comradery of dining companions? Would it be incumbent on one in such a state to eat only a healthy, balanced diet, or would it be permissible to binge on chocolate to one's heart's content? Would it be necessary (as Sabl asks) 'to go on eating beets and tofu because this would be the kind of eating which, "as eating," is suitable for a human being' though useless to the digestively-impaired individual? A moral injunction of 'healthy' eating, in this case, would appear to make no sense, though it might provide psychological comfort.

Moral judgement on the new natural law view is a blunt instrument, inattentive to the good of those who differ from the majority of the species. Why should we be required to generalize—or over-generalize—our ethical judgements in this way?[33] In the political realm, of course, we have practical reasons—not a function of the pursuit of justice or rightness—to govern by general rules. We want to put people on notice as to what they must do to avoid running afoul of the law, and we simply lack the resources to decide each case on its individual merits. But why should our ethical judgements labour under such constraints?

The new natural law's moral injunctions are, in some respects, too broad. The new natural law's account of valuable sexual activity is, in other ways, too narrow. The decisive feature of valuable sex on the natural lawyers' account is its openness to procreation and the great good of new life. Even accepting this questionable claim for the moment, we might say that gays and lesbians can, in effect, share the same openness to real goods beyond mere physical pleasure. In effect, gays can have sex in a way that is open to procreation, and to new life. They can be, and many are, prepared to engage in the kinds of loving relations that would result in procreation—were conditions different. Like sterile married couples, many would like nothing more than this. All we can say is that conditions would have to be more radically different in the case of gay and lesbian couples than sterile married couples for new life to result from sex . . . but what is the moral force of that? The new natural law does not make moral judgements based on natural facts. It is hard to see how this double standard can be reconciled within the new natural law framework.

For Finnis and Grisez everything turns on 'biological unity' and the 'organic complementarity' of men and women. Sodomy is an incomplete realization of the 'body's capacity'. All of this sounds perilously close to deriving an 'ought' from an 'is', or at least from certain selective 'is's': from the 'organic complementarity' of (some) heterosexuals, from the observation (reminiscent of the old natural law) that the male member and the female opening were obviously made for each other. Meanwhile, other 'natural facts' are simply left aside, such as the mutual attraction of homosexuals (why is homosexual activity an incomplete realization of the 'body's capacity' for one who is homosexual by nature, especially when compared with the celibacy the new natural lawyers would enjoin on homosexuals). If this is the real ground for the different treatment of infertile heterosexuals and homosexuals, then the much vaunted advances of the new natural law are a mirage.

Finnis ridicules the argument mentioned above (and made previously elsewhere[34]), namely, that gays and lesbians can have sex that is, in a sense, open to procreation. 'Here,' Finnis charges, 'fantasy has taken leave of reality. Anal or oral intercourse, whether between spouses or males, is no more a biological union "open to procreation" than is intercourse with a goat by a shepherd who fantasizes about breeding a faun.'[35] This is very clever but misses the point. The sterile heterosexual couple's 'openness to procreation' is as much a fantasy as that of Finnis's kinky shepherd. Sterile heterosexuals have as great a chance of breeding a child as the shepherd and his goat do a faun. Surely, the crucial thing about the loving sexual acts of sterile couples is not their openness to the sheer fantasy that their sexual acts are procreative, the crucial thing must be that their sex is open to goods such as friendship, mutual care, and so on. Surely, that is, their sterile union is valuable not because of goods that are absolutely *unavailable* to them and that they cannot share (procreation) but rather because of goods that they can attain and share (friendship, mutual help, etc.). Finnis's argument leads, absurdly, to the opposite conclusion.

The most that can be said for sterile heterosexual couples is that they can have loving sex in a way that is open to goods beyond mere physical gratification. All of the goods that can be shared by sterile heterosexuals can also be shared by committed homosexual couples. Homosexuals do not choose against the good of procreation any more than do the elderly or sterile. Finnis fails, therefore, to damage the conclusion that homosexuals can—every bit as much as sterile heterosexual couples—have sex that is open to goods beyond mere self-gratification.

The new natural law's sexual morality is caught in a bind of its own making. It does not want to describe the goods of sex purely in terms of procreation. It holds that sex is good within marriage (itself now considered a basic good), when sexual acts are open to new life: the good of new life must not be chosen against. So the circle of valuable sexuality is widened beyond the narrowly procreative, to bring in sterile and elderly couples. But how then can the circle exclude committed gay couples as well? The basis of the distinction drawn by new natural lawyers is the presence of a penis and vagina. But sterile non-working sexual organs that give only the appearance of biological unity cannot bear the weight of this important moral distinction. Finnis and Grisez mislocate the proper ground for drawing a distinction of moral goodness. The appropriate ground is the degree of mutual commitment and stable engagement in shared goods beyond the mere physical pleasures of sex.

The real point of a natural law prepared to endorse sex as a good in sterile unions must be that sex is a good so long as it is bound up in enduring intimacies, love, and shared commitments. Finnis and Grisez have broken the link between procreation and permissible sexual activity. That done, it is hard to fathom their continued insistence on the overwhelming moral significance of a biological complementarity that is necessary for procreation but that is not necessary for the other goods that sterile couples (and homosexuals) can share. It is absurd to allocate these valuable properties on the basis of irrelevant biological facts (non-working complementary organs). The attempt to ascribe value only to heterosexual couples fails.

The inconsistencies of the new natural law should not be allowed to obscure the valuable insight that sexual pleasure just for the sake of sexual pleasure—brute gratification—may well tend toward the masturbatory, and may well tend to undermine the reciprocity necessary to loving relations. We may well, therefore, have good reason to encourage people to integrate their sexual activities into stable commitments to monogamous relationships. All this is as true for homosexuals as it is for heterosexuals.

Finnis himself signals the failure of his argument by falling back on unsupported empirical generalizations about homosexual relationships. Homosexual acts are likened, as we have seen, to 'solitary masturbation', to sex between strangers, and to a quick trick with a prostitute.[36] No one remotely familiar with the variety of homosexual lives could engage in such gross generalizations, reminiscent of nothing so much as radical feminist Catherine Mackinnon's equation of all heterosexual sex with rape and violence against women.[37] Simplistic as they are, Finnis's generalizations are revealing. Given the implausibility of the insistence that biological complementarity is all important, Finnis must count on it being the case that homosexual relationships embody no real goods: none of the goods that might be shared by sterile heterosexuals. These sweeping generalizations are the only ground left to Finnis as a basis for condemning homosexual conduct as such. Homosexual conduct must be nothing more than solitary masturbation or sex with a prostitute, or else the new natural lawyers' wholesale condemnations make no sense. Heterosexual activity must be uniquely capable of expressing shared goods; otherwise, the radically different treatment of sterile heterosexuals and homosexuals hangs on nothing more than the all too obviously flawed biological complementarity argument.

Finnis provides no evidence whatsoever to support his account of the nature of homosexual intimacy: no reports or investigations into how homosexuals experience their sexual relations. Instead of evidence Finnis provides only offhanded references to 'the modern "gay" ideology', an ideology that 'treats sexual capacities, organs, and acts as instruments to be put to whatever suits the purposes of the individual "self" who has them'.[38] Here again, Finnis signals his argument's dependence on unexamined stereotype and over-generalization. Millions of homosexual lives and relationships are taken to be epitomized by a promiscuous,

liberationist 'gay lifestyle', which rejects all sexual restraints and value judgements.[39] In the end, Finnis's argument boils down to nothing more than this stereotype, for it is the only ground that really could support his sweeping moral condemnations, rendered without regard for the complexity, ambiguity, or diversity of actual lives.

If the crude stereotype is not true then the new natural law's sexual teaching falls apart. Promiscuity is the core of the stereotype, so one might have thought that Finnis would at least say something about the apparently substantial differences in behaviour between gay males and lesbians. Richard Posner cites evidence showing that lesbians have quite stable relationships and have intercourse less frequently than heterosexual couples.[40] Even if one were to conclude—and this is certainly a point of scholarly controversy—that men tend by nature to be more promiscuous than women and that gay men will tend to have a more difficult time than heterosexuals settling down in stable relationships, we would still have to let lesbians off the hook.

Of course, as I have already said, a tendency toward promiscuity would hardly justify lumping all gay men and all homosexual conduct into one category, defined by the least admirable homosexual behaviour. Gay sex may tend toward the masturbatory and promiscuous somewhat more than heterosexual relationships (which may tend that way more than lesbian relationships). But what would we conclude from this? That homosexuality as such is to be condemned? Men tend to be more violent than women, but this does not justify the condemnation of men in general. It would be wrong to regard the essence of 'maleness' (or indeed, heterosexuality) as captured by its worst forms (domestic violence and rape). It is no better to characterize homosexuality in this way. We expect reasonable public policy not to condemn men as a class but to address the issue of domestic violence as such. With respect to sexuality we should, similarly, think seriously about working to curb promiscuity, whether gay or straight, and about how to elevate and stabilize sexual relationships in general. Relying on the stereotype of gay promiscuity is not only unjust to non-promiscuous gays but a serious impediment to sound policy.

The inconsistent treatment of sterile heterosexuals and homosexuals is the thread that unravels the new natural law's sexual teaching. The garment might be repaired, and the new natural law's position made consistent, either through exclusion or inclusion. The exclusive strategy would extend the category of valueless sexual activity to cover sex between elderly and sterile couples. The natural lawyers could save their proscriptions against homosexuality in this way by arguing that, like gays and lesbians, elderly couples can enjoy mutual helping and friendship, but sex adds nothing to these goods, indeed it distracts from and destroys them. Sex between elderly and infertile couples would no longer be morally permissible, and they would be denied the right to marry. It is surely the case that the vast majority of elderly couples marry, after all, with the expectation that they will not bear children: indeed, if they thought they might some would not get married. If the natural lawyers want to remain steadfast in their attitude toward gays, then public policy should deter fornication by the elderly, deny them the right to marry, prohibit the 'promotion, commendation, or facilitation' of sex among the elderly (though not, as with gays, criminalizing sexual acts committed by the elderly in secret), and otherwise drive elderly and sterile fornicators into the closet and underground, along with gays and lesbians. This path to consistency is not completely without precedent.[41]

There is, luckily, an alternative path to reasoned consistency, and that is to broaden the scope of legitimate sexuality to include committed gay couples. Given the implausibility of the new natural law's narrow analysis of the valuable forms of sexuality, the path of inclusion is surely to be preferred. As we have seen, the new natural lawyers have furnished no grounds for supposing that the goods shared by infertile and elderly couples cannot be shared by gays in committed relationships. They provide no reasonable grounds for regarding loving sex within committed relationships as morally equivalent to the most casual and promiscuous sex among strangers. The path of inclusion would acknowledge all this, and allow that even if being gay will be regarded by some (not completely without reason) as a kind of disability, it is no more so than infertility or age. Sexual activity within committed and loving relationships can, then, be endorsed as a genuine good for all.

The new natural law's position on sexual morality falls on two counts. It falls first because of its extremely narrow account of valuable sexuality (so deeply at odds with the judgements of virtually everyone outside the Catholic hierarchy): an account that is unreasonably reductionist and puritanical. Secondly, the new natural law fails to offer any rational ground for treating sex within sterile heterosexual marriages differently from sex within committed homosexual relationships. While broad and fairminded in many respects, the new natural law's sexual teaching founders on an arbitrariness tailored to the interests of the heterosexual majority.

To reject Finnis's unreasonably narrow and (in part) arbitrarily defined strictures on sexuality does not require that one embrace a completely 'non-judgemental' attitude with respect to sexuality. There are reasonable elements within the natural law tradition that constitute good grounds for public measures to elevate and improve people's sexual lives, both for their own good and the good of society.

While rejecting Finnis's narrow prescriptions, we can still acknowledge that sexual desire can be a problem. There is something to the observation of Plato, Aristotle, and others that the relative intensity of the 'animal pleasures' means that most people will tend toward overdoing rather than underdoing not only sex but food, at least absent efforts at self-control and a well-developed character. Self-control and character development—crucial to a healthy and happy life—benefit greatly from social support, such as the inducements to stability that flow from the institution of marriage.[42]

Extending marriage to gays and lesbians is a way of allowing that the natural lawyers are not all wrong: promiscuous sex may well have the essentially masturbatory and distracting and valueless character that Finnis describes. We have legitimate public reasons to favour certain institutions that help order, stabilize and elevate sexual relations. But we should offer these inducements even-handedly to all whose real good can thereby be advanced: we offer them to the elderly and the sterile, to gays and lesbians, and not only to fertile heterosexuals. We provide everyone with help to stabilize and elevate their sexual relationships, and so to achieve the benefits that natural lawyers rightly claim for marriage. This allows us to accept and deploy a reasoned and defensible version of natural law.

IV. Conclusion: liberalism, the good life, and abortion

We should reject the new natural law's narrow sexual teaching, but not its deeper conviction that we can make judgements about the good life, and that such judgements have a legitimate role to play in the public policy of the liberal state. Respect for individual choice and freedom is one central imperative of liberal politics, but it is far from exhausting the legitimate public policy aims of a liberal state. I have endorsed, for example, attaching benefits to the status of marriage on the ground that we have good reasons for encouraging people to settle down in long-term relationships. The vice of the new natural law's sexual teaching is not the wholesale illegitimacy of embodying reasonable, secular judgements about better and worse lives in public policy; it is, rather, the clear weakness of

the substantive case with respect to sexual morality.

The best way of thinking about political power in a democratic constitutionalist regime such as ours is as the shared property of reasonable citizens, who should be able to offer one another reasons that can publicly be seen to be good to justify the use of that power.[43] Many natural law arguments (including those discussed above) are indeed acceptably public, as Finnis asserts: the reasons and evidence on which they are based are not overly complex or vague, and they can be shared openly with fellow citizens. The vice of the new natural law position described above is not its vagueness, complexity, or lack of public accessibility but, as we saw, its unreasonable narrowness and arbitrary extension. The new natural lawyers are right, therefore, to deny that liberalism is best identified with that straw man who is the principal exhibit and easy target of so many critics of liberalism, namely, neutralist liberalism.[44]

Rawls is nevertheless right, I think, to insist that we should avoid invoking reasonably contestable comprehensive moral and religious claims when fashioning the most basic principles that will inform the constitutional framework. This does not mean that Rawls—or liberalism properly understood—is similarly committed to excluding all such claims from politics as a whole. Though some of his critics have missed the point, Rawls develops his account of public reason as an appropriate basis for what he calls the 'basic structure' of society, not for politics as a whole.[45]

Even with respect to the 'basic structure' or the constitutional essentials, it would be a mistake to describe Rawls as committed to working without reference to human goods: he insists only that the conceptions of the good on which we rely when fashioning basic principles of justice should be widely acceptable to reasonable people. The constraints of wide acceptability may be, moreover, at least somewhat relaxed with respect to mere policy questions that do not touch on fundamental rights and interests (just how much they are relaxed and in what way we need not consider here). Museums can be subsidized, the arts can be funded, marriage can be given a special status, and churches can be granted tax exemptions, even though all of these policies rest on judgements about human goods that are subject to reasonable disagreement. Marriage, museums, and many other policy issues, are not matters of basic justice. The sorts of arguments adduced in this chapter are (I believe) perfectly legitimate grounds for publicly supporting marriage within a liberal order: no one's fundamental liberties are at stake and the goods appealed to (such as the value of an institution that encourages stable intimate relationships), while perhaps contestable, do not depend on a particular, highly sectarian religious view or secular ideal of human perfection.

If public support for marriage is permissible in the liberal state, that support is also subject to principled constraints. The basic liberties of those who choose not to marry, for example, must not be infringed upon, and the opportunity to marry must be made fairly available to all who can benefit. Public officials including judges should, moreover, take special measures to insure that the good of marriage and other public goods are not unfairly denied to some groups who we know are often victims of long-standing prejudice and discrimination.

Public provision of a good, such as marriage, while within the realm of legislative discretion may not be provided on discriminatory grounds. On this score, unfortunately, public policy in the United States stands accused of injustice. It would not be a basic injustice if marriage were altogether abolished (though I believe that would be a bad thing), but it is a basic injustice (and one worthy of judicial remedy) that gays and lesbians are being denied the good of marriage on grounds of prejudice abetted by weak philosophical arguments.

A closing word about abortion, by way of place-holder, perhaps, for a more adequate dis-

cussion. Finnis takes issue with my argument that a principled case for compromise may exist on some issues, such as abortion, which are difficult precisely because one finds powerful moral considerations on both sides.[46] On such issues, I have suggested, it might be hasty to join Ronald Dworkin in concluding that the side with the strongest case has the right to win.[47] On a matter such as abortion, this conclusion would be simplistic: when there really are weighty arguments and reasons on both sides (and not simply reasons that are strongly held) winning properly might require the law to acknowledge and express the fact that the 'losing' side was far from being all wrong.

On this basis, I have endorsed and continue to endorse attempts to fashion something like the sort of compromise that the Supreme Court allowed to stand in Pennsylvania.[48] One can argue about the propriety of state-mandated waiting periods or doctors' consultations for women who want abortions. Nevertheless, it seems to me that the law-makers ought to do something to express the fact that opponents of abortion have weighty and serious moral concerns on their side. Doing so expresses the virtue—too often neglected in this morally-charged area of our politics—of moderation and the good of comity.

Finnis is simply all too ready to characterize the arguments of his opponents in the abortion debate (the pro-choice side) as 'manifestations of prejudice'.[49] In this he is the mirror image of zealots on the pro-choice side who believe that concern for the human foetus in its early stages must reflect religious conviction or a lack of concern for women's freedom and equality. Zealots on both sides of the abortion debate view this area of moral world as too simple and stark. I admire Finnis's unflinching pursuit of the moral truth, and his transparent desire to get these difficult matters right. The sweep of his moral judgements, here as elsewhere, seem to me inadequate to the complexity of the moral world.

Notes

Robert George (ed.) *Natural Law, Liberalism and Morality* (Oxford 1996), pp. 27–48.

My thanks to Andy Koppelman and Andy Sabl for their generous comments on earlier drafts.

2 Germain Grisez, *The Way of the Lord Jesus*, vol. 2, *Living a Christian Life*, Quincy, Ill., Franciscan Press (Quincy 1993), p. 662.

3 John Finnis, 'Natural Law and Limited Government', ch. 1, p. 6.

4 Ibid., pp. 5–6.

5 Ibid., p. 7.

6 For an uncharacteristically lucid statement of his position, see Dewey, *A Common Faith* (New Haven, Conn., Yale U.P., 1934).

7 Ch. 1, p.3.

8 *Second Treatise of Government*, ch. 14.

9 Isaiah Berlin, *Four Essays on Liberty* (Oxford, 1979), see the Introduction and 'Two Concepts of Liberty'; Thomas Nagel, 'The Fragmentation of Value', in *Moral Questions* (Cambridge, 1981); Bernard Williams, 'Conflicts of Values', in *Moral Luck* (Cambridge, 1983).

10 At least so long as we faced an expansionist power such as the old Soviet Union, rightly characterized by President Reagan as an 'evil empire'.

11 As Russell Hittinger suggests in 'Does Natural Law Require Theological Justification?', paper presented at the American Public Philosophy Institute Conference, 'Liberalism, Modernity and Natural Law', Washington, D.C. (Sept. 1993). A divinely-inspired teleology may be the only way to salvage the new natural law's sexual teaching.

12 Strauss, *Natural Right and History* (University of Chicago, 1953), p. 159, Strauss's critique of Thomism seems to me cogent, esp., pp. 162–3.

13 Ch. 1, p. 6.

14 Ibid., p. 17, *see also* pp. 8–9.

15 Ibid., p. 9.

16 See Grisez, pp. 653–4. Finnis's moral argument is replete with references to ancient authors which I will not take up here. A lively debate has developed on these matters, see Finnis, 'Law, Morality, and "Sexual Orientation"', *Notre Dame University Law Review*, v. 69 (1994) p. 1049, and Martha Nussbaum, 'Platonic Love and Colorado Law: The Relevance of Ancient Greek Norms to Modern Sexual Controversies', *Virginia Law Review*, v. 80, pp. 1515–1651 (1994).

17 Ch. 1, p. 15.

18 Ibid., pp. 13–16, for Grisez's elaborate account see *Living a Christian Life*, pp. 553–752.

19 Ch. 1, p. 12, Grisez, *Christian Life*, p. 653.

20 Grisez, pp. 653–4.

21 Richard Posner, *Sex and Reason* (Cambridge, Mass., Harvard U.P., 1992), p. 306, and see ch. 11 generally.

22 Ch. 1, p. 15.

23 Ibid., p. 16.

24 Ibid., p. 15.

25 Grisez, *Christian Life*, p. 573.

26 I have benefited from his development of this analogy in 'Homosexuality, Nature, and Morality', unpublished, and from his important work, *The Antidiscrimination Project* (Yale U.P., 1996).

27 Grisez, *Christian Life*, pp. 572–3.

28 Ch. 1, pp. 15 and 16.

29 Ibid., n. 76.

30 I heard a stand-up comedian say this, but I cannot remember who. The analogy of sterility to unloaded guns is Koppelman's, 'Homosexuality'.

31 As in Finnis's insistence that good sex must have not only the 'generosity of acts of friendship but also the procreative significance,' Ch. 1, p. 15.

32 I am greatly indebted in this paragraph to a private communication from Sabl, 13 June 1994. See also Koppelman's 'Homosexuality'.

33 And of course, even our political judgements should be sensitive to false generalizations that ignore morally serious differences among people. I discuss these matters in 'The Rule of Law, Justice, and the Politics of Moderation'. *Nomos XXXVI: The Rule of Law* (New York U.P., 1994), pp. 148–77.

34 'The New Natural Lawyers', *Harvard Crimson*, 28 Oct., 1993.

35 Ch. 1, n. 76, p. 25.

36 Ch. 1, pp. 14–15.

37 See *Toward a Feminist Theory of the State* (Cambridge, Mass., Harvard U.P., 1989), p. 146 passim.

38 Ch. 1, pp. 14 and 16–17.

39 Ibid., pp. 16–17.

40 Posner, *Sex and Reason*, pp. 91–2.

41 Fustel de Coulange notes (as Sabl pointed out to me) that in some ancient cities it may have been obligatory for a man to divorce a wife who proved to be sterile, see *The Ancient City* (Johns Hopkins U.P.,

Baltimore, 1980). Philo of Alexandria condemned sex with an infertile partner (as Koppelman pointed out to me), likening it to copulation with a pig, see John Boswell, *Homosexuality, Christianity, and Social Tolerance* (University of Chicago Press, 1980), p. 148.

42 I have benefited from Andrew Sullivan's excellent 'Here Comes the Groom: A (Conservative) Case for Gay Marriage', *The New Republic*, 28 Aug. 1989, pp. 20, 22.

43 Which I argued in *Liberal Virtues: Citizenship, Virtue, and Community in Liberal Constitutionalism* (Oxford, Clarendon Press, 1990), mainly following Rawls, whose views have come together in *Political Liberalism* (Columbia, 1993).

44 See, for example, Michael Sandel's contribution to [the original] volume, and his review of *Political Liberalism, Harvard Law Review*, vol. 107 (May 1994), pp. 1765–94. I criticize and reject neutralist liberalism in *Liberal Virtues*, pp. 67, 73–4, 260–3.

45 Rawls, *Political Liberalism*, p. 11. Sandel makes this mistake in his contribution to [the original] volume.

46 *Liberal Virtues*, pp. 72–3.

47 See Ronald Dworkin, *Taking Rights Seriously* (Harvard U.P., 1977), and my discussion in *Liberal Virtues*, pp. 72–3, 84–95, and passim.

48 *Planned Parenthood of Southeastern Pennsylvania v. Casey* 112 S. Ct. 2791 (1992).

49 Ch. 1, p. 18.

PART 3

Rights

VI. THE NATURE OF RIGHTS

Introduction

THE LAW OF ANY DECENT legal system will be replete with a wide array of rights: for example, rights of bodily integrity, reflected in its criminal prohibitions on murder and rape and in the liability that its tort law assigns to battery and negligence; rights of free expression and association, captured in its constitutional law; and rights to the exclusive use of land, as outlined in its property law. What moral rights a legal system should recognize and incorporate as legal rights is of course a question of fundamental practical importance. But there is a philosophically prior question to this one, also having practical implications, regarding the *nature* of rights. The question "What are rights?", which concerns the nature of rights, is different from the questions "What rights are there?" or "What rights should there be?" Having some grasp of the nature of rights may help to answer those latter questions, to be sure, but an exploration of the nature of rights seeks an understanding of what a right is or indeed must be, and thus prescinds from the local facts about specific legal systems or particular social conditions that illuminate what rights there are or should be. The nature of rights is invariant in this way, and to explore the nature of rights is thus to seek out those features that all particular rights have in common.

Rights have many dimensions and for this reason there are many different approaches that one can take in exploring the nature of rights. One consists in delineating the logical structure of rights. Following this route, Wesley Newcomb Hohfeld famously argued that the notion of a right can be any or all of four distinct "elements": a claim, a privilege, a power, and an immunity.[1] Each of these, moreover, has "correlatives": if some person A has a claim, some other person B has a duty; if A has a privilege, B has a no-claim; if A has a power, B has a liability; and if A has an immunity, B has a disability. So if I have a full Hohfeldian right to my bicycle, the claim to it that I have correlates to a duty in everyone else not to use it, I have a privilege to use it myself such that others have no claim that I not use it, I have a power to waive or otherwise alter my right to it which makes everyone else liable to the change, and I have an immunity against anyone else being able to waive or otherwise alter my right, thus disabling them. Hohfeld's schema has been enormously influential, even if not universally accepted, and it is worth noting that although he presented it as an analysis of legal rights, it has proven to be influential in the analysis of moral rights as well.

The possibility that the natures of legal and moral rights might be illuminated by the same forms of analysis should not be surprising. Moral and legal rights are distinct, to be sure, but they are also closely related. H. L. A. Hart, for example, was loathe to conflate law and morality if anyone was (see Section I above) but maintains in "Are There Any Natural Rights?" that "the concept of a right belongs to that branch of morality which is specifically concerned to determine when one person's freedom may be limited by another's and so to determine what actions may appropriately be made the subject of coercive legal rules."[2] This claim is clearly consonant with Hart's rejection of legal moralism (see the introduction to Section V), but Hart here is not so much denying the state's authority to enforce conceptions of moral virtue as he is maintaining that whatever the appropriate boundary of state coercion, surely it encompasses the legal codification of moral rights. And this is all that one need recognize to understand why the analysis of legal rights will yield insights about moral rights and vice versa. Examination of the nature of rights, then, can safely proceed without specifying whether the object of study is legal or moral rights in particular.

Hohfeld's typology of rights is in the background of both Hart's "Are There Any Natural Rights?" and Neil MacCormick's "Rights in Legislation", and indeed one must understand Hohfeld's conception of rights to grasp fully the debate between Hart and MacCormick. Theirs is not a debate about Hohfeld's schema itself, however, but about the *explanation* of rights: Hart is a proponent of the "will" or "choice" theory of rights, while MacCormick defends the "interest" or "benefit" theory of rights. On MacCormick's characterization of the opposing positions,

> [the will theory] asserts that an individual's having a right of some kind depends upon the legal (or, *mutatis mutandis*, moral) recognition of his will, his choice, as being preeminent over that of others in relation to a given subject matter and within a given relationship. The 'interest theory', by contrast, contends that what is essential to the constitution of a right is the legal (or moral) protection or promotion of one person's interests as against some other person or the world at large, by the imposition on the latter of duties, disabilities, or liabilities in respect of the party favoured.[3]

Rights on the will theory thus provide one with a kind of normative control over how one may be treated, whereas on the interest theory, rights provide normative protection of one's especially important interests or one's well-being. Both theories have much to recommend them, and indeed each continues to have loyal contemporary advocates. Each theory also has its apparent difficulties. For example, Hart argues that the interest theory cannot make sense of the right that a promisee holds against a promisor when the beneficiary of the promise is a third party. It may be in the third party's interest that the promise be kept, but that fact is inapposite in a way that the interest theory cannot accept, for the obligation to keep the promise is owed not to the third party but to the promisee. On the other hand, MacCormick argues that the will theory cannot make sense of the inalienability of the right not to be deprived of one's freedom. For if the supposed right-holder lacks the power to alienate the right, as seems to be the case, then it follows according to the logic of the will theory that there is, paradoxically, no such right in the first place—normative control is, after all, the *sine qua non* of the will theory. And these points just scratch the surface of the debate.

Whether one accepts the will or interest theory has significant practical implications for questions about the possibility of, for example, animal rights, children's rights, and rights of the mentally impaired. Such questions concern who can have rights and, more generally, the existence conditions of rights. But assuming that we know what explains the existence of rights and thus who can have them, there remains the further question of what having rights does for the right-holder. This is a question about what we might call the *function* of rights, and it marks another aspect of the nature of rights.

Rights are, in the central case, possessed by individuals. This fact has inspired a widespread belief that the purpose of rights is to stand as a bulwark against socially expedient policies that would serve the many at the expense of the few. On this view, there are limits to the burdens that the many may ask individuals to bear in the service of valuable social goals, and those limits are imposed by individual rights. This, famously, is Ronald Dworkin's position. Drawing on a metaphor from the game of bridge, he argues in "Rights as Trumps" for "the right to moral independence as a trump over utilitarian justifications."[4] Where the invocation of rights is appropriate, according to Dworkin, rights are fundamentally opposed to and indeed override considerations of overall utility. But is so stark an opposition tenable? Joseph Raz thinks not. In "Rights and Individual Well-Being", Raz grants that it is individuals who possess rights first and foremost, but none the less argues that "[t]he protection of many of the most cherished civil and political rights in liberal democracies is justified by the fact that they serve the common or general good."[5] There is, Raz maintains, a mismatch between the importance of core political rights and their importance to any particular right-holder, and this suggests that the importance of such rights derives not so much from their protection of individuals as from the value of the liberal culture that they help to foster. If these rights are justified mostly by their contribution to the common good, as Raz maintains, however, then it makes little sense to follow Dworkin in conceiving of rights as individualistic trumps over considerations of social welfare. Dworkin and Raz both agree that rights protect individuals. Their debate here instead concerns whether rights protect individuals *in spite* or *in virtue* of the wider good.

Notes

1 Wesley Newcomb Hohfeld, "Fundamental Legal Conceptions as Applied in Juridical Reasoning", *Yale Law Journal* 23 & 26, 1913 & 1917, 16 & 710, later published as the book *Fundamental Legal Conceptions*, New Haven, CT: Yale University Press, 1923.
2 H. L. A. Hart, "Are There Any Natural Rights?", p. 312.
3 Neil MacCormick, "Rights in Legislation", p. 323.
4 Ronald Dworkin, "Rights as Trumps", p. 343.
5 Joseph Raz, "Rights and Individual Well-Being", p. 351.

Further reading

William Edmundson, *An Introduction to Rights*, New York: Cambridge University Press, 2004.

Wesley Newcomb Hohfeld, *Fundamental Legal Conceptions*, New Haven, CT: Yale University Press, 1923.

F. M. Kamm, *Morality, Mortality, Volume II: Rights, Duties, and Status*, New York: Oxford University Press, 1996.

F. M. Kamm, *Intricate Ethics: Rights, Responsibility, and Permissible Harm*, New York: Oxford University Press, 2007.

Matthew Kramer, N. E. Simmons, and Hillel Steiner, *A Debate Over Rights: Philosophical Enquiries*, New York: Oxford University Press, 1998.

John Oberdiek, "Lost in Moral Space: On the Infringing/Violating Distinction and its Place in the Theory of Rights", *Law and Philosophy* 23, 2004, 325–346.

John Oberdiek, "Specifying Rights Out of Necessity", *Oxford Journal of Legal Studies* 28, 2008, 1–20.

Russ Shafer-Landau, "Specifying Absolute Rights", *Arizona Law Review* 37, 1995, 209–224.

Hillel Steiner, *An Essay on Rights*, Oxford: Blackwell Publishers, 1994.

Judith Jarvis Thomson, *The Realm of Rights*, Cambridge, MA: Harvard University Press, 1990.

Jeremy Waldron, "Rights in Conflict", in *Liberal Rights: Collected Papers*, New York: Cambridge University Press, 1993, pp. 203–224.

Jeremy Waldron (ed.), *Theories of Rights*, New York: Oxford University Press, 1984.

Carl Wellman, *Real Rights*, New York: Oxford University Press, 1995.

Leif Wenar, "The Nature of Rights", *Philosophy and Public Affairs* 33, 2005, 223–253.

Questions

1. Can the interest theory of rights recognize a promisee's right to the performance of a promise that benefits a third party?
2. Can the will theory of rights recognize animal rights, children's rights, or the rights of the mentally incapacitated?
3. In what ways, if at all, can the interest and will theories of rights accommodate each other's insights?
4. Can there be a right to do wrong?
5. Can rights conflict?
6. Do rights exist merely to protect individuals from socially expedient policies?
7. Do rights that are based in part on the common good afford sufficient protection to individuals against socially expedient policies?

Chapter 18

H. L. A. Hart

ARE THERE ANY NATURAL RIGHTS?

I SHALL ADVANCE the thesis that if there are any moral rights at all, it follows that there is at least one natural right, the equal right of all men to be free. By saying that there is this right, I mean that in the absence of certain special conditions which are consistent with the right being an equal right, any adult human being capable of choice (1) has the right to forbearance on the part of all others from the use of coercion or restraint against him save to hinder coercion or restraint and (2) is at liberty to do (i.e., is under no obligation to abstain from) any action which is not one coercing or restraining or designed to injure other persons.[2]

I have two reasons for describing the equal right of all men to be free as a *natural* right; both of them were always emphasized by the classical theorists of natural rights. (1) This right is one which all men have if they are capable of choice; they have it *qua* men and not only if they are members of some society or stand in some special relation to each other. (2) This right is not created or conferred by men's voluntary action; other moral rights are.[3] Of course, it is quite obvious that my thesis is not as ambitious as the traditional theories of natural rights; for although on my view all men are *equally* entitled to be free in the sense explained, no man has an absolute or unconditional right to do or not to do any particular thing or to be treated in any particular way; coercion or restraint of any action may be justified in special conditions consistently with the general principle. So my argument will not show that men have any right (save the equal right of all to be free) which is "absolute," "indefeasible," or "imprescriptible." This may for many reduce the importance of my contention, but I think that the principle that all men have an equal right to be free, meager as it may seem, is probably all that the political philosophers of the liberal tradition need have claimed to support any program of action even if they have claimed more. But my contention that there is this one natural right may appear unsatisfying in another respect; it is only the conditional assertion that if there are any moral rights then there must be this one natural right. Perhaps few would now deny, as some have, that there are moral rights; for the point of that denial was usually to object to some philosophical claim as to the "ontological status" of rights, and this objection is now expressed not as a denial that there are any moral rights but as a denial of some assumed logical similarity between sentences used to assert the existence of rights and other kinds of sentences. But it is still important to remember that there may be codes of conduct quite properly termed moral codes (though we can of course say they are "imperfect") which do not employ the notion of *a* right, and there is nothing contradictory or otherwise absurd in a code or morality consisting wholly of prescriptions or in a code which prescribed only what should be done for the realization of happiness or some ideal of personal perfection.[4] Human actions in such systems would be evaluated or criticised as compliances with prescriptions or as *good* or *bad*, *right* or *wrong*, *wise* or *foolish*, *fitting* or *unfitting*, but no one in such a system would have, exercise, or claim rights, or violate or infringe them. So those who lived by such systems could not of course be committed to the recognition of the equal right of all to be free; nor, I think (and this is one respect in which the notion of a right differs from other moral notions), could any parallel argument be constructed to show that, from the bare fact that actions were recognized as ones which ought or ought not to be done, as right, wrong, good or bad, it followed that some specific kind of conduct fell under these categories.

I

(A) Lawyers have for their own purposes carried the dissection of the notion of a legal right some distance, and some of their results[5] are of value in the elucidation of statements of the form "X has a right to . . ." outside legal contexts. There is of course no simple identification to be made between moral and legal rights, but there is an intimate connection between the two, and this itself is one feature which distinguishes a moral right from other fundamental moral concepts. It is not merely that as a matter of fact men speak of their moral rights mainly when advocating their incorporation in a legal system, but that the concept of a right belongs to that branch of morality which is specifically concerned to determine when one person's freedom may be limited by another's[6] and so to determine what actions may appropriately be made the subject of coercive legal rules. The words "droit," "diritto," and "Recht," used by continental jurists, have no simple English translation and seem to English jurists to hover uncertainly between law and morals, but they do in fact mark off an area of morality (the morality of law) which has special

characteristics. It is occupied by the concepts of justice, fairness, rights, and obligation (if this last is not used as it is by many moral philosophers as an obscuring general label to cover every action that morally we ought to do or forbear from doing). The most important common characteristic of this group of moral concepts is that there is no incongruity, but a special congruity in the use of force or the threat of force to secure that what is just or fair or someone's right to have done shall in fact be done; for it is in just these circumstances that coercion of another human being is legitimate. Kant, in the *Rechtslehre*, discusses the obligations which arise in this branch of morality under the title of *officia juris*, "which do not require that respect for duty shall be of itself the determining principle of the will," and contrasts them with *officia virtutis*, which have no moral worth unless done for the sake of the moral principle. His point is, I think, that we must distinguish from the rest of morality those principles regulating the proper distribution of human freedom which alone make it morally legitimate for one human being to determine by his choice how another should act; and a certain specific moral value is secured (to be distinguished from moral virtue in which the good will is manifested) if human relationships are conducted in accordance with these principles even though coercion has to be used to secure this, for only if these principles are regarded will freedom be distributed among human beings as it should be. And it is I think a very important feature of a moral right that the possessor of it is conceived as having a moral justification for limiting the freedom of another and that he has this justification not because the action he is entitled to require of another has some moral quality but simply because in the circumstances a certain distribution of human freedom will be maintained if he by his choice is allowed to determine how that other shall act.

(B) I can best exhibit this feature of a moral right by reconsidering the question whether moral rights and "duties"[7] are correlative. The contention that they are means, presumably, that every statement of the form "X has a right to . . ." entails and is entailed by "Y has a duty (not) to . . .," and at this stage we must not assume that the values of the name-variables "X" and "Y" must be different persons. Now there is certainly one sense of "a right" (which I have already mentioned) such that it does not follow from X's having a right that X or someone else has any duty. Jurists have isolated rights in this sense and have referred to them as "liberties" just to distinguish them from rights in the centrally important sense of "right" which has "duty" as a correlative. The former sense of "right" is needed to describe those areas of social life where competition is at least morally unobjectionable. Two people walking along both see a ten-dollar bill in the road twenty yards away, and there is no clue as to the owner. Neither of the two are under a "duty" to allow the other to pick it up; each has in this sense a right to pick it up. Of course there may be many things which each has a "duty" not to do in the course of the race to the spot—neither may kill or wound the other—and corresponding to these "duties" there are rights to forbearances. The moral propriety of all economic competition implies this minimum sense of "a right" in which to say that "X has a right to" means merely that X is under no "duty" not to. Hobbes saw that the expression "a right" could have this sense but he was wrong if he thought that there is no sense in which it does follow from X's having a right that Y has a duty or at any rate an obligation.

(C) More important for our purpose is the question whether for all moral "duties" there are correlative moral rights, because those who have given an affirmative answer to this question have usually assumed without adequate scrutiny that to have a right is simply to be capable of benefiting by the performance of a "duty"; whereas in fact this is not a sufficient condition (and probably not a necessary condition) of having a right. Thus animals and babies who stand to benefit by our performance of our "duty" not to ill-treat them are said *therefore* to have rights to proper treatment. The full consequence of this reasoning is not usually followed out; most have shrunk from saying that we have rights against ourselves because we stand to benefit from our performance of our "duty" to keep ourselves alive or develop our talents. But the moral situation which arises from a promise (where the legal-sounding terminology of rights and obligations is most appropriate) illustrates most clearly that the notion of having a right and that of benefiting by the performance of a "duty" are not identical. X promises Y in return for some favor that he will look after Y's aged mother in his absence. Rights arise out of this transaction, but it is surely Y to whom the promise has been made and not his mother who *has* or *possesses* these rights. Certainly Y's mother is a person concerning whom X has an obligation and a person who will benefit by its performance, but the person *to whom* he has an obligation to look after her is Y. This is something *due to* or *owed to* Y, so it is Y, not his mother, whose right X will disregard and to whom X will have done *wrong* if he fails to keep his promise, though the mother may be physically injured. And it is Y who has a moral *claim* upon X, is *entitled* to have his mother looked after, and who can *waive* the claim and *release* Y from the obligation. Y is, in other words, morally in a position to determine by his choice how X shall act and in this way to limit X's freedom of choice; and it is this fact, not the fact that he stands to benefit, that makes it appropriate to say that he has *a right*. Of course often the person to whom a promise has been made will be the only person who stands to benefit by its performance, but this does not justify the identification of "having a right" with "benefiting by the performance of a duty." It is important for the whole logic of rights that, while the person who stands to benefit by the performance of a duty is discovered by considering what will happen if the duty is not performed, the person who has a right (to whom performance is *owed* or *due*) is discovered by examining the transaction or antecedent situation or relations of the parties out of which the "duty" arises. These considerations should incline us not to extend to animals and babies whom it is wrong to ill-treat the notion of a right to proper treatment, for the moral situation can be simply and adequately described here by saying that it is wrong or that we ought not to ill-treat them or, in the philosopher's generalized sense of "duty," that we have a duty not to ill-treat them.[8] If common usage sanctions talk of the rights of animals or babies it makes an idle use of the expression "a right," which will confuse the situation with other different moral situations where the expression "a right" has a specific force and cannot be replaced by the other moral expressions which I have mentioned. Perhaps some clarity on this matter is to be gained by considering the force of the preposition "to" in the expression "having a duty to Y" or "being under an obligation to Y" (where "Y" is the name of a person); for it is significantly different from the meaning of "to" in "doing something to Y" or "doing harm to Y," where it indicates the person affected by some action. In the first pair of expressions, "to" obviously does not have this force, but indicates the person to whom the person morally bound is bound. This is an intelligible development of the figure of a bond (*vinculum juris: obligare*); the precise figure is not that of two persons bound by a chain, but of *one* person bound, the other end of the chain lying in the hands of another to use if he chooses.[9] So it appears absurd to speak of having duties or owing obligations to ourselves—of course we may have "duties" not to do harm to ourselves, but what could be meant (once the distinction between these different meanings of "to" has been grasped) by insisting that we have duties or obligations *to* ourselves not to do harm to ourselves?

(D) The essential connection between the notion of a right and the justified limitation of one person's freedom by another may be thrown into relief if we consider codes of behavior which do not purport to confer rights but only to prescribe what shall be done. Most natural law thinkers down to Hooker conceived of natural law in this way: there were natural duties compliance with which would certainly benefit man—things to be done to achieve man's natural end—but not natural rights. And there are of course many types of codes of behavior which only prescribe what is to be done, e.g., those regulating certain ceremonies. It would be absurd to regard these codes as conferring rights, but illuminating to contrast them with rules of games, which often create rights, though not, of course, moral rights. But even a code which is plainly a moral code need not establish rights; the Decalogue is perhaps the most important example. Of course, quite apart from heavenly rewards human beings stand to benefit by general obedience to the Ten Commandments: disobedience is wrong and will certainly harm individuals. But it would be a surprising interpretation of them that treated them as conferring rights. In such an interpretation obedience to the Ten Commandments would have to be conceived as due to or owed to individuals, not merely to God, and disobedience not merely as wrong but *as a wrong to* (as well as harm to) individuals. The Commandments would cease to read like penal statutes designed only to rule out certain types of behavior and would have to be thought of as rules placed at the disposal of individuals and regulating the extent to which *they* may demand certain behavior from others. Rights are typically conceived of as *possessed* or *owned by* or *belonging to* individuals, and these expressions reflect the conception of moral rules as not only prescribing conduct but as forming a kind of moral property of individuals to which they are as individuals entitled; only when rules are conceived in this way can we speak of *rights* and *wrongs* as well as right and wrong actions.[10]

II

So far I have sought to establish that to have a right entails having a moral justification for limiting the freedom of another person and for determining how he should act; it is now important to see that the moral justification must be of a special kind if it is to constitute a right, and this will emerge most clearly from an examination of the circumstances in which rights are asserted with the typical expression "I have a right to. . . ." It is I think the case that this form of words is used in two main types of situations: (A) when the claimant has some special justification for interference with another's freedom which other persons do not have ("I have a right to be paid what you promised for my services"); (B) when the claimant is concerned to resist or object to some interference by another person as having no justification ("I have a right to say what I think").

(A) *Special rights.* When rights arise out of special transactions between individuals or out of some special relationship in which they stand to each other, both the persons who have the right and those who have the corresponding obligation are limited to the parties to the special transaction or relationship. I call such rights special rights to distinguish them from those moral rights which are thought of as rights against (i.e., as imposing obligations upon)[11] everyone, such as those that are asserted when some unjustified interference is made or threatened as in (B) above.

(i) The most obvious cases of special rights are those that arise from promises. By promising to do or not to do something, we voluntarily incur obligations and create or confer rights on those to whom we promise; we alter the existing moral independence of the parties' freedom of choice in relation to some action and create a new moral relationship between them, so that it becomes morally legitimate for the person to whom the promise is given to determine how

the promisor shall act. The promisee has a temporary authority or sovereignty in relation to some specific matter over the other's will which we express by saying that the promisor is under an obligation to the promisee to do what he has promised. To some philosophers the notion that moral phenomena—rights and duties or obligations—can be brought into existence by the voluntary action of individuals has appeared utterly mysterious; but this I think has been so because they have not clearly seen how special the moral notions of a right and an obligation are, nor how peculiarly they are connected with the distribution of freedom of choice; it would indeed be mysterious if we could make actions morally good or bad by voluntary choice. The simplest case of promising illustrates two points characteristic of all special rights: (1) the right and obligation arise not because the promised action has itself any particular moral quality, but just because of the voluntary transaction between the parties; (2) the identity of the parties concerned is vital—only this person (the promisee) has the moral justification for determining how the promisor shall act. It is *his* right; only in relation to him is the promisor's freedom of choice diminished, so that if he chooses to release the promisor no one else can complain.

(ii) But a promise is not the only kind of transaction whereby rights are conferred. They may be *accorded* by a person consenting or authorizing another to interfere in matters which but for this consent or authorization he would be free to determine for himself. If I consent to your taking precautions for my health or happiness or authorize you to look after my interests, then you have a right which others have not, and I cannot complain of your interference if it is within the sphere of your authority. This is what is meant by a person surrendering his rights to another; and again the typical characteristics of a right are present in this situation: the person authorized has the right to interfere not because of its intrinsic character but because *these* persons have stood in this relationship. No one else (not similarly authorized) has any right[12] to interfere in theory even if the person authorized does not exercise his right.

(iii) Special rights are not only those created by the deliberate choice of the party on whom the obligation falls, as they are when they are accorded or spring from promises, and not all obligations to other persons are deliberately incurred, though I think it is true of all special rights that they arise from previous voluntary actions. A third very important source of special rights and obligations which we recognize in many spheres of life is what may be termed mutuality of restrictions, and I think political obligation is intelligible only if we see what precisely this is and how it differs from the other right-creating transactions (consent, promising) to which philosophers have assimilated it. In its bare schematic outline it is this: when a number of persons conduct any joint enterprise according to rules and thus restrict their liberty, those who have submitted to these restrictions when required have a right to a similar submission from those who have benefited by their submission. The rules may provide that officials should have authority to enforce obedience and make further rules, and this will create a structure of legal rights and duties, but the moral obligation to obey the rules in such circumstances is *due to* the co-operating members of the society, and they have the correlative moral right to obedience. In social situations of this sort (of which political society is the most complex example) the obligation to obey the rules is something distinct from whatever other moral reasons there may be for obedience in terms of good consequences (e.g., the prevention of suffering); the obligation is due to the co-operating members of the society as such and not because they are human beings on whom it would be wrong to inflict suffering. The utilitarian explanation of political obligation fails to take account of this feature of the situation both in its simple version that the obligation exists because

and only if the direct consequences of a particular act of disobedience are worse than obedience, and also in its more sophisticated version that the obligation exists even when this is not so, if disobedience increases the probability that the law in question or other laws will be disobeyed on other occasions when the direct consequences of obedience are better than those of disobedience.

Of course to say that there is such a moral obligation upon those who have benefited by the submission of other members of society to restrictive rules to obey these rules in their turn does not entail either that this is the only kind of moral reason for obedience or that there can be no cases where disobedience will be morally justified. There is no contradiction or other impropriety in saying "I have an obligation to do X, someone has a right to ask me to, but I now see I ought not to do it." It will in painful situations sometimes be the lesser of two moral evils to disregard what really are people's rights and not perform our obligations to them. This seems to me particularly obvious from the case of promises: I may promise to do something and thereby incur an obligation just because that is one way in which obligations (to be distinguished from other forms of moral reasons for acting) are created; reflection may show that it would in the circumstances be wrong to keep this promise because of the suffering it might cause, and we can express this by saying "*I ought not to do it though I have an obligation to him to do it*" just because the italicized expressions are not synonyms but come from different dimensions of morality. The attempt to explain this situation by saying that our real obligation here is to avoid the suffering and that there is only a prima facie obligation to keep the promise seems to me to confuse two quite different kinds of moral reason, and in practice such a terminology obscures the precise character of what is at stake when "for some greater good" we infringe people's rights or do not perform our obligations to them.

The social-contract theorists rightly fastened on the fact that the obligation to obey the law is not merely a special case of benevolence (direct or indirect), but something which arises between members of a particular political society out of their mutual relationship. Their mistake was to identify *this* right-creating situation of mutual restrictions with the paradigm case of promising; there are of course important similarities, and these are just the points which all special rights have in common, viz., that they arise out of special relationships between human beings and not out of the character of the action to be done or its effects.

(iv) There remains a type of situation which may be thought of as creating rights and obligations: where the parties have a special natural relationship, as in the case of parent and child. The parent's moral right to obedience from his child would I suppose now be thought to terminate when the child reaches the age "of discretion," but the case is worth mentioning because some political philosophies have had recourse to analogies with this case as an explanation of political obligation, and also because even this case has some of the features we have distinguished in special rights, viz., the right arises out of the special relationship of the parties (though it is in this case a natural relationship) and not out of the character of the actions to the performance of which there is a right.

(v) To be distinguished from special rights, of course, are special liberties, where, exceptionally, one person is *exempted* from obligations to which most are subject but does not thereby acquire a *right* to which there is a correlative obligation. If you catch me reading your brother's diary, you say, "You have no right to read it." I say, "I have a right to read it—your brother said I might unless he told me not to, and he has not told me not to." Here I have been specially *licensed* by your brother who had a right to require me not to read his diary, so I am exempted from the moral obligation not to read

it, but your brother is under no obligation to let me go on reading it. Cases where *rights*, not liberties, are accorded to manage or interfere with another person's affairs are those where the license is not revocable at will by the person according the right.

(B) *General rights*. In contrast with special rights, which constitute a justification peculiar to the holder of the right for interfering with another's freedom, are general rights, which are asserted defensively, when some unjustified interference is anticipated or threatened, in order to point out that the interference is unjustified. "I have the right to say what I think."[13] "I have the right to worship as I please." Such rights share two important characteristics with special rights. (1) To have them is to have a moral justification for determining how another shall act, viz., that he shall not interfere.[14] (2) The moral justification does not arise from the character of the particular action to the performance of which the claimant has a right; what justifies the claim is simply—there being no special relation between him and those who are threatening to interfere to justify that interference—that this is a particular exemplification of the equal right to be free. But there are of course striking differences between such defensive general rights and special rights. (1) General rights do not arise out of any special relationship or transaction between men. (2) They are not rights which are peculiar to those who have them but are rights which all men capable of choice have in the absence of those special conditions which give rise to special rights. (3) General rights have as correlatives obligations not to interfere to which everyone else is subject and not merely the parties to some special relationship or transaction, though of course they will often be asserted when some particular persons threaten to interfere as a moral objection to that interference. To assert a general right is to claim in relation to some particular action the equal right of all men to be free in the absence of any of those special conditions which constitute a special right to limit another's freedom; to assert a special right is to assert in relation to some particular action a right constituted by such special conditions to limit another's freedom. The assertion of general rights directly invokes the principle that all men equally have the right to be free; the assertion of a special right (as I attempt to show in Section III) invokes it indirectly.

III

It is, I hope, clear that unless it is recognized that interference with another's freedom requires a moral justification the notion of a right could have no place in morals; for to assert a right is to assert that there is such a justification. The characteristic function in moral discourse of those sentences in which the meaning of the expression "a right" is to be found—"I have a right to . . .," "You have no right to . . .," "What right have you to . . .?"—is to bring to bear on interferences with another's freedom, or on claims to interfere, a type of moral evaluation or criticism specially appropriate to interference with freedom and characteristically different from the moral criticism of actions made with the use of expressions like "right," "wrong," "good," and "bad." And this is only one of many different types of moral ground for saying "You ought . . ." or "You ought not. . . ." The use of the expression "What right have you to . . .?" shows this more clearly, perhaps, than the others; for we use it, just at the point where interference is actual or threatened, to call for the moral title of the person addressed to interfere; and we do this often without any suggestion at all that what he proposes to do is otherwise wrong and sometimes with the implication that the same interference on the part of another person would be unobjectionable.

But though our use in moral discourse of "a right" does presuppose the recognition that interference with another's freedom requires a moral justification, this would not itself suffice to establish, except in a sense easily trivialized, that in the recognition of moral rights there is implied the recognition that all men have a right to equal freedom; for unless there is some restriction inherent in the meaning of "a right" on the type of moral justification for interference which can constitute a right, the principle could be made wholly vacuous. It would, for example, be possible to adopt the principle and then assert that some characteristic or behavior of some human beings (that they are improvident, or atheists, or Jews, or Negroes) constitutes a moral justification for interfering with their freedom; *any* differences between men could, so far as my argument has yet gone, be treated as a moral justification for interference and so constitute a right, so that the equal right of all men to be free would be compatible with gross inequality. It may well be that the expression "moral" itself imports some restriction on what can constitute a moral justification for interference which would avoid this consequence, but I cannot myself yet show that this is so. It is, on the other hand, clear to me that the moral justification for interference which is to constitute a *right* to interfere (as distinct from merely making it morally good or desirable to interfere) is restricted to certain special conditions and that this is inherent in the meaning of "a right" (unless this is used so loosely that it could be replaced by the other moral expressions mentioned). Claims to interfere with another's freedom based on the general character of the activities interfered with (e.g., the folly or cruelty of "native" practices) or the general character of the parties ("We are Germans; they are Jews") even when well founded are not matters of moral right or obligation. Submission in such cases even where proper is not *due to* or *owed to* the individuals who interfere; it would be equally proper whoever of the same class of persons interfered. Hence other elements in our moral vocabulary suffice to describe this case, and it is confusing here to talk of rights. We saw in

Section II that the types of justification for interference involved in special rights were independent of the character of the action to the performance of which there was a right but depended upon certain previous transactions and relations between individuals (such as promises, consent, authorization, submission to mutual restrictions). Two questions here suggest themselves: (1) On what intelligible principle could these bare forms of promising, consenting, submission to mutual restrictions, be either necessary or sufficient, irrespective of their content, to justify interference with another's freedom? (2) What characteristics have these types of transaction or relationship in common? The answer to both these questions is I think this: If we justify interference on such grounds as we give when we claim a moral right, we are in fact indirectly invoking as our justification the principle that all men have an equal right to be free. For we are in fact saying in the case of promises and consents or authorizations that this claim to interfere with another's freedom is justified because he has, in exercise of his equal right to be free, freely chosen to create this claim; and in the case of mutual restrictions we are in fact saying that this claim to interfere with another's freedom is justified because it is fair; and it is fair because only so will there be an equal distribution of restrictions and so of freedom among this group of men. So in the case of special rights as well as of general rights recognition of them implies the recognition of the equal right of all men to be free.

Notes

64 *Philosophical Review* 175 (1955)

1 I was first stimulated to think along these lines by Mr. Stuart Hampshire, and I have reached by different routes a conclusion similar to his.

2 Further explanation of the perplexing terminology of freedom is, I fear, necessary. *Coercion* includes, besides preventing a person from doing what he chooses, making his choice less eligible by threats; *restraint* includes any action designed to make the exercise of choice impossible and so includes killing or enslaving a person. But neither coercion nor restraint includes *competition*. In terms of the distinction between "having a right to" and "being at liberty to," used above and further discussed in Section I, B, all men may have, consistently with the obligation to forbear from coercion, the *liberty* to satisfy if they can such at least of their desires as are not designed to coerce or injure others, even though in fact, owing to scarcity, one man's satisfaction causes another's frustration. In conditions of extreme scarcity this distinction between competition and coercion will not be worth drawing; natural rights are only of importance "where peace is possible" (Locke). Further, freedom (the absence of coercion) can be *valueless* to those victims of unrestricted competition too poor to make use of it; so it will be pedantic to point out to them that though starving they are free. This is the truth exaggerated by the Marxists whose *identification* of poverty with lack of freedom confuses two different evils.

3 Save those general rights (cf. Section II, B) which are particular exemplifications of the right of all men to be free.

4 Is the notion of *a* right found in either Plato or Aristotle? There seems to be no Greek word for it as distinct from "right" or "just" (δικαίον) though expressions like τὰ ἐμά δικαία are I believe fourth-century legal idioms. The natural expressions in Plato are τὸ ἑαύτου (ἔχειν) or τὰ τιν ἱ ὀφειλόμενα, but these seem confined to property or debts. There is no place for a moral right unless the moral value of individual freedom is recognized.

5 As W. D. Lamont has seen: cf. his *Principles of Moral Judgment* (Oxford, 1946); for the jurists, cf. Hohfeld's *Fundamental Legal Conceptions* (New Haven, 1923).

6 Here and subsequently I use "interfere with another's freedom," "limit another's freedom," "determine how another shall act," to mean either the use of coercion or demanding that a person shall do or not do some action. The connection between these two types of "interference" is too complex for discussion here; I think it is enough for present purposes to point out that having a justification for demanding that a person shall or

shall not do some action is a necessary though not a sufficient condition for justifying coercion.

7 I write " 'duties' " here because one factor obscuring the nature of a right is the philosophical use of "duty" and "obligation" for all cases where there are moral reasons for saying an action ought to be done or not done. In fact "duty," "obligation," "right," and "good" come from different segments of morality, concern different types of conduct, and make different types of moral criticism or evaluation. Most important are the points (1) that obligations may be voluntarily incurred or created, (2) that they are *owed to* special persons (who have rights), (3) that they do not arise out of the character of the actions which are obligatory but out of the relationship of the parties. Language roughly though not consistently confines the use of "having an obligation" to such cases.

8 The use here of the generalized "duty" is apt to prejudice the question whether animals and babies have rights.

9 Cf. A. H. Campbell, *The Structure of Stair's Institutes* (Glasgow, 1954), p. 31.

10 Continental jurists distinguish between "*subjektives*" and "*objektives Recht*," which corresponds very well to the distinction between *a* right, which an individual has, and what it is right to do.

11 Cf. Section (B) below.

12 Though it may be *better* (the lesser of two evils) that he should.

13 In speech the difference between general and special rights is often marked by stressing the pronoun where a special right is claimed or where the special right is denied. "You have no right to stop him reading that book" refers to the reader's general right. "You have no right to stop *him* reading that book" denies that the person addressed has a special right to interfere though others may have.

14 Strictly, in the assertion of a general right both the *right* to forbearance from coercion and the *liberty* to do the specified action are asserted, the first in the face of actual or threatened coercion, the second as an objection to an actual or anticipated demand that the action should not be done. The first has as its correlative an obligation upon everyone to forbear from coercion; the second the absence in any one of a justification for such a demand. Here, in Hohfeld's words, the correlative is not an obligation but a "no-right."

Chapter 19

D. N. MacCormick

RIGHTS IN LEGISLATION

THERE MUST BE many for whom the beginnings of wisdom in the understanding and analysis of legal systems and legal concepts have been found in the lectures and the writings of H. L. A. Hart. Being one of whom that is true, I take particular pleasure in joining in the tributes to him in this *Festschrift* by presenting an essay on the subject of 'Rights', upon which subject he has had so many illuminating things to say during his career.[1] While I shall here advance a thesis which is fundamentally at variance with Hart's own account of rights, I cannot claim to be doing more than applying techniques learned from Hart in criticizing and (I hope) transcending that account of his.

I

The first point to be made about legal rights must seem, when made, to be of breath-taking banality. The point is that legal rights are conferred by legal rules, or (if you will) by laws.[2] What could be more obvious? Obvious as it may be, the point is one which has not been given sufficient weight in much of what has been written by legal theorists. The point being made that legal rights are conferred by legal rules, it should at once lead any jurist of the school of Hart to ask the question: 'What are the general characteristics of those legal rules which confer rights upon individuals—as distinct from imposing duties, granting powers, or whatever?'

(In *The Concept of Law*, for example, Hart quite rightly contends that to expound the meaning of terms such as 'duty' and 'obligation' one must first show that any particular obligation or duty arises in virtue of some legal rule, and one must then complete one's exposition by elucidating the general characteristics of those rules which impose duties or obligations.)[3]

That question which ought to be asked has not been asked and answered with clarity, partly indeed because of a false trail laid by the master himself in 'Definition and Theory in Jurisprudence', in which he based a famous account of the meaning and use of the term 'right' upon the supposition that the term was standardly used in sentences such as 'x has a legal right to . . .' which, as he put it, express 'conclusions of law'. The meaning of the phrase was thus best elucidated by explaining the conditions in which the statement 'x has a legal right' can be appropriately used as expressing a *true* conclusion of law. Such conditions are presupposed by, though not expressed in, the statement itself.[4]

All that depended upon a view which Hart used to state in his (unpublished) lectures on 'Legal Rights and Duties', delivered in Oxford in the early 1960s, the view that 'right' is a term used in discourse *about* the law, used for making statements *about* individual's positions as seen in terms of the law, rather than a term used in the law itself. 'Right' in this view is a term or concept used by the jurist or the commentator upon the law, used discursively, but not used dispositively in the law. The derivation from that view of the theory that 'expressing conclusions of law' is the *standard* use of the term is obvious enough.

At a quite simple empirical level, these assumptions underlying the early Hartian analysis can be falsified completely. The term 'right' and its congeners is in fact used regularly and frequently in dispositive legal utterances and documents. Consider for example section 2(1) of the Succession (Scotland) Act 1964:

> Subject to the following provisions of this Part of this Act—
>
> (a)   where an intestate is survived by children, they shall have right to the whole of the intestate estate.
>
> (b)   . . .

Of that Act, indeed, the first eight sections alone, comprising Part I of the Act, use the word 'right' twenty-four times, a tally which would be greatly swollen were one to incur the labour of counting its appearances throughout the whole Act. And if it were desired to demonstrate that this is by no means an entirely Caledonian eccentricity of the Scottish draftsman, one might cite a plethora of examples from the English property legislation of 1925, such as section 96(1) of the Law of Property Act 1925 which indeed piles entitlement *expressis verbis* on top of no less explicit 'right'.

> A mortgagor, so long as his right to redeem subsists, shall be entitled from time to time, at reasonable times, on his request, and at his own cost, and on payment of the mortgagee's costs and expenses in this behalf, to inspect and make copies or abstracts of or extracts from the documents of title relating to the mortgaged property in the custody or power of the mortgagee . . .

There is no need for further multiplication of examples such as these; they show conclusively that the language of 'rights' and of being 'entitled' is as well adapted to stating general premises of law (and indeed to establishing them by legislation) as it is to expressing particular conclusions of law. In fact to establish the conclusion that A (a Scotsman) has the right to a certain 'intestate estate' or that B (an Englishman) is entitled to make copies of certain documents of title held by a Building Society as mortgagee, one would have to refer to the rules of law in s.2(1) of the Succession (Scotland) Act and s.96(1) of the Law of Property Act. If the 'investitive facts' as set out in these and related provisions are satisfied in A's or in B's case, then each has indeed the right in question. But the premises from which the conclusions as to individual rights follow are rules which expressly purport to confer the postulated right on persons in general whenever the relevant investitive facts are realized. An inquiry into the nature of rights must therefore be an inquiry into the nature and character of the legal rules which concern the conferment of legal rights.

One characteristic which it would be a mistake to postulate as a necessary distinguishing feature of rules which confer rights would be that of expressly using the term 'right'. Consider section 46(ii) of the Administration of Estates Act 1925, which is in the following terms:

> The residuary estate of an intestate shall be distributed in the manner or be held on the trusts mentioned in this section, namely:
>
> . . .
>
> (ii)   If the intestate leaves issue but no husband or wife, the residuary estate of the intestate shall be held on the statutory trusts for the issue of the intestate.

The effect of that provision is very broadly similar to the effect of section 2(1)(a) of the Succession (Scotland) Act quoted above. But in this case the statute confers a right without saying so *expressis verbis*. While it is wrong to suppose that legislative provisions never speak of 'rights', it would be equally wrong to suppose that they always do whenever rights are being conferred.

II

Legal theorists have traditionally divided into two camps on the issue of the proper explanation of rights.[5] One line of thought, which may be called the 'will theory', asserts that an individual's having a right of some kind depends upon the legal (or, *mutatis mutandis*, moral) recognition of his will, his choice, as being pre-eminent over that of others in relation to a given subject matter and within a given relationship. The 'interest theory', by contrast, contends that what is essential to the constitution of a right is the legal (or moral) protection or promotion of one person's interests as against some other person or the world at large, by the imposition on the latter of duties, disabilities, or liabilities in respect of the party favoured. It is against the background of this clash of theories that we must pursue the question announced as to the general characteristics of those rules which confer legal rights. Are these to be conceived primarily in terms of giving a special status to the choice of one individual over others in relation to a given subject matter, or primrily in terms of the protection of the interests of individuals against possible forms of intrusion (or the advancement in other ways of individuals' interests)?

The answer which I shall offer to that question will be that the 'interest theory' is the more acceptable, though not to be accepted without modification. The essential feature of rules which confer rights is that they have as a specific aim the protection or advancement of individual interests or goods. The reasons for holding that view, and the necessary refinements of the view itself, can best be set out by showing the defects of the rival view, and so I shall proceed to expound, and criticize, what seems

to me the strongest version of the 'will theory', that advanced by Professor Hart[6] (appropriately enough to the present occasion).

(i) One class of rights is the class of rights which have correlative duties. Duties exist when there exist legal or social rules of a particular kind, in virtue of which individuals in certain circumstances are required to act or abstain from acting in certain ways. For any individual whose circumstances are an instance of those specified in the rule, it is true to say that he has a duty to act or abstain from acting as specified.

Of those rules which impose duties, some provide that the performance of the duty-act is to be conditional upon some other person's choice, either in the sense that it is to be performed only if and when he so requests, or in the sense that the other person can waive the requirement, and, if he does, the act (or abstention) need not be performed. When A's duty is in either sense made conditional upon B's choice, B may properly be said to have a right against A, a right that A act or abstain in the manner laid down in the rule. So also, when it is the case that in the event of A's breach of duty B has the power to take appropriate remedial action at law, at least if B has a discretion as to the use or non-use of that power.

Thus, for this class of right (sometimes called 'claim rights'[7] or 'rights of recipience')[8] the 'will theory' asserts that what is constitutive of rights is the way in which the law confers on certain individuals or classes of individuals power to waive or enforce the duties of other individuals, or other classes of individuals.

(ii) There are other classes of rights, for example liberty rights and power rights, in case of which the right-holder is, so to say, the active rather than the passive subject of the law. In so far as the law imposes no duty on me not to do so, I have a right to speak my mind (and you have no right that I should hold my tongue)— and that is a 'liberty right', a right constituted by freedom from legal duty to act or abstain in some specified way. What is more, it is sometimes the case that my acting in a certain way is not merely not impeded by the law, but is indeed recognized by law as achieving a certain change in the legal position of myself, or others, or both; for example, when an utterance of mine (intended as such) is recognized as a declaration of trust in favour of some other person over certain property. Such is a case of 'power right'.

In both these cases, yet more obviously than in the case of 'claim right' it is the law's recognition of the freedom or the legal efficacity of the choices of individuals which is central to the notion of 'a right'.

(iii) A further class of 'right', the so-called 'immunity right' presents on the face of it more difficulty for the will theory. This is the right which corresponds to lack of power in others. It may be the case not only that I have a (liberty) right to enter my place of work and to do my job, and a (claim) right to be paid for it, but also that I have a right not to be dismissed save on certain specified grounds proven by certain stipulated processes, and that because my employer cannot *validly* dismiss me from my job, because he has a disability to sack me. And so by way of general characterization of immunity rights we may say that whenever A's legal position is in certain respects protected from change by any act of B, in the sense that B lacks power to change it, A has an immunity (as against B) from having his legal position changed in that respect.

Professor Hart admits to a certain difficulty in accommodating 'immunity rights' within his over-all theory.[9] But he suggests that the characteristic manifestation of immunity rights within the law is their manifestation in constitutionally entrenched 'Bills of Rights' which protect various claims and freedoms against derogation or abrogation even by acts of legislation. He therefore regards these as being beyond the ordinary interests of the lawyer and belonging more to the province of the political or moral theorist. While some theory of rights other than that given by will theorists might be necessary

to account for such entrenched immunities, the fact (it is alleged) remains that the specific terminology of 'rights' is of peculiar utility to lawyers only when restricted to those instances of 'small-scale sovereignty' which the will theory takes to be constitutive of the notion of 'a right'—and to be the unifying thread among various types of right.

(iv) Subject to that qualification, it is asserted that what gives the concept 'right' its particular function and utility in legal language is that it draws attention to those relationships in which rules of law confer on one individual special recognition of his will or choice as predominating over that of others in the relationship. Such are the outlines of the theory which in the succeeding sections of the present essay I intend to refute.

III

There is something, on the face of it, odd about Hart's concession that immunities cannot be properly taken into account within the four corners of the 'will theory' as propounded by himself. For it is often the case that A's immunity is waivable by A's choice. If A owns a car, B cannot divest him of ownership by any unilateral act (if B is another private citizen); in other words, A's rights over the car are in this respect protected by (or do they simply include?) an immunity against B. But, of course, A's immunity from being divested of ownership in favour of B is not absolute, but conditional on his own choice to transfer or not transfer the property—otherwise sale, exchange, and gift would be impossible.

That being so, it follows that there is a class of immunities which could comfortably be brought within the Hartian version of the will theory, namely, the whole class of those immunities in relation to which the immunity-holder has a power of waiver. Looked at from the other party's point of view, from the point of view of the party B who is under a disability to alter A's legal position in some respect, such a disability may be absolute (B cannot enslave A, even if A should consent to be enslaved); or it may be conditional upon A's will; A has a right not to be assaulted by B, and B can't take that away from A, unless A agrees—for example, in a boxing match.

In the light of those facts, the reasonable extrapolation to make from Hart's thesis in relation to claims, liberties, and powers would be along the lines of including within the genus 'rights' only those immunities which lie within the immunity-holder's own power, those which he can waive or assert at will. Such would be 'immunity rights' (a species of the genus 'rights'); unwaivable immunities would belong outside of the genus 'rights'.

But surely the moment we make that extrapolation we hit upon the fundamental implausibility of the 'will theory'. It seems to me unproblematic to say that I have (legally and morally) a right not to be deprived of my personal freedom and a right not to be deprived of my property. The two rights seem to me to be on all fours with each other, at any rate when we are concerned with the propriety of using the noun 'right' in the statement of such propositions of law (or of morals); in my view, which I believe to be widely held, the former right is of greater importance than the latter—I would rather, if it came to the bit, be propertyless than be a slave. The laws of the U.K. certainly place a higher value on the right of freedom than on the right of property in a certain highly important respect: the former is regarded as absolute in the sense that no person can enslave any other, not even a person willing to be enslaved; whereas the latter is conditional upon the property-holder's will—no person can deprive another of his property *without his consent*.

Let us take note of the point. A's right to personal freedom involves B in having (a) a duty not to reduce A to a servile condition, e.g. by clapping him in irons; and (b) a disability to impose upon A the status of a slave; and (c) a

disability to change the relation (a) and (b) *even with A's consent*. A does not himself have power to waive his immunities in these respects—he too is under disability here, though it may well be said that the disability is to his own advantage in preventing him ever from bartering away his freedom, whatever the temptation. That, indeed, is one of the grounds upon which untutored common sense would found the assertion that the right to personal freedom is yet more securely protected in our law than any right of property.

But there's the rub, there, for the 'will theory', the paradox. For it appears that this legal dispensation, be it ever so advantageous from the point of view of securing liberty, is so forceful as to thrust liberty beyond the realm of 'right' altogether. If there be no power to waive or assert the immunity, the claim, or whatever, upon some matter, upon that matter there is, *by definition*, no right either. In the matter of non-enslavement no person in any contemporary western legal system can *de jure* waive his immunity; the same is true of other interests characteristically protected by Bills of Rights (whence, perhaps, Hart's embarrassment over these in connection with the notion of 'immunity'). Are we really to conclude that here the terminology of 'rights' is inapposite? Really to conclude that the language of the practical lawyer does such violence to common understanding as to extrude such protections of human interests, when arguably at their most efficacious, from the category which it is interesting or useful to describe as 'rights'? The paradox would seem to me altogether too violent; the ascription of concerns to the practical lawyer, unconvincingly ethnocentric.

Admittedly, we are to some extent in the realms of stipulative definition when we enter into contention over the essential characteristics of the concept 'right'. Yet we are entitled to ask somebody who stipulates that there shall be held to be 'rights' only where there are choices, whether that stipulation does not go wholly against common understanding, and whether there is any profit derived from it.

What seems to me strangest is the way in which the will theory seems to cut off the use of 'rights'-language at a predetermined point on the scale of protection which the law may confer upon people's interests. To take a somewhat trivial case: the law relating to assault prohibits any person from offering or inflicting physical interference or harm on another. A has a duty not to interfere with B. So far as concerns the 'will theory', B has a 'right not to be harmed' only if and in so far as he, B, can in some way regulate A's duty not to interfere with him. That seems all very well: in relation to minor interference, or manly sports, or bona-fide surgical operations, B can waive A's duty. So, for the 'will theory', B has a right not to be trivially assaulted, or assaulted in the course of manly sports, or assaulted by a surgeon conducting an operation. Yet in relation to serious assaults, or 'unmanly' pastimes (e.g. flagellation by or of a prostitute),[10] or operations by unqualified persons, no valid consent can be given which releases the assaulting party from the duty of non-interference.[11] It is rather bewildering to suppose that none of us has a right not to be thus grievously assaulted, simply because for various reasons of policy the law denies us the power to consent to these graver interferences with our physical security.

Students of Dicey's *Law and Opinion* will recall his ill-disguised disapproval of those collectivist measures which were introduced in the later nineteenth century in order to protect various elements in the poorer sections of the population.[12] The technique which he deplored was as follows: first, the legislature conferred protection on people which they could have conferred on themselves by contract, e.g. in matters of safety at work; secondly, the legislators, discovering that too many of the protected class exercised the power 'voluntarily' to contract out of the protection, removed the matter from the option of the protected party altogether by depriving of legal effect such waivers of the statutory pro-

tection. Perhaps such legislation was as disgracefully paternalistic as Dicey so evidently thought it (though it cannot be said that this century has seen any reversal of its increase, far from it) but can it really be said that the second stage of protection is a stage at which a 'right' disappears? At stage one, the employer is obliged to take certain steps to protect his employee's safety, unless his employee 'contracts out'—here, for the 'will theory' is a classic case of 'right'. At stage two, the employer's duty is made unconditional upon the employee's will, and that with a view to protecting better the interests of employees individually and as a class—and now, for the will theory, the 'right' has gone. How odd that, as the protection is strengthened, the right disappears![13]

There is no point in multiplying such examples, of which there is certainly an abundance; the ones here given reinforce the particular case of the legal and moral protections of children which I have discussed in my recent paper on 'Children's Rights'.[14] If I may immodestly quote, and adopt from, that argument, I should like to repeat what I said in relation to what I conceive to be a child's (legal and moral) right to care and nurture:

> We are put . . . to our election. Either we abstain from ascribing to children a right to care and nurture [on the ground that no one has discretion to waive the responsible adult's duty of care and nurture] or we abandon the will theory. For my part I have no inhibitions about abandoning the latter. It causes me no conceptual shock or mental cramp to say that children have that right. What is more, I will aver that it is *because* children have that right that it is good that legal provision should be made in the first instance to encourage and assist parents to fulfil their duty of care and nurture, and secondarily to provide for its performance by alternative foster parents when natural parents are disqualified by death, incapacity, or wilful and persistent

neglect. *Ubi ius, ibi remedium.* So far from its being the case that the remedial provision is constitutive of the right, the fact is rather that recognition of the right justifies the imposition of the remedial provision.

We are all accustomed to talking and thinking about some rights as 'inalienable'. But if the will theory is correct, the more they are inalienable, the less they are rights. So far at least as concerns claim rights and immunities, I find the paradoxes with which the will theory is faced so great that, rather than swallow them, I am driven to seek an alternative. As a first step towards doing so, I should like to probe some of the grounds which have been suggested as foundations for the will theory with a view to showing that they are not as sound as they sound. In doing so I shall resume consideration of the statutory provisions referred to in my opening section.

IV

The principal advocates of benefit or 'interest' theories of rights correlative to obligations have shown themselves sensitive to the criticism that, if to say that an individual has such a right means no more than that he is the intended beneficiary of a duty, then 'a right' in this sense may be an unnecessary, and perhaps confusing, term in the description of the law; since all that can be said in a terminology of such rights can be and indeed is, best said in the indispensable terminology of duty.[15]

In that statement we find one of the principal grounds of Hart's case in favour of this theory, and against any version of interest theory. By introducing 'the idea . . . of one individual being given by the law exclusive control, more or less extensive, over another person's duty so that in the area of conduct covered by that duty the individual who has the right is a small-scale sovereign to whom the duty is owed', Hart claims to have shown us an idea by reference to which the 'terminology of . . . rights' can be used without redundancy to say things which cannot be said in the 'indispensable terminology of duty' by itself.[16]

This argument of Hart's perhaps has a certain force as against Bentham's account of rights—even in the brilliantly polished version of it expounded by Hart in his essay thereon. To rest an account of claim rights *solely* on the notion that they exist whenever a legal duty is imposed by a law intended to benefit assignable individuals (in which case all the beneficiaries of the law have rights as against all the duty bearers) is to treat rights as being simply the 'reflex' of logically prior duties. Accordingly, for any statement about rights there could always be substituted a statement about duties which would be at a more fundamental level analytically and which yet would say just the same as the 'rights statement'.

It is however no part of my intention here to advance a theory according to which even 'claim rights' are conceived as being merely the reflex of duties,[17] as though the latter must always be understood as being in every way prior to rights. Here I return to the importance of my introductory point, that legal rights are conferred by laws, and that scrutiny of those laws which confer rights must therefore be profitable, not to say essential, for understanding rights. In relation to the point in hand, let me refer again to section 2(1) of the Succession (Scotland) Act 1964: '(a) Where an intestate is survived by children, they shall have right to the whole of the intestate estate.'

It is worth taking a few moments (and repeating a point which I have made elsewhere)[18] in explaining the context and effects of that provision. Under it, whenever a person domiciled in Scotland dies intestate leaving children, there automatically vests in those children a right to the whole of that part of his estate statutorily entitled 'the intestate estate' (i.e. the residue after certain statutorily established prior claims have been satisfied). At the moment at which the right vests, it is not a 'real right' involving ownership of the estate or any particular assets included in it. Rather, each child's right is a right to receive in due course an equal share in the assets remaining in the executor's hands after satisfaction of prior claims. So it seems that we have a normal right–duty relationship, which could as well have been stated in the 'indispensable terminology of duty' as in the terminology which commended itself to the draftsman.

The problem, however, is that whereas the right vests at the moment of the intestate's death, there is not at that moment an executor to bear a correlative duty. Vesting of the right is temporally prior to the vesting in any other individual of the correlative duty, which can occur only when an executor has in due course been judicially confirmed or appointed. The executor dative has then the duty to wind up the estate and to transfer appropriate shares in the intestate estate to those having right thereto. What is more, when the question of confirmation of an executor dative is raised before the relevant court, a person who has beneficial rights in the estate is normally *on that ground* to be preferred to other parties, at least if the estate appears to be solvent. So one of the intestate's children may, *because of this right conferred on him by the Act*, have a resultant preferential right to be confirmed as executor. His confirmation as such will in turn result in his incurring the duties of executor, including the duty of distributing the intestate estate to those (including himself) who have right thereto under section $2(1)(a)$ of the 1964 Act.

In this case, therefore, it is not only the case that the vesting of a given right is temporally prior to the vesting of the correlative duty, but it is also the case that the vesting of the right in a given individual is a ground for confirming him in that office to which is attached the duty correlative to the like rights of his brothers and sisters; so that in this context right is logically prior to duty as well. Here then we have a concrete instance of a 'right of recipience' which

correlates with 'duty' indeed, but in a much more interesting way than as being a mere 'reflex' of a duty which the legislator might have as readily imposed in simpler and more straightforward terms. An 'interest theory' of rights which can take account of such subtleties as this may well avoid the reproach of redundancy, as well as escaping the paradoxes in which (as the last section showed) the will theory is inevitably drawn.

In drafting a law to deal with intestate succession, a legislator might indeed be very likely to regard the crucial and primary question, as being who is to take the benefit of the estate left by the intestate, and to treat as secondary the means (appointment of executors or administrators, and imposition of appropriate duties upon them) of securing that the benefit in view should actually reach the hands of the intended beneficiary. It is the end which makes sense of the means, not vice versa. This is as obvious in relation to section 46 of the (English) Administration of Estates Act 1925, which likewise confers rights of succession on intestacy though without saying so expressly, as in relation to Section 2 of the Succession (Scotland) Act 1964.

In such a case, given that the legal system recognizes and establishes a system of private property, there is necessarily a vacant 'estate' whenever somebody dies possessed of property. The system must make *some* provision as to the destination of that estate. Whoever gets it, to him will be owed all the duties which are owed to property owners, and to him will ensue also the various liberties, powers, and immunities which accrue to property owners, but *that* person gets all that only because—only if—the law has already vested in him the right of ownership of the property in question. And the step before that is the conferment on some generically identified type of person(s) of the right to have ownership of some part of or share of the property comprising the estate invested in him. What is essentially at stake is, who is to get the more or less substantial advantage of inheriting what share of what part of the estate. It is a quite secondary question to settle by what precise means (imposition of duties and disabilities on *whom?*) that advantage shall be secured to him.

It seems obviously—even trivially—true that at least one function, and that a prominent one, of such laws as those concerning succession, is that they are concerned with the conferment and securing of advantages to individuals; or, rather, to members of given classes severally.[19] To explain the idea of 'members of given classes severally': section 2(1)(a) of the Succession (Scotland) Act protects and promotes the interests of a certain class, the class of children of a parent who has died intestate but possessed of some property. But the protection is not of the interests of the class indiscriminately, taking them all together as a group—as, perhaps, aircraft-noise-control legislation indiscriminately protects everybody living or working or doing anything else in the near vicinity of airports. The protection, in the succession case, is rather of each and every individual who is within that class each in respect of some separate share of an identified estate.

It is not necessarily the case that each individual acquiring a right under the law should experience it as a benefit, an advantage, an advancement or protection of his interests. Perhaps there are some people who have been more harmed than benefited by an inheritance. Perhaps in some cases property inherited—e.g. slum properties subject to statutory tenancies at controlled rents—are literally more trouble than they are worth, and, besides, something of an embarrassment to their proprietor. None of that is in any way inconsistent with the proposition that the function of the law is to confer what is considered to be normally an advantage on a certain class by granting to each of its members a certain legal right.

The case of the mortgagor's entitlement (under s.96(1) of the Law of Property Act 1925) to inspect and make copies of title-deeds, also quoted as an example in the introductory section of the present paper, further indicates the way in which a legislator's concern with protecting what are conceived to be legitimate interests of the members of a given class of individuals leads naturally to the framing of legislation in terms of the rights or entitlements of the given class rather than in terms of the correlative obligations of the mortgagee. In just this sense, what is essential to a clear and comprehensible law relating to mortgages is that the relevant legislation should make clear the respective advantages, protections, and powers accruing to each of the parties to any mortgage. Judicial enforcement of the legislation may then proceed by elucidation and enforcement of duties etc. as necessarily consequential upon conferment of the relevant rights.

By contrast with this branch of the law, the criminal law is no doubt primarily concerned with duties,[20] with laying down in clear and precise terms the prohibitions infraction of which may expose the citizen to prosecution and punishment. This of course follows from a respect for the right of individuals to freedom from interference by the state save for breach of clear rules of the criminal law. Thus, in so far as it is an important function of the criminal law to protect important individual rights—to freedom, to physical and mental security, and so on—it is nevertheless not surprising that the law is not expressly framed in terms of rights, but rather in terms of duties, or through the imposition of duties by the denomination of offences. Even at that, however, there is a large part of the criminal law which deals with crimes against property, and which therefore necessarily presupposes the existence of that elaborate and interlocking set of laws which define and regulate the institution of property and the many and various rights in relation thereto which the law confers. Rights of, and rights in relation to, property—e.g. a mortgagor's right to redeem, a child's right of intestate succession—are on the face of it much too complex to be dissoluble into a set of bare reflexes of correlative duties. But that is not an objection to the thesis that right-conferring laws are best understood in terms of a standard intention to confer some form of benefit or advantage or protection of interests upon the members of a class severally rather than collectively. There may indeed be simple cases in which some general duty—e.g. a duty not to assault—is imposed upon everyone at large with a view to protecting the physical security of each and every person in society, and where the 'right not to be assaulted' is simply the correlative of the duty not to assault; no doubt in such simple cases the 'terminology of rights' does not enable us to say very much more than can be said in the terminology of duty. But it may be well adapted even in this simple case to expressing a reason why people aggrieved by breaches of certain duties *should* be empowered to take various measures and actions at law to secure remedies therefor, and why they *should* be permitted, at least when there are no strong countervailing reasons of policy, to waive other people's duties in this respect. If I'm allowed to be the best judge of my own good, and if such laws (being right-conferring) are aimed at securing what's good for me, why should I not be allowed to have a say over their operation when only my own protection is at stake?

What is more, there are other, more complex, cases in which the legislative decision to confer certain benefits on individuals who satisfy certain generic qualifications ('institutive' or 'investitive' facts) is logically prior to the vesting or the enforcement of a correlative duty. Taken as a whole, there is no reason to suppose that an 'interest theory' so defines 'rights' as to make the term redundant.

In another context, I have expressed as follows the conclusion which follows from arguments such as the foregoing:[21]

To ascribe to all members of a class C a right to treatment T is to presuppose that T is, in all normal circumstances, a good for every member of C, and that T is a good of such importance that it would be wrong to deny it to or withhold it from any member of C. That as for moral rights; as for legal rights, I should say this: when a right to T is conferred by law on all members of C, the law is envisaged as advancing the interests of each and every member of C, and the law has the effect of making it legally wrongful to withhold T from any member of C.

That is certainly not a perfect or watertight formulation, nor am I sure that I can at present make it so. But it does bring out the three features which must be included in any characterization of rules which confer rights.

First, they concern 'goods' (or 'advantages', or 'benefit', or 'interests', or however we may express the point). Whatever x may be, the idea of anyone's having a right to x would be absurd unless it were presupposed that x is normally a good for human beings, at any rate for those people who qualify as having the 'right' in question. That does not mean that in every case the x which is subject matter of a right need be beneficial to a particular potential right-holder, or be thought so by him. Some *hereditates* may be *damnosae*, but our general view of the law of succession as conceding 'rights' of succession is founded on the firm supposition that most are not.

Secondly, they concern the enjoyment of goods by individuals separately, not simply as members of a collectivity enjoying a diffuse common benefit in which all participate in indistinguishable and unassignable shares. But since necessarily the qualifications and conditions which must be satisfied for the application of such a rule of law in favour of any given individual have to be expressible and expressed in generic terms, it is therefore correct to say that such rules of law must be concerned with classes of individuals, but the benefit secured is secured to each and every individual severally upon satisfaction of the 'institutive' or 'investitive' conditions.

Thirdly, benefits are secured to individuals in that the law provides normative protection for individuals in their enjoyment of them. No doubt it is too narrow to envisage such protection purely in terms of its being 'legally wrongful to withhold T from any member of C'. 'Normative protection' may be understood as involving any or all of the various modes identified by Hohfeld and others. Thus an individual A may in the relevant sense be 'protected' in his enjoyment of x if

(a)   some or all other people are under a duty not to interfere with him in relation to x or his enjoyment of x, or

(b)   he is himself not under any duty to abstain from enjoyment of, or avoid or desist from x (being therefore protected from any complaint as to alleged wrongful use, enjoyment, etc. of x), or

(c)   some or all other individuals lack legal power to change the legal situation to the prejudice of A's advantage in respect of x (the case of disability/immunity), or

(d)   A himself is in some respect enabled by law to bring about changes in legal relations concerning x in pursuit of whatever he conceives to be his advantage.

Not every right entails protection at all these levels or in all these modes simultaneously, though more than one may be and all sometimes are (this being contrary to the Hohfeldian picture of rights as atomic relations between paired individuals). Consider section 5(1) of the Trade Union and Labour Relations Act 1974: '. . . [E]very worker shall have the right not to be— (a) excluded from membership (b) expelled from membership, of a trade union . . . by way of arbitrary or unreasonable discrimination.' That confers protection of at least the first three kinds; it being presumed that membership of a union is beneficial to any worker in normal circumstances (a) people at large are put under a duty not to injure any worker by getting him excluded or expelled from a trade union, (b)

every worker is in law free to apply for membership of a union of his choice, and (c) any act of purported expulsion of a worker from his union lacks legal effect if it is judged to be 'by way of arbitrary or unreasonable discrimination'. Consequentially, of course, A has various legal remedies which he may pursue for alleged infractions of the primary right conferred by the Act.

Thus using the terminology (in my view indispensable) of 'rights' the legislature can in short and simple words achieve complex legal protections for the several members of a given class. What is more, it can do so in a way which draws attention to the end in view, the protection of those people in relation to a supposedly advantageous condition of things. This serves better than would any alternative formulation the function of conveying to the population in general and to the judiciary in particular the intended aim and object of the measure.

The example most recently used can be used to show why we should not accept the Hohfeldian view of 'rights' as being reducible without residue to atomic relationships (belonging to one or other of his four types) between pairs of identified individuals; or even to sets of such relations. During the whole period when the 1974 Act was in force, any individual who was a worker had the right conferred by Section 5(1) of the Act. For any worker at any moment of time his having that right would have entailed a large set of Hohfeld-type atomic relationships with other individuals in a position to affect his membership (actual or projected) of some union. But although such individual atomic relationships are derivable from the existence of the right conferred by the Act, the converse is not true. The legislature can establish that vast myriad of atomic relationships by establishing the right to non-exclusion and non-expulsion. It could not establish the latter by establishing the former. (Of course, the legislature could establish a whole set of such 'atomic' relationships, but no particular set would be equivalent to the right actually established, which, depending on the circumstances which emerge, results in a variable set of claims, powers, etc.).

Rights, in short, may be more or less simple or complex and might be ranged on a scale of relative complexity. The more complex they are, the more it is necessary, at least for practical understanding, to envisage them as 'institutional' concepts, as I have elsewhere analysed that term.[22] For any given right, e.g. a right of real security, it is (at least for practical comprehension) necessary to distinguish 'institutive' (per Bentham, 'investitive') provisions which establish the conditions upon which the right in question vests in qualified individuals; 'consequential' provisions establishing the various normative protections enjoyed by 'rightholders' as such; and 'terminative' or 'divestitive' provisions establishing the conditions in which the 'right' is 'lost' or 'transferred'. In the case of complex provisions of this kind, the concept of 'right' is for practical purposes indispensable. Even if it were theoretically the case that the whole set of rules comprising a developed legal system could be restated purely in terms of the imposition of duties and the conferment of powers, which I doubt, it would be of no advantage for the practical comprehension of the law were anyone to do so. (The difficulties can be gleaned from a scrutiny of Bentham's heroic attempt to show, by way of prolegomenon to a codification project, how it might in principle be done.)

Even in the case of very simple legal provisions expressed in the duty-imposing mode, the interpretation of such rules as also conferring rights is not wholly without point. First of all, if it be supposed that the law was made with a view to protecting the good of individuals severally, so that every qualified individual has a correlative right to the duty (a Hohfeldian 'claim right'), that would supply at least a prima facie reason for supposing that individuals adversely affected by anybody's breach of the duty imposed ought to be entitled to seek a private law remedy, 'Ubi ius, ibi remedium'; to interpret a law as right-conferring is to give a justifying reason why there should be a remedy at private law for its breach. Secondly, and by a similar line of argument, it would appear that when such a law is conceived as conferring individual rights, individuals ought normally to have the power of waiving the duty in particular cases affecting only themselves.

If it be accepted that the identifying feature of right-conferring laws is to secure certain goods to individuals, and if it be accepted (as liberals accept it) that people should have free choice as to the pursuit or not of their own good, that constitutes a reason why, when the law confers rights on people, they *ought* to have the kind of choice which the will theory conceives to be analytically entailed by the term 'right'. But surely it is better to conceive of such 'powers of waiver', like remedial powers, not as being essential to the definition of, but as being consequential on the recognition or conferment of, rights. Paternalistic legislation which seeks to protect people's rights by preventing them from waiving them may be objectionable, but that is for argument. Surely it cannot be the case that, by definition, it destroys as 'rights' the rights which it seeks better to protect? Freedom of choice is a good, but it is not necessarily the only good.

The more one considers the matter, and the more one looks at rights in legislation, the more implausible become the contentions of the 'will theory' as to the definition and elucidation of rights. Rights must be understood in terms of the type of 'interest theory' advanced in this essay. From that it may be seen that there are powerful reasons why people should be free to exercise or not exercise their rights. But these reasons are points of moral and political substance, not analytic truths about rights. What is more, the experience of the past century suggests that in contexts of economic inequality the value of freedom of choice (in its guise as freedom of contract) may justifiably be overridden by other values, at least sometimes. That gives a further reason for not erecting the liberal principle about freedom of choice into an analytic truth following from the definition of 'right'. To follow Hart's example by seeking to elucidate the character not of 'rights' directly, but of the laws that confer them, is to find grounds for rejecting his own theory of rights.

Endnote: *Ius quaesitum tertio*

Of the arguments adduced by Hart against the 'benefit theory', the only one not dealt with here is that which concerns contracts in favour of third parties.[23] If *A* and *B* make a contract which has a provision for the benefit of *C*, it follows that there is a duty under the contract, which is intended to be for the benefit of *C*. Therefore, if the benefit theory is true, *C* has a right under the contract, but in some (indeed most) legal systems the existence of third-party rights under contract is not recognized, so the benefit theory cannot be true.

Observe that the argument proves too much, for with an obvious modification it applies to the will theory too. If *A* and *B* make a contract containing a provision in favour of *C*, to be carried out by *B* if *C* requests, but not if *C* does not request, is there a right in favour of *C*? Not under English law, even though that duty of *B*'s has been set up so that its performance is at *C*'s option.

The point in both cases is that under English law (unlike Scots law in either case) *A* and *B* retain the power to alter the provisions of their contract without *C*'s consent. Since the term in *C*'s favour remains precarious until performed, it is not called a 'right'. What is crucial is the presence or absence of immunity. That embarrasses the will theory, but not the interest theory here propounded.

Notes

P. M. S. Hacker & Joseph Raz (eds.), *Law, Morality and Society* (Oxford 1977), pp. 189–209.

1 Hart's most interesting contributions on this subject in my opinion are: 'Definition and Theory in Jurisprudence', 70 *Law Quarterly Review* 37 (1954) at 47 f.; 'Bentham', *Proceedings of the British Academy* 48 (1962), 297; 'Are There Any Natural Rights', reprinted in *Political Philosophy*, ed. A. M. Quinton (Oxford, 1968); 'Bentham on Legal Rights' (hereinafter cited as 'B.L.R.') in *Oxford Essays in Jurisprudence*, 2nd series, ed. A. W. B. Simpson (Oxford, 1973).

2 Cf. J. Raz, *The Concept of a Legal System* (Oxford, 1970), pp. 175–83.

3 H. L. A. Hart, *The Concept of Law* (Oxford, 1961), esp. at pp. 82–6.

4 'Definition and Theory in Jurisprudence', pp. 49 f.

5 For a review of opposed theories see, e.g., G. W. Paton, *A Text-Book of Jurisprudence*, 4th edn (Oxford, 1972, ed. G. W. Paton and D. P. Derham), at pp. 285–90. Cf. also W. J. Kamba, 'Legal Theory and Hohfeld's Analysis of a Legal Right', [1974] *Juridical Review* 249–62.

In 'B.L.R.' Hart expounds Bentham's theory as an instance of 'interest theory' or (*per* Hart) 'benefit theory'; and he asserts the preferability of his own version of 'will theory' or, as he prefers to call it, 'choice theory'.

6 Variously in the works cited in n.1 above.

7 Cf. W. N. Hohfeld, *Fundamental Legal Conceptions* (New Haven, 1919; 3rd reprint, 1964); for variants of nomenclature, see W. J. Kamba, op. cit.

8 The term favoured by D. D. Raphael, in *Problems of Political Philosophy* (London, 1970), pp. 68–71.

9 See 'B.L.R.', pp. 198–200.

10 See *R. v. Donovan* [1934] 2 K.B. 498 for discussion of this instance, and of consent generally.

11 G. H. Gordon, *Criminal Law* (Edinburgh, 1967), pp. 773–6; J. C. Smith and B. Hogan, *Criminal Law*, 3rd edn (London, 1973), pp. 287–90.

12 A. V. Dicey, *Law and Opinion in England during the Nineteenth Century*, 2nd edn (London, 1924), pp. 260–9.

13 But note that in 'B.L.R.' at p. 192 Hart shows that the 'fullest measure of control' by one person over another's duty need not be present in every case of a right; there are several distinguishable elements in that 'fullest measure' of which powers of waiver or enforcement are only one (remedial powers and powers of waiver of remedial rights being others). But it must be at least embarrassing to him if measures conceived of as strengthening rights

standardly involve derogation from the fullest forms of control.

14 A paper read to the conference of the Association of Legal and Social Philosophy in Cambridge, April 1975, to be published in 1976 *Archiv für Rechts- und Sozialphilosophie*.

15 'B.L.R.', p. 190.

16 Ibid.

17 To this extent disagreeing with Geoffrey Marshall 'Rights, Options, and Entitlements' (in Simpson, ed., op. cit., pp. 228–41) with which otherwise I substantially agree. Cf. A. M. Honoré, 'Rights of Exclusion and Immunities against Divesting', 34 *Tulane Law Review* 453 (1959–60).

18 Op. cit. For a general account of the matters sketched here, see M. C. Meston, *The Succession (Scotland) Act 1964*, 2nd edn (Edinburgh, 1970).

19 For Hart's account of an essentially similar view of Bentham's, see 'B.L.R.', pp. 186–8. For another similar account, see John Austin on 'absolute' and 'relative' duties in the seventeenth chapter of *Lectures in Jurisprudence* (London, 1862).

20 Cf. 'B.L.R.', pp. 191–5.

21 Op. cit.

22 D. N. MacCormick, 'Law as Institutional Fact', 90 *Law Quarterly Review* 102 (1974).

23 'B.L.R.', pp. 195–6.

Chapter 20

Ronald Dworkin

RIGHTS AS TRUMPS

I. Rights and utility

RIGHTS ARE BEST understood as trumps over some background justification for political decisions that states a goal for the community as a whole.[1] If someone has a right to publish pornography, this means that it is for some reason wrong for officials to act in violation of that right, even if they (correctly) believe that the community as a whole would be better off if they did. Of course, there are many different theories in the field about what makes a community better off on the whole; many different theories, that is, about what the goal of political action should be. One prominent theory (or rather group of theories) is utilitarianism in its familiar forms, which suppose that the community is better off if its members are on average happier or have more of their preferences satisfied. There are, of course, many other theories about the true goal of politics. To some extent, the argument in favour of a political right must depend on which of these theories about desirable goals has been accepted; it must depend, that is, on what general background justification for political decisions the right in question proposes to trump. In the following discussion I shall assume that the background justification with which we are concerned is some form of utilitarianism which takes, as the goal of politics, the fulfilment of as many of people's goals for their own lives as possible.

This remains, I think, the most influential background justification, at least in the informal way in which it presently figures in politics in the Western democracies.

Suppose we accept then that, at least in general, a political decision is justified if it promises to make citizens happier, or to fulfil more of their preferences, on average, than any other decision could. Suppose we assume that the decision to prohibit pornography altogether does in fact, meet that test, because the desires and preferences of publishers and consumers are outweighed by the desires and preferences of the majority, including their preferences about how others should lead their lives. How could any contrary decision, permitting even the private use of pornography, then be justified?

Two modes of argument might be thought capable of supplying such a justification. First, we might argue that, though the utilitarian goal states one important political ideal, it is not the only important ideal, and pornography must be permitted in order to protect some other ideal that is, in the circumstances, more important. Second, we might argue that further analysis of the grounds that we have for accepting utilitarianism as a background justification in the first place—further reflection of why we wish to pursue that goal—shows that utility must yield to some right of moral independence here. The first form of argument is pluralistic: it argues for a trump over utility on the ground that though utility is always important, it is not the only thing that matters, and other goals or ideals are sometimes more important. The second supposes that proper understanding of what utilitarianism is, and why it is important, will itself justify the right in question.

I do not believe that the first, or pluralistic, mode of argument has much prospect of success, at least as applied to the problem of pornography. But I shall not develop the arguments now that would be necessary to support that opinion. I want instead to offer an argument in the second mode, which is, in summary, this. Utilitarianism owes whatever appeal it has to what we might call its egalitarian cast. (Or, if that is too strong, would lose whatever appeal it has but for that cast.) Suppose some version of utilitarianism provided that the preferences of some people were to count for less than those of others in the calculation how best to fulfil most preferences overall either because these people were in themselves less worthy or less attractive or less well-loved people, or because the preferences in question combined to form a contemptible way of life. This would strike us as flatly unacceptable, and in any case much less appealing than standard forms of utilitarianism. In any of its standard versions, utilitarianism can claim to provide a conception of how government treats people as equals, or, in any case, how government respects the fundamental requirement that it must treat people as equals. Utilitarianism claims that people are treated as equals when the preferences of each, weighted only for intensity, are balanced in the same scales, with no distinctions for persons or merit. The corrupt version of utilitarianism just described, which gives less weight to some persons than to others, or discounts some preferences because these are ignoble, forfeits that claim. But if utilitarianism in practice is not checked by something like the right of moral independence (and by other allied rights) it will disintegrate, for all practical purposes, into exactly that version.

Suppose a community of many people including Sarah. If the constitution sets out a version of utilitarianism which provides in terms that Sarah's preferences are to count for twice as much as those of others, then this would be the unacceptable, non-egalitarian version of utilitarianism. But now suppose that the constitutional provision is the standard form of utilitarianism, that is, that it is neutral towards all people and preferences, but that a surprising number of people love Sarah very much, and therefore strongly prefer that her preferences count for twice as much in the day-to-day political decisions made in the utilitarian calculus. When Sarah does not receive what she would have if her preferences counted for twice as much as those of others, then these people are unhappy, because their special Sarah-loving preferences are unfulfilled. If these special preferences are themselves allowed to count, therefore, Sarah will receive much more in the distribution of goods and opportunities than she otherwise would. I argue that this defeats the egalitarian cast of the apparently neutral utilitarian constitution as much as if the neutral provision were replaced by the rejected version. Indeed, the apparently neutral provision is then self-undermining because it gives a critical weight, in deciding which distribution best promotes utility, to the views of those who hold the profoundly un-neutral (some would say anti-utilitarian) theory that the preferences of some should count for more than those of others.

The reply that a utilitarian anxious to resist the right to moral independence would give to this argument is obvious: utilitarianism does not give weight to the truth of that theory, but just to the fact that many people (wrongly) hold that theory and so are disappointed when the distribution the government achieves is not the distribution they believe is right. It is the fact of their disappointment, not the truth of their views, that counts, and there is no inconsistency, logical or pragmatic, in that. But this reply is too quick. For there is in fact a particularly deep kind of contradiction here. Utilitarianism must claim (as I said earlier any political theory must claim) truth for itself, and therefore must claim the falsity of any theory that contradicts it. It must itself occupy, that is, all the logical space that its content requires. But neutral utilitarianism claims (or in any case presupposes) that no one is, in principle, any more entitled to have any of his preferences fulfilled than anyone else is. It argues that the only reason for denying the fulfilment of one person's desires, whatever these are, is that more or more intense desire must be satisfied instead. It insists that justice and political morality can supply no other reason. This is, we might say, the neutral utilitarian's *case* for trying to achieve a political structure in which the average fulfilment of preferences is as high as possible. The question is not whether a government can achieve that political structure if it counts political preferences like the preferences of the Sarah-lovers[2] or whether the government will in fact then have counted any particular preference twice and so contradicted utilitarianism in that direct way. It is rather whether the government can achieve all this without implicitly contradicting that case.

Suppose the community contains a Nazi, for example, whose set of preferences includes the preference that Aryans have more and Jews fewer of their preferences fulfilled just because of who they are. A neutral utilitarian cannot say that there is no reason in political morality, for rejecting or dishonouring that preference, for not dismissing it as simply wrong, for not striving to fulfil it with all the dedication that officials devote to fulfilling any other sort of preference. For utilitarianism itself supplies such a reason: its most fundamental tenet is that people's preferences should be weighed on an equal basis in the same scales, that the Nazi theory of justice is profoundly wrong, and that officials should oppose the Nazi theory and strive to defeat rather than fulfil it. A neutral utilitarian is in fact barred, for reasons of consistency, from taking the same politically neutral attitude to the Nazi's political preference that he takes to other sorts of preferences. But then he cannot make the case just described in favour of highest average utility computed taking that preference into account.

I do not mean to suggest, of course, that endorsing someone's right to have his preference satisfied automatically endorses his preference as good or noble. The good utilitarian, who says that the push-pin player is equally entitled to satisfaction of that taste as the poet is entitled to the satisfaction of his, is not for that reason committed to the proposition that a life of push-pin is as good as a life of poetry. Only vulgar critics of utilitarianism would insist on that inference. The utilitarian says only that nothing in the theory of justice provides any reason why the political and economic arrangements and decisions of society should be any closer to those the poet would prefer than those the push-pin player would like. It is just a matter, from the standpoint of political justice, of how many people prefer the one to the other and how strongly. But he cannot say that about the conflict between the Nazi and the neutral utilitarian opponent of Nazism, because the correct political theory, his political theory, the very political theory to which he appeals in attending to the fact of the Nazi's claim, does speak to the conflict. It says that what the neutral utilitarian prefers is just and accurately describes what people are, as a matter of political morality, entitled to have, but that what the Nazi prefers is deeply unjust and describes what no one is entitled, as a matter of political morality, to have. But then it is contradictory to say, again as a matter of political morality, that the Nazi is as much entitled to the political system he prefers as is the utilitarian.

The point might be put this way. Political preferences, like the Nazi's preference, are on the same level—purport to occupy the same space—as the utilitarian theory itself. Therefore, though the utilitarian theory must be neutral between personal preferences like the preferences for push-pin and poetry, as a matter of the theory of justice, it cannot, without contradiction, be neutral between itself and Nazism. It cannot accept at once a duty to defeat the false theory that some people's preferences should count for more than other people's and a duty to strive to fulfil the political preferences of those who passionately accept that false theory, as energetically as it strives for any other preferences. The distinction on which the reply to my argument rests, the distinction between the truth and the fact of the Nazi's political preferences, collapses, because if utilitarianism counts the fact of these preferences it has denied what it cannot deny, which is that justice requires it to oppose them.

We could escape this point, of course, by distinguishing two different forms or levels of utilitarianism. The first would be presented simply as a thin theory about how a political constitution should be selected in a community whose members prefer different kinds of political theories. The second would be a candidate for the constitution to be so chosen; it might argue for a distribution that maximized aggregate satisfaction of personal preferences in the actual distribution of goods and opportunities, for example. In that case the first theory would argue only that the preferences of the Nazi should be given equal weight with the preferences of the second sort of utilitarian in the choice of a constitution, because each is equally entitled to the constitution he prefers, and there would be no contradiction in that proposition. But of course the neutral utilitarian theory we are now considering is not simply a thin theory of that sort. It proposes a theory of justice as a full political constitution, not simply a theory about how to choose one, and so it cannot escape contradiction through modesty.

Now the same argument holds (though perhaps less evidently) when the political preferences are not familiar and despicable, like the Nazi theory, but more informal and cheerful, like the preferences of the Sarah-lovers who

think that her preferences should be counted twice. The latter might, indeed, be Sarahocrats who believe that she is entitled to the treatment they recommend by virtue of birth or other characteristics unique to her. But even if their preferences rise from special affection rather than from political theory, these preferences nevertheless invade the space claimed by neutral utilitarianism and so cannot be counted without defeating the case utilitarianism provides. My argument, therefore, comes to this. If utilitarianism is to figure as part of an attractive working political theory, then it must be qualified so as to restrict the preferences that count by excluding political preferences of both the formal and informal sort. One very practical way to achieve this restriction is provided by the idea of rights as trumps over unrestricted utilitarianism. A society committed to utilitarianism as a general background justification which does not in terms disqualify any preferences might achieve that disqualification by adopting a right to political independence: the right that no one suffer disadvantage in the distribution of goods or opportunities on the ground that others think he should have less because of who he is or is not, or that others care less for him than they do for other people. The right of political independence would have the effect of insulating Jews from the preferences of Nazis, and those who are not Sarah from the preferences of those who adore her.

The right of moral independence can be defended in a parallel way. Neutral utilitarianism rejects the idea that some ambitions that people might have for their own lives should have less command over social resources and opportunities than others, except as this is the consequence of weighing all preferences on an equal basis in the same scales. It rejects the argument, for example, that some people's conception of what sexual experience should be like, and of what part fantasy should play in that experience, and of what the character of that fantasy should be, are inherently degrading or unwholesome. But then it cannot (for the reasons just canvassed) count the moral preferences of those who do hold such opinions in the calculation whether individuals who form some sexual minority, including homosexuals and pornographers, should be prohibited from the sexual experiences they want to have. The right of moral independence is part of the same collection of rights as the right of political independence, and it is to be justified as a trump over an unrestricted utilitarian defence of prohibitory laws against pornography, in a community of those who find offence just in the idea that their neighbours are reading dirty books, in much the same way as the latter right is justified as a trump over a utilitarian justification of giving Jews less or Sarah more in a society of Nazis or Sarah-lovers.

It remains to consider whether the abstract right to moral independence, defended in this way, would nevertheless permit restriction of public display of pornography in a society whose preferences against that display were backed by the mixed motives we reviewed in the last part. This is a situation in which the egalitarian cast of utilitarianism is threatened from not one but two directions. To the extent to which the motives in question are moral preferences about how others should behave, and these motives are counted, then the neutrality of utilitarianism is compromised. But to the extent to which these are the rather different sort of motives we reviewed, which emphasize not how others should lead their lives, but rather the character of the sexual experience people want for themselves, and these motives are disregarded, the neutrality of utilitarianism is compromised in the other direction, for it becomes unnecessarily inhospitable to the special and important ambitions of those who then lose control of a crucial aspect of their own self-development. The situation is therefore not an appropriate case for a prophylactic refusal to count any motive whenever we cannot be sure that the motive is unmixed with moralism, because the danger of

unfairness lies on both sides rather than only on one. The alternative I described in the last part is at least better than that. This argues that restriction may be justified even though we cannot be sure that the preferences people have for restriction are untinged by the kind of preferences we should exclude, provided that the damage done to those who are affected adversely is not serious damage, even in their own eyes. Allowing restrictions on public display is in one sense a compromise; but it is a compromise recommended by the right of moral independence, once the case for that right is set out, not a compromise of that right.

II. Hart's objections

There are, then, good grounds for those who accept utilitarianism as a general background justification for political decisions also to accept, as part of the same package, a right of moral independence. I shall end this essay by considering certain objections that Professor H. L. A. Hart has made, in a recent article,[3] to a similar argument that I made some years ago about the connection between utilitarianism and these rights.[4] Hart's objections show what I think is a comprehensive misunderstanding of this argument, which my earlier statement, as I now see, encouraged, and it might therefore be helpful, as insurance against a similar misunderstanding now, to report these objections and my reasons for thinking that they misconceive my argument.

I suggested, in my earlier formulation of the present argument, that if a utilitarian counts preferences like the preferences of the Sarah-lovers, then this is a 'form' of double-counting because, in effect, Sarah's preferences are counted twice, once on her own account, and once through the second-order preferences of others that incorporate her preferences by reference. Hart says that this is a mistake, because in fact no one's preferences are counted twice, and it would under-count the Sarah-lovers' preferences, and so fail to treat them as equals, if their preferences in her favour were discarded. There would be something in this last point if votes rather than preferences were in issue, because if someone wished to vote for Sarah's success rather than his own, his role in the calculation would be exhausted by this gift, and if his vote was then discarded he might well complain that he had been cheated of his equal power over political decision. But preferences (as these figure in utilitarian calculations) are not like votes in that way. Someone who reports more preferences to the utilitarian computer does not (except trivially) diminish the impact of other preferences he also reports; he rather increases the role of his preferences overall, compared with the role of other people's preferences, in the giant calculation. So someone who prefers Sarah's success to the success of people generally, and through the contribution of that preference to an unrestricted utilitarian calculation secures more for her, does not have any less for himself—for the fulfilment of his more personal preferences—than someone else who is indifferent to Sarah's fortunes.

I do not think that my description, that counting his preferences in favour of Sarah is a form of double-counting, is misleading or unfair. But this description was meant to summarize the argument, not to make it, and I will not press that particular characterization. (Indeed, as Hart notices, I made it only about some of the examples I gave in which unrestricted utilitarianism produced obviously inegalitarian results.) Hart makes more substantial points about a different example I used, which raised the question of whether homosexuals have the right to practice their sexual tastes in private. He thinks I want to say 'that if, as a result of [preferences that express moral disapproval of homosexuals] tipping the balance, persons are denied some liberty, say to form some sexual relations, those so deprived suffer because by this result their concept of a proper or desirable form of life is despised by others, and this is tantamount to treating them as inferior to or of less worth than

others, or not deserving of equal concern, and respect'.[5]

But this misstates my point. It is not the result (or, as Hart later describes it, the 'upshot') of the utilitarian calculation that causes or achieves the fact that homosexuals are despised by others. It is rather the other way round: if someone is denied liberty of sexual practice by virtue of a utilitarian justification that depends critically on other people's moralistic preferences, then he suffers disadvantage in virtue of the fact that his concept of a proper life is already despised by others. Hart says that the 'main weakness' in my argument— the feature that makes it 'fundamentally wrong'—is that I assume that if someone's liberty is restricted this must be interpreted as a denial of his treatment as an equal. But my argument is that this is not inevitably or even usually so, but only when the constraint is justified in some way that depends on the fact that others condemn his convictions or values. Hart says that the interpretation of denial of liberty as a denial of equal concern is 'least credible' in exactly the case I discuss, that is, when the denial is justified through a utilitarian argument, because (he says) the message of that justification is not that the defeated minority or their moral convictions are inferior, but only that they are too few to outweigh the preferences of the majority, which can only be achieved if the minority is in fact denied the liberty it wishes. But once again this ignores the distinction I want to make. If the utilitarian justification for denying liberty of sexual practice to homosexuals can succeed without counting the moralistic preferences of the majority in the balance (as it might if there was good reason to believe what is in fact incredible, that the spread of homosexuality fosters violent crime) then the message of prohibition would, indeed, be only the message Hart finds, which might be put this way: 'It is impossible that everyone be protected in all his interests, and the interests of the minority must yield, regrettably, to the concern of the majority for its safety.' There is (at least in my present argument) no denial of treatment as an equal in that message. But if the utilitarian justification cannot succeed without relying on the majority's moralistic preferences about how the minority should live, and the government nevertheless urges that justification, then the message is very different, and, in my view, nastier. It is exactly that the minority must suffer because others find the lives they propose to lead disgusting, which seems no more justifiable, in a society committed to treating people as equals, than the proposition we earlier considered and rejected, as incompatible with equality, that some people must suffer disadvantage under the law because others do not like them.

Hart makes further points. He suggests, for example, that it was the 'disinterested' political preferences of liberals that tipped the balance in favour of repealing laws against homosexual relationships in 1967 in England, and asks how anyone could object that counting *those* preferences at that time offended anyone's rights to be treated as an equal. But this question misunderstands my point in a fundamental way. I do not argue—how could anyone argue?—that citizens in a democracy should not campaign and vote for what they think is just. The question is not whether people should work for justice, but rather what test we and they should apply to determine what is just. Utilitarianism holds that we should apply this test: we should work to achieve maximum possible satisfaction of the preferences we find distributed in our community. If we accepted this test in an unrestricted way, then we would count the attractive political convictions of the liberals of the nineteen-sixties simply as data, to be balanced against the less attractive convictions of others, to see which carried the day in the contest of number and intensity. Conceivably the liberal position would have won this contest. Probably it would not have.

But I have been arguing that this is a false test, which in fact undermines the case of utilitarianism, if political preferences of either the liberals

or their opponents are counted and balanced to determine what justice requires. That is why I recommend, as part of any overall political theory in which utilitarianism figures as a background justification, rights to political and moral independence. But the liberals who campaigned in the interests of homosexuals in England in the nineteen-sixties most certainly did not embrace the test I reject. They of course *expressed* their own political preferences in their votes and arguments, but they did not *appeal* to the popularity of these preferences as providing an argument in itself for what they wanted, as the unrestricted utilitarian argument I oppose would have encouraged them to do. Perhaps they appealed instead to something like the right of moral independence. In any case they did not rely on any argument inconsistent with that right. Nor is it necessary for us to rely on any such argument to say that what they did was right, and treated people as equals. The proof is this: the case for reform would have been just as strong in political theory even if there had been very few or no heterosexuals who wanted reform, though of course reform would not then have been practically possible. If so, then we cannot condemn the procedure that in fact produced reform on the ground that that procedure offended anyone's rights to independence.

Hart's misunderstanding here was no doubt encouraged by my own description of how rights like the right to moral independence function in a constitutional system, like that of the United States, which uses rights as a test of the legality of legislation. I said that a constitutional system of this sort is valuable when the community as a whole harbours prejudices against some minority or convictions that the way of life of that minority is offensive to people of good character. In that situation, the ordinary political process is antecedently likely to reach decisions that would fail the test we have constructed, because these decisions would limit the freedom of the minority and yet could not be justified, in political theory, except by assuming that some ways of living are inherently wrong or degrading, or by counting the fact that the majority thinks them so as itself part of the justification. Since these *repressive* decisions would then be wrong, for the reasons I offer, the constitutional right forbids them in advance.

Of course, the decision for reform that Hart describes would not—could not—be a decision justified only on these offending grounds. Even if the benign liberal preferences figured as data rather than argument, as I think they should not, no one would be in a position to claim the right to moral or political independence as a shield against the decision that was in fact reached. But someone might have been led to suppose, by my discussion, that what I condemn is any political process that would allow any decision to be taken if people's reasons for supporting one decision rather than another are likely to lie beyond their own personal interests. I hope it is now plain why this is wrong. *That* position would not allow a democracy to vote for social welfare programmes, or foreign aid, or conservation for later generations. Indeed, in the absence of an adequate constitutional system, the only hope for justice is precisely that people will vote with a disinterested sense of fairness. I condemn a political process that assumes that the fact that people have such reasons is itself part of the case in political morality for what they favour. Hart's heterosexual liberals may have been making the following argument to their fellow citizens. 'We know that many of you find the idea of homosexual relationships troubling and even offensive. Some of us do as well. But you must recognize that it would deny equality, in the form of moral independence, to count the fact that we have these feelings as a justification for penal legislation. Since that is so, we in fact have no justification for the present law, and we ought, in all justice, to reform it.' Nothing in this argument counts the fact that either the liberals or those they address happen to have any particular political preferences or convictions as itself an argument: the argument is made by appeal to

justice, not to the fact that many people want justice. There is nothing in that argument that fails to treat homosexuals as equals. Quite the contrary. But that is just my point.

I shall consider certain of the remaining objections Hart makes together. He notices my claim, that the rights people have depend on the background justification and political institutions that are also in play, because the argument for any particular right must recognize that right as part of a complex package of other assumptions and practices that it trumps. But he finds this odd. It may make sense to say, he remarks, that people *need* rights less under some forms of government than others. But does it make sense to say that they *have* fewer rights in one situation rather than another? He also objects to my suggestion (which is of course at the centre of the argument I made in the last section) that rights that have long been thought to be rights to liberty, like the rights of homosexuals to freedom of sexual practice or the right of pornographers to look at what they like in private, are in fact (at least in the circumstances of modern democracies) rights to treatment as an equal. That proposition, which Hart calls 'fantastic', would have the consequence, he says, that a tyrant who had forbidden one form of sexual activity or the practice of one religion would actually eliminate the evil rather than increase it if he broadened his ban to include all sex and all religions, and in this way removed the inequality of treatment. The vice in prohibitions of sexual or religious activity, he says, is in fact that these diminish liberty, not equal liberty; adding a violation of equality to the charge makes equality an empty and idle idea with no work to do.

These different objections are plainly connected, because they suppose that whatever rights people have are at least in large part timeless rights necessary to protect enduring and important interests fixed by human nature and fundamental to human development, like interests in the choice of sexual partners and acts and choice of religious conviction. That is a familiar theory of what rights are and what they are for, and I said that I would not give my reasons, in this essay, for thinking that it is in the end an inadequate theory of rights. I did say that this theory is unlikely to produce a defence of the right I have been considering, which is the right of moral independence as applied to the use of pornography, because it seems implausible that any important human interests are damaged by denying dirty books or films. But that is not much of an argument against the general fundamental-interests theory of rights, because those who accept that theory might be ready to concede (or perhaps even to insist) that the appeal to rights in favour of pornographers is an error that cheapens the idea of rights, and that there is nothing in political morality that condemns the prohibition of pornography altogether if that is what will best fulfil the preferences of the community as a whole.

My aim is to develop a theory of rights that is relative to the other elements of a political theory, and to explore how far that theory might be constructed from the exceedingly abstract (but far from empty) idea that government must treat people as equals. Of course that theory makes rights relative in only one way. I am anxious to show how rights fit into different packages, so that I want to see, for example, which rights should be accepted as trumps over utility if utility is accepted, as many people think it should be accepted, as the proper background justification. That is an important question because, as I said, at least an informal kind of utilitarianism has for some time been accepted in practical politics. It has supplied, for example, the working justification of most of the constraints on our liberty through law that we accept as proper. But it does not follow from this investigation that I must endorse (as I am sometimes said to endorse)[6] the package of utilitarianism together with the rights that utilitarianism requires as the best package that can be constructed. In fact I do not. Though rights are relative to packages, one package might still be

chosen over others as better, and I doubt that in the end any package based on any familiar form of utilitarianism will turn out to be best. Nor does it follow from my argument that there are no rights that any defensible package must contain—no rights that are in this sense natural rights—though the argument that there are such rights, and the explanation of what these are, must obviously proceed in a rather different way from the route I followed in arguing for the right to moral independence as a trump over utilitarian justifications.

But if rights figure in complex packages of political theory, it is both unnecessary and too crude to look to rights for the only defence against either stupid or wicked political decisions. No doubt Hitler and Nero violated whatever rights any plausible political theory would provide; but it is also true that the evil these monsters caused could find no support even in the background justification of any such theory. Suppose some tyrant (an Angelo gone even more mad) did forbid sex altogether on penalty of death, or banned all religious practice in a community whose members were all devout. We should say that what he did (or tried to do) was insane or wicked or that he was wholly lacking in the concern for his subjects which is the most basic requirement that political morality imposes on those who govern. Perhaps we do not need the idea of equality to explain that last requirement. (I am deliberately cautious here.) But neither do we need the idea of rights.

We need rights, as a distinct element in political theory, only when some decision that injures some people nevertheless finds prima-facie support in the claim that it will make the community as a whole better off on some plausible account of where the community's general welfare lies. But the most natural source of any objection we might have to such a decision is that, in its concern with the welfare or prosperity or flourishing of people on the whole, or in the fulfilment of some interest, widespread within the community, the decision pays insufficient attention to its impact on the minority; and some appeal to equality seems a natural expression of an objection from that source. We want to say that the decision is wrong, in spite of its apparent merit, because it does not take the damage it causes to some into account in the right way and therefore does not treat these people as equals entitled to the same concern as others.

Of course, that charge is never self-validating. It must be developed through some theory about what equal concern requires, or, as in the case of the argument I offered, about what the background justification itself supposes that equal concern requires. Others will inevitably reject any such theory. Someone may claim, for example, that equal concern requires only that people be given what they are entitled to have when their preferences are weighed in the scales with the preferences, including the political and moral preferences, of others. In that case (if I am correct that the right to sexual freedom is based in equality) he would no longer support that right. But how could he? Suppose the decision to ban homosexuality even in private is the decision that is reached by the balance of preferences that he thinks respects equality. He could not say that, though the decision treats homosexuals as equals, by giving them all that equal concern for their situation requires, the decision is nevertheless wrong because it invades their liberty. If some constraints on liberty can be justified by the balance of preferences, why not this one?[7] Suppose he falls back on the idea that sexual freedom is a fundamental interest. But does it treat people as equals to invade their fundamental interests for the sake of minor gains to a very large number of other citizens? Perhaps he will say that it does, because the fundamental character of the interests invaded have been

taken into account in the balancing process, so that if these are outweighed the gains to others, at least in the aggregate, were shown to be too large in all fairness to be ignored. But if this is so, then deferring to the interests of the outweighed minority would be giving the minority more attention than equality allows, which is favouritism. How can he then object to the decision the balancing process reached? So if anyone really does think that banning homosexual relationships treats homosexuals as equals, when this is the decision reached by an unrestricted utilitarian balance, he seems to have no very persuasive grounds left to say that that decision nevertheless invades their rights. My hypothesis, that the rights which have traditionally been described as consequences of a general right to liberty are in fact the consequences of equality instead, may in the end prove to be wrong. But it is not, as Hart says it is, 'fantastic'.

Notes

Jeremy Waldron (ed.), *Theory of Rights* (Oxford 1984), pp. 153–67.

1   See Ronald Dworkin, *Taking Rights Seriously* (London, 1978).

2   Though there are obvious dangers of a circle here. See Dworkin, 'What is Equality? Part I: Equality of Welfare', *Philosophy and Public Affairs* (1981).

3   Hart, 'Between Utility and Rights', *Col. L. Rev.*, 79 (1980), pp. 828, 836 ff.

4   See Dworkin, *Taking Rights Seriously*, Introduction, ch. 12, and Appendix, pp. 357–8. See also Dworkin, 'Liberalism', in Hampshire (ed.), *Public and Private Morality* (Cambridge, 1978); and Dworkin, 'Social Science and Constitutional Rights: the Consequences of Uncertainty', *J of L & Educ*, 6 (1977), p. 3.

5   Hart, *supra*, p. 842.

6   See, e.g, Hart, *supra*, p. 845 n. 43.

7   See Dworkin, *Taking Rights Seriously*, pp. 266–72.

Chapter 21

Joseph Raz

RIGHTS AND INDIVIDUAL WELL-BEING

GROUPS AND CORPORATIONS can and do have rights. Nations have a right to self-determination; Woolworth owns stores and has rights against its employees, etc. Yet there is a sense in which individual rights are the central case of rights. Corporate and collective rights are in that sense extensions of the institution beyond its primary terrain. When ascribing rights to groups and corporations, just as when holding them to be subject to duties, to be responsible, guilty, etc., one is treating them as individuals, applying to them concepts whose direct and primary application is to individuals, concepts which are comprehensible in these further applications only by extending to them features of their primary domain.

The primacy of individual rights is therefore not so much a special feature of rights as a fact about groups and corporations. They are individuals by extension, on sufferance only. Nevertheless, many have seized on the primacy of individual rights as one sign that the special role of rights, their special function or significance in moral and political thought, is that they represent the individual's perspective or interest against the general or public good or against the claims, demands, needs, or requirements of others generally. Challenging this view is the purpose of this essay. It has no specific target. It will not consider any of the many yet diverse writings which embraced the idea that in some such conflict between concern for the individual right-holder and the general good lies the key to the special role of rights in moral and political discourse. My target is rather a pervasive feeling, a generalized view of this nature which permeates much philosophical and some popular thought on the subject.

This being so, it may be surprising that I claim to be merely explicating the underlying features of our common culture. My contention is that the view that conflict between the individual and the general good is central to the understanding of rights misinterprets surface features of rights. The correction of such distortion will retain enough of the sources of the distortion to explain how it arises, and yet will avoid its misleading conclusions.

To the extent that the views to be outlined below can be here defended, the argument is phenomenological in style: it points to fundamental features of our common culture. No more than a gesture towards such an argument is possible here. But a word must be said in defence of relying on such an argument. Is it based on the complacent assumption that our moral beliefs and political arrangements are all right as they are? Not in the least. Though the conclusions are normative, they can and should be based on our common culture, for they do not defend a particular view about the proper distribution of rights or the specific grounds for the possession of rights. Such conclusions cannot rest on an examination of the status quo. What can be based on existing culture are conclusions about the nature of our concepts, their structure and general features, and about their role and function in moral and political thought. The question of the relation between concern for the right-holder and for the public good, and its significance to an understanding of the foundations of rights, belongs to this structural or conceptual level, hence the phenomenological approach.[1]

I. A problem to start from

There is a puzzle about rights which, even if not deep, is revealing of the motives for many of the common views about them. On the one hand, typically rights are to what is, or is thought to be, of value to the right-holder. On the other hand, quite commonly the value of a right, the weight it is to be given, or the stringency with which it is to be observed do not correspond to its value to the right-holder. Since rights are, generally speaking, to benefits, to what is in the interest of or is valuable for the right-holder, it is plausible to suppose that that interest is the basis of the right, i.e. that the reason for the right, its justification, is the fact that it serves the right-holder's interest. But in that case we would also expect the weight or importance of the right to correspond to the weight or importance of the interest it serves. Since this is clearly not the case, since the weight of rights diverges from the weight of the interests they serve, one would expect that the reasons for or justification of rights relate to considerations other than those interests. But if so, why do rights dovetail with interests? Why do we generally have rights only to what is in our interest? Can this be a mere coincidence?

The suggestion that no more than a coincidence is involved may be thought to be sustained by the cautious generalization stated that it is only generally the case that what one has a right to is in one's interest. But the possible exceptions to this rule are not ones which undermine the thought that there is a strong conceptual connection between a right and the interest of the right-holder. Most have to do with disputes about the nature of individual interest. Consider the view that offenders have a right to be punished. We find it odd precisely because being punished is not commonly thought to be in the interest of the punished. The defence of the right invariably includes showing that in fact it is, that it is not merely good that offenders are punished but that it is good to them to be punished. A person's interest will be understood to mean that which is good for him, i.e. that which makes his life intrinsically a better life, better not for others or for a cause but in itself as a human life. This familiar notion of personal well-being is the one that people use in deliberating about their own life, or aspects of it. The notion of the good life for a person is closely connected to the notion of the life that a person would (logically) desire for himself, be proud of or content with, etc. By and large it consists of the successful pursuit of and engagement in worthwhile pursuits, activities, and relationships, and in the absence of factors which impede such success. Once the notion of individual well-being is so understood we can remove the qualification and assert that rights are always to what is in the interest of the right-holder.[2]

It is, therefore, not accidental that rights are to what is in the interest of the owner, and it is implausible that that fact does not affect the reasons justifying the existence of rights. But saying this only restates the puzzle. For it seems equally clear that the importance of a person's right often bears little relation to the importance of his interest. One type of example is often produced to illustrate the point. I may own something which is of little value to me, say, an old shirt. Since it is my shirt, others have a duty to respect my right to it. Rights always justify the existence of duties on (some) others. This in itself shows that the right exceeds in importance the interest which it protects, since had I no right to it my interest in having the shirt would not have justified holding others to be duty-bound to let me have it.

The same conclusion can be reached by a different route. Imagine two people with an equal interest in having the shirt. It is clear that the one who owns it should have it. But as their interest gives them equal claim to it, this can only be because the right-holder's right to the shirt is a reason for giving it to him which is greater than his interest. His right does not merely reflect his interest, it adds to it an additional, independent reason.

II. Seizing the second horn: Sen's goal-rights

Faced with our mini-dilemma, Sen embraces the second horn with some gusto.[3] Pointing to the apparent lack of correspondence between the weight of rights and the weight of the interest in the object of the right, he concludes that rights are separate from a person's interests. In moral thought they represent independent moral goals with their own distinct weight. In considering what is to be done, we should act on the balance of reasons, which is based in part on a comparison of people's conflicting interests and in part on the additional, independent factor that some of them have rights.

Had morality been a hypothetical-deductive system designed to generate people's moral judgments, Sen's view might possibly be acceptable. It is possible that most of the moral judgments common in our society can be derived from an axiomatic system consisting of separate interest-promoting and rights-protecting principles. But morality resembles much more a system of reasoning or a network of intelligible connections between interconnected ideas. Moral theory is not committed to reproducing or vindicating common moral beliefs. It aims at displaying the connections between moral ideas and principles in ways which manifest their intelligibility. Sen's position leaves the puzzle we started from as perplexing as it was. It does not explain why rights are to benefits. This remains a mysterious coincidence, made even more mysterious by being a conceptually necessary coincidence. Sen cannot say that the point of rights is to protect and promote people's interests. According to him, while rights always serve the right-holder's interests, they do so by endowing the protection of these interests with importance greater than their intrinsic importance warrants. This mystery left unexplained raises the suspicion that if this is what rights are then no rights are ever justified.

I think that there is a second snag in Sen's account. It assumes that in reasoning what to do we normally add the weight of rights to the reasons arising from the interests those rights serve. When considering whether to take my friend's book without his consent, I am supposed to weigh as two separate and independent factors the value of the book to him and his right to the book. In fact, while the two factors figure in our reasoning, they figure as interdependent considerations. I will not take the book because it belongs to him and because it is important to respect this particular right more than (for instance) his right to the old shirt, because the book is of great value to him. The value of the book, in other words, figures in assessing the importance of the right, and is not an independent separate consideration.

III. Embracing the first horn: finessing the interest theory

The relevance of the interest promoted or protected by the right to the assessment of its importance is just what one would expect, given the close connection between rights and right-holders' interests. The trouble is that this merely returns us to the dilemma: if the two are that closely connected, why does the importance of rights so often fail to match the value of the interests of the right-holder that they are meant to protect? One response is to claim that in fact the alleged mismatch is merely illusory. A fuller, subtler understanding of the right-holders' interests will eliminate the worrying apparent discrepancy.

This response deserves to be taken seriously. Even if it fails to close the gap and to solve the puzzle, it may narrow the gap, instructing us in the process about the complex relationship between interests and values and the institutions which serve them. I refer to institutions deliberately, for one of the common arguments used to bridge the apparent gap between the weight of interests and that of rights is to the effect that rights belong to the ground level of practical thought in which we use simple-to-apply rules, whereas the interests protected by the rights are referred to at the more fundamental level of thought at which the justification for the ground-level rules are established. The need for ground-level rules to be simple to learn and apply is invoked to explain why they deviate from the accurate measure of the interest they are there to serve. This, however, does not after all show that there is a gap between the weights of rights and the right-holders' interests that they serve. The gap appears only if one has a blinkered view of the right-holders' interests that rights serve, a view which is blind to the interest in being able to guide one's action on the basis of simple and manageable rules.[4]

There is a second way in which the gulf between right-holders' interests and their rights may be claimed to be distorted by some superficial accounts of the question. They disregard people's interest in freedom, in being able to control a segment of their environment according to their will. Consider my interest in an old shirt or in a book. The previous remarks on such cases disregarded the fact that I have not only an interest in having the shirt or the book but also in being the one who decides whether I shall have them or destroy them.

The right-holder's interest in freedom is part of the justification of most rights and is the central element in the justification of some. It is, of course, particularly prominent in the justification of the great civil liberties. Freedom of religion, freedom of speech, freedom of association, of occupation, of movement, of marriage, and the like, are all important not because it is important that people should speak, should engage in religious worship, should marry or travel, etc., but because it is important that they should decide for themselves whether to do so or not.

While this point is obvious when we refer to these rights as 'freedom of such and such', or as civil liberties, it is less obvious when they are referred to as the right to marry, to travel, etc. Then we are liable to confuse the fact that the importance of the matters the rights deal with (speech, marriage, occupation) accounts for the importance of individual freedom in these matters with the different (and often much exaggerated) claim that individuals have an interest in exercising these rights in certain ways (getting married, speaking out, etc.). The confusion is all the more common in the case of some other rights. It is easy to overlook the role of the interest in freedom in the justification of property rights, and this accounts for much of the impression that there is a big gulf between the importance of the right-holder's interest and the importance of the right.

These remarks move us some way from our original puzzle. They lead to the rejection of the view that the interest of the right-holder in what he has a right to can be expected to be the reason for the right. While it is true that rights are to benefits, the justifying benefit need not be the benefit one has a right to. It is often the freedom to control the fate of that benefit. What the right is a right to, as the expression is here understood, depends on how the right is described, and often there are different ways of describing it, so that the same right can be said to be a right to marry and a right to have the freedom to marry, etc. What puzzles us, however, cannot be eliminated by verbal reformulations. It is the putative gap between the value of right-holders' interests on which a right is supposed to be based and the value of that right itself. The remarks above show that this gap is much smaller than often appears.

IV. The interest of others

While the gap may be narrower than it appears once the relations between rights and ground-level rules, and the importance of our interest in freedom, are taken into account, these considerations fail to bridge it. There are still the cases where you know not only that I do not need the book but that I do not mind and have no reason to mind your taking it without permission, i.e. that my interest in freedom is not at stake either. On such occasions, when all the facts are known and known to be known, there is no reason to follow a generalized simple rule. Rather, one would do better by acting on the basis of a more thorough and sensitive evaluation of the considerations underlying the rule.

Single-minded rights-holder interest theorists may not be deterred by the remaining mismatch between common evaluations of the importance of rights and their importance when judged according to their account of them. They may remind us that the appeal to common judgments concerning rights was not an end in itself. We were never set on vindicating common morality. Rather, we were looking for a better understanding of the concept of rights and its role in moral thought. The mismatch between common views about rights and the judgments generated by a theory was mere evidence that the theory missed some of the central features of the concept. If it did not, then the discrepancy in judgment is mere evidence of common fallacies about rights. Given that the remaining mismatch is not much, and is relatively sporadic and unsystematic, it seems consistent with the view that rights are indeed based exclusively on the interests of the right-holders, and that the notion is sometimes misapplied in practice.

In fact—and that is the snag in this argument—the remaining mismatch between the theoretical account we are examining and common judgments does include a systematic distortion of the role of rights in practical thought, and cannot be completely accounted for as a result of misapplying the concept. Though unusual, the right of a condemned pregnant woman not to be executed until after her child is delivered can serve as a point of departure. The right protects an interest of the woman, but the respect with which it is treated in some of the countries which maintain capital punishment is due to concern not for the woman but for her child. It is the child's interest which is the justifying reason for the woman's right. It is the woman's right none the less, for the child does not yet exist and has no rights, and because his interest in this respect is served by serving the interest of the woman.

Welfare law provides many similar examples. I, as a parent, have, in English law, a right to a periodic payment known as child benefit, which I receive because I am a parent and because benefiting me is a good way of benefiting my child. People who support invalid parents or spouses have similar rights to reductions in their tax liability, and there are many other examples. In all of them the weight of the right does not match the right-holder's interest which it serves, because in all of them the right is justified by the fact that by serving the interest of the right-holder it serves the interest of some others, and their interest contributes to determining the weight due to the right.

These examples indicate the road the argument should follow to solve the initial puzzle. How can rights both be based on the right-holders' interests and fail to match the weight and importance of these interests? They can since the right-holders' interests are only part of the justifying reason for many rights. The interests of others matter too. They matter, however, only when they are served by serving the right-holders' interests, only when helping the right-holder is the proper way to help others.

The examples mentioned have another

common feature which is, I suspect, of general significance. They are cases in which, so far as the rights in question extend, the interests of the right-holders and those of the others whose benefit is part of the justifying reason are doubly harmonious. Not only do the others benefit through the benefit to the right-holders but the right-holders themselves benefit from the service their rights do to those others.

All the examples have concerned benefits to dependent relations. People's success in pursuing worthwhile relationships contributes to their own well-being. Having rights which are designed to benefit one's children, spouse, or parents helps one in the conduct of one's relations with these people. Hence, by having rights for the benefit of others one does, in the cases we discuss, benefit oneself through benefiting others just as much as those others benefit from one's (financial) benefit secured by these rights.

Two clarificatory comments may help at this point. First, it is clear that the examples under discussion concern cases in which one is duty-bound to look after one's children, spouse, or parents. The right helps one in discharging one's duty, and it may be tempting to think that this shows that there is here a conflict between the right-holder's interest and that of his dependent relations. This would be to fall into the mistake of regarding a person's duties as essentially curtailing his freedom to pursue his own interest, and therefore as always in conflict with his interest. Far from this being so, duties often define avenues through which one's well-being can be promoted. The duties of friendship, for example, are part of what defines friendship and makes it a valuable option for people.[5] Second, two complementary points have been emphasized. On the one hand, rights are sometimes justified by the service they secure for people other than the right-holder. On the other, other people's interests count for the justification of the right only when they are harmoniously interwoven with those of the

right-holder, i.e. only when benefiting him is a way of benefiting them, and where by benefiting them the right-holder's interest is served. But this harmonious relation should not be thought to reduce the justification of the right to the interest of the right-holder alone. Though he gains from the benefit the right secures to others, the weight and importance of the right depends on its value to those others, and not on the benefit that this in turn secures to the right-holder. The dilemma of the relations between the right-holder's well-being and the right it justifies is solved by escaping between its horns, not by embracing one of them.

V. Rights and the common good

The examples we have considered are special, but they exemplify only one type of a general category, the most important and common type of which are rights which are based on the general interest, as well as on the interest of the right-holder. I shall refer variably to the 'general, or common good or interest' in its traditional sense, in which it refers not to the sum of the good of individuals but to those goods which, in a certain community, serve the interest of people generally in a conflict-free, non-exclusive, and non-excludable way.[6]

Oxford is even today a beautiful city. For the people of Oxford, its beauty is a common good in this sense, and so is the existence of those of its buildings, streets, town-planning regulations, etc., which lend it its beauty and preserve it. Living in a beautiful city, I am of course assuming, is in one's interest. It may conflict with some other aspects of one's interest. Some people leave beautiful cities to take a job, to look after their parents, to get married, etc. One may have conflicting interests, and one's interest in living in a beautiful city may not be one's greatest interest. So a person may have interests which conflict with his interest to live in a beautiful city. But even though not necessarily in their best interest all things considered, living in a beautiful city serves an aspect of everyone's interest, and therefore the beauty of a city is a good to its people. And it is a common good, for its enjoyment by one person does not detract from its enjoyment by others, and because none of its inhabitants can be denied that good. It is what I have called elsewhere a collective good, i.e. it is a conceptual truth that it is a public good in the currently common sense of the term among economists.

The protection of many of the most cherished civil and political rights in liberal democracies is justified by the fact that they serve the common or general good.[7] Their importance to the common good, rather than their contribution to the well-being of the right-holder, justifies the high regard in which such rights are held and the fact that their defence may involve a considerable cost to the welfare of many people. When people are called upon to make substantial sacrifices in the name of one of the fundamental civil and political rights of an individual, this is not because in some matters the interest of the individual or the respect due to the individual prevails over the interest of the collectivity or of the majority. It is because by protecting the right of that individual one protects the common good and is thus serving the interest of the majority.

The defence of this claim may start by observing that the common good often meets the condition of dual harmony with individual interest. Consider Juliet, an architect who is hired by Oxford City Council to devise a preservation scheme for central Oxford. She has a personal interest in being able to carry out the task. However, in doing her job she is serving the common good as well as her personal interest. If the public rises in uproar when property speculators scheme for her unjust dismissal, this is likely to reflect more than the public concern that an individual shall not be unjustly treated. It will also reflect the public interest in the beauty of the city. The evil is seen to be doubly great in being aimed against the common good as

well as being an injustice to an individual. In this case Juliet's interest displays the doubly harmonious relation to the public good. In protecting her interest one protects the common good, and, as always, the protection of the common good serves her interest since she is a member of the community.

Juliet's right is protected with particular vigour because of its importance to the common good. But hers is a special case. By dint of a combination of circumstances her interest in her contract of employment serves, for a time at least, the common good. The claim staked above is that a combination of private interest and the public good characterizes many of the fundamental civil and political rights and accounts for their centrality in our public culture.

The argument has two stages. The first establishes that the protection of individual civil and political rights serves the common good. The second shows that the common good served by those rights is, in the majority of cases, more important to individuals than the enjoyment of their own civil and political rights, and therefore that the status the rights enjoy in the liberal democracies is due to their contribution to the common good.

Consider freedom of contract. It is a vital means for assuring people a measure of control over the conduct of their affairs. Its value to individuals depends on protection from duress, deceit, misrepresentation, restraint of trade, etc. Hence individuals have rights securing them from such abuses. These rights also contribute greatly to the existence of an open market, i.e. an environment in which people can compete and make agreements free from the abuses we mentioned. The existence of such an environment is a common good. It serves not only those who make contracts. If you doubt this, think of young children. They do not make contracts, but they benefit from the fact that they live in a free society in which people generally have power to control the conduct of their own affairs, to the extent that that is guaranteed by freedom of contract and the existence of a free market. Furthermore, the existence of a free market and the institutions protecting it is a common good to all those who are thereby made able to make contracts, for our contractual relations are what they are because of the market and would have been very different but for it.

Here is a typical case of individual rights playing a major part in securing the existence of a common good. Similar relations between rights and the common good recur across a whole array of civil and political rights. Rights such as freedom of marriage and freedom of occupation are most like freedom of contract. They create an environment in which careers are freely chosen and family ties freely undertaken. In so doing they contribute to determining the character of marriage, and the significance of careers in the lives of individuals. For arranged marriages are, for the majority, a different kind of relationship from freely contracted ones, and the meaning for a skilled jeweller of his career differs depending on whether he engages in it out of his own free choice or because his father was a jeweller and he had virtually no choice but to follow in his footsteps. Freedom of contract, freedom of occupation, and freedom of marriage, by affecting the mode of entry into various relationships and enterprises, affect the nature, content, and significance of those enterprises. And their impact is not confined to those who make use of them. They affect everyone in the community where they prevail.

One last example will have to do here. Freedom of expression is among the foundation-stones of all political democracies. The right of free expression serves to protect the interest of those who have it and who may wish to use it to express their views. It also serves the interest of all those who have an interest in acquiring information from others. But here again the right serves the interests of those who are neither speakers nor listeners. Everyone who lives in a democracy is affected by the fact that this is a society enjoying a free exchange of information.

One may go one step further. If I were to choose between living in a society which enjoys freedom of expression, but not having the right myself, or enjoying the right in a society which does not have it, I would have no hesitation in judging that my own personal interest is better served by the first option. I think that the same is true for most people. Politicians, journalists, writers, etc., excepted, their right of free expression means little in the life of most people. It rightly means less to them than their success in their chosen occupation, the fortunes of their marriages, or the state of repair of their homes.

This explains why civil and political rights which are the prize of the official culture of liberal democracies do not enjoy a similar place in the estimation of most ordinary people. Many people judge them by their contribution to their well-being, and it is not much. Their real value is in their contribution to a common liberal culture. That culture serves the interests of members of the community. Given the great contribution that observance of the civil and political rights of individuals makes to the preservation of the common good, it would be irrational not to let that fact be reflected in the value of the rights. Given the doubly harmonious relation between the individual interest served by these rights and the public good they contribute to, and given that this mutually reinforcing relation is stable and secure, rather than coincidental, there is every reason to regard the value of the rights to the common good as part of their justification. That makes it also a factor in determining the weight of the rights. Here, then, we have arrived at the core of the explanation of our initial puzzle: in the case of the central civil and political rights of liberal societies, the main reason for the mismatch between the importance of the right and its contribution to the right-holder's well-being is the fact that part of the justifying reason for the right is its contribution to the common good.[8]

VI. The case for constitutional judicial review

Most of the liberal democracies have developed political systems which endow the courts with special responsibility for the protection of the fundamental civil and political life of the individual. Sometimes this is done through an attachment to a constitutional document with officially declared superior standing in which the fundamental rights are enshrined (as in the USA). Alternatively this is done in the name of fundamental doctrines of a common law; though formally the legislature can override such a law, the official assumption is that it will not intend to do so, and therefore legislative acts can be 'interpreted' beyond recognition to conform with the fundamental rights (as in the UK).[9] The question of the suitability of the courts to the task they are expected to perform raises many issues concerning the history of the countries concerned and their political culture and institutions, the exploration of which extends well beyond the province of political theory. The preceding reflections on the nature of rights do, however, throw some light on the question.

One of the ancient disputes concerning the role of constitutional review concerns the question of the relations between the courts and politics. Are the courts, in their constitutional adjudication, in charge of the creation and development of the law of the constitution in the light of political considerations of the kind which figure in ordinary and in constitutional law-making? Or are they to remain outside politics altogether? It is ancient wisdom that when both answers are repeatedly put to the critical test and are found, time and again, wanting, the fault lies with the question. Recent years have seen a new wave of attempts to escape the stifling barrenness of the question, and the preceding remarks point in the same direction.

Litigation concerning fundamental civil and political rights brings before the courts issues which inextricably combine issues of individual rights and issues of public policy concerning the common good. Any thought that the fact that the issues raised are matters of individual right keeps politics at bay is based on a profound misunderstanding of the nature of rights generally and of civil and political rights in particular.[10] Responsibility for fundamental rights brings the courts into the centre of the political arena, and makes their political involvement essential to their ability to discharge their functions.

Constitutional review is to be understood in relation to a model of a division of power between the different organs of government. But it is a division of political power—not a separation of powers which keeps the courts out of politics. It does not follow, however, that the courts merely duplicate the role of democratic or administrative law-making. There are many different kinds of political consideration, and constitutional review requires the courts to concentrate on one range of such considerations, while striving to steer clear of others.[11]

The politics of the common good, questions regarding what is and what is not in the public interest, are as controversial as other political issues. But they are relatively free from conflict. By and large they concern the question of what is in the interest of all. The controversy involved is that of people who share a common interest but disagree on the best way to pursue it. It is not unreasonable to develop a different political mechanism for handling controversies of this kind from that for controversies which fundamentally reflect conflicts of interests. In particular, there is more room for procedures which rely on open argument and less reason to rely on democratic procedures. To the extent that the democratic process is meant to establish what is in people's individual interests, and to encourage them to engage in trading some of their interests with others in return for reciprocal agreement, such procedures are particularly apt for the politics of conflicting interests. The reasons to use the same procedures in the politics of the common good are less compelling.

The fact that the politics of the common good differ from the politics of conflicting interests manifests itself in the fact that beliefs about the general principles defining the common good of a society constitute much of the common political culture of that society. Much as the details of the common good, including important details, are subject to controversy, its general principles are agreed upon at least by central sections of the population. This is no accident. A good cannot be a common good in a society, however much it deserves to be so, unless it is enshrined in its general practices and respected by its political culture.

The tie between the political traditions of a country and its common good provides the answer to one crucial objection to the preceding argument. It may be objected that I have exaggerated the degree to which controversies about the common good are free from conflict. They involve balancing the common good against other interests from individuals, and to that extent they too are affected by conflicts of interests. The point is valid. The actual degree of conflict involved depends to a considerable extent on the strength and limits of the common tradition underpinning belief in the common good.

We now have an outline of an account of the proper role of constitutional review in most liberal democracies, in matters of fundamental civil and political rights. Since these fundamental rights inextricably combine issues of individual interest with questions of the public interest, they can and should, like other issues of individual rights, be dealt with by the courts. But at the same time they inevitably involve the courts in politics, since they cannot be settled except by deciding questions concerning the public interest. Since, controversial though these issues are, they are relatively free from conflict of interests and are to be settled on the basis of the central tenets of the political tradition of the country

concerned, it is fitting that they should be removed from the ordinary democratic process and be assigned to a separate political process.

This means that the courts are political, but the political issues they deal with in constitutional review of fundamental rights differ for the most part in kind from the stuff that democratic politics is mostly concerned with. This does not mean, of course, that the job of the courts is to arrest the march of time and freeze the process of change which affects a country's political culture, and its common good, just as it affects everything else. All that is meant is that, in responding to change and in encouraging change, the courts should be attuned to the community's political traditions and to changes, which are normally continuous and gradual, in its common good, and not to short-term swings, however violent, in democratic politics.

The existence of a strong and independent judiciary and a legal profession imbued with the values of the liberal political culture of the country are necessary for the courts to be able to fulfil adequately this political role. When these and other necessary conditions obtain, one finds the familiar view of a judiciary which appears conservative and radical at the same time. It is conservative in its adherence to the persisting, only slowly changing tenets of a country's political culture. And yet it is radical in its willingness to ride political storms, to court unpopularity and the hostility of powerful groups in being loyal to those central traditions even in times when the tidal waves of politics make the majority or the powers that be blind to their value.

VII. Conclusion

A major theme of this essay is that the image of right as a bulwark of the right-holder's interest against the claim of others distorts the nature of the concept and its role in our thought. Little has been said to challenge directly theories such as Nozick's,[12] which start from first principles to derive propositions sustaining a view of rights in which their conflict with the interests and moral claims of others are central. But enough has been said to suggest that such views are radically revisionary. They gain no support from a balanced understanding of our concept of rights, nor from the role of rights in our moral and political culture.

The rejection of the picture of the fundamental conflict between the right-holder and the rest is premised on the rejection of another dichotomy, the dichotomy between self-interest and the moral claims of others, and alongside it the dichotomy between egoism and altruism. The traditional notion of the common good marks one crucial location where these distinctions fail. Instead of essentially competing with the well-being of the individual, the common good is presupposed by it. The range and nature of common goods determine the options available to individuals in their lives; they determine the channels which define the well-being of individuals. This leaves ample room for occasional conflict between individual well-being and the common good. But it marks the essential supportive connection between them.

Liberal political thought has often been guilty of overemphasizing the degree to which politics is a process of reconciling conflicting interests. The politics of the common good differs from the politics of conflict. The fact that it leads to heated public controversy should not obscure the difference, for we should not equate controversy with conflict of interests. This point is evident to academics, who naturally assume that no conflict of interest is essentially involved in the many academic controversies they engage in. The same is true of conflicts concerning the common good.

It is no accident that in the politics of the common good conflicting interests play a less important role than in other areas of politics. The existence of common goods depends on wide-ranging consensus. The relative absence of conflict of interests and the background of a common tradition makes the courts a suitable forum for the conduct of this branch of politics. Here, rights have a crucial role to play. Civil and political rights enjoy their centrality in our culture because they are effective means of protecting our liberal-democratic culture. The protection of rights is traditionally one of the central tasks entrusted to the courts. It is not surprising, therefore, that the courts have a central role to play in the politics of the common good. By serving individual rights they serve their community, in contributing to the protection and the development of its common culture.

Notes

First published in *Ratio Juris*, 5/2 (July 1992).

1 I do not mean to deny that a radical critique of our culture and its very concepts can sometimes be successful and play a legitimate role.

2 Several additional clarifications are called for but cannot be explored in detail here. One of them, the care one has to take in explaining the various common ways of stating what one has a right to, will be mentioned below. Another important clarification is obvious: what one can have a right to may be in one's interest to have in some respect but not in others. One may have a right to some valuable property which may make one a target for criminals or for temptation. It may be in one's overall interest not to have it, but as having the property is in one's interest in some respect one can have a right to it. Finally, sometimes the right-holder's interest, which is the reason or justification for his having the right, is not in what he has a right to but in the having of a right. Trivially, rights are assets. But only exceptionally is the fact that if I have a right to something I'll have an asset the justifying reason for my having that right. See *The Morality of Freedom* for a more thorough exploration of this as well as other aspects of the views expressed here.

3 A. Sen, 'Agency and Rights', *Philosophy and Public Affairs*, 11 (1982).

4 That interest is itself partly a derivative one. It is

the interest in having one's other interests reliably served, which cannot be done except by relying in most circumstances on simple rules. In part, however, it is a distinctive separate interest in having a life in which calculations and complicated evaluations play only a minor role. My remarks in the text above are consistent with the previous observation that the interests rights serve are used to determine the importance of rights. It is merely that only on relatively rare occasions would one avoid the general rule relating the average importance of an interest to the weight of the protecting right, and proceed to examine its importance to the individual concerned at the time in question.

5   On friendship, see Raz, *The Authority of Law*, ch. 15. There is no denying, of course, that commitments to friends and relations may well call for action contrary to self-interest on occasion.

6   For a particularly clear explanation of the notion see J. M. Finnis, *Natural Law and Natural Rights* (Oxford: Oxford Univ. Press, 1980), ch. 6.

7   Arguably the same is true of all rights, though the importance to the common good of protecting them varies from case to case.

8   I wish to claim that this is the only valid explanation of the puzzle, but this claim requires an extensive examination of alternative accounts of rights which cannot be undertaken here.

9   Far be it from me to suggest that the two types of protection of fundamental rights yield the same results. My only point is that the difference between them is often exaggerated, especially by those who overlook the degree to which the USA Supreme Court compromises with the legislative trends of the day. The difference in the practice of judicial review between the American court 100 years ago and the court today may well be greater than the difference between it and the British courts.

10   The comments in the text inevitably skirt round many issues. One of them is this: assume that the courts have to decide matters which concern the common good. It does not follow that it is for them to settle substantive questions concerning what is required by the common good. All they have to do is give effect to the legislator's understanding of what is required by the common good. This view is based on a misunderstanding of the nature of the law. While legislators have power to turn their views into binding law, they have to do so before their views become binding. Just entertaining certain thoughts, or even expressing them at cocktail parties, public lectures, or in newspaper articles does not make them into law. They have to be properly enacted. Legislators can and do bind the courts to give effect to their (the legislators') views on the common law when they enact them. But when they enact laws or bills of rights requiring the courts to give effect to people's right of free expression, or privacy, etc., what they enact is the duty of the court to ascertain what are the proper limits of such rights and enforce them. In doing so the legislators direct the courts to consider substantive issues concerning the common good, for the determination of the rights is impossible without this. For a similar argument see R. M. Dworkin, *Taking Rights Seriously*, 2nd edn (London: Duckworth, 1977).

11   Note that this is a matter of degree. In the practical world of politics no clean division of labour is possible.

12   R. Nozick, *Anarchy, State and Utopia* (New York: Basic Books, 1974).

VII. RIGHTS, TERRORISM, AND TORTURE

Introduction

TERRORISM IS NOT NEW. But since the bombing of the World Trade Center in New York on September 11th, 2001 and the subsequent bombings in London, Madrid and Bali, we know that terrorists are prepared to use ever more desperate measures to achieve their goals, including suicide bombers and the use of planes as missiles. Furthermore, terrorists are no longer largely contained in one geographical area—they now live and train in many different countries. In response to the atrocities of 9/11, the Bush administration declared a "war on terror." This began with an invasion of Afghanistan and subsequently Iraq with the declared mission of annihilating Al-Qaeda. But beyond this traditional warfare, the so-called "war on terror" had broader consequences for domestic law. In both the US and the UK, harsh anti-terrorism legislation was introduced which allowed for indefinite detention without trial for suspected terrorists.[1] Notoriously, the US government also constructed a detention camp at Guantanamo Bay in Cuba for foreigners it had captured in its military action in Afghanistan or arrested elsewhere in the world, and claimed the power to detain these prisoners indefinitely without trial as "unlawful enemy combatants" without granting them rights stipulated in the Geneva Conventions for prisoners of war and without allowing them access to lawyers or relatives.

These measures threaten the core human rights and liberties widely believed to be the hallmarks of a liberal, democratic country, most notably, the right to be free from arbitrary arrest, illegitimate detention and unfair treatment when in custody. This is not just a war in the classic sense, but also in the metaphorical sense of going all out (rather than piecemeal) against terrorist activity.[2] What justifies such breathtaking departures from cherished liberties? We are told that since 9/11, we have entered a "new era" where, in order to protect our security and prevent future attacks, government authorities need to be unshackled by the traditional constraints built into our criminal justice system.[3] If terrorists are using more drastic methods to achieve their ends, then we too need more drastic methods to deter them. Adhering to the standard criminal law requirements of protecting the rights of the accused, such as the presumption of innocence, undermines our ability to tackle terrorism effectively. As one British politician put it in parliamentary debate: "we cannot properly fight terrorism with one hand tied behind our backs, or give terrorists the unfettered right to defend themselves as they promote and prepare violent attacks on our society".[4]

The policies adopted to eradicate terrorism have tended to be justified on the basis that it is now necessary to strike a new balance between liberty and security, between the rights of those accused of murder and the safety of those who might be murdered. Jeremy Waldron dissects this political rhetoric about "balancing" and subjects it to probing analytic scrutiny. The challenge of responding to contemporary terrorism has become one of the defining issues of the present time. Waldron's analysis shows that beneath the urgently important practical questions about how we should respond to terrorism lie more abstract (but important) legal, political and ethical questions about the nature of rights and their limits, as well as the strength (and consequences) of our commitment to them. Clearly, the horrors of 9/11 generate immense fear about future terrorist threats. As Ronald Dworkin points out in a comment which is generalizable beyond the US, "people's respect for human and civil rights is very often fragile when they are frightened, and Americans are very frightened".[5] Waldron presents us with a number of reasons to be wary of succumbing too quickly to the idea that rights must be balanced against security. The very idea of balancing seems to run counter to Dworkin's influential claim that rights are "trumps" (see Section VI), namely, that they are not to be regarded as vulnerable to routine changes in social utility. At the very least, the law's response to terrorism forces us to question whether rights are as "resolutely anti-consequentialist"[6] as is sometimes believed, or whether it is legitimate to limit them when they come into conflict with more important interests or values. Beyond this jurisprudential discussion of the nature and limits of rights, Waldron notes that it is misleading to suggest that we are balancing *our* liberties against *our* security in the fight against terrorism. When we look more closely at the distribution of burdens and benefits entailed by this balancing exercise, it transpires that the proposed trade-off is actually between the rights and liberties of the few, against the alleged enhanced security of the vast majority of citizens whose liberties will in no way be threatened.

Terrorism and the law's response to it is an area of applied legal and political philosophy where many of the deepest jurisprudential questions come home to roost. Questions about the justifiability of torture, for example, prompt us to consider the classic natural law doctrine *lex iniusta non est lex*—that some legal edicts are too unjust to deserve the status of "law" (see Section I). It also requires that we think hard about the ideal of the rule of law and whether the relationship it posits between law and the state entails that torture cannot be legalised (see Section III).[7] It invites us to question whether a state subject to the rule of law is not only one where there are clear, predictable rules capable of guiding its subjects, but also one where the state's exercise of power and coercion is imbued with a "broader spirit of the repudiation of brutality".[8]

One of the consequences of 9/11 has been to make the question of the justifiability of torture a live political and legal issue. Whilst it would be naïve to think that torture was not practiced prior to 9/11 (even in democratic countries), what is different post 9/11 is that torture is more widely defended by politicians, lawyers and academics alike. It is no longer universally abhorred as an unthinkable option.[9] For example,

Harvard Law Professor Alan Dershowitz has argued that we should look again at the possibility of legalising torture by using "torture warrants".[10] These devices (last used in England in the 17th century) would permit a judge to licence the use of torture by the authorities when faced with the ticking-bomb hypothetical, which has long been a pedagogical favourite in law school and moral philosophy classes alike. In an updated variant of this hypothetical, Professor Dershowitz asks: what if on September 11th law enforcement officials had arrested terrorists boarding one of the planes and learned that other planes, then airborne, were heading towards unknown occupied buildings? Would they not have been justified in torturing the terrorists in their custody to get the information that would allow the target buildings to be evacuated?[11] This hypothetical beckons us to conclude that when the stakes are this high, torture cannot be out of the question.

Henry Shue firmly resists this conclusion and argues unequivocally that state-sponsored torture can never be justified. Moreover, he claims that ticking-bomb hypo-theticals are severely misleading because they rely on idealised and artificial features which are never present in reality, and therefore do not provide a useful guide for practical action: "The ticking bomb hypothetical is too good to be true—it is torture conducted by wise, self-restrained angels".[12] In other words, it is the eponymous "torture in dreamland". As empirical evidence shows that torture requires an insti-tutional and bureaucratic context in which to exist, is epidemic in nature, brutalizing, corrupting and not capable of being kept under rational control, we should not be seduced into supporting its legalisation because of over-simplified hypotheticals which obscure those features.[13] Jeff McMahan's article shows that one's views about what morality requires and one's views about what moral position should be enshrined in the law can come apart. McMahan does not believe that the prohibition on torture is a moral absolute. On the contrary, he argues that in certain rare circumstances, morality may permit or even require torture. However, he nonethe-less concludes that it should be *legally* prohibited because "the law also has to be formulated with a view both to the facts and to the expected consequences of its promulgation and enforcement".[14] In making this argument, McMahan shares some of Shue's pragmatic concerns about the nature and consequences of making torture legal.

One final issue not discussed directly by the writers in this section concerns the role of the courts when adjudicating state policies aimed at countering terrorism. The judicial record of opposing such policies in times of crisis is, at best, mixed. Rather than providing a meaningful challenge to such policies, the courts have often been overly deferential to the Executive branch of government.[15] Post 9/11, the question of the legality of many of the policies adopted by the US and UK governments has come before the courts and, in both countries, the courts have insisted that Executive detention without trial violates the rule of law and other constitutional requirements. Whilst not completely free of the charge of deference, these decisions may demon-strate that the courts can provide a check, however minimal, on a power-hungry Executive bent on violating rights. As such, they provide a useful heuristic for thinking about the value of entrenching rights and allowing the courts to enforce them, which is explored in Section VIII.

Notes

1 USA Patriot Act 2001 ("USA Patriot" is an acronym which stands for Uniting and Strengthening America by Providing Appropriate Tools Required to Intercept and Obstruct Terrorism); Anti-Terrorism, Crime and Security Act 2001 (UK).
2 Frances Kamm, "Terrorism and Several Moral Distinctions", *Legal Theory* 12, 2006, 19–69, 22.
3 Though many commentators are skeptical about the claim that the problems in countering contemporary terrorism are unprecedented, see e.g., David Feldman, "Human Rights, Terrorism and Risk: The Role of Politicians and Judges", *Public Law* 2006, 364–84.
4 Rt Hon. Charles Clarke M.P. (then Home Secretary), House of Commons, *Official Report*, October 26, 2005, cc.325–28.
5 Ronald Dworkin, "The Threat to Patriotism", *The New York Review of Books* 49, 2002, 328.
6 Jeremy Waldron, "Security and Liberty: The Image of Balance", p. 365.
7 For a consideration of this issue, see Waldron, "Torture and Positive Law: Jurisprudence for the White House", *Columbia Law Review* 105, 2005, 1681, 1739–43.
8 Waldron, "Torture and Positive Law", 1743.
9 David Luban, "Liberalism, Torture and the Ticking Bomb", *Virginia Law Rev* 91, 2005, 1425.
10 Alan Dershowitz, *Why Terrorism Works: Understanding the Threat, Responding to the Challenge*, New Haven, CT.: Yale University Press, 2002, pp. 156–63.
11 Dershowitz, *Why Terrorism* Works, 143–45.
12 Henry Shue, 'Torture in Dreamland', p. 381.
13 For reservations about the "ticking bomb" scenario along similar lines see David Luban, "Liberalism, Torture and the Ticking Bomb".
14 Jeff McMahan, "Torture, Morality and Law", p. 387.
15 See e.g., David Dyzenhaus, "Intimations of Legality Amid the Clash of Arms", *International Journal of Constitutional Law* 2, 2004, 244.
16 Case HCJ 5100/94, *Public Committee against Torture v. The State of Israel and the General Security Service* (1999) 7 BHRC 31, para. 39.

Further reading

Alan Dershowitz, *Why Terrorism Works: Understanding the Threat, Responding to the Challenge*, New Haven, Conn.: Yale University Press, 2002.

Ronald Dworkin, "The Threat to Patriotism", *The New York Review of Books* 49, February 28, 2002, 328.

Ronald Dworkin, "Terror & the Attack on Civil Liberties", *The New York Review of Books* 50, November 6, 2003.

Ronald Dworkin, "What the Court Really Said", *The New York Review of Books* 51, August 12, 2004.

David Dyzenhaus, "Intimations of Legality Amid the Clash of Arms", *International Journal of Constitutional Law* 2, 2004.

David Feldman, "Human Rights, Terrorism and Risk: The Roles of Politicians and Judges", *Public Law*, 2006, 364.

David Golove, "The Bush Administration's 'War on Terrorism' in the Supreme Court", *International Journal of Constitutional Law* 3, 2005, 128–46.

Sanford Levinson (ed.), *Torture: A Collection*, Oxford: Oxford University Press, 2004.

David Luban, "Liberalism, Torture, and the Ticking Bomb", *Virginia Law Review* 91, 2005, 1425.

Henry Shue, "Torture", *Philosophy and Public Affairs* 7, 1987, 124.

David Sussman, "What is Wrong with Torture?", *Philosophy and Public Affairs* 33, 2005, 1.

Jeremy Waldron, "Torture and Positive Law: Jurisprudence for the White House", *Columbia Law Review* 105, 2005, 1681.

The US cases

Boumediene v. Bush 553 US- (2008)

Rasul v. Bush 542 US-; 124 S.Ct 2686 (2004)

Hamdi v. Rumsfeld 542 US-; 124 S.Ct. 2633 (2004)

Rumsfeld v. Padilla 542 US-; 124 S.Ct. 2711 (2004)

The UK cases

A v. Secretary of State for the Home Department (no. 2) [2005] UKHL 71.

Questions

1. "Democracy must sometimes fight with one hand tied behind its back. Even so, a democracy has the upper hand. The rule of law and the liberty of an individual constitute important components in its understanding of security. At the end of the day, they strengthen it and this strength allows it to overcome the difficulties."

   President Aharon Barak, Supreme Court of Israel.

   Discuss the relationship between democracy, human rights and the rule of law posited by this statement.
2. Do you think that the metaphor of "balancing" is appropriate or helpful in thinking about the ways in which the law should respond to the threat of terrorism?
3. Is torture ever morally justified? Are there circumstances in which it ought to be legalised?

Chapter 22

Jeremy Waldron

SECURITY AND LIBERTY
The image of balance

I.

THERE SEEMS TO BE general acceptance in the wake of the terrorist attacks of September 11, 2001 that some adjustment in our scheme of civil liberties is inevitable. This is partly the product of political defeatism: the state is always looking to limit liberty, and a terrorist emergency provides a fine opportunity. People become more than usually deferential to the demands of their rulers in these circumstances and more than usually fearful that if they criticize the proposed adjustments they will be reproached for being insufficiently patriotic. There is also little likelihood that reductions in civil liberties will be opposed by the courts. Even in countries like the United States with strong judicial review, the courts have proved reluctant to oppose reductions in civil liberties in times of war or war-like emergency.[1] This makes it something of a mystery why legal scholars continue to defend the counter-majoritarian power of the judiciary on the ground that such a power will prevent panic-stricken attacks on basic rights by popular majorities. Those who make that argument know perfectly well that the judiciary is not immune from popular panic and that in times of emergency it usually proves itself "more executive-minded than the executive."[2] Anyway, with or without courts there is a dearth of serious political opposition to encroachments on civil liberty.

Political realism aside, there is also a sense that some curtailment of liberty might be *appropriate* in the wake of the terrorist attacks, and that it might be *unreasonable* to insist on the same restrictions on state action after September 11 as we insisted on before September 11.

A common suggestion invites us to think about this in terms of the idea of *balance*. According to this suggestion, it is *always* necessary—even in normal circumstances—to balance liberty against security. We always have to strike a balance between the individual's liberty to do as he pleases and society's need for protection against the harm that may accrue from some of the things it might please an individual to do. The former surely, cannot be comprehensive even under the most favorable circumstances—nobody argues for anarchy—and the latter has to be given some weight in determining how much liberty people should have. So there is always a balance to be struck. And—the suggestion continues—that balance is bound to change (and it is appropriate that it should change) as the threat to security becomes graver or more imminent. One newspaper columnist, Nicholas Kristoff, put it this way:

[T]errorist incidents in the 1970s (such as at the Munich Olympics) had maximum death tolls of about a dozen; attacks in the 1980s and 1990s raised the scale (as in the Air India and Pan Am 103 bombings) to the hundreds;

9/11 lifted the toll into the thousands; and terrorists are now nosing around weapons of mass destruction that could kill hundreds of thousands. As risks change, we who care about civil liberties need to realign balances between security and freedom. It is a wrenching, odious task, but we liberals need to learn from 9/11 just as much as the FBI does.[3]

This is the proposition I want to examine: a change in the scale and nature of the harms that threaten us explains and justifies a change in our scheme of civil liberties; and that process is best understood in terms of "striking a new balance between liberty and security."

II.

The idea of striking a new balance can be interpreted more or less literally. We know the language of balance is used in morality and politics when there are things to be said on both sides of an issue, values that pull us in opposite directions. But what does it mean to say that we confront this array of values or reasons by *balancing* the competing considerations? And what are we implying when we say the balance has shifted? Is it just a matter of our having thought of a new reason, or of new facts having given rise to new reasons, which weigh more on one side than the other? That we can make sense of: there is now (say, since September 11, 2001) something new to be said on one side of a familiar debate and nothing new to be said on the other. But "balance" also has connotations of quantity and precision, as when we use it to describe the reconciliation of a set of accounts or the relative weight of two quantities of metal. Where is the warrant for our reliance on this quantitative imagery when we say that the new consideration not only adds something to the debate but "outweighs" all considerations on the other side?

Here is one possibility. We know that liberty is in some respects a matter of more or less. For

example: I can range more or less widely without restrictions on my travel; or I may be permitted to come closer to or be kept back from important public sites or important public officials. So we may be able to make at least ordinal comparisons between different quantities of liberty L_x and L_y (for example, between one person's liberty and another's, or between my liberty one day and my liberty the following day).[4] And security may be conceived quantitatively, too, in terms of the extent of risk (R) faced by a person (where R equals the magnitude of a possible harm times the probability of its occurrence): we might say that a person is less secure the greater R is with regard to that person. With this primitive apparatus, we might then be able to express the idea of the security cost to a person A of another person B having a certain amount of liberty. The security cost to A of B's having a higher amount of liberty L_y rather than a lower amount L_x is the difference between two risks, the higher risk (let us call it R_n) to A from B's having the greater liberty (L_y) and the lower risk (R_m) to A of B's having the lesser liberty (L_x).

Now, if we assume (for the sake of argument) that the balance between security and liberty was exactly right on September 10, 2001, then maybe what happened the following day was that we became aware (or it became the case) that the risks of ceding a given amount of liberty were greater than we thought. Even on September 10, we knew that any amount of liberty carried with it a certain risk of harm. But we were prepared to accept a certain risk—say, R_n rather than a lower risk R_m—because any attempt to secure R_m would mean giving up something we valued at least as much as that extra security, namely, a certain degree of liberty: on September 10, we thought that to secure R_m we would have to diminish individual liberty from L_y to L_x; and we were not prepared to do that. However even on September 10 we were not prepared to cede a greater degree of liberty than L_y—say L_z—because we knew that that would carry a risk of harm greater than R_n.

And we were not prepared to accept a greater risk than R_n. However, it now turns out (in light of the events of September 11) that the cost of L_y (which we *were* prepared to concede) is much greater than we thought—say, R_o rather than R_n. Since we were prepared on September 10 to give up any degree of liberty that would pose a risk greater than R_n, consistency indicates that now we are going to have to settle for an amount of liberty much less than L_y—say, L_x—on September 12. That I think is what the case for "striking a new balance" is supposed to amount to. We have an idea of the maximum risk we are prepared to bear as a result of people's liberty, and we adjust their liberties downwards when it appears that the risk associated with a given quantum of liberty is greater than we thought (or greater than it used to be).

Of course it is possible that we could make the adjustment in the other direction. Instead of beginning with an idea of the maximum risk, R_n, we were prepared to bear as a result of people's liberty, we might begin with an idea of the minimum liberty, L_y, we were prepared to accept. The recalculation after September 11 would then require us not to accept less liberty but to brave a higher risk for the sake of the liberty we cherish. The appropriate changes in public policy, then, would be calls to greater courage, rather than diminutions of liberty. Most probably we work at the matter from both ends, and perhaps this is where talk of "balance" really comes into its own. Our liberties are not untouched. There has been a downward adjustment, to help address some of the graver risks. But even with the adjustments in civil liberties that have been put in place (and are likely to be put in place) since September 11, no one feels as secure as before: so everyone has to be a little braver for the sake of the modicum of liberty that is left.

III.

Readers may think all this is over-fussy. Surely everyone knows what we mean when we talk about the balance between liberty and security, and surely it is obvious that some adjustment has to be made after it becomes evident that terrorists can take advantage of our traditional liberties to commit murder on such a scale. Does it really need to be spelled out with this sort of algebra? Well, I think we *do* need to subject the balancing rhetoric to careful analytic scrutiny, and this for several reasons:

(i) *Objections to consequentialism.* Talk of balance—particularly talk of changes in the balance as circumstances and consequences change—may not be appropriate in the realm of civil liberties. Civil liberties are associated with rights, and rights-discourse is often resolutely anti-consequentialist. Maybe this imperviousness to consequences is something that rights-theorists need to reconsider. But that does not mean they should automatically buy into the sort of common-or-garden consequentialism involved in the argument set out in Section II.

(ii) *Difficulties with distribution.* Though we may talk of balancing our liberties against our security, we need to pay some attention to the fact that the real diminution in liberty may affect some people more than others. So, as well as the objection to consequentialism, justice requires that we pay special attention to the distributive character of the changes that are proposed and to the possibility that the change involves, in effect, a proposal to trade off the liberties of a few against the security of the majority.

(iii) *Unintended effects.* When liberty is conceived as *negative* liberty, a reduction in liberty is achieved by enhancing the power of the state. This is done so that the enhanced power can be used to combat terrorism. But it would be naive to assume that this is the only thing that that enhanced power can be used for. We need to consider the possibility that diminishing liberty might also diminish security against the state, even as it enhances security against terrorism.

(iv) *Real versus symbolic consequences.* Though talk of adjusting the balance sounds like hard-headed consequentialism, it often turns out that those who advocate it have no idea what difference it will actually make to the terrorist threat. Accordingly we must subject these balancing arguments to special scrutiny to see how far they are based on fair estimates of actual consequences and how far they are rooted in the felt need for reprisal, or the comforts of purely symbolic action.

I will discuss these concerns, one by one, in more detail in Sections IV through VII of this article, and I will try to show how they might apply to various issues of civil liberty.

As we pursue that discussion, we will need to bear in mind that the class of civil liberties at stake here is not necessarily a homogenous class of rights, principles, or guarantees. The term "civil liberties" represents a variety of concerns about the impact of governmental powers upon individual freedom. Because the issue of a change in the "balance" between civil liberties and security plays out slightly differently for different kinds of concern, let me briefly set out some distinctions.

(a) In its most straightforward meaning, "civil liberties" refers to certain freedoms understood as actions that individuals might wish to perform, which (it is thought) the state should not restrict. Free speech, religious freedom, freedom of travel fall into this category.

(b) We also use the phrase "civil liberties" to refer to more diffuse concerns about government power, which are not necessarily driven by any sense of a privileged type of action which individuals should be left free to perform. For example, the government's ability to listen in on telephone conversations is a civil liberties concern, even though the "liberty" in question—sometimes referred to as "privacy"—does not amount to very much more than the condition of not being subjected to this scrutiny.

(c) Sometimes "civil liberties" refers to procedural rights and powers which we think individuals should have when the state detains them or brings charges against them or plans to punish them. These are rights like the right not to be detained without trial, the right to a fair trial process, the right to counsel, etc.

This short list is by no means complete. A comprehensive account would also say something about (d) the rights associated with democracy and civic participation. Fortunately these rights have not been an issue in the current crisis. So for the rest of the article, I will focus mainly on (a), (b), and (c) and consider how the concerns I have outlined—(i) through (iv)—apply to them.

IV.

The first point—point (i)—is that we need a clear idea of what balancing is supposed to be so that we can determine whether it is even an appropriate tool to use with regard to civil liberties. The argument given in Section II assumes that an increase in risk is a *pro tanto* reason for diminishing liberty; maybe not a conclusive reason, but a reason that should count none the less. The argument assumes that the introduction of a new set of considerations (along the lines of "Now we have to worry about terrorism") or the perception that old reasons have greater weight ("Terrorists are more deadly than they used to be") *adds* something to one side of the balance of reasons that apply to the issue of liberty. It assumes that even though there are good reasons for protecting civil liberties, civil liberties must give way if the reasons in their favor remain the same while something is added to the reasons on the other side. But this may be misleading; for in certain contexts, it is not always appropriate to relate reasons to one another in this simple additive way.

Consider—as an analogy—the reasons associated with promise-keeping. If I have already promised to meet with a student to discuss his paper at 12.30 p.m., then I may not accept an invitation to lunch with a colleague at that time. There are good reasons not to inconvenience my student or disappoint his expectations, and those reasons outweigh the reasons associated with lunch. So far so good. But then what if I find out that it is going to be a *really delicious lunch* (which I did not know when I conceded that the obligation to the student "outweighed" the lunch invitation)? Does the introduction of this new factor change the balance? Not at all. The attractions of lunch and the importance of meeting my student are not to be weighed against one another, once the promise has been given. The existence of the promise provides a reason for not acting on considerations like the quality of the lunch; it provides what Joseph Raz has called an "exclusionary reason."[5]

Maybe something analogous is true of civil liberties. Maybe—like promises—they too are not supposed to be sensitive to changes on the scale of social costs. Certainly some have thought so. Civil liberties are often regarded as rights, and the idea of "rights as trumps"[6]—which many have found appealing, at least at the level of rhetoric—is precisely the idea that rights are not to be regarded as vulnerable to routine changes in the calculus of social utility.

Or consider a slightly different account—the proposition that civil liberties are best conceived as Nozickian side-constraints.[7] Perhaps the rule that the government must not imprison anybody it does not propose to charge with an offense is best understood on the model of the rule in chess that one may not move one's king into check. It would be like a side-constraint on the pursuit of one's goals, not something which is supposed to make the pursuit of one's goals more efficient overall. If this account were accepted, then the notion of a change in the pay-offs from detention without trial (greater security etc.) would be quite irrelevant; just as the change in pay-offs from moving one's king into check—"Just this once, it would really make a difference to my game"—is irrelevant in chess. (Or consider John Rawls's argument about the lexical priority accorded to the principle of basic liberties: if security falls into the domain of the principle governing social and economic goods, then a trade-off of liberty against security is simply ruled out.)[8]

None of this is conclusive against the balancing approach. "Rights as trumps" is so far just another piece of imagery to pit against "striking a new balance." And we must not be seduced by our technical familiarity with ideas like side-constraints or lexical priority into thinking that these can be applied unproblematically to civil liberties. On the contrary, there is much in our tradition of civil liberties thinking which cannot be modelled in this way. For instance, existing legal guarantees of civil liberties are always hedged around with explicit provisos to the effect that they may be limited "in the interests of national security, territorial integrity or public safety,"[9] and sometimes with implicit doctrines to the effect that the rights must be adapted to circumstances, the constitution is not a suicide pact, etc.[10] How far these should be regarded as political compromises to get the state to offer any guarantees at all, or how far they should be regarded as reasonable features of a well-thought-through theory of civil liberties is an open question.

Even apart from outright opposition to the trumping idea and the other models of special priority, there are various things that the proponents of "striking a new balance" can say in response to the concerns about consequentialism that I have raised in this Section.

They may say, first, that it is important to distinguish between two questions: (1) how is a given right defined? and (2) once defined, what sort of priority does it have over other goals and values? Even if the answer to question (2) is quite stringent—trumps, side-constraints, lexical priority, etc.—that is, even if balancing is precluded at that stage, still the idea of a balance may enter into the way we answer question (1). At the beginning of Section II, I said that liberty could be a matter of more or less. For example, I am free to move around the country but I am not free (unless invited) to come within touching distance of the President; and I could be made a little less free than that by being required to stand back, say, a hundred yards from the President. Where that boundary is drawn—from a few feet to a hundred yards—is surely a matter that requires consideration of consequences; it will be drawn differently in a republic with hand guns than in a republic where the weapon of choice for assassination is the stiletto. So we may say civil liberties are not even defined until some balancing exercise is undertaken. And all that is happening in a post-September 11 world is that our understanding of civil liberties is being made responsive to changes in the very factors that enter routinely into its definition. The balance does not affect the priority we accord to liberty: it affects only our discussion of what the appropriate liberty is. Admittedly this line is easier to take for those freedoms, like freedom of movement, that have no intrinsic definition and are obviously a matter of degree than for those—like free speech and freedom of religion—whose definition may be given in large part by the nature of the interests they embody. It will be quite implausible to say, for example, that ordinary political criticism does not count as "speech" in a time of crisis though it may count as "speech" in a time of peace.

Secondly, it should be noted that most of the philosophical theories which oppose routine trade-offs between rights and consequences nevertheless toy with the idea of some sort of "out" to avoid *ruat caelum* absolutism. Robert Nozick's caveat is typical:

> The question of whether these side constraints are absolute, or whether they may be violated in order to avoid catastrophic moral horror, and if the latter, what the resulting structure might look like, is one I hope largely to avoid.[11]

It may be thought that the events of September 11 do constitute exactly that—catastrophic moral horror—and that the occurrence of such horror should trigger whatever qualifications we are prepared to impose on our rights-absolutism. But it is important to notice that the *occurrence* of catastrophic horror is not the issue; the issue is whether the abrogation of rights is a plausible means of avoiding it. I shall say more about this in Section VII. For now, it is sufficient to point out that the balancing argument is supposed to turn on what we can achieve by diminishing liberty; it is not supposed to turn on the sheer fact of horror at what has happened nor of our fear at what might happen. Fear is only half a reason for modifying civil liberties: the other and indispensable half is a well-informed belief that the modification will actually make a difference to the prospect that we fear.

When Ronald Dworkin gave his version of the *ruat caelum* qualification—"Someone who claims that citizens have a right against the Government need not go so far as to say that the State is *never* justified in overriding that right"[12]—he suggested that the state may override a given right when this is necessary to protect the rights of others. This is a very common move in popular discussion of these matters. Someone worries aloud about changes in civil liberties and the rights of suspects etc., and people respond: "Well, what about the rights of those who might get blown up by terrorists?" Rights versus rights is a different ball-game from rights versus social utility. If security is also a matter of rights, then rights are at stake on both sides of the equation, and it might seem that there is no violation of the trumping principle or of the idea of lexical priority when some adjustment is made to the balance.

This business of conflicts of rights is a terribly difficult area—with which moral philosophers are only just beginning to grapple.[13] There are some who want to insist very strongly on distinctions between acts and omissions and on structures of agent-relativity that would make it quite wrong to posit an equivalence between a government violating someone's civil liberties and a government failing to save someone's life (because it refused to violate civil liberties).[14] Failing to do what is necessary to save P's life (because this would actively violate Q's rights) is not a way of disrespecting P; the responsibility rests with those—the terrorists—who kill P, not with the government that refuses to violate rights in order to stop them. Others, however, find the stringency of this approach unacceptable, either because they take a more consequentialist view of rights to begin with,[15] or because they accept that people do actually have certain rights to positive goods from their government—like the good of protection—which simply cannot be handled in the manner indicated in the previous sentence. But even those who find the acts/omissions and agent-relativity approach unacceptable are still nervous about treating the infringement of a right simply as a bad consequence to be minimized on the model of the utilitarian calculus. At the very least, they want conflicts of rights to be dealt with in a way that is sensitive to issues about the distribution of infringements. (Some argue, for example, that we should trade off rights-infringements against one another using a maximin model rather than a utilitarian model.)[16] Rights-talk is about respect for individuals, one-by-one; and these philosophers figure that if we abandon that distributive concern—which I discuss in more detail in the following section—then we forfeit

our entitlement to say that we are balancing conflicts of *rights* as opposed to simply maximizing the satisfaction of underlying interests.

It is not my intention to get very much further into this discussion. I only wanted to show the depth, the complexity, and the philosophically controversial character of the issues that open up when we start talking about balancing rights against interests that are included under the heading of "security" (whether we describe those too as rights or not). There is no consensus on any of these issues. But I think it is fair to say that even if there are very few who believe that rights should be utterly impervious to very large changes in social costs, there is almost nobody (who believes in rights) who thinks that they should be adjusted in every case where it appears that some other right-bearer has something to gain from the adjustment. Almost everyone believes that adjustments in rights require structured arguments for their justification—arguments that pay attention to their special character, to the ordered priorities of moral theory, and to the intricacies of various possible relations between one person's rights and another's.

So this should put us on warning that a peremptory use of the balancing idea—something has been added to one tray of the scale, so the balance must now be struck differently—will not do. If security outweighs liberty now in a way it did not outweigh it on September 10, then there must be complicated reasons (rather than simple consequentialist reasons) why that is so, reasons that are not necessarily captured in the straightforward additive connotations of the balancing argument in Section II.

V.

My second point is this: in order to evaluate the balancing argument, we have to ask tough questions about the *distribution* of the various changes envisaged in liberty and security. It is tempting to read the argument set out in

Section II in terms of a diminution in liberty for everyone—everyone's liberty is reduced from L_y to L_x—in order to secure the same amount of security for everyone. But often it does not work out that way.

The perpetrators of the September 11 attacks were foreigners, members of a foreign organization, and the U.S. government has taken that as grounds for drawing some quite sharp distinctions in its subsequent legislation between the protections accorded to the civil liberties of Americans and the protections accorded to others who are legally in the United States. Section 214 of the USA Patriot Act, for example, alters existing legislation concerning wire-tapping so that "investigation of a United States person is not conducted solely upon the basis of activities protected by the first amendment to the Constitution." (The class of "United States persons" includes American citizens and legally admitted permanent residents; but it does not include non-resident aliens legally present in the United States.) More importantly perhaps, the perpetrators of the September 11 attacks were not just non-residents but also members of a fairly visible ethnic group: and their actions mean that everyone (whether a United States person or not) who looks or dresses or speaks in any way like them is likely to face much greater levels of suspicion. Most of the changes in civil liberties are aimed specifically at suspected perpetrators or accomplices or persons who might be thought to have information about past or future terrorist actions, and most Americans assume that persons in these categories will look quite different from themselves.

True—as a legalistic matter, the changes in civil liberties may be formulated innocuously enough—"Anyone who is officially suspected of doing A or knowing B will have his or her liberty reduced from L_y to L_x"—and the "anyone" term seems universalizable. However, we must avoid a certain childish formalism in making the claim that civil liberties are diminished equally for everyone. As Ronald Dworkin points out,

None of the administration's decisions and proposals will affect more than a tiny number of American citizens: almost none of us will be indefinitely detained for minor violations or offenses, or have our houses searched without our knowledge, or find ourselves brought before military tribunals on grave charges carrying the death penalty. Most of us pay almost nothing in personal freedom when such measures are used against those the President suspects of terrorism.[17]

So perhaps the balance we ought to be discussing is not so much a balance between one thing we all like (liberty) and another thing we all like (security). It is more like the balance that is sometimes referred to when we say we should balance the interests of a dissident individual or minority against the interests of the community as a whole.

Ronald Dworkin has argued in a number of places that there is some confusion in the idea of a balance of interests between the individual and the community: "The interests of each individual are already balanced into the interests of the community as a whole, and the idea of a further balance, between their separate interests and the results of the first balance, is itself therefore mysterious."[18] But confusion is not the problem; the problem is moral, not logical. There are in fact two ways of parsing the idea of a balance between the interests of an individual and the interests of the community in the present context, neither of them reassuring.

First, talk of balancing the interests of the individual against the interests of the community may be a way of indicating that "the individual" in question is not really thought of as a member of the community at all: he is an alien, a foreigner, and so his interests have *not* already been counted in "the interests of the community." Alternatively, if we say that his interests *are* already counted in the interests of the community—for example, because he too is more secure from being blown up, as a result of what we do to the liberties of suspicious characters (like him)—we may mean to indicate that a balance must be struck between (i) what *justice* requires in the way of respect for his interests and (ii) what would best promote the aggregate interests—his included—calculated in a way that is indifferent to justice.

This second account is quite complicated, so let me explain it a little further. We know that "the interest of the community" is often calculated in a way that sidelines issues of justice and distribution: utilitarians do this all the time.[19] To take a very crude example: suppose that a choice between two policies (I and II) offers the following pay-offs to three individuals:

	I	II
A	20	30
B	20	10
C	20	30

Plainly policy II best promotes the interests of the community (comprising A, B, and C) in an aggregate sense: the total pay-off is higher and so is the average. But someone who believes this may also acknowledge that the outcome of policy I is more fair; and let us assume for the sake of argument that they are right. Now, since fairness is concerned particularly with what happens to individuals (rather than to arithmetical totals), and since A and C are both better off as individuals under the less fair policy, a concern about fairness and about the issue of sacrificing fairness to aggregate utility is likely to focus particularly on B. It would not be surprising if this concern were *abbreviated* as a concern about the balance between B's interests and the aggregate interests of the community, even though B's interests are actually counted in the aggregate interests of the community. Another way of putting it would be to say that the real issue is the relation between a concern for justice, on the one hand, and the prospect of gains (to some or to the aggregate) from ignoring justice, on the other.

Talk of "balance" here is quite insidious. Although it all sounds very moderate, the implication is that we should have *some* concern for justice but not too much: a proper sense of balance requires us to give up on justice when the costs of pursuing it (to those who would benefit from injustice) become too high. Now A and C might not think this in the choice between policy I and policy II above: there the cost to them of justice is not very great. But if we imagine that a new set of policy choices presents itself (say, on September 11), which greatly increases what A and C have to lose from sticking with justice—

	III	IV
A	10	30
B	10	5
C	10	30

—then we might be tempted to talk about "adjusting the balance" between justice and utility. After all, it is one thing to require A and C each to give up ten units of goodies for the sake of justice in the choice between I and II; it is quite another thing—and the afficionado of balance may say it is quite unreasonable—to expect them to give up twice that in the choice between III and IV.

I have put this provocatively—with what I hope is an ill-concealed sneer of outrage at the idea of "striking a new balance" between the demands of justice on the one hand, and what most members of a society could get for themselves if they were allowed to arrange their society unjustly on the other. But mainly what I am trying to establish is the need for care with the idea of balancing. If security-gains for most people are being balanced against liberty-losses for a few, then we need to pay attention to the few/most dimension of the balance, not just the liberty/security dimension. Given that the few/most dimension presents an issue of justice, it is by no means clear—I think it is clearly false—that simply adding something to the "most" side of the balance is sufficient by itself to justify taking something away from the "few".

Someone may respond by observing that the "few" in our present case are terrorists or persons suspected of participation or complicity in terrorism. No one believes that criminals should have the same rights as the rest of us, and even those who are suspected but not convicted of criminal activity have lesser rights even in ordinary times: they may be held pending trial, or required to surrender their passports, etc. The point may be accepted, but the issue is whether we should now make some additional downward adjustments to the scheme that already puts criminal suspects in a special position of more restricted liberty. The civil liberties in category (c) define the procedures and protections that are offered to those suspected of ordinary crimes, from the trivial to the heinous. Is there a good reason for changing these, in the light of the events of September 11?

Ronald Dworkin observes a temptation to think that the extraordinary gravity of the crimes that were committed on September 11 (or that terrorists are presently conspiring to commit) is itself a reason for diminishing the protections afforded to those who are charged with such offenses. But, as he said, that makes no sense: "If they are innocent, the injustice of convicting and punishing them is at least as great as the injustice in convicting some other innocent person for a less serious crime."[20] The "civil liberties" in category (c) are oriented in large part towards preventing such injustice, and the case for respecting them increases rather than diminishes the greater the crime that the suspect stands accused of. (This is because category (c) liberties are designed to protect people against condemnation and punishment, and both will be greater the more serious the charge.)

Can it not also be said, though, that the greater the crime the greater the dangers of a wrongful acquittal? It is not true in all cases, but it may be true with terrorists. Michael Dorf put the point this way:

The traditional way we balance these things is with the maxim, "It's better that 10 guilty men go free than one innocent man be in jail." I think people are a little nervous about applying that maxim where the 10 guilty men who are going to go free could have biological weapons.[21]

The implicit suggestion that the 1:10 ratio needs to be adjusted in light of the greater damage that the ten may do sounds reasonable enough. But we must not give the impression that it is only a matter of striking a different balance between this one (innocent) suspect and these ten (guilty) ones. That is not who the balance is between. We are not balancing the rights of the innocent against the rights of the guilty. We are balancing the interests in life or liberty of the one innocent man against the security interests of those of the rest of us (non-suspects) that will be served if the ten guilty men are convicted by the procedures that lead to the wrongful conviction of the innocent. The innocent man is being put to death or imprisoned, and his reputation drastically and wrongly besmirched, so that *we* may be safer. It may not be done intentionally, but the gist of the proposal is that it is something we are entitled to be reckless about. There was a way of taking care that it should not happen (or that it should happen less often)—that is what the civil liberties safeguards represent—but for our own benefit we have decided to take less care.

James Fitzjames Stephen remarked, in connection with this business of trading off a certain number of guilty acquittals against innocent convictions that "[e]verything depends on what the guilty men have been doing, and something depends on the way in which the innocent man came to be suspected."[22] The first point is like Dorf's. But Stephen's second point is relevant too. If the innocent persons who are sacrificed to security in this way are sacrificed because it was in the circumstances perfectly reasonable to suspect them of terrorist offenses (though, as it turned out, mistaken)—that is one thing. But if they were suspected in the first place because of appearance, ethnicity, or religion, and if the changes in the scheme of civil liberties facilitated suspicion on just that basis, and removed some of the safeguards that would prevent or mitigate that sort of suspicion—then, that is quite another thing. The injustice associated with the reckless conviction of one innocent man for the sake of the greater good becomes particularly acute—and the "balancing" talk that under-writes it becomes particularly objectionable—when it is associated with ethnic or religious prejudice. At that stage, our worrying has to go beyond the issue of individual costs and benefits and look to the moral corruption of the system as a whole.[23]

VI.

A third reason for taking care with balancing arguments is that one of the terms—"liberty"—is a relational term, so that it has ramifications for both sides of the balance.

When liberty is understood (as it usually is) in a negative sense, it is something that cannot be reduced without increasing something else, namely the powers and means and mechanisms that obstruct or punish the ability of individuals to do what they want.[24] Reducing liberty may prevent an action taking place which would otherwise pose a risk of harm. But it necessarily also increases the power of the state, and there is a corresponding risk that this enhanced power may also be used to cause harm.

It is important not to lose sight of this possibility. The protection of civil liberties is not just a matter of (a) cherishing certain freedoms that we particularly value. It is also a matter of suspicion of power, an apprehension that power given to the state is seldom ever used only for the purposes for which it is given, but is always and endemically liable to abuse. Category (b) of our civil liberties concerns picks this up precisely. Whether there is a freedom at stake or not, there are certain powers which we have traditionally thought it better that the state should not have.

Another way of putting this is to say that a commitment to civil liberties is born in part of a "liberalism of fear" (to use Judith Shklar's phrase),[25] that is, an apprehension about what may be done to us using the overwhelming means of force available to the state. True, the events of September 11 have heightened our fear of the worst that can be done to us by individuals and groups other than the state. And an increase in the power of the state may be necessary to prevent or diminish the prospect of that horror. But the existence of a threat from terrorist attack does not diminish the threat that liberals have traditionally appre-hended from the state. The former complements the latter; it does not diminish it, and it may enhance it. In this regard Shklar notes that the liberalism of fear owes a lot to the political philosophy of John Locke.[26] It will not do, said Locke, in justify-ing strong unconstrained government, to point to the perils that it might protect us from: "This is to think, that Men are so foolish, that they take care to avoid what Mischiefs may be done them by Pole-Cats, or Foxes, but are content, nay think it Safety, to be devoured by Lions."[27] We have to worry that the very means given to the govern-ment to combat our enemies will be used by the government against its enemies—and although these two classes "enemies of the people" and "enemies of the state" overlap, they are not necessarily co-extensive.

Nowhere is this point clearer than in our apprehensions about the use of torture. We all hope and pray that our government will not have resort to this expedient, although there have been suggestions from hitherto respectable civil libertarians that it should do so.[28] There are official assurances that its use is out of the question,[29] though that has to be balanced against the depressing precedent of two of our closest allies in the war against terrorism—the United Kingdom and Israel—having resorted in recent memory to methods very close to torture in dealing with their own terrorist emergencies.[30] And even if we could rely on the official assurances that torture will not be used—and to do so we would want governments that have been rather less mendacious than ours have been about their support for such practices by other regimes in the past—it is worth pondering why this expedient is unthinkable and what that should tell us about other areas where we are less reluctant to sacrifice civil liberties.

On the face of it, the prohibition against torture should be exactly the sort of thing that gives way in the present atmosphere of adjusting the balance between liberty and security. What we are desperate for in the war against terrorism is information—who is planning what—and torture is supposed to be an effective way of securing information. Philosophy classes studying consequentialism thrive on hypotheticals involving scenarios of grotesque disproportion between the pain that a torturer might inflict on an informant and the pain that might be averted by timely use of the information extracted from him: a little bit of pain from the electrodes for him versus five hundred thousand people saved from nuclear incineration. But now the hypotheticals are beginning to look a little less fantastic. Alan Dershowitz asks: what if on September 11 law enforcement officials had "arrested terrorists boarding one of the planes and learned that other planes, then airborne, were heading towards unknown occupied buildings"? Would they not have been justified in torturing the terrorists in their custody—just enough to get the information that would allow the target buildings to be evacuated?[31] How could anyone object to the use of torture if it were dedicated specifically to saving thousands of lives in a case like this?

The answer comes from Henry Shue: "I can see no way to deny the permissibility of torture in a case *just like this*."[32] But few cases are *just like this*: few have the certainty of Dershowitz's law school classroom formulation or the clean precision of the philosopher's hypothetical.

Think of the background conditions that need to be assumed:

> The torture will not be conducted in the basement of a small-town jail in the provinces by local thugs popping pills; the prime minister and chief justice are being informed; and a priest and doctor are present. The victim will not be raped or forced to eat excrement and will not collapse with a heart attack or become deranged before talking; while avoiding irreparable damage, the antiseptic pain will carefully be increased only up to the point at which the necessary information is divulged, and the doctor will then immediately administer an antibiotic and a tranquillizer. . . . Most important, such incidents do not continue to happen. There are not so many people with grievances against this government that torture is becoming necessary more often, and in the smaller cities, and for slightly lesser threats, and with a little less care, and so on.[33]

There is, as Shue notes, "considerable evidence of all torture's metastatic tendency."[34] In the last hundred years or so, it has shown itself not to be the sort of thing that can be kept under rational control. On the contrary—from a point near the beginning of the twentieth century in which it was thought it might disappear altogether, torture has returned and now flourishes on a colossal scale. What Judith Shklar calls the liberalism of fear is a response to this actuality—to the prospect that if we allow ourselves to be seduced into "adjusting the balance" in this regard, there is no telling what we will let ourselves in for.[35]

As I said, so long as there is no serious proposal to use it, the argument about torture is important mainly as an illustration of a more general misgiving, about the dangers of metastasis in regard to other powers which had previously been withheld from government now being fearfully assigned to it. One troubling example is the power of detention without trial. It seems now that the United States has a policy of detaining even its own nationals indefinitely as "enemy combatants," not in order to charge them with anything but to find out what they know.[36] It is not hard to think of scenarios where detention without trial is justified. But it is hard to think of methods of ensuring that this power is not abused, that it does not get out of hand, and that detention does not turn into "disappearance." Once again, one's confidence would be greater if we were dealing with governments that had resolutely opposed all such abuses by their allies and client-states in the past. But we know, on the contrary, that in the recent past the United States, for example, has been complicit in abuses of the detention power in Latin America and elsewhere. There is a sort of magical thinking that we are supposed to forget all about such abuses when we evaluate what is being presently proposed from a civil liberties perspective: it is as though we are supposed to think that now, for the first time, remarkably, we have a government that can be trusted to tell the truth about its intentions. (Another, sadder way of putting this is to say that there are costs to the sort of mendacity that in the past U.S. government officials have routinely indulged in: such mendacity leaves no basis for trust when, later, trust may be desperately needed.)

Against all this, some will say that the threat from a more powerful state as a result of a reduction in civil liberties is nothing but an hysterical hypothesis, whereas the threat from terrorism is *real*. In response we can say two things. First, no one but a fool thinks that the threat from the state is zero. Of course opinions about the magnitude of that threat may vary. But there is no reason to suppose that the introduction of a heightened threat from terrorism makes it *less* likely than it was (say on September 10) that the state will act oppressively. So unless we assume that the motivation to do so has somehow magically evaporated, we must assume that the net threat from the state goes up as the power accorded to

the state increases. Secondly, even though the terrorist threat is very real, the hypothesis that an increase in governmental power will diminish it is in many ways no less fanciful than the hypothesis that the government will abuse the extra power given to it. We must not confuse the means with the end. An enhanced ability to combat terrorism is not the same as an actual diminution in terrorist threat. This leads to the fourth of the grounds for caution that I mentioned in Section III.

VII.

The idea of balance supposes that we should consider civil liberties not just in and of themselves, but in terms of the consequences of their existence. If the consequence of a given degree of liberty is an enhanced level of risk, then we must take that into account when considering whether that degree of liberty should be maintained.

It is important to do these calculations honestly. The fact that a certain degree of liberty is associated in the public mind with a certain degree of risk is not itself a ground for diminishing the liberty given a concern for the risk. *We must also be sure that the diminution of liberty will in fact have the desired consequence.* Or, if the desired reduction in risk is only probable not certain, then we must be as clear as we can about the extent of the probability. In particular, it is never enough for government to show that reducing a given liberty is *necessary* for combating terrorism effectively. It may be a necessary condition, and yet— because sufficient conditions are unavailable— the terrorist threat may continue unabated. In other words, the case must be based on the actual prospect that security will be enhanced if liberty is reduced. It may be said—quite reasonably— that we cannot know what the prospect is. Fair enough: then what has to be inferred is that *we cannot know whether it is worth giving up this liberty,* and thus we cannot legitimately talk with any confidence about an adjustment in the balance.

It is not that we know nothing about the effects of the change in our liberties. The immediate effects on suspects and dissidents are quite clear. It is the long-range effects for the sake of which these costs are imposed that are less clear. In fact, given the record of the bumbling incompetence and in-fighting of American intelligence and law-enforcement agencies wielding the already very considerable powers that they had in the weeks leading up to September 11, there is no particular reason to suppose that giving them more power will make them more effective in this desperately difficult task. But it might make them more effective in the somewhat easier task of acting oppressively towards vulnerable political opponents at home.

Again, my intention is not to settle any argument with these considerations, but to insist on the importance of detailed scrutiny. The case for diminishing civil liberties is often presented as a hard-headed consequentialist alternative to the soft "pious moralism" of theorists of rights. But those who are used to this sort of Machiavellian abuse know that it becomes most vehement when hard *consequentialist* questions are asked about enhancements of state power that turn out to be purely symbolic in relation to the threat they purport to be dealing with, and deadly dangerous in relation to liberty and justice on the domestic front. In fact I suspect that much of the popular pressure for a change in liberties can be explained almost entirely at the level of symbolism. When they are attacked people lash out, or they want their government to lash out and inflict reprisals. To put it a little more kindly, people want to feel that something is being done, in response to the attacks and in response to the continuing threat—preferably something very, very violent (like the bombing of Afghanistan), or something new and drastic like the setting up of new forms of detention camp or new types of tribunal. People are less interested in the effectiveness of these devices than in *the sense that something striking and unusual is being done.* No doubt the psychological re-

assurance that people derive from this is a consequential gain from the loss of liberty. But whether it is the sort of gain that should count morally is another question.

The point can be illustrated with a consideration of due process issues. A reduction in due process guarantees may make it more likely that terrorist suspects will be convicted. And that, people will say, is surely a good thing. Is it? What reason is there to suppose that our security is enhanced by making the conviction and punishment of suspects more likely. We know that the conviction and punishment of an Al-Qaeda fanatic, for example, will have no general deterrent effect; if anything, it will have the opposite effect—making it more rather than less likely that the country punishing the suspect is subject to terrorist attack. Of course, this is not a reason for *not* punishing the perpetrators of murderous attacks, but the reasons for punishing them are reasons of justice, not security (via general deterrence); and those reasons of justice may not be as separable from the scheme of civil liberties that we are currently trading off as the "new balance" image might suggest. Maybe particular incapacitation is a means by which conviction might serve security, but for that it is especially important that we convict and punish the right people, and it may well be that limiting civil liberties in category (c) diminishes rather than enhances our assurance in this regard. Once again, undermining civil liberties—particularly the due process rights of terrorist suspects—may make us seem (at least to ourselves) more ferocious and vengeful in response to the atrocities of September 11. But it is less clear that the psychological benefit we derive from adopting this posture is the sort of value for which procedural rights are appropriately sacrificed.

VIII.

This article does not embrace any particular policy or proposal. It is intended mainly as a call for care and caution. We should be cautious about giving up our civil liberties. We should be even more careful about giving up our commitment to the civil liberties of a minority, so that we can enjoy our liberties in greater security. We should be worried about the enhanced power of the state (and we should reject as magical thinking the idea that the risk from that power goes down as the risk from terrorism goes up).[37] And finally, if we do remain receptive to the need to compromise civil liberty, we must insist that those who talk the balancing-talk step up to the plate with some actual predictions about effectiveness. We should not give up our liberties, or anyone else's liberties, for the sake of purely symbolic gains in the war against terrorism.

Notes

11 Journal of Political Philosophy 191 (2003).

1 For acknowledgment of this point by well-known defenders of judicial review, see Laurence Tribe, "Trial by fury: why Congress must curb Bush's military courts," The New Republic, December 10, 2001: "Historically, the judiciary has been so deferential to the executive in wartime as to provide virtually no meaningful check. . . . [I]t would be a terrible mistake for those who worry about civil rights and liberties to pin too much hope on the judiciary in times of crisis." See also Ronald Dworkin, "The threat to patriotism," New York Review of Books, February 28, 2002.

2 Lord Atkin's words, from his lonely dissent in Liversidge v. Anderson [1942] A.C. 206.

3 Nicholas Kristoff, "Liberal reality check: we must look anew at freedom vs. security," Pittsburgh Post-Gazette, June 3, 2002, p. A9.

4 Of course quantitative computations of liberty present enormous difficulties, many of them connected to the problem of the individuation of actions. For a discussion, see Hillel Steiner, "How free? Computing personal liberty," in Of Liberty, ed. A. Philips Griffiths (Cambridge: Cambridge University Press, 1983) and Hillel Steiner, An Essay on Rights (Oxford: Blackwell, 1994), pp. 42–54.

5 Raz, Practical Reason and Norms, new edn (Oxford: Clarendon Press, 1999), pp. 37 ff.

6 See Dworkin, Taking Rights Seriously (London: Duckworth, 1977), pp. xi and 190 ff.

7 Nozick, Anarchy, State and Utopia (Oxford: Blackwell, 1974), pp. 28 ff.

8 See Rawls, A Theory of Justice, rev. edn (Cambridge, Mass.: Harvard University Press, 1999), pp. 36–40 (lexical priority) and 214–20 (priority of liberty).

9 See, e.g., European Convention for the Protection of Human Rights and Fundamental Freedoms, Article 10 (2).

10 See Terminiello v. City of Chicago, 337 U.S. 1, at 37 (1949) (Jackson, J., dissenting) ("There is danger that . . . [the Court] will convert the constitutional Bill of Rights into a suicide pact."), and Kennedy v. Mendoza-Martinez, 372 U.S. 144, at 160 (1963) ("[W]hile the Constitution protects against invasions of individual rights, it is not a suicide pact").

11 Nozick, Anarchy, State and Utopia, p. 30 n.

12 Dworkin, Taking Rights Seriously, p. 191.

13 See the essays by F. M. Kamm, Philip Montague and Claire Finkelstein in a special symposium issue on "Conflicts of Rights" in Legal Theory, 7 (2001). See also Jeremy Waldron, "Rights in conflict," Ethics, 99 (1989), 503–19, reprinted in Waldron, Liberal Rights (Cambridge: Cambridge University Press, 1993).

14 Nozick, I think, would take this line. And Frances Kamm does too in "Conflicts of rights: typology, methodology and non-consequentialism," Legal Theory, 7 (2001), 239.

15 Amartya Sen, "Rights and agency," Consequentialism and its Critics, ed. Samuel Scheffler (Oxford: Oxford University Press, 1988), p. 186, esp. pp. 191–6.

16 Ibid., p. 193.

17 See Dworkin, "The threat to patriotism." See also Dworkin's more general discussion of the proposition that "[i]t is never true, at any time, that all members of a society are equally likely to be accused of any particular crime," in his essay "Principle, policy, procedure," in A Matter of Principle (Cambridge, Mass.: Harvard University Press, 1985), p. 87.

18 Dworkin, "Principle, policy, procedure," p. 73.

19 See the discussion in Rawls, Theory of Justice, pp. 19–22.

20 Dworkin, "The threat to patriotism."

21 As quoted in Pam Belluck, "Hue and murmur over

curbed rights," *New York Times*, Nov. 17, 2001, at B8.

22 James Fitzjames Stephen, *A History of the Criminal Law of England*, Vol. I, p. 438, quoted by Richard H. Menard, "Ten reasonable men," *American Criminal Law Review*, 38 (2001), 179 at p. 199.

23 A system of civil liberties should not be just conceived as an array of individual benefits. It has aspects of a public good—and there is a serious difference between having one's liberties secured in a system where the same liberties are scrupulously guaranteed to all (a system which resolutely turns its back on various forms of prejudice and discrimination) and having one's liberties secured as the artifact of a system that offers liberty to some but not others. (It may be less appropriate to describe the latter system as a scheme of civil liberties.) I am grateful to Neil Walker of the European University Institute, for conversation along these lines. "Public safety," says Walker, "is inexorably connected with the quality of our association with others. (See Ian Loader and Neil Walker, "Policing as a public good: reconstituting the connections between policing and the state," *Theoretical Criminology*, 5 (2001), 9, at p. 26.) Professor Walker's analysis suggests that, even though we might be individually safer, our security is degraded as a public good by distributive degradation in our scheme of civil liberties.

24 See Isaiah Berlin, "Two concepts of liberty," *Four Essays on Liberty* (Oxford: Oxford University Press, 1969), p. 122 ff.

25 See Judith Shklar, "The liberalism of fear," *Liberalism and the Moral Life*, ed. Nancy L. Rosenblum (Cambridge, Mass.: Harvard University Press, 1989), esp. pp. 26 ff.

26 Ibid., p. 30.

27 John Locke, *Two Treatises of Government*, ed. Peter Laslett (Cambridge: Cambridge University Press, 1988), II, section 93.

28 See Alan Dershowitz, *Shouting Fire: Civil Liberties in a Turbulent Age* (New York: Little, Brown, 2002), p. 477.

29 Eric Schmitt, "There are ways to make them talk," *The New York Times*, June 16, 2002 (Week in Review): "Military officials say torture is not an option. But, they said, under the Geneva Conventions, anything short of torture is permissible to get a hardened Qaeda operative to spill a few scraps of information that could prevent terrorist attacks."

30 For Israel, see Julian Borger, "Israeli government report admits systematic torture of Palestinians," *The Guardian* (U.K.), February 11, 2000. For the United Kingdom, see the ECHR decision in *Ireland v. United Kingdom*, Judgement of 18 January, 1978.

31 Dershowitz, op. cit., 477.

32 Henry Shue, "Torture," *Philosophy and Public Affairs*, 7 (1978), 124, at p. 141.

33 Ibid., p. 142.

34 Ibid., p. 143.

35 The formulations in this paragraph are adapted from Shklar, "Liberalism of fear," p. 27.

36 I infer this from the recent case of Jose Padilla, held for having talked about the possibility of detonating a radiological bomb in Washington D.C. See Benjamin Weiser with Dana Canedy, "Traces of terror: the bomb plot," *The New York Times*, June 12, 2002, p. A24.

37 We should see accusations of disloyalty which are used to slander those who raise these concerns for what they are—an attempt to distract us from careful public evaluation of these issues. (See Neil A. Lewis, "The Senate hearing; Ashcroft defends antiterror plan—says criticism may aid U.S. foes," *The New York Times*, December 7, 2001, p. A1: "Emboldened by public opinion surveys showing that Americans overwhelmingly support the administration's initiatives against terrorism, Mr. Ashcroft told the Senate Judiciary Committee, 'To those who scare peace-loving people with phantoms of lost liberty, my message is this: your tactics only aid terrorists.' ")

Chapter 23

Henry Shue

TORTURE IN DREAMLAND
Disposing of the ticking bomb

Nothing has changed. The body still trembles as it trembled before Rome was founded and after, in the twentieth century before and after Christ. Tortures are just what they were, only the earth has shrunk and whatever goes on sounds as if it's just a room away.[1]

TORTURE IS WRONG.[2] But sometimes we feel justified in doing what we know is wrong because the stakes are so very high. So the next question is: is torture so wrong that it is inexcusable no matter how high the stakes are? I will argue that all actual arrangements for torture are inexcusable, in spite of the fact that we can imagine hypothetical cases, like the notorious ticking-bomb cases in which it seems excusable.[3] Why are imaginary examples like ticking-bomb hypotheticals so badly misleading about how to plan for real cases? They mislead in two different ways that compound the error: idealization and abstraction.[4] Idealization is the addition of positive features to an example in order to make the example better than reality, which lacks those features. Abstraction is the deletion of negative features of reality from an example in order to make the example still better than reality. Idealization adds sparkle, abstraction removes dirt. Together they make the hypothetical superior to reality and thereby a disastrously misleading analogy from which to derive conclusions about reality.

The advocates of torture love a ticking bomb. But even the honest and thoughtful are mesmerized and bedeviled by the ticking-bomb hypothetical, with its suggestion of a catastrophic outcome avoidable only through torture. In a recent article Oren Gross writes:

> The foregoing discussion still leaves us with the question of what constitutes a truly "catastrophic case." I will attempt to answer this question, which clearly is significant to the overall tenability of my project, on a different occasion. For now, it is sufficient to acknowledge that *some* catastrophic case is possible.[5]

Two paragraphs earlier Gross has quoted Carl Schmitt, who declared in Germany in 1922, "For a legal order to make sense, a normal situation must exist;"[6] then concluded: "General norms are limited in their scope of application to those circumstances in which the normal state of affairs prevails. Catastrophes undermine this factual basis."[7]

Now, one problem is the easy assumption that no catastrophes occur in normal times. This is one of many reasons it is not true that "it is sufficient to acknowledge that *some* catastrophic case is possible."[8] We need to know a great deal about a specific catastrophe, especially one that has not actually happened yet, in order to determine whether it is evidence that times are not normal to such a degree that legal order does not make sense. But there are deeper problems here than circular definitions of 'normal' and 'catastrophe.'

Gross is sometimes flattering about my 1978 article, Torture,[9] but what he says about possible catastrophes possibly avoided by torture suggests that my fundamental methodological point concerning how to think about torture has not come across.[10] This emboldens me to repeat myself, attempting to be more lucid about argumentative methodology. I will not rehearse all the perfections built into the artificial case.[11] But note a few of the respects in which the standard hypothetical departs from reality through idealization.

Idealization

The right man. The ticking-bomb hypothetical is supposed to be the case in which the disaster that torture might prevent is so catastrophic that only the naive and the utopian would dream of choosing not to torture the person who is somehow known with certainty actually to be the person who planted the ticking bomb. He is not a suspected terrorist; it is built into the hypothetical that he *is a terrorist*—indeed, the terrorist—thus eliminating messy aspects of reality like uncertainty and probability. It is not that Central Intelligence Agency has kidnapped 100 people, some of whose names sound like the name of the bomber, which, luckily, they somehow happen to know. It is not that agents have arrested a Navajo who, they thought, "looked like an Arab."

Prompt and accurate disclosure. The torture victim talks in a timely and accurate fashion—he quickly divulges the crucial information before the bomb has had time to explode. He does not have a heart attack and pass out; he does not vomit on himself and have a psychotic break; he does not tell a plausible diversionary lie that wastes the time available.

Rare, isolated case. "Most important, such incidents [of torture] do not continue to happen."[12] Once the original 'right man' becomes too hysterical to provide coherent information, the torturers do not simply move on to, as it were,

the second-best 'right man.' And the torturers do not, operating on the principle that practice makes perfect, circulate from, say, Guantanamo to Bagram to Abu Ghraib to Romania to Poland.

Implicit in *Torture* were two different methodological theses that I did not explicitly separate. The weaker thesis was: do not base general policy on exceptional cases—roughly, hard cases make bad law. The stronger thesis was: do not base any institutional preparations on imaginary cases. Having quoted my proposed dictum, "artificial cases make bad ethics,"[13] Gross argues as follows:

> [I]ts problem lies in the fact that ticking bomb cases are not "artificial." They are real, albeit rare. Ignoring them completely, by rhetorically relegating them to the level of "artificial," is utopian or naive, at best. There is a difference between ignoring completely the truly catastrophic cases and focusing our attention elsewhere when designing general rules and policies.[14]

Because he earlier writes that we "must be mindful of the risk of creating bad law (and ethics) to answer to the particular needs of the hard case,"[15] I take it that Gross and I agree on the weaker thesis: do not base general policy on exceptional cases. But we disagree about the stronger thesis. We disagree about what else besides general policy, if anything, to base on the alleged exceptional case.

In part thanks to Gross's critique the multiple reasons why ticking-bomb hypotheticals seem "artificial" are clearer to me now. One reason is that they are idealized. They are not simply imaginary but unrealistic, like an imaginary alcoholic who drinks two beers only a night. There are former alcoholics, who do not drink at all, and active alcoholics. To think that there may be rare alcoholics who drink moderately is to fail to understand alcoholism. Similarly, history does not present us with a government that used torture selectively and judiciously.[16]

Are we to believe that America is likely to be the first alcoholic in history who can take only one drink? The first state apparatus that will use torture judiciously and selectively? Are American politicians so superior to mere mortals?

Gross is confident that what he calls "catastrophic cases" are "real, albeit rare."[17] If catastrophic cases had only the one feature of involving extremely high stakes in human life, yes, catastrophic cases would be "real, albeit rare"—perhaps not even so rare. But the high stakes are the only realistic feature in the ticking-bomb hypothetical. Its other features are all too good to be true, especially to be true in conjunction: the right man and the prompt right result and the judicious decision to refrain from all further torture until the next genuine catastrophe almost certainly looms. This happy conjunction is not rare—it is virtually impossible given the kind of people who rise to the top in politics. What would be "utopian or naive" would be to believe that the kind of people who are running the so-called "War on Terrorism" would, if they had discretion about using torture in secret—against "ghost detainees" in "black sites," say—choose to restrain themselves in spite of the impossibility of accountability.

The Alice-in-Wonderland character of the assumption that the use of torture will not be widespread throws into doubt the location of the catastrophe. Gross, along with most people who appeal to the ticking-bomb hypothetical, takes it to be beyond dispute that the catastrophe lies on the side of not torturing: we are too squeamish to torture the terrorist who planted the bomb, and the bomb explodes, bringing the catastrophe of death and destruction. One other possibility is that catastrophe lies on the side of undermining the taboo against torture. Then other nations will reason that if the superpower with its thousands of nuclear weapons and high-tech conventional forces cannot maintain its own security without the liberal use of secret torture, they can hardly be expected to defend their security without far more torture. And what currently passes for civilization may then slide backward in the general direction of the eighth century. That too would be a catastrophe, a civilizational catastrophe. I am not predicting a full return of barbarism. Yet it is clear that idealizations that cause the epidemic nature of torture to evaporate from view are no guide for practical action. My honest judgment is that stories that are too good to be true are not true rarely, but false. The ticking-bomb hypothetical is too good to be true—it is torture conducted by wise, self-restrained angels.

But what if I am mistaken in doubting that the perfect time for torture will arrive. I am certainly not appealing to conceptual necessities, but instead making empirical judgments about the nature of human beings and the effects of power without accountability, secret torture hidden from the citizens in whose name it is inflicted. What if I have the facts wrong?

Ironically, here Gross and I—at least as I reasoned in 1978—share a common problem. I think the exceptional case is probably in fact impossible, especially the feature stipulating that the torture does not metastasize throughout the body politic. Gross thinks the exceptional case is rare but clearly practically possible. Neither of us claims to have ruled it out. If it comes, what do we recommend? Here is where the unreality of abstraction, as distinguished from idealization, haunts us both.

Abstraction

Gross and I both think, it seems, that torture should remain, as it is, absolutely non-derogably illegal. But we both also wished that if a public official honestly, upon careful reflection, judged that the ultimate catastrophe loomed but that it could be prevented if and only if some one person—or even some small number of persons—were tortured, he could act on his conviction and conduct the torture outside the law. I say "outside the law" in order to fudge some differences between us that, although they are important, I do not want to pursue very far here. As his comments regarding the quotation from Carl Schmitt that I introduced at the beginning of this piece indicate, Gross believes that the arrival of what he calls the "catastrophic case" heralds, or perhaps simply constitutes, the suspension of normality that, Schmitt claimed, is a necessary condition for the rule of law. Schmitt seems to me to have matters backwards. It is when conditions are eroding that one really needs the rule of law. But that is a long story for another time.

Gross characterizes the non-normal situation as "extra-legal,"[18] which is worrisome because it seems much too wholesale. To be fair to him, however, he insists that any entry into the extra-legal be considered for "*ex post ratification*."[19] In his hypothetical, if the move to the extra-legal is not granted *ex post* ratification, then any official who ordered torture as an act of "official disobedience" may be punished criminally and sued civilly for violating the laws against torture.[20] My 1978 proposal was much more limited and simple: essentially, that the torture would be like an act of civil disobedience at least in the respect that the conscientious torturer would willingly submit to charges and trial. If the torture had demonstrably prevented the end of the world, the charges would presumably be dropped or the sentence suspended.

The difficulty, which seems equally severe for Gross's suggestion and mine, is that our reluctant torturer would probably also be an incompetent torturer, most unlikely to succeed at what might well be his first try at extracting information. Successful torturers must avoid sympathy and empathy, or they will go too easy. But they must also avoid anger and cruelty, or they will go too hard and merely knock the victim senseless, or drive him into a dissociative state, and learn nothing useful for the prevention of catastrophe. Torture is not for amateurs—successful torturers need to be real "pros", and no one becomes a "pro" overnight.

At a minimum, one must practice—perhaps do research, be mentored by the still more experienced. In short, torture needs a bureaucracy, with apprentices and experts, of the kind that torture in fact always has. Torquemada was not an independent consultant. Torture is an institution.[21]

Arrigo sums it up this way:

The use of sophisticated torture techniques by a trained staff entails the problematic institutional arrangements I have laid out: physician assistance; cutting edge, secret biomedical research for torture techniques unknown to the terrorist organization and tailored to the individual captive for swift effect; well trained torturers, quickly accessible at major locations; pre-arranged permission from the courts because of the urgency; rejection of independent monitoring due to security issues; and so on. These institutional arrangements will have to be in place, with all their unintended and accumulating consequences, *however rarely* terrorist suspects are tortured.... [T]he harm to innocent victims of the terrorist should be weighed against the breakdown of key social institutions and state-sponsored torture of many innocents.[22]

Now this actually further buttresses the earlier point about idealization: it is simply dreamy to think that all of a sudden we are simply going to stumble upon someone who happens to have the skills to make a man who planted a ticking bomb reverse the direction of his life and assist us in defusing his bomb. But this is very bad news for my attempt in 1978 and Gross's attempt now to allow the exceptional case. Our common problem is abstraction: we have abstracted from the social basis—the institutional context—necessary for the practice of torture. For torture is a practice. Practitioners who do not practice will not be very good at what they do. Who are we imagining that they will practice on? Practitioners without the best equipment will also not be very good. Where will they obtain their "cutting edge" equipment?[23] How will they test it in order to be sure it will work when the catastrophe looms?

Either "torturers" are just thugs who have no clue what they are doing, in which case we need not allow for exceptional cases in which they rapidly and effectively extract invaluable catastrophe-preventing information, or some can have genuine expertise. Arrigo cites one of her U.S. informants: "The Air Force interrogator said he tried to interview terrorist suspects 'before any heavy-handed ex-Turkish farmer slapped them around.' "[24] If expertise is available, we would certainly want it at hand in the exceptional, potentially catastrophic case. If we want it ready, we need to maintain, even nourish, the organizations and networks in which the expertise resides.

Here, then, is the really bad news. The moderate position on torture is an impractical abstraction—it is torture in dreamland. The only operationally feasible positions are toward the extremes. Gross and I (in 1978)—doubtless because we are moderate and reasonable people—have been trying to have it both ways.[25] I—and I leave Professor Gross to speak for himself—was like the recovering alcoholic dreaming of avoiding the extreme of total abstinence through the 'moderate' strategy of only a drink or two a night. That is not an option, and the alcoholic has only the extremes between which to choose. In the quarter-century since 1978 we have also learned that there is no moderate position on torture either. Torture is now rampant, and high-officials in the U.S. government are its poster-children. You cannot be a little bit pregnant, you cannot—if you are an alcoholic—have a drink only on special occasions, and you cannot—if your politicians are not angels—employ torture only on special occasions.

Michael Ignatieff, another reasonable and moderate person, hopes like Gross and me to have it both ways: "[A]n outright ban on torture creates the problem of the conscientious offender. This is a small price to pay for a ban on torture."[26] If the conscientious offender is to be an effective and competent torturer, or to have them on call, he must, because of the cascading corruption of key social institutions, like medicine and the courts, that Arrigo suggests, be the tip of a bureaucratic iceberg of institutionalized torture, an iceberg that will probably be replicated nation by nation around the world—not such a small price in fact. To try to leave a constrained loophole for the competent "conscientious offender" is in fact to leave an expanding loophole for a bureaucracy of routinized torture, as I misguidedly did in the 1978 article. What is truly "utopian or naïve" is trusting the state and its subservient lawyers not to exploit every loophole zealously, a lesson we should have learned from Orwell's 1984. The textbook for our remedial course is The Torture Papers.[27] One can imagine rare torture, but one cannot institutionalize rare torture. The suggestion of rare torture has no place in the real world of politics. It is an optimistic thought with no social embodiment.

As David Luban recently put it:

The real torture debate, therefore, isn't about whether to throw out the rulebook in the exceptional emergencies. Rather, it's about what the rulebook says about the ordinary interrogation. . . . [Senator] McCain has said that ultimately the debate is over who we are. We will never figure that out until we stop talking about ticking bombs, and stop playing games with words.[28]

So I now take the most moderate position on torture, the position nearest to the middle of the road, feasible in the real world: never again. Never, ever, exactly as international law indisputably requires. If the perfect time for torture comes, and we are not prepared to prevent a terroristic catastrophe, we will at least know that we have not sold our souls and we have not brutalized the civilization. These are catastrophes we actually can avoid. Some of us may, or may not, as a result of our refusal to tolerate secret torture bureaucracies and their gulags, die in some other catastrophe, but civilized principles will survive for members of future generations, who may be grateful for our sacrifice so that they could lead decent lives. About this price Ignatieff is correct: "Those of us who oppose torture should also be honest enough to admit that we may have to pay a price for our own convictions. Ex ante, of course, I cannot tell how high this price might be. . . . This is a risk I am prepared to take. . . ."[29] Meanwhile, our taxes fund secret detention centers into which people disappear but in which, we are assured on highest authority, in spite of a total lack of accountability no torture ever occurs.

Notes

"37 Case Western Reserve Journal of International Law 231 (2006)"

1 Wislawa Szymborska, Tortures, in Wislawa Szymborska, View with a Grain of Sand: Selected Poems 151 (Stanislaw Baranczak & Clare Cavanagh trans., 1995).

2 David Sussman provides a powerful explanation of why torture is wrong in his article [in the original volume]. David Sussman, Defining Torture, 37 Case W. Res. J. Int'l L. (2006).

3 David Luban, Torture, American-Style: This Debate Comes Down to Words vs. Deeds, Wash. Post, Nov. 27, 2005, at B1 (illustrating what a serious distraction from reality ticking-bomb cases are in the current U.S. debates).

4 My account of these two intellectual processes is roughly derived from Onora O'Neill, Ethical Reasoning and Ideological Pluralism, 98 Ethics 705, 711–12 (1988).

5 Oren Gross, The Prohibition on Torture and the Limits of the Law, in Torture: A Collection 229, 239 (Sanford Levinson ed., 2004).

6 Id. (quoting Carl Schmitt, Political Theology: Four Chapters on the Concept of Sovereignty 13 (George Schwab trans., 1985).

7 Id.

8 Oren Gross, Are Torture Warrants Warranted? Pragmatic Absolutism and Official Disobedience, 88 Minn. L. Rev. 1481, 1487 n.26 (2004).

9 Henry Shue, Torture, 7 Phil. & Pub. Aff. 124 (1978).

10 See id.

11 See id. at 141–42.

12 Id. at 142.

13 Gross, supra note 5, at 234 (quoting Henry Shue, Torture, 7 Phil. & Pub. Aff. 124 (1978)).

14 Id. at 234.

15 Id.

16 If anyone knows a case, I would appreciate an e-mail giving its name.

17 Gross, supra note 5, at 234.

18 Id. at 240.

19 Id. at 242.

20 Id. at 240–41. I do not entirely follow this reasoning. If the situation is extra-legal, the law has presumably been suspended; consequently it is difficult to see what violation the official could fairly be punished for. Nevertheless, I am glad the torturer will be punished if he gets it wrong.

21 See Jean Maria Arrigo, A Utilitarian Argument Against Torture Interrogation of Terrorists, 10 Science & Engineering Ethics 543 (2004) (portraying a realistic account of the practical prerequisites of torture based on serious research). See also Jessica Wolfendale, Training Torturers: A Critique of the 'Ticking Bomb' Argument, in 32 Social Theory and Practice (forthcoming 2006) (providing complementary arguments to a similar conclusion).

22 Id. at 564 (emphasis added). See Michael Hanna et al., The War on Medical Morality (forthcoming) (discussing the corrupting effects on the medical profession of physician assistance).

23 Id. at 552 (noting that the United States is "the largest international supplier of electro-shock weapons—stun guns, electro-shock batons, and the like—to governments that practice electro-shock torture") (citing Amnesty International, Stopping the Torture Trade 34 (2001)). This is of course the crude stuff.

24 Id. at 549 (withholding the identity of the Air Force interrogator).

25 Where violence and brutality seem necessary in a good cause, this is a constant, but often fatal,

attraction. *See* Henry Shue, *Having It Both Ways: The Gradual Wrong Turn in American Strategy, in Nuclear Deterrence and Moral Restraint: Critical Choices for American Strategy* 13 (Henry Shue ed., 1989) (presenting an analogous problem concerning nuclear weapons).

26 Michael Ignatieff, *Moral Prohibition at A Price, in Torture: Does It Make Us Safer? Is It Ever OK?* 25 (Kenneth Roth et al. eds, 2005).

27 *The Torture Papers: The Road to Abu Ghraib* (Karen J. Greenberg and Joshua L. Dratel eds, 2005).

28 Luban, supra note 3.

29 Ignatieff, supra note 26, at 27.

Chapter 24

Jeff McMahan

TORTURE, MORALITY, AND LAW

THE MORALITY OF TORTURE is similar to the morality of capital punishment in the following respect. There are in principle, and probably in practice, certain rare instances in which either would be morally justified. At the same time, morality itself demands that both be categorically banned in law.

Suppose that we have captured someone we know to have committed a series of daring and spectacular murders. The murderer is proud of these acts and boasts of them openly. He even had them video recorded. Suppose that because of the manner in which they were done, these murders are admired by certain people and that the evidence suggests that there are likely to be various series of "copycat" murders unless this murderer is executed. He has boasted that the state does not have the "guts" to execute him; therefore his execution will be regarded by his admirers as a defeat and a humiliation rather than a martyring.

By creating a threat of copycat murders, this man's acts have decreased the security of innocent people in his society. To the best of our knowledge, more innocent people will be murdered, partly as a result of what he has done, unless we kill him. In short, his own wrongful acts now force us to choose between killing him and allowing a number of wholly innocent but as yet unidentifiable people to be murdered. It is therefore a matter of justice that he should be the one to die—assuming that there are no other relevant considerations that bear on the case.

Notice that I do not claim that this is because he deserves to die. The justification for the claim that he ought morally to be executed makes no appeal to retribution. It appeals instead to the same considerations that justify self-defense in paradigm cases. This man has, through his own wrongful action, created a threat of unjust harm to innocent people. Granted, his own agency would not be the immediate cause of this harm. But he would share in the responsibility for it if it were to occur, and his execution, we are supposing, could prevent it. By sharing responsibility for this threat to innocent people that can best be averted by executing him, he has made himself liable to be killed in their defense.

But even if we have here a case in which execution would be morally justified, it does not follow that the law ought to permit capital punishment. Notice that in the case I have described, the threats to be deterred by the murderer's execution are ones for which he would be partly morally responsible. If that were not the case, the use of his execution to deter others from committing similar crimes would not be just—or at least not in the same way. The structure of justification, in any case, would not be the same as in paradigm instances of killing in self-defense.

It might be suggested, then, that capital punishment should be legally permitted only when it could be shown to be justified as a form of just defense rather than retribution. But the law also has to be formulated with a view both to the facts and to the expected consequences of its promulgation and enforcement. If in fact the death penalty does not deter serious crimes more effectively than life imprisonment, as many social scientists have argued, and if the practice of capital punishment inevitably involves the accidental execution of the innocent, it is likely that capital punishment will cause greater injustice than it can prevent. This is why it should be banned.

The argument about torture has much the same structure, though the details are obviously different. The wrongfulness of torture as it is actually practiced is almost always over-determined. There are features of torture—some of which are analyzed with insight in David Sussman's contribution [to the original] volume[1]—that may make it a uniquely awful thing to do to another person. And the reasons for which it is done are usually evil—because for decent people torture is virtually unthinkable as a means of achieving their ends. Torture is almost always, therefore, a despicable means to an immoral end.

Perhaps the worst form of torture is terrorist torture, whose instrumental function is fulfilled when the mutilated bodies of the victims are strewn in public places as a means of intimidating others. Retributive torture also lacks any justification other than in certain intuitions, which I think we should regard as the relics of an earlier stage of moral evolution—though it should give us pause to reflect that the gods of Christianity and Islam, whose holy texts were written during this earlier era, are widely believed by their worshipers to practice retributive torture extensively and everlastingly against sinners in the afterlife. Where a moral case *can* be made, along the lines of the case for capital punishment, is for what Henry Shue has called "interrogational torture"—torture not for the purpose of eliciting a confession but for the

extraction of information necessary to prevent a serious wrong.[2]

The example that is most frequently cited to demonstrate the permissibility of interrogational torture—an example that is now criticized, as it is in Henry Shue's illuminating contribution [to the original] volume,[3] with almost equal frequency—is the case of the "ticking bomb," in which a captured terrorist has planted a nuclear bomb in a city and our only chance of getting him to reveal its location before it detonates is to torture him.

There are indeed various aspects of this example that are misleading. It invites us to consider whether it can be permissible to engage in torture in order to prevent killing, but it is at least arguable that, even if it is in general less bad to be tortured than to be killed, torture is nevertheless morally more objectionable than killing. It also suggests that, if the constraint against torture can be overridden in this case, it is because of the sheer combined weight of the consequences of not doing so. The suggestion is, in other words, that any kind of action, even torture, can be justifiable on a relatively small scale if it can prevent something as catastrophic as the killing of millions of innocent people. Finally, people who object to what they see as the glib use of the example of the "ticking bomb" argue that because this kind of case never in fact arises, it is irrelevant to urgent and important issues of law and policy.[4]

All of these objections have merit. Here is an alternative hypothetical example that avoids at least the first two.

In various countries in which torture is practiced, theologians have expressed concern about the morally corrosive effect of the practice on those whose job it is to do the actual torturing. So scientists have addressed this problem by devising a machine that obviates the need for direct human involvement in the process of torture. This machine directly stimulates the pain centers in the brain and can be set to varying levels of intensity. It does not damage the victim's body. But it can be left running indefinitely. A terrorist has acquired one of these machines. He has taken one innocent hostage whom he has strapped into the machine, which has a timer that is set to begin inflicting great pain in 24 hours unless his demands are met. We have captured the terrorist but do not know where his machine is located. Our best chance of getting him to tell us is to put him into one of our torture machines. It is reasonable to expect that we will be able to extract the information from him, though because he is a tough character, we expect to have to set our machine at a higher level than that to which his is set.

In this example, we would not practice torture to prevent killing but to prevent torture. And because we would be torturing one person to prevent the torture of only one other person, our justification cannot be that torture is necessary to prevent a catastrophe. Indeed, because our machine would be set at a higher level than his and might have to run longer (since we would keep ours going as long as his continued to run), the harm we would cause would be greater than that which we would avert.

Still, it seems to me that we would be morally justified in torturing the terrorist in this example if that were the only way we might obtain from him the location of his torture machine. Indeed, I think we would be morally *required* to torture him. The form of justification is the same as in paradigm cases of self-defense. Through his own wrongful action, the terrorist has made it the case that either he or his innocent victim will be tortured. Our torturing him is a necessary and proportionate defense of his potential victim from an unjust harm that the terrorist will otherwise wrongfully inflict, albeit through action that is now completed. Because the terrorist is morally responsible for the threat of unjust harm that our defensive action is intended to avert, we will not wrong him, nor will he have any justified complaint against us, if we torture him. For he has acted in a way that makes him morally liable to our necessary and propor-

tionate defensive action. Note, finally, that it is within the terrorist's power to make it the case, merely by abandoning his own wrongful plan, that neither he nor anyone else is tortured.

The example is, of course, artificial and unrealistic, perhaps to an even greater extent than the case of the ticking bomb. But I believe that analogous cases can and do arise in practice, and that the structure of justification can be the same in these actual cases. There have been instances in which Israeli security forces have captured a suicide bomber with bombs strapped to his body before he could detonate them. And these forces have also captured persons in the process of making or transporting such bombs. In some of these cases, the persons captured have been tortured in order to force them to divulge information about other attacks that have been planned for the future. This information has then enabled the security forces to take preemptive action to thwart the planned attacks, thereby saving the lives of an indeterminate number of unidentifiable potential victims.[5]

In these cases, the persons captured have, through complicity in creating threats of unjust harm, made themselves liable to necessary and proportionate harm in defense of their potential victims. It is often argued, however, that torture is so heinous and vile an activity that relevant standards of necessity and proportionality simply cannot, in practice, be met. How, it is argued, can we be certain that the person we have in custody is really a terrorist? How can we be sure that there are further actions planned for the future, or, even if there are, that the person we have captured has any knowledge of them? And how can we be confident of the reliability of anything he might tell us under torture?

In the cases we are considering—which, again, I have reason to believe, but cannot prove, are actual cases—the evidence of the person's complicity in terrorism is very strong. It would normally be sufficiently compelling for a conviction in a court of law. But other questions—whether the person has knowledge that would enable us to save lives, whether torture is the best way to elicit it if he does—can seldom if ever be answered with certainty. With these questions, we are in the realm of risk. If we begin torturing the person, we are risking torturing a fellow human being to no purpose. For we may get nothing of sufficient value to justify the awful thing we will have done. If we refrain from torturing him, we risk allowing his collaborators to kill and maim innocent people. On whom should the burden of risk fall? I think there is much to be said for the claim that the terrorist's liability for complicity in the creation of threats of unjust harm makes it just that he rather than the potential victims of terrorist attacks should bear the costs. These terrible choices about the distribution of risks and harm would never have had to be made were it not for the wrongful activities of this person and his co-conspirators. Why should innocent people have to bear the costs of his wrongful action?

The idea that risks and costs should in general be imposed on those who are liable rather than on the innocent assumes that we can distinguish those who are liable from those who are not. In my examples involving people who are captured with bombs strapped to their bodies, or in the process of making such bombs, there can be little doubt of their liability. But matters are very seldom this clear. So one question that arises here is how stringent our standards of evidence should be in determining liability. It is striking, for example, that our requirements for determining liability to the death penalty are almost incomparably more exacting than our standards for determining liability to killing in war. We insist on a variety of safeguards to ensure that we do not execute an innocent person by mistake. But we take few precautions to ensure that in war we do not kill the innocent by mistake. I am not here referring to acts of war that kill the innocent as a side effect of attacking a military target. I am referring instead to intentional attacks against people who are believed to be legitimate targets but in fact may not be.

Some people argue that in defending our society against terrorism we should insist on standards of evidence of liability that are as stringent as the standards we employ in implementing the death penalty. If these people are right, cases in which torture might be morally justified by the same types of consideration that can justify killing in self-defense will be very rare. Other people argue, however, that even if social defense against terrorism is different from war in many ways, it is nevertheless like war in permitting a certain laxity in the standard of proof of liability. If this is right, it could be just in a broader range of cases to inflict harms on suspected terrorists, even when the evidence of their liability fails to meet the standards on which we insist in domestic law, rather than to allow people we know to be innocent to remain at greater risk.

Another possibility is that the positions I have described in the previous paragraph constitute a false dichotomy. For it can be argued that the reason we can accept a less stringent standard of proof of liability to attack in war is that in war there is virtually no scope for mistake. For in war it is sufficient for liability to attack merely to be a member of the enemy military. If a person wears a uniform, he is liable and may be killed even in the absence of evidence that killing him will be of military value.

Yet there are at least two reasons why the problem cannot be dissolved in this simple way. One is that even if we take the distinction between combatants and noncombatants to mark the boundary between those who are liable to attack in war and those who are not, the distinction between combatant and noncombatant is itself difficult to draw and in practice it is often quite difficult to determine who has combatant status and who does not. As a result, mistakes do occur: people who are in fact combatants are spared while those who are in fact noncombatants are attacked in the belief that they are combatants.

The other problem is that combatant status may not be sufficient for liability, nor non-combatant status sufficient for immunity. This is in fact my view. I think, for example, that those who fight in a just cause by permissible means cannot be liable to attack.

I will not, however, pursue this dialectic further. For I believe that there is a deeper issue here that decisively decides the practical question about torture and thus makes it unnecessary, as a matter of practice, to determine what the standards of evidence of liability should be in dealing with suspected terrorists.

It is not possible, at least at this stage in the evolution of international institutions, to formulate international law for the regulation of conflicts in a way that distinguishes, at least below the level of the political leadership, between those who have right or justice on their side and those who do not. The law of war, for example, cannot distinguish between soldiers who fight for a just cause and those whose cause is unjust, assigning one set of rights and protections to the former and another set to the latter. We have no choice, it seems, but to formulate neutral laws that are equally satisfiable by all belligerents. Because wars are inevitably going to be fought, because they cannot be fought without killing, and because they must nevertheless be regulated by law, it follows that the law of war must permit killing by both sides. This means that the law of war has to permit the killing of the just by the unjust.

Just as unjust wars of aggression will inevitably occur and will in many instances have to be countered by a just war of defense, so terrorist acts against our own society and against other societies are also inevitable. And just as killing in war cannot be legally permitted to one side but not to the other, so too, in the large area encompassing the overlapping spheres of war, counterterrorism, and international police work, the use of torture cannot be legally permitted to the just but not to the unjust. Killing cannot be banned in war; therefore it must be permitted to both sides. This is bad enough. It would be intolerable if torture were permitted, even in tightly circumscribed conditions, to the just and the unjust alike. I have not sought to identify the features of torture that make it uniquely morally repugnant; but whatever they are, they rule out the possibility that the law could ever permit wrong-doers to practice torture as a means of achieving unjust aims.

Fortunately, torture is unlike killing in war in that it can be legally banned. Since its use cannot in practice be legally restricted to the just, and since it must not be permitted to all, the only option is to prohibit it to all, absolutely and categorically.[6]

I argued earlier, however, that torture can on rare occasions be morally justified. What must an individual do in a situation in which torture seems morally required but is legally prohibited? What, for example, should people do if they have captured a person carrying irrefutable evidence of involvement in terrorist plots who refuses to reveal information that is necessary in order to thwart those plots? If, after taking into account the effect that engaging in torture might have on general respect for the law that forbids it, a person still has good reason to believe that morality requires that he engage in torture, because the person to be tortured is clearly liable and the torture would be a necessary and proportionate means of defending the innocent, then I think that person ought morally to engage in torture.

But this person, and the organization that authorizes his counterterrorist work, must remain accountable to the law. This person and his associates may plead for leniency, but they must submit themselves for punishment. They cannot claim a legal justification, in the way that someone who is charged with homicide may claim a justification of self-defense. For we do not want the law to contain provisions for the recognition of justified torture. Nor would it make sense for them to claim an excuse. Because they acted on the basis of a moral justification, none of the recognized excuses would seem to apply.

In paradigm instances of civil disobedience, a person breaks a law openly in order to challenge it, but nevertheless submits herself for punishment in order to demonstrate respect for the law in general, and for the rule of law. If the law that is challenged is in fact a bad law, this person sacrifices herself for the sake of morality. She willingly accepts penalties as a means of trying to bring about a morally better state of affairs.

The same must be true of someone who practices torture when it is morally required but legally prohibited (except, of course, that his reason for violating the law would not be to challenge it). We rightly regard torturers, in general, as the most morally degraded of human beings; but in these rare cases of morally justified torture, the torture would be, paradoxically, a martyr to a higher morality. He would, in fact, be doubly martyred, for there would be two dimensions to his sacrifice. He would have to accept punishment for having done what, in the circumstances, was morally necessary; but he would also have sacrificed something of importance in his own moral nature by having to override powerful inhibitions against a form of action that no decent person could engage in without the deepest moral revulsion.

Notes

37 *Case Western Reserve Journal of International Law* 241 (2006).

1 David Sussman, *Defining Torture*, 37 *Case W. Res. J. Int'l L.* 225 (2005).

2 *See* Henry Shue, *Torture*, 7 *Phil. & Pub. Aff.* 124 (1978).

3 Henry Shue, *Torture in Dreamland: Disposing of the Ticking Bomb*, 37 *Case W. Res. J. Int'l L.* 231 (2005) [hereinafter Shue, *Torture in Dreamland*].

4 *See id.*

5 The sources of my factual claims in this paragraph are personal and anecdotal. The persons who have supplied my information do not have first-hand knowledge of these matters. It is possible, therefore, though not likely, that my factual claims are unfounded. But they are not unrealistic. Even if they are false, we can see that they could easily be true. And that is sufficient for my purposes here. I will therefore continue to write on the assumption that these factual claims are true.

6 Although my argument here is quite different from his, I would like to go on record as registering emphatic agreement with the argument that Henry Shue movingly and compellingly develops in *Torture in Dreamland* against the practical possibility of an institution that would legalize torture but only in rare and exceptional cases. *See* Shue, *Torture in Dreamland, supra* note 3.

PART 4

Theorizing Areas of Law

VIII. CONSTITUTIONAL THEORY: INTERPRETATION AND AUTHORITY

Introduction

N**O ONE CAN DOUBT** the fundamental importance of constitutional law in any legal system. Often thought of as providing the legal framework of the state, the "constitution" consists of a set of rules or norms that define, regulate and structure the main organs of government and the general principles under which the country is governed. In this minimal sense, all states have constitutions. But there are also a variety of richer senses of the term "constitution". Most democratic countries have a written constitution, namely, a document enshrining the main features of the constitution in a canonical way in one written document. Typically this document is legally *supreme*, so that ordinary law which conflicts with it is invalid and is also *entrenched* such that constitutional amendments are more difficult to secure than ordinary legislation. These two central features of written constitutions raise a host of vexing questions of interest not only to lawyers and legal scholars, but also to anyone interested in exploring the legal and philosophical foundations of the state.

Constitutional theory comprises two major parts: an account of the legitimacy of constitutions and the institutions which implement them, and an account of the way constitutions should be interpreted. Clearly, both of these parts are interrelated: how one thinks judges should interpret constitutions depends crucially on how one conceives the nature, identity and authority of constitutions. Beyond questions which go to the legitimacy of the constitution itself, there are further concerns about who should be given the task of implementing it and how they carry out that task. Typically, a written constitution's superior status in the legal hierarchy is implemented by the courts. This gives rise to what Andrei Marmor refers to as "the uniquely problematic nature of constitutional interpretation",[1] namely, that it involves the power of the judiciary to determine issues of profound moral and political importance for society, resulting in legal decisions which are difficult if not impossible to change by regular democratic processes, on the basis of general, abstract provisions which offer minimal textual guidance on how those issues should be decided. As Marmor notes: "this tension between the scope of the power and the paucity of constraints informs the main concerns of constitutional interpretation".[2]

When surveying some of the rival theories of constitutional interpretation, Marmor notes that the widespread attraction of "originalism" is one of the main puzzles about theories of constitutional interpretation.[3] It should be clarified that the prominence of originalism and the politically-charged nature of the debate surrounding it is a particularly striking feature of *American* constitutional theory. Perhaps this is partly due to the symbolic status of the Framers of the US Constitution as Founding Fathers of the nation. But there may be other (more general) reasons for originalism's persistent appeal. The first is the basic fact that meaning is at least partly a result of human intentions and interpretation seeks to establish meaning. However, this perfectly valid conceptual point about the link between intention and meaning does not, in itself, establish the normative cogency of originalism as a valid doctrine of constitutional interpretation. Acknowledging the intentionality inherent in written constitutions does not necessarily lead us down the various originalist paths of deferring to what the Framers thought or believed or hoped when they enacted the US Constitution.

The second possible reason for originalism's persistent appeal draws on a general point which should be borne in mind when considering all rival theories of constitutional interpretation, namely, that the legitimacy of a method of constitutional interpretation is commonly thought to reside in the constraints which are placed on the interpretive activity. Given the immense power entrusted to judges when interpreting the constitution, we are concerned that the interpretive activity is not unbounded—and it is natural to look to the constitutional text and/or original intentions as a source of such constraints. However, by arguing that originalism is a constrained method of interpretation, one is not making any direct claim about the special role or status of the origination. Rather, originalism is then endorsed because of the vices it avoids rather than any of its distinctive virtues. Whether it actually succeeds in avoiding those vices is, of course, an important and contested question in constitutional theory.[4] But the widespread view that even if it does not succeed completely, it is a lesser evil compared to apparently less constrained methods of interpretation[5] may well account for the fact that originalism is often embraced, warts and all, by many practising judges and lawyers drawn from the highest echelons of the legal profession.

Justice Antonin Scalia of the United States Supreme Court is just one such figure. Both on and off the bench, Justice Scalia has attracted much attention for his particular brand of originalism and his fervent opposition to the idea of the "living constitution".[6] The metaphor of the constitution as a "living tree" gives expression to the normative claim that when judges interpret the constitution, they should do so dynamically, in a way which develops its content and updates and adapts it to modern needs and values. Justice Scalia reminds us that those who support the idea of a "living constitution", or indeed those like Marmor who argue that judges interpreting the constitution must engage in sound moral deliberation, face a difficult task, namely, to justify the legitimacy of "evolving" judicial interpretations when they seem, on the surface, so devoid of constraints.

The worry about the immensity of the power given to judges in constitutional interpretation underpins another pervasive concern in constitutional theory, namely, the need to justify the institution of constitutional judicial review in a democracy. It is often said that judicial review under an entrenched Bill of Rights is beset with the "counter-majoritarian difficulty", namely, that when judges strike down a law, they are opposing the choices made by elected representatives of the people. Jeremy Waldron has been one of the most influential opponents of American-style judicial review in recent legal and political theory. His case against judicial review (and in favour of unlimited participatory democracy) hinges on the fact that we disagree about the moral principles that should guide our political system. According to Waldron, the only acceptable way of responding to this fact, whilst simultaneously ensuring respect for citizens' differing views about justice, is to support democratic decision-making across the board. Waldron's central objection to judicial review is that by taking decisions about rights away from democratically accountable institutions, and placing them in the hands of the courts, judicial review involves an unjustifiable "disempowerment of ordinary citizens on matters of the highest moral and political importance".[7] It denies (or at least curtails) citizens' "right to democratic participation".

We should note two important features of Waldron's arguments. The first is that not only are they rooted in democratic values, they are also "right-based". On Waldron's view, if we believe that rights are important, we should have grave mis-givings about entrenching rights in a Bill of Rights, enforced by an unelected judiciary. Disabling citizens from "having a say" in questions about their rights is at variance with the reasons why we attribute rights to them in the first place, namely, because we respect them as autonomous persons with a capacity to reason morally. Thus, belief in the importance and value of human rights is a premise he shares with many supporters of judicial review. Secondly, Waldron's case against judicial review is process-oriented, rather than results-oriented. Waldron argues that a results-driven approach (whereby the decision-making mechanism most likely to deliver sound results is chosen) is unavailable to us, because we disagree about what those results should be. The only alternative, according to Waldron, is an account of political authority based solely on good procedures.[8]

Both of these features are challenged by Fabre. She argues, *contra* Waldron, that if we conceive of individuals as autonomous and confer on them rights protecting that autonomy, this commits us to constitutionalizing them, i.e. entrenching them in a Bill of Rights. She also makes the familiar charge that Waldron's favoured procedure of participatory-democracy suffers from the sort of disagreement he considers fatal to judicial review.[9] Participatory democracy could only survive a challenge posed in the terms Waldron uses to criticise judicial review, if it was itself an uncontroversial solution to the problem of rights protection. But this is clearly not the case. People disagree about whether majoritarianism is a desirable way of making political decisions, just as they disagree about the value of having constitutional judicial review. Waldron urges us to give the "right to participate" pride of place in both our understanding of rights and the justification of judicial review. The question is whether this special status is warranted.

Notes

1 Andrei Marmor, "Constitutional Interpretation", p. 403.
2 Ibid., p. 403.
3 Ibid., p. 411.
4 See further Ronald Dworkin, "The Forum of Principle", in *A Matter of Principle*, Cambridge, MA: Harvard University Press, 1985, pp. 33–72.
5 Antonin Scalia, "Originalism: The Lesser Evil", *Cincinnati Law Review* 57, 1989, 849.
6 For further examination of this idea, see Wil Waluchow, *The Common Law Theory of Judicial Review: The Living Tree,* Cambridge: CUP, 2007, and Aileen Kavanagh, "The Idea of a Living Constitution," *Canadian Journal of Law and Jurisprudence* 16, 2003, 55.
7 Waldron, "A Right-Based Critique of Constitutional Rights", p. 451.
8 For critiques of the process-orientated nature of Waldron's argument, see Aileen Kavanagh, "Participation and Judicial Review", *Law & Philosophy* 22, 2003, 451, 456ff; Joseph Raz, "Disagreement in Politics", *American Journal of Jurisprudence* 43, 1998, 25, 44–47; for Waldron's response, see "The Core of the Case Against Judicial Review", *Yale Law Journal* 115, 2006, 1346, 1369–1395.
9 See e.g. Thomas Christiano, "Waldron on Law and Disagreement", *Law and Philosophy* 19, 2001, 520.

Further reading

Paul Brest, "The Misconceived Quest for the Original Understanding", *Boston University Law Review* 60, 1980, 204–38.
Ronald Dworkin, *Freedom's Law*, Oxford: Oxford University Press, 1998.
Samuel Freeman, "Constitutional Democracy and the Legitimacy of Judicial Review", *Law and Philosophy* 9, 1990, 327–70.
Jeffrey Goldsworthy, "Originalism in Constitutional Interpretation", *Federal Law Review* 25, 1997, 1–50.
Mark Greenberg & Harry Litman, "The Meaning of Original Meaning", 86 *Georgetown Law Journal* 86, 1998, 569ff.
Aileen Kavanagh, "Original Intention, Enacted Text, and Constitutional Interpretation", *American Journal of Jurisprudence* 47, 2002, 255–98.
Aileen Kavanagh, "Participation and Judicial Review", *Law & Philosophy* 22, 2003, 451.
Aileen Kavanagh, "The Idea of a Living Constitution", *Canadian Journal of Law and Jurisprudence* 16, 2003, 55–89.
Stephen Munzer & James Nickel, "Does the Constitution Mean What It Always Meant?" *Columbia Law Review* 77, 1977, 1029–62.
Joseph Raz, "On the Authority and Interpretation of Constitutions", in L. Alexander (ed.) *Constitutionalism: Philosophical Foundations*, Cambridge: Cambridge University Press, 1998.
Antonin Scalia, *A Matter of Interpretation*, Princeton: Princeton University Press, 1996.
Jeremy Waldron, "The Core of the Case Against Judicial Review", *Yale Law Journal* 115, 2006, 1346.
Wil Waluchow, "Constitutionalism", *Stanford Encyclopedia of Philosophy* (last updated Feb 20, 2007 (12 pages).
Wil Waluchow, *A Common Law Theory of Judicial Review: the Living Tree*, Cambridge: Cambridge University Press, 2007.
Michael Walzer, "Philosophy and Democracy", *Political Theory* 9, 1981.

Questions

1. "Whilst it is often believed that the courts move between periods of activism and passivity, the truth is that both activism and restraint are constant features in constitutional interpretation."

   Discuss.

2. "The idea of the 'Living Constitution' is not a method of constitutional interpretation at all, but merely the name given to the view that judges can decide constitutional cases however they wish."

   Discuss.

3. How can a constitutionally-entrenched Bill of Rights be justified in a democracy?

4. Explain the sense in which Waldron's critique of judicial review is process-oriented rather than results-oriented. What impact does this have on the character of his critique?

Chapter 25

Andrei Marmor

CONSTITUTIONAL INTERPRETATION

1. Two basic questions

IN MOST CONSTITUTIONAL democracies, the interpretation of the constitution involves the power of the judiciary (typically the supreme or constitutional court) to determine issues of profound moral and political importance, on the basis of very limited textual guidance, resulting in legal decisions that may last for decades and are practically almost impossible to change by regular democratic processes. This unique legal power raises two main normative questions: One is about the moral legitimacy of the institution itself, and the other is about the ways in which it ought to be practiced. Both of these questions are actually more complex, of course, and the answers to them are bound to be related. It is one of the arguments of this chapter that the ways in which constitutional interpretation ought to be carried out must be sensitive to the main concerns about the moral legitimacy of a constitutional regime. First, however, we need a clearer picture of the issues.

Most democratic[1] countries have a 'written constitution', that is, a document (or a limited number of documents) enacted in some special way, containing the canonical formulation of that country's constitution. Other democracies, though by now very few,[2] have no such canonical document, and their constitution is basically customary. Thus, if by 'constitution' we mean the basic political structure of the legal

system, its basic law making and law applying institutions, then every legal system has a constitution. Every legal system must have, by necessity, certain rules or conventions which determine the ways in which law is made in that system and ways in which it is applied to particular cases. In stable legal systems we would also find rules and conventions determining the structure of sovereignty, the various organs of government, and the kinds of authority they have.

Nevertheless, a written constitution does make a crucial difference because it establishes a practice of judicial review. A written constitution typically enables a higher court, like the supreme court or a special constitutional court, to interpret the constitutional document and impose its interpretation on all other branches of government, including the legislature. I am not claiming that this power of judicial review is a necessary feature of legal systems with a written constitution.[3] Far from it. As a matter of historical development, however, with which we need not be concerned here, it has become the reality that in legal systems with written constitutions some higher court has the power of judicial review.

There are five main features of constitutional documents worth nothing here.

1   *Supremacy*. Constitutions purport to establish and regulate the basic structure of the

legal system, and thus they are deemed supreme over all other forms of legislation. The constitution, as we say, is *the supreme law of the land*.[4] Generally it is assumed that unless the constitutional provisions prevail over ordinary legislation, there is no point in having a constitutional document at all. I will therefore assume that this is a necessary feature of written constitutions.

2　*Longevity*. Constitutions, by their very nature, purport to be in force for a very long time, setting out the basic structure of the legal system for future generations. Ordinary statutes may happen to be in force for a very long time as well. But this is not an essential aspect of ordinary legislation. It is, however, an essential aspect of constitutions that they are meant to be lasting, that they are intended to apply to generations well beyond the generation in which they had been created.

3　*Rigidity*. The main technique by which constitutions can be guaranteed to be lasting for generations is their rigidity: Constitutions typically provide for their own methods of change or amendment, making it relatively much more difficult to amend than ordinary democratic legislation. The more difficult it is to amend the constitution, the more 'rigid' it is. Constitutions vary considerably on this dimension, but it is an essential aspect of constitutions that they are relatively secure from formal change by the ordinary democratic processes.[5] Without such relative rigidity, constitutions could not achieve their longevity. None of this means, however, that constitutions do not change in other ways. As we shall see in detail below, the main way in which constitutions change is by judicial interpretation. Whether they recognize it as such or not, judges have the power to change the constitution, and they often

do so. The question of whether this is an inevitable aspect of constitutional interpretation, or not, is an issue I will discuss in some detail below.

4　*Moral content*. Most constitutions regulate two main domains: the basic structure of government with its divisions of political power, and the area of human and civil rights. In the first domain we normally find such issues as the division of power between the federal and local authorities, if there is such a division, the establishment of the main legislative, executive and judicial branches of government and their respective legal powers, the establishment and control of the armed forces, and so on. In the second domain, constitutions typically define a list of individual and sometimes group rights which are meant to be secure from encroachment by governmental authorities, including the legislature. There is nothing essential or necessary in this two pronged constitutional content, and the reasons for it are historical. The moral content and moral importance of a bill of rights is obvious and widely recognized as such. It is worth keeping in mind, however, that many aspects of the other, structural, prong of constitutions involve moral issues as well. Determining the structure of government, legislation etc., is perhaps partly a matter of coordination, but many aspects of it are not without moral significance. After all, we are not morally indifferent to the question of who makes the law and how it is done.

5　*Generality and abstraction*. Many constitutional provisions, particularly in the domain of the bill of rights and similar matters of principle, purport to have very general application. They are meant to apply to all spheres of public life. This is one of the main reasons for the high level of abstraction in which constitutional provisions tend to be formulated.[6] The aspiration for longevity may be another reason for abstractly formulated principles. And of course, sometimes an abstract formulation is simply a result of compromise between competing conceptions of the relevant principle held by opposing parties of framers. Be this as it may, this need for generality and abstraction comes with a price: the more general and abstract the formulation of a constitutional provision, the less clear it is what the provision actually means, or requires.

These five features of written constitutions explain the uniquely problematic nature of constitutional interpretation. On the one hand, those who are entrusted with the authoritative interpretation of the constitution are granted considerable legal power, their decisions are often morally very significant, potentially long lasting, and, most importantly, with few exceptions, they have the final say on the matter.[7] On the other hand, these constitutional decisions are typically based on the interpretation of very general and abstract provisions, often enacted a very long time ago, by people who lived in a different generation. This tension between the scope of the power and the paucity of constraints informs the main concerns of constitutional interpretation.

One note of caution before we proceed. It would be a mistake to assume that there are no 'easy cases' in constitutional law. Not every provision of a written constitution is particularly abstract or problematic, nor is the whole constitution confined to such high-minded issues as basic rights or important moral or political principles. Many constitutional provisions can simply be understood, and applied, without any need for interpretation. It is certainly true that there are likely to be many more 'hard cases' in constitutional law than in the ordinary business of statutory regulation, but this is just a matter of proportion. There is nothing in the nature of constitutions which would preclude the existence of 'easy cases'.

With this rough outline of the uniqueness of constitutional interpretation, we can now formulate the main questions. So let us concentrate on a paradigmatic model, more or less along the lines of the US constitutional practice: we assume that there is a written constitutional document which is deemed the supreme law of the land, we assume that it has been enacted (and perhaps subsequently amended) some generations ago, we assume that there is a supreme court which is entrusted with the legal interpretation of the document and that this legal power includes the power of judicial review. I mentioned that there are two main normative questions that need to be addressed: Is a written constitution morally legitimate, and how should judges go about in their interpretation of the constitution?[8] Both questions are more complex. The first question is actually twofold: there is a question about the moral legitimacy of the constitution, and there is a separate question about the moral legitimacy of judicial review. Let me consider these questions in turn.

PART ONE: MORAL LEGITIMACY

2. The moral legitimacy of the constitution

Constitutions are often described as pre-commitment devices. Like Ulysses who tied himself to the mast, the constitution is seen as a device of self-imposed commitments and restrictions, guarding against temptations which may lead one off the track in the future.[9] But this Ulysses metaphor is very misleading. The most challenging moral question about the legitimacy of constitutions arises precisely because it is not like Ulysses who ties *himself* to the mast, but rather like a Ulysses who ties *others* to the mast with him. In other words, the inter-generational issue is central to the question about the very legitimacy of constitutions. The enactment of a constitution purports to bind the current and future generations by imposing significant constraints on their ability to make laws and govern their lives according to the ordinary democratic decision making processes. Thus the question arises: why should the political leaders of one generation have the power to bind future generations to their conceptions of the good and the right? It is crucial to note that the moral significance of this question is not confined to old constitutions. Even if the constitution is new, it purports to bind future generations. It is this intention to impose constitutional constraints for the future that is problematic, and thus it does not really matter how old the constitution is.

It may be objected that this formulation underestimates the significance of 'We the people', that it ignores the fact that constitutions tend to embody widely shared principles and ideals, representing, as it were, the nation's *raison d'etat*. But this would make very little difference. Even if at the time of the constitution's enactment its principles and ideals are really shared across the board, the intergenerational issue remains: perhaps no one, even an entire generation, should have the power to make important moral decisions for future generations. At least not deliberately so. It is true, of course, that a great number of our current practices and collective decisions are bound to affect, for better and worse, the fortunes of future generations. But these collective actions and decisions do not purport to have authority over future generations. They are not deliberately designed to bind future generations to our conceptions of the good and the just. On the other hand, if we think that constitutions are legitimate, we should be able to explain how it is legitimate to make authoritatively binding decisions on important matters of morality and politics, that are supposed to last for generations and difficult to change by ordinary democratic processes. I doubt that such an argument can be provided,

though I will not try to substantiate those doubts in any detail here.[10] But perhaps it is not necessary. There are several arguments which strive to avoid this inter-generational problem or mitigate it considerably.

First, it could be argued that the moral legitimacy of the constitution simply derives from its moral soundness. The constitution is valid because its content is morally good, that is, regardless of the ways in which it came into being. The claim would have to be that the principles concerning the form of government which the constitution prescribes and the rights and values it upholds are just the correct moral values under the present circumstances, and it is this moral soundness that validates the constitution. Needless to say, this argument cannot apply generally, to any constitution one encounters. It would only apply when it holds true, namely, when it is actually true that the content of the constitution is, indeed, morally sound. But even so, the argument is problematic. One could say that it misses the point of having a constitution at all. What would be the point of having a written constitution unless the constitutional document makes a normative-practical difference? It can only make such a difference if it constitutes reasons for action. But according to the argument under consideration, the only reasons for action the constitution provides are the kind of reasons we have anyway, regardless of the constitution, namely, that they are good moral reasons. According to the argument from moral soundness, then, it is very difficult to explain what difference the constitution makes.

This argument from moral soundness should not be confused, however, with a different and even more problematic argument for the legitimacy of constitutions, which draws not on the moral soundness of the constitution itself, but on the moral expertise of its framers. According to the latter, the constitution is legitimate because it had been enacted by people who, at least relative to us, are experts in those fields of political morality which are enshrined in the constitution. Thus, according to this argument, the legitimacy of the constitution derives from the moral authority of its framers. Notably, if this argument is sound, it could show how the constitutional document does make a practical difference. It would make a difference because it meets the conditions of *the normal justification thesis*: by following the constitutional prescriptions we are more likely to follow the correct moral reasons that apply to us than by trying to figure out those reasons for ourselves. But the argument clearly fails, and for two main reasons. First, because such an argument is bound to rely on a huge mystification of the moral stature of the framers, ascribing to them knowledge and wisdom beyond anything that would be historically warranted. More importantly, the argument fails because it assumes that there is expertise in morality, and this assumption is false. As I have mentioned in the previous chapter, there are good epistemic and moral reasons to hold that no one can possess expertise in the realm of basic moral principles.[11]

According to the third argument, the moral validity of the constitution is not a static matter, something that we can attribute to the constitutional document. Validity is dynamic, depending on the current interpretation of the constitution and its application to particular cases. As long as the particular content of the constitution is determined by its interpretation, and the authoritative interpretation at any given time correctly instantiates the values which ought to be upheld in the community, the constitution would be morally legitimate because its actual content is shaped by the pertinent needs and concerns of the community at the time of interpretation.[12] In other words, this argument, which I will call *the argument from interpretation*, renders the moral validity of the constitution entirely dependent on the particular uses to which it is put. These uses are determined by the particular interpretations and legal decisions rendered by the court at any given time. Thus, a

crucial assumption of this argument must be, that there is enough interpretative flexibility in constitutional documents to allow for the courts to adapt the constitutional prescriptions to current needs and values.

Before I consider the merit of the argument from interpretation, let me mention a fourth argument, recently suggested by Joseph Raz. According to Raz,

> *As long as they remain within the boundaries set by moral principles*, constitutions are self-validating in that their validity derives from nothing more than the fact that they are there.
>
> [P]ractice-based law is self-vindicating. The constitution of a country is a legitimate constitution because it is the constitution it has.
>
> (1998: 173)

As Raz himself points out, there is a whole range of practices which gain their moral validity from the fact of the practice itself. Social conventions are of such a nature. Conventions create reasons for action because they are practiced, and as long as the convention is not morally impermissible, the reasons for action it creates are valid reasons. The fact that we could have had a different, perhaps even better convention under the circumstances, does not entail that there is anything wrong with following the convention that we do have. Similarly, I presume, Raz wishes to claim that as long as the constitution we have is not immoral, the fact that we happen to have it is a good reason to abide by it. But we have to be more careful here. Our reasons for following a social convention are not entirely derivable from the fact that the convention is practiced, though they certainly depend on it. Conventions evolve either in order to solve a pre-existing co-ordination problem, or else they constitute their own values by creating a conventional practice which is worth engaging in.[13] Either way, there must be something valuable in the practice of following the convention for it to give rise to reasons for action, beyond the fact that the convention is there and just happens to be followed. Similarly, the fact that the constitution is there and happens to be followed cannot be the whole reason for following it. It must serve some values, either by solving some problems which were there to be solved, or by creating valuable practices worth engaging in. I think that Raz recognizes this when he points out that constitutions typically serve the values of stability and continuity of a legal system (1998: 174–75).[14]

There is another crucial assumption here about which Raz is quite explicit: the conclusion about the self-validating nature of constitutional practice can only follow 'if *morality underdetermines* the principles concerning the form of government and the content of individual rights enshrined in constitutions' (1998: 173). The same is true about social conventions, generally: unless their content is underdetermined by morality, they are not conventional rules. If morality *determines* the rule, say, R: 'All x's ought to φ under circumstances Cn', then the reason for φ-ing under circumstances Cn is a moral reason, irrespective of the fact that R is practiced.

I hope that we are now in a position to see that both Raz's argument and the argument from interpretation share a certain assumption about the nature of constitutions that is crucially important. Roughly, both arguments must assume that the written constitution, as such, actually makes less of a difference than one might have thought. Let me be more precise. The conditions for the legitimacy of a constitution must comprise the following conditions. First, the values and principles enshrined in it must be morally permissible. This goes without saying. (I am not suggesting that the constitution must be morally perfect, or optimal. Some moral errors a constitution contains may be outweighed by other values it promotes.) Second, when certain choices are made in particular cases, they would be legitimate if they are either morally underdetermined, or else, morally correct. The application of constitutional principles or values can

be morally underdetermined in two ways: either they concern issues which are simply not determined by moral considerations, such as solution to a coordination problem,[15] or else, if they do manifest moral choices, those would be the kind of choices which are made between incommensurable goods or values. However, in those cases in which the value choices are morally determinable, it is pretty clear that both the argument from interpretation and Raz's argument from self-validity must hold that only morally correct choices are valid. Therefore, either the constitution embodies choices which are morally underdetermined (in one of the two ways mentioned), or else, the constitution must be applied in a way which is morally sound. It follows from this that both arguments must assume that at least in those areas in which the constitution would make a moral difference, it can be interpreted to make the difference that it should, that is, according to the true moral principles that should apply to the particular case. To be sure, the thesis here is not that the constitutional document can be interpreted to mean just about anything we want it to mean. But the thesis must be that constitutional documents typically allow *enough interpretative flexibility* that makes it possible to apply their morally significant provisions in morally sound ways.

I do not wish to deny the truth of this last assumption. I will have more to say about it in the last section. For now, suffice it to point out one important implication of this thesis. Namely, that it makes the moral legitimacy of constitutions very much dependent on the practices of their interpretation. In other words, a great deal of the burden of moral legitimacy is shifted by these arguments to the application of the constitution, thus assuming that the constitution is legitimate only if the courts are likely to apply the constitution in a morally desirable way. This brings us to the second question about the legitimacy of constitutions, namely, the question about the legitimacy of judicial review.

3. The legitimacy of judicial review

Three points about judicial review are widely acknowledged. First, that it is not a necessary feature of a constitutional regime. As I have already mentioned, it is certainly conceivable to have a legal system with a written constitution without entrusting the power of its authoritative interpretation in the hands of the judiciary or, in fact, in the hands of anybody in particular. Therefore, secondly, it is also widely acknowledged that the desirability of judicial review is mostly a question of institutional choice: given the fact that we do have a constitution, which is the most suitable institution that should be assigned the role of interpreting it and applying it to particular cases? Finally, it is widely acknowledged that the courts' power of judicial review is not easily reconcilable with general principles of democracy. Even those who support the legitimacy of judicial review, acknowledge the existence of at least a tension between our commitment to democratic decision procedures and the courts' power to overrule decisions made by a democratically elected legislature.[16] This is a very complicated issue, and I cannot hope to expound here on the necessary elements of a theory of democracy to substantiate this point.[17] For our purposes, it should be sufficient just to keep this aspect of judicial review in mind, without assuming too much about any particular theory of democracy.

Lawyers sometimes find it difficult to understand why the normative justification of judicial review is separate from the question of the legitimacy of constitutions. For them the reasoning of *Marbury v. Madison* is almost tautological. We just cannot have it in any other way. If we have a written constitution which is the supreme law of the land, then surely it follows that the courts must determine what the law is and make sure that it is applied to particular cases. The power of the courts to impose their interpretation of the constitution on the legislature simply follows, so the argument goes, from the

fact that the constitution is legally supreme to ordinary legislation. But of course this is a *non sequitur*. Even if it is true that as a matter of law, constitutional provisions prevail over ordinary legislation, and it is also true that there must be some institution which has the power to determine, in concrete cases, whether such a conflict exists or not, it simply does not follow that this institution must be the supreme court, or any other institution in particular.[18] The argument must be premised on the further assumption that the court is the most suitable institution to carry out this task of constitutional interpretation. But why should that be the case?

One consideration which is often offered as a reply consists in the thesis that the constitution is a legal document and that therefore its interpretation is a legal matter. Since courts tend to possess legal expertise, they are the best kind of institution to be entrusted with constitutional interpretation. The problem with this argument is that it relies on a dubious inference: from the fact that the constitution is a legal document, and that its interpretation is, therefore, a legal matter, it does not follow that constitutional decisions are based on legal reasoning requiring legal expertise. Most constitutional decisions are based on moral and political considerations. That is so, because the kind of issues decided in constitutional cases are, mostly, moral and ethical in nature, such as determining the nature and scope of basic human and civil rights, or shaping the limits of political authorities and the structure of democratic processes.[19] Therefore, one of the crucial questions here is whether the supreme court is the kind of institution which is conducive to sound moral deliberation and decision making on moral issues. This question is not easy to answer. Partly, because it is a matter of culture that may vary from place to place. But also because there are conflicting considerations here. On the one hand, courts do have certain institutional advantages in this respect, having certain characteristics which are conducive to moral deliberation. (For example, the fact that deliberation in a courtroom is argumentative, that it is open to arguments from opposing sides, the requirement to justify decisions by reasoned opinions which are made public, and so forth.) On the other hand, courts are also under considerable pressure to conceal the true nature of the debate, casting it in legal language and justifying their decisions in legal terms, even if the choices are straightforwardly moral or political in nature. As we have noted in previous chapters, there is a constant pressure on judges faced with decisions in 'hard cases' to present their reasoning in legal language even if the decision is not based on legal reasons in any meaningful sense. Although perfectly rational from the judiciary's perspective, such a pretence is not necessarily conducive to sound moral deliberation.

There is a much more important issue here. Those who favor the courts' power of judicial review often rely on an argument which is less concerned with the nature of the institution, and more with the nature of the decisions in constitutional cases. According to this line of thought, which I will call *the argument from consensus*, the reasoning which supports the institution of judicial review is as follows:

1 The rights and principles entrenched in the constitution are those which are widely shared in the community, reflecting a deep level of moral consensus.

2 The constitutional entrenchment of these rights is required in order to protect them from the vagaries of momentary political pressures, from shortsighted political temptations.

3 Precisely because the supreme court is not an ordinary democratic institution, it is relatively free of political pressures and shortsighted populist temptations.

4 Therefore, by entrusting the power of judicial review to the supreme court, we are likely to secure, as far as possible, the protection of those rights and principles

which are, in fact, widely shared in the community.

Admittedly, there is a great deal to be said in favor of this argument. If its assumptions are sound, then it would not only justify the institutional choice of the court in deciding constitutional issues, but would also go a considerable way in mitigating the anti-democratic nature of judicial review. We could say that judicial review is anti-democratic only on its surface; at a deeper level, it secures the protection of those rights and principles which are actually held by the vast majority of the people.[20]

I think that this argument fails. And it fails mostly because it is based on a misconception of the nature of rights and the role of rights discourse in a pluralistic society. Explaining this point requires a small detour, exploring some crucial aspects of the nature of rights.[21] In what follows, I will assume that the most plausible account of the nature of rights is *the interest theory of rights*. Basically, according to this analysis, we would say that *A* has a right to φ if an aspect of *A*'s well being, that is, an interest of *A*, *justifies* the imposition of duties on others, those duties which would be required and warranted to secure *A*'s interest in φ.[22]

According to this analysis, rights are actually *intermediary conclusions* in arguments which begin with the evaluation of interests and end with conclusions about duties which should be imposed on other people. When we say that *A* has a right to φ, we say that *A*'s interest in φ justifies the imposition of duties on others in respect to that interest. From a strictly analytical point of view, however, the concept of a right is, in a sense, redundant; it is just an intermediary step in a moral argument leading from the values of certain human interests, to conclusions about the need to impose certain duties. Therefore, the question arises: Why do we need this intermediary step cast in the form 'a right'?

Joseph Raz gave two answers:[23] One partial answer might be, that it simply saves time and energy; it is often the case that practical arguments proceed through the mediation of intermediary steps, simply because there is no need to begin each and every practical argument from first premises; that would be too tedious.

There is, however, a much more important reason: intermediary steps, such as rights, enable us to settle on a set of shared intermediary conclusions, *in spite of considerable disagreement about the grounds* of those intermediary conclusions. In other words, people can settle on the recognition of rights, despite the fact that they would deeply disagree about the reasons for having those rights. Rights discourse enables a common culture to be formed around some intermediary conclusions, precisely because of their intermediary nature.

Furthermore, it is crucial to realize that there is an important asymmetry between rights and duties. Rights, unlike duties, do not entail that the right-holder has any particular reasons for action. The proposition: 'A has duty to φ' *entails* that A has a reason to φ. But having a right to do something does not entail that one has a reason to do it. (Your right to freedom of speech, for instance, does not give you any reasons to say something.) This analytical point is very important: it explains why people with different and competing sets of fundamental values are bound to disagree about the duties they have.[24] But this need not be the case with rights, since there is no immediate relation of entailment between rights and reasons for action. True, there is an indirect relation of entailment: rights justify the imposition of duties on others. But it is very often the case that people agree on the existence of a given right even if they actually disagree on the nature and scope of the duties which the right justifies. Thus, it is normally easier for people with different conceptions of the good to agree on a shared set of rights than duties, as rights do not entail immediate reasons for action.

It is, however, the intermediary nature of rights discourse which is quintessential. It explains why rights discourse is particularly fit for pluralistic societies. Societies where different groups of people are deeply divided about their conceptions of the good, need to settle on a set of rights they can all acknowledge, in spite of deep controversies regarding the grounds of those rights (and their ramifications). Hence it is not surprising or accidental that in homogeneous societies there is very little rights discourse; such societies normally share a common understanding of ultimate values, and consequently of the various duties people have, and they do not need this intermediary step from ultimate values to duties. Only in those societies where people do not share a common understanding of ultimate values, namely, in pluralistic societies, is rights discourse prevalent.[25]

But this social function of rights discourse also points to its own limits. The intermediary nature of rights discourse explains why determining the limits of rights, and their relative weight in competition with other rights or values, is bound to be a controversial matter. In order to determine in a reasoned manner the limits of a given right, or its relative weight in a situation of conflict, one would naturally need to go back to the reasons for having the right in the first place, and it is precisely at this point that agreement breaks down. As a matter of fact, more often than not we will discover that there was never an agreement there to begin with. In other words, precisely because of those reasons which explain the widespread consensus on the rights we have, there is bound to be disagreement over the boundaries of those rights and their desirable ramifications. Widespread consensus on how to resolve various conflicts between rights, or between rights and other values, is only possible in the framework of a shared culture of moral and political views, but it is typically in such cases that rights have relatively little cultural and political significance. If rights discourse is prevalent in a given society, it is mostly because there is little agreement on anything else, in particular, on the ultimate values people cherish.[26]

If this account of the nature of rights discourse is basically correct, then it should become clear why the argument from consensus is bound to fail. It fails because it relies on a widespread consensus which is illusory. It is true that in pluralistic societies we do tend to agree on the rights enshrined in the bill of rights, but this is a very tenuous agreement which breaks down as soon as a conflict comes to the surface. Since it is conflict between rights, or rights and other values, that gets litigated in the constitutional cases, we are bound to discover that there is not going to be any consensual basis on which such conflicts can be resolved.

At this point the interlocutor is likely to ask: but what is the alternative? If we do not entrust the resolution of such conflicts in the hands of the court, how else are we going to resolve them? The answer is, of course, that we can leave the resolution of such evaluative and ideological conflicts to the ordinary legislative and other democratic decision making processes. Not because they are more likely to be morally sound than the decisions of courts. But at least they have two advantages: for whatever its worth, they are democratic. And, not less importantly, perhaps, legislative decisions tend to be much more tentative than constitutional decisions of a supreme court. In fact, they are more tentative in two senses: First, legislative decisions on morally or ideologically controversial issues do not tend to last for too long. Those who have lost their case today may still gain the upper hand tomorrow.[27] Secondly, democratic decisions also tend to convey a more tentative kind of message than constitutional decisions of a supreme court. When the court decides a constitutional issue, it decides it in a sort of timeless fashion, declaring a timeless moral truth, as it were; such a message conveys to the losing party that it has got its profound moral principles wrong. As opposed to this, a democratic decision does not convey such a message; it tells the losing party no more than

that it simply lost this time, and may win at another. It does not necessarily convey the message that the loser is morally wrong, or at odds with the basic moral values cherished by the rest of the community.[28]

To be sure, none of this is meant to be conclusive. Ultimately, the desirability of judicial review is a matter of institutional choice, and a great many factors which figure in such a complex consideration are empirical in nature. Surely, one major consideration must concern the likelihood that a supreme court will get the moral decisions right, or at least, more frequently right than any other institution. Are there any reasons to believe that from an *instrumental* perspective, courts would do a better job in protecting our rights than, say, the democratic legislative assembly?

Supporters of judicial review think that there are plenty of such reasons. Jeremy Waldron (1999), however, is rather skeptical about this instrumental argument. This right-instrumentalism, he claims, faces the difficulty of taking for granted that we know what rights we should have, and to what extent, and then it is only an instrumental issue whether the courts, or the legislature, would do a better job in protecting them. But this is wrong, Waldron claims, because it assumes that we already possess the truth about rights, whereas the whole point of the objection to judicial review was that rights are just as controversial as any other political issue (1999: 252–53). Supporters of judicial review, however, need not make this obvious mistake. They can maintain that whatever our rights and their limits ought to be, they are of such a nature that legislatures are bound to get them wrong; or at least, judges are more likely to get them right. Even in the absence of knowledge or consensus about rights, there may be reasons to assume that some institutions are more likely to go right (or wrong) about such issues than others. Perhaps legislative assemblies do not have the appropriate incentives to even try to protect our rights, or they may be systematically biased about such issues, and so forth.

Waldron's reply to this, more plausible, version of rights-instrumentalism is that the assumptions it relies upon are just as controversial as the moral issues underlying rights discourse (1999: 253). But this is not a convincing reply. After all, how can we design political institutions, including legislative assemblies, unless we possess considerable knowledge about institutional constraints and the likely consequences of various institutional structures? Waldron should have confronted the institutional issue more directly, and perhaps he could show that rights-instrumentalism may actually fail on its own terms. Neither the long history of judicial review in the US, nor the institutional character of the courts, necessarily lend credence to the supporters of judicial review. It is certainly arguable that courts are essentially conservative institutions, typically lagging behind progressive movements in society,[29] severely circumscribed by adversary procedures, and most importantly, perhaps, constrained by the lack of any real political power which tends to limit severely their incentive and confidence in making progressive social changes. Perhaps legislative assemblies are not so diverse and progressive as Waldron depicts in his *Law and Disagreement* (1999), but he is certainly right to question whether courts are necessarily better suited to protect our rights. In any case, since judicial review is the constitutional practice in most contemporary democracies, and seems to be here to stay, I will move on to consider the second main issue about constitutional interpretation, namely, how should it proceed.

PART TWO: INTERPRETATION

4. Any sensible originalism?

The widespread attraction of 'originalism' is one of the main puzzles about theories of con-

stitutional interpretation. Admittedly, 'originalism' is not the title of one particular theory of constitutional interpretation but rather the name of a family of diverse ideas, some of which are actually at odds with each other. Nevertheless, the underlying theme, due to which it is warranted to subsume such diverse views under one title, is clear enough: Originalists claim that the interpretation of the constitution should seek to effectuate, or at least be faithful to, the understanding of the constitutional provisions which can be historically attributed to its framers. Such a general thesis must comprise both a normative and a descriptive element. The normative element pertains to the conditions of legitimacy of constitutional interpretation: It maintains that an interpretation of the constitution which would not be faithful to the ways in which the constitution was originally understood by those who enacted it, would not be a morally legitimate interpretation. This normative thesis, however, must be premised on the complex factual assumption that we can have a fairly sound conception of who the framers of the constitution are, and that their views on what the constitution means are sufficiently clear and discernible to allow for the kind of interpretative guidance that is needed to determine (at least some not insignificant number of) constitutional cases facing the supreme court. There are so many reasons to doubt both of these assumptions that it is quite a mystery why originalism still has the scholarly (and judicial) support that it does.

Consider the factual assumptions first. There are numerous ways in which constitutions come into being; sometimes they are enacted as a result of a revolution or a civil war striving to stabilize and legalize the new constitutional order, at other times as a result of a secession (which may be more or less orderly), and sometimes as a result of a legal reform that takes place within a well functioning legal system and according to its prescribed legal authority. In spite of this historical diversity, it is commonly the case that a very large number of political actors are involved in the process of creating (or amending) the constitution, and it is typically the case that our knowledge of their precise roles in the process, and their eventual impact on its result, is very partial, at best. Thus the term 'the framers of the constitution' usually refers to a very loose concatenation of a fairly large number of people and institutions, playing different legal and political roles in the constitution's enactment.[30] How likely is it that such a loose group of political actors would actually share a reasonably coherent moral and political philosophy underlying the various constitutional provisions? Or, indeed, that they would have any particular views about most of the constitutional issues which will come before the courts, often generations later?

But such factual doubts should be the least of our worries. The main problem with originalism is a moral one: Why should the framers of a constitution, or anyone for that matter, have the tremendous power of having their moral and political views about what constitutes good government and the nature of our basic rights, imposed on an entire nation for generations to come? Unless originalists can provide a moral justification for granting such a vast and lasting power on any particular person, or group of persons, their case for originalism cannot be substantiated. And the problem is that there are only two kinds of argument one can offer here, and both of them are bound to fail. The idea that the framers' views should inform constitutional interpretation can either be derived from the assumption that the framers somehow had known better what ought to be done, that they should be considered as moral experts, as it were, or else it must be based on the idea that any conceivable alternative is even worse, less legitimate.[31] Since I have already mentioned the doubts we should have about the idea that the framers can be regarded as moral experts, let me consider the second kind of argument.

Any alternative to originalism, so this argument runs, would involve the power of the judges of the supreme court to determine, on the basis of their own moral views, what the constitution actually means in controversial cases. In other words, the assumption is that unless judges are required to defer to the 'original' understanding of the constitution, they would simply impose their own moral and political views on us, and that would be illegitimate for various reasons. For example, because the supreme court is not a democratic institution, it is not accountable to the people, it does not necessarily reflect the wish of the people, and so forth. Once again, it should be noted that this argument rests on two limbs. It must assume that an original understanding of the constitution is actually capable of constraining, at least to some extent, the possible interpretations of the constitutional document, and it contends that such a constraint is, indeed, morally desirable.

Let me concentrate on the moral issue. Thus, to make the argument at least initially plausible, let us suppose that we do know who the framers of the constitution are, and suppose further that we can be confident that we know everything that there is to know about their purposes, intentions, and so forth. Framing this in terms of the intentions of the framers, let us follow the main distinction introduced in the previous chapter and divide the relevant intentions of the framers into those which constitute their *further intentions* and those which constitute their *application intentions*.

Now, most originalists would readily admit that deference to the framers' *application intentions* is very problematic. Or, at the very least, they would have to admit that the older the constitution, the less it would make sense to defer to the framers' *application intentions*.[32] Surely it makes no sense to rely on the views of people who lived generations ago about things they were completely unfamiliar with and could not have possibly imagined to exist. But if we think about this in a principled way, we must acknowledge that this conclusion cannot be confined to particularly old constitutions. Just as it makes no sense to bind the constitutional interpretation to *application intentions* of 'old' framers, because they could not have predicted the kind of concerns we face today, it would make no sense to bind any constitutional interpretation *for the future* by the *application intentions* of framers in our generation.

Thus, if originalism is to make any sense at all, it must be confined to the framers' *further intentions*. Even if we have no reason to speculate about the framers' thoughts and expectations with respect to the ways in which the relevant constitutional provisions should be applied to particular cases, so this argument runs, we do have reasons to understand and respect the general purposes that the framers' had had in enacting the constitutional provision which they did. Although not phrased in terms of this distinction between application and further intentions, this is basically the view about constitutional interpretation which Dworkin advocates. History should be consulted, Dworkin claims, in order to understand what is the general moral or political principle that the framers had sought to enact in the constitution. We must try to understand the 'very general principle, not any concrete application of it' (1996: 9). The latter should be left to the supreme court to figure out according to its best moral reasoning.

The main problem with this argument is, however, that it actually ignores Dworkin's own best insight about the nature of interpretation. Any interpretation, Dworkin (1986: 60–61) rightly claimed, must begin with certain views about the values which are inherent in the genre to which the text is taken to belong. Unless we know what it is that makes texts in that particular genre better or worse, we cannot even begin to interpret the particular text in hand. If I purport to offer an interpretation of a certain novel, for example, I must first have some views about the

kind of values which make novels good and worthy of our appreciation. Otherwise, I could hardly explain why we should pay attention to this aspect of the novel rather than to any other. A certain view about what makes instances of a given genre good or bad must inform any interpretation of a text within that genre. Dworkin is absolutely right about this. But then the same principle should apply to legal interpretation, including in the constitutional context. Before we decide to consult history, or intentions, or anything else for that matter, we must first form our views about the kind of values which are inherent in the relevant genre. In the constitutional case, we must rely on the correct views about what makes constitutions good or bad, what is it that makes a constitutional regime worthy of our appreciation and respect. But as soon as we begin to think about this question, the appeal of the framers intentions dissipates even before it takes any particular shape.

I do not intend to suggest that an answer to the general question of what makes constitutions valuable is easy to answer, or even that we can have satisfactory answers to it. But at least we know some of the problems, and the moral authority of the constitution's framers is one of them. As we have noted above, it is one of the main concerns about the legitimacy of constitutions that by following a constitution as the supreme law of the land, we in effect grant the framers of the constitution legal authority which exceeds the authority of our elected representatives to enact laws according to respectful democratic processes. This is a very considerable power that is not easy to justify, particularly when we take into account the fact that it is supposed to last for generations (and is typically guaranteed to do so by the constitution's rigidity). As we have noted earlier, the role of the framers in the enactment of a constitution is one of the most problematic aspects of the legitimacy of a constitutional regime. Once we discard any assumption about the framers' superior knowledge about matters of moral and political principle, as we should, not much remains to justify their particular role in legitimizing the constitutional framework that we have. Thus the more we tie our deference to the constitution to the framers' particular role in its enactment, the more acute the problem of moral legitimacy becomes. Whatever it is that makes constitutions good and worthy of our respect, could have very little to do with the moral or political purposes of its framers. The legitimacy of a constitution must reside in the solution it offers to the problems we face, not in the purposes, however noble and admirable, that the framers had had. And it is advisable to keep in mind that the framers of a constitution could also have had purposes and intentions which are not so noble and admirable. Either way, it should make no difference.

Consider, for example, one of Dworkin's own favorite cases: suppose that the question is whether the equal protection clause of the 14th amendment of the US Constitution rules out school segregation or not. Dworkin contends that this question should not be determined according to the application intentions of the framers; in fact, we probably know well enough that the framers of the 14th amendment would not have thought that it rules out anything like school segregation. Instead, Dworkin claims, we should consider the kind of general principle which the framers intended by the phrase 'equal protection of the laws'. Then we shall see that it must be a very general moral principle of excluding *any* form of unjustified discrimination, and not only some weaker principle of formal equality before the law. 'History seems decisive', Dworkin writes, 'that the framers of the Fourteenth Amendment did not mean to lay down only so weak a principle as that one . . .' (1996: 9). But it is just puzzling how Dworkin ignores the possibility of the opposite historical verdict here: What if it really turned out that history was decisive in supporting

the opposite conclusion? Suppose that it really was the case that the framers had in mind only, and exclusively, a very narrow principle of a formal equality before the law, and not anything as general as an anti-discrimination principle of equality.[33] Should that force us to the conclusion that *Brown v Board of Education* was wrongly decided? Or should it even mean that there is any consideration worth mentioning that counts against the moral legitimacy of *Brown*? We are just left to wonder why should we ever care about framers' purposes, as general or abstract as they may be.

I began this last discussion by suggesting that originalism is at least partly motivated by the fear of its alternative. I will get to this in a moment. However, it should be kept in mind that if originalism does not make any moral sense, the poor fate of its alternatives cannot provide it with any credentials either. Even if there is a problem of moral legitimacy with the supreme court's decisions on constitutional issues, it cannot be solved by striving to curtail the discretion of the court by means which are morally groundless. So what is the alternative? Perhaps this one: that the courts should strive to interpret the constitution according to their best possible understanding of the moral/ political issues involved, striving to reach the best possible moral decision under the current circumstances. To be sure, I do not mean to suggest that there is always, or even most of the time, one decision which is *the best*. There may be several conceivable decisions, equally, or incommensurably good (or bad). The point is that in constitutional interpretation on matters of moral or political principle, there is no substitute to sound moral reasoning. For better or worse, the courts are entrusted with the legal power to interpret the constitution and sound moral reasoning is the only tool at their disposal. This is only a conclusion at this stage, not an argument. Before it can be substantiated, we must consider a few more alternatives and modifications.

5. Alternative methods?

What is the legal authority of the court to rely on moral arguments in constitutional interpretation? The simple answer is that the constitution is phrased in moral terms, enshrining moral and political principles and individual or group rights. More precisely, however, the effect of the moral language and moral subject matter of constitutional clauses is to confer on the court a type of directed power.[34] This is a legal power, and it is directed in two respects: It is the kind of power that the courts ought to exercise, and it is constrained by certain prescribed aims and reasons. When the law grants a certain legal power to an agent, it typically leaves it entirely to the choice of the agent whether to exercise the power or not. However, the law frequently grants certain powers to various agents, mostly judges and other officials, which they are duty bound to exercise. This is one sense in which the power to interpret the constitution and, as I will argue below, actually to change it, is directed. When the constitution prescribes, for example, that 'cruel and unusual punishment' should be invalidated, it actually imposes a duty on the supreme court to determine what kinds of punishment are cruel and unusual, and therefore, invalid. Note, however, that this power is constrained in another crucial sense, since it limits the kind of purposes judges should take into account and the kind of reasons they can rely upon to justify their decision. Not any kind of consideration would justify invalidating certain penal practices, only those which are really cruel. And since cruelty is a moral concept, the reasons for such a decision must be moral ones, and not, say, economic efficiency or budgetary concerns.

The claim that judges have directed power to rely on moral arguments in their interpretation of constitutional clauses is not news, of course. Controversies abound, however, with respect to the kinds of moral argument which are legitimate and the boundaries of such interpretative reasoning. I will consider three such controversies: the question of whether judges should rely on the conventional conceptions of morality, the question of 'enumerated rights', and the question of whether there is a distinction between conserving and innovative interpretations.

5.1 Conventional morality?

It is difficult to deny that our constitutional regime has trapped us in a very uncomfortable situation. On the one hand, it is clear that constitutional cases involve decisions of profound moral importance and judges who are entrusted with the interpretation of the constitution must make decisions on very important issues of moral principle. But once we realize that the court's decisions in constitutional cases are, practically speaking, almost impossible to change by regular democratic processes, we are bound to feel very uneasy about the court's power to impose its moral views on the nation without any significant political accountability. Understandably, then, it is tempting to seek ways to mitigate such concerns. Now, there seems to be an obvious consideration which presents itself: judges should interpret the constitution on the basis of those moral and ethical values which are widely shared in the community, that is, even if they happen to believe that such moral views are mistaken and not critically defensible. So there seems to be an easy way out of the dilemma: as long as judges are confined to rely on conventional moral values, those values which are widely shared by the entire community, their decisions would not disrupt the democratic nature of the regime and thus we mitigate the problem of lack of accountability.[35]

This is not a very good idea, however, and for several reasons. To begin with, more often than not, it is not a real option. In a great number of cases which get litigated at the constitutional level, there is no widely shared view that can settle the interpretative question. Such cases tend to be litigated precisely because there is a widespread moral controversy and various segments of the population hold opposing views on the matter. Nor can we assume that controversies are only at the surface and that there is bound to be greater consensus at a deeper level. As I have already argued in section 3, quite the opposite is true. It is typically the case that only at a very superficial level we can all agree that a certain right should be protected, but when we begin to think about the deeper reasons for such normative conclusions we will soon realize that the disagreements are rather profound.

Secondly, and more importantly, the idea that constitutional interpretation should be grounded on those values which happen to be widely shared in the community would undermine one of the basic rationales for having a constitution in the first place. Values that are widely shared do not require constitutional protection. If we have a good reason to enshrine certain values in a constitution and thus remove their protection from the ordinary democratic decision making processes, it must be because we think that those values are unlikely to be shared enough, so to speak, as to allow their implementation without such constitutional protection. It is precisely because we fear the temptation of encroachment of certain values by popular sentiment that we remove their protection from ordinary democratic processes.[36] After all, the democratic legislature is the kind of institution which is bound to be sensitive to popular sentiment and widely shared views in the community. We do not need the constitutional courts to do more of the same. If we need constitutional protection at all, it is because we assume that ordinary legislation is all too sensitive to popular sentiment and widely shared views. And then we must think that even if a moral view is widely shared, it can still be mistaken and that it would be wrong to implement it. Without holding such a view on the limits of conventional morality, constitutionalism makes no sense.[37]

None of this means that the courts should ignore conventional morality altogether. In some cases there may be *good moral reasons* to take into account conventional morality, even if the latter is partly mistaken. But these are rare occasions. A typical case I have in mind concerns the phenomenon of moral change.[38] New values are sometimes discovered, or invented. We may come to realize new values of things or actions, hitherto unnoticed. Or things can lose their value when we come to realize that they are no longer valuable.[39] Such changes in evaluative judgments tend to involve a transitional period and such transition tends to be more difficult for some than for others. People differ in their capacities to adapt and internalize the need for change. Racial equality, and more recently, gender equality, are prominent examples that come to one's mind in this context. Thus, it may happen, as it often does, that the individuals who occupy the supreme court realize the need for change and would have good reasons to implement it. But if most people are not yet there, if it is the case that new values have not yet taken root in most of the population, it may be advisable to postpone constitutional change until a time when it would be better received and easier to implement. This is not a rule, and contrary conclusion is certainly warranted in some cases. Arguably, the *Brown* case is such a counter example, and the difficulties of implementing it, that lasted for decades, attest to it. But the fragility of this implementation process, and its tremendous cost, also point to the limits of innovation that courts can pursue. It is difficult to generalize here. Much depends on social context and a great many social variables that we can only hope to guess right.

5.2 Enumerated rights?

The phenomenon of moral change raises another important concern in constitutional interpretation. Very few constitutions explicitly grant to the supreme court the power to invent new constitutional rights as need arises. Constitutions tend to contain a specific list of individual (and, more recently, certain group) rights, mandating the court to enforce those rights and not others.[40] But when the constitution is relatively old, and social change brings with it new concerns and new values, social and moral pressure may build up to recognize a new basic right, not enumerated in the constitutional document.[41] Should then the courts simply incorporate the new right by their own innovation, or just wait for a formal constitutional amendment? An answer to this question partly depends on the specific legal and political culture. In some countries, the constitution is not particularly rigid and constitutional amendments are more frequent. Under such circumstances, there is likely to be an expectation, and perhaps a justified one, that new rights should be recognized only through the formal amendment process. In other places, particularly if the constitution is very rigid, there may be a greater amount of tolerance in allowing the courts to innovate and extend the constitution as need arises. But the question is not only a social-political one. It also pertains to the nature of legal interpretation and the morality of constitutional law.

There are two possible cases. Sometimes the constitutional document does not mention a specific right, but it can be derived by a moral inference from those rights and values which the constitution does mention. This is the easier case: If a given right can be derived from those rights and values which are listed in the constitution, there is a great deal to be said in favor of the conclusion that the courts should draw the correct moral inference and recognize the right in question. No other stance would be morally consistent. The main difficulty concerns the second type of case, where no such derivation is possible; cases in which it cannot be claimed that the new right in question is simply deducible from those which are already recognized in the constitution. In these latter type of cases, it seems

natural to claim that a recognition of a new right, un-enumerated in the constitution, amounts to changing the constitution itself, which is a legal power that the courts do not, and should not, have. Introducing any change in the constitution, this argument assumes, is exclusively within the domain of constitutional amendments according to the processes prescribed by the constitution, and not something that the courts should do within their power of rendering constitutional decisions.[42]

This sounds right, but under closer scrutiny, the argument turns out to be more problematic than it seems. The argument assumes that there is a distinction between the ordinary interpretation of constitutional clauses, which is presumed to be legitimate, and their change, which is not. But if any interpretation amounts to a certain change, then the distinction is, at best, a matter of degree and not a distinction between two kinds of activity. In other words, it is arguable that any interpretation of the constitution changes its meaning, and hence it would make no sense to claim that judges do not have the power to change the constitution. They do it all the time, and the only genuine concern is about the extent of the change which is legitimate, or desirable, under the pertinent circumstances.

I have already argued, in previous chapters, that any interpretation changes our understanding of the text, or the possible uses to which it is put. Interpretation, by its very nature, adds something new, previously unrecognized, to the ways in which the text is grasped. Let me reiterate briefly. In the ordinary use of a language, competent users just hear or read something, and thereby *understand* what the expression means. This does not amount to an interpretation of the expression. Interpretation comes into the picture only when there is something that is not clear, when there is a question, or a puzzle, something that needs to be clarified. There is always the possibility of misunderstanding, of course, but then again, misunderstanding does not call for an interpretation. We typically clarify a misunderstanding by pointing out the relevant fact, e.g. 'this is not what x means', or 'this is not what I meant' or such. Interpretation, on the other hand, is not an instance of clarifying a misunderstanding. You do not interpret anything simply by pointing out a certain fact (linguistic or other) about the text or its surrounding circumstances. Interpretation must always go beyond the level of the standard understanding of the meaning of the relevant expressions. When you offer an interpretation of a certain text, you strive to bring out a certain aspect of the text which could not have been grasped simply by, say, reading it and thereby understanding what the expression means. Thus, at least in one clear sense, interpretation always adds something, a new aspect of the text which had not been previously recognized or appreciated.

Does it mean that interpretation always changes the text, or would it be more accurate to say that it changes only our understanding of it? ('Understanding' here should be taken in a very broad sense, including such as what we value in the text, what uses it can be put to, and so on.) It seems natural, and generally quite right to say that it is the latter. The text, we should say, remains the same; its interpretation changes only what we make of it.[43] But there are two relevant exceptions. First, when we have a long series of successive interpretations of a given text, a point may be reached where the distinction between the original meaning of the text, and its meaning as it has been shaped by previous interpretations, may get very blurred. This is an actual, historical process, and it may, or may not, happen.

Be this as it may, the second exception is the important one: As opposed to interpretation in all other realms, legal interpretations which are exercised by the court, are *authoritative*. The court's interpretation of the law actually *determines what the law is* (that is, from the point of interpretation onwards). That is why in the legal case, authoritative interpretations of the text actually change it. When judges in their official capacity

express their interpretation of the law, it is the law. Judicial decisions attach new legal meanings, and thus new legal ramifications, to the text, and in this they change, in the legal sense, the text itself, not only our understanding of it. Needless to say, often these changes are minute and hardly noticeable; at other times, they are more evident, even dramatic. But once an authoritative interpretation of a law has been laid down, the law is changed, and the new law remains in force until it is changed again by a subsequent interpretation. All this is bound to be true about constitutional interpretation as well. In the legal sense, the constitution means what it is taken to mean by the supreme or constitutional court. And as their interpretation changes, so does the legal meaning of the constitution itself.[44] Thus the thesis we examined, according to which judges have the power to interpret the constitution but not to change it, is groundless. Any interpretation of the constitution changes its legal meaning, and therefore, the constitution itself.

A note of caution may be in place here. None of the above entails that judges cannot make mistakes in their constitutional interpretation. Surely, such an assumption would be absurd. There are better and worse interpretations, and there are mistaken interpretations as well. But the fact is that even erroneous interpretations make the law. I believe that the US supreme court has made an error, a huge error, in deciding that capital punishment does not violate the eighth amendment. I think that it was a mistaken interpretation of the constitution. Unfortunately, however, it is still the law. Capital punishment is constitutional in the US legal system.

All this being said, we are still not entitled to reach a conclusion about the courts' authority to invent new constitutional rights. We have only shown that one argument against it is not sound, but other arguments may still be valid. I doubt, however, that any general conclusion would be warranted. When a need for a certain constitutional change is present, the change ought to be made. The question of who should make it, and according to what procedures, is partly a question about the political culture of the relevant society, partly a question of institutional choice and, arguably, partly a matter of democratic theory. Perhaps in certain legal systems these considerations yield a fairly determinate conclusion. I cannot speculate on such matters here.

5.3 Conserving and innovative interpretations

In popular culture there is a conception of the courts' role in constitutional interpretation as one which moves between activism and passivity, sometimes leaning more towards the one than the other. Sometimes the courts come up with novel, even surprising decisions, at other times they manifest conservativism, passivity, or restraint. Judicial activism, however, can mean several different things.

First, there is a distinction which pertains to the content of the moral and political agenda of the court, to the extent that it has one. In this sense, we could say, for instance, that the Warren court was liberal and progressive, and the Rehnquist court is conservative. The moral and political agenda of the court, however, does not entail anything about the kind of constitutional interpretation which would be required to effectuate the relevant agenda. Sometimes, by exercising restraint or just not doing much, you get to advance a conservative agenda, at other times, you do not. The US supreme court during the Lochner era, for example, was activist in pursuing a very conservative agenda. It all depends on the base line and the relevant circumstances. The nature of the moral objective does not determine the nature of the constitutional interpretation strategy which is required to achieve it.

Another distinction which lawyers and political theorists often talk about concerns the willingness of the court to confront opposition and engage in a conflict with the other political

branches of the government or with certain segments of the population. The more the court is willing to impose its views in spite of (real or potential) opposition, the more it is an 'activist' court, we would say. But again, activism in this sense is neither related to the content of the moral views in question, nor does it entail anything about the nature of constitutional interpretation, as such. Both during the Lochner era, and the Warren court era, the US supreme court pursued an activist role, but driven by opposite moral/political agendas in these two cases. Furthermore, activism in this sense does not necessarily translate itself to any particular type or method of constitutional interpretation. Activism, in this sense, simply means the willingness to confront political opposition. What the opposition is, and what it takes to confront it, is entirely context dependent.

The distinction which does pertain to methods of constitutional interpretation is the one which divides interpretations of the constitution into those which conserve previous understandings of it, and those which strike out in a new direction, so to speak. Raz calls it the distinction between *conserving* and *innovative* interpretations. Both are inevitable in the interpretation of a constitution. In fact, constitutional interpretation, Raz suggests, 'lives in spaces where fidelity to an original and openness to novelty mix ... constitutional decisions are moral decisions that have to be morally justified, and the moral considerations that apply include both fidelity to the law of the constitution as it is, ... and openness to its shortcomings and to injustices its application may yield in certain cases, which leads to openness to the need to develop and modify it' (1998: 180–81).

I think that Raz would admit that just about any interpretation involves both a conserving and an innovative element. On the one hand, interpretation must be an interpretation of *a text*, which entails that it must be, to some extent, true to the original, defer to the text it strives to interpret. Otherwise, as Dworkin would say, it is just an invention of a new text, not an interpretation of one. But as we have already seen, every interpretation must also have an innovative element, it must add some new insight or understanding, something which is not obviously there already. In other words, every interpretation is a mix of a certain deference to the original and shedding new light on it, and if there is a distinction between conserving and innovative interpretations, it is a distinction between the proportions of these two elements. It is a difference in degree, not a distinction in kind.

Nevertheless, there is a sense in which the distinction is very familiar. Lawyers frequently refer to 'landmark decisions', and by this they usually refer to decisions which have introduced a major change in the law or, at the very least, have clarified an important aspect of it which had been confused or unclear before the decision was rendered. These would seem to be innovative interpretations. And then, of course, there are many decisions which do not qualify as 'landmark' decisions, in that they simply reaffirm an aspect of the law which was already known. Or, if they introduced a change, it was relatively small or marginal. I have no qualms about this distinction. But it may be worth asking what is it, exactly, that the court conserves in its 'conserving interpretation'? The constitution itself? Its 'original meaning'? And what would that be? What could be meant by Raz's expression 'fidelity to the law of the constitution as it is'?

In one sense, we know the answer: faced with a constitutional case, the court may decide to adhere to its previous interpretations of the relevant constitutional issue, or else, it may decide to change it. So when we speak about conserving interpretation, what we have in mind is the conservation of its *previous interpretations* by the court. Accordingly, innovative interpretation would be a form of overruling the court's own previous interpretation of the pertinent constitutional clause. This makes perfect sense.

The question is whether it would still make sense to speak of a conserving interpretation when it is not a previous *interpretation* which is supposed to be conserved, but somehow the constitution itself, or 'the constitution as it is', to use Raz's expression.

Before we explore this issue, let me reiterate a crucial point: even in constitutional law, there are 'easy cases'. Easy cases do not tend to reach constitutional courts, but it does not mean that the constitution cannot be simply understood, and applied, to countless instances in ways which do not involve any need for interpretation whatsoever. Governments operate on a day-to-day basis, elections are run, officials elected, and so on and so forth, all according to the provisions of the constitution. Almost invariably, however, constitutional cases get to be litigated and reach the supreme court in those 'hard cases' where the relevant constitutional clause is just not clear enough to determine a particular result. (Sometimes a case reaches the court in spite of the fact that there is, actually, a previous interpretation which would determine the result, but one of the parties manages to convince the court to reconsider its previous doctrine and potentially, overrule it. But even in those cases, there must be a plausible argument that the relevant constitutional clause could mean something different from what it had been previously thought to mean.) In other words, constitutional cases are almost always hard cases, arising because the constitution 'as it is' is just not clear enough. So what would it mean to conserve 'the meaning of the constitution as it is', when the litigation stems from the fact that it is not clear enough what the constitution requires in that particular case? Unless we want to revive a mythical originalism here, I think that there is nothing that a constitutional interpretation can conserve unless it is a previous interpretation. When there is no previous interpretation that bears on the case, and the case is respectable enough to have reached constitutional litigation, conserving interpretation is simply not an option because there is not anything to conserve there.

One final comment. I have been arguing here that in the realm of constitutional interpretation, there is hardly any alternative to sound moral deliberation. Constitutional issues are mostly moral issues, and they must be decided on moral grounds. On the other hand, I have also raised some doubts about the moral legitimacy of judicial review and, to some extent, about the very legitimacy of long lasting constitutions. So is not there a tension here? Yes there is, but it does not necessarily point towards a different conclusion. It would be a mistake to maintain that because the very legitimacy of constitutional interpretation is clouded in some moral doubts, judges should adopt a strategy of self-restraint, refraining from making the right moral decisions just because they might be considered bold, unpopular, or otherwise potentially controversial. Perhaps it is true that constitutional courts have too much political power in the interpretation of the constitution. But since they do have the power, they must exercise it properly. If the best way to exercise the power is by relying on sound moral arguments, then moral considerations are the ones which ought to determine, as far as possible, the concrete results of constitutional cases. Sometimes moral considerations may dictate caution and self-restraint and at other times they may not. But what the appropriate moral decision ought to be is rarely affected by the question of who makes it.

I should be more precise here. I do not intend to claim that courts should not exercise self-restraint. Far from it. There are many domains, including within constitutional law, where caution, self-restraint and avoidance of intervention is the appropriate strategy for courts to pursue. That is so, because there are many areas in which the courts are less likely to get things right than the particular agency or authority which they are required to review. This is basically a matter of comparative institutional competence. My argument above is confined to the nature of the moral considerations which ought to determine constitutional decisions. If the decision is of such a nature that it depends on relative institutional competence, then morality itself dictates that those who are more likely to have the better judgment should be left to make the relevant decision. Either way, the courts should rely on sound moral judgment.

None of this means that the doubts about the moral legitimacy of judicial review should be shelved away and forgotten. Far from it. The practical conclusions which follow from such concerns could justify the need for reform and amendment of our constitutional regime. Perhaps constitutions should be made less rigid, allowing for easier amendment procedures; perhaps certain powers of constitutional interpretation ought to be shifted from the judiciary to the legislative assembly; perhaps constitutions should mandate their own periodical revisions and re-confirmation by some democratic process. I am not sure about any of these suggestions, but I am confident that there is much room for innovation and improvement.

Notes

Excerpt from Andrei Marmor, *Interpretation and Legal Theory* (Hart 2005) pp. 141–69.

1 Most non-democratic countries have written constitutions as well. This chapter is confined, however, to a discussion of constitutional democracies. Another restriction on the scope of this essay is that it is confined to constitutions of sovereign states. I will not discuss sub-state or regional constitutions nor should it be assumed that the arguments presented here would straightforwardly apply to such cases.

2 These are, or perhaps just used to be, the UK, New Zealand and, until recently, Israel. (Israel does have some basic laws which are quasi-constitutional, and a few years ago the Israeli supreme court has ruled that it has the power of constitutional judicial

review.) Even the UK, however, is not entirely free of judicial review due to its submission to the European Convention on Human Rights and some other quasi-constitutional constraints the courts have recently recognized.

3 A written constitution is, however, practically necessary for judicial review. Without such a canonical document, it would be very difficult for a court to impose restrictions on the legislature's authority.

4 The constitution's normative supremacy should not be confused with the idea that all law derives its legal validity from the constitution. This latter thesis, famously propounded by Hans Kelsen, is probably false in most legal systems.

5 The US constitution is probably one of the most rigid constitutions in the Western world. At the other extreme, there are, for example, the constitution of India, which has already been amended hundreds of times, and the Swiss constitution, which is quite frequently amended by popular referenda.

6 Once again, constitutions vary considerably in this respect as well. Many constitutions contain very specific provisions even in the realm of rights and principles. (I would venture to guess that a high level of specificity tends to occur in those cases where the constitution allows for amendment by a relatively straightforward process of referendum.)

7 A very interesting and suggestive exception is section 33 of the *Canadian Charter of Rights and Freedoms* which allows the legislature to overrule constitutional decisions of the supreme court (both preemptively or *ex post*), as long as it is done so very explicitly and renewed every five years.

8 It would be a mistake to assume that only judges are in the business of constitutional interpretation. Surely, many other political actors, like legislators, lawyers, lobbyists, political activists etc., are also engaged in the interpretation of the constitution and their views may often have a considerable impact on how the constitution is understood in a given society. Nevertheless, for simplicity's sake, I will concentrate on the courts, assuming that it is the courts' authoritative interpretation which is the most important one.

9 See Jon Elster's *Ulysses Unbound* (2000); Elster himself has some doubts about the application of the precommitment idea to constitutions. Cf Waldron (1999).

10 There is one argument I would like to mention, though: it has been claimed that in the history of a nation, there are sometimes 'constitutional moments', when a unique opportunity arises to enshrine in a constitutional document moral principles of great importance. Since this is basically just a matter of unique historical opportunities, perhaps we should not attach too much weight to the intergenerational problem. The assumption is that the constitution legally enshrines values we would all see as fundamental as well, it's just that there is not always the political opportunity to incorporate those values into the law and render the values legally binding. This is an interesting point, but from a moral perspective, I think that it leaves the basic question in its place: either the constitutional protection of such values makes no practical difference, in which case it would be pointless, or else, if it does make a difference in being legally authoritative, then the intergenerational question remains: why should one generation have the power to legally bind future generations to its conceptions of the good government and the kind of rights we should have? An answer of the form: we just had the political opportunity to do it, is hardly a good one.

11 See also Raz (1998: 167).

12 This idea is usually expressed by the metaphor of the 'living constitution'. See, for example, Kavanagh (2003).

13 For a much more detailed account of the nature of social conventions see Marmor (2001: chs 1–2).

14 Constitutions may promote other values as well, such as educational values, social cohesion etc. It would be a mistake to assume, however, that every type of good promoted by a given institution legitimizes the need to have that institution in the first place. Those goods can often be achieved by other means as well, which may be more legitimate or desirable.

15 This is not to deny that there are cases in which there is a moral duty to solve a coordination problem. For a more detailed account, see Marmor (2001: 25–31).

16 It should be acknowledged that not every legal decision of the court about the interpretation of

the constitution amounts, technically speaking, to what we call 'judicial review', in the sense that not every constitutional decision is necessarily a review of an act of legislation. It may simply be a review of an administrative decision, or some other legal issue that may be affected by the constitution. However, it should be kept in mind that the practical effect of such constitutional decisions is basically the same: once rendered by the supreme (or constitutional) court, it cannot be changed by the ordinary processes of democratic legislation. Therefore, even if technically speaking, not every constitutional decision is an exercise of judicial review, for most practical purposes, the distinction is not morally/politically significant.

17 See Waldron (1999).

18 In fact there is another mistake here: even if the courts are assigned the role of constitutional interpretation, it does not necessarily follow that they should have the legal power to invalidate an act of legislation which is unconstitutional. The appropriate remedy could be much less drastic, e.g. a declaratory judgment, or there could be no remedy at all.

19 I do not wish to claim that all constitutional decisions are primarily concerned with moral issues; some constitutional decisions concern the structural aspects of government, in which case, often the issue is one of bureaucratic efficiency or such.

20 For a recent defense of this argument, see Harel (2003). Cf Alexander (2003).

21 I have presented the argument which follows in the next few paragraphs in Marmor (1997).

22 See Raz (1986: ch. 7).

23 See Raz (1986: 181). I do not intend to suggest that Raz would agree (or not) with the main thesis that I advocate here in the next few paragraphs.

24 Unless, of course, the duties in question are very abstract, like the duty not to cause unnecessary suffering, or the duty to respect others. I am not suggesting that people with conflicting conceptions of the good and of ultimate values cannot agree on some duties we should all have. My point is relative: that it is easier to agree on a list of relatively specific rights than duties.

25 Admittedly, this last point is actually a piece of armchair sociology. But not a particularly fancy one. I think that we are quite familiar with this phenomenon, namely, that rights discourse is much more prevalent in pluralistic societies than in homogenous ones. It is quite likely that there are other explanations for this difference, besides the one I offer here. I do not intend the explanation to be exhaustive.

26 It is probably true, though not universally so, that the prevalence of rights discourse in a given society does reflect a deeper level of consensus about the acceptance of pluralism and perhaps even individualism. But this deeper level of tacit consensus, to the extent that it exists, is very abstract and quite unlikely to have significant bearing on constitutional interpretation.

27 There is one important exception: some countries may have a persistent minority group which is unlikely to have its interests protected by an ordinary majoritarian decision making process. It would be a mistake to assume, however, that the only way to protect the interests of persistent minorities is by constitutional entrenchment of their rights. Often a more sophisticated democratic process (forcing, for example, political actors in the majority to take into account the interests of the minority) may be more efficient.

28 I heard this last argument in a lecture by Bernard Williams which he gave at Columbia Law School a few years ago. As far as I could ascertain, Williams has never published his lecture, which I deeply regret. However, it should be admitted that the observation underlying this argument is at least partly culture dependent; much depends on how the courts are actually perceived by the public.

29 Yes, of course there are exceptions. The Warren Court is a famous exception in the US supreme court's history, but it is precisely the point of it: the progressive agenda of the Warren Court (which only lasted, it should be recalled, for about two decades) is such a remarkable exception.

30 The problem of identifying the 'framers' is exacerbated in those cases in which there is an elaborate ratification process of the constitution.

31 In fact, there is a third argument which is often mentioned: originalists sometimes rest their case on the claim that the historical truths about framers' intentions are objective and thus allow

an objective constraint on judicial discretion in constitutional cases. But this is puzzling, at best. First, because one can think of countless other ways in which judges could decide cases, much more objective than this one; they could toss a coin, for example. Secondly, the assumption that the interpretation of history is somehow objective or free of evaluative considerations, or that it is free of bias and ideological prejudices, is just too naïve to be taken seriously.

32 See, for example, Goldsworthy (2003: 177).

33 In some of his writings Dworkin (1977: 134, but cf 1985: 49) seems to have suggested that *the only relevant evidence* of the framers' intentions in such cases is a linguistic one: the very abstract formulation of the pertinent constitutional provision attests to the further intention of the framers to enact the abstract principle as such, and not any specific principle which they may have hoped to achieve, but did not enact in the constitutional provision. But this is not a coherent argument: either the issue is an historical one, in which case no evidence can be excluded, or else, it is not an argument which refers to historical truths, in which case it is very unclear why we should speak about the framers here at all. To put it briefly, originalism cannot be derived from textualism.

34 See Raz (1994: ch. 10) and Marmor (2001: 67–68).

35 This is not an idle method invented by scholars only to be refuted in their articles. Many constitutional decisions are actually justified by such a reasoning. For example, it is often claimed that the US supreme court's decision to legalize capital punishment is justified because it gives effect to the views held by the vast majority of Americans. Recently, the court justified its decision to change its views on the constitutionality of the execution of retarded persons by appealing to changes in the popular sentiment. See *Atkins v Virginia* (536 US 304, 2002). Similarly, I am often told by my colleagues that it is impossible to change the current interpretation of the second amendment's so called 'right to bear arms' because it reflects widely shared popular beliefs.

36 I am not claiming here that, all things considered, this is a sound reason for constitutional protection of rights and principles. All I am saying is that, to the extent that there is such a sound reason, it

must assume this point. There is a sense, however, in which the argument should be more nuanced. Two people may share a certain value but differ in the ways in which they apply the value they share to particular cases. Shared values do not necessarily entail shared judgments on particular cases.

37 Perhaps this argument could also be used to reach the conclusion that democratic legislative assemblies are not to be trusted with the protection of constitutional rights. This might be too quick a move, however. Much depends on specific legislative procedures, and various institutional constraints. See, for example, Garrett and Vermeule (2001).

38 Another example, which is rarely relevant in constitutional cases, concerns those political choices in which the right decision is simply the one which is actually preferred by the majority. These are usually cases in which we must make choices about preferences of taste, where no particular preference is supported by any general reasons; in such cases it makes sense to maintain that the preferences of the majority should prevail, just because they are the majority. I have elaborated on this type of decision in my 'Authority, Equality, and Democracy' (forthcoming in *Ratio Juris*).

39 See Marmor (2001: 160–68).

40 Some lists of rights are more open ended and allow the courts to incorporate rights on the basis of new interpretations of existing rights. A good example is Article I of the German *Basic Law* which states that the right to human dignity is inviolable. The value of human dignity is broad and flexible enough to encompass a considerable range of rights and values thus allowing the German Constitutional Court a considerable amount of innovation.

41 A good example is the right to privacy in the US constitution. Privacy is not mentioned in the constitution, and there is certainly no right to privacy enumerated there, but as the court realized during the mid to late 1960s, a need to recognize and enforce such a right became apparent. Consequently, in a series of important and rather controversial decisions, the court recognized the right to privacy as a constitutional right. See: *Griswold v Connecticut* (381 US 479, 1965); *Katz v United States* (389 US 347 (1967) and others.

42 See, for example, Goldsworthy (2003).

43 Cf Raz (1995).

44 Lawyers would consider this quite obvious: when a question arises about the constitutionality of a certain issue, it is mostly the case law that lawyers would refer to.

References

Alexander, Larry, 'Is Judicial Review Democratic? A Comment on Harel' (2003) 22 *Law and Philosophy* 277–283.

Dworkin, Ronald, *Taking Rights Seriously* (London: Duckworth, 1977).

Dworkin, Ronald, *A Matter of Principle* (Cambridge, Mass.: Harvard University Press, 1985).

Elster, Jon, *Ulysses Unbound – Studies in Rationality, Precommitment, and Constraints* (Cambridge: Cambridge University Press, 2000)

Garrett, E., and Vermeule, A., 'Institutional Design of a Thayerian Congress' (2001) 50 *Duke Law Journal* 1277.

Goldsworthy, Jeremy, 'Raz on Constitutional Interpretation' (2003) 22 *Law and Philosophy* 167–193.

Harel, Alon, 'Right-Based Judicial Review: A Democratic Justification' (2003) 22 *Law and Philosophy*, 242–276.

Kavanagh, Aileen, 'The Idea of a Living Constitution' (2003) 16 *Canadian Journal of Law and Jurisprudence*, 55–89.

Marmor, Andrei, *Positive Law and Objective Values* (Oxford: Oxford University Press, 2001).

Marmor, Andrei, 'On The Limits of Rights' (1997) 16 *Law and Philosophy* 1–18.

Marmor, Andrei, 'Authority, Equality and Democracy' (2005) 18 *Ratio Juris* 315–345.

Raz, Joseph, 'On the Authority and Interpretation of Constitutions: Some Preliminaries', in Alexander (ed.) *Constitutionalism. Philosophical Foundations* (Cambridge: Cambridge University Press, 1998), 152–193.

Raz, Joseph, *The Morality of Freedom* (Oxford: Clarendon Press, 1986).

Raz, Joseph, *Ethics in the Public Domain: Essays in the Morality of Law and Politics* (Oxford: Clarendon Press, 1994).

Raz, Joseph, 'Interpretation Without Retrieval', in Marmor (ed.) *Law and Interpretation* (Oxford: Clarendon Press, 1995), 155–176.

Waldron, Jeremy, *Law and Disagreement* (Oxford: Oxford University Press, 1999).

Chapter 26

Antonin Scalia

INTERPRETING CONSTITUTIONAL TEXTS

WITHOUT PRETENDING to have exhausted the vast topic of textual interpretation, I wish to address a final subject: the distinctive problem of constitutional interpretation. The problem is distinctive, not because special principles of interpretation apply, but because the usual principles are being applied to an unusual text. Chief Justice Marshall put the point as well as it can be put in *McCulloch v. Maryland*:

> A constitution, to contain an accurate detail of all the subdivisions of which its great powers will admit, and of all the means by which they may be carried into execution, would partake of the prolixity of a legal code, and could scarcely be embraced by the human mind. It would probably never be understood by the public. Its nature, therefore, requires, that only its great outlines should be marked, its important objects designated, and the minor ingredients which compose those objects be deduced from the nature of the objects themselves.[1]

In textual interpretation, context is everything, and the context of the Constitution tells us not to expect nit-picking detail, and to give words and phrases an expansive rather than narrow interpretation—though not an interpretation that the language will not bear.

Take, for example, the provision of the First Amendment that forbids abridgment of "the freedom of speech, or of the press." That phrase does not list the full range of communicative expression. Handwritten letters, for example, are neither speech nor press. Yet surely there is no doubt they cannot be censored. In this constitutional context, speech and press, the two most common forms of communication, stand as a sort of synecdoche for the whole. That is not strict construction, but it is reasonable construction.

It is curious that most of those who insist that the drafter's intent gives meaning to a statute reject the drafter's intent as the criterion for interpretation of the Constitution. I reject it for both. I will consult the writings of some men who happened to be delegates to the Constitutional Convention—Hamilton's and Madison's writings in *The Federalist*, for example. I do so, however, not because they were Framers and therefore their intent is authoritative and must be the law; but rather because their writings, like those of other intelligent and informed people of the time, display how the text of the Constitution was originally understood. Thus I give equal weight to Jay's pieces in *The Federalist*, and to Jefferson's writings, even though neither of them was a Framer. What I look for in the Constitution is precisely what I look for in a statute: the original meaning of the text, not what the original draftsmen intended.

But the Great Divide with regard to constitutional interpretation is not that between

Framers' intent and objective meaning, but rather that between *original* meaning (whether derived from Framers' intent or not) and *current* meaning. The ascendant school of constitutional interpretation affirms the existence of what is called The Living Constitution, a body of law that (unlike normal statutes) grows and changes from age to age, in order to meet the needs of a changing society. And it is the judges who determine those needs and "find" that changing law. Seems familiar, doesn't it? Yes, it is the common law returned, but infinitely more powerful than what the old common law ever pretended to be, for now it trumps even the statutes of democratic legislatures. Recall the words I quoted earlier from the Fourth-of-July speech of the avid codifier Robert Rantoul: "The judge makes law, by extorting from precedents something which they do not contain. He extends his precedents, which were themselves the extension of others, till, by this accommodating principle, a whole system of law is built up without the authority or interference of the legislator."[2] Substitute the word "people" for "legislator," and it is a perfect description of what modern American courts have done with the Constitution.

If you go into a constitutional law class, or study a constitutional law casebook, or read a brief filed in a constitutional law case, you will rarely find the discussion addressed to the text of the constitutional provision that is at issue, or to the question of what was the originally understood or even the originally intended meaning of that text. The starting point of the analysis will be Supreme Court cases, and the new issue will presumptively be decided according to the logic that those cases expressed, with no regard for how far that logic, thus extended, has distanced us from the original text and understanding. Worse still, however, it is known and understood that if that logic fails to produce what in the view of the current Supreme Court is the *desirable* result for the case at hand, then, like good common-law judges, the Court

will distinguish its precedents, or narrow them, or if all else fails overrule them, in order that the Constitution might mean what it *ought* to mean. Should there be—to take one of the less controversial examples—a constitutional right to die? If so, there is.[3] Should there be a constitutional right to reclaim a biological child put out for adoption by the other parent? Again, if so, there is.[4] If it is good, it is so. Never mind the text that we are supposedly construing; we will smuggle these new rights in, if all else fails, under the Due Process Clause (which, as I have described, is textually incapable of containing them). Moreover, what the Constitution meant yesterday it does not necessarily mean today. As our opinions say in the context of our Eighth Amendment jurisprudence (the Cruel and Unusual Punishments Clause), its meaning changes to reflect "the evolving standards of decency that mark the progress of a maturing society."[5]

This is preeminently a common-law way of making law, and not the way of construing a democratically adopted text. I mentioned earlier a famous English treatise on statutory construction called *Dwarris on Statutes*. The fourth of Dwarris's Maxims was as follows: "An act of Parliament cannot alter by reason of time; but the common law may, since *cessante ratione cessat lex*."[6] This remains (however much it may sometimes be evaded) the formally enunciated rule for statutory construction: statutes do not change. Proposals for "dynamic statutory construction," such as those of Judge Calabresi and Professor Eskridge, are concededly avant-garde. The Constitution, however, even though a democratically adopted text, we formally treat like the common law. What, it is fair to ask, is the justification for doing so?

One would suppose that the rule that a text does not change would apply a fortiori to a constitution. If courts felt too much bound by the democratic process to tinker with statutes, when their tinkering could be adjusted by the legislature, how much more should they feel bound not to tinker with a constitution, when their tinkering is virtually irreparable. It certainly cannot be said that a constitution naturally suggests changeability; to the contrary, its whole purpose is to prevent change—to embed certain rights in such a manner that future generations cannot readily take them away. A society that adopts a bill of rights is skeptical that "evolving standards of decency" always "mark progress," and that societies always "mature," as opposed to rot. Neither the text of such a document nor the intent of its framers (whichever you choose) can possibly lead to the conclusion that its only effect is to take the power of changing rights away from the legislature and give it to the courts.

Flexibility and liberality of The Living Constitution

The argument most frequently made in favor of The Living Constitution is a pragmatic one: Such an evolutionary approach is necessary in order to provide the "flexibility" that a changing society requires; the Constitution would have snapped if it had not been permitted to bend and grow. This might be a persuasive argument if most of the "growing" that the proponents of this approach have brought upon us in the past, and are determined to bring upon us in the future, were the *elimination* of restrictions upon democratic government. But just the opposite is true. Historically, and particularly in the past thirty-five years, the "evolving" Constitution has imposed a vast array of new constraints—new inflexibilities—upon administrative, judicial, and legislative action. To mention only a few things that formerly could be done or not done, as the society desired, but now cannot be done:

- admitting in a state criminal trial evidence of guilt that was obtained by an unlawful search;[7]
- permitting invocation of God at public-school graduations;[8]

- electing one of the two houses of a state legislature the way the United States Senate is elected, i.e., on a basis that does not give all voters numerically equal representation;[9]
- terminating welfare payments as soon as evidence of fraud is received, subject to restoration after hearing if the evidence is satisfactorily refuted;[10]
- imposing property requirements as a condition of voting;[11]
- prohibiting anonymous campaign literature;[12]
- prohibiting pornography.[13]

And the future agenda of constitutional evolutionists is mostly more of the same—the creation of *new* restrictions upon democratic government, rather than the elimination of old ones. *Less* flexibility in government, not *more*. As things now stand, the state and federal governments may either apply capital punishment or abolish it, permit suicide or forbid it—all as the changing times and the changing sentiments of society may demand. But when capital punishment is held to violate the Eighth Amendment, and suicide is held to be protected by the Fourteenth Amendment, all flexibility with regard to those matters will be gone. No, the reality of the matter is that, generally speaking, devotees of The Living Constitution do not seek to facilitate social change but to prevent it.

There are, I must admit, a few exceptions to that—a few instances in which, historically, greater flexibility has been the result of the process. But those exceptions serve only to refute another argument of the proponents of an evolving Constitution, that evolution will always be in the direction of greater personal liberty. (They consider that a great advantage, for reasons that I do not entirely understand. All government represents a balance between individual freedom and social order, and it is not true that every alteration of that balance in the direction of greater individual freedom is necessarily good.)

But in any case, the record of history refutes the proposition that the evolving Constitution will invariably enlarge individual rights. The most obvious refutation is the modern Court's limitation of the constitutional protections afforded to property. The provision prohibiting impairment of the obligation of contracts, for example, has been gutted.[14] I am sure that We the People agree with that development; we value property rights less than the Founders did. So also, we value the right to bear arms less than did the Founders (who thought the right of self-defense to be absolutely fundamental), and there will be few tears shed if and when the Second Amendment is held to guarantee nothing more than the state National Guard. But this just shows that the Founders were right when they feared that some (in their view misguided) future generation might wish to abandon liberties that they considered essential, and so sought to protect those liberties in a Bill of Rights. We may *like* the abridgment of property rights and *like* the elimination of the right to bear arms; but let us not pretend that these are not *reductions of rights*.

Or if property rights are too cold to arouse enthusiasm, and the right to bear arms too dangerous, let me give another example: Several terms ago a case came before the Supreme Court involving a prosecution for sexual abuse of a young child. The trial court found that the child would be too frightened to testify in the presence of the (presumed) abuser, and so, pursuant to state law, she was permitted to testify with only the prosecutor and defense counsel present, with the defendant, the judge, and the jury watching over closed-circuit television. A reasonable enough procedure, and it was held to be constitutional by my Court.[15] I dissented, because the Sixth Amendment provides that "[i]n *all* criminal prosecutions the accused shall enjoy the right ... to be confronted with the witnesses against him" (emphasis added). There is no doubt what confrontation meant—or indeed means today. It means face-to-face, not watching from another room. And there is no

doubt what one of the major purposes of that provision was: to induce *precisely* that pressure upon the witness which the little girl found it difficult to endure. It is difficult to accuse someone to his face, particularly when you are lying. Now no extrinsic factors have changed since that provision was adopted in 1791. Sexual abuse existed then, as it does now; little children were more easily upset than adults, then as now; a means of placing the defendant out of sight of the witness existed then as now (a screen could easily have been erected that would enable the defendant to see the witness, but not the witness the defendant). But the Sixth Amendment nonetheless gave *all* criminal defendants the right to *confront* the witnesses against them, because that was thought to be an important protection. The only significant things that *have* changed, I think, are the society's sensitivity to so-called psychic trauma (which is what we are told the child witness in such a situation suffers) and the society's assessment of where the proper balance ought to be struck between the two extremes of a procedure that assures convicting 100 percent of all child abusers, and a procedure that assures acquitting 100 percent of those falsely accused of child abuse. I have no doubt that the society is, as a whole, happy and pleased with what my Court decided. But we should not pretend that the decision did not *eliminate* a liberty that previously existed.

Lack of a guiding principle for evolution

My pointing out that the American people may be satisfied with a reduction of their liberties should not be taken as a suggestion that the proponents of The Living Constitution *follow* the desires of the American people in determining how the Constitution should evolve. They follow nothing so precise; indeed, as a group they follow nothing at all. Perhaps the most glaring defect of Living Constitutionalism, next to its incompatibility with the whole antievolutionary purpose of a constitution, is that there is no agreement, and no chance of agreement, upon what is to be the guiding principle of the evolution. *Panta rei* is not a sufficiently informative principle of constitutional interpretation. What is it that the judge must consult to determine when, and in what direction, evolution has occurred? Is it the will of the majority, discerned from newspapers, radio talk shows, public opinion polls, and chats at the country club? Is it the philosophy of Hume, or of John Rawls, or of John Stuart Mill, or of Aristotle? As soon as the discussion goes beyond the issue of whether the Constitution is static, the evolutionists divide into as many camps as there are individual views of the good, the true, and the beautiful. I think that is inevitably so, which means that evolutionism is simply not a practicable constitutional philosophy.

I do not suggest, mind you, that originalists always agree upon their answer. There is plenty of room for disagreement as to what original meaning was, and even more as to how that original meaning applies to the situation before the court. But the originalist at least knows what he is looking for: the original meaning of the text. Often—indeed, I dare say usually—that is easy to discern and simple to apply. Sometimes (though not very often) there will be disagreement regarding the original meaning; and sometimes there will be disagreement as to how that original meaning applies to new and unforeseen phenomena. How, for example, does the First Amendment guarantee of "the freedom of speech" apply to new technologies that did not exist when the guarantee was created—to sound trucks, or to government-licensed over-the-air television? In such new fields the Court must follow the trajectory of the First Amendment, so to speak, to determine what it requires—and assuredly that enterprise is not entirely cut-and-dried but requires the exercise of judgment.

But the difficulties and uncertainties of determining original meaning and applying it to modern circumstances are negligible compared with the difficulties and uncertainties of the philosophy which says that the Constitution *changes*; that the very act which it once prohibited it now permits, and which it once permitted it now forbids; and that the key to that change is unknown and unknowable. The originalist, if he does not have all the answers, has many of them. The Confrontation Clause, for example, requires confrontation. For the evolutionist, on the other hand, every question is an open question, every day a new day. No fewer than three of the Justices with whom I have served have maintained that the death penalty is unconstitutional,[16] *even though its use is explicitly contemplated in the Constitution.* The Due Process Clause of the Fifth and Fourteenth Amendments says that no person shall be deprived of life without due process of law; and the Grand Jury Clause of the Fifth Amendment says that no person shall be held to answer for a capital crime without grand jury indictment. No matter. Under The Living Constitution the death penalty may have *become* unconstitutional. And it is up to each Justice to decide for himself (under no standard I can discern) when that occurs.

In the last analysis, however, it probably does not matter what principle, among the innumerable possibilities, the evolutionist proposes to determine in what direction The Living Constitution will grow. Whatever he might propose, at the end of the day an evolving constitution will evolve the way the majority wishes. The people will be willing to leave interpretation of the Constitution to lawyers and law courts so long as the people believe that it is (like the interpretation of a statute) essentially lawyers' work—requiring a close examination of text, history of the text, traditional understanding of the text, judicial precedent, and so forth. But if the people come to believe that the Constitution is *not* a text like other texts; that it means, not what it says or what it was understood to mean, but what it *should* mean, in light of the "evolving standards of decency that mark the progress of a maturing society"—well, then, they will look for qualifications other than impartiality, judgment, and lawyerly acumen in those whom they select to interpret it. More specifically, they will look for judges who agree with them as to what the evolving standards have evolved to; who agree with them as to what the Constitution *ought* to be.

It seems to me that that is where we are heading, or perhaps even where we have arrived. Seventy-five years ago, we believed firmly enough in a rock-solid, unchanging Constitution that we felt it necessary to adopt the Nineteenth Amendment to give women the vote. The battle was not fought in the courts, and few thought that it could be, despite the constitutional guarantee of Equal Protection of the Laws; that provision did not, when it was adopted, and hence did not in 1920, guarantee equal access to the ballot but permitted distinctions on the basis not only of age but of property and of sex. Who can doubt that if the issue had been deferred until today, the Constitution would be (formally) unamended, and the courts would be the chosen instrumentality of change? The American people have been converted to belief in The Living Constitution, a "morphing" document that means, from age to age, what it ought to mean. And with that conversion has inevitably come the new phenomenon of selecting and confirming federal judges, at all levels, on the basis of their views regarding a whole series of proposals for constitutional evolution. If the courts are free to write the Constitution anew, they will, by God, write it the way the majority wants; the appointment and confirmation process will see to that. This, of course, is the end of the Bill of Rights, whose meaning will be committed to the very body it was meant to protect against: the majority. By trying to make the Constitution do everything that needs doing from age to age, we shall have caused it to do nothing at all.

Notes

Excerpt from Antonin Scalia, *A Matter of Interpretation* (Princeton 1997) pp. 37–47.

1 McCulloch v. Maryland, 17 U.S. (4 Wheat.) 316, 407 (1819).

2 Rantoul, *supra* note 7, at 318.

3 *See* Cruzan v. Director, Mo. Dep't of Health, 497 U.S. 261, 279 (1990).

4 *See* In re Kirchner, 649 N.E.2d 324, 333 (III.), *cert. denied*, 115 S. Ct. 2599 (1995).

5 Rhodes v. Chapman, 452 U.S. 337, 346 (1981), quoting from Trop v. Dulles, 356 U.S. 86, 101 (1958) (plurality opinion).

6 Fortunatus Dwarris, *A General Treatise on Statutes, with American Notes and Additions by Platt Potter* 122 (Albany, N.Y. 1871).

7 *See* Mapp v. Ohio, 367 U.S. 643 (1961).

8 *See* Lee v. Weisman, 505 U.S. 577 (1992).

9 *See* Reynolds v. Sims, 377 U.S. 533 (1964).

10 *See* Goldberg v. Kelly, 397 U.S. 254 (1970).

11 *See* Kramer v. Union Free Sch. Dist., 395 U.S. 621 (1969).

12 *See* McIntyre v. Ohio Elections Comm'n, 115 S. Ct. 1511 (1995).

13 Under current doctrine, pornography may be banned only if it is "obscene," *see* Miller v. California, 413 U.S. 15 (1973), a judicially crafted term of art that does not embrace material that excites "normal, healthy sexual desires," Brockett v. Spokane Arcades, Inc., 472 U.S. 491, 498 (1985).

14 *See* Home Building & Loan Ass'n v. Blaisdell, 290 U.S. 398 (1934).

15 *See* Maryland v. Craig, 497 U.S. 836 (1990).

16 *See* Gregg v. Georgia, 428 U.S. 153, 227 (1976) (Brennan, J., dissenting); *id.* at 231 (Marshall, J., dissenting); Callins v. Collins, 114 S. Ct. 1127, 1128 (1994) (Blackmun, J., dissenting from denial of certiorari).

Chapter 27

Jeremy Waldron

A RIGHT-BASED CRITIQUE OF CONSTITUTIONAL RIGHTS

1 Introduction

'Individuals have rights, and there are things no person or group may do to them (without violating their rights).'[1] 'Each person possesses an inviolability founded on justice that even the welfare of society as a whole cannot override.'[2] 'There would be no point in the boast that we respect individual rights unless that involved some sacrifice, and the sacrifice in question must be that we give up whatever marginal benefits our country would receive from overriding these rights when they prove inconvenient.'[3]

These are familiar propositions of political philosophy. What do they imply about institutions? Should we embody our rights in legalistic formulae and proclaim them in a formal Bill of Rights? Or should we leave them to evolve informally in dialogue among citizens, representatives and officials? How are we to stop rights from being violated? Should we rely on a general spirit of watchfulness in the community, attempting to raise what Mill called 'a strong barrier of moral conviction' to protect our liberty?[4] Or should we also entrust some specific branch of government—the courts, for example—with the task of detecting violations and with the authority to overrule any other agency that commits them?

The advantages of this last approach continue to attract proponents of constitutional reform in the United Kingdom. Ronald Dworkin, for example, has argued that it would forge a decisive link between rights and legality, giving the former much greater prominence in public life. By throwing the authority of the courts behind the idea of rights, the legal system would begin to play 'a different, more valuable role in society'. Lawyers and judges might take on roles more akin to those of their counterparts in the United States:

> The courts, charged with the responsibility of creating . . . a distinctly British scheme of human rights and liberty, might think more in terms of principle and less in terms of narrow precedent. . . . Different men and women might then be tempted to the law as a career, and from their ranks a more committed and idealistic generation of judges might emerge, encouraging a further cycle in the renaissance of liberty.[5]

If these judges used their new powers well, Dworkin concludes, governments would no longer be free, as they are now, to treat liberty as a commodity of convenience or 'to ignore rights that the nation has a solemn obligation to respect'.[6]

What should a political philosopher say about these proposals? In discussions of constitutional reform, I find it commonly assumed that the aims of Charter 88 and similar groups are shared by philosophers whose normative theories of politics are organized around the idea of rights. Surely, it is said, anyone who believes in rights will welcome a proposal to institutionalize a Bill of Rights and give the courts power to strike down legislation that encroaches on basic liberties.[7]

In this paper, I shall question that assumption. I want to develop four main lines of argument. The first is a negative case: I shall show that there is no necessary inference from a right-based position in political philosophy to a commitment to a Bill of Rights as a political institution along with an American-style practice of judicial review.

Secondly, I shall argue that political philosophers should be more aware than other proponents of constitutional reform of the difficulty, complexity, and controversy attending the idea of basic rights. I shall argue that they have reason—grounded in professional humility—to be more than usually hesitant about the enactment of any canonical list of rights, particularly if the aim is to put that canon beyond the scope of political debate and revision.

Thirdly, I shall argue that philosophers who talk about rights should pay much more attention than they do to the processes by which decisions are taken in a community under circumstances of disagreement. Theories of rights need to be complemented by theories of authority, whose function it is to determine how decisions are to be taken when the members of a community disagree about what decision is right. Since we are to assume a context of moral disagreement, a principle such as 'Let the right decision be made' cannot form part of an adequate principle of authority. It follows from this that, if people disagree about basic rights (and they do), an adequate theory of authority can neither include nor be qualified by a conception of rights as 'trumps' over majoritarian forms of decision-making.

Finally, I shall argue that, in a constitutional regime of the sort envisaged by proponents of Charter 88, the courts will inevitably become the main forum for the revision and adaptation of basic rights in the face of changing circumstances and social controversies. (This of course is an extrapolation from the experience of constitutional politics in the United States.) I shall argue that a theorist of rights should have grave misgivings about this prospect. Some of us think that people have a right to participate in the democratic governance of their community, and that this right is quite deeply connected to the values of autonomy and responsibility that are celebrated in our commitment to other basic liberties. We think moreover that the right to democracy is a right to participate on equal terms in social decisions on issues of high principle and that it is not to be confined to interstitial matters of social and economic policy. I shall argue that our respect for such democratic rights is called seriously into question when proposals are made to shift decisions about the conception and revision of basic rights from the legislature to the courtroom, from the people and their admittedly imperfect representative institutions to a handful of men and women, supposedly of wisdom, learning, virtue and high principle who, it is thought, alone can be trusted to take seriously the great issues that they raise?[8]

2 Right-based theories

My first aim is to show that there is no necessary inference from the premises of a right-based moral theory to the desirability of constitutional rights as a particular political arrangement.

What is meant by '*right-based*' theory? The terminology is adapted from Dworkin's discussion in *Taking Rights Seriously*, proposing 'a tentative initial classification of political theories' into right-based, duty-based and goal-based types.[9] The idea is that in any but the most intuitionistic theory, it is possible to distinguish between judgments that are more or less *basic*, in the sense that the less basic judgments are derivable from or supported by the more basic ones.[10] Sometimes we may reach a level of 'basic-ness' below which it is impossible to go—a set of judgments which support other judgments in the theory but which are not themselves supported in a similar way. These will be the *fundamental* propositions of the theory or, as Dworkin has called them elsewhere, its '*constitutive*' positions.[11] Utilitarians pride themselves on the fact that their moral theory is organized explicitly in this way, and Dworkin's typology assumes that a structure of that kind can be discerned in many non-utilitarian theories as well.[12]

For the purposes of this article, nothing much hangs on the precise *distinction* between right-, duty- and goal-based theories. So I shall not go into the detail of Dworkin's classification.[13] What I want to work with is the idea that a concern for individual rights may lie in the foundations of a theory, leaving it an open question what those foundations entail at the level of political and constitutional construction.

Opinions differ as to whether the concerns at the basis of a theory of rights are exclusively concerns about freedom, exclusively concerns about independence, exclusively concerns about equality, or whether other material interests and needs may also be accorded basic importance in their own right. I hope to avoid that issue here as well (though it is one of the controversies whose significance I shall discuss later in the article).[14] Different theories will identify different individual rights—to freedom, independence, dignity, etc.—as having fundamental and abiding importance, and they will regard a sense of that importance as a general basis for normativity within the theory.

As premises, these concerns are liable to be fairly abstract in character.[15] One would not expect to find propositions like the Fourth Amendment to the US Constitution in the *foundations* of a theory of rights. A right to the protection of one's home against unreasonable searches is likely to be based on the importance accorded to a deeper individual interest such as privacy. A right to privacy may in turn be based on even deeper premises about the importance of autonomy and self-governance. Derivative conclusions will then be generated by working out what, in the circumstances of modern society, is required if the deepest interests in this series are to be respected. That is what normative argument amounts to in right-based political philosophy.

Sometimes in the development of such an argument, we may reach intermediate conclusions which enable us to say that some relatively concrete interest must be regarded as important if some deeper interest is to be properly respected. This is where *familiar* propositions about rights will figure in a well-thought-out political theory. As we move from deep abstract premises to particular concrete recommendations, we may find ourselves saying things like 'People have a right to free speech' or 'Everyone has a right to elementary education' or 'Suspects in police custody have a right not to be tortured'. Though these propositions indicate important individual interests, their importance is explained by their deeper connection to other, more abstract interests whose importance is ultimate in the theory.[16]

However, right-based theories are not always articulated in a linear structure of this kind, moving from abstract rights through a series of derivative rights, each one supported by and more concrete than the last. Sometimes the implications of abstract premises are teased out in a different structure. John Rawls's discussion of justice is an example. It seems plausible to say, as Dworkin has argued, that Rawls's theory is premised on some very deep assumption 'that individuals have a right to equal concern and respect in the design and administration of the institutions that govern them'.[17] But in trying to see the concrete implications of that premise, Rawls develops his model-theoretic device of the 'original position' leading to the choice of two lexically ordered principles to govern the basic structure of a society. At least one of these (the 'Difference Principle') is not formulated in terms of rights at all.[18] Maybe the further process of inferring policy recommendations from the Difference Principle will involve some re-introduction of the language of rights.[19] But there is nothing inevitable about that: everything depends on how the deep concerns of the theory are best articulated in the concrete circumstances in which they are applied. The fact that there are rights in the foundations does not mean that there must be rights, so to speak, all the way up.

The point is a general one and can be applied to other types of theory as well. Utilitarianism has, in or near its foundations, a sense that the basic aim of morality is the maximization of utility. Whenever there is a choice of actions, it is better, from the theory's point of view, that that action be chosen which secures the greatest balance of utility, all things considered. But though we find this 'act-utilitarian' formula in the foundations of the theory, it does not follow that the theory's practical recommendation for men and women in the real world is to adopt an act-utilitarian decision-procedure. 'Indirect' utilitarianism suggests that the basic aim may be better served if individuals follow certain rules which they treat more or less as absolute requirements in most of the circumstances they face.[20] Indeed, if a goal-based utilitarianism is articulated realistically, it may involve a commitment to rights at the surface even though rights do not figure at all in its deeper premises.[21] This example shows that we cannot infer much about the practical recommendations of a normative theory from the character of its fundamental premises.[22]

3 From moral rights to legal rights

So far we have considered only the relation between basic and derivative positions *within* a normative theory. The fact that, in a given theory, the basic premises (or even the intermediate theorems) are best formulated as rights

does not show that the derivative recommendations of the theory are best formulated as rights. But suppose, for the sake of argument, that the normative recommendations of a right-based theory *are* formulated as rights. Can we say anything about the relation between those recommendations and the actions that they call for in the real world? If someone believes in *moral* rights, does that mean she is to be taken as demanding *legal* rights?

Jeremy Bentham, for one, thought the answer was 'Yes'. Or rather, he thought this was the best we could make of what was really an oxymoron—the idea of a moral, i.e. non-legal, right.[23] Maybe, he thought, we can reinterpret natural rights claims as normative claims about the legal rights that ought to be established: 'In proportion to the want of happiness resulting from the want of rights, a reason exists for wishing that there were such things as rights.'[24] However, even Bentham's most sympathetic commentators have been bewildered by this insistence that the noun 'right' must necessarily refer (either descriptively or normatively) to *legal* rights. He did not take that view of 'duty', 'obligation', or 'right' (the adjective), each of which (he was prepared to say) had a normative meaning established by the principle of utility that was quite independent of the idea of positive law.[25]

One objection to Bentham's approach is that sometimes we talk of moral rights when we have no intention of saying anything about what the law ought to be. When my mother asks if I intend to remarry and adds 'I have a right to be told the truth', she is not saying anything about the law. She is saying I ought to tell her the truth and giving me some indication that I owe that duty *to her* in virtue of some interest she has at stake.

However, let us put those cases aside; suppose we accept H. L. A. Hart's suggestion that usually, when talk of rights is in the air, there is an implicit suggestion that the use of force (and thus the mechanisms of law) would not be inappropriate to secure what is required.[26] Even so, it does not follow that the normative claim

    (1) P has a (moral) right to X

entails

    (2) P (morally) ought to have a legal right to X.

If (1) entails anything about the law, it presumably entails

    (3) The law ought to be such that P gets X.

There may be all sorts of ways in which X may be secured legally for P, without her having a legal *right* to it.[27]

Here, of course, a lot will depend on exactly how one defines 'legal right'. Maybe, on a very broad definition of the term, *any* legal procedure by which X is secured for P amounts to the existence of P's legal right to X. I do not want to rule out such a broad definition, except to indicate that it will not advance the argument of this article one way or the other. Most jurists, however, think that the phrase 'legal right' has quite a narrow meaning. To say that P has a legal right is to indicate the existence of an articulated legal rule or principle entitling P to X. It indicates that P has standing to claim X and to bring suit for it in a court of law. And for most jurists, it indicates that officials have very limited discretion in determining who gets X and who does not. We distinguish, in other words, between (a) legal situations in which X is P's by right and she may peremptorily demand it and the law is such that her demand must be met unless there are extraordinary circumstances, and (b) legal situations in which some official has been vested with discretion to determine on a case by case basis how best to distribute a limited stock of resources like X to applicants like P. Students of public administration argue back and forth about whether it is better to have systems of rights in welfare law, for example; and these arguments presuppose that the existence of a legal right is a highly specific type of institutional arrangement along the lines of (a).

As far as I can see, nothing that institutionally specific is entailed by a claim like (1) above. I can imagine an advocate for the homeless saying, 'The homeless have a (moral) right to shelter', and certainly meaning that *something* legal should be done about it, but leaving it an open question whether that would be best achieved by a legal arrangement of type (a) or a legal arrangement of type (b). For suppose the following facts are known. There are many homeless people and, as things stand on any given night, only a limited stock of public housing, hotel rooms, and places in shelters that can be allocated to them. The circumstances of homeless individuals vary: some are with families, some are alone; some are sick, some are healthy; some have been homeless for months, others have just become homeless; some have the strength and morale to apply for a place, others wander helplessly in the streets. It is possible that an advocate who believes they all have a moral right to shelter will want to set up a rule whereby anyone who can prove she is homeless is assigned a place by a responsible official immediately, without further ado (until the available places run out). That would be clearly describable as a legal right to shelter. But it is equally possible that the homeless advocate will urge a more flexible arrangement than that—an arrangement that allows officials to match accommodation to need, to make quick judgments about who is sick and desperate and who is not, to hold some places in reserve for hapless folks found wandering in the rain late at night, and so on. And one can imagine that choice being made *on right-based grounds*: on the ground that, in the circumstances, this arrangement will better serve the moral principle that the homeless have a right to shelter.

To put the point strongly: a moral claim that people have the right to shelter is a claim about the importance of their getting shelter. It is not a claim about the importance of their being assigned shelter in accordance with a specific type of legal or bureaucratic procedure.

4 From legal rights to constitutional rights

Suppose everything I have said so far is wrong. Suppose the assertion of a moral right is always a moral demand for a legal right. Should we take the further step of saying that anyone who assents to (2), above, should also be committed to

> (4) P (morally) ought to have a constitutional right to X

if her support for (2) is wholehearted? Does a person who is in favour of a legal right always have a reason to demand that extra level of protection?

Not necessarily. There are practical reasons and reasons of principle to make her hesitate. To secure constitutional protection, the proponent of the right will either have to agitate for constitutional reform or, if there is already a Bill of Rights, persuade those entrusted with the task of interpreting it to recognize the new right under the heading of some existing provision. Either way, the political difficulties are considerable. The proponent of the right may well think that the process of securing constitutional protection would take too long or be too difficult, and that it may distract people from the more important task of actually making the legal provision that is called for.[28]

Those are strategic reasons for resisting the inference from (2) to (4). But suppose a political opportunity for constitutionalization has in fact arisen? What reasons of principle are there for hesitating in the face of that opportunity?

One point which is not *quite* as pragmatic as those already mentioned has to do with apprehensions about verbal rigidity. A legal right that finds protection in a Bill of Rights finds it under the auspices of some canonical form of words in which the provisions of the charter are enunciated. One lesson of American constitutional experience is that the words of each provision in the Bill of Rights tend to take on a life of their own, becoming the obsessive catch-phrase for expressing everything one might want to say about the right in question. For example, First Amendment doctrine in America is concerned to the point of scholasticism with the question of whether some problematic form of behaviour that the State has an interest in regulating is to be regarded as 'speech' or not. ('Is pornography speech?' 'Is burning a flag speech?' 'Is topless dancing speech?' 'Is pan-handling speech?' 'Is racial abuse speech?' and so on.) Yet surely this is not the way to argue about rights. Rights are principles of deep and pervasive concern. We may use the phrase 'freedom of speech' to pick out the sort of concerns we have in mind in invoking a particular right; but that is not the same as saying that the *word* 'speech' (as opposed to 'expression' or 'communication' etc.) is the key to our concerns in the area. The same is true for other formulae of American constitutional doctrine: 'cruel and unusual punishment', 'free exercise of religion', 'due process of law', etc.[29]

Of course, even statutory language will make use of some phraseology. The difference is that statutory language can readily be amended to meet our evolving sense of how best to get at the real issues at stake. If we think that one of the crucial tests for scrutinizing punishments is 'unusual-ness', we can write that into our statute. If later we see the merits of encouraging innovation in sentencing, we may want to express the proper constraints in some other way, and amend our criminal justice legislation accordingly. And of course this process of evolving phraseology is even easier if we are talking about legal recognition in the form of common law principles and precedents, and easier still if rights take the form of 'conventional' understandings subscribed to in the political community at large, as they have in Britain for many years. With that less articulate, less formulaic heritage of right-based concern, people can discuss issues of rights and limited government, issues of abortion, discrimination, punishment and toleration in whatever terms seem appropriate to them, free from obsession with the verbalism of a particular written charter.

For these reasons, then, the proponent of a given right may be hesitant about embodying it in a constitutionally entrenched Bill of Rights. She may figure that the gain, in terms of an immunity against wrongful legislative abrogation, is more than offset by the loss in our ability to evolve a free and flexible discourse.

But the deepest reasons of liberal principle have yet to be addressed. When a principle is entrenched in a constitutional document, the claim-right (to liberty or provision) that it lays down is compounded with an immunity against legislative change. Those who possess the right now get the additional advantage of its being made difficult or impossible to alter their legal position. That can sound attractive; but as W. N. Hohfeld emphasized, we should always look at both sides of any legal advantage.[30] The term correlative to the claim-right is of course the duty incumbent upon officials and others to respect and uphold the right. And the term correlative to the constitutional immunity is what Hohfeld would call a disability: in effect, a disabling of the legislature from its normal functions of revision, reform and innovation in the law. To think that a constitutional immunity is called for is to think oneself justified in disabling legislators in this respect (and thus, indirectly, in disabling the citizens whom they represent). It is, I think, worth pondering the attitudes that lie behind the enthusiasm for imposing such disabilities.

To embody a right in an entrenched constitutional document is to adopt a certain attitude towards one's fellow citizens. That attitude is best summed up as a combination of self-assurance and mistrust: self-assurance in the proponent's conviction that what she is putting forward really is a matter of fundamental right and that she has captured it adequately in the particular formulation she is propounding; and mistrust, implicit in her view that any alternative conception that might be concocted by elected legislators next year or the year after is so likely to be wrong-headed or ill-motivated that *her own* formulation is to be elevated immediately beyond the reach of ordinary legislative revision.

This attitude of mistrust of one's fellow citizens does not sit particularly well with the aura of respect for their autonomy and responsibility that is conveyed by the substance of the rights which are being entrenched in this way. The substantive importance of a given right may well be based on a view of the individual person as essentially a thinking agent, endowed with an ability to deliberate morally and to transcend a preoccupation with her own particular or sectional interests. For example, an argument for freedom of speech may depend on a view of people as 'political animals' in Aristotle's sense, capable of evolving a shared and reliable sense of right and wrong, justice and injustice, in their conversations with one another.[31] If *this* is why one thinks free speech important, one cannot simply turn round and announce that the products of any deliberative process are to be mistrusted.

If, on the other hand, the desire for entrenchment is motivated by a predatory view of human nature and of what people will do to one another when let loose in the arena of democratic politics, it will be difficult to explain how or why people are to be viewed as essentially bearers of rights. For in order to develop a theory of rights, we need some basis for distinguishing those interests which are characteristic of human dignity from those which are relatively unimportant in a person's activity and desires. If our only image of man is that of a self-seeking animal who is not to be trusted with a concern for the interests of others, we lack the conception of dignified moral autonomy on which such discriminations of interest might be based.

These are not intended as knock-down arguments against constitutionalization. All I have tried to show so far is that there is nothing obvious about combining a respect for rights with a profound mistrust of people in their democratic and representative capacities. Accordingly there is nothing perverse in saying: 'The reasons which make me think of the human individual as a bearer of rights are the very reasons that allow me to trust her as the bearer of political responsibilities. It is precisely because I see each person as a potential moral agent, endowed with dignity and autonomy, that I am willing to entrust the people *en masse* with the burden of self-government.' Once we see this as an intelligible set of attitudes, we might be more hesitant in expressing our enthusiasm for rights in terms of the disabling of representative institutions.

5 Doing philosophy

The attitudes we take towards our fellow citizens will depend in part on how easy we think it is to come up with an adequate conception of the rights that deserve protection. If someone has developed such a conception and if, moreover, she thinks it a relatively easy task, she will tend to distrust anyone who comes up with a conception of rights that differs from her own. She, after all, thinks of herself as acting in good faith and since the task presents no special difficulties, it is likely that her good faith will have yielded good results. The only explanation, then, of other people's contrary results is that they must have been acting for some ulterior motive. To put it another way, if we hold the truths that *we* have come up with to be 'self-evident', our only explanation of the contrary results arrived at by other people is that they are either simpletons or rogues. Either way, we have reason (on this conception of the task) to embody our self-evident

conclusions in immutable form as soon as possible in order to insulate them from the folly and chicanery of misguided revision or reformulation.

If, on the other hand, we take the view that the whole business of thinking about rights is fraught with difficulty and that it is something on which, with the best will in the world, people of good faith may differ, we will not evince the same distrust of our opponents' suggestions nor indeed the same dogmatic confidence in our own. Those who think it possible that they are mistaken should be less inclined to cast their conclusions in stone, and more open to the possibility that debate among their fellow citizens will from time to time produce conclusions that are better than theirs.

Which of these views of our task is correct? A theorist of rights has to work out what rights people have, how they are to be formulated, and how important they are in relation to other moral and political considerations. Is this an easy task or a difficult one?

There is some pressure to insist on its facility. Talk of individual rights is often supposed to be a way of registering fairly basic objections to the arcane computations of the utilitarian calculus. It is the utilitarian who is supposed to be telling us that everything is all very complicated, and that whether we allow horrible things like torture, censorship, or the execution of the innocent depends on all the circumstances, long-run calculations of probability, etc. The theorist of rights, by contrast, is supposed to be the one who can produce the trump card, the peremptory argument-stopper: '*Thou shalt not kill.*' The idea of rights has often been seized on precisely as a way of avoiding the casuistry of trade-offs and complex moral calculations—a way of insisting that certain basics are to be secured and certain atrocities prohibited, come what may. But if rights themselves are morally complicated, the spectre of casuistry reappears. Complicated problems presumably require complicated solutions; but it was the *simplicity* of right-based constraints that was supposed to be their main advantage over other more recondite and precarious modes of moral reasoning.[32]

The sad fact is, however, that this simplicity and moral certainty is simply unavailable. No one now believes that the truth about rights is self-evident or that, if two people disagree about rights, one of them at least must be either corrupt or morally blind. In the thirty years or so of the modern revival of the philosophical study of rights, there has been a proliferation of rival theories and conceptions.[33] Each of these has occasioned an outpouring of essays, articles and symposia discussing, elaborating and criticizing their accounts.[34] In addition there are hundreds of articles devoted to particular rights or making particular points about the idea of rights,[35] as well as a number of important books attacking the idea of rights and the individualist presuppositions of that idea.[36]

To believe in rights is to believe that certain key interests of individuals, in liberty and well-being, deserve special protection, and that they should not be sacrificed for the sake of greater efficiency or prosperity or for any aggregate of lesser interests under the heading of the public good. Now some people think this whole idea is misguided; but even those who propound it in political philosophy recognize its difficulty. Any theory of rights will face disagreements about the interests it identifies as rights, and the terms in which it identifies them. Those disagreements will in turn be vehicles for controversies about the proper balance to be struck between some individual interest and some countervailing social consideration. For example, in articulating and defending a right to free speech, we need to think through the congestion of values and principles that we find in crowded theatres that are not on fire, in public libraries where 'Silence' is enjoined, and in university lectures where racist hypotheses are being entertained. In addition, theories of rights have to face up to controversies about the forms of priority that they establish: lexical priorities, weighted

priorities, agent-relative side constraints, agent-relative prerogatives and so on. Our experience with these issues in moral philosophy indicates that their prominence in the literature is directly proportional to both their difficulty and their importance. Finally, theories of rights must develop accounts of who they take to be right-bearers: they must develop theories of the person, and articulate those into an account of the rights (or whatever) of foetuses, infants, the elderly, the comatose, the mentally ill, and so on. So even within the terms of a given theory of rights, its development and articulation is a complex and difficult task.

How should a philosopher approach these difficulties? The first and most obvious point is that, in her own work, she should recognize the possibility that she is mistaken. Robert Nozick noted in the preface to *Anarchy, State and Utopia* that each individual author tends to write as though mankind has been struggling for aeons with some philosophical or ethical problem, but 'he finally, thank God, has found the truth and built an impregnable fortress around it'.[37] In fact each of us is familiar with the business of argumentation, objections, answers to objections, rejoinders, and revisions. Indeed, we often use that apparatus to structure the way we write: here is my preliminary thesis; here is my account of the main objections; here are the answers to all but one of the objections; and here are the revisions that are needed to accommodate the unanswerable objection. That mode of presentation and the ethic of fallibility it evinces are the life-blood of the philosophical community.

Of course everyone thinks her own current position is correct; otherwise she would not be putting it forward. In the area of rights, where it is precisely questions of relative urgency and moral priority that are at stake, everyone will think that she has got the priorities right and that alternative views are wrong. Though each should think it possible she is mistaken, it is not necessarily a good idea for her to incorporate that misgiving into the substance of her theory. There is a difference between being modest about one's conclusion and modifying the conclusion to take account of that modesty. Modifying the conclusion may well diminish, rather than enhance, the proponent's conviction that it is correct. Still, though one may be convinced now that this, rather than some more modest formulation, is the correct one, it is part of philosophical maturity to be able to combine that conviction with a recollection of past occasions where similar beliefs have had to be abandoned in the face of philosophical difficulty, and with an openness to counter-argument and refutation in the future.[38]

Such fallibilism can be taken in a purely Cartesian spirit: a solitary thinker's openness to her own revisions, self-criticisms and reformulations. For most of us, however, it is an aspect of the way we do philosophy together, as members of a community of thinkers and critics. We accept and embrace the circumstance of a plurality of views and the trenchant disagreements they give rise to. Again, the discipline thrives on this. The interplay of arguments is expected to produce better theories that will form the basis for an even more vigorous debate, and so on. In these debates, each of us has a responsibility to take the perspective of the philosophical community as well as the perspective of the particular view she is defending. From the latter perspective, one is a passionate partisan of a particular theory. From the former perspective, however, one knows that it is wrong to expect any particular theory, no matter how attractive or well argued, to survive the process of debate unscathed. One recognizes that the debate has a point: to use collective interaction as a way of reaching towards complicated truth. Simple truths, self-evident truths may form in single minds, but complicated truths (in which category I include all propositions about individual rights) emerge, in Mill's words, only 'by the rough process of a struggle between combatants fighting under hostile banners'.[39]

6 Disagreement and authority

Politics, as Hannah Arendt once remarked, starts from the fact that not one man, but men, inhabit the earth.[40] One of the great problems of political philosophy is to explain how there can be a society, ordering and governing itself, taking initiatives and functioning as an agent, in the face of the plurality of its members and the disagreements they have with one another on the question of what is to be done.

Recent political philosophy with its emphasis on rights and justice has tended to neglect this topic. We have recognized (quite rightly) the importance of justice, and the importance of thinking hard about what justice requires in the way of distributions, structures, and respect for individuals and groups. However, given the inevitability of disagreement about all that, a theory of justice and rights needs to be complemented by a theory of authority. Since people disagree about what justice requires and what rights we have, we must ask: who is to have the power to make decisions, or by what processes are decisions to be taken, on the practical issues that the competing theories of justice and rights purport to address? Majoritarian democracy is the theory of authority with which most of us are familiar, but others include 'Toss a coin', 'Let the king decide', and 'Leave it to the judges'.

There are a few points to notice immediately about the problem of authority, before we consider how a right-based theorist should try to answer it.

First, the need is for us to complement our theory of rights with a theory of authority, not to replace the former with the latter. The issue of what counts as a good decision does not disappear the moment we answer the question 'Who decides?' On the contrary, the function of a theory of justice and rights is to offer advice to whoever has been identified (by the theory of authority) as the person to take the decision. If there are competing theories of justice and rights, then the authority is offered competing advice, each theory putting itself forward as the best product available.

Secondly, an answer to the question of authority must really settle the issue. It is no good saying, for example, that when people disagree about rights, the person who should prevail is the person who offers *the best conception of rights*. Each person regards her own view as better than any of the others; so this rule for settling on a social choice in the face of a disagreement is going to reproduce exactly the disagreement that called for the rule in the first place. The theory of authority must identify some view as the one to prevail, on criteria other than those which are the source of the original disagreement.[41]

It is important to notice how this point applies to disputes about rights. All of us want to see an end to injustice, oppression and the violation of human rights; none of us is happy with political procedures that allow such violations to take place. This enthusiasm sometimes leads people to qualify their views about authority with a rider to protect individual rights. For example, someone may say, 'If people in society disagree about anything, then a decision should be taken by majority voting, *provided individual rights are not violated thereby*.' But the emphasized rider will not work in a theory of authority, at least for a society in which rights themselves are a subject of political disagreement. People who disagree *inter alia* about rights will disagree about what that theory of authority requires, and that latter disagreement will be nothing but a reproduction of the problem about rights which evoked the need for a theory of authority in the first place.

Similarly, we cannot say, with Ronald Dworkin, that the whole *point* of rights is to 'trump' or override majority decisions.[42] For rights may be the very thing that the members of the society are disagreeing about, the very issue that they are using majority voting to settle. If we say, in a context where people disagree about rights, that rights may 'trump' a majority decision, it is incumbent on us to say which of the competing conceptions of rights is to do

the trumping, and how that is to be determined.

Thirdly, it follows from what has been said that there will sometimes be a dissonance between what one takes to be the just choice and what one takes to be the authoritative choice in political decision-making. A person who holds a complete political theory—one that includes a theory of authority as well as a theory of justice and rights—may find herself committed to the view that an unjust decision should prevail. Her theory of justice may condemn policy B and prefer policy A on right-based grounds, but her theory of authority may mandate a decision procedure (designed to yield a social choice even in the face of disagreement about the justice or injustice of A and B) which, when followed, requires that B be adopted.

Given the second point that I made, this prospect is simply unavoidable. In a famous article, Richard Wollheim called it 'a paradox in the theory of democracy'. He imagined citizens feeding their individual evaluations of policies into a democratic machine which would always choose the policy with the greatest number of supporters. The paradox arises from the fact that each citizen, if she is a democrat, will have an allegiance to the machine and its output, as well as to the evaluation which counts as her own whole-hearted individual input. It is the paradox that allows 'one and the same citizen to assert that A ought to be enacted, where A is the policy of his choice, and B ought to be enacted, where B is the policy chosen by the democratic machine'.[43] But Wollheim is wrong to describe this as a paradox of *democracy*. It is a general paradox in the theory of authority—a paradox which affects any political theory that complements its account of what ought to be done with an account of how decisions ought to be taken when there is disagreement about what ought to be done.

That point is important in the present context. American-style judicial review is often defended by pointing to the possibility that democratic majoritarian procedures may yield unjust or tyrannical outcomes. And so they may. But so may *any* procedure that purports to solve the problem of social choice in the face of disagreements about what counts as injustice or what counts as tyranny. The rule that the Supreme Court should make the final decision (by majority voting among its members)[44] on issues of fundamental rights is just such a procedural rule. It too may (and sometimes has) yielded egregiously unjust decisions.[45] Anyone whose theory of authority gives the Supreme Court power to make decisions must—as much as any democrat—face up to the paradox that the option she thinks is just may not be the option which, according to her theory of authority, should be followed.

Of course, as Wollheim argued at the end of his essay, the paradox does not really involve a contradiction. A person who believes that A is the right decision, but B the decision that should be implemented, is offering answers to two different, though complementary questions. That B should be implemented is her answer to the question, 'What are *we* to do, given that we disagree about whether A or B is just.' That A is the right decision is her contribution to the disagreement that calls forth that question.[46]

One final point. That we need a theory of authority to settle disagreements is in no way a concession to moral subjectivism or conventionalism or relativism. One can recognize the existence of disagreement in society, including disagreement on matters of rights and justice, and one can acknowledge that some disagreements are, for practical purposes, irresolvable, without staking the meta-ethical claim that there is no fact of the matter about the issue that the participants are disputing.[47] Earlier I argued that 'Choose the right answer' is not a useful rule for action in the face of disagreements. The rejection of that rule is not to be seen as a move away from moral realism towards some more relativist meta-ethic. It is simply a response to what must be for a realist the unhappy fact that people disagree implacably about what the objectively right answer is.[48]

7 Philosophical debate and political participation

Philosophers disagree among themselves and citizens disagree among themselves about issues of rights and justice. They disagree about welfare and taxation, about free speech and the rule of law, about equal opportunity and substantive equality. How should the philosophers regard the disagreements and discussions that take place among the citizens? I suggested in the previous section that the philosophers have a responsibility to think about the issue of authority: how is society to act when its members disagree? I now want to suggest that when we do so, we should think of the various people taking part in the social disagreement as being in many respects *just like us* when we disagree in a seminar or a journal. Or rather they are just like us with this one proviso: we have the luxury of not having to make a decision; they have to engage not only in hard thinking about what is just and what rights people have, but also in what we in the academy may too easily dismiss as the sordid and distasteful business of actual collective decision-making in the absence of moral consensus.

We pride ourselves, of course, that our thinking in books, articles and seminars is more reasoned and more profound than the thinking engaged in by working politicians and their constituents. And so it should be: in the social division of labour, it is our task to take time and energy to think these things through as carefully as it is possible to think them. But it is a mistake, I think, to regard our thought as different in kind from that of a citizen-participant in politics. Political philosophy is simply conscientious civic discussion without a deadline.[49]

To think that theoretical discussions are different in kind is not just an error of arrogance; it is a substantial philosophical mistake. At least since the seventeenth century, our conception of *argument* in political philosophy has been guided by the idea that social, political and legal institutions are to be, in principle, explicable and justifiable to all those who have to live under them. We have rejected the esoteric in political theory; we have rejected the idea of *arcana imperii*.[50] The model-theoretic ideas of consent and social contract, and the corresponding constraints of publicity and transparency, commit us to producing arguments that purport to be intelligible to anyone whose interests they affect, and that—in spirit, if not in idiom—are consonant with the arguments that they would find persuasive in their conversations with one another. There is, as I have argued elsewhere, an important connection between liberal argumentation and the Enlightenment conviction that everything real can in principle be explained, and everything right can in principle be justified, to everyone.[51] Modern philosophy evinces a commitment to the idea that theoretical argument aims not merely to justify laws or political proposals, but to justify them *to* the ordinary men and women whom they will affect.

For present purposes, the implication of this democratic model of political theory is that each of us should think of her conception of rights as a particularly well-worked out opinion or position which, in outline, might be held by any citizen. Similarly, we should think of the theoretical disagreements we have among ourselves as particularly civil, thoughtful and protracted versions of the disagreements that take place among citizens in the public realm. Conversely, when we come across a citizen or party of citizens holding a view about rights that differs from our own, we should think of that along the lines that we think of a colleague's contrary conception: something to be disagreed with but respected, treated as a good faith contribution to a debate in which nothing is self-evident.

These considerations should be sufficient to make us pause before adopting some of the more disrespectful images of democratic decision-making that one finds in constitutionalist writings. Cynics sometimes say that legislative and electoral politics is entirely a matter of self-interest, and that representatives and voters never raise their minds above the sordid question, 'What's in it for me?' This of course is an empirical issue, but I believe the cynicism is exaggerated.[52] Certainly the idiom of self-interest is not the idiom in which citizens' views about rights are normally expressed. Consider the debate about abortion. The pro-life and pro-choice factions cannot both be correct on the issues of whether foetuses have rights and whether women have the right to choose abortion, but it seems clear that both sides are engaged in good faith on exactly those general and difficult questions of ethics. Each group appears to be arguing for a particular view about what rights there are, and what sort of beings have them. We might, to sustain our cynicism, insist that these philosophical convictions are really only a cover for self-interest, in some less high-minded sense, so that the political debate should be discredited on that account. But then it will be hard to limit this cynicism. Why not say that about the opinions of judges? (Many people do.) Why not say it about constitution-framers? Why not say it about *anyone* who purports to think or write on such an issue. On the other hand, if we are willing, as most of us in our vanity are, to say that at least when *philosophers* write about abortion in professional journals they are not motivated by covert self-interest, why are we not prepared to say this about ordinary citizens, who certainly look and sound as earnest and high-minded as we do, when they disagree with one another?

8 The right to participate

Fortunately perhaps, our respect for the political thinking of ordinary citizens does not stem solely from our willingness to see similarities between what they are doing in political debate and what we are doing in our seminars. It stems also from our democratic principles, and from our conviction that self-government and participation in politics by ordinary men and women, on equal terms, is itself a matter of fundamental right.

I suppose one could imagine a theory of rights that accorded no great importance to the exercise of powers of political deliberation. It would be a rather Whiggish Lockean theory of the Augustan Age, emphasizing only rights to life, property and civil liberty, and regarding political participation in elections and so on as strictly one instrument among others to secure those ends. If it turned out that basic material interests could be secured better by non-participatory institutions, then the erstwhile electors would gratefully abjure politics forever and return to commerce or agriculture.

Some say this Lockean position is distinctive of modern 'liberalism' and that one has to be a civic republican to deny it.[53] I think that is false, but it does not matter. The point is that all interesting modern theories of individual rights *do* emphasize rights to political participation. These range from rights to political liberty—free speech, assembly, association, and the formation of parties—all the way through to what we may call the Hohfeldian *powers* of representative government—the right to stand for office and the right to have one's vote counted. More abstractly, they amount to the freedom to contribute to public deliberations and the power to have one's voice taken seriously in public decision-making. These have been the very stuff of rights, at least since 1789.[54]

Why do we demand respect for these rights? One answer is that we think of people as political animals on the Aristotelian model, and we believe that participation in the public realm is a necessary part of a fulfilling human life.[55] To deny people the opportunity for such participation is to deny part of their essence. Yet few would want to leave the matter there, saying that participation is important simply for the performance values associated with each person's contribution, as though the content of the participation did not matter.[56] Participation is valued

also as a mode of self-protection: each individual acts, to some extent, as a voice for those of her own interests that ought to be taken seriously in politics. We need not think of this in a crude utilitarian way, as though votes were inputs and the process were the institutional embodiment of a social welfare function. The heart of any theory of right is the insistence that certain individual interests are of paramount importance, and that their importance is to be appreciated at least in part from the point of view of those whose interests they are. More than anyone else, a rights-theorist should be uneasy about political arrangements that tend to silence such voices or that evince distaste for their clamour in a democratic forum.

Then there are arguments about the quality of public deliberation. The recognition of participatory rights is not just a grudging concession by those who have knowledge to the childish enthusiasms of those who do not. As my earlier remarks about philosophical debate indicated, the participation of the many acts as a useful corrective to the blinkered self-confidence with which one individual may hold her view.[57] Participation by all is valuable because of the importance of assembling diverse perspectives and experiences when public decisions are being taken; and it is valuable also because the sheer experience of arguing in circumstances of human plurality helps us develop more interesting and probably more valid opinions than we could manufacture on our own.[58]

In addition, there are points to be made about dignity, autonomy and self-government. I noted earlier that modern theories of rights are usually predicated on a view of the individual as essentially a thinking agent, endowed with the ability to deliberate morally and to govern her life autonomously. Connected with that is the view that the obligations that consort most deeply with our autonomy are those that are, in some sense, self-imposed. Pushed in one direction, this Kantian allegiance to autonomy leads to anarchy.[59] But if we take our situation in social life seriously, we may say with Rousseau that the only thing that 'self-imposed' can mean in a community is participation on equal terms with others in the framing of laws.[60] Or we can say at least what John Stuart Mill emphasized, that those who are to be required to comply with a decision are surely entitled to *some* sort of voice in that decision: 'If he is compelled to pay, if he may be compelled to fight, if he is required implicitly to obey, he should be legally entitled to be told what for; to have his consent asked, and his opinion counted at its worth. . . .'[61]

These paragraphs do not amount to a full theory of democracy but they are, I hope, enough to indicate the depth of the connection between the idea of civic participation and the ideas that lie at the heart of modern conceptions of rights. Both ideas represent people as essentially agents and choosers, with interests of their own to protect and, in their dignity and autonomy, as beings who flourish best in conditions that they can understand as self-government. The modern theory of democracy represents individuals not only as blind pursuers of self-interest, but as having the capacity to engage in thought and principled dialogue about the conditions under which everyone's interests may be served. An exactly similar moral optimism can be inferred from theories of rights. Each person's rights are matched by duties that she bears correlative to the rights of others: the rights that I have are universalizable and the principles they embody apply equally to all. This universality is at least partly determinative of their content: what my right is a right *to* depends partly on what can be guaranteed on equal terms, without mutual interference, to everyone. Since claiming and asserting a right is necessarily a self-conscious business, it follows that each right-bearer is already familiar with the idea of the common good at least in the sense of a universalized, mutually respectful and reciprocal *system* of rights. The rights of others are matters she already takes into account in working out the content of the rights she claims as her own.

Above all, the appearance of democratic participation on the list of rights that we value is a concession to human plurality. It is the recognition, in behalf of each person, that she too has a vision of how a human community may be organized, and that her vision is entitled not only to be respected in the sense of 'not suppressed', but also to *count* in whatever political decision-making goes on in the society in which she lives.

9 The proceduralist gambit

What about the constitutional importance of the participatory rights themselves? It may be thought that, according to the logic of my argument, these rights *at least* should be entrenched. Since it is the right to a say in the determination of what rights we have that is so important, surely *this* should be put beyond the reach of majoritarian revision. In the history of American attempts to square the circle of judicial review with the principles of democracy, this has been a common argument: democracy must protect itself from the majoritarian abrogation of its own constitutive structures; although there may be something undemocratic about entrenching substantive rights against majoritarian abrogation, there is nothing undemocratic about protecting the procedural rules of democracy in that way.[62]

Unfortunately, the proceduralist argument will not work. The truth about participation and process is as complex and disputable as anything else in politics, and the points made in previous sections apply equally to these issues. People disagree about how participatory rights should be understood and about how they should be balanced against other values. They have views on constituency boundaries, proportional representation, the frequency of elections, the funding of parties, the relation between free speech and political advertising, the desirability of referendums, and so on. Respect for their political capacities demands that their voices be heard and their opinions count on these matters, as much as on any matter. Honouring self-government does not stop at the threshold from substance to procedure.

I am not suggesting that we can afford to leave these matters open. Because we disagree, there have to be authoritative procedures for settling disputes about what should be our authoritative procedures. Now as we noticed in Section 6, the one option that is *not* open to us in settling these disputes is to lay down as an authoritative rule, 'Choose the best procedure'. That is a non-starter because it reproduces and does not settle the disagreement we began with. What we have to determine is who will choose the procedures we will use and what procedures they will use to choose them. Vesting that decisional power in a small group of judges is one solution; vesting it in the ordinary legislative process is another. Presumably we should choose between these two options in the same way as we make any decision of this kind. If we are partisans of democracy, holding the values that were sketched out in the previous section, we will I think opt to entrust these decisions about procedure to the people and their representatives, figuring that it is an insult to say that the issues are too important or perhaps too formalistic for them (rather than the judges) to decide.

But, it may be objected, in a dispute about *procedure*, are these not the very points at issue? If we really disagree about the proper scope of democratic decision-making, how can it be right to use democratic decision-procedures to settle that disagreement? The point seems a worrying one, but the worry dissolves when we realize that the same objection would apply to *any* solution of the problem of authority in the context of a disagreement about procedure. Since there are disagreements about how to settle disagreements (i.e. disagreements about authority), and since we need those disagreements settled too, we will always be in the uncomfortable position of using the procedures advocated by one or other of the disputants to settle the very dispute to which she

is a party. Though that may be uncomfortable, it is not question-begging. The use of decision-procedure A to settle the disagreement between those who think that decision-procedure A should be used and those who think we should use decision-procedure B does not necessarily load the dice in favour of the first of these outcomes. We are all familiar with political organizations that manage to reform their own decisional procedures: that means we are familiar with cases in which the use of decision-procedure A yields as an output the conclusion that, henceforth, procedure B, rather than A, should be used.

In addition, it is worth noting that the distinction between substance and democratic procedure is a notoriously difficult one to sustain in politics. Many of the values we affirm in our opinions about democratic procedures are also values which inform our views about substantial outcomes. For example, if we favour democratic participation on grounds of respect for individual autonomy—recognizing an element of self-authorship in one's participation in collective self-governance—we may well find it is the basis of many substantive outcome evaluations also. The strongest arguments for free religion (a liberty right which is not also a right of *political* participation) or public education (a welfare right rather than a political power) implicate that same basic consideration. Since the same fundamental values are implicated in both spheres, it will be difficult to keep constitutional jurisprudence apart from the consideration of other more obviously substantive concerns.

Moreover, we value participation not just as an end in itself but also because we think that this is one way to ensure that each person gets what is hers by right. Ronald Dworkin has argued that the case for one particular conception of the political process rather than another must always be based in the last resort on considerations of outcome: what ends up happening to people as a result of the operation of the institutions and procedures in question. 'The flight from substance', he says, 'must end in substance.'[63] I think he exaggerates that: there is a certain dignity in participation, and an element of insult and dishonour in exclusion, that transcends issues of outcome. When we are told, by those who would otherwise be our political masters, that some issue is to be decided by us, by a vote, there is an element of pride and egalitarian respect that is in principle separable from what we hope to achieve by voting. Still, even if Dworkin is half right, and particularly if the issues are tangled, we can say that any entrenchment of a set of putatively procedural principles would be *at least in part* the entrenchment of a particular view of the substantive outcomes to which each person is entitled. To that extent, it amounts to the political disempowerment of the proponents of any rival view on that matter of substance.

10 Imperfect democracy

It is time to descend now from ideal to reality. As a matter of fact, the enactment of a Bill of Rights need not involve the entrenchment of one particular view of individual rights beyond the reach of challenge or reform. A Bill of Rights can specify procedures for amendment; and certainly one upshot of the argument I have made is that we should insist on such opportunities for constitutional revision, for they give a politically empowered people the chance to think afresh about their understanding of individual rights.[64] However, even if the efforts of rights-proponents fall short of absolute entrenchment, there is a temptation to make the amendment process as difficult as possible, a temptation often motivated by the same self-assured mistrust of one's fellow citizens that I have been criticizing throughout this paper. At the very least, it is thought appropriate that any amendment to a Bill of Rights should require a super-majority, and often the procedural obstacles that are proposed are much more formidable than that.

The point of such super-majoritarian requirements is, presumably, to reduce the probability that any amendment will be successful. To the extent that that is the aim, one needs to ask: how is the Bill of Rights to be made responsive to changing circumstances and different opinions in the community over time about the rights we have and the way they should be formulated? Are the formulations of one generation to be cast in stone, and given precedence over all subsequent revisions, save for the rare occasion on which the obstacles to amendment can be surmounted? Or are there to be, in effect, other and even less democratic procedures for constitutional revision than these?

The experience of the United States indicates the importance of the latter possibility. For, of course, *there* it would be quite misleading to suggest that the formal amendment procedure exhausts the possibilities for constitutional revision. In addition to the processes specified in Article V of the US Constitution, changes in the American Bill of Rights have come about most often through the exercise of judicial power. The Supreme Court is not empowered to alter the written terms of the Bill of Rights. But the justices do undertake the task of altering the way in which the document is interpreted and applied, and the way in which individual rights are authoritatively understood—in many cases with drastic and far-reaching effects.

I shall not in this article consider the intriguing jurisprudential issue of how these alterations should be described: literary interpretation, constructive interpretation, or the raw exercise of legislative power by the courts. I shall use the general term 'revision' to refer to any substantial change in the official understanding of rights, whether or not it involves a change in constitutional wording. (Thus, for example, the decision in *Roe v Wade*,[65] whatever its merits, was undoubtedly a revision, notwithstanding the fact that none of the Articles in the Bill of Rights was changed in its wording thereby.)

Members of the higher judiciary in the

United States have the power to revise the official understanding of rights for that society and, when they do, their view prevails. The ordinary electors and their state and Congressional representatives do not have that power, at least in any sense that counts. A proposal to establish a Bill of Rights for Britain, judicially interpreted and enforced, is a proposal to institute a similar situation: to allow in effect routine constitutional revision by the courts and to disallow routine constitutional revision by Parliament. I hope it is easy to see, in the light of what I said in Section 8, why this arrogation of judicial authority, this disabling of representative institutions, and above all this quite striking political inequality, should be frowned upon by any right-based theory that stresses the importance of democratic participation on matters of principle by ordinary men and women.

Responses to this critique take three forms. First, it is argued that the judicial power of interpretation and revision is simply unavoidable. After all, it is the job of the courts to apply the law. They cannot do that except by trying to understand what the law says, and that involves interpreting it. As Dworkin put it (for the American context),

> If the Constitution, properly interpreted, does not prohibit capital punishment, then of course a justice who declared that it is unconstitutional for states to execute criminals would be changing the Constitution. But if the Constitution, properly interpreted, does forbid capital punishment, a justice who *refused* to strike down state statutes providing death penalties would be changing the Constitution by fiat, usurping authority in defiance of constitutional principle. The question of law, in other words, is inescapable.[66]

However, the inescapability of judicial interpretation does not settle the issue of whether *other* institutions should not also have the power to revise the official understanding of rights. On any account of the activity of the US Supreme Court over the past century or so, the inescapable duty to interpret the law has been taken as the occasion for serious and radical revision. There may not be anything wrong with that, but there is something wrong in conjoining it with an insistence that the very rights which the judges are interpreting and revising are to be put beyond the reach of *democratic* revision and reinterpretation.

In the end, either we believe in the need for a cumbersome amendment process or we do not. If we do, then we should be disturbed by the scale of the revisions in which the judges engage (inescapably, on Dworkin's account). They find themselves routinely having to think afresh about the rights that people have, and having to choose between rival conceptions of those rights, in just the way that traditional arguments for making amendment difficult are supposed to preclude. It is no answer to this that the amendment process focuses particularly on changes in constitutional *wording*, and that the judges are not assuming the power to make verbal alterations. For one thing, judicial doctrine in the US has yielded catch-phrases (such as 'clear and present danger', or 'substantive due process', or 'strict scrutiny') which have become as much a part of the verbalism of the American constitutional heritage as anything in the Constitution itself. For another thing, it cannot be that the *words* matter more—and so need more protection from change—than our substantive understanding of the content of the rights themselves.

If, on the other hand, we think it desirable that a Bill of Rights should be treated as 'a living organism . . . capable of growth—of expansion and of adaptation to new conditions',[67] then we do have to face the question of authority: who should be empowered to participate in this quotidian organic process? Now, if Dworkin is right, the question is not 'Who?' but 'The judges and who else?', for the judges' participation is inescapable. But if it is really thought to be necessary for society 'to adapt canons of right to situations not envisaged by those who framed them, thereby facilitating their evolution and preserving their vitality',[68] it is difficult to see why the ordinary people and their representatives should be excluded from this process. Or rather—and more disturbingly—it is all too easy to see why: those who want an adaptive constitution do not trust the people to participate in its adaptation. That distrust, it seems to me, is something we should recoil from, on the same right-based ground as we recoil from any attempt to exclude people from the governance of the society in which they live.

A second response is to appeal, not to the inescapability of judicial power, but to its democratic credentials. Judicial review, it may be said, is a form of democratic representation, albeit a rather indirect form. In the US, justices are nominated to the Supreme Court by the President and their appointment is ratified by the Senate, and in the United Kingdom appointments to the higher judiciary are made on the advice of the Prime Minister, who is of course head of the elected government. To that extent, the authority of a judge is an upshot of the exercise of elected representative power, and recent American experience shows that occasionally something of an electoral issue can be made of who a Presidential candidate's Supreme Court nominees are likely to be.

But it is not enough to show, as this argument does, a scintilla of democratic respectability in the constitution of judicial power. For that does not show that the courts should have prerogatives that the people and their directly elected representatives lack, nor does it establish that when judicial authority clashes with parliamentary authority, the former ought to prevail. The sponsors of a piece of legislation struck down by a court can also point to a democratic pedigree. They can say, moreover, that if the people disagree with their legislation, they can hold them accountable for it at the next election, throw them out of office, and elect MPs who are pledged to repeal it, and so on.

Nothing like that can be said in behalf of the judges.

In other words, the second response goes wrong by failing to see that the issue is essentially a *comparative* one. If a majority of judges in the House of Lords, for example, strikes down legislation passed by majoritarian processes in parliament, then the voting powers of a few judges are being held to prevail over the voting powers of the people's representatives. To provide a *democratic* justification for the judges' prevailing, one has to show not only that they have democratic credentials but that they have a *better* democratic claim than that asserted in the legislative action in question. I don't know of any jurist who can maintain that (with a straight face).[69]

Consider, moreover, how artificial this line of argument is. It is true that judges are appointed by elected officials. But the courts are not, either in their ethos or image, elective institutions, whereas parliament—whatever its imperfections—obviously is. Both in theory and in political practice, the legislature is thought of as the main embodiment of popular government: it is where responsible representatives of the people engage in what they would proudly describe as the self-government of the society. Now there are lots of dignified ways of describing the judiciary, but 'locus of representative authority' is unlikely to be one of them. Since my argument is in part about the respect and honour we accord to the people in our constitutional structures, it is important to understand that when a court strikes down a piece of legislation, a branch of the government that neither thinks of itself, nor is thought of, as a representative institution is striking down the act of an institution that is seen in more or less precisely that way.

Thirdly and perhaps most insidiously, it is argued that the objection to judicial power is a weak one, since both legislative and plebiscitary channels are rather imperfect forms of democracy. Now it is certainly true that the processes of election, representation, and legislation, as they actually exist in the United Kingdom, are quite imperfect by democratic standards. The executive dominates the House of Commons, leaving it weak as an independent institution; small or new parties are squeezed out by the plurality system; voters have to choose between whole packages of policies and cannot vote issue by issue; and as for deliberation, Prime Minister's Question-time and party political broadcasts on television hardly answer to the high-minded account of participation that we developed in Section 8. It is all very well to say that parliament has a democratic self-image. What are we to say about the numerous ways in which the corrupt reality falls short of this ideal?

We must remember, once again, what that argument is seeking to justify—the disempowerment of ordinary citizens, on matters of the highest moral and political importance. No one ever thought that the imperfection of existing representative institutions was a justification for not enfranchising women, or that in the United States it could be an argument to continue denying political rights to Americans of African descent. If someone were to meet *those* participatory demands with an argument like the one we are currently considering, the move would be rejected immediately as an insult. The response would be:

> Imperfect though those institutions are, we want to have our say. Our voices should have as much weight in this admittedly imperfect process as those of anyone else. If there is imperfection in the process, let us amend the process. But the imperfections are not mended by keeping half the people out. (And—to tell you the truth—we think you are raising this issue of the imperfections of the process purely as a ploy to justify the denial of our legitimate participatory rights.)

Offhand, I cannot think why a similar comment would not be in order in regard to the disenfranchisement of ordinary citizens, in favour of the judiciary, on the matters that are covered by a Bill of Rights.

The other thing to note about the argument from the imperfections of democracy is that it is still not an argument in favour of judicial power. The imperfection of one institution, by democractic standards, goes no way towards justifying the imperfection of another. One cannot, for example, legitimize the power of the monarchy or the unelected second chamber by pointing to the democratic imperfections of the House of Commons (egregious though they are); for the Lords and the monarchy are even *worse* from a democratic point of view. To empower those institutions is to compound rather than mitigate the imperfections of British democracy. The same applies to the courts. Even if we agree that parliament is not the epitome of democratic decision-making, the question is whether allowing parliamentary decisions to be overridden by the courts makes matters better or worse from a democratic point of view.

Ronald Dworkin has argued that '[i]f we give up the idea that there is a canonical form of democracy, then we must also surrender the idea that judicial review is wrong because it inevitably compromises democracy'.[70] Certainly there is no canonical form of democracy—no final or transcendently given set of answers to the question of what institutions can best embody the popular aspiration to self-government. But the argument against judicial reform does not depend on our access to a democratic canon. It depends solely on the point that, *whatever you say* about your favourite democratic procedures, decision-making on matters of high importance by a small elite that disempowers the people or their elected and accountable representatives is going to score lower than decision-making by the people or their elected and accountable representatives. It *may* score higher in terms of the substantive quality of the decision. But it will not score higher in terms of the respect accorded to ordinary citizens' moral and political capacities.

11 Democratic self-restraint

If a Bill of Rights is incorporated into British law it will be because parliament (or perhaps the people in a referendum) will have voted for incorporation. Ronald Dworkin has argued that this fact alone is sufficient to dispose of the democratic objections we have been considering. The objections, in his view, are self-defeating because polls reveal that more than 71 per cent of people believe that British democracy would be improved by the incorporation of a Bill of Rights.[71]

However, the matter cannot be disposed of so easily. For one thing, the fact that there is popular support, even overwhelming popular support, for an alteration in constitutional procedures does not show that such alteration therefore makes things more democratic. Certainly, my arguments entail that if the people want a regime of constitutional rights, then that is what they should have: democracy requires *that*. But we must not confuse the reason for carrying out a proposal with the character of the proposal itself. If the people wanted to experiment with dictatorship, principles of democracy might give us a reason to allow them to do so. But it would not follow that dictatorship is democratic. Everyone agrees that it is possible for a democracy to vote itself out of existence; that, for the proponents of constitutional reform, is one of their great fears. My worry is that popular support for the constitutional reforms envisaged by Dworkin and other members of Charter 88 amounts to exactly that: voting democracy out of existence, at least so far as a wide range of issues of political principle is concerned.

There is a debate going on in Britain about these issues. Citizens are deliberating about whether to limit the powers of parliament and enhance the powers of the judiciary along the lines we have been discussing. One of the things they are considering in this debate is whether such moves will make Britain more or less democratic. This article is intended as a contribution to that debate: I have offered grounds for thinking that this reform will make Britain less of a democracy. What the participants in that debate do *not* need to be told is that constitutional reform will make Britain more democratic if they think it does. For they are trying to work out *what to think* on precisely that issue.

Dworkin also suggests that the democratic argument against a Bill of Rights is self-defeating in a British context, 'because a majority of British people themselves rejects the crude statistical view of democracy on which the argument is based'.[72] But although democracy connotes the idea of popular voting, it is not part of the concept of democracy that its own content be fixed by popular voting. If a majority of the British people thought a military dictatorship was democratic (because more in tune with the 'true spirit of the people' or whatever), that would not show that it was, nor would it provide grounds for saying that democratic arguments against the dictatorship were 'self-defeating'. If Dworkin wants to make a case against 'the crude statistical view' as a conception of democracy, he must argue for it: that is, he must *show* that a system in which millions of votes cast by ordinary people are actually *counted*, and actually *count* for something when decisions are being made against a background of disagreement, is a worse conception of the values set out in Section 8 than a model in which votes count only when they accord with a particular theory of what citizens owe one another in the way of equal concern and respect.

However, Dworkin's comments do point the way to what is perhaps a more sophisticated answer to the democratic objection. We are familiar in personal ethics with the idea of 'pre-commitment'—the idea that an individual may have reason to impose on herself certain constraints so far as her future decision-making is concerned. Ulysses, for example, decided that he should be bound to the mast in order to resist the charms of the sirens, and he instructed his crew that 'if I beg you to release me, you must tighten and add to my bonds'.[73] Similarly, a smoker trying to quit may hide her own cigarettes, and a heavy drinker may give her car keys to a friend at the beginning of a party with strict instructions not to return them when they are requested at midnight. These forms of pre-commitment strike us as the epitome of self-governance rather than as a derogation from that ideal. So, similarly, it may be said, an electorate could decide collectively to bind itself in advance to resist the siren charms of rights-violations in the future. Aware, as much as the smoker or the drinker, of the temptations of wrong or irrational action under pressure, the people of a society might in a lucid moment put themselves under certain constitutional disabilities— disabilities which serve the same function in relation to democratic values as strategies like hiding the cigarettes or handing the car keys to a friend serve in relation to the smoker's or the drinker's autonomy.[74]

The analogy is an interesting one, but it is not ultimately persuasive. In the cases of individual pre-commitment, the person is imagined to be quite certain, in her lucid moments, about the actions she wants to avoid and the basis of their undesirability. The smoker knows that smoking is damaging her health and she can give a clear explanation in terms of the pathology of addiction of why she still craves a smoke notwithstanding her possession of that knowledge. The drinker knows at the beginning of the evening that her judgment at midnight about her own ability to drive safely will be seriously impaired. But the case *we* are dealing with is that of a society whose members disagree, even in their 'lucid' moments, about what rights they have, how they are to be conceived, and what weight they are to be given in relation to other values. They need not appeal to aberrations in rationality to explain these disagreements; they are, as we have seen, sufficiently explained by the subject-matter itself. A pre-commitment in these circumstances, then, is not the triumph of pre-emptive rationality that it appears to be in

the smoker's or in the drinker's case. It is rather the artificially sustained ascendancy of one view in the polity over other views whilst the philosophical issue between them remains unresolved.

A better individual analogy (than the case of the drinker or the smoker) might be the following. A person who is torn between competing religious beliefs opts decisively one day for the faith of a particular sect. She commits herself utterly to that religion and she abjures forever the private library of theological books in her house that had excited her uncertainty in the past. Indeed she locks the library and gives the keys to a friend with instructions never to return them, not even on demand. But the doubts in her own mind never go away ('Maybe Tillich was right after all . . .'), and a few months later she asks for the keys. Should the friend return them? It is clear, I think, for a number of reasons, that this is quite a different case from witholding the car keys from the drunk driver. Both involve forms of pre-commitment. But in the theological case, for the friend to sustain the pre-commitment would be, as it were, for her to take sides in a dispute between two or more conflicting selves (or two or more conflicting aspects of the self) of the agent in question, in a way that is simply not determined by any recognizable criteria of pathology or other mental aberration. To uphold the pre-commitment is to sustain the temporary ascendancy of one self (or one aspect of the self) at the time the library keys were given away, and to neglect the fact that the self that demands them back has an equal claim to respect for its way of dealing with the vicissitudes of theological uncertainty.[75]

Upholding another's pre-commitment may be regarded as a way of respecting her autonomy only if a clear line can be drawn between the aberrant mental phenomena the pre-commitment was supposed to override, on the one hand, and genuine uncertainty, changes of mind, conversions, etc., on the other hand. In the drunk driver case, we can draw such a line; in the theological case, we have much more difficulty, and that is why respecting the pre-commitment seems like taking sides in an internal dispute between two factions warring on roughly equal terms.

Clearly there are dangers in *any* simplistic analogy between the rational autonomy of individuals and the democratic governance of a community. The idea of a society binding itself against certain legislative acts in the future is particularly problematic in cases where the members of that society disagree with one another about the need for such bonds, or if they agree abstractly about the need, disagree about their content or character. It is particularly problematic where such disagreements can be expected to persist and to develop and change in unpredictable ways. If, moreover, the best explanation of these persisting disagreements is that the issues the society is addressing are just *very difficult issues*, then we have no justification whatever for regarding the temporary ascendancy of one or other party to the disagreement as an instance of full and rational pre-commitment on the part of the entire society. In these circumstances, the logic of pre-commitment must simply be put aside, and we must leave the members of the society to work out their differences and to change their minds in collective decision-making over time, the best way they can.

12 Conclusion

It is odd that people expect theorists of rights to support the institutionalization of a Bill of Rights and the introduction of American-style practices of judicial review. All modern theories of rights claim to respect the capacity of ordinary men and women to govern their own lives on terms that respect the equal capacities of others. It is on this basis that we argue for things like freedom of worship, the right to life and liberty, free speech, freedom of contract, the right to property, freedom of emigration, privacy and reproductive freedoms. It would be curious if nothing followed from these underlying ideas so far as the governance of the community was concerned. Most theories of rights commit themselves also to democratic rights: the right to participate in the political process through voting, speech, activism, party association, and candidacy. I have argued that these rights are in danger of being abrogated by the sort of proposals put forward by members of Charter 88 in the United Kingdom.

The matter is one of great importance. People fought long and hard for the vote and for democratic representation. They wanted the right to govern themselves, not just on mundane issues of policy, but also on high matters of principle. They rejected the Platonic view that the people are incapable of thinking through issues of justice. Consider the struggles there have been, in Britain, Europe and America—first for the abolition of property qualifications, secondly for the extension of the franchise to women, and thirdly, for bringing the legacy of civil rights denials to an end in the context of American racism. In all those struggles, people have paid tribute to the democratic aspiration to self-governance, without any sense at all that it should confine itself to the interstitial quibbles of policy that remain to be settled after some lawyerly elite have decided the main issues of principle.

These thoughts, I have argued, are reinforced when we consider how much room there is for honest and good faith disagreement among citizens on the topic of rights. Things might be different if principles of right were self-evident or if there were a philosophical elite who could be trusted to work out once and for all what rights we have and how they are to be balanced against other considerations. But the consensus of the philosophers is that these matters are not settled, that they are complex and controversial, and that certainly in the seminar room the existence of good faith disagreement is undeniable. Since that is so, it seems to me obvious that we should view the disagreements about rights that exist among citizens in exactly the same light, unless there is compelling evidence to the contrary. It is no doubt possible that a citizen or an elected politician who disagrees with my view of rights is motivated purely by self-interest. But it is somewhat uncomfortable to recognize that she probably entertains exactly the same thought about me. Since the issue of rights before us remains controversial, there seems no better reason to adopt my view of rights as definitive and dismiss her opposition as self-interested, than to regard me as the selfish opponent and her as the defender of principle.

Of course such issues have got to be settled. If I say P has a right to X and my opponent disagrees, some process has got to be implemented to determine whether P is to get X or not. P and people like her cannot be left waiting for our disagreements to resolve themselves. One of us at least will be dissatisfied by the answer that the process comes up with, and it is possible that the answer may be wrong. But the existence of that possibility—which is, as we have seen, an important truth about all human authority—should not be used, as it is so often, exclusively to discredit the democratic process. There is always something bad about the denial of one's rights. But there is nothing specially bad about the denial of rights at the hands of a majority of one's fellow citizens.

In the end, I think, the matter comes down to this. If a process is democratic and comes up with the correct result, it does no injustice to anyone. But if the process is non-democratic, it inherently and necessarily does an injustice, in its operation, to the participatory aspirations of the ordinary citizen. And it does *this* injustice, tyrannizes in *this* way, whether it comes up with the correct result or not.

One of my aims in all this has been to 'disaggregate' our concepts of democracy and majority rule. Instead of talking in grey and abstract terms about democracy, we should focus our attention on the individuals—the

millions of men and women—who claim a right to a say, on equal terms, in the processes by which they are governed. Instead of talking impersonally about 'the counter-majoritarian difficulty', we should distinguish between a court's deciding things by a majority, and lots and lots of ordinary men and women deciding things by a majority. If we do this, we will see that the question 'Who gets to participate?' always has priority over the question 'How do they decide, when they disagree?'.

Above all, when we think about taking certain issues away from the people and entrusting them to the courts, we should adopt the same individualist focus that we use for thinking about any other issue of rights. Someone concerned about rights does not see social issues in impersonal terms: she does not talk about 'the problem of torture' or 'the problem of censorship' but about the predicament of each and every individual who may be tortured or silenced by the State. Similarly, we should think not about 'the people' or 'the majority', as some sort of blurred quantitative mass, but of the individual citizens, considered one by one, who make up the polity in question.

If we are going to defend the idea of an entrenched Bill of Rights put effectively beyond revision by anyone other than the judges, we should try and think what we might say to some public-spirited citizen who wishes to launch a campaign or lobby her MP on some issue of rights about which she feels strongly and on which she has done her best to arrive at a considered and impartial view. She is not asking to be a dictator; she perfectly accepts that her voice should have no more power than that of anyone else who is prepared to participate in politics. But—like her suffragette forebears—she wants a vote; she wants her voice and her activity to count on matters of high political importance.

In defending a Bill of Rights, we have to imagine ourselves saying to her: 'You may write to the newspaper and get up a petition and organize a pressure group to lobby Parliament.

But even if you succeed, beyond your wildest dreams, and orchestrate the support of a large number of like-minded men and women, and manage to prevail in the legislature, your measure may be challenged and struck down because your view of what rights we have does not accord with the judges' view. When their votes differ from yours, theirs are the votes that will prevail.' It is my submission that saying this does not comport with the respect and honour normally accorded to ordinary men and women in the context of a theory of rights.

Notes

Jeremy Waldon, "A Rights-Based Critique of Constitutional Rights", 13 *Oxford Journal of Legal Studies* 18 (1993). Reprinted by permission of Oxford University Press.

1 Robert Nozick, *Anarchy, State and Utopia* (Oxford: Basil Blackwell, 1974), ix.

2 John Rawls, *A Theory of Justice* (Oxford: Oxford University Press, 1971), 3.

3 Ronald Dworkin, *Taking Rights Seriously*, New Impression (London: Duckworth, 1977), 193.

4 John Stuart Mill, *On Liberty*, ch 1, para 15 (Indianapolis: Bobbs-Merrill, 1955), 18.

5 Ronald Dworkin, *A Bill of Rights for Britain* (London: Chatto and Windus, 1990), 23.

6 Ibid, 12 and 21.

7 For example, Bruce Ackerman in a recent article suggests that scholars who have a philosophical commitment to fundamental rights—'rights foundationalists', as he calls them—take it for granted that democracy is to be constrained by this commitment. See Bruce Ackerman, 'Constitutional Politics/Constitutional Law' (1989) 99 *Yale Law Journal* 465–71.

8 My conception of this as an issue of respect is inspired by Aristotle, who confronted the prospect of tyrannical or unjust action by a majority under a democratic constitution in the following terms. 'If the poor, for example, because they are more in number, divide among themselves the property of the rich—is not this unjust? No, by heaven (will be the reply), for the supreme authority justly willed it. But if this is not extreme injustice, what is? . . . Then ought the good to rule and have supreme power? But in that case everybody else, being excluded from power, will be dishonoured. For the offices of a state are posts of honour; and if one set of men always hold them, the rest must be deprived.' Aristotle, *The Politics*, Bk III, ch. 10, 1281a29–32, translated by Benjamin Jowett, in the new Stephen Everson edition (Cambridge: Cambridge University Press, 1988), 15 (65–6).

9 See Dworkin, *Taking Rights Seriously*, 90–96. For further discussion of this typology, see J. L. Mackie, 'Can There be a Right-Based Moral Theory?' in Jeremy Waldron (ed.), *Theories of Rights* (Oxford: Oxford University Press, 1984).

10 Joseph Raz stresses that the relation is one of support not logical entailment. If we think for different reasons that there should be (i) a right to free political speech, and (ii) a right to free commercial speech, we may sum that up by saying there should be (iii) a right to free speech generally. But although (iii) entails (i), it does not support it on this account of our reasoning. See Joseph Raz, *The Morality of Freedom* (Oxford: Clarendon Press, 1986), 169.

11 See Ronald Dworkin, 'Liberalism', in *A Matter of Principle*, 186 ff.

12 Does this commit Dworkin or those who use his typology to 'foundationalism' in moral and political theory? The term has a wider and a narrower meaning. In its wider (and weaker) meaning, 'foundationalism' refers simply to the linear mode of organization that I have intimated: that there is some non-circular structure of support and justification within a theory, organized roughly on the model of an axiomatized theory in mathematics. The alternative to foundationalism in this sense is 'holism', where theorems are considered to be supported as much by what they imply as by what more general principles imply them. There is no doubt that a classification into right-based, duty-based, and goal-based types presupposes that the theories being classified are 'foundationalist' in this sense. When foundationalism is criticized, however, people often have in mind a stronger position than this. It is that the truth or assertibility of the 'basic propositions' or 'axioms' of such a theory can be immediately apprehended or intuited, and that the linear structure transmits this fundamental justifiability throughout the theory. The classification I have

in mind in this article is not committed to this epistemology, and it does not presuppose any such commitment on the part of the theories being classified.

13 For an unnecessarily protracted discussion, see Jeremy Waldron, *The Right to Private Property* (Oxford: Clarendon Press, 1988), 64–105.

14 See Section 5, below.

15 See n 11, above.

16 See the excellent discussion in Raz, *Morality of Freedom*, 168–70.

17 Dworkin, *Taking Rights Seriously*, 180.

18 Indeed it is important for Rawls that the principle governing economic inequalities will *not* be seen as a principle of particular entitlement. See Rawls, *Theory of Justice*, 64 and 88.

19 I have in mind the arguments intimated in Rawls, *Theory of Justice*, chapter V. See also Rex Martin, *Rawls and Rights* (Lawrence: University Press of Kansas, 1985) and Thomas Pogge, *Realizing Rawls* (Ithaca: Cornell University Press, 1989).

20 See R. M. Hare, *Moral Thinking: Its Levels, Method and Point* (Oxford: Clarendon Press, 1981), chs 2–3 and 9.

21 See the various discussions in R. G. Frey (ed.), *Utility and Rights* (Oxford: Basil Blackwell, 1984). However, for doubts about the utilitarian defence of rights, see David Lyons, 'Utility and Rights', in Waldron (ed.), *Theories of Rights*.

22 In addition to 'indirect' utilitarianism, there are also the complications discussed by Don Regan in his book, *Utilitarianism and Co-operation* (Oxford: Clarendon Press, 1980). Regan suggests that the fundamental aims of a utilitarian theory are best met by adopting a decision-procedure that bears very little affinity to traditional formulas of act-utilitarianism.

23 Jeremy Bentham, 'Supply without Burthern, or Escheat *vice* Taxation', in Jeremy Waldron (ed.), *Nonsense Upon Stilts: Bentham, Burke and Marx on the Rights of Man* (London: Methuen, 1987), 73: 'Right and law are correlative terms: as much so as son and father. Right is with me the child of law: from different operations of law result different sorts of rights. A natural right is a son that never had a father.'

24 Jeremy Bentham, 'Anarchical Fallacies', in Waldron (ed.), *Nonsense Upon Stilts*, 53. The passage continues: 'But reasons for wishing there were such things as rights, are not rights;—a reason for wishing that a certain right were established, is not that right—want is not supply—hunger is not bread.'

25 There is an excellent discussion in H. L. A. Hart, *Essays on Bentham: Jurisprudence and Political Theory* (Oxford: Clarendon Press, 1982), 85 ff.

26 H. L. A. Hart, 'Are There Any Natural Rights?' in Waldron (ed.), *Theories of Rights*, 79–80.

27 A similar point is made by Henry Shue, in his book *Basic Rights: Subsistence, Affluence and U.S. Foreign Policy* (Princeton: Princeton University Press, 1980), 16: '[A] right has not been fulfilled until arrangements are in fact in place for people to enjoy whatever it is to which they have the right. Usually, perhaps, the arrangements will take the form of law, making the rights legal ones as well as moral ones. But in other cases, well-entrenched customs, backed by taboos, may serve better than laws—certainly better than unenforced laws.'

28 The story of the Equal Rights Amendment in the United States would have been a sorrier one if all legislative initiatives against sex discrimination had rested on the success of this particular constitutional campaign. See Jane Mansbridge, *Why We Lost the ERA* (Chicago: University of Chicago Press, 1986).

29 I have discussed this a little more in Jeremy Waldron, *The Law* (London: Routledge, 1990), 83–4, and in *Nonsense Upon Stilts*, 177–81.

30 Wesley N. Hohfeld, *Fundamental Legal Conceptions* (New Haven: Yale University Press, 1923).

31 See Aristotle, *Politics*, Bk 1, ch. 2, 1253a1–18 (3).

32 I have discussed these points further in Jeremy Waldron, 'Rights in Conflict', *Ethics*, 99 (1989), 508.

33 As well as the works by Robert Nozick, John Rawls and Ronald Dworkin cited at the beginning of the article (see above, nn 1–3), one might mention the following major contributions: Bruce Ackerman, *Social Justice in the Liberal State* (New Haven: Yale University Press, 1980); John Finnis, *Natural Law and Natural Rights* (Oxford: Clarendon Press, 1980); David Gauthier, *Morals by Agreement* (Oxford: Clarendon Press, 1986); Alan Gewirth, *Human Rights: Essays on Justification and Applications* (Chicago: University of Chicago Press, 1982); and Raz, *Morality of Freedom*, op cit, n 10. This list is by no means complete.

34 See, for example, the following collections of essays: Marshall Cohen (ed.), *Ronald Dworkin and*

Contemporary Jurisprudence (Totowa: Rowman and Allenheld, 1983); Norman Daniels (ed.), *Reading Rawls: Critical Studies on Rawls 'A Theory of Justice'*, Second Edition (Stanford: Stanford University Press, 1989); Jeffrey Paul, *Reading Nozick: Essays on 'Anarchy, State and Utopia'* (Oxford: Basil Blackwell, 1982); Edward Regis, *Gewirth's Ethical Rationalism: Critical Essays* (Chicago: University of Chicago Press, 1984); Symposium on the work of Joseph Raz (1989) 62 *Southern California Law Review*, numbers 3 & 4.

35 Two recent anthologies (with bibliographies) are David Lyons (ed.), *Rights* (Belmont: Wadsworth, 1979) and Waldron (ed.), *Theories of Rights*, op cit, n 9.

36 See, for example, Alasdair MacIntyre, *After Virtue: A Study in Moral Theory* (London: Duckworth, 1981); Michael Sandel, *Liberalism and the Limits of Justice* (Cambridge: Cambridge University Press, 1982); and Mary Ann Glendon, *Rights Talk: The Impoverishment of Political Discourse* (New York: Free Press, 1991). For a critical discussion of some of this literature, see Waldron, *Nonsense Upon Stilts*, op cit, n 23, 166–209.

37 Robert Nozick, *Anarchy, State and Utopia* (Oxford: Basil Blackwell, 1974), xii.

38 The classic defence of such fallibilism is Mill, *On Liberty*, ch. 2. See also Karl Popper, *Conjectures and Refutations: The Growth of Scientific Knowledge* (London: Routledge and Kegan Paul, 1969), esp. chs 16–20.

39 J. S. Mill, *On Liberty*, ch. 2, para. 36 (58). The whole sentence reads: 'Truth in the great practical concerns of life, is so much a question of the reconciling and combining of opposites that very few have minds sufficiently capacious and impartial to make the adjustment with an approach to correctness, and it has to be made by the rough process of a struggle between combatants fighting under hostile banners.'

40 Hannah Arendt, *The Human Condition* (Chicago: University of Chicago Press, 1958), 234.

41 This point is due to Thomas Hobbes. Any theory that makes the authority of the sovereign depend on the moral goodness of his commands is self-defeating, for it is precisely because men *disagree* about good and evil that they need a sovereign. See Hobbes, *Leviathan*, C. B. Macpherson (ed.) (Harmondsworth: Penguin Books, 1968), ch. 18 and Hobbes, *De Cive: The English Version*, H. Warrender (ed.) (Oxford: Clarendon Press, 1983), VI. 6.

42 Dworkin, *Taking Rights Seriously*, 199–200.

43 Richard Wollheim, 'A Paradox in the Theory of Democracy', in P. Laslett & W. Runciman (eds), *Philosophy, Politics and Society*, Second Series (Oxford: Basil Blackwell, 1969), 84.

44 So it is a little misleading to describe the democratic objection to judicial review in the US as 'the counter-majoritarian difficulty'—cf Alexander Bickel, *The Least Dangerous Branch: the Supreme Court at the Bar of Politics* (New Haven: Yale University Press, 1962), 16. The US Supreme Court is a majoritarian institution; the problem is the very small number of participants in its majoritarian decision-making.

45 For an uncontroversial example of an egregiously unjust decision, see the 'Dred Scott' decision, *Scott v Sandford* 60 US (19 How) 393 (1857).

46 See also the discussion in Kim Scheppele and Jeremy Waldron, 'Contractarian Methods in Political and Legal Evaluation' (1991) 3 *Yale Journal of Law and the Humanities* 195, esp. 227–30.

47 For the contrary view, see Benjamin Barber, *Strong Democracy: Participatory Politics for a New Age* (Berkeley: University of California Press, 1984), 129: 'Where there is certain knowledge, true science, or absolute right, there is no conflict that cannot be resolved by reference to the unity of truth, and thus there is no necessity for politics.'

48 I have discussed this much more extensively in Jeremy Waldron, 'The Irrelevance of Moral Objectivity', in R. George (ed.), *Natural Law* (Oxford: Clarendon Press, 1992).

49 For a contrary view, see Hegel's Preface to the *Philosophy of Right*, trans T. M. Knox (Oxford: Oxford University Press, 1967), 5 ff.

50 Cf Peter Donaldson, *Machiavelli and Mystery of State* (Cambridge: Cambridge University Press, 1988).

51 See Jeremy Waldron, 'Theoretical Foundations of Liberalism' (1987) 37 *Philosophical Quarterly* 127, esp. 134 ff.

52 See further Waldron, 'Rights and Majorities', op cit, n (†) (p 18), 58–60.

53 See Mark Tushnet, *Red, White and Blue: A Critical Analysis of Constitutional Law* (Cambridge: Harvard University Press, 1988), 4–17.

54 See the French National Assembly's *Declaration of the Rights of Man and the Citizen*, 1789, Article 6: 'Legislation is the expression of the general will. All citizens have a right to participate in shaping

it either in person, or through their representatives.'

55 Aristotle, *Politics*, Bk 1, ch. 2, 1253a9 ff: 'Nature, as we say, does nothing without some purpose; and for the purpose of making man a political animal, she has endowed him with the power of reasoned speech.' (This is from the translation by T. A. Sinclair (Harmondsworth: Penguin Books, 1962), 28.)

56 Hannah Arendt comes close to this, in *On Revolution* (Penguin Books, 1973), 119, and is roundly criticized by J. Elster, *Sour Grapes: Studies in the Subversion of Rationality* (Cambridge: Cambridge University Press, 1985), 98.

57 See Section 5, above.

58 This theme can be traced from Aristotle's doctrine of 'the wisdom of the multitude' in *Politics*, Bk III, ch. 11 through to Mill, *On Liberty*, ch. 2, esp. para. 36 (57 ff).

59 See Robert Paul Wolff, *In Defense of Anarchism* (New York: Harper, 1976).

60 Jean-Jacques Rousseau, *The Social Contract*, edited by Maurice Cranston (Harmondsworth: Penguin Books, 1968), Bk I, ch. 6: ' "How to find a form of association which will defend the person and goods of each member with the collective force of all, and under which each individual, while uniting himself with the others obeys no-one but himself and remains as free as before." This is the fundamental problem to which the social contract holds the solution.' (60).

61 John Stuart Mill, *Considerations on Representative Government* (Buffalo, Prometheus Books, 1991), ch. VIII, 173.

62 The most eloquent recent expression of this doctrine is John Hart Ely, *Democracy and Distrust: A Theory of Judicial Review* (Cambridge: Harvard University Press, 1980). Ely concedes that the entrenchment of substantive values would be an affront to the process of democratic self-government, but he sees no such affront in the entrenchment of the process itself and of the values

and principles adjacent to it: 'substantive decisions are generally to be made democratically in our society and constitutional decisions are generally to be limited to policing the mechanisms of decision'. (ibid, 181.)

63 Dworkin, 'The Forum of Principle', in *A Matter of Principle*, 69; the argument is developed, ibid, 59–69.

64 The opportunity for constitutional amendment is celebrated, in the American context, in Bruce Ackerman, 'The Storrs Lectures: Discovering the Constitution' (1984) 93 *Yale Law Journal* 1013.

65 410 US 113 (1973), holding that the Constitution establishes a right to privacy that covers a woman's decision whether or not to have an abortion.

66 Ronald Dworkin, *Law's Empire* (Cambridge: Harvard University Press, 1986), 370–71.

67 Justice Brandeis, quoted in William Brennan, 'Why Have a Bill of Rights?' (1989) 9 OJLS 426.

68 Brennan, 'Why Have a Bill of Rights?' 426. (These are Brennan's own words now, not those of Brandeis.)

69 I shall not waste time with the argument that since judges live in the same community as the rest of us and read the newspapers, etc., their views about rights are therefore 'informally' in tune with, and representative of, the views prevalent in the community. Even if this is true, the same might be said of any dictator who inhabits the society that she dominates.

70 Dworkin, *A Matter of Principle*, 70.

71 Dworkin, *A Bill of Rights for Britain*, op cit, 36–7.

72 Ibid, 36.

73 Quoted in Jon Elster, *Ulysses and the Sirens: Studies in Rationality and Irrationality* (Cambridge: Cambridge University Press, 1984), 36.

74 I am grateful to Eric Rakowski for these analogies.

75 For an excellent discussion, see Thomas C. Schelling, *Choice and Consequences: Perspectives of an Errant Economist* (Cambridge: Harvard University Press, 1984), ch. 4. I am grateful to Carol Price for this reference.

Chapter 28

Cécile Fabre

THE DIGNITY OF RIGHTS

1

This article is a review of Jeremy Waldron's book Law & Disagreement and the page numbers in brackets refer to that book. The discussion focuses on Waldron's arguments about entrenching rights which were first published in 'A Right-Based Critique of Constitutional Rights'. – Eds.

2

Law and Disagreement rests on a central claim, which describes what Waldron calls the 'circumstances of politics'.[1]

> There is a recognizable need for us to act in concert on various issues or to coordinate our behaviour in various areas with reference to a common framework, and . . . this need is not obviated by the fact that we disagree among ourselves as to what our common course of action or our common framework ought to be (7).[2]

And later: 'the point of the law is to enable us to act in the face of disagreement' (7). The first part of the book is given over to answering the following question. Let us assume, following Raz, that an outcome is binding if citizens fare better if they accept it than if they follow their own judgment. In the face of disagreements about rights, which political procedures deliver outcomes which can be considered as binding on citizens, some

of whom will think that those outcomes are wrong? Waldron's answer, in a nutshell, is that disagreements about rights cannot be satisfactorily resolved by entrenching rights in the constitution and by asking the judiciary to adjudicate them. For the point is precisely that we disagree about rights, and so the only political mechanism which has authority to settle those issues is one where all views are represented and confronted with one another, and where decisions are made by majority rule, that is, through a procedure which treats each view, each vote, equally. Issues of rights, in short, can only be settled by a large assembly through democratic procedures (51, 72, 85, 111–16, 136–8).

I am not convinced that to appeal to those procedures is actually the only way to handle disagreements. For a start, in federal systems, where the allocation of rights and duties as between various levels of decision-making is a constant source of conflict, it is doubtful that one can dispense with the judiciary as the final arbiter in such conflicts.[3]

Moreover, it is unclear why one cannot handle such disagreements by invoking one's understanding of what justice requires. Waldron is not a relativist, and as such does not think that one has any right one thinks one has. As he claims, 'rape is wrong even in societies where it is a common practice' (105). But if one allows for the possibility that someone may be wrong about his and other people's rights, why not argue that in so far as he is wrong, his understanding of rights should not prevail? Since it is the case that individuals do not have the right to have sexual intercourse with others without their consent, and conversely that they have the right to refuse sexual intercourse, there is no reason why one must resort to democratic procedures to settle disagreements between those who deny that rape is wrong and those who think it is. Or consider discrimination on grounds of race. Since it is wrong to turn down individuals for a job on the grounds that they belong to a particular race and as such must be presumed to be incompetent (as Waldron undoubtedly would claim), there is no reason why one cannot say to the advocate of racial discrimination that his views, although sincerely held, are so mistaken that we cannot allow them to have legal and political authority. In both cases, it does make sense to claim that the legislature should not be allowed to pass laws condoning rape and the kind of racial discrimination I have just described.

Waldron, I think, would reply that there are many cases where we cannot be so confident that our understanding of rights is the correct one. Positive discrimination (to wit, racial or gender discrimination on the grounds that it rectifies historical injustices) is a paradigmatic example of a conflict between positions neither of which can, prima facie, be dismissed as unreasonable. In such cases where we do not have easy access to the underlying truth about rights, democratic procedures constitute a heuristic device whereby individuals settle what their rights and duties are.[4]

Waldron's line of argument calls for an account of the criteria whereby one can judge that an individual will do better by following Parliament's directives than by deciding for himself how he should act. Each citizen, or representative, brings his own view to the legislative table, has it confronted with everybody else's views, and in the process of doing so develops a

view which is a synthesis of the views on offer. Sometimes, even though none of the participants develops such synthesis, the group as a group does (137–8). I find the legislative process as described by Waldron rather mysterious: it is not clear at all that such synthesis will always operate. For a start, to talk about that which emerges from the process of discussion and deliberation as a synthesis presupposes that the various competing views on offer can be merged into a coherent one. This clearly is not often the case. There is no way an irreducible proponent of abortion can reconcile his view with the Pro Life militants' claim that abortion in all its forms is an instance of murder. What is likely to emerge from the confrontation of those two views is not a synthesis of both, but rather a winner and a loser.

Assuming that the competing positions are not so diametrically opposed that they cannot yield a compromise, it is unclear that the compromise in question will always be one under which all citizens do better than under other outcomes (recall that the outcome in question can be considered as binding only if citizens do better under it than if they followed their own judgment), and one which can be said to constitute a just position. In a trivial sense, citizens do better by accepting a decision reached by the democratic majority—a decision which they have good reasons to think everybody else will accept as well—than they do by engaging in civil disobedience every time they think that their conception of rights and justice, and not that of the majority, is the right one. Any settlement is better than none.[5] But it does not follow that any settlement reached through democratic procedures is always better, more likely to be just, than settlements reached through other procedures. Waldron does acknowledge that citizens may and will violate other people's rights, but does not attach to that point the importance it has. In fact, he simply says that 'although rights-bearers may on occasion be rights-violators, they are not themselves indifferent to that possibility' (258). Maybe not, but what about cases where they are, or where they conclude, *in bad faith*, that in voting for a given policy they are not, in fact, violating anyone's rights? Bills of rights, or so I shall argue in Section 4, are precisely meant to deal with such cases.

This is not to deny that proponents of bills of rights and judicial review very often present us with a naïve view of the judicial process. As Waldron rightly points out, Dworkin does not have much to say about the series of disastrously unjust (on Dworkin's own view) decisions handed down by the US Supreme Court in the first 30 years of the last century. Having said that, the point of a bill of rights protected by the judiciary is precisely to offer safeguards against mistakes committed by the majority, in cases where those mistakes can adversely and very seriously affect people's chances for a decent life. They offer a second chance to people who think that their rights have been violated to put their case forward to an independent institution such as the judiciary—independent in the sense that it is not a party in the conflict between the claimant and the democratic majority. To be sure, that institution may and will reach wrong decisions; in cases where it does, in so far as it is the final decision-maker about rights, no institution will in turn protect us from its mistakes. However, one appeal procedure is better than none at all.

3

In this section, I want to come back to the right to political participation, the 'right of rights', the importance of which Waldron defends as follows: 'it is impossible . . . to think of a person as a right-bearer and not think of him as someone who has the sort of capacity that is required to figure out what rights he has' (251). In short, if one thinks that people are autonomous and responsible and if one confers rights on them for those reasons, one must confer on them the

right to participate in political decision-making, including in decisions concerning rights themselves. If we take people seriously we have to take seriously what they have to say about their rights.

Now, if, as Waldron says, citizens disagree about important issues, there is no reason to doubt that they will also disagree about those very procedures which are meant to settle disputes about substantive issues. They are likely to disagree, that is, about three issues: (a) whether the best way to arrive at justice is through a set of political procedures or independently of any such procedure, by argument alone; (b) whether the right to political participation has preeminence over other rights, so that procedures in which it is pivotal should be used to solve issues about those other rights; (c) the modalities of the right to political participation itself. For example, should women and ethnic groups be given special representation rights? Should citizens be given the opportunity to settle important issues by referendums?

The latter question is actually quite crucial. Waldron does not draw a distinction between citizens and their representatives, between direct and indirect democracy: 'a representative's claim to respect is in large measure a function of his constituents' claims to respect; ignoring him, or slighting or discounting his views, is a way of ignoring, slighting, or discounting *them*. So let us deal direct' (109). But it is not difficult to think of many cases where citizens on the one hand and their representatives on the other hand will disagree about rights. For example, French MPs abolished capital punishment in 1981. There are good reasons to think that had citizens been given the opportunity to settle the issue by referendum, they would have decided against the abolition. Who, then, should have made the decision? And given that large democratic societies live under a representative regime, how should we decide when it is appropriate to make decisions about rights by referendum?

By which procedures, then, are citizens in turn going to settle *those* disagreements? Note that disagreements about (a) are deeper than disagreements about (b) since they pertain to the very nature of justice; as far as I can see, Waldron, who in any case, and as we have seen, is not very clear on that point, nowhere gives any guidance as to how they should be solved.

Disagreements about (b) in turn are deeper than disagreements about (c), since they pertain to the very nature of the regime. To claim that citizens should solve them by resorting to democratic means presupposes that they agree that democracy is the best regime. And yet, imagine that some citizens in the polity think that disagreements about rights can only be settled by a good understanding of God's law. It is quite plausible that they would invest priests, who by training and vocation are thought to be in the best position to understand God, with the authority to settle those disagreements. How is that conflict between the religious and the secular to be solved? In the light of recent events in the tumultuous political and legal history of North Africa and the Middle East, this is not merely an academic question.[6] Disagreements of type (c) pose the same problem. To say that in a country where only men vote, men should decide whether women should vote, implies that the procedure whereby men only vote is the right procedure; but that is exactly the problem we seek to solve.

In sum, to appeal to democracy and the right to participation in cases where those very values are at issue is question-begging. This is a familiar charge indeed, which Waldron unsatisfactorily seeks to rebut, in two steps (298–301): (1) it does not follow from the fact that the majority does not have the right to settle an issue pertaining to democracy itself that another institution, for example, the judiciary, has the right to do so; (2) there are compelling reasons for solving those issues by majority rule in the legislature instead of resorting to results-driven mechanisms: (a) for people disagree about

results anyway; and (b) democratic procedures are appealing from a pragmatic point of view.

Consider claim (1). Waldron concedes that 'a majority of men has no moral right to decide in the name of the whole community whether women shall have the right to vote' (299–300). Indeed not, for the very simple reason that as men are party to the conflict, for them to vote on that issue amounts to conferring on them the power to be judge in their own cause. Hence the claim, made by many, that, when there are such conflicts, another institution should settle them. Waldron rejects the principle *nemo iudex in sua causa* for two reasons. First, 'such decisions will inevitably be made by persons whose own rights are affected by the decision' (297). Note that it is not always true, and that in any case, even if it is, those persons are asked to reason in their official capacity, as members of that institution, not as persons whose rights are at stake. A judge who has to decide whether, on the basis of the constitution, women should have the right to vote, is constrained by the constitution, rules of interpretation, past jurisprudence etc. None of these considerations apply to citizens and their representatives.

Secondly, one cannot really invoke that principle 'in a situation where the community as a whole is attempting to resolve some issue concerning the rights of *all* the members of the community and attempting to resolve it on the basis of equal participation' (297). The last clause is problematic in those cases where what is at issue is precisely whether equal participation obtains. Setting that aside, it is misleading to aver that any debate about rights is a debate about rights *all* members have. When the legislature decides whether homosexuals should be granted all the rights heterosexuals have, they are discussing rights for *one* group of the population, to wit homosexuals. To deny that is to overlook the fact that serious conflicts are at stake between the majority and the minority and to paint a picture of a far more unified society than is warranted.

Suppose that I am wrong, and that claim (1) is valid. What about claim (2)? It says that, although one can question the legitimacy of using any procedure to make decisions pertaining to democracy, one should make such decisions through democratic procedures and not through result-driven procedures, on the grounds that people disagree about the results that are to be delivered by procedures. But, as we have seen, people do disagree about procedures themselves, so what reason is there to think that those disagreements are less problematic than disagreements about results?

Waldron, at this stage, appeals to pragmatism: we need a decision-making procedure, we happen to use majoritarian rules, so we might as well keep using them, 'without investing it with democratic legitimacy in any particularly question-begging way' (300). This does not amount to *privileging* that procedure, it simply amounts to *using* it, 'as we are stuck with [it] for the time being' (301). I do not see how we can avoid investing that procedure with democratic legitimacy; if we cannot do so, does that mean that anyone can contest its outcomes, on the grounds that the procedure whereby they were arrived at is not authoritative? Nor do I see how we can be said not to privilege the procedure in question. To employ an example Waldron uses in a different context, suppose that proportional representation (PR) is the most democratic electoral system, that the UK Parliament is torn between proponents of PR and advocates of the current system: bills and drafts go back and forth, without coming to a vote. The Queen takes the matter into her own hands and decides that henceforth PR will be used. On Waldron's view as expounded at 300–1, the Queen should have left Parliament to decide, a Parliament elected under the first-past-the-post system, on the grounds that this is after all the procedure we have. However, on grounds of pragmatism, there is no reason, in that instance, to claim that Parliament should have made the decision; in fact, there are reasons to endorse decision-

making by the Queen, which solved a deadlock. Waldron cannot avoid appealing to moral considerations pertaining to the value of democracy in order to argue convincingly against the Queen's decision to pre-empt Parliament's decision. But by appealing to such moral considerations, Waldron would be vulnerable to the charge that he is in fact pre-empting the expression by citizens of their conflicting views on those moral considerations themselves. In other words, Waldron's answer to the second question of political philosophy pre-supposes, indeed cannot but presuppose, an answer to the first.

4

Waldron, as we have seen, denies that rights should be protected under the constitution by the judiciary, yet acknowledges that rights violations do occur, even if the citizenry acts in good faith and with civic spirit. He does not seem to have anything constructive to say about such violations. As I shall argue in this section, a commitment to the view that individuals have rights by virtue of being autonomous entails a commitment to the constitutionalization of some of those rights, *even though some members of one's polity may disagree with one's conception of rights.*[7]

On the interest-based view of rights, which I adopt and which Waldron, as I understand, endorses, to say that P has a moral right to X against Y means that an interest of P is important enough to hold Y under some moral duty to provide P with X, if X furthers that interest.[8] It is not up to Y to decide whether he should do so. Note that interest-based moral rights are also powers, liberties, and immunities. The latter kind of right is particularly important in the present context. To say that P has a moral immunity with respect to X against Y means that Y is disabled from doing X or, as the case may be, from not doing X, to P.

If we are to take autonomy-protecting rights seriously, we must be committed to legalizing some of them, and to conceiving of them as rights we have not simply against private individuals but also against fellow citizens and representatives. Consider the first point. Simply to say that P has a moral right to freedom of speech, and thus that Y is under a moral duty not to silence him, without making any provision to ensure that Y performs that duty, is to fail to pay proper respect to the right in question.[9] To be sure, not all moral rights should be turned into legal rights. For example, if I promise to meet you at five o'clock, you have a right against me that I do so, but it would be absurd to seek to turn that right into a legal right. However, some rights clearly should be legal rights, and in particular those rights which secure goods and freedoms without which we cannot hope to lead an autonomous life; rights, for example, to freedom of speech, freedom of association, minimum income etc.

Secondly, we have those moral rights not only against private individuals but also against citizens. To claim that P has a moral right to X against Y only if Y is a private individual, even though Y is in a position, as a citizen, to secure X, is to drive an arbitrary wedge between what people can and ought to do as private individuals and what they can and ought to do as citizens and representatives.[10] Note that as a citizen and representative one respects others' rights by refraining from enacting laws which violate them, or by enacting laws which secure goods demanded by them. To claim that P has a moral right against citizen Y that he grant him freedom of speech amounts to saying that Y should refrain to pass laws censoring P's views.

If one is committed to the claims deployed in the last three paragraphs, one must be committed to the view that rights held against both private individuals and citizens and their representatives, and which are important enough to be turned into legal rights against private individuals, must also be turned into legal rights against citizens and their representatives. Simply saying that moral rights should be turned into legal rights is not enough, because it does not provide any legal guarantee that citizens and members of the legislature will respect those rights by refraining from enacting laws which violate them, or by enacting the laws necessary to implement them. But legal rights against citizens and representatives *are*, by definition, constitutional rights. The constitution, and more specifically the bill of rights, thus serve as such legal constraints on citizens and members of the legislature.

The foregoing argument works if it is true that a commitment to autonomy-protecting moral rights entails a commitment to legalizing those rights. Waldron actually disputes that it does, on the following grounds. To claim that P has a moral right to X does not entail that P (morally) ought to have a legal right to X; it only entails that the law ought to be such that P gets X. Waldron distinguishes (a) legal situations where there is 'an articulated legal rule or principle entitling P to X' (218), and (b) legal situations 'in which some official has been vested with discretion to determine on a case-by-case basis how best to distribute a limited stock of resources like X to applicants like P' (218). For example, if one thinks that homeless people have a right to shelter, one may think that they all have a legal right to get a place in a shelter. Or one may think that officials should decide who gets shelter on the basis of neediness, and so should be able, for example, to set aside some places for special cases (219). In the latter case, the principle that people have a right to shelter is respected, without the right being turned into a legal right.

The first thing to note is that Waldron circumscribes legal situations of type (b) to moral rights to distributable resources: it is unclear how the right to freedom of speech and association, the right not to be tortured, and generally rights which ground duties of non-interference would fit in. If the only reason for denying that a moral right to X should be turned into a legal right is that it is better to allow for flexibility in distributing material resources of type X, then rights which secure non-material goods such as freedoms can be turned into legal rights.

Moreover, to claim that individuals have a moral right to shelter does not mean that shelter places should be allocated indiscriminately. On the contrary, given that resources are scarce, and assuming for the sake of argument that helping people according to their needs is a requirement of justice, one should confer on the homeless a right to a place in a shelter subject to places being available and provided that, if there are not enough places available for everybody, places should go to the neediest. I do not see why a moral right to shelter formulated along those lines cannot be turned into a legal right. Clearly, in any given shelter, the official in charge will have to make discretionary decisions. But the right to shelter does not simply ground duties on such officials to allocate places in the most just way. It also grounds duties on the government to provide for shelters in the first instance, and to define the conditions under which people can use them, as well as a duty on government officials that they respect those conditions when making decisions as to whom to take in. It is quite appropriate to seek to turn those moral duties into legal rights, and thus to grant individuals the right to seek redress in court should they think that their right to shelter has been violated. To be sure, not all arrangements such that people get P are legal arrangements. In certain societies, people may very well get P through the enforcement of well-entrenched customs backed by taboos.[11] However, in societies ruled by laws, such arrangements ought to be legal, and enforced, as governments and courts will (mostly) do what the law asks them to do.[12]

I argued above that legal rights which we have against private individuals should be turned into legal rights against citizens and representatives, which amounts to turning them into constitutional rights. Waldron not only denies that

moral rights should be turned into legal rights, he also denies, unsurprisingly, that legal rights should be turned into constitutional rights. Rights, once constitutionalized, are cast in certain words, certain phrases, which, as shown by the American experience, 'tend to take a life of their own, becoming the obsessive catchphrase for expressing everything one might want to say about the right in question' (220). By contrast, although the phraseology used in statutes is more specific and therefore more rigid than the phraseology of the constitution, it can be amended very easily by Parliament itself. In so far as our understanding of rights is likely to change over time, legislative statutes, Waldron claims, are a better textual locus for its expression than a constitution.

Waldron is correct that the clauses of a bill of rights cannot be changed easily, but the picture he draws of constitutional interpretation in America—that of a rarefied debate about the exact meaning of the words used in the text—is rather hasty. Even if he were right on that latter account, however, one could still point out that constitutional adjudication need not have such effect. Waldron, like so many legal scholars steeped in the American tradition, seems to overlook the fact that other ways of enforcing the constitution are possible. Judicial review on the American model is not the be all and end all of constitutional protection of rights. I have argued at length for that conclusion elsewhere, but let me elaborate a little.[13]

When drafting a constitution, constitution-makers face the following dilemma. On the one hand, if the constitution is too vague, it is of very little help to policy-makers and to the judiciary. On the other hand, if it is too specific, it runs the risk of becoming irrelevant and of denying some people the resources and freedoms to which they should have constitutional rights. I suggest that a good way to protect constitutional rights is to draft the bill of rights in such a way as to leave scope for innovation, and to entrust a monitoring body, for example, a Human Rights

Commission, with the task of further delineating the scope of the government's obligations so as to take into account changing economic and social circumstances. For example, let us assume that everybody has a right to a minimum income. Such a right is understood as a right to the resources necessary to meet our basic needs, that is, the needs we have *qua* human beings, as well as those needs we have and which stem from the kind of society in which we live. Basic needs do not vary over time (we all need roughly the same quantity of food and liquids to survive) and the constitution can therefore specify them without running the risk of being obsolete. Socially determined needs, by contrast, should not be specified in the constitution. The latter should simply say that people should get the resources necessary for them to live a decent life given the kind of society that obtains. The role of the Human Rights Commission would be to assess what are these socially determined needs, and how much money people should have in order to meet both kinds of needs.

In adjudicating constitutional rights, the judiciary would be able to refer to the standards of compliance developed by the Human Rights Commission. Note, also, that in drafting policies, the government would be encouraged to cooperate with the Commission, so as to make sure that people's constitutional rights are not violated. Clearly, however, the Commission must be as independent as possible from the government. It should also include people from different walks of life: economists, jurists, representatives of the medical profession and of social workers' associations, of trade unions etc. Finally, it should have enough authority to request from the government that it submit regular reports on the steps taken to respect the bill of rights.[14]

The argument I have just deployed in favour of bills of rights is unlikely to convince a dedicated opponent of constitutional entrenchment. Waldron, after all, could argue against me that nothing I have said solves the problems stemming from the fact that whilst some citizens may agree with me, others are as likely to disagree. But my point is precisely that although not everybody will be convinced by the conception of rights enshrined in the constitution, one has to bite the bullet, and stand, in the face of others' disagreeing with us, for what is just. That is, one has to state what rights people have, as a matter of justice, and how those rights should be protected. Clearly, if a democratic majority is bent on violating rights, no legal or constitutional provision will hinder it: a bill of rights, if it is not to be useless, will have to be accepted by a democratic majority, if not on grounds of justice at least on grounds of expediency. However, if one thinks that autonomy is of crucial importance and that certain requirements, such as treating people in certain ways, can be shown to flow from it, that people, however genuinely, disagree about these requirements cannot invalidate the claim that it is just that they be enforced by way of a bill of rights.

5

Let me recapitulate. In this review article, I have expressed scepticism about Jeremy Waldron's rejection of bills of rights and, more generally, about his views on the authority of democratically enacted statutes, on the ways in which disagreements about rights amongst citizens should be solved, and, fundamentally, on how one should think of justice. Most importantly, I have denied that one can settle the question of which institution is best suited to handle questions of justice without appealing to one's view of what justice itself requires. But however strongly one might, quite fittingly, disagree with this book, its emphasis on that most neglected area of jurisprudence, to wit, legislation, and its exploration of issues which are relevant to moral, political, and legal philosophers alike, make it an invaluable contribution to the field.

Notes

20 *Oxford Journal of Legal Studies* 271 (2000).

1 The phrase 'the circumstances of politics' echoes Rawls' 'the circumstances of justice', which refers to the background conditions, such as scarcity of resources, under which it is necessary to devise principles of justice.

2 Throughout this review, the numbers bracketed in the text are page references to *Law and Disagreement*.

3 I owe this point to David Miller.

4 As textual evidence for my reading of Waldron's views on democratic procedures, consider the following statements: 'To say that ... justice is being subordinated to procedural values in political decision-making would be to beg the question of which of the positions competing for political support is to be counted as just' (161). And in addressing the claim that democratic procedures are instrumentally justified, justified, that is, only if they bring about just outcomes, Waldron writes that 'rights-instrumentalism seems to face the difficulty that it presupposes our possession of the truth about rights in designing an authoritative procedure whose point it is to settle that very issue' (253).

5 In some extreme situations, though, some people could do better by engaging in civil disobedience than by obeying the law: fugitive slaves might very well have held that view.

6 For example, secular Israelis are now demanding that marriages and divorces be handled by the state under democratically approved laws, rather than by Rabbinical courts under the *halacha*. Needless to say, orthodox Jews violently (sometimes literally) disagree.

7 The next four paragraphs are a very concise summary of Chapter 3 of my *Social Rights Under the Constitution* (2000).

8 The *locus classicus* for the definition of an interest-based right is J. Raz, *The Morality of Freedom* (1986) at 166.

9 H. L. A. Hart, 'Are There Any Natural Rights?' (1955) 64 *The Philosophical Review* 175 at 178. See also R. Martin, *A System of Rights* (1993) at 83.

10 Here, I am touching upon the complex question of the relationship between private morality and public morality. My point is not that private morality constrains public morality and that it is possible to determine everything that the State cannot do simply by determining everything that private individuals cannot do. Rather, my claim is that private and public morality stem from the same source, that in some cases we forbid private individuals and the State from harming people on the same grounds. For points along those lines, see W. Nelson, *On Democracy* (1980) at 100 ff and T. Nagel, 'Ruthlessness in Public Life' in S. Hampshire (ed.), *Public and Private Morality* (1978).

11 See H. Shue, *Basic Rights: Subsistence, Affluence and US Foreign Policy* (1980) at 16. Waldron actually refers to it on p. 218.

12 If legalizing the right will make the situation of the homeless worse then we have a good reason not to legalize it. But whether this is so or not cannot be decided *a priori*.

13 See my *Social Rights under the Constitution* (2000) ch. 5.

14 What I call the Human Rights Commission is modelled on the Committee of Experts and the Conference Committee of the International Labour Organization, which monitor the extent to which member states comply with the various conventions of the ILO; it is also drawn on the Committee of Independent Experts, which monitors the implementation of the European Social Charter. Both bodies gather evidence on State performances, levels of social and economic development etc.

IX. CRIMINAL LAW THEORY: PUNISHMENT

Introduction

SURELY ONE of the most salient features of any actual legal system is that it incorporates a body of criminal law, and in particular, an institution of punishment. This salience resides not in the fact that an institution of punishment is a necessary feature of a legal system, for it is not.[1] The salience is instead moral: no other legal institution calls for moral justification with the urgency that the institution of punishment does. This is because no other legal institution interferes so severely with the lives of people as does the institution of punishment. What greater interference with life is there, after all, than imprisonment or even death? In this light, it is not surprising that one of the central questions in criminal law theory, if not *the* central question, concerns the justification of punishment.

Punishment's justification has long been a subject of debate in philosophy. Immanuel Kant, for example, famously held that punishment was justified by *retribution*. Kant went so far as to argue that "[e]ven if a civil society were to be dissolved by the consent of all its members (e.g., if a people inhabiting an island decided to separate and disperse throughout the world), the last murderer remaining in prison would first have to be executed, so that each has done to him what his deeds deserve. . . ."[2] Kant, and those contemporary retributivists who follow him,[3] treats desert as both a necessary and sufficient condition for punishing a criminal. Thus, one must deserve punishment in order to be punished justifiably, and deserving punishment is reason enough to be punished.

Not all justifications of punishment give the pride of place to desert that retributivism does. Relying on his broader consequentialism, for example, Jeremy Bentham held that in so far as "all punishment in itself is evil", it could be justified only "in as far as it promises to exclude some greater evil."[4] Punishment is thus justified in the way that any conduct or institutional arrangement is justified on a consequentialist view; namely, by the extent that it promotes what is good and diminishes what is bad. In the context of punishment, this aim is typically explicated in terms of the *deterrence* that punishment effects: punishment is meted out to deter the particular criminal from committing a crime again (specific deterrence) and/or to make an example out of the criminal and thus to deter others from committing crime (general deterrence). According to such an account, crucially, desert is neither necessary nor sufficient for punishment. For on the one hand, punishing a deserving criminal will not necessarily reduce crime overall—a point made vivid by Kant's example of the disbanding island society. On the other hand, and much more troubling, it is in principle possible to "exclude some greater evil"—say, averting a vengeful mob's mayhem—by framing and punishing an innocent person.

Neither Kant's nor Bentham's accounts of punishment are entirely satisfactory, and yet each has appealing elements. Kant's retributivism seems draconian for insisting upon punishment even when no greater good will come of it, and yet the importance of desert to the justification of punishment is hard to deny. Bentham, for his part, seems right to acknowledge that the horror of punishment must be counter-balanced by some greater social good, but embracing the social good as the *sine qua non* of justification raises the specter that innocent people will be systematically vulnerable to abuse. For this reason, H. L. A. Hart's "Prolegomenon to the Principles of Punishment," first presented as a lecture in 1959 and later published in his 1968 book *Punishment and Responsibility*, was a great innovation, for it combined the attractive features of retributive and deterrence-based theories of punishment. "In regard to any social institution," Hart maintained, "after stating what general aim or value its maintenance fosters, we should inquire whether there are any, and if so what, principles limiting the unqualified pursuit of this aim or value."[5] Hart echoed Bentham in arguing that the reduction of crime overall, especially through deterrence, was punishment's general justifying aim, while maintaining with Kant that con-siderations of desert constrained who could be punished. Hart's was a broadly consequentialist account of punishment, but in conditioning punishment on desert, it was a constrained consequentialist account.

The elegance of Hart's "mixed" theory of punishment is manifest in even this thumbnail sketch, and so it should not be surprising that it has been enormously influential. Daniel Farrell's account of punishment in "The Justification of General Deterrence" is in many ways Hartian. Farrell begins by observing that capital punish-ment of convicted murderers may be justifiable on grounds of general deterrence, even though it is certainly not necessary for specific deterrence—life imprisonment, after all, would be just as effective in keeping a convicted murderer from killing again. That capital punishment may be justifiable under these circumstances, however, gives rise to the challenge of explaining "by what right we use convicted capital criminals in order to deter potential capital criminals."[6] The worry here is that capital punishment does not treat those who are put to death with sufficient respect even if it is otherwise justifiable on consequentialist grounds. One can thus see how Farrell's approach to the "problem" of punishment is broadly similar to Hart's. Farrell's project is, however, distinctive and arguably more ambitious. For whereas Hart argued that desert is a necessary condition of punishment, Farrell is reaching further, and seeks to show how a person's desert is a sufficient condition for using that individual to advance the social good. To show this, in turn, he invokes a kind of social right of self-defense and argues that a convicted murderer's legal guilt makes that criminal liable to being "used" for the greater good of social self-preservation.

Criminals occupy center stage in Farrell's discussion, for they are the ones whose claims put pressure on the justifiability of punishment, and in John Gardner's "Crime:

In Proportion and In Perspective", victims of crime join them at center stage. Victims are a focus because they are the ones who the criminal law must hold at bay. In the absence of a criminal law that punished wrongdoers, Gardner argues, victims of wrongdoing would be inclined to retaliate on their own behalf, and in doing so they would likely go too far. The justifiability of state punishment is therefore "closely connected to the *un*justifiability of our retaliating against those who wrong us."[7] Legal punishment, in short, is justified in large part because extra-legal personal retaliation rarely is. This "displacement function" is one of "the central pillars" of the criminal law's justification.[8] Still, criminals remain a focus as well, for even in its punitive practices the state must heed the duty of humanity that it owes to everyone over whom it has authority. And coupled with its duty of humanity is the state's duty of justice, which bears on the state's comparative and impartial treatment of its citizens. The task that Gardner sets for himself is to explain how the state can fulfill the criminal law's displacement function while at once discharging its duty of humanity and wearing "justice's blindfold."

In "Penal Communities", R. A. Duff takes a yet wider view, and asks whether legal punishment can be consistent with a normative, and specifically liberal, ideal of community. Among rival accounts of punishment, he argues, it is a communicative conception aiming to persuade offenders to repent and reform that coheres best with that community ideal. A purely deterrence-based account, in contrast, would fail to treat people as full members of the normative community, for it would address those whom it seeks to deter "as threatening outsiders against whom the community must protect itself."[9] A communicative account, while partially relying on deterrence, addresses those whom it would deter in terms of the communal values that it seeks to protect. In this way, Duff maintains, penal hard treatment should be "a part of a process of *moral communication* with the offender."[10] This account is retributive, in Duff's view, for punishment is held to be the fitting response to the crime. And yet punishment on this view is also goal-oriented, for it seeks to induce repentance. These two features of the position are, moreover, related: it is the goal of "repentant recognition of past wrongdoing" that makes communicating censure for that wrong-doing the appropriate way of achieving the goal of repentance.

Hart's influence is apparent in all three of these accounts, for Farrell, Gardner, and Duff each embrace one or another kind of mixed theory of punishment. Of course each does his mixing differently. In agreeing that *some* mixed theory is in order, however, all three follow Hart in recognizing that the institution of punishment is just too complex to be analyzed through a single lens and justified by recourse to a single value. Perhaps it also reflects agreement that, as Gardner puts it, criminal punishment "is such an extraordinary abomination, that it patently needs all the justificatory help it can get."[11]

Notes

1 For the denial that "coercive sanctions" are necessary to law or legal systems, see Hans Oberdiek, "The Role of Sanctions and Coercion in Understanding Law and Legal Systems", *American Journal of Jurisprudence* 21, 1976, 71–94.

2 Immanuel Kant, *The Metaphysics of Morals*, 1797 (Mary J. Gregor, trans. and ed.), New York: Cambridge University Press, 1996, p. 474.

3 See, for example, Herbert Morris, "Persons and Punishment", 52 *The Monist* (1968), pp. 475–501.

4 Jeremy Bentham, *An Introduction to the Principles of Morals and Legislation* (1789), p. 170.

5 H. L. A. Hart, "Prolegomenon to the Principles of Punishment", in *Punishment and Responsibility*, New York: Oxford University Press, 1968, pp. 1–27, p. 10.

6 Daniel M. Farrell, "The Justification of General Deterrence", p. 473.

7 John Gardner, "Crime: In Proportion and In Perspective", p. 490.

8 Ibid., p. 490.

9 R. A. Duff, "Penal Communities", p. 515.

10 Ibid., p. 517 (emphasis in the original).

11 Gardner, "Crime", p. 491.

Further reading

Larry Alexander, "The Doomsday Machine: Proportionality, Punishment and Prevention", *The Monist* 63, 1980, 199–227.

Jeremy Bentham, *An Introduction to the Principles of Morals and Legislation* (1789).

David Dolinko, "Some Thoughts About Retributivism", *Ethics* 101, 1991, 537–59.

R. A. Duff, *Trials and Punishments*, New York: Cambridge University Press, 1986.

Joel Feinberg, *Doing and Deserving*, Princeton, NJ: Princeton University Press, 1970.

Jean Hampton, "The Moral Education Theory of Punishment", *Philosophy and Public Affairs* 13, 1984, 208–38.

H. L. A. Hart, *Punishment and Responsibility*, New York: Oxford University Press, 1968, pp. 1–27.

Doug Husak, "Why Punish the Deserving?", *Nous* 26, 1996, 447–64.

Immanuel Kant, *The Metaphysics of Morals* (1797) (Mary J. Gregor, trans. and ed.), New York: Cambridge University Press, 1996.

Michael S. Moore, *Placing Blame: A General Theory of the Criminal Law*, New York: Oxford University Press, 1997.

Herbert Morris, "Persons and Punishment", 52 *The Monist* (1968), pp. 475–501.

Hans Oberdiek, "The Role of Sanctions and Coercion in Understanding Law and Legal Systems", *American Journal of Jurisprudence* 21, 1976, 71–94.

Warren Quinn, "The Right to Threaten and the Right to Punish", *Philosophy and Public Affairs* 14, 1985, 327–73.

Questions

1. Is punishment always bad (even if justified), or does punishing the deserving actually constitute a good?
2. Does punishing in order to effect general deterrence necessarily involve treating the person who is punished as a mere means to that socially useful end?
3. Can capital punishment be justified?
4. What role does the victim of crime play in the justification of punishment?
5. In what sense is "penal community" possible or desirable?

Chapter 29

Daniel M. Farrell

THE JUSTIFICATION OF GENERAL DETERRENCE

ASIDE FROM ANY "backward-looking" or retributivistic aims we may happen to have, there are at least two things we are typically trying to do when we punish someone for disobeying the law: we are trying to keep *them* from disobeying the law again, and we are trying to keep others from following their example. In many cases, we may have reason to believe that both of these aims will be served quite effectively by one and the same penalty: the "two-to-five" that we give the mugger for his first offense may arguably be likely both to deter him and to serve as an effective warning to others not to do likewise. In other cases, though, what we think is necessary for effectively deterring potential wrongdoers may be considerably more than what we think is necessary in order to keep the wrongdoer we are punishing from doing wrong again. The most dramatic example of this latter sort of case, of course, is capital punishment. For holding aside complications that are irrelevant to the present point, it seems that the most we would ever have to do to keep a convicted murderer from murdering again would be to imprison him for life. If, however, we had reason to believe that certain potential murderers could be deterred from murdering if we executed those convicted of the relevant sorts of murders, we might be tempted to resort to execution despite the fact that we are willing to concede that this is not necessary in order to keep the person executed from murdering again.

It is sometimes said that in treating convicted capital criminals in this way we would be wronging them, since we would be "using" them as a means to our own social ends. We may believe, of course, on retributive grounds, that capital criminals *deserve* to die, so that might be our reason for executing them. The effect our action has on potential murderers would then be just a happy side-effect. If, however, we do not accept this retributive rationale, and yet do believe that capital punishment is both necessary and morally justifiable as a way of reducing capital crime, we will face the challenge that is implicit in our remarks above: that of explaining by what right we use convicted capital criminals in order to deter potential capital criminals.

In what follows I want to suggest what I think is a novel way of meeting this challenge. I shall begin by showing why so-called "special" or "individual" deterrence is immune to doubts of the sort just imagined for the justification of general deterrence. I shall then show why the sorts of considerations that justify special deterrence are apparently unable to provide us with a justification of general deterrence. Finally, I shall show how it is that general deterrence may nonetheless be upheld. In doing all this, I shall take the liberty of extending ordinary usage, at least to a degree. I shall call the view that wrongdoers may be punished beyond what is necessary to keep them from doing wrong again—if so punishing them can plausibly be said to be likely to deter others from doing wrong themselves—a form of "weak retributivism." Obviously, weak retributivism, thus conceived, is nothing like the retributivism of the "classical" or "fierce" retributivist, who holds that the guilty may be punished simply because of what they have done. Still, inasmuch as it suggests that, in and of itself, wrongdoing makes a crucial moral difference with respect to how one may justifiably be treated—makes one, that is to say, a suitable object of social use—the view implicit in our ordinary thinking about the justification of general deterrence does appear to have at least something in common with certain forms of the retributive view. For it suggests that one's wrongful choices make one liable, morally, to treatment to which one would ordinarily not be liable. And this, as I explain below, might plausibly be thought of as introducing a kind of weak or watered-down retributivism into what is otherwise a clearly non-retributive approach to punishment.[1]

I

Suppose we ignore for a moment the problem of justifying the institution of punishment and reflect, instead, on the problem of articulating the rights and wrongs of various defensive actions in something like a Lockean state of nature. One right most of us would claim in such a situation is the right to resist, directly, others' attempts to violate our rights. If, for example, in a situation of the sort we have in mind, we imagine someone coming at me with a meat-cleaver, with the express intention of killing me so as to make it easier to rob me, most of us would say I have the right to resist him, even, if necessary, with deadly force. I shall call this presumed right my right to *direct self-defense*.

More problematic, I think, but equally widely accepted, is what I shall call the right to *indirect self-defense*. Suppose the offender described above has come at me with the aforementioned meat-cleaver on a good number of occasions in

the past, and it has become clear to me that he is going to continue these attacks. And suppose, as well, I have discovered that this particular individual has an intense aversion to physical pain. In particular, suppose I have learned that if I can make him believe that I will subject him to a certain amount of pain if he continues his attacks, he will discontinue them.

In these circumstances, it seems to me, I have a right to threaten the offender with the infliction of serious physical suffering if he continues his attacks. What's more, if it transpires that I cannot convince him that I am in earnest without actually inflicting such suffering, subsequent to one of his attacks, I have, I believe, a right to inflict it. After all, we are supposing that short of killing him, this is the only way of keeping him from continuing to try to kill me. And why should I have to run the risk of thus being killed, unjustifiably, if I can obviate that risk by subjecting him to a certain amount of physical pain?

Someone might deny that I have the right in question, his argument being that I have no right to harm an attacker in the required way given that by hypothesis doing so is not necessary for preventing the current attack (we are supposing I have already prevented it). Let him consider, then, the following sort of case. Suppose the circumstances are exactly as above, except that at the time of the most recent (unsuccessful) attack, I know exactly when the next attack will be and also that, when it occurs, I will be incapacitated by some recurrent illness. All I have time to do, let us suppose, as I resist the current attack, is either rebuff the attacker as I usually do or rebuff him and subject him to some intense physical pain. I know, let us suppose, that if subjected to the additional physical pain, he will not attack again, but that if not subjected to this pain, he will attack again, at a time when I will be sick with fever and unable to resist. If I am justified in resisting him during any given attack—with death, if necessary—how can it be that I may not do what I have to do to prevent his next attack, given that I know I will be unable to defend myself when he launches that attack?

Suppose it is granted that under the appropriate circumstances one has the right to both "direct" and "indirect" self-defense. What are the implications for the theory of punishment? Obviously, it might be thought that if the claims above are right, they can be applied more or less straightforwardly to that side of the institution of punishment that concerns itself with what is usually called "special" or "individual" deterrence: with the enterprise, that is, of trying to prevent convicted criminals from repeating their crimes. For if, in a Lockean state of nature, I would have the right to what we have called indirect self-defense, surely society, acting as my agent, can exercise that right on my behalf.

I think the analogy suggested here is sound: attempts at special deterrence are indeed instances of what I have called indirect self-defense. What is problematic is the question of whether the intuitions suggested above are themselves sound—that is, whether so-called "indirect self-defense" really is justifiable—and also the question of whether the defense of punishment along these lines really is free of any "backward-looking" or weakly retributivistic elements. That it might seem to be free of such elements, of course, is due to the fact that we have justified it, if we have, strictly on grounds of self-defense. And it is not clear, offhand, that there is anything "backward-looking," or even weakly "retributivistic," about acting in self-defense.

Upon reflection, however, it should be clear that the proposed principles of self-defense are certainly "backward-looking" in at least this sense: we would not ordinarily say that one is justified in doing just anything—to anyone—in defense of her life or liberty; we would say that one is justified in resisting *an unjust aggressor*, in certain ways, in defense of her life or liberty. Thus, to take just one example, it is not at all clear that we would feel justified in killing an aggressor's children, even if that were the only way of keeping her from killing us. And we would certainly say that we are much more clearly justified in killing the murderous aggressor, in order to protect ourselves from her, than in killing her children, even if the latter would do the job just as well as the former.

What this suggests, of course, is that we intuitively believe that self-defense, like punishment, must be "aggressor-oriented." We believe, that is to say, for reasons to be discussed below, that in unjustly aggressing against us, an aggressor loses her right not to be treated in certain ways. We do not believe, however, that *anyone else* loses those rights—the aggressor's children, for example—even if we also believe that by treating them in the relevant ways we can save ourselves from that aggressor.

All of this is connected, I think, in a fairly straightforward way, with the question of whether the principles of self-defense—and, thereby, the principles for justifiable special deterrence—are in some sense "retributivistic." For just as the pursuit of general deterrence seems to require the assumption that wrongdoers are morally liable for "social use"—in ways in which those who have not done wrong are not held to be liable—so too, we might say, special deterrence seems to require a somewhat similar assumption. For as we have seen, even in cases of self-defense, and hence in cases of special deterrence, we think of unjust aggressors as more appropriately treated in certain ways than nonaggressors, even when we believe that treating the nonaggressors in those ways will serve exactly the same purposes as treating the aggressors in those ways. Of course, we would not say that we are "using" aggressors when we treat them as we do, for purposes of indirect self-defense, and this is due to a significant difference between special and general deterrence. It is the case, however, as we have just seen, that the initiation of unjust aggression makes a person liable to certain sorts of treatment: treatment to which other, nonaggressing individuals are not ordinarily thought to be liable.

But now why should we suppose that our intuitions about justifiable self-defense are anything more than that—intuitions—and why, in particular, should we suppose that they are deserving of anything more than anthropological interest? The most insightful answer to this question, it seems to me, is that in the sorts of situations we have been imagining, self-defense is a matter of distributive justice.[2] To see this, notice that in cases of the relevant sort, the victim is faced with a choice of two ways of distributing certain harms: she can refrain from resisting the aggressor, thereby sparing the aggressor harm while suffering harm herself, or she can resist, thereby saving herself from harm (at least if her resistance is successful) by subjecting the aggressor to harm. Now if one is inclined to think, as I believe most of us are, that in a situation of this sort the victim is entitled to take the latter tack, one must say, at least roughly, why one believes that this is so. And one not implausible way of doing this, I think, is to argue as follows: inasmuch as it is the aggressor who has (knowingly and willingly) brought it about that the victim must make the relevant choice, justice entitles the victim to choose that the aggressor, rather than the victim, will suffer the harm that, by hypothesis, one or the other of them must suffer.

The principle that is implicit here is by no means uncontroversial.[3] Notice, though, that it has at least this much to be said for it: it explains our intuitions about ordinary cases of self-defense, and it explains as well our intuitions about defense of the innocent against unjust aggression. The first of these points will be clear from our remarks above. To appreciate the second point, we simply need to imagine a case where, as bystanders, we are in a position of either intervening on behalf of a potential victim of aggression or standing by and letting the victim be wronged. I think most of us would say that in such a case one has a right to intervene. We would call this, of course, not "self-defense" but "defense of the innocent against unjust

aggression." We do believe that it is justifiable, however, and it is not implausible to suppose that we believe this for precisely the reasons the account above suggests.

Suppose one agrees that this appeal to the notion of distributive justice provides a plausible basis for the intutions that underlie our thinking about the justifiability of actions taken in self-defense and also about the justifiability of actions taken in defense of others. It should be clear that far from removing the suspicion that there is something weakly retributivistic in our thinking about these matters, this account actually reinforces those suspicions and to some extent explains them. For what this account tells us is that a person's (informed) choices make her liable to suffering certain harms if, in light of those choices, it is inevitable that someone be harmed and she is one of the individuals who can be harmed in order that someone else be saved. And this, I shall say, is one version of the thesis of "weak retributivism": one must suffer, once one has done wrong, not (simply) because of one's decision to do wrong, as in classical or "fierce" retributivism; rather, one must suffer if one's decision to do wrong makes it necessary that someone must suffer and that sufferer must either be the wrongdoer or some innocent victim.

II

Thus far I have argued that special deterrence can plausibly be thought of as a form of self-defense, and I have argued as well that even if this is so, punishment with this end has an interestingly retributivistic aspect. I now want to consider punishment in the interests of general deterrence—capital punishment, for example, where what we hope to achieve is not merely prevention of a like offense by the offender in question but prevention of such offenses by other, likeminded individuals as well. Offhand, it seems clear that if general deterrence is morally permissible, this is not because it is permissible on grounds of distributive justice exactly like those suggested above. After all, our argument above was that we are justified in special deterrence because the aggressor is the one responsible for our having to choose between her suffering or our suffering and because in cases like this justice entitles us to choose that she suffer rather than that we suffer. In the case of general deterrence, by contrast, it would seem to be just false to suppose that any given offender can plausibly be said to be responsible for the choice we have to make. We do indeed have to decide, if the assumptions behind the pursuit of general deterrence are sound, between harming convicted criminals or letting innocent victims be harmed. However, we cannot say, straightforwardly, that this choice was forced on us by any particular criminal. It is, to be sure, a choice we face because of the existence of people *like* her—that is, because of the existence of her and of like-minded individuals. But to say this is quite different from saying that it is a choice we face because of an unjustifiable choice that she made and as a result of which we have apprehended her.[4]

There are, of course, a number of other tacks that we might take in attempting to justify the pursuit of our general-deterrence aims. One approach would be to modify the principle of distributive justice mentioned above, so that it extends to cases like those that now interest us: to allege, for example, that we may justifiably act to harm not just those who have faced us with the choice of harms but those, also, who have done the *sort* of thing that requires us to concern ourselves with this distribution-problem in the first place. Thus, we would allege, on this account, that justice allows us to "use" those who have perpetrated certain harms and that it allows us to do this simply because they have perpetrated those harms. There is no attempt to explain this claim, or otherwise defend it, on this approach; it is simply taken to be obvious that this is something that justice allows.

I shall call this view *undefended extensive weak-retributivism*. I introduce it here not because, at present, I propose to defend or to attack it, but because it provides us with a convenient point of reference for the evaluation of certain other views. The point is that if this is as much as we can say about the justification of general-deterrence penalties, there really is something deeply—though still "weakly"—retributivistic about this side of our institution of punishment. For what this view is saying is that, in the nature of things, it is simply *more appropriate* that those who have perpetrated certain wrongs should suffer than that those who would otherwise be the victims of similar wrongs should suffer, and that it is *more appropriate* simply because the members of the one group have done that kind of thing while the members of the other group have not.[5]

Another possibility, of course, is Herbert Morris's view, according to which our right to say and do the sorts of things we have in mind here is a corollary of the rights we have as a result of what might be called "the principle of fair play."[6] Very briefly, Morris's idea is a development of Hobbes's suggestion in *Leviathan*: we assume that unless most of us restrain ourselves in certain ways most of the time, we will all be worse off than we would otherwise be. And we argue that if, in light of this, most of us restrain ourselves in the relevant ways, it follows that those of us who have restrained ourselves have the right to take action against those who take advantage of this restraint. In particular, Morris argues, we have a right to announce and enforce a schedule of penalties for violations of the principles of restraint that the rest of us are following in order to reap the benefits that general restraint makes possible.

There are two serious problems with Morris's account, it seems to me. First, in supposing that we have a right to do whatever is necessary to secure general compliance with the relevant principles of restraint, Morris's account begs just the question that interests us: namely, the question by what right we "use" some in order to deter others. No doubt, if Morris's other assumptions are sound, fairness allows us to do some things to offenders that we are not ordinarily entitled to do to people. But why should we suppose it entitles us to do exactly what general deterrence requires?

Secondly, though, and perhaps more importantly, Morris's account seems to me to point us in the wrong direction. To see this, suppose we ask whether we would have the right to use a general-deterrence strategy against people who are clearly not willing to restrain themselves in the appropriate ways and who are quite candid about their unwillingness to do so. Suppose, for example, that we are a small group of individuals who have left the Lockean state of nature in order to form a civil society but that we are surrounded by—and still in the state of nature in relation to—a group of individuals who have chosen not to leave the state of nature. Surely we would have a right to defend ourselves against their aggression, and surely we would have this right even if these individuals had made it clear that they had no intention of restraining themselves in the relevant ways. We could not claim this right, however, by appealing to Morris's principle of fair play, according to which one gets the right to punish others as a result of their defaulting on an implicit agreement to try to reap the rewards of mutual restraint, since, by hypothesis, the individuals in question have never agreed, explicitly or implicitly, to restrain themselves in the relevant ways.[7]

Another approach, is that which is suggested by the work of John Rawls and some of his recent followers. The idea here is that even if the offenders in question have not agreed to restrain themselves in the relevant ways, they would have agreed to do so in an appropriately conceived position of ignorance and equality. Since, on Rawls's view, what we would have agreed to in such a situation is something that we are in fact bound to go along with in real life, it follows, for Rawls, that in real life we are bound to restrain ourselves in the relevant ways and also that we are liable for the penalties to which we would have agreed in "the original position." If we suppose, therefore, that the penalties to which we would have agreed in the original position are equivalent to the penalties that are required for general deterrence, we may say that justice requires us to restrain ourselves in the relevant ways and also that justice allows us to punish, in the appropriate ways, those who do not so restrain themselves.[8]

Now, clearly, Rawls's approach is vulnerable in whatever ways and to whatever degree the idea of arguing from the so-called "original position" is vulnerable. It is possible, of course, that doubts about Rawls's use of this mode of argument would be misplaced. Given the amount of controversy that surrounds this matter, however, it seems reasonable to at least consider some other, perhaps less controversial way of meeting the challenge we have set ourselves—a way like that which we used above, for example, in defending our intuitions about the justifiability of direct and indirect self-defense, where our appeal was not to a general and very controversial theory of morality but to a deep-seated and quite plausible intuition about what, in some cases at least, distributive justice allows.[9] Such an approach will suffer, of course, even if it succeeds in yielding a plausible basis for the justification of general deterrence, from the fact that, unlike a more systematic approach, it will rest ultimately on an undefended first-order moral principle, a principle that has whatever appeal it has simply because it strikes us as intuitively hard to resist. If, however, like the principle suggested above, our new principle has the virtue of explaining our intuitive views about a wide range of cases and of being, as already indicated, intuitively hard to resist, we will be able to say at least this much in our behalf: we will have managed to provide an alternative to the dominant contemporary theories of the justification of general deterrence which, given the features just alleged, is surely worthy of being taken seriously and of being studied, in its own right, in greater depth.

III

Let us begin by calling to mind a fact about the institution of punishment that we have so far ignored: in the institution of punishment as we know it, people who are "used" for the purpose of general deterrence are not people who just happen to have done things such that, once they have been done, the rest of us see that by punishing the doers of these deeds we can prevent other people from doing similar sorts of things in future. Rather, in the institution of punishment as we know it, potential criminals are warned, in advance of their crimes, that if they perpetrate those crimes, we will hold them liable for "use" in the appropriate ways. And this, I think most us would say, is crucial to that institution. It might indeed be wrong to use a person as general deterrence requires us to use him, if we have not in fact warned him that we will thus use him if he does wrong to us. If he *has* been warned, however, he can hardly object to our carrying out our threats when he ignores them—or so it might be said—especially if we have good reason to believe that thus warning and punishing people will serve the ends we intuitively believe that this will serve.

Holding aside for a moment any merits it may have, the view suggested here is clearly problematical in at least one rather obvious way: in suggesting that the crucial element in the justification of general deterrence is the fact that the relevant criminals have been forewarned in the relevant ways, it at least appears to beg exactly the question that interests us. We do not ordinarily think that telling someone we will do X if they do Y justifies us in actually *doing* X, if they do Y, unless we believe that we have a right to do X, if they do Y, in the first place. That is to say, if we have reason to believe that we are not justified in doing X to someone, should they do Y, then it is not at all clear that we are justified in

doing X to them, if they do Y, simply because we have told them, in advance of their doing Y, that we would do X if they did Y. To suppose otherwise, it would seem, would be to suppose that we can justify what we otherwise would have no right to do simply by telling the relevant parties that we intend to do it.[10]

Of course, it seems relevant, intuitively, that the persons in question have no right to do things like Y in the first place. And we shall have more to say about the relevance of this fact below. Notice, though, that it is not at all clear, offhand, exactly how this is relevant. We are supposing that despite the fact that a murderer had no right to murder, it is problematic as to whether or not we have a right to kill him in order to prevent other potential murderers from murdering. And if all we can say, by way of showing that we have this right, is that we have told him we would kill him if he killed, it seems we have not said nearly enough. For our question is exactly what makes us think we have a right to tell him this, meaning to do what we say we will do if *he* does what we have warned him not to do.

Now notice, by way of attempting an answer to this question, that our aim in making the relevant threats is not what one very simple-minded view would suggest: in making such threats, we are not *simply* trying to put ourselves into a position of being able to rationalize the application of the threatened penalties if and when our threats are ignored. No doubt, if and when we have to keep our threats, we will feel that our having threatened the relevant penalties is one thing that justifies us in applying them. Nonetheless, to think that our aim in making the threats is simply to justify thus carrying them out would be to overlook the fact that our real aim in making them could conceivably be achieved even if our threats were never ignored and hence never had to be carried out. For our real aim is to convince potential wrongdoers that their prospective wrongdoing would be a bargain. And this, of course, could conceivably be achieved, and with complete success, even if no one ever ignored our threats and hence even if no one ever had to be punished.

Suppose we gloss this way of thinking about the point of our general-deterrence threats as follows: suppose we say that in making the relevant threats we are attempting to restrain certain sorts of conduct by *putting a price* on actions of the relevant sorts. It will be clear from what we have already said that there are at least two very different moral problems that might be said to be associated with the use of such a "pricing system" in the control of people's conduct: the problem of saying what it is that justifies us in *making* the relevant threats—or setting the relevant prices—in the first place, thereby effectively limiting the freedom of choice of the persons threatened; and the problem of saying what it is that justifies us in actually carrying out these threats in cases where they are ignored. It would be a mistake, of course, to suppose that these are entirely independent problems. For now, however, it will be useful to think of them as if they were: to think of the relevant threats, that is, as comprised of things that we *say* we will do rather than as things that we necessarily intend to do, and to think of the carrying out of those threats as something that is itself not necessarily justified just because the threats were justified when we made them.

It might appear that the first of these problems is fairly easy to meet. No doubt, threats do need to be justified, even when, for all the person threatened knows, they are bluffs. For threats, if they are believed, are a way of limiting a person's freedom of action, and this, we generally suppose, is something which is *prima facie* wrong. In cases of the sort that interest us, however, coercive control of some sort is itself at least *prima facie* warranted, since in such cases we are dealing with potential violations of innocent persons' rights. If we suppose, therefore, as we are doing, that threats of harm are likely to reduce such violations and, moreover, are necessary if we are to reduce them to a tolerable level, it would seem that such threats are perfectly justifiable. After all,

our threats are directed only to potential wrong-doers—that is, they are threats to do harm only to those who wrong us in certain ways—and, for all we have said so far, they are not threats that will necessarily be carried out.

The problem with this, of course, is that it overlooks the fact that the threats we will be making will be "uniform" or "generic" threats rather than what we might call "individualized" threats: we will be threatening everyone with the same penalty (or spectrum of possible penalties) for each kind of crime, that is to say, basing our threats on considerations discussed below, rather than threatening specific persons with specific penalties, these latter being based on estimates of what seems necessary to deter each particular person from wronging us in some particular way. And this might be said to be objectionable, even by those who accept the basic thrust of the argument above, since we might be said to have no right even to so much as *threaten* a person with anything more than is arguably necessary to deter *him* or *her* from wronging us.

Now let us suppose that in a very simple social setting, we might very well be obligated to individualize our threats in the way this objection requires. It certainly does not follow that in a society like our own, the justification of generic threats is impossible, with the result that our argument for general deterrence cannot even get off the ground. For in a society as complex as our own, it would be virtually impossible, consistent with ever doing anything else, to individualize our threats in the way the objection above requires. If we simplify things for a moment, therefore, and suppose that, realistically, we must either issue uniform threats or else construct, at incalculable expense, an unimaginable bureaucracy that does nothing but issue particular threats to particular people, it seems reasonable to suppose that we are, after all, justified in issuing uniform threats.[11]

But now what about the justifiability of carrying out our threats, supposing they have been justifiably made? Obviously, our threats will sometimes be ignored. And given that all the argument above purports to show is that we are justified in *saying* we will do thus and such to those who wrong us, we now need an argument for the justifiability of actually doing it once our threats have been ignored.

Superficially, of course, the case for the justifiability of keeping threats which we have justifiably made seems clear enough. For if we suppose that in cases of the sort that interest us we have to carry out our threats, when they are ignored, in order for them to be effective in other cases, it would seem that we have a right to carry them out in order to keep them credible. For if they are not credible, we are not defended. And we have supposed that we have a right to be defended.

This argument obviously won't do, however, at least as it stands. For our critic could rightly contend that we have got things backwards here. If, as he contends, there are independent grounds for believing that there are certain things we have no right to do, we cannot justify the doing of them simply by showing we had a right to *say* we would do them—at least if what this latter right comes down to is just a right literally to say something, with no implication at all, for all we have said so far, about whether we would be justified in saying it *meaning to do it*.[12]

Now our critic's objection presumably rests on the fact that, using generic threats, we will, in some cases at least, have threatened to do more than we will actually have to do, to any particular wrongdoer once she has been apprehended, in order to keep that particular wrongdoer from wronging us again. It is not entirely clear, however, when one reflects on the matter, why this is supposed to make it wrong for us to carry out our threats. On one way of understanding it, of course, the objection might be put as follows: in doing more to any given wrongdoer than special deterrence requires, we are invariably wronging that wrongdoer because we are thereby "using" her for our own ends. This formulation of the critic's point is not very compelling, however, at

least as it stands. No doubt, there is a straight-forward sense in which, on the pricing-system model, we are indeed "using" convicted criminals when we carry out our threats: we are, having announced that we would do so, using the fact of their conviction as an occasion for making an example of them, with the hope, thereby, of deterring similar wrongdoing on the part of others. Whether or not in doing this we are thereby *wronging* convicted criminals, however, and in that sense "using" them, is precisely what is at issue here. Thus, while the point about how we are "using" people when we resort to our pricing system is sound, it is not a point that can be turned against that system until it is shown that to use people in this way is wrong.

Our critic could, of course, take a slightly different tack here and just *assert*—what is no doubt at the back of his mind in all this—that we simply have *no right* to do more, in any given case, than is necessary to deter the offender in question from acting similarly again and, more-over, that we have no right to do more even when we have warned him that we would do more if he acted against us. Unfortunately, in the absence of any argument, this claim simply begs the question that interests us, which is precisely the question of whether we ever *do* have a right to do more, in any given case, than is necessary to prevent the wrongdoer in question from wronging us again.

If this were all that could be said about the matter, of course, we would simply have reached a standoff, with our critic alleging that we do not have a right to use people in the relevant ways, even if we have warned them that they will be so used, while we allege that, sometimes at any rate, we do. There is, however, something more that we can say. Imagine that you are attacked by someone, unjustifiably, in a Lockean state of nature, and suppose that as a result of her attack you are in a condition which will not only make you unable to resist *her* subsequent attacks but which will also make you unable to resist the attacks of other (potential) attackers as well. We have already seen that if our principle of distributive justice is sound, you are justified in such a case in harming the original attacker in order to prevent her from initiating another attack. If this is so, however, why are you not also justified in harming her in order to prevent *others* from doing what they would not have been able—or inclined—to do except for the damage that she has inflicted on you? If, that is to say, you are more vulnerable—*to attacks from others*—because of her attack, and if you can counter just this degree of added vulnerability by harming her now that she has harmed you, then, by the principle of distributive justice introduced above, it seems you would, at least within certain limits, be justified in harming her in order to prevent harms that she has brought it about that you will suffer if you do *not* harm her.[13]

It might be objected to this, of course, that it is unreasonable—and not at all consonant with our earlier principle—to hold an attacker liable for harms she had no way of knowing she would instigate by her wrongful conduct. At best, it might be said, we can justly penalize such a person—in the way general deterrence requires—only if we can convincingly expand our earlier principle to include both harms that are created knowingly and those that are not. And this, of course, would be a radical extension of that principle and one that is not at all as intuitively plausible as our earlier principle appeared to be.

We can avoid this objection, however, if we can put ourselves into the position of being able to say, to any given wrongdoer, that she did indeed have plenty of reason to believe that, by wronging us, she was increasing our vulnerability to harm from others. And this we can do by calculating, in advance of any actual wrongdoing, the approximate degree of harm to which we will have been made vulnerable by any given attack, and then publicly announcing the results of our calculations. To be sure, these calculations will be rough ones, and, moreover, any given wrongdoer may be able to say that she was unaware of the fact that by acting against us

she would be putting us in a position of the relevant sort. Still, if we can plausibly say that the attacker *ought* to have known what we know—if we can say, for example, that there was plenty of available evidence and that any reasonable person would have known what we know—then, it seems to me, we will justly hold her liable despite her claims of ignorance.

So the critic of general-deterrence penalties is wrong to say that we may never do, to any given offender, more than we have to do in order to keep that offender from wronging us again: if, by not penalizing an offender to some degree beyond what special deterrence would warrant, we will be vulnerable to wrongdoing, from others, which we would not have faced in the absence of this particular wrongdoer's attack, and if we can plausibly say that the wrongdoer in question either knew or ought to have known that this would be so, we may, within certain as yet unexplored limits, justifiably harm that wrongdoer beyond what is necessary to keep him or her from wronging us again. And this, of course, if it is right, not only suggests that the critic of general-deterrence penalties is wrong in this particular respect; it also suggests a general conception of what we are doing in announcing and applying general-deterrence penalties and why we are justified in doing it. For if our argument is right, we are, contrary to our tentative conclusion in Section II above, justified in imposing at least *some* penalties, over and above what special deterrence warrants, *by virtue of the same principle that justifies our special-deterrence efforts themselves*: namely, the principle of distributive justice introduced above, which tells us that when someone wrongfully (and wittingly) puts us in the position of having to decide whether they shall suffer or some innocent party shall suffer, we are entitled to choose that they should bear the suffering.

Have we shown, then, that the pursuit of general deterrence can be vindicated by the principle of distributive justice introduced above? Unfortunately, we have not. For, clearly, our argument thus far presupposes that the wrongdoer in question is both causally and morally responsible for our increased vulnerability to others' wrongdoing. Suppose that in a certain set of circumstances this is not the case. Suppose, for example, that while my vulnerability will not be heightened as a result of a given wrongdoer's attack—if, that is, I do not retaliate against her—I have good reason to believe that if I do retaliate, I will increase my overall security. Or suppose that while my vulnerability *has* been heightened by her attack, I realize that I can enhance my previous level of security, vis-à-vis others, by doing even more to her than I need to do to bring myself back to where I was, "security-wise," prior to her attack. It will be tempting, of course, to retaliate, in the first sort of case, and, in the second, to do more than I have to do in order to get back to where I was. If I do retaliate, however, in the one case, or do in fact do more, in the other, than our principle of distributive justice allows, and if I wish to say that I am justified in doing so, this can only be, for all we have said so far, because I am implicitly relying on the view that we earlier called "undefended extensive weak-retributivism." For by hypothesis the wrongdoer in question is not responsible for my being in a position where I have to decide either to harm her (at least to the degree to which I am tempted to harm her) or let myself be harmed by others. If we assume, therefore, that I may justifiably harm her as a means of reducing the probability that I will be harmed by others, it must be, for all we have said so far, simply because she is a wrongdoer the harming of whom will do me some good. And this, of course, is simply undefended extensive weak-redistributivism. This doctrine may be sound, and it may not be in need of further defense. Our hope, however, was to provide some further defense, showing, thereby, either that general deterrence is not as retributivistic as it seems or, at any rate, that, if it is, it is justifiable nonetheless. And this is something we have thus far not been able to do.

IV

Let us call the approach to the justification of general deterrence that rests upon our special principle of distributive justice "the less radical approach," and let us call the approach that would allow us to set and enforce deterrent penalties beyond what this less radical approach allows "the more radical approach." Although I shall not be able to show it here, I think it can be shown that the latter approach really does require us to embrace a form of "extensive" weak-retributivism which cannot itself be grounded on any deeper or more general moral basis—a basis like that provided by our special principle of distributive justice, for example, which underlies the less radical of our strategies, which has intuitive appeal in its own right, and which is capable of accounting for all sorts of cases in addition to the sorts of cases that interest us here. Our thought, of course, was that this approach might be shown to be justifiable by virtue of the fact that its implementation is preceded by threats or "warnings," these latter having been issued on the assumption that issuing and enforcing them would significantly reduce the number of wrongful attacks to which we would be subjected. As we have seen, however, in the absence of an account of why it is that what may not be done *without* threats may sometimes be done once threats have been made, it is not at all clear how our having threatened a penalty justifies us in imposing it if and when it is ignored. An account of the relevant sort may be forthcoming, of course, but, unfortunately, nothing that we have been able to say here suggests how such an account would go. Rather, what we have seen here is that those penalties that may be threatened, and then imposed, are precisely those that, in theory at least, might have been imposed even in the absence of the relevant threats.[14]

There is, of course, still before us, the very important problem of attempting to say something about the limits that must be observed, on either of these approaches, in the pursuit of our general-deterrence aims. And in a moment I shall go on to discuss this question in connection with what I am calling the less radical approach to the justification of general deterrence. Notice here, though, that as far as the more radical approach is concerned, it would seem that in the absence of a general moral principle grounding this approach, it will be rather difficult to say anything convincing about the limits within which we must stay when pursuing general deterrence on the grounds that this approach suggests. The most that one could hope to do here, it seems to me, would be to produce more or less plausible intuitions about what those limits are. And, obviously, the problem with thus resting one's claims on intuition is that someone else could just as well summon up opposing intuitions in defense of an opposing view.

In connection with what I am calling the "less radical" approach, by contrast, I think we can say something rather more compelling about the limits to which we may justifiably go in pursuit of our general-deterrence aims. For, of course, on this approach we *do* have a general moral principle to guide us in what we say: the principle of distributive justice introduced above, according to which we have a right to protect ourselves—and other innocents—against harms that some wrongdoer's actions have made it necessary that either the wrongdoer himself must suffer or that some innocent party must suffer instead. Our question here is simply what limits this principle entails for the sorts of cases that interest us.

Now in attempting to answer this question, it will be useful to begin by calling to mind a fact that we have thus far ignored: the harms that the less radical approach to general deterrence allows us to impose do not *have* to have been threatened, or otherwise announced in advance, in order to be justifiably imposed. This, of course, is because that approach, being based on our special principle of distributive justice, allows us to impose suffering on someone who

has wrongfully (and wittingly) confronted us with a certain choice—namely, to hurt them or to run the risk of being hurt ourselves—even if we have not previously told them that we would choose their suffering, rather than our suffering, if it came down to this. Of course, it may be that we are obligated to warn people that we plan to act on this principle if there is time to warn them and if thus warning them will not entail any avoidable disadvantages to ourselves. And, in any case, it will certainly make sense to warn them that we plan to act on this principle, since just warning them of this may be enough to dissuade some of them from wronging us. Still, it is important to note that, in principle, we are free to act against wrongdoers in the rather extensive ways our special principle of distributive justice allows, even if we have not warned them that we would do so.[15]

But, now, suppose we ask what our situation would be like if we did not say, in advance of any wrongdoing against us, that we plan to act against wrongdoers in the relevant ways *and* if we did not say, in advance, roughly what we thought this would involve. We will be wronged at some point, we may suppose, and hence will have to decide what steps to take once we have been wronged. Presumably, one limit on what we may do in a situation like this will be set by the fact that, ordinarily, at any rate, we think of ourselves as being entitled to do no more, when we are acting to prevent avoidable harms on the basis of our special principle of distributive justice, than we *have* to do in order to protect ourselves against the harms made likely by any given wrongdoer's attack. How, then, will we calculate what we thus have to do in order to protect ourselves against these harms? Obviously, this is an empirical matter: we need to ask what harms we will face, if we do not react to a given degree, that we would not have faced if we had never been attacked in the first place. Notice, though, that in any given case this is likely to be an empirical question that it will be very hard to answer. Indeed, it seems fair to say that in many cases it will be impossible to answer. Of course, it is reasonable to assume, in light of this, that we are entitled, in such cases, to *estimate* what is required for protecting ourselves against the relevant sorts of harms. Notice, though, that our estimates, given that we have made no threats, must be estimates based on the details of each particular case. And these, while in principle quite possible, will themselves be extremely difficult to make.

Now suppose we were to try to get around these difficulties in an obvious way: by announcing, in advance of any actual wrongdoing against us, exactly what we intend to do in response to acts of wrongdoing—where acts are classified into categories in some appropriate way—in order to ensure that we are none the worse off by virtue of these acts having occurred. There will certainly be limits on what we may thereby announce (and enforce) as penalties— limits, it seems to me, which will be set by two very different sorts of considerations. On the one hand, it is clear that since we are basing our right to retaliate on the principle of distributive justice suggested above, there will be certain "absolute" or "*a priori*" limits, which will be set by the fact that we do not have a right to do just *anything*, no matter how severe, to avoid an evil that someone else has made it necessary for us to avoid, but, rather, that we have a right to do *certain* things to avoid evils that others have set for us but not to do other things. An example will make this clear. If we suppose that someone, by his wrongful action, has made it inevitable that either I (an innocent person) must die or that he must die, our principle tells us that I may choose that he die rather than I. If, by contrast, he has made it inevitable that either I suffer a mild inconvenience or he dies, most of us would say that I would be wrong to cause his death just so that I may be spared the mild inconvenience.

The question, of course, is exactly what I may and may not do in thus defending myself (and other innocents) against the likely consequences of others' wrongdoing. Unfortunately, this is a question to which I have, at present, no useful answer. Different people will no doubt have radically different intuitions about what is and is not appropriately done—in defense of oneself (and others) against various degrees of wrongdoing—and I am currently not in possession of a general account that would enable us to sort through these intuitions in order to create a cohesive whole. Notice, though, that the problem of resolving these difficulties is not *simply* a problem for the defender of general deterrence, as we are conceiving the latter here. Rather, it is a problem that is endemic to the general theory of self-defense and, even more generally, to that part of the theory of distributive justice that deals with the distribution of harms made inevitable by someone's wrongful conduct. Thus, while there are indeed large and very pressing problems here, they are not problems that are created by the approach to general deterrence that we are exploring here.

There are other considerations, though, which are relevant to what we may justifiably threaten when we make the threats that I am supposing the less radical approach to the justification of general deterrence allows, and these are considerations which might be thought to raise difficulties that are peculiar to the approach to general deterrence that we are following here. These latter considerations have to do with the fact, to which we have alluded above, that in defending ourselves against the harmful consequences of others' wrongful actions, we are entitled, or so we ordinarily suppose, to do only as much as we have to do, in any given case, in order to prevent those consequences. In cases of the sort that interest us, of course, the relevant consequences include the likely acts of those who might be affected by what we do or do not do in light of the current attack. Hence, in such cases a great deal more will be justified, at least in principle, than the ordinary picture of justifiable self-defense intuitively suggests. Still, there are definite limits here which are quite distinct, in theory at least, from the absolute or *a priori* limits discussed above. We might call these second sorts of limits "case-relative" or "a posteriori" limits, inasmuch as they seem to be set by the exigencies of each particular case.[16]

Now if we were supposing that, on the less radical approach that currently interests us, the pursuit of general deterrence would be effected on a case-by-case basis—with estimates of what's necessary for "self-defense" being made subsequent to any given attack and being tailored to the ascertainable facts of the particular case at hand—the existence of limits of this second or a posteriori kind would pose no special theoretical problems. We are supposing, of course, that it will generally be impossible to say, in any given case, exactly what we have to do in order to keep ourselves from suffering increased vulnerabilities as a result of the wrongdoer's attack in that particular case. But this difficulty can be handled, I think, without compromising the principles on which our current approach is grounded, by supposing, as we did above, that our right to defend ourselves in such situations allows us to estimate the penalties that are required, at least when it is impossible to determine them exactly. This is no different, it seems to me, than saying that in cases of direct self-defense we are entitled to estimate what we have to do to stop an immediate attack if, under the circumstances, it is impossible to determine exactly what we have to do to stop it.

The real problem that is raised by limits of this second (a posteriori) sort is a rather different one. To see this, we need to notice that, proceeding as we are supposing we will proceed, it will sometimes happen that what we have threatened to do, vis-à-vis a given type of crime, will be more than we in fact need to do in order to protect ourselves against avoidable vulnerabilities created by the person who has wronged us in the case at hand. If, in such cases, we apply the penalty that was threatened, rather than limiting ourselves to what is in fact required for "self-defense," it would seem that we will be violating the principle with which our current reflections

began: the principle that tells us that in defending ourselves against the harmful consequences of others' wrongful actions, we are justified in doing, within the a priori limits discussed above, only as much as we need to do in order to protect ourselves against vulnerabilities created by any given wrongdoer's wrongdoing in any given case.

It may well be that this line of argument is essentially correct: ideally, we ought not to do, in any given case, anything more than we need to do in order to block avoidable vulnerabilities that have been created by that particular case. Suppose it could be shown, though, that, as a matter of fact, we are actually likelier to prevent the relevant sorts of vulnerabilities, even as they arise in any given case, if we react to wrongful aggression not on a case-by-case basis but on the basis of a pre-announced schedule of penalties which has itself been established on the basis of an honest empirical estimate of what we must do to contain the likely effects of such aggression. This is a big assumption, of course, and an entirely empirical one. However, if we suppose that it is sound, we may ask whether we are not, in light of it, entitled to resort to the sort of strategy we have been favoring, despite the fact that such a strategy will inevitably require us to do more, in certain cases, than we need to do in order to protect ourselves from vulnerabilities that we face because of the particular case at hand. And the answer, it seems to me, is that we are entitled, on these assumptions, to choose the one strategy over the other and that we are so entitled not (simply) on utilitarian grounds but (also) on grounds provided by the principle of distributive justice that has guided our reflections in everything we have said above. For at the heart of that principle is the idea that in cases of the sort that interest us, we have a right to protect ourselves, and other innocents, against the harmful consequences of others' wrongful acts. And how could this right, properly interpreted, not include a right to announce and enforce fixed penalties of the sort we are supposing might be necessary if we (and other innocents) are to be protected against the relevant sorts of harms?

Suppose these last assertions are accepted as sound. I do not think that in accepting them we undermine the distinction between the so-called "less radical" and "more radical" approaches to the justification of general deterrence. For that distinction has to do with whether we are aiming, in our general-deterrence efforts, at preventing harmful consequences of particular wrongful acts, or at preventing wrongful acts as such, independently of their connection with any other wrongful act. And this distinction remains, it seems to me, despite our concession that, even on the former approach, we will occasionally be inflicting penalties, in any given case, that are somewhat more severe than those we actually need to inflict in order to prevent the harmful consequences that would otherwise be caused by the agent's actions in that particular case. No doubt, if, on the former approach, our threatened penalties generally tend to be considerably beyond what is actually required, in any given case, for the purpose of "self-defense," we would not be justified in continuing to impose them. If, however, our penalties are not typically beyond the relevant limits, and if, moreover, when they are over those limits, they are not egregiously so, it seems to me there is no objection to them, on grounds of moral principle, and that in holding them unobjectionable we have not deprived ourselves of being able to distinguish the less radical approach to general deterrence from the more radical approach described above.

V

I have suggested, in the previous section, that there are two different sorts of limits that our general-deterrence penalties must honor, at least if we follow the less radical approach to the justification of general deterrence suggested above, and I have tried to show, as well, how, consistent with the recognition of these limits, we could justifiably announce the relevant penalties in advance and then impose them, after the fact, once they are ignored. It is perhaps worth emphasizing, in concluding, that penalties that honor the spirit of our principle of distributive justice, and that consequently are aimed at making up only for whatever added vulnerability we would face in the absence of such penalties, might themselves be considerably less rigorous than those penalties that would be necessary to protect us from attacks that the given wrongdoer is not responsible for but that we *could* prevent if we were willing to do enough to him and to people like him. Thus, it could be, as a matter of empirical fact, that capital punishment is never necessary for controlling vulnerabilities that are created by any particular capital criminal but that capital punishment is necessary if we are to prevent certain capital crimes. In that case, we would have a very dramatic illustration of the difference between what can be justified on our less radical approach to the justification of general deterrence and what can be justified on the more radical approach.

It will perhaps be obvious, then, that a theory of general deterrence that is based on our principle of distributive justice will be less "retributivistic" than one that is not and that allows itself to go beyond what that principle allows, at least in this sense: on the latter, but not on the former, people may be "used" not just to prevent vulnerabilities that *they themselves* have created but also to prevent vulnerabilities that exist independently of their actions. If general deterrence is objectionable, therefore, on the grounds that it requires us to wrongfully harm some people—namely, convicted criminals—as a way of helping others, perhaps it will be precisely when we thus resort to harming some in order to help others without the excuse of doing so because of the fact that the former have made it necessary for us to harm them or to see innocent people be harmed. Whether or not general deterrence is objectionable when thus pursued, and is objectionable on the grounds suggested here, is, unfortunately, a question that must be left for another time.

Notes

94 *The Philosophical Review* 367 (1985).

1 Note that what makes the pursuit of general deterrence "weakly retributivistic," at least on the view suggested here, is not the fact that the advocate of general-deterrence penalties makes legal guilt a necessary condition of the imposition of such penalties but, rather, that the advocate of such penalties makes legal guilt a sufficient condition for "using" people in ways in which we would not use *innocent* people even if we believed that so using them would have results that would be just as beneficial, socially, as the results of similarly using convicted criminals. As I understand his argument in "Prolegomenon to the Principles of Punishment" (*Punishment and Responsibility* [New York: Oxford University Press, 1968], pp. 1–27), H. L. A. Hart makes much of the *necessity* of (legal) culpability for just punishment but nothing at all of the fact, explored here, that in the pursuit of general deterrence we are inclined to think of culpability as also sufficient, given certain empirical facts, for the justification of using the culpable individual for the advancement of our social ends.

2 Here I follow Philip Montague in "Punishment and Societal Self-Defense," in *Criminal Justice Ethics*, Vol. 2, No. 1 (Winter/Spring, 1983).

3 For some tentative and admittedly inconclusive reflections on the bases of this principle, see Judith Jarvis Thomson, "Remarks on Causation and Liability," *Philosophy and Public Affairs*, 13 (1984), pp. 101–133, which came to my attention only after the present paper was substantially completed.

4 I am simplifying here in ways that are explained below. It might in fact happen that a given offender *is* responsible for my being vulnerable to attacks from others—or, at any rate, for my being more vulnerable than I would otherwise have been—in which case the principle to which we have appealed above would be relevant. Our interest at the moment, however, is not in cases such as these but in cases where no one attacker is responsible for the other (potential) attacks with which I am faced but where I can diminish the likelihood of these other attacks occurring by doing more harm to any given attacker than is required for defending myself—directly or indirectly—*from her*. This, as we shall see, is the sort of case that presents the most difficult challenge for the defender of general deterrence as a form of social control.

5 This is not, of course, an uncommon view, nor is it, intuitively, an implausible one. For an oblique but rather compelling statement of it, see Steven Goldberg, "Does Capital Punishment Deter?" in Richard A. Wasserstrom (ed.), *Today's Moral Problems*, second edition (New York: Macmillan Publishing Co., 1979), pp. 547–548.

6 See Herbert Morris, "Persons and Punishment," *The Monist*, 54 (1968), esp. pp. 476–480.

7 For more on this, and on its relevance to the problem of justifying the use of force in international relations, see my "Coercion, Consent, and the Justification of Political Power: A New Look at Locke's Consent Claim," *Archiv fur Rechts- und Sozialphilosophie*, 65 (1979), pp. 521–543.

8 See John Rawls, *A Theory of Justice* (Cambridge, Mass.: Harvard University Press, 1971), esp. pp. 17–22. See also Jeffrie G. Murphy, "Marxism and Retribution," *Philosophy and Public Affairs*, 2 (1973), pp. 217–243.

9 On the critique of Rawls's "contractualism," see especially Robert Nozick, *Anarchy, State, and Utopia* (New York: Basic Books, 1974), pp. 183–231, and Ronald Dworkin, *Taking Rights Seriously* (Cambridge, Mass.: Harvard University Press, 1978), pp. 150–183.

10 See Alan Goldman, "The Paradox of Punishment," *Philosophy and Public Affairs*, 9 (1979), pp. 54–56, and also Richard W. Burgh, "Do the Guilty Deserve Punishment?" *The Journal of Philosophy*, 79 (1982), pp. 198 ff.

11 I return to this question below and remove the simplifying assumption. Notice here, though, that the present argument is merely intended to be an in-principle argument for the permissibility of uniform threats. It leaves open the question, considered immediately below, of whether we are justified in *carrying out* such threats, once they are ignored, and also the question, considered at length in Section IV, of whether these threats may be as harsh as maximally effective general deterrence requires. The point is simply that in our

special sense of "threat," generic threats seem to be justifiable, and they seem to be justifiable, given certain empirical assumptions, on grounds of self-defense.

12 Things are actually somewhat more complicated than I am allowing here, since someone might argue that we are sometimes entitled not only to *say* we will do what (we know) we may not do but also to say we will do it *meaning to do it* (i.e., fully intending to do it). I argue against this view in "Strategic Planning and Moral Norms: The Case of Deterrent Nuclear Threats" (unpublished ms.).

13 Notice that this reasoning can actually take us much further than is indicated in the text. For suppose the wrongdoer in question makes you more vulnerable not by incapacitating you but by making it the case that others are likelier to attack you if you do not harm her beyond what is necessary to deter *her* from subsequent attacks. If the wrongdoer is both causally and morally responsible for the situation in which you are thus placed—and, of course, in certain situations she will be and in others she will not—it would seem that our principle of distributive justice would justify your harming her beyond what is necessary for preventing her from harming you again.

Notice, too, that I am speaking of your saving *yourself* here, rather than some other innocent party, only for the sake of simplicity. Exactly the same points as were made in Section I above also apply here: our principle is one that justifies us in saving innocents from harms that wrongdoers have brought it about that either the innocents must suffer or that the wrongdoers must suffer. It is, that is to say, a principle governing the defense of the innocent against unjust aggression and not simply a principle of self-defense.

14 We did say, of course, that under certain circumstances we might have to have made certain information available to potential wrongdoers if we were going to be clearly justified in harming them—for purposes of general deterrence—on the basis of our special principle of distributive justice. (See above, p. 482.) Our point, however, was not that we needed to have announced the relevant penalties in advance in order to be justified in imposing them but, rather, that we might need to have done certain other things, in advance, in order to ensure that wrongdoers could rightly be said to have known, when they acted, that they were endangering us in so acting. See below, p. 484 ff., for further reflections that are relevant here.

15 See above, however, note 14, for an important *caveat*.

16 We might think of limits of the first sort as setting an *a priori* "upper bound" on what we may do, in any given case, in pursuit of the relevant general-deterrent aims and of limits of the second sort as varying, within the limits set by the first, depending on what is *in fact* required, in any given case, to keep us from being made more vulnerable than we would have been if we had never been wrongfully attacked in the first place.

Chapter 30

John Gardner

CRIME
In proportion and in perspective

1. The displacement function

WHAT IS THE criminal law for? Most explanations nowadays focus exclusively on the activities of criminal offenders. The criminal law exists to deter or incapacitate potential criminal offenders, say, or to give actual criminal offenders their just deserts. In all this we seem to have lost sight of the origins of the criminal law as a response to the activities of victims, together with their families, associates, and supporters. The blood feud, the vendetta, the duel, the revenge, the lynching: for the elimination of these modes of retaliation, more than anything else, the criminal law as we know it today came into existence.[1] It is important to bring this point back into focus, not least because one common assumption of contemporary writing about punishment, including criminal punishment, is that its justifiability is closely connected with the justifiability of our retaliating (tit-for-tat, or otherwise) against those who wrong us.[2] The spirit of the criminal law is, on this assumption, fundamentally in continuity with the spirit of the vendetta. To my mind, however, the opposite relation holds with much greater force. The justifiability of criminal punishment, and criminal law in general, is closely connected to the unjustifiability of our retaliating against those who wrong us. That people are inclined to retaliate against those who wrong them, often with good excuse but rarely with adequate justification,

creates a rational pressure for social practices which tend to take the heat out of the situation and remove some of the temptation to retaliate, eliminating in the process some of the basis for excusing those who do so. In the modern world, the criminal law has become the most ubiquitous, sophisticated, and influential repository of such practices. Indeed, it seems to me, this displacement function of the criminal law always was and remains today one of the central pillars of its justification.

This is not to deny the justificatory importance of the criminal law's many other functions, several of which obviously do focus on the activities of offenders. As students of criminal law, we have all been brought up on the idea that the various arguments for having such an institution are rivals, each of which takes the wind out of the others' sails. We must therefore decide whether we are retributivists, or rehabilitationists, or preventionists, or reintegrationists, or whatever else may be the penological flavour of the month. If we insist on an intellectual pick-and-mix, we are told, we can maybe get away with allocating different arguments strictly to different stages of the justification, e.g. deterrence to the purpose of criminal law in general and retribution to the justification of its punitive responses in individual cases.[3] Still, we must make sure the rival arguments are kept strictly in their separate logical spaces, or else, according to received wisdom, they tend to use up their force in clashes with each other.[4] To my way of thinking, however, this supposed rivalry among justifications for criminal law and its punitive responses is illusory. The criminal law (even when its responses are non-punitive) habitually wreaks such havoc in people's lives, and its punitive side is such an extraordinary abomination, that it patently needs all the justificatory help it can get. If we believe it should remain a fixture in our legal and political system, we cannot afford to dispense with or disdain any of the various things, however modest and localized, which can be said in its favour.[5] Each must be called upon to make whatever justificatory contribution it is capable of making. If and to the extent that the criminal law deters wrongdoing, that is one thing to be said in its favour. If and to the extent that it leads wrongdoers to confront and repent their wrongs, then that counts in its favour too. Likewise, the power of the criminal law, such as it is, to bring people with mental health problems into contact with those who can treat their conditions, to settle and maintain the internal standards of success for social practices such as marriage and share-dealing, and to stand up for those who cannot stand up for themselves. Even apparently trivial factors such as the role of the criminal law in validating and invalidating people's household insurance claims must be given their due weight. All of these considerations, and many others besides, add up to give the institution whatever justification it may have, and to the extent that any of them lapse or fail, the case for abolition of the criminal law comes a step closer to victory.

It is true, of course, that sometimes the considerations conflict, i.e. in some cases some of the considerations which support the criminal law's existence point to its reacting in one way while others point to its reacting in a dramatically different way, or not reacting at all. Sometimes it is even the case that considerations which partly support the criminal law's existence turn against it, and partly support its eradication. The only general thing that can be said of such conflict cases is that they reinforce still further the need for the criminal law to muster whatever considerations it can in its own defence, since by their nature these cases pit additional arguments against whatever course the law adopts for itself. So the existence of such cases strengthens, rather than weakens, my main point. It is also true that different arguments contribute to justifying different aspects or parts of the criminal law to greater or lesser extents. Considerations of deterrence do not support the criminalization of activities which cannot effectively be deterred by criminalization, and considerations of rehabilitation do not support the criminal conviction of people who cannot effectively be rehabilitated. In similar vein, the criminal law's function of displacing retaliation by or on behalf of victims does not support the criminalization of victimless wrongs, or of wrongs whose victims do not offer or inspire retaliatory responses. Criminalizing these wrongs will fall to be justified on an accumulation of other grounds, or else not at all. That still leaves the displacement function, however, as a central pillar of the criminal law's justification. By describing it as a central pillar, I mean only that some core parts of the edifice of the modern criminal law cannot properly remain standing, in spite of the existence of other valid supporting arguments, in the absence of the law's continuing ability to pre-empt reprisals against wrongdoers. In this chapter, accordingly, I want to sketch some of the major and (I believe) escalating difficulties of principle and practice faced by the modern criminal law in attempting to fulfil this displacement function and keep the heart of its edifice intact.

2. Humanity and justice

To continue fulfilling its displacement function satisfactorily has always been a grave challenge for the criminal law, because by the nature of the endeavour there is very little margin for error. On the one hand, the criminal law's medicine must be strong enough to control the toxins of bitterness and resentment which course through the veins of those who are wronged, or else the urge to retaliate in kind will persist unchecked. On pain of losing a central pillar of its justification, therefore, the criminal law cannot afford to downplay too much its punitive ingredient, the suffering or deprivation which it can deliberately inflict on the offender in response to the wrong. In the end, particularly in the absence of genuine contrition from the offender, that deliberate infliction of suffering or deprivation may be all the law can deliver to bring the victim towards what the psychotherapists now call 'closure', the time when she can put the wrong behind her, finally laying to rest her retaliatory urge. On the other hand, the law's medicine against that same retaliatory urge cannot be allowed to become worse than the affliction it exists to control. It must stop short of institutionalizing the various forms of hastiness, cruelty, intemperance, impatience, vindictiveness, self-righteousness, fanaticism, fickleness, intolerance, prejudice and gullibility that the unchecked desire to retaliate tends to bring with it. On pain of sacrificing a central pillar of its justification, therefore, the criminal law cannot simply act as the proxy retaliator any more than it can simply dilute its punitive side to the point where it is incapable of pacifying would-be retaliators.

As if this perennial predicament were not difficult enough for the criminal law, two further rational constraints upon the modern State have only served to compound the problem as we face it today. The first is the modern State's powerful duty of humanity towards each of its subjects. To avoid surrendering the whole basis of its authority—as the servant of its people—the modern State in all of its manifestations is bound to treat each of those over whom it exercises that authority as a thinking, feeling human being rather than, for instance, an entry on a computer, a commodity to be traded, a beast to be tamed, a social problem, an evil spirit, a pariah, or an

untouchable. The anonymous bureaucratic machinery of the modern State which came into existence to honour this duty is also, notoriously, the main contemporary cause of its violation. It is a depressingly short step from stopping thinking of someone as a serf to starting thinking of them as a statistic. But even if the pitfalls of bureaucratization are avoided, the practice of punishing criminal offenders inevitably calls the State's humane record into question, because of the element of deliberately inflicted suffering or deprivation which punishment by definition imports. Such an infliction of suffering or deprivation by the State cannot be justified solely on the ground that worse suffering or deprivation will be avoided as a result, even if the suffering which will be avoided as a result is suffering that would otherwise be deliberately inflicted on that very same person by other people's reprisals against her. The State's duty of humanity to each person has an agent-relative aspect, i.e. it emphasizes the State's own inhumanity towards a person and not just the sum total of inhumanity towards her which occurs within the State's jurisdiction or under its gaze.[6] This means that, other things being equal, the State's proper response to the fact that a wrongdoer is faced with the threat of retaliation is to protect the wrongdoer rather than to punish her, even if, thanks to the ruthlessness and cunning of the would-be retaliators, punishing her promises to be more effective in reducing her overall suffering.[7]

For punishment to be a morally acceptable alternative to protection, the State has to assure itself not only that the measure of punishment controls retaliation while stopping short of becoming a mere institutionalization of the retaliator's excesses, but also that the act of punishment affirms, rather than denies, the punished person's status as a thinking, feeling human being. That is not impossible. Many familiar features of modern criminal law, including some important substantive doctrines of the general part as well as many procedural, evidential and sentencing standards, reflect the State's successive efforts to meet this condition. Together, these features are supposed to ensure that trial and punishment for a criminal offence affirms the moral agency and moral responsibility of the offender, and in the process (since moral agency and moral responsibility represent a significant part of what it is to be a human being) affirms the offender's humanity.[8] For the reasons just outlined, I regard the constancy of this affirmation as a *sine qua non* of the criminal law's legitimacy. In saying this I am not retreating from my earlier claim that the function of displacing reprisals against wrongdoers is a central pillar of the criminal law's justification. I am only adding the complication that, for better or worse, this function cannot always be legitimately performed by the criminal law.

That point is reinforced when we move from the State's duty of humanity to its parallel, and no less important, duty of justice. Questions of justice, unlike questions of humanity, are questions about how people are to be treated *relative to one another*. Some contemporary political philosophers imagine that all questions dealt with by the institutions of the modern State should be dealt with, first and foremost, as questions of justice. 'Justice,' as John Rawls put it, 'is the first virtue of social institutions.'[9] The basic thought behind this view is the sound liberal one that under modern conditions the State should keep its distance from its people, leaving them free to make their own mistakes. Casting all questions for the State in terms of justice is one possible way to ensure this distance because, as the old adage goes, justice is blind. To do its relativizing work, justice must isolate criteria (although not necessarily the same criteria in every context) for differentiating among those who come before it. And to give these criteria of differentiation some rational purchase, they must be implemented against a background of assumed, but often entirely fictitious, uniformity. The just person, if you like, refuses to take sides in order to take sides;

she artificially blinds herself to some qualities of people and aspects of their lives in order to be able to make something of the other differences between them. Rawls memorably conveyed the idea when he spoke of 'the veil of ignorance' behind which just policies are conceived.[10] Now, as many of Rawls's critics have demonstrated, it is very doubtful whether cultivating this kind of artificial blindness to some of our qualities and some aspects of our lives is the proper way for the modern State as a whole to keep its distance from us. It leads to the wrong kind of distance, a remote and sometimes callous disinterest in people's well-being, which the State cannot legitimately, or even (some say) intelligibly, maintain across the board.[11] On the other hand, there is very good reason to think that at least one set of institutions belonging to the modern State, viz. the courts of law, should normally keep their distance from us in precisely this way. Courts are law-applying institutions, and it is in the nature of modern law, with its rule of law aspiration to apply more or less uniformly to all of those who are subject to it, that questions of how people are to be treated relative to one another always come to the fore at the point of its application. If we pursue this line of thinking, which of course calls for much more detailed elaboration, justice does turn out to be the first virtue of the courts even though not of other official bodies. The courts' primary business becomes, as the law itself puts it, 'the administration of justice'.

In the criminal law context, where (if the rule of law is being followed) the substantive law is relatively clear and certain, the most obvious everyday impact of the court's role as administrator of justice is in the procedural and evidential conduct of the trial—in determining, for example, the probative relevance and prejudicial effect of certain background information about offenders and witnesses, or the acceptability of certain modes of examination-in-chief and cross-examination. In these matters the court's first priority is to specify the density of its own veil of ignorance, the scope of its own blindness, the limits of forensic cognizance.[12] And it must do the very same thing once again at the sentencing stage of the trial where the law, rightly attempting to adjust for the inevitable rigidity and coarseness of its own relatively clear offence-definitions, typically leaves the court's options more open. Of course, in approaching these sentencing options, the court cannot ignore the State's duty of humanity, in the fulfilment of which the State's law-applying institutions must also do their bit. This is a duty which also has implications for sentencing. In the name of humanity, there must always be space for something like a plea in mitigation to bring out the offender's fuller range of qualities, the wider story of his life, some of which was necessarily hidden behind the 'veil of ignorance' during the earlier parts of the trial. But we may well ask: what is it, exactly, that falls to be mitigated when a plea in mitigation is presented to the court? If I am right so far, what falls to be mitigated is none other than the sentence which is, in the court's opinion, required by justice. Identifying a just sentence is thus the proper starting point. A court which begins from some other starting point, some other prima facie position, is a court which fails to observe its primary, and indeed one may be tempted to say definitive, duty.

Again, nothing in this proposal detracts from my original claim that the control of reprisal is a central pillar of the criminal law's justification. The proposal merely introduces a further troublesome complication. The complication is that, while the control of reprisal forms a key part of the argument for having criminal law and its punitive responses in the first place, those who must implement the criminal law and its punitive responses cannot legitimately make the control of reprisal part of their argument for doing so.[13] Displacement of retaliation is a reason for punishment which cannot be one of the judge's reasons for punishing. Judges cannot begin their reasoning at the sentencing stage by asking: what sentence would mollify the victim

and his sympathizers? Instead they should always begin by asking: what sentence would be just? I should stress that I am not assuming at the outset that these two questions are unconnected. At this stage I mean to leave open the possibility that, for example, victims and their supporters might want nothing more than the very justice which it is the court's role to dispense, so that doing justice will reliably serve that ulterior purpose. My only point is that the courts should not share in this ulterior purpose themselves; they should insist on thinking in terms of justice irrespective of whether doing so serves the further purpose of pacifying retaliators. For the criminal court, justice is an end, and that remains true even if, for the criminal justice system as a whole, justice is at best a means. In this respect the criminal court in a modern State is a classic bureaucratic institution. It has certain functions which cannot figure in its mission, and which therefore cannot directly animate its actions.

It is not surprising that this distinctively bureaucratic aspect of courts, and especially criminal courts, has been a cause for much complaint, particularly among victims of crime and their sympathizers, who accuse the courts of leaving them out in the cold, being out of touch with their concerns, stealing their cases away from them, etc. I already mentioned the challenge of maintaining a humane bureaucracy, and maintaining humanity towards victims is an aspect of that challenge to which I will return at the very end of this chapter. But in the context of the criminal law, the pre-eminence of the court's duty of justice creates a prior difficulty, which this discussion was designed to highlight, and aspects of which will occupy our attention over the next few pages. As I explained before, in fulfilling its displacement function the criminal law must always walk a fine line between failing to pacify would-be retaliators and simply institutionalizing their excesses. What we have just added is that under modern conditions an extended section of this fine line, the section which passes through the domain of the courts, must be walked wearing justice's blindfold. What hope can we have for the criminal law's fulfilment of its displacement function under these conditions?

3. The proportionality principle

In exploring this question, I want to focus attention on one particular principle of justice which is of profound moral importance for the criminal courts in their sentencing decisions, namely the principle that the punishment, if any, should be in proportion to the crime. I choose this principle not only because of its moral importance (to the explanation of which I will return presently), but also because so many people apparently read it as a principle which focuses on how the offender is to be treated relative to her victim or victims, and thus see it as a straightforward way of having the retaliatory impulses of victims systematically reflected in the administration of justice. To my mind, this victim-oriented reading is a serious misreading of the proportionality principle. The State's duty of justice, like the State's duty of humanity, has an important agent-relative aspect. The relativities with which the modern courts must principally contend under the rubric of justice are relativities between the State's treatment of different people, not relativities between how the State treats someone and how that someone treated someone else.[14] Therefore the question of proportionality in sentencing which concerns a modern criminal court is primarily the question of whether this offender's sentence stands to his crime as other offenders' sentences stood to their crimes. This means that the proportionality principle does not in itself specify or even calibrate the scale of punishments which the State may implement, but simply indicates how different people's punishments (or to be exact their prima facie punishments before any mitigating factors are brought to bear) should stand vis-à-vis one another on that scale.[15]

It does not automatically follow from this, however, that the victim's predicament or perspective cannot properly be introduced into the court's deliberations under the heading of proportionality. According to the proportionality principle, the sentence in a criminal case should be proportionate to the crime. If the court can point to features of the crime committed in the case at hand which make it more or less grave than other comparable crimes that have been dealt with by the courts, then the proportionality principle plainly points to a corresponding adjustment of the prima facie sentence. It means that everything turns on the applicable conception of 'the crime' and the specification of its axes of gravity. Now it may be thought that the law itself sets these parameters, so that the matter is simply a technical legal one. Crime, some will say, is a purely legal category, and a crime is none other than an action or activity which meets the conditions set by law for criminal conviction.[16] Thus 'the crime' referred to in the principle of proportionality can be none other than the crime as legally defined. It would follow that whether the victim's predicament or perspective is relevant under the heading of proportionality would depend only on whether the legal definition of the crime made specific mention of it. A crime defined in terms of the suffering or loss inflicted upon its victim would leave space for, even perhaps require, the degree of that suffering or loss to be brought to bear on the sentence under the proportionality principle, thus giving some aspects of the victim's predicament or perspective a role in the court's deliberations under the heading of justice. But a crime without such a definitional feature would naturally leave no such space and offer no such role to victim-centred considerations.

In fact, the problem is much more complicated than this. It is true that crimes are, in one ('institutional') sense, just activities which meet the conditions for criminal conviction. But criminal conviction is an all-or-nothing business. Questions of gravity can certainly be a relevant factor, on occasions, in determining which of a number of related crimes the accused should be convicted of, e.g. whether he is a murderer or a manslaughterer, a robber or a thief, etc. But for any *single* criminal offence considered by the jury or magistrate, the ultimate answer can only be guilty or not guilty; gravity is neither here nor there.[17] What is more, where the rule of law is properly observed, criminal offences are defined so as to facilitate exactly this kind of all-or-nothing decision-making. Rape, in England, is sexual intercourse without consent undertaken in the knowledge of, or reckless as to, the lack of consent. Grey areas and borderline cases of consent, sexual intercourse, knowledge and recklessness have all been, so far as possible, defined out.[18] There is nothing in the definition of rape, apart perhaps from the difference between the knowing rapist and the reckless one,[19] that could conceivably afford a sentencing judge any significant axis of gravity. So does the proportionality principle, by itself, prescribe the same sentence for all knowing rapists, irrespective of their brutality, treachery, bigotry, cowardliness, arrogance, and malice? This challenge cannot be avoided by observing that most crimes do harbour some residual questions of degree in their definitions—that grievous bodily harm is more grievous in some cases than in others, that some acts of dishonesty are more dishonest than others, etc. That is not the point. The point is that, where the rule of law is observed, individual criminal offences are not defined in law so as to retain a topography of gravity for the sentencing stage, but rather so as to flatten that topography, so far as possible, for the all-or-nothing purposes of conviction and acquittal. There is no reason to think that a definition crafted primarily for one purpose, viz. that of flattening the rational variation between different cases of the same wrong, should be regarded as authoritatively determining the scope of the court's veil of ignorance when its job turns, at the sentencing stage, from eliminating such rational variation to highlighting it.

There is no reason to assume that the court will find all, or any, of the relevant variables still inscribed on the face of the crime's definition.

It follows that, for the purpose of the principle that the sentence should be in proportion to the crime, we need to go beyond a purely institutional conception of the crime. I do not mean to write off all institutional circumscriptions. It seems to me to be a sound rule of thumb, for example, that evidence which was inadmissible in the trial on grounds of its irrelevance to the charge before the court should not be taken into account when the gravity of the crime is being assessed for the purposes of proportionate sentencing. That an act of dangerous driving caused death should be treated as irrelevant to the gravity of the crime if the crime charged is dangerous driving rather than causing death by dangerous driving. No doubt this is bound to frustrate victims of crime and their sympathizers who may have little patience with the due process principle that people should only be tried for the crimes with which they are charged and sentenced for the crimes which were proved against them at trial—recall that the predictability of such impatience was among the factors which justified the State in monopolizing retaliatory force to begin with. But be that as it may, the due process principle *itself* requires that we go beyond a merely institutional conception of the crime. To implement the principle of due process, just as to implement the principle of proportionality in sentencing, we need some grasp not only of the crime's legal definition but equally of what counts as the *substance* or the *gist* or the *point* of the crime as legally defined—and that is an unavoidably evaluative, non-positivistic issue.[20]

Here, for example, are a couple of classic due process questions. Apart from the charge spelt out in the indictment or summons, were there other lesser offences with which the accused was also implicitly being charged, which did not need to be spelt out? And when does the defendant's previous wrongdoing pass the 'similar fact' test, so that evidence of it is relevant for the purposes of proving the offence charged on the present indictment? Lawyers have often struggled to answer these questions in institutional terms, by pointing to features of crimes which figure in the positive legal definitions.[21] But that, as we should all have realized by now, was always a false hope. One cannot apply or even adequately understand these questions without developing what we may like to call the moral map of the crime, highlighting evaluative significances which may be missing from the law's pared down definition. Thus even if, as I suggested, the principle of proportionality in sentencing does usefully borrow some institutional circumscriptions from the due process principle, that ultimately just reiterates rather than eliminates the fundamentally evaluative, non-positivistic question of what counts as 'the crime' for the purposes of assessing the proportionate prima facie sentence. One still needs a moral map of the crime, and the question remains, after all this, of whether the predicament or perspective of the victim can figure anywhere on that map.

4. Perspectives on crime

One significant strand of the literature on criminal law and criminal justice proceeds from the thought that many, if not all, crimes are covered by one and the same moral map. This is the map of the offender's *blameworthiness* or *culpability*. Following this map leads to a specific interpretation of the principle of proportionality, according to which making the sentence proportionate to the crime means making the sentence proportionate to the offender's blameworthiness or culpability in committing the crime.[22] Let's call this the 'blameworthiness interpretation' of the proportionality principle. In the minds of many adherents as well as many critics, the proportionality principle in its blameworthiness interpretation systematically excludes victim-centred considerations from

the proper scope of the court's prima facie sentencing deliberations. The pivotal thought behind this is that a person's blameworthiness in acting as she did is a function of how things seemed to her at the time of her action.[23] It may of course be a more or less complex function. On some accounts of the function, blameworthiness increases or decreases according to how much of the evil of her action the agent appreciated. For others, it is a question of how much the agent should have appreciated, given the various other things she knew at the time. Either way, the crucial manoeuvre so far as blameworthiness is concerned is supposedly to look at the situation *ex ante*, from the perspective of the perpetrator. But that perspective, it is often claimed or assumed, is fundamentally at odds with the perspective of the victim, who looks at the wrong *ex post* and is interested not so much in how things may have seemed to the perpetrator, but rather in how things actually occurred or turned out.[24] On this view, the victim and those who sympathize with him are aggrieved first and foremost because of what he suffered or lost at the perpetrator's hands, whether or not the perpetrator appreciated or could have appreciated the full extent of this loss or suffering at the time of acting. If that is so, then the conception of the crime which lies at the heart of the proportionality principle on its blameworthiness interpretation is not the victim's conception. In fact it is diametrically opposed to the victim's conception. If anything, the proportionality principle in this interpretation seems to oblige courts systematically to *compound* the frustration of victims and their sympathizers, and hence to *aggravate* their retaliatory instinct, by insisting on seeing things the offender's way and hence (through the already aggrieved eyes of victims and their sympathizers) doggedly taking the offender's side in the whole conflict. Thus, on this view of the matter, fidelity to the proportionality principle scarcely militates in favour of the sentencing process making a systematic positive contribution to the fulfilment of the criminal law's displacement function.

There is, however, a great deal of confusion in this line of thinking. I can only scratch the surface of a few of the problems here. The problems start with a failure to spell out what blameworthiness or culpability is, which leads to an oversimplification of the principles on which it is incurred. Blameworthiness has a four-part formula. To be blameworthy, one must: (a) have done something wrong and (b) have been responsible for doing it, while lacking (c) justification and (d) excuse for having done it. Each of elements (a), (b), (c) and (d) can undoubtedly be sensitive, to some extent and in some respects and on some occasions, to how things seemed to the blameworthy person at the time of her action. Elements (c) and (d) in fact incorporate an across-the-board partial sensitivity to the *ex ante* perspective of the perpetrator. Take element (c) first. An action is *justifiable* if the reasons in favour of it are not defeated by the reasons against; but it is *justified* only if the agent acts for one or more of those undefeated reasons.[25] It follows that a purported justification based on considerations unknown to and unsuspected by the agent at the time of the action is no justification at all. Thus justification always does depend, in part, on how things seemed to the agent at the time of the action. Conversely, justification also depends, in part, on how things actually were. No matter how things seemed to the agent, if the reason for which she acted was not in fact an undefeated one then she has no justification. If she fails the test of justification on this score, the agent must retreat to element (d), the excuse element, to resist the allegation of blameworthiness. Here we find an additional sensitivity to the *ex ante* perspective of the perpetrator: here the agent can rely on what she mistakenly took to be undefeated reasons for her action, provided only that she was justified in her mistake. But again this last proviso shows that even excuses are not entirely insensitive to how things actually were; for whether the agent was excused by her

mistakes depends on whether her mistakes were justified, and that in turn depends, like any justification, on whether there really were undefeated reasons for her to see the world as she did.[26] So in both elements (c) and (d) we have questions which focus on how things seemed to the agent *as well as* questions which focus on how things really were. Justification and excuse have some across-the-board agent-perspectival dimensions, but are neither of them a pure function of how things seemed to the agent at the time of the action.

Things get more complicated still when we add elements (a) and (b) to the stew. It is tempting to think that wrong action is the mirror image of right or justified action, so that, adapting from the account of right or justified action just outlined, whether one's action is wrong depends on whether the reasons in favour of performing it were defeated by the reasons against and whether one acted for one of the latter reasons. Thus obviously no action could be wrong if the agent had no inkling of anything that made it wrong. But right and wrong are in fact dramatically asymmetrical. There are many more ways of doing the wrong thing than there are of doing the right thing. In particular, there is no general sensitivity of wrongdoing to the reasons for which one acted. It is perfectly true that some wrongs, e.g. deceit and betrayal, cannot be committed without certain knowledge or belief on the part of the person who commits them, and others, such as torture and extortion, require a certain intention. But this is not true of all wrongs. One may do wrong by breaking a promise or neglecting one's children quite irrespective of what one knew or had reason to know, and *a fortiori* quite irrespective of why one did it. The same holds true, I believe, of killing people or wounding them, damaging their property, poisoning them, and countless other wrongs which are of enduring importance for the criminal law. It is wrong to kill people or wound them, and one may kill someone or wound them by playing with intriguing buttons or switches which were none of one's proper concern, quite irrespective of whether one knew or had grounds to know the true awfulness of what one was doing. If one's *ex ante* perspective is to be relevant to one's blameworthiness in respect of such killings or woundings, on this view, it must be relevant by virtue of some other element of blameworthiness, such as the justification or excuse element. To be sure, it may also be relevant to one's responsibility, element (b) of the blameworthiness equation. But again its relevance here can only be occasional and limited. To deny that one was a responsible agent one must not only deny that one knew what one was doing, but also point to some underlying explanation such as psychotic delusion, infancy, or (on some views of the phenomenon) hypnosis which puts one temporarily or permanently out of reach of reason so that normal rational standards of justification and excuse do not apply to one. This is a very limited (and decidedly bottom-of-the-barrel) opening for one's ignorance to affect one's blameworthiness. So again, there is nothing here to make blameworthiness, in general, into a function of how things seemed to the agent at the time of his or her action. In fact, the influence of elements (a) and (b) in the blameworthiness equation fragments and complicates the conditions of blameworthiness even further, so that very few things can be said, in general, about the balance of agent-perspectival and non-agent-perspectival factors which will bear on the net blameworthiness of the agent.

Whatever one may think about the details of this elaboration of the conditions of blameworthiness, it draws attention to one crucial point which is far too easily overlooked. The crucial point is that there is no such thing as blameworthiness at large, or blameworthiness *tout court*. Our blameworthiness is necessarily our blameworthiness in respect of some specific action or activity we engaged in, such as killing, wounding, deceiving, betraying, torturing, or breaking a promise.[27] And whether and to what extent our blameworthiness is a function of how things seemed to us at the time of our action depends in very large measure on *which* action or activity we are supposed to be blameworthy in respect of, since different agent-perspectival conditions for blameworthiness evidently come into play for different actions and activities. Now there are those who try to make the determination of which action or activity we engaged in *itself* a function of the way things seemed to us at the time when we acted. Their response to my example of the person who kills unwittingly by playing with intriguing buttons and switches is to deny that it involves a killing, not because killing in particular is held to be, like deceit, an action with some definitive knowledge requirement, but rather because the scope of agency is always, so to speak, in the eyes of the agent. Fundamentally, we do only whatever we take ourselves to be doing.[28] Personally, I find this a deeply counterintuitive account of human agency.[29] But more importantly for present purposes, if this account of human agency is accepted, it makes a mockery of the process of determining blameworthiness which I outlined in the previous paragraph. We cannot ask, as I asked in the last paragraph, whether the killer was a responsible agent when he killed, or whether he had any justifications or excuses for doing it. For on this account of human agency *there was no killing*. The most the agent did was press buttons, or fiddle with things that didn't concern him. Having no possible inkling of the death-dealing aspect of what he was doing, he didn't kill anyone. All the hard work which the piecemeal doses of subjectivity in the separate elements of blameworthiness were supposed to do is thus pre-empted by a massive and all-consuming injection of subjectivity in the doctrine of human agency to which it is applied. We are not deprived of our (admittedly controversial and seriously under-specified) answer to the question of whether the button-presser was a blameworthy killer. *We are summarily deprived of the question itself.*

If we rescue the question, as I am sure we should, by jettisoning the extremely restrictive account of human agency which put it out of bounds, we can instantly see that the juxta-position with which this section began was grievously exaggerated. There is no automatic and comprehensive opposition between assess-ing the gravity of a crime in terms of the offender's blameworthiness and assessing the gravity of a crime according to the way it impacts upon its victim. That is because, to assess the offender's blameworthiness we must begin by asking 'blameworthiness in respect of which action?' and this requires us to interrogate our account of human agency. Since on any plausible account of human agency there can be actions which are, like killing and wounding, defined at least partly in terms of their actual impact upon other people independently of the way things seemed *ex ante* to the perpetrator, it follows that an inquiry into the perpetrator's blame-worthiness cannot be made independent of this impact. In fact, if we were to examine more thoroughly the so-called 'victim perspective' with which we started, I think we would find that the link between the blameworthiness of an offender and what irks the victim or her sympathizers is even more intimate than this last remark suggests. I believe it is the action of killing or wounding, complete with (but not limited to) the death or wound it involves, that normally aggrieves victims and their sympa-thizers and sparks their retaliation. Thus the starting point of the blameworthiness inquiry—the action which was wrongful—is also the normal trigger for retaliatory responses on behalf of the victim. Of course there may be differences of perception and emphasis. It is true, for example, that *excuses* tend to be looked upon less generously by victims and their supporters than their importance for blameworthiness would indicate. Victims and their supporters may also have trouble with some justifications where their interests were not among the main reasons in favour of the justified action, and they

may be more doubtful than the court might be, especially under the influence of psychiatric testimony, about a wrongdoer's supposed lack of responsibility. This means that the blame-worthiness inquiry could certainly drive some wedges between the court's proportionality-driven thinking on matters of prima facie sentencing and the demands of victims and their supporters. But one only drives wedges between surfaces which are in their original tendency attached to one another. On my account, that is exactly the situation with the offender's blame-worthiness and the victim's grievance. It follows that there is no fundamental opposition of per-spectives, no chasm of understanding, dividing the blameworthiness interpretation of the pro-portionality principle from the demands of those whose retaliation must be displaced if the criminal law is to fulfil its displacement function.

Here I am talking as if the blameworthiness interpretation of the proportionality principle came out basically unscathed from the process of correcting the analysis of blameworthiness which went into it. But of course it did not. What we have discovered in the process of explaining the concept and conditions of blameworthiness is that it makes no sense to prescribe, simply, that the sentence in a criminal trial should be in proportion to the offender's blameworthiness in committing the crime. For that prescription falls into the trap of presenting blameworthiness as an independent quantity, something that one can have more or less of *tout court*. Now that we have brought to mind the important point that blameworthiness is always blameworthiness in respect of some action, the blameworthiness interpretation in its original form should be replaced by a sharper ('modified blameworthi-ness') interpretation of the proportionality principle according to which the sentence should be in proportion to the offender's wrongful action, adjusted for his blameworthi-ness in respect of it.[30] This reinterpretation, with the slightly more complex moral map of a crime it implies, makes several important advances over the simpler blameworthiness interpretation it replaces. Let me mention just two of them here.

First, the modified blameworthiness interpretation helps to bring out what *justifies* the proportionality principle, and lends it the moral importance in the courtroom that I so confidently spoke of earlier. Although a principle of justice, the proportionality principle also contributes directly and powerfully to the court's compliance with the State's duty of humanity, and it takes much of its moral force from that contribution. As already mentioned, the State's duty of humanity requires it to affirm the moral agency and moral responsibility of those whom it punishes. The proportionality principle in its modified blameworthiness interpretation puts both the offender's agency and her responsibility centre stage. To ask about the offender's blameworthiness is to emphasize her responsibility. That is not only because element (b) of the blameworthiness equation is the element of responsibility. It is also because questions of justification and excuse—elements (c) and (d)—are applicable only to responsible agents, so that applying standards of justification and excuse to people is an assertion of their responsibility. But on top of that, the modified blameworthiness interpretation brings out the importance of questions about the offender's agency which are not highlighted in the simple blameworthiness interpretation. It reminds us that treating someone as an agent is of importance quite apart from treating them as responsible. Even someone who is not responsible for their actions is an agent, and should still be treated as one. True, the duty of humanity as I expressed it goes further, and demands that offenders be treated as *moral* agents and as *morally* responsible. This arguably introduces further complications which point to a need for some further modification of the modified blameworthiness interpretation. Nevertheless, the complications do not alter the main point, which is that by punishing people in proportion

to their crimes, where those crimes are mapped according to the action which made them wrongful adjusted for the offender's blameworthiness in respect of them, the court contributes decisively to the affirmation of the offender's humanity which is a *sine qua non* of the legitimacy of any modern State punishment. But remember that this is a function of the modern State's special duty of humanity towards its people, which comes of its claim to authority and its associated role as servant of its people. Those of us who stake no similar claim to authority and have no similar role in other people's lives are not covered by the same strict humanitarian duty towards them.[31] Thus the strictness of the court's attention to questions of moral agency and moral responsibility need not, rationally, be mirrored in all interpersonal transactions between wrongdoers and people they wronged, or supporters, or even onlookers. That is one important reason why the victim of a crime and his or her sympathizers may sometimes *quite properly* (i.e. independently of their various impatiences, hastinesses, prejudices, etc.) have less time for the niceties of blameworthiness than the court is morally required to have.

Second, the modified blameworthiness interpretation has the advantage that it alerts us to the *limitations* of the proportionality principle as a principle of justice for scaling criminal sentences. The principle's usefulness depends first on the court's ability to discern what is supposed to be the wrongful action in the crime, and then the court's ability to compare this action with other actions, before it can even start to settle degrees of blameworthiness as between them. This may not always be possible. Some pairs of wrongful actions are incommensurable. It means that the proportionality scale will not always be perfectly transitive.[32] The adjustments for differential blameworthiness required by the modified blameworthiness interpretation of the proportionality principle can only take effect within the transitive parts of the scale. It may be possible to compare a less blameworthy robbery with a more blameworthy theft. But it will not necessarily be possible, even in principle, to assess a more blameworthy theft alongside, say, a more blameworthy assault. Here, sentencing practice may have to move in relatively independent grooves, with guidelines that do not add up to a comprehensive code. The axes of gravity that operate at the sentencing stage will not necessarily, or even typically, allow the gravity of each crime to be plotted relative to that of every other crime. That, in my view, is no violation of the proportionality principle, nor on the other hand, an indictment of it, but rather one of its welcome implications. The idea that all crimes are covered by a single moral map has, on closer inspection, very little to recommend it.[33]

5. Filling the displacement gap

The foregoing does something to explain how the courts, as blindfolded administrators of justice, can in spite of their blindfolds systematically help to fulfil the criminal law's displacement function. Even though the justice that victims and their sympathizers want (which is primarily justice between offender and victim) is not the justice that courts are licensed and required to provide by the proportionality principle (which is primarily justice between offender and offender), the proportionality principle, correctly interpreted, nevertheless shares some of its basic moral geography with the retaliatory logic of victims and their sympathizers. For some distance, courts and retaliators travel on the same path even though the former cannot, consistent with their mission, deliberately track the latter. But as I have also attempted to show, the two paths do diverge at certain obvious points. First, as I started Section 2 ('Humanity and Justice') by explaining, to preserve the legitimacy of the criminal law's monopolization of retaliation, the courts must stop short of institutionalizing the excusable but unjustifiable retaliatory

excesses of victims and their sympathizers. Second, as I explained in Section 3 ('The Proportionality Principle'), the principle of due process means that the wrongful action at the heart of the offender's crime cannot always, in the eyes of the law, and notably for the purposes of sentencing, be the same wrongful action which inspires retaliation by or on behalf of victims. The need to restrict the trial to the substance of the charges with which it began may lead to some differences between the victim's perception and the law's rendition of what the offender has done, even when the victim is not driven to retaliatory excess. Finally, the requirement to adjust the sentence for the offender's blameworthiness may, as I just explained in Section 4 ('Perspectives on Crime'), drive some extra wedges between the court's sense of proportionality and the victim's retaliatory inclinations, even where those inclinations are not excessive and there are no due process impediments to their reflection in law. The court, as an agent of the State, owes a duty of humanity to all which may often exceed the duty each of us owes to other people, and which therefore requires the court to affirm each offender's moral agency and moral responsibility more conscientiously than need be the case in many of our ordinary interpersonal transactions, including transactions with those who wrong us. These three factors add up to constitute what I will call the 'displacement gap' in criminal sentencing: the gap between what retaliators want and what the courts can, in good conscience, deliver.

Traditionally, this displacement gap has been filled by the law's own wealth of symbolic significances. What was confiscated from victims and their sympathizers in point of retaliatory force has traditionally been compensated by the ritual and majesty of the law, and by the message of public vindication which this ritual and majesty served to convey. At one time it was the ritual of the punishment itself which made the greatest contribution. The pillory, the stocks, the carting, the public execution and various other modes of punishment involving public display allowed the State to close the displacement gap by exhibiting the offender in all his shame and humiliation, in all his remorse and regret, while the proceedings remained under some measure of official control to limit retaliatory excess.[34] But of course a new penal age dawned in the nineteenth century which put the offender out of reach and out of sight in the prison, where measured punishment and control of retaliation could be more successfully combined, both with each other and with the new disciplinary ambitions of supervision and rehabilitation.[35] From then on, the burden of providing ritual and majesty to fill the displacement gap was to a large extent shifted off the shoulders of the punishment system (which was now practically invisible to the general public except in the gloomy expanse of the prison walls) and onto the shoulders of the trial system instead. The courts themselves now had to offer the would-be retaliator the kind of public vindication which would once have been provided by the act of punishment, and the ritual and majesty of the courtroom had to substitute for the ritual and majesty of the recantation at the gallows. Of course the pressure to get this substitution exactly right was eased by the fact that the prison would to some extent protect the offender against the retaliator even if the displacement gap had not been successfully filled by the court. But it was still crucial that the trial itself should offer the victim and his sympathizers some symbolic significances which would divert them from taking the matter into their own hands, e.g. if the offender was acquitted, or if a custodial sentence was not used, or once the custodial sentence had expired. For this purpose the court could only rely on continuing respect, indeed deference, for its own heavily ceremonial processes and practices. If the court's processes and practices were to fall into disrepute, if they came to be seen as just distracting frippery, then the vindicatory symbolism of the trial would be lost and the

displacement gap would open wide for all to see. We would then face a major legitimation crisis in the system of criminal justice.

My view is that we now face this crisis in Britain, and for the very reason I have just given. During the 1980s and 1990s, the steady creep of the ideology of consumerism has led people to regard the courts, along with many other key public institutions, as mere 'service providers' to be judged by their instrumental achievements. League tables, customer charters, satisfaction surveys, outcome audits and efficiency scrutiny became the depressing norm. Respect for valuable public institutions declined at the same time as expectations of them increased. Even among those who took themselves to be anti-individualistic, the demand that institutions should become more 'transparent' and 'accountable' came to be regarded as orthodoxy, and euphemistic talk of 'cost-effectiveness' became acceptable. All this was, essentially, a corruption of a sound idea, which I mentioned at the outset—the idea that modern government is the servant of its people. It was mistakenly assumed that since public bureaucracies existed to serve social functions, ultimately serving people, they ought to be judged by the purely instrumental contribution they could make to those social functions, and hence their instrumental value for people. But it was forgotten that many social functions were not purely instrumental functions, i.e. many institutions made an intrinsic or constitutive contribution to their own social functions. The mission of such institutions, to return to my earlier expression, was partly integral to their function. The National Health Service and other organs of Beveridge's Welfare State are the most familiar examples in Britain; people who regard themselves as collectivists should rue the day they ever tried to defend these in purely instrumental terms, which was the day they surrendered to the creeping individualism of the consumer society. But the criminal courts exemplify the point even more perfectly. Historically, they filled the displacement gap in criminal justice by their own (to the public eye) bizarre and almost incomprehensible processes, their own special black magic if you like, which lent profound symbolic importance to their work. But armed with new consumerist ideas people came to see all these processes as mere frippery. They came to ask what the courts were *achieving* by their black magic, and whether it was giving them the *product* they wanted, whether this was the *service* they were looking for, and of course those questions quickly broke the spell. The courts could no longer fill the displacement gap from their own symbolic resources, since their own symbolic resources had been confiscated by the popular expectation of raw retaliatory results.

The consequence of this rapid social change is that the displacement gap is now an open and suppurating social wound, and the threat of retaliation by or on behalf of aggrieved victims of crime looms ever larger. The courts themselves sometimes feel the pressure and feel constrained to penetrate their own veil of ignorance, abandoning their mission to do justice where, as increasingly often, it parts company with their function to displace retaliation. That seriously violates their duty as courts, which is above all the duty of justice, and which positively requires them to stay 'out of touch with public opinion' on matters of sentencing policy. Meanwhile, populist politicians pander to retaliatory instincts by threatening to publish names and addresses of ex-offenders, to force ex-offenders to reveal old criminal records, even to license vigilantes in the form of private security guards—all in order 'to hand justice back to the people'. What they do not appear to appreciate is that all of this makes the justification for the criminal law less stable, not more so. For if the criminal law cannot successfully displace retaliation against wrongdoers, but instead collaborates with it, then a central pillar of its justification has collapsed.

I do not mean to suggest that the courts' recent well-documented waking up to the existence of victims is in every way a bad thing. There has been for as long as anyone can remember a tendency for criminal courts, with typical bureaucratic abandon, to pretend that nobody was concerned in their processes but themselves. Victims of crime, in particular, were kept badly informed and given no quarter at all in the operation of the system. Except insofar as they were witnesses, they were expected to find out for themselves where and when the trial would take place, to queue for the public gallery, to sit with the accused in the cafeteria, etc. In their capacity as witnesses, meanwhile, no concessions were made for the special difficulty of confronting those who had wronged them. Much of this amounted to a violation of the State's duty of humanity towards the victims of crime, and to the extent that it still goes on it still does.[36] The courts should remember that victims, as well as offenders, are thinking, feeling human beings. But this has absolutely no connection with the far more sinister contemporary campaigns to turn victims into parties to the criminal trial or administrators of criminal punishments, or in some other way to hand their grievances back to them.[37] That victims do not try, convict, sentence or punish criminal offenders, and have no official part in the trial, conviction, sentencing and punishment of criminal offenders, is not an accident of procedural history. It is, on the contrary, one of the main objects of the whole exercise.

Notes

Andrew Ashworth and Martin Wasik (eds.), *Fundamentals of Sentencing Theory* (Oxford 1998) pp. 31–52.

1 For those who accept that ancient criminal law had this *raison d'être* but who doubt whether it has done much to shape criminal law 'as we know it today', I commend J Horder, 'The Duel and the English Law of Homicide', *Oxford Journal of Legal Studies* 12 (1992), 419.

2 For instance, PF Strawson, 'Freedom and Resentment', *Proceedings of the British Academy* 48 (1962),

187; JM Finnis, 'Punishment and Pedagogy', *The Oxford Review* 5 (1967), 83; JG Murphy and J Hampton, *Forgiveness and Mercy* (1988); MS Moore, 'The Moral Worth of Retribution' in F Schoeman (ed), *Responsibility, Character, and the Emotions* (1987).

3 The classic version of such a structured hybrid justification is HLA Hart, 'Prolegomenon to the Principles of Punishment' reprinted in his *Punishment and Responsibility* (1968). A different variation is to be found in A von Hirsch, *Censure and Sanctions* (1993).

4 For more or less frank expressions of this anxiety, see N Lacey, *State Punishment: Political Principles and Community Values* (1988), 46ff, especially at 52; PH Robinson, 'Hybrid Principles for the Distribution of Criminal Sanctions', *Northwestern University Law Review* 82 (1987), 19, especially at 31–34; ND Walker, *Why Punish?* (1991), 135–136; RA Duff, 'Penal Communications: Recent Work in the Philosophy of Punishment', *Crime and Justice* 20 (1996), 1 at 8. More theoretically puritanical critics go further, and argue that mixing different arguments for the justification of punishment is doomed irrespective of attempts to keep them in separate logical spaces, e.g. J Morison, 'Hart's Excuses: Problems with a Compromise Theory of Punishment' in P Leith and P Ingram (eds), *The Jurisprudence of Orthodoxy* (1988); A Norrie, *Law, Ideology and Punishment* (1991), 125–135.

5 Contrast the position recommended by AGN Flew in 'The Justification of Punishment' in HB Acton (ed), *The Philosophy of Punishment* (1969), where the justification of punishment is held to be 'over-determined' by the many reasons which count in favour of punishment.

6 I cannot offer a proper defence of this claim here. For those who are interested, the basis of such a defence lies in the fact that the moral duties under discussion in this section occupy the lower level of a two-level approach to moral reasoning. They summarize and organize certain ultimate moral considerations, but are not ultimate moral considerations themselves.

7 That might include, e.g., providing a safe house, or taking criminal libel proceedings against those who make public accusations in a way which will incite reprisal. The demand for protection applies *a fortiori* to those who did wrong but who were acquitted at law, where reprisals not only threaten the wrongdoer but also challenge the law's own authority to deal with the wrong.

8 I have discussed some aspects of the substantive criminal law which contribute to this aim in J Gardner, 'On the General Part of the Criminal Law' in RA Duff (ed), *Philosophy and the Criminal Law* (1998).

9 J Rawls, *A Theory of Justice* (1971), 3. Rawls's slogan can bear various interpretations apart from the rather literal one I have adopted in the text. On one very different interpretation, Rawls was only saying that justice is the *last resort* of social institutions, i.e. when all else fails social institutions should at the very least be just. See J Waldron, 'When Justice Replaces Affection', *Harvard Journal of Law and Public Policy* 11 (1988), 625.

10 *A Theory of Justice*, at n 9 above, 136ff.

11 Both the conceptual and the moral objections are represented in M Sandel, *Liberalism and the Limits of Justice* (1982), 24–28 and 135–147. Likewise, with a strikingly different twist, in J Raz, *The Morality of Freedom* (1986), 110–133 and 369ff.

12 Isn't there a basic problem with letting an institution decide what it shall take notice of? Doesn't it have to know what it should not know in order to know whether it should know it? True enough. That is why, in trial by indictment, the *voir dire* exists to separate the function of determining what will be hidden by the veil of ignorance from the function of deliberating about guilt and innocence behind the veil of ignorance. This double-insulation against unwitting prejudice provides a major part of the case for retaining a right to jury trial whenever serious criminal charges are laid. On the question of a criminal charge's seriousness, see sections 3 and 4 below.

13 This helps us to see why as theorists we should not fear the multiplicity of considerations which add up to justify the practice of criminal punishment. As administrators of justice, judges are heavily restricted in their access to many of these considerations, and thus do not have to face all the conflicts among them in their raw form. I have discussed this in greater depth in J Gardner, 'The Purity and Priority of Private Law', *University of Toronto Law Journal* 46 (1996), 459.

14 See n 6 above.

15 Thus I am going to be writing about what von

Hirsch calls 'ordinal proportionality' rather than 'cardinal proportionality': Avon Hirsch, *Censure and Sanctions* (1993), 18–19. As it happens I also believe in a principle of cardinal proportionality, but it has a very different foundation and applies to the legislative business of setting sentencing maxima rather than to the sentencing stage of criminal trials. It is also worth mentioning that both cardinal and ordinal principles of proportionality need to be applied with the State's duty of humanity in mind, since this forbids cruel or brutalizing punishments even when these would be proportionate. None of this affects the substance of my argument.

16 G Williams, 'The Definition of Crime', *Current Legal Problems* 8 (1995), 107.

17 It is true that the Scots allow for 'not proven' as a *tertium quid*, but of course it still has nought to do with the gravity of the crime. The US solution of 'first degree' and 'second degree' crimes may look at first like another counterexample, but all it does in reality is multiply the number of separate crimes to which the all-or-nothing guilty/not guilty decision must be applied.

18 *R v Olugboja* (1981) 73 Cr App Rep 344 and *R v Linekar* [1995] 2 Cr App Rep 49 illustrate the law's attempts to turn certain grey areas between consent and non-consent into brighter lines. *Kaitamaki v R* [1985] AC 147 does the same with respect to 'sexual intercourse'. The *mens rea* elements were hotly debated in the early 1980s, but the debate was simply between two different ways of artificially stripping grey areas from the concept of recklessness, the broader contrived definition in *R v Pigg* [1982] 2 All ER 591 giving way to the narrower one in *R v Satnam S* (1983) 78 Cr App Rep 149.

19 cf *R v Bashir* (1982) 77 Cr App Rep 327.

20 This is not a criticism of legal positivism. Legal positivists hold that validity of a law turns on its sources rather than its merits. That does not prevent them from holding that legal reasoning reflects on the merits as well as the sources of laws, since there is no reason to suppose that legal reasoning is only reasoning about legal validity. See J Raz, 'On the Autonomy of Legal Reasoning', *Ratio Juris* 6 (1993), 1.

21 See *R v Novac* (1977) 65 Cr App Rep 107 and *R v Barrington* [1981] 1 All ER 1132 to see how the issue arises in relation to the similar fact doctrine;

concerning counts in an indictment, the issue is well-illustrated in the leading case of *R v Wilson* [1984] 1 AC 242.

22 A random selection: H Gross, 'Culpability and Desert' in RA Duff and N Simmonds (ed), *Philosophy and the Criminal Law* (ARSP Beiheft 19, 1984), 59; CL Ten, *Crime, Guilt, and Punishment* (1987), 155ff; A Ashworth, 'Taking the Consequences' in S Shute, J Gardner and J Horder (eds), *Action and Value in Criminal Law* (1994), 107 at 116–120. Von Hirsch also makes culpability the only axis of crime-seriousness when he introduces the proportionality principle on p 15 of *Censure and Sanctions* (1993). But contrast the more complex 'harm-plus-culpability' standard used for proportionality on p 29 of the same volume, and elsewhere in von Hirsch's work, e.g. in his *Past or Future Crimes* (1985), 64ff. See further n 30 below.

23 Among diverse writers who allocate blameworthiness on these terms, we find D Parfit, *Reasons and Persons* (1986), 24–25; S Sverdlik, 'Crime and Moral Luck', *American Philosophical Quarterly* 25 (1988), 79; R Swinburne, *Responsibility and Atonement* (1989), 34–35; D Husak and A von Hirsch, 'Culpability and Mistake of Law' in *Action and Value in Criminal Law*, at n 22 above; A Ashworth, 'Belief, Intent and Criminal Liability' in J Eekelaar and J Bell (eds), *Oxford Essays in Jurisprudence: Third Series* (1987), 1 at 7.

24 Talk of the 'victim perspective' and the 'perpetrator perspective' on wrongdoing will be familiar to those conversant with the literature on anti-discrimination law. See AD Freeman, 'Legitimizing Racial Discrimination through Antidiscrimination Law: A Critical Review of Supreme Court Doctrine', *Minnesota Law Review* 62 (1978), 1049. The version of the distinction relied upon here is slightly less ambitious than Freeman's, although the two are closely related. The distinction I am speaking of figures prominently in Sverdlik, 'Crime and Moral Luck' and in A Ashworth, 'Punishment and Compensation: Victims, Offenders and the State', *Oxford Journal of Legal Studies* 6 (1986), 86 at 96. cf also J Coleman, 'Crimes, Kickers and Transaction Structures' in JR Pennock and JW Chapman (eds), *Nomos XXVII: Criminal Justice* (1985), 313 on the contrasting 'economic' and 'moral' perspectives of tort law and criminal law.

25 I have defended this account of justification in

J Gardner, 'Justifications and Reasons' in AP Simester and ATH Smith (eds), *Harm and Culpability* (1996), 103.

26 ibid, at 118–122.

27 While we are blameworthy only in respect of actions, we are *to blame* in respect of consequences. To be to blame for a given consequence, we must be *responsible for* that consequence. Doesn't this complicate element (b) of my blameworthiness equation, which spoke only of responsibility for *actions* and therefore (you may say) swept under the carpet the further agent-perspectival conditions of responsibility for consequences? The answer is no. Whether we are responsible for consequences is already taken into account in element (a) of the blameworthiness equation. In the relevant sense, we are responsible for those consequences which contribute constitutively to the wrongness of our doing as we do. We are *to blame* for those consequences, accordingly, when that condition is met and elements (b), (c) and (d) of blameworthiness are also present. There is thus no further question, on top of those already anticipated in my blameworthiness equation, of whether our responsibility or blame extends to a particular unforeseen or unforeseeable consequence of our actions. Much effort in moral and legal philosophy has been wasted thanks to the mistaken assumption that one has two bites at the cherry: first one can deny that one was blameworthy in respect of the action and then one can deny, separately, that the blameworthiness extended to a given consequence of the action. In fact the correct answer to the first question necessarily settles the second.

28 cf Elizabeth Anscombe's misleading remark in *Intention* (2nd edn, 1963), 53: 'What happens must be given by observation; but . . . my knowledge of what I do is not by observation.' A Ashworth's 'Taking the Consequences', above n 22, is an example of a work which rigorously implements the highly subjectivized account of agency which this remark may be taken to support.

29 I also believe it is incoherent: see 'On the General Part of the Criminal Law', above n 8.

30 Compare this with von Hirsch's more complex version of the proportionality principle, mentioned in n 22 above, which requires the crime to be in proportion to blameworthiness-plus-harm.

Von Hirsch's principle comes close to mine in several ways, but still seems to leave blameworthiness as a free-floating quantity. It may be said that it does not float free because it is now attached to a harm. But harms cannot be blameworthy. Only *doing* harm can be blameworthy. If von Hirsch's principle is that the sentence should be in proportion to the harmdoing adjusted for the harmdoer's blameworthiness in respect of it, then the only thing which divides us is that I refuse to reduce all wrongdoing to harmdoing. This has consequences: see n 32 below.

31 Although, as I have assumed throughout this paper, we all have various more limited duties of humanity towards each other. Extra-judicial punishers such as teachers and parents are covered by the State's stricter duty to the extent that they echo the State's claim to authority and its basis.

32 In their classic article 'Gauging Criminal Harm: A Living-Standard Analysis', *Oxford Journal of Legal Studies* 11 (1991), 1, A von Hirsch and N Jareborg argued that all harms with which the criminal law should be concerned are commensurable, allowing a transitive sentencing scale under the proportionality principle. I think they are wrong about the commensurability of harms, and about the commensurability of living-standards on which their argument was based. But even if they are right, it is a long way from the doctrine that all harms are commensurable to the doctrine that all *wrongs* are commensurable, since a wrong is an action, and even when it is an action defined in terms of the harm done, the harm done is only one constituent of the wrong. This means that von Hirsch and Jareborg still have some way to go to show that the proportionality scale is transitive. And here I am granting the generous assumption that elements (b), (c) and (d) of the blameworthiness equation do not introduce yet further incommensurabilities. On the proliferation of incommensurability in an action-centred view of morality, see J Raz, *The Morality of Freedom* (1986), 321ff.

33 See J Gardner, 'On the General Part of the Criminal Law', above n 8, for a much closer inspection.

34 How could the death penalty ever have been consistent with limiting retaliatory excess? Surely nothing could ever have exceeded death?

Wrong. That one died with one's soul cleansed by confession or recantation was one mercy. That one died after judicial proceedings in which one was able to put one's defence, and therefore treated as a responsible agent, was another. On the mistaken assumption that the widespread availability and use of the death penalty in early-modern England was a sign of *sheer* brutality in criminal justice policy, see JA Sharpe, *Judicial Punishment in England* (1990), 27ff.

35 The line of thinking in this paragraph obviously owes something to M Foucault's *Discipline and Punish: The Birth of the Prison* (1977). I hesitate to specify exactly what.

36 On which, see H Fenwick, 'Rights of Victims in the Criminal Justice System: Rhetoric or Reality?', *Criminal Law Review* [1995], 843.

37 A prescient manifesto for criminological consumerism was N Christie, 'Conflicts as Property', *British Journal of Criminology* 27 (1977), 1, which spoke of conflicts being 'stolen' by criminal law and needing to be 'returned' to the parties through procedures which were 'victim-oriented' as well as 'lay-person-oriented'.

Chapter 31

R. A. Duff

PENAL COMMUNITIES

The penal rhetoric of 'community'

THE PERVASIVE POLITICAL rhetoric of 'community' often appears in discussions of crime and punishment (see Nelken, 1985; Lacey and Zedner, 1995). The community figures as the *victim* of crime: we must build safer communities and protect them against criminal depredations. It figures as an *agent* of crime prevention (Nelken, 1985): it should involve itself in 'situational crime prevention' and help to police itself. It figures as a *locus of* punishment: more punishments should be administered 'in the community', rather than in prison (Home Office, 1988; see Dean-Myrda and Cullen, 1998). It figures as the *beneficiary of* punishment: it is protected by punishment; and 'punishments in the community' like Community Service Orders enable offenders to make reparation to the community (Home Office, 1988: paras 1.5, 2.3). It also figures, less frequently, as the offender's proper place: even if rehabilitation is no longer a central penal purpose, one supposed benefit of 'punishment in the community' is that it allows offenders to retain their place in the community – a place that imprisonment threatens to destroy (Home Office, 1988). This concern to preserve the offender's place in the community is often displaced, in the dominant rhetoric of 'law and order', by an emphasis on the need to protect 'the (law-abiding) community' against criminals: but it will be central to this paper.

We must of course treat such invocations of 'community' with proper scepticism. Too often, they amount to little more than rhetorical appeals to vague but currently resonant ideas, or to romanticized images of a pre-modern golden age of small, stable communities. Too often, 'community' actually signifies only a geographical location. Criminals are punished outside the walls of the prison; the mentally disordered are cared for – or neglected – outside the walls of psychiatric institutions: but such people are not in any substantial sense in or of the 'community' whose members pass them by with distaste or averted eyes; and what drives policies of decarceration is often not a vision of the importance of community for human well-being, but a cruder economic calculation that these are cheaper ways of appearing to pursue the aims of crime reduction or psychiatric care (see Scull, 1984; Cohen, 1985).

Nonetheless, it is worth taking the idea of community seriously in such contexts. This is one way of exposing the hollowness of the rhetoric in which strategies of decarceration are often garbed; but it can also illuminate the problem of criminal punishment.

The question I want to discuss can be crudely expressed as – 'Can criminal punishment be consistent with community?'; or – 'Can criminal punishment treat the person punished as a full member of the community?' This question is of course vacuous without a substantial account of 'community': but I will sketch a normative conception of community which gives it substantive bite and which challenges some orthodox understandings of the justification of criminal punishment; and I will discuss two possible answers to it.

There is another penological tradition in which the idea of community is invoked – but to argue that criminal punishment *cannot* be consistent with community. A central theme among 'abolitionist' theorists is that 'communities' can resolve (or dissolve) 'the problem of crime': not because criminals should be *punished* in or by 'the community', but because what penal orthodoxy conceptualizes as 'crimes' requiring punishment by the state should rather be conceptualized as 'troubles' or 'conflicts' to be resolved by the local communities in which they arise. Instead of the formal, professionalized modes of retributive justice which characterize the criminal justice system, we should look to informal, participatory modes of conflict resolution which seek reparative or restorative justice within local communities (see, for example, Christie, 1977; Hulsman, 1986). On this view, state punishment has no place within a civilized community: it destroys the bonds of community. However, I will argue that we can, in principle, reconcile punishment with community.

A normative conception of community

The first task is to provide a suitable account of community – of a political community living under the law. I will begin, however, with a simpler example, of an academic community. I will sketch an account of the idea of an academic community as that idea is used by those who insist on its importance, or bewail its passing in our contemporary university system.

Those who talk in such terms are not giving 'community' a merely geographical sense; geographical contiguity is not, we will see, a necessary condition of community. Nor are they referring simply to a certain institutional structure: the existence of the institutional structure of a university does not suffice to create an academic community, since universities should aspire, and can fail, to be academic communities. What then do they mean?

There are two related aspects to this idea of community: first, a shared commitment by the community's members to certain defining values that structure their common activities; and, second, a regard for each other as fellow members of the community, a regard which is itself structured by those defining values. Both these aspects require further explanation.

This is obviously a *normative* conception of community: the community is defined by a shared commitment to certain values – the pursuit of knowledge and understanding within the various intellectual disciplines. Those values define the community's goods – the goods of pursuing and gaining such knowledge and understanding. Two features of these goods are important.

First, whilst those goods might be understood in partly instrumental terms, in terms of ends external to the university (for instance as providing useful skills for the wider society), they cannot be *merely* instrumental goods: there must be *intrinsic* goods *internal* to the community's academic activity; it must constitute a 'practice' (see MacIntyre, 1985, ch. 14).[1]

Second, they are *communal* goods: they are seen by members of the community as 'our' goods, in that their very character as goods depends on their being shared. Of course, there are individual goods within such a community: I can enhance my own understanding (and my career and reputation) by the work I do; and I can properly claim some kind of property in 'my' ideas and 'my' publications. But such individual goods take their character as goods – as goods internal to the practice – from their place within the shared academic pursuits of the community; and they count as goods internal to the practice only if they contribute, and are understood as contributing, to the shared goods of the community – to the common advancement of knowledge and understanding in which all its members share.

The members of the community must understand their own and each other's good, as members, in terms of the values and goods which define the community. The mutual regard which community requires is a regard for each other as being committed to those values, and as finding their good in those goods. This regard involves a willingness to help each other, to co-operate, in their academic activities; a refusal to exploit each other simply as means to their own ends (see Reitan, 1996: 58–61); and a readiness to treat each other in ways that are consistent with the defining values of the community. (This raises the question of just who count as members of the community. We should simply note here that only members of the community can be bound by the demands that its values make – by, for instance, the demands of intellectual commitment and honesty.)

I hope that this conception of an academic community is a plausible ideal. My aim in sketching it is to highlight some general features of the idea of community that I want to use in relation to the law. To that end, we should note some further aspects of this conception.

First, community of this kind is clearly a matter of aspiration as much as of fact. To see ourselves as members of such a community is to see ourselves as subject to the demands of its defining values – demands that we often fail to satisfy. We may hope to avoid the grosser forms of academic wrongdoing, but must recognize our frequent deficiencies in academic virtue and commitment – in our relations to the values we are supposed to serve and to our fellow academics. Community as thus conceived is an ideal towards which we should aspire, and in whose light we must judge ourselves and our activities.

Second, even if we agree on the structural features of community (mutual regard and a commitment to shared intrinsic values), we can disagree fiercely about just what those values are, about what that regard requires, about who should count as members of the community. Some such disagreements can render community impossible: we can no longer respect each other as being committed to the same goals and values. But not all such disagreements, even if profound, destroy community.

Third, academic communities like universities have formal structures of authority and rules. Such structures should express the community's defining values and assist the pursuit of its distinctive goods; its members must be able to accept the rules as being thus justified. They must be able to see them as 'our' rules – as rules in which they are at home and which suitably order their academic activities. If they cannot accept the rules, as embodying at least a reasonable conception of the community and its goods, they must instead see them as alien impositions, which they might have to obey, but cannot accept as theirs.

Fourth, an academic community is not typically the only community in which its members live. Its goods are not the only goods they pursue, its relationships not their only significant relationships. They also live in other (sometimes overlapping) communities which have their own distinct structures of values, goods and relationships.

Fifth, academic community is *partial*, rather than total: there are limits to the interest which its members properly take in each other's lives – limits determined by the values that define the community. There are two sides to such limits. On the one hand, there are limits to the kinds of support that members can *claim* from each other. I can expect my colleagues to take a sympathetic interest in my academic activities: but I cannot demand that they take such an interest in other aspects of my life – in my financial or marital problems for instance. Such interest is not (at least if invited) forbidden, and might often be forthcoming: but it is not expected simply in virtue of our fellow membership of an academic community. On the other hand, there are limits to the interest that members can properly insist on taking in each other's lives and thoughts: the nature of the community defines a distinction between the 'public' and the 'private' – between those aspects of our lives that are of proper interest and concern to our fellows and those that are not. I am answerable to my colleagues for my philosophical thoughts and for my performance of my academic duties: they can insist on discussing my ideas and challenge me about my teaching; these are 'public' aspects of my academic life. But if they seek to inquire into my personal life, or my moral or political views (insofar as these do not directly impinge on my academic activities), I can reply that that is not their business: I need not, simply as a member of this academic community, open myself to such – as it would now be – intrusive interest. (Note, however, that the distinction between the 'public' and the 'private' is relative to the community: what counts as 'public' or 'private' depends on the character of the community; and what is 'public', or 'private', in this context might not be so in the context of other communities to which I belong.)

Sixth, geographical contiguity is not necessary for community. Whilst most academics find their closest community in a university where they work in physical proximity to their colleagues, this is not essential. The geographically dispersed character of the British Open University does not preclude its constituting an academic community; and as a philosopher I can see myself as a member not just of my own department, but also of the wider community of Scottish philosophers, or British philosophers, or philosophers. To see myself thus is to see myself as engaged, with these others, in a common practice (though we may have different conceptions of its precise point and meaning);

to see my philosophical activity as part of, as contributing to, our common pursuit; and to recognize other philosophers as fellow members of this community – a recognition manifested in how I treat them, their work and ideas.

Seventh, membership of academic communities is typically voluntary: members choose to join (though perhaps under pressure) and can choose to leave (though often at significant cost). This fact, and the fact that there is life outside the academy, may make it easier to say, with a clear conscience, that those who are unwilling to accept the community's demands can leave, or to expel those who persistently flout its demands. We should not suppose, however, that only voluntary communities can bind their members; we have commitments as members of communities which we never chose to join and cannot choose to leave. The family is one such community: we can argue about the claims that members of my family have on me, and about the conditions (if any) under which I can free myself of those claims, but we cannot plausibly say that I am bound by them only if I choose to remain in the family. Our moral commitments are also grounded in moral communities into which we are born and inducted without choice; though we may rebel against them, such rebellion must appeal to shared values which we did not choose (see Beardsmore, 1969; also Dworkin, 1986: 195–202).

It might seem a piece of typical academic conceit to suppose that this (as some would say, romanticized) sketch of academic community can illuminate the realm of criminal law and punishment. However, by drawing on the central structural features of this normative idea of community, we can provide a plausible account of a legal community – a community defined by the values embodied in its laws; and this account should quieten at least some of the anxieties aroused in liberals by talk of 'community' in this context.

Legal community

Talk of 'community' in political discourse often conjures up images of small and close-knit communities, their members bound together by an all-embracing set of values defining the good life, and taking an intimate interest in every aspect of each other's lives. Liberal critics have two objections to taking such an idea of community as a model for the life of a political society. First, it is utterly unrealistic. Second, and more important, anyone who cares for such central liberal values as autonomy, freedom and the pursuit of diverse conceptions of the good could value such communities only insofar as they are themselves both diverse and optional. Individuals should be free to choose to live their private lives in such communities: but a liberal polity should protect them against being forced to join or remain in them. We should be free to choose our friends and neighbours, and to relate to other citizens, if we wish, as strangers rather than as friends. Hence the attractions of the social contract model: for contracts define the dealings of strangers, whose relationships are regulated not by bonds of affection or common goods, but simply by the formal terms of the contract.

I sympathize with this liberal response to some of the more extreme forms of normative communitarianism: but the previous section showed that we need not understand community in this way. For communitarians can be liberals. They can argue that a political community should be structured by (versions of) the values dear to liberal hearts: it should recognize individual autonomy as a central value, a central human good; individuals, and the smaller communities which they form and in which they find their specific goods, should be allowed extensive spheres of freedom and privacy within which to pursue a variety of such specific goods; the state's proper role is not to enforce one substantive conception of the good, but to respect and foster individual autonomy and freedom, and a diversity of substantive conceptions of human good.

How does this type of communitarianism differ from the kinds of liberalism which are often contrasted with communitarianism? One recent feature of the 'communitarian–liberal' debate has been a blurring of the boundaries between these supposedly opposed schools – a realization of the various ways in which one can be a 'communitarian–liberal', or a 'liberal–communitarian' (see Kymlicka, 1989; Taylor, 1989; Mulhall and Swift, 1992: Parts II–III): but communitarian liberalism still differs significantly from some other familiar kinds of liberalism. It differs in its underlying metaphysical conception of the relation between individual and society – individuals and their goods can be identified only within, and are part-constituted by, their social context and relations (Sandel, 1982; Mulhall and Swift, 1992: 10–13, 45–55); in its insistence that political association and obligation cannot be founded on the idea of a contract between pre-social individuals, since contracts themselves presuppose a normative community within which they can be made or even understood; in its denial that the right can be given absolute priority over the good in political theory, or that the state can remain wholly neutral between different conceptions of the good – autonomy and freedom at least must be taken as basic goods to be respected and promoted (Mulhall and Swift, 1992: 118–25); and in its account of such concepts as autonomy, freedom and privacy – as goods which are socially constituted and situated,[2] and which are also collective in the sense that they are properly of value only insofar as they are shared in by all.[3]

Now members of such a community will be related to most of their fellows as (relative) strangers; community does not entail intimacy. They constitute a community insofar as they aspire – and know that they aspire – to share the community-defining values of autonomy and freedom (values that themselves underpin a plurality of specific, substantive conceptions of the good, which not all will share); and insofar as they aspire – and know that they aspire – to an appropriate mutual concern for each other in the light of those values. That mutual concern will involve a readiness to assist each other in pursuing and preserving the community's distinctive goods – though such assistance will often be organized and directly provided by the state; and, more crucially for present purposes, a respect for each other as fellow members of the community which precludes simply exploiting others for one's own ends, or treating them in ways that are inconsistent with the community's defining values. Such concern and respect must also, of course, inform the state's institutions and activities.

What role will the criminal law play in such a community? In its central aspects, those concerning obvious *mala in se*, it will deal with those kinds of wrongdoing which flout the community's basic and essential values, which thus concern not just the immediate victim (as justifying a civil suit), but the whole community.[4] Three points about the function and scope of the criminal law are important here.

First, it is misleading to say that the law *forbids* such wrongdoing. For this implies that the law offers the citizens *content-independent* reasons for refraining from such conduct – reasons grounded in the law's power or authority – which they would not otherwise have. This is indeed how traditional positivism portrays the law, and is how the law *should* be portrayed insofar as it should be understood as a set of edicts imposed by a sovereign on their subjects.[5] But it is not how we should understand the criminal law of a liberal polity. Just as the rules of an academic community should be 'our' rules as members of that community, embodying the defining values to which we are committed, the law of a political community should be 'our' law as members of that community: it should embody the values to which we are already committed, as members of the community; it should be in that sense a genuinely 'common'

law.[6] But, if it is 'our' law, its specifications of certain kinds of conduct as crimes do not offer us *new*, content-independent reasons to refrain from such conduct: for it is conduct that we should already recognize as being wrong in terms of the shared values which the law embodies. Rather, the law *declares* these kinds of conduct to constitute 'public' wrongs, which must be formally recognized and condemned by the whole community.[7]

Second, there will be strict limits on the *scope* and the *depth* of the criminal law. As to scope, there will be limits on the kinds of conduct that should fall under its rules: given the need to encourage diverse conceptions of the good and the potentially oppressive character of the criminal law, the core of the criminal law should condemn only those kinds of conduct which threaten the basic values or conditions of social life. As to depth, there will be limits on the extent to which the law's definitions of crimes, and the courts' investigations of guilt, should be concerned with agents' underlying motives or attitudes – on how far the criminal law should delve into moral character: for a liberal law must allow its citizens as extensive as possible a sphere of privacy of thought and feeling. It will be concerned with *actions* which attack or threaten protected values or interests; and, whilst 'action' here involves *more* than mere bodily movements with their circumstances and consequences (since it includes the intentions and attitudes manifested in the agent's conduct), it involves *less* than the agent's entire moral character.[8]

Third, the law will not just declare certain kinds of conduct to constitute public wrongs. It will also provide for some response to such conduct: a community would not take crimes seriously, as public wrongs, if it ignored their commission. Furthermore, there are good reasons why that response should be a formal response, through something like a system of criminal trials: this protects actual or suspected offenders against what might otherwise be the excessive or over-hasty informal responses of other citizens,[9] and makes clear that such wrongdoing is the concern of the whole community – a concern expressed through courts which speak for the community. Now, such a response will properly consist, initially, in calling suspected wrongdoers to answer for their alleged wrongdoing to the community, through its courts; and in condemning them, by a formal conviction, if the charge is proved against them (see Duff, 1986: ch. 4). But our systems of criminal justice go further than this: they provide for punishments, involving 'hard treatment' (Feinberg, 1970), to be imposed on convicted offenders. We must, therefore, ask, at last, how criminal punishment could be consistent with such a community.

Deterrence and community

How can we inflict penal hard treatment on offenders, while still treating and respecting them as a member of the liberal community whose laws they have broken, but to whom we still owe respect and concern as fellow citizens? We can see the force of this question by considering two extreme examples.

Suppose, first, that the *sole* purpose of punishment was to incapacitate offenders from committing further crimes. Now, if responsible agents were liable to such punishment only if and when they had culpably broken the law, they would be treated as fellow citizens until that point: they would be left free, as a liberal society which values autonomy must leave its citizens free, to decide for themselves whether to obey the law. But, once they broke the law, they would be treated not as members of the community, but as dangerous enemies against whom 'we' – the law-abiding – must protect ourselves by caging or otherwise incapacitating them. (It might be said that offenders *forfeit* their standing as members of the community (see Morris, 1991): but my question is whether we can justify punishment *without* forfeiture.)

Second, suppose that the *sole* purpose of punishment was rational deterrence: to provide potential offenders with prudential reason to obey the law. Now, such a penal system could be appropriate for a society (if one could be imagined) of rational egoists, who all realize that they will benefit from a social contract whose terms are thus enforced: the law specifies the penalty clauses in the contract; the sole point of such penalties is to give agents prudential reason to obey the terms of the contract. But it cannot be appropriate to a liberal political community. For the law of that community, as its 'common' law, must address its members in terms of the values which it embodies – values to which they should, as members of the community, already be committed: it portrays criminal conduct as wrongful in terms of those values; and the reasons which citizens have to refrain from such conduct, the reasons to which the law refers and on which it depends, are precisely the moral reasons which make such conduct wrong. A purely deterrent law, however, addresses those whom it seeks to deter, not in terms of the communal goods and values which it aims to protect, but simply in the brute language of self-interest. It thus addresses them, not as members of the normative community of citizens, but as threatening outsiders against whom the community must protect itself; it implicitly *excludes* them from membership of the citizen community, by no longer addressing them in terms of that community's values.[10]

However, this is not yet to say that deterrence could have *no* proper role in a liberal polity. There are certainly some kinds of community within which deterrence has no place – in which attempts to modify others' conduct by deterrent threats would be inconsistent with the normative character of the community: consider, for instance, someone who bullies their academic colleagues by threats into accepting the policies they favour, or who uses deterrent threats to try to modify a friend's or a spouse's behaviour. But this does not show that a liberal polity cannot have a system of punishment whose function is *partly* deterrent.

Such a community's law must indeed address its members in terms of the shared values which it embodies: it declares that certain kinds of conduct are public wrongs; in convicting offenders it communicates to them (and to others) the censure that their crimes deserve. Now, penal hard treatment can also communicate censure; it can give material form to the censure which a conviction directly expresses. The first move for someone who wants to justify punishment in partly deterrent terms is thus to insist that its function is not *purely* deterrent: it must also express the censure that criminals deserve – thus reminding criminals and others of the wrongdoing which justifies their punishment. But, if we ask why that censure should be communicated through penal hard treatment, rather than simply through a formal conviction, an obvious answer is that such hard treatment adds to the law's initial moral appeal a prudential, deterrent incentive for obedience.[11]

Ideally, in a community of citizens more virtuous than ourselves, that moral appeal would suffice by itself: citizens would generally refrain from crime because they saw it to be wrong; and any who did occasionally succumb to criminal temptation would need no more than a formal censure to remind them of the error of their ways. But, in a society more like our own, whose members are not so unanimously or wholeheartedly committed to its central values, such methods of purely moral persuasion will be intolerably ineffective: not because they would not prevent *all* crime – a liberal society must accept a certain level of crime as the price of freedom; but because they would not prevent *enough* crime to preserve the social structures within which autonomy and freedom can be protected, and individuals can pursue their own goods.

Surely, then, it is consistent with – indeed required by – the values of such a community to use penal hard treatment as a deterrent for those who would not otherwise obey the law, if certain conditions are satisfied. So long as punishment is predicated on proved guilt; is not disproportionate to the seriousness of the crime punished; and still communicates the censure which the wrongdoer deserves: it surely does address those who are punished, and those who are threatened with punishment (who would not obey the law without that deterrent threat), as members of the political community – albeit as members whose commitment to the community's values is deficient. They share in the protection that an effective criminal law provides: if they are not willing to guide their own conduct by the values which the law embodies and protects, it is legitimate to try to persuade them to behave as they should by offering them prudential reasons which will motivate them.

This account of criminal punishment is not, I think, fully consistent with the ideal of a liberal political community. Insofar as the law addresses those whom it threatens with punishment, not just in the appropriate language of the shared values in which it is grounded, but in the coercive language of deterrence; insofar, furthermore, as it does not just remind them of prudential reasons which they already have to obey the law, but rather *creates* new and coercive reasons for them by its threat of sanctions: it ceases to address them as members of the normative community (and note how easy it is to talk of what 'we' must do to deter 'them' from breaking the law). A more plausible justification for this account is that it marks a realistic recognition of the limits of community – of the extent to which our own societies fall short of constituting genuine normative communities whose members all share in their defining values. It is the best that we can hope to do (and the least that we must do) in societies in which the normative bonds of community are insufficient to keep the peace that is required to make a tolerable social life, and the development of community, possible: societies in which some people do not see themselves as members of such a normative political community at all, whilst others are only tenuously or inconstantly committed to its values.

Now, our existing political societies do indeed fall very far short of constituting political communities of the kind I have sketched – though that falling short threatens to undermine *any* plausible justification of criminal punishment in such societies, by undermining the essential preconditions of just punishment (see my 1998a, 1998b). But I want now to focus on a different argument in favour of this kind of account, which insists that punishment as thus conceived is actually *more* consistent with the values of liberal community than is the alternative account which I have argued for elsewhere, since it is *more* respectful of the autonomy and privacy of individual citizens.

Penitential punishment and community

On that alternative account, penal hard treatment should not simply add a new, deterrent reason for obedience to the moral reasons by which citizens should ideally be moved: rather, it should still be part of a process of *moral communication* with the offender. Its aim should ideally be to bring offenders to understand and repent the wrong they have done: it tries to direct their attention on to their crime, to bring them to understand that crime's character as a wrong, and to persuade them to accept as deserved the censure that punishment communicates – an acceptance which must involve repentance. Punishment also provides a vehicle through which they can strengthen or deepen that repentant understanding of their wrongdoing and express it to others: a vehicle both for the attempt at self-correction and self-reform that sincere repentance involves, and for the communication to others (those they have wronged, their fellow citizens) of that repentance. Finally, by undergoing such penitential punishment, wrongdoers can reconcile themselves with their

fellow citizens, thus reinforcing their membership of the community from which their wrongdoing threatened to exclude them. Punishment is, in other words, a secular species of (enforced) penance. This account is retributivist, in that punishment is focused on and justified by the crime for which the offender is punished, as an appropriate response to that crime: but, unlike classical versions of retributivism, it also gives punishment the forward-looking goal of inducing repentance. This future-oriented purpose, however, is not to be understood in consequentialist terms, since the relationship between punishment and its proper goal is not – as it is for a consequentialist – instrumental, but internal: it is the nature of the goal (the repentant recognition of past wrongdoing) that makes punishment (the communication of censure for that wrongdoing) the appropriate way of achieving it (see my 1986: chs 9–10, 1996b).

Now there are plenty of objections to this even as an ideal account of what punishment ought to be (it is clearly not an account of punishment as it is actually imposed or suffered in our existing penal systems): I will focus on one objection, which reflects a liberal concern for individual privacy and freedom, and aims to make a system of deterrent punishment of the kind sketched above look more attractive to liberal eyes.

Punishment as penance, as an attempt to persuade offenders to repent their wrongdoing, seems to presuppose, or try to create, a rather *intimate* community between the punished and the punisher (the idea of penance, after all, seems most at home in the context of a close-knit, spiritually inquisitive religious community). It attempts to reach, to break through to, 'the inner citadels of his soul' (Lucas, 1968/9: 215); it intrudes coercively into the deepest aspects of their moral character. Such an insistent concern for a wrongdoer's moral condition might be appropriate between close friends, or within a family or religious community. It is surely not, however, a proper task for the penal institutions of a liberal state: even those 'perfectionists' who think that the state has *some* proper interest in 'making men moral' (see George, 1993) could argue that it should not use criminal punishment as a direct means to this end (Murphy, 1985; George, 1993: 42–7, 75–6). The law declares certain kinds of conduct to constitute public wrongs; through conviction and punishment it seeks to communicate the censure that such wrongs deserve to those who commit them: it thus offers citizens moral reasons for refraining from crime, in the *hope* that they will heed and be moved by those reasons; and it *invites* offenders to attend to the wrongfulness of what they have done. But penitential punishment goes further, seeking to *invade* the offender's conscience and moral character; and this is something that a state concerned to respect the privacy and autonomy of its citizens should not do, since it is something that the offender's fellow citizens, simply as fellow citizens, should not do. Though, as fellow citizens of the political community, they are not *mere* strangers, they are not their friends or family; they should maintain a suitable distance, unless the offenders themselves choose to enter into a more intimate relationship.

A deterrent system of punishment of the kind sketched above, by contrast, maintains such a respectful moral distance from offenders. It gives them the *option* to treat their punishment as a penance, but leaves them free to regard it simply as a prudential deterrent, and the laws under which they are punished simply as external demands on their conduct; it does not insist on a coercive inquiry into their moral character. It thus respects the privacy of offenders' moral personality, and their autonomy as agents who must be left to determine their own moral attitude to the law and its demands, as penitential punishment does not.

Now, penitential punishments are certainly demanding, and may be seen as intrusive by those who resent them, in a way that merely deterrent punishments are not. If I am caught for

drunken driving, I accept that I will be fined and disqualified: my punishment might be seriously inconvenient, and gives me good prudential reason to obey the law. But suppose instead that the court insists on engaging in moral discussion of the wrongfulness of my conduct, on challenging me to recognize it; and that my punishment, instead of a fine and disqualification, involves attending meetings with victims of drunken driving, visiting accident units dealing with such victims and watching graphic films of the effects of car crashes. This might not be more burdensome than a fine and disqualification, in that it need not involve greater costs to me in money, time or energy: but it might be more disturbing, and less welcome, as involving a demanding moral challenge; I might prefer to accept a fine and disqualification, which do not in the same – as I see it, intrusive – way strike at my conscience and invade my moral being. So, too, other, more serious, offenders might prefer the harsher deterrent punishments which the sophisticated deterrent account I sketched above would impose, to the kinds of punishment that seek to induce a repentant confrontation with the character and implications of their wrongdoing.

Such concerns about the intrusive character of penitential punishments might not be allayed by a reminder of the limits that a liberal society must place on the scope and depth of the criminal law (see at note 8 above): even if the law and its penal institutions were concerned only with actions which attacked or threatened important values or interests, and with the attitudes directly manifested in such actions, the coercive interest that it took in such actions and attitudes would still be seen as improperly intrusive. Nor might such concerns be allayed by a reminder that, whilst penitential punishments are indeed coercive, imposed on offenders regardless of their will, they must not aim to coerce the offenders' understanding or moral attitudes: that, whilst they are forced to *hear* the message which their punishment aims to communicate to them, and to undergo a penal process which is intended to persuade them to accept it, they are not forced to listen to the message or to be persuaded by it – they are left free to reject it, or to refuse to attend to it in the repentant spirit which it seeks to induce. For, apart from the danger that what are officially intended as exercises in forceful moral persuasion will in fact constitute oppressive attempts to coerce offenders into moral submission, liberal critics might still insist that moral beliefs and attitudes, like all matters of conscience, are not the proper concern of the criminal law – that they belong in the private sphere of individual freedom which the state must respect.

But what justifies this conception of the 'private'? The 'private' is not a metaphysical *given* (see page 511 above): what counts as 'public' or 'private' depends on the nature of the community in which the distinction is drawn. Those who object that penitential punishments invade the 'private' realm of conscience thus cannot ground the objection on some a priori conception of the 'private' according to which such matters *must* count as private: they must rather claim that a liberal polity *should* define such matters as private. But why should it?

Freedom of conscience, of thought and belief, of speech are indeed crucial values for a liberal community: my conscience, thoughts and beliefs are 'private' in the context of my dealings with my fellow citizens unless and until I choose to make them public by publishing them; and, even when published in speech, they generally remain 'private' as far as the law is concerned. Even here, of course, there are familiar (if controversial) limits to privacy: some kinds of speech, some kinds of expression of attitude and belief, properly concern the law. However, a familiar way to express the liberal concern about the implications of penitential punishment is to say that the criminal law should generally be concerned only with (external) conduct, not with (inner) attitude; and to cite the 'Harm Principle' – that the criminal law should be

concerned only with conduct which harms protected interests (see Feinberg, 1984). On a standard understanding of this principle, 'harms' of the kind that concern the criminal law are always identifiable independently of the human actions which might cause them (thus the harm which concerns the homicide laws is that of death). The law's interest in prohibiting and preventing harmful conduct is therefore an interest in conduct qua causing, or liable to cause, harm as thus understood – not in whatever intentions or attitudes might lie behind such conduct: it needs to refer to agents' intentions or attitudes only in order to determine whether they can properly be held responsible for their harmful or dangerous conduct.

What the law owes its citizens, as potential victims of crime, is that it should seek to prevent harmful or dangerous conduct. What it owes its citizens, as potential victims of its own coercive attention, is that it should pursue those harm-preventive aims by means which respect their standing as autonomous, responsible agents. Such aims are achieved by a system of deterrent punishments of the kind sketched above. Now, penitential punishments can protect citizens as potential victims against future crime: an offender who is brought to repentance is less likely to reoffend. But this method of pursuing the aim of preventing future crimes is inconsistent with respect for the offender's privacy and autonomy. Penitential punishment can also be of moral benefit to offenders: it is for their good, as members of the community, that they recognize and repent the wrongs they have done, and reconcile themselves to their fellow citizens. But, even if the state can have *some* proper concern for its citizens' moral good, it should not pursue that concern through the coercive, intrusive methods of criminal punishment.

This argument founders, however, on its inadequate conception of harm (see my 1996a: 363–74). The harm suffered by the victims of central kinds of *mala in se* crimes (such as murder, rape, theft, violent assault) consists not just in the physically, materially or psychologically damaging *effects* of such crimes, but in the fact that they are victims of an *attack* on their legitimate interests – on their selves; the harmfulness, and wrongfulness, of such attacks lie not just in their effects, but in the malicious, contemptuous or disrespectful intentions and attitudes which they manifest. The agents' intentions and practical attitudes (the attitudes directly manifest in their conduct) are thus relevant not merely as conditions of liability – conditions for holding them liable for conduct which causes or threatens to cause harm: they are an important aspect of the wrongfulness of the conduct – of what makes such conduct a proper concern of the criminal law.[12] That is why I said earlier that the criminal law is properly concerned with *actions* – 'action' being understood to include the intentions and attitudes which it directly actualizes.

What the law therefore owes the citizens, as potential victims of crime, is to protect them against wrongful actions of various kinds: it is concerned not merely with 'conduct' externally conceived in terms of its actual or likely consequences, but with actions as thus more richly conceived. Its response to crimes must also be a response to them as wrongs of this kind: not merely as extrinsically harmful conduct, but as wrongful actions. It owes such a response both to the victims, as a response which recognizes the character of the harm they have suffered; and to the offenders, as a response focused on that about their conduct which made it and them a proper object of the law's attention. Similarly, what the offenders owe their victims, and their fellow citizens, is an apology which recognizes the wrong they have done. Compensation can help to make up for the material harm caused: but only apology, a public expression of repentance, can begin to make up for the moral harm done.[13]

Offenders, therefore, cannot claim that the intentions and attitudes manifested in their criminal action are 'private' – that they are no business of the criminal law. The rapist's action manifests a contemptuous disregard for their victim's sexual integrity – a disregard viciously actualized in their attack on their victim; drunken drivers actualize in their conduct a culpable disregard for the safety of other road users. These are the kinds of (practical, actualized) attitude on which penitential punishment focuses, as being culpably harmful to the offenders' fellow citizens: they are answerable for them to their fellows, through the courts; they are censured for them by their conviction; and their punishment aims to bring them to recognize and repent their wrongfulness. What justifies this is not the claim that the state can properly take, through the criminal law, a coercive interest in its citizens' general moral character: but the claim that it can properly hold them answerable for, and demand that they themselves attend to, those attitudes which, as manifested in their criminal conduct, flout the central values of the legal community. Those attitudes, as thus actualized, cannot be said to belong in the 'private' realm of individual thought or conscience in which the law has no proper interest.

I conclude, therefore, that a system of communicative, would-be penitential punishment does not improperly seek to invade the autonomy or privacy of the offender; and that it is, as even a sophisticated system of deterrent punishment is not, consistent with and expressive of a proper regard for the offender as a member – albeit perhaps a recalcitrant or unwilling member – of a liberal political community.

I have sketched, with the broadest of broad brush strokes, a conception of a liberal political community within which criminal punishment would serve a communicative and penitential purpose. Central features of this account have been dogmatically asserted, rather than being given the extensive justification that they require; much more work is needed to spell out its implications for penal practice – for the modes and levels of punishment that it would sanction.[14] But I hope I have done enough to show how punishment as thus conceived and justified could be consistent with (could, indeed, express) the defining values of a liberal political community.

I should end, however, by emphasizing that this account is *not* offered as a description or justification of our existing penal systems. It is, rather, an *ideal* account of what a system of criminal punishment should *aspire* to be. Furthermore, any pursuit of that ideal requires attention not only to the character of punishment itself, as it is administered within the penal system, but also to the *preconditions* of just punishment, in particular to those concerning the existence of the kind of political community within which criminal punishment could have the meaning and justification given to it here (see page 517 above): does there exist a political community, of which all those supposedly bound by the law are full members, against which they do wrong in breaking the law, to which they are answerable through the courts for their crimes, and to which their punishment could reconcile them? However, whether these preconditions are satisfied, and what should follow from a recognition that they are not satisfied, are topics for another occasion.

Acknowledgements

Grateful thanks for helpful comments are due to audiences at Aberdeen and Stirling; to the referees for *Punishment & Society*; and especially to Sandra Marshall.

Notes

1 *Punishment and Society* 27 (1999)

1 Practices can of course, as MacIntyre points out, be immoral and vicious – in which case the 'goods' internal to them should not be seen as genuine goods: but I assume here that the practices of academic communities and of political communities *can* be moral.

2 On autonomy, see especially Raz, 1986: 369–429 (usefully discussed in Mulhall and Swift, 1992: 249–88); George 1993: ch. 6. On privacy see Sypnowich, forthcoming.

3 See Taylor, 1989; also Dworkin, 1986: 195–216; Dworkin, 1989. I cannot comment here on the differences between the various versions of 'liberal communitarianism'.

4 See Marshall and Duff, 1998; and my 1996b: 71–7. I cannot deal here with the role of *mala prohibita* in the criminal law.

5 See Cotterrell, 1995: ch. 11, on the *imperium* model of law.

6 On this idea of the 'common' law see Postema, 1986: chs 1–2; my 1998a; also Cotterrell, 1995: ch. 11 on the 'community' model of law.

7 The claims in this paragraph are in at least two respects seriously oversimplified. First, the law can provide even those who are fully committed to the values it embodies with authoritative guidance, when the precise meaning or implications of those values are controversial or unclear. Second, the law also provides those not thus committed to the values it embodies with more obviously content-independent reasons for obedience, consisting in the prospect of conviction and punishment; see following section.

8 For a more detailed explanation of these elliptical remarks, see my 1996a: chs 7, 9–11.

9 See Gardner, 1998 on the 'displacement function' of the criminal law.

10 This is a communitarian version of the Kantian objection that a purely deterrent system of punishment fails to treat those whom it threatens as autonomous agents: see my 1986: 178–86.

11 See, for example, Feinberg, 1970; von Hirsch, 1985: ch. 5. I cannot discuss here von Hirsch's later, subtler account of penal hard treatment as a 'prudential supplement': von Hirsch, 1993: ch. 2; see my 1999; von Hirsch, 1999.

12 Similarly, the wrongfulness of reckless conduct which endangers but does not attack the interests of others consists not just in the fact that the agent knowingly creates a risk, but in the attitude of practical indifference which their conduct manifests: see my 1990: ch. 7.

13 The relationship between apology and repentance, and the possible moral significance even of apologies which are not sincere expressions of

repentance, clearly requires more discussion than I can offer here: some of the material for that discussion can be found in Murphy, 1997.

14 It is worth emphasizing, however, that such an account would give a much reduced role to imprisonment (which would be reserved only for the most serious crimes, crimes that make it morally impossible for the offenders to live in a normal community with their fellow citizens), and to fines (the current sentence of choice for very many offences in Britain); and a much larger role to sentences such as Community Service Orders and probation, as well as more 'creative' sentences which aim to confront offenders with the nature and implications of their crime: see further my 1996b: 63–6.

References

Beardsmore, R.W. (1969) Moral reasoning. London: Routledge.

Christie, N. (1977) 'Conflicts as property', British Journal of Criminology 17: 1–15.

Cohen, S. (1985) Visions of social control. Cambridge: Polity Press.

Cotterrell, R. (1995) Law's community. Oxford: Clarendon Press.

Dean-Myrda, M.C. and Cullen, F.T. (1998) 'The panacea pendulum: an account of community as a response to crime', in J. Petersilia (ed.) Community corrections, pp. 3–18. New York: Oxford University Press.

Duff, R.A. (1986) Trials and punishments. Cambridge: Cambridge University Press.

Duff, R.A. (1990) Intention, agency and criminal liability. Oxford: Blackwell.

Duff, R.A. (1996a) Criminal attempts. Oxford: Clarendon Press.

Duff, R.A. (1996b) 'Penal communications', Crime and Justice 20: 1–97.

Duff, R.A. (1998a) 'Law, language and community: some preconditions of criminal liability', Oxford Journal of Legal Studies 18: 189–206.

Duff, R.A. (1998b) 'Inclusion and exclusion: citizens, subjects and outlaws', Current Legal Problems 51: 241–66.

Duff, R.A. (1999) 'Punishment, communication and community', in M. Matravers (ed.) Punishment and political theory, pp. 48–68. Oxford: Hart Publishing.

Dworkin, R. (1986) Law's empire. London: Fontana.

Dworkin, R. (1989) 'Liberal community', California Law Review 77: 479–504.

Feinberg, J. (1970) 'The expressive function of punishment', in J. Feinberg Doing and deserving, pp. 95–118. Princeton, NJ: Princeton University Press.

Feinberg, J. (1984) Harm to others. New York: Oxford University Press.

Gardner, J. (1998) 'Crime: in proportion and in perspective', in A.J. Ashworth and M. Wasik (eds) Fundamentals of sentencing theory, pp. 31–52. Oxford: Clarendon Press.

George, R.P. (1993) Making men moral. Oxford: Clarendon Press.

Home Office (1988) Punishment, custody and the community (Cmnd. 424). London: HMSO.

Hulsman, L. (1986) 'Critical criminology and the concept of crime', Contemporary crises 10: 63–80.

Kymlicka, W. (1989) Liberalism, community and culture. Oxford: Clarendon Press.

Lacey, N. and Zedner, L. (1995) 'Discourses of community in criminal justice', Journal of Law and Society 22: 301–25.

Lucas, J.R. (1968/9) 'Or else', Proceedings of the Aristotelian Society 69: 207–22.

MacIntyre, A. (1985) After virtue, 2nd edn, London: Duckworth.

Marshall, S.E. and Duff, R.A. (1998) 'Criminalization and sharing wrongs', Canadian Journal of Law and Jurisprudence 11: 7–22.

Morris, C.W. (1991) 'Punishment and loss of moral standing', Canadian Journal of Philosophy 21: 53–79.

Mulhall, S. and Swift, A. (1992) Liberals and communitarians. Oxford: Blackwell.

Murphy, J.G. (1985) 'Retributivism, moral education, and the liberal state', Criminal Justice Ethics 4: 3–11.

Murphy, J.G. (1997) 'Repentance, punishment, and mercy', in A. Etzioni and D.E. Carney (eds) Repentance: A comparative perspective, pp. 143–70. Totowa, NJ: Rowman & Littlefield.

Nelken, D. (1985) 'Community involvement in crime control', Current Legal Problems 38: 239–67.

Postema, G.J. (1986) Bentham and the common law tradition. Oxford: Clarendon Press.

Raz, J. (1986) The morality of freedom. Oxford: Clarendon Press.

Reitan, E. (1996) 'Punishment and community: the reintegrative theory of punishment', Canadian Journal of Philosophy 26: 57–81.

Sandel, M. (1982) *Liberalism and the limits of justice.* Cambridge: Cambridge University Press.

Scull, A. (1984) *Decarceration*, 2nd edn, Cambridge: Polity Press.

Sypnowich, C. (forthcoming) 'The civility of law: between public and private', in M.P. D'Entreves and U. Vogel (eds) *Public and private: legal, political and philosophical perspectives.* London: Routledge.

Taylor, C. (1989) 'Cross-purposes: the liberal-communitarian debate', in N.L. Rosenblum (ed.) *Liberalism and the moral life*, pp. 159–82. Cambridge, MA: Harvard University Press.

von Hirsch, A. (1985) *Past or future crimes.* Manchester: Manchester University Press.

von Hirsch, A. (1993) *Censure and sanctions.* Oxford: Clarendon Press.

von Hirsch, A. (1999) 'Punishment, penance and the state', in M. Matravers (ed.) *Punishment and political theory*, pp. 69–83. Oxford: Hart Publishing.

X. TORT THEORY: CORRECTIVE JUSTICE

Introduction

A S A BRANCH of private law, tort law is fundamentally different from either constitutional law or criminal law, which are branches of public law. Private law governs the legal relationships of private individuals, and tort law in particular enables private parties to seek redress as plaintiffs against defendant parties who have, broadly speaking, harmed them in certain ways. A plaintiff can invoke any number of distinct torts in seeking this redress, depending upon the nature of the defendant's conduct, and that redress almost always takes the form of compensatory damages—that is, money. Lawsuits for negligence and battery, for example, are quite different from each other in that the former is predicated on harm that is carelessly caused while the latter is predicated on harm that is intentionally caused, yet they each serve as a plaintiff's recourse for shifting harm back to the party who caused it through monetary remuneration. It is in this sense that the metaphor of "making whole" a wrongfully harmed plaintiff characterizes tort law's fundamental aim. And it is this picture, in turn, that gives credence to the widespread view among legal philosophers that tort law aspires to effect *corrective justice*, in contrast to *distributive* or *retributive justice*: tort law is a mechanism available to private individuals for "correcting" losses that they have been wrongfully dealt.

The nature of tort law has been the subject of sophisticated treatment by philosophers of tort law for a number of years now, yet their attention was initially piqued by the claims of those who subscribed to the economic analysis of law. In the early 1970s, with Guido Calabresi and Richard Posner leading the way, law and economics scholars maintained that tort law could best be understood through the lens of efficiency.[1] On this view, tort law in fact largely achieved efficient outcomes by holding liable the party who best could absorb the liability—what Calebresi termed the "cheapest cost-avoider" – and this was, further, all to the good. The economic model of tort law was and certainly remains very influential in the wider legal academy, especially in the United States where the law and economics movement has always been most dominant, but it has been mostly rejected by legal philosophers. And that is due in large part to Jules Coleman's withering early attack on it and concomitant defense of a corrective justice model of tort law.[2] Focusing on the signature tort of negligence, Coleman argued convincingly that the economic model failed to capture the importance of causation to negligence, for after all the cheapest cost-avoider might not be the one who caused the compensable injury. It is an uncontroversial commitment of tort law, however, that only the party who caused some injury can be liable to the plaintiff for the injury—tort law exhibits what Coleman called a "bi-lateral" structure. That the economic model could not explain this basic fact of tort law, Coleman argued, thwarted the economic account's descriptive aspirations. The normative arm of law and economics—holding that whatever the actual doctrine of tort law actually *is*, tort law *ought* to promote economic efficiency—has also not gained much credibility among legal philosophers, who have exposed its implicit but undefended crude and unsophisticated consequentialism.

Most philosophers of tort law, following Coleman, cleave to a corrective justice account of tort law, holding that it best satisfies the two desiderata of descriptive accuracy and normative appeal. But what is corrective justice and what is the source of its normative appeal? These are the questions that animate Tony Honoré's and Stephen Perry's essays.

Following H. L. A. Hart, who warned against a reductive account of the institution of punishment (see the introduction to Section IX), Honoré isolates several distinct questions about the law of torts that warrant separate treatment. The single issue that he devotes the most attention to concerns the justification of a plaintiff's compensatory claim against a defendant. Honoré maintains that corrective justice plays a foundational role in the justification of tort claims, to be sure, but he argues that it is only part of the story. For one needs an account "of the responsibility of one who causes another harm"[3] if one is to emphasize, as corrective justice theories of torts do, righting a defendant's wrong. While tort law is founded upon an ideal of corrective justice, then, corrective justice is in turn supported by a conception of responsibility that Honoré calls "outcome-responsibility". But if one digs yet deeper, he argues, one discovers that "the justification for imposing outcome-responsibility on those who cause harm to others rests not on corrective but on distributive justice."[4] Outcome-responsibility rests on distributive justice, claims Honoré, because it holds people responsible for, and thus distributes to them, the benefits but (most importantly in the context of tort law) also the burdens caused by their conduct. And it follows from this that corrective justice is in at least one sense dependent upon distributive justice, for "to justify corrective justice involves appealing at a certain stage to the just *distribution of risk* in a society."[5] Still, Honoré admits, there is a sense in which corrective justice does not depend upon distributive justice, for after all, "[t]he filthy rich can appeal to corrective justice if their holdings are filched by the grinding poor."[6] Corrective justice, in his view, does not turn a blind eye to otherwise tortious harms just because they have a positive distributive effect.

Honoré's discussion suggests that corrective and distributive justice bear a complex relationship to one another, and it is precisely that relationship that is the focus of Perry's scrutiny. Whereas some hold that it cannot be just to "correct" people's holdings so that they are less rather than more distributively just, and who would therefore employ tort law to achieve distributive justice (or at least not to undermine it), Perry demurs, rejecting the "distributive priority" view according to which corrective justice depends upon distributive justice. Perry undertakes searching reviews of theories of corrective and distributive justice, and he argues that "correct-ive justice is a general moral principle that is concerned, not with maintaining a just distribution, but rather with repairing harm."[7] In situating corrective justice relative to other domains of justice, then, Perry helps to explicate the nature of corrective justice and indeed of the law of torts.

Running throughout Honoré's and Perry's respective discussions is the recognition that tort law is largely distinguished by its focus on correcting wrongfully imposed harms and the liability regime that such a focus seems to entail. Equally important and distinctive, though, is the tortfeasor's role in that liability regime. Honoré and Perry each highlight, albeit in different ways, the conception of personal responsibility that tort law expresses, and which accounts for the role of the tortfeasor in tort law. (Indeed, taking seriously the tortfeasor, Honoré's ecumenical theory conditions a defendant's requirement to pay compensation on compliance with retributive justice, for otherwise compensation that a defendant would be liable to pay to a plaintiff would be "disproportionate to what is often a minor fault".)[8] It is especially important to draw out tort law's embrace of personal responsibility and to underscore the value of having such an institution in light of the occasional but serious calls for leaving tort law behind and adopting a no-fault state compensation scheme in its place. It is arguable, at least, that the ideal of personal responsibility at the heart of tort law would be lost if the law of torts were simply jettisoned in favor of a regulatory solution. And yet even if tort law is the only vehicle that expresses the valuable form of personal responsibility that it does express, perhaps it is, as Honoré says, a matter of "political judgment"[9] whether that value is worth the cost.

Tort theory is among the most active and dynamic branches of philosophical inquiry into legal doctrine. The questions touched upon in this section constitute only a small fraction of those that tort theory explores. Honoré's and Perry's respective investigations nevertheless illuminate the broad concerns about the nature and limits of agency, responsibility, and liability, to which corrective justice theories of tort law attempt to respond and, more broadly, that animate tort theory in all of its diverse manifestations.

Notes

1 See Guido Calabresi, *The Cost of Accidents*, New Haven, CT: Yale University Press, 1970, and Richard Posner, "A Theory of Negligence", *Journal of Legal Studies* 1, 1972, 29–96.

2 See Jules Coleman, *Risks and Wrongs*, New York: Cambridge University Press, 1992, and *The Practice of Principle*, New York: Oxford University Press, 2001.

3 Tony Honoré, "The Morality of Tort Law – Questions and Answers", p. 533.

4 Ibid., p. 535.

5 Ibid., p. 535.

6 Ibid., p. 535.

7 Stephen R. Perry, 'On the Relationship Between Corrective and Distributive Justice', p. 546.

8   Honoré, 'Tort Law', p. 539.
9   Ibid., p. 542.

Further reading

Guido Calabresi, *The Cost of Accidents*, New Haven, CT: Yale University Press, 1970.

Jules Coleman, *Risks and Wrongs*, New York: Cambridge University Press, 1992.

Jules Coleman, *The Practice of Principle*, New York: Oxford University Press, 2001.

John Oberdiek, "Philosophical Issues in Tort Law", *Philosophy Compass* 3, 2008.

Stephen Perry, "The Moral Foundations of Tort Law", *Iowa Law Review* 77, 1992, 449–514.

Stephen Perry, "Responsibility for Outcomes, Risk, and the Law of Torts", in Gerald Postema (ed.) *Philosophy and the Law of Torts*, New York: Cambridge University Press, 2001, pp. 72–130.

Richard Posner, "A Theory of Negligence", *Journal of Legal Studies* 1, 1972, 29–96.

Arthur Ripstein and Benjamin C. Zipursky, "Corrective Justice in an Age of Mass Torts", in Gerald Postema (ed.) *Philosophy and the Law of Torts*, New York: Cambridge University Press, 2001, pp. 214–49.

Christopher Schroeder, "Causation, Compensation, and Moral Responsibility", in David Owen (ed.) *Philosophical Foundations of Tort Law*, New York: Oxford University Press, 1995, pp. 347–62.

Hanoch Sheinman, "Tort Law and Corrective Justice", *Law and Philosophy* 22, 2003, 21–73.

Jeremy Waldron, "Moments of Carelessness and Massive Loss", in David Owen (ed.) *Philosophical Foundations of Tort Law*, New York: Oxford University Press, 1995, pp. 387–408.

Ernest Weinrib, *The Idea of Private Law*, Cambridge, MA: Harvard University Press, 1995.

Benjamin C. Zipursky, "Civil Recourse, Not Corrective Justice", *Georgetown Law Journal* 91, 2003, 695–756.

Questions

1. What are the essential features of corrective justice?
2. How is the form of distributive justice that Honoré believes underlies corrective justice similar to and different from the form of distributive justice that Perry denies is "prior" to corrective justice?
3. Does corrective justice depend upon distributive justice?
4. How, if at all, does tort law, on a corrective justice account, express concern for personal responsibility?

Chapter 32

A. M. Honoré

THE MORALITY OF TORT LAW
Questions and answers[1]

In relation to any social institution, after stating what general aim or value its maintenance fosters, we should inquire whether there are any, and if so what, principles limiting the unqualified pursuit of this aim or value.[2]

H. L. A. Hart

1. The questions posed

HART WAS WRITING about punishment. In his view, those who are puzzled about the justification of punishment should begin by disentangling a number of questions about the criminal process. It is a mistake to search for a single justification (deterrence or retribution) for the system as a whole. Moreover, once we see that a single aim will not justify every aspect of the system, we should not replace the single aim by a compound aim. We should not, for example, say that the justification of punishment is a mixture of deterrence, retribution, reform and denunciation. At least six questions about punishment need to be answered separately: (1) Why are certain kinds of conduct forbidden by law on pain of punishment? (2) What is the definition of punishment? (3) What general aims justify us in having a system of criminal law? (4) Who may properly be punished? (5) Subject to what mental and other conditions may a person be punished? and (6) How much punishment are we justified in inflicting? The answers to questions (4) to (6), which concern

the "distribution" of punishment, limit the extent to which it is proper to pursue the general aims that emerge in answer to (3).

Hart's remark was meant to apply to institutions other than criminal law, and it can certainly be applied to tort law. The theory of tort law is now the subject of a sophisticated debate, especially in North America.[3] But has enough groundwork been done in distinguishing the various questions to be answered? This essay tries to unravel some of the questions and to suggest some answers.

Tort law and criminal law have common features. Each aims to eliminate or reduce undesirable behaviour, each provides for sanctions to be imposed on those whose conduct is undesirable, and each poses difficult questions about the conditions for imposing sanctions and the extent of liability of wrongdoers. On the other hand the aims of the tort system are in some ways wider than those of the criminal justice system; and, corresponding to this, the definition of tort liability differs from that of punishment.

Here are some questions about tort law corresponding to those put by Hart about criminal law. We may ask (1) Why are certain types of conduct made tortious? (2) What is the definition of tort liability? (3) What general aims justify the state in maintaining a system of tort law? (4) What justifies the person whose rights have been infringed in claiming compensation from the wrongdoer? (5) Subject to what conditions may one who by his conduct has infringed the rights of another be required to pay compensation? and (6) What limits should be placed on the amount of compensation payable?

Only the moral aspect of these questions will be examined. Efficiency, and its elaboration by Richard Posner,[4] are left on one side, as are problems of proof. Tort law, like the rest of law, must satisfy several values, of which efficiency in pursuing worthwhile objectives is only one.[5] Efficiency must be pursued within a morally defensible framework;[6] so we must ask, and ask first, what aims it is morally defensible to pursue by imposing tort liability.

2. The questions answered

A. The descriptive framework of tort law

The first two questions listed, though concerned with norms, call for descriptive, not normative answers.

1. Why are certain types of conduct made tortious?

The first question Hart asked in his analysis of criminal law was why certain kinds of conduct are forbidden by law and so made crimes or offences. He gave the answer "to announce to society that these actions are not to be done and to secure that fewer of them are done".[7] The same may be said of the conduct that by common law or statute is made a tort. When the legislature or courts make conduct a tort they mean, by stamping it as wrongful, to forbid or discourage it or, at a minimum, to warn those who indulge in it of the liability they may incur. It is true that the terms used to describe it, "tortious" or "wrongful", are not as strong as the term "offence" in criminal law, and do not carry the same stigma. But that is a matter of degree. In tort law not only actions but omissions are at times treated as wrongful; that is also

the case in criminal law, for example in the law of homicide. Again, tort law sometimes treats as wrongful not an action or omission as such but the causing of harm by conduct of a potentially dangerous sort, for example selling a defective product or setting off explosives. In such cases the harm-causing action itself need not be wrongful, though it is done at the agent's risk. Criminal law also uses this technique, mostly with the implication that the conduct is wrongful even apart from its consequences. Think of the crime (in the UK) of causing death by dangerous driving, dangerous driving being itself an offence, though a less serious one. The word that best covers all these cases (actions, omissions, causing untoward consequences) is "conduct". If conduct is understood to include them all, we can say that tort law, like criminal law, announces that certain conduct is forbidden and tries to secure that less of it takes place. Tortious conduct is generally wrongful in itself, though if no harm results no liability may be incurred. When strict liability is imposed the conduct is generally not wrongful in itself, but the wrong consists in causing harm by engaging in risky activities.

But that is not the only reason why the state and its courts make conduct tortious. One point of creating a tort, as opposed to a crime, is to define and give content to people's rights by providing them with a mechanism for protecting them and securing compensation if their rights are infringed.

2. What is the definition of tort liability?

The second question follows naturally from the first. It concerns the definition of tort liability. Liability in tort is imposed, (a) if the dispute cannot be resolved without litigation, by the courts of the legal system having jurisdiction (b) at the instance of an individual whose right has been infringed (c) on a person who has committed a civil wrong (tort) against that person and (d) normally imposes on one who has committed the wrong an obligation to pay money by way of compensation to the person whose right has been infringed.[8] One may treat as subsidiary, though theoretically important, other remedies in tort law such as mandatory orders or injunctions and, outside tort law, administrative measures that may impose pecuniary penalties for such conduct.

B. The justifying aims of tort law

The first two questions called for a description of how the system of tort law operates. The answers did not serve to justify the existence of tort law, still less any particular part of it. The third question concerns the justification of tort law:

3. What general aims justify the state in maintaining a system of tort law?

Two different aspects of this question need to be dealt with here: (a) is the state entitled to take steps to discourage undesirable behaviour? and (b) if so, may it do so by treating certain interests of individuals as rights and giving them the legal power to protect those rights and obtain compensation if they are violated?

The tort system is one means by which the state, on behalf of the community, seeks to reduce conduct that it sees as undesirable. Others include the criminal law, education, administrative means such as licensing and inspection, differential taxes and many more. The state not only may but must, if a society is to be viable, try to minimize at least some types of disruptive conduct. Is tort law, like criminal law, a suitable means to this end? What tort and criminal law have in common, and what distinguishes them from some other means of social control, is that they work by marking out conduct, or the failure to attain a required standard of conduct, as wrongful. On the other hand licensing, inspection, differential taxation and rationing discourage behaviour, not by marking it as wrongful but by limiting opportunities to

indulge in it, for example by refusing licences for sex shops; or by denying benefits to those who do indulge in it, for example by charging more for leaded petrol. Other branches of the law of civil responsibility, such as the law of contracts or restitution, though they provide remedies for what are seen as wrongs, act primarily not by treating conduct as wrongful but in other ways. Contract law mainly marks out the conditions in which agreements will be enforceable and the law of restitution mainly specifies what is to count as an unjust benefit.

The technique of tort law is therefore to label certain things as not to be done or omitted or brought about, though in a less stigmatic way than criminal law. If the state is justified in making conduct criminal and attaching to it penalties that may include prison, it must also be justified in marking conduct as tortious and attaching to it the lesser sanction of compensation. In all societies some people behave disruptively or, without meaning to be disruptive, expose others to undue risks of injury. The state must have the right and duty to minimize the risks and remedy the disruption.

But it does not follow that the legislature or courts are right to make any particular sort of conduct tortious. That must depend on factors like those familiar in the debate about criminal law. Is the state justified in rendering tortious (or criminal) only conduct that threatens harm to others? If so, must the harm be physical/economic, or should inroads on personal, emotional and immaterial interests count as harm? This is not the place to pursue this important debate.

Assuming that the state can rightly make conduct tortious, is it entitled to do so by treating individual interests as rights and threatening economic sanctions against those who infringe the rights? Can the state properly use its resources, prestige and power for this purpose? The question goes deep into political theory. A supporter of the rule of law, and hence of the *Rechtstaat*[9] idea, is driven to a positive answer. The rule of law depends, among other factors, on a framework of individual rights that must be respected by others and by the state itself. This gives people a degree of independence from one another and from the power of government. One who accepts this ideal will think the state justified in trying to minimize undesirable behaviour by a technique that treats some interests as rights and gives those who have the rights the power to avert or redress the unwanted conduct.

Assuming that this is a proper role for the state, it may also be justified, within limits, in subsidizing right-holders by setting up and paying for a framework of civil courts for the enforcement of tort claims. But even a critic who is not in principle opposed to the rule of law can argue that to subsidize private rights in this way is not a proper use of the state's resources. While, so far as I know, there is no state in which this view has so far been taken, it may be rash in an age of privatization to assume that none will in future refuse to subsidize the use of its courts to give effect to the tort system. In such a state, those who pursue tort claims in the courts would have to pay the cost of judicial enforcement. It would be morally and politically objectionable for a state to go even further and refuse access to its courts to those wishing to bring claims in tort. Closing the courts to tort claims would be to give up an important technique for lessening undesirable conduct, and would jettison a central element in the structure of rights that underlies the rule of law. Of course in some societies (past and present), more emphasis is placed on reducing bad conduct by social pressures and administrative means than by the enforcing of individual rights. But these societies tend to be less committed to the rule of law.

Assuming that the arguments in favour of the rule of law are persuasive, the state is justified in maintaining a system of tort law that seeks to reduce the incidence of undesirable conduct by treating certain interests of individuals as rights and providing those who have them with the legal power to avert inroads on those rights and, if they are infringed, to obtain compensation for their violation.

C. The distribution of tort liability

4. What justifies the person whose rights have been infringed in claiming compensation from the wrongdoer?

What was said in answer to question (3) is incomplete. To justify the tort system, it is not enough to show that the state is entitled to take steps to minimize undesirable behaviour and to give individuals the power to protect their rights and obtain compensation if they are violated. It must also be shown that some principle or principles of justice entitle the right-holders (tort-plaintiffs) to sue the wrongdoers (tort-defendants) for compensation. For though the state may be entitled to designate certain interests as rights and certain sorts of conduct as wrongs, it cannot thereby make it just for the right-holders to sue the wrongdoers for compensation. It cannot by fiat create a principle of justice linking the two. The issue here is then whether there are one or more independent principles that justify tort claims against tort-defendants.

a. Corrective justice

The principle most often cited is that of corrective justice.[10] This can be put in various ways. On a wide view it requires those who have without justification harmed others by their conduct to put the matter right.[11] This they must do on the basis that harm-doer and harm-sufferer are to be treated as equals, neither more deserving than the other. The one is therefore not entitled to become relatively better off by harming the other. The balance must be restored.

I have said "without justification" rather than "wrongfully", not because the latter is incorrect, but to put aside the question whether to harm someone without justification is a wrong in itself[12] or whether it is a wrong only if the person doing the harm was at fault. "Putting the matter right" (reparation)[13] is a concept that may, according to the circumstances, require the harm-doer to restore something to the person harmed, or to repair a damaged object or (when the unharmed position cannot be restored, as it usually cannot) to compensate the harm-sufferer. Compensating in turn means doing something conventionally regarded as restoring the harm-sufferer to his unharmed position. "Compensate" is used to cover whatever may be done to make good the loss when reparation is not literally possible; what counts as compensation is largely a matter of convention. Nothing in the idea of corrective justice requires the compensation to be in money. Though in tort law it nearly always takes that form, outside of tort law various forms of substitute provision in kind or services are treated as proper ways of making good the harm to the sufferer.[14]

The claim to put things right lies against the harm-doer, and sometimes only the harm-doer can satisfy it, for example because what is called for includes an apology. But in other cases, for instance when the claim is purely for money, the harm-doer can arrange for someone else to pay, perhaps through third-party insurance or the generosity of a friend. If the matter is put right in that way, the harm-doer satisfies the demands of corrective justice.[15] Moreover, the loss may be covered by the harm-sufferer's own insurance, or through a state scheme, in which case the harm-doer may to that extent be freed from the need to compensate the harm-sufferer. The harm-doer has wrongfully caused the physical harm but, ultimately, not an economic loss. But then the harm-doer, not having satisfied the liability personally, may not unjustly be required to compensate the insurer or the state instead of compensating the harm-sufferer. In law this takes the form of subrogation.

From what has been said it will be clear that in my view corrective justice is a relational principle. It can exist only when the harm-doer's wrong violates the harm-sufferer's right; the two cannot be dissociated. On this point I agree with Weinrib and disagree with the view formerly embraced by Jules Coleman. For Coleman at one time thought that there could be wrongful losses, calling for redress, in the abstract, even though one could not point to any particular wrongdoer as the person who ought to put them right.[16]

Corrective justice presupposes that the defendant has caused harm to the plaintiff. It is this doing of harm that needs to be corrected. So there must be a causal link between the defendant's conduct and the plaintiff's loss. The conduct need not be *the* cause of the harm.[17] It is enough that it is *a* cause, and there can be more than one human cause of the harm in question, in which case both (or all) harm-doers can be responsible.[18] The existence of the causal link is a *necessary* condition of corrective justice and of the duty to compensate in a tort action. It is not a *sufficient* condition, however, for two reasons. First, for compensation to be rightly claimed, there must have been no justification for inflicting the harm. If there was a justification, the person harmed cannot on the same facts be justified in claiming compensation. Secondly, though someone who harms another without justification must in principle make the harm good as a matter of corrective justice, what form his responsibility should take, whether legal or extra-legal, and subject to what further conditions,[19] remains an open question.

Since a causal link is necessary to both corrective justice and tort liability, much turns on the view we take of the responsibility of one who causes another harm. A widespread view is that a person who harms another is responsible for the harm only when he is at fault.[20] If this view is accepted, corrective justice has to be defined more narrowly than in my earlier formulation. It will require reparation or compensation only if the person causing the harm was at fault in doing so. This view would set a narrower limit to corrective justice and, in particular, would exclude strict liability in tort law.[21] On the wider view, which I favour, the importance of fault is not denied, but the fault requirement operates, so far as it does, as an independent limit to the pursuit of corrective justice rather than as an element in it. If so, it falls to be discussed under the next question (5), which concerns the conditions for imposing tort liability.

b. Outcome responsibility

The view that those who cause harm are responsible for it even in the absence of fault fits what I have elsewhere termed outcome responsibility.[22] On this view we are, if of full capacity and hence in a position to control our behaviour, responsible for the outcome of our conduct, whether act or omission.[23] This responsibility is an essential constituent of our character and identity, without which we would lack both achievements and failures. Lacking a positive history of what we had done (and its outcome), we should at most be half-persons.[24] Outcome responsibility figures prominently in our sense of our own agency and is important for both the theory of agency and moral theory.[25] This is not to say that we are responsible for everything that would not have happened had we not acted, or refrained from acting, as we did.[26] That would be a misconception. The conduct that grounds outcome responsibility includes what we do, but does not include our not doing all that we do not do. Under non-doing it comprises only omissions, and an omission is the violation of a norm.[27]

There is nothing mysterious about this limitation of our responsibility to actions and those omissions that violate norms. When we act we launch ourselves upon the world and implicitly choose to be responsible for what we do, including its outcome. When we do not act we are responsible only so far as responsibility is thrust upon us, because society requires of us certain actions that we omit to do. Moreover, the outcomes to which outcome responsibility applies do not consist of everything that would not have happened but for the conduct in question, but are limited to consequences properly attributable to the conduct rather than to later voluntary or abnormal interventions by other people and events.

Outcome responsibility serves to foster a sense of identity because it does not stretch indefinitely into the future but enables each of us to claim for ourselves, or to share with a few others, outcomes of limited extent, whether successes or failures.[28] Yet outcome responsibility for harm to another does not by itself create a duty to compensate. The form that our responsibility for an outcome should take remains an open question. An apology or telephone call will often be enough. But outcome responsibility is a basis on which the law can erect a duty to compensate if there is reason to do so. There will be some reason to do so if the conduct in question is socially undesirable and if there is also reason to treat the harm suffered as the infringement of a right.

If the outcome of conduct is harmful to another, the next question is whether in the context there was a *justification* for inflicting the harm. We are sometimes justified in injuring others, for example in self-defence. When we compete we are justified in inflicting losses or setbacks on our rivals. Whether those injuries, losses or setbacks count as "harm" depends on whether that protean word is thought to carry with it the implication that the injury or loss has not been justifiably inflicted.[29] I win the one hundred metres and you lose. Outcome responsibility makes me responsible for your defeat as well as for my victory. But the nature of the race justifies me in inflicting that setback on you. The same is true of other forms of competition, for example in trade, business, politics, literature, and love. If some succeed, others fail. When, however, there is no justification for inflicting a loss on another, outcome-responsibility supports the claims of corrective justice. Since I am responsible for a loss inflicted on you without justification, I have a duty to answer for what I have done, and to make whatever amends are appropriate to the situation. It will then be in order for the state to impose tort liability to compel me to make good your loss, if my conduct was undesirable and your loss an infringement of your rights, provided that to do so is not inconsistent with other values important to maintain.[30]

c. Distributive justice

But if outcome responsibility supports the wider view of corrective justice,[31] we must note that the justification for imposing outcome responsibility on those who cause harm to others rests not on corrective but on distributive justice. Perry rightly points to the distinction between outcome responsibility from the agent's point of view – something that helps him foster a sense of his personal identity, character and history – and outcome responsibility as a justification for holding people liable to others for the harmful outcome of their conduct.[32] But I do not agree with him that these two aspects of outcome responsibility are inconsistent. The argument for holding people responsible to others for harmful outcomes is that it is fair to make the person to whom the advantages will flow from an uncertain situation over which he has some control (or which he has chosen to enter into) bear the losses that may equally flow from that situation. It is fair to treat the agent as if he had made a bet on the outcome of his action. This argument, somewhat loosely expressed, tries to spell out what justice requires in situations of uncertainty. It is a familiar notion in legal and extra-legal contexts. For example, the person to whom the income of property or a business will accrue if it does well has normally also to bear the risk of loss if it does badly. In the law of sales, when the right to income or fruits normally passes to the buyer, the risk of deterioration or destruction normally passes to him as well.

Aristotle and other philosophers who have developed the theory of distributive justice do not expressly mention this principle of risk, no doubt because it has arisen mainly in legal contexts. But, despite appearances, the risk principle rests on a form of distributive justice.[33] Though this form of justice is generally concerned with the distribution of goods, it also covers the distribution of losses and burdens. For example, it applies to the incidence of taxation. The just distribution of burdens and losses among the members of a society requires that a criterion be found (say benefit or capacity) according to which they may fairly be allocated. There is no reason why the distribution of the risk of gains or losses in a situation of uncertainty should not equally be part of distributive justice. To be specific, we can speak of the just distribution of risks as risk-distributive justice. It might seem at first sight that this sort of justice is not distributive, because the benefit of success and the risk of failure fall on the same person, whereas distributive justice is concerned with the allocation of assets and burdens among all or many of the members of a community. But the risk principle is entirely general. It places on every member of the community the burden of bearing the risk that his conduct may turn out to be harmful to others, in return for the benefit to himself that will accrue should his conduct turn out as he plans. It distributes throughout society the risks of harm attributable to human conduct.

d. The blend of corrective and (risk-) distributive justice

I therefore take corrective justice to be in one way distinct from distributive justice and in another dependent on it. It is distinct in the sense that the interests (holdings) that corrective justice protects need not be just from a distributive point of view. The filthy rich can appeal to corrective justice if their holdings are filched by the grinding poor. But to justify corrective justice involves appealing at a certain stage to the just *distribution of risk* in a society. In that respect corrective justice depends on distributive justice. Corrective justice is a genuine form of justice only because the just distribution of risks requires people of full capacity to bear the risk of being held responsible for harming others by their conduct even when they are not at fault in doing so.[34] For this reason, corrective justice is a substantive, not a merely formal principle. It needs, and can be given, a moral basis.

This principle of risk distribution has an intuitive appeal. It may rest on the sort of moral intuition that one cannot go behind; or it may be that deeper analysis will show that it turns on something more fundamental. At any rate, risk distribution serves to justify outcome responsibility, and outcome responsibility opens the door to imposing a duty of reparation in suitable cases, and so to corrective justice. This conclusion is welcome, since it puts some parts of tort liability on a morally sound basis. But it does so only when the defendant has personally infringed the plaintiff's rights. For it is only when this is the case, and the harm-sufferer sues the person who is outcome responsible for the harm, that corrective justice by itself justifies the claim.

In criminal law, the offender is nearly always held responsible for what he has done personally. Vicarious liability or, what comes to the same thing, the liability of corporations and other bodies for the conduct of their members, is exceptional. Tort liability is different. Many tort actions give effect to personal responsibility. But others follow a different pattern. They are brought, for example, against an employer for the act of an employee who, in working for him, has harmed the plaintiff. In that case, outcome responsibility and corrective justice do not serve to justify an action against the employer,[35] though they may justify one against the employee. Is some other justification available? The conventional reasons given for holding that the employer ought to bear the risk of loss within certain limits for the employee's harmful conduct are that the employer (a) has control over the business, including the work of employees, and (b) stands to profit from the employee's services. A combination of these reasons, it is generally thought, justifies us in imposing vicarious responsibility on the employer. As in outcome responsibility, the person who, in a situation of uncertainty, has a degree of control over how it will turn out, and who stands to gain if it goes in his favour, must bear the risk that it will turn out to harm another. This reasoning appeals once more to a principle of justice based on risk distribution. The justification of tort liability is, as before, a combination of corrective and distributive justice. But distributive justice now appears at two points rather than one. It does so, first, to support the outcome responsibility of the employee and, second, to support the action against the employer, who has not personally harmed the plaintiff.

In the end, the justification of tort liability both against the harmdoer personally and against secondary defendants, such as employers held to be vicariously liable, rests on both corrective and (risk-) distributive justice.

5. Subject to what conditions may one who by his conduct has infringed the rights of another be required to pay compensation?

The main questions are whether fault is, morally speaking, a necessary condition of tort liability, and whether modern conditions justify using loss spreading to support liability that may be out of proportion to the blameworthiness of a defendant's conduct. The second question is not strictly about the legal conditions of tort liability but about a background state of affairs that may be necessary if the pursuit of corrective justice by tort law is to be morally defensible. Both questions raise the issue of how far, if at all, corrective justice should be tempered by considerations of retributive justice.

a. Retributive justice and fault in criminal law

To begin with fault, there is no doubt that, however this complex notion is interpreted, it is in general a necessary condition of conviction for a criminal offence, at any rate for a serious offence for which imprisonment is possible. One reason is that the law's prohibitions are meant to guide the potential offender's choices. Their aim is to influence conduct and their sanctions are directed at those who choose to do what the law forbids, not those who do the forbidden action without choosing to do it. If, therefore, the defendant had no choice, but was compelled to act as he did, for example if he was forced to steal against his will, it cannot be said that he *disregarded* the prohibition. He contravened it but, since he did not disregard or defy it, he should not be subject to punishment.

But the focus on choice does not stop there. If, though not compelled, the offender did not intend to do the wrong that the law forbids, he again cannot be said to have defied the prohibition. For example, if he did not mean the victim he assaulted to die, or if, oddly, he did not realise that the woman with whom he was having intercourse did not consent to it, he cannot be said to have flouted the prohibition of murder or rape, though he may have defied some lesser prohibition, say of assault or sexual harassment.

This condition of punishment, that the offender should have flouted the law, by intentionally doing what it forbids, is well settled for serious cases that carry heavy penalties. This remains true though the offender, given the difficulties of proof and the desire not to reward ignorance of the law, need not have known the exact terms in which the prohibition is couched. When the wrongdoer's fault is less serious, say recklessness or negligence,[36] most legal systems will still permit lesser degrees of punishment. In these latter types of cases, the offender need not have deliberately flouted the prohibition. It is sufficient that he behaved in a way that displayed too much self-regard and too little concern for the interest of others. Indifference or unconcern, falling short of defiance, is enough. Moreover, when the penalty is only a modest fine, fault even in the sense of indifference or unconcern may be dispensed with altogether and strict liability imposed. Yet even in the case of strict liability,

the defendant must have chosen to act as he did. Compulsion will exclude punishment. But given the element of choice, the case for punishment here depends on the just distribution of risks. The criminal law may properly be used to ensure that those who, acting in their own interest, create a risk to others should suffer a modest penalty for the harm that their activity brings about. For example, the seller of milk which, unknown to him, is adulterated may properly be fined a modest sum for selling adulterated milk. There is therefore in practice a rough correlation between the type of fault or conduct and the weight of the punishment imposed. For the most serious penalties the offender must have chosen to defy the law, for the somewhat less serious he must have chosen to act with indifference to the interests of others, and for the relatively minor he must at least have chosen to do something that is potentially harmful to others.

What has been said describes in outline the correlation between fault/conduct and penalty in most systems of criminal justice. Can this rough correlation be morally justified? It has a certain intuitive appeal. The principle on which it seems to rest is retributive. The retributive principle has, however, two aspects. One *requires* that a sanction be imposed that is roughly proportionate to the moral gravity of the conduct. The other *forbids* that a sanction be imposed that is out of proportion to the gravity of the conduct. It is this second, limiting, aspect of the retributive principle that is in play here. The limiting principle requires the sanction to be no greater than is justified by the gravity of the conduct, of which the degree of fault is an important ingredient. Of course, the correlation is extremely rough.

It may be objected that talk of the retributive principle is out of place. According to some versions of retributive justice, there can be no punishment in the absence of fault, since conduct that is free from fault does not possess even a minor degree of moral gravity. Hence there should be no strict liability in criminal law. But a person who freely does something chooses to intervene in the world and, while what he does may display neither defiance of nor indifference to the interests of others, it may, in pursuit of his own interests, put others at risk. It seems reasonable to put conduct that exposes others to a risk that materializes – for example selling milk that may possibly be and in fact is adulterated – at a fairly low point on the scale of misconduct on which showing indifference to and defiance of the interests of others occupy the higher reaches. The behaviour located low on the scale is not morally bad, and does not amount to fault, but neither is it morally indifferent; conduct that may affect others cannot be that. It is taking a chance of harming others.[37] Suitably extended, therefore, the retributive principle can surely treat as just, and not merely expedient, the imposition of minor sanctions for risk-creating conduct that goes wrong. The retributive principle, thus modified, would still require the gravity of the conduct to be roughly proportionate to the sanction.

Of course, even without this suggested extension, retribution as a theory intended to justify the criminal process has been fiercely attacked. But it has its defenders so far as sentencing is concerned, and every system of criminal justice, so far as I know, pays some attention to it in that context. This is not the place for a detailed discussion of the case for it; I merely assume that, in its limiting form, it has some merit. And if it is right to require the conduct to be of sufficient moral gravity to correspond roughly to the severity of the penalty imposed in criminal law, something similar must in principle be true in tort law as well.

b. Retributive justice and fault in tort law

How should the retributive principle apply in tort law? First, the tortfeasor, like the criminal offender, presumably ought not to be made to pay unless he has chosen to do what the law forbids. There should be no tort liability for an act done under compulsion. So much seems to be required by the fact that tort law, like criminal law, is meant to influence conduct by inducing people to abstain from undesirable behaviour. But, as tort law does not impose imprisonment, there is on the retributive principle no strong case for requiring that a tortfeasor should have intended to defy the law, though, if he did, the case for a sanction is strengthened.[38] Provided his behaviour was selfish or inconsiderate, which negligent conduct often is, he may properly be made liable in tort. But the burdens of tort liability, though less grave than losing one's physical freedom, can be very serious, especially if the defendant is not insured.[39] In such cases, the retributive principle will not merely justify but require fault as a condition of tort liability.

In other cases, however, fault will not be necessary. A tort defendant is often insured and in some of the commonest types of tort liability, such as motoring accidents, insurance is compulsory. Hence the defendant does not have to pay the damages personally, except to the extent that he pays them indirectly through his insurance premium. Provided that the insurance premium is modest, therefore, there seems no moral reason to require fault as a condition of liability in these cases.[40] In practice many countries, such as France and Germany, impose strict liability for transport accidents, relying on insurance to minimize the burden on individual defendants. Again, when the defendant is vicariously liable for the conduct of an employee,[41] the retributive principle may not require that his liability be confined to cases where the employee is at fault. Since the profit that falls to the employer is not always merely the amount that he deserves to make, but may include windfalls, an employer's vicarious liability need not be confined to accidents caused by fault on the part of the employee, but may sometimes extend to harm that is purely accidental.[42]

Often, therefore, there should in principle be no moral objection to strict liability in tort law,[43] provided that it does not impose an undue burden on the defendant personally. Hence it is not surprising that the degree of care and skill required in tort law is a stringent one. The standard of negligence is nearly always objective. The defendant may therefore be held liable for faults that a reasonable person would not have committed but that he could not help because he was too rash, clumsy or stupid.[44] Though nominally the liability is for fault, the defendant is in effect subject to strict liability. Of course, often fault is actually present, but the faults in question may be rather minor ones of inattention and slowness to react.

What has been said so far shows that corrective justice as tempered by the retributive principle supports some strict liability, but not universal strict liability. But it also shows that the line between fault and strict liability is often blurred. And even when fault is genuinely a condition of tort liability, and still more when liability is objective or strict, the compensation payable may be disproportionate to what is often a minor fault. To avoid this disproportion, the retributive principle insists that defendants should not be exposed to disproportionately heavy losses. If the claims of corrective justice are to be morally viable, ways must therefore be found of spreading such losses.

Insurance provides a mechanism for spreading losses, and helps at the same time to protect the plaintiff's claim to compensation. Loss spreading is indeed often achieved by a form of distributive justice that allocates burdens roughly in proportion to benefits. Those who benefit from some activity, say motoring, are made to bear a proportionate share of the losses that the activity causes, for example through compulsory third-party insurance. This is certainly not an infallible instrument of justice, since insurance premiums may be exorbitant. Nevertheless, it helps to ensure that tort damages are in most cases not grossly disproportionate to the fault of the defendant who has caused the harm. Hence, though loss spreading (through third-party insurance) is distributive, the reason

why it is needed as an adjunct to the tort system is, in part at least, to satisfy the demands of retributive justice. It serves to cushion losses which, whether the defendants are at fault or not, are out of scale with the gravity of their conduct. This does not entail that loss spreading is an aim of the tort system as such, merely that it is essential if a system of corrective justice is to operate fairly in modern conditions. Corrective justice can operate as a morally defensible system only in harness with retributive justice. This is turn may require recourse to a form of justice that distributes burdens equitably.

So, while corrective justice in isolation warrants holding people strictly liable to make good the loss to those whom they harm without justification, the tort system is not bound to translate this into a legal liability to compensate, when to do so would be unduly burdensome to the defendant. On the contrary, the retributive principle requires that the burden be made roughly proportionate to the gravity of the conduct. In many instances this can to some extent be achieved by making fault a condition of liability. In others, the personal burden on the defendant must be reduced, whether he is at fault or not, by a system that redistributes losses among those who benefit from the activities that cause them. In that way full compensation can be achieved, as corrective justice demands, provided that the personal liability of the defendant is tempered by loss distribution.

6. What limits should be placed on the amount of compensation payable?

Retributive and distributive justice are not the only moral considerations that may limit the untrammelled pursuit of corrective justice. Three other reasons are commonly given for restricting the compensation payable in tort actions: the scope of the rule violated, the foreseeability of the harm for which compensation is sought, and the conduct of the plaintiff. A fourth is more radical. It is sometimes said that tort liability should be replaced, entirely or above a certain amount, by a state compensation scheme, at least in certain areas of life.[45] What is the moral status of these arguments?

a. The scope of the rule violated

A rule making conduct tortious, for example requiring dangerous machinery to be fenced, may have a limited scope. It may be that, properly interpreted, the aim of the rule is to prevent parts of the employee's body or clothes catching in the machinery rather than to prevent parts of the machinery flying out and injuring someone. There is nothing special to tort law about this need for interpretation. Every rule that makes conduct wrongful, whether in criminal law, tort law, the law of contract, trust law or whatever, requires interpretation and the interpretation will set limits to the scope of the rule in question. When the interpretation excludes certain types of harm, the pursuit of corrective justice by the use of state machinery is to that extent ruled out. But is it just to exclude, for example, certain of the plaintiff's economic, psychological or emotional interests from the scope of a tort law rule or from tort law as a whole?

It seems that the state must be justified in imposing some limits on the type of harm for which compensation may be claimed. To require compensation for every type of harm in the context of every rule of tort law would to be impose a burdensome liability on defendants. It would be inefficient when, as is likely to be the case with some types of harm difficult to ascertain, the cost of imposing tort liability would much exceed the likely benefit. The legislature and courts must be entitled to take the view that some interests – say, wrongfully inflicted but trivial psychological harm – do not deserve the status of a right. Of course, the state may make mistakes in these matters, but it must surely be justified, indeed bound, to mark out such limits on liability. If the state is bound to decide what conduct should be made criminal or tortious, fallible as its judgment may be, it must also be bound to fix the limits of responsibility for various types of harm.

b. The foreseeability of the harm

The foreseeability of the harm for which compensation is claimed is often put forward, particularly in tort claims based on negligence, as an independent ground for limiting the extent of the defendant's liability. The ground for this limitation is sometimes said to be that, when the liability is based on negligently failing to foresee and take steps to avoid harm, the resulting liability should logically be restricted to the harm, or type of harm, that should have been foreseen. Thus, if the defendant should have foreseen harm by impact alone, he should not be liable for the harm by fire or explosion that unexpectedly results. This argument assumes that there is never a case for placing the risk of an unexpected outcome on the person at fault in creating the risk.[46] The argument is no more convincing than the view that, where it is a condition of liability that the defendant intended harm, the harm for which he is liable should be confined to what he intended. The conditions of liability (question (5) above) and the extent of liability (this question (6)) present somewhat different moral and policy issues. But the retributive principle does require a rough proportion to be preserved between the degree of fault and the burden of the sanction. To rule out recovery for unforeseeable harm, or harm of an unforeseeable type, enables courts to limit the extent of the burden, though in a somewhat arbitrary way given the fluidity of the criteria used to identify unforeseeable harm after the event. But it must be stressed that the argument for proportionality weakens when the defendant does not pay the compensation personally, as in cases of insured, vicarious and organizational liability, which bulk large in tort liability for negligence.

c. Conduct and fault of the plaintiff

Corrective justice suggests that the defendant's duty to compensate the plaintiff should be limited when the plaintiff's conduct, along with that of the defendant, is a cause of the harm. In that case the plaintiff as well as the defendant is responsible for the outcome. If they are both responsible the plaintiff should bear part of the loss himself. How great that part should be will depend on whether causal contribution can be quantified. The question is controversial, though in my view the notion of causal contribution is a coherent one.[47] If causal contribution can be assessed, the plaintiff's claim, from the view-point of corrective justice, should be reduced proportionately to that contribution. If not, retributive principles must be taken into account.

Suppose that the plaintiff's conduct has not merely been a cause of the harm along with the conduct of the defendant, but that the plaintiff has been at fault in behaving as he did, or has acted with deliberation. Should the plaintiff's fault or deliberation bar or reduce his compensation? The plaintiff may be morally disentitled to sue, for instance because he consented to the defendant's conduct or intentionally provoked it. More difficult is the question how far his recovery should be affected by the fact that, short of intentional provocation, his fault contributed to the harm done. Does the existence of contributory fault modify the claim to compensation on the basis of corrective justice? To reduce the plaintiff's claim from what corrective justice on its own would warrant is to impose a loss on him. The retributive principle requires the loss to be not disproportionate to his fault. This sets a limit to the possible extent of the reduction, but does not settle the question whether a reduction proportionate to fault is morally required. If both plaintiff and defendant were at fault in causing the harm, the straightforward retributive principle would make both plaintiff and defendant responsible to an extent roughly proportionate to the gravity of their respective faults. Putting these considerations together, the plaintiff's claim, when both he and defendant are at fault, should be reduced by an amount that results in plaintiff and defendant bearing a share of the loss roughly proportionate to their respective faults, but not so as to impose on the plaintiff a loss disproportionate to his fault considered in isolation. In practice, those legal systems that admit the apportionment of damages for contributory negligence adopt these criteria, or something rather like them.

d. The replacement of tort liability by a state scheme of compensation

According to Richard Wright, the replacement of tort liability by a compulsory no-fault state compensation scheme would be inconsistent with corrective justice.[48] It would fail to impose the duty to compensate on the party who ought to bear it and impose it on persons who, from the point of view of corrective justice at least, have no duty to bear it. The effect of such a scheme is to transfer the whole or part of the duty to compensate from the harm-doer to the taxpayer or the contributors to an insurance fund.

There is, however, an argument for doing precisely this, based on the just distribution of risks. If it is fair for everyone to have to contribute through taxes to the defence of the country, since everyone in the country benefits from its being defended, so it is fair for everyone who owns or drives a vehicle, or who benefits from the existence of a transport system, to contribute to the accident costs that such a system carries with it. To argue in this way is simply to extend to a wider group the sort of argument that leads to an employer being held liable for the harm done by his employee when engaged in working for him. Of course there is a technical difference in that, under the imagined state scheme, the harm-doer would not be liable in tort, while in the law of vicarious liability as it stands in most countries, the employee remains liable even when his employer is vicariously liable. But in practice the employee is not sued, because he will usually not be able to pay the damages, or not so easily as the employer, and usually he does not even pay the insurance premium that covers the employer's potential liability for his harmful conduct. It would hardly be an injustice to take from the harm-sufferer (who is entitled to compensation from another source) a technical right to sue the harm-doer.

That is not to say that there is a morally compelling case for replacing tort liability by a state compensation scheme. To do so would tend to undermine the sense of personal responsibility of some potential harm-doers, just as vicarious liability tends to undermine the sense of personal responsibility of some employees. But to introduce a state compensation scheme would not in my view violate corrective justice. The propriety of corrective justice depends, I have argued, on our taking a certain view about the just distribution of risks in a society, a view for which individual outcome responsibility provides a basis. But it is possible to take a wider view about how risk should be distributed, at least in certain areas of life. One can argue that the distribution of risks should, for example as regards motoring, take place at the level not of the individual but of the vehicle-owning population or the whole community. The level at which risks should be distributed in a particular area of community life seems pre-eminently a matter of political judgment.

3. The answers summarized

A brief summary of the suggested answers to the six questions discussed may be helpful:

(1) and (2) By the tort system the state aims to reduce the incidence of undesirable conduct by treating certain individual interests as rights, and giving the right-holder the power to protect his rights and obtain compensation if they are infringed by undesirable conduct marked as a civil wrong.

(3) The state is justified in maintaining, and probably in subsidizing, a tort system and an institutional framework, including courts, to give effect to it.

(4) Subject to (5) and (6) below, tort-plaintiffs in principle are morally entitled, on the basis of corrective justice, to recover damages from tort-defendants who have without justification personally caused them harm. On a wide view, corrective justice requires those who have without justification harmed others by their conduct to put the matter right, even if they were not at fault. The reason is that we are responsible for the outcome of our conduct (outcome responsibility), and that a just distribution of risks requires us to make good the harm our conduct causes to others in return for the benefit and credit that accrues to us when our plans come off. The case for imposing vicarious liability in tort on employers and organizations who have not personally caused the harm also rests on the just distribution of risks.

(5) But the pursuit of corrective justice must be tempered by the need to keep a proportion between the burden of compensation that falls on a defendant personally and the gravity of his conduct. There are cases in which it is unjust to hold the defendant liable in the absence of fault and in which, even if he is at fault, the extent of his personal liability should be limited by loss spreading. The moral basis of the need for proportionality is the retributive principle, which requires that the sanction should not be disproportionate to the gravity of the conduct for which it is imposed. The argument for proportionality does not apply, or applies more weakly, when the liability is vicarious rather than personal.

(6) The pursuit of corrective justice is also tempered by the duty and power of the state to decide which harms are to count as infringing legal rights. The state is justified in reducing or refusing compensation when the harm lies outside the scope of the rule of law on which the plaintiff relies, or was of an unforeseeable type the risk of which should not be imposed on the defendant. When the plaintiff's conduct contributes to the harm he suffers, the extent to which his claim should be reduced, if any,

should be settled according to the principles of corrective justice and the retributive principle. Lastly, it would not be unjust, though it might be unwise, for the state to replace tort liability in certain areas by a scheme of no-fault insurance based on the just distribution of losses. The principle of corrective justice that justifies the straightforward cases of tort liability, in which the defendant has personally done the harm, has therefore to be tempered by considerations of distributive and retributive justice that limit the extent to which it can properly be applied.

Notes

1 First published in *Philosophical Foundations of Tort Law* (ed. David G. Owen, Oxford, 1995) pp. 73–95.

2 H. L. A. Hart, *Punishment and Responsibility. Essays in the Philosophy of Law* 10 (Oxford, 1968) [hereafter *Punishment and Responsibility*].

3 See Richard W. Wright, "Substantive Corrective Justice", 77 *Iowa Law Rev.* 625 (1992) (discussing the work of Jules L. Coleman and Ernest J. Weinrib). See generally Symposium, "Corrective Justice and Formalism – The Care One Owes One's Neighbours", 77 *Iowa Law Rev.* 403 (1992).

4 See e.g. Richard Posner, "What has Pragmatism to Offer Law?", 63 *S. Cal. Law Rev.* 1653, 1657, 1662–3 (1990).

5 "Tort law implements a variety of different principles and policies": Jules L. Coleman, "The Mixed Conception of Corrective Justice", 77 *Iowa Law Rev.* 427, 427 (1992) [hereafter *Mixed Conception*]; cf. Jules L. Coleman, "Tort Law and the Demands of Corrective Justice", 67 *Ind. Law J.* 349, 357 (1992) [hereafter *Tort Law and Demands*].

6 Ernest J. Weinrib, "The Case for a Duty to Rescue", 90 *Yale Law J.* 247, 263 (1980); Guido Calabresi, *The Cost of Accidents. A Legal and Economic Analysis* (1970) pp. 24–6, 291–308. For a view that this leaves minimal room for the pursuit of efficiency, see Richard W. Wright, "The Efficiency Theory of Causation and Responsibility: Unscientific Formalism and False Semantics", 63 *Chi.-Kent Law Rev.* 552, 562–7 (1987).

7 Hart, above n.2, p. 6.

8 See Wright, above n.3, at p. 634 n.38.

9 The idea that the state has a duty to set out and enforce certain rights of the citizen, even against itself.

10 Wright, above n.3, pp. 627–31.

11 The application of corrective justice to unjust gains is not dealt with here, though a similar analysis would be possible.

12 On the wrong-in-itself view, which I prefer, the defendant's conduct may not be *wrongful in itself*, but causing harm without justification is nevertheless a *wrong* that grounds a claim for compensation. Jules Coleman expresses it differently: "the duty to repair . . . wrongful losses is grounded not in the fact that they are the result of wrongdoing, but in the fact that the losses are the injurer's responsibility, the result of the injurer's agency". Coleman, *Mixed Conception*, above n.5, at p. 443. Unlike Coleman, I regard the two as correlative: the losses are wrongful if and only if caused by the agent without justification.

13 Neil MacCormick, *Legal Right and Social Democracy* (1982), p. 212.

14 Contrary to Coleman, *Tort Law and Demands*, above n.5, at p. 366, Wright argues that in cases where corrective justice requires the rightful position to be restored, the mode of rectification is implicit in the grounds of recovery and liability: see Wright, above n.3, at p. 683. But, unless settled by a particular legal system, the precise content of the victim's right and the appropriate mode of giving effect to it against the harm-doer seems an open question, though the rectification must be adequate in context.

15 Wright, *Corrective Justice*, above n.3, at p. 703.

16 Not entirely abandoned in his *Mixed Conception*, above n.5.

17 Stephen R. Perry, "The Moral Foundations of Tort Law", 77 *Iowa Law Rev.* 449, 464, n.58 (1992) [hereafter *Moral Foundations*].

18 See below, question (6).

19 See below, question (6).

20 E.g. Coleman, *Mixed Conception*, above n.5, 442–43; Perry, above n.17, at p. 497.

21 I take strict liability to be liability without fault, whether or not the defendant was engaged in a dangerous activity. To engage in a dangerous activity gives the law a reason to impose strict liability on the person engaging in it, but does not form part of the definition of strict liability.

Wright, interpreting Aristotle, takes a different view, distinguishing between strict liability for risk and absolute liability: Wright, above n.3, at p. 697 n.335. But are Aristotle's "unjust losses" not simply those caused by another without justification, for example by accident, even if the conduct did not apparently carry with it any special risk?

22 Honoré, "Responsibility and Luck", in *Responsibility and Fault* (Hart 2002) pp. 27, 31–2.

23 Cf. Perry, above n.17, pp. 488–9. My thesis can stand on its own feet. But it is arguable that Aristotle took a similar view viz. that wrongful, mistaken and accidental conduct (covering both fault and strict liability) causing harm to others obliges the harm-doer to repair the harm as a matter of corrective justice. Wright, above n.3, at pp. 697–8.

24 The other "negative" half of our history concerns what has happened to us.

25 Perry, *Moral Foundations*, above n.17, at p. 490.

26 As argued by Wright, above n.3, at p. 682.

27 Honoré, "Are Omissions Less Culpable?", in *Responsibility and Fault* (Hart 2002) pp. 46–54.

28 The discussion of outcome responsibility here fits an analysis of causal concepts by Hart and myself that need not be repeated in this essay: see generally H. L. A. Hart and Tony Honoré, *Causation in the Law* (2nd ed. 1985), 68–83 [hereafter Hart and Honoré]. Stephen Perry treats this as an analysis of responsibility rather than causation: see Perry, above n.17, at p. 503. But since our approach is regularly criticized for containing normative elements that are foreign to causation, it is worth stressing that the analysis of causal concepts that we put forward, though not normative, is functional. These causal concepts take the shape they do because they are tailored (of course not consciously) to fit certain purposes, especially explanation and the attribution of responsibility. Those purposes require them to incorporate cut-off points. Without cut-off points, both backward and forward, causal concepts would not play the prominent role they do in everyday life, because they would not serve any worthwhile purpose. But these concepts are not normative: they are neutral between different ways of behaving and different assessments of conduct. Thus, the responsibility that they serve to identify is as much responsibility for good conduct and good outcomes as for bad conduct and bad outcomes.

29 According to Jules Coleman, the implication of "harm" is that a legitimate interest of the plaintiff has suffered: see Coleman, *Tort Law and Demands*, above n.5, at p. 350.

30 See below, question (5).

31 Wider in the sense that reasons other than fault may support a duty to compensate.

32 Perry, above n.17, at pp. 490–1.

33 This is not to accept Nickel's argument that corrective justice applies only to the impairment of distributively just holdings of goods: see James W. Nickel, "Justice in Compensation", 18 *Wm. & Mary Law Rev.* 379, 381–3, 385–8 (1976) cf. Jules L. Coleman, "Justice and the Argument for No-Fault", 3 *Social Theory & Practice* 161, 174, 180, n.19 (1975) [hereafter *Argument for No-Fault*]. Corrective justice applies to actual holdings, whether or not those actual holdings in justice ought to be redistributed in whole or part to other members of the community.

34 How far this responsibility should be translated into strict legal liability depends on the answers to questions (5) and (6) below.

35 Richard Wright argues that corrective justice requires the employer to compensate the victim "for injuries that are tortiously inflicted in pursuance of the employer's objectives": Wright, above n.3, at p. 674, n.219. But, as he himself recognizes, id. at p. 674, it is unjust to compel someone to be an insurer for the fault of another, unless he has undertaken to do so (or, I would add, the just distribution of risks requires him to do so). It seems a mere fiction to argue that the employee's act is really the employer's, or must be treated as such.

36 Offences of negligence such as negligent wounding and killing are of course commoner in civil law than common law systems, but they are by no means absent from the common law.

37 Stephen Perry says it is based on something resembling fault: see Perry, above n. 17, at p. 504. The difference is between what one should not in any case do and what one may do provided it does not turn out to be harmful to others.

38 See generally David G. Owen, "The Moral Foundations of Punitive Damages", 40 *Ala. Law Rev.* 705 (1989).

39 Or if his employer is vicariously liable for his

conduct but exercises rights of subrogation against him – in practice a rare event.

40 See generally Coleman, *Argument for No-Fault*, above n.33, at pp. 173–4; Jules Coleman, "Mental Abnormality, Personal Responsibility and Tort Liability", in *Mental Illness: Law and Public Policy* (ed. Baruch A. Brody and H. Tristram Engelhardt, Jr, 1980) pp. 107, 118–21, 123–4. Cf. Jules Coleman, "The Morality of Strict Liability", 18 *Wm. and Mary Law Rev.* 259, 283–4 (1976).

41 For whose conduct the employer properly bears the risk according to principles of distributive justice.

42 It is true that in practice legal systems tend to confine vicarious liability of employers to accidents attributable to employeee fault.

43 As Coleman has pointed out, the retributive arguments in favour of fault liability in tort law as it operates in practice are rather weak: *Argument for No-Fault*, above n.33, at pp. 162–72. But see David G. Owen, "The Fault Pit", 26 *Ga. Law Rev.*, 703 (1992).

44 Above pp. 16–17, 24.

45 As in New Zealand, with respect to accidents.

46 Hart and Honoré, above n.28, at pp. 259–75.

47 Hart and Honoré, above n.28, at pp. 225–35.

48 Wright, above n.3, at p. 704.

Chapter 33

Stephen R. Perry

ON THE RELATIONSHIP BETWEEN CORRECTIVE AND DISTRIBUTIVE JUSTICE

DISTRIBUTIVE JUSTICE is concerned with the just distribution of material resources, income, other forms of wealth, and perhaps certain other goods within a society. Corrective justice is concerned with the moral duty of repair, meaning the moral duty to pay compensation, that one individual can come to owe another as a result of having harmed him. In this essay, I inquire into the relationship between these two principles. More particularly, I ask whether corrective and distributive justice are independent principles, or whether they are related in either a conceptual or a normative sense.

One common view is that corrective justice requires a prior distribution of entitlements upon which to operate, and that its purpose or point is to maintain that distribution; for that reason, it is regarded as both conceptually and normatively ancillary to distributive justice. Another, less common, view holds that corrective and distributive justice operate on quite distinct kinds of entitlement, and hence are conceptually and normatively independent of one another. The position I defend is that corrective justice is a general moral principle that is concerned, not with maintaining a just distribution, but rather with repairing harm. Individuals can be harmed in a number of different ways, and corrective justice accordingly protects a number of different kinds of interest and entitlement. Distributive justice often contributes to

the legitimacy of an entitlement that corrective justice protects, and in that sense there is a normative connection between the two. But corrective justice does not protect the entitlement *qua* distributive share, and its purpose is not to maintain or preserve a distributive scheme as such. Rather it protects a legitimate entitlement because interference with the entitlement harms the entitlement-holder. In that sense, corrective and distributive justice are conceptually independent.

It may be helpful to have a concrete theory of corrective justice in view as we proceed. To sketch briefly my own account of these matters,[1] the duty to repair in corrective justice depends on a more general concept of responsibility for outcomes which, following Tony Honoré, I call outcome-responsibility.[2] Outcome-responsibility, which is a fundamental aspect of our understanding of our own agency, requires that an agent have had control, in some appropriate sense, over the outcome that he caused. Different conceptions of outcome-responsibility involve different understandings of what it means to have control of this kind. The particular conception I defend conceives of control in terms of avoidability: a person is outcome-responsible for a harmful outcome to which she causally contributed if and only if she had the capacity to foresee that outcome and the ability and opportunity to take steps to avoid it. Outcome-responsibility in this sense means that a harmful outcome is properly attributable to someone's agency, but this is only a necessary and not a sufficient condition for the existence of a duty to repair in corrective justice. For such a duty to exist, it must also be possible to say that the harm in question belongs, in a moral sense, to the injurer rather than to the victim. I argue that a harm belongs to the injurer if she acted faultily in bringing the harm about, or if, in acting, she imposed certain kinds of unusual risks on the victim. In the former circumstance, a standard of intention or negligence is warranted; in the latter circumstance, strict liability is the appropriate approach.

The view just sketched is one understanding of corrective justice, but there are of course others.[3] Very little, if anything, in the argument I present below turns on the acceptance of this particular view. The argument should apply to any conception of corrective justice that understands it as a general moral principle giving rise to a duty to repair, and that does not involve either of the following two suppositions: first, that the function of corrective justice is by definition to protect distributive entitlements or, secondly, that there exist entitlements in corrective justice that are conceptually and normatively distinct from other kinds of entitlements, including in particular distributive entitlements. It also bears mention that the argument does not, for the most part, depend on any assumptions about the content of corrective justice—whether, for example, it involves a fault-based standard, a standard of strict liability, or some combination of the two.

Finally, I should note that corrective justice theorists are generally interested in corrective justice because they think that it constitutes the normative foundation of tort law. While I share that view, I make no attempt to defend it here. This essay is primarily concerned with the conceptual and normative relationship between two moral principles, rather than with the positive law that gives effect to those principles.

I

It might be suggested that corrective and distributive justice must be conceptually and normatively independent of one another just by virtue of being very different sorts of principles. Distributive justice is a matter of social justice. Since the concern is with the general distribution of goods throughout an entire society, it is plausible to think, with John Rawls, that the subject of distributive justice is the basic structure of society.[4] If distributive justice gives rise to reasons for action for individuals, as opposed to the state, they are presumably agent-general reasons. Corrective justice, on the other hand, appears to be a matter of personal or individual justice. The concern is with agent-relative obligations that one person owes to another as a result of a prior interaction between them. The basic subject of corrective justice is, we might say, not society but rather the individual. Given that distributive justice is most plausibly construed as social justice, whereas corrective justice is most plausibly construed as justice between individuals, why would the question of their relationship to one another even be thought to arise?

Corrective justice gives rise to a duty to repair when persons have harmed one another in certain ways. The phrase 'in certain ways' refers not only to the nature of the injurer's conduct (e.g. was the conduct negligent or subject to strict liability), but also to the type of harm suffered by the victim. It is plausible to think that the principle of corrective justice applies, like the law of torts, to harm of several different types. Put another way, corrective justice protects several different interests against interference by other persons. These need not be enumerated in full here, but they certainly include the interest an individual has in preserving her life and bodily security, on the one hand, and the interest she has in maintaining the physical integrity of her tangible property, on the other. The argument sketched in the preceding paragraph, to the effect that corrective and distributive justice are conceptually distinct principles that operate in separate normative spheres, has, in the case of the interest in life and bodily integrity, a certain plausibility. At least within non-consequentialist moral theory, it makes sense to think of this interest as morally fundamental, and hence as falling outside the purview of distributive justice; our physical persons belong to us from the outset, and are accordingly not subject to a social distribution of any kind. In so far as corrective justice concerns harm to the person, it appears to be both conceptually and normatively independent of distributive justice.

Matters arguably stand differently when it comes to damage to tangible property. For purposes of corrective justice, a person cannot have a cognizable interest in a particular material resource unless he has an entitlement to that resource. The law of torts necessarily concerns itself with legal entitlements, but at the level of corrective justice the entitlement must presumably be a moral one. Unless a person is morally, and not just legally, entitled to a particular thing that has been damaged, it is difficult to see how he could have the moral standing to claim compensation under what is, after all, supposed to be a principle of justice. It is plausible, moreover, to think that the moral legitimacy of an entitlement to a particular item of tangible property depends, at least in part, on its being held under a distributively just scheme of property rights. This suggests in turn that the point of corrective justice is to protect entitlements *qua* distributive shares, i.e. its point is to protect the just distribution as such. This is in fact a fairly common contemporary view of the relationship between corrective and distributive justice. Often, it is presented as an interpretation of Aristotle's original discussion of corrective and distributive justice in the *Nicomachean Ethics*.[5] But several of the commentators defending this interpretation also suggest, either implicitly or explicitly, that this is also the correct understanding of the relationship between corrective and

distributive justice. Since this view clearly regards distributive justice as conceptually and normatively prior to corrective justice, let me refer to it as the distributive priority view.

James Gordley and Wil Waluchow are two scholars who defend the distributive priority view both as an interpretation of Aristotle and, it would seem, as a correct understanding of the relationship between corrective and distributive justice. Gordley, after first noting that distributive justice is concerned with determining the shares of various goods that citizens are entitled to receive within a society, continues as follows:

> [Commutative, i.e. corrective, justice] is concerned not with sharing resources, but with preserving each citizen's share. Therefore, the party who has lost resources to another has a claim for the amount necessary to restore the original position. It is the mathematics of addition and subtraction, of balancing accounts.[6]

Waluchow's view is to the same effect. He suggests that distributive justice is concerned with 'a distribution flowing from state to citizen', whereas in corrective justice the aim 'is to correct an imbalance which has resulted from an unwarranted private transaction whose unwarranted status . . . is determined independently of corrective justice'.[7] Such transactions are unwarranted independently of corrective justice because, according to Waluchow, they involve a departure from the antecedently given just distribution:

> Corrective justice . . . is in a sense parasitic. It presupposes an independently definable just status quo; a status quo of equality in which each party has, by law, his due—his entitlements—and which owing to the actions of the defendant has been disturbed. Those actions introduce an imbalance which must be rectified.[8]

John Rawls arguably holds a similar view of the relationship between corrective and distributive justice, although it is also arguable that he holds a view closer to the one I will develop in section III.[9]

Leaving aside the question whether the distributive priority view is a plausible interpretation of Aristotle's original text,[10] the account it offers of the relationship between corrective and distributive justice is problematic in its own terms.[11] According to the distributive priority view, corrective justice is conceptually and normatively ancillary to distributive justice; the point of corrective justice, on this approach, is simply to regulate and maintain the antecedently-given just distribution. On that understanding, however, it is not clear that there is logical room for a principle of corrective justice that is in any way distinct from distributive justice; the latter concept is not merely ancillary to, but completely subsumed by, the former. Why not simply speak of maintaining the just distributive pattern, and leave aside misleading talk of a separate principle of justice? Corrective justice is, moreover, supposed to be concerned with rectifying departures from the antecedent pattern that were brought about by human agency operating in a certain way. By the phrase 'operating in a certain way', I mean to refer to an assessment of the agent's conduct in accordance with whatever standard of liability, fault-based or strict, that the best understanding of corrective justice determines to be applicable in the circumstances. But once the object of the exercise is taken to be the preservation of an existing distributive pattern, the limitations on achieving that object that are created, first, by the requirement that a certain standard of liability be met and, secondly, by the even more fundamental requirement that departures from the pattern must, to be rectifiable, flow from human agency, seem quite arbitrary. From the point of view of maintaining the pattern, why should it matter whether a given departure was brought about by human agency or by, say, natural disaster or the expenses associated with illness?

Gordley has argued that, on what I am calling the distributive priority view, corrective justice is in fact conceptually distinguishable from distributive justice. The idea is that a person responsible for undertaking a distribution 'would violate distributive justice if he disregarded the principle of proportionality that was supposed to guide the distribution. He would violate the arithmetic equality of corrective justice if he gave [someone] less than the amount that had been determined to be due to him.'[12] To do distributive justice, according to Gordley, a person must know what needs to be distributed, to whom, and on what basis, and then must be willing to apply the distributive principle even-handedly. To do corrective justice, '[o]ne has to be willing to pay what is owed'.[13] In other words, distributive justice involves calculating each person's share, whereas corrective justice involves handing those shares over. This would appear, however, simply to be a distinction between the deliberative and executive stages of distributive justice. It is possible, to be sure, to draw such a distinction, but it does not seem to have any theoretical significance, nor does there seem to be any basis for labelling the executive stage a separate principle of justice. It is thus not clear how this move is supposed to show that corrective justice is, after all, conceptually distinct from distributive justice.

If, moreover, we follow Gordley's suggestion and stipulatively define corrective justice as the executive stage of distributive justice, this understanding seems quite removed from corrective justice as traditionally understood. To see this, we need only revisit our earlier point about the arbitrariness, on the distributive priority view, of singling out distribution-preserving moves that are necessitated by human agency. The executive stage of distributive justice would presumably include not just distribution-preserving moves of this kind, but also all initial allocations under the appropriate distributive scheme. This by itself goes well beyond the traditional understanding of corrective justice. In addition, the executive stage would presumably also include all subsequently required distribution-preserving moves, including those that were needed because, e.g., someone had suffered a loss due to natural disaster or disease. There does not appear to be any principled basis for singling out a more limited executive principle that applies only to deviations from the existing distribution that came about as a result of a human agent falling below a certain standard of liability. Traditionally, however, it is only cases of the latter sort that have been regarded as falling within the province of corrective justice.

On the point that the effects of natural events on distributive justice seem, on the distributive priority view, to be indistinguishable in principle from corrective justice, Gordley makes two arguments in response. The first takes as its starting-point the claim that the function of private property is, in the Aristotelian tradition, to provide an incentive to work and to prevent quarrels. Even if it were possible to distinguish chance gains and losses from those that were the result of labour and care, 'the attempt might lead to so many charges of arbitrariness as to give rise to the quarrels that a system of private property is supposed to prevent'.[14] Note first that this argument about the effect that natural events should or should not have on distributive justice depends on a more general claim about the function of private property. I discuss that claim below, where I suggest that it complicates our understanding of distributive justice in such a way as to render problematic the idea that corrective justice preserves antecedently-specified distributions. For now I will simply point out that it seems implausible to suppose that attributing this function to private property entails that distributive justice is impervious to all disastrous natural events. If any readjustments to a distributive pattern are ever required because, say, an unpredictably severe storm destroyed many people's property, those

readjustments will fall under Gordley's definition of corrective justice (i.e. corrective justice understood as the executive stage of distributive justice). For the reasons already given, this seems problematic.

A similar point applies to Gordley's second response to the argument that the effect of natural events on distributive justice will, on the distributive priority view, be indistinguishable in principle from corrective justice. This response is that, if everyone were fully compensated when his property was destroyed through bad luck, people would be more willing than they should be to put their property at risk. Again, however, this argument does not establish that disastrous natural events should never affect distributive justice, since not all such events give rise to moral hazard problems. If a readjustment to a distribution is ever required because of a natural event—the unpredictably severe storm mentioned earlier, for example—that readjustment will, as already noted, fall under Gordley's definition of corrective justice. In addition, Gordley's two responses to the disastrous-natural-event problem both seem misplaced, for the following reason. Both attempt to show that, for essentially practical reasons, natural events should not have any effect on distributive justice. If this claim is meant to be a generalization completely without exceptions, it seems highly implausible. Even if it were always true, however, that would still not address the conceptual difficulty that there does not seem to be anything special, on the distributive priority view, about corrective justice as traditionally understood (i.e. a principle that imposes a duty of repair on human agents who cause others losses). Even if, for practical reasons, natural events never affect allocations under distributive justice, the characterization of corrective justice as the executive stage of distributive justice still includes the possibility of such readjustments; for that reason it is, conceptually speaking, far too broad.

There are other problems with the distributive priority view in addition to those just enumerated. Assume for the moment that distributive justice requires what Nozick calls a simple patterned distribution of goods, i.e. a more or less static distribution based on a fixed formula such as, 'to each in equal shares', 'to each in accordance with his moral virtue', etc.[15] Aristotle's discussion of these matters in the *Nicomachean Ethics* is plausibly interpreted as envisaging distributive justice as taking very much this form.[16] For the sake of simplicity, assume further that the relevant pattern is an equal distribution of material resources, that the society in question consists of four persons, and that each person has ten units of goods.[17] Suppose first that A takes four of B's units. The initial pattern can be restored, and equality reinstated, by taking those same four units (or perhaps some other four of equal quality) from A and giving them to B. Restitutionary cases of this kind appear, in fact, to be Aristotle's paradigm of corrective justice: '[a]s though there were a line divided into two unequal parts, [the judge] takes away the amount by which the larger part is greater than half the line and adds it to the smaller'.[18] It is with respect to such cases, moreover, that the distributive priority view seems to have most plausibility.

Suppose next that, instead of taking four of B's units, A causes their destruction. Assuming that the appropriate standard of liability applies to A's conduct, corrective justice would presumably require A to compensate B by giving her four units. Doing this will not, however, restore the original equal distribution. Equality can only be restored if B receives one unit from each of the others in the society, thereby constituting a new distribution of nine units each.[19] There are a couple of points to be noted here. The first, which is specific to the Aristotelian restitutionary understanding of corrective justice, is that it is not clear how that approach can be extended to cover cases involving damage to or destruction of property. Quite apart from the normative difficulties that arise in trying to justify a duty to repair on the basis of restitutionary principles,[20]

it is far from evident what the analogue of restitution would be in a case like this. In the example discussed in the preceding paragraph, A gained four units and B lost four. Corrective justice, on the restitutionary model, in effect required A to give the four units back; this wiped out both A's gain and B's loss and, in the process, restored the original pattern of distribution. In the case in which A destroys rather than takes four of B's units, however, the idea of giving something back seems inapplicable. A may well have incurred a gain in destroying B's units—perhaps he burned them to keep himself warm—but that gain is logically distinct from B's loss. Corrective justice, of course, focuses on the loss rather than on the gain. On a restitutionary model, however, it is not obvious why that should be so.

The second and more important point that is illustrated by the example of A destroying four of B's units pertains to the distributive priority view in general, and not just the Aristotelian restitutionary variant. The concern here is with the fact that if A compensates B for her loss, the original equal distribution is not thereby restored. In general, doing corrective justice between particular persons will not reinstate a formerly existing distributive pattern, and it might well have the effect of introducing new distributive distortions. (To take an example of Jules Coleman's, imagine that a very poor person negligently drives his ancient heap into the luxury vehicle of an extremely wealthy person, and that the former is then obligated to compensate the latter.[21]) The reason that doing corrective justice will not restore a distributive pattern is that the maintenance of such a pattern is a global problem, the solution to which requires taking account of the shares of all persons within the relevant group. But corrective justice rectifies loss on a local scale, between two persons. As a general matter, the local mechanism cannot respond satisfactorily to the global problem. Moreover, this deficiency of process reflects a deeper difficulty. The reasons for action arising from distributive justice are agent-general: they pertain to all persons within society (or to society as a whole). Corrective justice, on the other hand, is most plausibly thought to create agent-relative reasons for action: it gives the injurer alone a reason to compensate the victim.[22] For both these reasons—the local nature of corrective justice versus the global requirements of distributive justice, on the one hand, and the different structures of practical reasoning that pertain to each of the two forms of justice, on the other—corrective justice cannot plausibly be regarded as having the function of maintaining a just distribution of material resources.

Gordley offers a further defence of the distributive priority view, which takes issue with the premise that distributive justice should be understood in terms of simple patterned distributions of resources. According to Gordley, the Aristotelian tradition rejected this premise:

> Private property was supposed to prevent quarrels and to provide incentives to work. Consequently, a citizen cannot demand more resources in a democracy simply because he has less than someone else or in an aristocracy simply because he has the same amount as someone less virtuous. To obtain the advantages of a system of private property, a society will have to tolerate some deviations from the principle of distributive justice it regards as ideal.[23]

In assessing this defence of the distributive priority view, it is important to ask how seriously we should take Gordley's claim that 'a society will have to tolerate some deviations from the principle of distributive justice it regards as ideal'. On the most straightforward reading of this statement, Gordley is suggesting that the theoretical ideal of distributive justice is indeed a simple patterned distribution of resources, but that for various pragmatic reasons which are external to distributive justice this ideal cannot,

and indeed should not, be attained in practice. If that is Gordley's argument, however, it is insufficient to save the distributive priority view. The various criticisms of that view that were offered in the preceding paragraphs were conceptual in nature, meaning they were offered precisely at the level of ideal theory. The general charge against the distributive priority view to which those criticisms point is that corrective justice cannot plausibly be understood as having the function of preserving just distributions of resources, if just distributions are taken to be simple patterned distributions. It is no answer to this charge to say that, even though distributive justice ideally calls for simple patterned distributions, these cannot be achieved in practice. Nor is it an answer to say that there are good moral reasons why such patterns should not be achieved—the need to create incentives, avoid quarrels, and so on—if those reasons are external to the theory of distributive justice.

Perhaps, then, Gordley should be understood as arguing, in the above-quoted passage, that distributive justice does not call for simple patterned distributions of resources even at the level of ideal theory. He is suggesting, rather, that because distributive justice must take account internally of such factors as the need to avoid quarrels and give people incentives to work, it must be conceived dynamically rather than statically. Although the particular factors of avoiding quarrels and creating incentives may not be the most important ones in a more complex conception of distributive justice—the desirability of permitting market exchanges seems much more significant, for example—the general claim that distributive justice is complex in this way is a very plausible one.

The most influential contemporary theories of distributive justice are dynamic rather than static. John Rawls, for example, explicitly rejects the idea of simple patterning, which he calls the allocative conception of justice.[24] Rawls' own theory takes distributive justice to be, within certain limits, a matter of pure procedural justice. This means that if certain institutions such as competitive markets, appropriate forms of taxation, and a reasonable social minimum are in place, and if together those institutions tend over time to satisfy the difference principle, then any particular distributive state that happens to emerge at a given point in time is acceptable.[25] There is no independent criterion for assessing the acceptability of such distributive states. Ronald Dworkin's theory of distributive justice holds that an equal share of resources should be devoted to the lives of each person, but it similarly rejects the idea that equality of resources is measured, in the manner of simple patterning, at particular moments of time.[26] Rather it is measured diachronically, across entire lives and against the background of such institutions as a free market and progressive taxation. Equality of resources is thus understood abstractly, in a way that is supposed to be unaffected by a person's talents but that takes account of choices that affect which resources are available to oneself and to others. These include choice of occupation, choice of how hard to work, choice of which risks to run, and choice of with whom to contract and on what terms. Robert Nozick's libertarian entitlement theory is very different from the egalitarian theories of Rawls and Dworkin, but by determining the legitimacy of entitlements on a purely historical basis it, too, embraces a dynamic rather than a static conception of justice in holdings.[27]

In so far as Gordley is saying that distributive justice must be understood dynamically rather than statically, he is undoubtedly correct. But that does not help his defence of the distributive priority view, since on a dynamic understanding of distributive justice it is no longer clear what it means to say that the point of corrective justice is to preserve a just distribution. The Rawlsian and Dworkinian conceptions of distributive justice operate through institutions and over time. Simple patterning is concerned directly with the holdings of individuals as these exist at particular moments in time. Let me call such

patterns of holdings momentary distributive states. The Rawlsian and Dworkinian theories are properly called patterned, but the patterns are abstract and involve general tendencies that develop through time. So far as momentary distributive states are concerned, it is clear that both the Rawlsian and Dworkinian theories give rise to a great deal of indeterminacy; dynamic conceptions of distributive justice like these are compatible with many different such states.[28] While there are problems with the distributive priority view even as applied to simple patterning, we at least have some understanding of what it means to preserve or restore a momentary distributive state. What does it mean, though, to say that when an individual injurer complies with his duty to repair, this helps to preserve the abstract patterns associated with Dworkin's equality of resources or Rawls' difference principle? It is perhaps possible that content can be given to this notion, but surely the onus in this regard is on the person who wishes to defend the idea that the distributive priority view can be applied to a dynamic conception of distributive justice. It is not enough to assert that the problems the distributive priority view faces on a simple patterned theory do not matter because distributive justice involves abstract patterns rather than simple ones. This is the starting-point for theorizing, not the end-point.

As for the Nozickian entitlement theory, it does not involve patterning of any kind, simple or abstract. Corrective justice is, in effect, built into the theory through Nozick's principles of rectification and justice in transfer. Since patterning plays no role in the theory it is not really about distributive justice at all, at least as that notion has traditionally been understood. (Nozick himself prefers the term 'justice in holdings'.) One is tempted to say that, on the entitlement theory, corrective justice comprises, together with the principle of justice in acquisition, all the justice there is. Such a view of justice in holdings is not likely to appeal to an Aristotelian like Gordley, but the distributive priority view clearly has no purchase on the entitlement theory in any event. If there is no patterning, then the idea of preserving or maintaining a pattern simply has no application. To put the point more bluntly, if there is no distributive justice, how can it take priority over anything?

There is one final point I would like to make about the distributive priority view, before moving on. As I mentioned at the beginning of this section, we tend to think of corrective justice as a general principle that protects a number of different interests against interference by other persons. In particular, corrective justice protects life and bodily security, on the one hand, and tangible property, on the other. Of these two interests, only tangible property is plausibly thought to be subject to distributive justice. Since the basic claim of the distributive priority view is that the point of corrective justice is to preserve just distributions, it faces a dilemma. Either it must say, in the face of strong intuitions to the contrary, that life and bodily integrity are, after all, subject to distributive justice. Or it must say, again contrary to strong intuitions, that corrective justice is not a single general principle but two, one of which protects the fundamental interest in life and bodily security, and the other of which protects just distributions of material resources.

II

In section III I will argue that, if we accept the premise that distributive justice is best understood dynamically rather than statically, corrective justice should be conceived as an independent moral principle that operates within the context of distributive justice, but not as a part of it. First, however, I would like to examine a different attempt to show that the moral duty of repair is, properly understood, a matter of distributive justice. The distributive priority view characterizes corrective justice as an instrument for preserving just distributions and, therefore,

as a principle ancillary to distributive justice. In fact, a better characterization of that view would be that it tries to do away with the concept of corrective justice altogether, arguing that the moral duty to repair can be explained entirely in distributive terms. Ronald Dworkin has also attempted to explain the moral duty to repair in distributive terms.[29] The attempt is interesting for a couple of reasons. First, it explicitly begins with a dynamic conception of distributive justice which is, taken on its own terms, quite plausible and attractive. This is the theory of equality of resources that was sketched in the preceding section. Secondly, it looks upon the duty of repair not as a means for preserving or restoring an antecedently-given, determinate distribution of holdings—this being, of course, the approach of the distributive priority view—but rather as a means for refining or making concrete a set of initially abstract distributive entitlements.

Dworkin begins by considering situations in which there is a conflict between what he calls abstract rights in property. An example would be a dispute between A and B over their respective rights to use their neighbouring apartments as they wish: A wants to play his trumpet and B wants to study algebra. Another would involve a conflict between A's right to run a train on his land at the speed that he chooses and B's right to plant corn on his adjoining land, when sparks from the speeding train might ignite and burn the corn. Dworkin makes the assumption that A and B have roughly equal wealth in both the abstract sense of the theory of equality of resources, which is measured across entire lives, and the more limited sense of equal current holdings.[30] He also assumes that 'neither is handicapped or otherwise has special needs or requirements'.[31] Dworkin states that when A's and B's abstract rights conflict they must each act as if the concrete rights that they both cannot exercise had not yet been distributed between them, and that they must distribute these themselves as best they can, 'in the way equality of resources commends'.[32] If compromise is not possible then each must act 'so as to minimize the inequality of the distribution [they] achieve, and this means so that the loser loses less'.[33] Dworkin maintains that this principle of comparative harm calls for market-simulating behaviour, since, given the assumption of roughly equal wealth, this will provide a plausible measure of the relative respective importance to A and B of their two conflicting activities. Thus in the trumpet/algebra situation, for example, the conflict should be resolved in an all-or-nothing way by asking whether A would pay more for B to stop playing his trumpet than B would pay for the opportunity to play it.

Dworkin is thus looking at harmful interactions mainly from the point of view of a forward-looking distribution of rights, but it is clear that he regards the backward-looking moral and legal treatment of a loss as a question to be decided in light of how the parties ought to have applied the comparative harm principle. If A would not have paid as much for the opportunity to inflict the loss (or to impose the risk of the loss occurring) as B would have paid to engage in his activities unimpeded, then A has a moral duty of repair and B a correlative moral right. For the most part I shall only be considering here such criticisms of Dworkin's theory that call into question this explication of the duty of repair, although I shall also make incidental note of various ways in which the theory does not seem to provide a very good fit with the actual doctrines of tort law.

The first point to be noticed is that Dworkin does not adequately take account of our strong pre-theoretical conviction that, absent special circumstances such as contributory fault or damages that are too remote, a moral duty of repair should make the victim whole and not just provide partial compensation. (This conviction, it should be noted, has always been reflected in the substantive doctrines of the law of torts.) Dworkin acknowledges that his approach seems to call for compromise among citizens, and remarks at one point that it is only 'practical circumstances' that force all-or-nothing decisions on citizens acting for themselves.[34] But if backward-looking allocations of loss ought to coincide with what citizens should have decided on a forward-looking basis, as Dworkin is apparently assuming, then he is simply ignoring our sense that a moral duty of repair ought to be an all-or-nothing affair. He is ignoring, that is to say, our sense that in ordinary circumstances either the plaintiff has a right to recover his entire loss or else the defendant does not have to pay anything. Moreover, whatever practical circumstances may force on citizens deciding these issues for themselves on a forward-looking basis, there does not seem to be any reason why judges, dealing with disputes *ex post facto*, cannot apportion a loss between plaintiff and defendant in such a way as to mirror the compromise that Dworkin says the parties should have reached if it had been practicable, and that better accords with the general principles of distributive justice to which he is ultimately appealing.

A second, related criticism of Dworkin's theory concerns the fact that distributive justice might not be best served by treating particular instances of conflicting rights as discrete cases to be considered in isolation from another. Dworkin recognizes that, ideally, individual decisions about the distribution of concrete rights should, on his approach, be treated as part of a continuing series of linked decisions that can be taken into account in a 'moral ledger'.[35] Once again, however, this runs counter to a strong pre-theoretical conviction that moral (and therefore legal) rights of repair should not directly depend on what else has transpired or will transpire between the parties, and that particular cases therefore ought to be treated in isolation from one another, at least so far as the determination of liability is concerned. (Set-off in the determination of damages is, of course, another matter.)

It is worth noting that the practical difficulties of treating individual decisions as linked do not, unlike the practical difficulties that are involved in allocating losses on an all-or-nothing basis, appear to be ones that can be overcome in the judicial context, since courts are presumably in no better a position than citizens to keep ongoing moral ledgers. (This is not to deny, of course, that on Dworkin's view they should nevertheless make the attempt.) Dworkin responds to the general impracticability of keeping ledgers by appealing to the hypothesis that 'if everyone treats [decisions that affect others generally, or a stranger only once] as isolated cases, this will work out roughly fairly for everyone in the long run'.[36] Such a hypothesis seems most plausible in situations involving regularly occurring, low-level nuisances of the sort represented by Dworkin's example of trumpet-playing versus algebra-studying. However, as a generalization about the sorts of disputes that are dealt with by the law of torts as a whole, it is almost certainly untrue. For example, serious personal injuries, unlike low-level nuisances, occur randomly and relatively infrequently, so that any distributive injustice that results from the legal treatment of a single accident considered in isolation is unlikely to be offset, for the individual affected, by some future judgment in his favour. This aspect of Dworkin's theory is thus doubly problematic. First, in principle the theory calls for a linking of cases, where linking seems morally suspect in itself. Secondly, as a practical matter, the law of torts is incapable either of creating such links or mimicking their effects (by means, for example, of Dworkin's proposed hypothesis that everything will work out in the long run). This suggests that tort law is not a very efficient instrument for accomplishing the goal of refining or perfecting a scheme of distributive justice.

A third criticism of Dworkin's theory of moral rights and duties of repair focuses on the initial assumption that persons who find themselves in a situation requiring a decision about the distribution of concrete rights have roughly equal wealth, where neither is handicapped or otherwise has special requirements. Dworkin recognizes that this assumption will often not hold, but argues that because equality of resources is an abstract conception of distributive justice—i.e. it applies over lifetimes rather than simply looking to momentary distributive states—we should generally act on the assumption that people have equal resources in the abstract sense unless we have good reason to think this is not true. Recall, however, that Dworkin assumes that the parties have equal wealth both in the abstract sense and also in the sense of current holdings. The assumption that the parties have roughly equal current wealth would arguably yield information that is relevant and useful in the settlement of disputes. This is because what seems to be more appropriately compared in cases like that of the trumpet-player and the algebra-studier is the relative potential damage to the parties' specific conflicting projects, rather than the relative potential damage to their entire life-plans. Given an assumption of equal current wealth, knowing whether the trumpet-player would pay more to the algebra-studier or vice versa presumably tells us something about the relative strengths of their preferences for engaging in these particular activities, and that information is arguably relevant to settling the immediate dispute between them.

Equality of resources in the abstract sense, as measured over lifetimes, is the distributively ideal state of affairs within Dworkin's theory. The assumption that such a state of affairs obtains between two given persons is thus perhaps defensible,[37] at least in the absence of any evidence to the contrary. The same cannot be said, however, for the assumption of equal current holdings. Not only is it not a normative ideal of the theory that current holdings should be equal, but the expectation within the theory is very much to the contrary. Actual holdings are supposed to reflect various life-choices, which in the usual course of affairs will lead to different and possibly quite disparate levels of wealth among persons. In addition, the fact that two persons do or do not have equal current wealth is usually relatively easy to ascertain, at least as compared to the assumption of equal wealth in the abstract sense. There is thus neither a normative basis nor, ordinarily, an empirical one, for assuming of any two persons that they are even roughly equally wealthy. The assumption of equal current wealth, although it is arguably attractive because of what it reveals about the parties' preferences, is not warranted under Dworkin's theory and should not be made. According to the theory, persons' preferences should be reflected in their actual life-choices and, ultimately, in the extent of their individual holdings. Unwarranted assumptions about the extent of their holdings should not be used to work backwards in order to ascertain their preferences.

Of the two assumptions we have been discussing, then, it is only the assumption of equal wealth in the abstract sense that can appropriately be made under Dworkin's theory. Such an assumption suggests, however, that the relevant conflict is one between entire life-plans rather than immediate projects. Under that assumption, it does not matter that at the time of the simulated bargain the parties have unequal amounts of money in their pockets. The upshot is that the market simulation test might well penalize the algebra-studier, say, because he chose to devote his life to the not particularly lucrative career of a mathematics teacher. Suppose that, as a result of that decision, he is now less wealthy than the trumpet-player, who became a commercially successful jazz musician. Why should the resolution of the present dispute turn in any way on these past career decisions? It was presumably in order to avoid undesirable wealth effects of this kind that Dworkin assumed not just that the parties had equal resources in the abstract sense, but also that they had roughly equal funds at their disposal at the time of the simulated bargain. But an assumption of equal current wealth is, as we have seen, inappropriate under Dworkin's theory. The correct assump-

tion, which is that the parties have equal resources only in the abstract sense, will inevitably create wealth effects of just this kind.

It is also important to remember that the assumption of equal wealth is, in the end, just an assumption. In particular circumstances, equality of wealth even in the abstract sense can be shown not to hold. Dworkin acknowledges that the appropriate distribution of concrete rights is in principle affected by the fact that one party has more than he should have, or that the other party has less than she should have, under the theory of equality of resources.[38] But he does not seem entirely comfortable with this conclusion when he states that 'it seems unjust that compensation to a victim should depend on the relative wealth of the actor, if for no other reason than the difficulty that would pose to someone anxious to insure against injury on sensible terms'.[39] The injustice in fact extends further than this observation suggests, since it is highly implausible to think that, in principle, the manner in which I ought to act toward others in my daily life is in any way a function of my or their wealth. How I treat others should remain constant even against a range of different possible background schemes of distributive justice and, indeed, at least in certain sorts of cases, it should transcend membership in any particular political community. These intuitions are especially strong where personal injury is concerned. It surely cannot be correct that the degree of risk of death or bodily harm that I can permissibly impose on another person depends in any way on the wealth of either of us.

Dworkin does say that his general approach must be qualified to take account of individual rights that protect fundamental interests,[40] and at one point he suggests this would mean that 'threats to life' should not be dealt with in terms of the comparative harm principle.[41] However, he does not say how he thinks losses associated with such threats should then be handled. Differential treatment of property damage and personal injury cases would seem to be consistent with his assertion elsewhere that '[though a person's physical and mental] powers are resources, they should not be considered resources whose ownership is to be determined through politics in accordance with some interpretation of equality of resources'.[42] Thus while Dworkin regards the existence of a disability as a factor that should be taken into account in the distribution of resources, he does not think that distributive justice involves trying to make people equal in physical and mental terms: '[t]he problem is, rather, one of determining how far the ownership of independent material resources should be affected by differences that exist in physical and mental powers, and the response of our theory [of distributive justice] should speak in that vocabulary'.[43] This is surely correct, but the upshot would seem to be that an individual's interest in life and bodily integrity should not be treated as an 'abstract property right' of the sort with which Dworkin's theory of tort law primarily concerns itself. This suggests in turn, as does Dworkin's rather cryptic observation concerning threats to life, that he requires a separate account of moral (and therefore legal) rights and duties of repair where injury to the person is at issue.

The question that then arises is whether a moral theory that views rights and duties of repair as based on two distinct principles, one of which applies to the interest in life and bodily security and the other of which applies to interests in property, is a satisfactory one. (As was mentioned at the end of the preceding section, a similar difficulty seems to arise for the distributive priority view.) For the most part tort law itself does not determine liability differently in property and personal injury cases, and it seems implausible to think that such a distinction has any significant place in the general moral theory of rights and duties of repair. This is an issue to which I return in section III, where I argue that the most appropriate way to develop a unified general theory of corrective justice is to take the principle of repair that applies in personal injury cases as one's starting-point, and then inquire whether that principle can be extended to cases of property damage.

One final series of observations about Dworkin's assumption of equal wealth is in order here. As was mentioned earlier, Dworkin says that persons who have to distribute concrete rights between themselves should ordinarily assume, for practical reasons, that they each have available roughly equal resources for the pursuit of their respective projects in life. Whatever practicality may demand in everyday life, however, if Dworkin's account of rights and duties of repair were correct then there would be no reason why courts, when required in tort actions to distribute actual losses *ex post*, should not make an effort to ascertain the relative wealth of the litigants and then take that information into account, in the determination of both liability and the measure of damages, to try to realize as adequately as possible the abstract ideal of equality of resources. In fact the courts generally consistently refuse, as a matter of principle, to try to do anything like this. So far as plaintiffs are concerned, damages are assessed on the basis of actual losses suffered, without reference to whether the victim has more or less than he should have under an appropriate conception of distributive justice. So far as defendants are concerned, the law adopts objective standards, such as the standard of the reasonable person, the whole point of which is to make a great deal of specific information about the defendant irrelevant in principle. At least when it comes to information about wealth, however, the thrust of Dworkin's theory is exactly the opposite. In principle, the determination of liability depends on specific facts about the relative holdings of the parties, and if that information is available it should, according to the theory, be employed. The theory only manages to approximate the courts' actual practices by relying on epistemic opacity, in the form of the the assumption of equal wealth. But something seems to have gone seriously wrong when such a wide gap between theory and practice has to be bridged in that manner.

III

In section I, I argued that the moral duty to repair cannot be understood as a means to preserve or maintain an antecedently-given, determinate scheme of distributive justice. In section II I argued that that duty cannot be understood as a means to refine or perfect an abstract and partially indeterminate scheme of distributive justice. The more general conclusion to which these arguments point is that a moral duty to repair cannot be justified in distributive terms. I have not fully established that conclusion, however, because I have not offered a comprehensive argument that a duty to repair cannot be justified within a dynamic conception of distributive justice. I have argued that Dworkin's particular attempt to offer such a justification, within the context of his own theory of equality of resources, does not succeed. I have also suggested that someone who wishes to combine the distributive priority view with a dynamic conception of distributive justice bears the onus of showing that this can be done. But I have not presented a general argument showing that such a combination is impossible, nor will I attempt to do so now. Instead, I will offer a general characterization of the principle of corrective justice—a characterization that is meant to apply to a number of more specific theories that can be found in the literature—and argue that corrective justice thus conceived is appropriately viewed as complementary to, although conceptually independent of, distributive justice. As we will see, this can only be true if distributive justice is understood in dynamic rather than in static terms, since no plausible conception of corrective justice can be reconciled with simple distributive patterning. The proper conclusion to be drawn from this is, so much the worse for simple patterning.

In what follows I will, in discussing abstractly patterned conceptions of distributive justice, leave aside Nozick's entitlement theory. The reason for doing so is that the entitlement theory is not, as was noted in section I, best conceived as an account of distributive justice to begin with. It is, in effect, a theory of corrective justice to which a principle of justice in acquisition has been appended. Dworkin and the distributive priority theorists might be described as attempting to get rid of the notion of corrective justice or, if not going quite that far, as at least attempting to subsume it, normatively and conceptually, within distributive justice. It is only a slight exaggeration to say that Nozick wants to do the reverse; he is attempting either to get rid of the notion of distributive justice or else to subsume it, normatively and conceptually, within corrective justice. I of course do not claim to have established that a theory of distributive justice in the strict sense—i.e. a theory based on simple or abstract patterning—is the correct theory of justice in holdings. But it is only on that assumption that the problem with which I am concerned in this essay is a genuine problem.

According to the general characterization I have in mind, then, corrective justice protects legitimate entitlements in tangible property, but it does not do so because such entitlements are distributively just shares. Nor does it do so in order either to preserve or to refine the distributive scheme itself. Rather, corrective justice protects legitimate entitlements simply because they are legitimate. It is perfectly true that, on most theories of private property (although not on the entitlement theory), considerations of distributive justice figure in the justification of entitlements to material resources. On the view of corrective justice I am sketching, however, once the moral legitimacy of an entitlement has been established, the justificatory role of distributive justice is no longer of central concern. The concern is rather this. Damage to a tangible object can harm someone who possesses or uses the object, and if the possessor or user has a morally legitimate entitlement to it then the harm is of moral significance. The moral focus of corrective justice is not on background distributive considerations but rather on harm to another person.

One might try to develop a general account of corrective justice along the lines suggested in the preceding paragraph in either of two different ways. One of these attempts to derive corrective justice from the concept of property, while the other begins with an independent moral principle of repair and tries to show why that principle is applicable to property interests. The first, property-based approach to corrective justice has sometimes been adopted by libertarians. Richard Epstein, for example, at one time argued that a moral duty to repair, based on a standard of strict liability, is directly entailed by the concept of property.[44] This is implausible, if only because there does not seem to be any contradiction in the idea of a property interest that is protected by a negligence standard or, for that matter, that is not protected by any liability rule at all. Epstein has also put forward a conceptual/normative argument that in effect makes the following two claims. First, a right of restitution is inherent in the concept of property and, secondly, a moral duty of repair is derivable from the right of restitution.[45] The first of these claims is plausible,[46] but, as I have argued elsewhere,[47] the second is not. The basic problem with the second step of the argument is that no analogue of restitution seems to apply when the gainer's gain is not equal to the loser's loss. (As we saw in section I, this is the same problem that is encountered by the Aristotelian restitutionary model of corrective justice.) There is in any event a more plausible libertarian conception of corrective justice, which begins not with the concept of property in the strict sense but rather with the looser notion of self-ownership.[48]

This brings us to the second possibility, which takes an independent moral principle of repair as its starting-point and tries to show why that principle is applicable to property interests. ('Independent' here means independent of distributive justice.) Since the underlying concern of such a theory is harm to other persons, let me call this the harm-based view of corrective justice. Particular theories of corrective justice that embody or are consistent with this view tend to invoke some conception of responsibility for the outcomes of one's actions. Jules Coleman equates such responsibility with a conception of objective fault.[49] The libertarian theory mentioned at the end of the preceding paragraph, which takes the notion of self-ownership as its starting-point, equates responsibility for outcomes with causation. I have argued elsewhere that the basis of this form of responsibility is the fact that an outcome was both foreseeable and avoidable.[50] It would not, however, be to the present purpose to enter into the details of this debate. Instead, let me try to bring out some general points about the moral duty of repair by focusing on the paradigm case of intentional harm to the person.

If, intentionally and without justification, I cause you personal injury, I assume most people will agree that I have a moral duty to compensate you for the harm. Whatever the precise nature of the underlying responsibility here may be, notice that this duty is independent of distributive justice. If your interest in life and bodily integrity is properly called an entitlement, it is not an entitlement that is subject to distributive justice. Nor is my duty to compensate you sensitive to how wealthy I am.[51] This is enough to establish that there is an independent moral principle giving rise to an agent-relative duty of repair. The issue then becomes how general is this principle. There are two separate questions that arise in this regard. First, to what other conduct, besides intentional wrongdoing, can the duty be extended? Can it be extended, for example, to advertent negligence, inadvertent negligence, or non-faulty forms of conduct that would require a standard of strict liability? Secondly, to what other interests, besides the interest in life and bodily integrity, can the duty be extended? In the present context, it is the second of these questions that is of concern.

The main reason that personal injury constitutes harm is that it interferes with personal autonomy. It interferes, that is to say, with the set of opportunities and options from which one is able to choose what to do in one's life.[52] Interference with autonomy is not the only way that personal injury can adversely affect someone, of course: pain and suffering, for example, are separate types of harm. But there is no doubt that interference with autonomy is an exceptionally important category of harm, and the independent principle of repair clearly offers redress for having suffered it in inappropriate ways (in the paradigm case, by being intentionally injured). Notice next that the harm involved in damaging or destroying tangible property also constitutes an interference with autonomy. The use-value and the exchange-value of property both represent opportunities for the owner, and adversely affecting either type of value harms the owner precisely because it diminishes her opportunities.[53] If her entitlement to the property is morally legitimate, then the interference with autonomy is morally significant and a remedy against inappropriate instances should be provided by the independent principle of repair. Notice, finally, that while it is no doubt true that at least one of the aims of distributive justice is to ensure that everyone has enough material resources to be able to pursue an autonomous life, corrective justice is not best envisaged, in property damage cases, as either protecting entitlements because they are distributive shares or preserving a just distribution of resources for its own sake. Corrective justice applies in such cases because the owner of damaged property has suffered harm. She has, in fact, suffered the same general type of harm as she would have suffered had she been injured in her person. Because corrective justice focuses, even in property damage cases, on harm rather than on distributive considerations, it is properly

regarded as conceptually independent of distributive justice.

It should be emphasized that the harm-based understanding of corrective justice can only be regarded as conceptually independent of distributive justice if distributive justice is conceived dynamically rather than statically, i.e. if it is conceived in terms of abstract rather than simple patterning. We saw in section I that the distributive priority view of corrective justice cannot be reconciled with a static conception of distributive justice, although that had as much to do with the problematic aspects of the distributive priority view as it had to do with anything about simple patterning. In fact, no plausible conception of corrective justice, including any grounded in the harm-based view, can be reconciled with a static conception of distributive justice. Let me return for a moment to the example of static patterning that I borrowed from Larry Alexander in section I. The relevant pattern is an equal distribution. The relevant society consists of four persons, and each person has 10 units of goods. Suppose that A intentionally destroys four of B's units. Any plausible conception of corrective justice will require A to compensate B by giving her four of his units. Alexander points out that this will upset the pattern of equality, which can only be restored if everyone other than B gives her one of their units. Alexander argues that this 'conflict' between corrective and distributive justice can only be resolved by jettisoning one or the other, and he concludes that it is corrective justice that has to go: '[s]ince distributive justice is logically prior to corrective justice—there must be a distribution relative to which loss and compensation are measured—the obvious principle to discard is that of corrective justice'.[54]

The obvious way to resolve this conflict, however, is not to discard either corrective or distributive justice, but to discard the idea that distributive justice is a matter of simple patterning. As we saw in section I, the most powerful and well-developed contemporary theories of distributive justice are dynamic rather than static. The difference between these two types of theory is qualitative, and not just a matter of degree. I will argue in what follows that the harm-based view of corrective justice is consistent with and complementary to, although it is conceptually independent of, an appropriate, abstractly-patterned theory of distributive justice. Alexander's example, based as it is on a static pattern, in no way calls this conclusion into question. His argument is, in many ways, reminiscent of Nozick's famous Wilt Chamberlain example,[55] which also begins with a static distributive pattern. Nozick observes that a significant deviation from the pattern will occur if a large number of individuals voluntarily choose to give Chamberlain a certain proportion of their distributive shares to watch him play basketball. From this Nozick concludes that liberty upsets patterns, but all that he is really entitled to conclude is that liberty upsets simple patterns. The example tells us nothing about the role of liberty in any plausible dynamic theory of distributive justice, for example those of Rawls and Dworkin.

The general approach to corrective justice that is exemplified by the harm-based view has not gone unchallenged. Although he does not address that view directly, Peter Benson has in effect argued that any understanding of corrective justice that possesses the following two characteristics will inevitably collapse into what I earlier called the distributive priority view: (1) it views corrective justice as protecting legitimate entitlements; and (2) it views the legitimacy of entitlements as determined by distributive justice. Benson argues that if distributive justice is postulated as the ground of the entitlements that corrective justice is supposed to protect, then there is nothing to preclude the injurer from claiming that his infringement of the entitlement is, from a distributive point of view, actually an improvement:

> If the injuring party can coherently frame the dispute in this way, the correction of the infringement should also properly be characterized as an act of distributive justice, seeing that it can be viewed as a decision made between two competing distributive claims. In short, once the initial entitlement is grounded in distributive justice, there is no reason why the violation of the entitlement as well as its correction should not be construed from the same distributive standpoint. It follows that there is no need to introduce, and indeed no basis for referring to a second, genuinely distinct form of justice such as corrective justice ... The distinctiveness of corrective justice is not made out.[56]

Benson goes on to argue that the understanding of corrective justice he is criticizing can only hope to distinguish corrective from distributive justice by treating the background distribution, and hence the injured party's holdings, as presumptively just. But, he continues, since there is no particular reason to think that the distributive arrangement that existed before the parties harmfully interacted was more just than the arrangement that came into existence afterwards, such a presumption preserves the distinctiveness of corrective justice at the cost of its being a principle of justice.[57] According to Benson, corrective justice can only be understood as truly distinct from distributive justice if it operates with respect to a structure of entitlement that is completely independent of the structure of distributive entitlement. His own, Hegelian theory of corrective justice adopts the following principle: '[a] person who, through an external manifestation of will, has brought something under his or her present and exclusive control prior to others is, relative to those others, entitled to it in corrective justice'.[58] Since such entitlements can either coincide with or be at odds with distributive entitlements, this view of corrective justice treats the notion as both conceptually and normatively independent of distributive justice. Each form of justice exists in its own self-contained normative sphere.

Benson's Hegelian theory of corrective justice is subtle and complex, and it is beyond the scope of the present essay to offer a critique of it here. Instead, I will try to show that his objections to such conceptions of corrective justice as the harm-based view are not well-founded. The first point to be made in this regard is that Benson seems to beg the question by implicitly assuming that the position he is criticizing incorporates the distributive priority view. Benson suggests that, if the initial entitlement is grounded in distributive justice, then the injuring party can argue that his infringement of the entitlement is a distributive improvement. Even if the injurer can make such an argument, however, he is, on an understanding of corrective justice like the harm-based view, at best making a normative claim that is dissimilar from, and in competition with, the victim's claim. The moral focus of the victim's claim is the harm she has suffered. She is saying: you harmed me, and therefore you have a moral obligation to compensate me. The injurer responds with the argument that, distributively speaking, it would be better if he did not have to pay compensation.[59] At most, we have two distinct kinds of moral claims which must be balanced against one another. Yet according to Benson, the decision whether or not to correct the infringement involves a choice 'between two competing distributive claims'. There is, however, simply no basis for treating the victim's as well as the injurer's claim as distributive in nature, unless one has implicitly rejected anything resembling the harm-based view and assumed instead that a non-Hegelian theory of corrective justice must adopt the distributive priority view.

The second and more serious problem with Benson's argument is that he seems to be assuming that the legitimacy of so-called 'distributive' entitlements is determined solely by considerations of distributive justice. Benson clearly conceives of distributive justice in terms of patterning, and he appears to allow for the possibility that patterns can be abstract as well as simple.[60] Even so, he apparently does not think that there can be any normative 'play' between the distributive justification of an entitlement and its ultimate moral legitimacy. While this might very well be true of a simple patterned theory, there are strong grounds for thinking that it will not be true of any plausible dynamic conception of distributive justice. An important observation by Jules Coleman is relevant in this regard.[61] Coleman points out that there are very good reasons, in addition to considerations of distributive justice, for having a system of private property rights, and this suggests that a set of entitlements that is not distributively ideal— Coleman speaks of a set of 'second best' entitlements—may nonetheless be morally legitimate and worth protecting. He mentions in particular the importance of property rights to sustaining markets, since markets contribute to overall social welfare in well-known ways, but there are many other, similarly consequentialist concerns that come into play here. Gordley's points about giving people incentives to work and preventing quarrels are examples.[62] As Coleman observes, 'within limits, the rights in place may help to sustain an institution that generally improves individual well-being and social stability, and that does so in ways that encourage individual fulfillment, initiative, and self-respect. Those rights would then be worthy of respect even if they did not exactly coincide with the best or most just distribution of resources.'[63]

To this point Benson might reply that, just because an entitlement is morally legitimate, it does not follow that the courts, say, should not take advantage of a tort action to make distributive improvements. Why should legitimacy be thought to confer immunity from morally-required redistribution? Perhaps the degree of protection that even a morally legitimate entitlement should receive from corrective justice and tort law is dependent on the status of the entitlement in distributive justice. This might mean, to revert to an earlier example, that an extremely poor person who negligently collides with the Mercedes of an exceptionally wealthy person does not have to pay the Mercedes' owner compensation, even though the latter is morally entitled to her car. Benson's counter-argument would then conclude that the existence of 'play' between the distributive justification of an entitlement and its moral legitimacy does not prevent the collapse of the harm-based view of corrective justice into the distributive priority view (or, more accurately, into distributive justice *tout court*).

This is where the dynamic nature of distributive justice enters the picture. On a dynamic, abstractly-patterned theory based on, e.g. Rawls' difference principle or Dworkin's notion of equality of resources, distributive justice does not operate at the level of momentary distributive states, let alone at the level of individual holdings. These theories are dynamic and abstractly-patterned precisely in order to allow people to enter into contracts, make gifts, and so on, without thereby creating distributive disparities. The result is that such theories are highly indeterminate with respect to momentary distributive states and the extent of individual holdings. It is possible, for example, for some individuals to become very wealthy without disrupting abstract equality or the difference principle. Who ends up at any given moment with which resources and how much wealth is, as Rawls says, a matter of pure procedural justice. Coleman's point tells us that the overall system of private property rights can be morally legitimate even if it is not ideally distributively just. The moral legitimacy of the system will presumably be transmitted to individual entitlements. It is far from clear, however, that it even makes sense to say of individual holdings that they embody distributive imbalances, or at least that they do so in such a way that would justify *ad hoc* adjustments by a judge in a tort action.

Consider the case of someone who has acquired vast wealth in business but who has always played by the rules; she has always observed applicable market norms, paid exactly what she owes in income tax, never stolen from anyone, and so on. No doubt it is possible to say of such a person that she is too wealthy, but notice what this does and does not mean under a dynamic conception of distributive justice. As the Coleman point makes clear, it does not mean, or at least it does not necessarily mean, that her holdings are morally illegitimate (although if the entire system is too askew distributively, that is at least a possibility). It does not mean that she has too much under the existing, perhaps less-than-ideal, scheme of distributive justice. (How could she, since by hypothesis she played by all the rules, including in particular the redistributive rules embodied in the taxation scheme?) It might mean that she has too much wealth to be justified under any plausible conception of distributive justice, in which case the extent of her holdings might well be morally illegitimate. What it probably means to say that she is too wealthy, though, is that her vast wealth is symptomatic of systemic distributive problems in the property regime as a whole. Systemic deficiencies must be dealt with systemically: perhaps anti-trust law must be tightened up, or the marginal tax rates increased, or the social minimum raised. Contrary to what Benson suggests, however, it is not possible to do distributive justice in any meaningful way by tinkering with individual levels of holdings on a case-by-case basis, through, say, tort law.[64] As was noted earlier, it is not clear that this notion even makes sense. This is a normative point, and perhaps a conceptual point, about dynamic theories of distributive justice; it is not just a matter of practicality. Part of the point of such theories is to enhance people's liberty by creating stable and enduring entitlements to property that are not subject to continuous, ongoing, or *ad hoc* redistribution.

The harm-based view of corrective justice operates at the level of individual entitlements that have been subjected to interference by another person. By contrast, dynamic conceptions of distributive justice operate systemically, institutionally, and over time. Such conceptions are, as we have seen, highly indeterminate with respect to momentary distributive states and the extent of individual holdings as these exist at any given time, and this creates the logical space within which corrective justice is able to function. Thus when impoverished A negligently rams the Mercedes of extremely wealthy B, then so long as B's entitlement to her Mercedes is morally legitimate, A owes B compensation for the damage.[65] The reason is that A has harmed B in an inappropriate way. Of course, neither the legitimacy of B's specific entitlement, nor the justifiability of the property system as a whole (this being the most likely source of legitimacy for the specific entitlement), entails that the system is ideally distributively just. Thus it might well be the case that welfare payments should be raised, which would benefit A. Perhaps it is also true that marginal tax rates should be increased, which would hurt B. None of this alters the fact that, right now, A has a moral duty to hand money over to B which is unaffected by the great disparity in wealth between them.

According to Benson's Hegelian theory of corrective justice, corrective and distributive justice operate on distinct kinds of entitlement, and for that reason they are, in both a conceptual and a normative sense, completely independent of one another. The harm-based view looks upon corrective justice as conceptually distinct from distributive justice, and also in large measure as normatively distinct, because the two principles have different normative functions. One is concerned with the just distribution of resources, while the other is concerned with remedying harmful interactions between persons. But that does not mean there are no normative connections between the two principles; they are not, as on Benson's view, completely independent from one another. Despite the possibility of a shortfall between moral legitimacy and ideal distributive

justice, a system of private property rights will generally only be morally legitimate if it is distributively just to at least some minimum degree. Thus, in the case of property interests, corrective justice generally operates on what we might loosely call distributive entitlements ('loosely', because of the possibility of shortfall). To that extent, corrective and distributive justice are normatively connected.

Benson argues that if there is a normative connection between corrective and distributive justice of the kind just discussed, then corrective justice can only be regarded as independent from distributive justice if the former adopts a presumption that the existing set of holdings is distributively just. But that seems to be wrong. The conceptual independence of corrective and distributive justice, as well as their partial normative independence, results not from any such presumption but from the fact that the two principles have different normative functions. Benson further suggests that there is no reason in any event to presume that a given set of holdings is distributively just. This is in a sense correct, but irrelevant. If Benson means that no property system in, say, any existing liberal democratic state is ideally distributively just, he is undoubtedly right. From the point of view of corrective justice, however, what matters is not ideal distributive justice but moral legitimacy. Given Coleman's point about the possible discrepancy between the two, it is by no means outlandish to suppose that the property systems in many liberal democratic states are in fact morally justified.[66] Even if that were not true, however, it would not follow that corrective and distributive justice are not conceptually independent. It would just mean that the principle of corrective justice would have no applicability to property interests.[67]

My defence of the independence of corrective from distributive justice might, finally, be challenged from a different quarter. Even if a proponent of Dworkin's theory of equality of resources were to acknowledge the problems with the comparative harm principle that were discussed in section II, he might nonetheless wish to argue that the harm-based view of corrective justice is not independent of distributive justice for the following reason. Even though corrective justice operates at the level of individual entitlements rather than at a systemic level, it does so in such a way as to preserve equality of resources in the abstract sense. In this respect corrective justice resembles the role in Dworkin's theory of market transactions and decisions involving so-called option luck, i.e., deliberate or calculated decisions to run certain risks. Dworkin argues, quite plausibly, that individuals should, against the background of general redistributive institutions, both take the benefits and bear the costs of market transactions and other kinds of calculated gambles. Equality of resources in the abstract sense is thus unaffected by such events, regardless of the outcome. The same would seem to be true of the operation of corrective justice, which might perhaps be regarded as just a special case of option luck. Since corrective justice preserves equality of resources in this way, the argument concludes, it is best conceived as one element of the larger distributive theory.

The phrase, 'corrective justice preserves equality of resources', is ambiguous. On one reading, it suggests that the function of corrective justice is to preserve equality of resources, in very much the same way that the function of corrective justice is taken to be, on the distributive priority view, to preserve determinate just distributions. On another reading, however, the phrase simply means that the abstract pattern of equality is unaffected by the operation of corrective justice. Corrective justice is, so to speak, transparent to distributive justice. In the present context, it is clearly the second meaning of the phrase that is relevant. The function of corrective justice has nothing to do with distributive justice, even though it sometimes operates on distributive entitlements, as these were loosely defined above. The function of corrective justice is, rather, to provide a remedy to persons who have been harmed in certain ways by other persons. While it is an interesting and perhaps theoretically significant fact that corrective justice is transparent to distributive justice, it is one that seems to confirm rather than to call into question the conceptual independence of the former principle from the latter.

Notes

Jeremy Horder (ed.), *Oxford Essays in Jurisprudence*, 4th edition (Oxford 2000), pp. 237–63.

1 S.R. Perry, 'Responsibility for Outcomes, Risk, and the Law of Torts' in G. Postema (ed.), *Philosophy and the Law of Torts* (Cambridge University Press, Cambridge, forthcoming).

2 T. Honoré, 'Responsibility and Luck' (1988) 104 *Law Quarterly Review* 530.

3 Three theories that meet the criteria stated in this para. are developed in the following works: J.L. Coleman, *Risks and Wrongs* (Cambridge University Press, Cambridge, 1992) 303–28; R.A. Epstein, 'A Theory of Strict Liability' (1973) 2 *Journal of Legal Studies* 151; G.P. Fletcher, 'Fairness and Utility in Tort Theory' (1972) 85 *Harvard L. Rev.* 537.

4 J. Rawls, *A Theory of Justice* (Harvard University Press, Cambridge, Mass., 1971) 7.

5 Aristotle, *Nicomachean Ethics* (trans. M. Ostwald, Bobbs-Merrill, Indianapolis, Ind., 1962) Book V.

6 J. Gordley, 'Equality in Exchange' (1981) 69 *California L. Rev.* 1587, 1589.

7 W.J. Waluchow, 'Professor Weinrib on Corrective Justice' in S. Panagiotou, *Justice, Law and Method in Plato and Aristotle* (Academic Printing and Publishing, Edmonton, Alberta, 1987) 153, 155.

8 Ibid. 156.

9 Rawls, n. 4 above, 10–11.

10 Gordley and Waluchow favour this interpretation. Opposing it are P. Benson, 'The Basis of Corrective Justice and Its Relation to Distributive Justice' (1992) 77 *Iowa L.Rev.* 515, 529–49, and E.J. Weinrib, *The Idea of Private Law* (Harvard University Press, Cambridge, Mass., 1995) 76–80.

11 S. Perry, 'The Moral Foundations of Tort Law' (1992) 77 *Iowa L. Rev.* 449, 451–2.

12 J. Gordley, 'Tort Law in the Aristotelian Tradition' in D.G. Owen, *Philosophical Foundations of Tort Law* (Oxford University Press, Oxford, 1995) 131, 136.

13 Ibid.

14 Ibid. 136–7.

15 R. Nozick, *Anarchy, State, and Utopia* (Basic Books, New York, 1974) 155–60.

16 I am neither advocating nor disavowing this interpretation of Aristotle, and nothing in my argument turns on whether or not it is correct. As we shall see later, Gordley's claim that the function of private property 'in the Aristotelian tradition' is to provide incentives and prevent quarrels is most plausibly understood as a denial that distributive justice should be understood in terms of simple patterned distributions. The fact remains that Aristotle is plausibly interpreted in this way, and many commentators have so interpreted him. Furthermore, many theorists discuss the theoretical question of the relationship between corrective and distributive justice on the assumption that distributive justice can be understood by reference to simple patterning. See, e.g., L. Alexander, 'Causation and Corrective Justice: Does Tort Law Make Sense?' (1987) 6 *Law & Phil.* 1, 6–7. Much of Nozick's critical discussion of distributive justice also makes this assumption, at least if we are to judge by his examples: Nozick, n. 15 above, 155–64. Thus, although I ultimately reject this understanding of distributive justice, there is reason to give it serious consideration.

17 The example is taken from Alexander, n. 16 above, 6–7.

18 Aristotle, n. 5 above, 1132a25–27.

19 Cf. Alexander, n. 16 above, 6–7.

20 Cf. Perry, n. 11 above, 452–61.

21 Coleman, n. 3 above, 304.

22 Cf. S.R. Perry, 'Comment on Coleman: Corrective Justice' (1992) 67 *Indiana L.J.* 381, 389–90, 396–400; Coleman, n. 3 above, 319, 374.

23 Gordley, n. 12 above, 136.

24 Rawls, n. 4 above, 88.

25 Rawls, n. 4 above, 86–8.

26 R. Dworkin, 'What is Equality? Part 2: Equality of Resources' (1981) 10 *Philosophy and Public Affairs* 283, 304–7.

27 Nozick, n. 15 above, 150–3.

28 Cf. Dworkin, n. 26 above, 334.

29 R. Dworkin, *Law's Empire* (Harvard University Press, Cambridge, Mass., 1986) 276–312.

30 Ibid. 302, 305.

31 Ibid. 302.

32 Ibid.

33 Ibid. 303.

34 Ibid. 311.

35 Ibid. 305–6.

36 Ibid. 306.

37 This is, however, subject to the argument of section III below, where I suggest that, on a plausible dynamic conception of distributive justice such as equality of resources, it may not even make sense to say of individual holdings that they embody distributive imbalances. Distributive disparities are, rather, necessarily systemic in character.

38 Ibid. 305. Dworkin leaves open the question of what exactly citizens should do in situations of clear distributive injustice: ibid. 446, nn. 15, 18.

39 Ibid. 308.

40 Ibid. 307.

41 Ibid. 309.

42 Dworkin, n. 26 above, 301.

43 Ibid.

44 R.A. Epstein, 'Causation and Corrective Justice: A Reply to Two Critics' (1979) 8 *Journal of Legal Studies* 477, 500–1. Notice that, if corrective justice is to be a general principle that applies to more than one interest and, in particular, to the interest in life and bodily security as well as to the interest in tangible property, this position requires that the libertarian language of self-ownership be taken more or less literally. Self-ownership must be construed as a property right identical in its incidents to the right of ownership one can have in a material resource. Epstein has at times seemed willing to bite this particular bullet. See ibid. 500. However, it is possible to characterize self-ownership somewhat more plausibly as a set of rights that in a loose sense are property-like and that give rise, because no one else besides me 'owns' my person and my powers, to a general right to liberty. This general right to liberty then serves as the basis for deriving property rights in the strict sense. See G.A. Cohen, *Self-Ownership, Freedom, and Equality* (Cambridge University Press, Cambridge, 1995), 69–89, 112–14; S.R. Perry, 'Libertarianism, Entitlement, and Responsibility' (1997) 26 *Philosophy and Public Affairs* 351, 358–63.

45 R.A. Epstein, *Takings: Private Property and the Power of Eminent Domain* (Harvard University Press, Cambridge, Mass., 1985) 38.

46 Cf. A.M. Honoré, 'Ownership' in A.G. Guest, *Oxford*

Essays in Jurisprudence (1st series, Oxford University Press, Oxford, 1961) 107, 114.

47 Perry, n. 11 above, 452–61.

48 On the looser sense of self-ownership, see n. 44 above. On the more plausible libertarian conception of corrective justice, see Perry, n. 44 above, 363–73.

49 Coleman, n. 3 above, 345–7, 486 n. 17. More recently, Coleman has argued that the concept of responsibility underlying corrective justice is 'political' in nature: J. Coleman and A. Ripstein, 'Mischief and Misfortune' (1995) 41 *McGill L.J.* 91. This understanding of corrective justice, unlike the view presented in *Risks and Wrongs*, is in danger of collapsing into the distributive priority view. See S.R. Perry, 'The Distributive Turn: Mischief, Misfortune, and Tort Law' in B. Bix (ed.), *Analyzing Law: New Essays in Legal Theory* (Oxford University Press, Oxford, 1998) 141. Coleman responds in J.L. Coleman, 'Second Thoughts and Other First Impressions' in B. Bix (ed.), *Analyzing Law* 301–16.

50 Perry, n. 1 above.

51 The *existence* of the duty does not depend on how wealthy I am, although the normative consequences of my inability to pay is a separate question. Perhaps, as was once suggested in a Seinfeld episode, if I cannot compensate you with money then I have a duty to become your butler. As this example suggests, compensation for harm need not be in the form of monetary payments or the transfer of property. The possibility of repair therefore does not depend on the existence of property rights. Of course, there are good reasons of liberal political theory, rooted in considerations of personal autonomy, why monetary compensation is preferable to any form of forced labour.

52 Cf. J. Raz, *The Morality of Freedom* (Clarendon Press, Oxford, 1986), 413–14.

53 Ibid. Interference with non-tangible forms of property, such as pure economic interests, also adversely affects autonomy. The law of torts has never offered extensive protection for such interests, however, and there are good reasons for this. See S.R. Perry, 'Protected Interests and Undertakings in the Law of Negligence' (1992) 42 *U. Toronto L.J.* 247, 262–70. It is an interesting question to which interests other than autonomy the principle of corrective justice can be extended, but it is a question beyond the scope of the present essay.

54 Alexander, n. 16 above, 6.

55 Nozick, n. 15 above, 160–4.

56 Benson, n. 10 above, 530–1.

57 Ibid. 531–2. For similar arguments, see also J. W. Neyers, 'The Inconsistencies of Aristotle's Theory of Corrective Justice' (1998) 11 *Can. J. of Law & Juris.* 311, 315–19. Neyers, unlike Benson, thinks that Aristotle's original account of corrective justice cannot accommodate a Kantian/Hegelian interpretation and is, for that reason, defective.

58 Benson, n. 10 above, 543. Ernest Weinrib holds a roughly similar view of corrective justice and of its relationship to distributive justice. See Weinrib, n. 10 above, 80–3, 104, 128–9.

59 As we shall see below, there is a difference between a set of entitlements being morally legitimate and its being distributively ideal. Perhaps the injurer might be understood as saying that the victim did not even have a morally legitimate entitlement to the damaged property. That is different from arguing that leaving the victim uncompensated is a distributive improvement. The claim is, in effect, that the victim was not harmed, or at least that her harm was not of significant moral concern.

60 Benson, n. 10 above, 537.

61 Coleman, n. 3 above, 350–4.

62 The formulation 'preventing quarrels' understates the significance of Gordley's point, which is perhaps better captured by saying that the existence of property rights contributes to preventing social chaos.

63 Coleman, n. 3 above, 354.

64 The core problem with Dworkin's theory of rights of repair might be expressed by saying that he tries to combine a dynamic conception of distributive justice with the fundamentally incompatible idea that distributive adjustments can be made at the level of individual entitlements.

65 Corrective justice, as a moral principle, presumably only operates on morally legitimate entitlements. Tort law is another matter, since it is plausible to think that the law must either refuse to look past the fact of legal entitlement, or else must incorporate a very strong and perhaps irrebuttable presumption that legal entitlements are always also moral entitlements.

66 Cf. Coleman, n. 3 above, 354.

67 It would still apply, of course, to the interest in life and bodily integrity.

PART 5

Critical Approaches to Law

XI. CRITICAL LEGAL STUDIES, CRITICAL RACE THEORY, AND FEMINIST THEORY

Introduction

"**C**RITICAL LEGAL STUDIES**" (CLS) is the name given to a diverse body of legal scholarship which used ideas associated with Left politics to challenge established legal institutions and doctrines. As an intellectual movement, CLS coalesced around a group of American law professors in the 1970s and 1980s who were self-consciously at odds not only with mainstream jurisprudential traditions, but also with mainstream legal scholarship as a whole. They criticized what they perceived to be the atheoretical and uncritical nature of much legal scholarship which they saw as merely legitimating the status quo.[1] Iconoclastic in spirit, they set out to assail or, as one CLS scholar famously put it, "trash"[2] commonly-held beliefs about the determinacy, coherence, intelligibility, and legitimacy of the law. But their critical target was much broader than scholarly or theoretical disputes. CLS scholars also challenged what they perceived to be the essentially conservative tendencies of legal practice and legal education. They sought to expose the political presuppositions lying behind seemingly neutral legal procedures and methods of adjudication.

Beyond a shared left-wing political stance and a common desire to challenge legal orthodoxy, writers associated with CLS espoused a richly diverse range of ideas and arguments, some of which were actually at odds with each other.[3] However, despite this diversity of perspective, it is nonetheless possible to discern some common themes, which became some of the central (though by no means unanimous or uncontroversial) preoccupations of the group. Among the most well-known themes were: first, the indeterminacy of the law; second, the political or ideological nature of law; third, the idea that law promotes the interests of the powerful and legitimates injustice; and fourth, the claim that rights-rhetoric may be dangerous to the interests of subordinated groups. These themes require some elaboration.

CLS scholars generated controversy and debate about the law's indeterminacy. In general terms, we can say that the law is indeterminate on some point when the legal materials are insufficient to determine or justify a unique outcome on that point. CLS theorists hotly debated both the *degree* of indeterminacy prevalent in the law, as well as what its *causes* are and what *consequences* follow from it. Although some CLS writers believed that the law was *radically* indeterminate, that is to say, indeterminate in all or almost all cases,[4] many others subscribed to the more moderate view that the level of legal determinacy was "relatively low"[5]—and certainly lower than was commonly believed by mainstream legal scholars. It should be noted that many of the legal theories presented in this book, most notably modern legal positivism, did not fail to notice the partial indeterminacy of the law or the fact that the interpretation of indeterminate legal rules involves the exercise of some political discretion on the part of judges (see Sections I and II). In fact, one of the leading CLS scholars, Duncan Kennedy, noted that CLS "accepts fully the positivist idea that the law is sometimes determinate and sometimes indeterminate".[6] What he wished to emphasise was that it is not the words of legal rules that produce or determine judicial decisions, but rather other factors such as the political bias of the interpreter.[7] Like many other CLS scholars, Kennedy highlighted the strategic and often consciously ideological activity involved in interpreting legal materials and argued that the law was indeterminate if it was possible for an interpreter to "destabilise" conventional understandings of legal norms.[8] For writers like Kennedy, law's determinacy was contingent on the skill, strategy, time and politics of the interpreter.

Another theme in CLS writings was the inescapably political nature of law. Many CLS writers argued that "law is politics"—not just in the sense that it is possible to have a "liberal" or "conservative" perspective on various legal issues, but in the deeper sense that legal rules and principles are formed as a result of, and constituted by, the broader ideological battles within society.[9] They argued that politics was the dominant motivator of judicial decisions such that there could be no meaningful distinction between so-called "legal" reasoning and political debate. The pervasively political nature of law was also extended to legal education. Duncan Kennedy famously argued that law schools themselves were intensely political places which use systems of domination such as that of professors over students, in order to train lawyers to accept and reinforce later the hierarchies of the legal system.[10]

Roberto Unger develops some of these familiar CLS themes. He is scathingly critical of orthodox legal thinkers whom he disparages as "toadying jurists"[11] who fail to acknowledge the subversive implications of the idea that the normative ideas underpinning the law are indeterminate. At the core of Unger's critique is his attack on "objectivism" which he defines as the belief that "the authoritative legal materials . . . embody and sustain a defensible scheme of human association" and are "not merely the outcome of contingent power struggles or of practical pressures lacking in rightful authority".[12] The falsity of objectivism is evidenced by the ubiquitous pull of principle and counter-principle in the contents of case-law and legal doctrine more generally. The privileging of one "dominant" principle in the work of traditional legal scholarship reflects, according to Unger, a conscious or unconscious suppression of an alternative principle or explanation of an area of law, which is in truth equally supportable. What justifies the privileging of one principle over another is ideology or political choice rather than any "objective" requirement of legal reasoning. Unger urges us to face up to the way in which the law "already incorporates conflict over the desirable forms of human association"[13] and, as such, gives rise to ineliminable tensions between rival principles within the law.

While there are a number of "Crits" in the US and UK[14] who work on new and familiar CLS themes, much of the energy associated with the CLS movement has been transferred to other branches of legal scholarship, most prominently critical race theory and feminist legal theory. Critical race theory explores the extent to which the law reflects the perspective and values of whites and the impact this has on racial minorities. One of the most prominent critical race scholars, Richard Delgado, questions whether the CLS critique of rights-rhetoric is helpful to the interests of subordinated groups. Many CLS scholars denounced rights as myths designed to mask fundamental social, political and economic inequalities.[15] They pointed out that the powerful can (and do) use rights against the disadvantaged. Whilst not dismissing the validity of these insights, Delgado ultimately supports rights and rights-discourse as a way of meeting the needs of minorities most effectively. In so doing, he questions whether CLS is able to deliver (either intellectually or practically) on the type of radical social and legal reform it seems to advocate.

Like critical race theory, feminist legal theory is concerned with issues of disempowerment and exclusion. Many feminists share the belief that law (and/or our theoretical accounts of the nature of law) has been distorted towards the perspectives and interests of men. From a jurisprudential point of view, the claim that the law is "gendered" (i.e. biased in favour of patriarchal interests and values), naturally gives rise to an important critique of law's claim to be neutral, impartial or objective.[16] On a more practical level, feminist jurisprudence shares with critical race theory a focus on proposals for legal reform, i.e. on ways of reconstructing and improving the law so as to remove bias and discrimination. Of course, there are many feminist legal theories and many disagreements between them. One of the most fundamental of these disagreements concerns the question of whether there are inherent differences between men and women and the consequences this might have for legal reform. Anne Phillips provides background to these debates by articulating the pros and cons for feminists of emphasising their differences from men, but also of moving beyond an exclusive focus on women's oppression to encompass the broader concerns of other oppressed groups. By highlighting the common features shared by racial and sexual inequality, Phillips acknowledges the common intellectual resources available to marginal and oppressed groups in challenging their oppression. But she is also wary of subsuming feminist concerns within a more generalized "politics of difference". Both Delgado's and Phillips's pieces are deeply concerned with how our theoretical understandings of these issues can contribute to the practical aim of achieving greater justice for racial minorities and women and greater equality overall.

Notes

1 Alan Hunt, "The Theory of Critical Legal Studies", *Oxford Journal of Legal Studies* 6, 1986, 1; Duncan Kennedy, "Critical Labour Theory: A Comment", *Industrial Relations Law Journal* 4, 1981, 503, 506.
2 Mark Kelman, "Trashing", *Stanford Law Review* 36, 1984, 293.
3 Thus, Mark Tushnet (a major protagonist of CLS) characterized CLS broadly as a "political location for a group of people on the Left" rather than as a "movement" or "school" as such, see "Critical Legal Studies: A Political History", *Yale Law Journal* 100, 1990–91, 1515, 1516.

4 See James Boyle, "Introduction", in J. Boyle (ed.) *Critical Legal Studies,* New York: NYU Press, 1994; see further Duncan Kennedy, "Freedom and Constraint in Adjudication: A Critical Phenomenology", *Journal of Legal Education* 36, 1986, 518.

5 Tushnet, "Critical Legal Studies", 1538.

6 Kennedy, "A Left Phenomenological Critique of the Hart/Kelsen Theory of Legal Interpretation", in E. Caceres, I.B. Flores, J. Saldana, and E. Villaneuva (eds) *Problemas Contemporaneos de law Filosofia del Derecho*, National University of Mexico, 2005, p. 371, p. 376; see also Neil MacCormick, "Reconstruction after Deconstruction: A Response to CLS", *Oxford Journal of Legal Studies* 10, 1990, 539, 553.

7 MacCormick, "Reconstruction after Deconstruction", 553.

8 Kennedy, "A Left Phenomenological Critique", 381.

9 Mark Tushnet, "Critical Legal Studies", 1526.

10 Kennedy, "Legal Education as Training for Hierarchy", in David Kairys (ed.) *The Politics of Law,* New York: Pantheon, 1990, pp. 54–75.

11 Roberto Unger, "The 'Critical Legal Studies' Movement", p. 581.

12 Ibid., p. 578.

13 Ibid., p. 584.

14 UK-based CLS writers often publish in the journal *Law & Critique*. See also Peter Fitzpatrick & Alan Hunt, *Critical Legal Studies*, Oxford: Blackwell, 1987. Many UK "Crits" are known for their attempts to apply the ideas of European literary theorists, social theorists and philosophers (e.g., Derrida, Foucault, and Lacan) to an analysis of the law.

15 See, e.g., Mark Tushnet, "An Essay on Rights", *Texas Law Review* 62, 1983–4, 1363, 1371.

16 Patricia Smith, "Feminist Jurisprudence", in Dennis Patterson (ed.) *A Companion to the Philosophy of Law and Legal Theory*, Oxford: Blackwell, 1996, pp. 302–3; see also Emily Jackson and Nicola Lacey, "Introducing Feminist Legal Theory", in J. Penner, D. Schiff & R. Nobles (eds) *Jurisprudence and Legal Theory: Commentary and Material*, London: Butterworths, 2002, pp. 779–855.

Further reading

On Critical Legal Studies

John Finnis, "On 'The Critical Legal Studies' Movement' ", *American Journal of Jurisprudence* 30, 1985, 21.

Alan Hunt, "The Theory of Critical Legal Studies", *Oxford Journal of Legal Studies* 6, 1986, 1.

David Kairys (ed.) *The Politics of Law* (Pantheon, NY, 1990) 54–75.

Mark Kelman, *A Guide to Critical Legal Studies*, Cambridge, Mass.: Harvard University Press, 1987.

Duncan Kennedy, "Freedom and Constraint in Adjudication: A Critical Phenomenology", *Journal of Legal Education* 36, 1986, 518.

Neil MacCormick, "Reconstruction after Deconstruction: A Response to CLS" (1990) 10 OJLS 539.

Mark Tushnet, "An Essay on Rights", (1983–4) 62 Texas LR 1363, 1371

Mark Tushnet, "Critical Legal Studies: A Political History" (1990–91) 100 Yale LJ 1515.

On feminist legal theory

Susan James & Stephanie Palmer (eds) *Visible Women: Essays on Feminist Legal Theory*, Oxford and Portland, Oregon: Hart Publishing, 2002.
Emily Jackson and Nicola Lacey, "Introducing Feminist Legal Theory", in J. Penner, D. Schiff & R. Nobles (eds) *Jurisprudence and Legal Theory: Commentary and Material*, London: Butterworths, 2002.
Patricia Smith, "Feminist Jurisprudence", in Dennis Patterson (ed.) *A Companion to the Philosophy of Law and Legal Theory*, Oxford: Blackwell, 1996.

On Critical Race Theory

Peggy Davis, "Law as Microaggression", *Yale Law Journal* 98, 1989, 1559.
Richard Delgado and Jean Stefancic, "Critical Race Theory: an Annotated Bibliography", *Virginia Law Review* 79, 1993, 461.

Questions

1. Do you agree with Unger's view that the "dominant legal theories" engage in a "daring and implausible sanctification of the actual" which is, in turn, "tacitly presupposed by the unreflective common sense of orthodox lawyers" (p. 582)?
2. If the law is substantially indeterminate (as some CLS scholars claim), does it follow that court decisions are no more than disguised political decisions?
3. "To say that rights are politically useful is to say that they *do* something, yet to say that rights are indeterminate is to say that one cannot know whether a claim of right will do anything"; Mark Tushnet, "An Essay on Rights", 1384.

     Discuss this statement with regard to the ability of CLS to mount what Richard Delgado refers to as a "positive program" for reforming the law and our understanding of it.
4. Does critical race theory embody an affirmation and extension of CLS themes, or alternatively, a substantial departure from them?
5. Do you think that Anne Phillips's concerns about the dangers of subsuming feminist arguments within a broader "politics of difference" are valid? What, if any, might be the dangers for feminists of avoiding such assimilation?

Chapter 34

Roberto Mangabeira Unger

THE CRITICAL LEGAL STUDIES MOVEMENT

I. Introduction: the tradition of leftist movements in legal thought and practice

THE CRITICAL LEGAL STUDIES movement has undermined the central ideas of modern legal thought and put another conception of law in their place. This conception implies a view of society and informs a practice of politics.*

The ideas and activities of the movement respond to a familiar situation of constraint upon theoretical insight and transformative effort. This situation is exemplary: its dangers and opportunities reappear in many areas of contemporary politics and thought. Our response may, therefore, also have an exemplary character.

One of the most important obligations anybody has toward a movement in which he participates is to hold up before it what, to his mind, should represent its highest collective self-image. My version of this image of critical legal studies is more proposal than description. It may meet with little agreement among the critical legal scholars. But I have unequivocally preferred the risks of repudiation to those of indefinition. In this, if in nothing else, my statement will exemplify the spirit of our movement.

It may help to begin by placing critical legal studies within the tradition of leftist tendencies in modern legal thought and practice. Two over-riding concerns have marked this tradition.

The first concern has been the critique of formalism and objectivism. Let me pause to define formalism and objectivism carefully, for these ideas will play an important role in later stages of my argument. By formalism I do not mean what the term is usually taken to describe: belief in the availability of a deductive or quasi-deductive method capable of giving determinate solutions to particular problems of legal choice. What I mean by formalism in this context is a commitment to, and therefore also a belief in the possibility of, a method of legal justification that can be clearly contrasted to open-ended disputes about the basic terms of social life, disputes that people call ideological, philosophical, or visionary. Though such conflicts may not be entirely bereft of criteria, they fall far short of the rationality that the formalist claims for legal analysis. The formalism I have in mind characteristically invokes impersonal purposes, policies, and principles as an indispensable component of legal reasoning. Formalism in the conventional sense—the search for a method of deduction from a gapless system of rules—is merely the anomalous, limiting case of this jurisprudence.

You might add a second distinctive formalist thesis: that only through such a restrained, relatively apolitical method of analysis is legal doctrine possible. By legal doctrine or legal analysis, in turn, I mean a form of conceptual practice that combines two characteristics: the willingness to work from the institutionally defined materials of a given collective tradition and the claim to speak authoritatively within this tradition, to elaborate it from within in a way that is meant, at least ultimately, to affect the application of state power. Doctrine can exist—the formalist says or assumes—because of a contrast between the more determinate rationality of legal analysis and the less determinate rationality of ideological contests.

This thesis can be restated as the belief that lawmaking and law application differ fundamentally, as long as legislation is seen to be guided only by the looser rationality of ideological conflict. Lawmaking and law application diverge in both how they work and how their results may properly be justified. To be sure, law application may have an important creative element. But in the politics of lawmaking the appeal to principle and policy—when it exists at all—is supposed to be both more controversial in its foundations and more indeterminate in its implications than the corresponding features of legal analysis. Other modes of justification allegedly compensate for the diminished force and precision of the ideal element in lawmaking. Thus, legislative decisions may be validated as results of procedures that are themselves legitimate because they allow all interest groups to be represented and to compete for influence or, more ambitiously, because they enable the wills of citizens to count equally in choosing the laws that will govern them.

By objectivism I mean the belief that the authoritative legal materials—the system of statutes, cases, and accepted legal ideas—embody and sustain a defensible scheme of human association. They display, though always imperfectly, an intelligible moral order. Alternatively they show the results of practical constraints upon social life—constraints such as those of economic efficiency—that, taken together with constant human desires, have a normative force. The laws are not merely the outcome of contingent power struggles or of practical pressures lacking in rightful authority.

The modern lawyer may wish to keep his formalism while avoiding objectivist assumptions. He may feel happy to switch from talk about interest group politics in a legislative setting to invocations of impersonal purpose, policy, and principle in an adjudicative or professional one. He is plainly mistaken; formalism presupposes at least a qualified objectivism. For if the impersonal purposes, policies, and principles on which all but the most mechanical versions of the formalist thesis must rely do not come, as objectivism suggests, from a moral or practical order exhibited, however partially and ambiguously, by the legal materials themselves, where could they come from? They would have to be supplied by some normative theory extrinsic to the law. Even if such a theory could be convincingly established on its own ground, it would be a sheer miracle for its implications to coincide with a large portion of the received doctrinal understandings. At least it would be a miracle unless you had already assumed the truth of objectivism. But if the results of this alien theory failed to overlap with the greater part of received understandings of the law, you would need to reject broad areas of established law and legal doctrine as "mistaken." You would then have trouble maintaining the contrast of doctrine to ideology and political prophecy that represents an essential part of the formalist creed: you would have become a practitioner of the free-wheeling criticism of established arrangements and received ideas. No wonder theorists committed to formalism and the conventional view of doctrine have always fought to retain some remnant of the objectivist thesis. They have done so even at a heavy cost to their reputation among the orthodox, narrow-minded lawyers who otherwise provide their main constituency.

Another, more heroic way to dispense with objectivism would be to abrogate the exception to disillusioned, interest group views of politics that objectivist ideas at least implicitly make. This could be accomplished by carrying over to the interpretation of rights the same shameless talk about interest groups that is thought permissible in a legislative setting. Thus, if a particular statute represented a victory of the sheepherders over the cattlemen, it would be applied, strategically, to advance the former's aims and to confirm the latter's defeat. To the objection that the correlation of forces underlying a statute is too hard to measure, the answer may be that this measurement is no harder to come by than the identification and weighting of purposes, policies, and principles that lack secure footholds in legislative politics. This "solution," however, would escape objectivism only by discrediting the case for doctrine and formalism. Legal reasoning would turn into a mere extension of the strategic element in the discourse of legislative jostling. The security of rights, so important to the ideal of legality, would fall hostage to context-specific calculations of effect.

If the criticism of formalism and objectivism is the first characteristic theme of leftist movements in modern legal thought, the purely instrumental use of legal practice and legal doctrine to advance leftist aims is the second. The connection between these two activities—the skeptical critique and the strategic militancy—seems both negative and sporadic. It is negative because it remains almost entirely limited to the claim that nothing in the nature of law or in the conceptual structure of legal thought—neither objectivist nor formalist assumptions—constitutes a true obstacle to the advancement of leftist aims. It is sporadic because short-run leftist goals might occasionally be served by the transmutation of political commitments into delusive conceptual necessities.

These themes of leftist legal thought and practice have now been reformulated in the course of being drawn into a larger body of ideas. The results offer new insight into the struggle over power and right, within and beyond the law, and they redefine the meaning of radicalism.

II. The criticism of legal thought

We have transformed the received critique of formalism and objectivism into two sets of more specific claims that turn out to have a surprising relation. The two groups of critical ideas state the true lesson of the law curriculum—what it has actually come to teach, rather than what the law professors say it teaches, about the nature of law and legal doctrine. The recitation of this lesson carries the critique of formalist and objectivist ideas to an unprecedented extreme. This very extremism, however, makes it possible to draw from criticism elements of a constructive program.

A. The critique of objectivism

Take first the way we have redefined the attack upon objectivism. Our key idea here is to reinterpret the situation of contemporary law and legal doctrine as the ever more advanced dissolution of the project of the classical, nineteenth century jurists conceived in a certain way. Because both the original project and the signs of its progressive breakdown remain misunderstood, the dissolution has not yet been complete and decisive. The nineteenth century jurists were engaged in a search for the built-in legal structure of the democracy and the market. The nation, at the Lycurgan moment of its history, had opted for a particular type of society: a commitment to a democratic republic and to a market system as a necessary part of that republic. The people might have chosen some other type of social organization. But in choosing this one, in choosing it for example over an aristocratic and corporatist polity on the old-European model, they also chose the legally defined institutional structure that went along with it. This structure provided legal science with its topic and generated the purposes, policies, and principles to which legal argument might legitimately appeal. Thus, two ideas played the central role in this enterprise. One was the distinction between the foundational politics, responsible for choosing the social type, and the ordinary politics, including the ordinary legislation, operating within the framework established at the foundational moment. The other idea was the existence of an inherent and distinct legal structure of each type of social organization.

Many may be tempted to dismiss out of hand as wholly implausible and undeserving of criticism this conception of a logic of social types, each type with its intrinsic institutional structure. It should be remembered, however, that in less explicit and coherent form the same idea continues to dominate the terms of modern ideological debate and to inform all but the most rigorous styles of microeconomics and social science. It appears, for example, in the conceit that we must choose between market and command economies or at most combine into a "mixed economy" these two exhaustive and well-defined institutional options. The abstract idea of the market as a system in which a plurality of economic agents bargain on their own initiative and for their own account becomes more or less tacitly identified with the particular set of market institutions that triumphed in modern Western history. Moreover, the abandonment of the objectivist thesis would leave formalism, and the kinds of doctrine that formalism wants to defend, without a basis, a point to which my argument will soon return. The critique of objectivism that we have undertaken is essentially the critique of the idea of types of social organization with a built-in legal structure and of the more subtle but still powerful successors of this idea in current conceptions of substantive law and doctrine. We have conducted this assault on more than one front.

Historical study has repeatedly shown that every attempt to find the universal legal language of the democracy and the market revealed the falsehood of the original idea. An increasing part of doctrinal analysis and legal theory has been devoted to containing the subversive implications of this discovery.

The general theory of contract and property provided the core domain for the objectivist attempt to disclose the built-in legal content of the market just as the theory of protected constitutional interests and of the legitimate ends of state action was designed to reveal the intrinsic legal structure of a democratic republic. But the execution kept belying the intention. As the property concept was generalized and decorporealized, it faded into the generic conception of right, which in turn proved to be systematically ambiguous (e.g., Hohfeld) if not entirely indeterminate. Contract, the dynamic counterpart to property, could do no better. The generalization of contract theory revealed, alongside the dominant principles of freedom to choose the partner and the terms, the counterprinciples: that freedom to contract would not be allowed to undermine the communal aspects of social life and that grossly unfair bargains would not be enforced. Though the counterprinciples might be pressed to the corner, they could be neither driven out completely nor subjected to some system of metaprinciples that would settle, once and for all, their relation to the dominant principles. In the most contested areas of contract law, two different views of the sources of obligation still contend. One, which sees the counterprinciples as mere ad hoc qualifications to the dominant principles, identifies the fully articulated act of will and the unilateral imposition of a duty by the state as the two exhaustive sources of obligation. The other view, which treats the counterprinciples as possible generative norms of the entire body of law and doctrine, finds the standard source of obligations in the only partially deliberate ties of mutual dependence and redefines the two conventional sources as extreme, limiting cases. Which of these clashing conceptions provides the real theory of contract? Which describes the institutional structure inherent in the very nature of a market?

The development of constitutional law and constitutional theory throughout the late nineteenth and the twentieth centuries tells a similar story of the discovery of indeterminacy through generalization. This discovery was directly connected with its private law analogue. The doctrines of protected constitutional interests and of legitimate ends of state action were the chief devices for defining the intrinsic legal-institutional structure of the scheme of ordered liberty. They could not be made coherent in form and precise in implication without freezing into place, in a way that the real politics of the republic would never tolerate, some particular set of deals between the national government and organized groups. Legitimate ends and protected interests exploded into too many contradictory implications; like contract and property theory, they provided in the end no more than retrospective glosses on decisions that had to be reached on quite different grounds.

The critique of this more specific brand of objectivism can also be pressed through the interpretation of contemporary law and doctrine. The current content of public and private law fails to present a single, unequivocal version of the democracy and the market. On the contrary, it contains in confused and undeveloped form the elements of different versions. These small-scale variations, manifest in the nuances of contemporary doctrine, may suggest larger possible variations.

The convergent result of these two modes of attack upon objectivism—the legal-historical and the legal-doctrinal—is to discredit, once and for all, the conception of a system of social types with a built-in institutional structure. The very attempt to work this conception into technical legal detail ends up showing its falsehood. Thus, the insight required to launch the attack against objectivism—the discovery of the indeterminate content of abstract institutional categories like democracy or the market—with its far-reaching subversive implications, was partly authored by a cadre of seemingly harmless and even toadying jurists. Those who live in the temple may delight in the thought that the priests occasionally outdo the prophets.

B. The critique of formalism

We have approached the critique of formalism from an angle equally specific. The starting point of our argument is the idea that every branch of doctrine must rely tacitly if not explicitly upon some picture of the forms of human association that are right and realistic in the areas of social life with which it deals. If, for example, you are a constitutional lawyer, you need a theory of the democratic republic that would describe the proper relation between state and society or the essential features of social organization and individual entitlement that government must protect come what may.

Without such a guiding vision, legal reasoning seems condemned to a game of easy analogies. It will always be possible to find, retrospectively, more or less convincing ways to make a set of distinctions, or failures to distinguish, look credible. A common experience testifies to this possibility; every thoughtful law student or lawyer has had the disquieting sense of being able to argue too well or too easily for too many conflicting solutions. Because everything can be defended, nothing can; the analogy-mongering must be brought to a halt. It must be possible to reject some of the received understandings and decisions as mistaken and to do so by appealing to some background normative theory of the branch of law in question or of the realm of social practice governed by that part of the law.

Suppose that you could determine on limited grounds of institutional propriety how much a style of doctrinal practice may regularly reject as mistaken. With too little rejection, the lawyer fails to avoid the suspect quality of endless analogizing. With too much, he forfeits his claim to be doing doctrine as opposed to ideology, philosophy, or prophecy. For any given level of revisionary power, however, different portions of the received understandings in any extended field of law may be repudiated.

To determine which part of established opinion about the meaning and applicability of legal rules you should reject, you need a background prescriptive theory of the relevant area of social practice, a theory that does for the branch of law in question what a doctrine of the republic or of the political process does for constitutional argument. This is where the trouble arises. No matter what the content of this background theory, it is, if taken seriously and pursued to its ultimate conclusions, unlikely to prove compatible with a broad range of the received understandings. Yet just such a compatibility seems to be required by a doctrinal practice that defines itself by contrast to open-ended ideology. For it would be strange if the results of a coherent, richly developed normative theory were to coincide with a major portion of any extended branch of law. The many conflicts of interest and vision that law-making involves, fought out by countless minds and wills working at cross-purposes, would have to be the vehicle of an immanent moral rationality whose message could be articulated by a single cohesive theory. This daring and implausible sanctification of the actual is in fact undertaken by the dominant legal theories and tacitly presupposed by the unreflective common sense of orthodox lawyers. Most often, the sanctification takes the form of treating the legal order as a repository of intelligible purposes, policies, and principles, in abrupt contrast to the standard disenchanted view of legislative politics.

This argument against formalism may be criticized on the ground that the claimed contrast between the game of analogy and the appeal to a background conception of right is untenable; from the outset analogy is guided by such a conception, so the criticism would suggest. But for the analogy to be guided by such a conception would require precisely the miracle to which I just referred: the pre-established harmony between the content of the

laws and the teachings of a coherent theory of right. Or, again, it may be objected that in law such background views benefit from a self-limiting principle: the principle introduced by the constraints of institutional context. Such a principle, however, must rely either upon a more or less tacit professional consensus about the rightful limits of institutional roles or upon an explicit and justifiable theory of institutional roles. Even if a consensus of this sort could claim authority, it simply does not exist. The proper extent of the revisionary power—the power to declare some portion of received legal opinion mistaken—remains among the most contested subjects of legal controversy, as the American debates about judicial "activism" and "self-restraint" show. An explicit theory of institutional roles can make sense and find support only within a substantive theory of politics and rights. We thus return to the initial implausibility of a widespread convergence of any such theory with the actual content of a major branch of law.

Having recognized this problem with doctrine, modern legal analysis tries to circumvent it in a number of ways. It may, for example, present an entire field of law as the expression of certain underlying theoretical approaches to the subject. These implicit models, it is suggested, fit into some coherent scheme or, at least, point toward a synthesis. In this way it seems possible to reconcile the recognition that legal analysis requires an appeal to an underlying theory of right and social practice with the inability to show that the actual content of law and doctrine in any given area coincides, over an appreciable area of law, with a particular theory. But this recourse merely pushes the problem to another level. No extended body of law in fact coincides with such a metascheme, just as no broad range of historical experience coincides with the implications of one of the evolutionary views that claim to provide a science of history. (That this counts as more than a faint resemblance is a point to which I shall return.) It is always possible to find in actual legal materials radically inconsistent clues about the range of application of each of the models and indeed about the identity of the models themselves.

Once the lawyer abandons these methods of compensation and containment, he returns to a cruder and more cynical device. He merely imposes upon his background conceptions—his theories of right and social practice—an endless series of ad hoc adjustments. The looseness of the theories and the resulting difficulty of distinguishing the ad hoc from the theoretically required make this escape all the easier. Thus, there emerges the characteristic figure of the modern jurist who wants—and needs—to combine the cachet of theoretical refinement, the modernist posture of seeing through everything, with the reliability of the technician whose results remain close to the mainstream of professional and social consensus. Determined not to miss out on anything, he has chosen to be an outsider and an insider at the same time. To the achievement of this objective he has determined to sacrifice the momentum of his ideas. We have denounced him wherever we have found him, and we have found him everywhere.

One more objection might be made to this attack upon formalism and upon the type of doctrinal practice that formalism justifies. According to this objection, the attack succeeds only against the systematic constructions of the most ambitious academic jurists, not against the specific, problem-oriented arguments of practical lawyers and judges. It is hard, though, to see how such arguments could be valid, how indeed they might differ from rhetorical posturing, unless they could count as tentative fragments of a possible cohesive view of an extended body of law.

The implication of our attack upon formalism is to undermine the attempt to rescue doctrine through these several stratagems. It is to demonstrate that a doctrinal practice that puts its hope in the contrast of legal reasoning to ideology, philosophy, and political prophecy ends up as a collection of makeshift apologies.

C. The critiques of objectivism and formalism related: their significance for current legal theories

Once the arguments against objectivism and formalism have been rendered in these specific ways, their relation to each other gains a new and surprising clarity. As long as the project of the nineteenth century jurists retained its credibility, the problem of doctrine did not emerge. The miracle required and promised by objectivism could take place: the coincidence of the greater part of substantive law and doctrine with a coherent theory, capable of systematic articulation and relentless application. The only theory capable of performing the miracle would have been one that described the inner conceptual and institutional structure of the type of social and governmental organization to which the nation had committed itself at its foundational moment. Such a theory would not have needed to be imported from outside. It would not have been just somebody's favorite system. It would have translated into legal categories the abiding structure of ordinary political and economic activity. Once the objectivist project underlying the claim to reveal the inherent content of a type of social organization ceased to be believable, doctrine in its received form was condemned to the self-subversion that our critique of formalism has elucidated. But because the nature and defects of the project appeared only gradually, the permanent disequilibrium of doctrine became manifest little by little.

This view of the flaws in objectivism and formalism and of the close link between the two sets of ideas and the two critiques explains our approach to the most influential and symptomatic legal theories in America today: the law and economics and the rights and principles schools. Each of these theories is advanced by a group that stands at the margin of high power, that despairs of seeing its aims triumph through the normal means of governmental politics, and that appeals to some conceptual mechanism designed to show that the advancement of its program is a practical or moral necessity. The law and economics school has mainly addressed private law; the rights and principles school, public law. The law and economics school has invoked practical requirements (with normative implications) that supposedly underlie the legal system and its history; the rights and principles school, moral imperatives allegedly located within the legal order itself. The law and economics school has chiefly served the political right; the rights and principles school, the liberal center. But both theoretical tendencies can best be understood as efforts to recover the objectivist and formalist position. It is as restatements of objectivism and formalism that we have rejected them.

The chief instrument of the law and economics school is the equivocal use of the market concept. These analysts give free rein to the very mistake that the increasing formalization of microeconomics was largely meant to avoid: the identification of the abstract market idea or the abstract circumstance of maximizing choice with a particular social and institutional complex. As a result, an analytic apparatus intended, when rigorous, to be entirely free of restrictive assumptions about the workings of society and entirely subsidiary to an empirical or normative theory that needs independent justification gets mistaken for a particular empirical and normative vision. More particularly, the abstract market idea is identified with a specific version of the market—the one that has prevailed in most of the modern history of most Western countries—with all its surrounding social assumptions, real or imagined. The formal analytic notion of allocational efficiency is identified with a specific theory of economic growth or, quite simply, with the introduction, the development, or the defense of this particular institutional and social order. Such are the sophistries by which the law and economics school pretends to discover both the real basis for the overall evolution of the legal order and the relevant standard by which to

criticize occasional departures of that order from its alleged vocation. From this source supposedly come the purposes and policies that do and should play the paramount role in legal reasoning.

The rights and principles school achieves similar results through very different means. It claims to discern in the leading ideas of the different branches of law, especially when illuminated by a scrupulous, benevolent, and well-prepared professional elite, the signs of an underlying moral order that can then serve as the basis for a system of more or less natural rights. This time, the objective order that guides the main line of legal evolution and serves to criticize the numerous though marginal aberrations is a harshly simplified version of moral ideas supposedly expressed in authoritative legal materials. No longer able to appeal to the idea of the built-in institutional structure of a type of social organization, this school alternates confusedly between two options, both of which it finds unacceptable as a basis for legal theory. One option is that moral consensus (if only it could actually be identified) carries weight just because it exists. The alternative view is that the dominant legal principles count as the manifestations of a transcendent moral order whose content can be identified quite apart from the history and substance of a particular body of law. The third, mediating position for which the school grasps—that consensus on the received principles somehow signals a moral order resting mysteriously upon more than consensus—requires several connected intellectual maneuvers. One is a drastic minimization of the extent to which the law already incorporates conflict over the desirable forms of human association. Another is the presentation of the dominant legal ideas as expressions of higher moral insight, an insight duly contained and corrected by a fidelity to the proprieties of established institutional roles, a fidelity that must itself be mandated by the moral order. Yet another is the deployment of a specific method to reveal the content and implications of this order: generalize from particular doctrines and intuitions, then hypostasize the generalizations into moral truth, and finally use the hypostasis to justify and correct the original material. The intended result of all this hocus-pocus is far clearer than the means used to achieve it. The result is to generate a system of principles and rights that overlaps to just the appropriate extent with the positive content of the laws. Such a system has the suitable degree of revisionary power, the degree necessary to prove that you are neither an all-out and therefore ineffective apologist nor an irresponsible revolutionary.

The law and economics and the rights and principles schools supply a watered-down version of the enterprise of nineteenth century legal science. The endeavor of the classical nineteenth century jurists in turn represented a diluted version of the more common, conservative social doctrines that preceded the emergence of modern social theory. These doctrines pretended to discover a canonical form of social life and personality that could never be fundamentally remade and reimagined even though it might undergo corruption or regeneration. At each succeeding stage of the history of these ideas, the initial conception of a natural form of society becomes weaker: the categories more abstract and indeterminate, the champions more acutely aware of the contentious character of their own claims. Self-consciousness poisons their protestations. Witnessing this latest turn in the history of modern legal thought, no one could be blamed for recalling hopefully Novalis' remark that "when we dream that we dream we are about to awake."

A large part of this history consists in the attempt to deflect the critique of formalism and objectivism by accepting some of its points while saving increasingly less of the original view. The single most striking example in twentieth century American legal thought has been the development of a theory of legal process, institutional roles, and purposive legal

reasoning as a response to legal realism. Perhaps the most creditable pretext for these endless moves of confession and avoidance has been the fear that, carried to the extreme, the critique of objectivism and formalism would leave nothing standing. The very possibility of legal doctrine, and perhaps even of normative argument generally, might be destroyed. Thus, ramshackle and plausible compromises have been easily mistaken for theoretical insight. For many of us, the turning point came when we decided, at the risk of confusion, paralysis, and marginality, to pursue the critical attack *à outrance*. When we took the negative ideas relentlessly to their final conclusions, we were rewarded by seeing these ideas turn into the starting points of a constructive program. . . .

Note

* Two main tendencies can be distinguished in the critical legal studies movement. One tendency sees past or contemporary doctrine as the expression of a particular vision of society while emphasizing the contradictory and manipulable character of doctrinal argument. Its immediate antecedents lie in antiformalist legal theories and structuralist approaches to cultural history. Examples include Kennedy, *The Structure of Blackstone's Commentaries*, 28 *Buffalo L. Rev.* 205 (1979), and Kelman, *Interpretive Construction in the Substantive Criminal Law*, 33 *Stan. L. Rev.* 591 (1981). Another tendency grows out of the social theories of Marx and Weber and the mode of social and historical analysis that combines functionalist methods with radical aims. Its point of departure has been the thesis that law and legal doctrine reflect, confirm, and reshape the social divisions and hierarchies inherent in a type or stage of social organization such as "capitalism." But this thesis has been increasingly modified by the awareness that institutional types or stages lack the cohesive and foreordained character that received leftist theory attributes to them. *See* M. Horwitz, *The Transformation of American Law, 1780–1860* (1977); Trubek, *Complexity and Contradiction in the Legal Order: Balbus and the Challenge of Critical Social Thought About Law*, II *Law & Soc'y Rev.* 527 (1977). Many of the essays in *The Politics of*

Law: A Progressive Critique (D. Kairys ed. 1982) also exemplify this perspective.

Both tendencies criticize the dominant style of legal doctrine and the legal theories that try to refine and preserve this style. Both repudiate in the course of this critique the attempt to impute current social arrangements to the requirements of industrial society, human nature, or moral order. Both have yet to take a clear position on the method, the content, and even the possibility of prescriptive and programmatic thought, perhaps because some of the assumptions inherited from the radical tradition make it hard to turn constructive proposals into more than statements of commitment or anticipations of history.

The significance of the contrast between these tendencies should not be overstated. The actual works often differ less than the abstract interpretations placed upon them. And many writings do not fall into either of the two groups mentioned. *See* Gordon, *Historicism in Legal Scholarship,* 90 *Yale L.J.* 1017 (1981); Parker, *The Past of Constitutional Theory — And Its Future,* 42 *Ohio St. L.J.* 223 (1981); Simon, *The Ideology of Advocacy: Procedural Justice and Professional Ethics,* 1978 *Wis. L. Rev.* 29; Stone, *The Post-War Paradigm in American Labor Law,* 90 *Yale L.J.* 1509 (1981).

Though the view of critical legal studies presented here cannot be reconciled with much in the way these and other tendencies in the movement understand their own critical practice, I hope it remains faithful to a shared intention and direction.

Chapter 35

Richard Delgado

THE ETHEREAL SCHOLAR
Does Critical Legal Studies have what minorities want?

Introduction

WHAT DOES CRITICAL LEGAL STUDIES (CLS) have to offer racial minorities in their quest for social justice? More generally, what legal theory or program best meets the needs and desires of minorities? Any acceptable theory must be radical, or at any rate progressive, one would think, since minorities want to change the world. Although CLS purports to be a radical theory,[1] minorities have not flocked to it. And CLS has not paid much attention to minorities, not placing racial questions on its agenda until this year, ten years after its formation as a legal movement.[2]

This article suggests that the current schism between CLS and minorities results from a fundamental difference between what CLS proposes and what minorities seek in a legal theory. Part I describes what may be called the negative and positive aspects of the CLS program, and explains why they are troublesome for minorities. Part II reveals how a common theme of the CLS critique—the advocacy of informality—ignores the need for structure in containing and eliminating racism. The last section of the article describes what a radical political program must include to serve the interests of minorities, and outlines the social arrangements that could best provide the safe and decent conditions necessary for minorities to flourish.

I. CLS themes—from a minority perspective

The CLS program has both negative and positive features. The negative themes include a far-ranging attack on American legal and social institutions,[3] while the positive themes describe an alternative, utopian society.[4] What follows is an analysis of those elements of the CLS negative and positive programs that minorities find unappealing and worrisome.

A. The CLS negative program

I admit at the outset that the CLS negative program contains much that is useful for minorities. Its attack on the public/private distinction breaks down the artificial barrier between the public sphere, in which conduct is highly regulated, and the private sphere, in which it is not.[5] The CLS critique of the social order demonstrates that current arrangements and distributions of power are neither necessary nor natural,[6] and that hierarchy irrationally places some at the top while it sacrifices those at the bottom.[7] More generally, CLS challenges and decodes "Euromyths" that rule the lives of minorities and consign us to lowly fates.[8]

At the same time, however, the CLS negative program contains elements that repel and in fact threaten minorities. These elements include: (i) disparagement of legal rules and rights,[9]

(ii) rejection of piecemeal change,[10] (iii) idealism,[11] and (iv) use of the concept of false consciousness.[12] Much of CLS scholarship in these areas is either risky, since it asks minorities to give up something of value, or unreliable, because it is based on presuppositions that do not correspond to our experience.[13]

1. The CLS critique of legal rules and rights

The CLS critique of legal rules and reasoning is well known. Rules, since they are indeterminate and manipulable, can generate practically any result in a given situation.[14] Rules invite the savvy to operate near their borders while the uninitiated remain well inside.[15]

Rights, a special kind of rule, receive particularly harsh criticism from Critical Legal Scholars (Crits).[16] Rights legitimize society's unfair power arrangements, acting like pressure valves to allow only so much injustice.[17] With much fanfare, the powerful periodically distribute rights as proof that the system is fair and just, and then quietly deny rights through narrow construction, nonenforcement, or delay.[18]

Rights, Crits argue, are never promulgated in genuinely important areas such as economic justice.[19] They protect only ephemeral things, like the right to speak or worship.[20] When even these rights become threatening, they are limited.[21]

For CLS, rights reinforce a soulless, alienating vision of society made up of atomized individuals whose only concern is to protect their own security and property.[22] Crits argue that rights are alienating since they force one to look at oneself and others as isolated rights-bearers ("I got my rights") rather than as interdependent members of a community, and make it impossible for us even to imagine what a non-hierarchical society founded on cooperation and love would be like.

The CLS critique of rights and rules is the most problematic aspect of the CLS program, and provides few answers for minority scholars and lawyers.[23] We know, from frequent and sad experience, that the mere announcement of a legal right means little. We live in the gap between law on the books and law in action. We have no difficulty imagining a better world; for us, eliminating racism would be a good start.

Even if rights and rights-talk paralyze us and induce a false sense of security, as CLS scholars maintain, might they not have a comparable effect on public officials, such as the police? Rights do, at times, give pause to those who would otherwise oppress us; without the law's sanction, these individuals would be more likely to express racist sentiments on the job.[24] It is condescending and misguided to assume that the enervating effect of rights talk is experienced by the victims and not the perpetrators of racial mistreatment.

Second, CLS scholars are often hazy about what would provide minorities comparable protection if rights no longer existed.[25] The CLS positive program, or Utopia, discussed below,[26] is both far from adequate and far off in time.

Third, Crits argue that rights separate and alienate the individual from the rest of the human community.[27] This may be so for the hard-working Crits who spend much of their lives in their studies and law offices.[28] For minorities, however, rights serve as a rallying point and bring us closer together.[29] On the other hand, any distance rights place between us and others may be beneficial; there is at least safety in distance.[30]

One explanation for the CLS position on rights may be that the average Crit, a white male teaching at a major law school, has little use for rights.[31] Those with whom he comes in contact in his daily life—landlords, employers, public authorities—generally treat him with respect and deference. Rarely is he the victim of coercion, revilement, or contempt.[32] In the mind of the average Crit, rights offer relatively little security, while they promote a shrunken, atrophied, and unsatisfying social existence.[33] Rights transform those governed by them into lone, deformed stick figures vulnerable to pressures emanating from large corporations or faceless bureaucracies.[34] Yet, when Crits are treated insensitively or unfairly, or are coerced into giving up something of value—such as an academic appointment in a tenure battle tinged by anti-Crit bias—they have been as quick as anyone to resort to the language of rights.[35] Their behavior in such situations exemplifies the universal tendency of beleaguered persons and groups to revert to rights-talk.

For minorities, however, that rights minimize many forms of coercion is of enormous importance. At the same time, the psychic rewards that Crits believe will result from a rightless inter-racial "community" are far from our experience. Even if such rewards were achievable, they would necessarily rank lower than simple security on our scale of need. Of course, a utopian community of the sort Crits advocate might provide minorities with both security and psychic satisfaction. As will be shown later, however, that hope is probably vain.[36]

In short, the two groups see rights differently. White CLS members see rights as oppressive, alienating and mystifying. For minorities, they are invigorating cloaks of safety that unite us in a common bond. Instead of coming to grips with the different function of rights for the two groups, Crits insist that minorities adopt their viewpoint, labeling disagreement on our part false consciousness[37] or a lack of political sophistication.

2. The CLS critique of piecemeal reform

Critical scholars reject the idea of piecemeal reform. Incremental change, they argue, merely postpones the wholesale reformation that must occur to create a decent society.[38] Even worse, an unfair social system survives by using piecemeal reform to disguise and legitimize oppression.[39] Those who control the system weaken resistance by pointing to the occasional concession to, or periodic court victory of, a black plaintiff or worker as evidence that the system is fair and just.[40] In fact, Crits believe that teaching the common law or using the case method in law school is a disguised means of preaching incrementalism and thereby maintaining the current power structure.[41] To avoid this, CLS scholars urge law professors to abandon the case method, give up the effort to find rationality and order in the case law, and teach in an unabashedly political fashion.[42]

The CLS critique of piecemeal reform is familiar, imperialistic and wrong. Minorities know from bitter experience that occasional court victories do not mean the Promised Land is at hand.[43] The critique is imperialistic in that it tells minorities and other oppressed peoples how they should interpret events affecting them.[44] A court order directing a housing authority to disburse funds for heating in subsidized housing may postpone the revolution, or it may not. In the meantime, the order keeps a number of poor families warm. This may mean more to them than it does to a comfortable academic working in a warm office. It smacks of paternalism to assert that the possibility of revolution later outweighs the certainty of heat now, unless there is evidence for that possibility. The Crits do not offer such evidence.

Indeed, some incremental changes may bring revolutionary changes closer, not push them further away. Not all small reforms induce complacency; some may whet the appetite for further combat. The welfare family may hold a tenants' union meeting in their heated living room. CLS scholars' critique of piecemeal reform often misses these possibilities, and neglects the question of whether total change, when it comes, will be what we want.

3. CLS' idealism

The CLS program is also idealistic.[45] CLS scholars' idealism transforms social reality into a mental construct.[46] Facts become intelligible only through the categories of thought that we bring to experience. Crits argue that the principal impediments to achieving an ideal society are intellectual. People are imprisoned by a destructive system of mental categories that blocks any vision of a better world.[47] Liberal-capitalist ideology so shackles individuals that they willingly accept a truncated existence and believe it to be the best available. Changing the world requires primarily that we begin to think about it differently.[48] To help break the mental chains and clear the way for the creation of a new and better world, Crits practice "trashing"—a process by which law and social structures are shown to be contingent, inconsistent and irrationally supportive of the status quo without good reason.[49]

CLS scholars' idealism has a familiar ring to minority ears. We cannot help but be reminded of those fundamentalist preachers who have assured us that our lot will only improve once we "see the light" and are "saved."

Are our chains really mental? They may be so for members of privileged groups. They are much less so for minorities. Imagine that the Crits' trashing program succeeded and that all laws were repealed. Would our lot improve? That proposition is open to serious doubt. The forces that hold us back are not largely mental, legal, nor even political. What holds us back is, simply, racism—the myriad of insults, threats, indifference, and other "microaggressions" to which we are continually exposed.[50]

Because the Crits are intellectuals, they assign a large role to reason and ideology. Yet reason and ideology do not explain all evil. Telling an individual that he or she harbors racism will not make it go away; telling a black person that a rebuff was racially motivated will not ease its sting. Racism will not go away simply because Crits show that legalisms are indeterminate, that rights are alienating and legitimizing, and that law is a reflection of the interests of the ruling class. Whatever utility these concepts may have

in other settings and in attempting to explain the angst of CLS members,[51] they have limited application in helping to understand, much less cure, racism.

4. The CLS concept of false consciousness

The concept of false consciousness is the final aspect of Crit scholarship that minorities find problematic.[52] Workers and minorities buy into a system that degrades and oppresses them, and vehemently defend that system with a kind of "false honor."[53] These groups accept their own subordination because they believe that the constitutional system protects their property against takings by the state, and that it elevates their status above that of the lowest class.[54] Thus, oppressed people not only accept the liberal ideology and the mental shackles described in the preceding section, but also embrace it loyally and reject the proffered assistance of revolutionaries.

Some CLS writers even argue that the Framers intended false consciousness to exist. While extolling the virtues of freedom, the Framers set out to achieve ideological hegemony for themselves and their class by providing for separate classes and by protecting the property and prerogatives of employers and slave owners.[55]

False consciousness rationalizes the lowly status of workers, women, minorities and other oppressed groups.[56] According to capitalist-liberal ideology, society consists of individuals who express political preferences through voting and achieve economic results through the marketplace.[57] The system is formally fair; therefore, if one is poor, reviled, hungry, or out of work, it is one's own fault.[58] At the same time, the person who occupies a position of power deserves it. In a meritocratic society, the cream rises to the top. The duty of everyone else is to obey.

Ideologically achieved domination becomes a self-generating spiral. The masses are persuaded that they are of little merit. Demoralized, they take little interest in elections or in the way political and economic life is run.[59] Thus, false consciousness blinds them to the alienation, lack of justice, conflict and unfairness inherent in political life.

Civil rights law is subject to particularly scathing criticism. Crits argue that the purpose of civil rights is to reconcile minorities to subordination by convincing us that the system is fair; our lowly status is simply the result of our inferiority.[60] The legal system protects society's investment in the subordination of minorities by assuring everyone that the status quo is inevitable.[61] It accomplishes this by doling out the occasional victory, such as *Brown v. Board of Education*,[62] and by ensuring that most civil rights are formal, rather than substantive.[63]

As with the other elements of the negative program, one should begin by asking whether the concept of false consciousness holds true for minorities. Much of what Crits criticize as false consciousness evinces their distrust of liberal legalisms and the elusive promises of court victories. Most of us have already acquired this distrust; society has provided us with more than adequate tutelage.[64] We know from Derrick Bell[65] and from personal experience not to place too much reliance on liberal attorneys who say they know exactly what we want. We know, indeed we live, the bogus public-private distinction.[66]

Moreover, it is worth questioning the extent to which our current subordination is caused by uncritical absorption of self-defeating ideologies, as opposed to other forces. Much more of our current plight is due to other factors: coercion by the dominant group; exclusion from clubs, networks, information, and needed help at crucial times; microaggressions; and the paralysis and hopelessness caused by the majority culture's denial of our pain and reality. (Who among us has not been asked by a white person, naively or almost incredulously, "Do you really, in this day and age, suffer on account of your race?"[67])

Ultimately, the CLS false-consciousness analysis raises more questions than it answers. If false consciousness exists and is so powerful, why are only minorities and workers afflicted by it, and not white radicals? Is there not something patronizing in diagnosing an intellectual disease that exclusively afflicts persons of color?[68] Is not "false consciousness" an expression, like "incompetent" or "insane," that gives others the authority to treat the victim as if he lacks humanity, autonomy, or will?[69] Is not false consciousness an excuse for white radicals to assert and retain power they would otherwise have to explain and justify? Does not the CLS program create its own false consciousness within the law schools which employ CLS radicals, and ultimately within society at large? Unless coupled with practical action to storm trenches and organize workers, something CLS members have been remarkably slow to do,[70] the CLS reform program allows society to validate myths about free speech and the right to dissent.[71]

B. The CLS positive program

Critical Legal Studies, to date, has devoted much less effort to developing a positive program than to criticizing rules and social structures.[72] In general, the Crits' positive aim is to establish a Utopia in which true community would prevail.[73] Decisionmaking would be decentralized; rules would be set by small groups such as factory workers, farm workers, and students,[74] and would remain subject to constant renegotiation.[75] Hierarchy would not exist; everyone would be equal.[76] There would be no need for rights—at least not so many as we recognize today. Instead, everyone would share work, goods and responsibilities.[77]

Individuals would benefit from the deemphasis on individualism in Utopia. In contemporary society, the individual lacks depth and character because of his isolation and lack of commitment to others.[78] He may be free in a formal sense, but he is also stunted and barely human. In a non-hierarchical, non-repressive society, on the other hand, the human personality would flourish.[79]

The Crits' positive program would poorly serve the needs of minorities. Some radical theoreticians may indeed be lonely. Most minority lawyers and law professors are not: we have each other. We meet, share experiences, recount horror stories, laugh and cry together. Victimization brings us together, building in us a community. It is much more problematic to accept the invitation, if it is that, to join Crits and other whites in mixed-race communities lacking in structure or rules.

Two immediate difficulties confront any serious discussion of incorporating minorities into the utopian communities envisioned by the Crits. First, one must be a self who is fully recognized as a member of a community of selves before one can merge into such a community, and certainly before the lines between self and others can safely begin to blur. How can this happen unless society first recognizes us as coequal members, something it has yet to do?[80]

Second, there are no guarantees that racism would not resurface in the CLS communities. To date, Crits have not articulated a psychological or political theory of the origin of racism or of how it could be eradicated. If racism were to surface in a CLS-style Utopia, there would be no rules, rights, federal statutes, or even courts to counteract it. Even if there were tribunals or people's commissions of some kind, would they be guided by strict scrutiny[81] in examining cases of prejudice? Probably not, since the once-oppressed and politically powerless groups would presumably have been empowered by the egalitarian Utopia. Perhaps these difficulties could be overcome. In the meantime, however, the costs of moving to a utopian society would be borne by minorities, since the dismantling of formal structures would initially lead to an increase in racist behavior.[82]

Ostensibly, the CLS choice of structure for the post-revolutionary community is neutral and based on those arrangements with the greatest potential for humanity. However, that choice is not value-free. Utopian society would empower whites, giving them satisfaction currently denied,[83] and disempower minorities, making life even less secure than it is today. As a black leader is supposed to have said, "Community don't look like me."

II. Informality—the source of the trouble

Much of the misfit between the CLS program and the aspirations of minorities is due to the informality of the CLS program.[84] CLS themes and approaches criticize formal structures such as rights, rules and bureaucracies, while opting for consciously informal processes that rely on good will, intersubjective understanding and community. The CLS positive and negative programs exemplify this informality; they illustrate the Crits' preference for holistic approaches that sweep everything at once into their scope.[85]

Whatever sense informal, small-scale politics may make for the CLS membership, it is bad news for minorities. Discretionary judgments colored by racism or other forms of prejudice are made possible by replacing rules, guidelines and rights with fluid, informal decisionmaking. In fact, structureless processes affirmatively increase the likelihood of prejudice. CLS theorists have avoided confronting these risks, since CLS lacks a political and psychological theory of racism. CLS theory simply assumes that racism is just another form of class-based oppression, a product of a hierarchal social structure.[86]

The Crits' focus on informality also ignores the influence that rules have on an individual's character and action. A society that enacts rules and provides structures to curb racism announces that racism is unacceptable behavior. By committing ourselves to norms of fairness we become fairer people. By changing the structure, we change the setting in which we act and ultimately change ourselves. If we jettison rules and structures, we risk losing the gains we have made in combatting racism.

The psychological-political analysis that follows explains and illustrates the interaction among rules, conduct and character. I outline the principal social scientific theories of racism and then develop a consensus position which explains the circumstances in which most people are likely to behave in a discriminatory fashion. I apply this view to the highly informal Crit program to demonstrate that the CLS program exposes minorities to an increased risk of prejudicial treatment.

A. Theories of race and racism

Most Americans harbor some degree of racial prejudice.[87] Indeed, individuals rarely come to grips with their racist impulses and bring them completely under control.[88] Most deal with them through a variety of mechanisms: displacement, denial, rationalization, overcompensation and compromise.[89]

Social scientists have developed a number of overlapping theories to explain the origin of prejudice based on race, ethnicity, sex, or other immutable characteristics.[90] The principal approaches are: psychoanalytic theories, which explain prejudice in terms of unconscious forces and deep-seated syndromes, such as the authoritarian personality;[91] socioeconomic theories, which explain prejudice through historical trends, social group clashes and scape-goating;[92] and social-psychological theories, which explain racism by means of social conditioning and in-group/out-group categories.[93] It is likely that each of these theories partly explains the multifaceted aspects of racist behavior.

On the other hand, racism runs counter to the body of public principles that form our national ethos, including fairness, egalitarianism and humanitarianism.[94] The conflict between racist impulses and the American creed causes many people to act inconsistently—fairly and humanely on one occasion, thoughtlessly or with prejudice on another.[95] Racism and racial egalitarianism are thus maintained in equipoise. Americans are influenced by both public and private norms with respect to race.[96] The highly principled public norm exhorts us to treat others in an unprejudiced, evenhanded fashion.[97] The private norms, the standards that guide us during moments of intimacy or familiarity, are much less noble.[98] In private settings, prejudicial behavior and speech are much more likely to appear. The same individual may thus act quite differently on different occasions, depending on whether he sees himself as governed by public or private values.

The "situational specificity"[99] of the racist impulse supplies the best means for its control. Most people suppress their prejudices when environmental features remind them that racism will not be tolerated and that the American creed demands a high standard of conduct. Although there are other theories and approaches to racism,[100] the "confrontation" approach—where prejudice is publicly confronted and discouraged through formal structures—is the most widely accepted means of controlling prejudice in the legal and political literature.[101] The theory is supported by empirical studies of legal decisionmaking, including reviews of alternative dispute resolution and comparisons between the adversarial and inquisitorial modes of presenting evidence.[102]

Little of this will surprise minority readers. We know by a kind of instinct that there are times when our white friends can be trusted and times when they cannot. We know that there are occasions—when the flag is flying, the bands are playing, and public values are foremost in everyone's minds—when we are comparatively safe, and that there are other occasions when we must be careful.

The bottom line is that formal public settings are relatively safe for minorities, while informal private settings present risks. To minimize racism, one should structure settings so that public norms are enforced, and prejudice openly confronted and discouraged. Society should avoid creating intimate, unguided settings where highly charged interracial encounters can take place. It remains to be considered what the confrontation theory, and the formality/informality axis generated by that theory, implies for the CLS program.

B. Applying the theory of race to the CLS program

The confrontation theory helps to explain why the open-ended features of the CLS program worry minority scholars. For example, the CLS positive program, which calls for small communities that function without written agendas, statutes, rules or rights,[103] would allow for discretionary judgments based on racial prejudice, and contain few of the structural features that confront and check racism. The lack of confrontation mechanisms would likely ensure the invasion of racism into the community.

CLS scholars' rejection of incrementalism also illustrates the dangers of informality. By insisting that everything must change at once, CLS rejects the slow, painstaking process of establishing and refining precedent, replacing that relatively formal process with a mercurial vision of social change with no clear direction and undefined ends.

Similar considerations hold true, although not quite so strongly, for CLS scholars' idealism and their use of the concept of false consciousness. The Crits' emphasis on mental constructs reveals their preference for free-form change over the concrete reform accomplished by litigation, labor activism and community organizing. CLS prefers the broad reach of thought to the measured progression that occurs through new jobs, better housing, court victories and school desegregation.

C. The laboratory of daily life: applying the theory of race to the CLS organization and its mode of operation

Theories, according to pragmatic philosophy, must be tested by their consequences, and by the ways in which they modify the behavior of their adherents.[104] Thus, one should examine the organizational and personal behavior of the members of the Critical Legal Studies Conference on matters of race in order to determine the possible impact of their theories on minorities, particularly since many members of the Conference believe in the inseparability of politics and daily life.[105] If the Conference's reform program holds promise for minorities, one should find a heightened racial sensitivity among the organization and its members.

An examination of the Conference on racial matters does not yield a clear-cut answer to the question. The organization, as is predictable from its theories and program, is highly informal. There are no bylaws, elections, procedures, officers, membership cards or committees.[106] Annual meetings and summer workshops are organized by ad hoc groups who decide that they have something to say. The informality of the structure allows the "white male heavies," most of whom are at Harvard, to wield a disproportionate amount of power.[107] Few women or minorities wield significant influence.[108]

The record of individual members of the Conference is better than that of the organization itself. At least three of its well-known members wrote powerful and influential articles supporting minority causes.[109] Many Crits welcome minority colleagues on their faculties, and support affirmative action in law school admissions and appointments.[110] Yet few Crits took an active role in the aftermath of an incident in which the competence of a leading black scholar was challenged by students and colleagues.[111] In addition, there have been sporadic reports of racist language and stereotyping in Crits' scholarship,[112] and of rude treatment of minority panelists by Crits.[113] One would conclude that the Conference's record on racial justice matters is good, but not outstanding—perhaps 3.4 on a 4.0 point scale. If racism manifests itself among CLS members, it is frightening to imagine what would occur in a similarly unstructured group with a less progressively-minded membership.

III. Beyond CLS—toward a radical minority social-legal agenda

It is axiomatic that any social reform program that minorities would find appealing would be based on the express need for understanding and coping with racism. It is not enough to subsume racism under some other category, such as class struggle, that fails to understand racism's subtlety and complexity. The program should incorporate some variant of the confrontation approach to containing racism.[114] The new society, and its transitional predecessor, would create structures for detecting and punishing racism and for reminding community members that such conduct will not be tolerated. Because of these structures, such a society would be relatively formal.

Any society consciously designed to promote minority well-being must initially include a strong central authority founded on a healthy skepticism both of human nature and of the possibilities of change through appeals to idealism. Tempering romanticism with watch-fulness, it would instead effect change through appeals to citizens' self-interest by arguing that power and resource realignments benefit everyone.[115]

The need for centralized authority stems from the necessity for counter-coercive measures on behalf of minorities. One cannot rely on local authority to redistribute power and physical resources because it is too close to the community and unlikely to upset the status quo. The further authority is from the community, the better.

Our principal worry is not the abuse of corporate or bureaucratic power (CLS' foe), but rather the simple next-door, one-on-one micro-aggressions by whites.[116] It is a sad truth that, even today, many minorities find success and relative relief from racism only in highly structured, rule-bound environments such as the Army.[117] Group membership may force Crits and other majority-group members to reflect on politics and the nature of the common good, but unless such reflection is accompanied by formal barriers against racism, it is meaningless.

Conclusion

This article asked what minorities would like to see in a legal and political theory, and whether the CLS program matches that vision. The answer is that CLS does not provide what minorities seek.

Although some of the features of the CLS program are attractive to minorities, others increase our vulnerability to oppressive or degrading treatment by the majority. A number of these difficulties arise from CLS scholars' ironic failure to articulate a satisfactory theory of either the genesis or the treatment of racism.

The views of various scholars on racism coalesce to form a "confrontation theory," which describes the best means of confining and combatting racism. Many of the intuitive reservations and fears minorities have about the Crits' program arise from the Crits' desire to eliminate those formal societal structures which, according to the confrontation theory, are needed to curb racist impulses in society. In contrast, the radical social reform program out-lined here can provide minorities the protection and security they need to function in a world dominated by persons of a race and heritage different from their own.

This reform program may be a tall order, but it is no taller than the CLS vision of an informal Utopia. Indeed, compared to the Crits' proposed society, it is a great deal more humane, safe and protective for those of us who have been denied humanity, safety and protection for so long.

Notes

1 *See, e.g.,* Hutchinson & Monahan, *Law, Politics and the Critical Legal Scholars: The Unfolding Drama of American Legal Thought,* 36 Stan. L. Rev. 199, 199–202 (1984); Sparer, *Fundamental Human Rights, Legal Entitlements, and the Social Struggle: A Friendly Critique of the Critical Legal Studies Movement,* 36 Stan. L. Rev. 509, 509–10 (1984).

2 Approximately 40 minority lawyers, law students and law professors, out of a total of approximately 150 people, attended the 1987 annual meeting of the Conference on Critical Legal Studies. (The minority attendance at previous meetings has been much smaller.) The topic of the 1987 annual meeting was race. The program was entitled "The Sounds of Silence: Racism and the Law."

3 Among the targets of the CLS program are legal education, the bar, legal reasoning, rights (including civil rights), precedent, doctrine, hierarchy, meritocracy, the prevailing liberal political vision, and conventional views of labor and the free market. *See, e.g.,* Gordon, *Critical Legal Histories,* 36 Stan. L. Rev. 57 (1984); Hutchinson & Monahan, *The "Rights" Stuff: Roberto Unger and Beyond,* 62 Tex. L. Rev. 1477 (1984); Stick, *Can Nihilism Be Pragmatic?,* 100 Harv. L. Rev. 332 (1986). *See generally* Brosnan, *Serious But Not Critical,* 60 S. Cal. L. Rev. 259 (1986). Admittedly, this article contains a number of generalizations about a body of literature which has more than one strand of thought. Although the description herein may not apply equally to all Critical Legal Scholars, common themes do appear, and I feel I have fairly summarized the field.

4 *See infra* notes 72–83 and accompanying text; Unger, *The Critical Legal Studies Movement,* 96 Harv. L. Rev. 561 (1983); R. Unger, Knowledge and Politics (1975).

5 *See, e.g.,* Frug, *The City as a Legal Concept,* 93 Harv. L. Rev. 1057 (1980); Kairys, *Freedom of Speech,* in The Politics of Law: A Progressive Critique 140, 163–65 (D. Kairys ed. 1982); Kairys, *Introduction,* in id. at 1, 3; Sparer, *supra* note 1, at 529–31.

6 *See, e.g.,* Kennedy, *Legal Education as Training for Hierarchy,* in The Politics of Law: A Progressive Critique,

supra note 5, at 40, 50; Mensch, *The History of Mainstream Legal Thought,* in The Politics of Law: A Progressive Critique, *supra* note 5, at 18.

7 *See* Kennedy, *supra* note 6; *see also* D. Kennedy, Legal Education and the Reproduction of Hierarchy: A Polemic Against the System (1983); Klare, *Judicial Deradicalization of the Wagner Act and the Origins of Modern Legal Consciousness,* 62 Minn. L. Rev. 265 (1978) (attacking workplace hierarchies and judicial support thereof).

8 *See* Williams, *Taking Rights Aggressively: The Perils and Promise of Critical Legal Theory for Peoples of Color,* Inequal. & the L. J. (forthcoming in 1987) (attacking the Euromyths that whites rule by manifest destiny, being culturally and intellectually superior to third world persons, and that minorities must become westernized in order to gain power and control over their lives).

9 *See infra* notes 14–22 and accompanying text.

10 *See infra* notes 38–42 and accompanying text.

11 *See infra* notes 45–49 and accompanying text.

12 *See infra* notes 52–63 and accompanying text.

13 Moreover, the CLS movement may be reaching out to women and minorities now, *see supra* note 2 and accompanying text, in part because it is under attack by the right and needs allies. *See infra* note 35 and accompanying text. Coalition-building may thus serve the temporary interest of all of these groups. *See* Bell, *Brown v. Board of Education and the Interest-Convergence Dilemma,* 93 Harv. L. Rev. 518 (1980).

14 *See, e.g.,* Frug, *The Ideology of Bureaucracy in American Law,* 97 Harv. L. Rev. 1276, 1292 (1984); Kennedy, *supra* note 6, at 48–49; Kennedy, *Form & Substance in Private Law Adjudication,* 89 Harv. L. Rev. 1685, 1766–74 (1976); Trubek, *Max Weber on Law and the Rise of Capitalism,* 1972 Wis. L. Rev. 720, 748–49 (1972).

15 *See* Kennedy, *Form & Substance in Private Law Adjudication, supra* note 14.

16 *See generally* Symposium: *A Critique of Rights,* 62 Tex. L. Rev. 1363 (1984). Among the CLS writers who criticize reliance on rights are: Freeman, *Legitimating Racial Discrimination Through Antidiscrimination Law: A Critical Review of Supreme Court Doctrine,* 62 Minn. L. Rev. 1049 (1978); Hutchinson & Monahan, *supra* note 3, at 1482–83; Klare, *Labor Law as Ideology: Toward a New Historiography of Collective Bargaining Law,* 4 Indus. Rel. L.J. 450, 468–80 (1981); Tushnet, *An Essay on Rights,* 62 Tex. L. Rev. 1363 (1984).

17 See, e.g., Freeman, *Antidiscrimination Law: A Critical Review*, in The Politics of Law: A Progressive Critique, *supra* note 5, at 96, 112–14; Freeman, *supra* note 16; Klare, *The Quest for Industrial Democracy and the Struggle Against Racism: Perspectives from Labor Law and Civil Rights Law*, 61 Or. L. Rev. 157 (1982).

18 Freeman, *Antidiscrimination Law,* *supra* note 17.

19 E.g., Kennedy, *supra* note 6, at 49; Kairys, *Freedom of Speech*, *supra* note 5, at 164.

20 See Kennedy, *supra* note 6, at 48–49.

21 E.g., Kairys, *Freedom of Speech*, *supra* note 5, at 164–65 (freedom of expression is limited when it becomes powerful enough to be threatening, as in the "fighting words" or "clear and present danger" cases).

22 See Gordon, *New Developments in Legal Theory*, in The Politics of Law: A Progressive Critique, *supra* note 5, at 281, 287; Kennedy, *supra* note 6, at 49; Tushnet, *supra* note 16, at 1384. But see Singer, *The Player and the Cards: Nihilism and Legal Theory*, 94 Yale L.J. 1, 65–68 (1984) (describing rights-like features of proposed Crit society); Unger, *The Critical Legal Studies Movement*, *supra* note 4, at 597 (drawing distinction between property rights, which tend to make some individuals dependent on others, and political/ civil rights, which do not pose this threat).

23 See, e.g., Williams, *Alchemical Notes: Reconstructing Ideals from Deconstructed Rights*, 22 Harv. C.R.-C.L. L. Rev. 435 (1987); Williams, *supra* note 8; G. Torres, Address at Conference on Critical Legal Studies Annual Meeting (Jan. 7, 1987) (unpublished manuscript on file with Harvard Civil Rights-Civil Liberties Law Review).

24 See G. Allport, The Nature of Prejudice 472 (1954); Delgado, *Words that Wound: A Tort Action for Racial Insults, Epithets and Name-Calling*, 17 Harv. C.R.-C.L. L. Rev. 133, 148–49 (1982); P. van den Berghe, Race and Racism 20–21 (2d ed. 1978) (law's sanction has some effect in discouraging expression of racist sentiments).

25 See *infra* notes 67–73 and accompanying text (describing CLS' positive program); Brosnan, *supra* note 3, at 264–67 (CLS' critiques of rights lack a theory of justice); id. at 268 (describing CLS as politically passive).

26 See *infra* notes 80–83 and accompanying text.

27 See *supra* note 22; Sparer, *supra* note 1, at 529–30.

28 See Dalton, *The Clouded Prism*, 22 Harv. C.R.-C.L. L. Rev. 435 (1987) (describing critical scholars, typically white males who spend their lives in books, as being out of touch with the minority experience).

29 See *generally* D. Bell, Race, Racism and American Law 279–361 (2d ed. 1980) (describing black movement and struggle for civil rights).

30 Compare Kennedy, *The Structure of Blackstone's Commentaries*, 28 Buff. L. Rev. 205, 217 (1979) (we need, but fear, community; observing that a single look from a friend can reduce a victim to misery), with Abortion, Moral and Legal Perspectives (J. Garfield & P. Hennessy, eds. 1985) (close—especially sexual—relationships with men are risky and ill-advised because of power disparities between men and women and the oppression of women in society). Minorities run comparable risks. See, e.g., Delgado, *supra* note 24 (minorities frequently subject to slights, rebuffs, and slurs); C. Pierce, Unity in Diversity: Thirty-Three Years of Stress, Solomon Carter Fuller Lectures, American Psychiatric Ass'n Meeting, Washington, D.C. (May 12, 1986) (transcript on file with Harvard Civil Rights-Civil Liberties Law Review) (blacks frequent victims of "microaggressions"). See *generally* A. Higginbotham, In the Matter of Color (1978).

31 See *generally* Williams, *supra* note 23 (describing differing attitudes of the author and a white male colleague regarding an apartment lease in New York City); Dalton, *supra* note 28; Gabel, *The Phenomenology of Rights-Consciousness and the Pact of the Withdrawn Selves*, 62 Tex. L. Rev. 1563 (1984).

32 I use "rarely" in a relative sense. See Delgado, *supra* note 24, at 135–49 (frequency and severity of race-based harms greatest in minority populations).

33 See *supra* note 22.

34 These are the forms of mistreatment most white communitarians seem principally concerned about. See, e.g., Bush, *Between Two Worlds: The Shift from Individual to Group Responsibility in the Law of Causation of Injury*, 34 UCLA L. Rev. (forthcoming in 1987). See *generally* M. Sandel, Liberalism and the Limits of Justice (1982).

35 For example, when two Crits at an eastern law school were experiencing tenure difficulty, allegedly because of their politics and innovative teaching, CLS members around the country wrote to the university's president, urging him to investigate charges that the law school's personnel

procedures were biased and infringed the Crits' rights of academic freedom.

36 See infra notes 75–79 and accompanying text (critique of the CLS positive program).

37 For an explanation of the term "false consciousness," see infra notes 52–63 and accompanying text. See also Gabel, Reification in Legal Reasoning, 3 Res. in L. & Soc. 25, 25–27 (1980) (defining false consciousness as reification).

38 See Schwartz, With Gun and Camera Through Darkest CLS-Land, 36 Stan. L. Rev. 413, 421–23 (1984). See generally Brest, The Fundamental Rights Controversy: The Essential Contradictions of Normative Constitutional Scholarship, 90 Yale L.J. 1063 (1981).

39 See Gordon, supra note 22, at 286. See also Freeman, supra note 16; Klare, supra note 7.

40 See Freeman, supra note 16.

41 See Kennedy, supra note 6.

42 See D. Kennedy, supra note 7; Kennedy, supra note 6.

43 See, e.g., D. Bell, supra note 29, at 2–51; see also M. Jorrin, Governments of Latin America 120 (1953) (citing slogan, "Hecha la ley, hecha la trampa"—every law generates its own loophole).

44 See generally Delgado, The Imperial Scholar: Reflections on a Review of Civil Rights Literature, 132 U. Pa. L. Rev. 561 (1984).

45 I use the word "idealism" in its philosophic sense, whereby explanations of social reality are in the realm of thought or consciousness, rather than in material forces or concrete actions. See The Random House Dictionary of the English Language 707 (J. Stein ed. 1971) (definition 5a of "idealism").

46 See Schwartz, supra note 38, at 422, 426–28; Gordon, supra note 22, at 291.

47 See Gordon, supra note 22, at 288–89; Kelman, Interpretive Construction in the Substantive Criminal Law, 33 Stan. L. Rev. 591, 671–72 (1981); Kennedy, Antonio Gramsci and the Legal System, 6 A.L.S.A. Forum 32 (1982); Kennedy, Critical Labor Law: A Comment, 4 Indus. Rel. L.J. 503, 506 (1981).

48 See Gordon, supra note 22, at 291 (individuals' principal limitations are their own imagination and thought, but the article concedes that, for example, "propensities for evil" and "finite resources" might also play some part in limiting life possibilities of the poor).

49 See Gordon, supra note 22, at 289 (thinking one's way through the veil of ideological mystification spun by the dominant culture); Kairys, Legal Reasoning, in The Politics of Law: A Progressive Critique, supra note 5, at 11–17. See generally Kelman, Trashing, 36 Stan. L. Rev. 293 (1984).

50 See C. Pierce, supra note 30 (describing microaggressions as those "subtle, minor, stunning, automatic assaults . . . by which whites stress blacks unremittingly and keep them on the defensive, as well as in a psychologically reduced condition"); Pettigrew, New Patterns of Racism: The Different Worlds of 1984 and 1964, 37 Rutgers L. Rev. 673, 687, 690 (1985).

51 Rights-based talk may distress white professionals who hunger for a more communitarian, fulfilling lifestyle than is currently attainable within their professional lives and social class.

52 See generally Lukacs, History and Class Consciousness (1968); Freeman, supra note 16; Kairys, Introduction, supra note 5; Kennedy, Antonio Gramsci and the Legal System, supra note 47.

53 See Gabel & Kennedy, Roll Over Beethoven, 36 Stan. L. Rev. 1, 26–27, 33–34 (critique of illusory rights) (1984); Johnson, Do You Sincerely Want to Be Radical?, 36 Stan. L. Rev. 247, 255–56 (1984). See generally Kennedy, supra note 6 (hierarchy sets up artificial and false sense of self); Kennedy, supra note 30 (structure of society made possible by consciousness of society); Kennedy, Form and Substance in Private Law Adjudication, supra note 14.

54 See supra note 52.

55 Sparer, supra note 1, at 537. See D. Bell, supra note 29, at 16–29. Bell does not subscribe to the Crits' theory of black subordination via false consciousness.

56 See Hyde, The Concept of Legitimation in the Sociology of Law, 1983 Wis. L. Rev. 379 (1983); see also supra note 52.

57 See Kairys, Freedom of Speech, supra note 5, at 164; cf. Johnson, supra note 53, at 255–56.

58 See Freeman, supra note 16, at 1075; Klare, Law-Making as Praxis, 40 Telos 123, 134 (Summer, 1979).

59 See Pettigrew, supra note 50, at 674–75.

60 See Kennedy, Antonio Gramsci and the Legal System, supra note 47, at 8.

61 See supra note 47 and accompanying text.

62 347 U.S. 483 (1954).

63 See generally Freeman, supra note 16 (antidiscrimination laws actually perpetuate discrimination through formality).

64 See *supra* notes 23, 43 and accompanying text; *see generally* Pettigrew, *supra* note 50 (formal condemnation of racism by courts and legislators since 1964 has reduced blatant, violent acts of racism, but other forms persist).

65 Bell, *Serving Two Masters: Integration Ideals and Client Interests in School Desegregation Litigation*, 85 Yale L.J. 470 (1976) (conflicts of interest between minority clients and their lawyers).

66 See Kairys, *Freedom of Speech*, *supra* note 5, at 163–164.

67 See Pettigrew, *supra* note 50, at 690–97 (many whites believe racial problem has been solved, but continue to engage in subtle forms of racism).

68 Cf. Schwartz, *supra* note 38, at 438 (describing elements of paternalism in CLS scholarship).

69 Cf. M. Shapiro & R. Spece, Bioethics and Law: Cases, Materials and Problems 168–73 (1980) (terms like "ill" taken as justifying nonconsensual treatment of those so inflicted, when such treatment would otherwise be intolerable).

70 See Brosnan, *supra* note 3, at 264–68 (CLS politically passive, concentrates on doctrinal and conceptual manipulation at the expense of developing a theory of justice). *See also* Johnson, *supra* note 53, at 281–83 (program for action hazy and platitudinous); *but see* D. Kennedy, *supra* note 7 (proposing concrete reforms to law school structure and operation); Gabel & Harris, *Building Power & Breaking Images*, 11 N.Y.U. Rev. L. & Soc. Change 369 (1982) (urging revolutionary legal activism); Sparer, *supra* note 1, at 565–73 (urging progressive social action).

71 See *supra* notes 19–21 and accompanying text (CLS criticizes free speech as an ephemeral right).

72 See Sparer, *supra* note 1, at 565–71; Schwartz, *supra* note 38, at 426–28 (theoretical utopianism); *id.* at 448–52 (grotesque and irresponsible proposals).

73 See Brest, *supra* note 38, at 1109; Gabel, *supra* note 37, at 45–46; Kennedy, *Form and Substance in Private Law Adjudication*, *supra* note 14, at 1771.

74 See Hutchinson & Monahan, *supra* note 1, at 230.

75 *Id.*; *see also* Kennedy, *supra* note 53, at 1771.

76 See, e.g., Klare, *supra* note 7 (equality in the workplace); Simon, *The Ideology of Advocacy: Procedural Justice and Professional Ethics*, 1978 Wis. L. Rev. 29, 133 (1978) (equality of lawyer and client).

77 See Abel, *A Socialist Approach to Risk*, 41 Md. L. Rev. 695 (1982) (shared risks among workers and managers); Gabel, Book Review, 91 Harv. L. Rev. 302, 315 (1977) (shared selves—merging of sense of self with sense of others so as to blur lines among persons); Kennedy, *Form and Substance in Private Law Adjudication*, *supra* note 14, at 1771.

78 See Gabel and Kennedy, *supra* note 53, at 46; cf. C. Gilligan, In a Different Voice 173 (1983) (identifying in women a morality of connectedness). *See generally* Bush, *supra* note 34.

79 See Unger, *The Critical Legal Studies Movement*, *supra* note 4, at 579–85. *See generally* Bush, *supra* note 34.

80 On the difficulty of achieving selfhood in a racist society, see, e.g., G. Allport, *supra* note 24, at 142–62; W. Grier & P. Cobbs, Black Rage (1968).

81 Inability of a group to fend for itself in the political marketplace is a principal justification for applying strict scrutiny under the equal protection clause to state action. See San Antonio Indep. School Dist. v. Rodriguez, 411 U.S. 1, 28 (1972); cf. United States v. Carolene Products Co., 304 U.S. 144, 152 n. 4 (1938).

82 Cf. D. Bell, *supra* note 29, at 29–30, 40–46 (costs of racial remedies always placed on blacks or poor whites); Bell, *Minority Admissions and the Usual Price of Racial Remedies*, 67 Calif. L. Rev. 3 (1979).

83 See G. Torres, *supra* note 23.

84 For a discussion of formalism and nonformalism in the context of adjudicatory processes, see Delgado, Dunn, Brown, Lee & Hubbert, *Fairness and Formality: Minimizing the Risk of Prejudice in Alternative Dispute Resolution*, 1985 Wis. L. Rev. 1359 (1985).

85 See, e.g., *supra* notes 14–22 and accompanying text (rejection of rights in favor of principles, shared love and cooperation); *supra* notes 33–42 and accompanying text (rejection of incremental reform; insistence on global change).

86 I was unable to locate any CLS articles or books on the psychology of racism. The relatively few treatments of race discuss it in political or class terms. See, e.g., Freeman, *supra* note 16; Hutchinson & Monahan, *supra* note 1, at 227–36 (utopian proposals center almost exclusively on reforming social arrangements to eliminate hierarchy, lessen alienation, and increase community and sharing); cf. Pettigrew, *supra* note 50, at 685–86 (current theorists tend to confuse race problems with class struggle).

87 See Is the Dream Over?, Newsweek on Campus, Feb. 1987, at 10, 12 (black students "treated like aliens"; "[t]ales of insults abound"); Friedrich, Racism on the Rise, Time, Feb. 2, 1987, at 18, 21 (survey of attitudes); Racism Flares on Campus, Time, Dec. 8, 1980, at 28 (changes in national mood; prejudice now considered "acceptable" in some quarters); Less Tolerance for Cults, Broad Pattern of Prejudice Revealed, San Francisco Chronicle, Mar. 9, 1987, at 4, col. 3 (reporting results of Gallup poll).

For classic studies of the nature and extent of ethnic prejudice among Americans, see G. Allport, supra note 24, at 79–80, 197–202. For a recent study of the more subtle forms of prejudice, see generally Pettigrew, supra note 50.

88 See G. Allport, supra note 24, at 338; I. Katz, Stigma—A Social Psychological Analysis 97 (1981); Pettigrew, supra note 50, at 688–89 (many avoid outward expressions of racism, but without internalizing norms against it).

89 See Delgado, supra note 84, at 1384 (discussing the principal psychological methods by which individuals deal with tension between racist impulses and public norms condemning racism); Pettigrew, supra note 50, at 690 (discussing avoidance and displacement mechanisms).

90 Some of these theories are summarized in Delgado, supra note 84, at 1375–83. See generally P. van den Berghe, supra note 24.

91 For an excellent summary of psychoanalytic theories of racism, see Lawrence, The Id, The Ego and Equal Protection: Reckoning with Unconscious Racism, 39 Stan. L. Rev. 317, 331–36 (1987); see also G. Allport, supra note 24, at 199; T. Adorno, E. Frenkel-Brunswik, D. Levinson & R. Sanford, The Authoritarian Personality (1950); Simpson & Yinger, The Personality Functions of Prejudice and Discrimination, in Racial and Cultural Minorities: An Analysis of Prejudice and Discrimination (G. Simpson & J. Yinger 4th ed. 1972).

92 See G. Allport, supra note 24, at 224–25 (historical scapegoating); id. at 234–38 (unconscious use of racism and scapegoating to maintain group loyalty); J. Kovel, White Racism—A Psychohistory 44 (1984) (psychology of a people a product of historical forces); Delgado, supra note 84, at 1378–79; see also Handlin, Prejudice and Capitalist Exploitation, 6 Commentary 79 (1948) (psychological explanation of racism incomplete; explanation must reach out to include social forces).

93 See G. Allport, supra note 24, at 22, 29–47, 139; K. Clark, Prejudice and Your Child 17 (2d ed. 1963); J. Kovel, supra note 92, at 132. See generally Snyder, On the Self Perpetuating Nature of Social Stereotypes, in Cognitive Processes in Stereotyping and Intergroup Behavior 183 (D. Hamilton ed. 1981); Delgado, supra note 84, at 1380 (summarizing social-psychological theories of prejudices).

94 For the classic statement of this view, see G. Myrdal, An American Dilemma: The Negro Problem and Modern Democracy (1962).

95 See I. Katz, supra note 88, at 23; P. van den Berghe, supra note 24, at 20–21; Delgado, supra note 84, at 1384–85; Fairchild & Gurin, Traditions in the Social-Psychological Analysis of Race Relations, 21 Am. Behav. 757, 764 (1978).

96 See G. Myrdal, supra note 94, at LXXI, 80.

97 Id.

98 See supra notes 87–89 and accompanying text.

99 See I. Katz, supra note 88, at 23; J. Kovel, supra note 92, at 54–55; Fairchild & Gurin, supra note 95, at 764.

100 The leading contender is the "social contact" theory, which supports much of the push for social integration through, for example, school desegragation. This theory argues that prejudice arises from the individual's mistaken belief that minority group members hold beliefs and values different from one's own. Consequently, the belief may be dispelled through demonstration, via close contact, that it is erroneous. According to the social contact theorists, however, not all kinds of contact reduce discrimination. The contact must be among individuals of equal status and sanctioned by social supports, such as law and custom. See G. Allport, supra note 24, at 261–81; Delgado, supra note 84, at 1382, 1385–86; Simpson & Yinger, The Reeducation of Prejudice and Discrimination: Changing the Prejudiced Person, in Racial and Cultural Minorities: An Analysis of Prejudice and Discrimination, supra note 91, at 673.

101 See, e.g., I. Katz, supra note 88, at 16, 109. See generally Delgado, supra note 84, at 1385–87.

102 See generally Lind, Thibaut and Walker, A Cross-Cultural Comparison of the Effect of Adversary and Inquisitorial Process on Bias in Legal Decisionmaking, 62 Va. L. Rev. 271 (1976); Mnookin and Kornhauser, Bargaining in the Shadow of the Law: The Case of Divorce, 88 Yale L.J. 950 (1979); Nader, Disputing Without the

Force of Law, 88 Yale L.J. 998 (1979); Thibaut and Walker, *Discovery and Presentation of Evidence in Adversary and Non-Adversary Proceedings*, 71 Mich. L. Rev. 1129 (1973); Thibaut, Walker, LaTour and Houlden, *Procedural Justice as Fairness*, 26 Stan. L. Rev. 1271 (1974); Thibaut, Walker and Lind, *Adversary Presentation & Bias in Legal Decisionmaking*, 86 Harv. L. Rev. 386 (1972).

103 *See supra* notes 73–77 and accompanying text.

104 *See* W. James, Pragmatism, and Four Essays From the Meaning of Truth 133 (1975); *see generally* C. Peirce, *How to Make Our Ideas Clear*, in The Philosophy of Peirce: Selected Writings 23 (J. Buchler ed. 1940).

105 *See, e.g.*, Boyle, Critical Legal Studies: A Young Person's Guide 18 (1983) (unpublished manuscript on file with Harvard Civil Rights-Civil Liberties Law Review).

106 *Id.* at 20.

107 *Id.* at 18–28.

108 *Id.* at 28.

109 Brest, *The Federal Government's Power to Protect Negroes and Civil Rights Workers Against Privately Inflicted Harm, Part I*, 1 Harv. C.R.-C.L. L. Rev. 2 (1966); Brest, *The Federal Government's Power to Protect Negroes and Civil Rights Workers Against Privately Inflicted Harm, Part II*, 2 Harv. C.R.-C.L. L. Rev. 1 (1966); Freeman, *supra* note 16; Klare, *supra* note 17; *see also* Sparer, *supra* note 1.

110 Boyle, *supra* note 105, at 18.

111 *See* Bell, *The Price and Pain of Racial Perspective*, Stan. L. Sch. J., Apr., 1986, at 1, col. 1.

112 *See* J. Bracamonte, R. Delgado & G. Torres, Statement at the Minority Critique Panel, Critical Legal Studies Annual Meeting (Jan. 1987) (unpublished manuscript on file with Harvard Civil Rights-Civil Liberties Law Review).

113 *See* N. Gotanda, Statement at the Critical Legal Studies Annual Meeting (Jan. 1987) (on file with Harvard Civil Rights-Civil Liberties Law Review) (describing treatment of minority panelists at an earlier meeting).

114 *See supra* notes 100–02 and accompanying text.

115 Cf. Bell, *supra* note 82, at 17 (whites permit social remedies only when these coincide with their self-interest).

116 *See supra* note 50 and accompanying text.

117 Blacks and other minorities have often found professional advancement in the relatively formal environment of the armed forces. *See* Moskos, *Success Story: Blacks in the Army*, Atlantic Monthly, May 1986, at 64.

Chapter 36

Anne Phillips

FEMINISM AND THE POLITICS OF DIFFERENCE

Or, where have all the women gone?

Personally, I am a feminist, and an Old Feminist, because I dislike everything that feminism implies. I desire an end of the whole business, the demands for equality, the suggestions of sex warfare, the very name of feminist. I want to be about the work in which my real interests lie, the study of inter-race relationships, the writing of novels and so forth. But while the inequality exists, while injustice is done and opportunity denied to the great majority of women, I shall have to be a feminist and an Old Feminist, with the motto Equality First. [1]

WINIFRED HOLTBY, NOVELIST, journalist, harsh critic of South Africa's racial policies, and active if reluctant feminist, wrote this in 1926 in the context of a debate then raging between old and new Feminism. The old feminism she defended pursued equality between the sexes in education and politics and employment; the "new feminism" challenging this focused on policies to improve the condition of women as mothers. A similar debate surfaced in the 1980s, when feminists found themselves embroiled in a rather unhelpful opposition between either equality or difference. When women claimed equality with men, did this mean they were accepting male conventions about what constitutes a good life, like the equal right to sacrifice one's children to one's career advancement, or the equal right to brutalise oneself in the army? If they insisted instead on what made their lives different from men's, did this confirm traditional stereotypes about the sexes— notions about women finding their fulfilment in motherhood not employment, or caring more about their nearest and dearest than any abstract justice claims? These are not the questions I focus on here, for my perception of the current state of feminist debate is that it has moved beyond that dichotomy between either equality or difference. What interests me in Holtby's comment is the reluctance it suggests about having to keep going on about the women.

There is a curious cycle within feminism that starts with exposing the once-invisible woman (attacking the many ways in which her needs, concerns, or interests have been submerged under those of men or mankind), but then gets frustrated with what comes to be experienced as an obsessive preoccupation with sex difference, and wishes it could submerge those women again. In mid-nineteenth century Britain, women were literally obliterated as legal persona on entering marriage. They were subsumed under fathers or husbands for the purposes of political representation, prevented from addressing public audiences that included men, and through a combination of legal and customary practices, denied access to education and many fields of employment. Much of the campaigning activity of nineteenth-century feminism was devoted to putting these women back on the map, challenging the practices that had rendered their needs and claims invisible, and asserting their independent rights within employment, politics, and marriage. In later arguments, feminists have focused on the divisions between public and private that continued to obscure women from view even after the achievements of formal equality, and much contemporary analysis deals with the apparently inclusive categories (like humanity or citizenship) whose masculine provenance still keeps women out.

A great deal of feminism is about breaking the silence on women: disentangling the supposed unities of the family that conceal relationships of power and subordination; identifying the new issues that arise when we turn from the abstractions of humanity to put the spotlight on women themselves; drawing attention to conflicts of interest between the sexes; battling on behalf of women's rights or needs. In one particularly strong formulation of this, Carole Pateman has argued that our understanding of citizenship has to be reformulated "to open up space for two figures: one masculine, one feminine".[2] Instead, that is, of subsuming women under the false universalisms of humanity, feminists have sought to reframe views on freedom, equality, or democracy with the knowledge that there are both women and men.

This has always been a key moment in the feminist cycle, and yet the preoccupation with women never seems to last very long. It is as if we lose heart with what we come to see as an over-emphasis on women, begin stretching out towards broader implications, towards pacifism, perhaps eco-feminism, or as in the example discussed here, towards a more generalised politics of difference. This process can be extraordinarily productive, but it also threatens to return feminism to the beginning of the cycle. Women may then drop out of the picture, to become invisible again.

There are a number of reasons for this, and my own guess is that there are three particularly important contributory factors. One is that women have trouble insisting on their own special needs and interests (self-denial being part of the construction of femininity), and that feminists have proved no better at dealing with

this than other groups of women. In the history of feminist campaigning, there has always been an attempt to associate women's needs with the broader needs of humanity as a whole, and it is only in rare moments that feminists have felt tough enough—or angry enough—to insist on their own "selfish" concerns. The case for women's suffrage was typically argued in terms of the way women would civilise and moralise politics, and even the most ardent of suffragists found it hard to say she wanted the vote just to make life better for herself. When Britain entered the First World War, the Women's Social and Political Union immediately suspended its militant campaign for the vote, and in the aftermath of the War, many erstwhile feminists found it hard to continue to define themselves in these terms. This was less, in my view, because they felt their own battles were now won (British women did get the vote in 1918, but the franchise was still restricted to those over thirty), and more because the devastation of the War had been borne primarily by men. Focusing on women seemed hardly appropriate, when so many men had died.

The second reason is that sexual equality comes to seem so obvious, and it is boring to have to keep making the same old points. Writing in 1927 (and from a perspective very close to that of Winifred Holtby), Vera Brittain commented on the feelings of the typical feminist:

> The fight for acknowledgement now bores rather than enthralls her; its postponement seems illogical, an anachronism, a waste of precious time ... she continues to agitate, often a little wearily, only because she desires to abolish the need for agitation.[3]

In our own time, I am often struck by the disjunction between the theoretical sophistication and innovation of feminist writing and the policy recommendations most feminists support. However varied their views on psychoanalysis, postmodernism, post-colonialism, the nature of subjectivity, or whether it makes sense to talk of "women" at all, most tend to agree that there should be more nurseries, equal pay, protection against sexual harassment and domestic violence, non-sexist education, more women in positions of power. The disagreement is largely in the details, and the real difficulty is that progress is so slow. There has been no great theoretical challenge working out what needs to be done; the more intellectually exciting areas have been those where feminism stretches beyond its initial preoccupation with women to develop new connections.

The third point is that it is hard to sustain a politics on the margins. There are exceptional periods when this becomes both possible and desirable: the typical feminist of the 1970s had little fear of marginalisation, both because she took a pride in her "outsider" status, and because she was sustained by an active community in the women's movement. Thirty years on, there is a more palpable anxiety about remaining on the margins, and this often surfaces in a dislike of feminist "ghettos" or a need to show that feminism is not "just" about women. My own work falls within what would be described as feminist political theory. When asked what I work on, however, I commonly say I deal with issues of democracy or representation or political equality: it is as if I like to think of myself as a feminist who works on democracy, rather than someone defined and delimited by a field called "feminist political theory".[4] Offering oneself up to the accusation of focusing "only" on women suggests a narrowing of focus that most of us would prefer to avoid. One consequence is that the moments of dissidence can be distinctly short-lived.

I begin then with a warning. When looking at developments in feminist political theory, it is possible to trace a powerful movement that takes feminism beyond an exclusive preoccupation with women to link analyses of sexuality and gender to analyses of race, ethnicity, the politics

of multiculturalism, and what has come to be called the politics of difference. This is an impressive achievement. It also poses a challenge. The movement testifies to the power of feminism, demonstrating that its insights can illuminate far more than the condition of women. But it also fits—rather too closely for comfort—into a cycle that begins with making women visible and ends with concealing them again. In the course of the 1980s, feminists sometimes talked confidently of a movement "from margin to mainstream"; my question in this paper is whether that consolidation might not prove to be a capitulation as well. I start with a brief indication of what I understand by the politics of difference, and identify three problems that can arise with this. My conclusion is that there are indeed risks associated with the generalisation of feminism into a politics of difference, but that these are currently more apparent in the non-feminist than feminist literature.

The politics of difference

The "politics of difference" has been widely used in recent years, partly as an analytical, partly as a normative category. It seeks to capture the complexities of identity in societies where class is no longer (if it ever was) the predominant source of political identification but has given way to multiple axes of identity organised around sex, race, ethnicity, age, religion, language and culture. A politics of difference stresses the importance of recognising rather than obliterating these differences: this may be because recognising people's (differential) identities has come to be regarded as a necessary component in human well-being; more pragmatically, it may be because moves towards greater equality tend to fail when difference is not taken into account. In some versions, the key point is that identity is always forged in relations of difference, and that this uneasy mutual interdependence should encourage us to review notions of women as an identity group. In others, there is a substantive claim about the vitality and value of difference: the idea that heterogeneity is richer and more dynamic than homogeneity, and that we should welcome rather than fear our differences.

In the development of this tradition, Iris Marion Young's *Justice and the Politics of Difference* has been particularly influential.[5] Young has attacked a trend in contemporary political theory that is well exemplified in the work of John Rawls: a tendency to treat problems of social justice as a matter of what people should have rather than what they do. Her point is that focusing on questions of distribution (what do the principles of justice tell us about how goods should be distributed?) leads towards a politics from on-high, a politics without the politics, in which different social groups play no noticeable part in defining the principles of justice. Her related argument criticises the ideal of impartiality: the notion that it is possible to arrive at correct principles of justice by abstracting from what is particular to one's own or group position and repressing differences of gender, race, ethnicity, sexuality, culture or class. Young challenges what she sees as the assumption of a homogeneous public. She argues that this assumption renders invisible social groups whose values or practices do not fit with the dominant norms, and delivers all of us to an idealist fiction that represents the partial preoccupations of dominant groups as the last word in impartial interest. The better alternative is to recognise more rigorously the heterogeneous nature of contemporary life. This means attending to group-specific needs rather than denying them in some grand rhetoric about human equality. It also implies group-specific representation for oppressed groups so as to provide them with the empowerment and recognition that will enable them to challenge dominant norms.

In her introduction, Young describes her personal political passion as beginning with feminism, and says it was her participation in women's movement politics that first taught her to identify oppression. But it was also this participation that compelled her beyond an exclusive focus on women, for it was discussions within the women's movement on the importance and difficulty of acknowledging differences among women—differences of race, sexuality, age or culture—that ignited her reflections on the politics of difference. These discussions, as she puts it:

> compelled me to move out of a focus specifically on women's oppression, to try to understand as well the social position of other oppressed groups.[6]

The connections Young makes have been repeated in many other works, and the politics of gender is increasingly theorised in the wider context of what have come to be called "new social movements". In recent work on political representation, I have focused on the exclusions practised against groups defined by their gender, ethnicity and race, and have argued the importance of a politics of presence in dealing with these exclusions.[7] In doing so, I have claimed that it is incoherent to promote gender parity in politics without also promoting the fairer representation of racial and ethnic minorities, and have treated these in tandem as examples of the political representation of difference. In *Justice Interruptus*, Nancy Fraser explores what she sees as a shift from a politics of redistribution, most commonly associated with class and class interest, to a politics of recognition, fuelled by "groups mobilised under the banners of nationality, ethnicity, 'race', gender and sexuality".[8] While noting important distinctions between these last groups, she argues that the politics associated with gender and race, in particular, share crucial common features. A collection edited by Seyla Benhabib invited the contributors "to reflect upon the theory and practice of democracy after the experiences of identity politics in their 'new social movements' form",[9] and brought together essays on feminism, multi-culturalism, and the rights of indigeneous peoples under a general rubric of *Democracy and Difference*. There is a perception that these share important common features: most notably, that they complicate traditional views about abstract, universal rights by stressing the heterogeneity of political life.

The idea that racial and sexual inequality share common features is not new. Many of those who became active in the nineteenth-century women's movement came from a prior involvement in anti-slavery agitation, while many of those who became active in the con-temporary women's movement took it for granted that racism and sexism formed a com-mon enemy. The more unexpected alliance has been that between feminism and the defence of minority cultures, though here too one can readily identify connections. Feminists have written extensively on the relationship between equality and difference, and one of the points recurrently made is that policies of sex-blindness may not be as progressive as was traditionally assumed. Refusing to differentiate between women and men looks, on the face of it, the route to a more equal society: no more dis-crimination against women, no more differential treatment on the basis of sex. But in the frame-work of an unequal society, that refusal to recognise difference can have perverse effects. Without the sex-specific legislation that allows pregnant women to take maternity leave, for example, women are set at a disadvantage in the labour market; without the sex-specific policies that require political parties to take the sex of the candidates into account, women will continue to be grossly under-represented in politics. The refusal to recognise difference can become a covert way of elevating one group alone as the norm. Men then stand in for humanity, and humanity adopts a masculine form.

Arguments such as these have provided an important resource in addressing relationships between minority and majority cultures, for if sex-blindness is not unambiguously progressive, neither is the kind of "culture-blindness" that accommodates minority cultures only on con-dition that they keep their differences to a protected private zone. The pursuit of sexual equality sometimes requires differential treat-ment for women and men. In similar fashion, the pursuit of equal citizenship in a multicultural society may sometimes require differential rights or differential facilities for members of minority cultures. (One relatively uncontentious example is the exemption of Sikh men from the legal requirement to wear a safety helmet while riding a motorbike; another would be the pro-vision of public funding to establish cultural centres for minority groups.) Will Kymlicka, best known for his writings on *Multicultural Citizenship*,[10] argues that the "same attitudes and habits of mind which enabled liberals to ignore the just claims of women have also enabled them to ignore the just claims of ethnocultural minorities".[11] Both feminism and multicultural-ism take issue with the inadequacy of the traditional liberal conception of individual rights. Both see liberalism as blinding itself to grave injustice: in the first case by operating as if the citizen is a man; in the second, as if all citizens share the same language and national culture. Both traditions stress the institutional structures that have to be addressed in order to give meaning to an equality of rights. Both challenge the assumption that equality means identical treatment.

So when feminists defend affirmative action as necessary to deal with the deep structures of inequality that prevent women taking up their so-called equal opportunities, the argument points towards a parallel defence of affirmative action for members of racial and ethnic minorities. When feminists argue that legislation has been framed without reference to women's experience, and that giving women an equal voice would alter the prevailing norms, this points towards parallel charges that have been made by members of minority cultures. A feminism that focuses on experiences of marginalisation and exclusion has obvious points of contact with other groups that face a similar experience. This suggests a close alliance between all groups that have felt themselves defined out of the dominant norms.

The suggestions are, in my view, correct, for there are strong parallels between sexual and racial equality, and a close family resemblance between the issues posed by feminism and those that have to be addressed to achieve equality in multicultural societies. But the shift towards this more generalised politics of diversity and difference also carries certain risks. The first is that the preoccupation with difference can make it harder to sustain a politics focused around women or women's identity. The second is that alliances between feminism, multiculturalism, and the politics of indigenous groups can promote a conception of women's politics that pushes it too far into a paradigm derived from cultural minorities. The third is that the connections rightly made between women and other excluded groups can make it harder to articulate a critique of sexual inequality. These are substantially different points, and the fact that each can be made of something termed "the politics of difference" indicates something of the slipperiness of this term.

Identity/differences and the disappearing woman

The first point is that the recognition of difference can make it hard to articulate any clear sense of "women". At its most straightforward, this is because differences between women come more evidently to the fore. In the Anglo–American literature, it has become hard to sustain strong notions of "women" or "women's experience" or "women's interests": if we draw on such notions to criticise the false abstractions of "mankind" or "humanity" or "men", we may find ourselves deconstructing one set of fictions only to put another set in their place. Women are

indeed women, and most women are probably different from most men. But sexual identities intersect with racial identities, class identities, regional or national identities, and these make it hard to articulate a strong sense of women's identity or needs.

When this critique was first developed, many feminists continued to operate with notions of group identity or group interest, but refined these to address more precise sub-groupings, like working class women or women of colour. The supposed "interests of women" then fragmented into the interests of multiple groups, and just as men could not legitimately claim to speak to or represent the interests of women, so now, it was argued, middle class women could not speak to or represent the interests of working class women, white women the interests of black women, or first world women the interests of women from the Third World. This was felt by many to be a politics of despair, for if "women" dissolves into all these sub-categories, each of which is then open to further sub-division, there seems no stopping place short of a unique description of each unique individual. This typology of differences also failed to capture the way political identities are formed, for if no-one regards herself simply as "woman", it is also the case that no-one regards herself simply as a working class woman, or simply as a black woman. It is not so much that there are many identity groups, but that each person lives in a complex of identities, some elements of which may become more important than others depending on political context.

Under the impact of such arguments, the first attack on the homogeneity of women spawned a second, this time more indebted to a post-structuralist deconstructionism that stresses the ambiguity of all identities. In the literature associated with this, the search for identity is sometimes presented as a search for false security in what is necessarily an insecure world: an attempt to close down or close off a sense of things that do not fit, instead of embracing the uncertainty and dealing with the complications that then ensue. When we define ourselves as different from others (this may be women defining themselves as different from men, or one group of women defining themselves as different from another), we are trying to fix our own identity by pushing into some other camp the unruly elements we cannot make sense of. We are trying to impose order on a turbulent existence. Think, for example, of what is happening when women define themselves as different from men because of their greater capacity for empathy or care. There may well be differences between the sexes in this respect, but when we allow ourselves to define women through this more caring identity, we close off our troubled perception of other elements that co-exist with this—a sense, perhaps, that women can be very aggressive, or that part of what women want is simply to insist on their own personal needs. We are trying, that is, to fix identity by expunging what is contradictory or different.

For those working in this tradition, the search for women's identity is always problematic, even when pluralised to take into account multiple differences between women. It is not just that we now have to fill in all the additional details about race or class or age or ethnicity; as Judith Butler argues, even if we were to do so, we still could not expect to end up with a meaningful category of "women".[12] For Butler, the term is a permanent site of contest; it is what we battle over rather than who we are. For Bonnie Honig, we miss the point about difference if we treat it merely as a reminder that there are different groups: that there are men and women, black people and white, Muslims and Catholics and Jews. The real point about difference is that it prevents any of us from having a secure identity, either as an individual or as a member of a group. Taking difference seriously means giving up on the dream of an identity or culture or group vision that is "unmarked or unriven by difference";[13] it means recognising conflict as built into our identities and not just as conflict

between "us" and "them". From this perspective, identity can be more a source of oppression than a means to empowerment. Rather than organising around our so-called identities, we would do better to recognise that the subject is always "decentred" and identity always incomplete.

Many find this talk of the decentred subject hard to take: we might, under pressure, agree with Stuart Hall that "the fully unified, completed, secure and coherent identity is a fantasy",[14] but that seems to set an impossibly high standard for what counts as identity; to quote Hall from another context, "identity is not fixed, but it's not nothing either".[15] Yet whatever position people reach on this, few would now want to present "women" as either a pre-existing or soon-to-be-generated identity group, and much contemporary theory draws on a more troubled understanding of identity formation as organised around binary exclusions that always threaten to suppress differences on each side. The binary differences have come to seem particularly implausible, and the perhaps unexpected outcome is that what started as a pluralisation of differences (not just male or female, black or white, straight or gay) generates what many have felt to be an over-individualised conception of political agency.[16] This is the charge that has been levelled at Judith Butler, for example, who has been criticised for substituting individual acts of parody or transgression for the kind of political mobilisation that relies on a notion of social groups; for exaggerating the de-stabilising effects of cross-dressing as a subversion of norms of masculinity or heterosexuality, and playing down the possibilities of more traditional forms of collective action. She regards this as an unfair criticism, and I'm sure did not intend her drag example to be taken as such a paradigm for political action. It does, however, seem one consequence of the turn towards difference that any systemic differences between one group (say, women) and another group (say, men) that continue to shape and curtail our actions become less apparent. The argument builds on scepticism about the coherence of individual identity, but it also returns us, rather unexpectedly, to that individual. Women as a group drop out of the picture.

The reification of difference

A second problem arises in a very different part of contemporary literature, where notions of collective subjects remain almost too alive and well. Consider James Tully's *Strange Multiplicity*, which focuses on "the demands of the 250 million Aboriginal and Indigenous peoples of the world for the recognition and accommodation of their twelve thousand diverse cultures, governments and environmental practices",[17] and argues for reconciliation through dialogue and mutual respect rather than an assimilationist imposition of a uniform constitution. In this work, Tully draws on a tradition he describes as "cultural feminism", making frequent parallels between feminist critiques of the authoritative, dominant culture and the arguments put forward by Aboriginal peoples or members of linguistic and ethnic minorities.

The feminism he incorporates is one that stresses women's cultural difference, sees women as speaking "in a different voice" from men and appealing to different normative traditions. The parallels between this and the politics of Aboriginal peoples are obvious enough. In both cases, Tully suggests, the problem is how to "enter into a dialogue on equal footing with members from the authoritative tradition without being marginalised or assimilated":[18] how, that is, to claim an equal footing, but how to do this while still holding on to one's cultural distinctiveness. Many feminists will not recognise themselves in this description, will argue, on the contrary, that their feminism derives from the authoritative traditions of liberalism or democracy, and will see their task as making those traditions live up to their promises to women. But the fact that Tully draws

on only one strand of a variegated tradition is not a decisive objection. The larger problem is that the assimilation of women into the category of "cultural group" has unfortunate consequences for feminist critique.

Treating women as a cultural group overstates the homogeneity of "women's culture". It also presumes that the characteristics that have come to be associated with women's way of thinking or women's way of being are ones we will want to sustain and protect, in much the same way that one might want to sustain and protect minority cultures from forced assimilation into majority values.[19] So far as women's culture is concerned, this strikes me as a dubious presumption. Women are, in my view, different from men, do tend to have different ways of talking or relating to others, do tend towards different sets of priorities and values. It would be distinctly odd if this were not the case, given the markedly different treatment of boys and girls as they grow up, and the markedly different roles allocated to the sexes in carework, relationships and employment. If, with all this, men and women ended up just the same kind of people, they would have to be extraordinarily immune to the social influences acting upon them: inhuman, almost, in their detachment from social conditions. So I have no objection to the notion that women are, on average, different from men. But I cannot see that differences that derive from historical inequality or relationships of power and subordination can be treated as objects of veneration, differences one would seek to sustain.

Femininity and masculinity alike are tainted by the processes that create them, and neither, in my view, is entitled to the kind of respect that might more legitimately be accorded to traditions that have developed over centuries inside Aboriginal communities, or traditions that migrant groups have brought with them from their countries of origin. In any contest between them, I find it plausible enough that the qualities associated with femininity will win out over those associated with masculinity: that the responsibilities women carry for the care of the young, weak and old can generate a finer set of priorities than a more typically masculine experience; or that a history of subordination can generate greater sympathy for those in pain or suffering than a lifetime of being in control. But "women's culture" is formed in relations of dependency and subordination, and what is positive in it is almost inextricably intertwined with aspects that are less attractive. One of Simone de Beauvoir's complaints about women was that they were particularly prone to "bad faith", and that living in conditions of relative powerlessness, they were always inclined to blame other people or fate for the things that went wrong in their lives. Neither the master nor the slave ends up with a model culture, and while the assimilation of "women's culture" into "men's culture" is hardly a desirable objective, we cannot simply celebrate the characteristics of "women's culture" as if these were unproblematic.

The other side to this is what the analogy between women and "other" cultural groups does to the status of "men's culture". In Tully's analysis, feminism becomes "the struggles of women for the recognition and accommodation of their gender-related differences",[20] and this is taken to mean that women need something more or other than an equal say in the institutions or traditions established by men. They also need an equal say "in their own voice", which seems to imply an equal standing in a dialogue that women join from their own distinct organisations and with their own distinct traditions of interpretation. There is something rather odd in the scenario this conjures up. It suggests a dialogue between "women's culture" and "men's culture", something akin to the proposed dialogue between indigenous and settler peoples, which each party enters into in relations of mutual respect and where each comes to recognise the salience of the other's point of view. Whatever sense one might make of

this in considering the relationship between minority and majority cultures, it seems peculiarly inappropriate to relations between women and men, who always live side by side with one another—and if feminism is right, in a relationship of subordination and inequality. When feminism is presented as claiming an equal standing for women's culture alongside men's, this not only treats women's culture as less problematic than it is; it also gives far too much credence to the claims of "men's culture".

Feminism and multiculturalism

This leads to the third problem, which is that the connections made between gender and other kinds of difference can make it harder to articulate a critique of sexual inequality. The alliance between feminism and multiculturalism has been forged out of a common dissatisfaction with liberalism, contesting the excessive confidence liberalism places in a formal equality of rights, and its tendency to treat difference as something best ignored. This alliance, however, is fraught with difficulties, and this is particularly so when we consider the centrality of conventions regulating familial relationships to the definition of most cultures. What distinguishes one culture from another is very often the principles it adopts regarding the relative position of women and men: whether it regards marriage, for example, as a free contract between consenting individuals, as something that deprives women of their independent legal standing (as was the case in nineteenth century Britain), or as something best arranged by parents acting on what they conceive to be the true interests of their children. Cultures vary in their attitudes to sexuality (the most dramatic illustration being the importance some cultural groups have attached to the genital mutilation of young women), and in their willingness to recognise women as civic equals. One of the main concerns of cultural groups in their contestations with other groups or the state is to retain their authority to decide who is a group member: to decide, for example, who counts as a Jew, or who is to be recognised as a member of a particular indigenous group. As Ayelet Shachar has argued, this authority typically operates through family law, and in many cases, the criteria for membership have been self-evidently discriminatory, as when Indian tribes in North American reservations have recognised the children of men who marry outside the group as full members, but not the children of women who marry outside.[21]

The further point is that where religion is a prominent defining element in a culture, the principles regulating sexual relationships are almost always inequitable. All religions experience difficulty with sexual equality, and despite some notable exceptions (including the many early feminists who belonged to the Unitarian Church), most feminists experience difficulty with religion. That this should be so is hardly surprising, for religions tend to build into their moral prescriptions part of what have been the customs and conventions in the societies from which they arise. They then weight these customs with all the power of religious prescription. Since no society has yet operated on the basis of full sexual equality, it is only to be expected that religions will tend towards conservatism on the position of women. To say this is not to say that religion is intrinsically misogynist, for every religion contains within itself a variety of traditions, and these have included a variety of positions on the appropriate roles and relationships of the sexes. But religion is not, on the whole, associated with a strong defence of sexual equality. What then happens to the alliance between feminism and multiculturalism when feminists find themselves defending the rights of minority cultures?

Some of the literature sidesteps this problem by overlooking religion. One of the criticisms levelled at Iris Young is that there seems to be little space in her heterogeneous public for religious groups, and that the examples she typically offers are rather too obviously drawn

from what have been seen as the "progressive" end of the "new social movements" spectrum.[22] In principle, however, it is hard to see why a politics of difference should not apply equally to groups excluded or vilified because of their religious identities. The most recent survey of ethnic minorities in Britain suggests that it is people of Asian rather than African or Caribbean origin who currently bear the brunt of racial attacks and racial abuse, and the majority of Asians interviewed in the survey felt that this prejudice was primarily a prejudice against Muslims.[23] The current demonisation of Islam seems to fall well within the remit of any politics of difference—but Islam is not at its best on the question of women.

In a number of recent contributions, Susan Moller Okin sets out to prise feminism apart from its alliance with multiculturalism. "I think we—especially those of us who consider ourselves politically progressive and opposed to all forms of oppression—have been too quick to assume that feminism and multiculturalism are both good things which are easily reconciled".[24] When minority cultures lay claim to special exemptions, or argue for group rights in order to sustain their traditional practices, the cultural practices they are defending are often antagonistic to sexual equality: the examples Okin discusses include polygamy, forced marriages, female genital mutilation, and the veiling of women. The self-proclaimed leaders of these minority cultures are typically composed of their older and male members, and unless the women in these cultures speak out forcibly for the specific interests of women—and are supported in this by others committed to sexual equality—then the supposed common ground between feminism and multiculturalism will end up suppressing women's interests, making women invisible once again.

I agree with Okin on this last point, though I also think she weights the argument unfairly by focusing on practices that are widely condemned inside minority cultures (polygamy, female genital mutilation), or ones that are already extensively contested and no longer in general use. It is easy to overstate the tensions between feminism and multiculturalism, and in so doing, to reaffirm stereotypical misrepresentations of minority cultures that contribute to their marginality. But it is also, as Okin argues, possible to exaggerate their compatibility, and one of the dangers in a radical pluralism that lists women alongside ethnic minorities, linguistic minorities, indigenous peoples, lesbians and gay men, is that the focus on heterogeneity versus homogeneity can take the edge off sexual equality.

The problem here is almost the opposite to the first one discussed, for where some have used the language of difference to dissolve the coherence of any collective identity (no more "women", no more "blacks", no more Asians or lesbians or Jews), others employ it to describe what then seem rather too solid group identities. Yet "the ethnic minority", like "the Aboriginal people" or "the lesbian and gay community", is made up of women and men, old and young, rich and poor: people often engaged in conflict and disagreeing about the interpretation of their supposedly shared culture. In some cases, these conflicts will become so acute that individuals will choose to dissociate themselves from their supposed group and redefine themselves in different ways. A more common experience, perhaps, is that dissidents position themselves for contest on two fronts: simultaneously challenging the external disparagement of "their" culture or community and the internal representations of that culture or community that reproduce inequalities and injustice. The double nature of this contest is not always fully recognised in the literature on feminism and multiculturalism, which tends to represent cultural claims as the exclusive provenance of men in the community and counterposes these to the rights and protections of women members. But it is also not well recognised in the literature on multiculturalism, some of

which operates with an overly unified notion of "the community", and thinks of dialogue as taking place between rather than within and across the constituent groups.

Beyond the binary of female and male

In a variety of ways, the movement from "women's issues" to a more general analysis of difference can mean that questions once central to feminist politics become submerged under broader themes. In the first case, this is because "difference" comes to be viewed almost as a constitutive part of the human condition, associated with a lengthy (perhaps infinite) list of possible axes of differentiation, but thereby detached from any thesis about one group wielding or another group contesting power. In the second case, it is the assimilation of women into the category of "cultural group" that is the source of the problem. This encourages a perception of women as yet another culturally marginalised or threatened group, and in the process exaggerates the integrity of both "women's" and "men's" culture. In the third case, the alliance between similarly beleaguered outsiders can make it harder for feminists to articulate their critique of sexual inequality. The connections (rightly) made between gender and other kinds of difference can then end up silencing women.

At this point in the argument, many readers may feel my diagnosis is far too gloomy. After all, the assimilation of women into the category of cultural group has been more characteristic of the non-feminist than feminist literature; and if the recent voicing of concerns over the relationship between feminism and multiculturalism tells us anything, it is that feminists have retained a very healthy awareness that women in minority cultural groups can have different interests from men, and a very determined commitment to sexual equality. At this stage, indeed, one might want to stress the opposite risk. There is, of course, a danger that well-intentioned moves towards recognising the diversity and legitimacy of many cultures could encourage public authorities to turn a blind eye to practices that institutionalise women's subordination, could strengthen the power of self-styled community leaders—almost always male—who represent a very partial and often oppressive view of "their" community's most cherished traditions, and lead to a paralysed cultural relativism that puts cultural sensitivity over the rights or needs of women. But there is also a risk on the other side that the sexual equality agenda could be employed to dismiss out of hand the validity of any multicultural claims. There is a rather unsavoury strand of racism around today that uses the situation of women—"look what these people do to their women"—to characterise ethnic minority groups as backward, violent, or abusive, and then employs this stereotype to justify an arrogant assimilationism.[25] The sexual equality agenda can be adopted in a rather dishonest way—by people who otherwise show little interest in women's equality—as a means of disparaging or stereotyping the groups they regard as inferior. If this is so, we should perhaps be equally worried about the feminist challenge to the "wrong" kind of multiculturalism inadvertently encouraging a backlash against all such initiatives, or the abuse of the sexual equality agenda to promote an oppressively monocultural world. It may be that these pose a greater contemporary danger than any failure to speak out about women.

The object of my argument is not to reverse the movement from a politics centred around women to a more generalised focus on difference, for like many of those who now take difference as their central organising concept, I have found this movement enormously fruitful. It enables us to identify common patterns in processes of exclusion or marginalisation; it brings into sharper focus the connections between racial and sexual equality; it also establishes what I see as a close family relationship between feminist and multicultural concerns. But the

process simultaneously makes feminism both more and less central: more central, because the analysis of gender difference becomes one of the prototypes for addressing many axes of difference; less central, because the unravelling of group identity makes it hard to continue to speak of women as a distinct group. Once one moves from a simpler binary of female and male to a wider theorisation of difference, it does seem that generalisations about "women" and "men" miss the point: either they misread the complexities and ambiguities in the formation of identities; or they postulate an unproblematic and unified "women's culture"; or they treat women as a category outside of culture or ethnicity, and deal with culture or ethnicity as if these were exclusively male. Each of these points has a long prehistory in feminist theory and politics—there was no naïve early moment when we all thought of "women" as a simple description—but the movement that has linked analyses of gender and sexuality to the broader politics of difference helps bring them into sharper relief. In some cases it has done so by compounding the errors, as when women are listed alongside ethnic, racial, linguistic, cultural or religious minorities as the key groups challenging the presumptions of a homogeneous society: this ignores what was a central theme of feminist politics from the late 1970s, which is that women are not "just" women but make up half the membership of all the "other" minority groups.[26] In most cases, however, the very naming of the groups makes it clear that each of them intersects and shares membership with the others, for once one starts thinking about difference, it is hard to sustain for long the notion of mutually exclusive groups. What began as a heterogeneity of distinct and different groups, linked together by common experiences of marginalisation or exclusion, ends up as a more complex heterogeneity within them.

The resulting unravelling of group identity is, on the whole, a positive development—and certainly more beneficial to feminism than an uncritical reification of "women's culture" or uncritical defence of a supposedly unitary "minority culture". But the movement returns us to the problem posed earlier, which is that the logic of difference—particularly if linked to an analysis of identity formation as suppressing rather than enabling—can make it hard to talk about women. Perhaps more precisely (because we do all continue to talk about women whatever our theoretical take on the term), it can encourage an over-individualised understanding of political agency that attaches too little weight to structural differences between women and men. It is as if we either end up with a listing that places women alongside a range of minority groups as exemplars of the excluded "other" (failing therefore to recognise any specificity to gender, but also overlooking the women within each of these excluded groups); or else we dispense with these fragile group categories to fall back on the individual again. In either case, the capacity to address sexual inequality can be seriously compromised.

I have cited little so far in the way of evidence from feminist literature, and my argument has been rather short on illustrations of this supposed turn-around in feminist thought. This fits, as it happens, with my reading, for I see the dangers discussed here as more likely to mar the reception of a politics of difference outside feminist circles than characterise its development within. It would certainly be inappropriate to describe Iris Young's work as a case of the vanishing woman, for she has consistently argued against any tendency to submerge conflicts between women and men, and a recent collection of her essays is explicitly organised around issues of gentler.[27] The problem is not so much what happens in feminism. The problem, rather, is that the politics of difference can become one of the tickets of entry into mainstream debate, but what gets taken from feminism is its critique of universalism or emphasis on diversity and difference rather than its commitment to sexual equality.

So far as feminist work is concerned, the cycle has not been completed; women have not been rendered invisible again. But in pursuing the implications of the turn towards difference, it is important to continue to theorise that complex relationship between individual and group, and to do so in a way that retains a meaningful politics of sexual equality. The stretching beyond "women" to a more generalised focus on difference has been an extraordinary achievement. In measuring that achievement, however, we have to be aware of the challenge. Like Winifred Holtby, I believe we must continue to be feminists—and keep those women still firmly in view.

Notes

1 W. Holtby, "Feminism Divided" 1926, reprinted in P. Berry and A. Bishop (eds), *Testament of a Generation: The Journalism of Vera Brittain and Winifred Holtby* (London, Virago, 1985) 48.
2 C. Pateman, *The Sexual Contract* (Cambridge, Polity Press, 1988) 224.
3 V. Brittain, from a Six Point Group Pamphlet, 1927, reprinted in Berry and Bishop, *supra* n. 1, at 99.
4 In similar vein, Nicola Lacey has commented on her studious avoidance of the field of sexual offences, and linked this to the way that work on sexual offences in general, and the law of rape in particular, became pigeonholed as a peculiarly feminine or feminist concern. She makes this observation in the context of an essay that breaks with her previous practice to focus on the way that criminal law constructs the wrong of rape. See N. Lacey, "Unspeakable Subjects, Impossible Rights: Sexuality, Integrity and Criminal Law" in N. Lacey, *Unspeakable Subjects; Feminist Essays in Legal and Social Theory* (Oxford, Hart Publishing, 1998).
5 I. M. Young, *Justice and the Politics of Difference* (Princeton, NJ, Princeton University Press, 1990).
6 *Ibid.*, at 13–14.
7 A. Phillips, *The Politics of Presence* (Oxford, Clarendon Press, 1995).
8 N. Fraser, *Justice Interruptus: Critical Reflections on the "Postsocialist" Condition* (London, Routledge, 1997) 11.

9 S. Benhabib, *Democracy and Difference: Contesting the Boundaries of the Political* (Princeton, NJ, Princeton University Press, 1996) 5.

10 W. Kymlicka, *Multicultural Citizenship: A Liberal Theory of Minority Rights* (Oxford, Clarendon Press, 1995).

11 W. Kymlicka, "Liberal Complacencies", in S. M. Okin with respondents (eds), *Is Multiculturalism Bad For Women?* (Princeton, NJ, Princeton University Press, 1999) 34.

12 J. Butler, *Gender Trouble: Feminism and the Subversion of Identity* (London, Routledge, 1989).

13 B. Honig, "Difference, Dilemmas, and the Politics of Home" in S Benhabib (ed.), *supra* n. 9, at 258.

14 S. Hall, "New Ethnicities" in J. Donald and A. Rattansi (eds), *"Race", Culture and Difference* (London, Sage, 1992) 277.

15 S. Hall, "Interview on Culture and Power" (1997) 33 *Radical Philosophy* 86.

16 See L. McNay, *Gender as Agency* (Cambridge, Polity Press, 2000).

17 J. Tully, *Strange Multiplicity: Constitutionalism in an Age of Diversity* (Cambridge, Cambridge University Press, 1995) 3.

18 *Ibid.*, at 53.

19 Since these, too, are tainted by the processes that produce them, there is also a question mark over the respect due to any "tradition".

20 Tully, *supra* n. 17, at 178.

21 A. Shachar, "The Paradox of Multicultural Vulnerability: Individual Rights, Identity Groups, and the State" in C. Joppke and S. Lukes (eds), *Multicultural Questions* (Oxford, Oxford University Press, 1999); see also A. Shachar, "Group Identity and Women's Rights in Family Law: The Perils of Multicultural Accommodation" (1998) 6 *Journal of Political Philosophy* 285 at 285–305.

22 The list she offers in *Justice and the Politics of Difference* does make one reference to religion—"women, Blacks, Chicanos, Puerto Ricans and other Spanish-speaking Americans, American Indians, Jews, lesbians, gay men, Arabs, Asians, old people, working class people, and the physically and mentally disabled"—but the criticism is not entirely unjust. Young, *supra* n. 5, at 40.

23 T. Modood et al., *Ethnic Minorities in Britain: Diversity and Disadvantage* (London, Policy Studies Institute, 1997).

24 Okin and respondents, *supra* n. 11, at 10; See also "Feminism and Multiculturalism: Some Tensions" (1998) 108/4 *Ethics* 661–84.

25 This move is not unique to race: there has been a similar stereotyping of working class communities as peculiarly violent or abusive towards women, and one of the battles feminists have engaged in over the years is to get people to recognise that domestic violence is not an exclusively working-class phenomenon.

26 This is particularly powerfully argued in E. Spelman, *Inessential Woman: Problems of Exclusion in Feminist Thought* (Boston, Beacon Press, 1988).

27 I. M. Young, *Intersecting Voices: Dilemmas of Gender, Political Philosophy, and Policy* (Princeton, NJ, Princeton University Press, 1997).

Index